Caravan & Camping Europe 2011

AA Lifestyle Guides

This edition published 2011

To contact us:
Advertisement Sales: advertisingsales@theAA.com
Editorial: lifestyleguides@theAA.com

The Automobile Association would like to thank the following photographers, companies and picture libraries for their assistance in the preparation of this book.

Abbreviations for the picture credits are as follows: (t) top; (b) bottom; (l) left; (r) right; (c) centre; (AA) AA World Travel Library.

Front Cover (t) AA/J Smith; (bl) AA/I Dawson; (br) AA/J Smith; Back Cover (l) AA/A Baker; (c) AA/P Kenward; (r) AA/T Carter

Every effort has been made to trace the copyright holders, and we apologise in advance for any accidental errors. We would be happy to apply any corrections in the following edition of this publication.

Typeset by Keenes, London UK
Printed and bound by Printer Trento Srl, Italy

Published by AA Publishing, a trading name of
AA Media Limited, whose registered office is:
Fanum House, Basing View, Basingstoke,
Hampshire, RG21 4EA
Registered number 06112600

A CIP catalogue record for this book is available from the British Library

ISBN 978-0-7495-6834-4
A04585

Mapping prepared by the Mapping Services Department of AA Publishing

Contents

Countries

Using the Guide

Many of the countries in this guide are divided into regions, within which the site locations are listed in alphabetical order. Those not divided into regions are in alphabetical order of location. Regions and locations are shown on the country maps at the back of the book, and are listed in the index. For route planning you should use a road atlas, such as AA Road Atlas Europe. AA road atlases are also available for France, Germany, Italy, Spain and Portugal. The AA Route Planner Europe on theAA.com covers many of the countries in the guide.

Campsite entries

In order to update our information we send a questionnaire each year to every campsite. Inevitably a number of the questionnaires are not returned in time for publication, in which case the campsite name is printed in italics, and prices are omitted. Most of the sites accept both tents and caravans unless otherwise stated.

Websites

Campsite web addresses are included where available. The AA cannot be held responsible for the content of any of these websites.

Opening times

Dates shown are inclusive. All information was correct at the time of going to press, but we recommend you check with the site before arriving. Sometimes only restricted facilities are available between October and April.

Prices

Prices are given per night, and include two adults, a car, and caravan or tent. We also quote prices for weekly hire of static caravans/mobile homes. Prices are given in euros except for Switzerland (Francs), Bulgaria (Leva), Czech Republic (Koruny), Hungary (Forint), and Poland (New Złotych).

Booking

It is best to book well in advance for peak holiday seasons, or for your first and last stop close to a ferry crossing port. However, we do find that some sites do not accept reservations. Specimen booking letters in English, French, German, Italian and Spanish are on page 8. **Please note** that, although it is not common practice, some campsites may regard your deposit as a booking fee which is not deductible from the final account.

Complaints

If you have any complaint about a site, discuss the problem with the site proprietor immediately so that the matter can be dealt with promptly. We regret that the AA cannot act as intermediary in any dispute, or attempt to gain refunds or compensation. Your comments, however, help us to update new editions. Please use the Reader's Report Form at the back of the guide.

Disabled

We have asked each campsite if it is fully accessible for wheelchair users. Where a site has answered "yes" to this question we have included a wheelchair symbol (♿) in their entry. If you require further information on the site's suitability for wheelchair use, or any other disability, please contact the site directly.

Symbols

Abbreviations and symbols are explained at the foot of the gazetteer pages. Please note also:

CM camping municipal, parque municipal de campismo, or parque de la camara municipal (local authority site)

Sat Nav / GPS

Each site was asked to supply GPS positioning data for use in Sat Nav programming. Where this data could be verified by us, we have printed it. These coordinates can be entered into navigation devices to allow routeing to the campsite location. For more details regarding how to enter coordinates please refer to your device manual.

Camping and Caravanning Club

For the 2011 edition of the Guide, the Camping and Caravanning Club has inspected over a hundred of the sites in the guide, and these are highlighted by a tinted background and feature the Camping and Caravanning Club logo.

Online Information

This selection of websites contains useful travel information.

Camping

Official site of Calor Gas
www.calorgas.co.uk

Official site of LP Gas, suppliers of liquid petroleum gas
www.lpga.co.uk

Britain's major caravan clubs
www.campingand caravanningclub.co.uk
www.caravanclub.co.uk

Caravan news/info
www.practicalcaravan.com
www.motorcaravanmagazine.co.uk
www.caravanmagazine.co.uk
www.caravantimes.co.uk

Suppliers of camping & outdoor gear
www.tentastic.co.uk
www.outdoorgear.co.uk
www.campmania.co.uk
www.outdoorworlddirect.co.uk
www.outdoorworld.org.uk
www.gear-zone.co.uk
www.gooutdoors.co.uk
www.blacks.co.uk

European Federation of Campingsite Organisations and Holiday Park Associations
www.campingeurope.com

UK Government

The Foreign & Commonwealth Office travel information
www.fco.gov.uk/travel

HM Revenue & Customs
www.hmrc.gov.uk

Home Office Identity & Passport Office
www.direct.gov.uk/en/TravelAndTransport/Passports

Pet travel information and quarantine regulations
www.defra.gov.uk/wildlife-pets/pets/travel/pets/

EU, Euro, Currency

The European Union
europa.eu
www.ecb.int

Tourism

Andorra
www.andorra.ad

Austria
www.austria.info

Belgium
www.belgiumtheplaceto.be
www.visitbelgium.com
www.visitflanders.co.uk

Bulgaria
www.bulgariatravel.org
www.bulgarian-tourism.com

Czech Republic
www.czechtourism.com

Croatia
www.croatia.hr
www.croatiatouristcenter.com

France
uk.franceguide.com
www.francetourism.com

Germany
www.germany-tourism.de

Greece
www.gnto.gr
www.greek-tourism.gr

Holland
www.holland.com/uk

Hungary
www.hungary.com

Italy
www.italiantourism.com
www.enit.it

Luxembourg
www.luxembourg.co.uk
www.visitluxembourg.com

Poland
www.poland.travel

Portugal
www.visitportugal.com

Romania
www.romaniatourism.com

Slovenia
www.slovenia.info

Spain
www.spain.info
www.tourspain.org/

Switzerland
www.myswitzerland.com

Turkey
www.tourismturkey.org
www.turkeytourism.com
www.gototurkey.co.uk

Low Emission Zones (LEZs) in Europe

www.lowemissionzones.eu

Booking Letters

Please use capitals and enclose an International Reply Coupon, obtainable from a Post Office. Be sure to include your name, address, post code, email address and country.

English

Dear Sir

I intend to stay at your site for ... days, arriving on ... (date and month) and departing on ... (date and month). We are a party of ... people, including ... adults and ... children (aged ...) and would like a pitch for... tent(s) and/or parking space for our car/caravan/caravan trailer. We would like to hire a tent/caravan/bungalow. Please quote full charges when replying and advise on the deposit required, which will be forwarded without delay.

French

Monsieur

Je me propose de séjourner à votre terrain de camping pour ... jours, depuis le ... jusqu'au ...

Nous sommes ... personnes en tout, y compris ... adultes et ... enfants (âgés de ...) et nous aurons besoin d'un emplacement pour ... tente(s), et/ou un parking pour notre voiture/caravane/remorque.

Nous voudrions louer une tente/caravane/bungalow. Veuillez me donner dans votre réponse une idée de vos prix, m'indiquant en même temps le montant qu'il faut payer en avance, ce qui vous sera envoyé sans délai.

German

Sehr geehrter Herr!

Ich beabsichtige, mich auf Ihrem Campingplatz ... Tage aufzuhalten, und zwar vom ... bis zum ...

Wir sind im ganzen ... Personen, ... Erwachsene und ... Kinder (in Alter von ...), und benötigen Platz für Zelt(e) und/oder unseren Wagen/Wohnwagen/Wohnwagenanhänger.

Wir möchten ein Zelt/Wohnwagen/Bungalow mieten. Bitte, geben Sie mir in Ihrem Antwortschreiben die vollen Preise bekannt, und ebenso die Höhe der von mir zu leistenden Anzahlung, die Ihnen alsdann unverzüglich überwiesen wird.

Italian

Egregio Signore

Ho intenzione di remanere presso di voi per ... giorni. Arriverò il ... e partirò il ...

Siamo un gruppo di ... persone in totale, compreso ... adulti e ... bambini (de età ...) e vorrremo un posto per ... tenda(tende) e/o spazio per parcheggiare la nostra vetture/carovana/roulette.

Desideriamo affittare una tenda/carovana/bungalow. Vi preghiamo di quotare i prezzi completi quando ci risponderete, e darci informazioni sul deposito richiesto, che vi sarà rimesso senza ritardo.

Spanish

Muy señor mio

Desearia me reservara espacio por ... dias, a partir del ... hasta el ...

Nuestro grupo comprende .....personas todo comprendido, ... adultos y ... niños (... de años de edad). Necesitarimos un espacio por ... tienda(s) y/o espacio para apacar nuestro choche/caravana/remolque. Deseariamos alquilar una tienda de campana/caravan/bungalow.

Le ruego nos comunique los precios y nos informe sobre el depósito que debemos remitirle.

Visiting Europe

Planning your journey

Before leaving

General advice for driving in Europe is available at www.theaa.com/motoring_advice/overseas/index.html.
You can also buy AA European Breakdown Cover online at the website or call 0800 072 3279.
Before departure, it may be worth having your car checked by AA Vehicle Inspections.
For more information and charges visit www.theaa.com/motoring-advice/vehicle-inspections.html
or call 0800 056 8040.

AA UK travel news

When heading for your UK port of departure, check the traffic on the AA's information line 090688 84322 (land line) or 84322 ('theaa') from your mobile (calls cost up to 60p per minute).
Or click on to Travel or Traffic at theAA.com.

BBC World Service

The international radio arm of the BBC broadcasts in English and 32 other languages. World news is on the hour every hour and there are regular bulletins of British news. If you want to listen to the World Service when you are abroad, go to www.bbc.co.uk/worldservice or write for information to:

BBC World Service, Bush House, Strand
London WC2B 4PH
Tel 020 7240 3456
Email worldservice@bbc.co.uk

Camping Card International

A CCI is recognised at most campsites in Europe. At some campsites a reduction to the advertised charge may be allowed on presentation of the card. The CCI, which is valid for 12 months, provides third-party insurance cover for up to 11 people camping away from home, staying in rented accommodation or at a hotel.
AA personal members may purchase a CCI from the Camping & Caravanning Club, or the Caravan Club. If you require further information please call:
Camping & Caravanning Club on 0845 130 7701
or Caravan Club on 01342 327410 (Mon-Fri 9.15-5.15).
In either case, be prepared to quote your AA membership number.

Caravans & trailers

Take a list of contents, especially if any valuable or unusual equipment is being carried, as this may be required at some frontiers.
In some countries, a towed vehicle - boat trailer, caravan or trailer - must have a unique chassis number. The identification plate should be in an accessible position and show the name of the maker of the vehicle and the production or serial number.

Direction indicators

Most standard car-flasher units will be overloaded by the extra lamps of a caravan or trailer, and a special heavy duty unit or relay device should be fitted.

Disabled travellers

The AA Disability Helpline provides information on a range of disability related subjects, such as motoring in the UK and overseas. AA members can call this service free on 0800 26 20 50. The comprehensive *AA Disabled Traveller's Guide* is also free to all members of the public and contains information on motoring. Call free on 0800 26 20 50 to claim a copy. A pdf version of the guide is available for download at www.theAA.com/breakdowncover/disabilities_information.html.

Visiting Europe

A standard blue parking badge for disabled people has been introduced throughout the EU. All EU member states with reciprocal arrangements in place, operate the Blue Badge parking scheme. Badge holders across the participating EU states can enjoy the same parking concessions provided in the host country by displaying the badge issued under their own national scheme. (Badge holders should check local notices to ensure that they are parking within the law.) These arrangements apply only to badge holders themselves and are not for the benefit of non-disabled companions. Wrongful display of the badge may incur a fine.

For details of the Blue Badge parking scheme or for planning a trip abroad contact:
Department for Transport,
Great Minster House,
76 Marsham Street,
London SW1P 4DR
Tel 020 7944 8300
www.dft.gov.uk/transportforyou/access/
www.direct.gov.uk/DisabledPeople

Information on the Blue Badge scheme in 29 European countries is also available from the AA's website:
www.theAA.com/public_affairs/reports/blue_badge_abroad.pdf

Documents & insurance

Always carry your national driving licence (and International Driving Permit if necessary), the original vehicle registration document and your passport. Remember, if the registration document is not in your name, ask the registered keeper to provide you with a letter of authority. If the vehicle is hired or leased ask the company concerned to supply you with a Vehicle on Hire Certificate.

The IDP, for which a statutory charge is made, is issued by the AA to applicants who holds a valid full British driving licence and who are aged 18 and over.

Go to www.theAA.com/getaway/idp/index.html or call 0870 600 0371.

When driving abroad you must carry your certificate of motor insurance with you at all times. Third-party is the minimum legal requirement in most countries. Before taking a vehicle, caravan or trailer abroad, contact your insurer or broker to notify them of your intentions and ask their advice. Check that you are covered against damage in transit (e.g. on the ferry) when the vehicle is not being driven. Motorists can obtain all types of insurance at www.theAA.com or call 0800 316 2456.

Electrical

The electricity supply in Europe is usually 220 volts (50 cycles) AC (alternating current), but can be as low as 110 volts. In some isolated areas, low voltage DC (direct current) is provided. Continental circular two-pin plugs and screw-type bulbs are usually the rule. Check for correct polarity when using a mains hook-up on a touring caravan.

Electrical adaptors (not voltage transformers), which can be used in Continental power sockets, shaver points and light bulb sockets, are available in the UK from electrical retailers or from on-board ferry shops.

Euro

The currency of the majority of countries in this guide is the euro. For further information visit the European Central Bank at www.ecb.int.

Notes have denominations of 5, 10, 20, 50, 100, 200 and 500 euros; the coins 1 and 2 euros, and 1, 2, 5, 10, 20 and 50 cents.

There is no limit to the amount of sterling notes you may take abroad. Some countries have currency import or export restrictions and you should check this with your bank or currency supplier.

Credit and debit cards can be used abroad. Their use is subject to the conditions set out by the issuing bank. Establishments display the symbols of cards that they accept. However, it is recommended that you don't rely exclusively on any one payment method. A combination of traveller's cheques, a payment card and a small amount of local currency is suggested. Traveller's cheques can often be used like cash. Your bank will be able to recommend currency traveller's cheques for the countries you are visiting.

Countries in this guide that do not have the Euro as their national currency are: Switzerland (Francs), Bulgaria (Leva), Croatia (Kuna), Czech Republic (Koruny), Hungary (Forint), Poland (Złotych), Romania (New Lei), and Turkey (New Lira). Campsites in Croatia, Romania and Turkey have given their prices in Euros.

Visiting Europe

Fire extinguisher/first aid kit

In some countries it is compulsory to equip your vehicle with these items (see country introductions). A fire extinguisher is not required for two-wheeled vehicles.

Foodstuffs

Most countries have regulations governing the types and quantities of foodstuffs that may be imported. Although they are usually not strictly applied, visitors should know that they exist and only take reasonable quantities of food with them.

Lights

When driving on the Continent, you must adjust the headlamp beam pattern to suit driving on the right so that the dipped beam doesn't dazzle oncoming drivers. Never go without adjusting the headlamp pattern, as it is an offence to dazzle oncoming traffic.

Headlamp beam convertor kits are widely available, but don't leave adjustment to the last minute, as it may need to be made by your dealer.

Some models feature an internal 'shutter' that can be moved into place by a screw or lever adjustment at the back of the headlamp unit. Some designs are less convenient so the dealer will need to do it.

Some modern halogen-type headlamps, HID headlights and Xenon headlamps require external masks of such complex design that many motorists struggle to follow the instructions on where and how the mask should be applied. Check with your dealer or car handbook for advice.

Remember to remove your convertors as soon as you return to the UK.

AA Headlamp Beam Converters and/or AA Bulb Kits, or an AA Eurotravel Kit, which includes a highviz vest, first aid kit, GB magnetic plate, headlamp beam converters and warning triangle, can be purchased from the AA's Dover shop (Eastern Docks Terminal), the AA's Folkestone shop (Eurotunnel Passenger Terminal)
or online at www.theAA.com/shop

Medical treatment

EU/EEA nationals temporarily visiting another country in the European Economic Area (EEA) or Switzerland are entitled to receive state-provided medical care in the case of illness or an accident. A European Health Insurance Card (which replaced the E111 form in 2004) entitles you to reduced-cost or free public medical treatment for an illness or accident while you're in a European Economic Area (EEA) country or Switzerland. The EHIC can be obtained online via www.ehic.org.uk, or call 0845 606 2030, or pick up a EHIC form from the Post Office.

Nationality plate

Vehicles must display a nationality sticker of the approved design on a vertical surface at the rear (and caravan or trailer). Fines are imposed for failing to display the correct distinguishing sign.

UK registration plates displaying the GB Euro-symbol (Euro-Plates) must comply with British Standard AU 145d. These plates make display of a conventional sticker unnecessary when circulating within the EU. The Euro-Plate is only legally recognised in the EU; it is still a requirement to display a GB sticker when travelling outside the EU.

A GB sign can be purchased from the AA's Dover shop (Eastern Docks Terminal), the AA's Folkestone shop (Eurotunnel Passenger Terminal) or online at www.theAA.com/shop

Passports

Each person must hold a valid passport. Always carry your passport and a separate note of the number, date and place of issue. The only type of passport now is the standard UK passport.

All passports issued to children under the age of 16 years are for 5 years only. After 5 years a new application must be made.

To obtain a passport application call 0300 222 0000 or visit the UK Passport Service at www.passport.gov.uk.

Pet Travel Scheme

For information on how to bring pet cats and dogs back into the UK from certain countries without quarantine contact the Pets Helpline on 0870 241 1710 or visit the Department for Environment, Food & Rural Affairs (DEFRA) website
www.defra.gov.uk/animalh/quarantine/pets/

Vehicle licence

When taking a vehicle out of the UK for a temporary visit, the vehicle licence (tax disc) must be valid throughout your journey and on your return.

Agreement within the EU provides for the temporary use of foreign-registered vehicles within the member states. A vehicle which is properly registered and taxed in its home country should not be subject to the domestic taxation and registration laws of the host country during a temporary stay.

Visas

EU citizens travelling within the EU do not require visas. A visa is not normally required by United Kingdom and Republic of Ireland passport holders when visiting non-EU countries within western Europe for periods of three months or less. However, if you hold a passport of any other nationality, a UK passport not issued in this country, or if you are in any doubt at all, check with the embassies or consulates of the countries you intend to visit.

Warning triangle & reflective jacket

The use of a warning triangle is compulsory in most European countries in the event of accident or breakdown. In certain circumstances two triangles are required. Additionally, reflective jackets/waistcoats are now compulsory in several European countries.

Warning triangles and reflective jackets or waistcoats can be purchased from the AA's Dover shop (Eastern Docks Terminal), the AA's Folkestone shop (Eurotunnel Passenger Terminal) or online at www.theAA.com/shop

Weather

For weather information on the Continent visit www.metoffice.gov.uk
or call the Met Office on 0870 900 0100, from outside the UK on +44 (0)1392 885680.

During your journey

Accidents

If you are in an accident you must stop. A warning triangle should be placed on the road at the appropriate distance; the use of hazard warning lights does not affect the regulations governing the use of warning triangles. The accident must be reported to the police if the accident has caused death or bodily injury; or if an unoccupied vehicle or property has been damaged (see country openers for emergency telephone numbers). If the accident necessitates calling the police, leave the vehicle in position. If it obstructs other traffic, mark the position of the vehicle on the road and get the details confirmed by independent witnesses before moving it. Notify your insurance company (by letter) within 24 hours, making sure all the essential particulars are noted (see the conditions of your policy).

If a third party is injured, contact your insurers for advice or, if you have a Green Card, notify the company or bureau given on the back of your Green Card; this company or bureau will deal with any compensation claim from the injured party.

It is useful to take photographs of the scene. Include the other vehicles involved, their registration plates and any background that could help later enquiries or when completing the insurance company's accident form.

Emergency Numbers

All the countries in this guide use 112 as the principal emergency telephone number that can be dialled free of charge from any telephone or any mobile phone in order to reach emergency services (ambulances, fire-fighters and the police). Turkey only uses 112 for medical services. Other Turkish numbers are listed in Turkey's opening section.

Breakdown

Try to move the car to the side of the road so that it does not obstruct traffic flow. Place a warning triangle to the rear of the vehicle at the appropriate distance. Find the nearest telephone to call for assistance. On motorways emergency telephones are generally located every 2km and automatically connect you to the official motorway breakdown service.

Visiting Europe

Motorists are advised to take out *AA European Breakdown Cover* and travel insurance from the AA. They are available at www.theaa.com/breakdown-cover/european-breakdown-cover.jsp or call 0800 072 3279.

Beaches

Pollution of seawater at certain Continental coastal resorts can represent a health hazard. Countries of the European Union publish detailed information on the quality of their bathing beaches, including maps, which are available from national authorities and the European Union.

In many (though not all) popular resorts where the water quality may present risk, signs (generally small) forbid bathing:

France

No bathing	Défense de se baigner
Bathing prohibited	Il est défendu de se baigner

Italy

No bathing	Vietato bagnarsi
Bathing prohibited	Evietato bagnarsi

Spain

No bathing	Prohibido bañarse
Bathing prohibited	Se prohibe bañarse

Germany

Bathing prohibited	Baden verboten

British Embassies/Consulates

Many Continental countries have at least one British consulate in addition to the British embassy. British consulates (and consular sections in embassies) can help British travellers in distress overseas but there are limitations to what they can do. For example, they cannot pay your hotel, medical or any other bills, nor will they do the work of a travel agent, information bureau or the police.

Report any loss or theft of property to the local police in the first instance, not to the consular offices. If you need to obtain an emergency passport or guidance on how to transfer funds from the UK, contact the nearest British embassy or consulate. Note that the hours and functions of honorary consuls are more restricted than full consular posts.

For up-to-date advice on travelling abroad, visit www.fco.gov.uk/knowbeforeyougo or call 0845 850 2829.

Cycle carriers

If you are taking bicycles on a rear-mounted cycle rack, make sure that they do not obstruct rear lights and/or number plate, or you risk an on-the-spot fine.

N.B. Rear-mounted cycle racks are illegal in Portugal.

When travelling in Spain or Italy a reflectorised sign has to be placed on the back of a rear-mounted carrier.

For further information please see www.theaa.com/motoring_advice/overseas/countrybycountry.html

Crash helmets

The wearing of crash or safety helmets by motorcyclists and their passengers is compulsory in all countries.

Customs regulations

People travelling within the EU are free to take not only personal belongings but a motor vehicle, boat, caravan or trailer across the internal frontiers without being subject to customs formalities. The EU countries are Austria, Belgium, Bulgaria, Cyprus, Czech Republic, Denmark, Estonia, Finland, France, Germany, Greece, Hungary, Republic of Ireland, Italy, Latvia, Lithuania, Luxembourg, Malta, the Netherlands, Poland, Portugal, Romania, Slovakia, Slovenia, Spain (but not the Canaries), Sweden and the UK (but not the Channel Islands). Gibraltar is part of the EU, but customs allowances for outside the EU apply.

When you return to the UK, use the blue exit reserved for EU travellers. You do not have to pay any tax or duty in the UK on goods you have bought in other EU countries

Visiting Europe

for your own use. The law sets out guidelines for the amount of alcohol and tobacco you can bring into the UK. If you bring in more, you must be able to satisfy the customs officer that the goods are for your own use.
If you cannot, the goods may be taken from you, and your vehicle may also be seized.
The guidelines are:
3,200 cigarettes, 400 cigarillos, 200 cigars, 3kg smoking tobacco, 10 litres spirits, 20 litres fortified wine, 90 litres wine, 110 litres beer. (Bulgaria and Romania have a limit of 200 cigarettes, but there are no limits on other tobacco products as long as they are for your own use.)
People under 17 are not allowed to bring in alcohol or tobacco.
When you enter the UK from a non-EU country, or from an EU country having travelled through a non-EU country, you must pass through customs. If you have any goods over the allowance, or if you are not sure what to declare you must use the red exit. If you do not declare items on which you should pay duty you are breaking the law.
Customs allowances for travellers from outside the EU are:
200 cigarettes or 100 cigarillos or 50 cigars or 250g tobacco; 4 litres still table wine; 16 litres of beer; 1 litre of spirits or strong liqueurs over 22% volume or 2 litres fortified wine, sparkling wine or other liqueurs; £390 worth of all other goods including perfume, gifts and souvenirs.
For more information, see the HM Revenue & Customs website www.hmrc.gov.uk/customs/arriving/index.htm or call 0845 010 9000.

Fines

Some countries impose on-the-spot fines for minor traffic offences. Fines are paid in the currency of the country concerned to the police or local post office against a ticket issued. A receipt should be obtained as proof of payment. If you drink, don't drive - the laws are strict and the penalties severe.

Horn

In built-up areas, the general rule is that you should not use it unless safety demands it. In many large towns and resorts, and in areas indicated by the international sign (a horn inside a red circle, crossed through) use of the horn is banned.

Hot weather

In hot weather and at high altitude, excessive heat can cause engine problems. If towing a caravan, consult the manufacturers of your vehicle about the limitations of the cooling system, and the operating temperature of the gearbox fluid for automatics.

Journey times

As there are many factors to consider when travelling abroad it is extremely difficult to estimate how long a journey will take. Volume of traffic, road and weather conditions will all affect calculations. On motorways the average speed will be about 60mph, on all-purpose roads out of town the average can be about 45mph, and in urban areas it may be as low as 15-20mph. Remember to allow for refreshments, petrol and toilet stops, and if making for a port or airport to add extra time for checking in and unforeseen delays.
At peak travel periods delays may occur on some main routes and at frontier crossing points. Mountain passes and alpine roads may be closed during the winter months.

Mobile phones

The use of hand-held mobile phones while driving is prohibited in most countries. In Spain the use of an earpiece or headphones while driving is banned. Only fully hands-free phone systems are permitted.

Off-site camping

Off-site camping may contravene local regulations. You are strongly advised never to camp by the roadside or in isolated areas.

Parking

Heavy fines are imposed for parking offences and unaccompanied offending cars can be towed away. Make sure you understand all parking related signs. Always park on the right-hand side of the road or at an authorised place. If possible, park off the main carriageway.

Petrol & diesel

You will find familiar brands and comparable grades of petrol along the main routes in most countries. However, leaded petrol is no longer generally available in northern European countries. Diesel fuel is generally known as diesel or gas-oil.

While you may wish to carry a reserve can of fuel, remember that all ferry and some rail operators will either forbid the carriage of fuel in spare cans or insist that spare cans must be empty. In Luxembourg motorists are forbidden to carry petrol in cans in the vehicle.

Road signs

Most road signs throughout Europe conform to international standards and most will be familiar. Watch for road markings - do not cross a solid white or yellow line marked on the road centre. In Belgium there are three official languages, and signs will be in Dutch, French or German. In the Basque and Catalonian areas of Spain local and national place names appear on signposts. Road signs also indicate priority or loss of priority, and tourists must be sure that they understand such signs. Particular care should be exercised when circulating anti-clockwise on a roundabout. It is advisable to keep to the outside lane if possible, to make your exit easier.

Rule of the road

In all countries in this guide, drive on the right and overtake on the left.
When overtaking on roads with two lanes or more in each direction, signal in good time, and also signal your return to the inside lane. Do not remain in any other lane. Failure to comply with this regulation, particularly in France, will incur an on-the-spot fine (immediate deposit in France).
Do not overtake at level crossings, intersections, the crest of a hill or pedestrian crossings. When being overtaken, keep to the right and reduce speed if necessary.

Seat belts

All countries in this guide require seat belts to be worn. Regulations relating to children and seat belts are generally strict and should be checked in advance of travel. See country openers.

Signposting

Signposting between major towns and along main roads is generally efficient, but on some secondary roads and in open country advance direction signs may be less frequent. Signs are often of the pointer type and placed on walls or railings on the far side of the turn; they tend to point across the road they indicate which can be confusing at first. Difficulties may arise with spellings when crossing frontiers, and place names may not be so easily recognised when written in a different language. Extra difficulties may arise in countries with two or more official languages or dialects, although some towns may have both spellings, eg San Sebastian - Donostia in Spain, Antwerpen - Anvers in Belgium, Basel - Bâle in Switzerland.

Speed limits

Speed limits for individual countries are listed in the country openers. Lower limits may apply to motorcycles and new drivers in some countries and also generally when towing a trailer unless indicated otherwise. It can be an offence to travel so slowly as to obstruct traffic flow without good reason or in poor weather conditions.

Tolls

Tolls are payable on most motorways in Croatia, France, Greece, Italy, Portugal, Spain and on sections in Austria and Poland. Over long distances, charges can be considerable.
Always have some local currency ready to pay the tolls, as traveller's cheques are not accepted at toll booths. Credit cards are accepted at toll booths in France and Spain. In Austria, Czech Republic, Hungary, Slovakia and Switzerland, authorities levy a tax for using motorway networks. See country openers.
In some countries a "vignette" (tax sticker) may be required for the use of motorways, major roads or for entering environmental zones.
In Portugal, on some sections of motorway, an electronic device is required. This must be pre-loaded with currency. See country openers. Further info at www.theaa.com/allaboutcars/overseas/european_tolls_select.jsp

Trams

Trams take priority over other vehicles. Always give way to passengers boarding and alighting. Never position a vehicle so that it impedes the free passage of a tram. Trams must be overtaken on the right, except in one-way streets.

Channel Crossings

Brittany Ferries

Tel: 0871 244 0744
www.brittany-ferries.com
Cork to Roscoff
Plymouth to Roscoff
Plymouth to Santander
Portsmouth to Caen
Poole to Cherbourg
Portsmouth to Bilbao
Portsmouth to Cherbourg
Portsmouth to St Malo
Portsmouth to Santander

Condor Ferries

Tel: 0845 609 1024
www.condorferries.co.uk
Poole to St Malo
(via Channel Islands)
Weymouth to St Malo
(via Channel Islands)
Portsmouth to Cherbourg (seasonal)
Portsmouth to St Malo
(via Channel Islands)

Eurotunnel

Tel: 08705 35 35 35
www.eurotunnel.com
Folkestone to Calais

Irish Ferries

Tel: 0818 300 400 (from ROI)
08717 300 400 (from GB)
www.irishferries.com
Rosslare to Cherbourg
Rosslare to Roscoff

Stena Line

Tel: 08705 70 70 70
www.stenaline.co.uk
Harwich to Hook of Holland

LD Lines/ Transmanche Ferries

Tel: 0844 576 8836
www.ldlines.co.uk
Portsmouth to Le Havre
Newhaven to Dieppe
Dover to Boulougne
Ramsgate to Ostend
Rosslare to Le Havre
Rosslare to Cherbourg

Norfolkline Ferries

www.norfolkline.com
Dover to Dunkerque
Rosyth to Zeebrugge
Newcastle to Amsterdam

P&O Ferries

Tel: 08716 645 645
www.poferries.com
Portsmouth to Bilbao
Dover to Calais
Hull to Zeebrugge
Hull to Rotterdam

Seafrance

Tel: 0871 423 7119
www.seafrance.com
Dover to Calais

The Camping and Caravanning Club

History of the C&CC

The Camping and Caravanning Club is the world's oldest and largest club for people who enjoy camping, however they choose to camp.

If you love the great outdoors, you'll love The Camping and Caravanning Club. Whether you like striking out on your own, or you want the reassurance of a great place to stay, The Club can provide you with as much or as little of your camping needs as you want.

The Camping and Caravanning Club was founded in 1901 by six young men camping at Wantage, Berkshire. The Club celebrated its centenary in 2001 – little did those founder members realise how big their club would grow.

A number of notable people have been associated with the history of The Club. Captain Robert Falcon Scott – Scott of the Antarctic – was an early President. Legend has it that he took his Club pennon (pennant) on his tragic journey to the South Pole. Another President was Lord Baden-Powell, the father of Scouting. His grandson, the third Lord Baden-Powell, was also President of The Club for a decade. The current President, Professor David Bellamy OBE, is highly respected and known throughout the world for his environmental campaigning.

Proud of its history as an innovator and pioneer of camping trends, The Club constantly looks at what campers need to make the most of their outdoor lifestyle adventures. As it's a Club owned and run by its members – people who love the outdoors as much as you do – it's a not-for-profit organisation which means that any money made, is ploughed back into

providing better site facilities, locations and services for members.

There's nothing quite like getting out in the open: fresh air; freedom; new destinations; old and new friends. The Camping and Caravanning Club exists to help you and your family get even more out of the great outdoors. Whether taking the kids on a weekend's camping just half an hour from where you live, or going it alone to explore Europe, the USA or even Australia and New Zealand, The Club can help to make it a real adventure.

Member benefits

In addition to providing members with a foreign travel service which can offer individually tailored holidays, The Club also offers members over 100 award-winning UK Club Sites - all with a reputation for cleanliness and friendliness. There is also a choice of 1,400 smaller and often more rural sites which are exclusive to members. Thanks to a partnership with The Forestry Commission, Forest Holidays now offers over 20 Camping and Caravanning Sites and seven Cabin Sites in some of the UK's most beautiful and secluded woodland locations.

Club members can also benefit from publications which help you make the most out of your camping adventures plus products and services including tent, caravan and motorhome insurance – designed by campers, for campers.

Family membership of The Camping and Caravanning Club costs just £37.00 per year. And with special site rates you soon recoup your membership fee with just a few nights' stay at UK Club Sites

Once you become a member of The Camping and Caravanning Club, we're always here to help. If you have a query, a technical problem or simply need some reliable advice, you can call us on 0845 130 7632, Monday to Friday between 8:00am and 4:45pm (from 10am on Wednesdays). For a more detailed reply, you're also more than welcome to email us from the Club's website.

To see what other benefits are available to members or to join or find out more about The Club go to: www.thefriendlyclub.co.uk or speak to an advisor on: 0845 130 7632

The Club in Europe

Carefree, the overseas travel service from The Camping and Caravanning Club are experts in providing holidays for people who enjoy spending their time camping throughout Europe. Carefree now sends over 75,000 people abroad each year. Regardless of whether you're a first time camper or an expert overseas explorer, it provides a one-stop-shop travel service.

Peace of mind is assured. Carefree holiday packages are ABTA protected (or ATOL protected if you're taking a fly-drive motorhome holiday outside of Europe). Also, each European campsite suggested for your trip is personally inspected by Carefree's dedicated team against standards agreed with The Royal Society for the Prevention of Accidents (RoSPA). All of this means that you can be assured that your holiday will be one to remember – for all the right reasons.

Abroad for the first time

However you choose to camp, going overseas for the first time is made simpler and safer with The Club. The Carefree brochures have pages

of helpful ideas and tips for those travelling abroad with a tent, motorhome or caravan. You will find help on a multitude of subjects - from whether or not to take a universal travel sink plug, to how to take your pet with you, both safely and legally. The AA and Carefree's helpful European Driver's Handbook, along with this AA Caravan & Camping Europe guide, are the perfect partnership to help you find your way around Europe.

One excellent way to take advantage of other Club members' experience of travelling outside the UK is to visit a Carefree Holiday Rally. Here, campers can meet up with other Club members on site, secure in the knowledge that there will be an experienced Holiday Steward on hand to help if there are any problems. Please go to: www.thefriendlyclub.co.uk/travelabroad/rallies for an up to date list.

Carefree staff are experienced and incredibly knowledgeable about Carefree destinations. They are able to give campers travelling abroad for the first time the most up-to-date information at their fingertips, and you can talk to team members who have visited the sites themselves. You can speak to a European Travel Specialist on 0845 130 7701.

Summer holidays

The summer months are a great time to see much of Europe. From fabulous regional variations in France to the fascinating East of Europe, there is an ever-increasing array of campsites for you to choose from. European campsites can be simple or include a vast array of facilities, restaurants and activities. Swimming pools offer a cooling break from the summer heat or from trekking, shopping or other pastimes. Many allow you to hire bikes or boats etc depending on what adventures inspire you to get out and enjoy the area around the site.

The sites featuring a CCC report in this guide guarantee a good standard of facilities and are inspected regularly by CCC staff. Look for the sites with CCC report and you'll be guaranteed quality.

Be aware too of the differences between high season and low season. High season across Europe is geared to family holidays, family activities and on many coastal sites in particular this includes lively nighttimes. Each country's high season tends to tie in with the school holiday dates for that country. Children stay up late on many Spanish, Italian and lively French sites – be prepared, be local and go with the flow!

Low season is the ideal time for couples looking to explore abroad, or for families with young children who will also appreciate the peace and quiet on offer. Facilities on many sites in low season run at an absolute minimum – there are often simply not enough people on site to justify opening facilities. If a particular facility is important to you it is always recommended you establish whether or not this is available before you book a site.

Winter sun holidays

When the weather gets colder, this is your chance to travel to sunnier climes for camping opportunities. A large number of sites operate during the winter months across European destinations such as France, Spain and Portugal, each helping you to create new memories and providing a base for exploration. Many northern Europeans – British, Dutch,

German and Scandinavian in particular – have been wintering here for years and have got the art of 'snowbirding' down to a fine art.

European campsites – what to expect

Most British campers are amazed at the quality of continental sites when they travel abroad. You can definitely leave behind any notions of the 1950s and 'holes in the ground'! The vast majority of continental campsites have swimming pools for their campers. These can range from small traditional swimming pools, to Californian-style pools with waterslides and 'magic rivers', right through to amazing complexes with indoor and outdoor pools, Jacuzzis and steam rooms. Sites with pools nearly always have a paddling pool for babies and toddlers. Further sports facilities can include tennis courts, fitness rooms, cycle hire, crazy-golf, multisports courts and of course, in France, the almost obligatory boules pitch.

Similarly, forget any worries about dated wash block facilities. Continental wash blocks are modern and well equipped, with modern toilets, warm showers, and nearly always, washbasins in cubicles. The further south you go, the more open the wash blocks become, benefitting from the warmer climate. You might like to visit Camping la Paz at Vidiago in northern Spain where you can enjoy a view of the Picos de Europa mountain range from the showers. Travel to Germany and Austria and you will see some wash blocks worthy of a 5-star hotel, with superb quality bathroom fittings and ceramic tiling. Some sites even offer family bathrooms that you can rent for your exclusive use during your stay on site. Many sites also have great children's facilities, with baby baths and mini-showers, mini-loos and mini-basins, all at children's height.

On many sites you won't need to go far for an evening meal. Lots of sites have take-aways or snack bars, and most of the highest quality sites have very nice restaurants too. You can sample the local specialities just a short stroll

The Camping and Caravanning Club

away from your pitch. Bars are found on most sites too, ranging from either just a small set of optics and a few bottles behind reception to fabulous terraces overlooking beaches, lakes or the surrounding countryside.

Summer Camping 2011

The Camping and Caravanning Club
Carefree Travel

Great adventures abroad
The definitive guide to European camping

campingandcaravanningclub.co.uk
Telephone 0845 130 7701 or 024 7642 2024
The Friendly Club

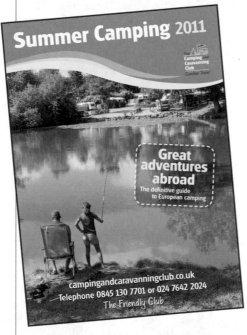

In high season, many of Europe's biggest and most popular sites, offer fabulous activity and entertainment programmes. You can join in with as much or as little as you like, and often it's completely free of charge. Activities might range from Children's Clubs, with sports and craft activities, to walks and bike rides in the local area, to coach excursions to places of interest, to musical evenings and dances. When the French, Spanish and Italians go on holiday, expect them to let their hair down and watch the whole family party until late at night (or early in the morning!). If you go to Germany, Holland or any other northern European country, expect the nighttimes to be rather more like campsites at home.

In terms of pitches, campers and caravanners travelling abroad for the first time will find one significant difference to many British campsites. Pitches on the continent are usually quite clearly marked out by either hedges, shrubs or trees. They can range in size from as small as $60m^2$ to as spacious as $200m^2$. So for the most part you will find that you are pitched much closer to your neighbour than you would generally be in the UK. Electric hook-up supplies are generally good, with a typical choice of a 6, 10 or sometimes 16 amp supply.

There are an increasing number of sites now that offer 'premium' pitches too, aimed specifically at the British tourer with a large caravan or motorhome. The style of these pitches vary from site to site but always offer the largest pitches available. Electricity, water and drainage are standard, but there are also a variety of added extras such as garden furniture, barbecue, washbasin, fridge and free Wi-fi access.

However, should you wish to leave all the facilities and sophisticated camping behind, throughout Europe you will find some of the simplest and most delightful little sites you could wish to experience. Surrounded by countryside, adjacent to small villages, or heading up to the mountains, Europe's sheer range of campsites is quite superb. There is bound to be something out there for you. With the help of this guide you are guaranteed fun in exploring and finding it.

Country Regions

Most of the countries in this guide are divided into regions. See the country maps at the end of the guide. The lists below of country regions show the corresponding national departments, districts or administrative areas.

Austria

TIROL — Tirol
CARINTHIA — Kärnten
STYRIA — Steiermark
LOWER AUSTRIA — Niederösterreich, Burgenland
UPPER AUSTRIA — Oberösterreich, Salzburg
VORARLBERG VIENNA — Wien

Belgium

SOUTH WEST/COAST — Hainaut, West-Vlaanderen
NORTH/CENTRAL — Brabant, Oost-Vlaanderen
NORTH EAST — Antwerpen, Limburg
SOUTH EAST — Liège, Luxembourg, Namur

France

ALPS/EAST — Ain, Doubs, Hautes-Alpes, Haute Saône, Haute Savoie, Jura, Isère, Savoie, Territoire-de-Belfort
ALSACE/LORRAINE — Bas-Rhin, Haut-Rhin, Meurthe-et-Moselle, Meuse, Moselle, Vosges
BURGUNDY/CHAMPAGNE — Aube, Ardennes, Côte-d'Or, Haute-Marne, Marne, Nièvre, Saône-et-Loire, Yonne
SOUTH WEST/ PYRENEES — Ariège, Dordogne, Gers, Gironde, Haute-Garonne, Hautes-Pyrénées, Landes, Lot, Lot-et-Garonne, Pyrénées-Atlantiques, Tarn, Tarn-et-Garonne
LOIRE/CENTRAL — Charente, Charente-Maritime, Cher, Corrèze, Creuse, Deux-Sèvres, Eure-et-Loir, Haute-Vienne, Indre, Indre-et-Loire, Loire-Atlantique, Loiret, Loir-et-Cher, Maine-et-Loire, Mayenne, Sarthe, Vendée, Vienne
BRITTANY/NORMANDY — Calvados, Côtes-d'Armor, Eure, Finistère, Ille-et-Vilaine, Manche, Morbihan, Orne, Seine-Maritime
PARIS/NORTH — Aisne, Essonne, Hauts-de-Seine, Nord, Oise, Paris, Pas-de-Calais, Seine-et-Marne, Seine-St-Denis, Somme, Val-de-Marne, Val d'Oise, Yvelines
AUVERGNE — Allier, Aveyron, Cantal, Haute-Loire, Loire, Lozère, Puy-de-Dôme, Rhône
SOUTH COAST/RIVIERA — Alpes-Maritimes, Alpes-de-Haute-Provence, Ardèche, Aude, Bouches-du-Rhône, Drôme, Gard, Hérault, Monaco, Pyrénées-Orientales, Var, Vaucluse
CORSICA — Corse-du-Sud, Haute-Corse

Germany

SOUTH EAST — Bayern
SOUTH WEST — Baden-Württemberg
BERLIN AND EASTERN PROVINCES — Brandenburg, Sachsen, Thüringen
CENTRAL — Hessen, Nordrhein-Westfalen, Rheinland-Pfalz, Saarland
NORTH — Bremen, Hamburg, Niedersachsen, Schleswig-Holstein

Italy

NORTH WEST/ALPS/LAKES — Aosta, Alessandria, Asti, Beramo, Bolzano, Brescia, Como, Cremona, Cuneo, Mantova, Milano, Novara, Pavia, Sondrio, Trento, Torino, Varese, Vercelli
VENICE/NORTH — Belluno, Gorizia, Padova, Pordenone, Rovigo, Treviso, Trieste, Udine, Venezia, Verona, Vicenza,
NORTH WEST/MED COAST — Arezzo, Firenze, Genova, Grosseto, Imperia, Livorno, Lucca, Massa Carrara, Pisa, Pistoia, Savona, Siena, La Spezia
NORTH EAST/ADRIATIC — Ancona, L'Aquila, Ascoli Piceno, Bologna, Campobasso, Chieti, Ferrara, Forli, Iserina, Macerata, Modena, Parma, Perugia, Pescara, Pesaro & Urbino, Piacenza, Ravenna, Reggio nell'Emilia, Teramo, Terni
ROME — Frosinone, Latina, Roma, Rieti, Viterbo
SOUTH — Avellino, Bari, Benevento, Brindisi, Caserta, Catanzaro, Cosenza, Foggia, Lecce, Matera, Napoli, Potenza, Reggio di Calabria, Salerno, Taranto
SARDINIA — Cagliari, Nuoro, Oristano, Sassari
SICILY — Agrigento, Caltanissetta, Catania, Enna, Messina, Palermo, Ragusa, Siracusa, Trapani

Netherlands

NORTH — Ameland, Drenthe, Friesland, Groningen
CENTRAL — Flevoland, Gelderland, Noord-Holland, Overijssel, Utrecht
SOUTH — Limburg, Noord-Brabant, Zeeland, Zuid-Holland

Portugal

SOUTH — Algarve, Baixo-Alentejo
NORTH — Costa Verde, Douro Litoral, Minho, Tras os Montes, Alto Douro
CENTRAL — Alto Alentejo, Beira Alta, Beira Baixo, Beira Litoral, Costa de Prata, Estremadura, Ribatejo

Spain

NORTH EAST COAST — Barcelona, Girona
CENTRAL — Albacete, Avila, Badajoz, Cáceres, Ciudad Real, Cuenca, Guadalajara, Madrid, Salamanca, Segovia, Soria, Teruel, Toledo
SOUTH EAST COAST — Alicante, Castellón, Tarragona, Valencia
NORTH COAST — Asturias, Cantabria, Guipúzcoa, La Coruña, Lugo, Vizcaya
NORTH EAST — Alava, Burgos, Huesca, Lleida, La Rioja, Navarra, Zaragoza
NORTH WEST — Léon, Logrono Orense, Palencia, Pontevedra, Valladolid, Zamora
SOUTH — Almeria, Cádiz, Cordoba, Granada, Huelva, Jaén, Málaga, Murcia, Sevilla
ISLANDS — Ibiza, Mallorca Menorca

Switzerland

NORTH — Aargau, Basel, Solothurn
NORTH EAST — Appenzell, Liechtenstein, St Gallen, Schaffhausen, Thurgau, Zürich
NORTH WEST/CENTRAL — Bern, Jura, Luzern, Neuchâtel, Nidwalden, Obwalden, Schwyz, Uri, Zug
EAST — Glarus, Graubünden
SOUTH — Ticino
SOUTH WEST — Fribourg, Genève, Valais, Vaud

Austria

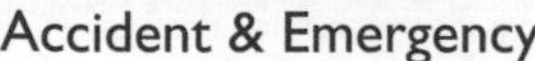

Accident & Emergency

Fire 122 Police 133 Ambulance 144

European emergency call number also in use – dial 112 and ask for the service required.

Drinking and Driving:

The maximum permitted level of alcohol in the bloodstream is 0.049%. Between 0.05% and 0.079% a fine will be imposed; 0.08% or more, a severe fine and/or driving ban for Austria are imposed. A lower limit of 0.01% is applicable to those who have held their licence under 2 years.

Driving Licence

Minimum age 18 for UK licence holder driving temporarily imported car, 16 for motorcycle (up to 50cc) with a maximum speed of 45km/h, and 18 for motorcycle (over 50cc). NOTE UK driving licences that do not have a photograph are only valid when accompanied by photographic proof of identity, e.g. passport.

Fines

On-the-spot. The officer collecting the fine should issue an official receipt. For higher fines the driver will be asked to pay a deposit and the rest within 2 weeks. Parked vehicles obstructing traffic may be towed away.

Lights

Passing lights (dipped headlights) must be used when visibility is poor due to bad weather conditions. It is prohibited to drive with side lights (position lights only).

Motorcycles

Wearing of crash helmets compulsory for both the driver and passenger. The use of dipped headlights during the day is compulsory.

Motor Insurance

Third-party compulsory, including trailers.

Passengers & Children

Children under 14 and less than 1.50 metres in height cannot travel as a front or rear seat passenger unless using suitable restraint system for their height/weight. Vehicles without such protection e.g. two-seater sports cars or vans/lorries may not be used at all to transport children under 14 years of age. Children under 14 years but over 1.50 metres in height must use the adult seat belt. Children 14 or over and over 1.35 metres in height are allowed to use a 'Dreipunktgurt' (three point seat belt) without a special child seat, if the belt does not cover the throat/neck of the child.

Seat Belts

Compulsory for front and rear seat occupants to wear seat belts, if fitted. Fine for non-compliance €35.

Speed Limits

Unless signed otherwise:

Private vehicles without trailers.

In built-up areas	50km/h
Outside built-up areas	100km/h
Motorways	130km/h

Vehicles not capable of sustaining a minimum speed of 60 km/h, are not permitted on motorways.

Mopeds	45km/h

vehicle towing a trailer not exceeding 750kg

Motorways	100km/h
Other roads	100km/h

When the weight of the trailer does not exceed that of the vehicle and the maximum weight of both vehicles does not exceed 3,500kg

Motorways	100km/h
Other roads	80km/h

Over 3,500kg

Motorways	70km/h
Other roads	60km/h

The maximum recommended speed limit for vehicles with snow chains is 40km/h. Vehicles equipped with spiked tyres must not exceed 100km/h on motorways and 80km/h on other roads.

Additional Information

Compulsory equipment in Austria: Warning triangle – Must conform to EC regulation 27 (for vehicles with more than two wheels); First-aid kit - Must be in a strong dirt proof box; Reflective Jacket/Waistcoat - Every car driver must carry one, compliant with European regulation EN471, to be used in the case of a breakdown or accident and even when setting up a warning triangle on the road. This regulation does not apply to mopeds/motorcycles, however it is recommended.

Winter equipment: all motorists are legally obliged to adapt their vehicle to winter weather conditions. Between 1 Nov and 5 Apr vehicles must be fitted with winter tyres (which must be marked M&S (mud and snow) on the side walls and have a minimum tread depth of 4mm), or all-season tyres (which must be marked M&S), and if roads have a covering of snow, slush or ice outside these dates.Theoretically snow chains on summer tyres can be used as an alternative to winter tyres where the road is heavily covered with snow and no damage to the road surface is caused by the snow chains. In practice, because road conditions and the weather

cannot be predicted, use of winter tyres is effectively compulsory.
Note: It is the driver's legal responsibility to carry the required winter equipment; therefore, it is essential to check that it is included in any hire car.

Other Rules & Requirements

All vehicles using Austrian motorways and expressways must display motorway tax sticker (vignette). The stickers, which are valid for one calendar year, two months or 10 days, may be purchased at some petrol stations located close to the border in neighbouring countries and in Austria: at the frontier, at petrol stations, post offices or in ÖAMTC offices. A special vignette, the 'Korridor Vignette' is required for vehicles travelling from Hohenehms to Horbranz on the German Border if a standard vignette has not been purchased. Fines for driving without a vignette can be severe, minimum €120. Tolls are also payable when passing through certain motorway tunnels.
The use of the horn is generally prohibited in Vienna and in the vicinity of hospitals.
When a school bus has stopped to let children on and off, indicated by a yellow flashing light, drivers travelling in the same direction are not permitted to overtake.
Spiked tyres may be used from the 1 Oct until 31 May, special local regulations may extend this period.
It is prohibited to use radar detectors.
If a voucher is required for parking they can be obtained from most tobacconists, banks and some petrol stations.

Tolls Vignette Currency Euro (€)	Car	Car Towing Caravan/Trailer
10 day vignette	€7.70	€7.70
2 month vignette	€22.20	€22.20
Annual vignette	€73.80	€73.80
A10 Tauern Autobahn	€9.50	€9.50
A13 Innsbruck-Brenner Pass	€8.00	€8.00
A16 (S16) Arlberg Expressway (Arlberg tunnel)	€8.50	
Gross Glockner Alpine Road	€28.00	
Bridges and Tunnels		
On A9 Bosruck Tunnel	€4.50	€4.50
On A9 Gleinalm Tunnel	€7.50	€7.50
On A11 Karawanken Tunnel	€6.50	€6.50

TIROL

ASCHAU **TIROL**

Aufenfeld

Aufenfeldweg 10, 6274
☎ 05282 2916 🖹 05282 291611
e-mail: info@camping-zillertal.at
web: www.camping-zillertal.at

A well-equipped family site on level meadowland backed by thickly wooded slopes.

dir: *Signed from Aschau road.*

Open: 8 Dec-2 Nov **Site:** 12HEC **Prices:** 27-34.70 **Facilities:** Wi-fi (charged) Kids' Club Play Area **Services:** **Leisure:** L P **Off-site:**

EHRWALD **TIROL**

Dr Lauth

Zugspitzstr 34, 6632
☎ 05673 2666 🖹 05673 26664
e-mail: info@campingehrwald.at
web: www.campingehrwald.at

On undulating grassland, surrounded by high conifers, below the Wetterstein mountain range. Cars may park by tents in winter.

dir: *To right of access road to Zugspitz funicular.*

Open: All Year. **Site:** 1HEC **Facilities:** **Services:** **Off-site:** P

Tiroler Zugspitze

Obermoos 1, 6632
☎ 05673 2309 🖹 05673 230951
e-mail: camping@zugspitze-resort.at
web: www.zugspitze-resort.at

A well-equipped site on several grassy terraces surrounded by woodland. Modern sanitary installations with bathrooms.

dir: *Near Zugspitz funicular station.*

Open: All Year. **Site:** 5HEC **Facilities:** **Services:** **Leisure:** P

FIEBERBRUNN TIROL

Tirol-Camp

6391
☎ 05354 56666 🖷 05354 52516
e-mail: office@tirol-camp.at
web: www.tirol-camp.at

A summer and winter site in pleasant Alpine surroundings.

Open: 6 Dec-Apr & 20 May-6 Nov **Site:** 7HEC **Prices:** 28.50-42 **Facilities:** Kids' Club Play Area **Services:** **Leisure:** L P

FÜGEN TIROL

Zillertal

Gageringerstr 1, 6263
☎ 05288 62203 🖷 05288 622034
e-mail: info@zillertal-camping.at
web: www.zillertal-camping.at

Meadow setting around a farm with fine views of the surrounding mountains. Dogs are welcome except July to 15 August.

dir: *1km N of Fügen on B169.*

GPS: 47.3592, 11.8517

Open: All Year. **Site:** 4HEC **Prices:** 22.90-35.50 **Facilities:** Wi-fi (charged) Kids' Club Play Area **Services:** **Leisure:** P **Off-site:** L

HAIMING TIROL

Center Oberland

Bundestr 9, 6425
☎ 05266 88294 🖷 05266 882949
e-mail: camping-oberland@qmx.at
web: www.camping-oberland.at

On a sloping meadow in a picturesque mountain setting. A variety of sports facilities are available.

dir: *Off B171 at Km485.*

Open: May-Oct **Site:** 4HEC **Prices:** 21.40-25 **Facilities:** Wi-fi (charged) Play Area **Services:** **Off-site:** L P R

HALL IN TIROL TIROL

Camping Schwimmbad Hall

Scheidensteinstr 26, 6060
☎ 0699 15855268
e-mail: h.niedrist@hall.ag
web: www.hall.ag/tourismus

400m from the historic town, this tidy site has leisure facilities including mini-golf and tennis court.

GPS: 47.2839, 11.5003

Open: May-Sep **Site:** 1.2HEC **Prices:** 17.50-19.50 **Facilities:** Wi-fi Play Area **Services:** **Leisure:** P **Off-site:**

HEITERWANG TIROL

Heiterwangersee

Hotel Fischer am See, 6611
☎ 05674 5116 🖷 05674 5260
e-mail: hotel@fischeramsee.at
web: www.fischeramsee.at

A quiet meadow location beside a lake behind the hotel.

dir: *By Hotel Fischer am See.*

Open: All Year. **Site:** 1HEC **Prices:** 26 **Facilities:** Play Area **Services:** **Leisure:** L

HUBEN TIROL

Ötztaler Naturcamping

6444
☎ 05253 5855 🖷 05253 5538
e-mail: info@oetztalernaturcamping.com
web: www.oetztalernaturcamping.com

A well-kept site in a beautiful wooded location beside a mountain stream.

dir: *S of town, signed from Km27 on B186.*

Open: All Year. **Site:** 0.5HEC **Prices:** 20.40-22 **Facilities:** Wi-fi (charged) **Services:** **Off-site:** P

IMST TIROL

Campingpark Imst-West

Langgasse 62, 6460
☎ 05412 66293 🖷 05412 6629319
e-mail: fink.franz@aon.at
web: www.imst-west.com

On open meadowland in the Langgasse area.

dir: *Off bypass near turning for the Pitztal.*

GPS: 47.2286, 10.7433

Open: All Year. **Site:** 1HEC **Prices:** 15-19 **Facilities:** Wi-fi Play Area **Services:** **Off-site:** L P R

INNSBRUCK TIROL

Camping Kranebitterhof

Kranebitter Allee 216, 6020
☎ 0512 279558 🖷 0512 279558 140
e-mail: info@camping-kranebitterhof.at
web: www.camping-kranebitterhof.at

A comfortable and functional site located ten minutes from Innsbruck's historical city centre, between the river Inn and the massive mountain ranges of Tirol.

Open: All Year. **Site:** 1.5HEC **Prices:** 25-30 **Facilities:** Wi-fi Play Area **Services:** **Off-site:** L R

ITTER TIROL

Schlossberg

Brixentalerstr 11, 6305
05335 2181 05335 2182
e-mail: info@camping-itter.at
web: www.camping-itter.at

A family site on terraced meadowland below Schloss Itter on the Brixental Ache. Good leisure facilities.

dir: *2km W on B170.*

Open: Dec-15 Nov **Site:** 4HEC **Prices:** 19-28 **Facilities:** Wi-fi (charged) Kids' Club Play Area **Services:** **Leisure:** P R **Off-site:** L

KITZBÜHEL TIROL

Schwarzsee

6370
05356 62806 05356 6447930
e-mail: office@bruggerhof-camping.at
web: www.bruggerhof-camping.at

Meadowland site on the edge of a wood behind a large restaurant.

dir: *B170 from town towards Wörgl, 2km turn right, 400m after Schwarzsee railway station.*

Open: All Year. **Site:** 6HEC **Facilities:** **Services:** **Leisure:** L P

KÖSSEN TIROL

Wilder Kaiser

Kranebittau 18, 6345
05375 6444 05375 2113
e-mail: info@eurocamp-koessen.com
web: www.eurocamp-koessen.com

Situated in a lovely position below Unterberg. The level site is adjoined on three sides by woodland. Kids' club in July and August.

dir: *Road to Unterberg lift & turn right for 200m.*

GPS: 47.6539, 12.415

Open: 8 Dec-6 Nov **Site:** 5HEC **Prices:** 20.40-24.40 **Facilities:** Wi-fi (charged) Kids' Club Play Area **Services:** **Leisure:** P **Off-site:** L

KRAMSACH TIROL

Seeblick Toni

The Camping and Caravanning Club The Friendly Club

Moosen 46, 6233
05337 63544 05337 63544305
e-mail: info@camping-seeblick.at
web: www.camping-seeblick.at

Rural site near the Brantlhof above Lake Reintaler. A kids' club is available during high season.

C&CC Report *A simply beautiful base for some Tyrolean relaxation, for hiking and for day trips to Innsbruck, Kitzbühel and Italy. With both summer and winter activities, a lakeside location, great places to visit and excellent washblocks, Seeblick Toni is top-notch at any time of year. The panoramic traditional restaurant offers superb local cuisine.*

dir: *From Inntal Motorway (Rattenberg/Kramsach exit) follow signs 'Zu den Seen' for about 3km, then drive through Seehof site.*

GPS: 47.4633, 11.9003

Open: All Year. **Site:** 4.5HEC **Prices:** 29.50-37.50 **Facilities:** Wi-fi (charged) Kids' Club Play Area **Services:** **Leisure:** L

Stadlerhof

6233
05337 63371 05337 65311
e-mail: camping.stadlerhof@chello.at
web: www.camping-stadlerhof.at

A pleasant, year-round site on the Reintaler See with well-defined pitches and good leisure facilities.

dir: *Via A12.*

Open: All Year. **Site:** 3HEC **Prices:** 24-27.50 **Facilities:** Wi-fi (charged) Play Area **Services:** **Leisure:** L P **Off-site:** R

KUFSTEIN TIROL

Kufstein

Salurner Str 36, 6330
05372 62229 05372 636894
e-mail: kufstein@hotelbaeren.at
web: www.hotelbaeren.at

A pleasant location with a variety of sports facilities.

dir: *1km W of Kufstein between River Inn & B171.*

Open: May-Oct **Site:** 1HEC **Facilities:** **Services:** **Off-site:** L P R

Parkcamping Hager

Kufsteinerstrasse 38, 6336
☎ 05372 64170 ▤ 05332 7296635
e-mail: office@hager-stb.at
Site situated on level meadowland.
Open: All Year. **Site:** 0.5HEC **Prices:** 22-25 **Facilities:** Play Area **Services:** **Off-site:** L R

LANDECK TIROL

Riffler

6500
☎ 05442 64898 ▤ 05442 648984
e-mail: lorenz.schimpfoessl@aon.at
web: www.camping-riffler.at
Site on meadowland between residential housing and the banks of the Sanna.
Open: Jun-Apr **Site:** 0.2HEC **Prices:** 22.10 Mobile home hire 175 **Facilities:** **Services:** **Leisure:** R
Off-site: P

LÄNGENFELD TIROL

Camping Ötztal

6444
☎ 05253 5348 ▤ 05253 53484
e-mail: info@camping-oetztal.com
web: www.camping-oetztal.com
Meadowland with some tall trees on the edge of woodland.
dir: *Turn right off E186 at fire station.*
GPS: 47.0723, 10.9640
Open: All Year. **Site:** 2.6HEC **Facilities:** Wi-fi (charged) Play Area **Services:**
Off-site: P

LERMOOS TIROL

Happy Camp Hofherr

Garmischer Str 21, 6631
☎ 05673 2980 ▤ 05673 29805
e-mail: info@camping-lermoos.com
web: www.camping-lermoos.com
Well-equipped site in a wooded location with fine views of the surrounding mountains.
dir: *0.5km from town, off B187 towards Ehrwald.*
Open: 16 Dec-Oct **Site:** 0.8HEC **Facilities:**
Services: **Off-site:** P R

LEUTASCH TIROL

Holiday-Camping

6105
☎ 05214 65700 ▤ 05214 657030
e-mail: info@holiday-camping.at
web: www.holiday-camping.at
A modern site on level grassland screened by trees on the Leutascher Ache.
dir: *Off B313 Mittenwald-Scharnitz towards Leutasch.*
GPS: 47.3984, 11.1797
Open: 7 Dec-5 Nov **Site:** 2.6HEC **Prices:** 18-28
Facilities: Wi-fi (charged) Play Area
Services: **Leisure:** P R

LIENZ TIROL

Falken

Falkenweg 7, 9900
☎ 04852 64022 ▤ 04852 640226
e-mail: camping.falken@tirol.com
web: www.camping-falken.com
On open ground on the outskirts of the town with modern sanitary facilities.
dir: *S of Lienz, signed from B100.*
Open: 21 Dec-19 Oct **Site:** 2.5HEC **Facilities:**
Services: **Off-site:** L P R

MAURACH TIROL

Karwendel

6212
☎ 05243 6116 ▤ 05243 20036
e-mail: info@karwendel-camping.at
web: www.karwendel-camping.at
On a level meadow with fine views of the surrounding mountains.
dir: *Off B181 in town onto Pertisau road.*
Open: All Year. **Site:** 1.8HEC **Facilities:**
Services: **Off-site:** L P

MAYRHOFEN TIROL

Mayrhofen

Laubichl 125, 6290
☎ 05285 6258051 ▤ 05285 6258060
e-mail: camping@alpenparadies.com
web: www.alpenparadies.com
A modern site with good facilities, a short walk from the village.
dir: *Near farm at N entrance to village.*
Open: 21 Dec-Oct **Site:** 2HEC **Prices:** 20.60-25.80
Facilities: Wi-fi (charged) Play Area **Services:**
Leisure: P **Off-site:** R

AUSTRIA

NATTERS TIROL

Natterer See

Natterer See 1, 6161
☎ 0512 546732 🖷 0512 54673216
e-mail: info@natterersee.com
web: www.natterersee.com

A terraced site beautifully situated among woodland and mountains. Extensive entertainments programme.

dir: *Brenner motorway exit Innsbruck Süd, via Natters, onto B182 & signed.*

GPS: 47.2383, 11.3389

Open: All Year. **Site:** 9HEC Wi-fi (charged) Kids' Club Play Area **Prices:** 19.90-35.10 **Facilities:** Wi-fi (charged) Kids' Club Play Area **Services:** **Leisure:** L P

NAUDERS TIROL

Alpencamping Nauders

6543
☎ 05473 87217 🖷 05473 8721750
e-mail: alpencamping@tirol.com
web: www.camping-nauders.at

A year-round family site in a delightful Alpine location with good recreational facilities.

dir: *Via B315.*

Open: 17 Dec-Oct **Site:** 3HEC **Facilities:** **Services:** **Off-site:** L

PETTNEU AM ARLBERG TIROL

Arlberg

6574
☎ 05448 22266 🖷 05448 2226630
e-mail: info@camping-arlberg.at
web: www.camping-arlberg.at

Site in the Tyrolean mountains suitable for hiking and mountaineering in summer and close to winter sports resorts.

dir: *S16 exit for Pettneu.*

Open: All Year. **Site:** 4.8HEC **Facilities:** **Services:** **Leisure:** P R

PILL TIROL

Plankenhof

6136
☎ 05242 641950 🖷 05242 72344
e-mail: m.khuen-belasi@tirol.com

Site in meadow.

dir: *On B171 near Gasthof Plankenhof.*

Open: May-1 Oct **Site:** 0.6HEC **Prices:** 24-27 **Facilities:** **Services:** **Off-site:** L P R

PRUTZ TIROL

Aktiv-Camping Prutz

Pontlatzstrasse 22, 6522
☎ 05472 2648 🖷 05472 26484
e-mail: info@aktiv-camping.at
web: www.aktiv-camping.at

A pleasant site in a beautiful mountain setting, close to the Inn River and Kaunertal Glacier, with modern facilities.

dir: *From E60 onto B180, via Reschen Pass.*

GPS: 47.0803, 10.6594

Open: All Year. **Site:** 1.5HEC **Prices:** 17.40-29.50 **Facilities:** Wi-fi (charged) Play Area **Services:** **Leisure:** R **Off-site:** L P

REUTTE TIROL

Seespitze

6600
☎ 05672 78121 🖷 05672 63372
e-mail: agrar.breitenwang@aon.at
web: www.camping-plansee.at

A quiet location on the shore of Plansee lake.

GPS: 47.4739, 10.7869

Open: May-15 Oct **Site:** 2HEC **Prices:** 19-20 **Facilities:** Play Area **Services:** **Leisure:** L **Off-site:**

Sennalpe

6600
☎ 05672 78115 🖷 05672 63372
e-mail: agrar.breitenwang@aon.at
web: www.camping-plansee.at

A quiet location next to the lake.

dir: *On Reutte-Oberammergau road 200m from Hotel Forelle.*

Open: 15 Dec-15 Oct **Site:** 4HEC **Prices:** 18-20 **Facilities:** Play Area **Services:** **Leisure:** L **Off-site:**

RIED BEI LANDECK TIROL

Dreiländereck

6531
☎ 05472 6025 🖷 05472 60254
e-mail: camping-dreilandereck@tirol.com
web: www.tirolcamping.at

Level site in centre of village beside a lake with spectacular views.

Open: All Year. **Site:** 1HEC **Facilities:** **Services:** **Off-site:** L P R

RINN TIROL

Judenstein

Judenstein 40, 6074
05223 78098 05223 7887715
e-mail: kommunalgmbh@rinn.tirol.gv.at
web: www.tiscover.at/camping.judenstein
A wooded location with fine views.
dir: *From motorway exit Hall.*
Open: May-Sep **Site:** 0.6HEC **Facilities:**
Services: **Off-site:**

ST JOHANN TIROL

Michelnhof

Weiberndorf 6, 6380
05352 62584 05352 625844
e-mail: camping@michelnhof.at
web: www.camping-michelnhof.at
dir: *1.5km S via B161 St-Johann-Kitzbühel.*
Open: All Year. **Site:** 3HEC **Facilities:**
Services: **Off-site:** P R

SEEFELD TIROL

Alpin

Leutascher Str 810, 6100
05212 4848 05212 4868
e-mail: info@camp-alpin.at
web: www.camp-alpin.at
Terraced site on an alpine plateau with fine mountain views, open for summer vacations and winter sports.
Open: All Year. **Site:** 3HEC **Prices:** 15-32.70
Facilities: Wi-fi (charged) Kids' Club Play Area
Services: **Off-site:** L P

SÖLDEN TIROL

Sölden

Wohlfahrtstr 22, 6450
05254 26270 05254 26275
e-mail: info@camping-soelden.com
web: www.camping-soelden.com
Situated on meadowland on the Ötztaler tributary. Beautiful views of the surrounding mountains.
dir: *By Grauer Bär Inn at Km36 on the B186.*
Open: Jan-Apr, Jul-Dec **Site:** 1.3HEC
Prices: 23.20-25.40 **Facilities:** Play Area
Services: **Off-site:** L P

THIERSEE TIROL

Rueppenhof

Seebauern 8, 6335
05376 5694
e-mail: rueppenhof@gmail.com
web: www.rueppenhof.com
Site made up of several meadows surrounding a farm that lies on the banks of the lake.
dir: *A12 exit Kufstein-Nord, signed Thiersee.*
Open: 15 Apr-15 Oct **Site:** 1.5HEC **Prices:** 15.50-18.70
Facilities: Play Area **Services:** **Leisure:** L
Off-site: P

UMHAUSEN TIROL

Ötztal Arena

6441
05255 5390 05255 5390
e-mail: info@oetztal-camping.at
web: www.oetztal-camping.at
dir: *Signed from B186.*
Open: All Year. **Site:** 1HEC **Prices:** 19.40-20
Facilities: **Services:**
Leisure: L R

UNTERPERFUSS TIROL

Farm

6175
05232 2209 05232 22094
e-mail: brangerbrau@aon.at
web: www.brangeralm.at
Modern site on gently sloping meadow in a beautiful mountain setting.
dir: *W end of village near Amberg railway & main road.*
Open: All Year. **Site:** 1.5HEC **Facilities:**
Services: **Off-site:**

VÖLS TIROL

Völs

Bahnhofstr 10, 6176
0512 303533
dir: *Motorway exit Innsbruck-Kranebitten.*
Open: Apr-Nov **Site:** 0.4HEC **Facilities:**
Services: **Off-site:** L P R

WAIDRING TIROL

Steinplatte

Unterwasser 43, 6384
☎ 05353 5345 05353 5406
e-mail: camping-steinplatte@aon.at
web: www.camping-steinplatte.at

On a level meadow with fine panoramic views of the surrounding mountains.

Open: All Year. **Site:** 4HEC **Facilities:** **Services:** **Leisure:** L **Off-site:** P R

WALCHSEE TIROL

Seespitz

Seespitz 1, 6344
☎ 05374 5359 05374 5845
e-mail: info@camping-seespitz.at
web: www.camping-seespitz.at

Pleasant surroundings beside the Walchsee with good recreational facilities.

dir: *Between B172 & lake.*

Open: All Year. **Site:** 4HEC **Prices:** 18.80-20.23 **Facilities:** Play Area **Services:** **Leisure:** L **Off-site:** P

Terrassencamping Süd-See

Seestr 76, 6344
☎ 05374 5339 05374 5529
e-mail: campingwalchsee@aon.at
web: www.camp-sud-see.com

A lakeside site in wooded surroundings with extensive terracing and fine mountain views.

dir: *0.5km W on B172 onto no through road, continue 1.5km.*

Open: All Year. **Site:** 11HEC **Prices:** 19.50-21.50 **Facilities:** **Services:** **Leisure:** L **Off-site:** P

WEER TIROL

Alpencamping Mark

Bundesstrasse 12, 6114
☎ 05224 68146 05244 681466
e-mail: alpcamp.mark@aon.at
web: www.alpencampingmark.com

Situated on meadowland by a farm on the edge of a forest.

dir: *Off B171.*

GPS: 47.3061, 11.6494

Open: Apr-Oct **Site:** 2HEC **Prices:** 15-22.70 **Facilities:** Wi-fi (charged) Kids' Club Play Area **Services:** **Leisure:** P **Off-site:**

WESTENDORF TIROL

Panorama

Mühltal 70, 6363
☎ 05334 6166 05334 6843
e-mail: info@panoramacamping.at
web: www.panoramacamping.at

A beautiful Alpine setting with modern facilities.

dir: *B170 W towards Wörgl.*

Open: 14 Dec-Oct **Site:** 2.2HEC **Facilities:** **Services:** **Off-site:** P

ZELL AM ZILLER TIROL

Hofer

Gerlosstr 33, 6280
☎ 05282 2248 05282 22488
e-mail: info@campingdorf.at
web: www.campingdorf.at

On meadowland with some fruit trees.

dir: *Site at end of Zillertal off road to Gerlos Pass.*

Open: All Year. **Site:** 1.5HEC **Facilities:** **Services:** **Leisure:** P

CARINTHIA

DELLACH KÄRNTEN

Neubauer

9872
☎ 04766 2532 04766 25324
e-mail: info@camping-neubauer.at
web: www.camping-neubauer.at

A terraced site with direct access to the Millstättersee.

dir: *Off B100 Leinz-Spittal, signed in village.*

Open: May-15 Oct **Site:** 1.5HEC **Facilities:** **Services:** **Leisure:** L **Off-site:**

DELLACH IM DRAUTAL KÄRNTEN

Waldbad

9772
☎ 04714 288 04714 2343
e-mail: info@camping-waldbad.at
web: www.camping-waldbad.at

A small site in a delightful wooded setting with two large swimming pools.

dir: *Off A10 at Spittal onto B100.*

Open: May-Sep **Site:** 3HEC **Prices:** 16-25 **Facilities:** Wi-fi (charged) Play Area **Services:** **Leisure:** P **Off-site:** R

Site 6HEC (site size) grass sand stone little shade partly shaded mainly shaded bungalows for hire (static) caravans for hire tents for hire no dogs site fully accessible for wheelchairs
Prices amount quoted is per night, for 2 adults and car, plus tent or caravan. Mobile home hire is a weekly rate.

DÖBRIACH KÄRNTEN

Brunner am See

Glanzerstr 108, 9873
☎ 04246 7189 🖹 04246 718914
e-mail: office@camping-brunner.at
web: www.camping-brunner.at

A tidily arranged site with award-winning facilities. Situated on the banks of Lake Millstatt with a private bathing area.

dir: *Off A10, at E end of Lake Millstatt.*

GPS: 46.7676, 13.6485

Open: All Year. **Site:** 3.5HEC **Prices:** 12.60-35 **Facilities:** Wi-fi (charged) Kids' Club Play Area **Services:** **Leisure:** L **Off-site:** P

Burgstaller

Seefeldstr 16, 9873
☎ 04246 7774 🖹 04246 77744
e-mail: info@burgstaller.co.at
web: www.burgstaller.co.at

A quiet site 100m from the lake, with modern facilities.

dir: *From B98 towards SE end of Lake Millstatt for 1km.*

GPS: 46.7697, 13.6481

Open: 15 Apr-6 Nov **Site:** 12HEC **Prices:** 17.90-42.50 **Facilities:** Wi-fi (charged) Kids' Club Play Area **Services:** **Leisure:** L P

DÖLLACH KÄRNTEN

Zirknitzer

9843
☎ 04825 451 🖹 04825 451
e-mail: camping.zirknitzer@utanet.at
web: web.utanet.at/zirknitp

Beside the River Möu.

dir: *Between Km8 & Km9 on B107 Glocknerstr.*

Open: All Year. **Site:** 0.6HEC **Prices:** 17.60 Mobile home hire 280 **Facilities:** **Services:** **Leisure:** R **Off-site:** P

FAAK AM SEE KÄRNTEN

Strandcamping Arneitz

Seeuferlandesstrasse 53, 9583
☎ 04254 2137 🖹 04254 3044
e-mail: camping@arneitz.at
web: www.arneitz.at

On a wooded peninsula jutting into the Faakersee with good sports facilities.

Open: 28 Apr-Sep **Site:** 6HEC **Prices:** 31.90-41.40 **Facilities:** Wi-fi (charged) Play Area **Services:** **Leisure:** L

Strandcamping Sandbank

Badeweg 3, 9583
☎ 04254 2261 🖹 04254 3943
e-mail: info@camping-sandbank.at
web: www.camping-sandbank.at

A partially shaded site between the lakeside and the road.

dir: *From road by Hotel Fürst.*

Open: May-25 Sep **Site:** 5HEC **Facilities:** **Services:** **Leisure:** L **Off-site:**

FELDKIRCHEN KÄRNTEN

Seewirt-Spiess

Maltschach am See 2, 9560
☎ 04277 2637 🖹 04277 26374
e-mail: office@seewirl-spiess.com
web: www.seewirl-spiess.com

A pleasant wooded location on the shore of the Maltschacher See.

dir: *Off B95 towards Klagenfurt.*

Open: May-Sep **Site:** 1.2HEC **Facilities:** **Services:** **Leisure:** L **Off-site:** P

HEILIGENBLUT KÄRNTEN

Grossglockner

9844
☎ 04824 2048 🖹 04824 24622
e-mail: nationalpark-camping@heiligenblut.at
web: www.heiligenblut.at/nationalpark-camping

Meadowland site surrounded by woodland within a national park.

dir: *Signed.*

Open: May-Oct & Dec-Apr **Site:** 2.5HEC **Prices:** 20-25 **Facilities:** Wi-fi (charged) Play Area **Services:** **Leisure:** R **Off-site:** P

HERMAGOR KÄRNTEN

Naturpark Schluga Seecamping

9620
☎ 04282 2760 🖹 04282 288120
e-mail: camping@schluga.com
web: www.schluga.com

A well-equipped family site 200m north of a lake in meadowland with some terraces and fine views.

dir: *6km E of Hermagor.*

Open: 10 May-20 Sep **Site:** 8.8HEC **Facilities:** Wi-fi (charged) Kids' Club Play Area **Services:** **Leisure:** L **Off-site:** R

Schluga Camping

9620
☎ 04282 2051 ▤ 04282 288120
e-mail: camping@schluga.com
web: www.schluga.com

Well-equipped family site in a rural setting 4km from Presseger See.

Open: All Year. **Site:** 5.5HEC **Facilities:** Wi-fi (charged) Kids' Club Play Area **Services:** **Leisure:** L P **Off-site:** R

KEUTSCHACH KÄRNTEN

Camping Reichmann

Reauz 5, 9074
☎ 0664 1430437
e-mail: info@camping-reichmann.at
web: www.camping-reichmann.at

On the east bank of Rauschelesee Lake, with a pebble beach. Sporting facilities include football, swimming and fishing.

Open: May-Sep **Site:** 3.2HEC **Facilities:** Wi-fi (charged) Play Area **Services:** **Leisure:** L

Strandcamping Süd

9074
☎ 04273 2773 ▤ 04273 2773-4
e-mail: info@strandcampingbruecklersued.at
web: www.keutschachsued.at

A pleasant setting among shrubs and trees on south side of the Keutschachersee.

dir: *Motorway exit Valden, towards Keutschacher-Seental.*

Open: May-Sep **Site:** 2HEC **Facilities:** **Services:** **Leisure:** L

KLAGENFURT KÄRNTEN

Strandbad

9020
☎ 0463 5216391 ▤ 0463 5216395
e-mail: camping@stw.at
web: www.camping-klagenfurt.at

Large site divided into sections by trees and bushes.

dir: *B83 from town centre towards Velden, left just outside town towards bathing area.*

Open: 15 Apr-Sep **Site:** 4HEC **Facilities:** **Services:** **Leisure:** L

KÖTSCHACH-MAUTHEN KÄRNTEN

Alpencamp Kötschach-Mauthen

9640
☎ 04715 429 ▤ 04715 429
e-mail: info@alpencamp.at
web: www.alpencamp.at

On level meadowland beside River Gail with good facilities for water sports.

dir: *In S of village, off B110, 0.8km towards Lesachtal.*

Open: 15 Dec-Oct **Site:** 1.8HEC **Prices:** 17.40-25.60 Mobile home hire 329-502 **Facilities:** Wi-fi (charged) Play Area **Services:** **Off-site:** P R

MALTA KÄRNTEN

Maltatal

9854
☎ 04733 2340 ▤ 04733 23416
e-mail: info@maltacamp.at
web: www.maltacamp.at

On a gently rising alpine meadow with breathtaking views of the surrounding mountains.

dir: *Off B99 in Gmünd for 5.5km through Malta Valley.*

GPS: 46.9497, 13.5094

Open: 31 Mar-Oct **Site:** 3.5HEC **Prices:** 21.50-30.90 **Facilities:** Wi-fi (charged) **Services:** **Leisure:** P R

OBERVELLACH KÄRNTEN

Activ Sport Erlebnis Camp

9821
☎ 04782 2727 ▤ 04782 27274
e-mail: info@sporterlebnis.at
web: www.sporterlebnis.at

Family campsite specialising in leisure activities such as rafting, kayaking etc.

dir: *A10 at Spittal exit onto B100 signed Lienz-Mallnitz then B106 signed Obervellach.*

Open: May-Sep **Site:** 10HEC **Prices:** 16-21 **Facilities:** Wi-fi Play Area **Services:** **Leisure:** R **Off-site:** P

OSSIACH KÄRNTEN

Ossiach

9570
04243 436 04243 8171
e-mail: martinz@camping.at
web: www.terrassen.camping.at
Divided into pitches with generally well-placed terraces.
dir: *Off B94 on E bank of Kale Ossiacher.*
Open: May-Sep **Site:** 10HEC **Facilities:** **Services:** **Leisure:** L

Parth

9570
04243 27440 04243 274415
e-mail: camping@parth.at
web: www.parth.at
On hilly ground on S shore of the lake. Steep, but there are some terraces.
dir: *Off B94 on S bank of Lake Ossiach.*
Open: 27 Dec-6 Nov **Site:** 1.8HEC **Facilities:** **Services:** **Leisure:** L **Off-site:**

Seecamping Berghof

Ossiachersee-Süduferstr 241, 9523
04242 41133 04242 4113330
e-mail: office@seecamping-berghof.at
web: www.seecamping-berghof.at
Attractive terraced meadowland with a 0.8km-long promenade with bathing areas.
dir: *E shore of Lake Ossiacher.*
Open: Apr-17 Oct **Site:** 10HEC **Facilities:** **Services:** **Leisure:** L

SACHSENBURG KÄRNTEN

Drau Camping

Ringmauergasse 8, 9751
04769 3131 04769 292520
e-mail: info@draucamping.at
web: www.draucamping.at
A modern family site with good facilities in a delightful mountain setting.
dir: *A10 between Spittal & Lienz.*
Open: May-Sep **Site:** 1.3HEC **Prices:** 19-25 **Facilities:** Wi-fi (charged) Play Area **Off-site:** P

ST PRIMUS KÄRNTEN

Strandcamping Turnersee Breznik

9123
04239 2350 04239 235032
e-mail: info@breznik.at
web: www.breznik.at
A quiet site in a picturesque mountain setting with a variety of recreational facilities. Kids' club available in high season.
dir: *B70 Klagenfurt-Graz towards Klopeinersee.*
Open: 17 Apr-2 Oct **Site:** 7.5HEC
Prices: 17.10-27.60 Mobile home hire 280-686 **Facilities:** Wi-fi (charged) Kids' Club Play Area **Services:** **Leisure:** L **Off-site:**

SEEBODEN KÄRNTEN

Strandcamping Winkler

Seepromenade 33, 9871
04762 81822 04762 81822
web: www.campsite.at/strandcamping-winkler
On the lake Millstätter See, pitches are reached by asphalt paths. Ideal for exploring the surrounding mountainous countryside.
Open: May-1 Oct **Site:** 0.7HEC **Prices:** 24-31.40
Facilities: **Services:** **Leisure:** L
Off-site:

SPITTAL AN DER DRAU KÄRNTEN

Draufluss

Schwaig 10, 9800
04762 2466 04762 2466
e-mail: drauwirt@aon.at
web: www.drauwirt.com
A long, narrow riverside site, partly surrounded by a hedge.
dir: *From town centre to river towards Goldeckbahn.*
Open: May-Sep **Site:** 0.7HEC **Facilities:** **Services:** **Leisure:** R **Off-site:** P

STOCKENBOI KÄRNTEN

Ronacher

Möse 6, 9714
04761 256 04761 2564
e-mail: info@campingronacher.at
web: www.campingronacher.at
Situated on meadow between forest slopes, gently sloping to the shore of Weissensee.
dir: *Approach for caravans via Weissensee.*
Open: May-10 Oct **Site:** 1.7HEC **Facilities:** Wi-fi (charged) Play Area **Services:**
Leisure: L

VILLACH — KÄRNTEN

Camping Gerli

St Georgenerstr 140, 9500
☎ 04242 57402 🖷 04242 582909
e-mail: gerli.meidl@utanet.at
web: www.campgerli.com

Level, isolated site with a heated swimming pool.

dir: *Off B100, turn right just before Villach & continue 2km.*

Open: All Year. **Site:** 2.3HEC **Prices:** 15-18.90 **Facilities:** Wi-fi Play Area **Services:** **Leisure:** P **Off-site:** P

Seecamping Berghof

Ossiacher See Süduferstr 241, 9523
☎ 04242 41133 🖷 04242 41133 30
e-mail: office@seecamping-berghof.at
web: www.seecamping-berghof.at

On the southern shore of Lake Ossiach, pitches overlook the lake or have wonderful mountain views. Wide range of leisure facilities including a sailing and surfing school and live evening entertainment. Dogs allowed except July and August.

GPS: 46.6533, 13.9333

Open: 15 Apr-16 Oct **Site:** 10HEC **Prices:** 18.80-28.30 Mobile home hire 370-685 **Facilities:** Wi-fi (charged) Kids' Club Play Area **Services:** **Leisure:** L

WERTSCHACH — KÄRNTEN

Alpenfreude

9612
☎ 04256 2708 🖷 04256 27084
e-mail: camping.alpenfreude@aon.at
web: www.alpenfreude.at

With wonderful views of the surrounding mountains, well-established family site with large swimming pool area.

Open: May-Sep **Site:** 5HEC **Prices:** 12.90-19 Mobile home hire 285-385 **Facilities:** Wi-fi Play Area **Services:** **Leisure:** P **Off-site:**

STYRIA

AUSSEE, BAD — STEIERMARK

Camping An Der Traun

Grundlseer Str 21, 8990
☎ 03622 54565 🖷 03622 52427
e-mail: office@staudnwirt.at
web: www.staudnwirt.at

Pleasant wooded surroundings.

dir: *2.5km from Bad Aussee towards Grundlsee.*

Open: All Year. **Site:** 0.4HEC **Prices:** 17.20 **Facilities:** Wi-fi Play Area **Services:** **Leisure:** R **Off-site:** L

GROSSLOBMING — STEIERMARK

Camping Murinsel

Teichweg 1, 8734
☎ 0664 3045045 🖷 03512 600884
e-mail: office@camping-murinsel.at
web: www.camping-murinsel.at

Located next to a lake, a peaceful and secure site.

dir: *4km from S36.*

GPS: 47.1933, 14.8067

Open: 1wk before Etr-15 Oct **Site:** 5HEC **Prices:** 15-22 **Facilities:** Wi-fi Play Area **Services:** **Leisure:** L R

HIRSCHEGG — STEIERMARK

Hirschegg

8584
☎ 03141 2201
e-mail: info@camping-hirschegg.at
web: www.camping-hirschegg.at

Delightful Alpine setting.

dir: *A2 towards Klagenfurt, exit Modriach.*

Open: All Year. **Site:** 2HEC **Prices:** 17.80-20.80 **Facilities:** **Services:** **Off-site:** L R

LANGENWANG-MÜRTZAL — STEIERMARK

Europa Camping

Siglstr 5, 8665
☎ 03854 2950
e-mail: europa.camping.stmk@aon.at
web: www.campsite.at/europa.camping.langenwang

On level meadow with some trees, surrounded by hedges. The site occupies an attractive alpine setting.

dir: *B306 (E7) bypasses town. Exit 6km S of Mürzzuschlag.*

Open: All Year. **Site:** 0.55HEC **Prices:** 16.40 **Facilities:** Play Area **Services:** **Off-site:** L R

LEIBNITZ STEIERMARK

Leibnitz

R-H-Bartsch-Gasse 33, 8430
☎ 03452 82463 🖷 03452 71491
e-mail: camping@leibnitz.at
web: www.camping-steiermark.at

A well-equipped site in pleasant wooded surroundings with plenty of leisure facilities.

dir: *Signed W of town.*

Open: May-15 Oct **Site:** 0.7HEC **Facilities:** **Services:** **Leisure:** P R **Off-site:** L

MARIA LANKOWITZ STEIERMARK

Piberstein

Am See 1, 8591
☎ 03144 7095910 🖷 03144 7095974
e-mail: office@piberstein.at
web: www.piberstein.at

Large well-equipped site surrounding a series of lakes. Plenty of sports facilities.

dir: *S of Maria Lankowitz towards Pack.*

Open: May-15 Oct **Site:** 5.6HEC **Facilities:** **Services:** **Leisure:** L **Off-site:**

MITTERNDORF, BAD STEIERMARK

Camping & Pension Grimmingsicht

8983
☎ 03623 2985 🖷 03623 29854
e-mail: camping@grimmingsicht.at
web: www.grimmingsicht.at

Small, friendly campsite, quietly situated near a village with beautiful views of the surrounding mountains.

dir: *Off B145.*

GPS: 47.5551, 13.9224

Open: All Year. **Site:** 0.6HEC **Prices:** 18.42-20.92 Mobile home hire 275-325 **Facilities:** Play Area **Services:** **Leisure:** R **Off-site:** P

MÜHLEN STEIERMARK

Camping am Badesee

Hitzmannsdorf 2, 8822
☎ 03586 2418 🖷 03586 2204
e-mail: office@camping-am-badesee.at
web: www.camping-am-badesee.at

A small family site with direct access to the lake. Ideally located fo fishing and hiking.

dir: *N via B92, signed.*

GPS: 47.0369, 14.4875

Open: 30 Apr-Sep **Site:** 1.5HEC **Prices:** 16-21.40 **Facilities:** Wi-fi Kids' Club Play Area **Services:** **Leisure:** L **Off-site:** P

OBERWÖLZ STEIERMARK

Rothenfels

8832
☎ 0664 1412514
e-mail: camping@rothenfels.at
web: www.camping-rothenfels.at

Set in the grounds of a castle with picturesque Alpine surroundings. Good recreational facilities.

dir: *On SE outskirts.*

Open: All Year. **Site:** 8HEC **Facilities:** **Services:** **Leisure:** L **Off-site:** P R

ST GEORGEN STEIERMARK

Olachgut

8861
☎ 03532 2162 🖷 03532 21624
e-mail: office@olachgut.at
web: www.olachgut.at

On a level meadow, surrounded by beautiful mountain scenery. The site owns a farm with a riding school.

dir: *Signed.*

Open: All Year. **Site:** 10HEC **Prices:** 22-23 **Facilities:** Wi-fi (charged) Play Area **Services:** **Leisure:** L **Off-site:** P R

ST SEBASTIAN STEIERMARK

Erlaufsee

Erholungszentrum, Erlaufseestr 3, 8630
☎ 03882 4937 🖷 03882 214822
e-mail: gemeinde@st-sebastian.at
web: www.st-sebastian.at

A picturesque Alpine setting in woodland, 100m from the lake.

dir: *Signed.*

Open: May-15 Sep **Site:** 1HEC **Prices:** 16.50 **Facilities:** **Services:** **Off-site:** L P R

SCHLADMING STEIERMARK

Camping-Restaurant Zirngast

Linke Ennsau 633, 8970
☎ 03687 23195 🖹 03687 231954
e-mail: camping@zirngast.at
web: www.zirngast.at

Meadowland site on the River Enns next to the railway.

dir: *Off B308 towards town, site by fuel station.*

Open: All Year. **Site:** 1.5HEC **Facilities:** Wi-fi (charged) **Services:** **Leisure:** R **Off-site:** P

UNGERSDORF BEI FROHNLEITEN STEIERMARK

Lanzmaierhof

Ungersdorf 16, 8130
☎ 03126 2360 🖹 03126 4174
e-mail: lanzmaierhof@tele2.at
web: www.camping-steiermark.at

A quiet site and an ideal base for walking and climbing.

dir: *Signed 2km S of Frohnleiten on Graz road.*

GPS: 47.1512, 15.1907

Open: Apr-15 Oct **Site:** 0.5HEC **Prices:** 17.70-20.20 **Facilities:** Play Area **Services:** **Off-site:** P

WEISSKIRCHEN STEIERMARK

50Plus Campingpark Fisching

Fisching 9, 8741
☎ 03577 82284 🖹 03577 822846
e-mail: campingpark@fisching.at
web: www.camping50plus.at

A modern site with fine sanitary and sports facilities, catering for over-50s. 6km from the Formula 1 circuit (A1-Ring) in Zeltweg.

dir: *S36 exit Zeltweg-Ost for Obdach & signs for B78, signed from centre of Fisching.*

Open: Apr-15 Oct **Site:** 1.5HEC **Facilities:** **Services:** **Leisure:** P **Off-site:**

WILDALPEN STEIERMARK

Wildalpen

8924
☎ 03636 342 & 341 🖹 03636 313
e-mail: camping@wildalpen.at
web: www.wildalpen.at

Located in a nature reserve beside the River Salza with good canoeing facilities.

Open: Apr-Oct **Site:** 0.8HEC **Prices:** 14-16 **Facilities:** Wi-fi (charged) **Services:** **Leisure:** R **Off-site:** P

LOWER AUSTRIA

GMÜND NIEDERÖSTERREICH

Sole-Felsen-Bad

Albrechtser Str 10, 3950
☎ 02852 202030 🖹 02852 202033
e-mail: info@sole-felsen-bad.at
web: www.sole-felsen-bad.at

A pleasant location with a variety of recreational facilities.

dir: *Signed off B41.*

Open: Apr-Oct **Site:** 0.5HEC **Facilities:** **Services:** **Off-site:** L P

JENNERSDORF BURGENLAND

Jennersdorf

Freizeitzentrum 3, 8380
☎ 03329 46133 🖹 03329 4626121
e-mail: post@jennersdorf.bgld.gv.at
web: www.jennersdorf.eu

A pleasant site in wooded surroundings.

dir: *A2 exit Fürstenfeld.*

Open: 16 Mar-Oct **Site:** 1HEC **Facilities:** **Services:** **Leisure:** P **Off-site:** R

KAUMBERG NIEDERÖSTERREICH

Paradise Garden Camping

Hoefnerbraben 2, 2572
☎ 0676 4741966 🖹 02765 3883
e-mail: grandl@camping-noe.at
web: www.camping-noe.at

In a picturesque valley setting surrounded by meadows where sheep graze and the proprietor grows 120 varieties of fruit. Quiet site with nearby cycle paths and walking trails for exploring the countryside.

dir: *B18.*

Open: Apr-Sep **Site:** 5HEC **Prices:** 17-21 **Facilities:** Wi-fi (charged) Play Area **Services:** **Leisure:** R **Off-site:** L P

MARBACH NIEDERÖSTERREICH

Marbacher

3671
☎ 07413 20733 07413 20733
e-mail: info@marbach-freizeit.at
web: www.marbach-freizeit.at

A pleasant location beside the River Danube.

dir: *A1 exit Pöchlarn.*

Open: Apr-Oct **Site:** 0.35HEC **Prices:** 16.20-22.70 **Facilities:** Wi-fi **Services:** **Leisure:** R **Off-site:** P

MARKT ST MARTIN BURGENLAND

Markt St Martin

Mühlweg 2, 7341
☎ 02618 2239 02618 22394
e-mail: post@markt-st-martin.bgld.gv.at
web: www.marktstmartin.at

On a level meadow with plenty of trees and bushes.

dir: *A2 exit Krumbach/Schäffern.*

Open: May-Sep **Site:** 0.5HEC **Prices:** 16.50 **Facilities:** Play Area **Services:** **Leisure:** L R **Off-site:** P

RECHNITZ BURGENLAND

GC

Hauptpl 10, 7471
☎ 03363 79202 03363 7920222
e-mail: post@rechnitz.bgld.gv.at
web: www.rechnitz.at

On an artificial lake in the heart of the beautiful Faludi Valley.

Open: Jun-Aug **Site:** 1HEC **Facilities:** **Services:** **Leisure:** L **Off-site:**

SCHÖNBÜHEL NIEDERÖSTERREICH

Stumpfer

3392
☎ 02752 8510 02752 851017
e-mail: office@stumpfer.com
web: www.stumpfer.com

A small site in a wooded location attached to a guesthouse close to the River Donau.

dir: *SW of town.*

Open: Apr-Oct **Site:** 1.5HEC **Prices:** 17-21.90 **Facilities:** Wi-fi (charged) **Services:** **Leisure:** R

TRAISEN NIEDERÖSTERREICH

Terrassen-Camping Traisen

Kulmhof 1, 3160
☎ 02762 62900 02762 629004
e-mail: info@camping-traisen.at
web: www.camping-traisen.at

Set out in a circular formation around the main buildings with plenty of trees around the pitches. There is a wonderful view.

dir: *0.6km W via B20.*

GPS: 48.0424, 15.6029

Open: 15 Feb-15 Nov **Site:** 2.1HEC **Prices:** 18-21 **Facilities:** Wi-fi Play Area **Services:** **Leisure:** P **Off-site:** R

TULLN NIEDERÖSTERREICH

Donaupark-Camping Tulln

Donaulánde 76, 3430
☎ 02272 65200 02272 65201
e-mail: camptulln@oeamtc.at
web: www.campingtulln.at

A modern site in a peaceful location with good facilities, close to the River Danube. Summer bus service to Vienna and guided cycling tours.

dir: *20km from the A1. Exit 41 St Christopher.*

GPS: 48.3325, 16.0719

Open: 15 Apr-15 Oct **Site:** 10HEC **Prices:** 20.60-27.60 Mobile home hire 315-385 **Facilities:** Wi-fi (charged) **Services:** **Leisure:** L **Off-site:** P R

WAIDHOFEN AN DER THAYA NIEDERÖSTERREICH

Thayapark

Badgasse 9, 3830
☎ 0664 5904433 02842 50399
e-mail: info@waidhofen-thaya-stadt.at
web: www.waidhofen-thaya.at

A family site in wooded surroundings close to the River Thaya.

dir: *Signed from village.*

Open: May-Sep **Site:** 10HEC **Facilities:** **Services:** **Leisure:** R **Off-site:** P

UPPER AUSTRIA/SALZBURG

ABERSEE — SALZBURG

Seecamping Wolfgangblick

Seestrasse 115, 5342
06227 3475 06227 3664
e-mail: camping@wolfgangblick.at
web: www.wolfgangblick.at
A pleasant position on the Wolfgangsee.
dir: *Signed from village. 6km from St Gilgen via B1598.*
GPS: 47.7367, 13.4328
Open: 20 Apr-Sep **Site:** 2HEC **Facilities:** Play Area **Services:** **Leisure:** L R **Off-site:**

ABTENAU — SALZBURG

Oberwötzlhof

Erlfeld 37, 5441
06243 2698 06243 269855
e-mail: oberwoetzlhof@sbg.at
web: www.oberwoetzlhof-camp.at
A summer and winter site on a level meadow with panoramic views of the surrounding mountains.
dir: *NW of Abtenau.*
Open: All Year. **Site:** 2HEC **Facilities:** **Services:** **Leisure:** P **Off-site:** R

BRUCK AN DER GROSSGLOCKNERSTRASSE — SALZBURG

Sportcamp Woferlgut

The Camping and Caravanning Club The Friendly Club

Kroessenbach 40, 5671
06545 73030 06545 73033
e-mail: info@sportcamp.at
web: www.sportcamp.at
Set in a beautiful valley beside a lake with extensive recreational facilities included in the camping price.
C&CC Report *An exceptional family site in outstanding scenery, justly renowned for its range of high quality facilities. All but fishing, solarium, canoe lessons and massages are free, while the private bathrooms are pure camping luxury. The Salzburg Summer Joker Card gives entry to nearly 200 attractions, from wildlife parks to cable cars; but a visit in late August and early September is highly recommended, for the many local farmers' festivals.*
dir: *Via Bruck-Süd or Grossglockner on B311.*
Open: All Year. **Site:** 17HEC
Prices: 22.30-31.80 **Facilities:** Wi-fi (charged) Kids' Club Play Area **Services:**
Leisure: L P **Off-site:** R

ESTERNBERG — OBERÖSTERREICH

Pyrawang

4092
07714 6504 07714 6504
dir: *On B130 Passau-Linz at Km45.5.*
Open: Apr-Oct **Site:** 3HEC **Facilities:**
Services: **Off-site:** R

GLEINKERAU — OBERÖSTERREICH

Pyhrn Priel

4582
07562 7066
e-mail: pyhrn-priel@aon.at
web: www.pyhrn-priel.at
A year-round site with a variety of facilities.
dir: *A9 exit 52 signed Gleinkerau.*
Open: All Year. **Site:** 1HEC **Prices:** 20.30-24.30
Facilities: **Services:** **Off-site:** R

KAPRUN — SALZBURG

Mühle

N-Gassner Str 66, 5710
06547 8254 06547 825489
e-mail: muehle@kaprun.at
web: www.muehle-kaprun.at
A pleasant family site on long stretch of meadow by the Kapruner Ache.
dir: *S end of village towards cable lift.*
Open: All Year. **Site:** 1.5HEC **Facilities:**
Services: **Leisure:** P

MAISHOFEN — SALZBURG

Kammerlander

Oberreit 18, 5751
06542 68755 06542 687555
e-mail: landhaus-christa@sbg.at
web: www.sbg.at/landhaus-christa
Quiet, family friendly site, ideal for hiking or cycling in the surrounding countryside.
dir: *On B168.*
Open: May-15 Sep **Site:** **Facilities:**
Off-site: L

Site 6HEC (site size) grass sand stone little shade partly shaded mainly shaded bungalows for hire (static) caravans for hire tents for hire no dogs site fully accessible for wheelchairs
Prices amount quoted is per night, for 2 adults and car, plus tent or caravan. Mobile home hire is a weekly rate.

MAUTERNDORF — SALZBURG

Camping Mauterndorf

5570
06472 72023 06472 7202320
e-mail: info@camping-mauterndorf.at
web: www.camping-mauterndorf.at

Located in an area ideal for hiking and skiing, a family friendly site with health spa. Swimming pool available in summer. Charge for dogs.

dir: *On B99.*

Open: All Year. **Site:** 2.5HEC **Prices:** 17.50-34 **Facilities:** Wi-fi (charged) Kids' Club Play Area **Services:** **Leisure:** P R

MONDSEE — OBERÖSTERREICH

Mond-See-Land

Punzau 21, 5310
06232 2600 06232 27218
e-mail: austria@campmondsee.at
web: www.campmondsee.at

A picturesque and peaceful site between the lakes Mondsee and Irrsee with good facilities.

dir: *A1 exit Mondsee, B154 towards Strasswalden for 1.5km, onto Haider-Mühle road for 2km.*

Open: Apr-Oct **Site:** 3HEC **Prices:** 15-23 **Facilities:** Play Area **Services:** **Leisure:** P

NUSSDORF — OBERÖSTERREICH

Gruber

Dorfstr 63, 4865
07666 80450 07666 80456
e-mail: office@camping-gruber.at
web: www.camping-gruber.at

On fairly long meadow parallel to the promenade.

dir: *S of village. Off B151 at Km19.7 towards Attersee.*

Open: 15 Apr-15 Oct **Site:** 2.6HEC **Facilities:** **Services:** **Leisure:** L P **Off-site:**

PERWANG AM GRABENSEE — OBERÖSTERREICH

Perwang

5166
06217 8288 06217 824715
e-mail: gemeinde@perwang.ooe.gv.at
web: www.perwang.at

Site beside lake.

Open: Apr-Oct **Site:** 1.5HEC **Facilities:** **Services:** **Leisure:** L **Off-site:**

RADSTADT — SALZBURG

Forellencamp

Gaismairallee 51, 5550
06452 7861 06452 5092
e-mail: info@forellencamp.com
web: www.forellencamp.com

Flat meadowland near town.

dir: *SW via B99.*

Open: All Year. **Site:** 1HEC **Prices:** 16.40-18.50 **Facilities:** Play Area **Services:** **Off-site:** P R

ST JOHANN IM PONGAU — SALZBURG

Hirschenwirt

Bundesstr 1, 5600
06412 6012 06412 60128
e-mail: hirschenwirt@aon.at
web: www.hirschenwirt.com

A small, pleasant, flat and open site well placed for the Salzburg-Badgastein road or as a base for exploring the surrounding region of mountains and lakes. A small pool is available in summer. Being on a major route there is traffic noise.

dir: *Behind Gasthof Hirschenwirt at St Johann im Pongau on B311.*

GPS: 47.3346, 13.1892

Open: 8 Dec-Oct **Site:** 0.8HEC **Prices:** 17-22 **Facilities:** Wi-fi Play Area **Services:** **Leisure:** P **Off-site:** L R

Wieshof

Wieshofgasse 8, 5600
06412 8519 06412 82929
e-mail: info@camping-wieshof.at
web: www.camping-wieshof.at

On gently sloping meadow behind pension and farmhouse. Modern facilities. Big spa house with massage facilities and health bars, adjacent to site.

dir: *Off B311 towards Zell am Zee.*

Open: All Year. **Site:** 1.6HEC **Prices:** 18 **Facilities:** Wi-fi Play Area **Services:** **Off-site:** L P

ST MARTIN BEI LOFER SALZBURG

Park Grubhof

5092
06588 8237 06588 82377
e-mail: home@grubhof.com
web: www.grubhof.com

Situated in meadowland on the banks of the River Saalach. Separate sections for dog owners, families, teenagers and groups. Extra large pitches available with mountain views.

dir: *B311 S of Lofer, 1.5km turn left.*

Open: All Year. **Site:** 10HEC **Prices:** 18-23 **Facilities:** Wi-fi (charged) Play Area **Services:** **Leisure:** R **Off-site:** P

ST WOLFGANG OBERÖSTERREICH

Appesbach

Au 99, 5360
06138 2206 06138 220633
e-mail: camping@appesbach.at
web: www.appesbach.at

On sloping meadow facing lake with no shade at upper end.

dir: *0.8km E of St Wolfgang between lake & Strobl road.*

Open: Mar-Oct **Site:** 2.2HEC **Facilities:** **Services:** **Leisure:** L **Off-site:**

Berau

Schwarzenbach 16, 5360
06138 2543 06138 25435
e-mail: camping@berau.at
web: www.berau.at

A family-run site in a picturesque setting on the edge of the Wolfgangsee. Spacious, level pitches and modern facilities. There is a kids' club during July and August.

dir: *A1 exit Talgau, N158 signed Hof/Bad Ischl, through Strobl towards St Wolfgang & signed.*

Open: All Year. **Site:** 2HEC **Prices:** 17.40-27 **Facilities:** Wi-fi (charged) Kids' Club Play Area **Services:** **Leisure:** L

SALZBURG SALZBURG

Camping Nord Sam

Samstr 22A, 5023
0662 660494 0662 660494
e-mail: office@camping-nord-sam.com
web: www.camping-nord-sam.com

Pitches divided by trees and shrubs with cycle route directly from site to city centre. Cycle rental available.

dir: *Salzburg Nord autobahn exit, site 400m.*

GPS: 47.8269, 13.0631

Open: 15 Apr-2 Nov, 7-11 Dec, 27 Dec-8 Jan **Site:** 1.4HEC **Prices:** 23-30 **Facilities:** Wi-fi (charged) Play Area **Services:** **Leisure:** P **Off-site:**

Kasern

C-Zuckmayerstr 26, 5101
0662 450576 0662 450576
e-mail: campingkasern@aon.at
web: www.camping-kasern-salzburg.com

dir: *A1 exit Salzburg-Nord.*

Open: 21 Apr-10 Oct **Site:** 0.9HEC **Facilities:** **Services:** **Off-site:**

Panorama Camping Stadtblick

Rauchenbichlerstr 21, 5020
0662 450652 0662 458018
e-mail: info@ panorama-camping.at
web: www.panorama-camping.at

A terraced site affording spectacular views of the surrounding mountains.

dir: *Motorway exit Salzburg-Nord & signed.*

Open: 20 Mar-5 Nov, 5-15 Dec & 27 Dec-6 Jan **Site:** 0.8HEC **Prices:** 20-26 **Facilities:** Wi-fi (charged) Play Area **Services:** **Off-site:** L

Schloss Aigen

5026
0662 622079 0662 622079
e-mail: camping.aigen@elsnet.at
web: www.campingaigen.com

Site divided into pitches in partial clearing on mountain slope.

dir: *Motorway exit Salzburg-Süd, Anif & Glasenbach.*

GPS: 47.7806, 13.0899

Open: May-Sep **Site:** 25HEC **Prices:** 17 **Facilities:** Play Area **Services:** **Off-site:** P R

SCHLÖGEN OBERÖSTERREICH

Freizeitanlage Schlögen

4083
☎ 07279 8241 🖷 07279 824122
e-mail: schloegen.freizeit@netway.at
web: www.schloegen.at

On level ground beside the River Donau, backed by woods and mountains.

Open: Apr-20 Oct **Site:** 2.8HEC **Prices:** 10-14 **Facilities:** **Services:** **Leisure:** P R

SEEKIRCHEN SALZBURG

See-camping Zell am Wallersee

Bayrham 40, 5201
☎ 06212 4080 🖷 06212 4080
e-mail: info@seecamping.at
web: www.see-camping.at

Level meadowland separated from the lake by the lido.

dir: *A1 exit Wallersee, via Seekirchen to Zell.*

Open: Apr-Oct **Site:** 3HEC **Prices:** 9-21 **Facilities:** Wi-fi (charged) Play Area **Services:** **Leisure:** L

Strandcamping Seekirchen

Seestr 2, 5201
☎ 06212 4088 🖷 06212 4088
e-mail: info@camping-seekirchen.at
web: www.camping-seekirchen.at

Beside the Wallersee in a beautiful meadow.

Open: 15 Apr-15 Oct **Site:** 2HEC **Prices:** 18-22 **Facilities:** Wi-fi Play Area **Services:** **Leisure:** L P R **Off-site:**

UNTERACH AM ATTERSEE OBERÖSTERREICH

Insel Camping

4866
☎ 07665 8311 🖷 07665 83115
e-mail: camping@inselcamp.at
web: www.inselcamp.at

Quiet family site on the shore of Lake Attersee, divided into two by the River Seeache. Fishing available.

dir: *Entrance below B152 towards Steinbach at Km24.5, 300m from B151 junct.*

Open: May-15 Sep **Site:** 1.8HEC **Prices:** 15-19 **Facilities:** **Services:** **Leisure:** L R **Off-site:**

WALD SALZBURG

S.N.P

Lahn 65, 5742
☎ 06565 84460 🖷 06565 84464
e-mail: info@snp-camping.at
web: www.snp-camping.at

A small family site in a beautiful Alpine setting.

dir: *W of town.*

Open: All Year. **Site:** 0.7HEC **Facilities:** **Services:** **Off-site:** L P

ZELL AM SEE SALZBURG

Camping & Appartements Südufer

Seeuferstr 196, 5700
☎ 06542 56228 🖷 06542 562284
e-mail: zell@camping-suedufer.at
web: www.campinginfo.at

A family site on level ground in a picturesque spot on the southern bank of the Zeller See. Ideal starting point for hiking and bike tours in the summer, as well as cross-country skiing and alpine skiing in the winter.

dir: *S via B311 exit for Thumersbach before tunnel entrance, after 500m, turn left. Follow road to S of lake, site on right.*

Open: All Year. **Site:** 1HEC **Prices:** 19-27.10 **Facilities:** Wi-fi (charged) **Services:** **Off-site:** L P R

Seecamp Zell am See

Thumersbacherstr 34, 5700
☎ 06542 72115 🖷 06542 7211515
e-mail: zell@seecamp.at
web: www.seecamp.at

Pleasant wooded location beside the lake with excellent site and recreational facilities.

dir: *B311 N of lake towards Thumersbach, signed.*

Open: All Year. **Site:** 3.2HEC **Prices:** 24.20-31.60 **Facilities:** Wi-fi (charged) **Services:** **Leisure:** L **Off-site:** P

AUSTRIA

AUSTRIA

VORARLBERG

BEZAU VORARLBERG

Bezau

Ach 206, 6870

☎ 05514 2964

e-mail: campingplatz.bezau@aon.at

web: www.campingfuehrer.at

Small family-owned site with modern sanitary facilities.

dir: *S via B200 Dornbirn-Warth.*

Open: All Year. **Site:** 0.5HEC **Facilities:** **Off-site:** P R

BRAZ VORALBERG

Traube

Klostertalerstr 12, 6751

☎ 05552 28103 05552 2810340

e-mail: office@traubebraz.at

web: www.campingtraube.at

On sloping grassland in the picturesque Klostertal Valley with modern facilities.

dir: *7km SE of Bludenz. Off S16 near railway, signed.*

Open: All Year. **Site:** 2HEC **Prices:** 22.80-34.60 **Facilities:** Wi-fi Play Area **Services:** **Leisure:** P **Off-site:** R

DALAAS VORARLBERG

Erne

Klostertalerstr 64, 6752

☎ 05585 7223 05585 20049

e-mail: info@etpc.at

web: www.etpc.at

Site in the town, attached to a guesthouse and next to the swimming pool.

dir: *S16 exit Dalass.*

Open: All Year. **Site:** 0.6HEC **Prices:** 24-26 **Facilities:** Wi-fi (charged) **Services:** **Leisure:** R **Off-site:** P

DORNBIRN VORARLBERG

In der Enz

6850

☎ 05572 29119

e-mail: camping@camping-enz.at

web: www.camping-enz.at

A municipal site beside a public park, in a wooded area 100m beyond the Karren cable lift.

dir: *Autobahn exit Dornbirn-Süd.*

Open: Apr-Sep **Site:** 10HEC **Facilities:** **Services:** **Off-site:** P R

LINGENAU VORARLBERG

Feurstein

Haidach 185, 6951

☎ 05513 6114 05513 61144

A small site located in a meadow adjacent to farm buildings with sufficient facilities for a pleasant stay.

dir: *B200 for Müselbach, then B205.*

Open: All Year. **Site:** 1HEC **Prices:** 18.60 **Facilities:** Wi-fi **Services:** **Off-site:**

NENZING VORARLBERG

Alpencamping Nenzing

6710

☎ 05525 62491 05525 624916

e-mail: office@alpencamping.at

web: www.alpencamping.at

A well-appointed site in magnificent Alpine scenery. There are fine sports facilities which include indoor and outdoor swimming pools, sun terrace and sauna. Also modern sanitary blocks.

dir: *Signed from B190 from Nenzing, 2km towards Gurtis.*

Open: All Year. **Site:** 3HEC **Prices:** 18-29 **Facilities:** Wi-fi (charged) Kids' Club Play Area **Services:** **Leisure:** P

NÜZIDERS VORALBERG

Terrassencamping Sonnenberg

Hinteroferst 12, 6714

☎ 05552 64035 05552 33900

e-mail: sonnencamp@aon.at

web: www.camping-sonnenberg.com

Clean site with modern facilities with terraces and splendid mountain scenery. Kids' club in high season.

dir: *E60 (A14), exit 57 via Bludenz-Nüziders road, at 1st fork go up hill.*

Open: May-3 Oct **Site:** 1.9HEC **Prices:** 19-27 **Facilities:** Wi-fi (charged) Kids' Club Play Area **Services:** **Off-site:** P R

RAGGAL-PLAZERA VORARLBERG

Grosswalsertal

6741
☎ 05553 209 📠 05553 2094
e-mail: info@camping-grosswalsertal.at
web: www.camping-grosswalsertal.at

A family site in a quiet location on gently sloping terrain, with pleasant views. Leisure facilities include beach volleyball.

dir: *On NE outskirts.*

Open: May-Sep **Site:** 0.8HEC **Prices:** 17-21.50 **Facilities:** Wi-fi (charged) Play Area **Services:** **Leisure:** P **Off-site:**

TSCHAGGUNS VORARLBERG

Zelfen

6774
☎ 0664 2002326
e-mail: kunsttischlerei.tschofen@utanet.at
web: www.camping-zelfen.at

Partly uneven, grassy site in a wooded location beside River Ill. Good recreational facilities.

dir: *A14 to Bludenz, then B188 to Tschagguns.*

Open: All Year. **Site:** 2HEC **Facilities:** **Services:** **Leisure:** R **Off-site:** P

VIENNA (WIEN)

WIEN (VIENNA) WIEN

Donaupark Camping Klosterneuburg

In der Au, 3400
☎ 02243 25877 📠 02243 25878
e-mail: campklosterneuburg@oeamtc.at
web: www.campingklosterneuburg.at

A modern site in delightful wooded surroundings with fine recreational facilities and within easy reach of the city centre.

dir: *A1 onto B19 to Tulln then B14 to Klosterneuburg.*

GPS: 48.3106, 16.3272

Open: Apr-Oct **Site:** 2.25HEC **Prices:** 18.60-38.10 **Facilities:** Wi-fi (charged) **Services:** **Off-site:** P R

Neue Donau

Am Kleehäufel, 1220
☎ 01 2024010 📠 01 2024020
e-mail: neuedonau@campingwien.at
web: www.campingwien.at

Situated in a meadow surrounded by trees beside the Danube within a leisure park.

dir: *On E bank of river via A4 & A22.*

Open: Etr-Sep **Site:** 3.3HEC **Facilities:** **Services:** **Off-site:** L P R

Rodaun

An der Au 2, Rodaun, 1230
☎ 01 8884154 📠 01 8884154

dir: *Between An der Au str & Leising River dam, via Breitenfürter Str N492.*

Open: Jun-12 Oct **Site:** 0.8HEC **Facilities:** **Services:** **Off-site:**

Wien West

Hüttelbergstr 80, 1140
☎ 01 9142314 📠 01 9113594
e-mail: west@campingwien.at
web: www.campingwien.at

30 minutes from the city centre by bus or underground, with facilities including satellite TV and bicycle rental.

dir: *End of A1 Linz-Wien to Bräuhausbrücke, turn left & across road to Linz for 1.8km.*

Open: Jan & Mar-Dec **Site:** 2.5HEC **Prices:** 18.10-28.60 **Facilities:** Wi-fi Play Area **Services:**

Accident & Emergency

Fire 100 Police 101 Ambulance 100
European emergency number also in use - dial 112 and ask for service required.

Drinking and driving

Maximum permitted level of alcohol in the bloodstream is 0.049%. If the level is between 0.05% and 0.08% you will be banned from driving for three hours and issued an on the spot fine of €137.50. If you refuse to pay, you will be prosecuted and the fine may go up to €2,750. 0.08% or more brings an on the spot fine of up to €550 and a ban from driving for at least six hours; if more than 0.15%, a fine up to €11,000 and a licence suspension up to five years. However, if you have held your licence for less than two years an on the spot fine will not be imposed, you will automatically be prosecuted.

Driving Licence

Minimum age 18 for UK licence holder driving temporarily imported car and/or motorcycle.

Fines

On-the-spot. The officer collecting the fine must issue an official receipt showing the amount of the fine. Motorists can refuse to pay an on-the-spot fine; a foreign motorist refusing to do so may be invited to make a consignation (deposit) and if he does not his vehicle will be impounded by the police, and permanently confiscated if the deposit is not paid within 96 hours. Fines can be paid for in cash euros or debit/credit card.

Lights

Dipped headlights should be used in poor daytime visibility.

Motorcycles

Use of dipped headlights during the day compulsory. Wearing of crash helmets compulsory for both driver and passenger.

Motor Insurance

Third-party compulsory. The police can impound an uninsured vehicle.

Passengers & Children

Children under 18 and less than 1.35m must use a suitable child-restraint system whether seated in the front or rear seat of a vehicle. Exception: When two child restraint systems are being used on the rear seats and there isn't adequate room to place a third child restraint system, then the third child may travel on the back seat protected by the adult seat belt. A child under three can not be transported in a vehicle without a child seat/restraint. It is prohibited to use a rear facing child seat on a front seat with a frontal airbag unless it is deactivated.

Seat Belts

Compulsory for occupants to wear seat belts, if fitted.

Speed Limits

Unless signed otherwise:

Car with or without trailers	
Built-up areas	50km/h
Outside built-up areas	90km/h
Motorways/dual carriageways	120km/h
Minimum speed on motorways	70km/h
Vehicles with spiked tyres	
Motorways/dual carriageways	90km/h
Normal roads	60km/h

Additional Information

Compulsory equipment in Belgium:
Reflective jacket - Drivers stranded on a Belgian motorway or on a major road (usually four-lane roads, called 'route pour automobiles' - sign E17), stopping on places where parking is not allowed, must wear a reflective safety jacket as soon as they leave their vehicle. Fine for non-compliance €50, but the amount can be much higher (€55 - €1,375) if the driver refuses to pay or in a circumstance where the driver has to go to court (for example in the event of an accident). The jacket is compulsory for vehicles registered in Belgium. Whilst a foreign registered vehicle will not be fined for not carrying a reflective jacket if there is a police check, he/she could be fined for not wearing a jacket in case the vehicle breaks down. Warning triangle - Compulsory for vehicles with more than two wheels.

Other rules/requirements in Belgium:
First-aid kit and fire extinguisher recommended as their carriage is compulsory for Belgian-registered vehicles.
The majority of roundabouts have signs showing that traffic on the roundabout has priority. If there is no sign present, (very few roundabouts) traffic joining from the right has priority.
A new road sign has been introduced banning the use of cruise control on congested motorways and can also appear during motorway road works. A white disc bordered in red, bearing the word 'Peage' in black indicates that drivers must stop. The Dutch word 'Tol' sometimes replaces 'Peage'.
Any vehicle standing must have its engine switched off, unless absolutely necessary.

A car navigation system with maps indicating the location of fixed speed cameras is permitted but equipment which actively searches for speed cameras or interferes with police equipment is prohibited.
The police can impound a vehicle with an unsafe load.
Spiked tyres are permitted from 1 Nov until 31 Mar on vehicles weighing up to a maximum of 3.5 tonnes.
Snow chains are only permitted on snow or ice covered roads. Winter tyres are permitted from 1 Oct until 30 Apr, a lower speed limit needs to be adhered to and the maximum designed speed for the tyres displayed on a sticker on the dashboard.
Vehicles with spiked tyres must display at the rear a white disc with a red reflectorised border showing the figure "60", when the spiked tyres are applied.

Tolls Vignette Currency Euro (€)	Car	Car Towing Caravan/Trailer
Tunnels		
On R2 Llefkenshoek Tunnel	€5.50	€18

SOUTH WEST/COAST

BLANKENBERGE — WEST-VLAANDEREN

Bonanza I

Zeebruggelaan 137, 8370
☎ 050 416658 [fax] 050 427349
e-mail: bonanza1@kmonet.be
web: www.bonanza1.be
A family site in wooded surroundings 1km from both the village and the sea.
Open: 15 Mar-15 Sep **Site:** 4.5HEC [symbols] **Facilities:** [shop] [shower] [razor points] [caravan points] [compulsory separate car park] **Services:** [café/restaurant] [bar] [Camping Gaz] [gas] [first aid] [laundry] **Off-site:** [swimming] L P S

Dallas

Ruzettelaan 191, 8370
☎ 050 418157 [fax] 050 429479
e-mail: campingdallas@skynet.be
web: www.campingdallas.com
Well-equipped family site near a large department store 50m from the beach.
Open: 15 Mar-1 Oct **Site:** 2.65HEC [symbols] **Facilities:** [shop] [shower] [razor points] [caravan points] Wi-fi (charged) Play Area [parking by tents] [compulsory separate car park] [disabled access] **Services:** [Camping Gaz] [gas] [first aid] [laundry] **Off-site:** [swimming] L P S [café/restaurant] [bar]

BREDENE — WEST-VLAANDEREN

Camping Astrid

Koningin Astridlaan 1, 8450
☎ 059 321247
e-mail: info@camping-astrid.be
web: www.camping-astrid.be
Family camp site 100m from the beach and dunes. Spacious pitches and cycle routes available.
Open: All Year. **Site:** 4.7HEC [symbols] **Prices:** 14-24 Mobile home hire 320-515 **Facilities:** [shower] [razor points] [caravan points] Wi-fi (charged) Play Area **Services:** [first aid] [laundry] **Leisure:** [swimming] S **Off-site:** [swimming] P [shop] [café/restaurant] [bar] [Camping Gaz] [gas]

JABBEKE — WEST-VLAANDEREN

Recreatiepark Klein Strand

Varsenareweg 29, 8490
☎ 050 811440 [fax] 050 814289
e-mail: info@kleinstrand.be
web: www.kleinstrand.be
A lakeside site with modern facilities and a variety of leisure activities.
dir: *Off Oostende-Brugge road.*
Open: All Year. **Site:** 28HEC [symbols] **Prices:** 16-35 Mobile home hire 165-625 **Facilities:** [shop] [shower] [razor points] [caravan points] Wi-fi (charged) Kids' Club Play Area [parking by tents] [compulsory separate car park] [disabled access] **Services:** [café/restaurant] [bar] [Camping Gaz] [gas] [first aid] [laundry] **Leisure:** [swimming] L P **Off-site:** [swimming] R

KNOKKE-HEIST — WEST-VLAANDEREN

De Vuurtoren

Heistlaan 168, 8301
☎ 050 511782
e-mail: kampvuurtoren@skynet.be
web: www.knokke-heist.be
On level meadow with tarred roads.
dir: *From Knokke to Oostende for 4km, turn S & signed.*
Open: 15 Mar-15 Oct **Site:** 6.6HEC [symbols] **Facilities:** [shower] [razor points] [caravan points] [parking by tents] **Services:** [café/restaurant] [bar] [first aid] [laundry] **Off-site:** [swimming] S [shop] [Camping Gaz] [gas]

Zilvermeeuw

Heistlaan 166, 8301
☎ 050 512726 [fax] 050 512703
e-mail: info.campingzilvermeeuw@skynet.be
web: www.camping-zilvermeeuw.be
Level site in wooded surroundings.
dir: *SW via N300.*
Open: Mar-1 Nov **Site:** 7HEC [symbols] **Prices:** 22.40-32 **Facilities:** [shop] [shower] [razor points] [caravan points] Wi-fi Kids' Club Play Area [parking by tents] [disabled access] **Services:** [café/restaurant] [Camping Gaz] [first aid] [laundry] **Off-site:** [swimming] L P S [bar]

KOKSIJDE WEST-VLAANDEREN

Blekker & Blekkerdal

Jachtwakerstr 12, 8670
058 511633 058 511307
e-mail: camping.deblekker@belgacom.net
web: www.deblekker.be

A peaceful location surrounded by trees. Good modern facilities.

dir: *Between Dunkerque & Oostende, 5km from Belgian frontier. Motorway exit towards Veurne.*

Open: Apr-30 Oct **Site:** 3HEC **Facilities:** **Services:** **Off-site:** P S

LOMBARDSIJDE WEST-VLAANDEREN

Lombarde

Elisabethlaan 4, 8434
058 236839 058 239908
e-mail: info@delombarde.be
web: www.delombarde.be

A well-equipped family site 400m from the sea and close to the centre of the village. 1 dog permitted per pitch.

dir: *E40 exit Nieuwpoort. At Nieuwpoort take N34 towards Oostende, site signed on right.*

GPS: 51.1564, 2.7537

Open: All Year. **Site:** 8.5HEC **Prices:** 17.50-31.50 **Facilities:** Wi-fi Play Area **Services:** **Off-site:** P S

Zomerzon

Elisabethlaan 1, 8434
058 237396 058 232817
web: www.zomerzon.be

A quiet location with good facilities, 0.8km from the dunes and beach.

Open: Mar-Oct **Site:** 10HEC **Facilities:** Wi-fi (charged) Play Area **Services:** **Off-site:** P S

MIDDELKERKE WEST-VLAANDEREN

Mijn Plezier

Duinenweg 489, 8430
059 300279 059 314503
e-mail: camping@mijnplezier.be
web: www.mijnplezier.be

Wooded surroundings close to the castle.

GPS: 51.175, 2.7922

Open: Apr-Sep **Site:** 3HEC **Prices:** 21.50 **Facilities:** Wi-fi (charged) Play Area **Services:** **Off-site:** S

MONS HAINAUT

Waux-Hall

av St-Pierre 17, 7000
065 337923 065 363848
e-mail: ot3@ville.mons.be
web: www.monsregion.be

A secluded position 1km from the town centre, with direct access to the Parc du Waux-Hall.

dir: *From town ring road exit for Beaumont/Binche, Charleroi, right at lights & sharp right.*

Open: All Year. **Site:** 1.44HEC **Facilities:** **Services:** **Off-site:** L P

NIEUWPOORT WEST-VLAANDEREN

Kompas Camping

Brugsesteenweg 49, 8620
058 236037 058 232682
e-mail: nieuwpoort@kompascamping.be
web: www.kompascamping.be

A family site in pleasant wooded surroundings. Plenty of recreational facilities including water sports and a kids' club is available during school holidays.

dir: *E40 exit 4 for Diksmuide & Nieuwpoort, signed from St Joris.*

Open: Apr-14 Nov **Site:** 24HEC **Prices:** 20.70-38.20 Mobile home hire 238-658 **Facilities:** Wi-fi (charged) Kids' Club Play Area **Services:** **Leisure:** P **Off-site:** L R S

OOSTENDE (OSTENDE) WEST-VLAANDEREN

Asterix

Duinenstr 200, 8450
059 331000 059 324202
web: www.camping-asterix.be

A family site in wooded surroundings, 0.5km from the sea.

dir: *N34 from Oostende towards Knokke-Heist, 7km right for Bredene-Dorp.*

Open: All Year. **Site:** 3HEC **Facilities:** **Services:** **Off-site:** L P S

TOURNAI HAINAUT

Orient

r JB Moens, 7500
069 222635 069 890229
e-mail: campingorient@tournai.be
web: www.tournai.be

A pleasant site in an area of woodland with good recreational facilities.

dir: *Motorway exit Tournai Est for town centre, left at 1st x-rds & signed.*

Open: All Year. **Site:** 20HEC **Facilities:** **Services:** **Leisure:** L P

WAREGEM — WEST-VLAANDEREN

Gemeentelijk

Zuiderlaan 13, 8790
☎ 056 609532 📠 056 621290
e-mail: toerisme@waregem.be
web: www.waregem.be
Set in a sports and leisure centre south-east of the town centre.
dir: *Via E17 Kortrijk-Gent.*
Open: Apr-Sep **Site:** 1HEC **Facilities:** **Services:** **Off-site:** P

NORTH/CENTRAL

BACHTE-MARIA-LEERNE — OOST-VLAANDEREN

Groeneveld

Groeneveldreef 14, 9800
☎ 09 3801014 📠 09 3801014
e-mail: info@campinggroeneveld.be
web: www.campinggroeneveld.be
Well-equipped, quiet site beside a fishing lake. One dog per pitch.
dir: *Approach via E17 or E40.*
Open: Apr-Sep **Site:** 1.7HEC **Prices:** 18.50-22 **Facilities:** Wi-fi **Services:** **Off-site:** P R

BEGYNENDYK — BRABANT

Roygaerden

Betekomsesteenweg 75, 3130
☎ 016 531087 📠 016 531087
e-mail: info@immovdb.be
web: www.camping-deroygaerden.be
Pitches are in wooded surroundings beside a lake.
dir: *A2 exit 22/N10 for Begijnendijk.*
Open: All Year. **Site:** 5HEC **Prices:** 11-16 **Facilities:** **Services:** **Off-site:** L P

BEVERE — OOST-VLAANDEREN

Kompas Camping Oudenaarde

Kortrijkstr 342, 9700
☎ 055 315473 📠 055 300865
e-mail: oudenaarde@kompascamping.be
web: www.kompascamping.be
A family site with good recreational facilities.
dir: *Signed from N453.*
Open: Apr-mid Nov **Site:** 24HEC **Facilities:** **Services:** **Leisure:** L P

GENT (GAND) — OOST-VLAANDEREN

Blaarmeersen

The Camping and Caravanning Club — The Friendly Club

Zuiderlaan 12, 9000
☎ 09 2668160 📠 09 2668166
e-mail: camping.blaarmeersen@gent.be
web: www.blaarmeersen.be
Pleasant wooded surroundings.
C&CC Report *Apart from being a very well located en-route site, this is great for families of all ages and anyone wanting to visit some of Belgium's most popular places, many of which are less than an hour's drive away. Historic Gent is a short bus ride from the site and there is loads to do in and around the adjacent leisure centre and lake.*
dir: *E17/E40/R4.*
Open: Mar-15 Oct **Site:** 10HEC **Prices:** 15-18.25 **Facilities:** Wi-fi (charged) **Services:** **Leisure:** L **Off-site:** P

GRIMBERGEN — BRABANT

Grimbergen

Veldkanstr 64, 1850
☎ 0479 760378 📠 02 2701215
e-mail: camping.grimbergen@telenet.be
dir: *Bruxelles ring road exit 7.*
Open: Apr-Oct **Site:** 1.5HEC **Prices:** 17 **Facilities:** **Services:** **Off-site:** P

TOURINNES-LA-GROSSE — BRABANT

Au Val Tourinnes

r du Grand Brou 16A, 1320
☎ 010 866642
e-mail: info@campingauvaltourinnes.com
web: www.campingauvaltourinnes.com
Scenic natural location in the Ardennes with two lakes.
dir: *Autoroute E40 exit 23 towards Wavre, Hamme-Mille. Autoroute E19 exit 19 towards Wavre, Leuven & Hamme-Mille.*
Open: 15 Jan-15 Dec **Site:** 5HEC **Prices:** 18 Mobile home hire 350 **Facilities:** Wi-fi **Services:** **Leisure:** L

WACHTEBEKE — OOST-VLAANDEREN

Puyenbroeck

Puyenbrug 1A, 9185
☎ 09 3424231 📠 09 3424258
e-mail: puyenbroeck@oost.vlaanderen.be
web: www.puyenbroeck.be
Open: Apr-Sep **Site:** 9HEC **Facilities:** **Services:** **Off-site:** P

NORTH EAST

EKSEL **LIMBURG**

Lage Kempen

Kiefhoek str 19, 3941
011 402243 011 348812
e-mail: info@lagekempen.be
web: www.lagekempen.be

Situated in the middle of a forest with a variety of recreational facilities.

dir: *Route 67 from Hasselt & signed left Lage Kampen.*

Open: 2 Apr-1 Nov **Site:** 3.75HEC **Prices:** 19.65-23 **Facilities:** **Services:** **Leisure:** P **Off-site:**

GIERLE **ANTWERPEN**

Lilse Bergen

The Camping and Caravanning Club The Friendly Club

Strandweg 6, 2275
014 557901 014 554454
e-mail: info@lilsebergen.be
web: www.lilsebergen.be

A very well-equipped family site surrounding a private lake.

C&CC Report *A very well-organised site with superb award-winning adventure park. Located in parkland, with many marked-out walks and cycle paths accessible from the site, De Lilse Bergen is a great holiday base both for exploring some beautiful Belgian cities – particularly Antwerp and Leuven – and for keeping the most active of children amused for days.*

dir: *E39 exit 22.*

Open: All Year. **Site:** 60HEC **Prices:** 20-26.50 **Facilities:** Play Area **Services:** **Leisure:** L

LANAKEN **LIMBURG**

Jocomo Parc

3620
089 722884 089 733087
e-mail: info@jocomo.be
web: www.jocomo.be

On the edge of Hoge Kempen National Park, there are both seasonal and touring pitches. Facilities include boating and fishing pond and tennis court.

Open: Apr-Oct **Site:** 31HEC **Prices:** 21 Mobile home hire 425 **Facilities:** Wi-fi (charged) **Services:** **Leisure:** P **Off-site:**

MOL **ANTWERPEN**

Provinciaal Recreatie Domein Zilvermeer

Zilvermeerlaan 2, 2400
014 829500 014 829501
e-mail: info@zilvermeer.provant.be
web: www.zilvermeer.be

A pleasant lakeside site with good recreational facilities.

Site: 45HEC **Facilities:** **Services:** **Leisure:** L **Off-site:** P

OPGLABBEEK **LIMBURG**

Wilhelm Tell

Hoeverweg 87, 3660
089 854444 089 810010
e-mail: receptie@wilhelmtell.com
web: www.wilhelmtell.com

A family site set in a vast nature reserve with heathland, woodland and marshlands. The large variety of water attractions on site includes a water chute and a swimming pool with a wave machine. Also an indoor family pool and bubble bath.

dir: *E313 exit 32 for Opglabbeek.*

GPS: 51.0283, 5.5978

Open: All Year. **Site:** 4HEC **Prices:** 22.40-32 Mobile home hire 340-710 **Facilities:** Wi-fi Kids' Club Play Area **Services:** **Leisure:** P

OPOETEREN **LIMBURG**

Camping Zavelbos

Kattebeekstr 1, 3680
089 758196
e-mail: receptie@zavelbos.com
web: www.zavelbos.com

Peaceful and child friendly site with table tennis and fishing available.

dir: *A2 exit Maaseik to Opoeteren, site on right towards Opglabbeek.*

GPS: 51.0581, 5.6292

Open: All Year. **Site:** 6HEC **Prices:** 21-30 **Facilities:** Wi-fi Play Area **Services:** **Off-site:** P

RETIE **ANTWERPEN**

Berkenstrand

Brand 78, 2470
014 377590 014 375139
e-mail: info@berkenstrand.be
web: www.berkenstrand.be

Wooded surroundings beside a lake.

dir: *3km NE on road to Postel.*

Open: Apr-Sep **Site:** 10HEC **Prices:** 11.25-19.25 Mobile home hire 250-325 **Facilities:** Kids' Club **Services:** **Leisure:** L

Site 6HEC (site size) grass sand stone little shade partly shaded mainly shaded bungalows for hire (static) caravans for hire tents for hire no dogs site fully accessible for wheelchairs
Prices amount quoted is per night, for 2 adults and car, plus tent or caravan. Mobile home hire is a weekly rate.

TURNHOUT ANTWERPEN

Baalse Hei

Roodhuisstr 10, 2300
☎ 014 448470 ▤ 014 448474
e-mail: info@baalsehei.be
web: www.baalsehei.be
An eco-friendly, family site in pleasant wooded surroundings with plenty of recreational facilities.
GPS: 51.3575, 4.9589
Open: 16 Jan-15 Dec **Site:** 30HEC **Prices:** 18-25 Mobile home hire 370-545 **Facilities:** Wi-fi (charged) Play Area **Services:** **Leisure:** L

VORST-LAAKDAL ANTWERPEN

Kasteel Meerlaer

Verboekt 115, 2430
☎ 013 661420 ▤ 013 667512
e-mail: camp.meerlaer@skynet.be
web: www.camping.be/campings
dir: *E313 exit 24 for Hasselt. Or exit 24 for Antwerp.*
Open: All Year. **Site:** 6HEC **Prices:** 18 **Facilities:** **Services:** **Off-site:**

ZONHOVEN LIMBURG

Holsteenbron

Hengelhoelseweg 9, 3520
☎ 011 817140 ▤ 011 441789
e-mail: camping.holsteenbron@skynet.be
web: www.holsteenbron.be
A rural family site in a wooded location.
dir: *E314 exit 29 for Zonhoven.*
Open: Apr-11 Nov **Site:** 4HEC **Prices:** 17-21 Mobile home hire 250-295 **Facilities:** **Services:**

SOUTH EAST

AISCHE-EN-REFAIL NAMUR

Manoir de lá Bas

rte de Gembloux 180, 5310
☎ 081 655353
e-mail: europa-camping.sa@skynet.be
web: www.camping-manoirdelabas.be
A beautiful location within the wooded grounds of a former manor house. Dogs accepted, please contact for details.
dir: *5km W of Eghezée, off E411.*
Open: Apr-Oct **Site:** 21HEC **Prices:** 13-18 **Facilities:** Wi-fi (charged) **Services:** **Leisure:** P **Off-site:**

AMBERLOUP LUXEMBOURG

Camping Tonny

r Tonny 35-36, 6680
☎ 061 688285 ▤ 061 688285
e-mail: camping.tonny@skynet.be
web: www.campingtonny.be
Set in a pleasant valley beside the River Ourthe with fine sports facilities.
dir: *E25 or A4 to Bastogne, then N826.*
Open: 15 Feb-15 Nov **Site:** 2.48HEC **Facilities:** Wi-fi (charged) **Services:** **Leisure:** R

BARVAUX-SUR-OURTHE LUXEMBOURG

Hazalles

Chainrue 77a, 6940
☎ 086 211642 ▤ 086 211642
Situated in an orchard beside a stream with well-maintained facilities, 0.6km from the village.
Open: Apr-Sep **Site:** 0.35HEC **Facilities:** **Services:** **Off-site:** P R

BERTRIX LUXEMBOURG

Ardennen Camping Bertrix

rte de Mortehan, 6880
☎ 061 412281 ▤ 061 412588
e-mail: info@campingbertrix.be
web: www.campingbertrix.be
Well-equipped family site in a pleasant wooded setting.
dir: *Via E411 exit 25 onto N89.*
Open: 14 Mar-3 Nov **Site:** 14HEC **Facilities:** **Services:** **Leisure:** P

BÜLLINGEN (BULLANGE) LIÈGE

Hêtraie

Rotheck 14, 4760
☎ 080 642413 ▤ 080 642413
This site is on a sloping meadow near a fish pond, surrounded by groups of beautiful beech trees and conifers.
dir: *From village towards Amel, left for 2km & signed.*
Open: Apr-15 Nov **Site:** 3HEC **Facilities:** **Services:** **Leisure:** P **Off-site:** R

BELGIUM

BELGIUM

BURE LUXEMBOURG

Parc la Clusure

30 Chemin de la Clusure, 6927
☎ 084 360050 📠 084 366777
e-mail: info@parclaclusure.be
web: www.parclaclusure.be

Pleasant site with good facilities in the centre of the Ardennes.

dir: *E411 & N846 from Tellin.*

Open: All Year. **Site:** 12HEC **Prices:** 16-32 Mobile home hire 259-840 **Facilities:** Wi-fi Kids' Club Play Area **Services:** **Leisure:** P R

BÜTGENBACH LIÈGE

Worriken

Worriken Center 1, 4750
☎ 080 446961 📠 080 444247
e-mail: info@worriken.be
web: www.worriken.be

Situated on the shores of a lake.

Open: All Year. **Site:** 8HEC **Facilities:** **Services:** **Leisure:** L **Off-site:** P R

CHEVETOGNE NAMUR

Domaine Provincial

5590
☎ 083 687211 📠 083 688677
e-mail: info.chevetogne@province.namur.be
web: www.domainedechevetogne.be

Located in the grounds of a castle and surrounded by fine ornamental gardens. There is a variety of leisure activities.

Open: All Year. **Site:** 0.5HEC **Facilities:** Play Area **Services:** **Off-site:** P

COO-STAVELOT LIÈGE

Cascade

Chemin des Faravennes 5, 4970
☎ 080 684312 📠 080 684312
e-mail: info@camping-coo.be
web: www.camping-coo.be

A small touring and holiday site beside the River Amblève.

dir: *Motorway exit 10 or 11, site 3km from Trois-Ponts.*

Open: Apr-30 Oct **Site:** 0.75HEC **Facilities:** **Services:** **Leisure:** R **Off-site:**

DOCHAMPS LUXEMBOURG

Panorama Camping Petite Suisse

Al Bounire 27, 6960
☎ 084 444030 📠 084 444455
e-mail: info@petitesuisse.be
web: www.petitesuisse.be

On a southern slope, terraced pitches with views over the surrounding area. Facilities include outdoor sports and mountain bike hire.

dir: *E25/A40.*

Open: All Year. **Site:** 7.5HEC **Prices:** 16-29 Mobile home hire 280-805 **Facilities:** Wi-fi Kids' Club Play Area **Services:** **Leisure:** P

FLORENVILLE LUXEMBOURG

Rosière

Rive Gauche de la Semois, 6820
☎ 061 311937 📠 061 314873
e-mail: larosiere@scarlet.be
web: www.larosiere.be

Wooded surroundings close to the town centre.

dir: *E411 exit 26 for Verlaine/Neufchâteau.*

Open: Apr-Oct **Site:** 10HEC **Facilities:** **Services:** **Leisure:** P

FORRIÈRES LUXEMBOURG

Pré du Blason

r de la Ramée 30, 6953
☎ 084 212867 📠 084 223650
e-mail: info@camping-predublason.be
web: www.camping-predublason.be

This well-kept site lies on a meadow surrounded by wooded hills and is completely divided into pitches and crossed by rough gravel drives.

dir: *Off N49 Masbourg road.*

Open: Apr-Oct **Site:** 3HEC **Prices:** 11 Mobile home hire 240 **Facilities:** Wi-fi (charged) Play Area **Services:** **Leisure:** R

GEMMENICH LIÈGE

Kon Tiki

Terstraeten 141, 4851
☎ 087 785973
e-mail: info@campingkontiki.be
web: www.campingkontiki.be

Open: All Year. **Site:** 12HEC **Facilities:** **Services:** **Leisure:** P R

GOUVY — LUXEMBOURG

Lac de Cherapont

Cherapont 2, 6670
080 517082 080 517093
e-mail: cherapont@skynet.be
web: www.cherapont.be
On an extensive lakeside tourist complex with a variety of recreational facilities.
dir: *E25 exit 51. Or E42 exit 15.*
Open: Apr-Oct **Site:** 10HEC **Prices:** 12.50-15 **Facilities:** Play Area **Services:** **Leisure:** L R **Off-site:**

GRAND-HALLEUX — LUXEMBOURG

Neuf Prés

av de la Résistance, 6698
080 216882
web: www.vielsalm.be
A family site in pleasant wooded surroundings beside a river.
dir: *Via E42.*
Open: Apr-Sep **Site:** 4HEC **Facilities:** **Services:** **Leisure:** P R **Off-site:**

HOGNE — NAMUR

Relais

16 r de Serinchamps, 5377
0475 423049
e-mail: info@camping lerelais.com
web: www.campinglerelais.com
A pleasant site in a wooded park beside a lake.
dir: *N4 from Courrière to Hogne via Marche.*
Open: Mar-4 Jan **Site:** 12HEC **Facilities:** **Services:** **Leisure:** L R

HOUFFALIZE — LUXEMBOURG

Chasse et Pêche

r de la Roche 63, 6660
061 288314 061 289660
e-mail: info@cpbuitensport.com
web: www.cpbuitensport.com
A pleasant site attached to a café-restaurant with good recreational facilities.
dir: *3km NW off E25.*
Open: All Year. **Site:** 2HEC **Prices:** 17-20 **Facilities:** **Services:** **Leisure:** R

Moulin de Rensiwez

Moulin de Rensiwez 1, 6663
061 289027 061 289027
A good stopover site on a series of terraces beside the River Ourthe close to an old water-mill.
Open: All Year. **Site:** 5HEC **Prices:** 19 **Facilities:** **Services:** **Leisure:** R

LOUVEIGNÉ — LIÈGE

Moulin du Rouge-Thier

Rouge-Thier 8, 4141
041 608341 041 608341
A well-equipped site in a pleasant wooded location.
dir: *S of town towards Deigné.*
Open: Apr-30 Oct **Site:** 8HEC **Facilities:** **Services:**

MALONNE — NAMUR

Trieux

Les Tris 99, 5020
081 445583 081 445583
e-mail: camping.les.trieux@skynet.be
web: www.campinglestrieux.be
Open: Apr-30 Oct **Site:** 2.2HEC **Facilities:** **Services:** **Off-site:** P R

MARCHE-EN-FAMENNE — LUXEMBOURG

Euro Camping Paola

r du Panorama 10, 6900
084 311704 084 314722
e-mail: camping.paola@skynet.be
web: www.campingpaola.be
A long site on a hill with beautiful views. The only noise comes from a railway line that passes the site.
dir: *Towards Hotton, right after cemetery for 1km.*
Open: All Year. **Site:** 13HEC **Facilities:** **Services:** **Off-site:** P

NEUFCHÂTEAU — LUXEMBOURG

Spineuse

r de Malome 7, rte de Florenville, 6840
061 277320 061 277104
e-mail: info@camping-spineuse.be
web: www.camping-spineuse.be
dir: *2km from Florenville towards Neufchâteau.*
Open: All Year. **Site:** 2.5HEC **Facilities:** **Services:** **Leisure:** L P R

BELGIUM

OLLOY-SUR-VIROIN NAMUR

Try des Baudets

r de la Champagne, 5670
☎ 060 390108 🖷 060 390108
e-mail: trydesbaudets@breeboscampings.be
web: www.breeboscampings.be

A peaceful location on the edge of a forest. Plenty of facilities for children including a big playground and water-park on site.

dir: *N5.*

GPS: 50.0688, 4.5964

Open: All Year. **Site:** 12HEC **Prices:** 12.50-20.50 Mobile home hire 325 **Facilities:** Kids' Club Play Area **Services:** **Leisure:** P **Off-site:** R

OTEPPE LIÈGE

Hirondelle

r de la Burdinale 76A, 4210
☎ 085 711131 🖷 085 711021
e-mail: info@lhirondelle.be
web: www.lhirondelle.be

Ideal family site with modern facilities in the picturesque Burdinale Valley.

dir: *Signed N of town between E40 & E42.*

Open: Apr-Sep **Site:** 45HEC **Prices:** 13.75-21 Mobile home hire 300-630 **Facilities:** Wi-fi Play Area **Services:** **Leisure:** P **Off-site:**

RENDEUX LUXEMBOURG

Camping "Le Festival-Floreal"

rte de la Roche 89, 6987
☎ 084 477371 🖷 084 477364
e-mail: camping.festival@florealclub.be

Unspoiled surroundings beside the River Ourthe.

GPS: 50.2256, 5.5261

Open: Jan-Sep **Site:** 11HEC **Prices:** 13.75-21.75 **Facilities:** Wi-fi (charged) Kids' Club **Services:** **Leisure:** R

ROBERTVILLE LIÈGE

Plage

33 rte des Bains, 4950
☎ 080 446658 🖷 080 446178
e-mail: info@campinglaplage.be
web: www.campinglaplage.be

Open: All Year. **Site:** 1.8HEC **Facilities:** **Services:** **Leisure:** L P R

ROCHE-EN-ARDENNE, LA LUXEMBOURG

Lohan

20a rte de Houffalize, 6980
☎ 084 411545 🖷 084 411545

Set in a park surrounded by woodland, on the N bank of the River Ourthe.

dir: *3km E of La Roche towards Maboge & Houffalize.*

Open: Apr-1 Nov **Site:** 4HEC **Prices:** 13-15.50 **Facilities:** Play Area **Services:** **Leisure:** R

Ourthe

6980
☎ 084 411459
e-mail: info@campingdelourthe.be
web: www.campingdelourthe.be

Well-kept site beside the River Ourthe.

dir: *On SW bank of Ourthe below N34.*

Open: 15 Mar-15 Oct **Site:** 2HEC **Facilities:** **Services:** **Leisure:** R **Off-site:** P

SART-LEZ-SPA LIÈGE

Touring Club

Stockay 17, 4845
☎ 087 474400 🖷 087 475277
e-mail: info@campingspador.be
web: www.campingspador.be

Located on the banks of the river Wayai, with good leisure facilities. Kids' club available in July and August.

dir: *Signed E of Spa.*

Open: Apr-Oct **Site:** 6HEC **Prices:** 15.50-24.50 Mobile home hire 245-1029 **Facilities:** Wi-fi (charged) Kids' Club Play Area **Services:** **Leisure:** P **Off-site:** L

SIPPENAEKEN LIÈGE

Vieux Moulin

114 Tebruggen, 4851
☎ 087 784255 🖷 087 883497
web: www.camping-vieuxmoulin.be

A family site with good recreational facilities, set in a pleasant wooded location close to a nature reserve.

dir: *E40 exit Battile for Aubel-Hombourg-Sippenaeken.*

Open: Apr-Sep **Site:** 6HEC **Facilities:** **Services:** **Leisure:** P R

SPA — LIÈGE

Parc des Sources

r de la Sauvenière 141, 4900
087 772311 087 475965
e-mail: info@parcdessources.be
web: www.parcdessources.be

On the outskirts of the town close to a forest.

dir: *S of town centre on N32 towards Malmédy.*

Open: Apr-Oct **Site:** 2.5HEC **Facilities:** **Services:** **Leisure:** P **Off-site:**

SPRIMONT — LIÈGE

Tultay

r de Tultay 22, 4140
04 3821162 04 2658721
e-mail: sprimont@rcccb.com
web: www.rcccb.com

A pleasant site in wooded surroundings on the edge of a nature reserve.

dir: *E25 exit 45.*

GPS: 50.5117, 5.6638

Open: All Year. **Site:** 1.5HEC **Prices:** 10-14 **Facilities:** Wi-fi (charged) Play Area **Services:** **Off-site:** P

STAVELOT — LIÈGE

Domaine de l'Eau Rouge

Cheneux 25, 4970
080 863075 080 863075
web: www.eaurouge.eu

A pleasant riverside site with good sports facilities. 3km from the Formula 1 circuit at Spa.

dir: *Via E42 to Francorchamps or Malmédy.*

Open: All Year. **Site:** 4HEC **Prices:** 14.50-17 Mobile home hire 455 **Facilities:** Wi-fi Play Area **Services:** **Leisure:** R **Off-site:** P

TENNEVILLE — LUXEMBOURG

Pont de Berguème

r Berguème 9, 6970
084 455443 084 456231
e-mail: info@pontbergueme.be
web: www.pontbergueme.be

A peaceful wooded setting in the beautiful Ardennes area with modern facilities.

dir: *Off N4 towards Berguème, then turn right.*

GPS: 50.0756, 5.5556

Open: All Year. **Site:** 3HEC **Prices:** 15 **Facilities:** Wi-fi (charged) **Services:** **Leisure:** R **Off-site:**

THOMMEN-REULAND — LIÈGE

Hohenbusch

Grüfflingen 44, 4791
080 227523 080 420807
e-mail: info@hohenbusch.be
web: www.hohenbusch.be

A well-appointed family site on a wooded meadow with plenty of recreational facilities.

dir: *E42 exit 15, take N62 to the right.*

GPS: 50.2417, 6.0931

Open: Apr-Oct **Site:** 5HEC **Prices:** 14-20 Mobile home hire 295-535 **Facilities:** Play Area **Services:** **Leisure:** P

BELGIUM

VIELSALM — LUXEMBOURG

Salm

chemin de la Vallée, 6690
080 216241 080 217266
web: www.vielsalm.be

Open: All Year. **Site:** 2.5HEC **Facilities:** **Services:** **Leisure:** R **Off-site:** L P

VIRTON — LUXEMBOURG

Colline de Rabais

clos des Horles 1, 6760
063 571195 063 583342
e-mail: info@collinederabais.be
web: www.collinederabais.be

A secluded family site in the heart of the Gaume region close to a lake, with good recreational facilities.

dir: *NE of Virton between N87 & N82.*

Open: All Year. **Site:** 8HEC **Facilities:** **Services:** **Leisure:** P **Off-site:** L

WAIMES — LIÈGE

Anderegg

Bruyères 4, 4950
080 679393
e-mail: campinganderegg@skynet.be
web: www.campinganderegg.be

A peaceful location beside the Lac de Robertville, the site has modern sanitary facilities.

GPS: 50.4392, 6.1181

Open: All Year. **Site:** 1.5HEC **Prices:** 14.70 **Facilities:** Wi-fi (charged) Play Area **Services:** **Off-site:** L

Facilities shop shower electric points for razors electric points for caravans parking by tents permitted compulsory separate car park **Services** café/restaurant bar Camping Gaz International gas other than Camping Gaz first aid facilities laundry **Leisure** swimming L-Lake P-Pool R-River S-Sea **Off-site** All facilities within 5km

Croatia

Drinking and driving

Forbidden for drivers under 24 years - 0 percentage of alcohol allowed in blood. Drivers 24 years and over; alcohol in blood 0.05%. Exceptions to this rule apply to professional drivers. Tests for narcotics may be performed. If tests prove positive consequences may include confiscation of vehicle, heavy fine and loss of licence. It is prohibited to drive after taking medicine whose side effects may affect the ability to drive.

Driving licence

Minimum age at which a UK licence holder may drive temporarily imported car and/or motorcycle (exceeding 125cc): 18.

Fines

On the spot; fines to be paid within 8 days at a post office or bank. Police may hold your passport until evidence of payment is produced. The licence of a foreign motorist can be suspended for up to 8 days for driving with excess alcohol, driving without prescribed medical aids e.g. glasses, driving in a state of exhaustion or whilst ill.

Lights

Dipped headlights are compulsory in reduced visibility, and in the daytime from the last Sunday in October to the last Sunday in March. Fine for non compliance.

Motorcycles

Use of dipped headlights during the day, and wearing of crash helmet(s) is compulsory. Children under 12 cannot travel as a passenger.

Motor insurance

Third-party compulsory. It is recommended that all visitors obtain a green card prior to travel to facilitate insurance formalities in case of an accident. The green card must cover Croatia (HR) as well as Bosnia Herzegovina if travelling on a 20km section of coastline at Neum, along the Dalmatian coastal highway.

Passengers/children in cars

Children under 12 cannot travel as a front seat passenger, with the exception of a child under 2 years seated in a suitable child seat. The seat must be fitted facing in the opposite direction of travel with passenger airbags turned off. Children from 2 to 5 must be in a suitable child seat; other children must use a suitable child restraint, with a booster seat where necessary.

Seat belts

Compulsory for all occupants to wear seat belts, if fitted.

Speed limits

Unless signed otherwise:

Vehicles without trailers.	
Built-up areas	50km/h
Outside built-up areas	90km/h
Expressways	110km/h
Motorways	130km/h
Private vehicles with a trailer/caravan	
Roads	80km/h
Expressways	80km/h
Motorways	90km/h
Motorists under 24 years of age	
Outside built-up areas	80km/h
Expressways	100km/h
Motorways	120km/h
Minimum speed on motorways	60km/h

Additional Information

Compulsory equipment: Spare bulbs (but not for xenon, neon, LED or similar lights); First-aid kit (excluding motorcycles); Warning triangle - two triangles required if towing a trailer. (excludes motorcycles); Snow chains, Nov-Apr, especially in Gorski Kotar and Lika regions; Reflective jacket (EN-471) - This must be worn if the driver has to get out of the vehicle at the roadside, in an emergency. Be aware however that car hire companies may not supply them to persons hiring vehicles.
Use of spiked tyres and radar detectors is prohibited.
Authorities at the frontier must certify any visible damage to a vehicle entering Croatia and a certificate obtained; this must be produced when leaving the country.

Tolls Currency: Kunas (HRK)	Car	Car Towing Caravan/Trailer
A1 (E65) Zagreb - Split - Dubrovnik	187HRK	309HRK
A6 (E65) Zagreb - Rijeka	60HRK	99HRK
A3+A5 (E70) Zagreb - Lipovac	93HRK	139HRK
A4 (E71) Zagreb - Gorican	36HRK	60HRK
A7 Rupa - Rijeka	5HRK	8HRK
Zagreb- Macelj (Zapresic Tollgate) A2 (E59)	42HRK	69HRK
Bridges and Tunnels		
Krk Bridge	30HRK	40HRK
A8 Ucka Tunnel (Kanfanar-Matuiji)	28HRK	46HRK
A9 Mirna Bridge (Kastel-Pula)	14HRK	23HRK

Please note: Although the official currency of Croatia is the Croation kuna, the campsites featured in this guide have quoted their prices in Euros.

CROATIA

BIOGRAD NA MORU — ZADAR

Camping Park Soline

Put Solina 17, 23210
023 383351 023 384823
e-mail: info@campsoline.com
web: www.campsoline.com

Set among pine trees with access to the sea and a pebble beach (with a sandy beach close by).

Open: 15 Apr-Sep **Site:** 20HEC **Prices:** 25.10-35.20 Mobile home hire 315-945 **Facilities:** Wi-fi (charged) Kids' Club Play Area **Services:** **Leisure:** S **Off-site:** P

FAZANA — ISTRIA

Bi-Village

Dragonja 115, 52212
052 300300 052 380711
e-mail: info@bivillage.com
web: www.bivillage.com

Site set among pine trees near the sea. Fine beaches.

dir: *Follow camping signs approaching Pula/Fazana.*

Open: 4 Apr-10 Oct **Site:** 40HEC **Facilities:** **Services:** **Leisure:** P S **Off-site:**

KOLAN (ISLAND OF PAG) — ZADAR

Village Šimuni

Šimuni bb, 23251
023 697441 023 657442
e-mail: info@camping-simuni.hr
web: www.camping-simuni.hr

Situated in oak and pine woods near a small fishing village on the Island of Pag, one of the largest Adriatic islands. The beach extends for 4km.

dir: *A1 motorway Karlovac-Split, before Zadar exit at Posedarje to Pag. 11km towards Novalia, site signed.*

Open: All Year. **Site:** 35HEC **Prices:** 15-39 Mobile home hire 210-1120 **Facilities:** Wi-fi (charged) Kids' Club Play Area **Services:** **Leisure:** S

LOPAR (RAB) — GORSKI KOTAR

San Marino

Lopar bb, 51280
051 775133 051 775290
e-mail: ac-sanmarino@imperial.hr
web: www.rab-camping.com

Situated in shady pinewoods next to the sandy Paradise Beach on the Island of Rab. Easy access to the sea.

dir: *Paradise Beach is 3km S of ferry landing at Crnika Bay*

Open: Apr-Sep **Site:** 9HEC **Facilities:** **Services:** **Leisure:** S

OKRUG GORNJI (ISLAND OF ČIOVO) — DALMATIA

Camping Rožac

Šetalište Stjepana Radicá 56, 21220
021 806105 021 882554
e-mail: booking@camp-rozac.hr
web: www.camp-rozac.hr

On the island of Čiovo, reached by bridge from Trogir. Surrounded by beach, the site is in a wooded setting.

dir: *From 8/E65 to Trogir, pass two bridges, turn right to island, follow road to site.*

GPS: 43.5058, 16.2583

Open: Apr-Oct **Site:** 2.5HEC **Prices:** 26.80-34 Mobile home hire 350-805 **Facilities:** Wi-fi (charged) Play Area **Services:** **Leisure:** S **Off-site:**

PAKOŠTANE — ZADAR

Camping Kozarica

Brune Bušica bb, 23211
023 381070 023 381068
e-mail: kozarica@adria-more.hr
web: www.adria-more.hr

Shaded by pines, a family friendly site where water sports are available.

Open: 2 Apr-Oct **Site:** 6HEC **Prices:** 17.70-33.90 Mobile home hire 210-882 **Facilities:** Wi-fi Kids' Club Play Area **Services:** **Leisure:** S **Off-site:** L

Facilities shop shower electric points for razors electric points for caravans parking by tents permitted compulsory separate car park **Services** café/restaurant bar Camping Gaz International gas other than Camping Gaz first aid facilities laundry **Leisure** swimming L-Lake P-Pool R-River S-Sea **Off-site** All facilities within 5km

POREČ — ISTRIA

Lanterna

52440

☎ 52 404500

e-mail: lanterna@valamar.com

Large shady site on the beautiful Lanterna peninsula situated among pine and oak trees.

Open: Apr-11 Oct **Site:** 80HEC **Facilities:** **Services:** **Leisure:** P S **Off-site:**

PUNAT (ISLAND OF KRK) — GORSKI KOTAR

Pila

Šetalište Ivana Brusića 2, 51521

☎ 051 854020 051 854020

e-mail: pila@hoteli-punat.hr

web: www.hoteli-punat.hr

Site set among pine woods in the south of the island of Krk which is connected to the mainland by a bridge. A tree-fringed promenade divides it from the sea and the beach.

dir: *From mainland take bridge to Krk, past Punat towards Stara Baaka, campsite 1st right.*

Open: 22 Apr-16 Oct **Site:** 8.44HEC **Prices:** 20-34 **Facilities:** **Services:** **Leisure:** S **Off-site:**

ROVINJ — ISTRIA

Naturist Camping Valalta

Cesta Valalta - Lim bb, 52210

☎ 052 804800 052 811463

e-mail: valalta@valalta.hr

web: www.valalta.hr

Large naturist site on the coast with sand and shingle beaches, located at the entrance to the Lim channel nature reserve. Modern facilities, salt water swimming pools, supermarket, sauna, beauty salon and entertainment.

dir: *7km NW from Rovinj, follow signs Valalta*

Open: 30 Apr-1 Oct **Site:** 90HEC **Prices:** 18-36.50 **Facilities:** Wi-fi (charged) Kids' Club Play Area **Services:** **Leisure:** P S

see advert below

Polari

Polari bb, 52210

☎ 052 801501 052 811395

e-mail: polari@maistra.hr

web: www.campingrovinjvrsar.com

Located in a picturesque cove south of Rovinj. Extensive facilities with pitches shaded by evergreen trees. One part of the camp, Punta Eva, is reserved for naturists.

Open: 2 Apr-1 Oct **Site:** 60HEC **Prices:** 17-36.10 **Facilities:** Wi-fi **Services:** **Leisure:** P S

Site 6HEC (site size) grass sand stone little shade partly shaded mainly shaded bungalows for hire (static) caravans for hire tents for hire no dogs site fully accessible for wheelchairs

Prices amount quoted is per night, for 2 adults and car, plus tent or caravan. Mobile home hire is a weekly rate.

SPLIT DALMATIA

Camping Stobreč Split

Sv.Lovre 6, 21311
021 325426 021 325452
e-mail: camping.split@gmail.com
web: www.campingsplit.com

In the district of Stobreč, part of the city of Split, set in a forest. Surrounded on two sides by the sea and at the mouth of the Žrnovnica river, with both sandy and pebble beaches. Camping pitches are fenced and planted with seedlings.

Open: All Year. **Site:** 5HEC
Prices: 17.70-28.70 **Facilities:** Wi-fi (charged) Kids' Club Play Area **Services:** **Leisure:** R S
Off-site: P

UMAG ISTRIA

Campsite Finida

Krizine 55, 52470
052 700700 052 725969
e-mail: camp.finida@istraturist.hr
web: www.istracamping.com

Peaceful site located on the sea front in an area with secluded bays.

dir: *7km from centre of Umag towards Novigrad.*

Open: 23 Apr-25 Sep **Site:** 5HEC **Prices:** 14.60-31.40
Facilities: **Services:**
Leisure: S **Off-site:** P

Campsite Park Umag

Karigador bb, 52470
052 700700 052 725053
e-mail: camp.park.umag@istraturist.hr
web: www.istracamping.com

Large family campsite with many facilities for children including swimming pools with waterfalls, castles and a pirate ship.

dir: *9km from town centre of Umag towards Novigrad.*

Open: 23 Apr-25 Sep **Site:** 101HEC
Prices: 17.50-45.60 Mobile home hire 343-1050 **Facilities:** Wi-fi (charged) Kids' Club Play Area **Services:** **Leisure:** P S **Off-site:**

Campsite Pineta

Istarska bb, 52475
052 709550 052 709559
e-mail: camp.pineta@istraturist.hr
web: www.istracamping.com

Quiet site among pine trees located near the beach close to a picturesque fishing village.

dir: *9km from town centre of Umag, at foot of lighthouse near village of Savudrija.*

Open: 23 Apr-25 Sep **Site:** 11.30HEC
Prices: 14.10-28.40 **Facilities:** **Services:** **Leisure:** P S **Off-site:**

Campsite Stella Maris

Stella Maris 8, Monterol, 52470
052 710900 052 710909
e-mail: camp.stella.maris@istraturist.hr
web: www.istracamping.com

Meadowland site among pine trees and situated next to a picturesque lagoon with a fine beach.

dir: *2km from town centre of Umag.*

Open: 23 Apr-25 Sep **Site:** 5HEC **Prices:** 14.60-31.40
Facilities: Wi-fi (charged) Kids' Club Play Area
Services: **Off-site:** P S

Naturist Kanegra FKK

Kanegra bb, 52470
052 700700 052 709499
e-mail: camping@istraturist.com
web: www.istracamping.com

A naturist site located on the seafront, with a pebble beach, 10km from Umag. Leisure facilities include a tennis school and bike rental.

Open: 23 Apr-25 Sep **Site:** 4.8HEC
Prices: 14.60-31.40 **Facilities:** Wi-fi Play Area
Services: **Leisure:** S **Off-site:**

VRSAR ISTRIA

Porto Sole

Petalon, 52450
052 426500 052 426580
e-mail: portosole@maistra.hr
web: www.maistra.com

A small site by the shore in a sheltered bay set in sunny meadows and pinewoods. Extensive sports facilities.

Open: 26 Apr-3 Oct **Site:** **Facilities:**
Leisure: P

Czech Republic

Drinking and driving

Strictly forbidden. 0% of alcohol allowed in drivers' blood. Fine may be between 25,000 and 50,000 Czech crown (CZK) and withdrawal of the driving licence for up to two years. Frequent random testing takes place, driving under the influence of alcohol and drugs is considered a criminal offence.

Driving licence

Minimum age at which a UK licence holder may drive a temporarily imported car or motorcycle over 125cc (max 25kW): 18. Photo card licences accepted - non-photo licences must be accompanied by an International Driving Permit.

Fines

On-the-spot up to 5,000 CZK, maximum fine for traffic offence 100,000 CZK. An official receipt should be obtained. The police can retain your driving licence if you have committed a serious traffic offence. Illegally parked vehicles may be clamped or towed away.

Lights

Use of dipped headlights compulsory: during the day, all year. Fine for non-compliance: approximately 2,000 CZK. Any vehicle warning lights, other than those supplied with the vehicle as original equipment, must be made inoperative.

Motorcycles

Use of dipped headlights compulsory: during the day, all year. The wearing of crash helmets is compulsory for driver and passenger. It is forbidden for motorcyclists to smoke while driving.

Motor insurance

Third-party compulsory.

Passengers & children

All passengers must use seat belts. Children or persons under 36kg and 1.5m, are not permitted to travel in a vehicle unless using a suitable restraint system. A child in the front of a vehicle using a child restraint system where the airbag is activated, must travel facing forward.

Seat belts

Compulsory for all occupants to wear seat belts, if fitted.

Speed limits

Standard legal limits, (unless signed)

private vehicles without trailers

built-up areas 50km/h

outside built-up areas 90km/h

motorways 130km/h

expressways through built up areas 80km/h

Car with trailer or caravan 80km/h

Maximum speed with snow chains 50km/h. At railway crossings drivers must not exceed 30km/h for 50m before the crossing. The arrival of a train is indicated by red flashing lights/red or yellow flag. Vehicles that are constructed with a maximum speed of 80km/h or under are not permitted to travel on motorways.

Additional information

Compulsory equipment in Czech Republic: First-aid kit; Warning triangle (not required for two wheeled vehicles); winter tyres (which must be marked M&S) or snow chains between 1 Nov and 31 Mar. Dependant upon weather conditions this period may be extended. The minimum depth on winter tyres is 4mm; reflective jacket – EU standard EN471. The driver of a vehicle with 2 or more axles must carry a reflective waistcoat which has to be used in the event of a breakdown or emergency outside a built up area on expressways and motorways. The jacket must be kept within the car, and not in the boot. Waistcoat is also recommended for passengers and riders of mopeds and motorcycles.

Motorway tax is payable for the use of motorways and express roads. A windscreen sticker must be displayed on all four-wheeled vehicles up to 3.5t as evidence of payment. Stickers can be purchased at the Czech frontier, UAMK branch offices, petrol stations or post offices for periods of one year, one month or ten consecutive days. Fines imposed for non-display.

The authorities at the frontier must certify any visible damage to a vehicle entering the Czech Republic. If any damage occurs inside the country a police report must be obtained at the scene of the accident. Damaged vehicles may only be taken out of the country on production of this evidence.

The use of an audible warning device is only permitted in built up areas to avoid imminent danger, they are prohibited between 2000hrs and 0600hrs, and in Prague.

The use of spiked tyres is prohibited.

A GPS satnav which has maps indicating the location of fixed speed cameras must have that function deactivated.

The use of radar detectors is prohibited.

Motorway Tax Sticker Currency: Czech Koruna (CZK)	Car	Car Towing Caravan/Trailer
1 week	250CZK	250CZK
1 month	350CZK	350CZK
1 year	1,200CZK	1,200CZK

CZECH REPUBLIC

BÍTOV JIHOMORAVSKÝ

Camp Bítov - Vranovská Přehrada

67110
☎ 605 842965 📠 515 296204
e-mail: info@camp-bitov.cz
web: www.camp-bitov.cz
Surrounded by deciduous forests, this site's leisure facilities include fishing, table tennis and concerts.

Open: May-15 Sep **Site:** **Prices:** 184-270 **Facilities:** Wi-fi Play Area **Services:** **Leisure:** L

CERNÁ V POSUMAVÍ BOHEMIA

Camping Olsina

Ckyne 212, 38481
☎ 608 029982
e-mail: info@campingolsina.cz
web: www.campingolsina.cz
Partly forested campsite situated by the Lipen lake, near Cerná village.

dir: *From Cerná v Posumaví towards Ceský Krumlov, after 1km turn left, campsite signed.*

Open: 20 Apr-20 Oct **Site:** 5.5HEC **Prices:** 320-340 **Facilities:** Wi-fi **Services:** **Leisure:** L **Off-site:**

Villa Bohemia

Lipno, 38223
☎ 380 744004
e-mail: camp@villabohemia.cz
web: www.villabohemia.cz
Situated on the shores of Lake Lipno with a kilometre long private beach. Fine views of the lake and the mountains beyond. Good facilities and high standard sanitary installations.

dir: *Ceský Krumlov-Cerná v Posumaví road. Directly after dam on Lipno lake follow sign for Jestrabi, site 1.5km*

Open: May-Sep **Site:** 3.5HEC **Facilities:** **Services:** **Leisure:** L **Off-site:**

FRYMBURK BOHEMIA

Frymburk

38279
☎ 380 735284 📠 380 735283
e-mail: info@campingfrymburk.cz
web: www.campingfrymburk.cz
In an attractive location on the Lipno lake in southern Bohemia, Frymburk is ideal for swimming and water activities. Level pitches in terraces. A kids' club is available during high season.

dir: *On route 163, 1km S of Frymburk at Lipno Lake.*

Open: 29 Apr-1 Oct **Site:** 4.5HEC **Prices:** 509-669 Mobile home hire 9100-16800 **Facilities:** Wi-fi Kids' Club **Services:** **Leisure:** L **Off-site:** P

HLUBOKÉ MAŠŮVKY MORAVIA

Country

67152
☎ 515 255249 📠 515 255249
e-mail: camping-country@cbox.cz
web: www.camp-country.com
Attractively landscaped site, close to the historical town of Znojmo. In a rural location close to a National Park and the Austrian border. Suitable for family camping with lots of activities for children.

dir: *7km N of Znojmo. Take E59 (Jihlava-Vienna), near Kravsko turn left, site 6km.*

Open: May-Oct **Site:** 2HEC **Prices:** 360-410 **Facilities:** Wi-fi Play Area **Services:** **Leisure:** P **Off-site:** R

HLUK MORAVIA

Camping Babi Hora

68725
☎ 572 581180
e-mail: babihora@quick.cz
web: www.camping-babihora.com
Quiet meadowland site surrounded by woodland.

dir: *E50, take exit to Kunovice, then follow exit for Hluk & signs to campsite.*

Open: 15 May-15 Sep **Site:** 2.5HEC **Prices:** 420-510 **Facilities:** Wi-fi Play Area **Services:** **Leisure:** P

CZECH REPUBLIC

MARIANSKÉ LAZNĚ — ZÁPADOCESKY

Karolina

Brod nad Tichou, 34815
777 296990
e-mail: office@camp-k.cz
web: www.camp-k.cz

A quiet, comfortable, family-based camp site surrounded by forest and hills with a brook running through, on the edge of the West Bohemian spa region.

dir: *E50 motorway towards Plzen, exit 128 for Brod nad Tichou, 13km to campsite.*

Open: May-15 Oct **Site:** 2.8HEC **Facilities:** Play Area **Services:** **Leisure:** P R **Off-site:** L

NOVÉ STRAŠECÍ — BOHEMIA

Bucek

Trtice 170, 27101
313 564212
e-mail: info@campingbucek.cz
web: www.campingbucek.cz

Partly forested site beside a large lake with a sandy beach and suitable for all kinds of water sports. At peak times there is a small restaurant open in the grounds of the campsite. Modern sanitary facilities.

dir: *On E48/6 Prague-Karlovy Vary road, 4km past Nové Strašecí exit.*

Open: 25 Apr-15 Sep **Site:** 5HEC **Prices:** 460-600 Mobile home hire 9770-17470 **Facilities:** Wi-fi Play Area **Services:** **Leisure:** L P

PASOHLÁVKY — MORAVIA

Autocamp Merkur

69122
519 427751 519 427501
e-mail: camp@pasohlavky.cz
web: www.pasohlavky.cz

Situated by the upper Novomlynskas reservoir, also called the Palava lakes, with views of surrounding hills. Ideal for swimming, fishing and water sports.

dir: *35km from Brno on right of E461 (Brno-Vienna).*

Open: Apr-Oct **Site:** 4.5HEC **Facilities:** **Services:** **Leisure:** L P

PLZEŇ — ZÁPADOCESKY

Autocamping Ostende

Maly Bolevec, 32300
377 520194 377 520194
e-mail: atc-ostende@cbox.cz
web: www.cbox.cz/atc-ostende

By the shore of the Grand Boulevec lake, surrounded by woods and forests. Good location for swimming and walking.

dir: *N of Plzen, signposted on Plzen-Most road.*

GPS: 49.7772, 13.39

Open: May-Sep **Site:** 3HEC **Prices:** 380-560 **Facilities:** Play Area **Services:** **Leisure:** L **Off-site:** P

PRAHA (PRAGUE) — BOHEMIA

Family Camp Drusus

K Reporyjim 4, 15500
235 514391 235 514391
e-mail: drusus@drusus.com
web: www.drusus.com

Quiet site on outskirts of Prague within easy reach of the city.

GPS: 50.0439, 14.2844

Open: Apr-5 Oct **Site:** 1.2HEC **Prices:** 370-570 **Facilities:** Wi-fi Play Area **Services:** **Off-site:** P

Prager

V Ladech 3, 14900
244 912854 244 912854
e-mail: petrgali@login.cz
web: www.camp.cz/prager

Family run campsite in south-east Prague, within easy reach of the city centre.

dir: *E50 (Prague-Brno), exit 2/2A for Seberov.*

GPS: 50.0125, 14.5117

Open: Etr & May-Sep **Site:** 0.4HEC **Prices:** 400 **Facilities:** Wi-fi Play Area **Services:** **Leisure:** P **Off-site:** L

Triocamp

Ústecká (Obsluzná 43), 18400
☎ 283 850793 283 850793
e-mail: triocamp.praha@telecom.cz
web: www.triocamp.cz

On the northern edge of Prague and convenient for visiting the city. The ground is slightly sloping but most pitches are level and in the shade of mature trees.

dir: *D8/E55 towards Teplice, exit Zdiby, route 608 to Dolni Cabry, site 3km on right.*

Open: All Year. **Site:** 1HEC **Prices:** 690-850 Mobile home hire 10000-15000 **Facilities:** Wi-fi (charged) Play Area **Services:** **Leisure:** P **Off-site:**

PROTIVÍN — BOHEMIA

Blanice

Chelcického 889, 39811
☎ 721 589125
e-mail: info@campingblanice.nl
web: www.campingblanice.nl

Low-lying site in the pretty, flat valley of the Blanice river. Situated between two forks of the river, the site is accessed over a little bridge.

dir: *Take E49 from Ceske Budejovice-Pisek, site signed by exit for Protovín.*

Open: Apr-15 Sep **Site:** 1HEC **Facilities:** **Services:** **Off-site:** R

ROZNOV POD RADHOŠTĚM — MORAVIA

Roznov

Radhostska 940, 75661
☎ 571 648001/3 571 620513
e-mail: info@camproznov.cz
web: www.camproznov.cz

Level site set amid a variety of fruit and other trees. Some pitches are small although the newer landscaped pitches are bigger. Situated by a main road although the surrounding trees help to reduce the traffic noise.

dir: *Between Dolni Becva & Roznov on E442, on right.*

Open: Apr-Oct **Site:** 3.9HEC **Facilities:** **Services:** **Leisure:** P **Off-site:** R

SOBĚSLAV — BOHEMIA

ATC Karvánky

39201
☎ 381 521003
e-mail: karvanky@post.cz
web: www.karvanky.cz

Set in a wooded area where facilities include fishing.

dir: *E55.*

Open: May-Sep **Site:** 5HEC **Facilities:** Wi-fi (charged) Play Area **Services:** **Leisure:** L **Off-site:** R

STRÁZOV — SUMAVA

U Dvou Orechu

Splz 13, 34021
☎ 602 394496
e-mail: info@camping-tsjechie.nl
web: www.camping-tsjechie.nl

Partly terraced site in scenic forested surroundings with glacial lakes and fast flowing rivers.

dir: *Take route 191 (Nyrsko-Katovy), then route 171 to Strázov. In Strázov right towards Depoltice/Divisovice, site on left after 2km.*

GPS: 49.2814, 13.2400

Open: May-1 Oct **Site:** 1.5HEC **Prices:** 375-500 **Facilities:** Wi-fi **Services:** **Off-site:** P

TURNOV — LIBERECKÝ

Autocamp Sedmihorky

51101
☎ 481 389162 481 389160
e-mail: camp@campsedmihorky.cz
web: www.campsedmihorky.cz

With good transport links, the site grounds are grassy and divided by asphalt paths. There is a pond where swimming is available along with cycle rental and grass courts for volleyball or badminton.

GPS: 50.5580, 15.1867

Open: All Year. **Site:** **Prices:** 155-280 Mobile home hire 5110-11970 **Facilities:** Wi-fi Kids' Club Play Area **Services:** **Leisure:** L **Off-site:** R

CZECH REPUBLIC

VRCHLABI KRÁLOVÉHRADECKÝ

Holiday Park Lisci Farma

Dolní Branná 350, 54362
☎ 499 421473 499 421656
e-mail: info@liscifarma.cz
web: www.liscifarma.cz

Pitches are fairly flat, although the terrain is slightly sloping and some pitches are terraced. There is shade and the site is well equipped for the whole family with many facilities. Close to a sandy lakeside beach.

dir: *Route 295 (Vrchlabi-Studenec), site on right.*

Open: All Year. **Site:** 8HEC **Facilities:** **Services:** **Leisure:** P **Off-site:** L R

ZLATNIKY BOHEMIA

Oase Praha

The Camping and Caravanning Club The Friendly Club

25241
☎ 241 932044
e-mail: info@campingoase.cz
web: www.campingoase.cz

A mere 16 kilometres from historic, romantic Prague, the bus stops at the site entrance.

C&CC Report *This friendly, high quality, family-run site is on the edge of a village amid the gently rolling countryside of Bohemia, while access to the area from the Channel is by fast and cheap roads. For a small and cosy site, Oase Praha provides a surprisingly wide range of good quality facilities, and is particularly good for families who like relaxing and exploring. A mere five kilometres from historic, romantic Prague, the bus stops at the site entrance. Other great attractions within reach are Konopiste and Karlstejn castles, old Kutna Hora and Prague zoo, with Aquapalace waterpark only 16km away.*

dir: *S of Prague follow E50/E65 (Prague-Brno), exit 11 (Jesenice). In Jesenice follow camping signs to Zlatniky, turn left at x-rds before village, campsite on left.*

GPS: 49.9514, 14.4747

Open: 30 Apr-15 Sep **Site:** 2HEC
Prices: 410-520 Mobile home hire 8400-18200 **Facilities:** Wi-fi Kids' Club Play Area **Services:** **Leisure:** P **Off-site:** L

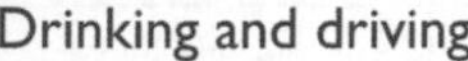

France

Drinking and driving

If the level of alcohol in the bloodstream is 0.05% or more, severe penalties include fine, imprisonment and/or confiscation of the driving licence. Saliva drug tests will be used to detect drivers under the influence of drugs – severe penalties as above.

Driving licence

Minimum age at which a UK licence holder may drive a temporarily imported car 18, motorcycle (up to 80cc) 16, motorcycle (over 80cc) 18.

Fines

On-the-spot fines or 'deposits' are severe. An official receipt should be issued. Vehicles parking contrary to regulations may be towed away and impounded.

Lights

Dipped headlights must be used in poor daytime visibility. It is highly recommended by the French Government that vehicles with more than 4 wheels use dipped headlights day and night.

Motorcycles

Dipped headlights during the day compulsory, as is wearing of crash helmets for both driver and passenger.

Motor insurance

Third-party compulsory.

Passengers and children

Children under the age of 10 are not permitted to travel in the front seats, unless there are no rear seats or the rear seats are already occupied with children under 10, or there are no seat belts. If a child under does travel in the front seat, the passenger airbag must be deactivated, and they must be in an approved child seat or restraint adapted to their size. A baby up to 13kg must be carried in a rear facing baby seat. A child between 9 and 18kg must be seated in a child seat and a child from 15kg up to 10 years can use a booster seat with seat belt or harness.

Seat belts

Compulsory for front/rear seat occupants to wear seat belts, if fitted.

Speed limits

unless signed otherwise,

private vehicles without trailers or trailer less than 3.5t

Built-up areas	50km/h
Outside built-up areas	90km/h
Urban motorways and dual carriageways separated by a central reservation	110km/h
Motorways	130km/h

Lower speed limits (wet weather & visiting motorists who have held a driving licence for less than 2 years)

Outside built-up areas	80km/h
Dual carriageways	100km/h
Motorways	110km/h
Minimum speed limit on motorways	80km/h

private vehicles with trailer of 3.5t to 12t

Motorways	90km/h
Priority roads/dual carriageways	90km/h
Other roads	80km/h

If the weight of the trailer exceeds that of the car, the speed limits are lower as follows:

- if the excess is less than 30%	65km/h
- if the excess is more than 30%	45km/h

In these cases, a disc showing maximum speed must be displayed on the rear of caravan/trailers. They may not be driven in the fast lane of a 3-lane motorway.

Additional information

Compulsory equipment in France/Monaco: Warning triangle (excludes motorcycles); snow chains - must be fitted to vehicles using snow-covered roads in compliance with the relevant road sign; reflective jackets (EN471) - one reflective jacket in the vehicle. This does not apply to drivers of two-wheeled and three-wheeled vehicles.

It is recommended that visitors equip their vehicle with a set of replacement bulbs.

In built-up areas give way to traffic coming from the right "priorité à droite". At signed roundabouts bearing the words "Vous n'avez pas la priorité" or "Cédez le passage" traffic on the roundabout has priority; where no such sign exists traffic entering the roundabout has priority.

Overtaking stationary trams is prohibited when passengers are boarding/alighting.

Parking discs for 'blue zone' parking areas can be obtained from police stations, tourist offices and some shops.

In built up areas the use of the horn is prohibited except in cases of immediate danger.

Apparatus with a screen which can distract a driver (such as television, video, DVD equipment) should be positioned in places where the driver is unable to see them. This excludes GPS systems. It is prohibited to touch or program the device unless parked in a safe place.

It is absolutely prohibited to carry, transport or use radar detectors. Failure to comply with this regulation involves a fine of up to €1500 and the vehicle and/or device may be confiscated.

Tolls, Tunnels & Bridges

Tolls Currency Euro (€)	Car	Car Towing Caravan/Trailer
A1 - Lille - Paris	€14.60	€21.50
A10 - Tours - Poitiers	€9.70	€16.00
A10 - Poitiers - Saintes	€11.30	€17.90
A10 - Paris - Tours	€22.80	€33.90
A10 - Tours - Bordeaux	€30.10	€47.40
A10/A71 - Paris - Clermont-Ferrand	€33.80	€54.30
A10/A837 - Bordeaux - La Rochelle	€12.60	€19.10
A11 - Angers - Nantes	€8.20	€12.40
A11 - Paris - Angers	€25.40	€39.00
A11/A81 - Paris - Rennes	€26.70	€40.80
A13 - Le Havre - St Saens	€7.20	€10.80
A13/A131 - Le Havre - Paris	€24.30	€39.10
A13/A14 - Rouen - Paris	€13.40	€24.10
A13/A14 - Caen - Paris	€21.60	€36.40
A14 - Orgeval - Paris (La defense)	€7.70	€15.40
A16 - Calais - Paris	€18.70	€27.30
A2/A1 - Valenciennes - Paris	€13.00	€19.10
A2/A26 - Valenciennes - Reims	€11.90	€17.80
A26 - Reims - Troyes	€10.20	€15.20
A26 - Calais - Reims	€20.20	€30.20
A26/A1 - Calais - Paris	€18.90	€27.30
A26/A5 - Reims - Lyon	€37.30	€57.00
A26/A5/A39/A40 - Reims - Mont Blanc Tunnel (Tunnel du Mont Blanc)	€51.10	€78.30
A29 - Le Havre - St Saens (A29)	€7.20	€10.80
A29/A16 - Neufchatel en Bray - Amiens	€6.30	€9.80
A29/A26 - Amiens - Reims	€12.10	€18.30
A31 - Langres - Dijon	€2.10	€3.10
A31 - Dijon - Beaune	€2.60	€3.80
A31 - Nancy - Langres	€7.90	€12.50
A36 - Belfort - Mulhouse (German Frontier)	€2.80	€4.10
A36 - Beaune - Besançon	€6.90	€10.60
A36 - Besançon - Belfort	€7.00	€10.70
A39 - Dijon - Dole	€2.80	€4.20

Tolls Currency Euro (€)	Car	Car Towing Caravan/Trailer
A39 - Dole - Bourg-en-Bresse	€8.20	€12.80
A4 - Paris - Reims	€9.70	€14.70
A4 - Metz - Strasbourg	€12.00	€18.60
A4 - Paris - Metz	€22.90	€34.90
A4 - Paris - Strasbourg	€34.90	€53.50
A40 - Geneve - Mont Blanc Tunnel (Tunnel Mont du Blanc)	€5.30	€9.20
A40 - Macon - Geneve	€14.60	€23.70
A41 - Grenoble - Chambery	€5.50	€7.90
A41 - Chambery - Geneve	€8.20	€12.40
A41/A40 - Chambery - Chamonix	€8.70	€14.20
A42/A40 - Lyon - Geneve	€14.40	€23.20
A43 - Lyon - Chambery	€10.30	€16.20
A43/A430 - Chambery - Albertville	€4.90	€7.60
A43/A48 - Lyon - Grenoble	€9.60	€15.50
A49 - Valence - Grenoble	€8.20	€12.90
A5/A31/A6 - Paris - Lyon (via Troyes)	€35.60	€55.10
A51 - Aix-en-Provence - La Saulce	€11.60	€17.60
A52/A50 - Aix-en-Provence - Toulon	€7.00	€10.70
A54/A7 - Montpellier - Aix-en-Provence	€10.10	€15.40
A57 - Toulon - Le Cannet de Maures	€2.30	€3.20
A6 - Paris - Beaune	€19.60	€30.40
A6 - Paris - Macon	€25.50	€39.80
A6 - Paris - Lyon	€30.90	€48.20
A61/A9 - Toulouse - Le Perthus (Spanish Frontier)	€17.90	€27.20
A61/A9 - Toulouse - Montpellier	€20.30	€30.70
A62 - Bordeaux - Toulouse	€16.70	€26.40
A63 - Bordeaux - Hendaye (Spanish Frontier)	€7.00	€10.70
A64 - Bayonne - Toulouse	€17.40	€27.80
A7/A8 - Lyon - Aix-en-Provence	€22.30	€35.30
A7/A9 - Lyon - Montpellier	€24.00	€37.50
A72 - Clermont-Ferrand - Lyon	€8.40	€12.90

Tolls	Car	Car Towing Caravan/Trailer
A8 - Nice - Menton (Italian frontier)	€2.10	€3.20
A8 - Cannes - Nice	€2.80	€4.30
A8 - Aix-en-Provence - Cannes	€13.20	€19.90
A83/A10 - Nantes - Bordeaux	€26.90	€40.90
A85 - Angers - Tours	€8.80	€12.40
A87 - Angers - Les Sables d'Olonne	€8.70	€14.10
A89 - Brive la Gaillarde - Clermont Ferrand	€9.30	€14.40
A89 - Bordeaux - Brive la Gaillarde	€15.60	€24.20
A9 - Orange - Montpellier	€1.10	€1.70
A9 - Montpellier - Le Perthus (Spanish frontier)	€12.60	€20.00
A9/A54 - Montpellier - Arles	€6.10	€9.40
E402 - Le Mans - Tours	€10.00	€15.50
E402 - Rouen - Le Mans	€18.60	€30.70
E604 - Tours - Bourges	€11.90	€18.20
E712 - Grenoble - Sisteron	€2.90	€4.50
E9 - Toulouse - Tunnel du Puymorens	€4.50	€6.80
E9 - Brive la Gaillarde - Toulouse	€13.90	€21.60

Bridges and Tunnels	Car	Car Towing Caravan/Trailer
Frejus Tunnel (Tunnel du Frejus) (French-Italian border)	€35.10	€46.40
A75 - Millau Viaduct (July & August)	€7.90	€11.80
A75 - Millau Viaduct (rest of the year)	€6.10	€9.20
Mont Blanc Tunnel (French-Italian border)	€35.10	€46.40
Pont de Normandie (Le Havre)	€5.00	€5.80
Pont de Tancarville (Le Havre)	€2.30	€2.90
Tunnel Prado Carenage (cars only) (Marseille)	€2.60	
A159 nr Colmar - Tunnel de Sainte Marie aux Mines	€7.70	€16.40
Tunnel du Puymorens (Andorra-Spanish border)	€6.00	€12.20

ALPS/EAST

ABRETS, LES — ISÈRE

Coin Tranquille

The Camping and Caravanning Club — The Friendly Club

6 chemin des Vignes, 38490
☎ 476321348 📠 476374067
e-mail: contact@coin-tranquille.com
web: www.coin-tranquille.com

Completely divided into pitches with attractive flower beds in rural surroundings. Kids' club available in July and August.

C&CC Report *This very pretty site is centrally located within easy reach of many favoured Alpine destinations. The nearby lakes, the Chartreuse (renowned as one of the finest walking areas of France) and the Vercors Regional Parks are favourites.*

dir: *2km E of village, 0.5km off N6.*

GPS: 45.5410, 5.6086

Open: Apr-1 Nov **Site:** 5HEC **Prices:** 15-29 **Facilities:** Kids' Club Play Area **Services:** **Leisure:** P **Off-site:** R

ALBENS — SAVOIE

Beauséjour

rte de la Rippe, 73410
☎ 479541520
web: www.campingbeausejour-albens.com

A peaceful wooded setting between Aix-les-Bains and Annecy.

dir: *SW via rte de la Chambotte, signed.*

Open: 15 Jun-20 Sep **Site:** 2HEC **Prices:** 9-12.80 Mobile home hire 260-380 **Facilities:** Play Area **Services:** **Off-site:** R

FRANCE

Facilities shop shower electric points for razors electric points for caravans parking by tents permitted compulsory separate car park **Services** café/restaurant bar Camping Gaz International gas other than Camping Gaz first aid facilities laundry **Leisure** swimming L-Lake P-Pool R-River S-Sea **Off-site** All facilities within 5km

ALLEVARD — ISÈRE

Clair Matin

20 rte de Pommiers, 38580
☎ 476975519 📠 476458715
e-mail: contact@camping-clair-matin.com
web: www.camping-clair-matin.com

Tranquil and shaded, gently sloping terraced site divided into pitches.

dir: *S of village, 300m off D525.*

Open: May-10 Oct **Site:** 5.5HEC **Prices:** 14.20-19.50 Mobile home hire 190-445 **Facilities:** Wi-fi (charged) Kids' Club Play Area **Services:** **Leisure:** P **Off-site:** L R

ARBOIS — JURA

Vignes

av Gl-Leclerc, 39600
☎ 384661412 📠 384661412
e-mail: reservation@rsl39.com
web: www.jura-campings.com

Terraced site.

dir: *E on D107 Mesnay road at stadium.*

Open: 16 Apr-2 Oct **Site:** 5HEC **Facilities:** **Services:** **Off-site:** L P R

ARGENTIÈRE — HAUTE-SAVOIE

Glacier d'Argentière

161 chemin des Chosalets, 74400
☎ 450541736
web: www.campingchamonix.com

Set on sloping meadowland in a beautiful location at the foot of the Mont Blanc Massif.

dir: *1km S of Argentière. Off N506 towards Cableway Lognan/ Grandes Montets & 200m to site.*

GPS: 45.9745, 6.9231

Open: 15 May-Sep **Site:** 1.5HEC **Prices:** 15.30-16.30 **Facilities:** **Services:** **Off-site:**

ARS-SUR-FORMANS — AIN

Bois de la Dame

Chemin du Bois de la Dame, 01480
☎ 474007723

Compulsory separate car park for arrivals after 22.00 hrs.

dir: *A6 exit Villefranche for Jassans-Riottier.*

Open: Apr-Sep **Site:** 1.5HEC **Facilities:** **Services:** **Leisure:** R **Off-site:**

AUTRANS — ISÈRE

Joyeux Réveil

38880
☎ 476953344 📠 476957298
e-mail: camping-au-joyeux-reveil@wanadoo.fr
web: www.camping-au-joyeux-reveil.fr

A beautiful location surrounded by woodland, with fine mountain views.

dir: *NE of town via rte de Montaud.*

Open: Dec-Mar & May-Sep **Site:** 1.5HEC **Prices:** 20-33 Mobile home hire 350-850 **Facilities:** Wi-fi Kids' Club Play Area **Services:** **Leisure:** P **Off-site:**

Le Vercors

Les Gaillards, 38880
☎ 476953188 📠 476953682
e-mail: camping.le.vercors@wanadoo.fr
web: www.camping-du-vercors.fr

Ideal for summer or winter holidays, situated in the heart of the Vercors with easy access to skiing.

dir: *0.6km S via D106 towards Méaudre.*

Open: 20 May-20 Sep, Dec-Mar **Site:** 1HEC **Prices:** 14.50-17.70 Mobile home hire 270-635 **Facilities:** Wi-fi (charged) Play Area **Services:** **Leisure:** P **Off-site:** R

BARATIER — HAUTES-ALPES

Verger

05200
☎ 492431587 📠 492434981
e-mail: campingleverger@wanadoo.fr
web: www.campingleverger.fr

Terraced site in plantation of fruit trees with fine views of Alps. Divided into pitches.

dir: *From N94 drive 2.5km S of Embrun, 1.5km E on D40.*

Open: All Year. **Site:** 4HEC **Facilities:** **Services:** **Leisure:** P **Off-site:** L R

Site 6HEC (site size) grass sand stone little shade partly shaded mainly shaded bungalows for hire (static) caravans for hire tents for hire no dogs site fully accessible for wheelchairs
Prices amount quoted is per night, for 2 adults and car, plus tent or caravan. Mobile home hire is a weekly rate.

BELFORT — TERRITOIRE-DE-BELFORT

Étang des Forges

r du Général Béthouart, 90000
384225492 384227655
e-mail: contact@camping-belfort.com
web: www.camping-belfort.com

Situated by Malsaucy lake in the regional nature reserve of Ballons des Vosges. Ideal terrain for hiking and water activities.

C&CC Report *Sitting next to a pretty leisure lake and within walking distance of the city centre, this is a very convenient base for visiting historic Belfort and exploring the famous Ballons regional park. The Territoire de Belfort département is a land of contrasts between the Vosges and Jura mountain ranges, so L'Étang des Forges has much to offer, with day trips also into Switzerland or the wine areas of Southern Alsace and Germany. Also recommended is a boat trip through the spectacular Doubs Gorge, just over an hour's drive away on the Swiss border.*

dir: *A36 exit 13, follow 'centre ville', then Offemont, then 'camping'.*

Open: 7 Apr-Sep **Site:** 3.5HEC **Facilities:** **Services:** **Leisure:** P **Off-site:** L

BOURG-D'OISANS, LE — ISÈRE

Caravaneige le Vernis

38520
476800268
e-mail: levernis.camping@wanadoo.fr
web: www.oisans.com/levernis

Well-kept site at foot of mountain in summer skiing area.

dir: *2.5km of N91, rte de Briançon.*

Open: Jun-10 Sep **Site:** 1.2HEC **Facilities:** **Services:** **Leisure:** P **Off-site:**

Cascade

rte de l'Alpe-d'Huez, 38520
476800242 476802263
e-mail: lacascade@wanadoo.fr
web: www.lacascadesarenne.com

Set at the foot of Alpe d'Huez with a waterfall and modern, very well-kept sanitary arrangements. TV lounge, open fireplace and snacks/pizzas available. Booking recommended.

Open: 15 Dec-Sep **Site:** 2.5HEC **Prices:** 20-26.50 **Facilities:** Wi-fi **Services:** **Leisure:** P R **Off-site:**

Colporteur

le Mas du Plan, 38520
476791144 476791149
e-mail: info@camping-colporteur.com
web: www.camping-colporteur.com

Situated 200m from the centre of Bourg d'Oisans, in the centre of a plain surrounded by mountains. Activities for children.

Open: mid May-mid Sep **Site:** 4HEC **Prices:** 21-26 **Facilities:** Wi-fi (charged) Play Area **Services:** **Leisure:** R **Off-site:** P

Rencontre du Soleil

rte de l'Alpe-d'Huez, 38520
476791222 476802637
e-mail: rencontre.soleil@wanadoo.fr
web: www.alarencontredusoleil.com

Charming site in a lovely setting in the Dauphiné Alps at the foot of a mountain. Rustic common room with open fireplace. TV, playroom for children and a kids' club is available in July and August.

C&CC Report *A classic small family-run site – very friendly and in a spectacular alpine location. Bourg d'Oisans is a thriving village on the main route to Briançon and Italy. This is a favourite haunt for the Tour de France and ideal base for exploring this outstanding region, with the Venosc and Ecrins National Parks close by. Rafting, canoeing, mountain biking, walking trips; visits to an alpine botanical garden, a hydro-electric station, a mountain railway and a mountain museum are all possible, locally.*

dir: *At foot of hairpin road to L'Alpe-d'Huez, off N91 in Le Bourg d'Osians.*

Open: May-Sep **Site:** 1.6HEC **Facilities:** Wi-fi (charged) Kids' Club **Services:** **Leisure:** P **Off-site:** R

BOURG-EN-BRESSE — AIN

CM de Challes

5 allée du Centre Nautique, 01000
474453721 474455995
e-mail: camping_municipal_bourgenbresse@wanadoo.fr

Set in a football ground near the swimming pool.

dir: *Signed from outskirts of town.*

Open: Apr-14 Oct **Site:** 2.7HEC **Prices:** 16 **Facilities:** Wi-fi Play Area **Services:** **Leisure:** P **Off-site:** L

BOURGET-DU-LAC, LE — SAVOIE

CM Ile aux Cygnes

73370
479250176 479722825
e-mail: camping@lebourgetdulac.fr
web: www.lebourgetdulac.fr

A family site on the shore of the Lac Bourdeau with plenty of recreational facilities. First aid and kids' club available during July and August.

dir: *Via N514.*

Open: 28 Apr-Sep **Site:** 4.5HEC **Prices:** 12.15-15.70 **Facilities:** Kids' Club **Services:** **Leisure:** L R **Off-site:**

BOURG-ST-MAURICE — SAVOIE

Versoyen

rte des Arcs, 73700
479070345 479072541
e-mail: leversoyen@wanadoo.fr
web: www.leversoyen.com

Many secluded pitches in a wood with two communal sanitary blocks (one heated). Skiing facilities in winter.

dir: *Via RN90.*

Open: 28 May-2 Nov & 15 Dec-2 May **Site:** 4HEC **Prices:** 12.10-14.60 Mobile home hire 250-550 **Facilities:** Wi-fi (charged) Play Area **Services:** **Off-site:** P R

BOUT-DU-LAC — HAUTE-SAVOIE

International du Lac Bleu

rte de la Plage, 74210
450443018 450448435
e-mail: contact@camping-lac-bleu.com
web: www.camping-lac-bleu.com

Modern, well-kept site. Overflow area with own sanitary blocks.

dir: *On S shore of Lake Annecy via N508, opposite garage.*

Open: Apr-25 Sep **Site:** 4HEC **Prices:** 16.50-31.50 Mobile home hire 300-920 **Facilities:** Wi-fi Kids' Club Play Area **Services:** **Leisure:** L P **Off-site:**

CHALEZEULE — DOUBS

Plage

12 rte de Belfort, 25220
381880426 381505462
e-mail: laplage.besancon@ffcc.fr
web: www.laplage-besancon.com

A modern site with good facilities near the main roads and close to the River Doubs.

dir: *N83 towards Belfort.*

Open: Apr-Sep **Site:** 1.8HEC **Facilities:** **Services:** **Leisure:** P R **Off-site:**

CHAMONIX-MONT-BLANC — HAUTE-SAVOIE

Cimes

28 rte des Tissieres, 74400
450535893
e-mail: info@campinglescimesmontblanc.com
web: www.campinglescimesmontblanc.com

A wooded meadow at the foot of Mont Blanc Massif. Ideal for hiking and mountain tours.

Open: Jun-Sep **Site:** 0.8HEC **Facilities:** **Services:** **Leisure:** R **Off-site:** L

Deux Glaciers

80 rte des Tissières, 74400
450531584 450559081
e-mail: glaciers@clubinternet.fr
web: www.les2glaciers.com

A glacial stream runs through the site. Pitches shaded by trees, very modern, well-kept sanitary installations. Rustic common room with open fires.

dir: *Off N506 towards road underpass, 250m to site.*

Open: All Year. **Site:** 16HEC **Facilities:** **Services:** **Off-site:**

Mer de Glace

200 Chemin de la Bagna, 74400
450534403 450536083
e-mail: info@chamonix-camping.com
web: www.chamonix-camping.com

A forested setting with individual pitches separated by hedges or trees and with wonderful views of the Mont Blanc mountain range. Leisure facilities include walking, hiking and mountain biking trails.

dir: *2km NE to Les Praz. On approach to village (from Chamonix) turn right under railway bridge if less than 2m40 in height or continue to rdbt, right over railway line. After 500m right & right again, 200m on left.*

GPS: 45.9383, 6.89

Open: 29 Apr-2 Oct **Site:** 2.2HEC **Prices:** 19.40-22.90 **Facilities:** Wi-fi Play Area **Services:** **Off-site:** P

CHAMPAGNOLE JURA

CM Boyse

r G-Vallery, 39300
384520032 384520116
e-mail: camping.boyse@wanadoo.fr
web: www.camping.champagnole.com

Clean and tidy site in the grounds of a municipal swimming pool with asphalt drives and divided into pitches.

dir: *Onto D5 before town & 1.3km to site.*

Open: Jun-15 Sep **Site:** 8HEC **Facilities:** **Services:** **Leisure:** P R

CHÂTEAUROUX-LES-ALPES HAUTES-ALPES

Cariamas

Fontmolines, 05380
492432263
e-mail: p.tim@free.fr
web: les.cariamas.free.fr

On a meadow in an attractive mountain setting beside the River Durance.

dir: *1.5km SE.*

Open: All Year. **Site:** 6HEC **Prices:** 16.75 Mobile home hire 320-630 **Facilities:** Wi-fi Play Area **Services:** **Leisure:** P **Off-site:** L R

CHÂTILLON JURA

Domaine de l'Epinette

15 r de l'Epinette, 39130
384257144 384257596
e-mail: contact@domaine-epinette.com
web: www.domaine-epinette.com

A small campsite situated beside the Ain river in an area of lakes and mountains. Kids' club available in July and August.

Open: 2 Jun-15 Sep **Site:** 7HEC **Facilities:** Kids' Club Play Area **Services:** **Leisure:** P R

CHOISY HAUTE-SAVOIE

Chez Langin

74330
450774165 450774101
e-mail: contact@chezlangin.com
web: www.chezlangin.com

Pleasant wooded surroundings.

dir: *1.3km NE via D3.*

Open: 14 Apr-Sep **Site:** 3HEC **Facilities:** **Services:** **Leisure:** P

CHORANCHE ISÈRE

Gouffre de la Croix

38680
476360713 476360713
e-mail: camping.gouffre.croix@wanadoo.fr
web: www.camping-choranche.com

A quiet and charming location beside the River Bourne with fine views of the surrounding mountains and modern facilities.

dir: *A49 exit St-Marcellin or Hostun.*

Open: 30 Apr-15 Sep **Site:** 2.5HEC **Prices:** 14.33-18.83 Mobile home hire 325.83-440.83 **Facilities:** Play Area **Services:** **Leisure:** R

CLAIRVAUX-LES-LACS JURA

Fayolan

39130
820005593 384252620
e-mail: reservation@rsl39.com
web: www.jura-campings.com

Wooded location beside the lake.

dir: *1.2km SE via D118.*

Open: 6 May-4 Sep **Site:** 17HEC **Prices:** 15-38 Mobile home hire 203-1113 **Facilities:** Kids' Club Play Area **Services:** **Leisure:** L P **Off-site:**

Grisière et Europe Vacances

39130
384258048 384252234
e-mail: bailly@la-grisiere.com
web: www.la-grisiere.com

Fenced in meadowland with some trees, sloping down to the Grand Lac. The site is guarded during July and August.

dir: *From village centre off N78 onto D118 towards Châtel-de-Joux for 0.8km.*

Open: May-Sep **Site:** 11HEC **Facilities:** **Services:** **Leisure:** L

CLUSAZ, LA HAUTE-SAVOIE

Plan du Fernuy

1800, rte des Confins, 74220
450024475 450326702
e-mail: info@plandufernuy.com

Well placed for skiing or walking. Airing rooms. 30 ski-lifts nearby and several cable cars.

dir: *Off N50 E of La Clusaz towards Les Confins, 2km to site.*

Open: 17 Jun-2 Sep & 20 Dec-Apr **Site:** 1.31HEC **Facilities:** **Services:** **Leisure:** P **Off-site:**

CORMORANCHE-SUR-SAÔNE AIN

Camping du Lac

365 rte du Lac, 01290
385239710 385239711
e-mail: contact@lac-cormoranche.com
web: www.lac-cormoranche.com

8km S of Mâcon, the site is situated on a lake suitable for swimming, fishing and water sports. The beach is supervised and cleaned daily. Kids' club in July and August. Dogs accepted, restrictions apply.

dir: *A6 exit 29 Mâcon Sud then towards Cormoranche-sur-Saône.*

GPS: 46.2519, 4.8259

Open: May-Sep **Site:** 4.5HEC **Prices:** 13.60-17.50 Mobile home hire 220-485 **Facilities:** Wi-fi (charged) Kids' Club Play Area **Services:** **Leisure:** L **Off-site:**

DIVONNE-LES-BAINS AIN

Fleutron

Quartier Villard, 01220
450200195 450200035
e-mail: info@homair.com
web: www.camping-lefleutron.com

Set in wooded surroundings with large individual pitches.

dir: *A40 exit Bellegarde, then D984 to Divonne. A33 exit Poligny, then RN5 to Gex, then D984 to Divonne.*

Open: 30 Mar-21 Oct **Site:** 8HEC **Facilities:** **Services:** **Leisure:** P **Off-site:** L R

DOLE JURA

Pasquier

18 Chemin V et G Thévenot, 39100
384720261 384792344
e-mail: camping-pasquier@wanadoo.fr
web: www.camping-le-pasquier.com

Meadow site near River Doubs. Close to city centre.

dir: *0.9km SE of town centre.*

Open: 15 Mar-15 Oct **Site:** 2HEC **Prices:** 12-18.30 Mobile home hire 450 **Facilities:** Wi-fi (charged) Play Area **Services:** **Leisure:** P R **Off-site:** L

DOUCIER JURA

Domaine de Chalain

39130
384257878 384257006
e-mail: chalain@chalain.com
web: www.chalain.com

A large site beside Lake Chalain with a variety of recreational facilities.

dir: *3km NE.*

Open: 29 Apr-21 Sep **Site:** 20HEC **Prices:** 22-36.50 Mobile home hire 280-644 **Facilities:** Wi-fi (charged) Kids' Club Play Area **Services:** **Leisure:** L P

DOUSSARD HAUTE-SAVOIE

Ferme de la Serraz

r de la Poste, 74210
450443068
e-mail: info@campinglaserraz.com
web: www.campinglaserraz.com

Modern site divided into pitches with beautiful views of the surrounding mountains.

dir: *At E end of village, N508 onto D181 for 0.5km.*

Open: May-15 Sep **Site:** 4HEC **Facilities:** Wi-fi Kids' Club Play Area **Services:** **Leisure:** P **Off-site:** L R

Ravoire

The Camping and Caravanning Club The Friendly Club

rte de la Ravoire, 74210
450443780 450329060
e-mail: info@camping-la-ravoire.fr
web: www.camping-la-ravoire.fr

A well-appointed, modern site on level ground 0.8km from Lake Annecy. Spectacular mountain views.

C&CC Report *Small, high quality, welcoming and relaxed, with facilities open all season, La Ravoire has been made by Philippe and Florence into a site that is much loved by people who enjoy mountains and lakes, as well as the more adventurous who can join in with activities booked through reception. Picturesque Annecy is well worth a visit, as is a day trip to Chamonix and Mont Blanc.*

dir: *Autoroute exit Annecy Sud for Albertville, N508 to Duingt & signed.*

Open: 15 May-6 Sep **Site:** 2HEC **Prices:** 24.50-34.20 **Facilities:** Wi-fi Play Area **Services:** **Leisure:** P **Off-site:** L

FRANCE

EMBRUN — HAUTES-ALPES

CM Clapière

av du Lac, 05200
492430183 492435022
Well-managed site with shaded pitches on stony ground, on N shore of lake.
dir: *2.5km SW on N94.*
Open: May-Sep **Site:** 5.3HEC **Facilities:** **Services:** **Off-site:** L P R

ENTRE-DEUX-GUIERS — ISÈRE

Arc en Ciel

r des Berges, 38380
476660697 476660697
e-mail: info@camping-arc-en-ciel.com
web: www.camping-arc-en-ciel.com
A wooded location by the river with well-shaded pitches.
dir: *On D520, 300m from N6.*
Open: Mar-15 Oct **Site:** 1.2HEC **Facilities:** **Services:** **Leisure:** P R **Off-site:**

ÉVIAN-LES-BAINS — HAUTE-SAVOIE

Plage

304 rue de la Garenne, Amphion les Bains, 74500
450700046 450700046
e-mail: info@camping-dela-plage.com
web: www.camping-dela-plage.com
A pleasant site with good recreational facilities.
dir: *NW of town on N5, 150m from lake.*
Open: All Year. **Site:** 1HEC **Facilities:** **Services:** **Leisure:** P **Off-site:** L R

FERRIÈRE-D'ALLEVARD — ISÈRE

CM Neige et Nature

chemin de Montarmand, 38580
476451984
e-mail: contact@neige-nature.fr
web: www.neige-nature.fr
A beautiful location with spectacular mountain views and modern facilities.
dir: *From Allevard D525A towards Le Pleynet.*
Open: 15 May-15 Sep **Site:** 1.2HEC **Facilities:** **Services:** **Leisure:** P R **Off-site:**

GAP — HAUTES-ALPES

Alpes Dauphiné

rte Napoleon (RN85), 05000
492512995 492535892
e-mail: info@alpesdauphine.com
web: www.alpesdauphine.com
With panoramic views of the surrounding mountains, the site is in a natural meadowland setting with shaded pitches. Facilities include a weekly entertainment programme including a kids' club in July and August.
Open: 15 Apr-25 Oct **Site:** 6HEC **Prices:** 15.50-20.30 **Facilities:** Wi-fi Kids' Club Play Area **Services:** **Leisure:** P

GRESSE-EN-VERCORS — ISÈRE

4 Saisons

38650
476343027 476343952
e-mail: pieter.aalmoes@wanadoo.fr
web: www.camping-les4saisons.com
A picturesque mountain setting with good facilities.
dir: *A51 Grenoble-Sisteron exit at Monestier de Clermont, follow signs Gresse-en-Vercors.*
Open: May-Sep, 20 Dec-15 Mar **Site:** 2.2HEC **Prices:** 17.50 Mobile home hire 660 **Facilities:** Wi-fi (charged) Play Area **Services:** **Leisure:** P **Off-site:** R

GUILLESTRE — HAUTES-ALPES

Villard

Le Villard, 05600
492450654 492450052
e-mail: info@camping-levillard.com
web: www.camping-levillard.com
A magnificent location between the Ecrins and Queyras regional parks with good facilities.
dir: *2km W via D902A & N4 rte de Gap.*
Open: 15 Dec-1 Nov **Site:** 3HEC **Facilities:** Kids' Club Play Area **Services:** **Leisure:** P R **Off-site:** L

HUANNE-MONTMARTIN — DOUBS

Bois de Reveuge

25680
381843860 381844404
web: www.campingduboisdereveuge.com
A terraced site in a 20-hectare park surrounded by the Vosges and Jura mountains with good recreational facilities.
dir: *A36 exit Baumes-les-Dames.*
Open: 26 Apr-11 Sep **Site:** 24HEC **Facilities:** **Services:** **Leisure:** L P

ISLE-SUR-LE-DOUBS, L' — DOUBS

CM Lumes

10 r des Lumes, 25250
381927305 381927305
e-mail: contact@les-lumes.com
web: www.les-lumes.com
The site lies close to the town. Common room with TV.
dir: *Off N83. Entrance near bridge over the Doubs.*
Open: All Year. **Site:** 1.5HEC **Facilities:** **Services:** **Leisure:** R **Off-site:**

LANDRY — SAVOIE

Eden

73210
479076181 479076217
e-mail: info@camping-eden.net
web: www.camping-eden.net
A modern site with excellent sports and sanitary facilities, situated in the heart of the Savoie Olympic area.
Open: 18 Dec-8 May & Jun-15 Sep **Site:** 2.7HEC **Facilities:** **Services:** **Leisure:** P R **Off-site:**

LONS-LE-SAUNIER — JURA

Marjorie

640 bd de l'Europe, 39000
384242694 384240840
e-mail: info@camping-marjorie.com
web: www.camping-marjorie.com
Clean, tidy site with tent and caravan sections separated by a stream. Caravan pitches are gravelled and surrounded by hedges. Heated common room with TV, reading area, kitchen.
dir: *Near swimming stadium on outskirts of town.*
Open: Apr-15 Oct **Site:** 9HEC **Prices:** 11.50-20.60 Mobile home hire 230-580 **Facilities:** Kids' Club Play Area **Services:** **Off-site:** P

LUGRIN — HAUTE-SAVOIE

Myosotis

28 chemin du Grand Tronc, 74500
450760759
e-mail: campinglesmyosotis@wanadoo.fr
web: www.camping-les-myosotis.com
A terraced site with fine views over the lake and of the surrounding mountains.
dir: *Via D321.*
GPS: 46.3992, 6.6644
Open: 10 May-20 Sep **Site:** 0.9HEC **Prices:** 12.20-13.30 **Facilities:** **Services:** **Off-site:** L

Rys

Route le Rys, 74500
627491535 450760575
e-mail: jeanmichel.blanc@wanadoo.fr
Calm shady site with panoramic views of the lake and mountains. 10min walk from the beach
dir: *Signed W of town.*
Open: 30 Apr-1 Oct **Site:** 2.3HEC **Facilities:** **Services:** **Off-site:** L

Vieille Église

53 rte des Prés Parrau, 74500
450760195 450761312
e-mail: campingvieilleeglise@wanadoo.fr
web: www.camping-vieille-eglise.com
On rising meadow between lake and mountains with good views. Close to lake Léman and its beaches.
dir: *D24 to Neuvecelle, onto D21, 1km on right after Maxilly.*
GPS: 46.4006, 6.6467
Open: 10 Apr-20 Oct **Site:** 1.5HEC **Prices:** 15.90-19.50 Mobile home hire 310-740 **Facilities:** Wi-fi Play Area **Services:** **Leisure:** P **Off-site:** L

MALBUISSON — DOUBS

Fuvettes

25160
381693150 381697046
e-mail: les-fuvettes@wanadoo.fr
web: www.camping-fuvettes.com
Mainly level site with some terraces at an altitude of 900m in the Jura mountains, gently sloping towards a lake.
dir: *0.5km S on D437.*
Open: Apr-Sep **Site:** 6HEC **Prices:** 15-21 Mobile home hire 290-650 **Facilities:** Wi-fi (charged) Kids' Club Play Area **Services:** **Leisure:** L P

Site 6HEC (site size) grass sand stone little shade partly shaded mainly shaded bungalows for hire (static) caravans for hire tents for hire no dogs site fully accessible for wheelchairs
Prices amount quoted is per night, for 2 adults and car, plus tent or caravan. Mobile home hire is a weekly rate.

MARIGNY — JURA

Pergola

39130
384257003 384257596
e-mail: contact@lapergola.com
web: www.lapergola.com

A well-equipped, terraced family site with direct access to the lake. Situated in the middle of the lake area, close to waterfalls and beautiful villages.

dir: *S of Marigny off D27.*

Open: 14 May-18 Sep **Site:** 12HEC **Prices:** 21-37 Mobile home hire 296-985 **Facilities:** Wi-fi (charged) Kids' Club Play Area **Services:** **Leisure:** L P **Off-site:** R

MATAFELON-GRANGES — AIN

Gorges de l'Oignin

r du Lac, 01580
474768097 474768097
e-mail: camping.lesgorgesdeloignin@wanadoo.fr
web: www.gorges-de-loignin.com

Rural site on the banks of a lake surrounded by low mountains. Kids' club available during July and August.

dir: *A404 exit 11, site signed after 1.6km.*

GPS: 46.2553, 5.5569

Open: 15 Apr-Sep **Site:** 2.6HEC **Prices:** 14-21.80 **Facilities:** Wi-fi Kids' Club Play Area **Services:** **Leisure:** L P

MÉAUDRE — ISÈRE

Buissonnets

38112
476952104
e-mail: camping-les-buissonnets@wanadoo.fr
web: www.camping-les-buissonnets.com

A quiet, friendly site in the heart of the Vercors regional park, with modern sanitary blocks and a range of summer and winter recreational facilities.

dir: *200m from village centre.*

Open: 15 Dec-1 Nov **Site:** 2.7HEC **Facilities:** **Services:** **Off-site:** P R

MESNOIS — JURA

Beauregard

The Camping and Caravanning Club — The Friendly Club

2 Grande Rue, 39130
384483251 384483251
e-mail: reception@juracampingbeuregard.com
web: www.juracampingbeauregard.com

C&CC Report *A real gem of a family-run site – friendly, attractive and very well-kept, with some excellent pitches and a very good wash block, all set in the beautiful Jura countryside, an area of lakes, waterfalls and hills. Lots of fresh air, open spaces and informality. For a day trip, Switzerland is just a short drive away.*

Open: Apr-Sep **Site:** 6HEC **Facilities:** **Services:** **Leisure:** P R **Off-site:** L

MESSERY — HAUTE-SAVOIE

Relais du Léman

74140
450947111 450947766
e-mail: info@relaisduleman.com
web: www.relaisduleman.com

Well-equipped site in a wooded location on the shore of Lac Léman.

dir: *1.5km SW via D25.*

Open: Apr-Sep **Site:** 3.5HEC **Prices:** 21 Mobile home hire 350-755 **Facilities:** Wi-fi Play Area **Services:** **Leisure:** P **Off-site:** L P

MEYRIEU-LES-ÉTANGS — ISÈRE

Moulin

38440
474593034 474583612
e-mail: basedeloisirs.du.moulin@wanadoo.fr
web: www.camping-meyrieu.com

A quiet rural setting with good recreational facilities.

dir: *On D552 between Vienne & Bourgoin-Jallieu.*

Open: 15 Apr-Sep **Site:** 1.5HEC **Facilities:** **Services:** **Leisure:** L

MIRIBEL-LES-ÉCHELLES — ISÈRE

Balcon de Chartreuse

950 chemin de la Foret, 38380
476552853 476552853
e-mail: info@camping-balcondechartreuse.com
web: www.camping-balcondechartreuse.com

A peaceful site in the heart of the Parc Régional de Chartreuse, with fine views of the surrounding mountains.

dir: *400m from village centre.*

Open: Apr-Oct **Site:** 2.5HEC **Facilities:** **Services:** **Leisure:** P **Off-site:**

Facilities shop shower electric points for razors electric points for caravans parking by tents permitted compulsory separate car park **Services** café/restaurant bar Camping Gaz International gas other than Camping Gaz first aid facilities laundry **Leisure** swimming L-Lake P-Pool R-River S-Sea **Off-site** All facilities within 5km

MONTMAUR — HAUTES-ALPES

Mon Repos

05400
☎ 592580314
e-mail: campingmonrepos@gmail.com

Generally well-kept site on wooded terrain with shaded pitches.

dir: *1km E on D937 & D994.*

Open: May-Sep **Site:** 7HEC **Facilities:** **Services:** **Leisure:** L R

MONTREVEL-EN-BRESSE — AIN

Plaine Tonique

Base de Plein Air, 01340
☎ 474308052 474308077
e-mail: plaine.tonique@wanadoo.fr
web: www.laplainetonique.com

A well-equipped site divided into a series of self contained sections beside the lake. Entrance closed between 22.00 & 07.00 hrs.

dir: *0.5km E on D28.*

Open: Apr-24 Sep **Site:** 17HEC **Facilities:** **Services:** **Leisure:** L P **Off-site:** R

MURS-ET-GELIGNIEUX — AIN

Ile de la Comtesse

rte des Abrets, 01300
☎ 479872333 479872333
e-mail: camping.comtesse@wanadoo.fr
web: www.ile-de-la-comtesse.com

A stunning natural setting beneath the Alps next to Lake Cuchet (part of the Rhône), with direct access to the water.

dir: *A43 exit 10, D592 to La Bruyere, site off route to Belley.*

Open: 15 May-15 Sep **Site:** 3HEC **Prices:** 11.40-29.80 **Facilities:** Wi-fi (charged) Kids' Club Play Area **Services:** **Leisure:** P R **Off-site:** L

NEYDENS — HAUTE-SAVOIE

Colombière

74160
☎ 450351314 450351340
e-mail: la.colombiere@wanadoo.fr
web: www.camping-la-colombiere.com

A pleasant, friendly site with good recreational facilities.

dir: *Via A40.*

Open: Apr-Sep **Site:** 2.2HEC **Facilities:** **Services:** **Leisure:** P **Off-site:** R

ORNANS — DOUBS

Chanet

9 chemin de Chanet, 25290
☎ 381622344 381621397
e-mail: contact@lechanet.com
web: www.lechanet.com

Comfortable site with good facilities in the peaceful Loue Valley.

dir: *1.5km SW on D241, green signs.*

Open: Apr-Oct **Site:** 2.2HEC **Facilities:** **Services:** **Leisure:** P **Off-site:** R

ORPIERRE — HAUTES-ALPES

Princes d'Orange

05700
☎ 492662253 492663108
e-mail: campingorpierre@wanadoo.fr
web: www.campingorpierre.com

The site lies on a meadow with terraces.

dir: *N75 exit Eyguians onto D30.*

Open: Apr-Oct **Site:** 20HEC **Prices:** 16.50-23.10 Mobile home hire 325-605 **Facilities:** Wi-fi Kids' Club Play Area **Services:** **Leisure:** P **Off-site:** R

OUNANS — JURA

Plage Blanche

The Camping and Caravanning Club — The Friendly Club

39380
☎ 384376963 384376021
e-mail: reservation@la-plage-blanche.com
web: www.la-plage-blanche.com

Pleasant location with spacious pitches on the banks of the River Loue, with good recreational facilities. Outdoor activity centre close by.

C&CC Report *Stretching along the banks of the river Loue, La Plage Blanche provides the perfect spot for outdoor pursuits. And it's not just this enviable location in the Jura which sets La Plage Blanche apart, but the carefully planned out and lovingly looked after grounds and facilities too. Children will be in their element with canoeing, treetop ropes and guided bike rides all on the doorstep. This spacious site caters for more peaceful moments too; take a quiet walk in the forest or fish in the private lake. Off-site you could visit the historic town of Dole, the nearby UNESCO world heritage Royal Saltworks site, or the Haut-Jura National Regional Park.*

dir: *A39 exit 7 (from south), exit 6 (from north) signed Pontarlier then Ounans.*

Open: 18 Apr-Sep **Site:** 7HEC **Prices:** 13-20 Mobile home hire 350-660 **Facilities:** Wi-fi Kids' Club Play Area **Services:** **Leisure:** P R **Off-site:**

Site 6HEC (site size) grass sand stone little shade partly shaded mainly shaded bungalows for hire (static) caravans for hire tents for hire no dogs site fully accessible for wheelchairs
Prices amount quoted is per night, for 2 adults and car, plus tent or caravan. Mobile home hire is a weekly rate.

PARCEY — JURA

Bords de Loue

Chemin du Val d'Amour, 39100
384710382 384710342
e-mail: contact@jura-camping.fr
web: www.jura-camping.fr

A quiet site on the River Loue.

dir: *1.5km from village centre via N5, signed.*

Open: 20 Apr-10 Sep **Site:** 18HEC **Facilities:** **Services:** **Leisure:** P R **Off-site:**

PASSY — HAUTE-SAVOIE

Village Center Les Iles

245 rte des Lacs, 74190
499572121 467516389
e-mail: contact@village-center.com
web: www.village-center.com/rhones-alpes/camping-montagne-iles.php

With unrestricted views of Mont Blanc, Les Iles is located on the edge of a lake, 3km from the centre of Passy.

dir: *A41 exit 21.*

GPS: 45.9236, 6.6506

Open: 15 Dec-13 Mar & 15 Jun-11 Sep **Site:** 4.5HEC **Prices:** 14-18 Mobile home hire 192-707 **Facilities:** Wi-fi (charged) **Services:** **Leisure:** L **Off-site:**

PATORNAY — JURA

Moulin

39130
384483121 384447121
e-mail: contact@camping-moulin.com
web: www.camping-moulin.com

A modern site on a level meadow in a peaceful, wooded location on the banks of the River Ain.

dir: *NE via N78 rte de Clairvaux-les-Lacs.*

Open: 30 Apr-12 Sep **Site:** 5HEC **Prices:** 17-28 Mobile home hire 210-609 **Facilities:** Wi-fi (charged) Kids' Club Play Area **Services:** **Leisure:** P R **Off-site:** L

PLAGNE-MONTCHAVIN — SAVOIE

Montchavin les Coches

73210
479078323 479078018
e-mail: campingmontchavin@wanadoo.fr
web: www.montchavin-lescoches.com

A summer and winter site overlooking the Tarentaise Valley with modern facilities.

Open: Nov-Sep **Site:** 1.33HEC **Prices:** 14.50 **Facilities:** Wi-fi (charged) Play Area **Services:** **Off-site:** P

PONT-DE-VAUX — AIN

Ripettes

St Benigne, Chavannes sur Reyssouze, 01190
385306658
e-mail: info@camping-les-ripettes.com
web: www.camping-les-ripettes.com

Small, friendly site with very large pitches, in peaceful countryside, but convenient for A6 motorway.

C&CC Report *A small, very well-kept and very pretty site, Les Ripettes' friendly atmosphere sets you right in the calm of the south Burgundy countryside. While the smallest pitches are big by any standards and the biggest are truly vast, the very experienced owners, Marc and Isabelle, are keen to maintain the cosy and convivial atmosphere. Great for bird spotters too.*

dir: *At Pont-de-Vaux take D2 signed Saint Triviers de Courtes. After 4km take next left after water tower & immediately left again.*

GPS: 46.4446, 4.9806

Open: Apr-Sep **Site:** 2.5HEC **Prices:** 13.50-15 Mobile home hire 280-420 **Facilities:** Wi-fi Play Area **Services:** **Leisure:** P **Off-site:** R

Rives du Soleil

Port de Fleurville, 01190
385303365 385303123
e-mail: info@rivesdusoleil.com
web: www.rivesdusoleil.com

A family site beside the River Saône with good facilities. Kids' club available in July and August.

dir: *3km from Pont-de-Vaux via N6.*

Open: 22 Apr-17 Oct **Site:** 7HEC **Facilities:** Wi-fi Kids' Club Play Area **Services:** **Leisure:** P R

PORT-SUR-SAÔNE HAUTE-SAÔNE

CM Maladière

70170
☎ 384915132 384781809
e-mail: tourisme.portsaone@wanadoo.fr

A quiet, comfortable site with modern facilities, close to the River Saône.

dir: *S on D6, between River Saône & canal.*

Open: 15 May-15 Sep **Site:** 2HEC **Facilities:** **Services:** **Off-site:** P R

ROCHETTE, LA SAVOIE

Lac St-Clair

73110
☎ 479257355 479257825
e-mail: campinglarochette@orange.fr
web: www.la-rochette.com

At the foot of the Belledonne mountains, 1km from a lake with good fishing.

dir: *Via D925B Grenoble-Albertville.*

Open: Jun-Sep **Site:** 3HEC **Facilities:** **Services:** **Leisure:** L **Off-site:** P

ROSIÈRE-DE-MONTVALEZAN, LA SAVOIE

Forêt

73700
☎ 479068621 479401625
e-mail: campinglaforet@free.fr
web: www.campinglaforet.free.fr

A peaceful site in pleasant wooded surroundings, with modern facilities.

dir: *2km S via N90 towards Bourg-St-Maurice.*

Open: 20 Jun-15 Sep & 15 Dec-24 Apr **Site:** 2.7HEC **Facilities:** **Services:** **Leisure:** P **Off-site:** R

ROUGEMONT DOUBS

Val de Bonnal

Bonnal, 25680
☎ 381869087 381860392
e-mail: val-de-bonnal@wanadoo.fr
web: www.camping-valdebonnal.fr

Quiet woodland site beside the River Ognon. Supervised swimming in lake with beach.

Open: 30 Apr-5 Sep **Site:** 15HEC **Facilities:** **Services:** **Leisure:** L P R

ST-CLAIR-DU-RHÔNE ISÈRE

Daxia

rte du Péage, D4 - av du Plateau des Frères, 38370
☎ 474563920 474564557
e-mail: info@campingledaxia.com
web: www.campingledaxia.com

A riverside site with good sanitary and recreational facilities.

dir: *Via N7/A7.*

Open: Apr-Sep **Site:** 7.5HEC **Facilities:** **Services:** **Leisure:** L P R

ST-CLAUDE JURA

Camping du Martinet

39200
☎ 384450040
e-mail: contact@camping-saint-claude.fr
web: www.camping-saint-claude.fr

A wooded location close to the Centre Nautique.

dir: *2km SE beside river.*

GPS: 46.3716, 5.8724

Open: May-Sep **Site:** 3HEC **Facilities:** Play Area **Services:** **Leisure:** R **Off-site:** P

ST-GERVAIS-LES-BAINS HAUTE-SAVOIE

Dômes de Miage

197 rte des Contamines, 74170
☎ 450934596 450781075
e-mail: info@camping-mont-blanc.com
web: www.camping-mont-blanc.com

On a beautiful wooded plateau with fine views of the surrounding mountains.

dir: *2km S on D902.*

Open: May-12 Sep **Site:** 2.5HEC **Facilities:** **Services:** **Off-site:** P

ST-JEAN-DE-COUZ SAVOIE

International la Bruyère

73160
☎ 479657911 479657427
e-mail: camping-labruyere@orange.fr
web: www.campingsavoie.com

Wooded surroundings close to the Grande Chartreuse range with a variety of sports facilities.

dir: *15km S of Chambery, towards Les Echelles Valence.*

Open: 15 May-Sep **Site:** 1HEC **Prices:** 10.50 Mobile home hire 250-390 **Facilities:** Wi-fi Play Area **Services:** **Off-site:** P R

FRANCE

ST-JORIOZ — HAUTE-SAVOIE

Europa

1444 rte d'Albertville, 74410
450685101 450685520
e-mail: info@camping-europa.com
web: www.camping-europa.com
Well-equipped site in picturesque surroundings close to Lake Annecy.
dir: *1.4km SE.*
Open: 25 Apr-19 Sep **Site:** 4.2HEC **Facilities:** **Services:** **Leisure:** P **Off-site:** L

International du Lac d'Annecy

1184 rte d'Albertville, 74410
450686793 450090122
e-mail: contact@camping-lac-annecy.com
web: www.camping-lac-annecy.com
400m from Lake Annecy with direct access to cycle paths. There are two swimming pools and leisure facilities.
dir: *N508 towards Albertville.*
GPS: 45.83, 6.182
Open: 8 May-15 Sep **Site:** 2.5HEC **Prices:** 15-28 Mobile home hire 300-740 **Facilities:** Wi-fi (charged) Kids' Club **Services:** **Leisure:** P **Off-site:** L

ST-LAURENT-EN-BEAUMONT — ISÈRE

Belvédère de l'Obiou

rte Napoleon (RN85), Lieu-dit les Egats, 38350
476304080 476304486
e-mail: info@camping-obiou.com
web: www.camping-obiou.com
Terraced meadow site at the foot of mountains with hedge surrounds.
dir: *1.6km from Ortsteil Les Egats on N85, signed.*
Open: 15 Apr-15 Oct **Site:** 1HEC **Facilities:** **Services:** **Leisure:** P **Off-site:**

ST-MARTIN-SUR-LA-CHAMBRE — SAVOIE

Bois Joli

St Martin-sur-la-Chambre, 73130
479562128
e-mail: info@campingleboisjoli.com
web: www.campingleboisjoli.com
Well-kept site with pitches and individual washing cabins.
dir: *1km N of St-Avre, off N6-E70 via La Chambre.*
Open: 15 Apr-15 Oct **Site:** 4HEC **Prices:** 10-13 Mobile home hire 210-510 **Facilities:** Wi-fi Play Area **Services:** **Leisure:** P **Off-site:** L

ST-PIERRE-DE-CHARTREUSE — ISÈRE

Martinière

rte du Col de Porte, 38380
476886036 476886910
e-mail: camping-de-martiniere@orange.fr
web: www.campingdemartiniere.com
Small family run site set in the Chartreuse National Park with fine panoramic views. Restaurant open in July and August.
dir: *2km SW off D512.*
GPS: 45.3258, 5.7971
Open: 30 Apr-11 Sep **Site:** 2.5HEC **Prices:** 15.60-19.60 Mobile home hire 245-500 **Facilities:** Play Area **Services:** **Leisure:** P

SALLE-EN-BEAUMONT, LA — ISÈRE

Champ-Long

38350
476304181 476304721
e-mail: champlong38@orange.fr
web: www.camping-champlong.com
A beautiful Alpine setting at the entrance to the Ecrins park at an altitude of 700m. Mini-golf course due to open.
dir: *1.5km NW off N85.*
GPS: 44.8556, 5.8451
Open: All Year. **Site:** 5HEC **Prices:** 14-16 Mobile home hire 300-650 **Facilities:** Wi-fi (charged) Play Area **Services:** **Leisure:** P **Off-site:** L R

SCIEZ — HAUTE-SAVOIE

Camping du Chatelet

658 chemin des Hutins Vieux, 74140
450725260 450723767
e-mail: info@camping-chatelet.com
web: www.camping-chatelet.com
Flat, grassy pitches, 500m from the shores of Lake Genève (Geneva).
GPS: 46.3409, 6.3970
Open: Apr-15 Oct **Site:** 3.2HEC **Prices:** 12.50-16.50 **Facilities:** Wi-fi (charged) Play Area **Services:** **Off-site:** L

SÉEZ SAVOIE

Reclus

RN 90, 73700
☎ 479410105 🖹 479410105
e-mail: contact@campinglereclus.com
web: www.campinglereclus.com
Pleasant wooded location within easy reach of the ski slopes.

dir: *NW on N90.*

GPS: 45.6253, 6.7925

Open: All Year. **Site:** 2HEC **Prices:** 13.60-14 Mobile home hire 300-550 **Facilities:** Wi-fi Play Area **Services:** **Leisure:** R **Off-site:** L P

SERRES HAUTES-ALPES

Barillons

05700
☎ 492671735
e-mail: camping.les.barillons@wanadoo.fr
Well-laid out with terraces.

dir: *1km SE on N75.*

Open: mid May-mid Sep **Site:** 3HEC **Facilities:** **Services:** **Leisure:** P **Off-site:** L R

Domaine des 2 Soleils

05700
☎ 492670133 🖹 492670802
e-mail: dom.2.soleils@wanadoo.fr
web: www.domaine-2soleils.com
Well-kept terraced site in Buéch Valley.

dir: *S of town off N75, signed.*

Open: May-Sep **Site:** 12HEC **Facilities:** **Services:** **Leisure:** P **Off-site:** L R

SEVRIER HAUTE-SAVOIE

Coeur du Lac

3233 RD1508, 74320
☎ 450524645 🖹 450190145
e-mail: info@aucoeurdulac.com
web: www.campingaucoeurdulac.com
Site adjacent to Lake Annecy with direct access to the lake, beach and cycle path and fine views of the Alps. Dogs permitted in low season.

dir: *Leave autoroute at Annecy in direction of Le Lac-Albertville.*

GPS: 45.8548, 6.1439

Open: Apr-Sep **Site:** 2.7HEC **Facilities:** Wi-fi (charged) Play Area **Services:** **Leisure:** L **Off-site:**

TALLOIRES HAUTE-SAVOIE

Lanfonnet

948 rte d'Angon, 74290
☎ 450607212 🖹 450607212 & 450233882
e-mail: camping.le.lanfonnet@wanadoo.fr
web: www.camping-lanfonnet.com
A well-equipped site 100m from the lake.

dir: *1.5km SE.*

Open: May-Sep **Site:** 2.3HEC **Prices:** 18-25.80 Mobile home hire 290-680 **Facilities:** Wi-fi **Services:** **Leisure:** L

THOISSEY AIN

CM

01140
☎ 474040425
e-mail: campingthoissey@orange.fr
Situated between the rivers Saône and Chalaronne.

dir: *1km SW on D7.*

Open: Apr-Sep **Site:** 13HEC **Facilities:** Play Area **Services:** **Leisure:** P R **Off-site:**

TIGNES-LES-BRÉVIÈRES SAVOIE

Europeen des Brevieres

rte des Boisses, 73320
☎ 684812250
e-mail: campingdetignes@free.fr
A well-equipped site 1km from the centre of the village.

dir: *Signed from D902*

Open: 15 Jun-15 Sep **Site:** 4.5HEC **Facilities:** **Services:** **Off-site:** L P R

TREPT ISÈRE

3 Lacs du Soleil

La Plaine, 38460
☎ 474929206 🖹 474929395
e-mail: info@les3lacsdusoleil.com
web: www.les3lacsdusoleil.com
Situated at the gateway to the Alps, an undulating wooded area with small lakes.

dir: *2.5km W on D517.*

Open: May-10 Sep **Site:** 26HEC **Facilities:** **Services:** **Leisure:** L P

FRANCE

VERNIOZ — ISÈRE

Kawan Resort Le Bontemps

5 impasse du Bontemps, 38150
474578352 474578370
e-mail: info@camping-lebontemps.com
web: www.camping-lebontemps.com
A pleasantly landscaped site beside the River Varèze.
dir: *N7 onto D131.*
Open: 26 Mar-Sep **Site:** 6HEC **Facilities:** **Services:** **Leisure:** P R

VILLARD-DE-LANS — ISERE

L'Oursière

38250
476951477 476955811
e-mail: info@camping-oursiere.fr
web: www.camping-oursiere.fr
Peaceful site in the Vercors regional park. Summer and winter facilities.
dir: *N off D531 towards Grenoble.*
Open: 4 Dec-6 May & 22 May-Sep **Site:** 4.2HEC **Prices:** 16-18.50 **Facilities:** Wi-fi Play Area **Services:** **Leisure:** R **Off-site:** P

VILLARS-LES-DOMBES — AIN

Camping des Autières

164 av des Nations, 01330
474980021 474980582
e-mail: camping@parcdesoiseaux.com
web: www.campingendombes.fr
Clean and tidy park-like site divided into plots and pitches. Part reserved for overnight campers. Clean, modern sanitary installations.
dir: *SW off N83.*
GPS: 45.9969, 5.0308
Open: May-5 Sep **Site:** 4.5HEC **Facilities:** Play Area **Services:** **Leisure:** P R **Off-site:**

ALSACE/LORRAINE

ANOULD — VOSGES

Acacias

88650
329571106
e-mail: contact@acaciascamp.com
web: www.acaciascamp.com
Pleasant surroundings with well-defined pitches in the heart of the Hautes-Vosges region.
dir: *NE of town centre towards ski slopes.*
Open: 5 Dec-5 Oct **Site:** 2.5HEC **Prices:** 11.20 Mobile home hire 450 **Facilities:** Wi-fi Play Area **Services:** **Leisure:** P **Off-site:** R

AUBURE — HAUT-RHIN

CM La Ménère

68150
389739299 389739345
e-mail: aubure@cc-ribeauville.fr
A peaceful site at an altitude of 800m.
dir: *N415 or D416 onto D11.*
Open: 15 May-Sep **Site:** 1.8HEC **Facilities:** **Services:** **Off-site:**

BAERENTHAL — MOSELLE

Ramstein Plage

Base de Baerenthal, Ramstein Plage, 57230
387065073 387065073
e-mail: camping.ramstein@wanadoo.fr
web: www.baerenthal.eu
The River Zinsel runs through this rural wooded site close to the border with Germany.
dir: *W via r du Ramstein.*
Open: Apr-Sep **Site:** 14HEC **Prices:** 14.80-19 **Facilities:** Wi-fi **Services:** **Leisure:** L P **Off-site:** R

BIESHEIM — HAUT-RHIN

Ile du Rhin

Zone Touristique, 68600
389725795 389721421
e-mail: camping@paysdebrisach.fr
web: www.campingiledurhin.com
On the Ile du Rhin, between the Canal d'Alsace and the River Rhine in pleasant wooded surroundings.
dir: *From Colmar N415 to Rhine bridge.*
Open: early Apr-early Oct **Site:** 3HEC **Facilities:** **Services:** **Off-site:** P R

FRANCE

Facilities shop shower electric points for razors electric points for caravans parking by tents permitted compulsory separate car park **Services** café/restaurant bar Camping Gaz International gas other than Camping Gaz first aid facilities laundry **Leisure** swimming L-Lake P-Pool R-River S-Sea **Off-site** All facilities within 5km

BRESSE, LA — VOSGES

Belle Hutte

88250
☎ 329254975
e-mail: camping-belle-hutte@wanadoo.fr
web: www.camping-belle-hutte.com

Terraced site beside the River Moselotte.

dir: *D34 towards Col de la Schlucht.*

Open: Jan-15 Nov & 15-31 Dec **Site:** 4.5HEC **Prices:** 13.22-22.72 **Facilities:** Wi-fi (charged) **Services:** **Leisure:** P R **Off-site:** L

BURNHAUPT-LE-HAUT — HAUT-RHIN

Castors

4 rte de Guewenheim, 68520
☎ 389487858 389627466

A modern site in a rural setting close to a river and surrounded by woodland.

dir: *E of Burnhaupt on D466 towards Guewenheim.*

Open: 15 Feb-Dec **Site:** 2.5HEC **Facilities:** **Services:** **Leisure:** R **Off-site:**

BUSSANG — VOSGES

Domaine de Champé

14 Les Champs Navés, 88540
☎ 329616151 329615690
e-mail: info@domaine-de-champe.com
web: www.domaine-de-champe.com

Pleasant surroundings beside the River Moselle.

dir: *On N57.*

Open: All Year. **Site:** 3.5HEC **Facilities:** **Services:** **Leisure:** P R **Off-site:** L

FRANCE

CELLES-SUR-PLAINE — VOSGES

Village Vacances des Lacs

BP3, 88110
☎ 329412800 329411869
e-mail: camping@paysdeslacs.com
web: www.paysdeslacs.com/camping

Set among wooded hills in an extensive natural leisure area around the Lakes of Pierre-Percée.

dir: *Via D392A.*

Open: Apr-Oct **Site:** 3.5HEC **Facilities:** **Services:** **Leisure:** P R **Off-site:** L

CERNAY — HAUT-RHIN

CM Acacias

16 rue Réne Guibert, 68700
☎ 389755697 389397229
e-mail: campoland.cernay@orange.fr
web: www.camping-les-acacias.com

Clean, quiet site on the River Thur.

dir: *Off N83 between Colmar & Belfort.*

Open: 15 Apr-15 Oct **Site:** 3HEC **Facilities:** **Services:** **Off-site:** P R

COLMAR — HAUT-RHIN

Intercommunal de l'Ill

1 allée du Camping, 68180
☎ 389411594 389411594
e-mail: camping.ill@calixo.net
web: www.campingdelill.com

On a meadow beside the river with modern facilities. Separate sections for campers in transit.

dir: *2km E on N415.*

Open: 21 Mar-6 Jan **Site:** 4.7HEC **Facilities:** **Services:** **Leisure:** R **Off-site:** P

CORCIEUX — VOSGES

Clos de la Chaume

21 r d'Alsace, 88430
☎ 329507676 329507676
e-mail: info@camping-closdelachaume.com
web: www.camping-closdelachaume.com

Situated in the Parc Régional des Ballons des Vosges. 600m from the village, a flat and quiet site with both sunny and shaded pitches. Run by a British and French family, there is a new swimming pool and sanitary installations.

Open: 30 Apr-18 Sep **Site:** 3.5HEC **Prices:** 16-16.80 Mobile home hire 280-647 **Facilities:** Wi-fi (charged) Kids' Club Play Area **Services:** **Leisure:** P R **Off-site:** L

Domaine des Bans

r J-Wiese, 88430
☎ 329516467 329516469
e-mail: les-bans@domaines-des-bans.com
web: www.domaine-des-bans.fr

On meadowland divided into pitches with a variety of recreational facilities.

dir: *E of village off D8.*

Open: 30 Apr-3 Sep **Site:** 35HEC **Prices:** 15-39 Mobile home hire 273-805 **Facilities:** Wi-fi (charged) Kids' Club Play Area **Services:** **Leisure:** L P **Off-site:**

Site 6HEC (site size) grass sand stone little shade partly shaded mainly shaded bungalows for hire (static) caravans for hire tents for hire no dogs site fully accessible for wheelchairs
Prices amount quoted is per night, for 2 adults and car, plus tent or caravan. Mobile home hire is a weekly rate.

DABO — MOSELLE

Rocher

CD 45, 57850
☎ 387074751 387074751
e-mail: info@ot-dabo.fr
web: www.ot-dabo.fr
Beautiful position close to the historic town of Dabo in the Vosges mountains.
dir: *1.5km SW via D45.*
Open: 10 Apr-2 Nov **Site:** 0.5HEC **Facilities:** **Off-site:**

DAMBACH-LA-VILLE — BAS-RHIN

L'Ours

rte d'Ebersheim, 67650
☎ 388924860
e-mail: camping-de-l-ours@orange.fr
web: www.pays-de-barr.com/dambach-la-ville
A wooded location close to the town centre.
dir: *1km E via D120.*
Open: 15 Mar-Dec **Site:** 1.8HEC **Facilities:** Play Area **Services:** **Off-site:**

EGUISHEIM — HAUT-RHIN

Trois Châteaux

10 r du Bassin, 68420
☎ 389231939 389241019
e-mail: camping.eguisheim@wanadoo.fr
web: www.eguisheimcamping.fr
Peaceful location surrounded by vineyards at an altitude of 210m.
dir: *6km S of Colmar on N83.*
GPS: 48.0430, 7.3000
Open: Apr-25 Oct **Site:** 1.8HEC **Prices:** 12.50-14 Mobile home hire 295-495 **Facilities:** Wi-fi **Services:** **Off-site:**

FONTENOY-LE-CHÂTEAU — VOSGES

Fontenoy

r Colonel Gilbert, 88240
☎ 329363474
e-mail: marliesfontenoy@hotmail.com
web: www.campingfontenoy.com
Small family site set on a hill in peaceful, wooded surroundings.
dir: *2.2km S via D40.*
Open: 11 Apr-4 Oct **Site:** 1.2HEC **Prices:** 10.94-12.15 Mobile home hire 200-290 **Facilities:** Wi-fi Play Area **Services:** **Leisure:** P **Off-site:** R

GEMAINGOUTTE — VOSGES

CM Le Violu

88520
☎ 329577070 329517260
e-mail: mairie.gemaingoutte@wanadoo.fr
dir: *W beside river via N59.*
Open: May-Sep **Site:** 0.9HEC **Facilities:** **Services:** **Leisure:** R **Off-site:**

GÉRARDMER — VOSGES

Ramberchamp

21 chemin du Tour du Lac, 88400
☎ 329630382 329632609
e-mail: boespflug.helene@wanadoo.fr
web: www.camping-de-ramberchamp.com
On a level meadow on south side of Lac de Gérardmer.
dir: *2km from village centre via N417 or 486.*
Open: 13 Apr-18 Sep **Site:** 3.5HEC **Prices:** 16 Mobile home hire 345-520 **Facilities:** **Services:** **Leisure:** L **Off-site:** P

GRANGES-SUR-VOLOGNE — VOSGES

Château

2 Les Chappes, 88640
☎ 329575083
e-mail: camping-du-chateau@wanadoo.fr
A terraced site with good sports facilities 1km from the village, next to the forest.
Open: 15 Jun-15 Sep **Site:** 2HEC **Prices:** 12.50 Mobile home hire 320 **Facilities:** **Services:** **Leisure:** P **Off-site:** R

Gina-Park

88460
☎ 329514195
web: www.ginapark.com
A pleasant park at the foot of a wooded mountain. Streams cross the site and there is a lake and facilities for a variety of sports.
dir: *1km SE of town centre.*
Open: All Year. **Site:** 4.5HEC **Facilities:** **Services:** **Leisure:** P R **Off-site:**

FRANCE

HEIMSBRUNN — HAUT-RHIN

Chaumière

62 r de la Galfingue, 68990
389819343 389819343
e-mail: reception@camping-lachaumiere.com
web: www.camping-lachaumiere.com
A pleasant wooded location with modern facilities.
dir: *Signed from village centre.*
Open: All Year. **Site:** 1HEC **Prices:** 10.90 Mobile home hire 250-490 **Facilities:** Wi-fi **Services:** **Leisure:** P **Off-site:** R

HOHWALD, LE — BAS-RHIN

CM

67140
388083090 388083090
e-mail: lecamping.herrenhaus@orange.fr
A well-equipped terraced site in beautiful wooded surroundings.
dir: *W via D425.*
Open: All Year. **Site:** 2HEC **Prices:** 12.20 **Facilities:** **Services:** **Off-site:**

ISSENHEIM — HAUT-RHIN

Florival

rte de Soultz, 68500
389742047 389742047
e-mail: contact@camping-leflorival.com
web: www.camping-leflorival.com
Level meadowland site, situated in a regional park and surrounded by a forest.
dir: *N83 Colmar-Mulhouse exit for Issenheim, site signed.*
Open: Apr-Oct **Site:** 3.5HEC **Prices:** 13.40-14.50 **Facilities:** Play Area **Services:** **Off-site:** P

KAYSERSBERG — HAUT-RHIN

CM

r des Acacias, 68240
389471447 389471447
e-mail: camping@ville-kaysersberg.fr
Between a sports ground and the River Weiss. Subdivided by low hedges.
dir: *200m from N415, signed.*
Open: Apr-Sep **Site:** 1.5HEC **Prices:** 12.85 **Facilities:** Wi-fi Play Area **Services:** **Leisure:** R **Off-site:** P

KRUTH — HAUT-RHIN

Schlossberg

r du Bourbach, 68820
389822676 389822017
e-mail: contact@schlossberg.fr
web: www.schlossberg.fr
A quiet location in the heart of the Parc des Ballons with modern facilities.
dir: *2.3km NW via D13b.*
GPS: 47.9436, 6.9544
Open: Etr-1 Oct **Site:** 5.2HEC **Prices:** 13.50 **Facilities:** Wi-fi Play Area **Services:** **Leisure:** R **Off-site:** L

LAUTERBOURG — BAS-RHIN

CM des Mouettes

chemin des Mouettes, 67630
388546860 388546860
e-mail: camping-lauterbourg@wanadoo.fr
A level site on the shores of a lake.
dir: *D63 from Haguenau.*
Open: 19 Apr-Nov **Site:** 3HEC **Facilities:** **Services:** **Leisure:** L **Off-site:** R

LIÈPVRE — HAUT-RHIN

Camping du Haut Koenigsbourg

rte de la Vancelle, 68660
389584320 389589829
e-mail: camping.haut.koenigsbourg@orange.fr
web: www.liepvre.fr/camping
Tranquil and shady site, ideal for exploring the local wine-growing region.
GPS: 48.2731, 7.2906
Open: 15 Mar-15 Oct **Site:** 1HEC **Prices:** 9.50 **Facilities:** Wi-fi Play Area **Services:** **Off-site:** R

LUTTENBACH — HAUT-RHIN

Amis de la Nature

4 r du Château, 68140
389773860 389772572
e-mail: camping.an@wanadoo.fr
web: www.camping-an.fr
Situated on a long strip of land, in the heart of Luttenbach countryside. Divided into pitches.
dir: *D10 from Munster for 1km.*
Open: All Year. **Site:** 7HEC **Prices:** 9.90-11 **Facilities:** Wi-fi Play Area **Services:** **Leisure:** P R **Off-site:** P

MASEVAUX HAUT-RHIN

Masevaux

3 r du Stade, 68290
389824229 389824229
e-mail: contact@camping-masevaux.com
web: www.camping-masevaux.com
Wooded surroundings beside the River Doller, 200m from small picturesque town.

Open: All Year. **Site:** 3.5HEC **Prices:** 12.50 **Facilities:** Wi-fi **Services:** **Off-site:** P R

MITTLACH HAUT-RHIN

Camping Municipal

68380
389776377 389777436
e-mail: camping@mittlach.fr
web: www.mittlach.fr
Very quiet forested area by a small village.

dir: *From Munster signs for Metzeral then Mittlach D10.*

Open: May-Oct **Site:** 3HEC **Prices:** 10.65 **Facilities:** Play Area **Services:** **Leisure:** R **Off-site:**

MOOSCH HAUT-RHIN

Mine d'Argent

r de la Mine d'Argent, 68690
389823066
A well-established site in a peaceful wooded setting.

dir: *1.5km SW off N66.*

GPS: 47.8506, 7.0306

Open: 15 Apr-15 Oct **Site:** 2.5HEC **Prices:** 9.50 Mobile home hire 210-375 **Facilities:** Play Area **Services:** **Leisure:** R **Off-site:** L P R

MULHOUSE HAUT-RHIN

CM de L'Ill

av P-de-Coubertin, 68100
389062066 389611834
e-mail: campingdelill@wanadoo.fr
web: www.camping-de-lill.com
Set in the park between the canal and the River Ill, a short walk from the city centre.

dir: *From town centre signs for Fribourg & Allemagne, signed at Ile Napoléon.*

Open: Apr-15 Oct **Site:** 5.5HEC **Prices:** 11.80-15.25 Mobile home hire 310-540 **Facilities:** Wi-fi (charged) **Services:** **Leisure:** P **Off-site:** R

MUNSTER HAUT-RHIN

Village Center Le Parc de la Fecht

rte de Gunsbach, 68140
499572121 467516389
e-mail: contact@village-center.com
web: www.village-center.com/alsace/camping-montagne-parc-fecht.php
Quiet and friendly site close to the town centre.

dir: *On D417 via Colmar (direction of Epinal).*

GPS: 48.0396, 7.1425

Open: 15 Dec-13 Mar & 15 Jun-11 Sep **Site:** 4.5HEC **Prices:** 14-16 Mobile home hire 167-672 **Facilities:** Play Area **Services:** **Leisure:** R **Off-site:** P

OBERBRONN BAS-RHIN

CM Oasis

3 r du Frohret, 67110
388097196 388099787
e-mail: oasis.oberbronn@laregie.fr
web: oasis67110.jimdo.com
Site with 139 pitches, plus chalets with leisure facilities including a health spa.

dir: *Signed W from D28 Oberbronn-Zinswiller.*

Open: Apr-Sep **Site:** 9HEC **Prices:** 15.45-19.75 **Facilities:** Wi-fi (charged) Play Area **Services:** **Leisure:** P **Off-site:**

OBERNAI BAS-RHIN

CM

rue de Berlin, 67210
388953848 388483147
e-mail: camping@obernai.fr
web: www.obernai.fr
Partly terraced site in a park. Vaccination book required for dogs.

dir: *W on D426 towards Ottrott.*

GPS: 48.4645, 7.4678

Open: All Year. **Site:** 3HEC **Facilities:** Wi-fi Play Area **Services:** **Off-site:** P

FRANCE

REHAUPAL — VOSGES

Barba

The Camping and Caravanning Club
The Friendly Club

45 le Village, 88640
☎ 329663557 329663557
e-mail: barba@campingdubarba.com
web: www.campingdubarba.com

Small, quiet, friendly site in beautiful hill country.

C&CC Report *For a well-run, small, peaceful, relaxing and friendly site, look no further than Le Barba. Agnès and Gilles Lalevée's welcome is much appreciated and they also offer lots of information, from walking and cycling routes – some direct from the site – to other activities and places to visit within easy reach. No matter how energetic you choose to be, you have the peace and quiet of a friendly site to return to, plus the option of a wholesome meal from the next door auberge.*

dir: *In Epinal D11 direction Gérardmer, before Tendon left (D30) direction Rehaupal.*

GPS: 48.1190, 6.7323

Open: May-Sep **Site:** 2HEC **Prices:** 12-14 Mobile home hire 280-530 **Facilities:** Wi-fi **Services:** **Off-site:** L P

RIBEAUVILLE — HAUT-RHIN

Pierre de Coubertin

23 r de Landau, 68150
☎ 389736671
e-mail: camping.ribeauville@wanadoo.fr
web: www.camping-alsace.com/ribeauville/index.htm

Peaceful location.

dir: *Via D106.*

GPS: 48.1947, 7.3365

Open: 15 Mar-14 Nov **Site:** 3.5HEC **Prices:** 12-13 **Facilities:** Wi-fi Play Area **Services:** **Off-site:** P

RIQUEWIHR — HAUT-RHIN

Inter Communal

rte des Vins, 68340
☎ 389479008 389490563
e-mail: campingriquewihr@wanadoo.fr
web: www.camping-alsace.com/riquewihr/

Extensive site overlooking vineyards.

dir: *2km E on D16. Turn W off N83 at Ostheim.*

Open: Apr-Dec **Site:** 4HEC **Facilities:** **Services:** **Off-site:**

ST-MAURICE-SUR-MOSELLE — VOSGES

Deux Ballons

17 r du Stade, 88560
☎ 329251714
e-mail: stan@camping-deux-ballons.fr
web: www.camping-deux-ballons.fr

Well-maintained site beside a stream and surrounded by woodland and mountains.

dir: *1km W on N66 near fuel station.*

Open: 28 Apr-16 Sep **Site:** 4HEC **Prices:** 15-18 **Facilities:** Wi-fi (charged) Play Area **Services:** **Leisure:** P **Off-site:** R

ST-PIERRE — BAS-RHIN

Beau Séjour

r de l'Église, 67140
☎ 388085224 388085224
e-mail: camping.saintpierre@laposte.net
web: www.pays-de-barr.com/beau-sejour/

Situated midway between Strasbourg and Colmar with modern facilities.

Open: 15 May-1 Oct **Site:** 0.6HEC **Facilities:** **Services:** **Leisure:** R **Off-site:**

STE-CROIX-EN-PLAINE — HAUT-RHIN

Clair Vacances

rte de Herrlisheim, 68127
☎ 389492728 389493137
e-mail: clairvacances@wanadoo.fr
web: www.clairvacances.com

A pleasant woodland setting with good facilities for a family holiday.

dir: *On D1 towards Herrlisheim.*

GPS: 48.0160, 7.3500

Open: Etr-17 Oct **Site:** 3.5HEC **Prices:** 15-20 **Facilities:** Wi-fi Play Area **Services:** **Leisure:** P **Off-site:**

SAVERNE — BAS-RHIN

CM

67700
☎ 388913565 388913565
e-mail: camping.saverne@ffcc.fr
web: www.ffcc.fr

A pleasant site at the foot of the Rocher du Haut Barr.

dir: *1.3km SW via D171.*

Open: Apr-Sep **Site:** 2.5HEC **Facilities:** **Services:** **Off-site:**

FRANCE

Site 6HEC (site size) grass sand stone little shade partly shaded mainly shaded bungalows for hire (static) caravans for hire tents for hire no dogs site fully accessible for wheelchairs
Prices amount quoted is per night, for 2 adults and car, plus tent or caravan. Mobile home hire is a weekly rate.

SÉLESTAT BAS-RHIN

CM Cigognes

r de la 1-er DFL, 67600
☎ 388920398

Rural setting at an altitude of 175m.

dir: *0.9km from town centre.*

Open: May-Sep **Site:** 0.7HEC **Prices:** 13.55-15.45
Facilities: **Services:** **Off-site:** P

SEPPOIS-LE-BAS HAUT-RHIN

Village Center Les Lupins

1 r de la Gare, 68580
☎ 499572121 467516389
e-mail: contact@village-center.com
web: www.village-center.com/alsace/camping-campagne-lupins.php

Picturesque site close to the German and Swiss borders.

dir: *From Colmar/Mulhouse, through Altkirch in direction of Férette.*

GPS: 47.5377, 7.1825

Open: 24 Jun-4 Sep **Site:** 4HEC **Prices:** 14-16
Facilities: Wi-fi Play Area **Services:**
Leisure: P **Off-site:**

SIVRY-SUR-MEUSE MEUSE

Brouzel

26 r du Moulin, 55110
☎ 329748155
e-mail: lebrouzel@gmail.com

Quiet site on the banks of a canal.

Open: Apr-1 Oct **Site:** 1.5HEC **Prices:** 11-14.50
Facilities: Play Area **Services:** **Leisure:** R
Off-site: R

THOLY, LE VOSGES

Noir Rupt

15 chemin de l'Étang de Noirrupt, 88530
☎ 329618127 329618305
e-mail: info@jpvacances.com
web: www.jpvacances.com

A peaceful site in a beautiful wooded location, 1km from Tholy. With plenty of facilities an ideal base whatever the season.

dir: *2km SE on D417.*

GPS: 48.0888, 6.7289

Open: May-15 Oct **Site:** 3HEC **Prices:** 14.70-21
Facilities: Wi-fi (charged) Play Area
Services: **Leisure:** P **Off-site:** R

TURCKHEIM HAUT-RHIN

Cigognes

68230
☎ 389270200
e-mail: municipc@calixo.net
web: www.turckheim-alsace.com

Relaxing site with recreational facilities on site or nearby. Folk events occasionally held.

dir: *N417 from Colmar to Wintzenheim then Turckheim, left before bridge, pass railway station & stadium.*

Open: 15 Mar-20 Dec **Site:** 2.5HEC **Prices:** 11.90
Facilities: **Services:** **Leisure:** R **Off-site:**

VAGNEY VOSGES

CM du Mettey

88120
☎ 329621686 329618236
e-mail: ccvbr@wanadoo.fr

dir: *1.3km E on road to Gérardmer.*

Open: Jun-15 Sep **Site:** 2HEC **Facilities:**
Services: **Off-site:**

VERDUN MEUSE

Breuils

allée des Breuils, 55100
☎ 329861531 329867576
e-mail: contact@camping-lesbreuils.com
web: www.camping-lesbreuils.com

A family site in peaceful surroundings. Pitches are divided by trees and bushes and the sanitary facilities are well-maintained.

dir: *SW via D34, signed.*

Open: Apr-Sep **Site:** 5.5HEC **Facilities:**
Services: **Leisure:** P **Off-site:** L R

FRANCE

VILLERS-LÈS-NANCY — MEURTHE-ET-MOSELLE

Campéole le Brabois

The Camping and Caravanning Club — The Friendly Club

av Paul Muller, 54600
☎ 383271828 📠 383400643
e-mail: campeoles.brabois@orange.fr
web: www.camping-brabois.com

Beautiful wooded surroundings with well-defined pitches and good recreational facilities.

C&CC Report *Good facilities, a British manager, a restaurant often featuring the site's own fresh produce, a location handy for Nancy's lovely historic centre – all these mean that this small and well-run site attracts both long and short stays. Nancy itself, the hub of the Art Nouveau movement, makes for a very rewarding visit. In Place Stanislas, a splendid UNESCO World Heritage Site, evenings from mid-June to mid-September present a spell-binding free sound and light show, with the region's history told by images projected onto the buildings.*

dir: *Motorway A33 junct 2b, follow signs. From centre of Nancy follow sign to Technopole de Brabois.*

Open: Apr-15 Oct **Site:** 6HEC **Facilities:** **Services:** **Off-site:** P

VITTEL — VOSGES

Vittel

270 r Claude Bassot, 88800
☎ 329080271 📠 386379583
e-mail: aquadis1@wanadoo.fr
web: www.aquadis-loisirs.com

Friendly site located in this spa town in the Vosges mountains.

dir: *NE via D68 rte de Domjulien.*

Open: Apr-Sep **Site:** 3HEC **Facilities:** **Services:** **Off-site:** P

WASSELONNE — BAS-RHIN

CM

Rue Des Sapins, 67310
☎ 388870008 📠 388684890
e-mail: camping-wasselonne@wanadoo.fr

On a level meadow adjoining the local sports complex.

dir: *1km W on D224.*

Open: Apr-15 Oct **Site:** 2.5HEC **Facilities:** **Services:** **Leisure:** P **Off-site:**

WATTWILLER — HAUT-RHIN

Sources

rte des Crêtes, 68700
☎ 389754494 📠 389757198
e-mail: camping.les.sources@wanadoo.fr
web: www.camping-les-sources.com

A family site on the edge of the Vosges forest close to the Route du Vin. A kids' club is available in July and August. Touring pitches from 22 April.

dir: *N83 exit Cernay Nord.*

Open: 9 Apr-Sep **Site:** 15HEC **Prices:** 10.40-30 Mobile home hire 240-770 **Facilities:** Wi-fi Kids' Club Play Area **Services:** **Leisure:** P

WIHR-AU-VAL — HAUT-RHIN

Route Verte

13 r de la Gare, 68230
☎ 389711010
e-mail: info@camping-routeverte.com
web: camping-routeverte.com

Near the centre of the village at an altitude of 320m.

dir: *Approach via D10.*

Open: end Apr-Sep **Site:** 1HEC **Prices:** 9.15-12.05 **Facilities:** **Services:** **Off-site:** P R

XONRUPT/LONGEMER — VOSGES

Camping Les Jonquilles

rte du Lac, 88400
☎ 329633401 📠 329600928
e-mail: info@camping-jonquilles.com
web: www.camping-jonquilles.com

A delightful wooded lakeside setting.

dir: *2km SE on D67A beside Lac de Longemer.*

Open: 23 Apr-2 Oct **Site:** 4HEC **Prices:** 9.50-13.50 **Facilities:** Wi-fi **Services:** **Leisure:** L **Off-site:**

L'Eau-Vive

2799 rte de Colmar, 88400
☎ 329630737
e-mail: campingeauvive@wanadoo.fr
web: www.campingaleauvive.com

On a meadow surrounded by trees, close to the ski slopes.

dir: *2km SE on D67A next to Lac de Longemer.*

Open: All Year. **Site:** 1HEC **Facilities:** **Services:** **Leisure:** R **Off-site:** L

BURGUNDY/CHAMPAGNE

ACCOLAY — YONNE

Moulin Jacquot

rue de Ste Pallaye, 89460
386815687 386815687
e-mail: dominique-tilmant0971@orange.fr
A well-equipped site in a pleasant rural setting, close to the village.
dir: *W to Canal du Nivernais.*
Open: Apr-Sep **Site:** 0.8HEC **Prices:** 8.60-10.80
Facilities: Play Area **Services:** **Off-site:** R

ANCY-LE-FRANC — YONNE

CM

rte de Cusy, 89160
386751321
A sheltered position just beyond the village.
dir: *Via Montbard road.*
Open: 15 Jun-15 Sep **Site:** 0.8HEC **Facilities:** **Services:** **Off-site:** R

ANDRYES — YONNE

Au Bois Joli

89480
386817048 386817048
e-mail: info@campingauboisjoli.com
web: www.campingauboisjoli.com
Family friendly site, but suitable for all ages, set in pleasant Burgundian countryside.
dir: *0.6km SW via N151.*
Open: Apr-Oct **Site:** 5HEC **Prices:** 14.35-20.50
Facilities: Wi-fi **Services:**
Leisure: P **Off-site:** L

ARNAY-LE-DUC — CÔTE-D'OR

Fouché

r du 8 mai 1945, 21230
380900223 380901191
e-mail: info@campingfouche.com
web: www.campingfouche.com
A quiet location beside a lake with good recreational facilities, close to the medieval town of Arnay-le-Duc.
dir: *0.7km E on CD17.*
Open: Apr-15 Oct **Site:** 8HEC **Facilities:** Wi-fi Kids' Club Play Area **Services:**
Leisure: L P

AUXERRE — YONNE

CM

8 rte de Vaux, 89000
386521115 386511754
e-mail: camping.mairie@auxerre.com
dir: *SE towards Vaux.*
Open: 15 Apr-Sep **Site:** 3HEC **Prices:** 8.20-10
Facilities: Play Area **Services:**
Off-site: P R

AUXONNE — CÔTE-D'OR

Arquebuse

rte d'Athée, 21130
380310689 380311302
e-mail: camping.arquebuse@wanadoo.fr
web: www.campingarquebuse.com
Clean, well-equipped site on the River Saône, near a bathing area.
dir: *N5 W from Auxonne for 3km, N onto D24 towards Athée & Pontailler-sur-Saône.*
Open: All Year. **Site:** 5HEC **Facilities:**
Services: **Off-site:** P R

AVALLON — YONNE

Sous-Roches

1 r Sous-Roche, 89200
386341039 386341039
e-mail: campingsousroches@ville-avallon.fr
web: www.ville-avallon.fr
In a riverside setting within Morvan Regional Natural Park.
dir: *2km SE by D944 & D427.*
Open: Apr-15 Oct **Site:** 2HEC **Prices:** 12.20
Facilities: **Services:** **Leisure:** R
Off-site: P

BANNES — HAUTE-MARNE

Hautoreille

52360
325848340 325848340
e-mail: campinghautoreille@orange.fr
web: www.campinghautoreille.com
Small grassy site with modern facilities, offering large pitches, many in shaded positions. Separate car park for late arrivals.
dir: *D74, S towards Langres.*
Open: All Year. **Site:** 3.5HEC **Prices:** 14.90-19.90
Facilities: Wi-fi Play Area **Services:**
Off-site: L R

Facilities shop shower electric points for razors electric points for caravans parking by tents permitted compulsory separate car park **Services** café/restaurant bar Camping Gaz International gas other than Camping Gaz first aid facilities laundry **Leisure** swimming L-Lake P-Pool R-River S-Sea **Off-site** All facilities within 5km

BEAUNE — CÔTE-D'OR

CM Cent Vignes

10 rue August Dubois, 21200
☎ 380220391 📠 380201551
e-mail: campinglescentvignes@mairie-beaune.fr

On outskirts of town. Site divided into pitches, clean, well-looked after sanitary installations.

dir: *On N74 on Savigny-les-Beaune road.*

Open: 15 Mar-Oct **Site:** 2HEC **Prices:** 13.20 **Facilities:** Wi-fi **Services:** **Off-site:** L P

BOURBON-LANCY — SAÔNE-ET-LOIRE

St-Prix

r du St-Prix, 71140
☎ 385892098 📠 386379583
e-mail: aquadis1@wanadoo.fr
web: www.aquadis-loisirs.com

A well-equipped family site close to an extensive water-sports centre.

dir: *By swimming pool off D979a.*

Open: Apr-Oct **Site:** 2.5HEC **Facilities:** **Services:** **Leisure:** P **Off-site:** L

BOURBONNE-LES-BAINS — HAUTE-MARNE

Montmorency

r du Stade, BP N7, 52400
☎ 325900864 📠 325842374
e-mail: c.montmorency@wanadoo.fr
web: www.camping-montmorency.com

A well-equipped site in a pleasant natural setting.

Open: Apr-Oct **Site:** 2HEC **Prices:** 16.60-17.10 **Facilities:** Play Area **Services:** **Off-site:** L P

BOURG — HAUTE-MARNE

Croix d'Arles

rte de Dijon D974, 52200
☎ 325882402 📠 325882402
e-mail: croix.arles@yahoo.fr
web: www.croixdarles.eu

A peaceful site in flat wooded surroundings close to Langres. Kids' club available in July and August.

dir: *A31 exit 6, D428 towards Langres, onto RN74 for Dijon, site 2km on right.*

Open: 15 Mar-1 Nov **Site:** 7HEC **Prices:** 13-16 Mobile home hire 238-518 **Facilities:** Wi-fi Kids' Club Play Area **Services:** **Leisure:** P **Off-site:**

BOURG-FIDÈLE — ARDENNES

Camping de la Murée

35 r Catherine de Clèves, 08230
☎ 324542445
e-mail: campingdelamuree@wanadoo.fr
web: www.campingdelamuree.com

A lakeside site in wooded surroundings.

dir: *1km N via D22.*

Open: 15 Jan-15 Dec **Site:** 1.3HEC **Prices:** 14.50-18.50 **Facilities:** **Services:** **Off-site:** L P

BUZANCY — ARDENNES

Samaritaine

The Camping and Caravanning Club — The Friendly Club

08240
☎ 324300888 📠 324302939
e-mail: info@campinglasamaritaine.com
web: www.campinglasamaritaine.com

Site set in a peaceful location in a small village in the heart of the Ardennes. The forests in the area are well-suited for walking, horse-riding or cycling. Kids' club available in summer months.

C&CC Report *A very attractive site with large pitches separated by flowering shrubs, beautifully kept grounds and facilities, and a friendly atmosphere, in the lovely Ardennes countryside. Worth visiting are weekly farmers' markets, a beer museum, a zoo where day is turned into night, a historic iron furnace with a dazzling multimedia show, the Great War sites of the Maginot Line and Verdun, the Museum of War and Peace – and in Belgium, a brewery in a Trappist monastery.*

dir: *D12 onto D947 towards Buzancy for 17km.*

Open: May-20 Sep **Site:** 2.5HEC **Prices:** 18.20-20.20 Mobile home hire 294-497 **Facilities:** Kids' Club Play Area **Services:** **Off-site:** L

CHAGNY — SAÔNE-ET-LOIRE

Pâquier Fané

20 r de Paquier, 71150
☎ 385872142
e-mail: camping-chagny@orange.fr
web: www.camping-chagny.com

A clean site 0.6km west of the church, close to village.

dir: *D974 from village centre.*

Open: 15 Apr-Oct **Site:** 1.8HEC **Prices:** 13.50-16.50 **Facilities:** Wi-fi **Services:** **Leisure:** R **Off-site:** P

FRANCE

CHÂLONS-EN-CHAMPAGNE MARNE

Camping de Châlons en Champagne

r de Plaisance, 51000
326683800 386379583
e-mail: aquadis1@orange.fr
web: www.aquadis-loisirs.com

Pleasant wooded location with good recreational facilities.

dir: *N44 NE/N77 S.*

Open: Apr-Oct **Site:** 7.5HEC **Prices:** 18.90-22.35 **Facilities:** Wi-fi Play Area **Services:** **Off-site:** P

CHAROLLES SAÔNE-ET-LOIRE

CM

rte de Viny, 71120
385240490
e-mail: camping.charolles@orange.fr

Pleasant wooded surroundings with modern sanitary facilities.

dir: *NE of town on D33 towards Viry, signed.*

Open: Apr-5 Oct **Site:** 0.6HEC **Prices:** 9 **Facilities:** Wi-fi **Services:** **Leisure:** P R **Off-site:**

CHÂTILLON-SUR-SEINE CÔTE-D'OR

CM Louis Rigoly

espl St-Vorles, 21400
380910305 380912146
e-mail: tourism-chatillon-sur-seine@wanadoo.fr

Hilly shaded site near the historic Renaissance church of St Vorles.

dir: *SE of town off D928 rte de Langres.*

Open: Apr-Sep **Site:** 0.8HEC **Facilities:** **Services:** **Off-site:** P

CHEVIGNY NIÈVRE

Hermitage de Chevigny

58230
386845097

A pleasant site with good facilities in wooded surroundings within the Morvan nature reserve. There is direct access to the lake and water sports are available.

dir: *On left bank of Lake Chevigny.*

Open: 15 Apr-Sep **Site:** 2.5HEC **Prices:** 16.50 **Facilities:** Play Area **Services:** **Leisure:** L R

CLAMECY NIÈVRE

Pont Picot

rte de Chenoches, 58500
386270597

A pleasant location between the River Yonne and the Canal du Nivernais.

Open: Apr-Sep **Site:** 1.2HEC **Prices:** 12-14.50 Mobile home hire 300-400 **Facilities:** Wi-fi Play Area **Services:** **Leisure:** R **Off-site:** P

CLAYETTE, LA SAÔNE-ET-LOIRE

Bruyères

9 rte de Gibles, 71800
385280915 386379583
e-mail: aquadis1@wanadoo.fr
web: www.aquadis-loisirs.com

Peaceful, friendly site well located for visiting the Beaujolais region and 50km from Lyon. Situated close to an historic location.

dir: *A6 exit for Macon, take N88 to La Clayette.*

Open: Apr-Sep **Site:** 3HEC **Facilities:** **Services:** **Off-site:** P

COSNE-SUR-LOIRE NIÈVRE

Camping de L'Ile

Ile de Cosne, 18300
386282792 386281810
e-mail: campingile18@orange.fr
web: www.restaurantcamping.com

Site borders River Loire.

dir: *D955 W towards Sancerre.*

Open: Etr-15 Oct **Site:** 10HEC **Prices:** 12-14.70 Mobile home hire 370-605 **Facilities:** **Services:** **Leisure:** P R **Off-site:**

CRÊCHES-SUR-SAÔNE SAÔNE-ET-LOIRE

CM Le Port d'Arciat

71680
385371183 385365791
e-mail: camping-creches.sur.saone@orange.fr
web: pagesperso-orange.fr/campingduportdarciat

Wooded location beside the River Saône.

dir: *1.5km E via D31.*

Open: 15 May-15 Sep **Site:** 6HEC **Prices:** 10.90-14.70 **Facilities:** Wi-fi Play Area **Services:** **Leisure:** L R **Off-site:**

FRANCE

DECIZE — NIÈVRE

Camping des Halles

Allee Marcel Merle, 58300
386251405 386379583
e-mail: aquadis1@orange.fr
web: www.aquadis-loisirs.com
Located by the River Loire.
dir: *NW of town centre.*
Open: May-Sep **Site:** 4HEC **Prices:** 11.50-13.80 **Facilities:** **Services:** **Off-site:** P R

DIGOIN — SAÔNE-ET-LOIRE

CM Chevrette

r de la Chevrette, 71160
385531149 385885970
e-mail: lachevrette@wanadoo.fr
web: www.lachevrette.com
On the banks of the river Loire set in peaceful countryside.
dir: *W of village on N79 exit 23/24.*
Open: 15 Mar-15 Oct **Site:** 1.5HEC **Prices:** 15.10-18.50 **Facilities:** Wi-fi Play Area **Services:** **Leisure:** P R **Off-site:**

DIJON — CÔTE-D'OR

Lac Kir

3 bd Chanoine Kir, 21000
380435472 380455706
e-mail: campingdijon@wanadoo.fr
web: www.camping-dijon.com
A well-maintained site in natural surroundings, an ideal base for exploring the historic town of Dijon.
dir: *1.5km W on N5.*
Open: Apr-15 Oct **Site:** 2.5HEC **Facilities:** **Services:** **Off-site:** L P

DOMPIERRE-LES-ORMES — SAÔNE-ET-LOIRE

Village des Meuniers

71520
385503660
e-mail: contact@villagedesmeuniers.com
web: www.villagedesmeuniers.com
A well-equipped site in the heart of the southern Burgundy countryside. Kids' club available in July and August.
dir: *Via N79, signed.*
Open: 15 Mar-1 Nov **Site:** 4HEC **Prices:** 21-27.50 Mobile home hire 280-770 **Facilities:** Wi-fi Kids' Club Play Area **Services:** **Leisure:** P

ÉCLARON-BRAUCOURT — HAUTE-MARNE

Presqu'Ile de Champaubert

52290
325041320 325943351
e-mail: ilechampaubert@free.fr
web: www.lescampingsduder.com
Situated on a lake peninsula.
Open: Apr-Sep **Site:** 3.5HEC **Facilities:** **Services:** **Off-site:** L

EPINAC — SAÔNE-ET-LOIRE

Pont Vert

Rue de la Piscine, 71360
385820026 385821367
e-mail: info@campingdupontvert.com
web: www.campingdupontvert.com
Wooded location on the banks of the river. Modern facilities and motel within the site.
dir: *S via D43 beside River Drée.*
Open: Apr-Oct **Site:** 4HEC **Facilities:** **Services:** **Leisure:** R **Off-site:**

FRONCLES — HAUTE-MARNE

Deux Ponts

r des Ponts, 52320
325023121 325020980
e-mail: mairie.froncles@wanadoo.fr
A peaceful location beside the River Marne.
Open: 15 Mar-15 Oct **Site:** 3HEC **Facilities:** **Off-site:** R

GIBLES — SAÔNE-ET-LOIRE

Château de Montrouant

Montrouant, 71800
385845113
e-mail: campingdemontrouant@wanadoo.fr
web: www.chateau-de-montrouant.com
A small site in the Charollais hill region with access to extensive parkland.
dir: *1.6km NE beside lake.*
Open: Jun-9 Sep **Site:** 1HEC **Facilities:** **Services:** **Leisure:** L P R **Off-site:**

Site 6HEC (site size) grass sand stone little shade partly shaded mainly shaded bungalows for hire (static) caravans for hire tents for hire no dogs site fully accessible for wheelchairs
Prices amount quoted is per night, for 2 adults and car, plus tent or caravan. Mobile home hire is a weekly rate.

GIFFAUMONT — MARNE

Plage

Chemin de la Cachotte, Station Nautique, 51290
608513824

A well-maintained site at the Station Nautique.

dir: *2km from village.*

Open: May-10 Sep **Site:** 1.5HEC **Prices:** 16.50-20
Facilities: **Services:** **Off-site:** L

GIGNY-SUR-SAÔNE — SAÔNE-ET-LOIRE

Château de l'Epervière

The Camping and Caravanning Club The Friendly Club

71240
385941690 385941697
e-mail: info@domaine-eperviere.com
web: www.domaine-eperviere.com

Peaceful site in the park surrounding a 16th-century château. Close to the River Saône for fishing and sailing. Kids' club available in July and August.

C&CC Report *A beautiful site, with excellent services and a great location, in a lovely, fascinating region. Most services operate for most of the season, which makes l'Epervière an attractive base for exploring the beautiful Burgundian wine areas and countryside at any time. Popular and well-known by campers seeking both traditional France and a restful and high quality camp site.*

dir: *N6 to Sennecey-le-Grand & signed.*

Open: Apr-Sep **Site:** 10HEC **Prices:** 24.30-34.40
Facilities: Wi-fi Kids' Club Play Area
Services: **Leisure:** P **Off-site:** R

GRANDPRÉ — ARDENNES

CM

08250
324305071

A peaceful riverside site.

dir: *150m from village centre on D6.*

Open: Apr-Sep **Site:** 2HEC **Facilities:**
Services: **Leisure:** R **Off-site:**

ISSY-L'ÉVÊQUE — SAÔNE-ET-LOIRE

Flower Camping de l'Étang Neuf

71760
385249605
e-mail: info@issy-camping.com
web: www.issy-camping.com

A fine position beside the lake, with views of the château.

Open: 13 May-15 Sep **Site:** 4HEC **Facilities:**
Wi-fi Play Area **Services:** **Leisure:** L P
Off-site:

LAIVES — SAÔNE-ET-LOIRE

Lacs La Heronnière

Rte de la Ferté, Les Bois de Laives, 71240
385449885 385449885
e-mail: contact@camping-laheronniere.com
web: camping-laheronniere.com

A family site, quiet and shady, in a pleasant environment surrounded by nature, very close to a leisure park. Between Chalon-sur-Saône and Mâcon, the campsite is surrounded by three lakes. Compulsory separate car park for arrivals after 22.00 hrs.

dir: *Autoroute exit Chalon Sud towards Mâcon.*

GPS: 46.6719, 4.833

Open: 19 May-15 Sep **Site:** 2HEC **Prices:** 18-20
Mobile home hire 294-385 **Facilities:** Play Area
Services: **Leisure:** P **Off-site:** L R

MÂCON — SAÔNE-ET-LOIRE

Camping Municipal de Mâcon

Route des Grandes Varennes, 71000
385381622 385393918
e-mail: camping@ville-macon.fr

Site divided into pitches with a water-sports centre and pool nearby.

dir: *A6 exit Mâcon Nord, follow signs for camp site.*

GPS: 46.3308, 4.8434

Open: 15 Mar-Oct **Site:** 5HEC **Prices:** 13.55-14.95
Facilities: Wi-fi **Services:**
Leisure: P **Off-site:** R

MARCENAY — CÔTE-D'OR

Grebes du Lac de Marcenay

Lac de Marcenay, 21330
380816172 380816199
e-mail: info@campingmarcenaylac.com
web: www.campingmarcenaylac.com

A peaceful site in unspoiled contryside with separate hedged pitches. Direct access to lake.

Open: 30 Mar-Sep **Site:** 3HEC **Facilities:**
Services: **Leisure:** L P **Off-site:** R

MATOUR — SAÔNE-ET-LOIRE

CM Le Paluet

Le Paluet, 71520
385597058 385597454
e-mail: lepaluet@matour.fr
web: www.matour.fr

Not far from the town centre in a pleasant countryside setting beside the river, pitches are shady and well-spaced. Family and large group gatherings can be facilitated.

Open: May-Sep **Site:** 2HEC **Facilities:** Wi-fi
Services: **Leisure:** P R **Off-site:**

FRANCE

MESNIL-ST-PÈRE AUBE

Kawan Village Camping Le Lac d'Orient

r du Lac, 10140
325406185 325709687
e-mail: info@camping-lacdorient.com
web: www.camping-lacdorient.com

Site set in wooded parkland leading down to a lake. The sheltered pitches have varying degrees of shade. During July and August an events programme, including a kids' club, takes place with occasional evening entertainment.

Open: 26 Mar-Sep **Site:** 10HEC **Facilities:** Kids' Club Play Area **Services:** **Leisure:** P **Off-site:** L

MEURSAULT CÔTE-D'OR

Grappe d'Or

2 rte de Volnay, 21190
380212248 380216574
e-mail: info@camping-meursault.com
web: www.camping-meursault.com

Clean terraced site on an open meadow. Mountain bikes are available for hire.

dir: *0.7km NE on D11b.*

Open: Apr-15 Oct **Site:** 5.5HEC **Prices:** 14-18 Mobile home hire 294-490 **Facilities:** Wi-fi (charged) **Services:** **Leisure:** P **Off-site:**

MONTAPAS NIÈVRE

CM La Chênaie

La Chênaie, 58110
386583432 386582905
e-mail: mairiedemontapas@orange.fr
web: www.camping-nievre-montapas.net

Wooded location beside a lake with plenty of recreational facilities.

dir: *0.5km from town centre via D259, beside lake.*

Open: Apr-Oct **Site:** 1HEC **Prices:** 5.60 **Facilities:** **Services:** **Leisure:** L **Off-site:**

MONTBARD CÔTE-D'OR

CM

r M-Servet, 21500
380926950 380922160

Quiet, shady location close to the canal and river.

dir: *NW via rte de Laignes.*

Open: Mar-27 Oct **Site:** 2.5HEC **Facilities:** **Services:** **Leisure:** P **Off-site:** R

MONTHERMÉ ARDENNES

Base de Loisirs Départementale

08800
324328161 324323766
e-mail: campinghaulme@cg08.fr

A pleasant wooded location.

dir: *0.8km NE beside the River Semoy.*

Open: Apr-Oct **Site:** 16HEC **Facilities:** **Services:** **Leisure:** R

MONTSAUCHE NIÈVRE

Mesanges

Lac des Settons, Rive Gauche, 58230
386845577 386845577
e-mail: campinglesmesanges@orange.fr

On Lac des Settons.

dir: *D193 towards Lac des Settons.*

Open: 15 May-15 Sep **Site:** 5HEC **Prices:** 16.50 **Facilities:** Play Area **Services:** **Off-site:** L P R

Plage du Midi

58230
386845197 386845731
e-mail: campplagedumidi@aol.com
web: www.settons-camping.com

Wooded setting on Lac des Settons with good facilities.

dir: *D193 from town centre to Les Settons and site.*

Open: Etr-15 Oct **Site:** 4HEC **Facilities:** **Services:** **Leisure:** L **Off-site:**

PARAY-LE-MONIAL SÂONE-ET-LOIRE

Mambré

19 rue du Gué-Léger, 71600
385888920
e-mail: bureau-reservations@orange.fr
web: www.campingdemambre.com

Peaceful site on a level meadow with modern facilities.

dir: *N70, exit at Paray-le Monial-Sud. Site signposted along Canal-du-Centre on the D979 direction Moulins.*

GPS: 46.4573, 4.1050

Open: 3 May-Sep **Site:** 4.5HEC **Prices:** 16.90-19.50 Mobile home hire 204-450 **Facilities:** Play Area **Services:** **Leisure:** P **Off-site:** R

PEIGNEY — HAUTE-MARNE

Lac de la Liez

The Camping and Caravanning Club The Friendly Club

r des Voiliers, 52200
☎ 325902779 📠 325906679
e-mail: campingliez@free.fr
Kids' club available in July and August.

C&CC Report *In a convenient location, 18km from the A5 and 20km from the A31 motorway exits, in the recently designated Parc Naturel de la Haute Marne. An ideal site both for short stays en-route to and from sites further south, and for longer stays, with good fishing, cycling and walking routes nearby. Enjoy views over the lake from many pitches, be sure to eat in the excellent on-site restaurant and visit the fascinating ancient hilltop town of Langres, where an audio tour explains its history.*

dir: *A31 exit 7, then N19 S, then follow Vesoul and Lac de la Liez.*

Open: Apr-2 Oct **Site:** **Prices:** 19.90-26.90 Mobile home hire 350-770 **Facilities:** Wi-fi (charged) Kids' Club Play Area **Services:** **Leisure:** P **Off-site:** L

PONT-SAINTE-MARIE — AUBE

CM de Troyes

7 r Roger Salengro, 10150
☎ 325810264 📠 325810264
e-mail: info@troyescamping.net
web: www.troyescamping.net
Wooded site a short walk from the town of Troyes, which has a large shopping centre. Ideally located for exploring the surrounding countryside.

dir: *Follow signs for 'Pont Saint Marie' and 'Municipal' through Troyes.*

Open: Apr-15 Oct **Site:** 3.8HEC **Prices:** 15.70-19.40 **Facilities:** Wi-fi Play Area **Services:** **Leisure:** P **Off-site:**

see advert on page 100

POUGUES-LES-EAUX — NIÈVRE

CM Chanternes

av de Paris, 58320
☎ 386688618
dir: *7km N of Nevers on N7.*

Open: Jun-Sep **Site:** 1.4HEC **Facilities:** **Services:** **Off-site:** P R

RADONVILLIERS — AUBE

Garillon

Rue des Anciens Combattants, 10500
☎ 325922146
e-mail: camping-le-garillon@hotmail.fr
Beside the river, 250m from the lake.

Open: May-14 Nov **Site:** 1HEC **Facilities:** **Leisure:** P **Off-site:** L R

RIEL-LES-EAUX — CÔTE-D'OR

Riel-les-Eaux

21570
☎ 380937276
A lakeside site with fishing and boating facilities.

dir: *2.2km W via D13.*

Open: Apr-Oct **Site:** 0.2HEC **Facilities:** **Services:** **Leisure:** L **Off-site:**

ST-HILAIRE-SOUS-ROMILLY — AUBE

Domaine de La Noue des Rois

The Camping and Caravanning Club The Friendly Club

chemin des Brayes, 10100
☎ 325244160 📠 325243418
e-mail: contact@lanouedesrois.com
web: www.lanouedesrois.com
A quiet site in a pine forest.

C&CC Report *In a lakeside, woodland setting, two and a half km from village, with an on-site restaurant.*

dir: *2km NE.*

Open: All Year. **Site:** 30HEC **Facilities:** **Services:** **Leisure:** L P

ST-HONORÉ — NIÈVRE

Bains

15 av J-Mermoz, 58360
☎ 386307344 📠 386306188
e-mail: camping-les-bains@wanadoo.fr
web: www.campinglesbains.com
A family site with good facilities close to the Morvan national park.

dir: *Via A6 & D985.*

Open: Apr-Oct **Site:** 4.5HEC **Facilities:** **Services:** **Leisure:** P **Off-site:**

FRANCE

FRANCE

Site 6HEC (site size) grass sand stone little shade partly shaded mainly shaded bungalows for hire (static) caravans for hire tents for hire no dogs site fully accessible for wheelchairs
Prices amount quoted is per night, for 2 adults and car, plus tent or caravan. Mobile home hire is a weekly rate.

ST MARCEL — SAÔNE-ET-LOIRE

Pont de Bourgogne

r Julien Leneveu, 71380
385482686 385485063
e-mail: campingchalon71@wanadoo.fr
web: www.camping-chalon.com

Situated on the banks of the river Saône, only a few minutes from the city centre of Chalon sur Saône, and within easy reach of the Autoroute.

dir: *A6 exit 26 (Chalon Sud), signed.*

GPS: 46.7843, 4.8723

Open: Apr-Sep **Site:** 3HEC **Prices:** 19.40-26.10 Mobile home hire 299-599 **Facilities:** Wi-fi Play Area **Services:** **Leisure:** R **Off-site:** P

ST-PÉREUSE — NIÈVRE

Manoir de Bezolle

58110
386844255 386844377
e-mail: info@camping-bezolle.com
web: www.camping-bezolle.com

A well-kept site divided by hedges in the grounds of a manor house, at the edge of a national park.

dir: *At x-rds of D11 & D978.*

Open: All Year. **Site:** 8HEC **Facilities:** **Services:** **Leisure:** P

STE-MENEHOULD — MARNE

CM de la Grelette

51800
326608021
web: www.ste-menehould.fr

A well-equipped municipal site.

dir: *E of town towards Metz, beside River Aisne.*

GPS: 49.0894, 4.9097

Open: May-Sep **Site:** 1HEC **Prices:** 6 **Facilities:** Play Area **Off-site:** P R

SAULIEU — CÔTE-D'OR

Camping le Perron

21210
380641619 386379583
e-mail: aquadis1@orange.fr
web: www.aquadis-loisirs.com

On level, open ground with good recreational facilities.

dir: *1km NW on N6.*

GPS: 47.2892, 4.2236

Open: All Year. **Site:** 3HEC **Prices:** 12-14 Mobile home hire 102-510 **Facilities:** Wi-fi Play Area **Services:** **Leisure:** P **Off-site:** L

SEDAN — ARDENNES

CM de la Prairie

bd Fabert, 08200
324271305 324271305

A well-equipped municipal site on the banks of the River Meuse, close to the centre of the village.

Open: Apr-Sep **Site:** 1.5HEC **Facilities:** **Services:** **Leisure:** R **Off-site:** L P

SEURRE — CÔTE-D'OR

Piscine

21250
380204922 380203401

A well-equipped municipal site with direct access to the river.

dir: *N73 W from town centre for 0.6km towards Beaune.*

Open: 15 May-15 Sep **Site:** **Facilities:** **Services:** **Leisure:** P R **Off-site:**

SÉZANNE — MARNE

CM

rte de Launat, 51120
326805700
e-mail: campingdesezanne@wanadoo.fr

dir: *1.5km W on D239.*

Open: Apr-1 Oct **Site:** 1HEC **Facilities:** **Services:** **Leisure:** P **Off-site:**

SIGNY-LE-PETIT — ARDENNES

Domaine de la Motte

Base de Loisirs, 08380
324535473 324535473
e-mail: campingprehugon@wanadoo.fr
web: www.domainedelamotte.eu

A pleasant site in wooded surroundings with a spa facility. Kids' club available in high season.

dir: *Via N43.*

Open: All Year. **Site:** 0.8HEC **Prices:** 14 Mobile home hire 250-425 **Facilities:** Wi-fi Kids' Club Play Area **Services:** **Leisure:** P **Off-site:** L R

Facilities shop shower electric points for razors electric points for caravans parking by tents permitted compulsory separate car park **Services** café/restaurant bar Camping Gaz International gas other than Camping Gaz first aid facilities laundry **Leisure** swimming L-Lake P-Pool R-River S-Sea **Off-site** All facilities within 5km

SOULAINES-DHUYS — AUBE

La Croix Badeau

10200
☎ 325270543
e-mail: steveheusghem@hotmail.com
web: www.croix-badeau.com
Open: Apr-Sep **Site:** 1.5HEC **Facilities:** **Services:** **Off-site:** R

TAZILLY — NIÈVRE

Château de Chigy

58170
☎ 386301080 386300922
e-mail: reception@chateaudechigy.com.fr
web: www.chateaudechigy.com.fr
A beautiful location within the extensive grounds of a magnificent château. Good sports facilities and entertainment programme.
dir: *4km from Luzy on D973 Luzy-Moulins.*
Open: May-Sep **Site:** 7HEC **Facilities:** **Services:** **Leisure:** L P

THONNANCE-LES-MOULINS — HAUTE-MARNE

Forge de Ste-Marie

The Camping and Caravanning Club The Friendly Club

52230
☎ 325944200 325944143
e-mail: info@laforgedesaintemarie.com
web: www.laforgedesaintemarie.com
Partially terraced, on the site of an 18th-century forge containing a lake.
C&CC Report *This fabulous site, makes for a lovely restful setting. The welcome and helpfulness of Angela and Jacco and the beauty of the area make it impossible not to relax. Low season here is especially good, with a programme of walks, painting, cheese and wine tasting and other activities, plus the delicious restaurant meals.*
dir: *Via N67 & D427.*
Open: 24 Apr-10 Sep **Site:** 11HEC **Facilities:** **Services:** **Leisure:** P R

TOULON-SUR-ARROUX — SAÔNE-ET-LOIRE

CM du Val d'Arroux

rte d'Uxeau, 73120
☎ 385795122 385796217
e-mail: mairie.toulon@wanadoo.fr
On western outskirts beside the River Arroux.
dir: *D985 onto Uxeau road.*
Open: 18 Apr-18 Oct **Site:** 0.62HEC **Facilities:** **Services:** **Leisure:** R **Off-site:**

TOURNUS — SAÔNE-ET-LOIRE

Tournus

14 r des Canes, 71700
☎ 385511658 385511658
e-mail: reception@camping-tournus.com
web: www.camping-tournus.com
Friendly campsite with large, grassy pitches which are easily accessible. Most offer semi-shade but some are more sunny.
dir: *A6 autoroute, exit 27 for Tournus, follow RN6, campsite signposted.*
GPS: 46.5737, 4.9093
Open: Apr-Sep **Site:** 1.5HEC **Prices:** 19.10-24.50 **Facilities:** Wi-fi Play Area **Services:** **Leisure:** R **Off-site:** P R

UCHIZY — SAÔNE-ET-LOIRE

National 6

71700
☎ 385405390 385405390
e-mail: camping.uchizylen6@wanadoo.fr
web: www.camping-lenational6.com
Site surrounded by poplar trees on banks of river.
dir: *Off N6 towards Saône, 6km S of Tournus & continue 0.8km.*
Open: Apr-1 Oct **Site:** 6HEC **Facilities:** **Services:** **Leisure:** P R

VAL-DES-PRÉS — MARNE

Gentianes

La Vachette, 05100
☎ 492212141 492212412
A delightful wooded location bordered by a river and backed by imposing mountains.
dir: *On edge of village, 3km SE of Briançon.*
Open: All Year. **Site:** 2HEC **Facilities:** **Services:** **Leisure:** P R **Off-site:**

VANDENESSE-EN-AUXOIS — CÔTE-D'OR

Lac de Panthier

21320
☎ 380492194 380492580
e-mail: info@lac-de-panthier.com
web: www.lac-de-panthier.com
A pleasant location beside a lake with plenty of facilities for families. Kids' club available in July and August.
dir: *A6 or A38 exit at Pouilly-en-Auxois towards Créancey.*
GPS: 47.2368, 4.6282
Open: 9 Apr-8 Oct **Site:** 7HEC **Prices:** 19-28 Mobile home hire 280-777 **Facilities:** Wi-fi (charged) Kids' Club Play Area **Services:** **Leisure:** L P

FRANCE

VENAREY-LES-LAUMES — CÔTE-D'OR

Alésia

r Dr-Roux, 21150

380960776 380960776

e-mail: camping.venarey@wanadoo.fr

web: www.alesia-tourisme.net

A peaceful site close to the lake and river.

Open: Apr-15 Oct **Site:** 2HEC **Facilities:** **Services:** **Off-site:** L R

VERMENTON — YONNE

Coullemières

89270

386815302 386815302

e-mail: camping.vermenton@orange.fr

web: www.camping-vermenton.com

A peaceful meadowland site with good facilities.

dir: *On N6 S of Auxerre.*

Open: Apr-Sep **Site:** 1.5HEC **Facilities:** **Services:** **Leisure:** R **Off-site:**

VIGNOLES — CÔTE-D'OR

Bouleaux

The Camping and Caravanning Club The Friendly Club

11 r Jaune, 21200

380222688

Small, immaculately-kept site handy for A6 motorway.

C&CC Report *A small and pretty site suitable for short or long stays, in an excellent location. Always lovingly well-kept by the attentive and welcoming owners, Les Bouleaux is a good base for visits to any number of vineyards, or for ambling through the many wine villages in the lovely countryside of Burgundy. The unique old town of Beaune, with its ancient hospices, its decorated tiled roofs and its wine museums, whose names are so familiar from many a wine bottle label, is always worth a visit.*

dir: *From Beaune onto RD973 (towards Dole), turn left to Vignoles. 3km from Beaune centre.*

Open: All Year. **Site:** 1.4HEC **Prices:** 14 **Facilities:** **Services:** **Off-site:** L P

VILLENEUVE-LES-GENÊTS — YONNE

Bois Guillaume

89350

386454541 386454920

e-mail: camping@bois-guillaume.com

web: www.bois-guillaume.com

Wooded surroundings with modern facilities. Heated swimming pool from mid June to mid September.

dir: *A77 exit Briare follow signs Blèneau on D22.*

Open: All Year. **Site:** 8HEC **Prices:** 14.30-19.20 Mobile home hire 320-525 **Facilities:** Wi-fi (charged) Play Area **Services:** **Leisure:** P **Off-site:** R

VINCELLES — YONNE

Ceriselles

rte de Vincelottes, 89290

386425047 386423939

e-mail: camping@cc-payscoulangeois.fr

web: www.campingceriselles.com

Rural location beside the river Yonne, close to the local village.

dir: *D606 exit between Avallon & Auxerre, signed.*

Open: Apr-Oct **Site:** 2.5HEC **Prices:** 15-19 Mobile home hire 280-450 **Facilities:** Wi-fi Play Area **Services:** **Leisure:** P **Off-site:** R

SOUTH WEST/PYRÉNÉES

AIGNAN — GERS

Castex

32290

562092513 562092479

e-mail: info@domaine-castex.com

web: www.domaine-castex.com

Wooded site in peaceful surroundings.

dir: *0.8km from D48.*

Open: 15 Mar-15 Oct **Site:** 3HEC **Facilities:** **Services:** **Leisure:** P **Off-site:** L R

AIRE-SUR-L'ADOUR — LANDES

Ombrages de l'Adour

r des Graviers, 40800

558717510 558713259

e-mail: hetapsarl@yahoo.fr

web: www.camping-adour-landes.com

A clean, tidy site next to a sports stadium beside the river. Clean sanitary installations.

Open: Apr-Oct **Site:** 2HEC **Prices:** 13.90-16.90 Mobile home hire 275-385 **Facilities:** Wi-fi (charged) Play Area **Services:** **Leisure:** R **Off-site:** P

FRANCE

Facilities shop shower electric points for razors electric points for caravans parking by tents permitted compulsory separate car park **Services** café/restaurant bar Camping Gaz International gas other than Camping Gaz first aid facilities laundry **Leisure** swimming L-Lake P-Pool R-River S-Sea **Off-site** All facilities within 5km

ALBI — TARN

Albirondack Park Camping Lodge & Spa

1 allée de la piscine, 81000
☎ 563603706
e-mail: ballario.andre.ballario@orange.fr
web: www.albirondack.fr

Shaded by 100 year old oak trees, the site's restaurant is based on an American Lodge with cathedral ceiling. Kids' club available in July and August. Dogs accepted but restrictions apply.

dir: *N99 from village towards Millau, left onto D100, left to site.*

GPS: 43.9337, 2.1663

Open: All Year. **Site:** 18HEC **Prices:** 15-28 **Facilities:** Wi-fi (charged) Kids' Club **Services:** **Leisure:** P **Off-site:**

ALLAS-LES-MINES — DORDOGNE

Domaine Le Cro Magnon

The Camping and Caravanning Club The Friendly Club

24220
☎ 553291370 📠 553291579
e-mail: contact@domaine-cro-magnon.com
web: www.domaine-cro-magnon.com

Spacious pitches in a generously wooded estate.

C&CC Report *The Léger family is rightly proud that this well-run, high quality and popular site is also noted by campers for its informal and friendly family atmosphere. The beautiful hilltop setting includes a viewpoint over the river, while its location makes the site a perfect base for visiting the very best of the wonderful villages and prehistoric sites for which the Dordogne is so famous. Large pitches, open and covered pools, a waterslide and excellent site facilities make this a great place for relaxation, too.*

dir: *D25 southwards exit Marnac Berbiguières.*

Open: 25 Jun-3 Sep **Site:** 22HEC **Prices:** 9.40-25.70 Mobile home hire 288-958 **Facilities:** (charged) Kids' Club Play Area **Services:** **Leisure:** P **Off-site:** R

ALLES-SUR-DORDOGNE — DORDOGNE

Port de Limeuil

24480
☎ 553632976 📠 553630419
e-mail: didierbonvallet@aol.com
web: www.leportdelimeuil.com

Situated in a conservation area at the confluence of the Dordogne and Vézère rivers, with a 400m-long beach.

dir: *Signed off D51.*

Open: May-Sep **Site:** 7HEC **Prices:** 14-26.50 Mobile home hire 190-840 **Facilities:** Wi-fi **Services:** **Leisure:** P R

ANDERNOS-LES-BAINS — GIRONDE

Fontaine-Vieille

4 bd du Colonel Wurtz, 33510
☎ 556820167 📠 556820981
e-mail: fontaine-vieille-sa@wanadoo.fr
web: www.fontaine-vieille.com

On level ground in sparse forest. Dogs allowed except in mobile homes.

dir: *S of village centre.*

Open: Apr-Sep **Site:** 12.6HEC **Facilities:** Wi-fi Kids' Club Play Area **Services:** **Leisure:** P S

ANGLARS-JUILLAC — LOT

Floiras

46140
☎ 565362739
e-mail: campingfloiras@aol.com
web: www.campingfloiras.com

A quiet level site beside the River Lot, surrounded by vineyards in a hilly landscape dotted with villages, castles and caves. Facilities for boating.

dir: *SW via D8.*

Open: Apr-15 Oct **Site:** 1HEC **Prices:** 12.50-17.50 **Facilities:** **Services:** **Leisure:** R **Off-site:**

ANGLET — PYRÉNÉES-ATLANTIQUES

Parme

Quartier Brindos, 64600
☎ 559230300 📠 559412955
e-mail: campingdeparme@wanadoo.fr
web: www.campingdeparme.com

Wooded area with good facilities on the outskirts of Biarritz.

dir: *3km SW off N10.*

Open: Apr-30 Oct **Site:** 3.5HEC **Prices:** 17.50-35 Mobile home hire 245-850 **Facilities:** Wi-fi (charged) Kids' Club Play Area **Services:** **Leisure:** P **Off-site:** L R S

FRANCE

ARCACHON GIRONDE

Camping Club d'Arcachon

av de la Galaxie, Les Abatilles, 33120
556832415 557522851
e-mail: info@camping-arcachon.com
web: www.camping-arcachon.com
A delightful wooded position 0.8km from the town and 1km from the beaches.

dir: *1.5km S.*

Open: 13 Dec-11 Nov **Site:** 6HEC **Prices:** 13-36 Mobile home hire 240-910 **Facilities:** Wi-fi (charged) Kids' Club Play Area **Services:** **Leisure:** P **Off-site:** S

ARCIZANS-AVANT HAUTES-PYRÉNÉES

Lac

29 chemin d'Azun, 65400
562970188 562970188
e-mail: campinglac@campinglac65.fr
web: www.campinglac65.fr
Set in delightful Pyrenean surroundings on outskirts of village. Quiet and peaceful, with spacious and grassy pitches.

dir: *S on N21, onto D13 through St-Savin.*

Open: 15 May-Sep **Site:** 4HEC **Prices:** 16.90-24.50 **Facilities:** Wi-fi Play Area **Services:** **Leisure:** P **Off-site:** L R

ARÈS GIRONDE

Canadienne

rte de Lège, 82 r du Gl-de-Gaulle, 33740
556602491 557704085
e-mail: info@lacanadienne.com
web: www.lacanadienne.com
A family site surrounded by pine and oak trees with good facilities.

dir: *1km N off D106.*

Open: Feb-Nov **Site:** 2HEC **Facilities:** **Services:** **Leisure:** P **Off-site:** L

La Cigale

The Camping and Caravanning Club The Friendly Club

rte de Lège, 33740
556602259 557704166
e-mail: contact@camping-lacigale-ares.com
web: www.camping-lacigale-ares.com
Clean tidy site among pine trees. Grassy pitches and good recreational facilities.

C&CC Report *A small, immaculately kept site with a convivial family atmosphere, close to the magnificent Atlantic beaches and within walking distance of the town centre. The attention to detail shown by the friendly owners is apparent throughout the site. Nature lovers will want to visit the bird sanctuary at La Teste, while more energetic visitors may prefer the Dune du Pyla, the highest sand dune in Europe.*

dir: *0.5km N on D106, between sea & Arcachon Basin.*

Open: 23 Apr-Sep **Site:** 2.8HEC **Prices:** 20-31 **Facilities:** Wi-fi Play Area **Services:** **Leisure:** P **Off-site:** S

Goëlands

av de la Libération, 33740
556825564 556820751
e-mail: camping-les-goelands@wanadoo.fr
Situated among oak trees 200m from the beach with good facilities.

dir: *1.7km SE.*

Open: Mar-Oct **Site:** 10HEC **Prices:** 17-28 **Facilities:** Wi-fi Kids' Club **Services:** **Leisure:** P **Off-site:** L

Pasteur

1 r du Pilote, 33704
556603333
web: www.atlantic-vacances.com
Comfortable family site with friendly atmosphere.

dir: *S of D3, 300m from the sea.*

Open: Apr-Sep **Site:** 1HEC **Facilities:** **Services:** **Leisure:** P **Off-site:** S

ARREAU HAUTES-PYRÉNÉES

Refuge International

RD 929, 65240
562986334 562986334
e-mail: camping.international.arreau@wanadoo.fr
Enclosed terrace site.

dir: *2km N on D929.*

Open: All Year. **Site:** 15HEC **Facilities:** **Services:** **Leisure:** P R **Off-site:** L

FRANCE

Facilities shop shower electric points for razors electric points for caravans parking by tents permitted compulsory separate car park **Services** café/restaurant bar Camping Gaz International gas other than Camping Gaz first aid facilities laundry **Leisure** swimming L-Lake P-Pool R-River S-Sea **Off-site** All facilities within 5km

ASCARAT — PYRÉNÉES-ATLANTIQUES

Europ' Camping

64220
☎ 559371278 559372982
e-mail: europcamping64@orange.fr
web: www.europ-camping.com
Rural surroundings of mountains and vineyards, 300m from the River Nive.
dir: *1km W of St-Jean-Pied-de-Port on D918.*
Open: Etr-Sep **Site:** 2HEC **Facilities:** **Services:** **Leisure:** P **Off-site:** R

ATUR — DORDOGNE

Grand Dague

24750
☎ 553042101 553042201
e-mail: info@legranddague.fr
web: www.legranddague.fr
Well-equipped family site in the heart of the Dordogne region, with pitches divided by bushes and hedges.
dir: *NE of Atur via D2.*
Open: 29 Apr-25 Sep **Site:** 22HEC **Facilities:** **Services:** **Leisure:** P **Off-site:** R

AUREILHAN — LANDES

Village Center Aurilandes

1001 promenade de l'Étang, 40200
☎ 499572121 467516389
e-mail: contact@village-center.com
web: www.village-center.com/aquitaine/camping-mer-aurilandes.php
Quiet site on the banks of Lake Aureilhan.
dir: *D626, 2km before Mimizan, on right.*
GPS: 44.2230, -1.2036
Open: 24 Jun-4 Sep **Site:** 8HEC **Prices:** 13-24 Mobile home hire 167-854 **Facilities:** Wi-fi Kids' Club Play Area **Services:** **Leisure:** L P **Off-site:**

Village Center Eurolac

Promenade de l'Étang, 40200
☎ 499572121 467516389
e-mail: contact@village-center.com
web: www.village-center.com/aquitaine/camping-eurolac.php
At the edge of Aureilhan Lake with exceptional views.
dir: *Off N10 at exit 16 to Mimizan onto D626 to Aureilhan.*
GPS: 44.2228, -1.2039
Open: 27 May-18 Sep **Site:** 7HEC **Prices:** Mobile home hire 192-924 **Facilities:** Wi-fi Kids' Club Play Area **Services:** **Leisure:** L P **Off-site:**

AZUR — LANDES

Camping Azu' Rivage

720 Route des Campings, Au bord du lac, 40140
☎ 558483072 558483072
e-mail: info@campingazurivage.com
web: www.campingazurivage.com
A family site in wooded surroundings close to Lac de Soustons and 8km from the coast.
dir: *2km S of Azur.*
Open: 15 Jun-15 Sep **Site:** 7HEC **Facilities:** **Services:** **Leisure:** L P R

BAGNÈRES-DE-BIGORRE — HAUTES-PYRÉNÉES

Bigourdan

rte de Tarbes, 65200
☎ 562951357
web: www.camping-bigourdan.com
A level site recommended for caravans in a beautiful Pyrenean setting.
dir: *2.5km NW at Pouzac.*
Open: 31 Mar-21 Oct **Site:** 1HEC **Facilities:** **Services:** **Leisure:** P **Off-site:** R

Parc des Oiseaux

RD26, 65200
☎ 562953026
Clean, well-kept site with large pitches.
Open: All Year. **Site:** 2.8HEC **Facilities:** **Services:** **Leisure:** R **Off-site:** P

Tilleuls

12 av Maréchal Alan Brooke, 65200
☎ 562952604
A well-equipped site at an altitude of 500m. There are good recreational facilities and a bakery operates during July and August.
Open: May-Sep **Site:** 2.6HEC **Facilities:** **Services:** **Off-site:** P

FRANCE

BASTIDE-DE-SEROU, LA — ARIÈGE

Arize

rte de Nescus, 09240
☎ 561658151 📠 561658334
e-mail: camparize@aol.com
web: www.camping-arize.com

A well-run site with a friendly atmosphere and offering a range of facilities in a peaceful wooded location at the foot of the Pyrénées. Available nearby, horse riding, trout fishing and hiking.

GPS: 43.0018, 1.4454

Open: 11 Mar-13 Nov **Site:** 3HEC **Prices:** 16.40-32.60 Mobile home hire 294-749 **Facilities:** Wi-fi (charged) Kids' Club Play Area **Services:** **Leisure:** P R **Off-site:**

BEAUCENS-LES-BAINS — HAUTES-PYRÉNÉES

Viscos

65400
☎ 562970545

A secluded location at the foot of the Pyrénées.

dir: *1km N on D13 rte de Lourdes.*

Open: 10 May-Sep **Site:** 2HEC **Facilities:** **Services:** **Off-site:** R

BELVÈS — DORDOGNE

Hauts de Ratebout

24170
☎ 553290210 📠 553290828
e-mail: ratebout@franceloc.fr
web: www.camping-hauts-ratebout.fr

A well-equipped site on an old Périgord farm, set in extensive grounds on top of a hill.

dir: *D710 to Fumel, after Vaurez-de-Belvès onto D54 to Casals.*

Open: 28 Apr-12 Sep **Site:** 12HEC **Facilities:** **Services:** **Leisure:** P

Nauves

Bos Rouge, 24170
☎ 553291264
e-mail: campinglesnauves@hotmail.com
web: www.lesnauves.com

Located on a site with 40 different species of trees. A good base for touring the Perigord Noir.

dir: *4.5km SW via D53.*

Open: 13 Apr-24 Sep **Site:** 7HEC **Prices:** 10.80-28.90 Mobile home hire 224-707 **Facilities:** Wi-fi (charged) Kids' Club Play Area **Services:** **Leisure:** P **Off-site:** R

RCN Le Moulin de la Pique

24170
☎ 553290115 📠 553282909
e-mail: info@rcn-lemoulindelapique.fr
web: www.rcn-campings.fr

A quiet well-equipped site set out around an imposing villa and a small lake. There are fine entertainment facilities and modern sanitary installations.

dir: *0.5km S on D710.*

Open: 10 Apr-2 Oct **Site:** 12HEC **Facilities:** Wi-fi (charged) Play Area **Services:** **Leisure:** L P R

BEYNAC-ET-CAZENAC — DORDOGNE

Capeyrou

24220
☎ 553295495 📠 553283627
e-mail: lecapeyrou@wanadoo.fr
web: www.campinglecapeyrou.com

Situated beside the River Dordogne close to the gates of the picturesque medieval town of Beynac. Great view of the castle.

dir: *Via D703.*

GPS: 44.8383, 1.1486

Open: 15 Apr-Sep **Site:** 5HEC **Prices:** 14.70-22.50 **Facilities:** Wi-fi Play Area **Services:** **Leisure:** P R **Off-site:**

BEZ, LE — TARN

Plô

81260
☎ 563740082
e-mail: info@leplo.com
web: www.leplo.com

A pleasant small family site in wooded surroundings.

dir: *0.9km W via D30.*

GPS: 43.6081, 2.4713

Open: May-Sep **Site:** 4.2HEC **Prices:** 11-17.60 **Facilities:** Wi-fi Play Area **Services:** **Leisure:** P **Off-site:** R

FRANCE

BIARRITZ — PYRÉNÉES-ATLANTIQUES

Biarritz

28 r d'Harcet, 64200
559230012 559437467
e-mail: biarritz.camping@wanadoo.fr
web: www.biarritz-camping.fr

A pleasant site with spacious pitches, 200m from the beach.

dir: *2km from town centre on N10, signed Espagne.*

Open: 6 May-16 Sep **Site:** 2.6HEC **Facilities:** **Services:** **Leisure:** P **Off-site:** S

BIAS — LANDES

CM Le Tatiou

40710
558090476 558824430
e-mail: campingletatiou@wanadoo.fr
web: www.campingletatiou.com

Well-equipped family site in a forested setting, 4km from the sea.

dir: *2km W towards Lespecier.*

Open: Apr-Oct **Site:** 10HEC **Facilities:** **Services:** **Leisure:** P **Off-site:** S

BIDART — PYRÉNÉES-ATLANTIQUES

Ilbarritz

rte de Biarritz, 64210
559230029 559412459
e-mail: contact@camping-ilbarritz.com
web: www.camping-ilbarritz.com

Terraced site with numbered pitches, 0.8km from the sea.

C&CC Report *A great location for a site, with the beaches of Biarritz close at hand. The owners are constantly seeking to improve the site with a new outdoor fun pool with water slides and sanitation block planned for 2011. The Basque country is perfect for active families, with many walks and cycle paths in the area, whilst Biarritz is the surf capital of France.*

dir: *2km N on N106 Biarritz road.*

Open: Apr-Sep **Site:** 7.7HEC **Prices:** 15-42 Mobile home hire 279-945 **Facilities:** Wi-fi Kids' Club **Services:** **Leisure:** P **Off-site:** S

Oyam

Ferme Oyamburua, 64210
559549161 559547687
e-mail: accueil@camping-oyam.com
web: www.camping-oyam.com

Level meadow site near farm. Views of the Pyrénées. Simple but pleasant site. Shop, bar and restaurant open July and August.

dir: *Turn off beyond church onto N10 towards Arbonne for 1km.*

Open: Jun-Sep **Site:** 7HEC **Prices:** 13-30 Mobile home hire 250-714 **Facilities:** Play Area **Services:** **Leisure:** P **Off-site:** S

Pavillon Royal

av Prince de Galles, 64210
559230054 559234447
e-mail: info@pavillon-royal.com
web: www.pavillon-royal.com

A beautiful, well-kept site beside a sandy beach, divided into pitches, most of which have a sea view.

dir: *2km N.*

Open: 15 May-Sep **Site:** 5HEC **Prices:** 24-51 **Facilities:** Wi-fi (charged) Play Area **Services:** **Leisure:** P **Off-site:** S

Ruisseau

rte d'Arbonne, 64210
559419450 559419573
e-mail: francoise.dumont3@wanadoo.fr
web: www.camping-le-ruisseau.fr

A well-equipped family site in wooded surroundings set out around two lakes. There is a mini-farm for children.

dir: *2km E on D255.*

Open: 22 May-19 Sep **Site:** 15HEC **Prices:** 16-38 Mobile home hire 280-1040 **Facilities:** Wi-fi (charged) Kids' Club Play Area **Services:** **Leisure:** P **Off-site:** S

Sunêlia Berrua

r Berrua, 64210
559549666 559547830
e-mail: contact@berrua.com
web: www.berrua.com

A well-equipped family site 1km from the beach and 0.5km from the village. In a peaceful, shaded setting among trees, easy to get to and offering a view of the Pyrénées. The holiday park has a family atmosphere and lots of activities.

dir: *A63 exit Bayonne Nord for Pau.*

Open: 2 Apr-25 Sep **Site:** 5HEC **Prices:** 20-41.60 Mobile home hire 264.60-1106 **Facilities:** Wi-fi **Services:** **Leisure:** P **Off-site:** S

Ur-Onéa
r de la Chapelle, 64210
559265361 559265394
e-mail: uronea@wanadoo.fr
web: www.uronea.com
A well-equipped site lying at the foot of the Pyrénées with good recreational facilities.
dir: *Off RN10.*
Open: 9 Apr-17 Sep **Site:** 5HEC **Prices:** 15.50-27.50 Mobile home hire 210-780 **Facilities:** Play Area **Services:** **Leisure:** P **Off-site:** R S

Rive
rte de Bordeaux, 40600
558781233 558781292
e-mail: info@larive.fr
web: www.larive.fr
Level site in tall pine forest on eastern side of lake. Private port and beach. A restaurant and take away will be available during 2011.
dir: *N of town off D652 Sanguinet road.*
Open: 8 Apr-11 Sep **Site:** 15HEC **Prices:** 24.50-47 **Facilities:** Wi-fi (charged) Kids' Club Play Area **Services:** **Leisure:** L P

BIRON DORDOGNE

Moulinal
24540
553408460 553408149
e-mail: lemoulinal@perigord.com
web: www.lemoulinal.com
A pleasant location beside a lake close to the former mill of Château de Biron. The modern holiday village has a variety of recreational facilities.
dir: *2km S on the Lacapelle-Biron road.*
Open: 22 Mar-22 Sep **Site:** 18HEC **Facilities:** **Services:** **Leisure:** L P

BISCARROSSE LANDES

Camping les Petits Ecureuils
254 chemin Crastail, 40600
558780197 556884727
e-mail: bisca.petits.ecureuils@wanadoo.fr
web: www.les-petits-ecureuils.com
Family site, with facilities including a snack bar and ping-pong.
GPS: 44.4052, -1.1485
Open: 3 Apr-15 Oct **Site:** 1.7HEC **Prices:** 15-24 Mobile home hire 220-480 **Facilities:** Play Area **Services:** **Leisure:** P **Off-site:** L S

Ecureuils
Port Navarrosse, 40600
558098000 558098121
e-mail: reception@ecureuils.fr
web: www.ecureuils.fr
A pleasant wooded location 200m from the lake. Plenty of recreational facilities.
dir: *Via D652.*
GPS: 44.4294, -1.1669
Open: Apr-Sep **Site:** 7HEC **Prices:** 25-43 Mobile home hire 350-850 **Facilities:** Wi-fi Kids' Club Play Area **Services:** **Leisure:** P **Off-site:** L

BOURNEL LOT-ET-GARONNE

Ferme de Bourgade
47210
553366715
e-mail: bourgade.gites@nordnet.fr
web: www.bourgade-holidays.co.uk
A small, tranquil site with good, clean facilities.
dir: *Signed from N21 between Castillonnès & Villeréal.*
Open: 15 Jun-15 Sep **Site:** 1HEC **Prices:** 12-14 **Facilities:** **Services:** **Leisure:** L **Off-site:**

BRETENOUX LOT

Bourgnatelle
46130
565108904 565108918
e-mail: contact@dordogne-vacances.fr
web: www.dordogne-vacances.fr
A pleasant location beside the River Cére. Separate car park for arrivals after 22.30hrs.
dir: *D940 towards Rocamadour.*
Open: May-Sep **Site:** 3HEC **Prices:** 12-18 Mobile home hire 650 **Facilities:** Wi-fi Play Area **Services:** **Leisure:** P R **Off-site:**

BRUGES GIRONDE

Le Village du Lac
blvd Jacques Chaban, Delmas, 33520
557877060 557877061
e-mail: contact@camping-bordeaux.com
web: www.camping-bordeaux.com
Situated 8km from the centre of Bordeaux, with spacious pitches. Bike rental available. Shop on site open 15 June to 15 September.
GPS: 44.8974, -0.5827
Open: All Year. **Site:** 6HEC **Prices:** 16.80-31 Mobile home hire 490-1050 **Facilities:** Wi-fi (charged) Play Area **Services:** **Leisure:** P
Off-site: L R

FRANCE

BUGUE, LE — DORDOGNE

Brin d'Amour

Saint Cirq, 24260
☎ 553072373 📠 553072373
e-mail: campingbrindamour@orange.fr
web: www.campings-dordogne.com/brindamour

A fine location overlooking the Vézère Valley with good facilities.

Open: Apr-10 Oct **Site:** 3.8HEC **Facilities:** **Services:** **Leisure:** P **Off-site:** L R

Rocher de la Granelle

rte du Buisson, 24260
☎ 53072432
e-mail: info@lagranelle.com
web: www.lagranelle.com

Surrounded by woodland with pitches set out among trees and bushes on the banks of the Vézère with a variety of leisure facilities.

dir: *From Le Bugue centre over bridge & signed.*

Open: Apr-Sep **Site:** 8HEC **Facilities:** **Services:** **Leisure:** P R

St-Avit Loisirs

St-Avit-de-Vialard, 24260
☎ 553026400 📠 553026439
e-mail: contact@saint-avit.loisirs.com
web: www.saint-avit-loisirs.com

A pleasant site in natural wooded surroundings.

dir: *W of town via C201.*

Open: Apr-Sep **Site:** 7HEC **Facilities:** **Services:** **Leisure:** P **Off-site:** R

CAHORS — LOT

Rivière de Cabessut

r de la Rivière, 46000
☎ 565300630
e-mail: contact@cabessut.com
web: www.cabessut.com

1.5km from Cahors with quiet, shaded pitches.

dir: *N of town via Cabessut Bridge over River Lot.*

Open: Apr-Sep **Site:** 3HEC **Prices:** 17-19 Mobile home hire 210-540 **Facilities:** Wi-fi **Services:** **Leisure:** P R **Off-site:**

CALVIAC — LOT

Trois Sources

Le Peyratel, 46190
☎ 565330301 📠 565330301
e-mail: info@les-trois-sources.com
web: www.les-trois-sources.com

Wooded location, family site with plenty of leisure facilities.

dir: *D653 onto D25 to Calviac.*

Open: 28 Apr-Sep **Site:** 7.5HEC **Facilities:** **Services:** **Leisure:** L P R

CAP FERRET — GIRONDE

Truc Vert

rte Forestière, 33970
☎ 556608955 📠 556609947
e-mail: camping.truc-vert@worldonline.fr
web: www.trucvert.com

A very pleasant location on a slope in a pine wood close to the beach.

dir: *On D106 towards Cap Ferret to Petit Piquey, turn right & signed.*

Open: May-Sep **Site:** 11HEC **Prices:** 13.50-21.50 **Facilities:** Wi-fi **Services:** **Off-site:** S

CARLUCET — LOT

Château de Lacomté

The Camping and Caravanning Club — The Friendly Club

46500
☎ 565387546 📠 565331768
e-mail: chateaulacomte@wanadoo.fr
web: www.campingchateaulacomte.com

Set in wooded surroundings with good size, fully serviced pitches and a variety of recreational facilities.
Site for adults only.

C&CC Report *Popular with returning customers from all over Europe, this British-owned adults only site is a peaceful, rustic, rural retreat. A good base for trips to the Gouffre du Padirac, Rocamadour, Sarlat and Cahors, Lacomté has also delighted nature lovers with its swallowtail butterflies, rare orchids, three species of woodpecker and sightings of birds of prey, as well as the occasional visiting hare or deer. You can also take in the peaceful surroundings either while enjoying Sheila's cooking on the terrace or during a swim in the pool.*

dir: *Signed from D807/D32.*

Open: 15 May-Sep **Site:** 12HEC **Prices:** 18-31 Mobile home hire 150-300 **Facilities:** Wi-fi **Services:** **Leisure:** P

CASTELJALOUX — LOT-ET-GARONNE

CM de la Piscine

rte de Marmande, 47700
☎ 553935468 📠 553934807
dir: *NW on D933 Marmande road.*

Open: Apr-Nov **Site:** 1HEC **Facilities:** shower, electric points for razors, electric points for caravans, parking by tents permitted **Services:** laundry **Off-site:** swimming P R shop café/restaurant bar Camping Gaz International gas other than Camping Gaz first aid facilities

Sarl Castel Chalets

rte de Mont-de-Marsan, 47700
☎ 553930745 📠 553939309
e-mail: castel.chalets@orange.fr
web: www.castel-chalets.com

A large site with direct access to the 17-hectare Lac de Clarens and good recreational facilities.

Open: Apr-Nov **Site:** 2HEC **Prices:** 10 **Facilities:** shower, electric points for razors, electric points for caravans, Wi-fi Play Area, parking by tents permitted **Services:** café/restaurant bar **Leisure:** swimming L R **Off-site:** swimming P shop first aid facilities

CASTELNAUD-LA-CHAPELLE — DORDOGNE

Maisonneuve

24250
☎ 553295129 📠 553302706
e-mail: contact@campingmaisonneuve.com
web: www.campingmaisonneuve.com

Picturesque surroundings 0.8km from the village, close to the River Céou in the Périgord Noir region.

dir: *10km S of Sarlat on D57.*

GPS: 44.8056, 1.1644

Open: 27 Mar-2 Nov **Site:** 6HEC **Prices:** 15-21.20 Mobile home hire 275-675 **Facilities:** shop shower, electric points for razors, electric points for caravans, Wi-fi Play Area, parking by tents permitted, disabled access **Services:** café/restaurant bar Camping Gaz International first aid facilities laundry **Leisure:** swimming P R **Off-site:** Camping Gaz International gas other than Camping Gaz

CLAOUEY — GIRONDE

Airotel les Viviers

rte du Cap Ferret, 33950
☎ 176767010 📠 557703777
e-mail: reception@lesviviers.com
web: www.lesviviers.com

Extensive site in a beautiful forest divided by seawater channels.

dir: *On D106 1km S of the town.*

Open: 8 Apr-1 Oct **Site:** 33HEC **Facilities:** shop shower, electric points for razors, electric points for caravans, parking by tents permitted **Services:** café/restaurant bar first aid facilities laundry **Leisure:** swimming L P S

CONTIS-PLAGE — LANDES

Lous Seurrots

40170
☎ 558428582 📠 558424911
e-mail: info@lous-seurrots.com
web: www.lous-seurrots.com

Well-equipped site in a pine forest on outskirts of village between a road and a stream.

dir: *Via D41.*

Open: Apr-Sep **Site:** 15HEC **Facilities:** shop shower, electric points for razors, electric points for caravans, parking by tents permitted **Services:** café/restaurant bar Camping Gaz International gas other than Camping Gaz first aid facilities laundry **Leisure:** swimming P R S

CORDES — TARN

Moulin de Julien

81170
☎ 563561110

A beautiful valley with good pitches for caravans and tents and plenty of modern facilities.

dir: *0.9km E on D600 & D922.*

Open: May-Sep **Site:** 6HEC **Facilities:** shower, electric points for razors, electric points for caravans, parking by tents permitted **Services:** café/restaurant bar Camping Gaz International first aid facilities laundry **Leisure:** swimming P **Off-site:** swimming R shop gas other than Camping Gaz

COUX-ET-BIGAROQUE — DORDOGNE

Clou

Meynard, 24220
☎ 553316332 📠 553316933
e-mail: info@camping-le-clou.com
web: www.camping-le-clou.com

Separate section for dog owners.

dir: *Via D703 Le Bugue-Delve road.*

Open: 18 Apr-4 Oct **Site:** 3.5HEC **Facilities:** shop shower, electric points for razors, electric points for caravans, parking by tents permitted **Services:** café/restaurant bar Camping Gaz International gas other than Camping Gaz first aid facilities laundry **Leisure:** swimming P

Valades

Les Valades, 24220
☎ 553291427
e-mail: info@lesvalades.com
web: www.lesvalades.com

Wooded surroundings within a pleasant valley. Well-equipped pitches available. Every comfortable pitch has its own individual toilets, including a shower, toiler and sink. The site is also equipped with a sink for dishes, a refrigerator, a barbecue and a wooden table.

dir: *5km N of town off N703.*

GPS: 44.8606, 0.9639

Open: Apr-Sep **Site:** 12HEC **Facilities:** shop shower, electric points for razors, electric points for caravans, Wi-fi Play Area, parking by tents permitted **Services:** café/restaurant bar first aid facilities laundry **Leisure:** swimming L P **Off-site:** swimming R Camping Gaz International gas other than Camping Gaz

FRANCE

CRÉON GIRONDE

Bel Air

33670

☎ 556230190 556230838

web: www.camping-bel-air.com

A well-equipped, roomy site on a level meadow shaded by tall trees.

dir: *1.6km W of Créon on D671.*

Open: All Year. **Site:** 2HEC **Facilities:** **Services:** **Leisure:** P

DAGLAN DORDOGNE

Moulin de Paulhiac

24250

☎ 553282088 553293345

e-mail: info@moulin-de-paulhiac.com

web: www.moulin-de-paulhiac.com

Picturesque wooded surroundings with wide, well-marked pitches and modern facilities.

dir: *4km N via D57 beside the Céou.*

Open: 15 May-15 Sep **Site:** 5HEC **Facilities:** **Services:** **Leisure:** P R

DAX LANDES

Chênes

Au Bois-de-Boulogne, 40100

☎ 558900553 558904243

e-mail: camping-chenes@wanadoo.fr

web: www.camping-les-chenes.fr

A wooded park on the edge of the Bois-de-Boulogne with good facilities.

dir: *1.5km W of town beside River Adour.*

GPS: 43.7116, -1.0731

Open: 19 Mar-5 Nov **Site:** 5HEC **Prices:** 13.70-16 Mobile home hire 261-521 **Facilities:** Wi-fi (charged) **Services:** **Leisure:** P **Off-site:** R

DOMME DORDOGNE

Perpetuum

Au Bord de la Dordogne, 24250

☎ 553283518 553296364

e-mail: leperpetuum.domme@wanadoo.fr

web: www.campingleperpetuum.com

Situated on the edge of the Dordogne, a friendly, family site with flat, green pitches and leisure activities.

Open: May-10 Oct **Site:** 4.5HEC **Prices:** 11.62-19 Mobile home hire 210-700 **Facilities:** Wi-fi Kids' Club Play Area **Services:** **Leisure:** P R

DURAS LOT-ET-GARONNE

Le Cabri

The Camping and Caravanning Club The Friendly Club

rte de Savignac, 47120

☎ 553838103 553830891

e-mail: holidays@lecabri.eu.com

web: www.lecabri.eu.com

C&CC Report *Highly recommended for short breaks, with village centre services and château within 500 metres.*

dir: *A89 exit 12, or A62 exit 5, then D708 to Duras.*

Site: 6.47HEC **Facilities:** Play Area **Services:** **Leisure:** P

DURAVEL LOT

Club de Vacances

Port de Vire, 46700

☎ 565246506

e-mail: info@clubdevacances.eu

web: www.clubdevacances.eu

A pleasant site with good facilities beside the River Lot.

dir: *2.3km S via D58.*

Open: 25 Apr-Sep **Site:** 7HEC **Facilities:** **Services:** **Leisure:** P R

DURFORT ARIÈGE

Bourdieu

09130

☎ 561673017 561672900

e-mail: lebourdieu@wanadoo.fr

web: www.location-chalet-camping-ariege.com

Well-equipped site in a picturesque setting with fine views of the Pyrénées.

dir: *Off D14 Le Fossat-Saverdun.*

Open: All Year. **Site:** 20HEC **Prices:** 17-32 Mobile home hire 385-847 **Facilities:** Wi-fi (charged) Play Area **Services:** **Leisure:** P **Off-site:**

ESQUIÈZE-SÈRE HAUTES-PYRÉNÉES

Camping Airotel Pyrénées

The Camping and Caravanning Club The Friendly Club

65120

☎ 562928918

e-mail: airotel.pyrenees@wanadoo.fr

C&CC Report *A superb setting, much enjoyed by campers of all ages. Whether you want to be active or just relax in the breathtaking scenery, this mountain location takes some beating – and it's only a short walk into the town, too. Visit mountains and passes made famous by the Tour de France, or try more adventurous activities such as white water rafting.*

dir: *Access directly off N927.*

Open: All Year. **Site:** 2.5HEC **Facilities:** **Services:** **Leisure:** P **Off-site:**

Site 6HEC (site size) grass sand stone little shade partly shaded mainly shaded bungalows for hire (static) caravans for hire tents for hire no dogs site fully accessible for wheelchairs

Prices amount quoted is per night, for 2 adults and car, plus tent or caravan. Mobile home hire is a weekly rate.

ESTAING — HAUTES-PYRÉNÉES

Pyrénées Natura

rte du Lac, 65400
☎ 562974544 Fax 562974581
e-mail: sarl.ruysschaert@wanadoo.fr
web: www.camping-pyrenees-natura.com

A well-run site at an altitude of 1000m, situated on the edge of the national park with views of the surrounding mountains.

dir: *8km from Argeles-Gazost turn left on D13 to Bun, cross the river then right on D103 to site.*

Open: May-20 Sep **Site:** 2.5HEC **Prices:** 16.50-34 **Facilities:** Play Area **Services:** **Leisure:** R **Off-site:** L P

ÉYZIES-DE-TAYAC, LES — DORDOGNE

Pech Charmant

24620
☎ 553359708 Fax 553359709
e-mail: info@lepech.com
web: www.lepech.com

Located on the side of a wooded hill and contains a small farm with donkeys, goats, horses and chickens.

Open: 15 Apr-15 Sep **Site:** 17HEC **Facilities:** **Services:** **Leisure:** P **Off-site:** R

FIGEAC — LOT

Rives du Célé

Domaine du Surgie, 46100
☎ 561648854 Fax 561648917
e-mail: contact@marc-montmija.com
web: www.lesrivesducele.com

A pleasant wooded location on the banks of the River Célé with plenty of leisure facilities. The site lies within a large recreation area. Separate car park for late arrivals. Gîtes are available for rental.

Open: Apr-Sep **Site:** 2HEC **Prices:** 14-22 Mobile home hire 250-610 **Facilities:** Kids' Club Play Area **Services:** **Leisure:** L P R **Off-site:**

FOIX — ARIÈGE

Camping du Lac

RN 20, 09000
☎ 561651158 Fax 561651998
e-mail: camping-du-lac@wanadoo.fr
web: www.campingdulac.com

On well-kept meadow beside the Lac de Labarre.

dir: *3km N on N20.*

Open: All Year. **Site:** 5HEC **Prices:** 13.50-24 Mobile home hire 280-525 **Facilities:** Wi-fi Play Area **Services:** **Leisure:** L P **Off-site:**

FONTRAILLES — HAUTES-PYRÉNÉES

Fontrailles

65220
☎ 562356252
e-mail: detm.paddon@orange.fr
web: www.fontraillescamping.com

Set in a peaceful location, next to a shady oak wood and small fishing lake.

dir: *2km N of Trie-sur-Baise, left off D939 Tarbes-Mirande, signed.*

Open: Jul-Sep **Site:** 1.5HEC **Prices:** 13.50-15 **Facilities:** Wi-fi **Services:** **Leisure:** P **Off-site:**

FUMEL — LOT-ET-GARONNE

Domaine de Guillalmes

Fumel, 47500
☎ 553710199 Fax 553710257
e-mail: info@guillalmes.com
web: www.holidayvillagelot.com

Attractive site on the banks of the River Lot with limited touring pitch area on spacious hardstandings divided by small hedges. Small trees offer some shade.

dir: *From Fumel take D911 signed Cahors, then follow signs to Domaine de Guillalmes. Turn right 150m before Soturac, site signed.*

Open: All Year. **Site:** **Facilities:** **Services:** **Leisure:** P R **Off-site:**

FRANCE

Facilities shop shower electric points for razors electric points for caravans parking by tents permitted compulsory separate car park **Services** café/restaurant bar Camping Gaz International gas other than Camping Gaz first aid facilities laundry **Leisure** swimming L-Lake P-Pool R-River S-Sea **Off-site** All facilities within 5km

Villagecenter
Le Moulin de David ****
Green site very close to nature
Artificial lake filled with non-saline water and waterslide
96 places - 64 rental accomodations - 16 ha
24540 MONPAZIER-GAUGEAC
+33 (0)4 99 57 21 21 - www.village-center.com/C08

GAUGEAC — DORDOGNE

Village Center le Moulin de David

D2, 24540
☎ 499572121 🖷 467516389
e-mail: contact@village-center.com
web: www.village-center.com/aquitaine/camping-campagne-moulin-david.php

Situated in a wooded valley alongside a small stream, with well-defined pitches and good recreational facilities.

dir: *3km from town towards Villeréal.*

GPS: 44.6596, 0.8798

Open: 24 Jun-4 Sep **Site:** 16HEC **Prices:** 16-24 Mobile home hire 216-784 **Facilities:** Wi-fi Kids' Club Play Area **Services:** **Leisure:** L P

see advert on this page

GOURDON — LOT

Paradis

La Peyrugue, 46300
☎ 565416501 🖷 565416501
e-mail: contact@campingleparadis.com
web: www.campingleparadis.com

On a pleasant wooded meadow surrounded by hills.

dir: *1.6km SW off N673.*

Open: May-15 Sep **Site:** 2HEC **Prices:** 14 Mobile home hire 400 **Facilities:** Play Area **Services:** **Leisure:** P **Off-site:** L R

GOURETTE — PYRÉNÉES-ATLANTIQUES

Ley

64440
☎ 559051147 🖷 559051147

Terraced site with gravel and asphalt caravan pitches. TV, common room.

dir: *E from Laruns to Eaux-Bonnes & uphill to Gourette.*

Open: Dec-Apr & Jul-Aug **Site:** 2HEC **Facilities:** **Services:** **Leisure:** R **Off-site:** L

GRADIGNAN — GIRONDE

Beausoleil

The Camping and Caravanning Club The Friendly Club

371 cours Gén de Gaulle, 33170
☎ 556891766 🖷 556891766
e-mail: campingbeausoleil@wanadoo.fr
web: www.camping-gradignan.com

C&CC Report *Small friendly site in a good location not far from the Bordeaux ring-road, convenient transport links to Bordeaux.*

dir: *Off Bordeaux ring road, exit 16.*

Open: All Year. **Site:** 0.5HEC **Facilities:** **Services:** **Off-site:**

GRAULGES, LES — DORDOGNE

Crozes les Graulges

24340
☎ 553607473
e-mail: info@lesgraulges.com
web: www.lesgraulges.com

A picturesque setting in woodland beside a lake.

dir: *Off D939 between Angoulême & Périgueux.*

Open: Apr-Sep **Site:** 8HEC **Facilities:** **Services:** **Leisure:** L P R

GROLÉJAC — DORDOGNE

Granges

24250
☎ 553281115 🖷 553285713
e-mail: contact@lesgranges-fr.com
web: lesgranges-fr.com

Beautifully situated terraces on a hill with big pitches. The site has been constructed around a disused railway station, incorporating the old ticket office and the bridge into the modern design. Facilities for sports and entertainment. Kids' club available in high season.

dir: *Off D704 in village towards Domme.*

Open: 30 Apr-10 Sep **Site:** 6.5HEC **Prices:** 14-24.30 Mobile home hire 291-870 **Facilities:** Wi-fi Kids' Club Play Area **Services:** **Leisure:** P R **Off-site:** L

FRANCE

HASPARREN PYRÉNÉES-ATLANTIQUES

Chapital

rte de Cambo, 64240
559296294

On level ground, surrounded by woodland. Good facilities for families.

dir: *0.5km W via D22. Or via A64 exit 3 for 10km.*

Open: May-Sep **Site:** 2.58HEC **Prices:** 14-16 **Facilities:** Play Area **Services:** **Off-site:** P R S

HAUTEFORT DORDOGNE

Camping du Coucou

Le Bois du Coucou, 24390
553508697 553508697
e-mail: campingducoucou@orange.fr
web: www.campingducoucou.com

Located at the foot of the Château de Hautefort in rural countryside with modern amenities on site.

dir: *2km SW via D72 & D71, 100m from Coucou lake.*

GPS: 45.2477, 1.1379

Open: 23 Apr-15 Oct **Site:** 4HEC **Prices:** 11.70-15.10 Mobile home hire 190-590 **Facilities:** Wi-fi Play Area **Services:** **Leisure:** P **Off-site:** L R

HENDAYE PYRÉNÉES-ATLANTIQUES

Acacias

64700
559207876 559207876
e-mail: info@les-acacias.com
web: www.les-acacias.com

A pleasant family site in parkland, 5 minutes from the beach.

dir: *1.8km E (rte de la Glacière).*

Open: Apr-Sep **Site:** 5HEC **Facilities:** **Services:** **Leisure:** L **Off-site:** S

HOURTIN GIRONDE

Acacia

Ste-Hélène, 33990
556738080
e-mail: camping.lacacia@orange.fr
web: www.camping-lacacia.com

Pleasant, quiet site on the edge of a forest with good sanitary facilities. Compulsory car park for arrivals after 23.30hrs.

dir: *Off D3 towards lake.*

Open: Jun-Sep **Site:** 5HEC **Prices:** 14.34-16.34 Mobile home hire 260-380 **Facilities:** Play Area **Services:** **Off-site:** L

Ourmes

90 av du Lac, 33990
556091276 556092390
e-mail: info@lesourmes.com
web: www.lesourmes.com

A family campsite in wooded surroundings close to the beach and 0.5km from the largest freshwater lake in France.

dir: *D4 towards lake.*

Open: May-20 Sep **Site:** 7HEC **Prices:** 14-31.50 Mobile home hire 240-755 **Facilities:** Wi-fi Kids' Club Play Area **Services:** **Leisure:** P **Off-site:** L S

HOURTIN-PLAGE GIRONDE

Côte d'Argent

33990
556091025 556092496
e-mail: info@camping-cote-dargent.com
web: www.camping-cote-dargent.com

Set in a pine and oak forest with good facilities, 300m from the beach.

dir: *D101 from Hourtin.*

Open: 14 May-18 Sep **Site:** 20HEC **Prices:** 21-46 Mobile home hire 196-938 **Facilities:** Wi-fi (charged) Kids' Club Play Area **Services:** **Leisure:** L P S

LABENNE LANDES

Pins Bleus

av de l'Océan, 40530
559454113 559454470
e-mail: camping@lespinsbleus.com
web: www.lespinsbleus.com

Tranquil, family site located close to the beach.

dir: *On RN10.*

Open: Apr-4 Nov **Site:** 6.5HEC **Facilities:** **Services:** **Leisure:** P **Off-site:** L R S

LABENNE-OCÉAN LANDES

Boudigau

40530
559454207 559457776
e-mail: info@boudigau.com
web: www.boudigau.com

Situated in a pine forest.

dir: *Turn right after bridge into site.*

Open: 15 May-15 Sep **Site:** 6HEC **Facilities:** **Services:** **Leisure:** P **Off-site:** S

FRANCE

Côte d'Argent

60 av de l'Océan, 40530
☎ 559454202 559457331
e-mail: info@camping-cotedargent.com
web: www.camping-cotedargent.com
Very well-managed modern site attached to holiday village.
dir: *3km W on D126.*
Open: Apr-Oct **Site:** 4HEC **Facilities:** **Services:** **Leisure:** P **Off-site:** R S

Mer

rte de la Plage, 40530
☎ 559454209 559454307
e-mail: campinglamer@wanadoo.fr
web: www.campinglamer.com
Set in a pine forest 0.5km from the beach. A kids' club is available in July and August.
dir: *On D126 rte de la Plage.*
Open: 8 Apr-2 Oct **Site:** 11HEC **Prices:** 11-30.75 Mobile home hire 240-850 **Facilities:** Wi-fi (charged) Kids' Club Play Area **Services:** **Leisure:** P R **Off-site:** S

Yelloh Village Le Sylvamar

av de l'Océan, 40530
☎ 559457516 559454639
e-mail: camping.sylvamar.fr
web: www.sylvamar.fr
Situated in a tranquil location in a pine forest. Paddling pool and heated spa area.
dir: *Access via D126.*
Open: 9 Apr-3 Nov **Site:** 21HEC **Prices:** 15-44 **Facilities:** Wi-fi (charged) Kids' Club Play Area **Services:** **Leisure:** P **Off-site:** L S

LACANAU-OCÉAN GIRONDE

Airotel de l'Océan

24 Rue du Répos, 33680
☎ 556032445 557700187
e-mail: web-airotel@wanadoo.fr
web: www.airotel-ocean.com
On rising ground in a pine forest, 0.8km from the beach.
Open: 8 Apr-24 Sep **Site:** 9.5HEC **Facilities:** **Services:** **Leisure:** P **Off-site:** S

Talaris

rte de l'Océan, 33680
☎ 556030415 556262156
e-mail: talarisvacances@free.fr
web: www.talaris-vacances.fr
A family site in delightful wooded surroundings 1.2km from the lake. Separate car park for arrivals after 22.30hrs.
dir: *2km E on rte de Lacanau.*
Open: 7 Apr-15 Sep **Site:** 8.25HEC **Facilities:** **Services:** **Leisure:** P **Off-site:** L

Tedey

rte de Longarisse, 33680
☎ 556030015 556030190
e-mail: camping@le-tedey.com
web: www.le-tedey.com
Quiet site in pine forest, on edge of Lake Lacanau. Private bathing area.
dir: *Off D6 onto narrow track through forest for 0.5km.*
Open: 23 Apr-17 Sep **Site:** 14HEC **Prices:** 17-26 Mobile home hire 330-715 **Facilities:** Wi-fi (charged) **Services:** **Leisure:** L

Yelloh Village Grands Pins

Plages Nord, 33680
☎ 556032077 557700389
e-mail: reception@lesgrandspins.com
web: www.lesgrandspins.com
On very hilly terrain in woodland, 350m from the beach through dunes.
dir: *A10 exit 7, D6 to Lacanau.*
Open: 16 Apr-24 Sep **Site:** 12HEC **Prices:** 15-47 **Facilities:** Wi-fi (charged) Kids' Club Play Area **Services:** **Leisure:** P **Off-site:** S

LACAPELLE-MARIVAL LOT

CM Bois de Sophie

Route d'Aynac, 46120
☎ 565408259
e-mail: lacapelle.mairie@wanadoo.fr
A pleasant wooded location with a variety of sports facilities.
dir: *1km NW via D940.*
Open: Mar-Sep **Site:** 2HEC **Prices:** 12.10-15.30 Mobile home hire 50-440 **Facilities:** **Services:** **Leisure:** P **Off-site:** L R

LANTON GIRONDE

Roumingue

33138
556829748 556829609
e-mail: contact@romingue.fr
web: www.roumingue.fr

Level terrain under a few deciduous trees partially in open meadow on the Bassin d'Arcachon. During July and August, shop, bar, café, restaurant, swimming pool bungalows/chalets are all available.

dir: *1km NW of village towards sea.*

GPS: 44.704, -1.048

Open: 15 Mar-15 Nov **Site:** 10HEC **Prices:** 12.90-23.90 Mobile home hire 280-670 **Facilities:** Wi-fi Kids' Club Play Area **Services:** **Leisure:** P S **Off-site:**

LARNAGOL LOT

Ruisseau de Treil

46160
565312339 565312327
e-mail: lotcamping@wanadoo
web: www.lotcamping.com

A quiet site within a small valley on the southern edge of the Massif Central with large well-defined pitches and good leisure facilities.

dir: *0.6km E of Larnagol off D662 towards Cajarc.*

Open: 15 May-11 Sep **Site:** 3.2HEC **Facilities:** Wi-fi (charged) Play Area **Services:** **Leisure:** P **Off-site:** R

LARUNS PYRÉNÉES-ATLANTIQUES

Gaves

64440
559053237 559054714
e-mail: campingdesgaves@wanadoo.fr
web: www.campingdesgaves.com

On the bank of the Gave d'Ossan amid beautiful Pyrenean scenery. Some pitches reserved for caravans.

dir: *1km S.*

GPS: 42.9823, -0.4173

Open: All Year. **Site:** 2.5HEC **Prices:** 14.80-20.40 Mobile home hire 252-630 **Facilities:** Wi-fi Play Area **Services:** **Leisure:** R **Off-site:** P

LECTOURE GERS

Lac des Trois Vallées

32700
562688233 562688882
web: www.lacdes3vallees.fr

This rural site is part of a large park and lies next to a lake. It has spacious marked pitches.

dir: *3km SE on N21.*

Open: 20 May-10 Sep **Site:** 40HEC **Facilities:** **Services:** **Leisure:** L P

LÉON LANDES

Airotel Lou Puntaou

Avenue du Lac, 40550
558487430 558487042
e-mail: reception@loupuntaou.com
web: www.loupuntaou.com

Set in an oak wood with separate sections for caravans.

dir: *Off N652 in village onto D142 towards lake for 1.5km.*

Open: Apr-1 Oct **Site:** 8HEC **Facilities:** **Services:** **Leisure:** P **Off-site:** L R S

St-Antoine

St-Michel-Escalus, 40550
558487850
e-mail: campingstantoine@wanadoo.fr
web: www.camping-stantoine.com

A pleasant, well-equipped site beside a river in peaceful wooded surroundings.

Open: Apr-Sep **Site:** 6HEC **Facilities:** **Services:** **Leisure:** R

LESCAR PYRÉNÉES-ATLANTIQUES

Terrier

av du Vert Galant, 64230
559810182 559812683
e-mail: camping.terrier@wanadoo.fr
web: www.camping-terrier.com

Meadowland site divided in two with pitches surrounded by hedges in foreground.

dir: *From Pau N117 towards Bayonne for 6.5km, left onto D501 towards Monein to site towards bridge.*

Open: All Year. **Site:** 4HEC **Prices:** 13.65 Mobile home hire 440-570 **Facilities:** Play Area **Services:** **Leisure:** P **Off-site:** L

FRANCE

LINXE — LANDES

CM Le Grandjean

rte de Mixe, 40260
☎ 558429000 558429467

A modern family site on the edge of a forest.

dir: *Off Castets road onto D42 towards Linxe.*

Open: 25 Jun-27 Aug **Site:** 2.7HEC **Facilities:** **Services:** **Off-site:**

LIT-ET-MIXE — LANDES

Village Center les Vignes

rte du Cap de l'Homy, 40170
☎ 499572121 467516389
e-mail: contact@village-center.com
web: www.village-center.com/aquitaine/camping-mer-les-vignes.php

5km from the ocean, set in a pine forest with good sanitary and sports facilities.

dir: *N10 exit 13 onto D41.*

GPS: 44.0234, -1.2796

Open: 8 Apr-2 Oct **Site:** 15HEC **Prices:** 14-40 Mobile home hire 216-1155 **Facilities:** Wi-fi (charged) Kids' Club Play Area **Services:** **Leisure:** P **Off-site:** S

LIVERS-CAZELLES — TARN

Rédon

81170
☎ 563561464 563561464
e-mail: info@campredon.com
web: www.campredon.com

A quiet site with modern facilities, and fine views over the surrounding area.

dir: *4km SE of Cordes on D600.*

Open: 28 Mar-30 Oct **Site:** 4HEC **Facilities:** **Services:** **Leisure:** P **Off-site:** R

LOUPIAC — LOT

Hirondelles

46350
☎ 565376625 565376665
e-mail: camp.les-hirondelles@wanadoo.fr
web: www.les-hirondelles.com

A natural setting in the heart of the Quercy region with a variety of recreational facilities.

dir: *3km N via N20.*

Open: Apr-15 Sep **Site:** 2.5HEC **Facilities:** **Services:** **Leisure:** P

LOURDES — HAUTES-PYRÉNÉES

Arrouach

9 r des Trois Archanges, Quartier Biscaye, 65100
☎ 562421143 562420527
e-mail: camping.arrouach@wanadoo.fr
web: www.camping-arrouach.com

Pleasant wooded surroundings on N outskirts.

dir: *On D947 Soumoulou road.*

Open: 15 Mar-Oct **Site:** 13HEC **Prices:** 13 **Facilities:** Wi-fi **Services:** **Off-site:** L P R

Domec

rte de Julos, 65100
☎ 562940879 562940879
e-mail: campingdomec@free.fr
web: www.camping-domec-lourdes.com

In a quiet area near the city centre. Leisure facilities include a games room.

dir: *Off N21 Tarbes road N of town centre.*

Open: Etr-Oct **Site:** 2HEC **Facilities:** **Services:** **Off-site:** L P R

LUZ-ST-SAUVEUR — HAUTES-PYRÉNÉES

Bergons

rte de Barèges, 65120
☎ 562929077
e-mail: info@camping-bergons.com
web: www.camping-bergons.com

A beautiful setting on a level meadow surrounded by woodland close to the main Pyrenean ski resorts.

dir: *0.6km E on D618 Barèges road.*

Open: 3 Dec-24 Apr, 9 May-23 Oct **Site:** 1HEC **Prices:** 10.14-10.44 Mobile home hire 230-490 **Facilities:** Play Area **Services:** **Off-site:** P R

Pyrénées International

rte de Lourdes, 65120
☎ 562928202 562929687
e-mail: camping.international.luz@wanadoo.fr
web: www.international-camping.fr

Set in a wooded valley at an altitude of 700m with panoramic views of the surrounding mountains.

dir: *1.3km NW on N21.*

Open: 15 Dec-20 Apr & Jun-Sep **Site:** 4HEC **Facilities:** **Services:** **Leisure:** P **Off-site:** R

Pyrénévasion

rte de Luz-Ardiden, Sazos, 65120
562929154 562929834
e-mail: camping-pyrenevasion@wanadoo.fr
web: www.campingpyrenevasion.com

A quiet site in an idyllic mountain setting close to the ski-runs. The pitches are well-defined and all facilities are clean and modern.

dir: *2km from town on Luz-Ardiden road.*

Open: 20 Nov-20 Oct **Site:** 3HEC **Prices:** 12-24 **Facilities:** Wi-fi Play Area **Services:** **Leisure:** P **Off-site:** R

MARCILLAC-ST-QUENTIN DORDOGNE

Tailladis

24200
553591095 553294756
e-mail: tailladis@wanadoo.fr
web: www.tailladis.com

Well-maintained family site with good recreational facilities.

dir: *2km N near D48.*

GPS: 44.9742, 1.1872

Open: Mar-Nov **Site:** 4HEC **Prices:** 13-20 Mobile home hire 245-600 **Facilities:** Wi-fi (charged) Play Area **Services:** **Leisure:** L P

MARTRES-TOLOSANE HAUTE-GARONNE

Moulin

31220
561988640 561986690
e-mail: info@campinglemoulin.com
web: www.campinglemoulin.com

A beautiful wooded location beside the River Garonne at the foot of the Pyrénées. Well maintained with a variety of recreational facilities. Kids' club available in July and August.

dir: *1.5km SE off N117.*

Open: Apr-Sep **Site:** 12HEC **Prices:** 16-27.80 Mobile home hire 273-770 **Facilities:** Wi-fi Kids' Club Play Area **Services:** **Leisure:** P R **Off-site:** L

MAULÉON-LICHARRE PYRÉNÉES-ATLANTIQUES

Camping Uhaitza Le Saison

rte de Libarrenx, 64130
559281879 559280623
e-mail: camping.uhaitza@wanadoo.fr
web: www.camping-uhaitza.com

A peaceful site beside the river, near the town centre.

dir: *1.5km S on D918.*

Open: Mar-Oct **Site:** 1.13HEC **Prices:** 13-19.60 **Facilities:** Wi-fi Play Area **Services:** **Leisure:** R **Off-site:** P

MAZION GIRONDE

Tilleuls

33390
557421813 557421301
e-mail: chateau_alberts@hotmail.com
web: www.chateau-les-alberts.com

In a shady setting amongst the vineyards of Château les Alberts.

dir: *5.5km NE on N937*

Open: May-Oct **Site:** 0.5HEC **Prices:** 15 **Facilities:** **Services:** **Off-site:** P

MESSANGES LANDES

Acacias

The Camping and Caravanning Club The Friendly Club

Quartier Delest, Route d'Azur, 40660
558480178 558482312
e-mail: lesacacias@lesacacias.com
web: www.lesacacias.com

Quiet family site, close to sandy beaches, cycle paths and the forest of Landes.

C&CC Report *In an area with many large, busy sites, this is a small, friendly, more relaxed and traditional alternative which is generally very peaceful in low season. The welcoming owners, proximity to superb beaches, and well-sized pitches make the site ideal for younger families and couples. The local beaches, traditional surrounding Basque architecture, and towns of Bayonne and Dax, are a further delight.*

Open: 25 Mar-25 Oct **Site:** 3.36HEC **Prices:** 10.30-16 Mobile home hire 240-630 **Facilities:** Wi-fi **Services:** **Off-site:** L S

FRANCE

Albret Plage

rte Plagesud, 40660
☎ 558480367 558482191
e-mail: albretplage@wanadoo.fr
web: www.albretplage.fr

Site with direct access to beach (300m). 1km from town of Vieux Boucau.

GPS: 43.7970, -1.4010

Open: Apr-Sep **Site:** 6HEC **Prices:** 12-17.20 Mobile home hire 220-570 **Facilities:** Wi-fi (charged) **Services:** **Leisure:** S **Off-site:** L P R

see advert on this page

Côte

BP 37, 40660
☎ 558489494 558489444
e-mail: info@campinglacote.com
web: www.campinglacote.com

A picturesque wooded area 1km from the beach.

dir: *2.3km S via D652.*

Open: Apr-Sep **Site:** 4HEC **Prices:** 10.70-20.50 **Facilities:** Wi-fi Play Area **Services:** **Leisure:** P **Off-site:** L S

Moïsan

rte de la Plage, 40660
☎ 558489206 558489206
e-mail: camping.moisan@orange.fr
web: www.camping-moisan.com

Family site set in a pine forest 0.8km from the sea with modern facilities.

GPS: 43.8161, -1.3908

Open: Apr-3 Oct **Site:** 7HEC **Prices:** 9-18.50 **Facilities:** Wi-fi Play Area **Services:** **Off-site:** P S

Vieux Port

Plage Sud, 40660
☎ 176767000 558480169
e-mail: contact@levieuxport.com
web: www.levieuxport.com

A family site in the heart of the Landes forest with direct access to the beach. Good recreational facilities, including a large pool area.

dir: *2.5km SW via D652.*

Open: 2 Apr-25 Sep **Site:** 30HEC **Prices:** 15-48.50 Mobile home hire 200-1764 **Facilities:** Wi-fi (charged) Kids' Club Play Area **Services:** **Leisure:** P S **Off-site:** L R

MÉZOS LANDES

Sen Yan

40170
☎ 558426005 558426456
e-mail: reception@sen-yan.com
web: www.sen-yan.com

A pleasant site in exotic tropical gardens, surrounded by a pine wood. Dogs accepted but may be restricted on some pitches. Kids' club available for children aged 5-10.

dir: *1km E.*

Open: May-12 Sep **Site:** 8HEC **Prices:** 20-38 Mobile home hire 400-1100 **Facilities:** Wi-fi (charged) Kids' Club Play Area **Services:** **Leisure:** P **Off-site:** R

MIERS LOT

Pigeonnier

46500
☎ 565337195 565337195
e-mail: camping-le-pigeonnier@orange.fr
web: www.campinglepigeonnier.com

Peaceful, shady site close to the River Dordogne amid spectacular scenery.

dir: *400m E via D91.*

Open: Apr-1 Oct **Site:** 1HEC **Facilities:** **Services:** **Leisure:** P **Off-site:** L

FRANCE

MIMIZAN — LANDES

Club Marina-Landes

rue Marina, 40200
558091266 558091640
e-mail: contact@clubmarina.com
web: www.marinalandes.com

Set in a pine wood 0.5km from the beach.

dir: *D626 from Mimizan Plage.*

GPS: 44.2040, -1.2909

Open: 14 May-17 Sep **Site:** 9.5HEC **Prices:** 16.83-43.83 Mobile home hire 203-1140 **Facilities:** Wi-fi Kids' Club Play Area **Services:** **Leisure:** P **Off-site:** R S

Plage

bd de l'Atlantique, 40200
558090032 558094494
e-mail: contact@mimizan-camping.com
web: www.mimizan-camping.com

Well equipped secure site with thoughtfully divided areas and good facilities.

Open: 8 Apr-25 Sep **Site:** 16HEC **Facilities:** Wi-fi (charged) Play Area **Services:** **Off-site:** S

MIRANDOL-BOURGNOUNAC — TARN

Clots

Les Clots, 81190
563769278
e-mail: campclots@wanadoo.fr
web: www.campinglesclots.info

A campsite for nature lovers lying in a wooded area within the Viaur Valley with good facilities.

dir: *5.5km N via D905, rte de Rieupeyroux.*

GPS: 44.1772, 2.1791

Open: May-Sep **Site:** 7HEC **Prices:** 15-20 **Facilities:** Wi-fi Play Area **Services:** **Leisure:** P R **Off-site:**

MOLIÈRES — DORDOGNE

Lac du Malivert

Centre de Loisirs du Malivert, 82220
563677637 563676216
e-mail: molieres.82@wanadoo.fr
web: www.cdg82.fr/molieres

A pleasant lakeside setting.

dir: *To Molières from S, towards Centre de Loisirs & Lac Malivert.*

Open: Jun-Sep **Site:** 0.7HEC **Prices:** 9 Mobile home hire 310-410 **Facilities:** Play Area **Services:** **Leisure:** L **Off-site:**

MOLIETS-PLAGE — LANDES

Cigales

av de l'Océan, 40660
558485118 558483527
e-mail: reception@camping-les-cigales.fr
web: www.camping-les-cigales.fr

On undulating ground in pine trees.

dir: *300m from beach.*

Open: Apr-Sep **Site:** 23HEC **Prices:** 12.84-18.74 **Facilities:** Wi-fi (charged) **Services:** **Off-site:** L R S

Le Saint Martin

av de l'Océan, 40660
558485230 558485073
e-mail: contact@camping-saint-martin.fr
web: www.camping-saint-martin.fr

Large site on the Atlantic coast with direct access to the largest sandy beach in the region. Wi-fi free out of season. Kids' club in July and August.

C&CC Report *A large, family-oriented site in a fantastic location, right on a huge beach and in the busy little holiday village of Moliets-Plage, offering a quiet beach holiday in low season, with free indoor heated pool, or the full seaside experience in the busier times. If you want a change from the beach, take to the forest roads or cycle tracks and golfers get special discounts for using the local golf club.*

dir: *Between village & beach.*

Open: 8 Apr-1 Nov **Site:** 18.5HEC **Prices:** 18.80-43.30 **Facilities:** Wi-fi (charged) Kids' Club Play Area **Services:** **Leisure:** P S **Off-site:**

MONCRABEAU — LOT-ET-GARONNE

Mouliat

Le Mouliat, 47600
553654328 553654328
e-mail: campinglemouliat@free.fr

A small site in a wooded location on the banks of the River La Baïse.

dir: *On D219, 200m from D930.*

Open: May-25 Sep **Site:** 1.3HEC **Facilities:** **Services:** **Leisure:** P R

FRANCE

MONTCABRIER — LOT

Moulin de Laborde

46700
☎ 565246206
e-mail: moulindelaborde@wanadoo.fr
web: www.moulindelaborde.com

Well-equipped site, set by a 17th-century watermill, surrounded by woods and hills, in a picturesque valley on the River Thèze.

dir: *NW off D673.*

GPS: 44.5478, 1.0836

Open: 25 Apr-8 Sep **Site:** 12HEC **Prices:** 16.44-21.80 **Facilities:** Wi-fi Play Area **Services:** **Leisure:** L P R **Off-site:**

MONTIGNAC — DORDOGNE

Moulin du Bleufond

av Aristide Briand, 24290
☎ 553518395 553511992
e-mail: le.moulin.du.bleufond@wanadoo.fr
web: www.bleufond.com

Situated beside a river in the grounds of a 17th-century mill.

dir: *0.5km off D65 Montignac to Sergeac road.*

Open: Apr-12 Oct **Site:** 1.3HEC **Facilities:** **Services:** **Leisure:** P **Off-site:** R

NAGES — TARN

Village Center Rieumontagné

Lac du Laouzas, 81320
☎ 499572121 467516389
e-mail: contact@village-center.com
web: www.village-center.com/midi-pyrenees/camping-rieumontagne.php

Wooded location beside the Laouzas lake with good recreational facilities.

dir: *4.5km S via D62.*

GPS: 43.6487, 2.7781

Open: 24 Jun-4 Sep **Site:** 11HEC **Prices:** 14-24 Mobile home hire 241-833 **Facilities:** Wi-fi (charged) Kids' Club Play Area **Services:** **Leisure:** P **Off-site:** L

see advert on this page

OLORON-STE-MARIE — PYRÉNÉES-ATLANTIQUES

Gite du Stade

chemin de Lagravette, 64400
☎ 559391126 559391126
e-mail: camping-du-stade@wanadoo.fr
web: www.camping-du-stade.com

Peaceful shady site in the Pyrénées with a sports complex nearby.

dir: *A64 exit for Pau, take direction Oleron-Saragossa.*

GPS: 43.1788, -0.6233

Open: May-Sep **Site:** 3HEC **Facilities:** Play Area **Services:** **Leisure:** R **Off-site:** P

ONESSE-ET-LAHARIE — LANDES

Bienvenu

259 route de Mimizan, 40110
☎ 558073049 558073049
e-mail: campingbienvenu.landes@orange.fr

A family site situated in a forest.

dir: *0.5km from village centre on D38.*

Open: 15 Mar-30 Oct **Site:** 1.2HEC **Facilities:** **Services:** **Leisure:** P **Off-site:** L R S

OUSSE — PYRÉNÉES-ATLANTIQUES

Sapins

64320
☎ 559817421
e-mail: lessapins64@orange.fr

dir: *N117 exit Pau. Or A64 exit Soumoulou.*

Open: All Year. **Site:** 1HEC **Prices:** 10 Mobile home hire 320 **Facilities:** **Services:** **Off-site:**

PAUILLAC — GIRONDE

CM Les Gabarreys

rte de la Rivière, 33250
☎ 556591003 556733068
e-mail: camping.les.gabarreys@wanadoo.fr
web: www.pauillac-medoc.com
A municipal site with good sports facilities plus a sauna and spa.
dir: *RN 215/D2.*
Open: 3 Apr-10 Oct **Site:** 2HEC **Prices:** 13-15 Mobile home hire 290-490 **Facilities:** Wi-fi Play Area **Services:** **Off-site:** P R

PAYRAC — LOT

Flower Camping les Pins

46350
☎ 565379632 565379108
e-mail: info@les-pins-camping.com
web: www.les-pins-camping.com
A well-managed site, partly in forest, partly on meadowland. Sheltered from traffic noise.
dir: *S of village off D820.*
GPS: 44.7893, 1.4730
Open: 16 Apr-11 Sep **Site:** 3.5HEC **Prices:** 17.50-32 Mobile home hire 196-749 **Facilities:** Wi-fi Kids' Club Play Area **Services:** **Leisure:** P **Off-site:**

Panoramic

rte de Loupiac, 46350
☎ 565379845
e-mail: info@campingpanoramic.com
web: www.campingpanoramic.com
A peaceful family site 5km from the River Dordogne with good recreational facilities.
dir: *Off D820 N of Payrac.*
Open: All Year. **Site:** 1.85HEC **Prices:** 11 Mobile home hire 170-395 **Facilities:** Wi-fi Play Area **Services:** **Off-site:** P

PÉRIGUEUX — DORDOGNE

Barnabé

80 r des Bains, Boulazac, 24750
☎ 553534145 553541662
e-mail: contact@barnabe-perigord.com
web: www.barnabe-perigord.com
A well-appointed site in a wooded park-like location beside the river.
dir: *Signed from N89, 2km E of town centre.*
Open: Mar-Oct **Site:** 1.5HEC **Prices:** 15.60-19.70 **Facilities:** **Services:** **Off-site:** P

PETIT-PALAIS — GIRONDE

Pressoir

Queyrai Petit-Palais, 33570
☎ 557697325 557697736
e-mail: contact@campinglepressoir.com
web: www.campinglepressoir.com
An old farm in the rolling countryside around St-Emilion.
dir: *N89 Bordeaux-Périgeux, exit St-Médard de Guizières & signed.*
Open: All Year. **Site:** 2HEC **Facilities:** **Services:** **Leisure:** P **Off-site:**

PEZULS — DORDOGNE

Forêt

24510
☎ 553227169 553237779
e-mail: camping.laforet@wanadoo.fr
web: www.camping-la-foret.com
Set in extensive grounds on the edge of the forest with modern facilities.
dir: *3km from village centre, site 0.6km off D703.*
GPS: 44.9153, 0.8211
Open: Apr-Oct **Site:** 9HEC **Prices:** 12.90-17.80 Mobile home hire 192-440 **Facilities:** Play Area **Services:** **Leisure:** P

PONT-ST-MAMET — DORDOGNE

Lestaubière

Pont-St-Mamet, 24140
☎ 553829815 553829017
e-mail: lestaubiere@cs.com
web: www.lestaubiere.com
Secluded site in an attractive part of the Dordogne, occupying the former outbuildings and wooded grounds of the adjacent château. Fine views of the surrounding countryside.
dir: *Off N21. 0.5km N of Pont-St-Mamet.*
Open: 26 Apr-1 Oct **Site:** 22HEC **Facilities:** **Services:** **Leisure:** L P

PUYBRUN — LOT

Sole

46130
☎ 565385237 565109109
e-mail: camping.la.sole@wanadoo.fr
web: www.la-sole.com
A well-run site in pleasant wooded surroundings with good facilities.
dir: *D703 from village towards Bretenoux, 1st turning after garage.*
Open: Apr-Sep **Site:** 2.1HEC **Facilities:** **Services:** **Leisure:** P **Off-site:** L R

FRANCE

PYLA-SUR-MER GIRONDE

Camping de la Dune

rte de Biscarrosse, 33115
☎ 556227217 556227401
e-mail: reception@campingdeladune.fr
web: www.campingdeladune.fr

A beautifully situated and quiet site located at the base of the highest sand dune in Europe.

dir: *Dune du Pyla following signs for camping - route de Biscarrosse.*

GPS: 44.5813, -1.2127

Open: Mar-Oct **Site:** 6HEC **Facilities:** Wi-fi (charged) Kids' Club Play Area **Services:** **Leisure:** P **Off-site:** L S

Pyla Camping

rte de Biscarrosse, 33115
☎ 556227456 556221031
e-mail: reception@pylacamping.fr
web: www.pyla-camping.com

Located at the southern end of the Dune du Pyla, a well-equipped family site with good recreational facilities and direct access to the sea. Kids' club in season.

GPS: 44.5779, -1.2135

Open: Apr-2 Oct **Site:** 10HEC **Prices:** 16-36 Mobile home hire 315-925 **Facilities:** Wi-fi (charged) Kids' Club Play Area **Services:** **Leisure:** P S

Sunêlia Petit Nice

rte de Biscarrosse, 33115
☎ 556227403 556221431
e-mail: info@petitnice.com
web: www.petitnice.com

Sandy terraced site, partly steep slopes in pine woodland, mainly suitable for tents. Paths and standings are strengthened with timber, and there are 220 steps down to the beach.

dir: *6km S on D218.*

Open: 4 Apr-Sep **Site:** 5.5HEC **Facilities:** **Services:** **Leisure:** P S

Village Center la Forêt

rte de Biscarrosse, 33115
☎ 499572121 467516389
e-mail: contact@village-center.com
web: www.village-center.com/aquitaine/camping-la-foret.php

Located in an ancient forest at the foot of the Dune du Pyla.

GPS: 44.5848, -1.2092

Open: 8 Apr-2 Oct **Site:** 12HEC **Prices:** 16-34 Mobile home hire 241-980 **Facilities:** Wi-fi (charged) Kids' Club Play Area **Services:** **Leisure:** P S

Yelloh Village Panorama du Pyla

rte de Biscarrosse, 33115
☎ 556221044 556221012
e-mail: mail@camping-panorama.com
web: www.camping-panorama.com

Partially terraced site among dunes, on the edge of the 100m high Dune du Pyla. Views of the sea from some pitches.

dir: *Signed on D218.*

Open: 15 Apr-3 Oct **Site:** 15HEC **Prices:** 15-43 **Facilities:** Wi-fi Kids' Club Play Area **Services:** **Leisure:** P S

RAUZAN GIRONDE

Vieux Château

Route Départementale 123, 33420
☎ 557841538 557841834
e-mail: hoekstra.camping@wanadoo.fr
web: www.vieux-chateau.com

A family site in a peaceful valley surrounded by vineyards and overlooked by the ruined 12th-century Rauzan castle.

dir: *1.5km from D670.*

Open: Apr-Oct **Site:** 2.5HEC **Facilities:** **Services:** **Leisure:** P **Off-site:**

REYREVIGNES LOT

Domaine de Vacances Papillon

46320
☎ 565401240 565401718
e-mail: info@domaine-papillon.com
web: www.domaine-papillon.com

A wooded park in the heart of the Haut-Quercy region with modern facilities.

dir: *Via N653.*

Open: May-Sep **Site:** 3HEC **Facilities:** **Services:** **Leisure:** P **Off-site:** L R

ROCAMADOUR LOT

Relais du Campeur l'Hospitalet

46500
☎ 565336328 565106821
e-mail: lerelaisducampeur@orange.fr
web: www.lerelaisducampeur.com

Shady, level site with well-marked pitches and good facilities. Fine views of Rocamadour.

dir: *On D36.*

Open: 15 Feb-10 Nov **Site:** 1.7HEC **Prices:** 11-13.50 **Facilities:** Wi-fi (charged) **Services:** **Leisure:** P **Off-site:**

Site 6HEC (site size) grass sand stone little shade partly shaded mainly shaded bungalows for hire (static) caravans for hire tents for hire no dogs site fully accessible for wheelchairs
Prices amount quoted is per night, for 2 adults and car, plus tent or caravan. Mobile home hire is a weekly rate.

FRANCE

Le Roc

Pech-Alis, 46500
☎ 565336850
e-mail: campingleroc@wanadoo.fr
web: www.camping-leroc.com

Shady, spacious pitches located close to the medieval city of Rocamadour. Guided walks of the city are offered.

GPS: 44.8194, 1.6544

Open: Apr-Oct **Site:** 2HEC **Prices:** 11.60-16.60 Mobile home hire 247-557 **Facilities:** Wi-fi (charged) Play Area **Services:** **Leisure:** P

ROCHE-CHALAIS, LA — DORDOGNE

Gerbes

r de la Dronne, 24490
☎ 553914065 553903201
e-mail: campinggerbes@orange.fr
web: www.larochechalais.com

Well-appointed family site on banks of River Dronne.

dir: *Off D674 in village centre, signed.*

Open: 15 Apr-Sep **Site:** 3.5HEC **Facilities:** **Services:** **Off-site:** P R

ROMIEU, LA — GERS

Camp de Florence

32480
☎ 562281558 562282004
e-mail: info@lecampdeflorence.com
web: www.lecampdeflorence.com

Well-equipped site in rural surroundings. Spaciously laid out with large pitches, many with views of the Gascony countryside.

dir: *D931 towards Agen-Condom, 3km before Condom left to La Romieu.*

GPS: 43.9828, 0.5017

Open: Apr-10 Oct **Site:** 10HEC **Prices:** 15.90-32.50 Mobile home hire 280-910 **Facilities:** Wi-fi (charged) Kids' Club Play Area **Services:** **Leisure:** P **Off-site:**

ROQUEFORT — LANDES

CM de Nauton

Cité Nauton, 40120
☎ 558455046 558455363
e-mail: mairie.roquefort@wanadoo.fr

A small municipal site with good facilities.

dir: *1.6km N on D932 towards Bordeaux.*

Open: Jun-Aug **Site:** 1.35HEC **Facilities:** **Services:** **Off-site:** L P R

ROQUELAURE — GERS

Talouch

32810
☎ 562655243 562655368
e-mail: info@camping-talouch.com
web: www.camping-talouch.com

A family site in picturesque wooded surroundings in the heart of Gascony. There are good sports and entertainment facilities.

dir: *N21 onto D148.*

Open: Apr-Sep **Site:** 9HEC **Facilities:** **Services:** **Leisure:** P

ST-ANTOINE-D'AUBEROCHE — DORDOGNE

Pélonie

La Pélonie, 24330
☎ 553075578 553037427
e-mail: lapelonie@aol.com
web: www.lapelonie.com

In a picturesque rural location in the heart of the Perigord.

dir: *Off N89 between St Pierre de Chignac & Fossmagne.*

GPS: 45.13, 0.93

Open: 20 Apr-10 Oct **Site:** 3HEC **Prices:** 12.20-16.30 **Facilities:** Wi-fi Kids' Club Play Area **Services:** **Leisure:** P

ST-ANTOINE-DE-BREUILH — DORDOGNE

Riviere Fleurie

180 r Théophile Cart, lieu dit St Aulaye de Breuilh, 24230
☎ 553248280 553248280
e-mail: info@la-riviere-fleurie.com
web: www.la-riviere-fleurie.com

Relaxing, friendly site with swimming pool and fishing available on the River Dordogne, 50m away.

dir: *Off D936 W of St-Antoine & 3km towards River Dordogne.*

GPS: 44.8289, 0.1225

Open: Apr-Sep **Site:** 2.4HEC **Prices:** 15.90-21.90 Mobile home hire 195-735 **Facilities:** Wi-fi Play Area **Services:** **Leisure:** P R **Off-site:**

FRANCE

ST-ANTONIN-NOBLE-VAL TARN-ET-GARONNE

Trois Cantons

82140
☎ 563319857
e-mail: info@3cantons.fr
web: www.3cantons.fr

Divided into pitches, partly on sloping ground in an oak forest, near St Antonin Noble Val. Separate section for teenagers. Kids' club available mid July to mid August.

dir: *8.5km NW near D926, signed.*

Open: 15 Apr-Sep **Site:** 15HEC **Prices:** 14.50-22 Mobile home hire 245-695 **Facilities:** Wi-fi Kids' Club Play Area **Services:** **Leisure:** P **Off-site:** R

ST-BERTRAND-DE-COMMINGES HAUTE-GARONNE

Es Pibous

chemin de St-Just, 31510
☎ 561883142 561956383
e-mail: es.pibous@wanadoo.fr
web: www.es-pibous.fr

A quiet, shaded site in an elevated position with good facilities.

dir: *A64 exit 17 onto RN125. Right towards Valcabrère on RD26.*

Open: Apr-Oct **Site:** 1.8HEC **Prices:** 16.02-17.50 Mobile home hire 370-400 **Facilities:** Play Area **Services:** **Leisure:** P **Off-site:** L R

ST-CÉRÉ LOT

CM le Soulhol

The Camping and Caravanning Club The Friendly Club

quai A-Salesse, 46400
☎ 565381237 565381237
e-mail: info@campinglesoulhol.com
web: www.campinglesoulhol.com

A family site bordered by two rivers with good recreational facilities.

C&CC Report *Le Soulhol is a great site for exploring the lovely, unspoiled and fascinating Lot. There's a relaxing riverside setting, a friendly atmosphere, swimming pool, the town centre a short stroll away and more places to visit than can be fitted into one stay, including Figeac, Rocamadour, Cahors and Beaulieu-sur-Dordogne.*

dir: *Via A20, exit 52/54.*

GPS: 44.8581, 1.8977

Open: May-Sep **Site:** 4HEC **Prices:** 14.20-15.20 Mobile home hire 190-490 **Facilities:** Wi-fi (charged) Play Area **Services:** **Leisure:** P R **Off-site:**

ST-CIRQ-LAPOPIE LOT

Plage

46330
☎ 565302951 565302333
e-mail: camping-laplage@wanadoo.fr
web: www.campingplage.com

Site beside the River Lot with well-defined pitches and modern facilities. Boat and bicycle hire available.

dir: *Via D41 from N. Or D42 from S.*

Open: All Year. **Site:** 3HEC **Facilities:** **Services:** **Leisure:** R **Off-site:**

ST-CRICQ GERS

Lac de Thoux Saint Cricq

32440
☎ 562657129 562657481
e-mail: contact@camping-lacdethoux.com
web: www.camping-lacdethoux.com

A family site with good facilities on the edge of the lake, 50m from the beach.

Open: Apr-15 Oct **Site:** 3HEC **Facilities:** **Services:** **Leisure:** L P

ST-CYPRIEN DORDOGNE

CM Garrit

24220
☎ 553292056 553292056
e-mail: pbecheau@aol.com
web: www.campingdugarritendordogneperigord.com

A peaceful location beside the River Dordogne with safe bathing.

dir: *1.5km S on D48.*

Open: May-Sep **Site:** 2HEC **Facilities:** **Services:** **Leisure:** P R **Off-site:** R

ST-ÉMILION GIRONDE

Domaine de la Barbanne

2 lieu dit les Combes, 33330
☎ 557247580 557246968
e-mail: barbanne@wanadoo.fr
web: www.camping-saint-emilion.com

A peaceful country setting among vineyards, close to a 5-hectare lake.

dir: *3km N via D122.*

Open: 16 Apr-24 Sep **Site:** 10HEC **Prices:** 15-39 Mobile home hire 203-1113 **Facilities:** Wi-fi (charged) Kids' Club Play Area **Services:** **Leisure:** P

ST-GENIES DORDOGNE

Bouquerie

24590
553289822 553291975
e-mail: labouquerie@wanadoo.fr
web: www.labouquerie.com
A family site in wooded surroundings with a variety of facilities.
dir: *N of village on D704.*
Open: 19 Apr-19 Sep **Site:** 8HEC **Facilities:** **Services:** **Leisure:** L P

ST-JEAN-DE-LUZ PYRÉNÉES-ATLANTIQUES

Atlantica

Quartier Acotz, 64500
559477244 559547227
e-mail: info@campingatlantica.com
web: www.campingatlantica.com
A family site with good facilities at the foot of the Pyrénées close to the Spanish border, and 0.5km from the beach.
dir: *N10 exit St-Jean-de-Luz Nord for Biarritz, 1km on left.*
Open: Apr-Sep **Site:** 3.5HEC **Facilities:** **Services:** **Leisure:** P **Off-site:** S
see advert on this page

Ferme d'Erromardie

64500
559263426 559512602
e-mail: contact@camping-erromardie.com
web: www.camping-erromardie.com
Site by the sea with several sections divided by roads and low hedges.
dir: *N to N10, over railway bridge & sharp right, signed.*
Open: 15 Mar-2 Oct **Site:** 2HEC **Facilities:** **Services:** **Leisure:** R S **Off-site:**

Tamaris Plage

quartier d'Acotz, 64500
559265590 559477015
e-mail: tamaris1@wanadoo.fr
web: www.tamaris-plage.com
Level family site with good facilities divided into sections by drives and hedges. Kids' club available 10 July to 12 August.
dir: *Signed from N10 towards sea.*
Open: All Year. **Site:** 1.3HEC **Prices:** 18-27 Mobile home hire 350-780 **Facilities:** Wi-fi Kids' Club Play Area **Services:** **Leisure:** S **Off-site:**

ST-JEAN-PIED-DE-PORT PYRÉNÉES-ATLANTIQUES

Narbaïtz

rte de Bayonne, Ascarat, 64220
559371013 559372142
e-mail: camping-narbaitz@wanadoo.fr
web: www.camping-narbaitz.com
A quiet, comfortable site beside the River Berroua with heated swimming pool.
dir: *2km NW towards Bayonne.*
Open: May-mid Sep **Site:** 2.5HEC **Facilities:** Kids' Club Play Area **Services:** **Leisure:** P R **Off-site:**

ST-JULIEN-EN-BORN LANDES

Lette Fleurie

40170
558427409 558424151
e-mail: contact@camping-municipal-plage.com
web: www.camping-municipal-plage.com
On undulating ground in a pine wood with good facilities, 5 minutes from the beach.
Open: Apr-Sep **Site:** 18HEC **Facilities:** **Services:** **Leisure:** P **Off-site:** R S

ST-JUSTIN LANDES

Camping le Pin

rte de Roquefort, 40240
558448891 558448891
e-mail: camping.lepin@wanadoo.fr
web: www.campinglepin.com
A quiet family site with a kids' club during July and August.
dir: *2.3km N on D626.*
Open: Mar-Oct **Site:** 3HEC **Prices:** 11-18 Mobile home hire 190-580 **Facilities:** Wi-fi Kids' Club Play Area **Services:** **Leisure:** P **Off-site:**

Facilities shop shower electric points for razors electric points for caravans parking by tents permitted compulsory separate car park **Services** café/restaurant bar Camping Gaz International gas other than Camping Gaz first aid facilities laundry **Leisure** swimming L-Lake P-Pool R-River S-Sea **Off-site** All facilities within 5km

ST-LÉON-SUR-VÉZÈRE DORDOGNE

Paradis

24290

☎ 553507264 🖷 553507590

e-mail: le-paradis@perigord.com

web: www.le-paradis.fr

Situated on the river bank in the picturesque Vézère Valley. Kids' club available in July and August.

dir: *S of village off D706 Les Éyzies road.*

GPS: 45.0017, 1.0715

Open: Apr-19 Oct **Site:** 7HEC **Prices:** 18.40-27.50 Mobile home hire 322-910 **Facilities:** Wi-fi (charged) Kids' Club Play Area **Services:** **Leisure:** P R

ST-NICOLAS-DE-LA-GRAVE TARN-ET-GARONNE

Plan d'Eau

Base de Plein Air, et de Loisirs, 82210

☎ 563955002 🖷 563955001

e-mail: basedeloisirs.stnicolas@cg82.fr

web: www.cg82.fr

dir: *2.5km N via D15.*

Open: 15 Jun-15 Sep **Site:** 1.5HEC **Prices:** 10.50 **Facilities:** **Services:** **Leisure:** L P R **Off-site:** L P R

ST-MARTIN-DE-SEIGNANX LANDES

Lou P'tit Poun

The Camping and Caravanning Club – The Friendly Club

40390

☎ 559565579 🖷 559565371

e-mail: contact@louptitpoun.com

web: www.louptitpoun.com

A quiet site with well-defined pitches on terraces.

C&CC Report *One of the most friendly and lovingly kept sites around. A spacious, peaceful and relaxed site, with the Basque country's bustling resorts, lovely beaches, mountains and lively Bayonne all easily accessible. Many campers return here year after year to enjoy the distinctive culture of the region and Monsieur and Madame Sauvy's welcome.*

dir: *A63 exit Bayonne Nord for Pau.*

Open: Jun-11 Sep **Site:** 7HEC **Facilities:** **Services:** **Leisure:** P

ST-PARDOUX-LA-RIVIÈRE DORDOGNE

Kawan Village Château le Verdoyer

24470

☎ 553569464 🖷 553563870

e-mail: chateau@verdoyer.fr

web: www.verdoyer.fr

A small, well-equipped site in the grounds of a restored castle.

dir: *3km N via D96.*

Open: 23 Apr-4 Oct **Site:** 25HEC **Prices:** 18-23 Mobile home hire 240-700 **Facilities:** Wi-fi (charged) Kids' Club Play Area **Services:** **Leisure:** L P

ST-PAUL-LES-DAX LANDES

Pins du Soleil

RD459, 40990

☎ 558913791

e-mail: info@pinsoleil.com

web: www.pinsoleil.com

On a hotel complex with modern facilities.

dir: *SW via D954.*

GPS: 43.7205, -1.0936

Open: Apr-Oct **Site:** 6HEC **Prices:** 8-24 Mobile home hire 280-699 **Facilities:** Wi-fi Kids' Club Play Area **Services:** **Leisure:** P **Off-site:** R

ST-PÉE-SUR-NIVELLE PYRÉNÉES-ATLANTIQUES

Goyetchea

64310

☎ 559541959

e-mail: info@camping-goyetchea.com

web: www.camping-goyetchea.com

Quiet, peaceful site in a wooded location at the foot of the Pyrénées.

dir: *2km from St Pée via D918.*

Open: 6 Jun-19 Sep **Site:** 4HEC **Prices:** 14-21 Mobile home hire 210-740 **Facilities:** Wi-fi (charged) Play Area **Services:** **Leisure:** P **Off-site:** L R

Ibarron

64310

☎ 559541043

e-mail: camping.dibarron@wanadoo.fr

web: www.camping-ibarron.com

A pleasant wooded location with level pitches and modern facilities.

dir: *2km W on D918.*

Open: May-Sep **Site:** 2.88HEC **Prices:** 14.16-20.26 Mobile home hire 230-600 **Facilities:** Wi-fi Play Area **Services:** **Leisure:** P R **Off-site:** L P R

FRANCE

ST-PIERRE-LAFEUILLE LOT

Les Graves

46090
565368312 565368312
e-mail: infos@camping-lesgraves.com
web: www.camping-lesgraves.com
On a small hill on the northern outskirts of the village providing fine views over the surrounding countryside.
dir: *A20 exit 57, 10km N of Cahors.*
GPS: 44.5262, 1.4601
Open: 15 Apr-Sep **Site:** 1.5HEC **Prices:** 14-16.10 Mobile home hire 175-546 **Facilities:** Play Area **Services:** **Leisure:** P **Off-site:**

Quercy-Vacances

Le Mas de Lacombe, 46090
565368715
e-mail: quercyvacances@wanadoo.fr
web: www.quercy-vacances.com
A well-equipped site in pleasant wooded surroundings.
dir: *On N20. 12km N of Cahors.*
Open: Apr-Sep **Site:** 3HEC **Prices:** 12.90-19.10 Mobile home hire 250-590 **Facilities:** Wi-fi Play Area **Services:** **Leisure:** P **Off-site:** L R

ST-SERNIN-DE-DURAS LOT-ET-GARONNE

Moulin de Borie Neuve

47120
553207073
e-mail: info@borieneuve.com
web: www.borieneuve.com
A pleasant site in the Dourdèze Valley close to an old mill.
dir: *D244 towards St-Astier-de-Duras.*
Open: 15 May-1 Oct **Site:** 1HEC **Facilities:** **Services:** **Leisure:** P R **Off-site:**

ST-SEURIN-DE-PRATS DORDOGNE

Plage

24230
553586107
e-mail: enquiries@dordognecamping.co.uk
web: www.dordognecamping.co.uk
A peaceful wooded setting beside the Dordogne with a variety of recreational facilities.
dir: *0.7km on D11.*
Open: 15 May-15 Sep **Site:** 4.5HEC **Facilities:** **Services:** **Leisure:** P R **Off-site:**

STE-EULALIE-EN-BORN LANDES

Bruyères

chemin Laffont, 40200
558097336 558097558
e-mail: bonjour@camping-les-bruyeres.com
web: www.camping-les-bruyeres.com
Set in the middle of the Landes forest close to the lakes and the sea.
dir: *2.5km N via D652.*
Open: 14 May-29 Sep **Site:** 3HEC **Facilities:** **Services:** **Leisure:** P
Off-site: L R

STE-NATHALÈNE DORDOGNE

Camping la Palombière

24200
553594234 553284540
e-mail: la.palombiere@wanadoo.fr
web: www.lapalombiere.fr
Terraced pitches among pines and oaks. There is an aquatic complex and during high season sports activities run during the day with entertainment in the evening. Kids' club available in season.
dir: *8km NE of Sarlat.*
GPS: 44.9081, 1.2925
Open: 23 Apr-11 Sep **Site:** 11HEC **Prices:** 14.50-29.70 Mobile home hire 270-985 **Facilities:** Wi-fi Kids' Club Play Area **Services:** **Leisure:** P

Domaine des Mathevies

Les Mathevies, 24200
553592086 614109586
e-mail: mathevies@mac.com
web: www.mathevies.com
Suitable for young families, the terraced pitches are generous in size and all have electricity, in addition there are wooden chalets, mobile homes and a traditional stone Gîte. A shaded terrace offers stunning views over the valley and a beautiful Perigordine barn has been restored into a modern sanitary block and restaurant that offers local home cooked food.
dir: *7km NW of Sarlat-la-Caneda. A20, exit 55 (Souillac), follow signs to Routillac then signs to Carlux & continue to Ste Nathalène.*
Open: Apr-Sep **Site:** 2.5HEC **Prices:** 14.50-21.50 Mobile home hire 300-650 **Facilities:** Wi-fi Play Area **Services:** **Leisure:** P
Off-site: L R

FRANCE

SALIGNAC — DORDOGNE

Peneyrals

Le Poujol, St-Crépin Carlucet, 24590
553288571 553288099
e-mail: camping.peneyrals@wanadoo.fr
web: www.peneyrals.com

Extensive leisure facilities are available, swimming pools with waterslides, tennis, mini-golf etc. Entertainment from end of May to beginning of September with a kids' club during July and August.

dir: *10km N of Sarlat on D60.*

Open: 12 May-14 Sep **Site:** 13HEC **Prices:** 16.90-29.20 Mobile home hire 300-970 **Facilities:** Wi-fi (charged) Kids' Club Play Area **Services:** **Leisure:** P

see advert on this page

SALLES — LOT-ET-GARONNE

Bastides

47150
553408309 553408176
e-mail: info@campingdesbastides.com
web: www.campingdesbastides.com

Peaceful wooded surroundings overlooking the Lède Valley with good sports and entertainment facilities.

dir: *1km N via D150.*

GPS: 44.5524, 0.8813

Open: Etr-Sep **Site:** 6HEC **Prices:** 15-26.50 Mobile home hire 238-616 **Facilities:** Wi-fi (charged) Kids' Club Play Area **Services:** **Leisure:** P

Val de l'Eyre

8 rte de Minoy, 33770
556884703 556884727
e-mail: levaldeleyre2@wanadoo.fr
web: www.valdeleyre.com

A well-equipped family site in a pleasant wooded location between the Landes forests and Bordeaux vineyards.

dir: *SW on D108 rte de Lugos.*

Open: Apr-15 Oct **Site:** 13HEC **Facilities:** **Services:** **Leisure:** P R **Off-site:** P

SARLAT-LA-CANÉDA — DORDOGNE

Maillac

Ste-Nathalène, 24200
553592212 553296017
e-mail: campingmaillac@wanadoo.fr
web: www.campingmaillac.fr

Wooded surroundings in the heart of the Périgord Noir region with good facilities for a family holiday. Separate car park for arrivals after 23.00hrs.

dir: *7km NE on D47.*

Open: 15 May-Oct **Site:** 6HEC **Facilities:** **Services:** **Leisure:** P **Off-site:** L R

Moulin du Roch

rte des Éyzies, Le Roch, 24200
553592027 553592095
e-mail: moulin.du.roch@wanadoo.fr
web: www.moulin-du-roch.com

A picturesque location between the Dordogne and Vézère Valleys. Kids' club available in July and August.

dir: *10km NW via D704, D6 & D47.*

GPS: 44.9081, 1.1155

Open: 9 May-16 Sep **Site:** 8HEC **Prices:** 15-35 Mobile home hire 270-950 **Facilities:** Wi-fi (charged) Kids' Club Play Area **Services:** **Leisure:** P

Périères

rue Jean Gabin, BP98, 24203
553590584 553285751
e-mail: les-perieres@wanadoo.fr
web: www.lesperieres.com

Very well-kept terraced site in parkland and woods in the heart of the Périgord Noir, with fine views over the Sarlat Valley. There are good recreational facilities.

dir: *1km N of town on D47.*

GPS: 44.8939, 1.2275

Open: Etr-Sep **Site:** 11HEC **Prices:** 20-31.40 **Facilities:** Wi-fi **Services:** **Leisure:** P

Site 6HEC (site size) grass sand stone little shade partly shaded mainly shaded bungalows for hire (static) caravans for hire tents for hire no dogs site fully accessible for wheelchairs
Prices amount quoted is per night, for 2 adults and car, plus tent or caravan. Mobile home hire is a weekly rate.

Rocher de la Cave

24200
☎ 553281426 🖷 553282710
e-mail: rocher.de.la-cave@wanadoo.fr
web: www.rocherdelacave.com

Pleasant family site on a level meadow beside the Dordogne, set in beautiful countryside.

dir: *Via D703 & D704.*

Open: May-Sep **Site:** 4HEC **Prices:** 13-17.70 Mobile home hire 200-650 **Facilities:** Wi-fi Play Area **Services:** **Leisure:** P R

Val d'Ussel

La Fond d'Ussel, Proissans, 24200
☎ 553592873 🖷 553293825
e-mail: info@homair.com
web: www.camping-valdussel.com

A well-equipped site in woodland in the heart of the Périgord Noir region. Separate car park for late arrivals.

dir: *Off D704 or D56.*

Open: 25 Apr-19 Sep **Site:** 7HEC **Facilities:** **Services:** **Leisure:** P

Village Center Aqua Viva

rte de Sarlat-Souillac, Carsac-Aillac, 24200
☎ 499572121 🖷 467516389
e-mail: contact@village-center.com
web: www.village-center.com/aquitaine/camping-aqua-viva.php

6km from Sarlat on a sheltered site in beautiful wooded surroundings.

dir: *A20 exit 55.*

Open: 8 Apr-2 Oct **Site:** 13HEC **Prices:** 16-29 Mobile home hire 192-777 **Facilities:** Wi-fi (charged) Kids' Club Play Area **Services:** **Leisure:** P

see advert on this page

SAUVETERRE-LA-LEMANCE LOT-ET-GARONNE

Moulin du Périé

rte de Loubejac, 47500
☎ 553406726
e-mail: moulinduperle@wanadoo.fr

In a wooded valley close to an 18th-century watermill with good, modern facilities.

dir: *3km E of town off D710. Follow signposts from the entrance to the village and keep to the valley road*

Open: Apr-Sep **Site:** 5HEC **Facilities:** **Services:** **Leisure:** P R **Off-site:** L

SEIGNOSSE LANDES

Belambra vvf Club Les Estagnots

40510
☎ 558416850 🖷 558432326

A pleasant, quiet site 300m from the sea.

Open: 29 Jun-2 Sep **Site:** 11HEC **Facilities:** **Services:** **Leisure:** P **Off-site:** L S

Chevreuils

2388 rte de Hossegor, à Vieux Boucau, 40510
☎ 558433280 🖷 558433280
e-mail: info@chevreuils.com
web: www.chevreuils.com

Set in a pine forest close to the sea with good recreational facilities.

dir: *On CD79 rte de Hossegor.*

Open: May-27 Sep **Site:** 8HEC **Prices:** 15-27 Mobile home hire 231-987 **Facilities:** Kids' Club **Services:** **Leisure:** P **Off-site:** L S

Océliances

av des Tucs, 40510
☎ 558433030 🖷 558416421
e-mail: oceliances@wanadoo.fr
web: www.oceliances.com

Very clean and tidy site in a pine forest 0.6km from the sea.

dir: *200m from Seignosse town centre.*

Open: Apr-29 Sep **Site:** 13HEC **Facilities:** **Services:** **Leisure:** P **Off-site:** L S

FRANCE

Oyats

rte de la Plage des Casernes, 40510
☎ 558433794 558432329
e-mail: cployats@atciat.com
web: www.campeoles.fr

Level site, subdivided into fields and surrounded by woodland. Separate section for young people. Children's play area.

dir: *Off D79 in N outskirts towards Plage des Casernes.*

Open: 15 May-15 Sep **Site:** 17HEC **Facilities:** **Services:** **Leisure:** P **Off-site:** S

SEIX ARIÈGE

Haut Salat

09140
☎ 561668178 561669417
e-mail: camping.le-haut-salat@wanadoo.fr
web: www.ariege.com/campinglehautsalat

Very clean, well-kept site beside stream. Big gravel pitches for caravans. Common room with TV.

dir: *0.8km NE on D3.*

Open: 2 Jan-14 Dec **Site:** 3HEC **Facilities:** **Services:** **Leisure:** P R

SÉRIGNAC-PÉBOUDOU LOT-ET-GARONNE

Vallée de Gardeleau

47410
☎ 553369696 553369696
e-mail: valleegardeleau@wanadoo.fr
web: perso.wanadoo.fr/camping.valleegardeleau.fr

A shaded wooded position, offering peace and comfort in relaxing surroundings.

dir: *On RN21 between Lauzun & Castilonnès.*

Open: Mar-Oct **Site:** 2HEC **Facilities:** **Services:** **Leisure:** P

SOUILLAC LOT

Domaine de la Paille Basse

The Camping and Caravanning Club The Friendly Club

46200
☎ 565378548 565370958
e-mail: info@lapaillebasse.com
web: www.lapaillebasse.com

A family site in a picturesque wooded hilltop location in the grounds of an old farming hamlet.

C&CC Report *This classic Castels site, built on an old farmstead hamlet of great character and charm, offers modern facilities in an idyllic setting with open views. Busy, yet relaxed, the site has something for all nature-lovers – young children love the pet farm, while the active enjoy the group walks and cycling excursions. In low season this is a lovely haven and a convenient base for exploring the best parts of the Dordogne and Lot valleys, both within easy reach.*

dir: *6.5km NW off D15 Salignac-Eyvignes road.*

GPS: 44.9454, 1.4414

Open: 15 May-15 Sep **Site:** 12HEC **Prices:** Mobile home hire 750-850 **Facilities:** Wi-fi (charged) Kids' Club Play Area **Services:** **Leisure:** P

SOULAC-SUR-MER GIRONDE

Amélie-Plage

L'Amélie-sur-Mer, 33780
☎ 556098727 556736426
e-mail: camping.amelie.plage@wanadoo.fr
web: www.camping-amelie-plage.com

Hilly wooded terrain. Lovely sandy beach.

dir: *3km S on Soulac road.*

Open: Mar-Dec **Site:** 12.5HEC **Facilities:** **Services:** **Leisure:** P S

Club de Soube

8 allée Michel Montaigne, 33780
☎ 556097763 556099482
e-mail: contact@lelilhan.com
web: www.lelilhan.com

Located in an oak tree and pine forest, a short distance from the beach.

Open: Apr-Sep **Site:** 4HEC **Facilities:** **Services:** **Leisure:** P **Off-site:** S

Lacs

126 rte des Lacs, 33780
☎ 556097663 556099802
e-mail: info@camping-les-lacs.com
web: www.camping-les-lacs.com

Site with marked pitches within easy reach of fine Atlantic beaches.

Open: Apr-5 Nov **Site:** 5.8HEC **Facilities:** **Services:** **Leisure:** P

FRANCE

Palace

65 bld Marsan de Montbrun, 33780
556098022 556098423
e-mail: info@camping-palace.com
Well-kept site on sand dunes. Individual pitches, asphalt drives.
dir: *1km S from village centre. Access is via D1 and D101.*
Open: May-15 Sep **Site:** 16HEC **Facilities:** **Services:** **Leisure:** P **Off-site:** S
see advert on this page

Pins

213 passe de Formose, Lilian, 33780
556098252 5577365558
e-mail: contact@campingdespins.fr
web: www.campingdespins.fr
Situated in a beautiful pine forest close to the beach with plenty of sports facilities.
dir: *S on D101.*
Open: Apr-Oct **Site:** 3.2HEC **Facilities:** **Services:** **Leisure:** P **Off-site:** R S

Sables d'Argent

33 bd de l'Amèlie, 33780
556098287 556099482
e-mail: contact@sables-d-argent.com
web: www.sables-d-argent.com
Set in a pine forest bordered by dunes, with direct access to the beach.
dir: *1.5km SW of village.*
Open: Apr-Sep **Site:** 2.6HEC **Prices:** 16.40-25.70 Mobile home hire 257-989 **Facilities:** Wi-fi (charged) Kids' Club **Services:** **Leisure:** S **Off-site:** P

SOUSTONS LANDES

L'Airial

61 av Port d'Albret, 40140
558411248 558415383
e-mail: contact@camping-airial.com
web: www.camping-airial.com
Situated in a shady park with plenty of recreational facilities and modern installations. Heated, covered swimming pool.
dir: *2km W on D652.*
GPS: 43.7545, -1.3517
Open: Apr-15 Oct **Site:** 12HEC **Prices:** 17.50-29.20 Mobile home hire 300-830 **Facilities:** Wi-fi Kids' Club Play Area **Services:** **Leisure:** P **Off-site:** L S

TARASCON-SUR-ARIÈGE ARIÈGE

Camping Village Le Pré Lombard

BP 90148, 09400
561056194 561057893
e-mail: leprelombard@wanadoo.fr
web: www.prelombard.com
Beautiful wooded surroundings beside the River Ariège with modern facilities.
dir: *1.5km SE on D23.*
Open: 15 Mar-15 Oct **Site:** 3.5HEC **Prices:** 15-34 Mobile home hire 245-945 **Facilities:** Wi-fi Kids' Club Play Area **Services:** **Leisure:** P R

TEILLET TARN

Relais de l'Entre Deux Lacs

81120
563557445
e-mail: contact@campingdutarn.com
web: www.campingdutarn.com
Shady terraced site. Various activities arranged. Beautiful views.
dir: *Off D81 towards Lacaune.*
Open: 9 Apr-Sep **Site:** 4HEC **Facilities:** Wi-fi Play Area **Services:** **Leisure:** P **Off-site:** L R

FRANCE

THIVIERS DORDOGNE

CM Le Repaire

24800
☎ 553526975 📠 553526975
e-mail: campingthiviers@wanadoo.fr
web: www.thiviers.fr

A well-appointed family site in a wooded valley in the Périgord Vert region of the Dordogne, a short walk from the ancient village of Thiviers.

dir: *On D707 1.5km towards Lanouaille.*

Open: May-Sep **Site:** 11HEC **Facilities:** **Services:** **Leisure:** P **Off-site:** L R

TOUZAC LOT

Ch'Timi

46700
☎ 565365236 📠 565365323
e-mail: info@campinglechtimi.com
web: www.campinglechtimi.com

A well-equipped site overlooking the River Lot. Entertainment available in summer.

dir: *0.8km from Touzac on D8.*

Open: Apr-Sep **Site:** 3.5HEC **Prices:** 16.50-22.10 Mobile home hire 180-565 **Facilities:** Wi-fi (charged) Kids' Club Play Area **Services:** **Leisure:** P R

Clos Bouyssac

46700
☎ 565365221 📠 565246851
e-mail: camping.leclosbouyssac@wanadoo.fr
web: www.leclosbouyssac.eu

On the fringe of a wooded hillside by the sandy shore of the River Lot with most pitches having direct river access. Good for walking.

dir: *S of Touzac on D65.*

Open: Apr-Sep **Site:** 1.5HEC **Facilities:** Wi-fi Play Area **Services:** **Leisure:** P R

TURSAC DORDOGNE

Pigeonnier

24620
☎ 553069690 📠 553069690
e-mail: campinglepigeonnier@wanadoo.fr
web: www.campinglepigeonnier.fr

A small, peaceful site in the heart of the Dordogne countryside.

dir: *Via D706 between Le Moustier & Les Éyzies.*

Open: Jun-Sep **Site:** 1.14HEC **Prices:** 15.90 **Facilities:** Play Area **Services:** **Leisure:** P **Off-site:** R

Vézère Périgord

The Camping and Caravanning Club — The Friendly Club

route de Montignac, 24620
☎ 553069631 📠 553067966
web: www.levezereperigord.com

A well-equipped site in wooded surroundings close to the river.

C&CC Report *Expect a warm and friendly welcome at this peaceful site, only a short walk from the River Vézère with its fishing, canoeing and river beach, while close by are many of the unique prehistoric dwellings, paintings and sculptures for which the Dordogne is world renowned. Most notable of these are La Roque-St.-Christophe's troglodyte dwellings, just 5km away – but there are plenty more prehistoric and natural wonders to keep you busy.*

dir: *0.8km NE on D706.*

Open: Etr-Oct **Site:** 6HEC **Facilities:** **Services:** **Leisure:** P **Off-site:** R

URRUGNE PYRÉNÉES-ATLANTIQUES

Juantcho

rte de la Corniche, Socoa, 64122
☎ 559471197 📠 559473179
e-mail: camping.juantcho@wanadoo.fr
web: www.camping-juantcho.com

dir: *2km W on D912.*

Open: 19 May-Sep **Site:** 6HEC **Facilities:** **Services:** **Off-site:** R S

Larrouleta

The Camping and Caravanning Club — The Friendly Club

210 route de Socoa, 64122
☎ 559473784 📠 559474254
e-mail: info@larrouleta.com
web: www.larrouleta.com

Hilly meadow with young trees.

C&CC Report *The Basque country is a fascinating area with its own identity that is separate from France and this friendly site is well placed to explore both Spanish and French areas. With the Atlantic beaches just a short drive away you are spoilt for choice with the swimming pool (covered in low season) and lake swimming on site. Why not try one of the free pedaloes?*

dir: *Via RN10 or A63.*

Open: All Year. **Site:** 10HEC **Facilities:** **Services:** **Leisure:** L P R **Off-site:** S

FRANCE

URT PYRÉNÉES-ATLANTIQUES

Etche Zahar

allée de Mesplès, 64240
559562736
e-mail: info@etche-zahar.fr
web: www.etche-zahar.fr

A small, privately owned site in a wooded location and within easy reach of local tourist areas. Separate car parking for arrivals 22.00-08.00 hrs. The owner speaks English and will help with any information needed. Special offers may be available.

dir: *A63 exit 8. Or A64 exit 4.*

GPS: 43.4917, -1.2966

Open: Mar-15 Nov **Site:** 2.5HEC **Prices:** 14-21.30 Mobile home hire 238-630 **Facilities:** Wi-fi (charged) Kids' Club Play Area **Services:** **Leisure:** P **Off-site:** R

VALEUIL DORDOGNE

Bas Meygnaud

D393 Brantome, 24310
553055844
e-mail: camping-du-bas-meygnaud@wanadoo.fr
web: www.basmeygnaud.fr

A quiet, shady site in the Dronne Valley. English spoken.

dir: *Off D939 at Lasserre.*

Open: Apr-15 Oct **Site:** 1.7HEC **Prices:** 13-19.50 Mobile home hire 200-405 **Facilities:** Play Area **Services:** **Leisure:** P **Off-site:** R

VARILHES ARIÈGE

Château

av du 8 Mai 45, 09120
561674284 561674284
e-mail: camping.du.chateau@orange.fr
web: www.campingdevarilhes.com

On the banks of the river and close to the town.

dir: *N on N20.*

Open: All Year. **Site:** 1.2HEC **Facilities:** **Services:** **Leisure:** P **Off-site:** R

VAYRAC LOT

Camping Les Chênes Clairs

Condat, 46110
565321632
e-mail: leschenesclairs@laposte.net
web: www.leschenesclairs.fr

With the Dordogne River a few kilometres to the south, this site has shaded pitches and a gite for rent.

dir: *Off D20 between Condat & Vayrac.*

Open: May-Oct **Site:** 4HEC **Prices:** 11.40-18 Mobile home hire 250-500 **Facilities:** Wi-fi Play Area **Services:** **Leisure:** P **Off-site:** L R

VENDAYS-MONTALIVET GIRONDE

Camping de Mayan

3 route de Mayan, 33930
556417651
e-mail: campingmayan@sfr.fr

A small site in a pine wood.

dir: *Via N215 & D102.*

Open: 15 Jun-15 Sep **Site:** 1HEC **Prices:** 9.30-11.70 Mobile home hire 185-230 **Facilities:** Wi-fi **Services:** **Off-site:** S

Chesnays

8 rte de Mayan, 33930
556417274 556417274
e-mail: lachesnays@camping-montalivet.com
web: www.camping-montalivet.com

Peaceful campsite, shaded by trees and situated between the sand beaches of the Atlantic shoreline and the Gironde Estuary.

dir: *Leave A10 at Saintes (junct 25) follow signs for Royan. Find Bac (ferry) to cross The Gironde. Follow N215 to Soulac, then D101 to campsite.*

GPS: 45.3758, -1.0822

Open: Apr-Sep **Site:** 2HEC **Prices:** 13.50-19.40 Mobile home hire 250-650 **Facilities:** Wi-fi Play Area **Services:** **Leisure:** P **Off-site:** R S

VERDON-SUR-MER, LE GIRONDE

Royannais

88 rte de Soulac, 33123
556096112 556737067
e-mail: camping.le.royannais@wanadoo.fr
web: www.royannais.com

Level, sandy terrain under high pine and deciduous trees.

dir: *S of Le Verdon-sur-Mer in Le Royannais district on D1.*

Open: Apr-15 Oct **Site:** 3HEC **Facilities:** Kids' Club Play Area **Services:** **Leisure:** P **Off-site:** R S

FRANCE

VÉZAC — DORDOGNE

Deux Vallées

La Gare, 24220
☎ 553295355 🖹 553310981
e-mail: contact@campingles2vallees.com
web: www.campingles2vallees.com

A level site in a picturesque location in the Dordogne Valley. Good facilities for families, with a kids' club available from July and August.

dir: *Via D57 from Sarlat. Or D703 from Bergerac.*

GPS: 44.8356, 1.1587

Open: All Year. **Site:** 3.8HEC **Prices:** 14.30-22 Mobile home hire 245-715 **Facilities:** Wi-fi Kids' Club Play Area **Services:** **Leisure:** P **Off-site:** R

Plage

La Roque Gageac, 24220
☎ 685232216
e-mail: campinglaplage24@orange.fr
web: www.camping-laplage.fr

Modest but attractive site in a pleasant riverside setting.

dir: *Via D703 beyond La Roque Gageac.*

Open: Apr-Sep **Site:** 3.5HEC **Facilities:** **Services:** **Leisure:** P R

VIELLE-ST-GIRONS — LANDES

Camping Campéole les Tourterelles

St-Girons-Plage, 40560
☎ 558479312 🖹 558479203
e-mail: tourterelles@campeole.com
web: www.camping-tourterelles.com

Large site situated close to the beach.

dir: *N10 exit Castets, Vielle-St-Girons.*

Open: 30 Apr-Sep **Site:** 19HEC **Prices:** 13.80-27.60 Mobile home hire 294-952 **Facilities:** Wi-fi (charged) Kids' Club Play Area **Services:** **Leisure:** P **Off-site:** S

Eurosol

rte de la Plage, 40560
☎ 558479014 🖹 558477674
e-mail: contact@camping-eurosol.com
web: www.camping-eurosol.com

Well-maintained family site in a pine forest, 0.7km from one of the finest beaches in the country. Kids' club available in July and August and dogs not permitted in chalets or mobile homes.

dir: *A63 exit Castets.*

GPS: 43.9517, -1.3521

Open: 14 May-10 Sep **Site:** 18HEC **Prices:** 14-29 Mobile home hire 315-840 **Facilities:** Wi-fi (charged) Kids' Club Play Area **Services:** **Leisure:** P **Off-site:** S

Sunêlia Col Vert

1548 route de l'Etang, 40560
☎ 890710001 🖹 558429188
e-mail: contact@colvert.com
web: www.colvert.com

Quiet site on lakeside in sparse pine woodland. Small natural harbour in the mouth of a stream.

dir: *Off D652 on N side of village, continue towards lake.*

GPS: 43.9026, -1.3104

Open: Apr-Sep **Site:** 30HEC **Prices:** 10-37.90 Mobile home hire 217-868 **Facilities:** Wi-fi (charged) Kids' Club Play Area **Services:** **Leisure:** L P

VIEUX-BOUCAU-LES-BAINS — LANDES

CM des Sablères

bd du Marensin, 40480
☎ 558481229 🖹 558482070
e-mail: camping-lessableres@wanadoo.fr
web: www.les-sableres.com

A family site with modern facilities and direct access to the beach.

dir: *Via N10 & D652.*

GPS: 43.7938, -1.4082

Open: Apr-15 Oct **Site:** 11HEC **Prices:** 15.20-22.20 Mobile home hire 210-600 **Facilities:** Wi-fi Play Area **Services:** **Off-site:** L S

VIGAN, LE — LOT

Rêve

Revers, 46300
☎ 565412520
e-mail: info@campinglereve.com
web: www.campinglereve.com

A modern family site in wooded surroundings.

dir: *D673 from Payrac towards Le Vigan & signed.*

Open: May-21 Sep **Site:** 10HEC **Prices:** 12.78-18.25 **Facilities:** Wi-fi (charged) Play Area **Services:** **Leisure:** P

FRANCE

Val de l'Arre

rte de Ganges, 30120
467810277 467817123
e-mail: valdelarre@wanadoo.fr
web: www.valdelarre.com

Wooded surroundings beside the River Arre. Compulsory separate car park for late arrivals.

dir: *2.5km E on D999.*

GPS: 43.9911, 3.6375

Open: Apr-Sep **Site:** 4HEC **Prices:** 13.90-18.40 Mobile home hire 189-651 **Facilities:** Wi-fi (charged) Play Area **Services:** **Leisure:** P R **Off-site:**

VILLEFRANCHE-DU-QUEYRAN LOT-ET-GARONNE

Moulin de Campech

The Camping and Caravanning Club The Friendly Club

47160
553887243 553880652
e-mail: camping@moulindecampech.co.uk
web: www.moulindecampech.co.uk

A beautiful site in a peaceful location beside a small lake stocked with trout.

C&CC Report *It's no wonder so many visitors return again and again, with very friendly British owners providing a real family welcome. The homely, picturesque old mill sets off the site's natural beauty, with a pretty bar terrace next to the fishing lake and a real sun trap at the heated pool. This is a greatly recommended, simple site where you can make friends, relax in peace and get out to explore the lovely locality, even as far as the Pyrenean foothills.*

dir: *D11 towards Casteljaloux.*

GPS: 44.2747, 0.1964

Open: Apr-15 Oct **Site:** 4HEC **Prices:** 16.20-23.20 **Facilities:** **Services:** **Leisure:** L P R

VILLERÉAL LOT-ET-GARONNE

Château de Fonrives

Rives, 47210
553366338 553360998
e-mail: chateau.de.fonrives@wanadoo.fr
web: www.campingchateaufonrives.com

A beautiful natural park in the grounds of a château with good facilities for all ages.

dir: *2.2km NW via D207.*

Open: 9 Apr-Sep **Site:** 20HEC **Prices:** 15-35.50 Mobile home hire 180-790 **Facilities:** Wi-fi (charged) Kids' Club Play Area **Services:** **Leisure:** L P **Off-site:**

VITRAC DORDOGNE

Bouysse

Caudon, 24200
553283305 553303852
e-mail: info@labouysse.com
web: www.labouysse.com

Well-appointed site in a wooded valley beside the Dordogne.

dir: *2km E, near the River Dordogne.*

Open: Apr-Sep **Site:** 3HEC **Prices:** 14.20-20.10 Mobile home hire 250-750 **Facilities:** Wi-fi Kids' Club Play Area **Services:** **Leisure:** P R **Off-site:**

Domaine de Soleil Plage

The Camping and Caravanning Club The Friendly Club

Caudon par Montfort, 24200
553283333 553283024
e-mail: info@soleilplage.fr
web: www.soleilplage.fr

Set out around an old farmhouse bordering the Dordogne with excellent facilities. Kids' club available in July and August.

C&CC Report *A high quality, renowned site in an outstanding location, perfectly situated for visiting lovely Sarlat and all the western Dordogne. With excellent facilities open nearly all season, it's a great place to relax and watch the meandering river wind past the cliffs, either from the river bank or from one of the site's canoes. Pitches are in two separate areas, each with advantages – those with full facilities are by the river, others are closer to the site's main facilities.*

dir: *4km E on D703, turn by Camping Clos Bernard.*

Open: 15 Apr-29 Sep **Site:** 8HEC **Prices:** 21-33.50 Mobile home hire 290-830 **Facilities:** Wi-fi (charged) Kids' Club Play Area **Services:** **Leisure:** P R

see advert on this page

FRANCE

LOIRE/CENTRAL

AIRVAULT — DEUX-SÈVRES

Camping de Courte Vallée

Courte Vallée, 79600
549647065 549941778
e-mail: camping@caravanningfrance.com
web: www.caravanningfrance.com
Small, family run site with large pitches and good facilities, situated in a river valley.
dir: *On NW outskirts of town, 0.5km towards Availles.*
Open: Apr-Oct **Site:** 12HEC **Facilities:** Wi-fi Play Area **Services:** **Leisure:** P **Off-site:** P R

ALLONNES — MAINE-ET-LOIRE

Pô Doré

Le Pô Doré, 49650
241387880 241387880
e-mail: camping.du.po.dore@wanadoo.fr
web: camping-lepodore.com
A family site in a pleasant rural setting in the heart of the Anjou region with good recreational facilities. Separate car park for arrivals after 22.00hrs.
dir: *D35 from Tours. Or N147 from Angers.*
Open: 15 Mar-15 Nov **Site:** 2HEC **Facilities:** **Services:** **Leisure:** P **Off-site:**

AMBRIÈRES-LES-VALLÉES — MAYENNE

Camping Le Parc de Vaux

35 rue des Colverts, 53300
243049025
e-mail: parcdevaux@camp-in-ouest.com
web: www.parcdevaux.com
Campsite with chalet, mobile homes and bungalows. Kids' club in July and August.
GPS: 48.3919, -0.6171
Open: All Year. **Site:** 4HEC **Prices:** 11.40-14 Mobile home hire 240-670 **Facilities:** Wi-fi Kids' Club Play Area **Services:** **Off-site:**

ANCENIS — LOIRE-ATLANTIQUE

Ile Mouchet

Impasse de L'Ile Mouchet, 44150
240830843 240831619
e-mail: camping-ile-mouchet@orange.fr
web: www.camping-estivance.com
Peaceful, wooded site located on the banks of the Loire.
dir: *Off N23 Nantes-Ancenis.*
Open: Apr-8 Oct **Site:** 3HEC **Facilities:** **Services:** **Leisure:** P **Off-site:** R

ANGERS — MAINE-ET-LOIRE

Lac de Maine

av du Lac de Maine, 49000
241730503 241730220
e-mail: camping@lacdemaine.fr
web: www.camping-angers.fr
Pleasant rural surroundings on the 100-hectare Lac de Maine. There are fine sports and entertainment facilities and the historic town of Angers is within easy reach.
dir: *A11 exit Lac de Maine.*
Open: 25 Mar-10 Oct **Site:** 4HEC **Facilities:** **Services:** **Leisure:** P **Off-site:** L R

ANGLES — VENDÉE

Moncalm et Atlantique

85750
251975580 251289109
e-mail: camping-apv@wanadoo.fr
web: www.camping-apv.com
Two distinct sites, but sharing the same recreational facilities in a wooded setting close to the beach.
Open: 31 Mar-22 Sep **Site:** 3HEC **Facilities:** **Services:** **Leisure:** P **Off-site:** R
see advert on opposite page

ANGOULINS-SUR-MER — CHARENTE-MARITIME

Chirats

rte de la Platère, 17690
546569416 546566595
web: www.campingleschirats.fr
Modern site with good facilities 100m from a small sandy beach and providing panoramic views over the Bay of Fouras. The more popular, larger beaches of the area are some 3km away.
dir: *7km S of La Rochelle.*
Open: Apr-Sep **Site:** 4.5HEC **Facilities:** **Services:** **Leisure:** P S

ARCES CHARENTE-MARITIME

Chez Filleux

17120
☎ 546908433 🖷 546908433
e-mail: laferme.chezfilleux@wanadoo.fr
web: www.camping-chezfilleux.com

A level meadow partly shaded by trees and bushes, with modern facilities, 10 minutes from the beaches.

Open: Jun-Sep **Site:** 3HEC **Facilities:** **Services:** **Leisure:** P

ARGENTAT CORRÈZE

Gibanel

Le Gibanel, 19400
☎ 555281011 🖷 555288685
e-mail: contact@camping-gibanel.com
web: www.camping-gibanel.com

Pleasant site in the grounds of a château next to a lake.

dir: *S from Tulle on N120.*

GPS: 45.1115, 1.9598

Open: Jun-3 Sep **Site:** 6.5HEC **Prices:** 15.20-20.60 Mobile home hire 240-720 **Facilities:** Wi-fi **Services:** **Leisure:** L P **Off-site:**

Saulou

Vergnolles, 19400
☎ 555281233 🖷 555288067
e-mail: le.saulou@wanadoo.fr
web: www.saulou.net

A peaceful site in a wooded location beside the River Dordogne. Ideal for families.

dir: *6km S on D116.*

Open: Apr-Sep **Site:** 7.5HEC **Facilities:** **Services:** **Leisure:** P R

Vaurette

Monceaux-sur-Dordogne, 19400
☎ 555280967 🖷 555288114
e-mail: info@vaurette.com
web: www.vaurette.com

In a sheltered valley on the banks of the River Dordogne with sporting facilities including heated swimming pool and tennis court.

dir: *On D12 between Argentat & Beaulieu.*

GPS: 45.0458, 1.8839

Open: May-21 Sep **Site:** 4HEC **Prices:** 15.80-25.80 Mobile home hire 335-690 **Facilities:** Wi-fi Kids' Club Play Area **Services:** **Leisure:** P R

ARGENTON-LES-VALLÉES DEUX-SÈVRES

CM du Lac d'Hautibus

79150
☎ 549659508 🖷 549657084
e-mail: marie-argenton-chateau@cegetel.net

Partly shaded, individually marked pitches on this site, close to the town.

dir: *0.4km S on D748.*

Open: Apr-Oct **Site:** 16.2HEC **Prices:** 8.30-8.95 **Facilities:** Play Area **Services:** **Off-site:** L P R

AUBAZINE CORRÈZE

Campéole le Coiroux

Centre Touristique du Coiroux, 19190
☎ 555272196 🖷 555271916
e-mail: coiroux@campeole.com
web: www.uk.camping-coiroux.com

Peaceful, shady site with large pitches, 300m from a lakeside beach. Sporting facilities include volleyball and tennis courts. Shop, bar, café and restaurant available during July and August.

Open: Apr-Sep **Site:** 11HEC **Prices:** 11-20.40 Mobile home hire 245-777 **Facilities:** Wi-fi Kids' Club Play Area **Services:** **Leisure:** L P **Off-site:** R

AUBETERRE SUR DRONNE CHARENTE

Camping Municipal d'Aubeterre

rte de Riberac, 16390
☎ 545986017
e-mail: camping.aubeterre-sur-dronne@orange.fr
web: www.camping-aubeterre.fr

200m from the village, grassy site bordered with hedges and trees. Kayak and canoe hire nearby.

GPS: 45.2705, 0.1731

Open: May-Sep **Site:** 4HEC **Prices:** 10-17.80 **Facilities:** Wi-fi **Services:** **Leisure:** R **Off-site:**

FRANCE

AVRILLÉ — VENDÉE

Domaine des Forges

rue des Forges, 85440
251223885 251909870
e-mail: contact@campingdomainedesforges.com
web: www.campingdomainedesforges.com

A pleasant position beside a lake, 300m from the town centre, the site has a variety of leisure facilities.

C&CC Report *As you approach Domaine des Forges along a country lane, by the fishing lake, and then see the pretty courtyard where you'll find the site services, you'll realise this is not a typical Vendéen campsite. Lying just outside the village of Avrillé, offering huge pitches in a peaceful parkland setting, this site provides a great base all year round for those who want the best of the Vendée without the high season coastal hassle. A 'sleeping beauty' that is being redeveloped, it is a delight to watch this site blossom.*

Open: All Year. **Site:** 14HEC **Prices:** 16-32 Mobile home hire 215-980 **Facilities:** Wi-fi Kids' Club Play Area **Services:** **Leisure:** P **Off-site:**

Mancellières

rte de Longeville-sur-Mer, 85440
251903597 251903931
e-mail: camping.mancellieres@wanadoo.fr
web: www.lesmancellieres.com

A pleasant site in a wooded park 5km from the fine beaches of south Vendée. Separate car park for arrivals after 23.00 hrs.

dir: *1.7km S on D105 towards Longeville.*

Open: May-15 Sep **Site:** 2.6HEC **Facilities:** **Services:** **Leisure:** P **Off-site:**

AZAY-LE-RIDEAU — INDRE-ET-LOIRE

Parc du Sabot

r du Stade, 37190
247454272 247454911
e-mail: camping.lesabot@wanadoo.fr

Site lies in a large meadow on the River Indre.

dir: *Near château in town centre.*

GPS: 47.2591, 0.4701

Open: Apr-Oct **Site:** 9HEC **Prices:** 10-11 **Facilities:** Wi-fi Play Area **Services:** **Leisure:** R **Off-site:** P

BALLAN-MIRÉ — INDRE-ET-LOIRE

Mignardière

22 av des Aubepines, 37510
247733100 247733101
e-mail: info@mignardiere.com
web: www.mignardiere.com

A well-maintained site with a variety of sports facilities.

C&CC Report *The facilities on site and across the quiet road make La Mignardière ideal for younger families. It's a great base for discovering the Loire châteaux and all of the central Loire valley. Buses to Tours centre stop very close to the site entrance. The welcoming and friendly owners provide tourist information and advice on the riverside cycle routes of the Loire and Cher valleys.*

dir: *2.5km NE*

Open: 10 Apr-Sep **Site:** 3.5HEC **Facilities:** **Services:** **Leisure:** P **Off-site:**

BARROU — INDRE-ET-LOIRE

Camping Les Rioms

lieu dit Les Rioms, 37350
247945307
e-mail: campinglesrioms@orange.fr
web: www.lesrioms.com

Small, friendly site in an attractive region.

Open: Apr-Oct **Site:** 1.6HEC **Prices:** 10-12 Mobile home hire 195-510 **Facilities:** Wi-fi Play Area **Leisure:** P R **Off-site:**

BATZ-SUR-MER — LOIRE-ATLANTIQUE

Govelle

10 rue de la Govelle, 44740
240239163

Direct access to the sea. Supervised beach and sea-fishing nearby.

dir: *On D45 between Le Pouliguen & Batz.*

Open: 20 Apr-Sep **Site:** 6.8HEC **Facilities:** **Services:** **Leisure:** S

BAULE, LA — LOIRE-ATLANTIQUE

Ajoncs d'Or

chemin du Rocher, 44500
240603329 240244437
e-mail: contact@ajoncs.com
web: www.ajoncs.com

A large wooded park with well-defined pitches, close to the beach.

dir: *Signed from entrance to town.*

Open: Apr-Sep **Site:** 6HEC **Facilities:** **Services:** **Leisure:** P **Off-site:** S

FRANCE

Site 6HEC (site size) grass sand stone little shade partly shaded mainly shaded bungalows for hire (static) caravans for hire tents for hire no dogs site fully accessible for wheelchairs
Prices amount quoted is per night, for 2 adults and car, plus tent or caravan. Mobile home hire is a weekly rate.

Bois d'Amour

av de Diane, 44500
☎ 0820 320751 🖷 473770506
e-mail: labaule@lesbalconsverts.com
web: www.lesbalconsverts.com
Site consists of two sections, one for caravans, one for tents, each with separate entrance.
dir: *On NE outskirts near railway.*
Open: Apr-Oct **Site:** 4HEC **Facilities:** **Services:** **Off-site:** P S

Camping l'Eden

13/15 rte de Ker Rivaud, 44500
☎ 240600323 🖷 240119425
e-mail: eden-caravaning@wanadoo.fr
web: www.campingeden.com
Pleasant rural surroundings with good sports and sanitary facilities. Kids' club in July and August.
dir: *1km NW via N171 exit La Baule-Escoublac.*
Open: 26 Mar-6 Nov **Site:** 5HEC **Prices:** 16-25 Mobile home hire 180-770 **Facilities:** Kids' Club Play Area **Services:** **Leisure:** P **Off-site:** S

Roseraie

20 av J-Sohier, 44500
☎ 240604666 🖷 240601184
e-mail: camping@laroserie.com
web: www.laroseraie.com
A well-planned site in wooded surroundings with good recreational facilities.
dir: *E of N171 towards bay.*
Open: Apr-Sep **Site:** 5HEC **Facilities:** **Services:** **Leisure:** P **Off-site:** S

BEYNAT CORRÈZE

Lac de Miel

19190
☎ 555855066 🖷 555855796
e-mail: info@camping-miel.com
web: www.camping-miel.com
A family site in a picturesque wooded setting close to the lake.
dir: *4km E on N121 Argentat road.*
Open: May-Sep **Site:** 42HEC **Facilities:** **Services:** **Leisure:** L P R

BOIS-DE-CENÉ VENDÉE

Bois Joli

2 r de Châteauneuf, 85710
☎ 251682005 🖷 251684640
e-mail: contact@camping-leboisjoli.com
web: www.camping-leboisjoli.com
C&CC Report *A traditional campers' and caravanners' site, with a warm welcome and good quality facilities. Tourers enjoy some very good-sized pitches and the recently rebuilt wash block is very good too. Le Bois Joli offers great value for money, and avoids the hustle and bustle of the coast, yet with the seaside not far away. Within easy reach too are Noirmoutier island, Challans and the beaches of St. Jean-de-Monts.*
dir: *From Nantes take A83, exit for Machecoul/Challans.*
Open: Apr-Sep **Site:** 5HEC **Prices:** 12.60-17.10 Mobile home hire 240-630 **Facilities:** Wi-fi (charged) Play Area **Services:** **Leisure:** P **Off-site:**

BONNAC-LA-CÔTE HAUTE-VIENNE

Château de Leychoisier

87270
☎ 555399343 🖷 555399343
e-mail: contact@leychoisier.com
web: www.leychoisier.com
A well-managed site of roomy pitches sloping gently towards woods.
dir: *1km S off A20, exit 27.*
GPS: 45.9330, 1.2900
Open: 15 Apr-20 Sep **Site:** 4HEC **Prices:** 26-29 **Facilities:** Wi-fi (charged) Play Area **Services:** **Leisure:** L P

BONNES VIENNE

CM

r de la Varenne, 86300
☎ 549564434 🖷 549564851
e-mail: camping_bonnes@hotmail.com
A quiet site with plenty of recreational facilities.
dir: *S beside River Vienne.*
Open: Jun-15 Sep **Site:** 1HEC **Facilities:** **Services:** **Leisure:** P R **Off-site:** L

BONNY-SUR-LOIRE LOIRET

Val

45420
☎ 238315771 🖷 238315771
Woodland site beside the Loire, near the town centre.
dir: *At junct of N7 & D965.*
Open: mid Apr-Sep **Site:** 0.8HEC **Facilities:** **Services:** **Leisure:** R **Off-site:**

FRANCE

BOURGES CHER

CM Robinson

26 bd de l'Industrie, 18000
☎ 248201685 🖷 248503239
e-mail: camping@ville-bourges.fr
web: www.ville-bourges.fr/english/tourism/camping.php

In the town near Lake Auron.

dir: *Via A71, N144 or N76.*

Open: 15 Mar-15 Nov **Site:** 2.2HEC **Prices:** 12.30-14.60 **Facilities:** Wi-fi (charged) **Services:** **Off-site:** L P R

BOUSSAC-BOURG CREUSE

Château de Poinsouze

rte de La Châtre - BP 12, 23600
☎ 555650221 🖷 555658649
e-mail: info@camping-de.poinsouze.com
web: www.camping-de-poinsouze.com

A picturesque location in the grounds of a château with modern facilities. Dogs accepted except mid July to mid August.

C&CC Report *It's all about space, quality and welcome at Château de Poinsouze – vast, spacious grounds, high-quality facilities in the beautifully restored château outbuildings, open green spaces, caring, attentive owners and very large pitches. The area is an unspoilt rural idyll, with many châteaux, forests and rivers to enjoy, ideal for anglers, walkers and cyclists, plus many quiet country lanes and footpaths. Easily reached from the A71 motorway, leading onto the free A75 motorway to the south of France, it's a lovely site for long and short stays alike.*

dir: *2km N via D917.*

GPS: 46.3706, 2.2072

Open: Jun-11 Sep **Site:** 22HEC **Prices:** 19-27 Mobile home hire 190-890 **Facilities:** Wi-fi (charged) Kids' Club Play Area **Services:** **Leisure:** L P **Off-site:** R

BRACIEUX LOIR-ET-CHER

CM des Châteaux

11 r Roger Brun, 41250
☎ 254464184 🖷 254464121
e-mail: campingdebracieux@wanadoo.fr
web: www.campingdeschateaux.com

A pleasant shady park close to the town centre and convenient for visiting the châteaux of Chambord, Cheverny and Villesavin.

Open: 28 Mar-Nov **Site:** 8HEC **Facilities:** **Services:** **Leisure:** P R **Off-site:**

BRAIN-SUR-L'AUTHION MAINE-ET-LOIRE

CM Caroline

49800 ☎ 241804218
e-mail: info@campingduportcaroline.fr
web: www.campingduportcaroline.fr

A modern site in a pleasant wooded setting close to the river.

Open: All Year. **Site:** 3.2HEC **Facilities:** **Services:** **Leisure:** P **Off-site:** R

BREM-SUR-MER VENDÉE

Chaponnet

85470
☎ 251905556 🖷 251909167
e-mail: campingchaponnet@wanadoo.fr
web: www.le-chaponnet.com

Situated 1.3km from the sea, a well-equipped site with good leisure facilities and swimming pool area.

C&CC Report *A super site all season round, with a great pool area and a popular high season activities programme to keep you well entertained. Here you can enjoy the best of all worlds; countryside and beach, peace and quiet, next to a busy little village. The local market is great, as is the local produce – try the wine from the vineyards surrounding Brem-sur-Mer. The cycle path network continues to grow in the Vendée, so why not cycle to Les Sables or St-Gilles-Croix-de-Vie and beat the traffic?*

Open: Apr-Sep **Site:** 6.7HEC **Prices:** 17.50-26.90 Mobile home hire 240-699 **Facilities:** Wi-fi (charged) Kids' Club Play Area **Services:** **Leisure:** P **Off-site:** R S

BRESSUIRE DEUX-SÈVRES

Puy Rond

Cornet, 79300 ☎ 685603726
e-mail: puyrondcamping@gmail.com
web: www.puyrondcamping.com

Small family friendly site with local interests.

Open: May-Sep **Site:** 2.5HEC **Facilities:** **Leisure:** P **Off-site:** L R

BRÉTIGNOLLES-SUR-MER VENDÉE

Dunes

Plage des Dunes, 85470
☎ 251905532 🖷 251905485
e-mail: infos@campinglesdunes.fr
web: www.campinglesdunes.com

Direct access to the beach. All plots surrounded by hedges. Kids' club available in July and August.

dir: *2km S turn right off D38, 1km across dunes, 150m from beach.*

Open: Apr-11 Nov **Site:** 12HEC **Prices:** 20-36 Mobile home hire 260-910 **Facilities:** Kids' Club Play Area **Services:** **Leisure:** P **Off-site:** L S

FRANCE

Motine

4 r des Morinières, 85470
251900442
e-mail: lamotine@free.fr
web: www.lamotine.com

Pleasant site 350m from the town centre and 400m from the beach, with good facilities.

Open: Apr-Sep **Site:** 1.8HEC **Prices:** 21-25 Mobile home hire 290-600 **Facilities:** **Services:** **Leisure:** P **Off-site:** L R S

Trevilliere

The Camping and Caravanning Club The Friendly Club

rte de Bellevue, 85470
251900965 251339404
e-mail: contact@chadotel.com
web: www.chadotel.com

Friendly, family site with many leisure activities and entertainment.

C&CC Report *This site offers the great combination of easy access to coast, countryside and village life. Tourers are well catered for and the upper part of the site has popular, sunny, good-sized pitches. High season life centres around the pool, slide and bar; the new covered pool is the perfect addition to the site. The bustling resort of Brétignolles, its shops, weekly market and services are all an easy stroll away. A bike ride or short drive takes you to the glorious beaches of Brétignolles.*

dir: *0.9km from town centre. 2km from beach.*

GPS: 46.6363, -1.8584

Open: Apr-Sep **Site:** 3.5HEC **Prices:** 9-24 Mobile home hire 150-799 **Facilities:** Wi-fi (charged) **Services:** **Leisure:** P **Off-site:** R S

Vagues

20 bd du Centre, 85470
251901948 240024988
e-mail: lesvagues@free.fr
web: www.campinglesvagues.fr

A family site in a delightful rural setting on the Côte de Lumière. Near shops and ocean.

dir: *N on D38 towards St-Gilles-Croix-de-Vie.*

Open: Apr-Sep **Site:** 5HEC **Prices:** 15-25 Mobile home hire 240-740 **Facilities:** Wi-fi Kids' Club Play Area **Services:** **Leisure:** P **Off-site:** L R S

BRISSAC-QUINCÉ — MAINE-ET-LOIRE

L'Étang

The Camping and Caravanning Club The Friendly Club

rte de St Mathurin, 49320
241917061 241917265
e-mail: info@campingetang.com
web: www.campingetang.com

A lakeside site in the heart of the Anjou countryside with good recreational facilities.

C&CC Report *A spacious and top quality site, in a peaceful setting to which the owning charity continue to add facilities. The luxury of its own vineyard, serving and selling its wines on site, and a fishing lake makes L'Etang an ideal place to unwind. Children are equally spoilt for choice owing to the two swimming pools on site and adjacent play park. The heritage and cuisine of the region are a delight to discover.*

dir: *D748 towards Poitiers.*

GPS: 47.3595, -0.4339

Open: 15 May-11 Sep **Site:** 6HEC **Prices:** 16-28 Mobile home hire 270-640 **Facilities:** Wi-fi (charged) Kids' Club Play Area **Services:** **Leisure:** P R **Off-site:** L

CANDÉ-SUR-BEUVRON — LOIR-ET-CHER

Grande Tortue

3 rte de Pontlevoy, 41120
254441520 254441945
e-mail: grandetortue@wanadoo.fr
web: www.la-grande-tortue.com

A family site in a peaceful wooded setting. Kids' club available in July and August.

dir: *A10 exit 17, cross Loire river, turn right just after bridge. Cande on D751.*

GPS: 47.4900, 1.2583

Open: 2 Apr-25 Sep **Site:** 5.8HEC **Prices:** 17-29 Mobile home hire 273-756 **Facilities:** Wi-fi (charged) Kids' Club Play Area **Services:** **Leisure:** P **Off-site:** R

CHALARD, LE — HAUTE-VIENNE

Vigères

Les Vigères, 87500
555093722 555099339
e-mail: lesvigeres@aol.com
web: www.lesvigeres.com

Generally level site in peaceful surroundings in an elevated position with fine views.

dir: *On D901 between Châlus & Le Chalard.*

GPS: 45.555, 1.1186

Open: All Year. **Site:** 20HEC **Prices:** 10.50-15.25 Mobile home hire 250-450 **Facilities:** Wi-fi (charged) Play Area **Services:** **Leisure:** L P **Off-site:** R

FRANCE

CHALONNES-SUR-LOIRE — MAINE-ET-LOIRE

CM Candais

rte de Rochefort, 49290
☎ 241780227 🖷 241741481
e-mail: camping@chalonnes-sur-loire.fr
On the banks of the River Loire at its confluence with the River Louet.
dir: *NE off D751 towards Rochefort.*
Open: 15 May-Sep **Site:** 3HEC **Facilities:** **Services:** **Off-site:** P

CHAPELLE HERMIER, LA — VENDÉE

Pin Parasol

The Camping and Caravanning Club — The Friendly Club

Lac du Jaunay, Chateaulong, 85220
☎ 251346472 🖷 251346462
e-mail: contact@campingpinparasol.fr
web: www.campingpinparasol.fr
Set in the heart of the Vendée on the shore of Lac du Jaunay with modern facilities.
C&CC Report *A truly excellent family-owned site, built and run to highest standards. Provides a superb location, away from coastal hassle, with the great indoor pool a real plus all season round. The relaxed atmosphere is perfect for couples, young families, anglers and canoeists alike.*
dir: *Between D6 & D12.*
Open: 25 Apr-25 Sep **Site:** 12HEC **Prices:** 12.50-29.50 Mobile home hire 200-772 **Facilities:** Wi-fi (charged) Kids' Club Play Area **Services:** **Leisure:** P **Off-site:** S

CHARTRES — EURE-ET-LOIR

CM des Bords de l'Eure

9 r de Launay, 28000
☎ 237287943 🖷 237282943
e-mail: camping-roussel-chartres@wanadoo.fr
web: www.auxbordsdeleure.com
Wooded surroundings beside the river.
dir: *Signed towards Orléans.*
Open: 10 Apr-10 Nov **Site:** 3.86HEC **Facilities:** **Services:** **Off-site:** P R

CHARTRE-SUR-LE-LOIR, LA — SARTHE

Vieux Moulin

chemin des Bergivaux, 72340
☎ 243444118 🖷 243442406
e-mail: camping@lachartre.com
web: www.le-vieux-moulin.fr
Open: Apr-Sep **Site:** 2.4HEC **Facilities:** **Services:** **Leisure:** P R **Off-site:** L P

CHARTRIER-FERRIÈRE — CORRÈZE

Magaudie

La Magaudie Ouest, 19600
☎ 555852606
e-mail: camping@lamagaudie.com
web: www.lamagaudie.com
A peaceful site covering 8 hectares, half consisting of forest, 3km from Lac du Causse with beaches and water sports. The 18th-century buildings on the site have been converted to hygenic sanitary facilities.
dir: *A20 exit 53, N20 for Cahors, at rdbt onto D19 for Chasteaux, D154 left for Chartrier & Nadaillac, 3rd right for La Magaudie, 1st right, site on left.*
Open: All Year. **Site:** 8HEC **Prices:** 11.90-15.40 **Facilities:** Play Area **Services:** **Leisure:** P

CHASSENEUIL-SUR-BONNIEURE — CHARENTE

CM Les Charmilles

r des Écoles, 16260
☎ 545395536 🖷 545225245
e-mail: mairie.chasseneuil@wanadoo.fr
web: www.chasseneuil-sur-bonnieure.fr
dir: *W of town via D27, beside River Bonnieure.*
Open: Jun-Sep **Site:** 1.5HEC **Facilities:** **Services:** **Leisure:** R **Off-site:** P

CHÂTELAILLON-PLAGE — CHARENTE-MARITIME

Deux Plages

17340
☎ 546562753 🖷 546435118
e-mail: reception@2plages.com
web: www.2plages.com
Pleasant wooded surroundings 200m from the beach.
Open: May-Sep **Site:** 4.5HEC **Facilities:** **Services:** **Leisure:** P **Off-site:** L S

CHÂTELLERAULT — VIENNE

Relais du Miel

rte d'Antran, 86100
☎ 549020627
e-mail: camping@lerelaisdumiel.com
web: www.lerelaisdumiel.com
Set in the grounds of Château de Valette, beside the River Vienne.
dir: *A10 exit 26 Châtellerault Nord.*
Open: 15 Jun-Aug **Site:** 7HEC **Facilities:** **Services:** **Leisure:** P R **Off-site:**

FRANCE

CHÂTRES-SUR-CHER LOIR-ET-CHER

CM des Saules

41320
254980455

Close to medieval city with opportunities to fish in local canals or visit nearby châteaux.

dir: *On N76 near bridge.*

Open: May-Aug **Site:** 2HEC **Facilities:**
Services: **Off-site:** R

CHAUFFOUR-SUR-VELL CORRÈZE

Feneyrolles

19500
0555 840958
e-mail: contact@camping-feneyrolles.com
web: www.camping-feneyrolles.com

A quiet wooded location with good facilities. Ideal for exploring the Dordogne Valley and surrounding area.

dir: *2.2km E.*

Open: 15 May-Sep **Site:** 3.5HEC **Prices:** 17.50 Mobile home hire 325-610 **Facilities:** Wi-fi
Services: **Leisure:** P

CHEF-BOUTONNE DEUX-SÈVRES

Moulin

The Camping and Caravanning Club The Friendly Club

Treneuillet, 1 rte de Niort, 79110
549297346 549297346
e-mail: info@campingchef.com
web: www.campingchef.com

Small, secluded family site, child and dog friendly. Located in a rural setting but within walking distance of local town.

C&CC Report *If your ideal is a friendly welcome from a family of British owners, on an intimate site on the edge of a market town, and in picturesque French countryside with lovely walks, then Camping Le Moulin is for you. With its popular restaurant and the nearby shops in Chef-Boutonne, you will be well looked-after at any time of the year. Make sure you find time to visit the Château de Javarzay in Chef-Boutonne, and remember that Niort, lovely La Rochelle, the brandy cellars of Cognac, plus Poitiers and Futuroscope all offer rewarding visits.*

dir: *1km NE via D740.*

Open: All Year. **Site:** 2.5HEC **Prices:** 15.90-18.50 Mobile home hire 180-460 **Facilities:** Play Area
Services: **Leisure:** P R
Off-site:

CHEMILLÉ-SUR-INDROIS INDRE-ET-LOIRE

Les Coteaux du Lac

Base de Loisirs, 37460
247927783
e-mail: lescoteauxdulac@wanadoo.fr
web: www.lescoteauxdulac.com

In peaceful countryside setting with leisure facilities including table-tennis and mountain bike rental.

Open: 26 Mar-15 Oct **Site:** **Prices:** 13.90-19
Facilities: Wi-fi Kids' Club Play Area
Services: **Leisure:** L P **Off-site:**

CHENONCEAUX INDRE-ET-LOIRE

Moulin Fort

37150
247238622 247238093
e-mail: lemoulinfort@wanadoo.fr
web: www.lemoulinfort.com

A peaceful site on the banks of the River Cher with well-maintained facilities. Booking recommended in high season.

dir: *2km SE*

GPS: 47.3272, 1.0883

Open: Apr-Sep **Site:** 3HEC **Prices:** 14-22 **Facilities:** Wi-fi (charged) **Services:**
Leisure: P R

CHÉVERNY LOIR-ET-CHER

Les Saules

The Camping and Caravanning Club The Friendly Club

rte de Contres, 41700
254799001 254792834
e-mail: contact@camping-cheverny.com
web: www.camping-cheverny.com

Set in the heart of the Val de Loire, bordered by a golf course and the Cheverny forest. Kids' club available July to 20 August.

C&CC Report *A very friendly, family-run site, excellent for adults and young families who want to visit the many châteaux and villages of the area. This is especially true for those who like to get around by bike; after the welcoming owners, Les Saules' biggest plus is its access to a huge network of cycle paths linking up some of the region's greatest châteaux, via some of its loveliest woodland.*

dir: *1.5km from town on D102 towards Contres.*

GPS: 47.4786, 1.4522

Open: Apr-Sep **Site:** 8HEC **Prices:** 16-26.50
Facilities: Wi-fi Kids' Club Play Area
Services: **Leisure:** P

FRANCE

CLOYES-SUR-LE-LOIR — EURE-ET-LOIR

Val Fleuri

rte de Montigny, 28220
☎ 237985053 🖹 237983384
e-mail: info@val-fleuri.fr
web: www.val-fleuri.fr

On the bank of the River Loir. Extensive leisure facilities. Separate section for teenagers.

dir: *N10 S from Châteaudun towards Cloyes, right onto Montigny-le-Gamelon road.*

Open: 15 Mar-15 Nov **Site:** 6HEC **Prices:** 15.50-21.15 Mobile home hire 295-679 **Facilities:** Wi-fi (charged) Play Area **Services:** **Leisure:** P R

COGNAC — CHARENTE

Camping de Cognac

rte de Ste-Sévère, bd de Chatenay, 16100
☎ 545321332 🖹 545321582
e-mail: infos@campingdecognac.com
web: www.campingdecognac.com

Wooded surroundings beside the River Charente with modern facilities.

dir: *2km N on D24.*

Open: May-Sep **Site:** 2HEC **Prices:** 13-20 Mobile home hire 275-490 **Facilities:** Wi-fi Play Area **Services:** **Leisure:** P R **Off-site:** P R

CONCOURSON-SUR-LAYON — MAINE-ET-LOIRE

Vallée des Vignes

The Camping and Caravanning Club — The Friendly Club

La Croix Patron, 49700
☎ 241598635 🖹 241590983
e-mail: campingvdv@wanadoo.fr
web: www.campingvdv.com

Family run site with leisure facilities including mini golf, table tennis and boules.

C&CC Report *Vallée des Vignes is a superbly maintained and spacious site with a fine array of facilities that have been developed to complement its rural surroundings. An ideal base for Saumur, Angers and the local wine villages, as well as Doué's rose gardens and World Wildlife Fund recognised zoo. The Nicols organise friendly barbecue evenings, trips to local vineyards, wine appreciation lessons and provide cycle maps of the local lanes and tracks. Le Puy du Fou is not far away either.*

dir: *Located just outside Concourson on D960 direction Cholet. Signposted.*

Open: Apr-Sep **Site:** 3.5HEC **Prices:** 16.50-24 Mobile home hire 300-650 **Facilities:** **Services:** **Leisure:** P **Off-site:** R

CONDAT SUR GANAVEIX — CORRÈZE

Moulin de la Geneste

Moulin de la Geneste, 19140
☎ 555989008 🖹 555989008
e-mail: la.geneste@lineone.net
web: www.lageneste.net

Undulating land with three small lakes and a small trout river. Part of the land and small wood have been left as a nature reserve with an abundance of wildlife.

dir: *From Limoges take A20 exit 44 Uzerche travelling S. Follow signs for Condat sur Ganaveix.*

Open: May-15 Sep **Site:** 4HEC **Facilities:** **Services:** **Off-site:**

CONTRES — LOIR-ET-CHER

Charmoise

Sassay, 41700
☎ 254795515 🖹 254795515

On a level meadow with good facilities.

dir: *N956.*

Open: Apr-Oct **Site:** 1HEC **Prices:** 8-10 Mobile home hire 150 **Facilities:** Play Area **Services:** **Off-site:** P R

CORRÈZE — CORRÈZE

Au Bois de Calais

r René Cassin, 19800
☎ 555262627
e-mail: auboisdecalais@orange.fr
web: www.auboisdecalais.com

Quiet, relaxing site in an attractive national park location close to a lake and river.

Open: Apr-Oct **Site:** 5HEC **Facilities:** **Services:** **Leisure:** P **Off-site:** L R

COUHÉ-VERAC — VIENNE

Peupliers

86700
☎ 549592116 🖹 549379209
e-mail: info@lespeupliers.fr
web: www.lespeupliers.fr

A family site in a forest beside the river.

dir: *N of village on N10 Poitiers road.*

GPS: 46.3118, 0.1800

Open: 2 May-Sep **Site:** 16HEC **Prices:** 17.25-26.50 Mobile home hire 175-1015 **Facilities:** Wi-fi (charged) Kids' Club Play Area **Services:** **Leisure:** P R **Off-site:**

see advert on opposite page

Site 6HEC (site size) grass sand stone little shade partly shaded mainly shaded bungalows for hire (static) caravans for hire tents for hire no dogs site fully accessible for wheelchairs
Prices amount quoted is per night, for 2 adults and car, plus tent or caravan. Mobile home hire is a weekly rate.

COURÇON-D'AUNIS CHARENTE-MARITIME

Garenne

21 r du Stade, 17170
546016050 546016359
e-mail: mairie.courcon@mairie17.com
Open: Jul-Aug **Site:** **Facilities:** **Services:**
Off-site: P

COUTURES MAINE-ET-LOIRE

Parc de Montsabert

Montsabert, 49320
241579163 241579002
e-mail: camping@parcdemontsabert.com
web: www.parcdemontsabert.com

The site is situated in the old Castle Montsabert Park (adjacent to campground). Quiet with a natural setting, the pitches are spacious and well separated by hedges. Good facilities and amenities.

dir: *Off D751 along River Loire between Angers and Saumur.*

Open: 9 Apr-11 Sep **Site:** 10HEC **Prices:** 15-29 Mobile home hire 273-735 **Facilities:** Wi-fi (charged) Kids' Club Play Area **Services:** **Leisure:** P
Off-site:

CROISIC, LE LOIRE-ATLANTIQUE

Océan

44490
240230769 240157063
e-mail: info@camping-ocean.com
web: www.camping-ocean.com

A quiet, well-appointed site 150m from the sea. In the heart of the peninsula of Le Croisic close to the town centre and harbour.

dir: *1.5km NW via D45.*

Open: Apr-Sep **Site:** 7.5HEC **Prices:** 17-42 Mobile home hire 350-1250 **Facilities:** Wi-fi Kids' Club Play Area **Services:** **Leisure:** P
Off-site: S

see advert on page 160

DISSAY VIENNE

CM du Parc

r du Parc, 86130
549628429 549625872
e-mail: accueil@dissay.fr
web: www.dissay.fr

Quiet, shady site at the foot of a 15th-century castle, close to Futuroscope, the lake of St-Cyr and the forest of Moulière.

GPS: 46.6983, 0.4258

Open: 14 Jun-Aug **Site:** 1.4HEC **Prices:** 9.90 **Facilities:** Play Area **Services:** **Off-site:** L P R

DURTAL MAINE-ET-LOIRE

International

9 r du Camping, 49430
241763180
e-mail: contact@camping-durtal.fr
web: www.camping-durtal.fr

A pleasant site beside the River Loire.

dir: *Near town centre, via N23 or A11.*

Open: 21 Mar-27 Sep **Site:** 3HEC **Facilities:** **Services:** **Off-site:** P

EYMOUTHIERS CHARENTE

Gorges du Chambon

16220
545707170 545708002
e-mail: info@gorgesduchambon.fr
web: www.gorgesduchambon.fr

A beautiful location on a wooded hilltop. Kids' club available in high season.

dir: *3km N via D163.*

Open: 23 Apr-17 Sep **Site:** 7HEC **Prices:** 18.40-31.90 Mobile home hire 266-567 **Facilities:** Kids' Club Play Area **Services:**
Leisure: P R

FRESNAY-SUR-SARTHE SARTHE

CM Sans Souci

r de Haut Ary, Allée André Chevalier, 72130
243973287 243337572
e-mail: camping-fresnay@wanadoo.fr
web: www.fresnaysursarthe.fr/camping

A family site with good facilities and direct access to the river.

dir: *1km SE on D310.*

Open: Apr-Sep **Site:** 2HEC **Facilities:** Play Area **Services:** **Leisure:** P R
Off-site:

FRANCE

FRIAUDOUR — HAUTE-VIENNE

Freaudour

87250
☎ 555765722 555712393
e-mail: lacsaintpardoux@wanadoo.fr
web: www.lac-saint-pardoux.com
A well-equipped site beside Lac de St-Pardoux.
dir: *A20 exit 25.*
Open: Jun-12 Sep **Site:** 3.5HEC
Facilities: **Services:**
Leisure: L P **Off-site:**

FROSSAY — LOIRE-ATLANTIQUE

Migron

Le Square de la Chaussée, 44320
☎ 240397272
A pleasant location beside the canal.
Open: Jul-Sep **Site:** 2.5HEC **Facilities:**
Services: **Leisure:** R **Off-site:**

GENNES — MAINE-ET-LOIRE

Au Bord de Loire

av des Cadets de Saumur, 49350
☎ 241380467 241380712
e-mail: auborddeloire@free.fr
web: www.camping-auborddeloire.com
Peaceful location on the river.
dir: *Via D952-D751.*
GPS: 47.3425, -0.2317
Open: May-Sep **Site:** 3HEC **Prices:** 9.60
Facilities: Wi-fi Play Area **Services:**
Leisure: R **Off-site:** L P

GIEN — LOIRET

Domaine Les Bois du Bardelet

rte de Bourges, Poilly, 45500
☎ 238674739 238382716
e-mail: contact@bardelet.com
web: www.bardelet.com
A family site with a variety of sports facilities.
C&CC Report *A picturesque setting, with lots to do both on and off site. There's plenty to occupy young families and the site's wide appeal also means it's popular with retired couples. In low season there's the benefit of heated indoor and outdoor pools, as well as the fitness room. An ideal base for exploring the countryside south of Paris and the eastern Loire region, but perfect for just relaxing on site too.*
dir: *D940 SW of Gien.*
GPS: 47.6415, 2.6153
Open: Apr-Sep **Site:** 18HEC **Prices:** 19.20-44
Mobile home hire 291-924 **Facilities:** Wi-fi (charged) Kids' Club Play Area **Services:**
Leisure: P

GUÉMENÉ-PENFAO — LOIRE-ATLANTIQUE

Hermitage

36 av du Paradis, 44290
☎ 240792348 240792348
e-mail: camping.hermitage@wanadoo.fr
web: www.campinglhermitage.com
A beautiful setting overlooking the Don valley with modern facilities.
dir: *1.5km E on rte de Châteaubriant.*
Open: Apr-Oct **Site:** 2.5HEC **Prices:** 15.50
Facilities: Kids' Club **Services:**
Leisure: P **Off-site:** R

GUÉRANDE — LOIRE-ATLANTIQUE

Domaine de Lévéno

rte de l'Étang de Sandun, 44350
☎ 240247930 240620123
e-mail: domaine.leveno@wanadoo.fr
web: www.camping-leveno.com
A pleasant location with good facilities.
dir: *3km E via rte de Sandun.*
Open: 4 Apr-Sep **Site:** 12HEC **Facilities:**
Services: **Leisure:** P

see advert on page 160

HÉRIC LOIRE-ATLANTIQUE

Pindière

44810
☎ 240576541 🖹 228022543
e-mail: contact@camping.la.pindiere.com
web: www.camping-la-pindiere.com

A relaxing family site on a level meadow with a wide range of good facilities.

dir: *1km from town on D16.*

Open: All Year. **Site:** 3HEC **Prices:** 12.90-14 Mobile home hire 225-435 **Facilities:** Play Area **Services:** **Leisure:** P **Off-site:** L R

HOUMEAU, L' CHARENTE-MARITIME

Au Petit Port de l'Houmeau

17137
☎ 546509082 🖹 546500133
e-mail: info@aupetitport.com
web: www.aupetitport.com

Quiet site with grassed and shaded pitches. 800m to the sea.

dir: *NE via D106.*

Open: Apr-Sep **Site:** 2HEC **Prices:** 15-19 Mobile home hire 310-730 **Facilities:** Wi-fi Play Area **Services:** **Off-site:** S

ILE DE NORMOUTIER, BOIS DE LA CHAISE

Indigo Noirmoutier

The Camping and Caravanning Club The Friendly Club

Bois de la Chaise, 23 Allée des Sableaux, 85330
☎ 251390624 🖹 251359763
e-mail: noirmoutier@camping-indigo.com
web: www.camping-indigo.com

A well equipped site in a pine wood close to the beach. 1 dog per pitch.

C&CC Report *For an authentic taste of France and a touch of 'retro' back-to-nature camping, Indigo Noirmoutier is a breath of fresh sea air. Approach the island of Noirmoutier via the Passage du Gois (only at low tide) or on the toll-free bridge. Famous for farming sea salt and oysters, the island has a distinctly separate character from the mainland. Look out for the oyster farmers at work on the beach by the site. The town of Noirmoutier-en-l'Ile, with its château and wide choice of seafood restaurants, is just a short drive away too.*

dir: *From town centre towards Plage des Sableaux.*

Open: Apr-2 Oct **Site:** 12HEC **Prices:** 13.30-19.90 **Facilities:** Play Area **Services:** **Leisure:** S **Off-site:** P

ILE DE NORMOUTIER, GUERINIERE, LA

Caravan'Ile

BP N4, 85680
☎ 251395029 🖹 251358685
e-mail: contact@caravanile.com
web: www.caravanile.com

Located near fine sand beaches. Swimming pool with aquatic toboggan.

Open: Mar-15 Nov **Site:** 9HEC **Facilities:** **Services:** **Leisure:** P S

ILE DE OLÉRON, BOYARDVILLE

Camping Signol

17190
☎ 546470122 🖹 546472346
e-mail: contact@signol.com
web: www.camp-atlantique.com

Attractive surroundings in a pine forest, close to the village centre and 0.8km from the beach. Spacious pitches and a wide range of leisure facilities.

dir: *D126 W from town by fuel station, signed for 0.6km.*

Open: 2 Apr-24 Sep **Site:** 8HEC **Prices:** 23-35 Mobile home hire 190-1250 **Facilities:** Kids' Club Play Area **Services:** **Leisure:** P **Off-site:** S

ILE D'OLÉRON, CHÂTEAU-D'OLÉRON, LE

Airotel d'Oléron

Domaine de Montreavail, 17480
☎ 546476182 🖹 546477967
e-mail: info@camping-airotel-oleron.com
web: www.camping-airotel-oleron.com

A peaceful, parklike setting 1km from the beach and the town centre.

dir: *Signed from town centre.*

Open: Mar-1 Nov **Site:** 4HEC **Facilities:** **Services:** **Leisure:** L P S

Brande

rte des Huîtres, 17480
☎ 546476237 🖹 546477170
e-mail: info@camping-labrande.com
web: www.camping-labrande.co.uk

A family site with good facilities in beautiful surroundings.

dir: *2.5km NW, 250m from sea.*

Open: 20 Mar-14 Nov **Site:** 5.5HEC **Facilities:** **Services:** **Leisure:** P **Off-site:** S

FRANCE

Facilities shop shower electric points for razors electric points for caravans parking by tents permitted compulsory separate car park **Services** café/restaurant bar Camping Gaz International gas other than Camping Gaz first aid facilities laundry **Leisure** swimming L-Lake P-Pool R-River S-Sea **Off-site** All facilities within 5km

ILE D'OLÉRON, DOLUS-D'OLÉRON

Ostréa

rte des Huitres, 17550
546476236 546752001
e-mail: camping.ostrea@wanadoo.fr
web: www.camping-ostrea.com
A well-equipped site in wooded surroundings close to the beach.
dir: *3.5km NE.*
Open: Apr-Sep **Site:** 2HEC **Facilities:** **Services:** **Leisure:** P S

ILE D'OLÉRON, ST-GEORGES-D'OLÉRON

Domaine d'Oléron

The Camping and Caravanning Club — The Friendly Club

La Jousselinière, 17190
546765497 251339404
e-mail: info@chadotel.com
web: www.chadotel.com
Pitches shaded by oak trees, site located 2.5km from the beach.
C&CC Report *The toll-free bridge to the Ile d'Oléron allows you to try island life yet remain within easy reach of the mainland, while nearly 100 miles of cycle tracks help you explore the island's lovely beaches, quiet villages, salt marshes and oyster parks. Try a boat trip around famous Fort Boyard, a visit to the world famous Zoo de la Palmyre or relax on the island's beautiful beaches.*
dir: *2km from centre of St Pierre d'Oléron.*
GPS: 45.9675, -1.3193
Open: Apr-Sep **Site:** 3HEC **Prices:** 9.40-24.90 Mobile home hire 280-850 **Facilities:** Wi-fi (charged) Play Area **Services:** **Leisure:** P **Off-site:** S

Gros Joncs

17190
546765229 546766774
e-mail: info@les-gros-joncs.fr
web: www.camping-les-gros-joncs.com
Quiet location on undulating land in lovely pine woodland. Spa facilities are available all year.
Open: Apr-Oct **Site:** 5.15HEC **Prices:** 15.70-43.70 **Facilities:** Wi-fi (charged) Kids' Club Play Area **Services:** **Leisure:** P S **Off-site:**

Signol

av de Albatros, Boyardville, 17190
546470122 546472346
e-mail: contact@signol.com
web: www.signol.com
Situated among pine and oak trees, 0.8km from a sandy beach.
Open: Apr-Sep **Site:** 8HEC **Facilities:** **Services:** **Leisure:** P **Off-site:** S

Suroît

rte Touristique Côte Ouest, l'Ileau, 17190
546470725 546750424
e-mail: info@camping-lesuroit.com
web: www.camping-lesuroit.com
Level ground sheltered by dunes with fine modern facilities.
dir: *5km SW of town.*
Open: Apr-Sep **Site:** 5HEC **Facilities:** **Services:** **Leisure:** P S **Off-site:**

ILE D'OLÉRON, ST-PIERRE-D'OLÉRON

Aqua Trois Masses

Le Marais Doux, 17310
546472396 546751554
e-mail: accueil@campingaqua3masses.com
web: www.campingaqua3masses.com
A well-equipped site in a picturesque location 2.5km from the beach.
Open: Apr-Sep **Site:** 3HEC **Facilities:** Wi-fi **Services:** **Leisure:** P **Off-site:** S

ILE DE RÉ, ARS-EN-RÉ

Cormoran

rte de Radia, 17590
546294604 546292936
e-mail: info@cormoran.com
web: www.cormoran.com
Situated on the edge of a forest 0.5km from village of Ars.
Open: 4 Apr-26 Sep **Site:** 3HEC **Facilities:** **Services:** **Leisure:** P **Off-site:** S

ILE DE RÉ, BOIS-PLAGE-EN-RÉ, LE

Sunêlia Interlude

8 rte de Gros Jonc, 17580
546091822 546092338
e-mail: infos@interlude.fr
web: www.interlude.fr
A pleasant wooded location 50m from the beach. The site has a fitness centre and can arrange guided tours of the area. Kids' club available during school holidays in April, July and August.
Open: 9 Apr-25 Sep **Site:** 7.5HEC **Prices:** 23-46 **Facilities:** Wi-fi (charged) Kids' Club Play Area **Services:** **Leisure:** P **Off-site:** S

Site 6HEC (site size) grass sand stone little shade partly shaded mainly shaded bungalows for hire (static) caravans for hire tents for hire no dogs site fully accessible for wheelchairs
Prices amount quoted is per night, for 2 adults and car, plus tent or caravan. Mobile home hire is a weekly rate.

ILE DE RÉ, COUARDE-SUR-MER, LA

Océan

50 rte d'Ars, 17670
546298770 546299213
e-mail: info@campingocean.com
web: www.campingocean.com
A fine position facing the sea with modern facilities.
dir: *3km NW on N735.*
Open: 16 Apr-24 Sep **Site:** 9HEC
Prices: 19.20-42.65 Mobile home hire 315-882 **Facilities:** Wi-fi (charged) Kids' Club Play Area **Services:** **Leisure:** P **Off-site:** S

Tour des Prises

rte d'Ars, B.P. 27, 17670
546298482 546298899
e-mail: camping@lesprises.com
web: www.lesprises.com
Located in the heart of the island, next to a wood, in a peaceful and quiet location. The trees dotted throughout the site offer many shady areas.
Open: 23 Mar-Sep **Site:** 2.5HEC **Facilities:** Wi-fi Play Area **Services:** **Leisure:** P **Off-site:** S

ILE DE RÉ, FLOTTE, LA

Camping la Grainetiere

rte de St Martin de Ré, D735, 17630
546096886 546095313
e-mail: la-grainetiere@orange.fr
web: www.la-grainetiere.com
1.5km from village centre, a wooded, family friendly site with a wide range of leisure activites including a games room and cycle hire.
Open: 2 Apr-Sep **Site:** 2.7HEC **Prices:** 15-28 Mobile home hire 235-765 **Facilities:** Wi-fi (charged) Play Area **Services:** **Leisure:** P **Off-site:** S

Camping Les Peupliers

17630
546096235 546095976
e-mail: camping@les-peupliers.com
web: www.camp-atlantique.com
Situated in a large, wooded park 0.8km from the sea with good sports and entertainment facilities.
dir: *1.3km SE.*
Open: 2 Apr-24 Sep **Site:** 4.4HEC **Prices:** 21-34 Mobile home hire 250-870 **Facilities:** Wi-fi (charged) Kids' Club Play Area **Services:** **Leisure:** P **Off-site:** S

ILE DE RÉ, LOIX

Ilates

Le Petit Boucheau, rte du Grouin, 17111
546290543 546290679
e-mail: ilates@wanadoo.fr
web: www.camping-loix.com
dir: *E towards Pointe du Grouin, 0.5km from sea*
Open: 21 Mar-4 Oct **Site:** 4.5HEC **Facilities:** **Services:** **Leisure:** P **Off-site:** S

ILE DE RÉ, ST-MARTIN-DE-RÉ

CM

r du Rempart, 17410
546092196 546099418
e-mail: camping.stmartindere@wanadoo.fr
Pleasant wooded surroundings at the foot of the 17th-century ramparts.
dir: *N, beyond La Flotte.*
Open: 15 Feb-15 Nov **Site:** 4HEC **Facilities:** **Services:** **Off-site:** S

ILE DE RÉ, STE MARIE-DE-RÉ

Camping les Grenettes

rte du Bois Plage, 17740
546302247 546302464
e-mail: contact@hotel-les-grenettes.com
web: www.campinglesgrenettes.com
Located 200m from the sea and set in pine woodland.
Open: All Year. **Site:** 7HEC **Prices:** 15-32 Mobile home hire 230-825 **Facilities:** Wi-fi **Services:** **Leisure:** P S

JARD-SUR-MER VENDÉE

Écureuils

The Camping and Caravanning Club The Friendly Club

rte des Goffineaux, 85520
251334274 251339114
e-mail: ecureuils@franceloc.fr
web: www.camping-ecureuils.com
Quiet woodland terrain 450m from the sea, with large pitches surrounded by hedges.
C&CC Report *A top quality site with very helpful staff, ideal for those seeking a peaceful, shady site close to beaches. Excellent programme of activities and excursions plus an on-site bakery point, offering fresh hot bread throughout the day. Jard village, port and beach are just a short walk away down quiet lanes, but some might prefer to stay in the popular site bar, complete with Sky Sports.*
Open: Apr-Sep **Site:** 4.3HEC **Facilities:** **Services:** **Leisure:** P **Off-site:** S

FRANCE

Océano d'Or

58 r G-Clemenceau, 85520
☎ 251336508 📠 251339404
e-mail: contact@chadotel.com
web: www.chadotel.com

A well-maintained site 1km from the beach and 0.5km from the town centre. An aqua park and entertainment caters for all ages.

dir: *Via D19, 400m from city centre.*

Open: Apr-Sep **Site:** 8HEC **Prices:** 9.40-24.90 Mobile home hire 199-850 **Facilities:** Wi-fi (charged) Play Area **Services:** **Leisure:** P **Off-site:** S

see advert on this page

JAUNAY CLAN — VIENNE

Croix du Sud

rte de Neuville, 86130
☎ 549625814
e-mail: camping@la-croix-du-sud.fr
web: www.la-croix-du-sud.fr

Within easy reach of Futuroscope, the European Park of the Moving Image.

dir: *Via A10 & D62.*

Open: 29 Mar-13 Sep **Site:** 4HEC **Facilities:** **Services:** **Leisure:** P **Off-site:**

LAGORD — CHARENTE-MARITIME

CM Parc

r du Parc, 17140
☎ 546676154 📠 546006201
e-mail: mairie.lagord@wanadoo.fr

Pleasant municipal site within easy reach of the coast.

dir: *Via N137/D735.*

Open: Jun-15 Sep **Site:** **Prices:** 9-12.50 **Facilities:** **Services:** **Off-site:** P

LIMERAY — INDRE-ET-LOIRE

Jardin Botanique

9 r de la Rivière, 37530
☎ 247301350 📠 247301732
e-mail: info@camping-jardinbotanique.com
web: www.camping-jardinbotanique.com

Set in wooded shady parkland.

dir: *6km NE of Amboise on N152.*

Open: All Year. **Site:** 1.5HEC **Prices:** 12.20-15.50 Mobile home hire 180-480 **Facilities:** Wi-fi Play Area **Services:** **Leisure:** P **Off-site:** R

LINDOIS, LE — CHARENTE

Étang

16310
☎ 545650267 📠 545650896
web: www.campingdeletang.com

Well-shaded site with a natural lake, ideal for swimming and fishing with a small beach.

dir: *From Rochefoucauld D13 towards Montemboeuf.*

Open: Apr-1 Nov **Site:** 10HEC **Facilities:** **Services:** **Leisure:** L **Off-site:**

LION D'ANGERS, LE — MAINE-ET-LOIRE

CM Frénes

49220
☎ 241953156

A municipal site on the banks of the River Oudon, 300m from the town centre.

dir: *NE on N162.*

Open: Jun-Aug **Site:** 2HEC **Facilities:** **Leisure:** R **Off-site:** P

LONGEVILLE — VENDÉE

Brunelles

Le Bouil, 85560
☎ 251335075 🖹 251339821
e-mail: camping@les-brunelles.com
web: www.camp-atlantique.com

A well-appointed site in a wooded location 0.7km from the beach. Indoor and outdoor pools, entertainments, spa and fitness, are available.

dir: *On coast between Longeville & Jard-sur-Mer.*

Open: 2 Apr-24 Sep **Site:** 13HEC **Prices:** 21-31 Mobile home hire 230-1140 **Facilities:** Wi-fi (charged) Kids' Club Play Area **Services:** **Leisure:** P **Off-site:** S

Clos des Pins

Les Conches, 85560
☎ 251903169 🖹 251903068
e-mail: info@campingclosdespins.com
web: www.campingclosdespins.com

A family run site with good facilities, 250m from a sandy beach.

dir: *Between Longeville & La Tranche.*

Open: Apr-Sep **Site:** 1.6HEC **Facilities:** **Services:** **Leisure:** P **Off-site:** S

LUCHÉ-PRINGÉ — SARTHE

CM de la Chabotière

Place des Tilleuls, 72800
☎ 243451000 🖹 243451000
e-mail: contact@lachabotiere.com
web: www.lachabotiere.com

Site by a river just 100m from the village and a short drive from several Loire chateaux. Large marked sites on terraces above the river, and most cars are kept in a car park to ensure safe play areas for children. Kids' club available in July and August.

dir: *From Le Mans, RN23 then D13 at Clermont-Créans. In village, turn left before monument.*

GPS: 47.7022, 0.0734

Open: Apr-15 Oct **Site:** 2.5HEC **Prices:** 8.80-12.96 **Facilities:** Wi-fi Kids' Club Play Area **Services:** **Leisure:** P **Off-site:**

LUSIGNAN — VIENNE

CM Vauchiron

chemin de la Plage, Vauchiron, 86600
☎ 549433008 🖹 549436119
e-mail: lusignan@cg86.fr
web: www.lusignan.fr

Close to a medieval city, a quiet wooded location beside the River Vonne with good facilities.

dir: *0.5km NE on RD611.*

Open: 15 Apr-Sep **Site:** 4HEC **Prices:** 9.60 Mobile home hire 201-253 **Facilities:** **Services:** **Leisure:** R **Off-site:**

LUYNES — INDRE-ET-LOIRE

Granges

Les Granges, 37230
☎ 247557905 🖹 247409243
e-mail: reception@campinglesgranges.fr
web: www.campinglesgranges.fr

Quiet site close to the village. Ideal for visiting historical sites, fishing, and wine tasting

dir: *S via D49.*

Open: May-Sep **Site:** 1.82HEC **Facilities:** **Services:** **Leisure:** P **Off-site:** R

MACHÉ — VENDÉE

Val de Vie

5 r du Stade, 85190
☎ 251602102 🖹 251602102
e-mail: campingvaldevie@aol.com
web: www.camping-val-de-vie.com

Traditional, quiet, family owned campsite.

dir: *Off D948 Aizenay-Challans, follow blue signs in 300m from village centre.*

Open: May-Sep **Site:** 2.2HEC **Prices:** 15-19 Mobile home hire 170-550 **Facilities:** **Services:** **Leisure:** P **Off-site:** L

MAGNAC-BOURG — HAUTE-VIENNE

Écureuils

rte de Limoges, 87380
☎ 555008028 🖹 555004909
e-mail: mairie.magnac-bourg@wanadoo.fr

A grassy site close to the historic village.

dir: *25km S on N20.*

Open: Apr-Sep **Site:** 1.3HEC **Facilities:** **Services:** **Off-site:**

FRANCE

MANSIGNÉ SARTHE

Plage

rte du Plessis, 72510
☎ 243461417
e-mail: camping-mansigne@orange.fr
web: www.atouvert.com

A holiday complex set in extensive parkland around a 24-hectare lake with good recreational facilities.

dir: *On D13, 4km from D307.*

Open: Apr-Oct **Site:** 3.4HEC **Prices:** 9-11.50 Mobile home hire 200-420 **Facilities:** Kids' Club Play Area **Services:** **Leisure:** L P **Off-site:**

MARANS CHARENTE-MARITIME

CM Le Bois Dinot

rte de Nantes, 17230
☎ 546011051 546660265
e-mail: campingboisdinot.marans@wanadoo.fr
web: www.ville-marans.fr

Separate car park for arrivals after 23.00 hrs.

dir: *Via N137.*

Open: Apr-Sep **Site:** 6HEC **Prices:** 10.40-20.90 **Facilities:** Wi-fi (charged) Play Area **Services:** **Leisure:** P **Off-site:** R

MARÇON SARTHE

Lac des Varennes

rte du Port Gauthier, 72340
☎ 243441372 243445431
e-mail: lacdesvarennes@camp-in-ouest.com
web: www.camp-in-ouest.com

An attractive site bordering the lake in the heart of the Loire Valley, with spacious pitches and well-maintained installations.

Open: 4 Apr-30 Oct **Site:** 9HEC **Facilities:** **Services:** **Leisure:** L R **Off-site:**

MATHES, LES CHARENTE-MARITIME

Estanquet

17570
☎ 546224732 546225146
e-mail: contact@campinglestanquet.com
web: www.campinglestanquet.com

Close to sandy beaches, site with shade provided by pine trees. Leisure activities include a swimming pool complex.

Open: Apr-Sep **Site:** 8HEC **Facilities:** Wi-fi Kids' Club Play Area **Services:** **Leisure:** P **Off-site:** S

Orée du Bois

225 rte de la Bouverie, La Fouasse, 17570
☎ 546224243 546225476
e-mail: info@camping-oree-du-bois.fr
web: www.camping-oree-du-bois.fr

A family site in a pine and oak forest, 5 minutes from the beach.

dir: *3.5km NW.*

Open: 28 May-10 Sep **Site:** 6HEC **Prices:** 18-40 **Facilities:** Wi-fi (charged) Kids' Club Play Area **Services:** **Leisure:** P **Off-site:** S

Pinède

2103 rte de la Fouasse, 17570
☎ 546224513 546225021
e-mail: contact@campinglapinede.com
web: www.campinglapinede.com

A modern family site in a wooded area around the large Aquatic Park. Excellent sports facilities. Entertainment available in July and August.

dir: *3km NW.*

Open: Apr-Sep **Site:** 7HEC **Facilities:** **Services:** **Leisure:** P

MAYENNE MAYENNE

CM du Gue St Leonard

r St-Léonard, 53100
☎ 243045714 243000199
e-mail: campingsaintleonard@orange.fr
web: www.paysdemayenne-tourisme.fr

Situated close to Mayenne town centre, on the banks of the river, the site offers attractive, shady grounds. Swimming pool available during July and August.

dir: *0.8km from town centre near N12.*

Open: 15 Mar-Sep **Site:** 1.8HEC **Facilities:** Wi-fi Play Area **Services:** **Leisure:** P **Off-site:**

MEMBROLLE-SUR-CHOISILLE, LA INDRE-ET-LOIRE

CM

rte de Fondettes, 37390
☎ 247412040
e-mail: mairie@ville-la-membrolle37.fr

On level meadow in sports ground beside River Choisille.

dir: *N on N138 Le Mans road.*

Open: May-Sep **Site:** 1.5HEC **Facilities:** **Services:** **Leisure:** R **Off-site:** L

FRANCE

Site 6HEC (site size) grass sand stone little shade partly shaded mainly shaded bungalows for hire (static) caravans for hire tents for hire no dogs site fully accessible for wheelchairs
Prices amount quoted is per night, for 2 adults and car, plus tent or caravan. Mobile home hire is a weekly rate.

MERVENT VENDÉE

Chêne Tord

34 chemin du Chêne Tord, 85200
251002063 251002063
e-mail: contact@camping-mervent.fr
web: www.camping-mervent.fr

A well-appointed site 200m from a large artificial lake in the heart of the Mervent forest.

dir: *Via D99 - autoroute.*

Open: Apr-Nov **Site:** 4HEC **Facilities:** Wi-fi Play Area **Services:** **Off-site:** L R

MESLAND LOIR-ET-CHER

Parc du Val de Loire

rte de Fleuray, 41150
254702718 254702171
e-mail: parcduvaldeloire@wanadoo.fr
web: www.parcduvaldeloire.com

A sheltered position among Touraine vineyards with good recreational facilities.

dir: *1.5km W between A10 & N152.*

Open: 8 Apr-11 Sep **Site:** 13.6HEC **Prices:** 15-34 Mobile home hire 250-500 **Facilities:** Wi-fi Kids' Club Play Area **Services:** **Leisure:** P

MESQUER LOIRE-ATLANTIQUE

Château de Petit Bois

44420
240426877 240426558
e-mail: info@campingdupetitbois.com
web: www.campingdupetitbois.com

Set in the extensive grounds of an 18th-century château with shaded, well-defined pitches.

Open: Apr-Sep **Site:** 10HEC **Facilities:** **Services:** **Leisure:** P **Off-site:** S

Praderoi

14 allée des Barges, Quimiac, 44420
240426672 240426672
e-mail: camping.praderoi@wanadoo.fr
web: mtger.debonne.pagesperso-orange.fr

On level ground 90m from Lanseria beach, 350m from shopping centre.

dir: *From Guérande on D774 onto D52.*

Open: 15 Jun-15 Sep **Site:** 0.5HEC **Prices:** 15-19.80 Mobile home hire 220-480 **Facilities:** Wi-fi Play Area **Services:** **Off-site:** S

CAMPING ★★★★ GRAND CONFORT
le Lac d'Orient
Champagne
Water park - Water slides
Heated indoor pool - Multisport
Bar - Restaurant - Supermarket
Very modern sanitary - Rentals ...
... in an exceptional natural setting near the lake!
www.camping-lacdorient.com

Welcome

r de Bel-Air, 44420
240425085 240425085
e-mail: contact@lewelcome.com
web: www.lewelcome.com

Pleasant wooded surroundings, 0.6km from the coast. Separate car park for arrivals after 22.30hrs.

dir: *1.8km NW via D352.*

Open: Apr-Oct **Site:** 2HEC **Facilities:** **Services:** **Leisure:** P **Off-site:** S

MESSÉ DEUX-SÈVRES

Grande Vigne

79120
549293993
e-mail: grande.vigne@orange.fr
web: www.grande-vigne.com

Flat orchard site bordered by fruit trees and set in rural countryside. No boundaries or marked pitches as only 5 pitches are let at any one time.

dir: *Off RN10 between Poitiers & Angouleme.*

GPS: 46.2561, 0.0886

Open: All Year. **Site:** 0.5HEC **Prices:** 15.50-18.50 **Facilities:** **Services:** **Leisure:** P

MISSILLAC LOIRE-ATLANTIQUE

CM des Platanes

10 r du Château, 44780
240883888

dir: *1km W via D2, 50m from the lake.*

Open: Jul-Aug **Site:** 2.04HEC **Facilities:** **Services:** **Off-site:**

FRANCE

MONTGIVRAY — INDRE

CM Solange Sand

2 r du Pont, 36400
254061036 254061039
e-mail: mairie.montgivray@wanadoo.fr

A pleasant riverside site in the grounds of a château.

Open: 15 Mar-15 Oct **Site:** 1HEC **Prices:** 7 **Facilities:** **Services:** **Leisure:** R **Off-site:** P

MONTLOUIS-SUR-LOIRE — INDRE-ET-LOIRE

Camping des Peupliers

RD 751, 37270
247508190 386379583
e-mail: aquadis1@orange.fr
web: www.aquadis-loisirs.com

On level meadow.

dir: *1.5km W on N751, next to swimming pool near railway bridge.*

Open: Apr-17 Oct **Site:** 4HEC **Prices:** 13.20-15.20 Mobile home hire 218-465 **Facilities:** Wi-fi Play Area **Services:** **Leisure:** P **Off-site:** R

MONTMORILLON — VIENNE

CM Allochon

av F-Tribot, 86500
549910233
e-mail: camping@ville-montmorillon.fr

A well-equipped municipal site close to the river and 1.5km from the town centre.

dir: *SE via D54.*

Open: Mar-Oct **Site:** 2HEC **Facilities:** Wi-fi Play Area **Services:** **Off-site:** P R

MONTSOREAU — MAINE-ET-LOIRE

Isle Verte

av de la Loire, 49730
241517660 241510883
e-mail: isleverte@cvtloisirs.fr
web: www.campingisleverte.com

Situated in a pretty village, in wooded surroundings beside the River Loire. Kids' club available in high season.

dir: *On D947 between road & river.*

GPS: 47.2181, 0.0528

Open: Apr-Sep **Site:** 2HEC **Prices:** 15-19 **Facilities:** Wi-fi (charged) Kids' Club Play Area **Services:** **Leisure:** P R **Off-site:**

MORTEROLLES-SUR-SEMME — HAUTE-VIENNE

CM

87250
555766018 555766845
e-mail: ot.bessines@wanadoo.fr
web: www.tourisme-bessines87.fr

A small, quiet country campsite with spacious pitches.

dir: *A20 exit 24.*

Open: All Year. **Site:** 8HEC **Prices:** 7-10 **Facilities:** **Services:** **Off-site:** L R

MOUTIERS-EN-RETZ, LES — LOIRE-ATLANTIQUE

Domaine du Collet

44760
240214092 240214512
e-mail: info@domaine-du-collet.com
web: www.domaine-du-collet.com

Site set in a large estate with leisure facilities including tennis courts and fishing.

Open: Apr-Oct **Site:** 12HEC **Prices:** 14-23 Mobile home hire 200-600 **Facilities:** Wi-fi (charged) Kids' Club Play Area **Services:** **Leisure:** L P R S

Village de la Mer

18 r de Prigny, 44760
240646590
e-mail: vdmer@hotmail.com
web: www.village-mer.fr

Quiet site close to a village and the beach.

dir: *9km S of Pornic on D97.*

Open: 15 Jun-15 Sep **Site:** 7HEC **Prices:** 17-32 **Facilities:** Wi-fi (charged) **Services:** **Leisure:** P **Off-site:** S

MUIDES-SUR-LOIRE — LOIR-ET-CHER

Château des Marais

27 r de Chambord, 41500
254870542 254870543
e-mail: chateau.des.marais@wanadoo.fr
web: www.chateau-des-marais.com

A wooded campsite set in the spacious grounds of an old stone manor house. The campsite retains the atmosphere of a country estate and the waterpark features waterslides and spacious sun terraces.

Open: 8 May-19 Sep **Site:** 12HEC **Facilities:** **Services:** **Leisure:** P **Off-site:** R

see advert on opposite page

FRANCE

NANTES — LOIRE-ATLANTIQUE

Petit Port

bd du Petit Port 21, 44300
☎ 240744794 🖷 240742306
e-mail: camping-petit-port@nge-nantes.fr
web: www.nge-nantes.fr/camping

A modern, well-kept park by a river.

dir: *In N of town near Parc du Petit Port. N137 Rennes road from town centre & signed.*

Open: All Year. **Site:** 8.5HEC **Facilities:** **Services:** **Off-site:** P R

NÉRET — INDRE

Camping le Bonhomme

Mulles, 36400
☎ 254314611
e-mail: info@camping-lebonhomme.com
web: www.camping-lebonhomme.com

Small site on a sunny hillside, sheltered by hedges.

Open: 15 Apr-Sep **Site:** 1.5HEC **Prices:** 16-18 **Facilities:** **Services:** **Leisure:** P

NEUVILLE-SUR-SARTHE — SARTHE

Vieux Moulin

72190
☎ 243253182 🖷 243253811
e-mail: info@lemanscamping.net
web: www.lemanscamping.net

Nearest campsite to the medieval town of Le Mans. A privately owned site of 12 acres, close to the village. Beautifully landscaped mature parkland bordering the river Sarthe. Good sized pitches, outdoor swimming pool. Ideal as a stop-over, short holiday or for the 24 hour Le Mans motor race.

dir: *Via N138 & D197.*

Open: Jul-Aug **Site:** 4.8HEC **Prices:** 13 **Facilities:** Play Area **Services:** **Leisure:** P **Off-site:** L R

NIBELLE — LOIRET

Nibelle

rte de Boiscommun, 45340
☎ 238322355 🖷 238320387
e-mail: info@camping-parcdenibelle.com
web: www.camping-parcdenibelle.com

Spacious, quiet, level site in the clearing of an oak woodland with a good range of leisure facilities.

dir: *Off D921 E to Nibelle, signed.*

Open: Mar-Nov **Site:** 10HEC **Prices:** 25-29 Mobile home hire 380-893 **Facilities:** Play Area **Services:** **Leisure:** P **Off-site:**

NOTRE-DAME-DE-MONTS — VENDÉE

Beauséjour

85690
☎ 251588388
e-mail: campingbeausejour85@orange.fr
dir: *2km NW on D38.*

Open: Apr-Sep **Site:** 1.34HEC **Facilities:** Play Area **Services:** **Off-site:** P R S

Grand Jardin

Le Grand Jardin, 50 r de la Barre, 85690
☎ 228112175
e-mail: contact@legrandjardin.net
web: www.legrandjardin.net

A family site in a picturesque location facing the Ile d'Yeu. Modern sanitary installations and plenty of sports facilities. 1km from the beach.

dir: *0.6km N.*

Open: All Year. **Site:** 4HEC **Facilities:** **Services:** **Leisure:** P R **Off-site:** S

FRANCE

Facilities shop shower electric points for razors electric points for caravans parking by tents permitted ompulsory separate car park **Services** café/restaurant bar Camping Gaz International gas other than Camping Gaz first aid facilities laundry **Leisure** swimming L-Lake P-Pool R-River S-Sea **Off-site** All facilities within 5km

NOTRE-DAME-DE-RIEZ VENDÉE

Domaine des Renardières

85270
☎ 251551417
e-mail: caroline.raffin@free.fr

Pleasant countryside site with sandy beaches close by.

Open: May-2 Sep **Site:** 3.5HEC **Facilities:** **Services:** **Leisure:** P **Off-site:** S

OLIVET LOIRET

CM Olivet

r du Pont Bouchet, 45160
☎ 238635394 238635896
e-mail: campingolivet@wanadoo.fr
web: www.camping-olivet.org

Site lies partly on shaded peninsula, partly on open lawns beside river.

dir: *2km E, signed from village.*

Open: Apr-14 Oct **Site:** 1HEC **Facilities:** **Services:** **Leisure:** R **Off-site:** P

OLONNE-SUR-MER VENDÉE

Domain de l'Oree

rte des Amis de la Nature, 85340
☎ 251331059 251331516
e-mail: loree@free.fr
web: www.l-oree.com
dir: *3km N.*

Open: 16 Apr-18 Sep **Site:** 7HEC **Prices:** 15.30-29 Mobile home hire 242-665 **Facilities:** Wi-fi Kids' Club Play Area **Services:** **Leisure:** P **Off-site:** S

Loubine

The Camping and Caravanning Club The Friendly Club

1 rte de la Mer, 85340
☎ 251331292 251331271
e-mail: camping.la.loubine@wanadoo.fr
web: www.la-loubine.fr

Situated on the edge of a forest bordering the beach.

C&CC Report *A lively site for older families and nightbirds, with many static units as well as tourers, and one of the best pool complexes in the area. Many people walk or cycle to the nearest sandy beach and Les Sables d'Olonne is a short drive away. Early booking is very strongly advised for the school holiday period, with the second halves of July and August best bets for availability.*

dir: *N via D87/D80*

Open: 2 Apr-24 Sep **Site:** 8HEC **Facilities:** **Services:** **Leisure:** P **Off-site:** S

ONZAIN LOIR-ET-CHER

Domaine de Dugny

rte de Chambon-sur-Cisse, 41150
☎ 254207066 254337169
e-mail: ld.reception@siblu.fr
web: www.siblu.fr

On a small lake, surrounded by farmland with well-marked pitches shaded by poplars. Entertainment programme 21 May-11 September. Dogs allowed on touring pitches.

dir: *CD45 from Onzain for Chambon-sur-Cisse.*

Open: 11 Feb-11 Nov **Site:** 10HEC **Prices:** 15-55 Mobile home hire 250-1000 **Facilities:** Wi-fi (charged) Kids' Club Play Area **Services:** **Leisure:** P

PERRIER, LE VENDÉE

Maison Blanche

85300
☎ 251493923
e-mail: campingmaisonblanche@yahoo.fr
web: www.campingmaisonblanche.fr

A family site on level ground, with pitches divided by trees. 6km from the coast.

Open: May-Sep **Site:** 3.2HEC **Facilities:** **Services:** **Leisure:** P R **Off-site:** S

PIERREFITTE-SUR-SAULDRE LOIR-ET-CHER

Parc des Alicourts

Domaine des Alicourts, 41300
☎ 254886334 254885840
e-mail: info@lesalicourts.com
web: www.lesalicourts.com

In wooded surroundings at the heart of an extensive park, this family site is exceptionally well equipped and provides a wide variety of recreational facilities.

dir: *6km NE via D126 beside the lake.*

GPS: 47.5444, 2.1914

Open: 29 Apr-6 Sep **Site:** 25HEC **Prices:** 20-52 **Facilities:** Kids' Club Play Area **Services:** **Leisure:** L P **Off-site:** R

see advert on opposite page

FRANCE

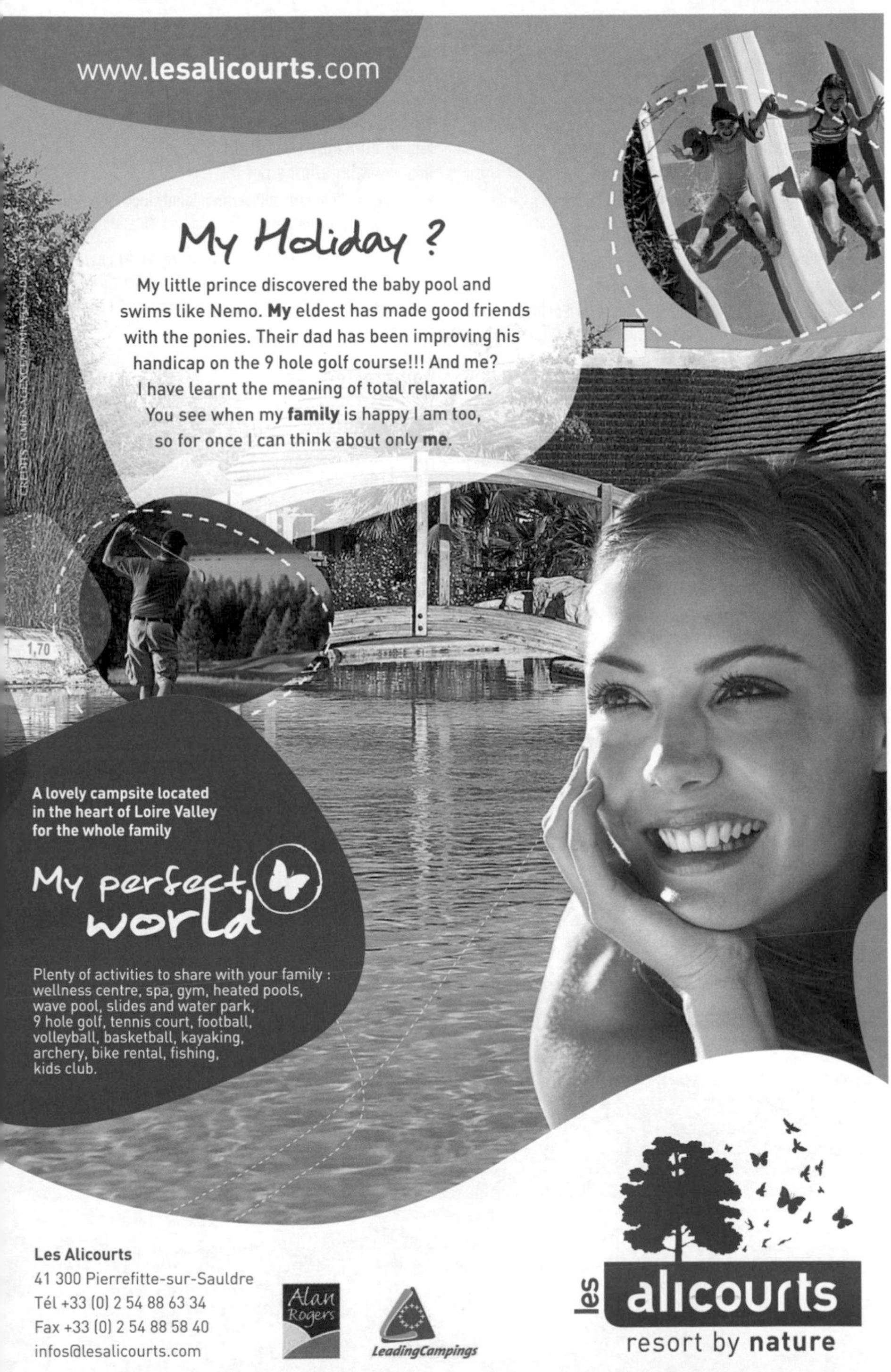
www.lesalicourts.com
My Holiday ?
My little prince discovered the baby pool and swims like Nemo. My eldest has made good friends with the ponies. Their dad has been improving his handicap on the 9 hole golf course!!! And me? I have learnt the meaning of total relaxation. You see when my family is happy I am too, so for once I can think about only me.
A lovely campsite located in the heart of Loire Valley for the whole family
My perfect world
Plenty of activities to share with your family : wellness centre, spa, gym, heated pools, wave pool, slides and water park, 9 hole golf, tennis court, football, volleyball, basketball, kayaking, archery, bike rental, fishing, kids club.
Les Alicourts
41 300 Pierrefitte-sur-Sauldre
Tél +33 (0) 2 54 88 63 34
Fax +33 (0) 2 54 88 58 40
infos@lesalicourts.com
Alan Rogers
LeadingCampings
les alicourts
resort by nature
FRANCE

PLAINE-SUR-MER, LA — LOIRE-ATLANTIQUE

Tabardière

44770

☎ 240215883 240210268

e-mail: info@camping-la-tabardiere.com

web: www.camping-la-tabardiere.com

A wooded, terraced site 3km from the sea.

dir: *Off D13 between Pornic & La Plaine-sur-Mer.*

GPS: 47.1406, -2.1533

Open: 16 Apr-25 Sep **Site:** 6HEC **Prices:** 15.50-28.60 Mobile home hire 220-800 **Facilities:** Wi-fi (charged) **Services:** **Leisure:** P **Off-site:** S

PONS — CHARENTE-MARITIME

Chardon

Chardon, 17800

☎ 546950125

e-mail: jacques.bier@cegetel.net

web: www.camping-chardon.fr

Quiet location on the edge of a small village, next to a farm.

dir: *D732 W from Pons towards Royan, site 2.5km on left. Or A10 exit 36, towards Pons, site 0.8km on right.*

Open: All Year. **Site:** 1.6HEC **Facilities:** **Services:** **Off-site:** R

PONT-L'ABBÉ-D'ARNOULT — CHARENTE-MARITIME

Parc de la Garenne

24 av Bernard Chambenoit, 17250

☎ 546970146

e-mail: info@lagarenne.net

web: www.lagarenne.net

Peaceful site in a parkland setting. Shady individual pitches.

dir: *Via A10, N137 & D18.*

Open: 15 May-Oct **Site:** 4.8HEC **Prices:** 14-21 Mobile home hire 499-599 **Facilities:** Wi-fi Kids' Club Play Area **Services:** **Leisure:** P **Off-site:** R

PONTS-DE-CÉ, LES — MAINE-ET-LOIRE

Ile du Château

rte de Cholet, av de la Boire Salée, 49130

☎ 241446205 241446205

e-mail: ile-du-chateau@wanadoo.fr

web: www.camping-ileduchateau.com

Situated on a small island in the Loire close to the Château des Ponts-de-Cé. Separate car park for arrivals after 21.00hrs.

dir: *SW of Angers towards Cholet.*

Open: Apr-Sep **Site:** 2.3HEC **Facilities:** **Services:** **Leisure:** P R **Off-site:**

Site 6HEC (site size) grass sand stone little shade partly shaded mainly shaded bungalows for hire (static) caravans for hire tents for hire no dogs site fully accessible for wheelchairs

Prices amount quoted is per night, for 2 adults and car, plus tent or caravan. Mobile home hire is a weekly rate.

'ORNIC LOIRE-ATLANTIQUE

'outinardière

de la Plage de la Boutinardière, 44210
☎ 240820568 📠 240824901
-mail: info@boutinardiere.com
/eb: www.camping-boutinardiere.com

family campsite, 200 metres from the beach, has indoor and utdoor pools with 10 water slides, as well as a sauna and team-room. Kids' club available in July and August.

'pen: Apr-Sep **Site:** 8HEC **Prices:** 16.50-38.50 'obile home hire 230-1150 **Facilities:** Kids' Club 'lay Area **Services:** **Leisure:** P **ff-site:** S

see advert on opposite page

'atisseau

9 rue de Patisseau, 44210
☎ 240821039 📠 240822281
-mail: contact@lepatisseau.com
'eb: www.lepatisseau.com

/ooded surroundings close to the beach with good recreational acilities. Shop open July and August.

ir: *3km E via D751.*

pen: 9 Apr-14 Sep **Site:** 4.3HEC **Prices:** 25-41 obile home hire 420-1050 **Facilities:** Wi-fi (charged) ds' Club Play Area **Services:** **Leisure:** P **ff-site:** S

ORNICHET LOIRE-ATLANTIQUE

el Air

v Bonne Source/av Chevissens, 44380
☎ 240611078
eb: www.belairpornichet.fr

pleasant wooded location 50m from the beach.

pen: Apr-Sep **Site:** 6HEC **Prices:** 20-38 Mobile ome hire 320-1000 **Facilities:** Wi-fi Kids' Club ay Area **Services:** **Leisure:** P **ff-site:** S

'orges

8 rte de Villes Blais, 44380
☎ 240611884 📠 240601184
-mail: camping@campinglesforges.com
eb: www.campinglesforges.com

'ooded surroundings with well-defined pitches and good creational facilities.

ir: *Via N171.*

pen: Jul-Aug **Site:** 2HEC **Facilities:** **ervices:** **Leisure:** P **Off-site:** L

PRAILLES DEUX-SÈVRES

Lambon

Plan d'eau du Lambon, 79370
☎ 549328511 📠 549329492
e-mail: lambon.vacances@wanadoo.fr
web: www.lelambon.com

A peaceful rural site by a stretch of water, with a beach for bathing. Activities include archery, canoeing and climbing.

dir: *D948 from Niort towards Limoges, signs for Celle-sur-Belle, site 6km N.*

Open: May-Sep **Site:** 1HEC **Prices:** 10.40-12.40 Mobile home hire 168-392 **Facilities:** Wi-fi Play Area **Services:** **Leisure:** L P **Off-site:** R

PRÉFAILLES LOIRE-ATLANTIQUE

Eléovic

rte de la Pointe Saint Gildas, 44770
☎ 240216160 📠 240645195
e-mail: contact@camping-eleovic.com
web: www.camping-eleovic.com

Small shady site in a fine location with good facilities and close to local beaches. Views across the Bay of Bourgneuf to the Ile de Noirmoutier.

dir: *Motorway A33, junct 2b & follow signs. From centre of Nancy follow signs to Technopole de Brabois.*

Open: 5 Apr-28 Sep **Site:** 3HEC **Facilities:** **Services:** **Leisure:** P **Off-site:** S

RILLE INDRE-ET-LOIRE

Huttopia Rille

Lac de Rillé, 37340
☎ 247246297 📠 247246361
e-mail: rille@huttopia.com
web: www.huttopia.com

Site located at the edge of a lake surrounded by forest in the chateaux area of the Loire. Home to some 190 species of birds. Spacious shady pitches. Kids' club available in July and August. 1 dog per pitch.

dir: *A85 exit 7, cross Langeais then D57 to Hommes, then Rille. Follow signs to lake.*

Open: 22 Apr-6 Nov **Site:** 4.5HEC **Prices:** 14.60-25.50 Mobile home hire 404.25-784 **Facilities:** Kids' Club Play Area **Services:** **Leisure:** L P

FRANCE

ROSIERS, LES — MAINE-ET-LOIRE

Val de Loire

6 r Ste-Baudruche, 49350
☎ 241519433 🖷 241518913
e-mail: contact@camping-valdeloire.com
web: www.camping-valdeloire.com

A comfortable site partly on the banks of the River Loire with good recreational facilities.

dir: *N via D59*

Open: Apr-Sep **Site:** 3HEC **Facilities:** **Services:** **Leisure:** P **Off-site:** R

ROYAN — CHARENTE-MARITIME

Clairfontaine

Campeole, r du C Lachaud, Pontaillac, 17200
☎ 546390811 🖷 546381379
e-mail: clairefontaine@campeole.com
web: www.campeole.com

A well-equipped site in wooded surroundings 300m from the beach with a variety of recreational facilities.

Open: May-26 Sep **Site:** 5HEC **Facilities:** **Services:** **Leisure:** P **Off-site:** S

SABLES-D'OLONNE, LES — VENDÉE

Dune des Sables

La Paracou - Route de l'Aubraie, 85100
☎ 251323121 🖷 251339404
e-mail: contact@chadotel.com
web: www.chadotel.com

A fine location facing the sea and with direct access to the beach. Various events take place during the summer season.

dir: *2km from town centre.*

GPS: 46.5123, -1.8146

Open: Apr-Sep **Site:** 5.5HEC **Prices:** 14-26.40 Mobile home hire 175-820 **Facilities:** Wi-fi (charged) Play Area **Services:** **Leisure:** P S **Off-site:**

Roses

1 r des Roses, 85100
☎ 251951042 🖷 251339404
e-mail: contact@chadotel.com
web: www.chadotel.com

A level site shaded by trees and bushes, 0.5km from the Remblai beach, set in the residential heart of les Sables-d'Olonne. Heated pool with water slide and a programme of entertainment.

dir: *Close to town centre off D949, 0.5km from the beach.*

GPS: 46.4914, -1.7658

Open: Apr-Nov **Site:** 3HEC **Prices:** 14-26.40 Mobile home hire 175-850 **Facilities:** Wi-fi (charged) **Services:** **Leisure:** P **Off-site:** S

SABLÉ-SUR-SARTHE — SARTHE

Hippodrome

allée du Quebec, 72300
☎ 243954261 🖷 243927482
e-mail: camping@sablesursarthe.fr
web: www.tourisme.sablesursarthe.fr

A peaceful wooded setting with a great variety of recreational facilities.

dir: *450m from town.*

Open: Apr-Oct **Site:** 3HEC **Prices:** 9.95-12.49 Mobile home hire 236-356 **Facilities:** Wi-fi Play Area **Services:** **Leisure:** P R **Off-site:**

ST-AIGNAN-SUR-CHER — LOIR-ET-CHER

Les Cochards

41110
☎ 254751559 🖷 254754472
e-mail: camping@lescochards.com
web: www.lescochards.com

On beautiful meadowland, completely surrounded by hedges. Activities for children in July and August.

dir: *1km from bridge on D17 towards Selles.*

Open: Apr-15 Oct **Site:** 4HEC **Prices:** 18.50-21.50 Mobile home hire 280-590 **Facilities:** Wi-fi (charged) Kids' Club **Services:** **Leisure:** P **Off-site:** R

ST-AMAND-MONTROND — CHER

CM Roche

chemin de la Roche, 18200
☎ 248960936 🖷 248960936
e-mail: camping-la-roche@wanadoo.fr
web: www.ville-saint-amand-montrond.fr

A lovely wooded location between the River Cher and the Berry Canal with modern facilities.

dir: *1.5km SW near river & canal.*

GPS: 46.7166, 2.4833

Open: Apr-Sep **Site:** 4HEC **Prices:** 10.40 Mobile home hire 107 **Facilities:** Wi-fi Play Area **Services:** **Leisure:** R **Off-site:** P

FRANCE

Site 6HEC (site size) grass sand stone little shade partly shaded mainly shaded bungalows for hire (static) caravans for hire tents for hire no dogs site fully accessible for wheelchairs
Prices amount quoted is per night, for 2 adults and car, plus tent or caravan. Mobile home hire is a weekly rate.

T-AVERTIN — INDRE-ET-LOIRE

M Rives du Cher

1 r de Rochepinard, 37550
247272760 247258289
-mail: contact@camping-lesrivesducher.com
eb: www.camping-lesrivesducher.com
unicipal site on the banks of the River Cher.
ir: *400m N of town centre. 4km from Tours.*
pen: Apr-15 Oct **Site:** 3HEC **Facilities:** **Services:** **Off-site:** L P R

T-BRÉVIN-LES-PINS — LOIRE-ATLANTIQUE

M Courance

00/110 av Ml-Foch, 44250
240272291 240272291
-mail: info@campinglacourance.fr
eb: www.campinglacourance.fr
et in a pine forest with direct access to the beach.
ir: *S off D305.*
pen: All Year. **Site:** 4HEC **Facilities:** **Services:** **Leisure:** S **Off-site:** P

ief

7 chemin du Fief, 44250
240272386 240644619
-mail: camping@lefief.com
eb: www.lefief.com
family site adjacent to a long sandy beach. The pitches are urrounded by trees and bushes and there are modern facilities.
ir: *From town centre onto Route Bleue to Centre Leclerc & 2nd ght to site.*
pen: 2 Apr-2 Oct **Site:** 7HEC **Prices:** 17-39
acilities: Kids' Club Play Area **Services:** **Leisure:** P S **Off-site:** S

T-BRÉVIN-L'OCÉAN — LOIRE-ATLANTIQUE

ierres Couchées

Ermitage, 44250
240278564 240849703
-mail: contact@pierres-couchees.com
eb: www.pierres-couchees.com
ktensive, well-screened terrain made up of three sites.
ir: *300m from sea. 2km on D213 toward Pornic.*
pen: Apr-8 Oct **Site:** 14HEC **Facilities:** **Services:** **Leisure:** P **Off-site:** S

ST-CYR — VIENNE

Lac de Saint Cyr

The Camping and Caravanning Club — The Friendly Club

86130
549625722 549522858
e-mail: contact@lacdesaintcyr.com
web: www.lacdesaintcyr.com
A delightful setting in a spacious park beside a lake. Futuroscope is within easy reach via the A10.

C&CC Report *A good modern site, convenient not only as a stopover between the ports and south-west France, but also for longer stays. It's great for both families and couples, with on-site leisure facilities as well as the nearby golf, fishing or watersports. It's also a good choice if all you want to do is relax or visit the local area, with Poitiers and the theme park of the moving image, Futuroscope, close by.*

dir: *1.5km NE via D4/D82.*
Open: Apr-Sep **Site:** 5HEC **Facilities:** **Services:** **Leisure:** L

SAINTES — CHARENTE-MARITIME

Au Fill de l'Eau

6 r de Courbiac, 17100
546930800
e-mail: contact@camping-saintes-17.com
web: www.camping-saintes-17.com
Site lies beside the River Charente, 0.9km from the town centre.
dir: *A10 exit 35 towards town centre on D128.*
Open: May-Oct **Site:** 7HEC **Prices:** 15.60-18.35
Facilities: **Services:**
Leisure: P R **Off-site:**

ST-FLORENT-LE-VIEIL — MAINE-ET-LOIRE

Ile Batailleuse

44370
240834501
e-mail: serge.rabec@tiscali.fr
web: campingilebatailleuse.com.chez-alice.fr
dir: *6km SE. N of Lac du Boudon.*
Open: Apr-16 Nov **Site:** 2.7HEC
Facilities: **Services:** **Leisure:** R
Off-site: P

FRANCE

ST-GEORGES-DE-DIDONNE CHARENTE-MARITIME

Bois Soleil

2 av de Suzac, 17110
546050594 546062743
e-mail: camping.bois.soleil@wanadoo.fr
web: www.bois-soleil.com

Pitches lie on different levels. Direct access to the beach.

dir: *2.5km S of town on D25 Meschers road.*

Open: 2 Apr-9 Oct **Site:** 10HEC **Prices:** 20-42 Mobile home hire 180-1130 **Facilities:** Wi-fi (charged) Kids' Club Play Area **Services:** **Leisure:** P S

Ideal Camping

16 Avenue de Suzac, 17110
546052904 546063236
e-mail: info@ideal-camping.com
web: www.ideal-camping.com

A well-equipped, peaceful site in a pine forest 200m from Suzac beach.

dir: *W of St-Georges-de-Didonne via D25.*

GPS: 45.5854, -0.9850

Open: 7 May-4 Sep **Site:** 8HEC **Prices:** 16.50-27.80 Mobile home hire 250-750 **Facilities:** Play Area **Services:** **Leisure:** P **Off-site:** S

Village Center les Catalpas

45 chemin d'Enlias, 17110
499572121 467516389
e-mail: contact@village-center.com
web: www.village-center.com/poitou-charentes/camping-mer-catalpas.php

Close to the town centre and beach with clearly marked-out pitches. Leisure facilities available during the day and evening.

GPS: 45.6151, -0.9946

Open: 24 Jun-4 Sep **Site:** 2HEC **Prices:** 14-23 Mobile home hire 167-833 **Facilities:** Wi-fi (charged) Play Area **Services:** **Leisure:** P **Off-site:**

ST-GEORGES-LÈS-BAILLARGEAUX VIENN

Futuriste

86130
549524752 549372333
e-mail: camping-le-futuriste@wanadoo.fr
web: www.camping-le-futuriste.fr

An elevated position having fine views over the Clain Valley.

C&CC Report *Small, family run, very friendly site, half a kilometre from the village centre and 4km from Futuroscope.*

Open: All Year. **Site:** 4HEC **Prices:** 20.40-27.40 Mobile home hire 480-650 **Facilities:** Play Area **Services:** **Leisure:** L P **Off-site:**

ST-GERMAIN-LES-BELLES HAUTE-VIENN

Camping de Montréal

r du Petit Moulin, 87380
555718620 555710083
e-mail: contact@campingdemontreal.com
web: www.campingdemontreal.com

With a lakeside setting, pitches separated by hedges with views of the surrounding hills.

dir: *A20 exit 42 towards St-Germain-les-Belles.*

GPS: 45.6114, 1.5011

Open: Apr-Oct **Site:** 2HEC **Prices:** 11-13 Mobile home hire 149-519 **Facilities:** Wi-fi (charged) Play Are **Services:** **Leisure:** L **Off-site:**

ST-GILLES-CROIX-DE-VIE VENDÉ

Bahamas Beach

168 rte des Sables, 85800
251546916 251339404
e-mail: contact@chadotel.com
web: www.chadotel.com

Site lies 0.6km from the beach. Sunny pitches, heated indoor and outdoor pools and varied entertainment.

C&CC Report *A modern, well-equipped site, very well situated on one of the most popular stretches of the Vendée coastline, just to the south of St-Gilles-Croix-de-Vie. There are many static units on site, yet touring pitches are still reasonably sized for such a good coastal location. A footpath direct from the site takes about 15 minutes to the beach while another path goes to St Gilles itself. There's a classic French holiday atmosphere on site, with English spoken at reception. Good pitches for sunseekers! Nearby St-Gilles-Croix-de-Vie is very popular for its shops and markets, including a high season evening market.*

dir: *2km from town centre.*

GPS: 46.6774, -1.9152

Open: Apr-Sep **Site:** 4.5HEC **Prices:** 9.40-24.90 Mobile home hire 199-850 **Facilities:** Wi-fi (charged) Play Area **Services:** **Leisure:** P **Off-site:** R S

FRANCE

)omaine de Beaulieu

;ivrand - rue du Parc, 85800
251555946 251339404
-mail: contact@chadotel.com
veb: www.chadotel.com
former farm, located 1km from the beach, this family site has acilities including a heated swimming pool and take away.
lir: *4km from town. 1km from beach.*
PS: 46.6718, -1.9041
pen: Apr-Sep **Site:** 7HEC **Prices:** 9-24 Mobile home ire 199-799 **Facilities:** Wi-fi (charged) Play Area **ervices:** **Leisure:** P **Off-site:** R S

ST-HILAIRE-DE-RIEZ VENDÉE

Biches

te de Notre-Dame-de-Riez, 85270
251543882 251543074
-mail: info@camping-les-biches.com
veb: www.camping-les-biches.com
well-equipped site in a pine forest and close to the sea.
lir: *2km N.*
pen: 15 May-15 Sep **Site:** 10HEC **Facilities:** **Services:** **Leisure:** P

Bois Tordu

4 av de la Pège, 85270
251543378 251540829
-mail: info@leboistordu.com
veb: www.leboistordu.com
Vooded location with good facilities.
lir: *5.3km NW.*
pen: 15 May-10 Sep **Site:** 2HEC **Prices:** 28-35 Mobile home hire 330-830 **Facilities:** Play Area **ervices:** **Leisure:** P **Off-site:** S

Chouans

108 av de la Faye, 85270
251540592
-mail: info@campingleschouans.com
veb: www.camping-leschouans.com
Vooded location on the edge of a national forest.
lir: *2.5km NW.*
pen: May-Sep **Site:** 5HEC **Facilities:** Wi-fi (charged) Kids' Club Play Area **Services:** **Leisure:** P **Off-site:** S

Ecureuils

100 av de la Pège, 85270
251543371 251556908
e-mail: info@camping-aux-ecureuils.com
web: www.camping-aux-ecureuils.com
Pleasant surroundings 250m from a fine sandy beach, with good recreational facilities.
dir: *D178 & D753 from Nantes to St-Hilaire-de-Riez.*
Open: May-15 Sep **Site:** 4HEC **Prices:** 26.60-36 Mobile home hire 322-742 **Facilities:** Wi-fi (charged) Play Area **Services:** **Leisure:** P **Off-site:** S

Padrelle

1 r Prévot, La Corniche de Sion/l'Océan, 85270
251553203
e-mail: contact@camping-la-padrelle.com
web: www.camping-la-padrelle.com
A rural setting 50m from the beach and 5 minutes from the town.
Open: May-15 Oct **Site:** 1.5HEC **Facilities:** **Services:** **Off-site:** S

Parée Préneau

The Camping and Caravanning Club The Friendly Club

23 av de la Parée Préneau, 85270
251543384 251552957
e-mail: contact@campinglapareepreneau.com
web: www.campinglapareepreneau.com
C&CC Report *A long-established and well-located site, great for beaches and lively high season resorts. Ideal for campers who prefer smaller scale sites and who prefer entertainment and services nearby but not right on site – the popular resorts of St-Gilles-Croix-de-Vie and St Jean-de-Monts are both just a few kilometres away. Nearby too is 'Feeling Forest', a tree-based adventure park with aerial slides and walkways - great fun for all ages.*
dir: *From D38 St-Hilaire and St-Gilles C-de-Vie, then St-Hilaire centre ville, Sion-l'Océan and signed.*
Open: May-10 Sep **Site:** 1.5HEC **Facilities:** **Services:** **Leisure:** P **Off-site:** S

Plage

106 av de la Pège, 85270
251543393 251559702
e-mail: campinglaplage@campingscollinet.com
web: www.campingscollinet.com
On a meadow with trees. Access to beach via dunes.
dir: *5.7km NW.*
Open: Apr-Sep **Site:** 5.5HEC **Facilities:** **Services:** **Leisure:** P S **Off-site:**

FRANCE

Prairie

chemin des Roselières, 85270
☎ 251540856 251559702
e-mail: campinglaprairie@campingscollinet.com
web: www.campingscollinet.com

A family site with pitches shaded by trees. A big swimming pool complex and entertainment for adults and children, in July and August.

dir: *5.5km NW, 0.5km from beach.*

Open: 15 May-10 Sep **Site:** 4.7HEC **Facilities:** Wi-fi Kids' Club Play Area **Services:** **Leisure:** P **Off-site:** L S

Puerta del Sol

7 chemin des Hommeaux, 85270
☎ 251491010 251498484
e-mail: info@campinglapuertadelsol.com
web: www.campinglapuertadelsol.com

A peaceful site with well-defined pitches in a wooded location. Good facilities for family recreation.

dir: *4.5km N.*

Open: Apr-Sep **Site:** 4HEC **Facilities:** **Services:** **Leisure:** P **Off-site:**

Sol-à-Gogo

61 av de la Pège, 85270
☎ 251542900 251548874
e-mail: info@solagogo.com
web: www.solagogo.com

A family site with good recreational facilities, including an aquaslide, with direct access to the beach.

dir: *4.8km NW of St-Hilaire, 6km S of St-Jean-de-Monts.*

Open: 15 May-13 Sep **Site:** 4HEC **Prices:** 28-35 Mobile home hire 350-850 **Facilities:** Wi-fi Kids' Club Play Area **Services:** **Leisure:** P S **Off-site:**

ST-HILAIRE-LA-FORÊT VENDÉE

Batardières

85440
☎ 251333385

A pleasant site surrounded by mature trees and shrubs, with large pitches separated by hedges.

dir: *W on D70.*

Open: Jul-Aug **Site:** 1.6HEC **Prices:** 20 **Facilities:** **Services:** **Off-site:**

Grand' Métairie

8 r de la Vineuse en Plaine, 85440
☎ 251333238 251332569
e-mail: info@camping-grandmetairie.com
web: www.la-grand-metairie.com

Site with flowers and trees with clearly marked pitches. Entertainment for children and teenagers. Free shuttle available to nearby sandy beach. Rental bikes, indoor and outdoor pool.

Open: Apr-Sep **Site:** 3.84HEC **Prices:** 17-22 Mobile home hire 210-847 **Facilities:** Wi-fi (charged) Kids' Club Play Area **Services:** **Leisure:** P **Off-site:** L S

ST-HILAIRE-PEYROUX CORRÈZE

Le Chazal

19560
☎ 555255248
e-mail: lechazal@neuf.fr
web: lechazal-19.perso.sfr.fr

A peaceful site on the edge of the Massif Central with fine views over the Couze Valley, good for walking holidays.

dir: *Off N89 at Malemort onto D141 at rdbt to Venarsal & 1.5m fo St-Hilaire-Peyroux, left onto C13 for site.*

Open: Apr-1 Nov **Site:** 1.5HEC **Prices:** 12 **Facilities:** Wi-fi **Services:** **Off-site:** R

ST JEAN-D'ANGELY CHARENTE-MARITIME

Val de Boutonne

56 quai de Bernouet, 17400
☎ 546322616
e-mail: info@valba.net
web: www.valba.net

Wooded location near the river.

dir: *NE of town.*

Open: Apr-Sep **Site:** 3.5HEC **Facilities:** **Services:** **Off-site:** P

FRANCE

Site 6HEC (site size) grass sand stone little shade partly shaded mainly shaded bungalows for hire (static) caravans for hire tents for hire no dogs site fully accessible for wheelchairs
Prices amount quoted is per night, for 2 adults and car, plus tent or caravan. Mobile home hire is a weekly rate.

;T-JEAN-DE-MONTS VENDÉE

Amiaux

The Camping and Caravanning Club The Friendly Club

223 rte de Notre-Dame de Monts, 85169
☎ 251582222 251582609
e-mail: accueil@amiaux.fr
web: www.amiaux.fr

A well-equipped site on the edge of a forest, 0.7km from the beach.

C&CC Report *A great family site, with excellent pitches, where tourers are preferred to static units. The swimming pools and waterslides are superb, particularly the large indoor pool, and it's only 15 minutes walk along a woodland path to the nearest sandy beach. The cycle paths are first-rate too throughout the Vendée – cycle into St-Jean-de-Monts or to the Grand-Plage.*

dir: *3.5km NW of D38.*

GPS: 46.8075, -2.1049

Open: 3 May-Sep **Site:** 16HEC **Prices:** 18.50-34.50 Mobile home hire 280-700 **Facilities:** Wi-fi (charged) Kids' Club Play Area **Services:** **Leisure:** P **Off-site:** S

3ois Dormant

.68 r des Sables, 85160
☎ 251586262 251582997
-mail: boisdormant@siblu.fr
veb: www.siblu.fr/leboisdormant

pen: 24 Apr-5 Sep **Site:** 11.5HEC **Facilities:** **Services:** **Leisure:** P
ff-site: S

ois Joly

:6 r de Notre-Dame-de-Monts, BP 507, 85165
☎ 251591163 251591106
-mail: campingboisjoly@wanadoo.fr
veb: www.camping-leboisjoly.com

pleasantly landscaped, terraced site set among pine trees. :lose to the beach and town centre, heated covered pool with lides and entertainment in July and August. Dogs allowed except 1 chalets/mobile homes.

PS: 46.7996, -2.0744

pen: 9 Apr-25 Sep **Site:** 7.5HEC **Prices:** 18-32 1obile home hire 230-900 **Facilities:** Wi-fi Kids' :lub Play Area **Services:** **Leisure:** P R
ff-site: S

Bois Masson

149 r des Sables, 85160
☎ 251586262 251582997
e-mail: boismasson@siblu.fr
web: www.siblu.com

A family site with a variety of facilities in a wooded setting near the beach. Aquatic complex includes covered and outdoor pools, water chutes, jacuzzi and sauna.

dir: *2km SE.*

Open: 27 Mar-18 Sep **Site:** 7.5HEC **Facilities:** **Services:** **Leisure:** P
Off-site: S

Clarys Plage

av des Epines, 85160
☎ 251581024 251595196
e-mail: info@leclarys.com
web: www.leclarys.com

A family site with good facilities including an indoor swimming pool and an outdoor pool with a water slide.

dir: *S of town 300m from beach.*

Open: 15 May-15 Sep **Site:** 8HEC **Prices:** 28-35
Facilities: Wi-fi Kids' Club Play Area
Services: **Leisure:** P **Off-site:** S

Forêt

190 chemin de la Rive, 85160
☎ 251588463 251588463
e-mail: camping-la-foret@wanadoo.fr
web: www.hpa-laforet.com

A well-equipped family site in a pleasant rural setting, with direct access to the beach.

dir: *Off D38.*

Open: Apr-25 Sep **Site:** 1HEC **Prices:** 15-28 Mobile home hire 279-689 **Facilities:** Wi-fi (charged) Play Area **Services:** **Leisure:** P **Off-site:** S

Yole

chemin des Bosses, Orouet, 85160
☎ 251586717 251590535
e-mail: contact@la-yole.com
web: www.la-yole.com

Set in rural surroundings, 1km from a fine sandy beach. Kids' club in July and August for 5 to 12 year olds.

dir: *Signed from D38 in Orouet.*

Open: 4 Apr-29 Sep **Site:** 7.5HEC **Prices:** 16-28.50 Mobile home hire 260-890 **Facilities:** Wi-fi (charged) Kids' Club Play Area **Services:** **Leisure:** P **Off-site:** S

FRANCE

Facilities shop shower electric points for razors electric points for caravans parking by tents permitted ›mpulsory separate car park **Services** café/restaurant bar Camping Gaz International gas other than Camping Gaz first aid facilities laundry **Leisure** swimming L-Lake P-Pool R-River S-Sea **Off-site** All facilities within 5km

Zagarella

rte des Sables, 85160
☎ 251581982 🖷 251593528
e-mail: zagarella@zagarella.fr
web: www.zagarella.fr

In pine woods close to the sea.

Open: May-26 Sep **Site:** 5.3HEC **Prices:** 11.50-32 Mobile home hire 221-866 **Facilities:** Wi-fi Kids' Club Play Area **Services:** **Leisure:** P **Off-site:** S

ST-JULIEN-DES-LANDES — VENDÉE

Château de la Fôret

85150
☎ 251466211
e-mail: camping@domainelaforet.com
web: www.domainelaforet.com

A picturesque setting in the grounds of a château with well-defined pitches and modern facilities.

dir: *NE on D55, rte de Martinet*

Open: 15 May-15 Sep **Site:** 50HEC **Facilities:** Wi-fi (charged) Kids' Club Play Area **Services:** **Leisure:** P **Off-site:**

Garangeoire

The Camping and Caravanning Club — The Friendly Club

85150
☎ 251466539 🖷 251466985
e-mail: info@garangeoire.com
web: www.camping-la-garangeoire.com

Family site set in 200-hectare estate with a variety of recreational facilities. Pitches separated by hedges.

C&CC Report *An extremely popular site, with a well-deserved reputation for quality. La Garangeoire is particularly popular with British families, not least because of the very spacious pitches, friendly English-speaking staff and wide range of services operating virtually all season. Should you ever leave the site during your stay – many families don't! – you'll find the nearest beaches just quarter of an hour's drive away, while inland there are châteaux to visit at nearby Apremont and Avrillé.*

dir: *2km N of village.*

Open: 9 Apr-24 Sep **Site:** 18HEC **Prices:** 14.50-29.50 **Facilities:** Wi-fi (charged) Kids' Club Play Area **Services:** **Leisure:** P **Off-site:** L

Village de la Guyonnière

La Guyonnière, 85150
☎ 251466259 🖷 251466289
e-mail: info@laguyonniere.com
web: www.laguyonniere.com

A pleasant site with pitches divided by hedges with good sanitary and recreational facilities. Kids' club available in July and August.

dir: *2km from town centre towards St-Gilles-Croix-de-Vie.*

Open: 23 Apr-2 Sep **Site:** 30HEC **Prices:** 14-36.90 Mobile home hire 200-844 **Facilities:** Wi-fi (charged) Kids' Club Play Area **Services:** **Leisure:** L P

ST-JUST-LUZAC — CHARENTE-MARITIME

Castel Camping Séquoia Parc

La Josephtrie, 17320
☎ 546855555 🖷 546855556
e-mail: info@sequoiaparc.com
web: www.sequoiaparc.com

Situated in a spacious park on the La Josephtrie estate, which contains an attractive château, 5km from the coast and the beaches. There is a swimming pool complex with water slides and a large paddling pool. Organised entertainment for children throughout the season, adult entertainment in July and August.

Open: 14 May-4 Sep **Site:** 45HEC **Prices:** 20-47 **Facilities:** Wi-fi (charged) Kids' Club Play Area **Services:** **Leisure:** P **Off-site:** S

ST-LAURENT-NOUAN — LOIR-ET-CHER

Camping Municipal de l'Amitié

r du Camping, 41220
☎ 254870152
e-mail: camping@stlaurentnouan.eu
web: www.stlaurentnouan.fr/fr/information/34193/camping-amitie

On the shore of the River Loire between Blois and Orléans, 6km from the château of Chambord.

dir: *On D951.*

GPS: 47.6866, 1.5581

Open: All Year. **Site:** 2HEC **Prices:** 10.40-11.75 Mobile home hire 255-335 **Facilities:** **Services:** **Off-site:** P

FRANCE

ST-LÉONARD-DE-NOBLAT HAUTE-VIENNE

Beaufort

87400
555560279 555560279
e-mail: info@campingdebeaufort.com
web: www.campingdebeaufort.com
Set in pleasant wooded surroundings with good facilities.
dir: *Off D39.*
Open: 14 Apr-Sep **Site:** 2HEC **Facilities:** **Services:** **Leisure:** R **Off-site:**

ST-MALÔ-DU-BOIS VENDÉE

La Vallee de Poupet

85590
251923145 251923865
e-mail: camping@valleedepoupet.com
web: www.valleedepoupet.com
A picturesque location beside the River Sèvre Nantaise, surrounded by woodland.
dir: *D72 from village, 1km left fork & signed.*
Open: 15 May-15 Sep **Site:** 3HEC **Facilities:** **Services:** **Leisure:** P R **Off-site:**

ST-MARC-SUR-MER LOIRE-ATLANTIQUE

Yukadi Village L'Eve

rte du Fort de L'Eve, 44600
546223822 240917659
e-mail: leve@yukadivillages.com
web: www.yukadivillages.com
Large, well-kept site on gentle slope. Divided into pitches. Access to sea through a private tunnel. Dogs allowed except in mobile homes.
dir: *On D292.*
Open: 13 May-4 Sep **Site:** 6HEC **Prices:** 14.50-30.50 Mobile home hire 210-885.50 **Facilities:** Wi-fi Kids' Club Play Area **Services:** **Leisure:** P S

ST-PALAIS-SUR-MER CHARENTE-MARITIME

Côte de Beauté

The Camping and Caravanning Club The Friendly Club

157 av de la Grande Côte, 17420
546232059
e-mail: campingcotedebeaute@wanadoo.fr
web: www.camping-cote-de-beaute.com
Situated facing sea.
C&CC Report *This is a quiet little site in an excellent location just across the road from the Atlantic Ocean. With a fine sandy beach within 500 metres, it is a beach lover's dream and cyclists will enjoy the cycle path along the coast which is adjacent to the site. The friendly owners ensure that the sanitation is immaculately kept and are always on hand to recommend one of the restaurants within walking distance.*
dir: *N of town on road to La Palmyre (D25).*
Open: May-Sep **Site:** 1HEC **Facilities:** **Off-site:** S

Ormeaux

44 av de Bernezac, 17420
546390207 546385666
e-mail: campingormeaux@tiscali.fr
web: www.camping-ormeaux.com
Well-equipped site in wooded surroundings, 0.5km from the beach.
dir: *1km N.*
Open: Apr-Oct **Site:** 3.5HEC **Facilities:** **Services:** **Leisure:** P **Off-site:** L S

Yukadi Village Le Logis

22 r des Palombes, 17420
546223822 546231061 & 546236510
e-mail: reservations@ yukadivillages.com
web: www.yukadivillages.com
Situated 300m from the sea.
dir: *2.5km NW on D25.*
Open: 12 May-5 Sep **Site:** 19HEC **Facilities:** **Services:** **Leisure:** P **Off-site:** S

ST-PARDOUX-CORBIER CORRÈZE

Le Domaine Bleu

Plan d'eau, 19210
555735989
e-mail: ledomainebleu@orange.fr
web: www.ledomainebleu.eu
A quiet, peaceful campsite on a fishing lake.
dir: *A20 exit 44 towards Lubersac. Follow signs for St-Pardoux-Corbier*
GPS: 45.4297, 1.4547
Open: Jul-Aug **Site:** 1.5HEC **Prices:** 11.50 **Facilities:** Play Area **Leisure:** L **Off-site:** P R

FRANCE

ST-REVÉRÉND — VENDÉE

Pont Rouge

av Georges Clémenceau, 85220
251546850 251546167
e-mail: camping.pontrouge@wanadoo.fr
web: www.camping-lepontrouge.com

Quiet site in the Vendée countryside within easy reach of the sea.

dir: *D6 E from St Gilles, turning to St-RevéréND.*

Open: Apr-Oct **Site:** 1.6HEC **Facilities:** **Services:** **Leisure:** P
Off-site: L R

ST-SATUR — CHER

St-Satur

Quai de la Loire, 18300
248540467 386379583
e-mail: aquadis1@orange.fr
web: www.aquadis-loisirs.com

Quiet, shady site alongside the Loire at the foot of vineyard covered hills.

dir: *A71 exit for Sancerre.*

Open: May-Sep **Site:** 1.6HEC **Facilities:** **Services:** **Off-site:** P R

ST-SORNIN — CHARENTE-MARITIME

Valerick

The Camping and Caravanning Club — The Friendly Club

1 Domaine de La Mauvinière, 17600
546851595
e-mail: campingvalerick@orange.fr
web: www.camping-le-valerick.fr

Small, peaceful site in quiet surroundings.

C&CC Report *The most relaxing way to enjoy the delightful Charente-Maritime, away from the busy seaside resorts. Begin at St. Sornin church for a rewarding start, then cross the sea bridge to the Ile d'Oléron on a weekday, or visit the Saturday market in Saintes. On site, all is picturesque and peaceful, with great warmth of welcome and personal attention from the resident site owners, Monsieur and Madame Vignaud. There is also plenty of wildlife around, such as the storks' nest visible from the site.*

Open: Apr-Sep **Site:** 1.5HEC **Prices:** 18.70 Mobile home hire 250-300 **Facilities:** Play Area **Services:** **Off-site:** R

ST TROJAN-LES-BAINS — CHARENTE-MARITIME

Indigo Oléron

11 av des Bris, 17370
546760239 546764295
e-mail: oleron@camping-indigo.com
web: www.camping-indigo.com

Spacious, shady and slightly sloping pitches set in a pine forest, 1.5km from the beach at Gatseau. Cycles are available to hire. Kids' club in July and August. One dog per pitch allowed.

dir: *A10 exit 33 signed La Rochelle then follow signs to Rochefort/Ile d'Oleron.*

GPS: 45.8363, -1.2097

Open: 22 Apr-2 Oct **Site:** 5HEC **Prices:** 12.90-19 **Facilities:** Kids' Club Play Area **Services:** **Leisure:** P **Off-site:** S

ST-USTRE — VIENNE

Petit Trianon de St-Ustre

1 r du Moulin, 86220
549026147 549026881
e-mail: chateau@petit-trianon.fr
web: www.petit-trianon.fr

Set in a beautiful park surrounding a small 18th-century château, the site has good entertainment and recreational facilities.

dir: *Off N10 at sign N of Ingrandes, site 1km.*

Open: 20 May-20 Sep **Site:** 7HEC **Facilities:** **Services:** **Leisure:** P
Off-site:

ST-VINCENT-SUR-JARD — VENDÉE

Bolée d'Air

rte du Bouil, 85520
251903605 251339404
e-mail: contact@chadotel.com
web: www.chadotel.com

A family site on level ground with pitches divided by hedges. Good recreational facilities, including two pools, sauna, tennis and mini-golf, and 0.9km from Bouil beach.

dir: *2km E via D21. 900m from the beach.*

GPS: 46.4184, -1.5279

Open: Apr-Sep **Site:** 6.5HEC **Prices:** 9-24 Mobile home hire 170-799 **Facilities:** Wi-fi (charged) Play Area **Services:** **Leisure:** P
Off-site: S

Site 6HEC (site size) grass sand stone little shade partly shaded mainly shaded bungalows for hire (static) caravans for hire tents for hire no dogs site fully accessible for wheelchairs
Prices amount quoted is per night, for 2 adults and car, plus tent or caravan. Mobile home hire is a weekly rate.

ST-XANDRE CHARENTE-MARITIME

Beaulieu

3 r du Treuil Gras, Puilboreau, 17138
☎ 546680438 🖹 546358595
e-mail: contact@camping-la-rochelle.com
web: www.camping-la-rochelle.com

Shady pitches with hedges.

Open: All Year. **Site:** 5HEC **Facilities:** **Services:** **Leisure:** P **Off-site:**

STE-CATHERINE-DE-FIERBOIS INDRE-ET-LOIRE

Parc de Fierbois

37800
☎ 247654335 🖹 247655375
e-mail: contact@fierbois.com
web: www.fierbois.com

Beside artificial lake, good bathing area. Kids' club available in July and August.

dir: *Off N10 onto D101, 1.5km SE.*

GPS: 47.1483, 0.6547

Open: 16 May-8 Sep **Site:** 40HEC **Prices:** 16-43 Mobile home hire 315-910 **Facilities:** Wi-fi (charged) Kids' Club Play Area **Services:** **Leisure:** L P

see advert on this page

STE-LUCE-SUR-LOIRE LOIRE-ATLANTIQUE

Belle Rivière

rte des Perrières, 44980
☎ 240258581 🖹 240258581
e-mail: belleriviere@wanadoo.fr
web: www.belle-riviere.com

Located close to Nantes, on the banks of the Loire river. A peaceful site with landscaped grounds.

C&CC Report *Rural setting, close to the village of Sainte Luce-sur-Loire, 8km from Nantes city centre, good for an overnight stay on the way south.*

dir: *Off Nantes eastern ring road.*

GPS: 47.2514, -1.4536

Open: All Year. **Site:** 4HEC **Prices:** 15.60-18.30 Mobile home hire 215-430 **Facilities:** Wi-fi (charged) Play Area **Services:** **Leisure:** R **Off-site:** P

FRANCE

STE-REINE-DE-BRETAGNE LOIRE-ATLANTIQUE

Château du Deffay

BP 18, 44160
240880057 240016655
e-mail: campingdudeffay@wanadoo.fr
web: www.camping-le-deffay.com

Set in the beautiful Parc de Brière providing fishing, walking and horse riding. Games and TV rooms.

dir: *4.5km W on D33 rte de Pontchâteau.*

GPS: 47.4410, -2.1598

Open: May-Sep **Site:** 13HEC **Prices:** 16.10-24.60 Mobile home hire 150-707 **Facilities:** Wi-fi (charged) Play Area **Services:** **Leisure:** P

SANTROP HAUTE-VIENNE

Camping de Santrop

87640
555710808 386379583
e-mail: aquadis1@orange.fr
web: www.aquadis-loisirs.com

A well-equipped family site on the shore of Lac de St-Pardoux with good facilities for water sports.

dir: *A20 exit 25.*

Open: May-Oct **Site:** 4.5HEC **Prices:** 10.30-16.40 **Facilities:** Play Area **Services:** **Leisure:** L **Off-site:** P

SAUMUR MAINE-ET-LOIRE

Chantepie

The Camping and Caravanning Club
The Friendly Club

49400
241679534 241679585
e-mail: info@campingchantepie.com
web: www.campingchantepie.com

A pleasant site with a fine view over the River Loire.

C&CC Report *A delightful family site perched in a prime position on the Loire. This high quality site provides a range of activities including wine-tasting, walks, canoeing and a childrens' club. The rustic charm of the site fits well with the local region where you can discover mushroom caves, châteaux and Saumur's vineyards.*

dir: *D751 towards Gennes.*

Open: 13 May-10 Sep **Site:** 10HEC **Facilities:** **Services:** **Leisure:** P

Ile d'Offard

bd de Verden, 49400
241403000 241673781
e-mail: iledoffard@cvtloisirs.fr
web: www.cvtloisirs.com

On an island in the middle of the Loire near municipal stadium, facing the "Chateau of Saumur". Kids' club in high season.

Open: Mar-mid Nov **Site:** 5.5HEC **Prices:** 16-29 **Facilities:** Wi-fi (charged) Kids' Club Play Area **Services:** **Leisure:** P R **Off-site:**

SELLE CRAONNAISE, LA MAYENNE

Rincerie

Base de Loisirs la Rincerie, 53800
243061752 243075020
e-mail: contact@la-rincerie.com
web: www.la-rincerie.com

A modern site offering a good selection of sports facilities and activities for children in July and August. Separate car park for arrivals after 22.00hrs.

dir: *N of La Selle-Craonnaise towards Ballots.*

GPS: 47.8644, -1.0669

Open: Mar-Oct **Site:** 5HEC **Prices:** 6.80-10.90 **Facilities:** Wi-fi **Services:** **Off-site:** P

SENONCHES EURE-ET-LOIRE

Huttopia Senonches

Etang de Badouleau, 28250
237378140 237377893
e-mail: senonches@huttopia.com
web: www.huttopia.com

Located in the Perche region, this site has pitches within a wooded area. A natural swimming pool is on offer and campers can watch films on a large open-air screen. Guided nature walks at dusk. Kids' club in July and August, 1 dog per pitch.

dir: *N12 onto D928 towards Digny then Senonches, follow Huttopia signs.*

GPS: 48.5531, 1.0386

Open: 22 Apr-6 Nov **Site:** 10HEC **Prices:** 13-21.90 **Facilities:** Kids' Club Play Area **Services:** **Leisure:** L P **Off-site:**

FRANCE

SILLÉ-LE-GUILLAUME — SARTHE

Indigo Les Molières

Sille Plage, 72140
☎ 243201612 🖹 243245684
e-mail: molieres@camping-indigo.com
web: www.camping-indigo.com

Situated in the national forest of Sillé, flat site, shaded by large trees. Swimming is available in both the lake and pool. Kids' club in July and August. 1 dog per pitch.

dir: *A11 exit 7 follow signs.*

GPS: 48.2034, -0.1287

Open: Jun-11 Sep **Site:** 8HEC **Prices:** 13-18 Mobile home hire 240.10-595 **Facilities:** Kids' Club Play Area **Services:** **Leisure:** L P **Off-site:**

SILLÉ-LE-PHILIPPE — SARTHE

Château de Chanteloup

72460
☎ 243275107
e-mail: chanteloup.souffront@wanadoo.fr
web: www.chateau-de-chanteloup.com

Set partly in wooded clearings and open ground within the park surrounding an old mansion. Good sanitary installations. Kids' club available from 15 July to 15 August.

C&CC Report *The spacious grounds around the owning family's château provide pitches in a peaceful and beautiful setting, while there's both a relaxed, sociable atmosphere and lots of space, with woodland walks, fishing, cycle routes and fun outdoor family activities. An idyllic site, with friendly, attentive and caring owners, especially for younger families and those who genuinely want to take it easy. Great too for visiting Le Mans for the free nightime sound and light shows (July and August Tue-Sat only).*

dir: *17km NE of Le Mans on D301.*

Open: 28 May-Aug **Site:** 20HEC **Prices:** 22.70-29.90 **Facilities:** Wi-fi Kids' Club Play Area **Services:** **Leisure:** L P

SONZAY — INDRE-ET-LOIRE

Camping l'Arada Parc

r de la Baratière, 37360
☎ 247247269 🖹 247247270
e-mail: info@laradaparc.com
web: www.laradaparc.com

Site with leisure facilities that include indoor and outdoor pools, plus spa and fitness room. Programme of events for both children and adults. Kids' club takes place in summer.

GPS: 47.5262, 0.4509

Open: 26 Mar-Oct **Site:** 1.7HEC **Prices:** 15-23 Mobile home hire 245-679 **Facilities:** Wi-fi (charged) Kids' Club Play Area **Services:** **Leisure:** P

SUÈVRES — LOIR-ET-CHER

Château de la Grenouillère

41500
☎ 254878037 🖹 254878421
e-mail: la.grenouillere@wanadoo.fr
web: www.camping-loire.com

A family site in the Loire region, close to the château of Chambord. A large selection of pitches, all with electricity, entertainment and swimming pools.

dir: *A10 exit 16 Mer/Chambord, RN152 towards Blois. Site 2km after Mer on right.*

Open: 9 Apr-10 Sep **Site:** 12HEC **Prices:** 26-45 **Facilities:** Wi-fi (charged) Kids' Club Play Area **Services:** **Leisure:** P

SULLY-SUR-LOIRE — LOIRET

Hortus Jardin de Sully

rte de St Benoit - D60, 45600
☎ 238363594 🖹 238363594
e-mail: info@camping-hortus.com
web: www.camping-hortus.com

On a level meadow beside the River Loire.

C&CC Report *Set on the banks of the Loire across the river from Sully-sur-Loire, with views of the nearby medieval château and bars, restaurants and shops within a couple of kilometres.*

dir: *W on D60 towards St-Benoît-sur-Loire.*

Open: All Year. **Site:** 5HEC **Facilities:** **Services:** **Leisure:** P R **Off-site:** L

TALMONT-ST-HILAIRE — VENDÉE

Yelloh Village Le Littoral

Le Porteau, 85440
☎ 251220464 🖹 251220537
e-mail: info@campinglelittoral.fr
web: www.campinglelittoral.fr

Situated near Port Bourgenay, 80m from the sea. Good facilities and entertainment available during the season. Bar, restaurant, grocery, bakery shop open from April to September. Servicing posts for motor homes.

dir: *In Talmont-St-Hilaire follow signs to aquarium, site close by.*

Open: 8 Apr-11 Sep **Site:** 8.5HEC **Prices:** 15-41 Mobile home hire 245-1365 **Facilities:** Wi-fi Kids' Club Play Area **Services:** **Leisure:** P **Off-site:** S

FRANCE

Villagecenter
Les Almadies ***
Indoor water park, heated with water slides
3 km from the beach
125 places - 387 rental accomodations - 11 ha
85360 LA TRANCHE SUR MER
+33 (0)4 99 57 21 21 - www.village-center.com/C37

TRANCHE-SUR-MER, LA — VENDÉE

Baie d'Aunis

10 r du Pertuis Breton, 85360
☎ 251274736 🖷 251274454
e-mail: info@camping-baiedaunis.com
web: www.camping-baiedaunis.com

On level land by the sea, 50m from the beach and 400m from the town centre with a variety of leisure activities.

dir: *300m E on D46.*

Open: 30 Apr-20 Sep **Site:** 2.4HEC **Prices:** 25.10-33.40 **Facilities:** Wi-fi Play Area **Services:** **Leisure:** P S **Off-site:**

Bel

r du Bottereau, 85360
☎ 251304739 🖷 251277281
e-mail: campbel@wanadoo.fr

A quiet, family-run site 450m from a magnificent beach and a marine lake. Plenty of sports and entertainment facilities.

C&CC Report *Abandon your car at this small family run campsite, within easy walking distance of the popular resort of La Tranche-Sur-Mer. The friendly owners take pride in their facilities, and families with smaller children are particularly welcome. As well as the site pool there is also a water park in the resort with indoor pools and waterslides, but it'll be the great beaches in this area that keep the whole family happy.*

dir: *Follow town centre direction.*

Open: 26 May-4 Sep **Site:** 3.5HEC **Prices:** 29 **Facilities:** Wi-fi (charged) Play Area **Services:** **Leisure:** P S **Off-site:**

Cottage Fleuri

La Grière-Plage, 85360
☎ 251303457 🖷 251277477

A level site with modern facilities.

dir: *2.5km E, 0.5km from beach.*

Open: Apr-Sep **Site:** 7.5HEC **Facilities:** **Services:** **Leisure:** P **Off-site:** S

Jard

123 bd de Lattre-de-Tassigny, 85360
☎ 251274379 🖷 251274292
e-mail: info@campingdujard.fr
web: www.campingdujard.fr

A family site on level ground with clearly defined pitches, 0.7km from the beach, with plenty of recreational facilities.

C&CC Report *Great for all the family, this site is well placed to enjoy the sandy beaches of the sunny Southern Vendée. A short walk will take you to La Grière beach, one of the local favourites, if you can drag yourself away from the excellent pool complex and activity programme. Camping du Jard is a popular site with British campers and caravanners, many of whom return here year after year.*

dir: *Via D747.*

Open: 20 May-12 Sep **Site:** 6HEC **Facilities:** **Services:** **Leisure:** P **Off-site:**

Village Center les Almadies

La Charrière des Bandes, 85360
☎ 499572121 🖷 467516389
e-mail: contact@village-center.com
web: www.village-center.com/pays-de-la-loire/camping-les-almadies.php

An 11 hectare park, 3km from beach.

dir: *A83 take exit for St Hermine, then onto D949 to Luçon, then D747 to La Tranche-sur-Mer.*

GPS: 46.3725, -1.4153

Open: 8 Apr-2 Oct **Site:** 11HEC **Prices:** 14-25 Mobile home hire 167-637 **Facilities:** Wi-fi (charged) Kids' Club Play Area **Services:** **Leisure:** P

see advert on this page

TROCHE — CORRÈZE

Domaine Vert

Les Magnes, 19230
☎ 555735989
e-mail: ledomainevert@orange.fr
web: www.ledomainevert.nl

Peaceful farm site surrounded by grass and woodland where campers can select their own pitch. Well-kept facilities and the opportunity to try the organic produce from the farm.

dir: *A20 exit 45, to Vigeois, after Vigeois right onto D50 for Lubersac, site 5km.*

GPS: 45.4086, 1.4788

Open: Apr-1 Oct **Site:** 3HEC **Prices:** 18 **Facilities:** Wi-fi **Services:** **Off-site:** L R

TROGUES INDRE-ET-LOIRE

Château de la Rolandière

37220
☎ 247585371
e-mail: contact@larolandiere.com
web: www.larolandiere.com

Situated in parkland surrounding a fine chateau. A good base for visiting the chateaux of the Loire.

dir: *A10 exit 25, road for Chinon for 6km.*

GPS: 47.1071, 0.5102

Open: 23 Apr-24 Sep **Site:** 4HEC **Prices:** 16.50-24.50 Mobile home hire 310-680 **Facilities:** Wi-fi (charged) Play Area **Services:** **Leisure:** P **Off-site:** R

Village Center le Parc des Allais

Les Allais, 37220
☎ 499572121 467516389
e-mail: contact@village-center.com
web: www.village-center.com/centre/camping-parc-les-allais.php

A natural environment site at the heart of the Loire châteaux. On the banks of the Vienne river and beside a fine lake.

dir: *A10 autoroute from Tours exit 25 Ste Maure de Touraine.*

GPS: 47.0974, 0.5020

Open: 8 Apr-2 Oct **Site:** 16HEC **Prices:** 16-26 Mobile home hire 192-889 **Facilities:** Wi-fi Kids' Club Play Area **Services:** **Leisure:** P

see advert on this page

TURBALLE, LA LOIRE-ATLANTIQUE

Parc Ste-Brigitte

Domaine de Bréhet, Chemin des Routes, 44420
☎ 240248891 240156572
e-mail: saintebrigitte@wanadoo.fr
web: www.campingsaintebrigitte.com

Parkland site in the grounds of a château, divided into pitches and surrounded by hedges.

dir: *E of village on D99 Guérande road.*

Open: Apr-Sep **Site:** 6HEC **Prices:** 23.90-30.80 Mobile home hire 440-770 **Facilities:** Wi-fi Play Area **Services:** **Leisure:** P **Off-site:** S

VARENNES-SUR-LOIRE MAINE-ET-LOIRE

Étang de la Brèche

5 Impasse de la Brèche, 49730
☎ 241512292 241512724
e-mail: etang.breche@wanadoo.fr
web: www.etang-breche.com

Relaxing site in the heart of the Loire Valley, ideal base for visiting sites of historical interest. A kids' club is available in high season.

dir: *4.5km NW via N152.*

Open: 15 May-11 Sep **Site:** 24HEC **Prices:** 16.50-37 Mobile home hire 248-1049 **Facilities:** Wi-fi Kids' Club Play Area **Services:** **Leisure:** P

VELLES INDRE

Grands Pins

Les Maisons Neuves, 36330
☎ 254366193
e-mail: contact@les-grands-pins.fr
web: www.les-grands-pins.fr

The site has individual pitches and has easy access to the countryside. Swimming pool only available July and August.

dir: *7km S of Châteauroux on D920 direction Les Maisons Neuves; between exits 14 & 15 of A20.*

Open: 10 Mar-15 Dec **Site:** 5HEC **Prices:** 15 **Facilities:** Wi-fi **Services:** **Leisure:** P

VENDÔME LOIR-ET-CHER

Grand Prés

r G-Martel, 41100
☎ 254770027 254894101
e-mail: campings@cpvendome.com

Site lies on a meadow, next to a sports ground.

dir: *E of town on right bank of Loire.*

Open: 21 May-7 Sep **Site:** 3HEC **Facilities:** **Services:** **Leisure:** P R **Off-site:**

FRANCE

VILLIERS-LE-MORHIER — EURE-ET-LOIR

Ilots de St Val

28130
237827130 237827767
e-mail: lesilots@campinglesilotsdestval.com
web: www.campinglesilotsdestval.com

A peaceful rural setting between Maintenon and Nogent-le-Roi, nestling above the Eure river. A haven for wildlife.

dir: *On D983.*

Open: All Year. **Site:** 10HEC **Facilities:** **Services:** **Off-site:** R

BRITTANY/NORMANDY

ALENÇON — ORNE

CM de Guéramé

65 r de Guéramé, 61000
233263495 233263495
e-mail: campingguerame@ville-alencon.fr

Set in open country near a stream, 0.5km from town centre.

dir: *Via boulevard Périphérique in SW part of town.*

Open: Apr-Sep **Site:** 1.5HEC **Prices:** 10.30 **Facilities:** Wi-fi Play Area **Services:** **Leisure:** R **Off-site:** P

ALLINEUC — CÔTES-D'ARMOR

Lac de Bosméléac

Bosméléac, 22460
296288788 296288097
e-mail: bosmeleac@orange.fr
web: bosmeleac.monsite-orange.fr

Wooded site beside a lake with a beach.

dir: *RN12 Brest-Paris exit Loudéac.*

Open: 15 Jun-Sep **Site:** 1.15HEC **Prices:** 8 **Facilities:** Play Area **Services:** **Leisure:** L **Off-site:** P R

ARRADON — MORBIHAN

Penboch

9 chemin de Penboch, 56610
297447129 297447910
e-mail: camping.penboch@wanadoo.fr
web: www.camping-penboch.fr

An well-appointed site in a pleasant wooded location 200m from the beaches of the Gulf of Morbihan. The swimming pool has a large chute with 4 waterslides, plus an indoor pool and jacuzzi.

dir: *Signed from N165.*

Open: 8 Apr-25 Sep **Site:** 4HEC **Prices:** 15.90-34.80 Mobile home hire 285-1190 **Facilities:** Wi-fi Play Area **Services:** **Leisure:** P S

ARZANO — FINISTÈRE

Ty Nadan

The Camping and Caravanning Club — The Friendly Club

rte d'Arzano, 29310
298717547 298717731
e-mail: infos@camping-ty-nadan.fr
web: www.camping-ty-nadan.fr

A quiet riverside site in attractive parkland in the Ellé Valley.

C&CC Report *An activity lover's paradise for all ages, all season through, with everything from horse-riding, archery, paint-balling, canoe trips and zip-lining to quad biking. You won't need to go off-site, but the local area is very pretty, and if you need a rest, head to the nearest beaches, just 20 minutes drive away.*

dir: *3km W. N165 exit Quimperlé for Arzano.*

Open: 27 Mar-2 Sep **Site:** 23HEC **Facilities:** **Services:** **Leisure:** P R

see advert on opposite page

AUDIERNE — FINISTÈRE

Loquéran

BP 55, 29770
298749506 298749114
e-mail: campgite.loqueran@free.fr
web: campgite.loqueran.free.fr

A terraced woodland site in calm and peaceful surroundings, a short distance from the sea.

Open: May-Sep **Site:** 1HEC **Prices:** 10.50 **Facilities:** Wi-fi **Services:** **Off-site:** S

BADEN MORBIHAN

Mané Guernehué

r Mane er Groez, 56870
☎ 297570206 297571543
e-mail: info@camping-baden.com
web: www.camping-baden.com

A pleasant location at the head of the Gulf of Morbihan with good recreational facilities including a large pool complex with indoor and outdoor pools and water slides plus an equestrian farm.

C&CC Report *With one of the best campsite pool complexes in France, Mané-Guernehué is more than just a campsite, it's an activities paradise. Busy and lively, on-site activities include pony rides for tiny tots through to adults, archery, a treetop adventure park and a spa facility worthy of a top-class hotel. The pretty rural location is also perfect for visiting the Morbihan Gulf islands, resorts of Carnac and La Trinité, as well as nearby Le Bono and Auray.*

dir: *1km SW via Mériadec road.*

GPS: 47.6141, -2.9254

Open: Apr-Oct **Site:** 10HEC **Prices:** 15-38 Mobile home hire 238-1281 **Facilities:** Kids' Club Play Area **Services:** **Leisure:** P **Off-site:** S

BARNEVILLE-CARTERET MANCHE

Yelloh Village Les Vikings

St-Jean-de-la-Rivière, 50270
☎ 233538413
web: www.camping-lesvikings.com

A family site with level terrain, 400m from the sea and a fine sandy beach.

dir: *SE of Barneville-Carteret off D904.*

Open: 15 Mar-15 Nov **Site:** 6HEC **Facilities:** **Services:** **Leisure:** P

BAYEUX CALVADOS

CM Calvados

bd d'Eindhoven, 14400
☎ 231920843 231920843
e-mail: campingmunicipal@mairiebayeux.fr
web: www.mairie-bayeux.fr

Very clean and tidy site with tarmac drive and hardstanding for caravans. Adjoins football field.

dir: *N side of town on Boulevard Circulaire.*

Open: May-Sep **Site:** 2.9HEC **Facilities:** **Services:** **Off-site:** P

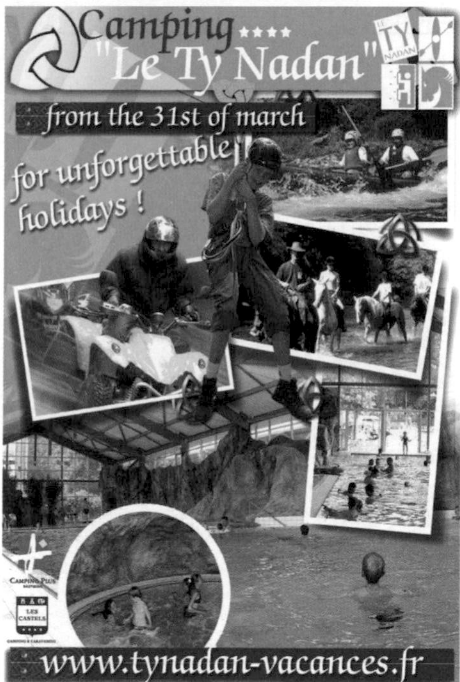

BEG-MEIL FINISTÈRE

Kervastard

chemin de Kervastard, 29170
☎ 298949152 298949983
e-mail: camping.le.kervastard@wanadoo.fr
web: www.campinglekervastard.com

A pleasant wooded site 250m from a fine sandy beach with plenty of leisure facilities, close to the village centre.

dir: *In village.*

Open: May-Sep **Site:** 2HEC **Prices:** 15.60-23.50 Mobile home hire 280-660 **Facilities:** Play Area **Services:** **Leisure:** P **Off-site:** R S

Roche Percée

29170
☎ 298949415 298944805
e-mail: contact@camping-larochepercee.com
web: www.camping-larochepercee.com

Wooded family site 400m from the Roche Percée beach.

dir: *1km from Beg Meil towards Fouesnant.*

GPS: 47.8694, -3.9918

Open: 2 Apr-24 Sep **Site:** 2.35HEC **Facilities:** Wi-fi (charged) Kids' Club Play Area **Services:** **Leisure:** P **Off-site:** S

FRANCE

BÉNODET FINISTÈRE

Letty

29950
☎ 298570469 🖷 298662256
e-mail: reception@campingduletty.com
web: www.campingduletty.com

Site bordering beach, divided into small paddocks. Good sanitary installations, ironing rooms and games room. Good beach for children. Use of car park compulsory after 23.00hrs.

C&CC Report *The best site in the popular resort of Bénodet, now about to be further enhanced with the addition of a superb new indoor and outdoor pool complex. An extremely well-run site, with no statics on site, you will always receive a warm welcome here and enjoy the high quality range of facilities which suit campers and caravanners of all ages.*

dir: *1km SE beside sea.*

Open: 11 Jun-6 Sep **Site:** 10HEC **Prices:** 19-32 **Facilities:** Wi-fi Kids' Club Play Area **Services:** **Leisure:** P S **Off-site:** P

Pointe St-Gilles

Corniche de la Mer, 29950
☎ 298570537 🖷 298572752
e-mail: sunelia@stgilles.fr
web: www.stgilles.fr

Holiday site south of village, on fields by beach. Divided into sectors with individual pitches. Well-equipped sanitary blocks and a range of facilities, including a covered pool complex and spa.

dir: *D34 Quimper-Bénodet, signed in town. From N165 take exit for Concarneau, turn right following signs for Bénodet, site signed.*

Open: 22 Apr-18 Sep **Site:** 10HEC **Prices:** 20-42 Mobile home hire 319-1225 **Facilities:** Wi-fi (charged) Kids' Club Play Area **Services:** **Leisure:** P S **Off-site:**

Yelloh Village Port de Plaisance

Lieu dit Prad Poullou, Clohars Fouesnant, 29950
☎ 298570238 🖷 298572525
e-mail: info@campingbenodet.fr
web: www.campingbenodet.fr

A well-equipped family site on the outskirts of the town, 0.5km from the harbour, 1km from the beach.

dir: *NE off D34 at entrance to town.*

GPS: 47.8821, -4.1033

Open: 8 Apr-18 Sep **Site:** 12HEC **Prices:** 15-40 Mobile home hire 224-1141 **Facilities:** Wi-fi Kids' Club Play Area **Services:** **Leisure:** P **Off-site:** R S

BÉNOUVILLE CALVADOS

Hautes Coutures

av de la Côte de Nacre, 14970
☎ 231447308 🖷 231953080
e-mail: info@campinghautescoutures.com
web: www.campinghautescoutures.com

Pleasant site with good facilities near the Canal Maritime and within easy reach of the Caen-Portsmouth ferry. Kids' club available in July and August.

C&CC Report *Extremely well placed to visit the historic D-Day beaches, Les Hautes Coutures is also close to the port of Ouistreham. Pegasus Bridge, its superb museum and the Café Gondrée are a short stroll away, while Caen's Peace Memorial museum, the D-Day beaches and Bayeux, with its famous Norman tapestry, are all an easy drive away. The swimming pool complex will be popular with the children after being taken to see the historic sites of the region.*

dir: *From Caen towards Ouistréham on dual carriageway, exit Zone Activités Benouville, site after Pegasus Bridge exit.*

Open: Apr-Oct **Site:** 7HEC **Prices:** 23-28.80 Mobile home hire 284-883 **Facilities:** Wi-fi Kids' Club Play Area **Services:** **Leisure:** P R **Off-site:** S

BINIC CÔTES-D'ARMOR

Palmiers

Kerviarc'h, 22520
☎ 296737259 🖷 296737259
e-mail: campingpalmiers.chantal@laposte.net
web: www.campingpalmiers.com

A well-equipped site within the Parc Tropical de Bretagne, just over 1km from the town centre.

dir: *Via N12/D786.*

Open: Jun-Sep **Site:** 2HEC **Facilities:** **Services:** **Leisure:** P **Off-site:** R S

FRANCE

BLANGY-LE-CHÂTEAU CALVADOS

Brévedent

Le Brévedent, 14130
☎ 231647288 📠 231643341
e-mail: contact@campinglebrevedent.com
web: www.campinglebrevedent.com

Situated in the grounds of an 18th-century manor house with good facilities.

C&CC Report *Perfect for young families and couples, this top quality site offers an idyllic rural château setting, a splendid restaurant and charming site owners. The friendly little café by the château and the family bathrooms are welcome enhancements to the relaxed, family atmosphere. Visits to Lisieux, Pont l'Evêque, Deauville, a local farm, a Calvados distillery and even Paris are possible and often organised by the site.*

dir: *3km SE on D51 beside lake.*

Open: May-18 Sep **Site:** 5.5HEC **Facilities:** **Services:** **Leisure:** P **Off-site:**

Domaine du Lac

rte du Mesnil, 14130
☎ 231646200 📠 231641591
e-mail: info@normandie-challenge.com

In natural parkland close to lake and river, the site has good facilities and is close to the village.

Open: Apr-Oct **Site:** 7HEC **Facilities:** **Services:** **Leisure:** L R **Off-site:**

BLANGY-SUR-BRESLE SEINE-MARITIME

CM

r des Étangs, 76340
☎ 235945565 📠 235945565

In the middle of the local leisure park comprising 80 hectares of woodland, lakes and streams.

dir: *300m on N28.*

Open: Apr-Sep **Site:** 8HEC **Prices:** 8.95-11.55 **Facilities:** **Services:** **Off-site:** R

BOURG-ACHARD EURE

Clos Normand

235 rte de Pont-Audemer, 27310
☎ 232563484
e-mail: eric.tanney@wanadoo.fr
web: www.leclosnormand.eu

A peaceful location within an apple orchard. Situated on the plateau of the Roumois, an ideal corner for those wanting to escape city life.

dir: *A13 exit Bourg-Achard, site 1km.*

Open: Apr-Sep **Site:** 1.5HEC **Prices:** 13-19.50 Mobile home hire 250-470 **Facilities:** (charged) Play Area **Services:** **Leisure:** P **Off-site:**

CAHAGNOLLES CALVADOS

Camping l'Escapade

r de l'église, 14490
☎ 231216359 📠 231920648
e-mail: escapadecamping@orange.fr
web: www.campinglescapade.net

Quiet site with wide pitches. Three ponds with fishing available. Only dogs below 10kg are accepted.

Open: Apr-Oct **Site:** 7HEC **Prices:** 13-16 Mobile home hire 231-686 **Facilities:** Wi-fi (charged) Play Area **Services:** **Leisure:** P

CALLAC CÔTES-D'ARMOR

CM Verte Vallée

BP58 Mairie de Callac, 22160
☎ 296455850

Between town and countryside, a few minutes' walk from the centre of Callac the site borders a pretty lake. There are facilities for tennis or mini-golf.

dir: *W on D28 towards Morlaix.*

Open: 15 Jun-15 Sep **Site:** 1HEC **Facilities:** **Services:** **Off-site:**

CAMARET-SUR-MER FINISTÈRE

Armorique

29570
☎ 298277733 📠 298273838
e-mail: contact@campingarmorique.com
web: www.campingarmorique.com

Situated beside the sea on the edge of the Armorique regional park with a variety of recreational facilities.

dir: *3km NE on D355 rte de Roscanvel.*

Open: 29 Mar-Sep **Site:** 2.5HEC **Facilities:** **Services:** **Leisure:** P **Off-site:** S

Grand Large

Lambezen, 29570
☎ 298279141 📠 298279372
e-mail: contact@campinglegrandlarge.com
web: www.campinglegrandlarge.com

Situated at the tip of the Armorique regional park, facing the sea.

dir: *Entering Camaret, at rdbt right onto D355, 2km turn right.*

Open: Apr-Sep **Site:** 2.8HEC **Facilities:** **Services:** **Leisure:** P **Off-site:** S

FRANCE

Plage de Trez Rouz

29570
☎ 298279396
e-mail: contact@trezrouz.com
web: www.trezrouz.com

On level ground 50m from the beach.

dir: *3km from Camaret-sur-Mer on D355 towards Pointe-des-Espagnols.*

Open: 15 Mar-15 Oct **Site:** 3.1HEC
Prices: 12.70-16.50 Mobile home hire 220-690 **Facilities:** Wi-fi Play Area **Services:** **Leisure:** S

CANCALE ILLE-ET-VILAINE

Notre Dame du Verger

35260
☎ 299897284 299896011

Terraced site overlooking the sea with direct access to the beach.

dir: *2km from Pointe-du-Grouin on D201.*

Open: 29 Mar-28 Sep **Site:** 2.2HEC **Facilities:** **Services:** **Off-site:** S

CARANTEC FINISTÈRE

Mouettes

The Camping and Caravanning Club The Friendly Club

50 rte de la Grande Grève, 29660
☎ 298670246 298783146
e-mail: camping@les-mouettes.com
web: www.les-mouettes.com

Level site divided by low shrubs and trees with extensive leisure facilities and activities for children.

C&CC Report *This very high quality, family-run, family-oriented and very busy site, is renowned for its range and quality of services, many being open all season. The superb water park, with an adults-only session at the start of each morning, comprises 1,000m2 of water, 180m of slides, sunbathing terraces and artificial river, with a bar terrace, shop and take-away adjacent. An entertainments room and second bar, a crêperie, plus a large stage and square now add to the picture, while on-site sports facilities are good and there are watersports in Carantec. Close by, St. Pol-de-Léon, Morlaix, the coast and the inland moors are recommended visits.*

dir: *1.5km SW on rte de St-Pol-de-Léon towards sea.*

Open: 13 May-11 Sep **Site:** 14HEC
Prices: 15-44 Mobile home hire 123-1477 **Facilities:** Wi-fi Kids' Club Play Area **Services:** **Leisure:** P **Off-site:** S

CARENTAN MANCHE

CM le Haut Dick

30 chemin du Grand-Bas Pays, 50500
☎ 233421689
e-mail: lehautdick@aol.com
web: www.camping-municipal.com

A level site in wooded surroundings with well-defined pitches.

dir: *Village road off N13 towards Le Port.*

Open: 15 Jan-1 Nov **Site:** 2.5HEC **Facilities:** **Services:** **Off-site:** P R

CARNAC MORBIHAN

Bruyères

Kerogile, 56340
☎ 297523057 971704647
e-mail: contact@camping-lesbruyeres.com
web: www.camping-lesbruyeres.com

Partly wooded site with modern facilities close to the local beaches.

dir: *N of Carnac on C4, 2km from Plouharnel.*

Open: Apr-Sep **Site:** 3.8HEC **Prices:** 14.70-18.40 Mobile home hire 246-670 **Facilities:** Wi-fi Kids' Club Play Area **Services:**

Druides

55 chemin de Beaumer, 56340
☎ 297520818 297529613
e-mail: contact@camping-les-druides.com
web: www.camping-les-druides.com

Family site with well-defined pitches, 400m from a fine sandy beach.

dir: *SE of town centre. Approach via D781 or D119.*

Open: May-13 Sep **Site:** 2.5HEC **Facilities:**
Services: **Leisure:** P **Off-site:** S

Étang

67 rte de Kerlann, 56340
☎ 297521406
web: www.camping-etang.fr

A rural setting with pitches divided by hedges, 2.5km from the coast.

dir: *2km N at Kerlann on D119.*

Open: Apr-15 Oct **Site:** 2.5HEC **Prices:** 18.40 Mobile home hire 540 **Facilities:** Wi-fi (charged) Play Area **Services:** **Leisure:** P

Grande Métairie

rte des Alignements, de Kermario, 56342
297522401 297528358
e-mail: info@lagrandemetairie.com
web: www.lagrandemetairie.com
Holiday site with modern amenities, completely divided into pitches. Kids' club available 21 May-10 Sep.

dir: *2.5km NE on D196.*

Open: 2 Apr-10 Sep **Site:** 15HEC **Prices:** 17.10-41.20 Mobile home hire 245-1100 **Facilities:** Kids' Club Play Area **Services:** **Leisure:** P S **Off-site:** L

see advert on this page

Men Dû

22 bis Chemin de Beaumer, 56340
297520423
e-mail: mendu@wanadoo.fr
web: www.camping-mendu.com
Peaceful site in a wooded setting close to the beach.

dir: *1km from Carnac Plage via D781 & D186.*

GPS: 47.5789, -3.0535

Open: Apr-Oct **Site:** 1.5HEC **Prices:** 15-23 Mobile home hire 190-620 **Facilities:** Wi-fi (charged) **Services:** **Off-site:** R S

Menhirs

The Camping and Caravanning Club The Friendly Club

allée St-Michel, 56343
297529467 297522538
e-mail: contact@lesmenhirs.com
web: www.lesmenhirs.com
A family site near the beach and shops with good recreational facilities and modern sanitary blocks, including toilets suitable for the disabled.

C&CC Report *Enjoying a superb location, just a short walk from the beach and shops, this bustling site has lots to do for active families – so forget about the car. Enjoy the pools, the waterslides, the bars and activity room complex. Carnac-Plage is a popular little resort, while the famous prehistoric standing stones, Quiberon peninsula and pretty Breton towns of Auray and Vannes should not be missed.*

Open: 25 Apr-26 Sep **Site:** 6HEC **Prices:** 24-46.90 Mobile home hire 275-953 **Facilities:** Wi-fi (charged) Kids' Club Play Area **Services:** **Leisure:** P **Off-site:** R S

see advert on this page

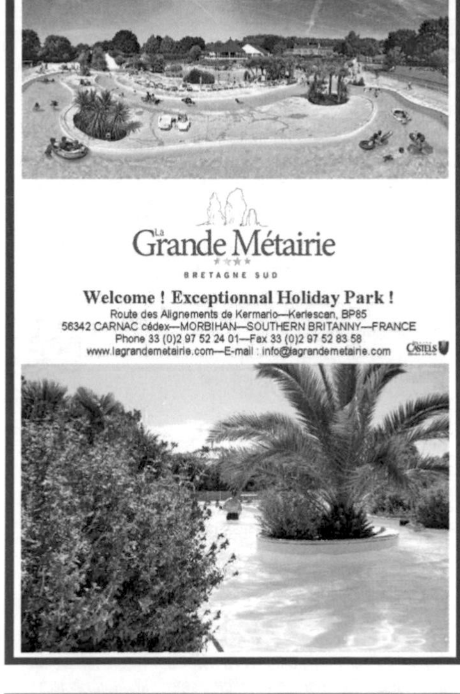

La Grande Métairie
BRETAGNE SUD
Welcome ! Exceptionnal Holiday Park !
Route des Alignements de Kermario—Kerlescan, BP85
56342 CARNAC cédex—MORBIHAN—SOUTHERN BRITANNY—FRANCE
Phone 33 (0)2 97 52 24 01—Fax 33 (0)2 97 52 83 58
www.lagrandemetairie.com—E-mail : info@lagrandemetairie.com
Castels

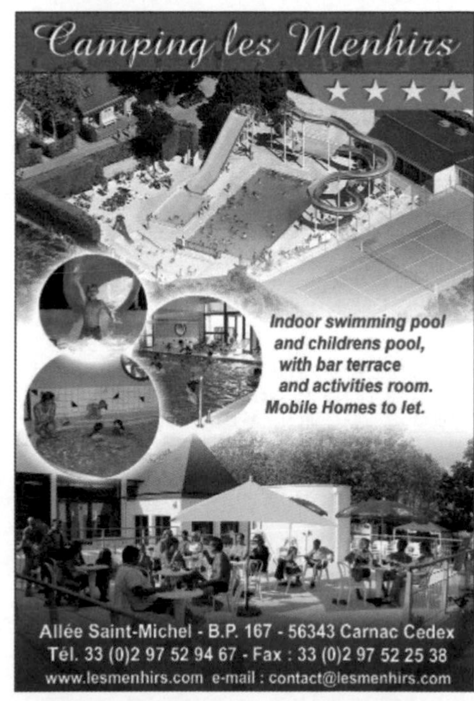

Camping les Menhirs
★★★★
Indoor swimming pool and childrens pool, with bar terrace and activities room.
Mobile Homes to let.
Allée Saint-Michel - B.P. 167 - 56343 Carnac Cedex
Tél. 33 (0)2 97 52 94 67 - Fax : 33 (0)2 97 52 25 38
www.lesmenhirs.com e-mail : contact@lesmenhirs.com

Facilities shop shower electric points for razors electric points for caravans parking by tents permitted compulsory separate car park **Services** café/restaurant bar Camping Gaz International gas other than Camping Gaz first aid facilities laundry **Leisure** swimming L-Lake P-Pool R-River S-Sea **Off-site** All facilities within 5km

Moulin de Kermaux

rte de Kerlescan, 56340
☎ 297521590 🖷 297528385
e-mail: moulin-de-kermaux@wanadoo.fr
web: www.camping-moulinkermaux.com

A quiet location surrounded by trees and bushes, with good facilities. Within easy reach of the coast and the local megaliths.

dir: *2.5km NE.*

Open: 9 Apr-17 Sep **Site:** 3HEC **Prices:** 17.70-26.90 **Facilities:** Wi-fi (charged) Kids' Club Play Area **Services:** **Leisure:** P **Off-site:** R S

Moustoir

The Camping and Caravanning Club The Friendly Club

71 rte du Moustoir, 56340
☎ 297521618 🖷 297528837
e-mail: info@lemoustoir.com
web: www.lemoustoir.com

Well-equipped site in a rural setting close to the sea. Kids' club in July and August.

C&CC Report *In a great location, just a short drive or bike ride away from Carnac resort, while enjoying a lovely countryside setting. There is so much for children to do on site; the waterslides, indoor pool, splashball, pony rides and zip-lines being hot favourites. An excellent family site with much to see and do in the surrounding area – Carnac, La Trinité, Quiberon and the rugged Côte Sauvage peninsula are all close by. Plus Carnac's standing stones are literally just down the road.*

dir: *3km NE of Carnac.*

GPS: 47.6087, -3.0674

Open: Apr-Sep **Site:** 5HEC **Prices:** 20-32 Mobile home hire 224-788 **Facilities:** Wi-fi Kids' Club Play Area **Services:** **Leisure:** P **Off-site:** S

Ombrages

56430
☎ 297521652

Wooded location with shaded pitches divided by hedges.

dir: *Rte Carnac to Auray, left at fuel station.*

Open: 10 Jun-20 Sep **Site:** 1HEC **Prices:** 15.60 Mobile home hire 210-500 **Facilities:** **Services:** **Off-site:** L S

CAUREL — CÔTES-D'ARMOR

Nautic International

The Camping and Caravanning Club The Friendly Club

rte de Beau Rivage, 22530
☎ 296285794 🖷 296260200
e-mail: contact@campingnautic.fr
web: www.campingnautic.fr

A terraced site in woodland on the edge of Lake Guerlédan with a variety of recreational facilities.

C&CC Report *A rare combination of relaxation, location and water activities is what makes this rustic site special. A short stroll to the pleasure cruisers, bars and eateries of the lakeside leaves the site an oasis of calm amid nearly 100 different species of tree and shrub. Children love the unique underwater arched windows of the site swimming pool. In the centre of Brittany, this is also a good base for day trips to almost anywhere in the region.*

dir: *N164 towards Beau Rivage.*

GPS: 48.2089, -3.0508

Open: 15 May-25 Sep **Site:** 3.6HEC **Prices:** 15.20-22.80 Mobile home hire 280-610 **Facilities:** **Services:** **Leisure:** L P **Off-site:**

CHAPELLE-AUX-FILZMÉENS, LA — ILLE-ET-VILAINE

Domaine du Logis

35190
☎ 299452545 🖷 299453040
e-mail: domainedulogis@wanadoo.fr
web: www.domainedulogis.com

A quiet, pleasant site in the wooded grounds of an 18th-century château. Restaurant and kids' club available in July and August.

dir: *NE of town towards Combourg.*

GPS: 48.3811, -1.8327

Open: Apr-1 Nov **Site:** 6HEC **Prices:** 16.40-23.40 Mobile home hire 280-640 **Facilities:** Wi-fi Kids' Club **Services:** **Leisure:** P **Off-site:** R

CHÂTEAULIN — FINISTÈRE

La Pointe

rte St-Coulitz, 29150
☎ 298865153
e-mail: lapointecamping@aol.com
web: www.lapointesuperbecamping.com

Set in a wooded valley close to the town with modern facilities. Pitches divided by hedges.

dir: *D770 S from Châteaulin centre for Quimper, 1km left to St-Coulitz, site 100m on right.*

Open: 11 Mar-15 Oct **Site:** 2.5HEC **Prices:** 14.50-16.50 **Facilities:** Wi-fi Play Area **Services:** **Leisure:** R **Off-site:** P

CLOÎTRE-ST-THEGONNEC, LE — FINISTÈRE

Bruyères

29410
☎ 298797176
web: www.camping-bruyeres.com

A small, secluded site in a picturesque setting within the Amorique regional park, 30km from Roscoff.

dir: *12km S of Morlaix via D769.*

Open: Jul-15 Sep **Site:** 2.5HEC **Prices:** 16 **Facilities:** Play Area **Services:** **Off-site:**

COMBOURG — ILLE-ET-VILAINE

Bois Coudrais

Cuguen, 35270
☎ 299732745
e-mail: info@vacancebretagne.com
web: www.vacancebretagne.com

A small family-run site with heated pool. Ideally located for exploring sites including Mont-St-Michel, St Malo, Rennes and Dinan.

dir: *Off D83.*

GPS: 48.4540, -1.6513

Open: May-Sep **Site:** 2.2HEC **Prices:** 16-20 **Facilities:** Wi-fi Play Area **Services:** **Leisure:** P **Off-site:**

CONCARNEAU — FINISTÈRE

Camping les Sables Blancs

av du Dorlett, 29900
☎ 298971644 298971644
e-mail: contact@camping-lessablesblancs.com
web: www.camping-lessablesblancs.com

150m from the beach and a 15 minute walk to the town, the swimming pool overlooks the sea. Entertainment includes concerts and karaoke.

Open: 2 Apr-Oct **Site:** 3HEC **Prices:** 13-20 Mobile home hire 200-700 **Facilities:** Wi-fi Kids' Club Play Area **Services:** **Leisure:** P S **Off-site:**

Les Prés Verts

Kernous Plage, BP612, 29900
☎ 298970974
e-mail: info@presverts.com
web: www.presverts.com

A landscaped site with good facilities overlooking Concarneau Bay.

dir: *1.2km NW.*

Open: May-Sep **Site:** 3HEC **Prices:** 16.10-23 **Facilities:** Wi-fi (charged) **Services:** **Leisure:** P S **Off-site:**

COURTILS — MANCHE

Saint Michel

The Camping and Caravanning Club — The Friendly Club

50220
☎ 233709690
e-mail: info@campingsaintmichel.com
web: www.campingsaintmichel.com

Well kept site located in a peaceful, rural setting, 8km from Mont-St-Michel. Pitches are shaded by many trees and shrubs. On site is a small enclosure of farm animals kept to entertain visitors.

C&CC Report *A beautifully kept, very friendly site, that is both great for holidays and highly convenient for all routes across the north of France. The attractive restaurant, bar, reception and shop are all run together to create a welcoming, community feel as soon as you arrive. There are lots of quiet lanes for cycling and Christophe and his staff are a mine of information. Though superbly located for visiting Le Mont-St-Michel, including its shellfish centres and even guided walks across the bay, just a little further afield are Europe's oldest medieval castle at Fougères, the picturesque copper-working centre of Villedieu-les-Poêles, and many scenic coastal paths.*

dir: *From Caen A84, exit 34 in direction Mont-St-Michel through Courtils village. From Rennes take exit 33.*

Open: 5 Feb-13 Nov **Site:** 5.2HEC **Facilities:** **Services:** **Leisure:** P **Off-site:** S

COUTERNE — ORNE

Clos Normand

rte de Bagnoles-de l'Orne, 61410
☎ 233379243
e-mail: france.doffemont@voila.fr
web: www.camping-clos-normand.fr

A pleasant site in rural surroundings in a sheltered position close to the thermal spa of Bagnoles-de-l'Orne.

dir: *Approach D916.*

Open: Mar-Oct **Site:** 1.3HEC **Prices:** 9.60 Mobile home hire 265-420 **Facilities:** Play Area **Services:** **Off-site:** L P R

CRACH — MORBIHAN

Fort Espagnol

rte de Fort Espagnol, 56950
☎ 297551488 297300104
e-mail: fort-espagnol@wanadoo.fr
web: www.fort-espagnol.com

A family site in a secluded, wooded location, with a variety of recreational facilities.

Open: Jun-10 Sep **Site:** 4.5HEC **Facilities:** **Services:** **Leisure:** P **Off-site:** R S

FRANCE

Facilities shop shower electric points for razors electric points for caravans parking by tents permitted compulsory separate car park **Services** café/restaurant bar Camping Gaz International gas other than Camping Gaz first aid facilities laundry **Leisure** swimming L-Lake P-Pool R-River S-Sea **Off-site** All facilities within 5km

CRIEL-SUR-MER — SEINE-MARITIME

Mouettes

r de la Plage, 76910
235867073
e-mail: contact@camping-lesmouettes.fr
web: www.camping-lesmouettes.fr

Small grassy site overlooking the sea.

Open: Apr-2 Nov **Site:** 2HEC **Facilities:** **Services:** **Off-site:** R S

Parc Val d'Albion

1 r de la Mer, Mesnil-Val-Plage, 76910
235862142 235867851

Terraced site in wooded parkland next to the sea.

dir: *3km S from Le Tréport on D126.*

GPS: 50.0433, 1.3311

Open: Jun-15 Sep **Site:** 3HEC **Prices:** 16.20 **Facilities:** **Services:** **Off-site:** S

CROZON — FINISTÈRE

Pen ar Menez

bd de Pralognan, 29160
298271236

On fringe of a pine wood. Water sports 5km away. Cycles for hire.

Open: All Year. **Site:** 2.6HEC **Facilities:** **Services:** **Off-site:** S

Plage de Goulien

Kernaveno, 29160
608434932 298262316
e-mail: camping.delaplage.degoulien@presquile-crozon.com
web: www.camping-crozon-laplagedegoulien.com

Grassy site in wooded surroundings 150m from the sea.

dir: *5km W on D308.*

Open: 10 Jun-15 Sep **Site:** 3HEC **Facilities:** **Services:** **Off-site:** S

DEAUVILLE — CALVADOS

Haras

chemin du Calvaire, Touques, 14800
231884484 231889708
e-mail: campingdesharas@orange.fr

A partially residential site in pleasant surroundings. Ideal for overnight stops.

dir: *N on D62, to Honfleur.*

Open: Feb-Nov **Site:** 4HEC **Facilities:** **Services:** **Off-site:** P

Vallée de Deauville

av de la Vallée, St Arnoult, 14800
231885817 231881157
e-mail: contact@campingdeauville.com
web: www.campingdeauville.com

A pleasant wooded setting with plenty of recreational facilities.

dir: *1km S via D27 & D275.*

Open: Apr-Oct **Site:** 19HEC **Prices:** 34.42 **Facilities:** **Services:** **Leisure:** L P R **Off-site:** S

DIEPPE — SEINE-MARITIME

La Source

63 r Tisserands, P Appeville, Hautot-sur-Mer, 76550
235842704 235822502
e-mail: reception@camping-la-source.fr
web: www.camping-la-source.fr

Quiet, green site with games room and fishing available.

Open: 15 Mar-15 Oct **Site:** 2.5HEC **Facilities:** Wi-fi (charged) Play Area **Services:** **Leisure:** P R **Off-site:** S

DOL-DE-BRETAGNE — ILLE-ET-VILAINE

Domaine des Ormes

35120
299735300 299735355
e-mail: info@lesormes.com
web: www.lesormes.com

Site in grounds of a château, with a large indoor water park including a wave pool. Horse riding also available.

dir: *7km S on N795 Rennes road.*

GPS: 48.49, -1.7267

Open: 21 May-3 Sep **Site:** 50HEC **Prices:** 23.90-55 Mobile home hire 378-1246 **Facilities:** Wi-fi Kids' Club Play Area **Services:** **Leisure:** P

Tendieres

r des Tendieres, 35120
299481468 299481869
e-mail: campinglestendieres@orange.fr
web: www.camping-lestendieres.com

On level meadow.

dir: *SW from town centre on rte de Dinan 400m.*

Open: 15 May-15 Oct **Site:** 1.7HEC **Facilities:** **Services:** **Leisure:** R **Off-site:** P

Vieux Chêne

The Camping and Caravanning Club The Friendly Club

Baguer-Pican, 35120
☎ 299480955 299481337
e-mail: vieux.chene@wanadoo.fr
web: www.camping-vieuxchene.fr

Spacious site in a pleasant lakeside location.

C&CC Report *Amid the beautiful countryside around the Bay of Mont-St-Michel, Vieux Chêne and its pretty fishing lake make a welcoming and comfortable base for children and adults alike. Spectacular Mont-St-Michel, a host of historic towns, picturesque coastline and the enchanting villages of Brittany are all within easy reach.*

dir: *5km E of Dol-de-Bretagne on D576.*

Open: 17 May-25 Sep **Site:** 12HEC **Prices:** 15.50-29 Mobile home hire 259-769 **Facilities:** Wi-fi (charged) Kids' Club Play Area **Services:** **Leisure:** P

DOUARNENEZ — FINISTÈRE

Kerleyou

Tréboul, 29100
☎ 298741303 298740961
e-mail: campingdekerleyou@wanadoo.fr
web: www.camping-kerleyou.com

Family site in wooded surroundings near the beach. Separate car park for arrivals after 23.00hrs.

dir: *1km W on rue de Préfet-Collignon towards sea.*

Open: 10 Apr-19 Sep **Site:** 3HEC **Prices:** 12.35-17.35 Mobile home hire 195-650 **Facilities:** Wi-fi Play Area **Services:** **Leisure:** P **Off-site:** S

Pil Koad

Poullan-Sur-Mer, 29100
☎ 298742639 298745597
e-mail: info@pil-koad.com
web: www.pil-koad.com

A natural wooded setting with a variety of recreational facilities.

dir: *E on D7 towards Douarnenez.*

Open: Apr-Sep **Site:** 5.5HEC **Prices:** 16.80-30.90 Mobile home hire 210-945 **Facilities:** Wi-fi (charged) Kids' Club Play Area **Services:** **Leisure:** P **Off-site:** S

ERDEVEN — MORBIHAN

Ideal

Route de la plage, 56410
☎ 297556766
e-mail: info@camping-l-ideal.com
web: www.camping-l-ideal.com

Open: Apr-Sep **Site:** 0.5HEC **Facilities:** **Services:** **Leisure:** P **Off-site:** R S

Sept Saints

56410
☎ 297555265 297552267
e-mail: info@septsaints.com
web: www.septsaints.com

Wooded surroundings with good recreational facilities.

dir: *2km NW via D781 rte de Plouhinec.*

Open: 15 May-15 Sep **Site:** 5HEC **Facilities:** **Services:** **Leisure:** P **Off-site:** L R S

ERQUY — CÔTES-D'ARMOR

Camping Bellevue

rte de la Libération, 22430
☎ 296723304
e-mail: campingbellevue@yahoo.fr
web: www.campingbellevue.fr

Situated 2km from a sandy beach and ideal for families. Pitches are separated by hedges, trees and plants. Dogs accepted, some restrictions apply.

GPS: 48.5943, -2.4848

Open: 6 Apr-20 Sep **Site:** 3HEC **Prices:** 15.50-21 Mobile home hire 270-690 **Facilities:** Wi-fi Kids' Club Play Area **Services:** **Leisure:** P **Off-site:** S

Hautes Greés

123 r St-Michel, 22430
☎ 296723478 296723015
e-mail: hautesgrees@wanadoo.fr
web: www.camping-hautes-grees.com

Good family site, 2km from the town centre and 400m from the beach.

dir: *0.5km from sea.*

Open: Apr-Sep **Site:** 3HEC **Facilities:** **Services:** **Leisure:** P **Off-site:** S

FRANCE

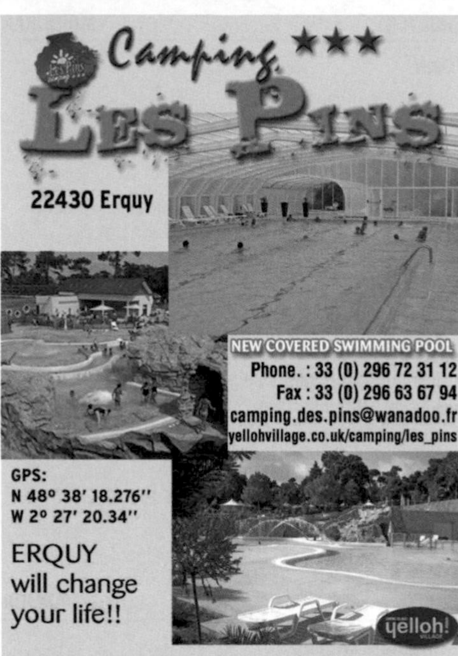

Pins

rte du Guen, 22430
☎ 296723112 📠 296636794
e-mail: camping.des.pins@wanadoo.fr

A well equipped family site situated in a pine forest 800mtrs from Erquy harbour and the Guen beach.

dir: *1km NE of village.*

Open: 12 Apr-15 Sep **Site:** 10HEC **Facilities:** **Services:** **Leisure:** P **Off-site:** S

see advert on this page

Roches

Caroual Village, 22430
☎ 296723290 📠 296635784
e-mail: info@camping-les-roches.com
web: www.camping-les-roches.com

A quiet site in a rural setting with well-marked pitches, 0.8km from the beach.

dir: *3km SW off D786.*

Open: Apr-Sep **Site:** 3.1HEC **Prices:** 12.50-15.40 **Facilities:** Wi-fi Play Area **Services:** **Off-site:** S

St-Pabu

22430
☎ 296722465 📠 296728717
e-mail: camping@saintpabu.com
web: www.saintpabu.com

On big open meadow with several terraces in beautiful, isolated location by sea. Divided into pitches.

dir: *W on D786, signed from la Coutre.*

Open: Apr-10 Oct **Site:** 5.5HEC **Prices:** 16-19.90 Mobile home hire 265-670 **Facilities:** Kids' Club Play Area **Services:** **Leisure:** S

Vieux Moulin

r des Moulins, 22430
☎ 296723423 📠 296723663
e-mail: camp.vieux.moulin@wanadoo.fr
web: www.camping-vieux-moulin.com

Clean tidy site divided into pitches and surrounded by a pine forest. Suitable for children.

dir: *On D783.*

Open: 9 Apr-11 Sep **Site:** 6.5HEC **Prices:** 19.80-33.30 Mobile home hire 310-995 **Facilities:** Wi-fi (charged) Kids' Club Play Area **Services:** **Leisure:** P **Off-site:** S

ÉTABLES-SUR-MER **CÔTES-D'ARMOR**

Abri Côtier

The Camping and Caravanning Club The Friendly Club

22680
☎ 296706157 📠 296706523
e-mail: camping.abricotier@wanadoo.fr
web: www.camping-abricotier.fr

A pleasant family site in a wooded location close to the sea.

C&CC Report *This friendly, very well-kept and relaxing little site is much appreciated for its quiet, family atmosphere, attractive location and proximity to the superb beaches and coves of Brittany's lovely north coast. Add in the very helpful Anglo-French owners and it makes for an ideal site for any time of the season, both for first-timers and returners alike.*

dir: *1km N of town centre on D786.*

Open: 5 May-9 Sep **Site:** 2HEC **Prices:** 15.60-21.20 Mobile home hire 280-600 **Facilities:** Wi-fi (charged) **Services:** **Leisure:** P **Off-site:** S

FRANCE

TRÉHAM CALVADOS

Reine Mathilde

14400
☎ 231217655
e-mail: camping.reine-mathilde@wanadoo.fr
web: www.camping-normandie-rm.fr
A quiet rural setting 4km from the sea.
dir: *1km W via D123*
Open: Apr-Sep **Site:** 6.5HEC **Facilities:** Wi-fi (charged) Play Area **Services:** **Leisure:** P **Off-site:**

FAOUËT, LE MORBIHAN

Beg Er Roch

rte de Lorient, 56320
☎ 297231511 297231166
e-mail: camping.lefaouet@wanadoo.fr
Pleasant surroundings on the banks of a river. A popular site with modern sanitary facilities and opportunities for many sports.
Open: 10 Mar-Sep **Site:** 3.5HEC **Prices:** 9.20-13.70 Mobile home hire 212-410 **Facilities:** Play Area **Services:** **Leisure:** R **Off-site:**

FIQUEFLEUR-EQUAINVILLE EURE

Domaine Catinière

rte d'Honfleur, 27210
☎ 232576351 232421257
e-mail: info@camping-catiniere.com
web: www.camping-catiniere.com
Picturesque site in a pretty valley.
dir: *From Le Havre E05/E44/D22.*
GPS: 49.4008, 0.3064
Open: 8 Apr-20 Sep **Site:** 5HEC **Prices:** 20-27 Mobile home hire 260-760 **Facilities:** Wi-fi Play Area **Services:** **Leisure:** P R **Off-site:**

FORÊT-FOUESNANT, LA FINISTÈRE

Camping Les Saules

rte de la Plage, 29440
☎ 298569857 298568660
e-mail: info@camping-les-saules.com
web: www.camping-les-saules.com
In a green shaded area with direct access to the beach, a swimming pool complex has slides.
GPS: 47.8987, -3.9612
Open: 3 Apr-2 Oct **Site:** 3.5HEC **Prices:** 15-27 Mobile home hire 195-890 **Facilities:** Wi-fi Kids' Club Play Area **Services:** **Leisure:** P S

Domaine du Saint Laurent

Kerleven, 29940
☎ 298569765 298569251
e-mail: info@camping-du-saint-laurent.fr
web: www.camping-du-saint-laurent.fr
On rocky coast. Divided into pitches.
dir: *3.5km SE of village.*
Open: Apr-Sep **Site:** 5.25HEC **Facilities:** **Services:** **Leisure:** P S **Off-site:**

Européen De La Plage

5 r de Port la Forêt, 29940
☎ 678077228
e-mail: laplage.camp@wanadoo.fr
web: www.cedlp.com
Pitches divided by hedges, close to the sea.
dir: *2.5km SE on D783.*
Open: 15 Mar-15 Oct **Site:** 1HEC **Prices:** 16 **Facilities:** **Services:** **Off-site:** S

Manoir de Penn Ar Ster

29940
☎ 298569775
e-mail: info@camping-pennarster.com
web: www.camping-pennarster.com
Well-tended site close to Port La Forêt, a major yachting arena.
dir: *NE off D44.*
Open: Feb-11 Nov **Site:** 3HEC **Prices:** 17-23 Mobile home hire 280-650 **Facilities:** Wi-fi (charged) Play Area **Services:** **Off-site:** P S

FOUESNANT FINISTÈRE

Domaine Le Grand Large

48 route du Grand Large, Pointe de Mousterlin, 29170
☎ 298560406 298565826
e-mail: grand-large@franceloc.fr
web: www.campings-franceloc.fr
A family site in a wooded setting with direct access to the beach. Plenty of modern facilities.
dir: *S of Fouesnant via D145.*
Open: 2 Apr-11 Sep **Site:** 6HEC **Prices:** 16-22 Mobile home hire 133-966 **Facilities:** Wi-fi Kids' Club Play Area **Services:** **Leisure:** P S **Off-site:**

Piscine

51 Hent Kerleya, 29170
☎ 298565606 🖹 298565764
e-mail: contact@campingdelapiscine.com
web: www.campingdelapiscine.com

A beautiful location 1.5km from the beach, a family friendly site with a swimming pool area including slides and a children's pool.

C&CC Report *The Caradec's family-run, friendly and spacious site is set in pretty countryside close to the lovely Finistère coast. It's a site well suited both to low season tourers and, with high season children's activities, to younger families. For 2011 the already impressive pool complex will be improved by the addition of a new covered pool complete with hydromassage, sauna and steam room. Océanoplis (the ocean discovery park) in Brest or boat trips to the Glénan islands are popular day trips.*

dir: *4km NW towards Kerleya.*

GPS: 47.8667, -4.0158

Open: 14 May-18 Sep **Site:** 5HEC **Prices:** 17-27.50 **Facilities:** Wi-fi (charged) Kids' Club Play Area **Services:** **Leisure:** P **Off-site:** S

Sunêlia Atlantique

rte de Mousterlin, 29170
☎ 298561444 🖹 298561867
e-mail: sunelia@latlantique.fr
web: www.latlantique.fr

Modern site with plenty of amenities 400m from the beach.

dir: *4.5km S on road to Mousterlin.*

Open: 27 Apr-12 Sep **Site:** 9HEC **Facilities:** **Services:** **Leisure:** P **Off-site:** S

see advert on this page

FOUGÈRES — ILLE-ET-VILAINE

CM Paron

rte de la Chapelle Janson, 35300
☎ 299994081 🖹 299942794

A well-managed site suitable for overnight stays.

dir: *1.5km E via D17.*

Open: Apr-Oct **Site:** 2.5HEC **Facilities:** **Services:** **Off-site:** P R

:UILLIGOMARC'H — FINISTÈRE

Bois des Ecureuils

:9300
298717098 298717098
-mail: bois-des-ecureuils@aliceadsl.fr
/eb: bois-des-ecureuils.com

ranquil 1.6-hectare wooded site set among oak, chestnut and eech trees. An ideal base for walking, cycling, horse riding and shing.

pen: Jun-1 Sep **Site:** 2.5HEC **Facilities:** **ervices:**

:UILVINEC — FINISTÈRE

'elloh Village La Plage

te de Penmarc'h, 29730
298586190 298588906
-mail: info@yellohvillage-la-plage.com
'eb: www.villagelaplage.com

n level meadow. Divided into pitches. Flat beach suitable for hildren.

pen: 9 Apr-12 Sep **Site:** 14HEC **rices:** 15-41 Mobile home hire 203-1071 **Facilities:** Wi-fi Kids' Club Play Area **Services:** **eisure:** P S

HAYE-DU-PUITS, LA — MANCHE

Étang des Haizes

50250
233460116 233472380
e-mail: info@campingetangdeshaizes.com
web: www.campingetangdeshaizes.com

A well-equipped family site bordering a lake, shaded by apple trees. Activities are organised in summer.

dir: *D903 from Carentan.*

Open: Apr-15 Oct **Site:** 5HEC **Prices:** 14-31 Mobile home hire 252-833 **Facilities:** **Services:** **Leisure:** P **Off-site:**

HOULGATE — CALVADOS

Vallée

88 r de la Vallée, 14510
231244069 231244242
e-mail: camping.lavallee@wanadoo.fr
web: www.campinglavallee.com

Site with good recreational facilities, 0.9km from the beach.

dir: *1km S.*

Open: Apr-Sep **Site:** 11HEC **Facilities:** **Services:** **Leisure:** P **Off-site:** S

see advert on this page

FRANCE

Facilities shop shower electric points for razors electric points for caravans parking by tents permitted mpulsory separate car park **Services** café/restaurant bar Camping Gaz International gas other than Camping Gaz first aid facilities laundry **Leisure** swimming L-Lake P-Pool R-River S-Sea **Off-site** All facilities within 5km

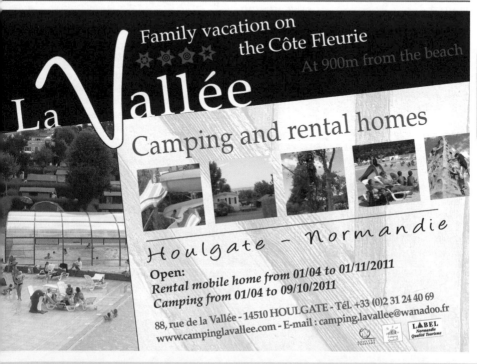

ISIGNY SUR MER — CALVADOS

Camping le Fanal

r du Fanal, 14230
231213320 231221200
e-mail: info@camping-lefanal.com
web: www.camping-normandie-fanal.fr

Family friendly site with swimming pool complex. Entertainment facilities include concerts and plays. Kids' club available in July and August. Dogs allowed except July and August.

Open: Apr-Sep **Site:** 8HEC **Prices:** 13-27 Mobile home hire 273-896 **Facilities:** Wi-fi (charged) Kids' Club Play Area **Services:** **Leisure:** L P **Off-site:** R

JULLOUVILLE — MANCHE

Chaussée

1 av de la Libération, 50610
233618018 233614526
e-mail: jmb@camping-lachaussee.com
web: camping-lachaussee.com

On large meadow, completely divided into pitches. Separated from the beach and coast road by a row of houses.

Open: 10 Apr-20 Sep **Site:** 6HEC **Facilities:** **Services:** **Leisure:** P **Off-site:** S

JUMIÈGES — SEINE-MARITIME

Forêt

The Camping and Caravanning Club — The Friendly Club

rue Mainberthe, 76480
235379343 235377648
e-mail: info@campinglaforet.com
web: www.campinglaforet.com

Located in the heart of the Brotonne regional park beside the Seine.

C&CC Report *Ideal starting point to discover the Seine valley, to visit the Abbey route and reach the medieval city of Rouen. The site offers pitches bordered with hedges in a calm and shady environment.*

dir: *A13 exit Bourg-Achard, site 10km.*

Open: 11 Apr-24 Oct **Site:** 2.5HEC **Prices:** 16.50-26 Mobile home hire 305-680 **Facilities:** Wi-fi (charged) Play Area **Services:** **Leisure:** P **Off-site:** L R

KERLIN — FINISTÈRE

Étangs de Trévignon

Pointe de Trévignon, Kerlin, 29910
298500041
e-mail: camp.etangdetrevignon@wanadoo.fr
web: www.camping-etangs.com

A family site with modern facilities including a covered pool and big waterslide. A path leads to the beach, 0.8km away.

Open: Jun-15 Sep **Site:** 3.5HEC **Prices:** 15-20.65 **Facilities:** Play Area **Services:** **Leisure:** P **Off-site:** S

LANDAUL — MORBIHAN

Le Pied-à-Terre

Branzého, 56690
297245270
e-mail: jimrolland@wanadoo.fr
web: www.lepiedaterre.net

A pleasant, quiet location, 15 minutes from the sea.

dir: *1km from N165, signed from Landaul.*

Open: 15 May-15 Sep **Site:** 2.6HEC **Prices:** 16 **Facilities:** **Services:** **Off-site:**

LANDÉDA — FINISTÈRE

Camping des Abers

The Camping and Caravanning Club — The Friendly Club

Dunes de Ste-Marguerite, S1 Toull Treaz, 29870
298049335 298048435
e-mail: info@camping-des-abers.com
web: www.camping-des-abers.com

Very quiet beautiful site among dunes with off-shore islands accessible at low tide. Ideal for children.

C&CC Report *A truly beautiful position perfectly complements the owners' friendly, personal care for every one of their campers. This traditional site transports you back in time with its strong sense of community. Popular open stage evenings are the social highlight, with eclectic contributions from returning and new campers alike. The Abers country reinvigorates all season, with the Vallée des Moulins tidal watermills, Folgoët's basilica, the Mene-ham artists' colony and a seaweed harvesting museum.*

dir: *2.5km NW on peninsula between bays Aber-Wrac'h & Aber Bernoît.*

Open: May-Sep **Site:** 4.5HEC **Prices:** 13.77-15.30 Mobile home hire 270-570 **Facilities:** Wi-fi Play Area **Services:** **Leisure:** S **Off-site:** R

FRANCE

ANLOUP — CÔTES D'ARMOR

amping le Neptune

erguistin 3, 22580
296223335
-mail: contact@leneptune.com
eb: www.leneptune.com

o minutes from the sea and beaches, this site has grassy, acious pitches separated by hedges. Entertainment includes ncerts, sports and a mini-farm.

PS: 48.7137, -2.9670

pen: Apr-17 Oct **Site:** 1.5HEC **Prices:** 14.70-19.70 obile home hire 220-710 **Facilities:** Wi-fi Play Area **Services:** **Leisure:** P **Off-site:** S

ESCONIL — FINISTÈRE

amping de la Grande Plage

r P-Langevin, 29740
298878827 298878827
mail: campinggrandeplage@hotmail.com
b: www.campinggrandeplage.com

ll-equipped level site, surrounded by woodland and 300m from e sea. Heated swimming pool with slides available.

en: May-Sep **Site:** 2.5HEC **Prices:** 19.60 Mobile me hire 300-650 **Facilities:** Wi-fi Play Area rvices: **Leisure:** P **Off-site:** S

unes

r P-Langevin, 29740
298878178 298822705
mail: campingdesdunes0556@orange.fr
b: www.camping-lesdunes-29.com

amily site on slightly sloping landscaped ground, 0.8km from e town centre and harbour.

en: May-15 Sep **Site:** 2.8HEC **Prices:** 20.80 cilities: Wi-fi Play Area **Services:** isure: S **Off-site:** R

LITTEAU — CALVADOS

Domaine de Litteau

14490
231222208 231218565
e-mail: hsm.dlt@siblu.fr
web: www.siblu.com/domainedelitteau

Open: 22 Mar-4 Nov **Site:** 19HEC **Facilities:** **Services:** **Leisure:** L P

LOUANNEC — CÔTES-D'ARMOR

CM Ernest Renan

rte de Perros-Guirec, 22700
296231178 293490447
e-mail: mairie-louannec@orange.fr

Site next to the sea. Takeaway food, games room.

dir: *1km W.*

Open: May-Sep **Site:** 4.5HEC **Facilities:** **Services:** **Leisure:** L P R S

LOUVIERS — EURE

Bel Air

rte de la Haye Malherbe, 27400
232401077
e-mail: campinglebelair@aol.com
web: www.camping-lebelair.fr

Small site on the edge of a forest with landscaped pitches and good facilities.

dir: *3km from town centre via D81.*

GPS: 49.2152, 1.1332

Open: Mar-Oct **Site:** 2.5HEC **Facilities:** Wi-fi **Services:** **Leisure:** P

FRANCE

LUC-SUR-MER CALVADOS

Capricieuse

2 r Brummel, 14530
☎ 231973443 231968278
e-mail: info@campinglacapricieuse.com
web: www.campinglacapricieuse.com

A large family site 100m from the beach.

dir: *On W outskirts. A13 exit Douvres.*

Open: Apr-Sep **Site:** 4.5HEC **Facilities:** Wi-fi Play Area **Services:** **Off-site:** P S

MARCILLY-SUR-EURE EURE

Domaine de Marcilly

rte de St André, 27810
☎ 237484542 237485111
e-mail: domainedemarcilly@wanadoo.fr

Overlooking the Eure valley, spacious pitches in wooded surroundings separated by hedges and shrubs.

dir: *On D52.*

GPS: 48.83, 1.3321

Open: Apr-Oct **Site:** 15HEC **Prices:** 21.50 Mobile home hire 410-610 **Facilities:** Wi-fi (charged) Play Area **Services:** **Leisure:** P **Off-site:**

MARTIGNY SEINE-MARITIME

2 Rivières

76880
☎ 235856082 235859516
e-mail: martigny.76@orange.fr
web: www.camping-2-rivieres.com

On the shore of a lake in pleasant surroundings 8km from Dieppe.

dir: *Via D154.*

Open: 26 Mar-10 Oct **Site:** 6.8HEC **Prices:** 12.10-15.15 **Facilities:** Play Area **Services:** **Off-site:** P

MARTRAGNY CALVADO

Château de Martragny

The Camping and Caravanning Club The Friendly Club

14740
☎ 231802140 231081491
e-mail: chateau.martragny@wanadoo.fr
web: www.chateau-martragny.com

Family site in grounds of a château, which also offers accommodation.

C&CC Report *An exclusively touring site with a rural feel, in impressive, spacious grounds. Martragny is an ideal base for either short or long stays, especially for younger families and couples. The D-Day beaches, sites and museums and the Caen Peace Memorial are close by, as is Bayeux with its famous Norman tapestry. The D-Day Festival takes place throughout the area in the days around 6 June, but amid all the history don't ignore the simple pleasures of the beautiful Norman countryside, its lovely villages and the delicious regional produce.*

dir: *N13 exit Martragny, through St-Léger, site on right.*

Open: May-12 Sep **Site:** 12HEC **Prices:** 25.50-29 **Facilities:** Wi-fi **Services:** **Leisure:** P **Off-site:** R S

MAUPERTUS-SUR-MER MANCH

Anse du Brick

50330
☎ 233543357 233544966
e-mail: welcome@anse-du-brick.com
web: www.anse-du-brick.com

Terraced site in a landscaped park between the sea and a fores

dir: *10km E of Cherbourg ferry terminal, 200m from beach.*

GPS: 49.667, -1.487

Open: Apr-Sep **Site:** 17HEC **Prices:** 18.50-36 Mobile home hire 350-790 **Facilities:** Wi-fi (charge Kids' Club Play Area **Services:** **Leisure:** P **Off-site:** S

MERVILLE-FRANCEVILLE CALVAD

Peupliers

Allée des Pins, 14810
☎ 231240507 231240507
e-mail: contact@camping-peupliers.com
web: www.camping-peupliers.com

A rural setting 300m from the beach. The sanitary facilities include a bathroom for babies.

dir: *2km E from sign on D514.*

Open: Apr-Oct **Site:** 3.6HEC **Prices:** 22.60 Mobile home hire 70.50-350 **Facilities:** Wi-fi Kids' Club Play Area **Services:** **Leisure:** P **Off-site:** R S

FRANCE

IONTERBLANC MORBIHAN

laras

ersimon, Vannes-Meucon, 56250
297446606 297444941
-mail: contact@campingvannes.com
eb: www.campingvannes.com
uiet well equipped family site with plenty of activities for hildren, close to Vannes and the Gulf of Morbihan.
ir: *4km from Vannes towards Aerodrome Vannes-Meucon.*
PS: 47.7303, -2.7279
pen: All Year. **Site:** 14HEC **Prices:** 14-20 Mobile ome hire 224-750 **Facilities:** Wi-fi Play Area **ervices:** **Leisure:** P **Off-site:**

see advert on this page

IONT-ST-MICHEL, LE MANCHE

iué de Beauvoir

rte du Mont-St-Michel, Beauvoir, 50170
233600923 233582175
-mail: nolleauyves@yahoo.fr
eb: www.hotel-gue-de-beauvoir.fr
level site in an orchard close to the River Couesnon.
ir: *4km S of Abbey on D776 Pontorson road.*
pen: Etr-Sep **Site:** 0.6HEC **Prices:** 15 **Facilities:** Wi-fi **Services:** **Leisure:** R S **Off-site:**

IORGAT FINISTÈRE

Bruyeres

e Bouis, 29160
298261487 298261487
-mail: info@camping-bruyeres-crozon.com
eb: www.camping-bruyeres-crozon.com
n a meadow surrounded by woodland with pitches divided by edges on the edge of the Parc Naturel Régional d'Armorique.
ir: *From Morgat D255 towards Cap de la Chèvre, 1.5km right owards Bouis.*
pen: May-Sep **Site:** 3HEC **Facilities:** ervices: **Off-site:**

IOYAUX CALVADOS

olombier

4590
231636308 231615017
-mail: chateau@camping-lecolombier.com
eb: www.camping-lecolombier.com
Vell-kept site in grounds of manor house.
ir: *3km NE on D143.*
pen: May-15 Sep **Site:** 10HEC **Prices:** 22-31 acilities: Wi-fi (charged) **Services:** **Leisure:** P

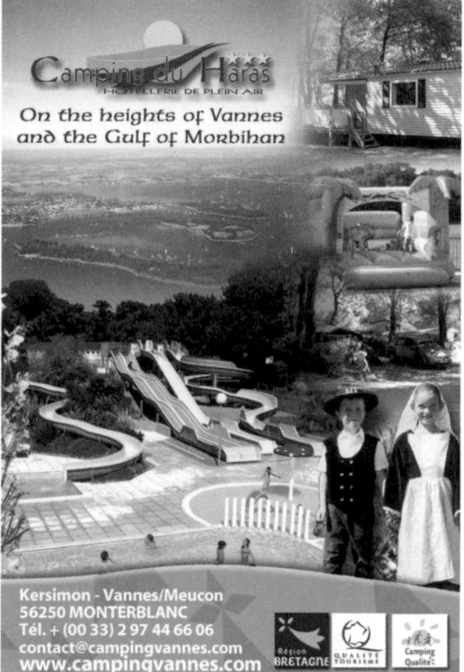

NÉVEZ FINISTÈRE

Deux Fontaines

Feuntelin Vehan, 29920
298068191 298067180
e-mail: info@les2fontaines.fr
web: www.les2fontaines.fr
Mainly level site, subdivided into several fields surrounded by woodland with good recreational facilities including an aquaslide and indoor swimming pool.
dir: *0.7km from Ragunès beach.*
Open: 7 May-11 Sep **Site:** 7HEC **Prices:** 16-31.90 Mobile home hire 174-904 **Facilities:** Wi-fi Kids' Club Play Area **Services:** **Leisure:** P **Off-site:** R S

NOYAL-MUZILLAC MORBIHAN

Moulin de Cadillac

Moulin de Cadillac, 56190
297670347 297670002
e-mail: infos@moulin-cadillac.com
web: www.camping-moulin-cadillac.com
A well-equipped family site in a pleasant wooded location with good facilities including an indoor swimming pool.
dir: *Via N165, N through Muzillac.*
Open: May-Sep **Site:** 5HEC **Prices:** 11.80-21.60 Mobile home hire 190-600 **Facilities:** Play Area **Services:** **Leisure:** P

FRANCE

PÉNESTIN-SUR-MER — MORBIHAN

Camping des Iles

La Pointe du Bile - BP4, 56760
☎ 299903024 299904455
e-mail: contact@camping-des-iles.fr
web: www.camping-des-iles.fr

A family site with direct access to the beach and a separate residential section. Kids' club available in July and August.

dir: *3km S on D201.*

Open: 9 Apr-2 Oct **Site:** 4HEC **Prices:** 17-36 Mobile home hire 250-990 **Facilities:** Wi-fi (charged) Kids' Club Play Area **Services:** **Leisure:** P S

Cénic

56760
☎ 299904565 299904505
e-mail: info@lecenic.com
web: www.lecenic.com

A forested area 2km from the sea. The spacious grassy pitches are ideal for families.

dir: *D34 from La Roche-Bernard.*

GPS: 47.4777, -2.4530

Open: Apr-Sep **Site:** 7HEC **Prices:** 15-28 **Facilities:** Kids' Club Play Area **Services:** **Leisure:** P **Off-site:** S

Yelloh Domaine d'Inly

rte de Couarne, 56760
☎ 299903509 299904093
e-mail: inly-info@wanadoo.fr
web: www.camping-inly.com

Set in the centre of a nature reserve close to the coast, with good recreational facilities.

dir: *2km SE via D201.*

Open: 3 Apr-20 Sep **Site:** 29HEC **Facilities:** **Services:** **Leisure:** L P **Off-site:** R S

PENMARC'H — FINISTÈRE

Camping les Genêts

r Gouesnac'h Nevez, 29760
☎ 298586693
e-mail: campinglesgenets29@orange.fr
web: www.camping-lesgenets.com

1.5km from a sandy beach, this family site has large pitches and offers lots of activities.

Open: Apr-Sep **Site:** 3.5HEC **Prices:** 12-19.50 Mobile home hire 210-680 **Facilities:** Wi-fi Kids' Club Play Area **Services:** **Leisure:** P **Off-site:** S

PENTREZ-PLAGE — FINISTÈRE

Ker-Ys

29550
☎ 298265395 298265248
e-mail: camping-kerys@wanadoo.fr
web: www.ker-ys.com

Level site divided into pitches 20m from the beach.

dir: *Via D887.*

Open: Apr-14 Sep **Site:** 3HEC **Facilities:** **Services:** **Leisure:** P S **Off-site:**

PIEUX, LES — MANCHE

Grand Large

The Camping and Caravanning Club — The Friendly Club

50340
☎ 233524075 233525820
e-mail: info@legrandlarge.com
web: www.legrandlarge.com

An unspoiled family site, with direct access to the sandy beach.

C&CC Report *Le Grand Large is a very well-run and well-established site in an outstanding location for great summer holidays. With direct access to the wonderful beach and its views over the Channel Islands, there are also many walking paths, a rugged coastline and historic towns, sites and battlegrounds of the Cotentin peninsula to explore. The site is also very handy for Cherbourg's ferry port and the amazing ocean attraction, Cité de la Mer.*

dir: *From Valognes, take D902. From Bricquebec towards Les Pieux, signed.*

GPS: 49.4936, -1.8425

Open: 9 Apr-18 Sep **Site:** 4HEC **Prices:** 17-31 Mobile home hire 250-870 **Facilities:** Wi-fi (charged) Play Area **Services:** **Leisure:** P S **Off-site:**

PLÉRIN — CÔTES-D'ARMOR

Mouettes

Les Rosaires les Mouettes, 22190
☎ 296745148

Open: 15 Jun-15 Sep **Site:** 1HEC **Facilities:** **Services:** **Off-site:** P R S

FRANCE

PLEUBIAN — CÔTES-D'ARMOR

Port la Chaîne

22610

☎ 296229238 Fax 296228792

e-mail: info@portlachaine.com

web: www.portlachaine.com

A peaceful and quiet terraced site on the Wild Peninsula, with direct access to the sea, with good facilities.

dir: *2km N via D20.*

Open: 5 Apr-13 Sep **Site:** 5HEC **Prices:** 20.20-31.60 **Facilities:** Wi-fi Play Area **Services:** **Leisure:** P S

PLOBANNALEC-LESCONIL — FINISTÈRE

Yelloh Village L'Océan Breton

The Camping and Caravanning Club The Friendly Club

29740

☎ 298822389 Fax 298822649

e-mail: info@yellohvillage-loceanbreton.com

web: www.oceanbreton.com

A peaceful site located in the grounds of a manor house some 2km from the beach.

C&CC Report *This busy, bustling site is a great family base for exploring stunning west Brittany. There is always something going on on-site and children of all ages are very welcome. The superb value Kerlut Pass helps keep little ones happy on site, while cultural and children's entertainments keep everyone occupied. A new, even better pool area is planned for 2011 too.*

Open: 28 May-18 Sep **Site:** 12HEC **Prices:** 15-40 Mobile home hire 203-1043 **Facilities:** Wi-fi Kids' Club Play Area **Services:** **Leisure:** P S **Off-site:**

PLOËMEL — MORBIHAN

Kergo

The Camping and Caravanning Club The Friendly Club

56400

☎ 297568066 Fax 297568066

e-mail: camping.kergo@wanadoo.fr

web: campingkergo.com

Pleasant wooded surroundings close to the beaches.

C&CC Report *This simple, peaceful alternative for visiting this ever-popular and busy area brings you a friendly welcome and beautiful natural surroundings. With attractive pitches and helpful owners, De Kergo is within easy reach of Carnac, La Trinité-sur-Mer, the Quiberon peninsula and the region's numerous prehistoric and other attractions.*

Open: May-Sep **Site:** 2.5HEC **Prices:** 12-14 Mobile home hire 230-560 **Facilities:** Wi-fi (charged) Play Area **Services:** **Off-site:**

PLOEMEUR — MORBIHAN

Ajoncs

Beg Minio, 56270

☎ 297863011 Fax 297863011

e-mail: ccdf.plo@cegetel.net

web: www.campingclub.asso.fr

A rural site set in an orchard.

dir: *From town centre towards Fort-Bloqué.*

Open: 18 Mar-Sep **Site:** 2HEC **Facilities:** **Services:** **Off-site:** L P S

PLOËRMEL — MORBIHAN

Lac

Les Belles Rives, Taupont, 56800

☎ 297740122

e-mail: camping.du-lac@wanadoo.fr

web: www.camping-du-lac-ploermel.com

A lakeside family site with plenty of facilities for water sports.

dir: *2km from village centre beside lake.*

Open: Apr-Oct **Site:** 3HEC **Facilities:** **Services:** **Leisure:** L

Vallée du Ninian

Le Rocher, 56800

☎ 297935301 Fax 297935727

e-mail: infos@camping-ninian.com

web: www.camping-ninian.com

Peaceful family site beside the River Ninian in the heart of Brittany. The owners specialise in homemade cider.

dir: *W of Taupont towards river.*

Open: 9 Apr-24 Sep **Site:** 2.7HEC **Prices:** 11.60-15.20 Mobile home hire 180-600 **Facilities:** **Services:** **Leisure:** P R **Off-site:** L

PLOMEUR — FINISTÈRE

Torche

Pointe de la Torche, 29120

☎ 298586282 Fax 298588969

e-mail: info@campingdelatorche.fr

web: www.campingdelatorche.fr

A family site with pitches surrounded by trees and bushes, 1.5km from the beach.

dir: *3.5km W.*

Open: 3 Apr-Sep **Site:** 4HEC **Facilities:** **Services:** **Leisure:** P **Off-site:** S

Facilities shop shower electric points for razors electric points for caravans parking by tents permitted compulsory separate car park **Services** café/restaurant bar Camping Gaz International gas other than Camping Gaz first aid facilities laundry **Leisure** swimming L-Lake P-Pool R-River S-Sea **Off-site** All facilities within 5km

PLOMODIERN — FINISTÈRE

Iroise

Plage de Pors-ar-Vag, 29550
298815272 298812610
e-mail: campingiroise@orange.fr
web: www.camping-iroise.fr

A family site with fine recreational facilities, providing magnificent views over the Bay of Douarnenez.

dir: *5km SW, 150m from the beach.*

Open: 2 Apr-1 Oct **Site:** 2.5HEC **Prices:** 16.90-24.90 Mobile home hire 285-600 **Facilities:** Wi-fi (charged) Play Area **Services:** **Leisure:** P S **Off-site:**

PLONÉVEZ-PORZAY — FINISTÈRE

Domaine de Kervel

29550
298925154 298925496
e-mail: camping.kervel@wanadoo.fr
web: www.kervel.com

One of the best sites in the region and 0.8km from the sea. Ideal for families.

dir: *SW of village on D107 Douarnenez road for 3km, turn at x-rds towards coast.*

Open: 30 Apr-10 Sep **Site:** 7HEC **Facilities:** **Services:** **Leisure:** P **Off-site:** S

Plage de Tréguer

Plage de Ste Anne la Palud, 29550
298925352 298925489
e-mail: camping-treguer-plage@wanadoo.fr
web: www.camping-treguer-plage.com

A level site with direct access to the beach.

dir: *1.3km N.*

Open: 7 Apr-29 Sep **Site:** 6HEC **Facilities:** **Services:** **Leisure:** P S **Off-site:**

see advert on this page

PLOUESCAT — FINISTÈRE

Village Center la Baie du Kernic

r de Pen An Théven, 29430
499572121 467516389
e-mail: contact@village-center.com
web: www.village-center.com/bretagne/camping-mer-baie-kernic.php

In a countryside setting, 100m from the beach between Roscoff and Plouescat.

dir: *From Plouescat follow signs for Pors Guen-Porsmeur.*

GPS: 48.6590, -4.2175

Open: 27 May-18 Sep **Site:** 6HEC **Prices:** 14-22 Mobile home hire 192-819 **Facilities:** Wi-fi (charged) Kids' Club Play Area **Services:** **Leisure:** P S

see advert on opposite page

PLOUÉZEC — CÔTES-D'ARMOR

Cap Horn

Port Lazo, 22470
296206428 296206388
e-mail: info@camping-capdesiles.com
web: www.lecaphorn.com

An elevated position overlooking the Ile de Bréhat with direct access to the beach.

dir: *2.3km NE via D77 at Port-Lazo.*

Open: Apr-Sep **Site:** 5HEC **Facilities:** **Services:** **Leisure:** P S **Off-site:**

PLOUEZOCH — FINISTÈRE

Baie de Térénez

Moulin de Caneret, 29252
298672680
e-mail: campingbaiedeterenez@wanadoo.fr
web: www.campingbaiedeterenez.com

A well-equipped site in a pleasant rural setting, 1.5km from the sea.

dir: *3.5km NW via D76.*

GPS: 48.6597, -3.8483

Open: Apr-Sep **Site:** 3HEC **Prices:** 10.80-15.70 Mobile home hire 190-650 **Facilities:** Wi-fi Play Area **Services:** **Leisure:** P **Off-site:** R S

FRANCE

PLOUGASNOU FINISTÈRE

Etangs de Mesqueau

26930
☎ 298673745
e-mail: domaine-de-mesqueau@orange.fr
web: www.camping-bretagne-mer.com
Large site with good recreational facilities.
dir: *3.5km S via D46.*
Open: Apr-Sep **Site:** 7HEC **Prices:** 8-15 Mobile home hire 180-650 **Facilities:** Wi-fi **Services:** **Leisure:** P R **Off-site:** S

Trégor

Kerjean, 29630
☎ 298673764
e-mail: bookings@campingdutregor.com
web: www.campingdutregor.com
A sheltered site with numbered, grassy pitches. Surrounded by hedges.
dir: *Off D46 towards Morlaix.*
Open: Etr-Oct **Site:** 1HEC **Prices:** 12-15 Mobile home hire 200-420 **Facilities:** Wi-fi (charged) **Services:** **Off-site:** S

PLOUGOULM FINISTÈRE

M du Bois de la Palud

The Camping and Caravanning Club The Friendly Club

29250
☎ 298298182 298299226
e-mail: mairie-de-plougoulm@wanadoo.fr
C&CC Report *A super, simple little site, very close to Roscoff town and ferry port. Although an ideal site for an overnight stop, people who stay longer confirm that both the area and this tranquil little site offer real rest and relaxation, far from the madding crowd. Both the coast and the inland moors are great for walking and a boat trip to the island of Batz is also recommended. Plougoulm provides all the basic local services while St. Pol-de-Léon is good for more extensive shopping.*
Open: 15 Jun-6 Sep **Site:** 2HEC **Facilities:** **Off-site:** S

PLOUHA CÔTES-D'ARMOR

Domaine de Keravel

rte de Port Moguer, La Trinité, 22580
☎ 296224913
e-mail: keravel@wanadoo.fr
web: www.keravel.com
Forested site built around an elegant country mansion, 1km from the sea.
Open: 15 May-Sep **Site:** 5HEC **Facilities:** **Services:** **Leisure:** P **Off-site:** S

PLOUHARNEL MORBIHAN

Kersily

Ste-Barbe, 56340
☎ 297523965 297524476
e-mail: camping.kersily@wanadoo.fr
web: www.camping-kersily.com
Open: Apr-Oct **Site:** 4HEC **Facilities:** **Services:** **Leisure:** P **Off-site:** S

Lande

Kerzivienne, 56340
☎ 297523148 297523148
e-mail: contact@campingdelalande.com
web: www.campingdelalande.com
On partially shaded terrain, 0.6km from the beach.
Open: Jun-27 Sep **Site:** 1HEC **Prices:** 14.50 Mobile home hire 320-450 **Facilities:** Wi-fi Play Area **Services:** **Off-site:** S

Loperhet

56340
☎ 297523468 297523468
e-mail: info@camping-loperhet.com
web: www.camping-loperhet.com
dir: *1km NW via D781.*
Open: Apr-Sep **Site:** 6HEC **Facilities:** **Services:** **Leisure:** P **Off-site:** S

PLOUHINEC MORBIHAN

Moténo

rte du Magouer, 56680
☎ 297367663 297858184
e-mail: info@camping-moteno.com
web: www.camping-le-moteno.com
On slightly sloping ground, subdivided into several fields in a wooded area, 0.8km from the beach.
Open: 2 Apr-25 Sep **Site:** 4HEC **Prices:** 32 Mobile home hire 640 **Facilities:** Wi-fi Kids' Club Play Area **Services:** **Leisure:** P **Off-site:** P R S

FRANCE

PLOUMANACH — CÔTES-D'ARMOR

Claire Fontaine

Toul ar Lann, Perros-Guirec, 22700
☎ 296230355 296490619
web: www.camping-claire-fontaine.com

Spacious, level site in a rural setting.

dir: *1.2km SW of town centre, 0.8km from Trestraou beach.*

Open: Etr-Sep **Site:** 3HEC **Facilities:** **Services:** **Off-site:** S

Yelloh Village Ranolien

22700
☎ 296916565 296914190
e-mail: info@yellohvillage-ranolien.com
web: www.leranolien.fr

The site is divided into pitches by hedges, with separate sections for caravans.

dir: *0.5km from village.*

GPS: 48.8284, -3.4754

Open: 9 Apr-17 Sep **Site:** 15HEC **Prices:** 15-41 Mobile home hire 273-1295 **Facilities:** Wi-fi (charged) Kids' Club Play Area **Services:** **Leisure:** P **Off-site:** S

PLOZÉVET — FINISTÈRE

Corniche

The Camping and Caravanning Club The Friendly Club

rte de la Corniche, 29710
☎ 298913394
e-mail: info@campinglacorniche.com
web: www.campinglacorniche.com

Peaceful rural site 1.5km from the sea.

C&CC Report *An absolutely immaculately kept site, with great coast both locally and within easy driving distance. The site is also very well situated for exploring some of lovely Finistère's best historic sites. An all-round favourite for those who like quiet relaxation on site, or getting out and about to lots of places of interest, all within under an hour's drive.*

Open: 3 Apr-2 Oct **Site:** 2HEC **Prices:** 18.30-21.70 **Facilities:** **Services:** **Leisure:** P **Off-site:** L R S

PONTAUBAULT — MANCHE

Vallée de la Sélune

7 rue Mal Leclerc, 50220
☎ 233603900 233603900
e-mail: campselune@wanadoo.fr
web: www.campselune.com

This site is in a quiet village near the River Sélune. Ideal base for exploring the Normandy/Brittany area.

dir: *Off N175 onto D43 towards Pontaubault. Site in village.*

GPS: 48.63, -1.3527

Open: Apr-20 Oct **Site:** 1.6HEC **Prices:** 13 Mobile home hire 140-350 **Facilities:** Wi-fi Play Area **Services:** **Off-site:** R

PONTORSON — MANCHE

Haliotis

chemin des Soupirs, 50170
☎ 233681159 233589536
e-mail: camping.haliotis@wanadoo.fr
web: www.camping-haliotis-mont-saint-michel.com

On the banks of a river, a short distance from Mont-St-Michel. Kids' club during July and August.

dir: *Off D976 towards Avranches.*

Open: 18 Mar-14 Nov **Site:** 6HEC **Prices:** 16.90-21.90 Mobile home hire 290-590 **Facilities:** Wi-fi Kids' Club Play Area **Services:** **Leisure:** P **Off-site:** R

PORDIC — CÔTES-D'ARMOR

Madières

rte le Vau Madec, 22590
☎ 296790248
e-mail: campinglesmadieres@wanadoo.fr
web: www.campinglesmadieres.com

A quiet coastal site in a well-shaded position.

dir: *1.5km from village on D786 towards St-Brieuc.*

Open: Apr-Oct **Site:** 2HEC **Prices:** 15-17.50 Mobile home hire 250-550 **Facilities:** **Services:** **Leisure:** P **Off-site:** S

FRANCE

PORT-EN-BESSIN CALVADOS

Port'land

14520
☎ 231510706 🖹 231517649
e-mail: campingportland@wanadoo.fr
web: www.camping-portland.com

Situated in rural surroundings near Omaha Beach, with an indoor heated swimming pool on site. Kids' club available during July and August.

Open: Apr-3 Nov **Site:** 8.6HEC **Prices:** 20.50-35 Mobile home hire 441-854 **Facilities:** Wi-fi Kids' Club Play Area **Services:** **Leisure:** P **Off-site:** S

PORT-MANECH FINISTÈRE

St-Nicolas

29920
☎ 298068975 🖹 298067461
e-mail: info@campinglesaintnicolas.com
web: www.campinglesaintnicolas.com

Divided into hedge-lined pitches in beautiful surroundings close to the beach.

Open: May-Sep **Site:** 3.5HEC **Prices:** 16.50-22 **Facilities:** Play Area **Services:** **Leisure:** P **Off-site:** S

POULDU, LE FINISTÈRE

Camping Les Embruns

1 r du Philosophe Alain, 29360
☎ 298399107 🖹 298399787
e-mail: camping-les-embruns@wanadoo.fr
web: www.camping-les-embruns.com

A pleasant site with good facilities and easy access to the beach. Separate car park for arrivals after 22.00hrs.

Open: 8 Apr-24 Sep **Site:** 6HEC **Facilities:** **Services:** **Leisure:** P **Off-site:** R S

QUETTEHOU MANCHE

Rivage

75 r Sainte Marie, 50630
☎ 233541376 🖹 233431042
web: www.camping-lerivage.fr

Quiet, sheltered site, 400m from the sea.

dir: *Via D14.*

Open: Apr-Sep **Site:** 2HEC **Facilities:** **Services:** **Leisure:** P **Off-site:** S

QUIBERON MORBIHAN

Bois d'Amour

rue St-Clement, 56170
☎ 297501352 🖹 297504267
e-mail: info@homair.com
web: www.camping-leboisdamour.com

A family site with plenty of recreational facilities close to the area's fine beaches.

Open: Apr-Oct **Site:** 5.5HEC **Facilities:** **Services:** **Leisure:** P **Off-site:** S

QUIMPER FINISTÈRE

Orangerie de Lanniron

The Camping and Caravanning Club The Friendly Club

Château de Lanniron,
Chemin de Lanniron, 29336
☎ 298906202 🖹 298521556
e-mail: camping@lanniron.com
web: www.lanniron.com

Set in the grounds of the former residence of the bishops of Quimper, beside the River Odet and surrounded by tropical vegetation.

C&CC Report *A top quality site, in an exceptional setting. The addition of the new heated aquapark, with its slides, fountains and spa will keep the chidren entertained, or you may want to simply relax in the extensive château grounds, where the rhododendrons in May are absolutely glorious. Quimper, the county's capital, can be reached by footpath directly from the site.*

dir: *2.5km from town centre via D34.*

Open: 15 May-15 Sep **Site:** 40HEC **Facilities:** **Services:** **Leisure:** P R

RAGUENÈS-PLAGE FINISTÈRE

Airotel International Raguenès-Plage

The Camping and Caravanning Club The Friendly Club

19 r des Iles, Raguenez, 29920
☎ 298068069 🖹 298068905
e-mail: info@camping-le-raguenes-plage.com
web: www.camping-le-raguenes-plage.com

Site with asphalt drives, 300m from beaches.

C&CC Report *Le Raguenès-Plage is a superbly-located, much-loved, family-run, traditional site. All season round it's a great base for some wonderful places to visit, with its proximity to the beach a huge plus. Families love the pools and waterslides, but the site appeals to anyone seeking relaxation on the coast. The charming artists' town of Pont-Aven is only a short drive away, as is the fortified harbour of Concarneau, while much of west and south Brittany is also easily within a day trip.*

dir: *From Pont-Aven to Nevez, signs to Raguenès.*

Open: Apr-1 Oct **Site:** 7HEC **Prices:** 16.50-31 Mobile home hire 280-820 **Facilities:** Wi-fi (charged) Kids' Club Play Area **Services:** **Leisure:** P S

FRANCE

RAVENOVILLE-PLAGE — MANCHE

Le Cormoran

50480
☎ 233413394 🖷 233951608
e-mail: lecormoran@wanadoo.fr
web: www.lecormoran.com

A pleasant family site with well-defined pitches, 20m from the sea. Kids' club during July and August. Facilities include indoor and outdoor pools and a goats' enclosure.

dir: *300m from town towards Utah Beach.*

Open: 2 Apr-25 Sep **Site:** 8.5HEC **Prices:** 20-32 Mobile home hire 238-847 **Facilities:** Wi-fi (charged) Kids' Club Play Area **Services:** **Leisure:** P **Off-site:** S

ROCHE-BERNARD, LA — MORBIHAN

CM Patis

3 chemin du Patis, 56130
☎ 299906013 🖷 299908828
e-mail: camping.lrb@gmail.com

On banks of River Vilaine.

dir: *100m from village centre, on the port.*

Open: Apr-15 Oct **Site:** 1HEC **Prices:** 12.50-15.40 **Facilities:** Wi-fi (charged) Play Area **Services:** **Leisure:** R **Off-site:** P

ROCHEFORT-EN-TERRE — MORBIHAN

Moulin Neuf

56220
☎ 297433752 🖷 297433545

A well-equipped site in wooded surroundings.

dir: *Signed from D744 in village.*

Open: May-Sep **Site:** 2.5HEC **Facilities:** **Services:** **Leisure:** P **Off-site:** L R

ROSTRENEN — CÔTES-D'ARMOR

Fleur de Bretagne

Kerandouaron, 22110
☎ 296291545 🖷 296291645
e-mail: contact@fleurdebretagne.com
web: www.fleurdebretagne.com

A spacious site in a picturesque, sheltered valley with modern facilities.

dir: *D764 from Rostrenen 1.5km towards Pontivy.*

Open: All Year. **Site:** 6HEC **Prices:** 12-19 Mobile home hire 150-250 **Facilities:** Wi-fi Play Area **Services:** **Leisure:** L P **Off-site:**

ST-ALBAN — CÔTES-D'ARMOR

St-Vrêguet

St-Vréguet, 22400
☎ 296329021
e-mail: vreguet@aliceadsl.fr
web: www.campingvreguet.fr

A peaceful site in a pleasant park with good sanitary and recreational facilities.

Open: Jun-Sep **Site:** 1HEC **Facilities:** **Services:** **Off-site:** R

ST-AUBIN-SUR-MER — CALVADOS

CM Mesnil

76740
☎ 235830283

A family site attached to a typical Norman farm.

dir: *2km W on D68.*

Open: Apr-Oct **Site:** 2.3HEC **Facilities:** **Services:** **Off-site:** S

Yelloh Village Côte de Nacre

17 r du General Moulton, 14750
☎ 231971445 🖷 231972211
e-mail: camping-cote-de-nacre@wanadoo.fr
web: www.camping-cote-de-nacre.com

A pleasant site with good recreational facilities. Separate car park for arrivals after 22.00hrs.

Open: 8 Apr-25 Sep **Site:** 10HEC **Prices:** 23-44 Mobile home hire 385-1253 **Facilities:** Wi-fi Kids' Club Play Area **Services:** **Leisure:** P **Off-site:** S

ST-BRIEUC — CÔTES-D'ARMOR

Vallées

Parc de Brézillet, 22000
☎ 296940505
e-mail: campingdesvallees@wanadoo.fr

Situated on the edge of the town in a plateau crossed by wooded valleys. Restaurant only open July and August.

Open: All Year. **Site:** 4.8HEC **Facilities:** Play Area **Services:** **Leisure:** R **Off-site:** P S

FRANCE

ST-CAST-LE-GUILDO CÔTES-D'ARMOR

Château de Galinée

The Camping and Caravanning Club The Friendly Club

22380
☎ 296411056 🖷 296410372
e-mail: contact@chateaudegalinee.com
web: www.chateaudegalinee.com

A family site with swimming pool complex including water slides and an indoor pool. Set in a wood incorporating the buildings of an old farm, 3km from the beaches.

C&CC Report *The large pitches and a spacious countryside setting appeal to seekers of peace and quiet, while younger families also love the leisure facilities, with the excellent indoor pool and the bar and terrace adding to everyone's enjoyment in both low and high season. Some of France's most beautiful and spectacular stretches of coastline are only a short drive away – if you don't yet know the stunning Côtes-d'Armor then a visit is long overdue.*

dir: *1km from CD786. Signed.*

Open: 14 May-10 Sep **Site:** 14HEC **Prices:** 16.50-32.60 Mobile home hire 350-917 **Facilities:** Wi-fi (charged) Kids' Club **Services:** **Leisure:** P **Off-site:** L S

ST-COULOMB ILLE-ET-VILAINE

Camping des Chevrets

La Guimorais, 35350
☎ 299890190 🖷 299890116
e-mail: campingdeschevrets@wanadoo.fr
web: www.campingdeschevrets.fr

Tranquil site with direct access to a sandy beach, pitches are individually marked. Events take place throughout the season.

Open: Apr-1 Nov **Site:** 21HEC **Prices:** 15-22 Mobile home hire 290-800 **Facilities:** Wi-fi (charged) Kids' Club Play Area **Services:** **Leisure:** P S

ST-EFFLAM CÔTES-D'ARMOR

CM

r de Ian-Carré, 22310
☎ 296356215
e-mail: campingmunicipalplestin@wanadoo.fr
web: www.camping-municipal-bretagne.com

On a level meadow with well-defined pitches, 100m from a magnificent beach.

Open: Apr-Sep **Site:** 4HEC **Facilities:** **Services:** **Off-site:** S

ST-GERMAIN-SUR-AY MANCHE

Aux Grands Espaces

50430
☎ 233071014 🖷 233072259
e-mail: auxgrandespaces@orange.fr
web: www.aux-grand-espaces.com

On slightly sloping ground among dunes, 0.5km from the sea. Children's play area.

dir: *Off D650 W of town onto D306 signed Plage.*

Open: May-15 Sep **Site:** 15HEC **Facilities:** **Services:** **Leisure:** P **Off-site:** S

ST-GILDAS-DE-RHUYS MORBIHAN

Menhir

The Camping and Caravanning Club The Friendly Club

rte de Port Crouesty, 56730
☎ 297452288
e-mail: campingmenhir@aol.com
web: www.camping-bretagnesud.com

A family site with good facilities, 1km from the beach.

C&CC Report *A lovely family site, with a warm welcome and great waterslides, guaranteed to keep youngsters happy. Le Menhir is ideal for people who enjoy beach holidays and getting out on the water, whether under their own steam or on boat trips. The excellent location, at the tip of the Rhuys peninsula on the Morbihan Gulf, means a boat trip to the Gulf islands is a must, as is a stroll past the yachts and a stop at a café at le Crouesty.*

dir: *3.5km N.*

Open: May-5 Sep **Site:** 3HEC **Prices:** 15-30.10 Mobile home hire 229-700 **Facilities:** Wi-fi Play Area **Services:** **Leisure:** P **Off-site:** S

ST-JOUAN-DES-GUÉRÊTS ILLE-ET-VILAINE

P'tit Bois

35430
☎ 299211430 🖷 299817414
e-mail: camping.ptitbois@wanadoo.fr
web: www.ptitbois.com

A pleasant family site in quiet wooded surroundings. At the centre of the Gulf of Saint Malo and just a few minutes away from the fine sandy beaches. Le P'tit Bois has spacious pitches with plenty of facilities and activities. Nearby are the beaches of the Rance River, and the sea is only 5km away.

dir: *Via N137 exit St-Jouan-des-Guérêts, take D4.*

Open: 8 Apr-1 Sep **Site:** 6HEC **Prices:** 18-35 Mobile home hire 259-994 **Facilities:** Wi-fi Kids' Club Play Area **Services:** **Leisure:** P **Off-site:** R

see advert on page 202

FRANCE

ST-LÉGER-DU-BOURG-DENIS — SEINE-MARITIME

Aubette

23 r Vert Buisson, 76160
☎ 235084769 235084769
Set in a wooded valley 3km E of Rouen.

Open: All Year. **Site:** 0.8HEC **Prices:** 9.10 **Facilities:** **Services:** **Off-site:** P R

ST-LUNAIRE — ILLE-ET-VILAINE

Longchamp

bd de St-Cast, 35800
☎ 299463398 299460271
e-mail: contact@camping-longchamp.com
web: www.camping-longchamp.com
A beautiful wooded setting, 100m from the sea on the Emerald coast, with a good range of facilities.

dir: *Off D786 towards St-Briac at end of village, site on left.*

Open: Jun-10 Sep **Site:** 5HEC **Prices:** 18.30-22.90 **Facilities:** Play Area **Services:** **Off-site:** S

Touesse

171 rue Ville Géhan, 35800
☎ 299466113 299160258
e-mail: camping.la.touesse@wanadoo.fr
web: www.campinglatouesse.com
A well-equipped family site, 300m from the beach.

dir: *2km E via D786.*

Open: Apr-29 Sep **Site:** 2.8HEC **Prices:** 16.90-22.10 Mobile home hire 245-679 **Facilities:** Wi-fi Play Area **Services:** **Off-site:** P S

ST-MALO — ILLE-ET-VILAINE

CM le Nicet

av de la Varde Rotheneuf, 35400
☎ 299402632 299219262
e-mail: camping@ville-saint-malo.fr
Site 100m from the beach, access via stairs. Water sports and other activities available.

Open: Jul-Aug **Site:** 2.9HEC **Facilities:** **Services:** **Leisure:** S **Off-site:**

Domaine de la Ville Huchet

rte de la Passagère, 35400
☎ 299811183 299815189
e-mail: info@lavillehuchet.com
web: www.lavillehuchet.com
A family campsite set around an old manor house. Leisure facilities include crazy golf and bike hire. Kids' club available in high season.

dir: *5km S via N137.*

GPS: 48.6153, -1.9864

Open: 8 Apr-18 Sep **Site:** 6.3HEC **Prices:** 21.95-34 Mobile home hire 224-903 **Facilities:** Wi-fi Kids' Club Play Area **Services:** **Leisure:** P **Off-site:** R S

ST-MARCAN — ILLE-ET-VILAINE

Balcon de la Baie

35120
☎ 299802295
web: www.lebalcondelabaie.com
A quiet, family site set in a beautiful location overlooking the bay of Mont-St-Michel.

dir: *10km NW of Pontorson on D797.*

Open: Apr-Oct **Site:** 2.7HEC **Prices:** Mobile home hire 300-520 **Facilities:** Play Area **Services:** **Leisure:** P **Off-site:**

ST-MARTIN-DES-BESACES CALVADOS

Camping le Puits

14350
231678002
e-mail: enquiries@lepuits.com
web: www.lepuits.com

A small family run site surrounded by a pleasant garden and lush fields.

dir: *A84 junction 41 for St Martin-des-Besaces.*

GPS: 49.0080, -0.86

Open: Mar-Oct **Site:** 3.6HEC **Prices:** 19 **Facilities:** Wi-fi (charged) Play Area **Services:** **Off-site:**

ST-MARTIN-EN-CAMPAGNE SEINE-MARITIME

Goélands

r des Grèbes, Saint Martin Plage, 76370
235838290 235832179
e-mail: domainelesgoelands@orange.fr
web: www.lesdomaines.org

A pleasant, comfortable campsite ideal for those who love the sea. Kids' club available in July and August.

dir: *NE of Dieppe, 2km from D925.*

Open: Mar-mid Nov **Site:** 4.5HEC
Prices: 18.50-21.50 Mobile home hire 390-610 **Facilities:** Wi-fi (charged) Kids' Club Play Area **Services:** **Off-site:** P S

ST-PAIR-SUR-MER MANCHE

Ecutot

50380
233502629 233506494
e-mail: camping.ecutot@wanadoo.fr
web: www.ecutot.com

Set in an orchard 1km from the sea.

dir: *On main road between Granville & Avranches.*

GPS: 48.8169, -1.5511

Open: Jun-15 Sep **Site:** 5HEC **Facilities:** **Services:** **Leisure:** P **Off-site:** S

Lez-Eaux

St-Aubin-des-Preaux, 50380
233516609 233519202
e-mail: bonjour@lez-eaux.com
web: www.lez-eaux.com

Situated in grounds of a château. Facilities include a bank, TV and reading room and swimming pools with water slides. On-site fishing and a kids' club is available in July and August.

dir: *7km SE via D973 rte d'Avranches.*

Open: Apr-18 Sep **Site:** 12HEC **Prices:** 20-44
Facilities: Wi-fi (charged) Kids' Club Play Area
Services: **Leisure:** P **Off-site:** S

Mariénée

50380
233906005 233906005

Set in the grounds of an old farm 2km from the sea.

dir: *2km S of town on D21.*

Open: Apr-Sep **Site:** 1.2HEC **Facilities:**
Services: **Off-site:** P S

ST-PIERRE-DU-VAUVRAY EURE

St-Pierre

1 r du Château, 27430
232610155
e-mail: eliane-darcissac@wanadoo.fr
web: www.lecampingdesaintpierre.com

Wooded surroundings with pitches divided by hedges, 50m from the River Seine.

dir: *Via A13/N15.*

Open: 7 Jan-20 Dec **Site:** 3HEC **Prices:** 13.10
Facilities: **Services:** **Leisure:** P **Off-site:** R

ST-QUAY-PORTRIEUX CÔTES-D'ARMOR

Bellevue

68 bd du Littoral, 22410
296704184 269705546
e-mail: campingbellevue22@orange.fr
web: www.campingbellevue.net

A terraced site adjacent to the sea with numbered pitches.

dir: *0.8km from town centre off D786.*

Open: 23 Apr-17 Sep **Site:** 4HEC **Prices:** 14-18.80
Facilities: Wi-fi (charged) Play Area
Services: **Leisure:** P S **Off-site:**

FRANCE

ST-VAAST-LA-HOUGUE — MANCHE

Gallouette

r de la Gallouette, 50550
233542057 233541671
e-mail: contact@camping-lagallouette.fr
web: www.camping-lagallouette.fr

A well-equipped site, 300m from the town centre and with direct access to the beach.

Open: Apr-Sep **Site:** 3.5HEC **Facilities:** **Services:** **Leisure:** P S

ST-YVI — FINISTÈRE

Village Center le Bois de Pleuven

rte de St-Yvi, 29140
499572121 467516389
e-mail: contact@village-center.com
web: www.village-center.com/bretagne/camping-mer-bois-pleuven.php

A peaceful site set in a forest between Quimper and Concarneau.

dir: *D765 towards Rosporden, last site before St-Yvi.*

GPS: 47.9504, -3.9705

Open: 24 Jun-4 Sep **Site:** 17HEC **Prices:** 14-22 Mobile home hire 241-833 **Facilities:** Wi-fi (charged) Kids' Club Play Area **Services:** **Leisure:** P **Off-site:** S

STE-MARIE-DU-MONT — MANCHE

Utah Beach

La Madeleine, 50480
233715369 233710711
e-mail: contact@camping-utahbeach.com
web: www.camping-utahbeach.com

On a level meadow 100m from the beach.

dir: *6km NE via D913 & D421.*

Open: Apr-Sep **Site:** 3.5HEC **Facilities:** **Services:** **Leisure:** P **Off-site:** S

STE-MARINE — FINISTÈRE

Hellès

55 r du Petit Bourg, 29120
298563146
e-mail: contact@le-helles.com
web: www.le-helles.com

Family site close to the beach and village of Sainte Marine.

dir: *400m from beach.*

Open: May-15 Sep **Site:** 3HEC **Prices:** 15.80-21.50 **Facilities:** Wi-fi **Services:** **Leisure:** P **Off-site:** S

SARZEAU — MORBIHAN

Bohat

56730
297417868 297417097
e-mail: campingbohat@wanadoo.fr

C&CC Report *A very pretty site, ideal for families or couples who enjoy traditional sites. Loads of space for children to play safely, with great new play areas throughout the site. A lovely part of Brittany, with cycle routes and boat trips to take you around the Morbihan Gulf, plus a foot and cycle path straight into Sarzeau village, avoiding traffic.*

dir: *Bypass Sarzeau, keeping on D780, following signs to Arzon. Turn left (S) at site sign after 2 km, site 300m on right.*

Open: Apr-Nov **Site:** **Facilities:** **Services:** **Leisure:** P

Ferme de Lann Hoedic

rte du Roaliguen, rue Jean de la Fontaine, 56370
297480173 297417287
e-mail: contact@camping-lannhoedic.fr
web: www.camping-lannhoedic.fr

Quiet site 0.8km from a sheltered beach, accessible by foot or bike by a forest path. Pitches in sunny or shady locations, some surrounded by landscaped hedges.

dir: *From Vannes exit for Sarzeau, continue towards Arzon, left at 1st rdbt by Super U, 2km left for Lann Hoedic.*

Open: Apr-Oct **Site:** 3.6HEC **Prices:** 16.80-21 Mobile home hire 240-650 **Facilities:** Wi-fi Play Area **Services:** **Off-site:** S

Trest

rte de la Plage du Roaliguen, 56370
297417960 297413621
web: www.an-trest.com

A family site with good facilities, 0.8km from Roaliguen beach.

dir: *2.5km S.*

Open: Jun-14 Sep **Site:** 5HEC **Facilities:** **Services:** **Leisure:** P **Off-site:** S

SUBLIGNY — MANCHE

Grand Chemin

50870
233513096

Small site in a rural setting with well-defined pitches within easy reach of the village.

dir: *N175 towards Avranches, onto D39 & signed.*

Open: All Year. **Site:** 2HEC **Facilities:** **Services:**

SURRAIN CALVADOS

Camping la Roseraie d'Omaha

14170
☎ 231211771 📠 231510220
e-mail: camping-laroseraie@orange.fr
web: www.camping-calvados-normandie.fr

Close to the Normandy landing beaches, relaxing site with indoor heated swimming pool and table tennis. Cycles can be hired.

Open: Apr-Sep **Site:** 2.6HEC **Prices:** 15.90-17.90 Mobile home hire 390-567 **Facilities:** Wi-fi (charged) Play Area **Services:** **Leisure:** P **Off-site:** S

TELGRUC-SUR-MER FINISTÈRE

Panoramic

130 rte de la Plage, 29560
☎ 298277841 📠 298273610
e-mail: info@camping-panoramic.com
web: www.camping-panoramic.com

Quiet terraced site with views across a wide sandy beach. Secluded pitches.

dir: *W on D887, S onto D208.*

Open: May-15 Sep **Site:** 4HEC **Facilities:** **Services:** **Leisure:** P **Off-site:** S

THEIX MORBIHAN

Rhuys

Le Poteau Rouge, r Duguay Trouin, 56450
☎ 297541477
e-mail: campingderhuys@wanadoo.fr

Site directly on the sea with modern facilities.

dir: *3.5km NW via N165.*

Open: 10 Apr-15 Oct **Site:** 2HEC **Prices:** Mobile home hire 175-630 **Facilities:** Wi-fi Play Area **Services:** **Leisure:** P **Off-site:**

THURY-HARCOURT CALVADOS

Vallée du Traspy

rue du Pont Benôit, 14220
☎ 231796180 📠 231796180
web: www.campingtraspy.com

Level meadow site near a small reservoir, 250m from Centre Aquatique de la Suisse Normande.

Open: 15 Apr-Sep **Site:** 1.5HEC **Facilities:** **Services:** **Leisure:** L P R **Off-site:**

TINTÉNIAC ILLE-ET-VILAINE

Peupliers

Manoir de la Besnelais, 35190
☎ 299454975
e-mail: camping.les.peupliers@wanadoo.fr
web: www.les-peupliers-camping.fr

A peaceful site in a wooded location with good facilities.

dir: *2km SE via N137.*

Open: Apr-Sep **Site:** 4.5HEC **Facilities:** **Services:** **Leisure:** P **Off-site:**

TOLLEVAST MANCHE

Village Vert

30 Les Pins, 50470
☎ 233430078
e-mail: campinglevillagevert@orange.fr
web: www.le-village-vert.com

A peaceful site in a pine grove within an extensive park.

dir: *From Cherbourg ferry terminal N13 to Auchan Hypermarket, site 200m on left.*

Open: All Year. **Site:** 5.5HEC **Facilities:** **Services:** **Off-site:**

TOURLAVILLE MANCHE

Espace Loisirs de Collignon

50110
☎ 233201688 📠 233448171
e-mail: camping-collignon@wanadoo.fr
web: www.mairie-tourlaville.fr

A pleasant site with good facilities, 1km from town centre.

Open: May-Sep **Site:** 2HEC **Facilities:** **Services:** **Leisure:** S **Off-site:** P

TOURNIÈRES CALVADOS

Picard Holidays

14330
☎ 231228244
e-mail: paulpalmer@orange.fr
web: www.normandycampsite.com

A quiet site between Cherbourg and Caen, with pleasant sheltered pitches.

dir: *Via N13 & D15/D5.*

Open: All Year. **Site:** 2HEC **Prices:** 18 Mobile home hire 450-585 **Facilities:** Wi-fi Play Area **Services:** **Leisure:** L P **Off-site:** R

FRANCE

TRÉBEURDEN — CÔTES-D'ARMOR

Armor-Loisirs

r de Kernévez-Pors-Mabo, 22560
☎ 296235231 🖷 296154036
e-mail: info@armorloisirs.com
web: www.armorloisirs.com

Modern site with individual pitches surrounded by hedges. Hardstandings for caravans.

dir: *0.5km S of Kernévez road.*

Open: Apr-Sep **Site:** 2.2HEC **Facilities:** **Services:** **Leisure:** P **Off-site:** R S

TRÉDREZ-LOCQUÉMEAU — CÔTES-D'ARMOR

Capucines

Kervourdon, 22300
☎ 296357228 🖷 296357898
e-mail: les.capucines@wanadoo.fr
web: www.lescapucines.fr

A peaceful setting near the beach with a large variety of facilities.

dir: *On D786 Lannion-Morlaix road.*

Open: 27 Mar-2 Oct **Site:** 4HEC **Prices:** 18-27 Mobile home hire 260-700 **Facilities:** Wi-fi Play Area **Services:** **Leisure:** P **Off-site:** S

TRÉGUNC — FINISTÈRE

Pommeraie

St-Philibert, 29910
☎ 298500273
e-mail: pommeraie@club-internet.fr
web: www.campingdelapommeraie.com

A well-equipped site with good facilities for children, 1.2km from the beach.

dir: *S via D1.*

Open: Apr-15 Oct **Site:** 7HEC **Prices:** 18-26.80 Mobile home hire 190-555 **Facilities:** Wi-fi (charged) Kids' Club Play Area **Services:** **Leisure:** P **Off-site:** R S

TRÉLÉVERN — CÔTES-D'ARMOR

Port l'Epine

10 Venelle de Pors-Garo, 22660
☎ 296237194 🖷 296237783
e-mail: camping-de-port-lepine@wanadoo.fr
web: www.camping-port-lepine.com

Well-shaded site directly on the sea.

Open: 8 May-25 Sep **Site:** 3HEC **Facilities:** **Services:** **Leisure:** P S

TRÉPORT, LE — SEINE-MARITIME

CM les Boucaniers

r Mendes-France, 76470
☎ 235863547 🖷 235865582
e-mail: camping@ville-le-treport.fr
web: www.ville-le-treport.fr

Well-kept site on flat meadow on E edge of village. Sports and games nearby. Kids' club available in July and August.

Open: Apr-Sep **Site:** 5.5HEC **Facilities:** Wi-fi (charged) Kids' Club Play Area **Services:** **Off-site:** P R S

Parc International du Golf

102 rte de Dieppe, 76470
☎ 227280150 🖷 227280151
web: www.campings-treport.com

Set in a park on the cliffs in a wooded retreat. Rediscover the pleasure of a comfortable and quiet area, near the city centre, port and the beach by the funicular.

dir: *1km W on D940.*

GPS: 50.0516, 1.3677

Open: Apr-20 Sep **Site:** 5HEC **Prices:** 12.40-15.60 **Facilities:** **Services:** **Off-site:** P S

TRÉVOU-TRÉGUIGNEC — CÔTES-D'ARMOR

Mât

38 r de Trestel, 22660
☎ 296237152
e-mail: camping-le-mat@wanadoo.fr

A family site on level ground, 50m from the beach.

dir: *Via D38.*

Open: Apr-Sep **Site:** 1.6HEC **Facilities:** **Services:** **Leisure:** P **Off-site:** L S

TRINITÉ-SUR-MER, LA — MORBIHAN

Baie

Plage de Kervillen, 56470
☎ 297557342 🖷 276013337
e-mail: contact@campingdelabaie.com
web: www.campingdelabaie.com

Several strips of land divided by tall trees on the edge of a fine sandy beach. Kids' club available in July and August.

dir: *Signed towards Kerbihan & Plage de Kervillen.*

Open: 21 May-18 Sep **Site:** 2.4HEC **Prices:** 17.70-42.40 Mobile home hire 224-819 **Facilities:** Wi-fi (charged) Kids' Club Play Area **Services:** **Leisure:** P **Off-site:** S

Kervilor

rte du Letz, 56470
297557675 297558726
e-mail: ebideau@camping-kervilor.com
web: www.camping-kervilor.com

A pleasant wooded location 1.5km from the port. Plenty of recreational facilities.

dir: *1.6km N.*

Open: Apr-28 Sep **Site:** 5HEC **Prices:** 15-28.95 Mobile home hire 265-895 **Facilities:** Wi-fi (charged) Kids' Club Play Area **Services:** **Leisure:** P **Off-site:** S

Plage

The Camping and Caravanning Club The Friendly Club

Plage de Kervilen, 56470
297557328 276013305
e-mail: contact@camping-plage.com
web: www.camping-plage.com

A family site divided into pitches behind dunes, with direct access to the beach. Kids' club during July and August.

C&CC Report *You simply cannot beat the location of this classic beachside site just outside the fishing port of La Trinité-sur-Mer, one of France's premier yachting centres. Access to some of the pitches can be a bit tight, but this is more than compensated for by the direct access to the safe and sandy beach. A short walk along the beach takes you to the site shop, bar and restaurant where you can dine on the terrace and enjoy views over Quiberon bay.*

dir: *1km S towards Carnac-Plage.*

GPS: 47.5756, -3.0290

Open: 15 May-18 Sep **Site:** 3HEC
Prices: 17.50-36.50 Mobile home hire 245-830 **Facilities:** Wi-fi (charged) Kids' Club Play Area
Services: **Leisure:** P S **Off-site:**

PARIS/NORTH

ACY-EN-MULTIEN **OISE**

Ancien Moulin

60620
344872128 344872128
e-mail: ccdf_acy@cegetel.net
web: www.campingclub.asso.fr

Situated beside a river and a small lake with good sports facilities.

Open: All Year. **Site:** 5HEC **Facilities:**
Services: **Leisure:** L R **Off-site:**

AMIENS **SOMME**

Parc des Cygnes

111, avenue des Cygnes, 80080
322432928 322435942
e-mail: camping.amiens@wanadoo.fr
web: www.parcdescygnes.com

A well maintained site on the outskirts of Amiens. Pitches are grassy and flat in varying sizes and some specially designed for motor homes.

dir: *A16 exit 20 Amiens Nord.*

Open: Apr-14 Oct **Site:** 3.2HEC **Prices:** 14.60-20.30
Facilities: Wi-fi (charged) **Services:**
Off-site: R

ARDRES **PAS-DE-CALAIS**

St-Louis

223 r Leulène, Autingues, 62610
321354683
e-mail: domirine@aol.com
web: www.campingstlouis.com

A well-equipped site in pleasant wooded surroundings.

dir: *Off N43 1km SE of Ardres onto D224 & signed.*

Open: Apr-Oct **Site:** 1.7HEC **Prices:** 21-22 **Facilities:** Wi-fi Play Area **Services:**
Off-site: L

BERCK-SUR-MER **PAS-DE-CALAIS**

Orée du Bois

chemin Blanc 251, Rang-du-Fliers, 62180
321842851 321842856
e-mail: oree.du.bois@wanadoo.fr
web: www.loreedubois.com

A modern site in wooded surroundings with good sports facilities.

dir: *2km NE.*

Open: Apr-Oct **Site:** 18.5HEC **Facilities:**
Services: **Off-site:**

BERNY-RIVIÈRE **AISNE**

Croix du Vieux Pont

2290
323555002 323550513
e-mail: lacroixduvieuxpont@wanadoo.fr
web: www.la-croix-du-vieux-pont.com

Wooded surroundings beside the River Aisne with good facilities.

dir: *N of N31. Over River Aisne, site 0.5km E of Vic-sur-Aisne on D91.*

Open: All Year. **Site:** 34HEC **Prices:** 25.50-30.50
Facilities: Wi-fi (charged) **Services:**
Leisure: P **Off-site:**

BERTANGLES **SOMME**

Camping du Château

r du Château, 80260
☎ 360656836
e-mail: camping@chateaubertangles.com
web: www.chateaubertangles.com

Site in an old orchard of a château.

dir: *Signed off Amiens-Doullens road.*

Open: 22 Apr-12 Sep **Site:** 0.8HEC **Prices:** 14.60 **Facilities:** Play Area **Services:** **Off-site:**

BOIRY-NOTRE-DAME **PAS-DE-CALAIS**

Paille Haute

145 r de Sailly, 62156
☎ 321481540 321220724
e-mail: lapaillehaute@wanadoo.fr
web: www.la-paille-haute.com

On a level meadow with a variety of recreational facilities.

dir: *A1 exit 15 towards Cambrai, site on D34. Or A26 exit 8 towards Arras.*

Open: Apr-Oct **Site:** 4.9HEC **Facilities:** **Services:** **Leisure:** P **Off-site:**

BOUBERS-SUR-CANCHE **PAS-DE-CALAIS**

Petit St Jean

27 rue de Frevent, 62270
☎ 321048520 321048520
e-mail: arielle.triart@wanadoo.fr
web: www.campingboubers.com

A peaceful rural setting within easy reach of the village.

dir: *E via D340 towards Frévent.*

Open: Apr-15 Oct **Site:** 1HEC **Facilities:** **Services:** **Off-site:** P R

BOULANCOURT **SEINE-ET-MARNE**

Ile de Boulancourt

6 allée des Marronniers, 77760
☎ 164241338 164241043
e-mail: camping-ile-de-boulancourt@wanadoo.fr
web: www.camping-iledeboulancourt.com

A peaceful site shaded by mature trees in a convenient location in the Essonne Valley.

dir: *Via D410.*

GPS: 48.2558, 2.435

Open: All Year. **Site:** 5HEC **Prices:** 13-13.50 Mobile home hire 152-280 **Facilities:** Wi-fi (charged) Kids' Club Play Area **Services:** **Off-site:** P

BRAY-DUNES **NORD**

Perroquet-Plage

59123
☎ 328583737 328583701
e-mail: contact@campingleperroquet.com
web: www.campingleperroquet.com

Situated among dunes with direct access to the beach. A site with many activities or the opportunity to relax.

dir: *3km NE towards La Panne.*

Open: Apr-Sep **Site:** 28HEC **Prices:** 19.70-20 **Facilities:** Wi-fi Kids' Club Play Area **Services:** **Leisure:** S **Off-site:** P

CHARLY-SUR-MARNE **AISNE**

Camping des Illettes

rte de Pavant, 02310
☎ 323821211 323821399
e-mail: mairie.charly@wanadoo.fr
web: www.charly-sur-marne.fr

Five minutes walk from the town centre, small site with some facilities for children.

GPS: 48.9735, 3.2820

Open: Apr-Sep **Site:** 1HEC **Prices:** 12-14.50 **Facilities:** Play Area **Services:** **Off-site:**

CONDETTE **PAS-DE-CALAIS**

Château

21 r Nouvelle, 62360
☎ 321875959 321875959
e-mail: campingduchateau@libertysurf.fr
web: camping-caravaning-du-chateau.com

Pleasant parkland bordered by a forest, 0.5km from the town centre. Separate car park for arrivals after 23.00hrs.

dir: *D940 towards Hardelot.*

GPS: 50.6464, 1.6253

Open: Apr-30 Oct **Site:** 1.2HEC **Prices:** 15.80-21 Mobile home hire 370-610 **Facilities:** Wi-fi (charged) Kids' Club Play Area **Services:** **Off-site:** L S

COUDEKERQUE **NORD**

Bois des Forts

59280
☎ 328610441

dir: *0.7km NW on D72.*

Open: All Year. **Site:** 4HEC **Facilities:** **Services:** **Off-site:** P R

CRÉVECOEUR-EN-BRIE SEINE-ET-MARNE

Des 4 Vents

The Camping and Caravanning Club The Friendly Club

r de Beauregard, 77610
☎ 164074111 🖷 164074507
e-mail: contact@caravaning-4vents.fr
web: www.caravaning-4vents.fr
Well-kept family run site in an excellent location.

C&CC Report *With the George family's welcome, the lovingly tended grounds and a peaceful location in easy striking distance of Disneyland® Resort Paris, Parc Astérix and Paris itself, this is an understandably popular site. Nearby medieval Provins is well worth a visit, with fabulous re-enactments of battles of the Middle Ages, while the châteaux at Vaux-le-Vicomte, Fontainebleau and Versailles are some of France's finest. And if all that isn't enough excitement, a superb big cats safari park is only five minutes drive away.*

dir: *A4 exit 13 in direction Provins D231.*

Open: Mar-1 Nov **Site:** 10HEC **Prices:** 27 **Facilities:** Wi-fi Play Area **Services:** **Leisure:** P **Off-site:**

CROTOY, LE SOMME

Aubépines

300 r de la Maye, Saint Firmin, 80550
☎ 322270134 🖷 322271366
e-mail: lesaubepines@baiedesommepleinair.com
web: www.camping-lesaubepines.com
A peaceful verdant location surrounded by hawthorn trees on the Picardy coast and Somme Bay. The nearest beach, 1km away, is part of a nature reserve. Kids' club available 15 July to 15 August.

dir: *D940 from Abbeville, follow signs for Le Crotoy at 1st rdbt straight over, 2nd rdbt turn right then 1st left.*

GPS: 50.2494, 1.6115

Open: Apr-Oct **Site:** 4HEC **Prices:** 16-25.50 Mobile home hire 220-714 **Facilities:** Kids' Club Play Area **Services:** **Leisure:** P **Off-site:** S

Ridin

Lieu dit Mayocq, 80550
☎ 322270322 🖷 322277076
e-mail: leridin@baiedesommepleinair.com
web: www.baiedesommepleinair.com
Situated in the heart of the Somme Bay, conveniently located for Paris and Lille. Kids' club available in July and August.

dir: *From Calais take A16 exit 24 towards Rue then Le Crotoy. At rdbt turn right, then 2nd right.*

Open: Apr-Nov **Site:** 4.5HEC **Prices:** 16.50-22 Mobile home hire 290-630 **Facilities:** Kids' Club Play Area **Services:** **Leisure:** P **Off-site:** L R S

DUNKERQUE (DUNKIRK) NORD

Licorne

1005 bd de l'Europe, 59240
☎ 328692668 🖷 328695621
e-mail: campinglalicorne@ville-dunkerque.fr
Open: Apr-Nov **Site:** 10HEC **Prices:** 17.50 **Facilities:** (charged) Play Area **Services:** **Off-site:** P S

ÉPERLECQUES PAS-DE-CALAIS

Château de Gandspette

62910
☎ 321934393 🖷 321957498
e-mail: contact@chateau-gandspette.com
web: www.chateau-gandspette.com
A peaceful site, surrounded by woodland.

dir: *11.5km NW on D943 & D207.*

GPS: 50.8189, 2.1775

Open: Apr-Sep **Site:** 11HEC **Prices:** 14-24 Mobile home hire 350-585 **Facilities:** Wi-fi (charged) **Services:** **Leisure:** P **Off-site:**

EQUIHEN-PLAGE PAS-DE-CALAIS

CM la Falaise

r C-Cazin, 62224
☎ 321312261 🖷 321805401
e-mail: camping.equihen.plage@orange.fr
web: www.ville-equihen-plage.fr
Between Boulogne and Le Touquet.

Open: Apr-Oct **Site:** 8HEC **Facilities:** Play Area **Services:** **Off-site:** S

FELLERIES NORD

CM La Boissellerie

r de la Place, 59740
☎ 327590650 🖷 327590288
e-mail: mairie.felleries@wanadoo.fr
Shaded site.

dir: *Take RN2 southbound.*

GPS: 50.1431, 4.0286

Open: 15 Apr-Sep **Site:** 1HEC **Prices:** 11.20 **Facilities:** **Off-site:** R

FRANCE

FERTÉ-SOUS-JOUARRE, LA — SEINE-ET-MARNE

Bondons

47/49 r des Bondons, 077260
☎ 160220098 🖷 160229701
e-mail: castel@chateaudesbondons.com
Set in a beautiful wooded park. Reserved for caravans.
dir: *2km NE via D402 & D70.*
GPS: 48.9478, 3.1483
Open: All Year. **Site:** 28HEC **Prices:** 27 **Facilities:** Play Area **Services:** **Off-site:** P R

FORT-MAHON-PLAGE — SOMME

Royon

rte de Quend, 80120
☎ 322234030 🖷 322236515
e-mail: info@campingleroyon.com
web: www.campingleroyon.com
A family site with good facilities and well-marked pitches, 2.5km from the beach.
Open: 10 Mar-1 Nov **Site:** 5.5HEC **Facilities:** **Services:** **Leisure:** P **Off-site:** S

GOUVIEUX — OISE

Le Mont César

rte de Toutevoie 10, 60270
☎ 344570205
e-mail: lemontcesar@wanadoo.fr
web: www.lemontcesar.com
On a hill overlooking the River Oise.
dir: *A1 to Gouvieux town centre, then towards Creil.*
Open: Apr-Oct **Site:** 6HEC **Prices:** 13.40 Mobile home hire 290 **Facilities:** Wi-fi Play Area **Services:** **Off-site:** P

GRAND-FORT-PHILIPPE — NORD

Camping de la Plage

r Ml-Foch, 59153
☎ 328653195 🖷 328653599
e-mail: campingdelaplage@campingnvpa.fr
web: www.camping-de-la-plage.info
On a level meadow separated from the beach (0.5km).
dir: *Via A16.*
Open: Apr-Oct **Site:** 1.5HEC **Facilities:** **Services:** **Off-site:** R S

GREZ-SUR-LOING — SEINE-ET-MARNE

CM Près

chemin des Près, 77880
☎ 164457275 🖷 164457275
e-mail: camping-grez@wanadoo.fr
web: www.camping-grez-fontainebleau.info
dir: *NE towards Loing.*
Open: end Mar-11 Nov **Site:** 6HEC **Facilities:** **Services:** **Off-site:** R

GUINES — PAS-DE-CALAIS

Bien Assise

The Camping and Caravanning Club The Friendly Club

62340
☎ 321352077 🖷 321367920
e-mail: castels@bien-assise.com
web: www.bien-assise.com
Rural site near to a forest and next to a charming little town.
C&CC Report *A pretty, well-established and very welcoming site with excellent facilities, close to the beautiful Opal Coast, with its impressive cliffs and golden beaches. Ideal for short breaks, first-time holidays abroad, long stays and overnight stops alike. As well as being very handy for Calais ferry port and the Channel Tunnel, time spent here lazily exploring the Picardy countryside, coast, towns and historic sites reaps many rewards.*
dir: *D231 towards Marquise.*
Open: 19 Apr-21 Sep **Site:** 12HEC **Facilities:** Play Area **Services:** **Leisure:** P **Off-site:**

ISQUES — PAS-DE-CALAIS

Cytises

chemin Georges Ducrocq, 62360
☎ 321311110 🖷 321311110
e-mail: campcytises@orange.fr
A pleasant rural setting beside the River Liane.
dir: *A16 exit 28.*
GPS: 50.6777, 1.6427
Open: Apr-15 Oct **Site:** 2.5HEC **Prices:** 13.20-14.60 Mobile home hire 275-420 **Facilities:** Wi-fi Play Area **Services:** **Off-site:** L R S

FRANCE

ABLINES SEINE-ET-MARNE

International de Jablines

Base de Loisirs, 77450
160260937 160264333
e-mail: welcome@camping-jablines.com
web: www.camping-jablines.com
Only 9km from Disneyland® Resort Paris.
dir: *A1 or A3 towards Marne-la-Vallée, onto N3.*
GPS: 48.9133, 2.7342
Open: 9 Apr-5 Nov **Site:** 3.5HEC **Prices:** 24-29 Mobile home hire 455-660 **Facilities:** Play Area **Services:** **Off-site:** L

LICQUES PAS-DE-CALAIS

Canchy

de Canchy, 62850
321826341 321826341
e-mail: camping.lecanchy@wanadoo.fr
web: www.camping-lecanchy.com
A quiet site on an open, level meadow. Well situated for the ferries and the Channel Tunnel.
Open: 15 Mar-Oct **Site:** 1HEC **Facilities:** **Services:** **Leisure:** R **Off-site:**

Pommiers des Trois Pays

273 r de Breuil, 62850
321350202 321350202
e-mail: contact@pommiers-3pays.com
web: www.pommiers-3pays.com
Small, relaxing site with large pitches separated by hedges.
dir: *D215 Guines-Licques/D224 Ardres-Licques, then follow D191.*
GPS: 50.7797, 1.9476
Open: Apr-Oct **Site:** 2.5HEC **Prices:** 16-19.50 Mobile home hire 280-600 **Facilities:** Wi-fi Play Area **Services:** **Leisure:** P **Off-site:** R

MAISONS-LAFFITTE YVELINES

International

r Johnson, 78600
139122191 139127050
e-mail: ci.mlaffitte@wanadoo.fr
web: www.campint.com
A well-kept site in a residential area on the banks of the Seine. Modern installations, heated in cold weather.
dir: *8km N of St-Germain-en-Laye. Or A86 exit Colombos-Ouest.*
GPS: 48.9402, 2.1451
Open: Apr-Oct **Site:** 6.5HEC **Prices:** 23.20-28.50 **Facilities:** Wi-fi (charged) Play Area **Services:** **Off-site:** P R

MAUBEUGE NORD

Camping Municipal de Clair de Lune

rte de Mons, 59600
327622548 327602594
e-mail: camping@ville-maubeuge.fr
web: www.ville-maubeuge.fr
Close to the town centre with pitches divided by hedges.
dir: *1.5km N via N2 Bruxelles road.*
Open: mid Feb-mid Dec **Site:** 2.13HEC **Prices:** 11-15.35 **Facilities:** Play Area **Services:** **Off-site:** P R

MELUN SEINE-ET-MARNE

Belle Étoile

Quai Maréchal Joffre, 77000
164394812 164372555
e-mail: info@campinglabelleetoile.com
web: www.campinglabelleetoile.com
Pleasant grassy site with two central blocks, in wooded, peaceful countryside and yet convenient for visiting Paris and Disneyland® Resort Paris.
dir: *At La Rochette on River Seine, 1km from town.*
Open: 26 Mar-15 Oct **Site:** 3.5HEC **Prices:** 16.50-19.50 Mobile home hire 294-600 **Facilities:** Wi-fi (charged) Kids' Club Play Area **Services:** **Leisure:** P **Off-site:** P R

MERLIMONT PAS-DE-CALAIS

St-Hubert

RD 940, 62155
321891010 321891012
e-mail: sthubert62@wanadoo.fr
web: www.sthubert62.com
Pleasant wooded surroundings with good recreational facilities.
dir: *3km S via D940, near Parc de Bagatelle.*
Open: Apr-Oct **Site:** 16HEC **Facilities:** **Services:** **Leisure:** P

FRANCE

MIANNAY SOMME

Clos Cacheleux

rte de Bouillancourt, 80132
☎ 322191747 🖷 322313533
e-mail: raphael@camping-lecloscacheleux.fr
web: www.camping-lecloscacheleux.fr

Situated in the grounds of an 18th-century castle, bordered with woodland and very large pitches. Organised activities plus a fishing pond and farm animals. Other facilities include use of a swimming pool at a neighbouring site under the same ownership.

dir: *From A28 exit 2 at Abbéville take D925 towards Eu & Le Tréport (not towards Moyenville). Left in Miannay on D86 towards Toeufles. Left to Bouillancourt-sous-Miannay after 2km, site signed in village.*

GPS: 50.0864, 1.7156

Open: 15 Mar-15 Oct **Site:** 8HEC **Prices:** 15.60-21.40 **Facilities:** Wi-fi Kids' Club Play Area **Services:** **Off-site:** L P R

MILLY-LA-FORÊT ESSONNE

Musardière

rte des Grandes Vallées, 91490
☎ 164989191 🖷 164989191
e-mail: lamusardiere91@orange.fr

Pleasant wooded surroundings.

dir: *4km SE via D948.*

Open: 16 Feb-20 Nov **Site:** 12HEC **Prices:** 20.60-22.80 Mobile home hire 445.20-550.20 **Facilities:** Play Area **Services:** **Leisure:** P **Off-site:** R

MONNERVILLE ESSONNE

Bois de la Justice

91930
☎ 164950534 🖷 164951731
web: campingboislajustice.pagesperso-orange.fr

Pitches separated by trees and hedges in beautiful natural woodland with good facilities.

dir: *N20 Orléans to Étampes.*

GPS: 48.3325, 2.0470

Open: Feb-Nov **Site:** 5.5HEC **Prices:** 19.50 Mobile home hire 368 **Facilities:** Play Area **Services:** **Leisure:** P

MONTREUIL-SUR-MER PAS-DE-CALAIS

CM Fontaine des Clercs

1, rue de l'Eglise, 62170
☎ 321060728
e-mail: desmarest.mi@wanadoo.fr
web: www.campinglafontainedesclercs.fr

Quiet, shady site, 15 minutes from beaches and 200m from railway station.

dir: *N of town on N1.*

Open: All Year. **Site:** 2HEC **Facilities:** **Services:** **Leisure:** R **Off-site:** P

MOYENNEVILLE SOMME

Val de Trie

Bouillancourt-sous-Miannay, 80870
☎ 322314888 🖷 322313533
e-mail: raphael@camping-levaldetrie.fr
web: www.camping-levaldetrie.fr

A small site in a picturesque wooded location with good facilities.

dir: *1km from D925. On A28, exit 3 (Moyennes16), signed.*

GPS: 50.0860, 1.7149

Open: Apr-15 Oct **Site:** 3HEC **Prices:** 15.60-21.40 Mobile home hire 312.55-714 **Facilities:** Wi-fi Kids' Club Play Area **Services:** **Leisure:** P **Off-site:** L R

NESLES-LA-VALLÉE VAL-D'OISE

Parc de Séjour de l'Étang

10 Chemin des Belles Vues, 95690
☎ 134706289
e-mail: brehinier1@hotmail.fr
web: www.campingparcset.fr

Level site near a small lake.

Open: Mar-Oct **Site:** 6HEC **Prices:** 15 **Facilities:** **Services:** **Off-site:** P R S

OYE-PLAGE PAS-DE-CALAIS

Oyats

272 Digue Vert, 62215
☎ 321851540 🖷 328603833
e-mail: billiet.nicolas@wanadoo.fr
web: www.les-oyats.com

dir: *4.5km NW on beach.*

Open: May-Sep **Site:** 5HEC **Facilities:** **Services:** **Leisure:** P S

FRANCE

ARIS

Bois de Boulogne

 allée du Bord de l'Eau, 75016
 145243000 142244295
-mail: paris@campingparis.fr
eb: www.campingparis.fr
his popular site is close to the city centre and it can be crowded uring the summer, as it is the only site in central Paris.
pen: All Year. **Site:** 7HEC **Facilities:**
ervices:

LESSIS-FEU-AUSSOUX — SEINE-ET-MARNE

Château-de-Chambonnières

7540
 164041585 164041336
-mail: campingchambonnieres@orange.fr
ir: *On D231 towards Provins.*
pen: Apr-Sep **Site:** 5HEC **Facilities:**
ervices: **Off-site:** P R

OIX-DE-PICARDIE — SOMME

Bois des Pêcheurs

te de Forges-les-Eaux, 80290
 322901171 322903291
-mail: camping@ville-poix-de-picardie.fr
eb: www.ville-poix-de-picardie.fr
 quiet riverside location with a high standard of sanitary acilities.
ir: *A29 exit 13.*
pen: Apr-Sep **Site:** 2.35HEC **Facilities:**
ervices: **Off-site:** P R

OMMEUSE — SEINE-ET-MARNE

Chêne Gris

4 pl de la gare de Faremoutiers, 77515
 164042180 164200589
-mail: info@lechenegris.com
eb: www.lechenegris.com
oodland site within easy travelling distance of Disneyland® esort Paris and the capital itself.
ir: *N34 towards Coulommiers-Crécy, onto D25 to Pommeuse, igned on right after station.*
pen: Apr-8 Nov **Site:** 6HEC **Facilities:**
i-fi (charged) Kids' Club Play Area **Services:**
eisure: P **Off-site:** R

PORT-LE-GRAND — SOMME

Chateau des Tilleuls

rte D40 A, 80132
322240775 322242380
On gently sloping meadow surrounding a farm.
dir: *1km SE on D40A.*
Open: Mar-Oct **Site:** 5HEC **Facilities:**
Services: **Leisure:** P **Off-site:** R

PROYART — SOMME

Loisir la Violette

rte de Mericourt, 80340
322858136 322851737
Close to the N29 and A29, this site overlooks marshes and fishponds.
Open: Apr-Oct **Site:** 1.8HEC **Prices:** 7.66 Mobile home hire 216.37 **Facilities:** **Off-site:**

QUEND-PLAGE-LES-PINS — SOMME

Roses

80120
322277617 322239306
e-mail: info@campingdesroses.com
web: www.campingdesroses.com
Well-kept site with trees and hedges surrounding individual pitches.
dir: *Off D940 at Quend onto D102, site 0.5km on left.*
Open: 15 Mar-23 Oct **Site:** 9HEC **Facilities:**
Services: **Leisure:** L P **Off-site:** S

Vertes Feuilles

25 rte de la Plage, Monchaux, 80120
322235512 322190752
e-mail: lesvertesfeuilles@baiedesommepleinair.com
web: www.baiedesommepleinair.com
Situated 3km from the sea between the Somme Bay and Authe Bay. Kids' club available in July and August.
dir: *A16 exit 24, follow D32 towards Quend Plage.*
GPS: 50.3198, 1.6063
Open: Apr-Oct **Site:** **Prices:** 14.50-24.50 Mobile home hire 305-658 **Facilities:** Wi-fi Kids' Club Play Area **Services:** **Leisure:** P
Off-site: L R S

RAMBOUILLET YVELINES

Huttopia Rambouillet

rte du Château d'Eau, 78120
☎ 130410734 🖹 130410017
e-mail: rambouillet@huttopia.com
web: www.huttopia.com

In the heart of the forest of Rambouillet, beside the Etang d'Or (Golden Pond). Kids' club available in July and August. 1 dog per pitch.

dir: *From Paris take A13, then A12 then N10.*

Open: 25 Mar-6 Nov **Site:** 8HEC **Prices:** 17.50-26.20 Mobile home hire 548.10-705.60 **Facilities:** Kids' Club Play Area **Services:** **Leisure:** L P **Off-site:**

ST-AMAND-LES-EAUX NORD

Mont des Bruyères

806 r Basly, 59230
☎ 327485687 🖹 327485687
e-mail: lemontdesbruyeres@orange.fr

A quiet site on the edge of a large forest. A discount may be available on presentation of this guide.

dir: *3.5km SE in forest of St-Amand*

Open: 15 Mar-30 Oct **Site:** 3.5HEC **Prices:** 18.50-22 Mobile home hire 220-270 **Facilities:** Wi-fi (charged) Play Area **Services:** **Off-site:** L P R

ST-CHÉRON ESSONNE

Parc des Roches

La Petite Beauce, 91530
☎ 164566550 🖹 164565450
e-mail: info@camping-parcdesroches.com
web: www.camping-parcdesroches.com

Set in a wooded park.

Open: 10 Apr-15 Oct **Site:** 23HEC **Facilities:** **Services:** **Leisure:** P **Off-site:**

ST-CYR-SUR-MORIN SEINE-ET-MARNE

Choisel

Courcelles la Roue, 77750
☎ 160238493 🖹 160248174
e-mail: campingduchoisel@wanadoo.fr
web: www.camping-du-choisel.com

A pleasant location. Separate car park for arrivals after 22.00hrs.

dir: *2km W via D31.*

Open: Mar-Nov **Site:** 3.5HEC **Facilities:** **Services:** **Off-site:** L P R

ST-LEU-D'ESSERENT OISE

Campix

The Camping and Caravanning Club The Friendly Club

60340
☎ 344560848 🖹 344562875
e-mail: campix@orange.fr
web: www.campingcampix.com

Set in wooded surroundings within easy reach of Chantilly.

C&CC Report *If you like to get back to nature and just relax, this simple green hide-away site, in its lush, irregular and rambling surroundings has a picturesque swimming pool, paddling pool and large sunbathing terrace that together provide its focus. Monsieur Ozon, the friendly, English-speaking owner is always around to help and advise. The château of Chantilly is just a short drive away; Parc Astérix, a short distance away, is a great fun day out, and all that Paris has to offer is just a train ride away from the village.*

dir: *3.5km NE via D12.*

Open: 7 Mar-1 Dec **Site:** 6HEC **Facilities:** **Services:** **Off-site:** L P

ST-VALÉRY-SUR-SOMME SOMME

Domaine du Château de Drancourt

80230
☎ 322269345 🖹 322268587
e-mail: chateau.drancourt@wanadoo.fr
web: www.chateau-drancourt.com

Set within the grounds of a former hunting lodge surrounded by woods, fields and lakes.

dir: *3.5km S via D48.*

GPS: 50.1533, 1.3809

Open: Apr-1 Nov **Site:** 15HEC **Prices:** 17-21 **Facilities:** Wi-fi (charged) Kids' Club **Services:** **Leisure:** P **Off-site:** L

SALENCY OISE

Étang du Moulin

54 r du Moulin, 60400
☎ 344099981

A small site opposite a trout fishing lake and recreational area under the ownership of the site proprietors.

dir: *3km from Noyon on N32 towards Chauny.*

Open: All Year. **Site:** 0.36HEC **Prices:** 14.60 **Facilities:** **Services:** **Off-site:** P R

Site 6HEC (site size) grass sand stone little shade partly shaded mainly shaded bungalows for hire (static) caravans for hire tents for hire no dogs site fully accessible for wheelchairs
Prices amount quoted is per night, for 2 adults and car, plus tent or caravan. Mobile home hire is a weekly rate.

FRANCE

ERAUCOURT-LE-GRAND AISNE

Pêche du Vivier aux Carpes

10 r Ch-Voyeux, 02790
☎ 323605010 323605169
e-mail: camping.du.vivier@wanadoo.fr
web: www.camping-picardie.com

A peaceful site bordered by lakes. Separate car park for arrivals after 22.00hrs.

C&CC Report *This pristine, immaculately kept little site is a paradise for anglers and makes for an ideal break not far from home. In the heart of the Somme region, nearer to Paris than Calais and close to many cathedral cities and Great War sites, it makes a superb base for exploring historic Picardy and further afield. There's a lot of useful advice and information available from the owners and cycle routes into this lovely area, straight from the site.*

dir: *A26 exit 11, left onto D1, onto D72 Essigny.*

Open: Mar-Oct **Site:** 3HEC **Facilities:** **Services:** **Off-site:** R

TELLA-PLAGE PAS-DE-CALAIS

amping la Forêt

49 blvd de Benck, 62780
321947501
mail: info@laforetstella.fr
eb: www.laforetstella.fr

3km from the sea, family friendly site with facilities including games room.

PS: 50.4734, 1.5918

pen: 11 Mar-7 Nov **Site:** 3HEC **Prices:** 17.50-21.50 obile home hire 380-670 **Facilities:** Wi-fi (charged) ay Area **Services:** **Off-site:** S

HIEMBRONNE PAS-DE-CALAIS

'ommiers

e de Desvres, 62560
321395019
mail: campinglespommiers62@orange.fr
eb: www.camping-pommiers.com

family site in pleasant wooded surroundings.

r: *NW on D132.*

pen: 15 Mar-15 Oct **Site:** 3HEC **Facilities:** **ervices:** **Leisure:** P **Off-site:** R

TOLLENT PAS-DE-CALAIS

Val d'Authie

rte de Berck, 62390
☎ 321471427 321471427

A pleasant wooded location with wide, well-marked pitches.

dir: *SE via D119.*

Open: Apr-Sep **Site:** 5.7HEC **Prices:** 78 Mobile home hire 470 **Facilities:** Wi-fi Play Area **Services:** **Leisure:** L P **Off-site:** R

TORCY SEINE-ET-MARNE

Parc de la Colline

rte de Lagny, 77200
☎ 160054232 164800517
e-mail: camping.parc.de.la.colline@wanadoo.fr
web: www.camping-de-la-colline.com

An ideal base for visiting Paris (30 minutes from the centre by Metro). Separate car park for arrivals after 22.00hrs.

dir: *A104 exit 10, onto D10E.*

Open: All Year. **Site:** 13HEC **Facilities:** **Services:** **Off-site:** L P

TOUQUIN SEINE-ET-MARNE

Étangs Fleuris

rte de la Couture, 77131
☎ 164041636 164041228
e-mail: contact@etangs-fleuris.com
web: www.etangsfleuris.com

Wooded surroundings with well-defined pitches and modern facilities.

dir: *A4 exit 13 towards Provins. In Touquin follow signs.*

GPS: 48.7331, 3.0470

Open: 15 Apr-15 Sep **Site:** 5.5HEC **Prices:** 19 Mobile home hire 390-640 **Facilities:** Wi-fi Play Area **Services:** **Leisure:** P **Off-site:**

TOURNEHEM PAS-DE-CALAIS

Hotel Bal Caravanning

500 r du Vieux Château, 62890
☎ 321356590 321351857
e-mail: hotelbal@yahoo.fr

A peaceful site in rural surroundings with modern facilities.

C&CC Report *A convenient location for an overnight stop. Set in the grounds of a hotel, half a mile from a medieval village and with an on-site restaurant.*

dir: *D218 from village centre*

Open: All Year. **Site:** 1.6HEC **Facilities:** **Services:** **Off-site:** R

FRANCE

Facilities shop shower electric points for razors electric points for caravans parking by tents permitted mpulsory separate car park **Services** café/restaurant bar Camping Gaz International gas other than Camping Gaz first aid facilities laundry **Leisure** swimming L-Lake P-Pool R-River S-Sea **Off-site** All facilities within 5km

VAILLY-SUR-AISNE — AISNE

Domaine de la Nature

chemin de Boufaud, Pont de Vailly, 02370
☎ 323547455
e-mail: domainedelanature@orange.fr
web: www.domainedelanature.fr

A pleasant rural setting alongside the canal with well-defined pitches and modern sanitary facilities.

dir: *4km W via D144 near canal & lake.*

Open: All Year. **Site:** 3HEC **Facilities:** Ⓟ **Services:** **Off-site:** R

VERNEUIL-SUR-SEINE — YVELINES

Val de Seine

chemin du Rouillard, 78480
☎ 139281620 139711860
e-mail: vds78@orange.fr
web: www.vds78.com

Set on the outskirts of Paris in a pine forest.

Open: Apr-Sep **Site:** 3.5HEC **Facilities:** **Services:** **Leisure:** L **Off-site:**

VERSAILLES — YVELINES

Huttopia Versailles

31 rue Berthelot, 78000
☎ 139512361 139536829
e-mail: versailles@huttopia.com
web: www.huttopia.com

Site in forest location 2.5km from the palace of Versailles. Very convenient for Paris.

dir: *A13 from Paris, exit Versailles centre, follow signs.*

GPS: 48.7946, 2.1612

Open: 25 Mar-6 Nov **Site:** 4HEC
Prices: 22.90-32.90 Mobile home hire 548.10-787.50
Facilities: Wi-fi Play Area Ⓟ **Services:**
Leisure: P **Off-site:**

VILLENNES-SUR-SEINE — YVELINES

Club des Renardières

rte de Vernouillet, 78670
☎ 139758897

Site for caravans only, in beautiful hilly park laid out with hedges, lawns and flower beds. Fully divided into completely separated pitches.

dir: *D113 to Maison Blanche, turn right for 3km.*

Open: All Year. **Site:** 7HEC **Facilities:**
Services: **Off-site:** L P R

VILLERS-SUR-AUTHIE — SOMM

Val d'Authie

20 rte de Vercourt, 80120
☎ 322299247 322299330
e-mail: camping@valdauthie.fr
web: www.valdauthie.fr

A well-designed site between the forest of Crécy and the sea.

dir: *Via N1.*

Open: Apr-11 Oct **Site:** 7HEC **Facilities:** Wi-fi Kids' Club Play Area Ⓟ **Services:**
Leisure: P **Off-site:** R

VILLIERS SUR ORGE — ESSONN

Camping le Beau Village de Paris

1 Voie des Prés, 91700
☎ 160161786 160163146
e-mail: le-beau-village@wanadoo.fr
web: www.beau-village.com

20 minutes by train from the centre of Paris and with a range of local amenities close by. Restaurant for guests' use between Jun and 20 September.

GPS: 48.6551, 2.3042

Open: All Year. **Site:** 2.5HEC **Prices:** 18-20 Mobile home hire 250-440 **Facilities:** Wi-fi Play Area Ⓟ **Services:** **Leisure:** R
Off-site: L

VIRONCHAUX — SOMM

Peupliers

221 r du Cornet, 80150
☎ 322235427
e-mail: les-peupliers3@orange.fr
web: www.campingpeupliers.fr

A peaceful site 3km from the forest of Crécy.

dir: *Via N1 & D938.*

Open: Apr-Oct **Site:** 2.5HEC **Facilities:** Ⓟ
Services:

WACQUINGHEN — PAS-DE-CALAI

Éscale

62250
☎ 321320069 321320069
e-mail: camp-escale@wanadoo.fr
web: www.escale-camping.com

A landscaped park with modern facilities close to the coast.

dir: *Via A16 & D231.*

Open: 15 Mar-15 Oct **Site:** 11HEC **Prices:** 17.50 Mobile home hire 290-510 **Facilities:** Wi-fi (charged) Play Area Ⓟ **Services:** **Leisure:** L
Off-site:

AUVERGNE

LLANCHE CANTAL

amping Les Gentianes

5160
471204587 471204181
-mail: campingallanche@orange.fr
ir: *1km S on D679 towards St-Flour.*
pen: 15 Jun-15 Sep **Site:** 3HEC **Prices:** 8-9.50
obile home hire 215-285 **Facilities:** **Services:**
eisure: R **Off-site:**

LLEYRAS HAUTE-LOIRE

M

3580
471575686 471575686
mail: mairie.camping-municipal@akeonet.com
easant surroundings on level ground beside the River Allier.
r: *2.5km NW.*
pen: 15 Apr-15 Oct **Site:** 1HEC **Prices:** 9.90
cilities: **Services:** **Off-site:** R

MBERT PUY-DE-DÔME

rois Chênes

e du Puy, 63600
473823468 473823468
mail: tourisme@ville-ambert.fr
eb: www.camping-ambert.com
the outskirts of Ambert the site is well presented with an
nphasis on green areas.
en: May-Sep **Site:** **Facilities:** Play Area
rvices: **Leisure:** P **Off-site:** L P

RNAC CANTAL

ineste

5150
471629190 471629272
mail: contact@village-vacances-cantal.com
eb: www.village-vacances-cantal.com
tuated on a peninsula in Lake Enchanet with modern facilities
d access to ski slopes.
r: *NW of Arnac towards lake.*
en: All Year. **Site:** 3HEC **Facilities:** Play
ea **Services:** **Leisure:** L P **Off-site:** R

ARPAJON-SUR-CÈRE CANTAL

Cère

r F-Ramond, 15130
471645507
e-mail: tourisme@caba.fr
web: www.caba.fr/camping
dir: *S towards Rodez on D920, site beside river.*
Open: Jun-Sep **Site:** 2HEC **Facilities:** **Services:** **Leisure:** P R **Off-site:**

BELLERIVE-SUR-ALLIER ALLIER

Acacias

r Claude-Decloître, 03700
470323622 470598852
e-mail: camping-acacias03@orange.fr
web: www.camping-acacias.com
Well-managed site, sub-divided into numbered pitches by hedges. Clean sanitary installations. Library, billiard room. Water sports are available on nearby lake.
dir: *From Vichy left after bridge beside fuel station & along river for 0.5km.*
Open: Apr-15 Oct **Site:** 3HEC **Prices:** 10.60-16.90
Mobile home hire 330-650 **Facilities:** Wi-fi Kids' Club Play Area **Services:** **Leisure:** L P R
Off-site:

Beau Rivage

r Claude Decloitre, 03700
470322685 470320394
e-mail: camping-beaurivage@wanadoo.fr
web: www.camping-beaurivage.com
Neat meadowland with marked out pitches. Well-kept sanitary installations.
dir: *Over bridge onto left bank of River Allier.*
Open: Apr-Oct **Site:** 1.5HEC **Facilities:** **Services:** **Leisure:** P R **Off-site:** L

BOURBON-L'ARCHAMBAULT ALLIER

C M de Bourbon L'Archambault

Parc Jean Bignon, 03160
470670883 470673535
Shady site in parkland.
dir: *1km SW on N153, rte de Montluçon, turn right.*
Open: Mar-Oct **Site:** 3HEC **Prices:** 7.09-7.44
Facilities: Wi-fi (charged) **Services:**
Off-site: P

FRANCE

BOURG-ARGENTAL LOIRE

Astrée

42220
☎ 477397297 🖷 477397621
e-mail: prl@bourgargental.fr
Pleasant surroundings with good recreational facilities.
dir: *Via N82.*
Open: All Year. **Site:** 2HEC **Facilities:** **Services:** **Leisure:** R **Off-site:** P

BRAIZE ALLIER

Champ de la Chapelle

03360
☎ 470061545
e-mail: champdelachapelle@wanadoo.fr
web: www.champdelachapelle.com
A family site in the centre of the Tronçais forest with good recreational facilities.
dir: *7km SE via D28 & D978.*
GPS: 46.6431, 2.6544
Open: mid Apr-end Oct **Site:** 5.6HEC **Prices:** 11.50-14.50 Mobile home hire 320-400 **Facilities:** Wi-fi (charged) Play Area **Services:** **Leisure:** P **Off-site:** L R

BRIVES-CHARENSAC HAUTE-LOIRE

Audinet

avenue des Sports, 43700
☎ 471091018 🖷 471091018
e-mail: camping.audinet@wanadoo.fr
web: www.brives-charensac.fr
A peaceful site in a wooded setting beside the River Loire with good recreational facilities.
dir: *E on N88.*
Open: 30 Apr-22 Sep **Site:** 4.5HEC **Facilities:** **Services:** **Leisure:** R **Off-site:** P

CANET-DE-SALARS AVEYRO

Le Caussanel

Lac de Pareloup, 12290
☎ 565468519 🖷 565468985
e-mail: info@lecaussanel.com
web: www.lecaussanel.com
Well-equipped site on the shore of Lake Pareloup. Kids' club in high season.
dir: *Via D911.*
GPS: 44.2150, 2.7645
Open: 23 May-17 Sep **Site:** 10HEC **Prices:** 14.50-29.2 Mobile home hire 308-994 **Facilities:** Wi-fi Kids' Club Play Area **Services:** **Leisure:** L P

Soleil Levant

Lac de Pareloup, 12290
☎ 565460365
e-mail: contact@camping-soleil-levant.com
web: www.camping-soleil-levant.com
A family site set on terraces on the shores of Lac de Pareloup wi good recreational facilities.
dir: *S of Canet-de-Salars on D933 towards Salles-Curan.*
GPS: 44.2149, 2.7779
Open: Apr-Sep **Site:** 11HEC **Prices:** 12-20 Mobile hom hire 180-625 **Facilities:** Wi-fi Kids' Club Play Area **Services:** **Leisure:** L **Off-site:**

CAPDENAC-GARE AVEYRO

CM Rives d'Olt

bd Paul-Ramadier, 12700
☎ 565808887
A quiet site on level ground with pitches divided by hedges on th bank of a river.
dir: *7km from Figeac via N140 towards Rodez, onto D35 to Capendac.*
Open: Apr-Sep **Site:** 1.3HEC **Facilities:** **Services:** **Leisure:** R **Off-site:** P

CEYRAT PUY-DE-DOM

Camping Le Chanset

The Camping and Caravanning Club — The Friendly Club

63122
☎ 473613073 🖷 473613073
e-mail: camping.lechanset@wanadoo.fr
web: www.campingdeceyrat63.com
Kids' club available in July and August.
C&CC Report *Six and a half kilometres from Clermont-Ferrand, with views over the village towards the surrounding hills and countryside and 800m to the village centre.*
Site: **Facilities:** Wi-fi Kids' Club Play Area **Services:** **Leisure:** P

FRANCE

HAMPAGNAC-LE-VIEUX HAUTE-LOIRE

'hanterelle

e Plan d'Eau, 43440
☎ 471763400 🖷 471763400
-mail: camping@champagnac.com
eb: www.champagnac.com
tuated in the heart of the Auvergne beside a wooded lake.
r: *1km N via D5.*
pen: Apr-Oct **Site:** 4HEC **Facilities:**
ervices: **Leisure:** L **Off-site:** R

HAMPS-SUR-TARENTAINE CANTAL

'arentaine

5270
☎ 471787125 🖷 471787509
-mail: contact@champs-marchal.org
n attractive location surrounded by lakes and woodland.
r: *1km SW via D679 & D22 beside River Tarentaine.*
pen: 15 Jun-15 Sep **Site:** 4HEC **Facilities:**
ervices: **Leisure:** R **Off-site:** P

HÂTEL-DE-NEUVRE ALLIER

eneuvre

Moulins, 03500
☎ 470420451
mail: campingdeneuvre@wanadoo.fr
eb: www.deneuvre.com
easant surroundings within a nature reserve beside the River ier.
r: *0.5km N via D9.*
pen: Apr-Sep **Site:** 1HEC **Facilities:**
ervices: **Leisure:** R **Off-site:**

HÂTEL GUYON PUY-DE-DÔME

los de Balanède

de la Piscine, 63140
☎ 473860247 🖷 473860564
mail: clos-balanede.sarl-camping@wanadoo.fr
eb: www.balanede.com
pleasant site set in an orchard.
r: *Via A71 & D685.*
pen: 15 Apr-Oct **Site:** 4.4HEC **Prices:** 20.10
obile home hire 290-400 **Facilities:** Wi-fi (charged)
ervices: **Leisure:** P **Off-site:** R

CHÂTEL-MONTAGNE ALLIER

Croix Cognat

03250
☎ 470593138
e-mail: campinglacroixcognat@hotmail.fr
web: www.campinglacroixcognat.com
Well-equipped family site at an altitude of 540m.
dir: *0.5km NW on D25 towards Vichy.*
Open: Jul-Aug **Site:** 1HEC **Prices:** 13 Mobile home hire 360-410 **Facilities:** Wi-fi Kids' Club Play Area **Services:** **Leisure:** P **Off-site:** R

CHAUDES-AIGUES CANTAL

CM du Couffour

15110
☎ 471235708 🖷 471235708
web: www.chaudesaigues.com
Tastefully sited around the town football pitch in the local leisure area.
dir: *2km S via D921.*
Open: May-20 Oct **Site:** 2.5HEC **Facilities:**
Services: **Off-site:** P R

CONDRIEU RHÔNE

Belle Rive

La Plaine, 69420
☎ 474595108
Wooded surroundings bordering the Rhône.
dir: *11km S of Vienne on N86.*
Open: Apr-Sep **Site:** 5HEC **Facilities:**
Services: **Leisure:** P R

CONQUES AVEYRON

Beau Rivage

12320
☎ 565698223
e-mail: camping.conques@wanadoo.fr
web: www.campingconques.com
Peaceful site beside the river with spacious, well-marked pitches.
dir: *On D901.*
Open: Apr-Sep **Site:** 1HEC **Prices:** 14-17.50 Mobile home hire 275-575 **Facilities:** Wi-fi Play Area
Services: **Leisure:** P R **Off-site:**

FRANCE

COURNON-D'AUVERGNE PUY-DE-DÔME

CM Pré des Laveuses

r de Laveuses, 63800
473848130 473846590
web: www.cournon-auvergne.fr/camping

A rural setting beside a 7-hectare lake, close to the River Allier.

dir: *1.5km E towards Billom.*

Open: Apr-Oct **Site:** 5HEC **Facilities:** **Services:** **Leisure:** L R **Off-site:** P

DALLET PUY-DE-DÔME

Ombrages

rte de Pont-du-Château, 63111
473831097
e-mail: lesombrages@hotmail.com
web: www.lesombrages.nl

Wooded location beside the River Allier, a family campsite with friendly staff and clean modern facilities including swimming pools. A short drive from many of the regions tourist attractions.

Open: 15 May-15 Sep **Site:** 4HEC **Prices:** 13-21 **Facilities:** Play Area **Services:** **Leisure:** P R **Off-site:**

DARDILLY RHÔNE

Indigo International Lyon

The Camping and Caravanning Club The Friendly Club

Porte de Lyon, 69570
478356455 472170426
e-mail: lyon@camping-indigo.com
web: www.camping-indigo.com

Generously arranged and equipped site divided into pitches. Ideal for overnight stays near motorway. Concrete platforms for caravans. 1 dog per pitch.

C&CC Report *Ideally situated, just off the A6 motorway north of Lyon, for a stopover on the road to the south. Buses leave from outside the site entrance so visits to Lyon and its UNESCO listed buildings are both easy and interesting. If you're not just stopping over en-route, take time to enjoy the history and gastronomy of one of France's finest cities.*

dir: *A6 exit north of Lyon signed Dardilly, follow signs to Porte de Lyon.*

GPS: 45.8195, 4.7617

Open: All Year. **Site:** 6HEC **Prices:** 16.30-18.40 Mobile home hire 191.10-442.40 **Facilities:** Play Area **Services:** **Leisure:** P **Off-site:**

EBREUIL ALLIE

Filature de la Sioule

Ile de Nieres, 03450
470907201
e-mail: camping.filature@aliceadsl.fr
web: www.campingfilature.com

A peaceful, well-equipped in an orchard beside the River Sioule.

dir: *A71 exit 12, site signed.*

Open: 30 Mar-1 Oct **Site:** 3.6HEC **Prices:** 12-18 **Facilities:** **Services:** **Leisure:** R **Off-site:**

FLAGNAC AVEYRO

Port de Lacombe

12300
565641008
e-mail: accueil@campingleportdelacombe.com
web: www.campingleportdelacombe.com

A shady site in the Lot Valley. Water activities including fishing and canoeing on the river and an aquatic area incorporating a large water chute.

dir: *A75 towards Rodez, turn for Decazeville/Flagnac.*

Open: Apr-Sep **Site:** 4HEC **Prices:** 11.90-21.90 Mobile home hire 196-609 **Facilities:** Wi-fi (charged) Play Area **Services:** **Leisure:** P R **Off-site:**

FLEURIE RHÔN

CM la Grappe Fleurie

69820
474698007 474698571
e-mail: camping@fleurie.org
web: www.camping-beaujolais.com

A good quality municipal site in a picturesque setting in the hea of the Beaujolais region.

dir: *0.6km SE on D119 E.*

Open: mid Mar-mid Oct **Site:** 2.46HEC **Facilities:** **Services:** **Leisure:** P **Off-site:**

GOUDET HAUTE-LOIR

Bord de l'Eau

Plaine du Chambon, 43150
471571682
e-mail: camping@campingauborddeleau.com
web: www.campingauborddeleau.com

Well-equipped site in wooded surroundings below the ruins of the castle.

dir: *W via D49, beside River Loire.*

Open: Mar-15 Oct **Site:** 4HEC **Facilities:** **Services:** **Leisure:** P R

Site 6HEC (site size) grass sand stone little shade partly shaded mainly shaded bungalows for hire (static) caravans for hire tents for hire no dogs site fully accessible for wheelchairs
Prices amount quoted is per night, for 2 adults and car, plus tent or caravan. Mobile home hire is a weekly rate.

SLE-ET-BARDAIS ALLIER

cossais

3360
470666257 470066399
-mail: campingecossais@aol.com
eb: www.campingstroncais.com

peaceful location in the heart of the forest of Tronçais, beside
ne Pirot lake.

ir: *Via A71/E11.*

pen: Apr-Sep **Site:** 25HEC **Facilities:**
ervices: **Leisure:** L **Off-site:**

ENZAT ALLIER

hamp de Sioule

te de Chantelle, 03800
470568635 470568538
-mail: camping-jenzat@orange.fr
eb: www.bassin-gannat.com

ituated close to the River Sioule, in a good location for canoeing
nd fishing.

ir: *From A71 exit signed Gannat, then onto RD2009. At Saulzet,
ft onto D42.*

PS: 46.1660, 3.1897

pen: May-25 Sep **Site:** 1HEC **Prices:** 8.40-10.30
acilities: Play Area **Services:**
ff-site: R

ACAPELLE-VIESCAMP CANTAL

uech des Ouilhes

5150
471464238 471464238
-mail: truyere@aol.com
eb: www.cantal-camping.fr

n a wooded peninsula on Lake St-Étienne-Cantalès.

pen: 15 May-15 Sep **Site:** 2HEC **Facilities:**
Services: **Leisure:** L P

ANGEAC HAUTE-LOIRE

orges de l'Allier

omaine du Prad'Eau, 43300
471770501 471772734
-mail: infos@campinglangeac.com
eb: www.campinglangeac.com

et in wooded surroundings within a nature reserve, 0.8km from
e river. Good recreational facilities.

r: *Off N102.*

pen: Apr-Oct **Site:** 14HEC **Prices:** 10.50-12.50
obile home hire 300-500 **Facilities:** Play Area
ervices: **Leisure:** P R **Off-site:**

LAPEYROUSE PUY-DE-DÔME

CM Les Marins

La Loge, 63700
473523706 473520389
web: 63lapeyrouse.free.fr

A modern, lakeside site with good facilities set among the rolling hills of the Combtaille.

dir: *2km E via D998.*

Open: 15 Jun-1 Sep **Site:** 2HEC **Prices:** 12.90
Facilities: Play Area **Services:**
Leisure: L **Off-site:** P

LEMPDES HAUTE-LOIRE

Pont d'Allagnon

43410
471765369
e-mail: centre.auvergne.camping@orange.fr
web: www.campingenauvergne.com

Close to the village and on the l'Allagnon river, quiet site ideal for activities such as hiking and canoeing.

Open: May-Sep **Site:** 2HEC **Prices:** 10-13.50
Mobile home hire 250-380 **Facilities:** Wi-fi Play Area
Services: **Leisure:** P R **Off-site:**

LOUBEYRAT PUY-DE-DÔME

Colombier

63410
473866694
web: www.campingducolombier.com

A welcoming campsite in parkland.

dir: *1.5km S via D16.*

Open: May-Sep **Site:** 1.3HEC **Facilities:**
Services: **Leisure:** P

MALZIEU-VILLE, LE LOZÈRE

Piscine

48140
466314763

Peaceful shaded site on the banks of a river near to the municipal sports complex.

Open: Jun-Aug **Site:** 1HEC **Facilities:**
Services: **Off-site:** P R

FRANCE

MARTRES-DE-VEYRE, LES PUY-DE-DÔME

Camping la Font de Bleix

r des Roches, 63730
473397272

A pleasant site beside the River Allier. A good centre for touring the surrounding area.

dir: *SE via D225 beside River Allier.*

Open: All Year. **Site:** 1.3HEC **Facilities:** **Services:** **Leisure:** R **Off-site:**

MASSIAC CANTAL

CM Allagnon

av de Courcelles, 15500
471230393 471230393
e-mail: camping.allagnon@orange.fr

A riverside site with plenty of facilities.

dir: *0.8km W on N122.*

Open: May-Sep **Site:** 2.5HEC **Facilities:** **Services:** **Leisure:** R **Off-site:** P

MENDE LOZÈRE

Tivoli

av des Gorges-du-Tarn, 48000
466650038 466650038
e-mail: camping.tivoli0601@orange.fr
web: www.campingtivoli.com

A level site in wooded surroundings beside the river.

dir: *2km from town via A75 or N88.*

Open: All Year. **Site:** 1.8HEC **Prices:** 15.90-19.50 Mobile home hire 250-560 **Facilities:** Wi-fi **Services:** **Leisure:** P R **Off-site:**

MEYRUEIS LOZÈRE

Ayres

rte de la Brêze, 48150
466456051 466456051
e-mail: campinglechampdayres@wanadoo.fr
web: www.campinglechampdayres.com

On a wooded meadow with well-defined pitches and modern sanitary installations within easy reach of the picturesque Gorges de la Jonte. Plenty of recreational facilities.

dir: *A75 sortie S44-1.*

Open: 7 Apr-17 Sep **Site:** 1.5HEC **Prices:** 10-21.50 Mobile home hire 390-640 **Facilities:** Wi-fi Kids' Club Play Area **Services:** **Leisure:** P **Off-site:** R

Capelan

48150
466456050 466456050
e-mail: camping.le.capelan@wanadoo.fr
web: www.campingcapelan.com

Set in picturesque surroundings alongside the Gorges de la Jonte with good sports facilities. Dogs not permitted in mobile homes.

dir: *Via A75.*

Open: 6 May-17 Sep **Site:** 4HEC **Prices:** 14.50-27 Mobile home hire 175-735 **Facilities:** Wi-fi Play Area **Services:** **Leisure:** P R **Off-site:**

MILLAU AVEYRON

CM Millau Plage

rte de Millau Plage, 12100
565601097 565601688
e-mail: info@campingmillauplage.com
web: www.campingmillauplage.com

Beside the River Tarn, flat shady parkland.

dir: *Via D187.*

Open: 28 Mar-Sep **Site:** 5HEC **Facilities:** **Services:** **Leisure:** P R

Côté Sud

av de L'Aigoual, 12100
565611883
e-mail: camping-cotesud@orange.fr
web: www.camping-cotesud.fr

dir: *1km E on D591 next to River Dourbie.*

Open: Apr-Sep **Site:** 3.5HEC **Prices:** 12.50-20.50 **Facilities:** Wi-fi **Services:** **Leisure:** P R

Rivages

av de l'Aigoual, 12100
565610107 565590356
e-mail: campinglesriveages@wanadoo.fr
web: www.campinglesrivages.com

A family site with good facilities beside the River Dourbie.

dir: *1.7km E via D991.*

Open: Apr-15 Oct **Site:** 7HEC **Facilities:** **Services:** **Leisure:** P R **Off-site:**

'iaduc

21 av de Millau Plage, 12100
565601575 565613651
-mail: info@camping-du-viaduc.com
eb: www.camping-du-viaduc.com
ocated on the banks of the River Tarn, site facilities include wimming pools, water slides and evening entertainment. Kids' 'ub available in July and August.

ir: *From North, A75 exit 45; from South, A75 exit 47.*

pen: 13 May-26 Sep **Site:** 5HEC **Prices:** 15-28 obile home hire 308-686 **Facilities:** Wi-fi harged) Kids' Club Play Area **Services:** eisure: P R

IIREMONT PUY-DE-DÔME

:onfolant

3380
473799806
'ell equipped site with a variety of recreational facilities.

ir: *7km NE via D19 & D19E*

pen: Jun-10 Sep **Site:** 2.5HEC **Facilities:** **Services:** **Leisure:** L

IONTAIGUT-LE-BLANC PUY-DE-DÔME

M

e Bourg, 63320
473967507 473957005
-mail: montaigut-le-blanc@wanadoo.fr
eb: www.ville-montaigut-le-blanc.fr
quiet, level municipal site with good recreational facilities.

pen: May-Sep **Site:** 1.5HEC **Facilities:** ervices: **Leisure:** P R **Off-site:** L

IONT-DORE, LE PUY-DE-DÔME

M du L'Esquiladou

e des Cascades, 63240
473652374 473652374
-mail: camping.esquiladou@orange.fr
eb: www.mairie-mont-dore.fr
ountainous location within a national park.

pen: 20 Apr-30 Oct **Site:** 2HEC **Prices:** 10.35-11.45 obile home hire 260-520 **Facilities:** Play Area ervices: **Leisure:** P **Off-site:** R

MORNANT RHÔNE

CM de la Trillonière

bd du Général-de-Gaulle, 69440
478441647 478449170
e-mail: accueil@ville-mornant.fr
web: www.ville-mornant.fr
A rural setting on the southern outskirts of the town at an altitude of 333m. 25km to Lyon, bus service available.

dir: *Off D30 towards La Condamine.*

GPS: 45.6166, 4.6710

Open: May-Sep **Site:** 1.6HEC **Prices:** 10.50-14 **Facilities:** Wi-fi Play Area **Services:** **Leisure:** R **Off-site:** L P R

MUROL PUY-DE-DÔME

Europe

63790
473397666 473397661
e-mail: europe.camping@wanadoo.fr
web: www.camping-europ.fr
A family site in rural surroundings on the slopes of a forested valley close to the banks of Lake Chambon.

dir: *Via A71/75 & D996.*

Open: 30 May-30 Aug **Site:** 5.5HEC **Facilities:** **Services:** **Leisure:** P **Off-site:** L R

Plage

Plage du Lac Chambon, 63790
473886004
e-mail: lac.chambre@wanadoo.fr
web: www.lac-chambon-plage.fr
Busy site beside lake. Caravan section divided into pitches, terraced area for tents. Asphalt drive.

dir: *1.2km from village centre. Onto allée de Plage before village & signed.*

Open: May-Sep **Site:** 7HEC **Facilities:** **Services:** **Leisure:** L R **Off-site:**

Pré-Bas

Lac Chambon, 63790
473886304 473886593
e-mail: prebas@lac-chambon.com
web: www.campingauvergne.com
On the side of Lake Chambon with direct access to beaches including one where windsurfing is possible.

dir: *SW off D996.*

Open: May-Sep **Site:** 3.5HEC **Prices:** 13.10-23.70 **Facilities:** Wi-fi Play Area **Services:** **Leisure:** L P **Off-site:** R

FRANCE

NANT — AVEYRON

Val de Cantobre

12230
☎ 565584300 🖹 565621036
e-mail: info@rcn-valdecantobre.fr
web: www.rcn-valdecantobre.fr

Beside the river in the picturesque Gorges de la Dourbie with fine views from the terraced pitches.

C&CC Report *This continues to be an exceptional site, in a stunningly beautiful area, with facilities being of the highest standard. An idyllic setting, any time of the season, with wonderful views from many pitches. You can choose just to relax on site, visit this geologically fascinating area or try one of the many activity sports available locally.*

dir: *4km N of Nant, off D991 towards Millau.*

GPS: 44.0447, 3.3023

Open: 9 Apr-1 Oct **Site:** 6.5HEC **Prices:** 19.90-43.90 Mobile home hire 131.95-973 **Facilities:** Wi-fi (charged) Kids' Club Play Area **Services:** **Leisure:** P R

NAUSSAC — LOZÈRE

Terrasses du Lac

Lac de Naussac, 48300
☎ 466692962 🖹 466692478
e-mail: info@naussac.com
web: www.naussac.com

Situated beside the lake at an altitude of 1000m with fine views.

dir: *Autoroute 75 exit 88 for Langogne.*

Open: 15 Apr-Sep **Site:** 5.8HEC **Facilities:** **Services:** **Leisure:** L P **Off-site:**

NÉBOUZAT — PUY-DE-DÔME

Domes

Les Quatre routes de Nébouzat, 63210
☎ 473871406
e-mail: camping.les-domes@wanadoo.fr
web: www.les-domes.com

A comfortable site with hard-standing for caravans.

dir: *Off RN89 Clermont-Bordeaux.*

Open: May-16 Sep **Site:** 1HEC **Facilities:** **Services:** **Leisure:** P **Off-site:** R

NÉRIS-LES-BAINS — ALLIER

Lac

av Marx-Dormoy, 03310
☎ 470032470 🖹 470037999
web: www.ville-neris-les-bains.fr

Situated in a spa town, close to the centre. Some pitches are close to a road, the remainder are in a shaded valley by a stream.

Open: 4 Apr-early Nov **Site:** 7.05HEC **Facilities:** **Services:** **Off-site:** P

NEUVÉGLISE — CANTAL

Belvédère du Pont de Lanau

15260
☎ 471235050 🖹 471235893
e-mail: belvedere.cantal@wanadoo.fr
web: www.campinglebelvedere.com

Located in the Truyère Valley in a peaceful location with south-facing pitches.

dir: *5km S on D921.*

Open: 24 Apr-16 Oct **Site:** 5HEC **Prices:** 14-27.50 Mobile home hire 200-640 **Facilities:** Wi-fi (charged) Kids' Club Play Area **Services:** **Leisure:** P **Off-site:** L R

OLLIERGUES — PUY-DE-DÔME

Chelles

63880
☎ 473955434
e-mail: info@camping-les-chelles.com
web: www.camping-les-chelles.com

A family site in wooded surroundings with good leisure facilities.

dir: *5km from town centre.*

GPS: 45.6904, 3.6327

Open: Apr-Oct **Site:** 3.5HEC **Prices:** 13.50 Mobile home hire 185-480 **Facilities:** Wi-fi Play Area **Services:** **Leisure:** P

FRANCE

RCET PUY-DE-DÔME

Clos Auroy

r de la Narse, 63670
☎ 473842697 📠 473842697
e-mail: contact@campingclub.info
web: www.camping-le-clos-auroy.com

Terraced site in a green valley next to a small river.

C&CC Report *Le Clos Auroy is great for younger families and anyone seeking tranquil camping in a region of outstanding natural beauty. The owners are eager to share their vast local knowledge, with lots of information on walks and touring. Some of the most unspoilt parts of France are a short drive away, with lakes, volcanoes, mountain rivers and beautiful villages to discover.*

dir: *A75 exit 5 to Orcet, signed.*

GPS: 45.7002, 3.1695

Open: 4 Jan-1 Oct **Site:** 2.5HEC **Prices:** 23.80 Mobile home hire 275 **Facilities:** Wi-fi Kids' Club Play Area **Services:** **Leisure:** P R **Off-site:** L

OLLIONNAY RHÔNE

ol de la Luère

hemin de Roche Coucou, 69290
 478458111
-mail: contact@camping-coldelaluere.com
eb: camping-coldelaluere.com

ituated in the Monts du Lyonnais, 20 minutes from Lyon.

PS: 45.7508, 4.6430

pen: All Year. **Site:** 5HEC **Prices:** 13.90 obile home hire 300-366 **Facilities:** Wi-fi Kids' ub Play Area **Services:** **Leisure:** P ff-site: R

OMEYS RHÔNE

amping d'Hurongues

one de Loisirs d'Hurongues, 69590
 478484429
-mail: campinghurongues@orange.fr
eb: www.camping-hurongues.com

ite bordered by oak trees, suitable for families, with large itches. Activities available close by include mountain biking, iking and canoeing.

pen: 17 Apr-17 Oct **Site:** 3.6HEC **Prices:** 9-16 acilities: Play Area **Services:** eisure: P **Off-site:** L R

PONT-DE-SALARS AVEYRON

Terrasses du Lac

rte du Vibal, 12290
☎ 565468818 📠 565468538
e-mail: campinglesterrasses@orange.fr
web: www.campinglesterrasses.com

Pleasant lake-side site with terraced pitches overlooking the Pont-de-Salars lake.

dir: *4km N via D523.*

Open: Apr-Sep **Site:** 6HEC **Prices:** 12.50-27.50 Mobile home hire 225-819 **Facilities:** Wi-fi Kids' Club Play Area **Services:** **Leisure:** L P

PONTGIBAUD PUY-DE-DÔME

CM

rte de la Miouze, 63230
☎ 473889699 📠 473887777
e-mail: mairie.pontgibaud@wanadoo.fr
web: www.ville-pontgibaud.fr

Set in a wooded area beside the River Sioule.

dir: *0.5km SW on D986 towards Rochefort-Montagne.*

Open: 15 Apr-15 Oct **Site:** 4.5HEC **Facilities:** **Services:** **Leisure:** R **Off-site:** L

PRADEAUX, LES PUY-DE-DÔME

Châteaux la Grange Fort

63500
☎ 473710593 📠 473710769
e-mail: chateau@lagrangefort.com
web: www.lagrangefort.com

Set in a park surrounding a château on the River Allier.

dir: *A75 exit 13 for Parentignat, onto D999 & signed.*

Open: Etr-15 Oct **Site:** 22HEC **Facilities:** **Services:** **Leisure:** P R **Off-site:**

PUY, LE HAUTE-LOIRE

Camping du Puy-en-Velay

43000
☎ 471095509 📠 471095509
web: www.camping-bouthezard-43.com

On a wooded meadow with a section reserved for motor caravans.

dir: *From town centre towards Clermont-Ferrand, right at lights by church of St-Laurent, signed, site 0.5km on left.*

Open: 15 Mar-15 Oct **Site:** 1HEC **Facilities:** **Services:** **Off-site:** P

FRANCE

Facilities shop shower electric points for razors electric points for caravans parking by tents permitted mpulsory separate car park **Services** café/restaurant bar Camping Gaz International gas other than Camping Gaz first aid facilities laundry **Leisure** swimming L-Lake P-Pool R-River S-Sea **Off-site** All facilities within 5km

Village center
Les Tours ****
Pitches with direct access to the lake
Tree-climbing and rock climbing
147 places - 128 rental accomodations - 15 ha
12460 SAINT-AMANS-DES-CÔTS
+33 (0)4 99 57 21 21 - www.village-center.com/C03

RIVIÈRE-SUR-TARN AVEYRON

Peyrelade

rte des Gorges-du-Tarn, 12640
☎ 565626254 📠 565626561
e-mail: campingpeyrelade@orange.fr
web: www.campingpeyrelade.com

Wooded surroundings close to the Gorges du Tarn.

dir: *2km E via D907, beside River Tarn.*

Open: 15 May-15 Sep **Site:** 4HEC **Prices:** 15-37 Mobile home hire 266-763 **Facilities:** Wi-fi Kids' Club Play Area **Services:** **Leisure:** P R

RODEZ AVEYRON

CM Layoule

12000
☎ 565670952 📠 565671143

Clean, tidy site in valley below town, completely divided into pitches.

dir: *NE of town centre, signed.*

Open: Jun-Sep **Site:** 3HEC **Facilities:** **Services:** **Off-site:**

ROYAT PUY-DE-DÔME

Indigo Royat

rte de Gravenoire, 63130
☎ 473359705 📠 473356769
e-mail: royat@camping-indigo.com
web: www.camping-indigo.com

A natural setting at the foot of the Puy de Dome and overlooking Clermont Ferrand. The pitches are laid out in terraces and are comfortably shaded. Kids' club available in July and August. 1 dog per pitch.

dir: *Off D941 SW of Royat.*

Open: Apr-29 Oct **Site:** 7HEC **Prices:** 14.40-21.90 Mobile home hire 325.50-693 **Facilities:** Kids' Club Play Area **Services:** **Leisure:** P **Off-site:** L R

RUYNES-EN-MARGERIDE CANTAL

Petit Bois

15320
☎ 471234226 📠 467363542
e-mail: contact@revea.vacances.com
web: www.revea-vacances.fr/campings

A pleasant, well-equipped, park-like site on the bank of the River Charente.

dir: *0.5km SW on D13 rte de Garabit, signed.*

Open: 5 May-14 Sep **Site:** 7HEC **Facilities:** **Services:** **Off-site:** P

SAIGNES CANTAL

Bellevue

15240
☎ 471406840 📠 471406165
e-mail: saignes.mairie@wanadoo.fr
web: saignes-mairie.fr

A pleasant rural site in the Sumène Valley.

Open: Jul-Aug **Site:** 0.9HEC **Facilities:** **Services:** **Off-site:** P

ST-ALBAN-SUR-LIMAGNOLE LOZÈRE

Galier

48120
☎ 466315880 📠 466314183
e-mail: accueil@campinglegalier.fr
web: www.campinglegalier.fr

Well-equipped site beside the river.

dir: *A75 exit 34.*

Open: Mar-Oct **Site:** 4HEC **Facilities:** **Services:** **Leisure:** P R **Off-site:**

ST-AMANS-DES-COTS AVEYRON

Village Center les Tours

12460
☎ 499572121 📠 467516389
e-mail: contact@village-center.com
web: www.village-center.com/midi-pyrenees/camping-campagne-les-tours.php

On the shore of Selves Lake with some pitches having direct access to the water. Comprehensive leisure facilities available.

dir: *From N A75 exit St Flour; from S A75 exit Séverac le Château*

GPS: 44.6676, 2.6812

Open: 27 May-18 Sep **Site:** 15HEC **Prices:** 16-3 Mobile home hire 216-889 **Facilities:** Wi-fi (charged Kids' Club Play Area **Services:** **Leisure:** P

see advert on this pa

ST-AMANT-ROCHE-SAVINE PUY-DE-DÔME

CM Saviloisirs

63890
☎ 473957360 📠 473957262
e-mail: saviloisirs@wanadoo.fr
web: www.saviloisirs.com

Run by the local tourist authority with plenty of sports facilities within easy reach.

Open: May-Sep **Site:** 1.5HEC **Facilities:** **Services:** **Off-site:** L R

ST-BONNET-TRONÇAIS ALLIER

Champ-Fossé

03360
☎ 470061130 📠 470061501
e-mail: champfosse@aol.com
web: www.campingstroncais.com

Set in the forest of Tronçais beside a lake with plenty of recreational facilities.

dir: *Via A71-E11.*

Open: Apr-Oct **Site:** 35HEC **Facilities:** **Services:** **Leisure:** L P **Off-site:**

ST-CLÉMENT-DE-VALORGUE PUY-DE-DÔME

Narcisses

63660
☎ 473954576 📠 473954576
e-mail: ptipois2@wanadoo.fr
web: www.campinglesnarcisses.com

A beautiful natural setting within the Livradois-Forez regional park.

Open: May-Sep **Site:** 1.3HEC **Facilities:** **Services:** **Leisure:** P R **Off-site:** L

ST-GAL-SUR-SIOULE PUY-DE-DÔME

Pont de St-Gal

63440
☎ 473974471
e-mail: campingdesaintgal@orange.fr

A pleasant site with shaded, well-defined pitches, and access to the river for boating and fishing.

dir: *E on D16 towards Ebreuil, beside River Sioule.*

Open: May-Sep **Site:** 1HEC **Facilities:** **Services:** **Leisure:** R

ST-GENIEZ-D'OLT AVEYRON

Marmotel

12130
☎ 565704651 📠 565463619
e-mail: info@marmotel.com
web: www.marmotel.com

Grassy family site on River Lot with a variety of recreational facilities.

dir: *A75 exit 41.*

Open: 2 May-17 Sep **Site:** 5HEC **Prices:** 18-35 Mobile home hire 210-790 **Facilities:** Wi-fi Kids' Club Play Area **Services:** **Leisure:** P R **Off-site:**

ST-GERMAIN-DE-CALBERTE LOZÈRE

La Garde

48370
☎ 466459482
e-mail: campinglagarde@orange.fr
web: www.causses-cevennes.com/lagarde

A pleasant location on the edge of the Cevennes national park.

dir: *Via A7 or A75.*

Open: Jun-Sep **Site:** 2.4HEC **Prices:** 21.50-23.50 **Facilities:** Wi-fi Play Area **Services:** **Leisure:** P **Off-site:** R

ST-GÉRONS CANTAL

Domaine du Lac

Espinet, 15150
☎ 471622798
e-mail: prldomainedulac@orange.fr
web: www.prl-domainedulac.fr

A relaxing stay is assured on the shores of Lake St Etienne Cantalès, where fishing is available.

GPS: 44.9351, 2.2301

Open: Apr-Oct **Site:** 4HEC **Prices:** Mobile home hire 250-550 **Facilities:** Wi-fi Play Area **Services:** **Leisure:** L P **Off-site:**

Les Rives du Lac

Espinet, 15150
☎ 625346289
e-mail: info@lesrivesdulac.fr
web: www.lesrivesdulac.fr

Wooded and shady site on the shore of Lake St Etienne Cantalès. Fishing is a popular activity here, with fishing permits available on site.

Open: 15 Apr-Oct **Site:** 4HEC **Prices:** 13-15 Mobile home hire 250-500 **Facilities:** Wi-fi Play Area **Services:** **Leisure:** L P

FRANCE

ST-GERVAIS-D'AUVERGNE PUY-DE-DÔME

CM de l'Étang Philippe

rte de St-Eloy-les-Mines, 63390
☎ 473857484
e-mail: campingstgervais@wanadoo.fr
web: www.camping-loisir.com

A small municipal site beside a small lake.

dir: *Via N987.*

Open: Apr-Sep **Site:** 5HEC **Facilities:** **Services:** **Leisure:** L **Off-site:**

ST-JACQUES-DES-BLATS CANTAL

CM des Blats

rte de la Gare, 15800
☎ 471470590 471470709
e-mail: i-tourisme-st-jacques@wanadoo.fr

A small site on the banks of the River Cère. A good centre for exploring the surrounding Volcanic Park area.

Open: May-Sep **Site:** 1HEC **Facilities:** **Services:** **Leisure:** R **Off-site:**

ST-JUST CANTAL

CM

Le Bourg, 15320
☎ 471737048 471737144
e-mail: commune.stjust@wanadoo.fr
web: www.saintjust.com

Set in the centre of the village beside the river. Children's activities take place during July and August.

dir: *A75 exit at juncts 31 or 32.*

GPS: 44.8896, 3.209

Open: Etr-Sep **Site:** 2HEC **Prices:** 8-10.20 Mobile home hire 225-407 **Facilities:** Wi-fi (charged) Play Area **Services:** **Leisure:** P **Off-site:** R

ST-MARTIN-VALMEROUX CANTAL

Moulin du Teinturier

Mont Joly, 15140
☎ 471694312 471692452
e-mail: lemoulinduteinturier@orange.fr

Wooded valley site close to a medieval market town.

dir: *Off D922 Aurillac-Mauriac.*

Open: Jun-Sep **Site:** 2.8HEC **Facilities:** Play Area **Services:** **Leisure:** R **Off-site:** P

ST-NECTAIRE PUY-DE-DÔME

Vallée Verte

rte des Granges, 63710
☎ 473885268
e-mail: lavalleeverte@libertysurf.fr
web: www.campinglavalleeverte.com

Wooded surroundings by a river within the Auvergne volcanic park.

dir: *On R146, 400m from R996.*

Open: 15 Apr-Sep **Site:** 2.5HEC **Facilities:** **Services:** **Leisure:** R **Off-site:** P R

ST-OURS PUY-DE-DÔME

Bel-Air

63230
☎ 473887214
e-mail: contact@campingbelair.fr
web: www.campingbelair.fr

In a park setting with spacious pitches. Facilities include an area for games and barbecues.

dir: *1km SW on D941.*

Open: May-Sep **Site:** 2HEC **Prices:** 14.10 **Facilities:** Wi-fi (charged) Play Area **Services:** **Off-site:**

ST-PIERRE-COLAMINE PUY-DE-DÔME

Ombrage

63610
☎ 473967787
e-mail: campombrage@orange.fr
web: www.campombrage.com

A pleasant site in peaceful wooded surroundings at an altitude of 800m on the edge of the Auvergne Volcano Park. All the usual services are provided and there are good recreational facilities.

dir: *300m from D978.*

GPS: 45.5381, 2.9778

Open: All Year. **Site:** 2HEC **Prices:** 11.24-13.95 **Facilities:** Wi-fi Play Area **Services:** **Leisure:** P **Off-site:** R

FRANCE

Site 6HEC (site size) grass sand stone little shade partly shaded mainly shaded bungalows for hire (static) caravans for hire tents for hire no dogs site fully accessible for wheelchairs
Prices amount quoted is per night, for 2 adults and car, plus tent or caravan. Mobile home hire is a weekly rate.

ST-RÉMY-SUR-DUROLLE PUY-DE-DÔME

CM Chanterelles

63550
☎ 473943171 473943171
e-mail: leschanterelles0549@orange.fr
web: www.revea-vacances.fr

Pleasant wooded surroundings close to the lake.

dir: *3km NE via D201.*

Open: May-Sep **Site:** 6HEC **Facilities:** **Services:** **Off-site:** L P

ST-ROME-DE-TARN AVEYRON

Cascade

12490
☎ 565625659 565625862
e-mail: contact@camping-cascade-aveyron.com
web: www.campingdelacascade.com

Terraced site beside the river Tarn.

dir: *0.3km N via D993.*

Open: All Year. **Site:** 4HEC **Facilities:** **Services:** **Leisure:** L P R **Off-site:**

ST-SALVADOU AVEYRON

Muret

12200
☎ 565818069 565818069
e-mail: info@lemuret.com
web: www.campinglemuret.com

A modern site in peaceful, rural surroundings beside the lake.

dir: *3km SE.*

Open: Apr-Oct **Site:** 3HEC **Facilities:** **Services:** **Leisure:** L **Off-site:**

STE-CATHERINE RHÔNE

CM du Châtelard

69440
☎ 478818060 478818773
e-mail: mairie-ste-catherine@wanadoo.fr

A quiet, well-equipped site providing magnificent views over the surrounding countryside.

dir: *2km S.*

Open: Mar-Nov **Site:** 4HEC **Facilities:** **Services:** **Off-site:** R

STE-SIGOLÈNE HAUTE-LOIRE

Kawan Village Camping de Vaubarlet

The Camping and Caravanning Club – The Friendly Club

rte de Grazac, Vaubarlet, 43600
☎ 471666495 471661198
e-mail: camping@vaubarlet.com
web: www.vaubarlet.com

Set in a beautiful wooded valley beside the River Dunières with a variety of supervised family activities including a kids' club in summer months.

C&CC Report *For those who love nature and want friendly welcoming site owners and a green-award winning camp site, le Vaubarlet is ideal. The hill walking and mountain bike routes, the on-site first category fishing river, heated pools and the relaxing atmosphere provide the makings of great holidays. Visits to the gorges of the Loire and their châteaux, the spectacular volcanic town of Le Puy-en-Velay, the local towns and markets and the various museums will remain long in the memory.*

dir: *D44 exit to Ste-Sigolène, D43 towards Grazac, signed after 10km.*

Open: May-Sep **Site:** 3.5HEC **Prices:** 16-20 Mobile home hire 180-620 **Facilities:** Wi-fi Kids' Club Play Area **Services:** **Leisure:** P R

SALLES-CURAN AVEYRON

Beau Rivage

Route des Vernhes, Lac de Pareloup, 12410
☎ 565463332
e-mail: camping-beau-rivage@orange.fr
web: www.beau-rivage.fr

A terraced site located on the shore of Lac de Pareloup. There are facilities for water sports and a kids' club in July and August.

dir: *A75 exit 44.1, follow D991.*

Open: Apr-Oct **Site:** 2HEC **Prices:** 14-28.50 Mobile home hire 180-700 **Facilities:** Wi-fi Kids' Club Play Area **Services:** **Leisure:** L P

Genêts

12410
☎ 565463534 565780072
e-mail: contact@camping-les-genets.fr
web: www.camping-les-genets.fr

On the edge of the Pareloup lake.

dir: *7km W via D577.*

Open: Jun-Sep **Site:** 3HEC **Prices:** 18-33 Mobile home hire 199-805 **Facilities:** Wi-fi (charged) Kids' Club **Services:** **Leisure:** L P

FRANCE

Facilities shop shower electric points for razors electric points for caravans parking by tents permitted compulsory separate car park **Services** café/restaurant bar Camping Gaz International gas other than Camping Gaz first aid facilities laundry **Leisure** swimming L-Lake P-Pool R-River S-Sea **Off-site** All facilities within 5km

SAZERET — ALLIER

Petite Valette

03390
☎ 470076457
e-mail: la.petite.valette@wanadoo.fr
web: www.valette.nl

A well-equipped site attached to a farm with well-defined pitches and organised activities for children.

dir: *A71 exit 11 & signed.*

Site: 4HEC **Facilities:** **Services:** **Leisure:** L P

SEMBADEL-GARE — HAUTE-LOIRE

Casses

43160
☎ 471009472 471009179

A family site in a rural setting at an altitude of 1000m, 2km from a lake.

dir: *1km W via D22.*

Open: Jul-20 Sep **Site:** 2.4HEC **Facilities:** **Services:** **Off-site:** L R

SÉNERGUES — AVEYRON

Étang du Camp

12320
☎ 565460195
e-mail: info@etangducamp.fr
web: www.etangducamp.fr

Well-equipped site, with spacious pitches and clean facilities, in a tranquil wooded setting beside the lake.

dir: *6km SW via D242.*

GPS: 44.5581, 2.4627

Open: Apr-Sep **Site:** 3HEC **Prices:** 12-16 **Facilities:** Wi-fi Kids' Club Play Area **Services:** **Off-site:** P

SÉVÉRAC-L'ÉGLISE — AVEYRON

Grange de Monteillac

Monteillac, 12310
☎ 565702100 565702101
e-mail: info@la-grange-de-monteillac.com
web: www.la-grange-de-monteillac.com

A family site in a quiet wooded location with good recreational facilities.

dir: *Via A75 & N88.*

Open: 15 May-15 Sep **Site:** 4.5HEC
Prices: 16.50-28.50 Mobile home hire 260-735 **Facilities:** Wi-fi Kids' Club Play Area **Services:** **Leisure:** P **Off-site:**

SINGLES — PUY-DE-DÔME

Moulin de Serre

Vallee de la Burande, 63690
☎ 473211606 473211256
e-mail: moulindeserre@orange.fr
web: www.moulindeserre.com

A spacious and well maintained campsite beside the River Burande with pitches raised and separated by hedges. Friendly atmosphere with activities for both adults and children.

dir: *1.7km S of La Guinguette via D73.*

Open: 9 Apr-18 Sep **Site:** 7HEC
Prices: 9.95-18.15 Mobile home hire 154-679 **Facilities:** Wi-fi Kids' Club Play Area **Services:**
Leisure: P R

THÉRONDELS — AVEYRON

La Source

Presqu'ile de Laussac, 12600
☎ 565660562 565662100
e-mail: info@camping-la-source.com
web: www.camping-la-source.com

A beautiful location beside Lake Sarrans.

Open: 27 May-9 Sep **Site:** 4.5HEC **Prices:** 17-28.50 Mobile home hire 230-798 **Facilities:** Wi-fi (charged) Kids' Club Play Area **Services:** **Leisure:** L P

TRIZAC — CANTAL

Pioulat

15400
☎ 471786420 471786540
e-mail: mairie.trizac@wanadoo.fr

In a tranquil setting the site has good facilities.

Open: 16 Jun-16 Sep **Site:** 4.71HEC **Facilities:** **Services:** **Leisure:** L R **Off-site:**

VARENNES-SUR-ALLIER — ALLIER

Château de Chazeuil

r de Moulins, 03150
☎ 470458326
e-mail: camping-dechazeuil@ifrance.com

On well-kept meadow within the château park.

dir: *3km NW on N7.*

Open: Apr-15 Oct **Site:** 1.5HEC **Facilities:** **Services:** **Leisure:** P **Off-site:**

FRANCE

Site 6HEC (site size) grass sand stone little shade partly shaded mainly shaded bungalows for hire (static) caravans for hire tents for hire no dogs site fully accessible for wheelchairs
Prices amount quoted is per night, for 2 adults and car, plus tent or caravan. Mobile home hire is a weekly rate.

ERRIÈRES-EN-FOREZ LOIRE

erme Le Soleillant

e Soleillant, 42600
477762273
-mail: camille.rival@wanadoo.fr
eb: www.le-soleillant.com

small terraced site within the grounds of a farm.

ir: *RD496 between Montbrison & St Anthème. Campsite signed.*

PS: 45.5777, 3.9944

pen: All Year. Site: 3.2HEC Prices: 10.50 Mobile ome hire 350 Facilities: Services: ff-site: R

IC-SUR-CÈRE CANTAL

ommeraie

5800
471475418 471496330
mail: pommeraie@wanadoo.fr
eb: camping-la-pommeraie.com

well-equipped family site in a peaceful location with good creational facilities.

r: *2km SE.*

pen: May-15 Sep Site: 2.5HEC Facilities: Services: Leisure: P Off-site: R

LLEFORT LOZÈRE

alhère

e du Mas de la Barque, 48800
466468063 466468063
mail: campinglapalhere@orange.fr
eb: www.everyoneweb.fr/campinglapalhere

well-equipped, peaceful site on the edge of the Parc National s Cévennes.

r: *4km SW via D66 beside river.*

en: May-Sep Site: 2HEC Facilities: Play Area Services: Leisure: P R f-site: L

LLEFRANCHE-DE-PANAT AVEYRON

antarelles

rance, 12430
565464035 565464035
mail: cantarelles@wanadoo.fr
eb: www.lescantarelles.com

level grassland by Lac de Villefranche-de-Panat.

: *On D25 3km N.*

en: May-Sep Site: 3.5HEC Facilities: rvices: Leisure: L

VILLEFRANCHE-DE-ROUERGUE AVEYRON

Camping du Rouergue

35 bis av de Fondies, 12200
565451624 565451624
e-mail: campingrouergue@wanadoo.fr
web: www.campingdurouergue.com

A comfortable site in a pleasant, shady location beside the River Aveyron.

dir: *1.5km SW via D47 rte de Monteils.*

GPS: 44.3406, 2.0264

Open: Apr-Sep Site: 2HEC Prices: 11.62-14.62 Mobile home hire 180-450 Facilities: Wi-fi Play Area Services: Leisure: P Off-site: R

YSSINGEAUX HAUTE-LOIRE

CM Choumouroux

43200
471655344
dir: *0.8km S of town off rte de Puy.*

Open: May-Sep Site: 0.8HEC Facilities: Services: Off-site: P R

SOUTH COAST/RIVIERA

AGAY VAR

Agay Soleil

1152 bd de la Plage, rte de Cannes D559, 83530
494820079 494828870
e-mail: camping-agay-soleil@wanadoo.fr
web: www.agay-soleil.com

A small site in a shady position directly on a sandy beach. The facilities are good and water sports are available nearby.

dir: *Between N98 & sea.*

Open: 25 Mar-5 Nov Site: 0.7HEC Facilities: Services: Leisure: S Off-site:

Estérel

avenue des Golfs, 83530
494820328 494828737
e-mail: contact@esterel-caravaning.fr
web: www.esterel-caravaning.fr

A pleasant family-site with provencal architecture. There is plenty to entertain all age groups day and evening. Riding and cycling can be enjoyed nearby in the surrounding hills and woods. Just 3km away from the sandy beach of Agay

dir: *3km N from Agay-Plage towards Valescure, near golf course.*

Open: Apr-Sep Site: 15HEC Prices: 18-343 Mobile home hire 200-2600 Facilities: Wi-fi (charged) Kids' Club Play Area Services: Leisure: P Off-site: R S

FRANCE

AGDE HÉRAULT

Champs Blancs

rte de Rochelongue, Rochelongue-Plage, 34300
☎ 467942342 🖷 467948781
e-mail: champs.blancs@wanadoo.fr
web: www.champs-blancs.fr

Quiet shady site with hedged pitches and surrounded by exotic vegetation. Good sports and entertainment facilities.

Open: 5 Apr-Sep **Site:** 4HEC **Prices:** 16-44
Facilities: Wi-fi (charged) Kids' Club Play Area
Services: **Leisure:** P **Off-site:** R S

Escale

rte de la Tamarissière, 34300
☎ 467212109 🖷 467211024
e-mail: info@camping-lescale.com
web: www.camping-lescale.com

A riverside site, 0.9km from the sea, with good recreational facilities.

Open: Apr-Sep **Site:** 3HEC **Facilities:**
Services: **Leisure:** P R **Off-site:** S

Mer et Soleil

chemin de Notre Dame, à Saint Martin, 34300
☎ 467942114 🖷 467948194
e-mail: contact@camping-mer-soleil.com
web: www.camping-mer-soleil.com

A modern, well-equipped family site within easy reach of the beach.

GPS: 43.2855, 3.4778

Open: 14 Apr-8 Oct **Site:** 7.9HEC **Facilities:** Wi-fi (charged) Kids' Club Play Area **Services:** **Leisure:** P **Off-site:** R S

Romarins

rte du Grau, 34300
☎ 467941859 🖷 467265880
e-mail: contact@romarins.com
web: www.romarins.com

Located in a busy Mediterranean fishing village south of the city of Agde. On the left bank of the Herault river with fine sandy beaches. Kids' club available in July and August. No dogs in mobile homes.

Open: 3 Apr-25 Sep **Site:** 2.2HEC **Facilities:** Wi-fi (charged) Kids' Club Play Area **Services:** **Leisure:** P **Off-site:** R S

Village Center Les 7 Fonts

Chemin de Baldy, 34300
☎ 499572121 🖷 467516389
e-mail: contact@village-center.com
web: www.village-center.com/languedoc-roussillon/camping-les-sept-fonts.php

Close to the Canal du Midi, Les 7 Fonts is set in a waterpark.

dir: *A9 exit 34, follow RN312 then RN112 towards Agde/Sète, the Agde, turn right after garden centre.*

GPS: 43.3112, 3.4992

Open: 27 May-18 Sep **Site:** 5.5HEC **Prices:** 14-34 Mobile home hire 192-952 **Facilities:** Wi-fi (charged) Kids' Club Play Area **Services:** **Leisure:** P

AIGUES MORTES GAR

Camping Fleur de Camargue

The Camping and Caravanning Club The Friendly Club

St-Laurent-d'Aigouze, 30220
☎ 466881542
e-mail: contact@fleur-de-camargue.com
web: www.fleur-de-camargue.com

1 dog per pitch, pets not permitted in mobile homes.

C&CC Report *This friendly, family site is a quieter alternative to the sites nearer the coast and there is much to see and do in the area. You can cycle along the canals, go to the beach, spot the flamingoes of the Camargue, visit Montpellier or venture into the beautiful Languedoc interior for a day out.*

GPS: 43.6111, 4.2089

Site: **Facilities:** Play Area **Leisure:** P

Camping Village La Petite Camargue

Quartier du Mole, 30220
☎ 466539898 🖷 466539880
e-mail: info@yellohvillage-petite-camargue.com
web: www.yellohvillage-petite-camargue.com

A grassy site among vineyards on the D62, 3.5km from the sea.

dir: *Autoroute exit Gallargues for La Grande Motte.*

GPS: 43.5669, 4.1558

Open: 22 Apr-18 Sep **Site:** 10HEC **Prices:** 15-44
Facilities: Wi-fi Kids' Club Play Area
Services: **Leisure:** P **Off-site:** S

FRANCE

Site 6HEC (site size) grass sand stone little shade partly shaded mainly shaded bungalows for hire (static) caravans for hire tents for hire no dogs site fully accessible for wheelchairs
Prices amount quoted is per night, for 2 adults and car, plus tent or caravan. Mobile home hire is a weekly rate.

AIX-EN-PROVENCE BOUCHES-DU-RHÔNE

Arc en Ciel

Pont de Trois Sautets, 50 av Malacrida, 13100
442261428
e-mail: camping-arcenciel@neuf.fr
web: www.campingarcenciel.com
A pleasant terraced site on both sides of a stream.
dir: *N7 exit 3 Sautets for Toulon, 3km SE near Pont des Trois Sautets.*
Open: Apr-Sep **Site:** 3HEC **Prices:** 19.20 **Facilities:** Wi-fi Play Area **Services:** **Leisure:** P R **Off-site:**

Chantecler

Val St Andre, 13100
442261298 442273353
e-mail: info@campingchantecler.com
web: www.campingchantecler.com
Extensive, uneven site on a hill with terraced pitches. A kids' club is available in July and August.
dir: *A8 exit Aix-Est, 2.5km SE of town.*
Open: All Year. **Site:** 8HEC **Prices:** 19-21.10 Mobile home hire 500-850 **Facilities:** Wi-fi (charged) Kids' Club Play Area **Services:** **Leisure:** P **Off-site:** S

ALBARON BOUCHES-DU-RHÔNE

Domaine du Crin Blanc

CD37 Hameau de Saliers, 13123
466874878 466871866
e-mail: camping-crin.blanc@wanadoo.fr
web: www.campingcrinblanc.com
Two swimming pools, plus a paddling pool for campers' use with many leisure and entertainment activities taking place during July and August.
Open: Apr-Sep **Site:** 5HEC **Prices:** 18-24 Mobile home hire 200-750 **Facilities:** Wi-fi Kids' Club Play Area **Services:** **Leisure:** P **Off-site:** R

ALET-LES-BAINS AUDE

Val d'Aleth

Chemin de la Paoulette, 11580
468699040
e-mail: camping@valdaleth.com
web: www.valdaleth.com
Picturesque surroundings beneath the historic ramparts, on the banks of the River Aude.
dir: *D118 S from Carcassonne, through Limoux, site 8km S off D118.*
Open: All Year. **Site:** 0.5HEC **Prices:** 15-16 **Facilities:** Wi-fi (charged) **Services:** **Leisure:** R **Off-site:** P

ANDUZE GARD

Arche

30140
466617408 466618894
e-mail: resa@camping-arche.fr
web: www.camping-arche.fr
A beautiful location on the River Gard in the Cevennes region.
dir: *A7 exit Bollène onto D907.*
Open: Apr-Sep **Site:** 10HEC **Prices:** 19-38 Mobile home hire 310-1025 **Facilities:** Wi-fi Kids' Club Play Area **Services:** **Leisure:** P R

Brise des Pins

rte de St-Félix de Pallières, 30140
466616339
A terraced site offering fine panoramic views over the surrounding countryside.
dir: *3km from Anduze.*
Open: Jun-15 Sep **Site:** **Facilities:** **Services:**

Castel Rose

610 chemin de Recoulin, 30140
466618015
e-mail: castelrose@wanadoo.fr
web: www.castelrose.com
A spacious, wooded and well-equipped site on the banks of the River Gardon.
dir: *1km NW on D907.*
Open: Apr-Sep **Site:** 7HEC **Prices:** 14.50-28 Mobile home hire 260-730 **Facilities:** Wi-fi Kids' Club Play Area **Services:** **Leisure:** P R **Off-site:**

Cévennes Provence

30140
466617310 466616074
e-mail: marais@camping-cevennes-provence.com
web: www.camping-cevennes-provence.com
Situated in a valley bordered by two rivers. A quiet site with a choice of pitches in varying levels of shade and terrain.
dir: *From Anduze take D907 towards St Jean du Gard for 3km, turn right to Corbes on D284.*
Open: 20 Mar-2 Oct **Site:** 30HEC **Prices:** 14.90-22.90 **Facilities:** Wi-fi Play Area **Services:** **Leisure:** R

FRANCE

ANNEYRON **DRÔME**

Flower Camping La Châtaigneraie

rte de Mantaille, 26140
475314333 475038467
e-mail: contact@chataigneraie.com
web: www.chataigneraie.com

Family site in peaceful surroundings with fine views of the Rhône Valley and the mountains of the Ardèche. Large grassy pitches, clearly marked with a choice of sunny or shady position and large secure play areas for children.

dir: *A7 exit 12 (Chanas), take N7 towards Valence/St Vallier. Before Le Creux de la Thine left onto D1 for Anneyron, site signed.*

GPS: 45.255, 4.904

Open: Apr-Sep **Site:** 2HEC **Prices:** 11.50-27 Mobile home hire 210-588 **Facilities:** Wi-fi (charged) Kids' Club Play Area **Services:** **Leisure:** P

ANTHÉOR-PLAGE **VAR**

Viaduc

bd des Lucioles, 83530
494448231

A quiet site 150m from a sandy beach, with good facilities.

dir: *Via N98.*

Open: Jun-Sep **Site:** 1.1HEC **Facilities:** **Services:** **Off-site:** S

ANTIBES **ALPES-MARITIMES**

Logis de la Brague

1221 rte de Nice, La Brague, 06600
493335472 493746257
e-mail: contact@camping-logisbrague.com
web: www.camping-logisbrague.com

On a level meadow beside a small river, 50m from the beach.

dir: *On N7, follow signs to Marineland.*

Open: 2 May-Sep **Site:** 1.7HEC **Prices:** 19.50-24 Mobile home hire 650 **Facilities:** (charged) Play Area **Services:** **Leisure:** R S **Off-site:** P

ARGELÈS-SUR-MER **PYRÉNÉES-ORIENTALES**

Criques de Porteils

La Corniche de Collioure, 66700
468811273 468958576
e-mail: contact@lescriques.com
web: www.lescriques.com

Terraced site with beautiful view of sea.

dir: *D914, exit 13. Turn right at Hotel du Golfe & follow signs.*

Open: 2 Apr-22 Oct **Site:** 5.5HEC **Prices:** 21-40 Mobile home hire 169-1289 **Facilities:** Wi-fi Kids' Club Play Area **Services:** **Leisure:** P S

Dauphin

The Camping and Caravanning Club – The Friendly Club

rte de Taxo à la Mer, 66704
468811754 468958260
e-mail: info@campingledauphin.com
web: www.campingledauphin.com

On a long stretch of grassland shaded by poplars, 1.5km from the sea.

C&CC Report *This very well-run site enjoys a superb location between beach and mountains, and the optional individual sanitation blocks are a great bonus. The new pool complex will be ready in time for the 2011 season and will provide a welcome retreat from the Mediterranean sun. Nearby Collioure, a picturesque harbour town and home to many artists, is a must-see.*

dir: *3km N of town, turn right at Taxo d'Avall.*

Open: 14 May-17 Sep **Site:** 8.5HEC **Prices:** 18-43.70 **Facilities:** Play Area **Services:** **Leisure:** P **Off-site:** L R S

Galets

rte de Taxo à la Mer, 66700
468810812 468816876
e-mail: lesgalets@campinglesgalets.fr
web: www.campmed.com

A well-equipped family site with trees, bushes and exotic plants.

dir: *4km N.*

Open: 4 Apr-Sep **Site:** 5HEC **Facilities:** **Services:** **Leisure:** P **Off-site:** R S

Marsouins

chemin de la Retirada, 66702
468811481 468959358
e-mail: marsouins@campmed.com
web: www.campmed.com

A large family site close to the sea, with good facilities and activities for both adults and children.

dir: *2km NE towards Plage Nord.*

Open: 16 Apr-24 Sep **Site:** 10HEC **Prices:** 16-37 Mobile home hire 210-1071 **Facilities:** Wi-fi Kids' Club Play Area **Services:** **Leisure:** P **Off-site:** S

Massane

66702
468810685 468815918
e-mail: camping.massane@infonie.fr
web: www.camping-massane.com

Shady, well-planned site, 1km from the sea.

dir: *Beside D618 near municipal sports field.*

Open: 15 Mar-15 Oct **Site:** 3HEC **Facilities:** **Services:** **Leisure:** P **Off-site:** S

FRANCE

Site 6HEC (site size) grass sand stone little shade partly shaded mainly shaded bungalows for hire (static) caravans for hire tents for hire no dogs site fully accessible for wheelchairs
Prices amount quoted is per night, for 2 adults and car, plus tent or caravan. Mobile home hire is a weekly rate.

Ombrages

av du Général-de-Gaulle, 66702
☎ 468812983 🖷 468958187
e-mail: contact@les-ombrages.com
web: www.les-ombrages.com
A picturesque wooded setting 300m from the beach. The well-equipped site has good recreational facilities and defined pitches.
Open: Jun-Sep **Site:** 4HEC **Prices:** 15.38-23.88 Mobile home hire 240-630 **Facilities:** Wi-fi **Services:** **Off-site:** L P R S

Pins

av du Tech, 66702
☎ 468811046
e-mail: camping@les-pins.com
web: www.les-pins.com
A peaceful family site on a narrow stretch of grassland with some poplar trees.
Open: May-Sep **Site:** 4HEC **Facilities:** **Services:** **Off-site:** P S

Pujol

rte du Tamariguer, 66700
☎ 468810025 🖷 468812121
A lush setting with a variety of recreational facilities.
dir: *0.5km from village, 1km from beach.*
Open: Jun-Sep **Site:** 6.3HEC **Facilities:** **Services:** **Leisure:** P **Off-site:** S

Sirène

rte de Taxo d'Avall, 66702
☎ 468810461 🖷 468816974
e-mail: contact@camping-lasirene.fr
web: www.camping-lasirene.fr
A well-appointed family site with good facilities in a delightful wooded setting.
dir: *4km NE.*
Open: 22 Apr-24 Sep **Site:** 17HEC **Prices:** 23-40 Mobile home hire 203-1680 **Facilities:** Kids' Club Play Area **Services:** **Leisure:** P **Off-site:** S

Soleil

rte du Littoral, Plage Nord, 66702
☎ 468811448 🖷 468814434
e-mail: camping.soleil@wanadoo.fr
web: campmed.com
Peaceful site in wide meadow surrounded by tall trees. Private beach, natural harbour.
dir: *N from town & 1.5km towards beach.*
Open: 14 May-17 Sep **Site:** 13HEC **Prices:** 23.59-36.30 Mobile home hire 273-840 **Facilities:** Wi-fi Kids' Club **Services:** **Leisure:** P R S

Village Center le Neptune

av de la Retirada - Plage Nord, 66702
☎ 499572121 🖷 467516389
e-mail: contact@village-center.com
web: www.village-center.com/languedoc-roussillon/camping-mer-neptune.php
Located 500 metres from the sea, a site with both sunny and shady pitches.
dir: *N114 exit 11, in Argelès follow signs to Plage Nord.*
GPS: 42.5653, 3.0367
Open: 8 Apr-2 Oct **Site:** 3.4HEC **Prices:** 18-42 Mobile home hire 265-1015 **Facilities:** Wi-fi (charged) Kids' Club Play Area **Services:** **Leisure:** P **Off-site:** S

ARLES — BOUCHES-DU-RHÔNE

Rosiers

145 Draile Marseillaise, Pont de Crau, 13200
☎ 490960212
e-mail: lesrosiers.arles@wanadoo.fr
web: www.arles-camping-club.com
On level ground, shaded by bushes.
dir: *Autoroute exit Arles Sud. Or via N443.*
Open: All Year. **Site:** 3.5HEC **Facilities:** **Services:** **Leisure:** P **Off-site:** L R

ARLES-SUR-TECH — PYRÉNÉES-ORIENTALES

Riuferrer

66150
☎ 468391106 🖷 468391209
e-mail: campingriuferrer@libertysurf.fr
web: www.campingduriuferrer.com
Quiet holiday site on gently sloping ground in pleasant area. Clean sanitary installations. Separate area reserved for overnight stops.
dir: *Signed from N115.*
Open: Mar-Oct **Site:** 4.5HEC **Facilities:** **Services:** **Leisure:** R **Off-site:** P

FRANCE

ARPAILLARGUES — GARD

Mas de Rey

rte d'Anduze, 30700
☎ 466221827 🖷 955681833
e-mail: info@campingmasderey.com
web: www.campingmasderey.com

Quiet wooded surroundings with pitches divided by trees and bushes. There are good sports facilities and modern sanitary arrangements.

dir: *3km from Uzès towards Anduze.*

Open: 15 Apr-15 Oct **Site:** 3HEC **Prices:** 15-21 **Facilities:** Play Area **Services:** **Leisure:** P **Off-site:**

AUBIGNAN — VAUCLUSE

Brégoux

410 chemin du Vas, 84810
☎ 490626250 🖷 490626521
e-mail: camping-lebregoux@ventoux-comtat.com
web: www.camping-lebregoux.fr

A level site with good views of Mont Ventoux. Right in the heart of Provence, at Aubignan, in the Ventoux-Comtat Venaissin district.

dir: *On S outskirts of town. D7 onto D55 towards Caromb for 0.5km.*

GPS: 44.0982, 5.0362

Open: Mar-Oct **Site:** 3.5HEC **Prices:** 10.45 Mobile home hire 290-500 **Facilities:** Wi-fi Play Area **Services:** **Off-site:** R

AUPS — VAR

International

rte de Fox-Amphoux, 83630
☎ 494700680 🖷 494701051
e-mail: info@internationalcamping-aups.com
web: www.internationalcamping-aups.com

Wooded surroundings with well-defined pitches and good recreational facilities. A good base for exploring the magnificent Gorges du Verdon.

dir: *0.5km W on D60 towards Fox-Amphoux.*

Open: Apr-Sep **Site:** 4HEC **Facilities:** **Services:** **Leisure:** P **Off-site:**

see advert on this page

AURIBEAU — ALPES-MARITIMES

Parc des Monges

635 chemin du Gabre, 06810
☎ 493609171 🖷 493609171
e-mail: contact@parcdesmonges.fr
web: www.parcdesmonges.com

Wooded setting on the banks of a good fishing river, surrounded by mimosa fields.

dir: *A8 exit Mandelieu for Grasse.*

GPS: 43.6061, 6.9025

Open: 23 Apr-24 Sep **Site:** 1.4HEC **Prices:** 16.90-24 Mobile home hire 280-680 **Facilities:** Wi-fi (charged) Play Area **Services:** **Leisure:** P R **Off-site:**

AVIGNON — VAUCLUSE

Bagatelle

25 Allee Antoine Pinay, Ile de la Barthelasse, 84000
☎ 490863039 🖷 490271623
e-mail: camping.bagatelle@wanadoo.fr
web: www.campingbagatelle.com

Pleasant site with tall trees on the Ile de la Barthelasse. All pitches are numbered, on hard standing and divided by hedges. Separate section for young people.

dir: *Along town wall & river to Rhône bridge (Nîmes road), signed on right.*

Open: All Year. **Site:** 4HEC **Facilities:** **Services:** **Off-site:** P R

CM Pont St-Bénézet

10 chemin de la Barthelasse, 84000
490806350 490852212
e-mail: info@camping-avignon.com
web: www.camping-avignon.com

Set on an island near the bridge with fine views of town. Several tiled sanitary blocks with individual wash cabins. Individual pitches with divisions for tents and caravans. Several playing fields for volleyball and basketball.

dir: *NW of town on right bank of Rhône, 370m upstream from bridge on right. (N100 towards Nîmes).*

Open: Mar-Oct **Site:** 7.5HEC **Facilities:** **Services:** **Leisure:** P

AXAT — AUDE

Crémade

11140
468205064
e-mail: lacremade@hotmail.fr
web: www.lacremade.com

A shady, peaceful site, ideal for water sports.

Open: May-Sep **Site:** 4HEC **Prices:** 12.50-17.50 Mobile home hire 230-370 **Facilities:** Wi-fi **Services:** **Off-site:** P R

Moulin du Pont d'Alies

11140
468205327 874762003
e-mail: contact@alies.fr
web: www.alies.fr

A picturesque location at the entrance to the Gorges de la Pierre.

dir: *Junct D117 & D118, 0.8km from Axat.*

Open: Apr-Oct **Site:** 2HEC **Facilities:** **Services:** **Leisure:** P R

BALARUC-LES-BAINS — HÉRAULT

Camping le Mas du Padre

4 chemin du Mas du Padre, 34540
467485341 467480894
e-mail: contact@mas-du-padre.com
web: www.mas-du-padre.com

2km from the centre of the village and Thau lake. Relaxing, family friendly site with facilities including ping-pong, volleyball and weekly discos. Kids' club in July and August. Dogs must be on a lead, no dangerous dogs.

GPS: 43.4522, 3.6924

Open: 2 Apr-23 Oct **Site:** 1.8HEC **Prices:** 12.35-30.30 Mobile home hire 266-700 **Facilities:** Wi-fi Kids' Club Play Area **Services:** **Leisure:** P **Off-site:** L

BANDOL — VAR

Vallongue

83150
494294955 494294955
e-mail: camping.vallongue@wanadoo.fr
web: www.campingvar.com

Parts of this terraced site have lovely sea views.

Open: Apr-Sep **Site:** 1.5HEC **Facilities:** **Services:** **Leisure:** P **Off-site:**

BARCARÈS, LE — PYRÉNÉES-ORIENTALES

Bousigues

av des Corbières, 66420
468861619 468862844
e-mail: lasbousigues@wanadoo.fr
web: www.camping-barcares.com

Well-equipped family site 1km from the sea. Bar and café only open July and August.

dir: *D83 exit 10.*

Open: 29 Mar-28 Sep **Site:** 3HEC **Facilities:** **Services:** **Leisure:** P **Off-site:** L R S

California

rte de St-Laurent, 66423
468861608 468861820
web: www.camping-california.fr

A friendly family site with regular organised entertainment in a pleasant wooded location close to the beach. Kids' club available in July and August.

dir: *1.5km SW via D90.*

Open: 23 Apr-2 Sep **Site:** 5.5HEC **Prices:** 13-35 Mobile home hire 336-980 **Facilities:** Wi-fi (charged) Kids' Club Play Area **Services:** **Leisure:** P **Off-site:** L R S

Europe

The Camping and Caravanning Club The Friendly Club

rte de St-Laurent, 66420
468861536 468864788
e-mail: reception@europe-camping.com
web: www.europe-camping.com

A holiday village type of site with good recreational facilities, 0.5km from the beach.

C&CC Report *Located in a summer resort, this site is a good stopover in winter for travelling into Spain, with an individual sanitation block on each pitch. The local area can be very quiet in winter.*

dir: *Via D90 2km SW, 200m from Agly.*

Open: All Year. **Site:** 6HEC **Facilities:** **Services:** **Leisure:** P **Off-site:** R S

FRANCE

Oasis

rte de St Laurent, 66420
468861243 466864683
e-mail: info@camping-oasis.com
web: www.camping-oasis.com

Site only 1000 metres from the sea and close to shops. The aquatic area has three swimming-pools, a 33 metre slide and a large sun terrace. Supervised activities for children.

dir: *A9 exit 41 Perpignan Centre/Nord, take D83 for Le Barcarès, exit 9 & D81 towards Canet. 1st exit passing St Laurent on right, under bridge for Le Bacarès, site on left.*

Facilities: **Services:** **Leisure:** P
Off-site: S

see advert on this page

Presqu'île

66420
468861280 468862509
e-mail: contact@lapresquile.com
web: www.lapresquile.com

A well-equipped family site on the edge of Lake Leucate and close to the beach.

dir: *2km on rte de Leucate, turn right.*

Open: 9 Apr-1 Nov **Site:** 3.5HEC **Facilities:** **Services:** **Leisure:** L P
Off-site: R S

Sable d'Or

r des Palombes, 66420
468861841 466743730

A wooded site between the sea and Lac Marin.

dir: *A9 exit 40 for Grand Plage.*

Open: Apr-30 Oct **Site:** 4HEC **Facilities:** **Services:** **Leisure:** P S **Off-site:** L

Tamaris

rte de St Laurent, 66420
468860818 468862309
e-mail: tamaris@altranet.fr
web: www.tamaris.com

Large, secure site with leisure facilities including pool area, karaoke and disco.

dir: *Off A9 motorway.*

Open: All Year. **Site:** 17HEC **Facilities:** **Services:** **Leisure:** P
Off-site: L R S

BÉNIVAY-OLLON DRÔME

Domaine de L'Ecluse

Quartier Barastrage, 26170
475280732 475281687
e-mail: camp.ecluse@wanadoo.fr
web: www.campecluse.com

Situated in the heart of a farm with fruit trees, olive fields and vineyards. A choice of sunny, shaded or semi-shaded pitches separated by hedges.

dir: *D538 (Nyons-Vaison la Romaine), after 11km take D46 to Buis-les-Baronnies, then left for D147 to Bénivay.*

Open: May-15 Sep **Site:** 3HEC **Facilities:** **Services:** **Leisure:** P

BIOT ALPES-MARITIMES

Antipolis

a du Pylone, La Brague, 06600
493339399 492910200
e-mail: contact@camping-antipolis.com
web: www.camping-antipolis.com

Site close to the sea. Shady pitches separated with hedges.

dir: *A8 exit Antibes-Biot, towards Marineland. Turn right after 800m.*

Open: Apr-Sep **Site:** 4.5HEC **Facilities:** **Services:** **Leisure:** P **Off-site:** S

Site 6HEC (site size) grass sand stone little shade partly shaded mainly shaded bungalows for hire (static) caravans for hire tents for hire no dogs site fully accessible for wheelchairs
Prices amount quoted is per night, for 2 adults and car, plus tent or caravan. Mobile home hire is a weekly rate.

Eden

chemin du Val-de-Pome, 06410
☎ 493656370 🖹 493655422
e-mail: campingeden@wanadoo.fr
Site on level meadowland.
dir: *On D4.*
Open: Apr-30 Oct **Site:** 2.5HEC **Prices:** 18-25 Mobile home hire 200-650 **Facilities:** Wi-fi **Services:** **Leisure:** P **Off-site:** S

Pylône

av du Pylone, La Brague, 06600
☎ 493335286 🖹 493333054
e-mail: camping.pylone@wanadoo.fr
web: www.campingdupylone.com
Situated between Cannes and Nice, a family site with good facilities.
dir: *N7 onto D4 for Biot, 1st left.*
Open: All Year. **Site:** 16HEC **Facilities:** **Services:** **Leisure:** P R **Off-site:** S

BOISSET-ET-GAUJAC GARD

Domaine de Gaujac

2406 chemin de la Madelaine, 30140
☎ 466616757 🖹 466605390
e-mail: contact@domaine-de-gaujac.com
web: www.domaine-de-gaujac.com
A family site in wooded surroundings on the banks of a river.
dir: *Via D910.*
Open: Apr-20 Sep **Site:** 10HEC **Facilities:** **Services:** **Leisure:** P R

BOISSON GARD

Château de Boisson

30500
☎ 466248561 🖹 466248014
e-mail: reception@chateaudeboisson.com
web: www.chateaudeboisson.com
A peaceful, well-equipped site in the beautiful Cevennes region. Painting and bridge courses are available. Kids' club in July and August. Dogs allowed except July and August.
dir: *D7 towards Fumades, Boisson 10km on right, site signed.*
GPS: 44.2093, 4.2568
Open: 9 Apr-24 Sep **Site:** 7.8HEC **Prices:** 21.10-51.10 Mobile home hire 178.50-1127 **Facilities:** Wi-fi (charged) Kids' Club Play Area **Services:** **Leisure:** P

BOLLÈNE VAUCLUSE

Barry

Lieu Dit St-Pierre, 84500
☎ 490301320 🖹 490404864
Well-kept site near ruins of Barry troglodyte village.
dir: *Signed from Bollène via D26.*
Open: All Year. **Site:** 3HEC **Facilities:** **Services:** **Leisure:** P **Off-site:** L R

Simioune

Quartier Guffiage, 84500
☎ 490304462
e-mail: la-simioune@orange.fr
web: www.la-simioune.fr
Pleasant wooded surroundings close to the River Rhône. Pony club and riding school available.
dir: *Off A7, 3rd right for Carpertras, at 3rd x-rds turn left for Lambisque, site is signed.*
Open: All Year. **Site:** 3HEC **Prices:** 14 **Facilities:** Wi-fi **Services:** **Leisure:** P **Off-site:** R

BORMES-LES-MIMOSAS VAR

Clau Mar Jo

895 chemin de Benat, 83230
☎ 494715339 🖹 494243873
e-mail: contact@camping-clau-mar-jo.fr
web: www.camping-clau-mar-jo.fr
A well-shaded site with good facilities 1.2km from the sea.
dir: *N98 onto D298.*
Open: 15 Mar-15 Oct **Site:** 1HEC **Facilities:** **Services:** **Off-site:** S

Domaine

La Faviere, 83230
☎ 494710312 🖹 494151867
e-mail: mail@campdudomaine.com
web: www.campdudomaine.com
A very attractive setting with a long sandy beach and numbered pitches. Fine views of sea and sports facilities. A kids' club is available in July and August.
dir: *0.5km E of Bormes-Cap Bénat road.*
Open: Apr-Oct **Site:** 45HEC **Prices:** 18-41 Mobile home hire 500-910 **Facilities:** Wi-fi (charged) Kids' Club Play Area **Services:** **Leisure:** S

FRANCE

Manjastre

150 chemin des Girolles, 83230
494710328 494716362
e-mail: manjastre@infonie.fr
web: www.campingmanjastre-com

A peaceful site 6km from the Mediterranean beaches. Dogs allowed out of season.

dir: *5km NW via N98 on road to La Môle/Cogolin.*

Open: All Year. **Site:** 8HEC **Prices:** 28.42 **Facilities:** Wi-fi (charged) Play Area **Services:** **Leisure:** P **Off-site:** S

BOULOU, LE — PYRÉNÉES-ORIENTALES

Mas Llinas

66165
468832546
e-mail: info@camping-mas-llinas.com
web: www.camping-mas-llinas.com

A family site in wooded surroundings with a variety of leisure facilities.

dir: *3km N via N9.*

GPS: 42.5431, 2.8319

Open: Feb-Nov **Site:** 15HEC **Prices:** 14.30-19.80 Mobile home hire 250-600 **Facilities:** Wi-fi Play Area **Services:** **Leisure:** P **Off-site:**

BOULOURIS-SUR-MER — VAR

Ile d'Or

rte de la Corniche, 83700
494945213 494945213

A quiet location with well-equipped pitches 50m from a private beach.

dir: *E off N98.*

Open: Apr-15 Nov **Site:** 10HEC **Prices:** 28 **Facilities:** Wi-fi (charged) **Services:** **Leisure:** S

BOURDEAUX — DRÔME

Couspeau

Quartier Bellevue, Le Poet-Celard, 26460
475533014 475533723
e-mail: info@couspeau.com
web: www.couspeau.com

A beautiful natural setting with well-maintained facilities.

dir: *1.3km SE via D328A.*

Open: 15 Apr-Sep **Site:** 8HEC **Facilities:** **Services:** **Leisure:** P

BROUSSES-ET-VILLARET — AUDE

Martinet Rouge

11390
619344160
e-mail: camping.lemartinetrouge@orange.fr
web: www.camping-lemartinetrouge.com

A pleasant, well-equipped site on gently sloping terrain. Terraced, with well-marked pitches.

dir: *Via D48.*

Open: Mar-Nov **Site:** 2.8HEC **Facilities:** **Services:** **Leisure:** P **Off-site:** L R

CADENET — VAUCLUSE

Val de Durance

Les Routes, 84160
490683775 490681634
e-mail: info@homair.com
web: www.camping-levaldedurance.com

A well-equipped family site on the shore of a lake and close to the River Durance.

Open: 30 Mar-Sep **Site:** 11HEC **Facilities:** **Services:** **Leisure:** L P **Off-site:** R

CAGNES-SUR-MER — ALPES-MARITIMES

Colombier

35 chemin de Ste-Colombe, 06800
493731277 493731277
e-mail: campinglecolombier06@wanadoo.fr
web: www.campinglecolombier.com

Well-equipped site in a wooded location, 2km from the sea.

Open: Apr-1 Oct **Site:** 0.6HEC **Prices:** 16-21 Mobile home hire 265-550 **Facilities:** Play Area **Services:** **Leisure:** P **Off-site:** R S

Green Park/Todos

159 bis, Vallon-des-Vaux, 06800
442204725 442950363
e-mail: info@homair.com
web: www.camping-greenpark.com

Modern sites with well-defined pitches in pleasant wooded surroundings with good recreational facilities.

dir: *A8 exit Cagnes-sur-Mer onto N7 for Nice.*

Open: 28 Mar-27 Sep **Site:** 5.4HEC **Facilities:** **Services:** **Leisure:** P S

Rivière

168 chemin des Salles, 06800
☎ 493206227 📠 493207253
web: www.campinglariviere06.fr

Secluded wooded surroundings with modern facilities.

dir: *4km N beside River Cagne.*

Open: 15 Mar-15 Oct **Site:** 1.2HEC **Facilities:** **Services:** **Leisure:** P

see advert on this page

CAMURAC AUDE

Sapins

11340
☎ 468203811 📠 468314123
e-mail: info@lessapins-camurac.com
web: www.lessapins-camurac.com

A picturesque wooded site on the edge of a forest with views of the surrounding mountains.

dir: *1.5km from village.*

Open: Apr-15 Oct **Site:** 3HEC **Facilities:** **Services:** **Leisure:** P
Off-site: L

CANET-EN-ROUSILLON PYRÉNÉES-ORIENTALES

Brasilia

Voie de la Crouste, Zone Technique du Port, 66140
☎ 468802382 📠 468733297
e-mail: info@lebrasilia.fr
web: www.brasilia.fr

Site near the beach, with pitches divided by bushes and flowerbeds in pine woods. Pitches are well maintained.

dir: *Off main road in village towards beach for 2km.*

GPS: 42.7090, 3.0369

Open: 15 Apr-Sep **Site:** 15HEC **Prices:** 20-50 Mobile home hire 259-1393 **Facilities:** Wi-fi (charged) Kids' Club Play Area **Services:** **Leisure:** P S
Off-site:

Ma Prairie

The Camping and Caravanning Club — The Friendly Club

av des Coteaux, 66140
☎ 468732617 📠 468732882
e-mail: ma.prairie@wanadoo.fr
web: www.maprairie.com

Peaceful grassland site in a hollow surrounded by vineyards at the entrance to Canet-en-Roussillon. Kids' club in July and August.

C&CC Report *A welcoming, family site with excellent facilities. Subject to demand, coach excursions are run weekly to Andorra, Barcelona and other local places of interest and a wine tasting visit is organised. The medieval Cathar castles, cave paintings and prehistoric remains are highlights of this captivating region, as is a visit to Collioure - a paradise for lovers of art in all its forms.*

dir: *N617 Perpignan-Canet-Plage onto D11 towards Elne.*

Open: 5 May-25 Sep **Site:** 4.5HEC **Prices:** 17-37 Mobile home hire 245-980 **Facilities:** Wi-fi (charged) Kids' Club **Services:** **Leisure:** P **Off-site:**

Peupliers

av des Anneaux de Rousillon, 66140
☎ 468803587 📠 468733875
e-mail: contact@camping-les-peupliers.fr

Quiet, level site divided into pitches by hedges with a variety of leisure facilities.

Open: Jun-Sep **Site:** 4HEC **Prices:** 24-39 Mobile home hire 182-777 **Facilities:** **Services:** **Leisure:** P S

CANET-PLAGE PYRÉNÉES-ORIENTALES

Mar Estang

1 rte de St-Cyprien, 66140
468803553 468733294
e-mail: contact@marestang.com
web: www.marestang.com

Close to a sandy beach, the site offers varied activities includes an art school and a water park with heated pool.

dir: *A9 exit 41 follow signs for Canet then towards St Cyprien.*

GPS: 42.6754, 3.0310

Open: 24 Apr-11 Sep **Site:** 15HEC **Prices:** 12-37 Mobile home hire 169-1029 **Facilities:** Wi-fi Kids' Club Play Area **Services:** **Leisure:** P S **Off-site:**

CANNES ALPES-MARITIMES

Parc Bellevue

67 av M Chevalier, 06150
493472897 493486625
e-mail: contact@parcbellevue.com
web: www.parcbellevue.com

Shaded park location with entertainment available in season.

dir: *A41 exit Cannes, right at 1st lights.*

Open: Apr-Sep **Site:** 4HEC **Facilities:** **Services:** **Leisure:** P **Off-site:** S

Ranch

chemin St-Joseph, L'Aubarède, 06110
493460011 493464430
web: www.leranchcamping.fr

On a wooded hillside 2km from the local beaches, with good facilities.

dir: *A8 exit 41 or 42.*

Open: 2 Apr-29 Oct **Site:** 2HEC **Facilities:** **Services:** **Leisure:** P **Off-site:** S

CARCASSONNE AUDE

Breil d'Aude

rte de Limoux, Preixan, 11250
468268818 468268507
e-mail: sudfrance@wanadoo.fr
web: www.camping-grandsud.com

Wooded location beside a private lake with free fishing.

dir: *1.5km N via D118.*

Open: Apr-Sep **Site:** 11HEC **Prices:** 19-32 Mobile home hire 370-810 **Facilities:** Wi-fi Play Area **Services:** **Leisure:** P R **Off-site:**

Cité

rte de St-Hilaire, 11000
468251177 468473313
e-mail: cpallacite@atciat.com
web: www.campeoles.fr

Wooded surroundings beside the River Aude. A good base for exploring the region.

dir: *Via A61 or A9.*

Open: 15 May-10 Oct **Site:** 7HEC **Facilities:** **Services:** **Leisure:** P **Off-site:** L R

CARPENTRAS VAUCLUSE

Lou Comtadou

rte de St Didier, 881 av P-de-Coubertin, 84200
490670316 490460181
e-mail: info@campingloucomtadou.com
web: www.campingloucomtadou.com

Near the Carpentras swimming pool in pleasant surroundings with modern facilities.

dir: *SE of town centre towards St-Didier.*

Open: Apr-Sep **Site:** 2.5HEC **Facilities:** **Services:** **Off-site:** P

CARQUEIRANNE VAR

Beau-Vezé

rte de la Moutonne, 83320
494576530 494576530
e-mail: info@camping-beauveze.com
web: www.camping-beauveze.com

Set in a beautiful wooded park with modern facilities.

dir: *2.5km NW via N559 & D76 between Hyères & Toulon.*

Open: May-Sep **Site:** 7HEC **Prices:** 20-33 Mobile home hire 310-777 **Facilities:** Wi-fi (charged) Kids' Club **Services:** **Leisure:** P S

CASTEIL PYRÉNÉES-ORIENTALES

Domaine St Martin

6 bd de la Cascade, 66820
468055209
e-mail: info@domainestmartin.com
web: www.domainestmartin.com

Quiet site situated in the attractive landscape of the Confluent Valley at the foot of the Massif Canigou in the Pyrénées.

dir: *D116 towards Vernet-les-Bains. Entering Vernet, turn right crossing main street & follow signs for Casteil.*

Open: Apr-15 Oct **Site:** 4.5HEC **Prices:** 13-24.45 Mobile home hire 260-590 **Facilities:** Wi-fi Play Area **Services:** **Leisure:** P **Off-site:** R

ASTELLANE ALPES-DE-HAUTE-PROVENCE

ollines de Castellane

e de Grasse Napoléon, Garde-Castellane, 04120
 492836896 492837540
mail: info@rcn-lescollinesdecastellane.fr
b: www.rcn-campings.fr
rraced site on wooded grassland with mountain views and fine creational facilities.
: *On Grasse road beyond La Garde.*
en: 20 Apr-23 Sep **Site:** 10HEC **Facilities:**
Services: **Leisure:** P

Domaine du Verdon

The Camping and Caravanning Club The Friendly Club

04120
 492836129 492836937
e-mail: contact@camp-du-verdon.com
web: www.camp-du-verdon.com
Flat, well-maintained site in gorge on banks of River Verdon.
C&CC Report *A wide range of facilities in the most spectacular but still easily reachable part of the gorge country, on the famous Route Napoléon and with an off-road path to pretty Castellane. A great site in low season for those wanting a peaceful base with many facilities open, but also at any time for active families, with early booking strongly advised. The very best stretches of the truly jaw-dropping Grand Canyon du Verdon, as well as some of the prettiest countryside, lavender fields and towns in lovely Provence, are all within very easy reach.*
dir: *Below D952 towards Gorges du Verdon.*
Open: 15 May-15 Sep **Site:** 14HEC
Prices: 14-34 **Facilities:** Wi-fi Play Area
Services: **Leisure:** P R **Off-site:** L

orges du Verdon

s d'Arémus, Chasteuil, 04120
 492836364 492837472
nail: aremus@camping-gorgesduverdon.com
b: www.camping-gorgesduverdon.com
uated beside the River Verdon at an altitude of 660m, rounded by mountains. Site divided into pitches and split two by a road. Bathing in river is not advised due to strong rent.
9.5km S of village.
en: 8 May-15 Sep **Site:** 7HEC **Prices:** 15
bile home hire 290-708 **Facilities:** Wi-fi Play Area
Services: **Leisure:** P R

International

rte Napoléon, 04120
 492836667 492837767
e-mail: info@camping-international.fr
web: www.camping-international.fr
Family site at the foot of the Col des Lèques and close to the Gorges du Verdon.
dir: *1km from village centre, signed.*
Open: Apr-Sep **Site:** 6HEC **Facilities:**
Services: **Leisure:** P **Off-site:** L R

Nôtre Dame

rte des Gorges du Verdon, 04120
 492836302
e-mail: camping-notredame@wanadoo.fr
web: www.camping-notredame.com
Meadowland site with deciduous and fruit trees.
dir: *0.5km from village centre on D952.*
GPS: 43.8457, 6.5048
Open: Apr-14 Oct **Site:** 0.6HEC **Prices:** 12-17
Mobile home hire 225-530 **Facilities:** Wi-fi
Services: **Off-site:** L P R

CASTRIES HÉRAULT

Fondespierre

chemin Rioch Viala, 34160
 467912003
e-mail: accueil@campingfondespierre.com
web: www.campingfondespierre.com
dir: *A9, exit 28 and take D610 towards Ales, 1.5 km after Castries turn left and follow signs.*
Open: All Year. **Site:** 3HEC **Prices:** 16.50-24.70
Mobile home hire 343-756 **Facilities:** Wi-fi (charged)
Play Area **Services:** **Leisure:** P
Off-site: L

CAVALAIRE-SUR-MER VAR

Cros de Mouton

83240
 494641087 494646312
e-mail: campingcrosdemouton@wanadoo.fr
web: www.crosdemouton.com
Terraced site with individual pitches, separated for caravans and tents. Good view of sea 1.5km away.
dir: *Off N559 in town centre & continue inland for 1.5km.*
Open: 15 Mar-4 Nov **Site:** 5HEC **Facilities:**
Services: **Leisure:** P
Off-site: S

FRANCE

Pinède

chemin des Mannes, 83240
494641114 494641925
web: www.le-camping-la-pinede.com
A family site with well-defined pitches, 0.5km from the sea.
dir: *300m from village centre.*
Open: 15 Mar-15 Oct **Site:** 2HEC **Facilities:** **Services:** **Off-site:** P S

CENDRAS GARD

Croix Clémentine

rte de Mende, 30480
466865269 466865484
e-mail: clementine@clementine.fr
web: www.clementine.fr
An extensive, partly terraced site, in wooded surroundings.
dir: *Signed W of town on D160 towards La Baume.*
GPS: 44.1519, 4.0431
Open: 31 Mar-12 Sep **Site:** 12HEC **Facilities:** Wi-fi Kids' Club Play Area **Services:** **Leisure:** P **Off-site:** R

CEYRESTE BOUCHES DU RHÔNE

Camping de Ceyreste

av Eugène Julien, 13600
442830768
e-mail: campingceyreste@yahoo.fr
web: www.campingceyreste.com
3km from beaches at La Ciotat, quiet and shady pitches with leisure activities including miniature golf and a fitness trail course. Shop, bar, café, Camping Gaz and kids' club all available in season.
dir: *N9 exit La Ciotat, then Ceyreste.*
GPS: 43.2168, 5.6302
Open: 30 Mar-11 Nov **Site:** 3HEC **Prices:** 19-32 Mobile home hire 350-760 **Facilities:** Wi-fi Kids' Club Play Area **Services:** **Leisure:** P **Off-site:** S

CHABEUIL DRÔME

Grand Lierne

Les Garalands, 26120
475598314 475598795
e-mail: grand-lierne@franceloc.fr
web: www.grandlierne.com
On the edge of the Vercors Regional Park.
dir: *A7 exit Valence Sud for Chabeuil, site signed.*
Open: 18 Apr-26 Sep **Site:** 7HEC **Facilities:** **Services:** **Leisure:** P **Off-site:** R

CHARLEVAL BOUCHES-DU-RHÔ

Orée des Bois

av du Bois, 13350
442284175 442284748
e-mail: oreedesbois@village-center.com
web: www.village-center.com
Spacious, well-shaded pitches 0.5km from the village.
dir: *A7 exit Sémas, from Charleval towards Cazan.*
Open: 5 Apr-14 Sep **Site:** 5HEC **Facilities:** **Services:** **Off-site:** P

CHÂTEAU-ARNOUX ALPES-DE-HAUTE-PROVEN

Salettes

04160
492640240 492640240
e-mail: info@lessalettes.com
web: www.lessalettes.com
dir: *1km E beside river.*
Open: Jun-Sep **Site:** 4HEC **Facilities:** **Services:** **Leisure:** P

CHÂTEAUNEUF-DE-GALAURE DRÔ

Château de Galaure

26330
475686522
Spacious, restful site within walking distance of village.
dir: *A7 exit 12 (Chanas), take N7 for St Valier, left for D51 towards Chateauneuf de Galaure.*
Open: 25 Apr-27 Sep **Site:** 12HEC **Facilities:** **Services:** **Leisure:** P R **Off-site:**

CHÂTEAUNEUF-SUR-ISÈRE DRÔ

Soleil Fruité

Les Peches, 26300
475841970 475780585
e-mail: contact@lesoleilfruite.com
web: www.lesoleilfruite.com
Situated in a 9 acre orchard of peach, apricot and olive trees a surrounded by the mountains of the Ardèche and the massif of the Vercors. Dogs allowed except 6 July to 20 August.
dir: *A7 exit 14 Valence Nord. Follow signs for Pont d'Isère/Tain l'Hermitage.*
Open: 28 Apr-15 Sep **Site:** 4HEC **Prices:** 16.10-23.90 Mobile home hire 298-625 **Facilities:** Wi-fi Kids' Club Play Area **Services:** **Leisure:** P

FRANCE

HAUZON ARDÈCHE

igue

7120
475396357 475397517
-mail: info@camping-la-digue.fr
eb: www.camping-la-digue.fr
beautiful wooded location with good recreational facilities.
r: *1km E, 100m from River Ardèche.*
pen: 20 Mar-30 Oct **Site:** 2.5HEC **Facilities:** **Services:** **Leisure:** P R

IOTAT, LA BOUCHES-DU-RHÔNE

liviers

e du Bord de Mer, 13600
442831504 442839443
eb: www.camping_lesolivers.com
terraced family site between the N559 and the railway line om Nice.
r: *Inland off N559 at Km34 (5km E of town centre) for 150m.*
pen: Apr-Sep **Site:** 10HEC **Facilities:** **Services:** **Leisure:** P **Off-site:** S

t Jean

0 av de St-Jean, 13600
442831301 442714641
te on the right side of the coast road in an excellent position th direct access to the beach.
r: *Between D559 & sea behind motel in NE part of town.*
en: 2 Jun-22 Sep **Site:** 9.9HEC **Facilities:** **Services:** **Leisure:** S **Off-site:**

oleil

51 av Emile Bodin, rte de Cassis, 13600
442715532
mail: contact@camping-dusoleil.com
eb: www.camping-dusoleil.com
small site, divided into pitches, 1.5km from the beach.
r: *A50 exit 9 La Ciotat.*
en: Apr-Sep **Site:** 0.5HEC **Prices:** 18-20 Mobile me hire 350-650 **Facilities:** Wi-fi **Services:** **Off-site:** P S

COGOLIN VAR

Argentière

chemin de l'Argentière, 83310
494546363 494540615
e-mail: camping-largentiere@wanadoo.fr
web: www.camping-argentiere.com
Landscaped, partly terraced site with leisure facilities and entertainment.
dir: *1.5km NW along D48 rte de St-Maur.*
GPS: 43.255, 6.5131
Open: Apr-Sep **Site:** 6HEC **Prices:** 14-30 Mobile home hire 220-800 **Facilities:** Wi-fi Kids' Club Play Area **Services:** **Leisure:** P **Off-site:** S

COLLE-SUR-LOUP, LA ALPES-MARITIMES

Castellas

rte de Roquefort, 06480
493329705 493329705
e-mail: lecastellas.camping@wanadoo.fr
web: www.camping-le-castellas.com
Wooded location with direct access to the river.
Open: All Year. **Site:** 1.2HEC **Facilities:** **Services:** **Leisure:** R S **Off-site:** P

Pinèdes

rte du Pont de Pierre, 06480
493329894 493325020
e-mail: info@lespinedes.com
web: www.lespinedes.com
Well-kept terraced site on steep slope with woodland providing shade, interesting walks and beautiful views. Kids' club available in July and August.
dir: *A8 exit Cagnes-sur-Mer, onto D6, right for La Colle-sur-Loup.*
Open: 15 Mar-Sep **Site:** 3.8HEC **Prices:** 15.50-32 Mobile home hire 280-790 **Facilities:** Wi-fi (charged) Kids' Club Play Area **Services:** **Leisure:** P **Off-site:** R

Vallon Rouge

rte Greolières, 06480
493328612 493328009
e-mail: info@auvallonrouge.com
web: www.auvallonrouge.com
A picturesque forest location close to the river with good facilities. Situated between Nice, Monaco and Cannes, 9km from beaches.
dir: *3km W of town. D6 towards Gréolières, site on right.*
Open: 4 Apr-25 Sep **Site:** 3HEC **Prices:** 14-28.50 Mobile home hire 195-750 **Facilities:** Wi-fi Kids' Club Play Area **Services:** **Leisure:** P R **Off-site:**

FRANCE

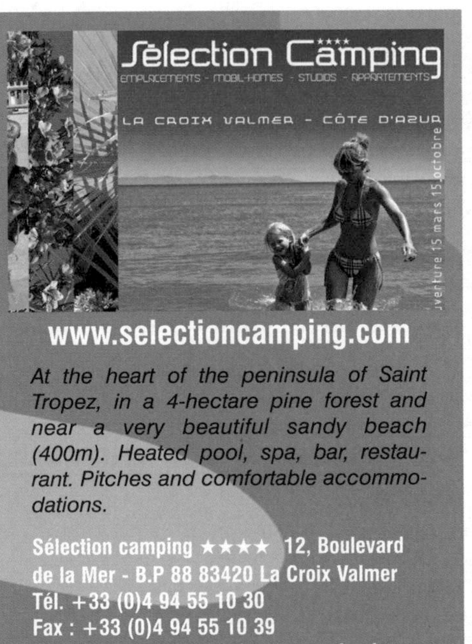

CRAU, LA — VAR

Bois de Mont-Redon

480 chemin du Mont-Redon, 83260
☎ 494667408 🖷 494660966
e-mail: mont.redon@wanadoo.fr
web: www.mont-redon.com

Set among oak and pine trees with well-defined pitches and plenty of recreational facilities.

dir: *3km NE via D29.*

Open: 15 Jun-15 Sep **Site:** 5HEC **Facilities:** **Services:** **Leisure:** P

CRESPIAN — GARD

Mas de Reilhe

30260
☎ 466778212 🖷 466802650
e-mail: info@camping-mas-de-reilhe.fr
web: www.camping-mas-de-reilhe.fr

Set in the grounds of a château, surrounded by pine trees with good recreational facilities.

dir: *On N110 for Lédignan, site on right before Crespian.*

Open: 3 Apr-19 Sep **Site:** 3HEC **Facilities:** **Services:** **Leisure:** P

CROIX-VALMER, LA — VA

Selection

12 bd de la Mer, 83420
☎ 494551030 🖷 494551039
e-mail: camping-selection@wanadoo.fr
web: www.selectioncamping.com

Site in a pine wood, protected from wind. Many terraces and divided into pitches. Kids' club available during July and August. No dogs permitted in July and August.

dir: *Off N559 at rdbt at Km78.5, 300m W.*

GPS: 43.1959, 6.5553

Open: 15 Mar-15 Oct **Site:** 3.8HEC **Prices:** 23-3 Mobile home hire 360-920 **Facilities:** Wi-fi (charged) Kids' Club Play Area **Services:** **Leisure:** P **Off-site:** S

see advert on this pa

DARBRES — ARDECH

Camping les Lavandes

Le Village, 07170
☎ 475942065
e-mail: sarl.leslavandes@free.fr
web: www.les-lavandes-darbres.com

Shaded terraces with large pitches. There are two children's playgrounds and a small shop in July and August. A restaurant i open from mid June to August.

dir: *RN102 to Darbres.*

GPS: 44.6478, 4.5036

Open: 15 Apr-Sep **Site:** 1.5HEC **Prices:** 12.50-19.80 **Facilities:** Play Area **Services:** **Leisure:** P **Off-site:** L R

DIE — DRÔM

Pinède

Quartier du Pont-Neuf, 26150
☎ 475221777 🖷 475222273
e-mail: pinedeclub@infonie.fr
web: www.camping-pinede.com

A picturesque mountain setting beside the River Drôme. Kids' club available in July and August.

dir: *W via D93, over railway line & river to site.*

Open: 8 Apr-15 Sep **Site:** 11HEC **Prices:** 15-34 Mobile home hire 240-595 **Facilities:** Wi-fi (charged) Kids' Club Play Area **Services:** **Leisure:** P R

LNE PYRÉNÉES-ORIENTALES

lorida

te de Latour Bas Elne, 66200
468378088 468378076
eb: www.campingleflorida.com
uiet location between sea and mountains but close to local
esorts and amenities.
pen: 5 Apr-8 Nov **Facilities:** **Leisure:** P

NTRECHAUX VAUCLUSE

on Crouzet

te de St-Marcelin, 84340
490460162 490460162
-mail: du.bon.crouzet@free.fr
eb: du.bon.crouzet.free.fr
n level ground with modern facilities beside the river.
r: *D938 exit Vaison-la-Romaine for St-Marcelin-les-Vaison for km.*
pen: Apr-Oct **Site:** 1.2HEC **Prices:** 12-16
acilities: Wi-fi **Services:**
eisure: P R

LEURY AUDE

ux Hamacs

es Cabanes de Fleury, 11560
468332222 468332223
-mail: info@cottagevillage.fr
eb: www.campingauxhamacs.com
large site beside the River Aude and 1km from the coast.
r: *A9 exit Béziers, 15km W.*
pen: Apr-17 Sep **Site:** 10HEC **Facilities:**
Services: **Leisure:** P R
ff-site: S

ONT-ROMEU PYRÉNÉES-ORIENTALES

uttopia Font-Romeu

e de Mont-Louis, 66120
468300932 468045639
mail: font-romeu@huttopia.com
eb: www.huttopia.com
pacious and shaded pitches set in a beautiful site with a
ackdrop of the Pyrénées. Kids' club in July and August.
r: *N20-E9 (Ax-les-Thermes to Bourg-Madame), take exit for 618.*
PS: 42.5117, 2.0497
pen: 27 May-11 Sep & 4 Dec-3 Apr **Site:** 7HEC
rices: 14.20-23.60 **Facilities:** Kids' Club Play Area
Services: **Leisure:** P **Off-site:** L R

FONTVIEILLE BOUCHES-DU-RHÔNE

CM Pins

r Michelet, 13990
490547869 490548125
e-mail: campingmunicipal.lespins@wanadoo.fr
Set in a pine wood close to the Moulin d'Alphonse Daudet.
dir: *1km from village via D17.*
Open: Apr-Sep **Site:** 3.5HEC **Facilities:**
Services: **Off-site:** P

FORCALQUIER ALPES-DE-HAUTE-PROVENCE

Indigo Forcalquier

rte de Sigonce, 04300
492752794 492751810
e-mail: forcalquier@camping-indigo.com
web: www.camping-indigo.com
5 minute walk from village centre, family campsite with high quality facilities.
dir: *A7 exit Avignon Sud onto RN100.*
GPS: 43.9620, 5.7874
Open: 22 Apr-2 Oct **Site:** 4HEC
Prices: 14.10-21.40 Mobile home hire 289.10-665 **Facilities:**
Kids' Club Play Area **Services:**
Leisure: P **Off-site:**

FRÉJUS VAR

Domaine du Colombier

1052 r des Combattants en Afrique du Nord, 83600
494515601 494515557
e-mail: info@clubcolombier.com
web: www.clubcolombier.com
Extensive site between Cannes and St Tropez, 4.5km from the beach. Good recreational facilities including heated swimming pools and water slides, jacuzzis and a fitness area. Plenty of activities and entertainment for adults and children.
dir: *A8 exit 38.*
Open: 9 Apr-10 Oct **Site:** 10HEC
Prices: 15-51 Mobile home hire 273-2205 **Facilities:**
Wi-fi (charged) Kids' Club Play Area **Services:**
Leisure: P **Off-site:** S

FRANCE

Holiday Green

rte de Bagnols-en-Forêt, 83600
☎ 494198830 📠 494198831
e-mail: info@holiday-green.com
web: www.holidaygreen.com
A family site in a beautiful wooded location, offering fine modern facilities and a variety of recreational and entertainment facilities.
dir: *6km N via D4.*
Open: Apr-Sep **Site:** 15HEC **Facilities:** **Services:** **Leisure:** P **Off-site:** L

Montourey

Quartier Montourey, 83600
☎ 494532641 📠 494532675
e-mail: montourey@wanadoo.fr
A well-equipped site close to the beach.
dir: *2km N.*
Open: Apr-Sep **Site:** 5HEC **Facilities:** **Services:** **Leisure:** P

Pierre Verte

rte de Bagnols, 83600
☎ 494408830 📠 494407541
e-mail: info@campinglapierreverte.com
web: www.campinglapierreverte.com
A large family site in a pine forest 8km from the coast.
dir: *Exit 38 (Frejus Centre) of the A8, towards Bagnols en Forêt.*
GPS: 43.4883, 6.7154
Open: 2 Apr-Sep **Site:** 28HEC **Prices:** 20-36 Mobile home hire 300-1020 **Facilities:** Wi-fi (charged) Kids' Club Play Area **Services:** **Leisure:** P

Pins Parasols

The Camping and Caravanning Club The Friendly Club

3360 rue des Combattants en Afrique du Nord, 83600
☎ 494408843 📠 494408199
e-mail: lespinsparasols@wanadoo.fr
web: lespinsparasols.com
A modern family site shaded by oaks and pines with spacious, well-defined pitches and good recreational facilities.
C&CC Report *An ideal family site for discovering the Riviera and Provence. None of the Côte d'Azur resorts are far away, but do take time to discover some of the beautiful Provençal villages that lie only a few kilometres inland – as well as the fantastic Gorges du Verdon. Unlike many coastal sites that are now almost static villages, Les Pins Parasols is still a predominantly traditional touring site.*
dir: *4km N via D4.*
Open: 2 Apr-24 Sep **Site:** 4.5HEC
Prices: 18.40-27.90 Mobile home hire 207-710 **Facilities:** Play Area **Services:** **Leisure:** P
Off-site:

FRONTIGNAN HÉRAUL

Soleil

60 av d'Ingril, 34110
☎ 467430202 📠 467533469
e-mail: campingdusoleil@wanadoo.fr
web: www.campingsoleil.fr
Family site bordering the beach.
dir: *NE via D60.*
Open: Apr-Sep **Site:** 1.2HEC **Facilities:** **Services:** **Leisure:** P S **Off-site:**

Tamaris

av d'Ingril, 34110
☎ 467434477 📠 467189790
e-mail: les-tamaris@wanadoo.fr
web: www.les-tamaris.fr
A family site on level ground with direct access to the beach. Good recreational facilities.
dir: *N112 onto D129 & D60/D50 for 6km.*
Open: Apr-Sep **Site:** 4.5HEC **Prices:** 45 Mobile hom hire 210-1060 **Facilities:** Wi-fi Kids' Club Play Area **Services:** **Leisure:** P S

GALLARGUES-LE-MONTUEUX GAR

Amandiers

30660
☎ 466352802
web: www.camping-lesamandiers.com
A family site with good facilities in a beautiful wooded location.
dir: *N113 from Lunel towards Nîmes.*
Open: May-10 Sep **Site:** 3HEC **Facilities:** **Services:** **Leisure:** P
Off-site: R

GALLICIAN GAR

Camping le Mas de Mourgues

30600
☎ 466733088 📠 466733088
e-mail: info@masdemourgues.com
web: www.masdemourgues.com
Situated in an old vineyard with some vines retained to separate pitches. Views overlooking the Camargue and ideal for touring th surrounding area including the historic town of Nîmes.
dir: *On D6572 between St-Gilles & Vauvert at road junct to Gallician.*
Open: Apr-Sep **Site:** 2HEC **Prices:** 11.50-19 Mobile home hire 260-655 **Facilities:** Wi-fi (charged Play Area **Services:** **Off-site:** L

ASSIN VAR

Parc St-James Gassin

te du Bourrian, 83580
494552020 494563477
ark-like site on slopes of a hill.
ir: *2.5km E of N559, via Km84.5 & Km84.9 on D89.*
ite: 32HEC **Facilities:** **Services:** **Leisure:** P

see advert on this page

IENS VAR

Mediterranée-Les Cigales

58 bd Alsace Lorraine, 83400
494582106 494589673
-mail: accueil@campinglemed.fr
veb: www.campinglemed.fr
well-kept site with numbered pitches. Special places for aravans.
ir: *300m E of D97.*
pen: Apr-Sep **Site:** 1.5HEC **Facilities:**
ervices: **Off-site:** S

GRASSE ALPES-MARITIMES

Paoute

160 rte de Cannes, 06130
493091142 493400640
e-mail: camppaoute@hotmail.com
web: www.campinglapaoute.com
A family site in a wooded location close to the town centre.
dir: *S of town ctr, E of the Cannes road just beyond Ctr Commercial.*
GPS: 43.6364, 6.9510
Open: Apr-Sep **Site:** 2.5HEC **Facilities:**
Services: **Leisure:** P

GRAU-DU-ROI, LE GARD

Abri de Camargue

rte du Phare de l'Espiguette, Port Camargue, 30240
466515483 466517642
e-mail: contact@abridecamargue.fr
web: www.abridecamargue.fr
A pleasant site near the beach on the edge of the Camargue with well-marked pitches and modern installations. Activities include petanque and multi-sports.
dir: *A9 exit Gallargues onto N313 then D979 to Grau-du-Roi.*
GPS: 43.5225, 4.1488
Open: Apr-Sep **Site:** 4HEC **Prices:** 27-56 Mobile home hire 399-917 **Facilities:** Kids' Club Play Area **Services:** **Leisure:** P **Off-site:** S

Eden

Port-Camargue, 30240
☎ 466514981 🖷 466531320
web: www.campingleden.fr

Quiet site on both sides of the access road, 300m from the beach.

dir: *On D626 towards Espiguette.*

Open: 7 Apr-Sep **Site:** 5.25HEC **Prices:** 21-47 Mobile home hire 245-1092 **Facilities:** Wi-fi (charged) Kids' Club Play Area **Services:** **Leisure:** P **Off-site:** L S

Jardins de Tivoli

rte de l'Éspiquette, 30240
☎ 466539700 🖷 466510981
e-mail: contact@lesjardinsdetivoli.com
web: www.lesjardinsdetivoli.com

A modern site with well-marked pitches in a wooded setting 0.6km from the beach. There are good recreational facilities including mountain bike hire.

dir: *A9 SE through Le Grau-du-Roi.*

Open: Apr-Sep **Site:** 7HEC **Facilities:** **Services:** **Leisure:** P **Off-site:** S

GRIGNAN — DRÔME

Truffières

Lieu-dit Nachony, 26230
☎ 475469362
e-mail: info@lestruffieres.com
web: www.lestruffieres.com

A family site opposite the Château Grignan with good facilities.

dir: *A7 exit Montélimar Sud & N7 E.*

Open: 20 Apr-Sep **Site:** 3HEC **Facilities:** **Services:** **Leisure:** P **Off-site:**

HYÈRES — VAR

Ceinturon III

L'Ayguade, 2 r des Saraniers, 83400
☎ 494663265 🖷 494664843
e-mail: contact@ceinturon3.fr
web: www.ceinturon3.fr

Well-kept site in wooded surroundings divided into numbered pitches. Individual washing cubicles.

dir: *4km SE of Hyères on D42.*

Open: 27 Mar-Sep **Site:** 3HEC **Facilities:** **Services:** **Leisure:** P S **Off-site:** S

International

1737 rte de la Madrague,
Presqu'ile de Giens, 83400
☎ 494589016 🖷 494589050
e-mail: thierry.coulomb@wanadoo.fr
web: www.international-giens.com

Site at the far end of the Almanarre beach, 400m from the village of Giens. A private solarium, sheltered from the wind, has direct access to the sea. Special play areas for children. Heated swimming pool. Ideal place for windsurfers.

Open: 22 Mar-3 Nov **Site:** 2.5HEC **Prices:** 20.50-23.50 **Facilities:** Wi-fi (charged) Play Area **Services:** **Leisure:** P S

Palmiers

r du Ceinturon, L'Ayguade, 83400
☎ 494663966 🖷 494664730
e-mail: camping-palmiers@orange.fr
web: www.camping-les-palmiers.fr

A popular site on level meadowland divided into pitches. 300m from the sea. Some individual washing cubicles.

dir: *4km SE of Hyères on D42.*

Open: 15 Mar-15 Oct **Site:** 4.8HEC **Facilities:** **Services:** **Leisure:** P **Off-site:** R S

ISLE-SUR-LA-SORGUE, L' — VAUCLUSE

Sorguette

rte d'Apt, 84800
☎ 490380571 🖷 490208461
e-mail: sorguette@wanadoo.fr
web: www.camping-sorguette.com

Tranquil wooded surroundings beside the River Sorguette with good sports and entertainment facilities. Kids' club available during high season.

dir: *N100 towards Apt.*

GPS: 43.9142, 5.0717

Open: 15 Mar-15 Oct **Site:** 2.5HEC **Prices:** 17.10-21.50 Mobile home hire 392-714 **Facilities:** Wi-fi (charged) Kids' Club Play Area **Services:** **Leisure:** R **Off-site:** P

FRANCE

ANUÉJOLS GARD

omaine de Pradines

te de Millau, 30750

☎ 467827385

eb: www.domaine-de-pradines.com

family-run site, situated at 3000ft in the Parc National des évennes, between Millau and the Mont Aigoual. Spacious itches and activities for children twice weekly. Touring pitches vailable Jun-15 Sep.

ir: *A75 exit Millau, follow towards Montpellier-le-Vieux then orges de la Dourbie. At rdbt after bridge turn left onto D41, follow owards Lanuéjols via D29/D28. At Roque St Marguerite take D991.*

pen: All Year. **Site:** 30HEC **Prices:** 6-8 Mobile ome hire 350-570 **Facilities:** Wi-fi Play Area **ervices:** **Leisure:** P **Off-site:** R

ARGENTIÈRE ARDÈCHE

Ranchisses

rte de Rocher, 07110

☎ 475883197 475883273

e-mail: reception@lesranchisses.fr

web: www.lesranchisses.fr

The Camping and Caravanning Club The Friendly Club

C&CC Report *Les Ranchisses' tranquil valley setting in this lovely part of the Ardèche complements a friendly, relaxing atmosphere and the excellent site facilities. Younger children and couples of all ages love it and the friendly owners Philippe and Véronique have lots of suggestions for visits and outdoor pursuits. Make sure you try the traditional Ardèche fare at the very picturesque locally renowned site restaurant, and try out their Wellness Centre.*

dir: *D104 road to Uzer, then follow signs for Largentière (D5). Through village and follow signs for Rocher/Valgorge, 2km to campsite.*

Open: 16 Apr-25 Sep **Site:** 7HEC **Prices:** 19-45 **Facilities:** Wi-fi (charged) Kids' Club Play Area **Services:** **Leisure:** P R **Off-site:**

AROQUE-DES-ALBÈRES PYRÉNÉES-ORIENTALES

amping des Albères

e Moulin de Cassagnes, 66740

☎ 468692364 468891430

mail: camping-des-alberes@wanadoo.fr

eb: www.camping-des-alberes.com

m from the sea at Argèles-sur-Mer and within the Massif des bères, an area known for its hiking and mountain bike trails. isure facilities include swimming and paddling pools and a mes room. Kids' club available in July and August. Charge ade for dogs.

pen: Apr-15 Oct **Site:** 7HEC **Prices:** 15-29 obile home hire 190-790 **Facilities:** Wi-fi (charged) Kids' ub Play Area **Services:** **Leisure:** P **f-site:**

Planes

117 av du Vallespir, 66740

☎ 468892136 468890142

e-mail: info@lasplanes.com

web: www.lasplanes.com

A picturesque setting surrounded by trees, bushes and flowers.

dir: *RD11.*

Open: 15 Jun-Aug **Site:** 2.5HEC **Prices:** 21-21.50 **Facilities:** **Services:** **Leisure:** P **Off-site:**

LÉZIGNAN-CORBIÈRES AUDE

CM Pinède

r des Rousillous, 11200

☎ 468270508 468270508

e-mail: campinglapinede@wanadoo.fr

web: www.campinglapinede.fr

Well-kept terraced site with numbered pitches and asphalt drives, decorated with bushes and flower beds. Shop only open July and August.

dir: *Signed from N113.*

Open: Mar-Oct **Site:** 3.5HEC **Facilities:** **Services:** **Leisure:** P **Off-site:**

LONDE-LES-MAURES, LA VAR

Moulières

83250

☎ 494015321 494015322

e-mail: camping.les.moulieres@wanadoo.fr

web: www.campingsmoulieres.com

Well-tended level meadowland in quiet location. 1km from the sea.

dir: *On W outskirts towards coast.*

Open: 12 Jun-5 Sep **Site:** 3HEC **Prices:** 20-29 **Facilities:** Wi-fi Play Area **Services:** **Off-site:** S

Pansard

83250

☎ 494668322 494665612

e-mail: pansardcamping@aol.com

web: www.provence-campings.com/azur/pansard

Beautiful, wide piece of land in a pine forest beside the beach.

dir: *Off N98.*

Open: Apr-Sep **Site:** 6HEC **Facilities:** **Services:** **Leisure:** S

FRANCE

Facilities shop shower electric points for razors electric points for caravans parking by tents permitted mpulsory separate car park **Services** café/restaurant bar Camping Gaz International gas other than Camping Gaz first aid facilities laundry **Leisure** swimming L-Lake P-Pool R-River S-Sea **Off-site** All facilities within 5km

LUC-EN-DIOIS DRÔME

Camping les Foulons

chemin de la Piscine, 26310
☎ 475213614
e-mail: mcsv@neuf.fr
web: www.camping-luc-en-diois.com

Located in an area known for climbing, a shaded site with facilities including tennis court, swimming pool and beach volleyball field.

Open: Apr-Oct **Site:** 2HEC **Prices:** 10.50-15.30 Mobile home hire 250-480 **Facilities:** Wi-fi Kids' Club Play Area **Services:** **Leisure:** P R **Off-site:** P

LUNEL HÉRAULT

Pont de Lunel

rte de Nîmes, 34400
☎ 467711022
e-mail: nb.pontdelunel@wanadoo.fr
web: www.campingdupontdelunel.com

A small, family site with shaded pitches. A games area for football, volleyball and mini-golf. Events include pétanque and ping-pong competitions.

dir: *A9 or RN113.*

GPS: 43.6854, 4.1519

Open: 15 Mar-15 Oct **Site:** 2.8HEC **Prices:** 13.90-18.40 Mobile home hire 250-500 **Facilities:** Wi-fi (charged) Play Area **Services:** **Off-site:** P R

MALLEMORT BOUCHES-DU-RHÔNE

Durance Luberon

Domaine du Vergon, 13370
☎ 490591336
e-mail: duranceluberon@orange.fr
web: www.campingduranceluberon.com
dir: *2.5km on D23c, 200m from canal*

Open: Apr-Sep **Site:** 4.37HEC **Prices:** 21.90 Mobile home hire 480-690 **Facilities:** **Services:** **Leisure:** P **Off-site:** R

MANDELIEU-LA-NAPOULE ALPES-MARITIMES

Cigales

505 av de la Mer, 06210
☎ 493432353 493433045
e-mail: campingcigales@wanadoo.fr
web: www.lescigales.com

A riverside site with well-defined pitches, 0.8km from the sea.

dir: *S on N7.*

Open: All Year. **Site:** 2HEC **Prices:** 31.50-47 Mobile home hire 360-925 **Facilities:** Wi-fi Play Area **Services:** **Leisure:** P **Off-site:** L R S

MARSEILLAN-PLAGE HÉRAULT

Beauregard Plage

250 chemin de l'Airette, 34340
☎ 467771545 467012178
e-mail: campingbeauregardplage@orange.fr
web: www.camping-beauregard-plage.com

A family camping site bordering a sandy beach sheltered by natural sand dunes. High standard sanitary facilities.

Open: 3 Apr-15 Oct **Site:** 3.3HEC **Prices:** 17-31 **Facilities:** Wi-fi Play Area **Services:** **Leisure:** S **Off-site:** L

Créole

74 av des Campings, 34340
☎ 467219269 467265816
e-mail: campinglacreole@wanadoo.fr
web: www.campinglacreole.com

A quiet family site with direct access to a pleasant sandy beach.

GPS: 43.3128, 3.5464

Open: Apr-Oct **Site:** 1.5HEC **Prices:** 13.50-32.50 **Facilities:** Wi-fi (charged) Play Area **Services:** **Leisure:** S **Off-site:**

Languedoc-Camping

117 chemin du Payrollet, 34340
☎ 467219255 467016375

A family site in wooded surroundings with direct access to the beach.

dir: *On coast road between Mediterranean & Bassin de Thau.*

Open: 15 Mar-Oct **Site:** 1.5HEC **Facilities:** **Services:** **Leisure:** S **Off-site:** L P R

FRANCE

'lage

9 chemin du Payrollet, 34340
467219254 467016357
-mail: info@laplage-camping.net
'eb: www.laplage-camping.net
family site with direct access to a sandy beach.
pen: 15 Mar-Oct Site: 1.3HEC Prices: 15-33.50 Mobile ome hire 265-620 Facilities: Wi-fi (charged) Play Area Services: Leisure: S Off-site:

'elloh Village les Méditerranées

v des Campings, 34340
467219449 467218105
-mail: info@nouvelle-floride.com
eb: www.lesmediterranees.com
uiet wooded surroundings with good sanitary facilities, 200m om the beach. The site comprises Charlemagne Zone and ouvelle Floride, with leisure facilities available. Dogs accepted ut restrictions apply.
ir: *Via N112 at Marseillan-Plage.*
pen: 15 Apr-1 Oct Site: 7.5HEC Prices: 15-50 acilities: Wi-fi Kids' Club Play Area ervices: Leisure: P S Off-site:

AUREILLAS PYRÉNÉES-ORIENTALES

al Roma Park

es Thermas du Boulou, 66480
468398813 468398813
mail: valromapark@wanadoo.fr
eb: valromapark.monsite.wanadoo.fr
mainly shaded site, 5km from the border with Spain.
r: *2.5km NE on N9.*
pen: May-Sep Site: 3.5HEC Prices: 14-18.60 obile home hire 200-500 Facilities: Play Area ervices: Leisure: P R Off-site: L

ÉOLANS-REVEL ALPES-DE-HAUTE-PROVENCE

omaine de Loisirs de l'Ubaye

4340
492810196 492819253
mail: info@loisirsubaye.com
eb: www.loisirsubaye.com
large terraced site in a delightful wooded valley. There is a nall lake and direct access to the river and good sports and creational facilities.
r: *7km NW of Barcelonnette.*
PS: 44.3966, 6.5455
pen: 2 Feb-9 Nov Site: 10HEC Prices: 12-22 acilities: Wi-fi Play Area Services: Leisure: L P R

MIRABEL-ET-BLACONS DRÔME

Gervanne Camping

26400
475400020 475400397
e-mail: info@gervanne-camping.com
web: www.gervanne-camping.com
A pleasant family site with scattered shade and plenty of facilities beside the River Drôme. Well located in the heart of the Drôme region, close to the natural park of the Vercors.
dir: *Via D164 Crest-Die.*
Open: Apr-Sep Site: 3.8HEC Prices: 13.70-21 Mobile home hire 287-749 Facilities: Wi-fi Kids' Club Play Area Services: Leisure: P R

MONDRAGON VAUCLUSE

Pinède en Provence

Les Massanes RD 26, 84430
490408298 959921656
e-mail: contact@camping-pinede-provence.com
web: www.camping-pinede-provence.com
Peaceful site with shady pitches located in a pine forest.
dir: *1km SW via N7.*
GPS: 44.2403, 4.7139
Open: All Year. Site: 3.5HEC Prices: 15.60-22.20 Mobile home hire 150-680 Facilities: Wi-fi Kids' Club Play Area Services: Leisure: P Off-site:

MONTBLANC HÉRAULT

Rebau

34290
467985078 467986863
e-mail: gilbert@camping-lerebau.fr
web: www.camping-lerebau.fr
Divided into pitches and surrounded by vineyards.
dir: *N113 from Pézenas to La Bégude de Jordy, onto D18 towards Montblanc for 2km.*
Open: Mar-Oct Site: 3HEC Facilities: Services: Leisure: P Off-site:

FRANCE

Facilities shop shower electric points for razors electric points for caravans parking by tents permitted npulsory separate car park **Services** café/restaurant bar Camping Gaz International gas other than Camping Gaz first aid facilities laundry **Leisure** swimming L-Lake P-Pool R-River S-Sea **Off-site** All facilities within 5km

Villagecenter
Le Coteau de la Marine ****
Direct access to the Verdon gorges
Watersports base at the foot of the campsite
76 places - 177 rental accomodations - 12 ha
04500 MONTAGNAC-MONTPEZAT
+33 (0)4 99 57 21 21 - www.village-center.com/C26

MONTCLAR — AUDE

Domaine d'Arnauteille

11250

☎ 468268453 🖹 468269110

e-mail: info@arnauteille.com

web: www.camping-arnauteille.com

A natural wooded park surrounded by mountains with panoramic views. Well maintained facilities include Roman Bath style aqua-complex with jacuzzi and solarium.

dir: *2.2km SE via D43.*

Open: 9 Apr-25 Sep **Site:** 12HEC **Prices:** 15-36 Mobile home hire 273-763 **Facilities:** Wi-fi Kids' Club Play Area **Services:** **Leisure:** P **Off-site:** R

MONTPELLIER — HÉRAULT

Floréal

rte de la 1ère écluse, 34970

☎ 467929305 🖹 467559244

e-mail: contact@campinglefloreal.com

web: www.campinglefloreal.com

On level ground surrounded by vineyards.

dir: *A9 exit Montpellier-Sud, site 0.5km. From town centre D986 for Palavas.*

Open: Apr-3 Nov **Site:** 1.55HEC **Facilities:** **Services:** **Off-site:** P R

MONTPEZAT — ALPES-DE-HAUTE-PROVENCE

Village Center le Coteau de la Marine

Coteau de la Marine, 04500

☎ 499572121 🖹 467516389

e-mail: contact@village-center.com

web: www.village-center.com/provence-cote-azur/camping-montagne-coteau-marine.php

A pleasant wooded site set within Verdon regional park, providing easy access to the Verdon Gorges and lavender fields of the Valensole.

dir: *Via D11 & D211.*

GPS: 43.7464, 6.1004

Open: 8 Apr-2 Oct **Site:** 12HEC **Prices:** 16-29 Mobile home hire 241-889 **Facilities:** Wi-fi (charged) Kids' Club Play Area **Services:** **Leisure:** P

see advert on this page

MOURIÈS — BOUCHES-DU-RHÔNE

Devenson

13890

☎ 490475201 🖹 490476309

e-mail: camping-devenson@orange.fr

web: www.camping-devenson.com

Terraced site among pine and olive trees in Parc Naturel des Alpilles.

dir: *Off N113 at La Samatane & N towards Mouriès, site in N of village.*

GPS: 43.7011, 4.8578

Open: 30 Apr-15 Sep **Site:** 3.5HEC **Prices:** 18.40 **Facilities:** Play Area **Services:** **Leisure:** P **Off-site:**

MOUSTIERS-STE-MARIE — ALPES-DE-HAUTE-PROVENCE

St-Jean

rte de Riez, quartier St Jean, 04360

☎ 492746685 🖹 492746685

Quiet and relaxing site located at the gateway to the Gorges du Verdon, close to Ste-Croix Lake.

dir: *Via D952.*

GPS: 43.8433, 6.2158

Open: Apr-16 Oct **Site:** 1.6HEC **Prices:** 14.90-16.50 Mobile home hire 290-575 **Facilities:** Wi-fi Play Area **Services:** **Leisure:** R **Off-site:** L P

FRANCE

Vieux Colombier

Quartier St-Michel, 04360
492746189
e-mail: contact@lvcm.fr
web: campinglevieuxcolombier.com

A family site near the entrance to the Gorges du Verdon at an altitude of 630m.

dir: *0.8km S on D952 towards Castellane.*

Open: Apr-Sep **Site:** 2.73HEC **Prices:** 15-16.50 Mobile home hire 298-575 **Facilities:** Wi-fi Play Area **Services:** **Off-site:** L R

MUY, LE — VAR

Cigales

1 chemin de Jas de la Paro, 83490
494451208 494458280
e-mail: contact@camping-les-cigales-sud.fr
web: www.camping-les-cigales-sud.fr

A family site set among Mediterranean vegetation with excellent facilities. Organised entertainment in summer. Kids' club available in July and August.

dir: *A8 exit Draguignan, after toll booth, take 1st rdbt to the left & follow road to the entrance of the site - signed.*

Open: 19 Mar-15 Oct **Site:** 13.5HEC **Prices:** 19.25-35 Mobile home hire 364-868 **Facilities:** Wi-fi Kids' Club Play Area **Services:** **Leisure:** P **Off-site:** R

Domaine de la Noguière

The Camping and Caravanning Club — The Friendly Club

83490
494451378
web: www.rcn-campings.fr/domainedelanoguiere

C&CC Report *A warm welcome awaits you at this friendly campsite just outside the Provençal town of Le Muy. Ideally situated between the sea and the mountains of the Massif de l'Estérel and the Massif des Maures, the site has an impressive view over the Roche de Roquebrune. Children of all ages will enjoy the pool complex complete with water slides, whilst adults will enjoy a relaxing drink in the welcoming bar and restaurant.*

dir: *A8, exit 37 towards Roquebrune sur Argens, then N7 Le Muy.*

Open: 19 Mar-29 Oct **Services/Facilities:** P Play Area Wi-fi **Off-site:** P

NANS-LES-PINS — VAR

Village Club La Sainte Baume

chemin du Camping, quartier Delvieux Sud, 83860
494789268 494786737
e-mail: ste-baume@wanadoo.fr
web: www.saintebaume.com

Located among pine and oak trees, pitches are flat and shaded. Ideal for families with facilities including a pool complex.

dir: *A8 exit 34 towards St Zacharie, then signs for Nans-les-Pins.*

GPS: 43.3769, 5.7881

Open: Apr-Sep **Site:** 8HEC **Prices:** 20-35 Mobile home hire 175-994 **Facilities:** Wi-fi (charged) Kids' Club Play Area **Services:** **Leisure:** P

NARBONNE — AUDE

Camping la Nautique

The Camping and Caravanning Club — The Friendly Club

11100
468904819 468907339
e-mail: info@campinglanautique.com
web: www.campinglanautique.com

Situated on the salt-water Étang de Bages et de Sigean, this site is particularly well-appointed, each pitch having its own washing and toilet facilities. There are good recreational facilities.

C&CC Report *The friendly owners of this well maintained lakeside site are keen to welcome you. The individual sanitary blocks on each pitch, which can take the largest of units, are a definite plus. Day trips to Cathar country will definitely include a trip to the Corbières and Minervois vineyards. The medieval fortified town of Carcassonne is also worth the trip.*

dir: *A9 exit Narbonne Sud.*

GPS: 43.1472, 3.0039

Open: 15 Feb-15 Nov **Site:** 16HEC **Prices:** 19.50-42 Mobile home hire 238-840 **Facilities:** Wi-fi Kids' Club Play Area **Services:** **Leisure:** P **Off-site:** L

NARBONNE-PLAGE — AUDE

CM Falaise

av des Vacances, 11100
468498077 468751200
web: www.campinglafalaise.com

On level ground at the foot of the Massif of the Calpe with modern facilities.

dir: *W of Narbonne Plage, 400m from beach.*

Open: Apr-22 Sep **Site:** 8HEC **Facilities:** **Services:** **Off-site:** S

FRANCE

Facilities shop shower electric points for razors electric points for caravans parking by tents permitted compulsory separate car park **Services** café/restaurant bar Camping Gaz International gas other than Camping Gaz first aid facilities laundry **Leisure** swimming L-Lake P-Pool R-River S-Sea **Off-site** All facilities within 5km

NÉBIAS AUDE

Fontaulié-Sud

11500
468201762
e-mail: lefontauliesud@free.fr
web: www.fontauliesud.com
A beautiful setting in the heart of the Cathar region.
dir: *0.6km S via D117.*
Open: Jun-15 Sep **Site:** 4HEC **Prices:** 16-18 Mobile home hire 270-520 **Facilities:** Play Area **Services:** **Leisure:** P **Off-site:** L R

NÎMES GARD

Domaine de la Bastide

rte de Generac, 30900
466620582 466620583
e-mail: immocamp@wanadoo.fr
web: www.camping-nimes.com
A rural setting with excellent facilities.
dir: *5km S of town centre on D13. A9 exit Nîmes-Ouest.*
Open: All Year. **Site:** 5HEC **Facilities:** **Services:** **Off-site:** L P

OLLIÈRES-SUR-EYRIEUX, LES ARDÈCHE

Domaine des Plantas

07360
475662153 475662365
e-mail: plantas.ardeche@wanadoo.fr
web: www.camping-franceloc.fr
Games room, disco and other leisure activities.
Open: 5 Apr-4 Oct **Site:** 10HEC **Facilities:** **Services:** **Leisure:** P R

ORAISON ALPES-DE-HAUTE-PROVENCE

Camping les Oliviers

chemin St Sauveur, 04700
492787000
e-mail: camping-oraison@wanadoo.fr
web: www.camping-oraison.com
Spacious, flat pitches amongst olive trees. Entertainment throughout the day in high season. During July and August, a bar, café, restaurant and kids' club are available.
GPS: 43.9232, 5.9246
Open: Apr-Sep **Site:** 2HEC **Prices:** 13-16 Mobile home hire 250-580 **Facilities:** Wi-fi Kids' Club Play Area **Services:** **Leisure:** P **Off-site:** L R

ORANGE VAUCLUSE

Jonquier

1321 r Alexis-Carrel, 84100
490344948 490511697
e-mail: info@campinglejonquier.com
web: www.campinglejonquier.com
dir: *On NW outskirts.*
Open: Apr-Sep **Site:** 2HEC **Facilities:** **Services:** **Leisure:** P **Off-site:** R

PALAU DEL VIDRE PYRÉNÉES-ORIENTALES

Haras

The Camping and Caravanning Club The Friendly Club

66690
468221450 468379893
e-mail: haras8@wanadoo.fr
web: www.camping-le-haras.com
C&CC Report *A delightful little site in this very popular area, away from the hurly-burly of the coast, run by the welcoming Gil family. Luxuriant plant and tree life abound on site. Nearby, in the small town of Palau you can watch glassmakers at work. Car excursions take you to the beaches of the Roussillon coast, its vineyards, the Albères massif, Andorra, Spain and all that Catalan France has to offer.*
dir: *A9, exit Perpignan Sud, then RN114 towards Argelès-Sur-Mer. Exit 9 for Palau del Vidre, site on left before village.*
Open: 20 Mar-20 Oct **Site:** 4.5HEC **Facilities:** **Services:** **Leisure:** P **Off-site:**

PEYREMALE-SUR-CÈZE GARD

Drouilhédes

30160
466250480 466251095
e-mail: info@campingcevennes.com
web: www.campingcevennes.com
A beautiful location beside the River Cèze surrounded by acacia trees
dir: *Via A6 & D17.*
Open: Apr-Sep **Site:** 2HEC **Prices:** 15-24.50 **Facilities:** Wi-fi Play Area **Services:** **Leisure:** R **Off-site:**

PONT-D'HÉRAULT GARD

Magnanarelles

Le Rey, 30570
467824013 467825061
e-mail: info@maxfrance.com
web: www.maxfrance.com
A pleasant mountain setting with well-defined pitches.
dir: *0.3km W via D999, beside river.*
Open: All Year. **Site:** 2HEC **Facilities:** **Services:** **Leisure:** P R

FRANCE

Site 6HEC (site size) grass sand stone little shade partly shaded mainly shaded bungalows for hire (static) caravans for hire tents for hire no dogs site fully accessible for wheelchairs
Prices amount quoted is per night, for 2 adults and car, plus tent or caravan. Mobile home hire is a weekly rate.

PORT-GRIMAUD VAR

Camping de la Plage

83310
☎ 494563115 📠 494564961
e-mail: campingplagegrimaud@wanadoo.fr
web: www.camping-de-la-plage.fr

Wide area of land on both sides of road beside sea. Partly terraced and divided into pitches.

dir: *N on N98.*

Open: 27 Mar-11 Oct **Site:** 18HEC **Facilities:** Wi-fi (charged) Play Area **Services:** **Leisure:** S **Off-site:** P

Club Holiday Marina

The Camping and Caravanning Club The Friendly Club

Le Ginestrel, 83310
☎ 494560843 📠 494562388
e-mail: info@holiday-marina.com
web: www.holiday-marina.com

Located close to beaches with diving tuition available. Kids' club in July and August.

C&CC Report *A great location near the Gulf of St. Tropez, with trendy, chic coastal resorts and exclusive hilltop villages within easy reach. Relaxing site facilities and the innovative private bathrooms make this a very comfortable and good quality site.*

dir: *On N98.*

Open: Mar-Dec **Site:** 3.5HEC **Facilities:** Wi-fi (charged) Kids' Club Play Area **Services:** **Leisure:** P **Off-site:** S

Domaine des Naiades

St-Pons-les-Mûres, 83310
☎ 494556780 📠 494556781
e-mail: info@lesnaiades.com
web: www.lesnaiades.com

Site on hilly land with terraces divided into pitches and with many modern facilities. A kids' club is available mid June to August.

dir: *N98 onto D244, turn right & continue uphill.*

Open: 9 Apr-5 Nov **Site:** 27HEC **Prices:** 26.20-53.20 Mobile home hire 343-1540 **Facilities:** Wi-fi (charged) Kids' Club Play Area **Services:** **Leisure:** P **Off-site:** S

PORTIRAGNES-PLAGE HÉRAULT

Camping Les Mimosas

34420
☎ 467909292 📠 467908539
e-mail: les.mimosas.portiragnes@wanadoo.fr
web: www.mimosas.com

A well-equipped family site located in a leisure park on the banks of the Canal du Midi, 1.3km from the sea.

dir: *A9 exit Béziers Centre direction of airport Béziers/Cap d'Agde, N112 & D37 towards coast.*

Open: Jun-4 Sep **Site:** 7HEC **Prices:** 22-40 Mobile home hire 217-1330 **Facilities:** Wi-fi (charged) Kids' Club Play Area **Services:** **Leisure:** P R **Off-site:** S

Sablons

rte de Portiragnes, 34420
☎ 467909055 📠 467908291
e-mail: contact@les-sablons.com
web: les-sablons.com

Large site subdivided into fields by fences. Beside beach. Night club and disco.

dir: *0.5km N on D37.*

Open: Apr-Sep **Site:** 15HEC **Facilities:** **Services:** **Leisure:** P S

PRADET, LE VAR

Mauvallon

chemin de la Gavaresse, 83220
☎ 494213173

A well-kept site divided into pitches among young trees.

dir: *Off N559 in Le Pradet onto D86 for 2.5km towards sea.*

Open: 15 Jun-15 Sep **Site:** 1.2HEC **Facilities:** **Services:** **Off-site:** S

PRAMOUSQUIER VAR

Pramousquier

83980
☎ 494058395 📠 494057504
e-mail: camping-lavandou@wanadoo.fr
web: www.campingpramousquier.com

A terraced site set in a wooded park 400m from a fine sandy beach. Good recreational facilities.

dir: *2km E via D559.*

Open: May-Sep **Site:** 3HEC **Facilities:** **Services:** **Off-site:** S

FRANCE

PRIVAS — ARDÈCHE

Ardeche

rte de Montélimar, 07000
475640580 475645968
e-mail: jcray@wanadoo.fr
web: www.ardechecamping.fr

A comfortable site with good facilities in the heart of the Ardèche region.

Open: Apr-Sep **Site:** 5.5HEC **Facilities:** **Services:** **Leisure:** P R **Off-site:** P

PUGET-SUR-ARGENS — VAR

Aubrèdes

408 chemin des Aubrèdes, 83480
494455146 494452892
e-mail: campingaubredes@wanadoo.fr
web: campingaubredes.com

Situated on undulating meadowland surrounded by pine trees with modern facilities.

dir: *A8 exit Puget-sur-Argens, site 0.85km.*

Open: 8 May-12 Sep **Site:** 3.8HEC **Facilities:** **Services:** **Leisure:** P

Bastiane

1056, chemin des Suvières, 83480
494555594 494555593
e-mail: info@labastiane.com
web: www.labastiane.com

Hilly site divided into numbered pitches in a pine and oak wood. Individual washing cubicles. Separate car park for arrivals after 23.00hrs. Kids' club in July and August.

dir: *Via A8 exit 37.*

GPS: 43.4685, 6.6765

Open: Apr-25 Oct **Site:** 3.05HEC **Prices:** 20.40-41.40 Mobile home hire 259-798 **Facilities:** Wi-fi (charged) Kids' Club Play Area **Services:** **Leisure:** P **Off-site:** L

QUINSON — ALPES-DE-HAUTE-PROVENCE

Village Center les Prés du Verdon

04500
499572121 467516389
e-mail: contact@village-center.com
web: www.village-center.com/provence-cote-azur/camping-montagne-pres-verdon.php

Ideal for exploring the Verdon gorges, the site has many leisure facilities with a nearby water sports centre offering canoeing and kayaking.

GPS: 43.6969, 6.0415

Open: 8 Apr-2 Oct **Site:** 3.5HEC **Prices:** 14-18 Mobile home hire 216-637 **Facilities:** Kids' Club Play Area **Services:** **Leisure:** P **Off-site:**

RACOU, LE — PYRÉNÉES-ORIENTALES

Bois de Valmarie

66700
468810992 468958058
e-mail: contact@camping-lasirene.fr
web: www.camping-lasirene.fr

A family site with plentiful recreational facilities.

dir: *N114 exit Perpignan Sud.*

Open: 22 Apr-24 Sep **Site:** 7HEC **Prices:** 23-40 Mobile home hire 238-1505 **Facilities:** Wi-fi Play Area **Services:** **Leisure:** P S **Off-site:**

RAMATUELLE — VAR

Yelloh Village Tournels

rte de Camarat, 83350
494559090 494559099
e-mail: info@tournels.com
web: www.tournels.com

Lovely views to Pampelonne Bay from part of this site. 1km to beach. Swimming pool area includes lazy river, slides and a children's pool.

dir: *Off D93 Croix-Valmer to St-Tropez, signs to Cap Camarat.*

GPS: 43.2058, 6.6507

Open: Apr-9 Jan **Site:** 20HEC **Prices:** 15-57 **Facilities:** Wi-fi (charged) Kids' Club Play Area **Services:** **Leisure:** P **Off-site:** S

see advert on opposite page

REMOULINS — GARD

Soubeyranne

rte de Beaucaire, 30210
466370321 466371465
e-mail: soubeyranne@franceloc.fr
web: www.soubeyranne.com

A picturesque location close to the River Gard with modern facilities.

dir: *S on D986.*

Open: Apr-23 Sep **Site:** 6HEC **Facilities:** **Services:** **Leisure:** P **Off-site:** R

FRANCE

Site 6HEC (site size) grass sand stone little shade partly shaded mainly shaded bungalows for hire (static) caravans for hire tents for hire no dogs site fully accessible for wheelchairs
Prices amount quoted is per night, for 2 adults and car, plus tent or caravan. Mobile home hire is a weekly rate.

Sousta

v du Pont-du-Gard, 30210
466371280 466372369
-mail: info@lasousta.fr
veb: www.lasousta.com
Picturesque forest site with access to the river, a short distance rom the Pont du Gard.

lir: *2km NW. A9 exit for Remoulins, right after bridge towards Pont de Gard.*

pen: Mar-Oct **Site:** 14HEC **Prices:** 13.90-23.90 **acilities:** Wi-fi Play Area **Services:** **Leisure:** P R

REVENS — GARD

Lou Triadou

Le Bourg, 30750
467827358
-mail: lou.triadou@wanadoo.fr
veb: site.voila.fr/camping_lou_triadou
. well-equipped site in the heart of the Causse Noir.

ir: *Via D159/D151.*

pen: 15 Mar-1 Sep **Site:** 0.78HEC **Prices:** 10 lobile home hire 200-300 **Facilities:** **Services:** **Leisure:** P

RIA — PYRÉNÉES-ORIENTALES

Bellevue

18 r Bellevue, 66500
468964896
e-mail: camping.bellevue@free.fr
web: www.camping-bellevue-riasirach.com
Beautifully terraced site beside a former vineyard. Very well-kept.

dir: *2km S on N116, onto road to Sirach, turn right for 0.6km up driveway.*

Open: 9 Apr-15 Oct **Site:** 2.5HEC **Prices:** 16.90 Mobile home hire 240-450 **Facilities:** Wi-fi Play Area **Services:** **Leisure:** P **Off-site:** L P R

ROQUEBRUNE-SUR-ARGENS — VAR

Domaine de la Bergerie

Valleé du Fournel, 83520
498114545 498114546
e-mail: info@domainelabergerie.com
web: www.domainelabergerie.com
A large, well-run family site set in pleasant Provençal countryside with fine recreational facilities.

dir: *A8 exit Le Muy, onto N7 & D7.*

Open: 23 Apr-Sep **Site:** 60HEC **Prices:** 20.50-49 **Facilities:** Wi-fi Kids' Club Play Area **Services:** **Leisure:** L P

FRANCE

Lei Suves

Quartier du Blavet, 83520
☎ 494454395 🖷 494816313
e-mail: camping.lei.suves@wanadoo.fr
web: www.lei-suves.com

Set in a picturesque forested area with good recreational facilities.

dir: *4km N via N7.*

GPS: 43.4778, 6.6389

Open: 2 Apr-15 Oct **Site:** 7.4HEC **Prices:** 21-40 Mobile home hire 340-910 **Facilities:** Wi-fi (charged) Kids' Club Play Area ℗ **Services:** **Leisure:** P **Off-site:** L

see advert on this page

Pêcheurs

83520
☎ 494457125 🖷 494816513
e-mail: info@camping-les-pecheurs.com
web: www.camping-les-pecheurs.com

A pleasant site with direct access to the river in a wooded location at the foot of the Roquebrune crag. Kids' club available mid June until end of August.

dir: *0.5km NW via D7, near lake.*

Open: Apr-Sep **Site:** 5HEC **Prices:** 17.50-39.50 Mobile home hire 450-1085 **Facilities:** Wi-fi (charged) Kids' Club Play Area ℗ ♿ **Services:** **Leisure:** L P R

ROQUE-D'ANTHÉRON, LA — BOUCHES-DU-RHÔNE

Silvacane

av de la Libération, 13640
☎ 499572121
e-mail: contact@village-center.com
web: www.silvacane-en-provence.com

Level gravelled ground with pitches of 100 sq m. Water-sports centre and stables nearby. Site in wood on slopes of hill.

Open: 16 Jun-2 Sep **Site:** 6HEC **Facilities:** ℗ **Services:** **Leisure:** P R **Off-site:** L R

Village Center le Domaine des Iscles

Le Plan d'Eau, 13640
☎ 499572121 🖷 467516389
e-mail: contact@village-center.com
web: www.village-center.com/provence-cote-azur/camping-campagne-les-iscles.php

On the banks of the River Durance.

dir: *A7 exit 26 (Sénas) towards Aix en Provence. At Pont Royal rdbt, exit towards Charleval, then La Roque d'Anthéron on D561.*

GPS: 43.7282, 5.3210

Open: 8 Apr-2 Oct **Site:** 10HEC **Prices:** 16-28 Mobile home hire 216-917 **Facilities:** Wi-fi (charged) Kids' Club Play Area ℗ **Services:** **Leisure:** L P

see advert on opposite pag

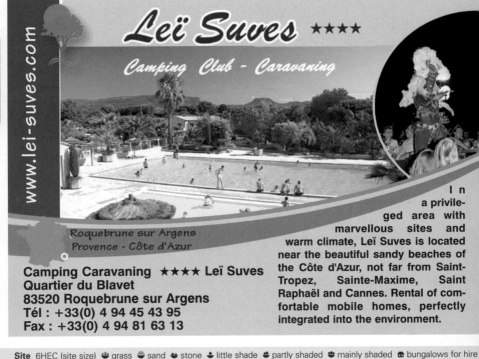

FRANCE

ROQUETTE-SUR-SIAGNE, LA ALPES-MARITIMES

Panoramic

1630 av de la République, Quartier St-Jean, 06550
☎ 492190777 🖷 492190777
e-mail: campingpanoramic@wanadoo.fr
web: www.campingpanoramic.fr

In the centre of a holiday resort, a well-equipped, modern site in a wooded location with shaded terraces, affording magnificent views of the surrounding hills.

dir: *N of village off D9.*

Open: All Year. **Site:** 1HEC **Prices:** 23-26 Mobile home hire 450-700 **Facilities:** Wi-fi (charged) Play Area **Services:** **Leisure:** P **Off-site:** R S

SAILLAGOUSE PYRÉNÉES-ORIENTALES

Cerdan

11 rte d'Estavar, 66800
☎ 468047046
e-mail: lecerdan@lecerdan.com
web: www.lecerdan.com

Picturesque setting in meadow with some terraces. Hot meals served during peak season.

dir: *Via N116.*

Open: Nov-Sep **Site:** 2.8HEC **Prices:** 12-13 Mobile home hire 300-600 **Facilities:** Wi-fi (charged) Play Area **Services:** **Off-site:** P R

ST-ALBAN-AURIOLLES ARDÈCHE

Ranc Davaine

07120
☎ 475396055 🖷 475393850
e-mail: camping.ranc.davaine@wanadoo.fr
web: www.camping-ranc-davaine.fr

Well-equipped, mainly level site with direct access to the River Chassezac and a variety of entertainment facilities.

dir: *2.3km SW via D58.*

Open: Apr-12 Sep **Site:** 13HEC **Facilities:** **Services:** **Leisure:** P R

ST-AMBROIX GARD

Beau-Rivage

Le Moulinet, 30500
☎ 466241017
e-mail: marc@camping-beau-rivage.fr
web: www.camping-beau-rivage.fr

A good location between the sea and the Cevennes mountains, set beside the River Cèze.

dir: *3.5km SE on D37.*

GPS: 44.2374, 4.2019

Open: Apr-Sep **Site:** 3.5HEC **Prices:** 24 **Facilities:** Wi-fi **Services:** **Leisure:** R **Off-site:**

Clos

30500
☎ 466241008 🖷 466602562
e-mail: campingleclos@wanadoo.fr
web: www.camping-saint-ambroix.fr

A quiet site in a pleasant setting beside the River Cèze with modern facilities.

dir: *Off Church Square.*

Open: Apr-Oct **Site:** 1.8HEC **Prices:** 8.50-17.50 Mobile home hire 210-700 **Facilities:** **Services:** **Leisure:** P R **Off-site:** L

ST-AYGULF VAR

Paradis des Campeurs

La Gaillarde Plage, 83380
☎ 494969355 🖷 494496299
web: www.paradis-des-campeurs.com

A quiet family site in a picturesque location with direct access to the beach.

dir: *2.5km towards Gaillarde-Plage between St-Aygulf & Ste-Maxime.*

Open: 29 Mar-16 Oct **Site:** 3.7HEC **Facilities:** **Services:** **Leisure:** S

FRANCE

Pont d'Argens

RN98, 83370
494511497 494512944
e-mail: campinglepontdargens@yahoo.fr
web: www.camping-caravaning-lepontdargens.com

A pleasant site with good facilities beside the river and sea.

Open: Apr-15 Oct **Site:** 7HEC **Prices:** 20-33 Mobile home hire 400-1000 **Facilities:** Wi-fi (charged) Kids' Club Play Area **Services:** **Leisure:** P R S

see advert on this page

St-Aygulf Plage

270 av Salvarelli, 83370
494176249 494810316
e-mail: info@camping-cote-azur.com
web: www.camping-cote-azur.com

A well-equipped family site in wooded surroundings with direct access to the beach.

dir: *Inland from N98 at Km881.3 N of town.*

Open: Apr-Oct **Site:** 22HEC **Facilities:** **Services:** **Leisure:** S

ST-CHAMAS — BOUCHES-DU-RHÔNE

Canet Plage

13250
490509689 490508751
e-mail: info@camping-lecanet.fr
web: www.camping-lecanet.fr

A well-equipped site beside the Étang de Berre with a range of recreational facilities.

dir: *On D10, S of Salon-de-Provence towards La Fare les Oliviers.*

Open: All Year. **Site:** 3HEC **Facilities:** **Services:** **Leisure:** L P **Off-site:**

ST-CYPRIEN — PYRÉNÉES-ORIENTALES

Cala Gogo

The Camping and Caravanning Club — The Friendly Club

av Armand Lanoux, Les Capellans, 66750
468210712 468210219
e-mail: camping.calagogo@wanadoo.fr
web: www.campmed.com

C&CC Report *The superb beach-side location of this lively camp site is complemented by the excellent range of modern facilities. It is very rare to find such large pitches so close to the beach on the Mediterranean coast. Located near the foothills of the Pyrénées, there is much to see in this Catalan part of France. The Aqualand Water park will be an attraction for children both young and old.*

dir: *4km S towards Les Capellans.*

GPS: 42.5994, 3.0373

Open: 14 May-17 Sep **Site:** 12HEC **Prices:** 22.93-35.30 Mobile home hire 273-840 **Facilities:** Wi-fi Play Area **Services:** **Leisure:** P S

Roussillon

Cami de la Mar, 66750
468210645 251339404
e-mail: contact@chadotel.com
web: www.chadotel.com

Close to the Spanish border, flanked on one side by the Mediterranean sea and on the other by the Pyrénées. Leisure facilities available along with a programme of entertainment.

GPS: 42.6188, 3.0160

Open: Apr-Sep **Site:** 3.05HEC **Prices:** 14-26.40 Mobile home hire 199-870 **Facilities:** Wi-fi (charged) Play Area **Services:** **Leisure:** P **Off-site:** S

ST-CYR-SUR-MER — VAR

Clos Ste-Thérèse

rte de Bandol, 83270
494321221 494322962
e-mail: camping@clos-therese.com
web: www.clos-therese.com

Located within an area of vineyards overlooking the sea. A well-shaded family site with well-defined pitches on terraces.

dir: *Autoroute A50.*

Open: Apr-Sep **Site:** 4HEC **Prices:** 16-23 Mobile home hire 215-820 **Facilities:** Wi-fi (charged) Play Area **Services:** **Leisure:** P **Off-site:** S

ST-JEAN-LE-CENTENIER ARDÈCHE

Camping les Arches

rte de Mirabel, 07580

475367545 475367545

e-mail: info@camping-les-arches.com

web: www.camping-les-arches.com

A family site in a wooded location with direct access to the river. Activities for children.

dir: *A7 exit Montélimar Nord, N102 to Mirabel, onto D458 for 0.5km.*

Open: 29 Apr-18 Sep **Site:** 4HEC **Prices:** 13.78-20.78 Mobile home hire 230-620 **Facilities:** Wi-fi Kids' Club Play Area **Services:** **Leisure:** R **Off-site:**

ST-JEAN-PLA-DE-CORTS PYRÉNÉES-ORIENTALES

Casteillets

66490

468832683 468833967

e-mail: jc@campinglescasteillets.com

web: www.campinglescasteillets.com

A family site between the sea and the mountains close to the River Tech.

dir: *A9 exit le Boulu.*

Open: All Year. **Site:** 5HEC **Prices:** 10.90-18.50 Mobile home hire 270-715 **Facilities:** Wi-fi (charged) Kids' Club Play Area **Services:** **Leisure:** P **Off-site:** L R

ST-JULIEN-DE-LA-NEF GARD

Isis en Cevennes

Domaine de St-Julien, 30440

467738028 467738848

e-mail: aa@isisencevennes.com

web: www.isisencevennes.fr

Set in wooded surroundings with direct access to the River Hérault. Plenty of sports facilities.

dir: *5km from Ganges towards Le Vigan.*

Open: Mar-Oct **Site:** 14HEC **Facilities:** **Services:** **Leisure:** P R

ST-LAURENT-DU-VAR ALPES-MARITIMES

Magali

1814 rte de la Baronne, 06700

493315700 492120133

e-mail: contact@camping-magali.com

web: www.camping-magali.com

A family site on level meadowland, surrounded by trees and bushes at the foot of the southern Alps.

dir: *A8 exit St-Laurent-du-Var, cross industrial zone turn left, after 100m turn right, site in 2km.*

Open: Feb-Oct **Site:** 1.2HEC **Prices:** 17-22.50 **Facilities:** Wi-fi **Services:** **Leisure:** P **Off-site:**

ST-MARTIN-D'ARDÈCHE ARDÈCHE

Indigo le Moulin

07700

475046620 475046012

e-mail: moulin@camping-indigo.com

web: www.camping-indigo.com

Site bordering the Ardèche river, with its own beach. Shady, spacious pitches are available. During the summer months, sports tournaments take place. Kids' club takes place in July and August. 1 dog per pitch.

dir: *A7 exit Bollene, then Pont St Esprit. Follow Gorges de l'Ardèche signs.*

Open: 22 Apr-2 Oct **Site:** 7HEC **Prices:** 14-20.10 Mobile home hire 264.60-630 **Facilities:** Kids' Club Play Area **Services:** **Leisure:** P R **Off-site:**

ST-MAXIMIN-LA-STE-BAUME VAR

Provençal

rte de Mazaugues, 83470

494781697

web: www.camping-le-provencal.com

A family site in wooded surroundings with plenty of recreational facilties. Bar, café and swimming pool only open July and August.

dir: *2.5km S via D64.*

Open: Apr-Sep **Site:** 5HEC **Prices:** 14.50-18.30 Mobile home hire 225-650 **Facilities:** Play Area **Services:** **Leisure:** P **Off-site:**

FRANCE

ST-PAUL-EN-FORÊT — VAR

Parc

83440
☎ 494761535 🖷 494847184
e-mail: campingleparc@wanadoo.fr
web: www.campingleparc.com
Quiet, fairly isolated site surrounded by woodland.

dir: *3km N on D4.*

Open: Apr-Sep **Site:** 3.1HEC **Facilities:** **Services:** **Leisure:** P
Off-site: L

ST-RAPHAËL — VAR

Dramont

83700
☎ 494820768 🖷 494827530
Located in a pine forest with direct access to the beach and modern facilities.

dir: *Via N98 at St-Raphaël, between Boulouris & Agay.*

Open: 15 Mar-15 Oct **Site:** 6.5HEC **Facilities:** **Services:** **Leisure:** S

ST-RÉMY-DE-PROVENCE — BOUCHES-DU-RHÔNE

Camping du Mas de Nicolas

av Plaisance du Touch, 13210
☎ 490922705 🖷 490923683
e-mail: camping-masdenicolas@nerim.fr
Close to the centre of St-Rémy-de-Provence, this secure site has a swimming pool with spa and fitness room.

Open: Mar-Oct **Site:** 3HEC **Prices:** 14.50-21.50 Mobile home hire 270-710 **Facilities:** Wi-fi Kids' Club Play Area **Services:** **Leisure:** P
Off-site: L

Monplaisir

chemin Monplaisir, 13210
☎ 490922270 🖷 490921857
e-mail: reception@camping-monplaisir.fr
web: www.camping-monplaisir.fr
Located in the middle of Alpilles Natural Regional Park, pitches are shady and screened with hedges. A bar and kids' club are available in July and August.

Open: 6 Mar-Oct **Site:** 2.8HEC **Facilities:** Wi-fi Kids' Club Play Area **Services:**
Leisure: P

Pégomas

av Jean Moulin, 13210
☎ 490920121 🖷 490920121
e-mail: contact@campingpegomas.com
web: www.campingpegomas.com
Well-tended grassland with trees and bushes. Divided into several fields by high cedars providing shade. Within easy walking distance to town centre.

dir: *0.5km E of village, signed.*

GPS: 43.7892, 4.8417

Open: 12 Mar-29 Oct **Site:** 2HEC **Prices:** 15-23 Mobile home hire 200-500 **Facilities:** Wi-fi Play Area **Services:** **Leisure:** P **Off-site:** L

ST-ROMAIN-EN-VIENNOIS — VAUCLUSE

Soleil de Provence

rte de Nyons, 84110
☎ 490464600 🖷 490464037
e-mail: info@camping-soleil-de-provence.fr
web: www.camping-soleil-de-provence.fr
Peaceful site on an uphill meadow 12km from the foot of Mont Ventoux, with superb views of the surrounding mountains. Large swimming pool with an island and palm trees.

dir: *4km from Vaison-la-Romaine.*

Open: 15 Mar-Oct **Site:** 5HEC **Facilities:** **Services:** **Leisure:** P

ST-SAUVEUR-DE-MONTAGUT — ARDÈCHE

Ardechois

Le Chambon, Gluiras, 07190
☎ 475666187 🖷 475666367
e-mail: ardechois.camping@wanadoo.fr
web: www.ardechois-camping.fr
Set in the grounds of a restored 18th-century farm in rolling countryside. Fine views of the surrounding hills.

dir: *8.5km W on D102, beside River Gluèyre.*

Open: 24 Apr-Sep **Site:** 5.5HEC **Facilities:** **Services:** **Leisure:** P R

ST-SORLIN-EN-VALLOIRE — DRÔME

Château de la Pérouze

26210
☎ 475317021 🖷 475317575
A well-appointed family site with a variety of recreational facilities.

dir: *2.5km SE via D1.*

Open: 15 Jun-15 Sep **Site:** 14HEC **Facilities:** **Services:** **Leisure:** L P

ST-THIBÉRY HÉRAULT

Pin Parasol

Le Causse, 34630
467778429 467778429
e-mail: campsite-pin-parasol@wanadoo.fr
web: www.campinglepinparasol.com
Pleasant wooded surroundings 1km from the River Hérault.
dir: *A9 exit Agde-Pézenas.*
Open: Jun-Sep **Site:** 2.7HEC **Facilities:**
Services: **Leisure:** P **Off-site:** R

ST-VALLIER-DE-THIEY ALPES-MARITIMES

Parc des Arboins

06460
493426389
Pleasantly terraced site on a hillside with some oak trees.
dir: *Off N85 at KmV36.*
Open: All Year. **Site:** 4HEC **Prices:** 18.10-22.60
Mobile home hire 238-523 **Facilities:** Play Area
Services: **Leisure:** P **Off-site:** R

STES-MARIES-DE-LA-MER BOUCHES-DU-RHÔNE

Clos-du-Rhône

BP 74, 13460
490978599 490977885
e-mail: info@camping-leclos.fr
web: www.camping-leclos.fr
A family site with direct access to the sea. Kids' club available in July and August.
dir: *2km W via D38, near beach.*
Open: Apr-5 Nov **Site:** 7HEC **Prices:** 14-24
Mobile home hire 317-944 **Facilities:** Kids' Club
Services: **Leisure:** P R S

CM Brise

13460
490978467 490977201
e-mail: info@camping-labrise.fr
web: www.camping-labrise.fr
A well-equipped family site with direct access to the beach, situated in the heart of the Camargue. Modern sanitary blocks and facilities for a variety of sports. Kids' club available in July and August.
dir: *NE on D85A towards beach.*
Open: 15 Dec-15 Nov **Site:** 19HEC **Prices:** 13-21
Mobile home hire 309-750 **Facilities:** Kids' Club
Services: **Leisure:** P S **Off-site:** R

SALAVAS ARDÈCHE

Chauvieux

40 chemin de la Plage, 07150
475880537 475880537
e-mail: camping.chauvieux@wanadoo.fr
web: www.camping-le-chauvieux.com
A popular site in a wooded location close to the River Ardèche with plenty of recreational facilities.
dir: *NE off D579.*
Open: 29 Apr-12 Sep **Site:** 2.3HEC
Prices: 14.90-22.90 Mobile home hire 309-645 **Facilities:** Wi-fi (charged) Play Area **Services:**
Leisure: P R

SALERNES VAR

Arnauds

Quartier des Arnauds, 83690
494675195 494707557
e-mail: lesarnauds@ville-salernes.fr
web: www.village-vacances-lesarnauds.com
Level site alongside a river and a lake.
dir: *Via D560 just beyond village.*
Open: 2 May-Sep **Site:** 3HEC **Prices:** 19.50-25.95
Facilities: Wi-fi (charged) Play Area **Services:**
Leisure: R **Off-site:**

SALINS-D'HYÈRES, LES VAR

Port Pothuau

101 chemin les Ourledes, 83400
494664117 494663309
e-mail: pothuau@free.fr
web: www.campingportpothuau.com
A peaceful holiday village, completely divided into pitches with good leisure facilities.
dir: *6km E of Hyères on N98 & D12.*
Open: 4 Apr-19 Oct **Site:** 6HEC **Facilities:**
Services: **Leisure:** P **Off-site:** R S

SALON-DE-PROVENCE BOUCHES-DU-RHÔNE

Nostradamus

rte d'Eyguières, 13300
490560836 490562341
e-mail: gilles.nostra@gmail.com
web: www.camping-nostradamus.com
Pleasant wooded surroundings with good sports facilities.
dir: *5km W on D17 towards Eyguières & Arles.*
Open: Mar-Oct **Site:** 2.2HEC **Prices:** 16-20 Mobile home hire 310-742 **Facilities:** Wi-fi (charged)
Play Area **Services:** **Leisure:** P R
Off-site:

FRANCE

SALVETAT, LA — HÉRAULT

Goudal

rte de Lacaune, 34330
467976044 467976268
e-mail: info@goudal.com
web: www.goudal.com
A natural mountain setting within the Haut Languedoc park.
dir: *Via D907.*
Open: May-Sep **Site:** 5HEC **Facilities:** **Services:** **Leisure:** L **Off-site:** R

SAMPZON — ARDÈCHE

Aloha-Plage

07120
608988503 475891026
e-mail: reception@camping-aloha-plage.fr
web: www.camping-aloha-plage.fr
A fine location beside the River Ardèche, midway between Ruoms and Vallon-Pont-d'Arc. The site has two private swimming pools.
dir: *50m from river.*
Open: Apr-20 Sep **Site:** 3HEC **Facilities:** **Services:** **Leisure:** P R **Off-site:**

Bastide en Ardèche

The Camping and Caravanning Club — The Friendly Club

07120
475396472 475397328
e-mail: info@rcn-labastideardeche.fr
web: www.rcn-campings.fr
Well-equipped family site in a pleasant wooded location.
C&CC Report *A top quality site, with excellent facilities in the heart of one of France's most beautiful and renowned areas, in a great position on the river Ardèche at the foot of Sampzon castle. Good for young families with its lovely pool, for walking in stunning countryside or for just relaxing amid outstanding scenery.*
dir: *4km SW on the banks of the Ardèche.*
Open: 16 Apr-8 Oct **Site:** 7HEC **Facilities:** **Services:** **Leisure:** P R

Riviera

07120
475396757 475939557
e-mail: leriviera@wanadoo.fr
web: www.campingleriviera.com
Located on the banks of the Ardèche river, just a short distance from the Pont d'Arc.
dir: *From Valence exit autoroute at Montelimar Nord for Le Teil/ Ruoms/Sampzon.*
Open: Apr-Sep **Site:** 6HEC **Facilities:** **Services:** **Leisure:** P R **Off-site:**

Soleil Vivarais

07120
475396756 475396469
e-mail: info@soleil-vivarais.com
web: www.soleil-vivarais.com
An exceptionally well-appointed, terraced site surrounded by the imposing scenery of the Ardèche Gorge. An excellent canoeing centre with opportunities for outdoor and water activities, and regular organised entertainment.
dir: *D579 from Vallon towards Ruoms for 5km & over River Ardèche.*
GPS: 44.4292, 4.3553
Open: 15 Apr-11 Sep **Site:** 12HEC **Prices:** 15-44 **Facilities:** Wi-fi Kids' Club **Services:** **Leisure:** P R **Off-site:** S

SANARY-SUR-MER — VAR

Pierredon

652 chemin Raoul Coletta, 83110
494742502 494746142
e-mail: pierredon@campasun.com
web: www.campasun.com
A well-equipped, wooded site providing a variety of family entertainment, 3km from the sea.
dir: *A50 exit Bandol or Sanary.*
Open: 5 Apr-15 Sep **Site:** 4HEC **Facilities:** **Services:** **Leisure:** P **Off-site:**

SAUVIAN — HÉRAULT

Gabinelle

34410
467395087
e-mail: info@lagabinelle.com
web: www.lagabinelle.com
A modern site in pleasant wooded surroundings with good facilities.
dir: *D19 from Sauvian towards Valras Plage.*
Open: 15 Apr-15 Sep **Site:** 4HEC **Facilities:** **Services:** **Leisure:** P **Off-site:** R S

FRANCE

SÉRIGNAN-PLAGE HÉRAULT

Aloha

34410 ☎ 467397130 467325815
e-mail: info@alohacamping.com
web: www.alohacamping.com
Situated by the sea with private access to the beach. Good facilities, including jacuzzi and childrens' pool. Entertainment available in summer.
GPS: 43.2683, 3.3356
Open: 23 Apr-18 Sep **Site:** 7HEC **Prices:** 15-48 Mobile home hire 245-1575 **Facilities:** Wi-fi (charged) Kids' Club Play Area **Services:** **Leisure:** P S

Clos Virgile

34410 ☎ 467322064 467320542
e-mail: contact@leclosvirgile.fr
web: www.leclosvirgile.com
Situated 400m from the beach, the site is on level meadowland with large pitches, heated pools and has three well-kept sanitary blocks.
GPS: 43.2699, 3.3312
Open: May-15 Sep **Site:** 5HEC **Prices:** 19-38 Mobile home hire 180-795 **Facilities:** Wi-fi (charged) Kids' Club Play Area **Services:** **Leisure:** P S

Yelloh Village Le Sérignan-Plage

34410 ☎ 467323533 467326839
e-mail: info@leserignanplage.com
web: www.leserignanplage.com
On a fine sandy beach, this is a family site with good recreational facilities.
dir: *A9 exit Béziers Est.*
Open: 29 Apr-26 Sep **Site:** 32HEC **Facilities:** **Services:** **Leisure:** P S

SÈTE HÉRAULT

Village Center le Castellas

RN112, 34200
☎ 499572121 467516389
e-mail: contact@village-center.com
web: www.village-center.com/languedoc-roussillon/camping-mer-le-castellas.php
Facing the sea, the site has a wide range of leisure activities and entertainment. Cycles can be hired and a mini-train operates in high season.
GPS: 43.3400, 3.5820
Open: 8 Apr-2 Oct **Site:** 24HEC **Prices:** 18-40 Mobile home hire 241-1022 **Facilities:** Wi-fi (charged) Kids' Club Play Area **Services:** **Leisure:** P S

SEYNE-SUR-MER, LA VAR

Mimosas

av M-Paul, 83500
☎ 494947315 494873613
e-mail: camping-des-mimosas@wanadoo.fr
web: www.camping-mimosas.com
Situated among pine trees facing the fortress of Six-Fours.
dir: *A50 exit 13 for La Seyne centre & towards Sanary-Bandol.*
Open: All Year. **Site:** 1.08HEC **Prices:** 13-16.80 Mobile home hire 210-590 **Facilities:** Wi-fi (charged) Play Area **Services:** **Off-site:** P

SILLANS-LA-CASCADE BOUCHES-DU-RHÔNE

Relais de la Bresque

chemin de la Piscine, 83690
☎ 494046489 494771954
e-mail: info@lerelaisdelabresque.com
web: www.lerelaisdelabresque.com
A beautiful setting among pine trees with good sanitary and recreational facilities.
Open: Apr-Oct **Site:** 3HEC **Facilities:** **Services:** **Off-site:** P R

SIX-FOURS-LES-PLAGES VAR

International St-Jean

av de la Collégiale, 83140
☎ 494875151 494062823
e-mail: campingstjean@gmail.com
web: www.campingstjean.com
Site with pitches, separated by hedges and reeds. Well managed, it lies just below the Fort Six-Fours.
dir: *Via N559 & D63, via chemin de St-Jean.*
Open: All Year. **Site:** 2HEC **Facilities:** **Services:** **Leisure:** P

Playes

419 r Grand, 83140
☎ 494255757 494071990
e-mail: camplayes@wanadoo.fr
Terraced site on north side of town. Trees abound in this excellent location.
dir: *Via N559 & D63, via chemin de St-Jean.*
Open: All Year. **Site:** 1.5HEC **Facilities:** **Services:** **Off-site:** P S

FRANCE

SOMMIÈRES — GARD

Camping de Massereau

rte d'Aubais, 30250
466531120 411715020
e-mail: info@massereau.fr
web: www.massereau.fr

Located between the Camargue and Mediterranean Sea, family owned site offering relaxation along with a swimming pool complex, sauna and jacuzzi.

dir: *A9/E15 exit 26 Gallargue then signed Sommières.*

Site: 10HEC **Facilities:** Play Area **Services:**
Leisure: P

see advert on this page

SOSPEL — ALPES-MARITIMES

Domaine St-Madeleine

rte de Moulinet, 06380
493041048
e-mail: camp@camping-sainte-madeleine.com
web: camping-sainte-madeleine.com

A peaceful site in beautiful, unspoiled surroundings.

dir: *4.5km NW via D2566.*

Open: 26 Mar-1 Oct **Site:** 3.5HEC **Prices:** 16.40-20
Facilities: Wi-fi (charged) **Services:**
Leisure: P **Off-site:** R

SOUBÈS — HÉRAULT

Les Rials

rte de Poujols, 34700
467441553
e-mail: lesrials@hotmail.fr
web: campinglesrials.free.fr

A terraced site in wooded surroundings on the banks of the River Lergue.

dir: *4km from Lodève. 10km from Lac du Salagou.*

GPS: 43.7725, 3.3275

Open: Jul-Aug **Site:** 3.5HEC **Prices:** 17.10 Mobile home hire 451 **Facilities:** Wi-fi **Services:**
Leisure: P R **Off-site:**

Sources

1445 chemin d'Aubaygues, 34700
467443202 467884875
e-mail: camping-sources@orange.fr
web: www.camping-sources.com

A small, friendly site in a quiet location beside a river.

dir: *5km NE, signed on N9.*

Open: Apr-15 Oct **Site:** 1.3HEC **Facilities:**
Services: **Leisure:** P R **Off-site:** L

TAIN-L'HERMITAGE — DRÔME

CM Lucs

24 av Prés-Roosevelt, 26600
475083282 475083282
e-mail: camping.tainlhermitage@wanadoo.fr
web: www.campingleslucs.fr

Good overnight stopping place but some traffic noise. Caravan limit 5.5m.

dir: *S of town near N7. Turn towards River Rhône at fuel station.*

GPS: 45.0699, 4.8391

Open: 15 Mar-Oct **Site:** 1.5HEC **Prices:** 14.30-17.20
Facilities: **Services:** **Leisure:** P
Off-site: R

THOR, LE — VAUCLUSE

Jantou

chemin des Coudelieres, 84250
490339007 490337984
e-mail: jantou@franceloc.fr
web: www.lejantou.com

Wooded surroundings beside a river.

dir: *Via N100.*

Open: 15 Mar-Oct **Site:** 6HEC **Facilities:**
Services: **Leisure:** P R

TORREILLES — PYRÉNÉES-ORIENTALES

Dunes

66440
468283829 468283257
e-mail: contact@camping-lesdunes.fr
web: www.camping-lesdunes.fr

A well-equipped site in wooded surroundings with direct access to the beach.

dir: *E of village off D81.*

Open: 15 Mar-15 Oct **Site:** 16HEC **Facilities:**
Services: **Leisure:** P S
Off-site: R

pa Marisol

lage de Torreilles, 66440
468280407 468281823
-mail: marisol@camping-marisol.com
eb: www.camping-marisol.com

family site with a variety of sports and entertainment facilities
a pleasant park-like setting 350m from the beach with direct
ccess from the site.

ir: *Off D81 towards sea.*

pen: Apr-Sep **Site:** 9HEC **Prices:** 15-54
obile home hire 203-1113 **Facilities:** Wi-fi Kids'
lub Play Area **Services:**
eisure: P S **Off-site:** R

rivoly

d des Plages, 66440
468282028 251339404
-mail: contact@chadotel.com
eb: www.chadotel.com

modern site with excellent facilities and well-defined pitches,
.8km from the beach.

ir: *Autoroute exit Perpignan Nord for Le Barcarès.*

pen: Apr-Sep **Site:** 5HEC **Facilities:**
ervices: **Leisure:** P **Off-site:** S

OURNON-SUR-RHÔNE ARDÈCHE

lanoir

te de Lamastre, 07300
475080250
-mail: info@lemanoir-ardeche.com
eb: www.lemanoir-ardeche.com

icturesque wooded surroundings with modern facilities.

ir: *Off N86 onto Lamastre road for 3km.*

PS: 45.0648, 4.7898

pen: Apr-Sep **Site:** 2HEC **Prices:** 12-19 Mobile
ome hire 300-565 **Facilities:** Wi-fi (charged) Play
rea **Services:** **Leisure:** P R

ournon HPA

promenade Roche de France, 07300
475080528 475080528
-mail: camping@camping-tournon.com
eb: www.camping-tournon.com

ell laid-out site in town centre beside River Rhône.

ir: *NW on N86.*

pen: All Year. **Site:** 1.1HEC **Facilities:**
ervices: **Leisure:** R **Off-site:** P

TOURRETTES-SUR-LOUP ALPES-MARITIMES

Camassade

523 rte de Pie Lombard, 06140
493593154 493593181
e-mail: courrier@camassade.com
web: www.camassade.com

Quiet site under oak trees and pines with several terraces.

dir: *From Vence turn left just after Tourrette.*

Open: All Year. **Site:** 2HEC **Prices:** 27 Mobile home hire 600 **Facilities:** Wi-fi Play Area **Services:** **Leisure:** P **Off-site:**

Rives du Loup

rte de la Colle, 06140
493241565 493245370
e-mail: info@rivesduloup.com
web: www.rivesduloup.com

Wooded riverside setting with modern facilities adjacent to a small hotel.

dir: *Between Vence & Grasse, 3km from Pont-du-Loup on road to La Colle-sur-Loup CD6.*

GPS: 43.6981, 7.0078

Open: Apr-Sep **Site:** 2.2HEC **Prices:** 15.50-25.50 Mobile home hire 195-730 **Facilities:** Wi-fi (charged) Play Area **Services:** **Leisure:** P R **Off-site:**

UCEL ARDÈCHE

Domaine de Gil

rte de Vais les Bains, Quartier Chamboulas, 07200
475946363 475940195
e-mail: info@domaine-de-gil.com
web: www.domaine-de-gil.com

Pleasant location on the River Ardèche, surrounded by beautiful countryside.

dir: *N of Aubenas off N104.*

Open: 17 Apr-19 Sep **Site:** 4.5HEC **Facilities:** **Services:** **Leisure:** P R

UR PYRÉNÉES-ORIENTALES

Gare

rte d'Espagne, 66760
468048095
e-mail: info@camping-cerdagne.com
web: www.camping-cerdagne.com/camping.html

A pleasant mountainous setting with well-defined pitches. 0.5km from the village.

Open: Nov-Sep **Site:** 1HEC **Facilities:**
Services: **Off-site:** R

FRANCE

UZÈS — GARD

Moulin Neuf

St Quentin-la-Poterie, 30700
☎ 466221721 466229182
e-mail: lemoulinneuf@yahoo.fr
web: www.le-moulin-neuf.fr
Quiet site on extensive meadowland within an estate.
dir: *4km NE on D982.*
Open: Etr-Sep **Site:** 5HEC **Prices:** 14.50-23 **Facilities:** Wi-fi Kids' Club Play Area **Services:** **Leisure:** P

VAISON-LA-ROMAINE — VAUCLUSE

Domaine Carpe Diem

rte de St-Marcellin, 84110
☎ 490360202 490363690
e-mail: contact@camping-carpe-diem.com
web: www.camping-carpe-diem.com
Wooded surroundings close to Mont Ventoux with a variety of leisure facilities.
dir: *S of town towards Malaucène.*
Open: 23 Mar-1 Nov **Site:** 10HEC **Facilities:** **Services:** **Leisure:** P **Off-site:** R

Théâtre Romain

Quartier des Arts, chemin du Brusquet, 84110
☎ 490287866 490287876
e-mail: info@camping-theatre.com
web: www.camping-theatre.com
A peaceful site with some leisure facilities.
dir: *0.5km from town centre near Roman theatre.*
GPS: 44.2446, 5.0793
Open: 15 Mar-5 Nov **Site:** 1.5HEC **Prices:** 14-21.50 Mobile home hire 300-650 **Facilities:** Play Area **Services:** **Leisure:** P **Off-site:** L R

VALENCE — DRÔME

Eperviėre

chemin de l'Epervière, 26000
☎ 475423200 475562067
e-mail: eperviere26@orange.fr
A well-equipped site bordering the Rhône.
dir: *A7 exit Valence Sud.*
Open: Feb-15 Dec **Site:** 3.5HEC **Facilities:** **Services:** **Leisure:** P **Off-site:**

VALLABRÈGUES — GAR

Lou Vincen

30300
☎ 466592129 466590741
e-mail: campinglouvincen@wanadoo.fr
web: www.campinglouvincen.com
A pleasant shady location in a Provençal village.
Open: 24 Mar-30 Oct **Site:** 1.4HEC **Prices:** 14.70-18.8 Mobile home hire 248-589 **Facilities:** Wi-fi (charged) **Services:** **Leisure:** P **Off-site:** L R

VALLERAUGE — GAR

Corconne

Pont d'Hérault, 30570
☎ 467824682
e-mail: contact@lacorconne.com
web: www.lacorconne.com
Unspoiled site in the Cevennes. Spacious terraced pitches blending into the wooded landscape. The river l'Hérault is suitable for swimming.
Open: All Year. **Site:** 7HEC **Facilities:** **Services:** **Leisure:** R

VALLON-PONT-D'ARC — ARDÈCH

Camping Nature Park L'Ardechois

07150
☎ 475880663 475371497
e-mail: ardecamp@bigfoot.com
web: www.ardechois-camping.com
A pleasant location in the Ardèche gorge. Good access for caravans and plentiful sports facilities.
dir: *D290 from Vallon towards St-Martin, site signed.*
Open: 15 Apr-Sep **Site:** 6HEC **Prices:** 25.50-47 **Facilities:** Wi-fi (charged) Kids' Club Play Area **Services:** **Leisure:** P R **Off-site:**

Camping La Roubine

rte de Ruoms, 07150
☎ 475880456 475880456
e-mail: roubine.ardeche@wanadoo.fr
web: www.camping-roubine.com
Family friendly site with large, separated and shady pitches on the banks of the River Ardèche. Leisure facilities include table tennis, volleyball and basketball. Kids' club in summer. Dogs allowed on leads.
dir: *D579 exit Vallon-Pont-d'Arc, direction Ruoms.*
GPS: 44.4081, 4.3782
Open: 23 Apr-15 Sep **Site:** 7HEC **Prices:** 18.50-43 Mobile home hire 400-1300 **Facilities:** Wi-fi Kids' Club Play Area **Services:** **Leisure:** R

FRANCE

londial

e des Gorges de l'Ardèche, 07150
475880044 475371373
-mail: reserv-info@mondial-camping.com
eb: www.mondial-camping.com
odernised site on the bank of the Ardèche with good sanitary rrangements.
pen: 20 Mar-Sep **Site:** 4.2HEC **Facilities:** **Services:** **Leisure:** P R
see advert on this page

lage Fleurie

es Mazes, 07150
475880115 475881131
-mail: info@laplagefleurie.com
eb: www.laplagefleurie.com
oliday site in an unspoiled village beside river.
r: *D579 towards Ruoms, 2.5km left towards Les Mazes.*
pen: 29 Apr-15 Sep **Site:** 12HEC **Facilities:** **Services:** **Leisure:** P R

ALRAS-PLAGE HÉRAULT

ou Village

hemin des Montilles, 34350
467373379 467375356
mail: info@louvillage.com
eb: www.louvillage.com
tuated along a sandy beach, bordered by dunes.
r: *2km SW, 100m from beach.*
en: May-14 Sep **Site:** 8HEC **Facilities:** rvices: **Leisure:** P S **Off-site:** R

ables du Midi

P29, 34350
467323386 467325820
mail: sablesdumidi@siblu.fr
b: www.siblu.fr
mily site on rising ground to the north of town, 1km from the ach.
: *A9 exit Béziers-Est for Valras.*
en: 31 May-8 Aug **Site:** 15HEC **Facilities:** **Services:** **Leisure:** P
-site: R S

Yole

34350
☎ 467373387 467374489
e-mail: info@campinglayole.com
web: www.campinglayole.com
Very comfortable site divided into pitches. Good sanitary installations with individual washing cubicles. Sailing boats for hire. Riding stables in village.
dir: *SW of D37E towards Vendres.*
Open: 24 Apr-18 Sep **Site:** 20HEC **Facilities:** **Services:** **Leisure:** P
Off-site: S

VEDÈNE VAUCLUSE

Flory

385 rte d'Entraigues, 84270
☎ 490310051
e-mail: infos@campingflory.com
web: www.campingflory.com
Well-kept site with good facilities on a pine covered hill.
dir: *Off motorway onto D942 for 0.8km.*
GPS: 43.9906, 4.9131
Open: 15 Mar-Sep **Site:** 6.5HEC **Prices:** 14-20.50 Mobile home hire 200-650 **Facilities:** Play Area **Services:** **Leisure:** P

FRANCE

VENCE — ALPES-MARITIMES

Domaine de la Bergerie

1330 chemin de la Sine, 06140
☎ 493580936 493598044
e-mail: info@camping-domainedelabergerie.com
web: www.camping-domainedelabergerie.com
Well-kept site on hilly land. Pitches near to a wood.
dir: *3km W on D2210.*
Open: 25 Mar-15 Oct **Site:** 13HEC **Prices:** 16.50-31.50 **Facilities:** Play Area **Services:** **Leisure:** P

VERCHENY — DRÔME

Acacias

26340
☎ 475217251 475217398
e-mail: infos@campinglesacacias.com
web: campinglesacacias.com
Pleasant site beside the River Drôme.
dir: *Via D93.*
Open: Apr-Sep **Site:** 3.7HEC **Prices:** 11-18 Mobile home hire 210-640 **Facilities:** Wi-fi Kids' Club Play Area **Services:** **Leisure:** R

VÉREILLES — HÉRAULT

La Sieste

Véreilles, 34260
☎ 467237296 467237538
e-mail: camping.sieste@orange.fr
web: pagesperso-orange.fr/camping.sieste
A rural setting on the River Orb.
dir: *NE of Bédarieux, 10km from Lodève.*
Open: 30 Apr-3 Sep **Site:** 2HEC **Prices:** 13-16 Mobile home hire 205-375 **Facilities:** **Services:** **Leisure:** P R

VERS-PONT-DU-GARD — GARD

Gorges du Gardon

762 chemin Barque Vieille, 30210
☎ 466228181 466229012
A peaceful wooded location beside the River Gardon.
dir: *1km from aqueduct on D981 Uzès road.*
Open: Apr-Sep **Site:** 4.2HEC **Facilities:** **Services:** **Leisure:** P R

VIAS — HÉRAUL

Air Marin

34450
☎ 467216490 467217679
e-mail: info@camping-air-marin.fr
web: www.camping-air-marin.fr
A well-equipped family site in wooded surroundings, a 10-minut walk from the beach. Facilities includes tennis and a fitness centre.
dir: *A6 exit Bierre-les-Semur/RN954.*
Open: 15 May-15 Sep **Site:** 7HEC **Prices:** 24-40 Mobile home hire 290-910 **Facilities:** Wi-fi Kids' Club Play Area **Services:** **Leisure:** P **Off-site:** R S

Californie Plage

34450
☎ 467216469
e-mail: californie.plage@wanadoo.fr
web: www.californie-plage.fr
Very tidy site completely divided into pitches beside sea.
dir: *S on D137 past bridge over Canal du Midi turn right and follow signposts.*
GPS: 43.2925, 3.4017
Open: Apr-Sep **Site:** 5.5HEC **Prices:** 14.50-37 Mobile home hire 175-930 **Facilities:** Wi-fi (charged) Kids' Club Play Area **Services:** **Leisure:** P S

Cap Soleil

Côte Ouest, 34450
☎ 467216477 467217066
e-mail: cap.soleil@wanadoo.fr
web: www.capsoleil.fr
On level land near sea. Divided into pitches.
dir: *Cross Canal du Midi, S of town, then turn W.*
Open: All Year. **Site:** 5HEC **Facilities:** **Services:** **Leisure:** P **Off-site:** S

Carabasse

rte de Farinette, 34450
☎ 467216401 467217687
e-mail: lacarabasse@siblu.fr
web: www.siblu.com
A lively camping park with a range of activites, especially for young families and teenagers, centred around a lagoon pool complex and entertainment terrace.
dir: *1.5m NE of Vias.*
Open: 15 Apr-14 Sep **Site:** **Facilities:** **Services:** **Leisure:** P **Off-site:**

FRANCE

Site 6HEC (site size) grass sand stone little shade partly shaded mainly shaded bungalows for hir (static) caravans for hire tents for hire no dogs site fully accessible for wheelchairs
Prices amount quoted is per night, for 2 adults and car, plus tent or caravan. Mobile home hire is a weekly rate.

élios

as-Plage, 34450
☎ 467216366 🖷 467216366
mail: franceschi.louis@wanadoo.fr
eb: www.campinghelios-viasplage.com
n level ground divided into pitches.
r: *On D137 S of village signed Farinette.*
pen: May-Sep **Site:** 3.5HEC **Facilities:** **Services:** **Off-site:** R S

nternational le Napoléon

171 av de la Mediterranée, 34450
☎ 467010780 🖷 467010785
mail: reception@camping-napoleon.fr
eb: www.camping-napoleon.fr
well-equipped family site surrounded by tropical vegetation ith direct access to the beach. Entertainment shows take place July and August.
r: *A9 exit 34, Agde-Vias.*
pen: 8 Apr-2 Sep **Site:** 3.4HEC **Facilities:** Wi-fi (charged) Kids' Club Play Area
rvices: **Leisure:** P S **Off-site:** R

lediterranee Plage

4450
☎ 467909907 🖷 467909917
mail: contact@mediterranee-plage.com
eb: www.mediterranee-plage.com
rect access to a fine sandy beach.
r: *A75/A9 exit Beziers Centre/Cabrials in direction of ortriagnes.*
pen: 2 Apr-Sep **Site:** 7HEC **Prices:** 16.90-40.50
cilities: Wi-fi Kids' Club Play Area
rvices: **Leisure:** P S

unêlia Domaine de la Dragonnière

D 612, 34450
☎ 467010310 🖷 467217339
mail: contact@dragonniere.com
eb: www.dragonniere.com
busy family site, located between the popular resorts of Vias d Portiragnes with three heated pools, one with slides and mes for children. In high season there is a lively entertainment ogramme and a free shuttle to the beach.
r: *From the A9, exit 34/36, onto the A75, take exit 64 towards éziers Centre. Follow signs for Aéroport Béziers Cap d'Agde. At ossroads by airport turn right.*
PS: 43.3139, 3.3606
pen: 9 Apr-18 Sep **Site:** 30HEC **Prices:** 14-51 obile home hire 215.60-1995 **Facilities:** Kids' Club ay Area **Services:** **Leisure:** P

Yelloh Village Farret

34450
☎ 467216445 🖷 467217049
e-mail: farret@wanadoo.fr
web: www.yellohvillage-club-farret.com
On level meadow beside flat sandy beach, ideal for children. A spa includes sauna, steam room and jacuzzi. Evening entertainment available.
dir: *A9 exit Agde-Vias.*
GPS: 43.2908, 3.4186
Open: 14 Apr-8 Oct **Site:** 14HEC **Prices:** 15-50 Mobile home hire 273-1113 **Facilities:** Wi-fi (charged) Kids' Club Play Area **Services:** **Leisure:** P S **Off-site:** R

VIC-LA-GARDIOLE — HÉRAULT

Village Center l'Europe

31 rte de Frontignan, 34110
☎ 499572121 🖷 467516389
e-mail: contact@village-center.com
web: www.village-center.com/languedoc-roussillon/camping-mer-l-europe.php
Close to the town centre, a Mediterranean-village style site with a relaxed atmosphere.
dir: *1.5km W via D114.*
GPS: 43.4916, 3.7792
Open: 24 Jun-4 Sep **Site:** 5HEC **Prices:** Mobile home hire 216-896 **Facilities:** Wi-fi (charged) Kids' Club Play Area **Services:** **Leisure:** P

VILLARS-COLMARS — ALPES-DE-HAUTE-PROVENCE

Haut-Verdon

04370
☎ 492834009 🖷 492835661
e-mail: campinglehautverdon@wanadoo.fr
web: www.lehautverdon.com
A comfortable site in a picturesque wooded location beside the River Verdon.
dir: *N on D908.*
Open: May-Sep **Site:** 3.5HEC **Prices:** 13-25 **Facilities:** Wi-fi Play Area **Services:** **Leisure:** P R **Off-site:**

FRANCE

VILLEMOUSTAUSSOU — AUDE

Pinhiers

chemin du Pont Neuf, 11620
468478190 468714349
e-mail: campingdaspinhiers@wanadoo.fr
web: www.camping-carcassonne.net
dir: *A61 towards Mazamet.*

Open: Mar-Nov **Site:** 2HEC **Facilities:** **Services:** **Leisure:** P **Off-site:**

VILLENEUVE-DE-BERG — ARDÉCHE

Domaine le Pommier

07170
475948281 475948390
e-mail: info@campinglepommier.com
web: www.campinglepommier.com

Holiday site in beautiful setting with terraces divided into pitches. Kids' club available where Dutch is spoken. Dogs admitted onto pitches.

dir: *On winding private road off N102, 2km from village.*

GPS: 44.5744, 4.5077

Open: 15 Apr-17 Sep **Site:** 20HEC **Prices:** 19.50-39.50 Mobile home hire 350-784 **Facilities:** Wi-fi (charged) Kids' Club Play Area **Services:** **Leisure:** P R

VILLENEUVE-DE-LA-RAHO — PYRÉNÉES-ORIENTALES

Rives-du-Lac

chemin de la Serre, 66180
468558351 468558637
e-mail: camping.villeneuveraho@wanadoo.fr

A quiet family site beside the lake.

dir: *Via RN9.*

Open: Apr-Oct **Site:** 2.5HEC **Facilities:** **Services:** **Off-site:** L

VILLENEUVE-LÈS-AVIGNON — GAR

Île des Papes

The Camping and Caravanning Club — The Friendly Club

30400
490151590 490151591
e-mail: ile-des-papes@campeole.com
web: www.avignon-camping.com

A well-equipped site on an island between the Rhône Canal and the River Rhône.

C&CC Report *This relaxing, well-maintained, modern Provençal site makes a convenient base for a terrific area rich in scenery and history. There's medieval Villeneuve, beautiful Avignon with its Pope's Palace, the famous vineyards of Châteauneuf-du-Pape, and breathtaking Roman sites such as the amphitheatre at Orange and the Pont du Gard aqueduct. Easy day trips include Van Gogh's Arles, the Camargue, the Ardèche, majestic Mont Ventoux and Provence's lavender-scented hills and gorges. In springtime, don't miss Fontaine de Vaucluse, where a fully formed river rises straight out of the ground.*

dir: *From A9 junct 22, follow Roquemaure, Sauveterre and Villeneuve-lès-Avignon. Before Volleneuve, D780 to site.*

GPS: 43.9936, 4.8177

Open: 27 Mar-6 Nov **Site:** 20HEC **Facilities:** Kids' Club Play Area **Services:** **Leisure:** P

VILLENEUVE-LOUBET — ALPES-MARITIME

Panorama

06270
493209153

Small terraced site, mainly for tents 0.8km, from the sea.

dir: *0.5km from Nice-Cannes autoroute.*

Open: All Year. **Site:** 1HEC **Facilities:** **Services:** **Off-site:** R S

Parc des Maurettes

730 av du Dr-Lefebvre, 06270
493209191 493737720
e-mail: info@parcdesmaurettes.com
web: www.parcdesmaurettes.com

Terraced site in a pine forest with modern facilities, including jacuzzi and sauna.

dir: *A8 exit Villeneuve-Loubet-Plage, N7 towards Antibes for 1km*

GPS: 43.6309, 7.1298

Open: 10 Jan-15 Nov **Site:** 2HEC **Facilities:** Wi-fi (charged) Play Area **Services:** **Off-site:** P S

'arc St-James Sourire

te de Grasse, 06270
493209611 493220752
-mail: lesourire@camping-parcsaintjames.com
eb: www.camping-parcsaintjames.com
'arkland dominated by an 11th-century monastery.
ir: *2km W on D2085.*
pen: 9 Apr-1 Sep Site: 5.5HEC Prices: 17-31
lobile home hire 284-833 Facilities: Play Area
ervices: Leisure: P Off-site: R

'ieille Ferme

96 bd des Groules, 06270
493334144 493333728
-mail: info@vieilleferme.com
eb: www.vieilleferme.com
'ooded park close to the sea.
ir: *Via A8/N7 from Antibes or Cagnes-sur-Mer.*
pen: All Year. Site: 2.8HEC Facilities:
Services: Leisure: P Off-site: S

'ILLEROUGE-LA-CRÉMADE AUDE

'inada

1200
468436788 468436861
-mail: lepinada@libertysurf.fr
eb: camping-le-pinada.com
leasant rural surroundings on edge of forest.
ir: *0.6km NW on D106.*
pen: Apr-15 Oct Site: 4.5HEC Facilities:
Services: Leisure: P Off-site:

'LLES-SUR-AUZON VAUCLUSE

erguettes

'e de Carpentras, 84570
490618818 490619787
-mail: info@provence-camping.com
eb: www.provence-camping.com
'ing at the foot of Mont Ventoux and Nesque Gorges in a pine rest.
ir: *W via D942.*
pen: Apr-15 Oct Site: 2HEC Prices: 17.10-21.20
obile home hire 253-684 Facilities: Wi-fi (charged)
ay Area Services: Leisure: P
ff-site: L

VITROLLES BOUCHES-DU-RHÔNE

Marina Plage

13127
442893146 442795990
e-mail: information@marina-plage.com
web: www.marina-plage.com
A family site in pleasant wooded surroundings with good recreational facilities.
dir: *A7 exit Vitrolles, RN113 for Roquac, left at 2nd rdbt.*
Open: All Year. **Site:** 11HEC **Facilities:** **Services:** **Leisure:** L

VIVIERS ARDÈCHE

Rochecondrie Loisirs

07220
475527466 475527466
e-mail: campingrochecondrie@wanadoo.fr
web: www.campingrochecondrie.com
A level site with good facilities beside the River l'Escoutay.
dir: *N of town on N86.*
Open: Apr-15 Oct **Site:** 1.8HEC **Prices:** 11.50-19
Mobile home hire 230-510 **Facilities:** Play Area
Services: **Leisure:** P R **Off-site:**

VOGÜÉ ARDÈCHE

Domaine du Cros d'Auzon

Hotellerie de Plein Air, 07200
475370414 475370102
e-mail: camping.auzon@wanadoo.fr
web: www.domaine-cros-auzon.com
Wooded surroundings close to the Gorges de l'Ardèche with good recreational facilities. Kids' club available in July and August.
dir: *2.5km via D579 bordering river.*
Open: 9 Apr-18 Sep **Site:** 20HEC
Prices: 16.50-29.50 Mobile home hire 210-895 **Facilities:** Wi-fi Kids' Club Play Area **Services:**
Leisure: P R **Off-site:**

VOLONNE ALPES-DE-HAUTE-PROVENCE

Hippocampe

rte Napoléon, 04290
492335000 492335049
e-mail: camping@l-hippocampe.com
web: www.l-hippocampe.com
Several strips of land, interspersed with trees, and running down the edge of lake. Surrounded by fields and gardens.
dir: *On S edge of town, 2km E of N85.*
Open: 16 Apr-Sep **Site:** 8HEC **Prices:** 13-43
Mobile home hire 294-1099 **Facilities:** Wi-fi (charged) Kids' Club Play Area **Services:**
Leisure: P

FRANCE

CORSICA

BONIFACIO CORSE-DU-SUD

Rondinara

Suartone, 20169
☎ 495704315 📠 495705679
e-mail: reception@rondinara.fr
web: www.rondinara.fr

A beautiful location 300m from the beach with modern facilities and opportunities for water sports.

dir: *On N198 midway between Porto-Vecchio & Bonifacio.*

GPS: 41.4731, 9.2625

Open: 15 May-Sep **Site:** 6HEC **Facilities:** **Services:** **Leisure:** P S

CALVI HAUTE-CORSE

Dolce Vita

Ponte Bambino, 20260
☎ 495650599 📠 495653125
web: www.dolce-vita.fr

Set in extensive woodland with defined pitches and modern facilities.

Open: May-Sep **Site:** 6HEC **Facilities:** Wi-fi (charged) Play Area **Services:** **Leisure:** R S **Off-site:** L

CARGESE CORSE-DU-SUD

Torraccia

Bagghiuccia, 20130
☎ 495264239 📠 495264239
e-mail: contact@camping-torraccia.com
web: www.camping-torraccia.com

Terraced site close to the Chiuni and Pero beaches and backed by some fine mountain scenery.

dir: *4km N on N199.*

Open: May-Sep **Site:** 3.5HEC **Facilities:** **Services:** **Off-site:** S

CASTELLARE DI CASINCA HAUTE-CORSE

Village Center le Domaine d'Anghione

20213
☎ 499572121 📠 467516389
e-mail: contact@village-center.com
web: www.village-center.com/corse/camping-domaine-anghione.php

With direct access to the sea and ideal for families. Leisure facilities include tennis, squash courts and horse riding (at an extra charge).

dir: *N193 then N198.*

GPS: 42.4765, 9.5296

Open: 8 Apr-2 Oct **Site:** 40HEC **Facilities:** Wi-fi (charged) Kids' Club Play Area **Services:** **Leisure:** P S

GALÉRIA HAUTE-CORSE

Deux Torrents

20245
☎ 495620067 📠 495620332
e-mail: 2torrents@corsica-net.com

A spacious, well-equipped site nestling between two torrents at the foot of the mountains.

dir: *5km E on D51 towards Calenzana.*

Open: Jun-Sep **Site:** 6.3HEC **Prices:** 16.70-19.10 Mobile home hire 290-700 **Facilities:** Wi-fi (charged) **Services:** **Off-site:** R

GHISONACCIA HAUTE-CORSE

Arinella-Bianca

20240
☎ 495560478 📠 495561254
e-mail: arinella@arinellabianca.com
web: www.arinellabianca.com

Wooded surroundings beside the beach with good recreational facilities.

Open: 11 Apr-10 Oct **Site:** 9HEC **Prices:** 23-39 Mobile home hire 190-1300 **Facilities:** Wi-fi (charged) Kids' Club Play Area **Services:** **Leisure:** R S

LOZARI HAUTE-CORSE

Clos des Chênes

rte de Belgodère, 20226
☎ 495601513 📠 495602116
e-mail: cdc.lozari@wanadoo.fr
web: www.closdeschenes.fr

A delightful wooded setting 1km from a fine sandy beach.

dir: *1.5km S on N197 towards Belgodère.*

Open: Etr-Sep **Site:** 5.5HEC **Facilities:** **Services:** **Leisure:** P **Off-site:** S

FRANCE

LUMIO — HAUTE-CORSE

Panoramic

rte de Lavataggio 1, 20260
495607313 495607313
e-mail: panoramic@web-office.fr
web: www.le-panoramic.com

Quiet site with friendly atmosphere close to beaches. Very clean and tidy, divided into pitches.

dir: *From Calvi, 12km on N197, 200m from main road.*

Open: May-20 Sep **Site:** 6HEC **Facilities:** **Services:** **Leisure:** P **Off-site:** S

OLMETO-PLAGE — CORSE-DU-SUD

Esplanade

20113
495760503 495761622
e-mail: campinglesplanade@orange.fr
web: www.camping-esplanade.com

A pleasant natural park, 100m from the sea. The campsite is located 5km from Propriano and Olmeto. Weight limit for dogs is 10kg.

Open: Apr-Oct **Site:** 4.75HEC **Prices:** 19.60-25.30 Mobile home hire 365-880 **Facilities:** **Services:** **Leisure:** P S **Off-site:** R

PIANOTTOLI — CORSE-DU-SUD

Kevano Plage

plage de Kevano, 20131
495718322 495718383

A beautiful setting in the middle of woodland with modern facilities, 400m from the beach.

Open: May-Sep **Site:** 6HEC **Facilities:** **Services:** **Off-site:** S

PISCIATELLO — CORSE-DU-SUD

Benista

20166
495251930 495259370
e-mail: camping.benista@orange.fr
web: www.benista.fr

A beautiful wooded setting 5 minutes from the beaches. Pitches are divided by hedges and there are good sports facilities.

Open: Apr-Oct **Site:** 5HEC **Facilities:** **Services:** **Leisure:** P R

PORTO-VECCHIO — CORSE-DU-SUD

Vetta

rte de Bastia, 20137
495700986 495704321
e-mail: info@campinglavetta.com
web: www.campinglavetta.com

Set in natural parkland with modern facilities, 3km from the sea.

dir: *5.5km N on N198.*

Open: Jun-Oct **Site:** 8HEC **Facilities:** **Services:** **Leisure:** P **Off-site:** S

ST-FLORENT — HAUTE-CORSE

U Pezzo

rte de la Roya, 20217
495370165 495370165
e-mail: contact@upezzo.com
web: www.upezzo.com

Pleasant site, partly level, partly terraced under eucalyptus trees. Private access to large beach.

dir: *S of town on road to beach.*

Open: Apr-15 Oct **Site:** 2HEC **Prices:** 16-18 Mobile home hire 350-1000 **Facilities:** Play Area **Services:** **Leisure:** S **Off-site:** R

SOTTA — CORSE-DU-SUD

U Moru

20114
495712340 495712619
e-mail: u-moru@wanadoo.fr
web: www.u-moru.com

A quiet family site 5 minutes from the beach.

dir: *4km SW via D859.*

Open: 15 Jun-15 Sep **Site:** 6HEC **Prices:** 22.30-23.20 **Facilities:** Wi-fi **Services:** **Leisure:** P

TIUCCIA — CORSE-DU-SUD

Couchants

rte de Casaglione, 20111
495522660 495593177
e-mail: camping.les-couchants@wanadoo.fr
web: camping-lescouchants.fr

A quiet location facing the vast Sagone bay and close to the Liamone River.

dir: *3km from sea.*

Open: May-Oct **Site:** 5HEC **Prices:** 25-28 **Facilities:** Wi-fi **Services:** **Off-site:** R S

FRANCE

Germany

Drinking and driving
If the level of alcohol in the bloodstream is 0.05% or more, penalties include fines and the licence holder may be banned from driving in Germany. The blood alcohol level is 0% for drivers aged under 21 or drivers who have held their licence for less than 2 years, should even a small amount of alcohol be detected in the blood the fine is €250.

Driving licence
Minimum age at which a UK licence holder may drive a temporarily imported car and/or motorcycle 18.

Fines
On-the-spot fine or deposit. Should a foreign motorist refuse to pay, their vehicle can be confiscated. Motorists can be fined for such things as exceeding speed limits, using abusive language, making derogatory signs and running out of petrol on a motorway. Wheel clamps are not used in Germany but vehicles causing obstruction can be towed away.

Lights
Dipped headlights or day time running lights recommended at all times, and compulsory during daylight hours if fog, snow or rain restrict visibility. Driving with sidelights (parking lights) alone is not allowed. Vehicles must have their lights on in tunnels.

Motorcycles
Use of dipped headlights at all times is compulsory. The wearing of a crash helmet is compulsory for both driver and passenger of a moped and motorcycle.

Motor insurance
Third-party compulsory.

Passengers and children
A child less than 1.5m and under 12 years old travelling in any type of vehicle must be seated in an approved child seat or child restraint. Where a child restraint/seat is not available because other children are secured by a child restraint/seat, a child 3 years and over must travel in the rear seat of the vehicle using a seat belt or other safety device attached to the seat. A child under 3 years old may not be transported in a vehicle without a suitable child restraint/seat.

Seat belts
Compulsory for front and rear seat occupants to wear seat belts, if fitted.

Speed limits
Unless signed otherwise

Private vehicles without trailers	
Built-up areas	50km/h
Outside built-up areas	100km/h
Dual carriageways & motorways	130km/h
Minimum speed on motorways	60km/h
In bad weather conditions	50km/h
Vehicles with snow chains	50km/h
Car towing a trailer	
Motorways/dual carriageways	100km/h
Other roads	80km/h
Camper van up to 3.5t, with trailer	
Motorways/dual carriageways	80km/h
Other roads	80km/h
Vehicle over 3.5t with a trailer	
Motorways/dual carriageways	80km/h
Other roads	60km/h

Additional information
It is not compulsory for visiting UK motorists to carry a warning triangle, but they are strongly advised to do so, as all drivers must signal their vehicle in case of breakdown, and it is a compulsory requirement for residents. It is recommended that visitors equip their vehicle with a first-aid kit and set of replacement bulbs. Slow-moving vehicles must stop at suitable places and let others pass. It is prohibited to overtake or pass a school bus that is approaching a stopping point. In all other cases of passing buses it has to be with caution. A fine will be imposed for non-compliance.

Spiked tyres are prohibited.

A GPS based navigation system which has maps indicating the location of fixed speed cameras must have this function deactivated. Should you be unable to deactivate this function the GPS system must not be carried. The use of radar detectors is prohibited.

All motorists have the obligation to adapt their vehicles to winter weather conditions. This includes but is not limited to winter tyres and anti-freeze fluid for the washer system. Extreme weather may additionally require snow chains. The law does not specify which type of tyre is 'appropriate' the general opinion is that any type of tyre except summer tyres is appropriate, including all-year tyres. Winter tyres must bear the mark M&S or display the snowflake on the side wall. Motorists, whose car is equipped with summer tyres while there is snow and ice may not take the car on the road. Motorists in violation face fines of €20. If they obstruct traffic, the fine is €40. Restrictions on the circulation of vehicles are enforced in several German cities, in order to reduce emission levels in some areas. The areas where restrictions apply will be indicated by signs "Umweltzone" showing coloured

vignettes ("Plakette") - green, yellow and red. To enter these areas, drivers will have to stick a vignette on their vehicle windscreen, this can be obtained from technical inspection centres or approved garages, fine for non-compliance €40.
The owner of the vehicle (German or foreign) is required to present the registration certificate of the vehicle and pay a fee of €5 to €10. The colour of the vignette issued will depend on the type of engine and the Euro classification of the vehicle.
The fee is a 'one-off' charge and remains valid in any Germany city as long as it stays fixed to the vehicle i.e. not transferred to another vehicle.
Owners of foreign-registered vehicles can obtain a sticker by sending an email to the Berlin vehicle registration authority at kfz-zulassung@labo.verwalt-berlin.de attaching a copy of the vehicle registration certificate specifying the emission code or a manufacturer's certificate (preferably pdf files).
Upon verification of the documents, the registration authority will send a payment request by advance email including the bank details to the applicant. A €6 administration/handling fee will be charged per sticker. The sticker will be sent to the applicant by direct mail. As order processing may take two to three weeks, the sticker should be ordered well in advance.
Alternatively you can now obtain a sticker from the Cologne vehicle registration office by sending an application including a copy of the vehicle documents and €5 (cash or crossed cheque) to Kfz-Zulassungsstelle, Max-Glomsda-Straße 4, D-51105 Köln. For further information, visit
http://www.stadt-koeln.de/3/umwelt/umweltzone/
For maps and detailed information of the environmental zone areas, please see;
http://www.umweltbundesamt.de/umweltzonen

SOUTH EAST

AACH BEI OBERSTAUFEN — BAYERN

Aach

87534
☎ 08386 363 🖷 08386 961721
e-mail: info@camping-aach.de
web: www.camping-aach.de
A terraced site with beautiful views of the mountains. Sauna, solarium, games room.
dir: *B308 from Oberstaufen towards Austrian border for 7km.*
Open: All Year. **Site:** 2.5HEC **Prices:** 21.60-25.60
Facilities: **Services:**
Off-site: R

AITRANG — BAYERN

Elbsee

Am Elbsee 3, 87648
☎ 08343 248 🖷 08343 1406
e-mail: info@elbsee.de
web: www.elbsee.de
On the E shore of the lake with good bathing facilities. Section reserved for campers with dogs.
dir: *NW from Marktoberdorf centre to Ruderatshofen & W towards Aitrang, site signed S of Aitrang (narrow winding road).*
Open: All Year. **Site:** 5HEC **Prices:** 23.20
Facilities: Wi-fi (charged) Play Area
Services: **Leisure:** L **Off-site:** P

ARLACHING — BAYERN

Kupferschmiede

Trostberger Str 4, 83339
☎ 08667 446 🖷 08667 16198
e-mail: campingkupfer@aol.com
web: www.campingkupferschmiede.de
On meadowland and close to forest. Partially gravel.
dir: *On Seebruck-Traunstein road.*
Open: Apr-Oct **Site:** 2.5HEC **Prices:** 19.90-21.30
Facilities: Wi-fi (charged) Play Area **Services:**
Leisure: L **Off-site:** P R

AUGSBURG — BAYERN

Augusta

Mühlhauser Str 54B, 86169
☎ 0821 707575 🖷 0821 705883
e-mail: info@caravaningpark.com
web: www.caravaningpark.com
Hard standings for caravans. Separate section for residential caravans.
dir: *E11 exit Augsburg-Ost, N towards Neuburg & 400m right.*
Open: All Year. **Site:** 6.6HEC **Facilities:**
Services: **Leisure:** L **Off-site:**

GERMANY

BAMBERG — BAYERN

Insel

Bug, 96049
☎ 0951 56320 Fax 0951 56321
e-mail: campinginsel@web.de
web: www.campinginsel.de
The site lies on the bank of the River Regnitz. Park and Ride scheme into Bamberg.

dir: *A73 exit Bamberg S, B505/B4 towards Bamberg, signed on left.*

Open: All Year. **Site:** 5HEC **Prices:** 18.60 **Facilities:** **Services:** **Leisure:** R

BERCHTESGADEN — BAYERN

Allweglehen

Allweggasse 4, 83471
☎ 08652 2396
e-mail: camping@allweglehen.de
web: www.allweglehen.de
A terraced site at the foot of the Untersalzberg Mountain surrounded by woods. There is also a steep and narrow asphalt access road with passing places. A truck is available for towing caravans.

dir: *B305 towards Schellenberg for 3.5km.*

Open: All Year. **Site:** 4HEC **Facilities:** **Services:** **Leisure:** P **Off-site:** R

BERGEN — BAYERN

Wagnerhof

Campingstr 11, 83346
☎ 08662 8557 Fax 08662 5924
e-mail: info@camping-bergen.de
web: www.camping-bergen.de
Level site.

dir: *München-Salzburg motorway exit Bergen, right at sawmill before town.*

Open: All Year. **Site:** 2.8HEC **Facilities:** **Services:** **Off-site:** L P

BISCHOFSWIESEN — BAYERN

Winkl-Landthal

Winkl bei Berchtesgaden, 83483
☎ 08652 8164 Fax 08652 979831
e-mail: camping-winkl@t-online.de
web: www.camping-winkl.de
Meadowland site between the B20 and the edge of woodland.

dir: *From Bad Reichenhall to Berchtesgaden for 8km.*

Open: Dec-Oct **Site:** 2.5HEC **Prices:** 21-24 **Facilities:** Wi-fi (charged) Play Area **Services:** **Leisure:** R

BRUNNEN FORGGENSEE — BAYERN

Brunnen

Seestr 81, 87645
☎ 08362 8273 Fax 08362 8630
e-mail: info@camping-brunnen.de
web: www.camping-brunnen.de
Situated on E shore of Lake Forggensee.

dir: *B17 from Füssen to Schwangau, then N on minor road.*

Open: 21 Dec-2 Nov **Site:** 6HEC **Facilities:** **Services:** **Leisure:** L **Off-site:** P

BUXHEIM — BAYERN

See International

Am Weiherhaus 7, 87740
☎ 08331 71800 Fax 08331 63554
web: www.camping-buxheim.de
Terraced site beyond public bathing area.

dir: *Leave Um-Kempten motorway at Memminger Kreuz then right to Buxheim.*

Open: May-15 Sep **Site:** 42HEC **Prices:** 19.50 **Facilities:** **Services:** **Leisure:** L **Off-site:** P R

DIESSEN — BAYERN

St-Alban

86911
☎ 08807 7305 Fax 08807 1057
e-mail: ivan.pavic@t-online.de
web: www.camping-ammersee.de
Clean site next to St-Alban, lakeside with private bathing beach and reserved section for residential campers. Good sanitary installations also used by the public.

dir: *B12 from München towards Landsberg/Lech, near Greifenberg turn left, continue via Utting to St-Alban.*

Open: Apr-Oct **Site:** 3.8HEC **Facilities:** **Services:** **Leisure:** L **Off-site:**

DINKELSBÜHL — BAYERN

Romantische Strasse

91550
☎ 09851 7817 Fax 09851 7848
e-mail: campdinkelsbuehl@aol.de
web: www.campingplatz-dinkelsbuehl.de
Terraced site with some hedges and trees. Separate field for young people. Good sports facilities.

dir: *Signed.*

Open: All Year. **Site:** 9HEC **Facilities:** **Services:** **Leisure:** L **Off-site:**

NDORF, BAD — BAYERN

Stein

lintersee 10, 83093
08053 9349 08053 798745
-mail: info@camping-stein.de
veb: www.camping-stein.de
family site in wooded surroundings on the shore of the Simsee.
pen: 15 May-Sep **Site:** 2.5HEC **Facilities:** **Services:** **Leisure:** L **Off-site:**

RLANGEN — BAYERN

angau

ampingstr 44, 91056
09135 8866 09135 724743
-mail: info@camping-rangau.de
eb: www.camping-rangau.de
ong stretch of land behind the sports ground, next to the echsendorfer Weiher lake in a nature reserve.
ir: *A3 exit Erlangen W.*
pen: Apr-Sep **Site:** 18HEC **Prices:** 20.50 **Facilities:** **Services:** **Off-site:** L

SCHERNDORF — BAYERN

scherndorf-Main

7332
09381 710945 09381 2889
-mail: info@campingplatz-mainschleife.de
eb: www.campingplatz-escherndorf.de
te lies on meadowland by the River Main, next to the ferry ation (River Ferry Nordheim).
r: *A7 exit Würzburg Estenfeld, E for Volkach.*
pen: Apr-Oct **Site:** 1.5HEC **Prices:** 22.50 **Facilities:** Wi-fi (charged) **Services:** **Leisure:** R
f-site: P

STENFELD — BAYERN

amping Estenfeld

aidbronner Str 38, 97230
09305 228 09305 8006
mail: cplestenfeld@freenet.de
eb: www.camping-estenfeld.de
meadowland next to sportsground and gardens on the tskirts of Estenfeld.
r: *A7 exit Würzburg/Estenfeld, B19 S for 1km.*
en: 10 Mar-23 Dec **Site:** 0.5HEC **Prices:** 15-20
bile home hire 105-210 **Facilities:** Play Area
rvices: **Off-site:** P

FEILNBACH, BAD — BAYERN

Tenda

Reithof 2, 83075
08066 884400 08066 8844029
e-mail: info@tenda-camping.de
web: www.tenda-camping.de
Well-organised site on level grassland with pitches laid out in circles and hardstandings for tourers near the entrance.
dir: *A8 exit Bad Aibling, 4km S on minor road.*
GPS: 47.7891, 12.0058
Open: All Year. **Site:** 14HEC **Prices:** 19-27
Facilities: Wi-fi (charged) Play Area
Services: **Leisure:** P **Off-site:** L

FICHTELBERG — BAYERN

Fichtelsee

95686
09272 801 09272 909045
e-mail: info@camping-fichtelsee.de
web: www.camping-fichtelsee.de
Gently sloping meadow amid pleasant woodland 100m from Lake Fichtelsee.
dir: *A9 exit Bad Berneck, B303 to Fichtelsee Leisure Centre turning.*
GPS: 50.0163, 11.8552
Open: 16 Dec-7 Nov **Site:** 2.6HEC **Prices:** 16.50-22.50
Facilities: Wi-fi (charged) Kids' Club Play Area
Services: **Off-site:** L P

FINSTERAU — BAYERN

Nationalpark-Ost

94151
08557 768 08557 1062
e-mail: berghof-frank@berghof.frank.de
web: www.camping-nationalpark.eu
Terraced site on edge of extensive woodland area at the entrance to a national park.
dir: *N of Freyung towards frontier.*
Open: All Year. **Site:** 3HEC **Facilities:**
Services: **Off-site:**

FRICKENHAUSEN BAYERN

KNAUS Camping Park Frickenhausen

Ochsenfurter Str 49, 97252
☎ 09331 3171 🖷 09331 5784
e-mail: frickenhausen@knauscamp.de
web: www.knauscamp.de
On level meadow in a small poplar wood beside River Main.
dir: *On N bank of River Main 0.5km E of Ochsenfurt.*
Open: 14 Mar-3 Nov **Site:** 3.5HEC **Facilities:** **Services:** **Leisure:** P **Off-site:** P R

FÜRTH IM WALD BAYERN

Einberg

Daberger Str 33, 93437
☎ 09973 1811 🖷 09973 803220
e-mail: camping@stadtwerke-furth.de
web: www.stadtwerke-furth.de
Municipal site in Daberger Str, near swimming pool.
dir: *NE of Cham on B20.*
Open: Mar-Oct **Site:** 2HEC **Facilities:** **Services:** **Leisure:** R **Off-site:** L P

FÜSSEN BAYERN

Hopfensee

Fischerbichl 17, 87629
☎ 08362 917710 🖷 08362 917720
e-mail: info@camping-hopfensee.com
web: www.camping-hopfensee.de
A quiet location beside a lake with a private beach. Ski-safari in winter.
dir: *4km N of Füssen.*
GPS: 47.6013, 10.6833
Open: 17 Dec-6 Nov **Site:** 8HEC **Prices:** 33.85-37.60 **Facilities:** Wi-fi (charged) Kids' Club Play Area **Services:** **Leisure:** L P **Off-site:**

FÜSSING, BAD BAYERN

Kur-Camping Fuchs

94072
☎ 08537 356 🖷 08537 912083
e-mail: info@kurcamping-fuchs.de
web: www.kurcamping-fuchs.de
On meadow divided into pitches and 1km from spa baths at Bad Füssing.
dir: *Turn at Passau end of Tutling on B12 to Kircham & signs to site on Egglfinger Strasse, 2km from Bad Füssing.*
Open: All Year. **Site:** 1.5HEC **Facilities:** **Services:** **Leisure:** P **Off-site:** R

Max I

Falkenstr 12, Egglfing, 94072
☎ 08537 96170 🖷 08537 961710
e-mail: info@campingmax.de
web: www.campingmax.de
On a level meadow with some trees. Good modern facilities.
dir: *S of Bad Füssing via B12.*
Open: All Year. **Site:** 3.5HEC **Prices:** 19.80 **Facilities:** Play Area **Services:** **Leisure:** L P

GADEN BAYERN

Schwanenplatz

Am Schwanenplatz 1, 83329
☎ 08681 281 🖷 08681 4276
e-mail: info@schwanenplatz.de
web: www.schwanenplatz.de
Site lies on a meadow, divided into sections beside Waginger See.
dir: *From Traunstein to Waging, right towards Freilassing for 1km, left to lake.*
GPS: 47.9366, 12.7607
Open: 30 Apr-4 Oct **Site:** 4HEC **Prices:** 18.10-23.10 **Facilities:** Wi-fi (charged) Kids' Club Play Area **Services:** **Leisure:** L R **Off-site:**

GARMISCH-PARTENKIRCHEN BAYERN

Zugspitze

Griesener Str 4, 82491
☎ 08821 3180 🖷 08821 947594
A beautiful setting at the foot of the Zugspitze between the road and the Loisach.
dir: *On B24 towards Austrian frontier.*
Open: All Year. **Site:** 2.9HEC **Facilities:** **Services:** **Leisure:** R **Off-site:** L P

GEMÜNDEN AM MAIN BAYERN

Saaleinsel

Duivenallee 7, 97737
☎ 09351 8574
The municipal site lies a short distance off the main road bordering the River Fränkische Saale. It is in the grounds of a sports field and has a swimming pool.
dir: *Signed off B26.*
Open: Apr-15 Oct **Site:** 7HEC **Prices:** 17 **Facilities:** Play Area **Services:** **Leisure:** P R **Off-site:**

GERMANY

GEMÜNDEN-HOFSTETTEN BAYERN

Schönrain

97737

09351 8645 09351 8721

e-mail: info@spessart-camping.de

web: www.spessart-camping.de

Slightly sloping, partly terraced meadowland east of River Main.

dir: *From Gemünden/Main along left bank of River Main, 3km downstream. Turn left off B26 through Hofstetten to site.*

Open: 15 Mar-Sep **Site:** 7HEC **Facilities:** **Services:** **Leisure:** P

GRIESBACH, BAD BAYERN

Kur-Und Feriencamping Dreiquellenbad

94086

08532 96130 08532 961350

e-mail: info@camping-bad-griesbach.de

web: www.camping-bad-griesbach.de

Pleasant wooded surroundings with modern facilities.

dir: *1km S of Griesbach Spa, on the Karpfham-Schwaim road.*

GPS: 48.4208, 13.1919

Open: All Year. **Site:** 4.5HEC **Prices:** 24.50-25 **Facilities:** Wi-fi (charged) Play Area **Services:** **Leisure:** P **Off-site:** R

HASLACH BAYERN

Feriencenter Wertacher Hof

87466

08361 770

Well-kept site on Lake Grüntensee.

dir: *Near Wertach-Haslach railway station.*

Open: All Year. **Site:** 3.5HEC **Facilities:** **Services:** **Leisure:** L

HOFHEIM BAYERN

Brugger am Riegsee

82418

08847 728 08847 228

e-mail: office@camping-brugger.de

web: www.camping-brugger.de

Lakeside site in a rural setting with modern facilities and a view of the mountain range Zugspitze and Alpspitze.

Open: Apr-15 Oct **Site:** 6HEC **Prices:** 15-25 **Facilities:** Wi-fi Kids' Club Play Area **Services:** **Leisure:** L

INGOLSTADT BAYERN

AZUR Camping Auwaldsee

85053

0841 9611616 0841 9611617

e-mail: ingolstadt@azur-camping.de

web: www.azur-camping.de/ingolstadt

Near to Auwaldsee, this site lies in a beautiful setting beside the München-Ingolstadt motorway.

dir: *A9 exit Ingolstadt-Süd.*

Open: All Year. **Site:** 10HEC **Facilities:** Play Area **Services:** **Leisure:** L **Off-site:** P

ISSIGAU BAYERN

Schloss Issigau

Altes Schloss 3, 95188

09293 7173 09293 933385

e-mail: schloss_issigau@t.online.de

web: www.schloss-issigau.de

Close to Issigau in a central position for a holiday or stopover site.

dir: *A9 exit Berg/Bad Steben, 5km W.*

GPS: 50.3738, 11.7211

Open: 15 Mar-Oct & Xmas-New Year **Site:** 2HEC **Prices:** 17.50 **Facilities:** Play Area **Services:** **Off-site:**

JODITZ BAYERN

Auensee

95189

09295 381 09281 1706666

e-mail: rathaus@gemeinde-koeditz.de

web: www.gemeinde-koeditz.de

Municipal site on partly terraced meadowland above lake.

dir: *München-Berlin motorway exit Berg-Bad Steben, site 4km E.*

Open: All Year. **Site:** 9HEC **Facilities:** Play Area **Services:** **Leisure:** L **Off-site:** P R

KIPFENBERG BAYERN

AZUR-Camping Altmühltal

Campingstr, 85110

08465 905167 08465 3745

e-mail: kipfenberg@azur-camping.de

web: www.azur-camping.de/kipfenberg

Well-equipped site in an unspoiled wooded location with good canoeing facilities.

Open: Apr-Oct **Site:** 4HEC **Facilities:** **Services:** **Leisure:** R **Off-site:** P

GERMANY

KIRCHZELL — BAYERN

AZUR-Camping Odenwald

Am Campingplatz 1, 63931
09373 566 09373 7375
e-mail: kirchzell@azur-camping.de
web: www.azur-camping.de/kirchzell

Site on natural terraced meadowland in wooded hilly country.

dir: *From Amorbach towards Eberbach road for 5km, site 1km from town.*

Open: Apr-Oct **Site:** 7HEC **Facilities:** **Services:** **Leisure:** P

KISSINGEN, BAD — BAYERN

Bad Kissingen

Euerdorfer Str 1, 97688
0971 5211 0971 6990820
e-mail: campingpark-badkissingen@web.de
web: www.campingpark-badkissingen.de

Set in a park beside the River Saale in central location for touring the area.

dir: *Near S bridge over the Saale.*

Open: Apr-30 Oct **Site:** 1.8HEC **Facilities:** Wi-fi (charged) Play Area **Services:** **Off-site:** P R

KITZINGEN — BAYERN

Schiefer Turm

Marktbreiter Str 20, 97318
09321 33125 09321 384795
e-mail: info@camping-kitzingen.de
web: www.camping-kitzingen.de

dir: *A3 exit Biebelried/Kitzingen.*

Open: Apr-15 Oct **Site:** 2.3HEC **Facilities:** **Services:** **Leisure:** R **Off-site:** P

KLINGENBRUNN — BAYERN

NationalPark

94518
08553 727 08553 6930
web: www.camping-nationalpark.de

Pleasant wooded surroundings set around the restaurant on southern slope between Klingenbrunn and Spiegelau.

dir: *Off B85 12km SE of Regen near Kirchdorf, 6km E towards Klingenbrunn.*

Open: All Year. **Site:** 5HEC **Prices:** 16 **Facilities:** Wi-fi **Services:** **Off-site:** L P

KÖNIGSDORF — BAYERN

Königsdorf

Am Bibisee, 82549
08171 81580 08171 81165
e-mail: mail@camping-koenigsdorf.de
web: www.camping-koenigsdorf.de

Unspoiled site in natural setting in meadowland. A number of individual pitches for tourers.

dir: *2km N of town off B11, just beyond edge of forest.*

Open: All Year. **Site:** 8.6HEC **Facilities:** **Services:** **Leisure:** L **Off-site:** P R S

KÖNIGSSEE — BAYERN

Mühlleiten

83477
08652 4584 08652 69194
e-mail: info@muehlleiten.eu
web: www.muehlleiten.eu

A pleasant site in wooded surroundings adjacent to a small guesthouse. Beautiful views of the Berchtesgaden mountains.

dir: *N of Königsee towards Berchtesgaden.*

Open: All Year. **Site:** 1.8HEC **Prices:** 25 **Facilities:** Wi-fi **Services:** **Leisure:** R **Off-site:** L P

KRUN — BAYERN

Tennsee

The Camping and Caravanning Club — The Friendly Club

82493
08825 170 08825 17236
e-mail: info@camping-tennsee.de
web: www.camping-tennsee.de

A partially terraced site with fine views of the Karwendel and Zugspitze mountains.

C&CC Report *A really friendly site with top-notch facilities, a beautiful Alpine setting and outstanding Bavarian cuisine. There are discounts for local attractions and a wealth of day trips. Fairytale castles including Neuschwanstein, of Chitty-Chitty-Bang-Bang fame, grace the lovely Alpine scenery, while Venice, Lake Garda, Innsbruck and the Dolomites can all be reached as day trips by car, or through the site with the local coach tour company.*

dir: *From München-Garmisch-Partenkirchen motorway B2 to Mittenwald & signed.*

Open: 15 Dec-7 Nov **Site:** 5.2HEC **Facilities:** **Services:** **Off-site:** L

GERMANY

ÜHNHAUSEN BAYERN

Stadler

trandbadstr 11, 83367
08686 8037 08685 1049
veb: www.camping-stadler.de
evel meadow on lake with private beach.
ir: *2m E shore of Lake Waginger.*
pen: Apr-Sep **Site:** 0.8HEC **Facilities:**
ervices: **Leisure:** L S **Off-site:**

ACKENHÄUSER BAYERN

Knaus Campingpark Lackenhäuser

ackenhäuser 127, 94089
08583 311 08583 91079
-mail: lackenhaeuser@knauscamp.de
eb: www.knauscamp.de
xtensive site with woodland parks, waterfalls. Many health esort facilities.
pen: 16 Dec-3 Nov **Site:** 15HEC **Facilities:** **Services:** **Leisure:** P
ff-site: L

ANGLAU BAYERN

anglau

eestr 30, Kleiner Brombachsee, 91738
09834 96969 09834 96968
-mail: mail@seecamping-langlau.de
eb: www.seecamping-langlau.de
n the shores of the Kleiner Brombachsee.
r: *From Gunzevhausen towards Pleinfield for 10km.*
pen: Mar-15 Nov **Site:** 12.4HEC **Facilities:** **Services:** **Off-site:** L

ENGFURT BAYERN

ain-Spessart-Park

pessartstr 30, 97855
09395 1079 09395 8295
mail: info@camping-main-spessart.de
eb: www.camping-main-spessart.de
te lies partly on terraced meadowland and partly on the eastern opes of the Main Valley. Some water sports and nearby private ooring on the River Main.
r: *A3 exit Markheidenfeld, N to Altfeld, 6km E to Lengfurt (NW dge of village).*
PS: 49.8183, 9.5886
pen: All Year. **Site:** 10HEC **Prices:** 18.60
cilities: Play Area **Services:**
f-site: P R

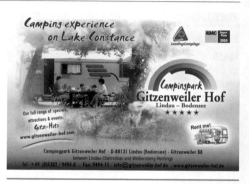

LINDAU BAYERN

Campingpark Gitzenweiler Hof

The Camping and Caravanning Club – The Friendly Club

Gitzenweiler 88, 88131
08382 94940 08382 949415
e-mail: info@gitzenweiler-hof.de
web: www.gitzenweiler-hof.de
Located in hilly meadow ground near Lake Constance surrounded with trees and hedges.

C&CC Report *This large, friendly and very well run site has great international appeal, plus a wide range of services and activities available most of the year, making it perfect for active families of all ages. Don't miss the lovely historic island town of Lindau and a boat trip on stunning Lake Constance, or the award-winning Friedrichshafen Zeppelin museum.*

dir: *A96 exit Weissensberg. B31a exit Lindau.*

Open: All Year. **Site:** 14HEC **Prices:** 21.10-32 Mobile home hire 420-630 **Facilities:** Wi-fi (charged) Kids' Club Play Area **Services:** **Leisure:** P

see advert on this page

Lindau am See

Fraunhoferstr 20, Zech, 88131
08382 72236 08382 976106
e-mail: info@park-camping.de
web: www.park-camping.de
Site lies on meadowland with trees, reaching down to the lake. Very large sanitary blocks. Common room, reading room, field for ball games and a separate common room for young people.

dir: *B31 from Lindau towards Bregenz, turn right (signed) before level crossing, site 0.5km.*

Open: 15 Mar-10 Nov **Site:** 5HEC **Prices:** 18-28
Facilities: Kids' Club Play Area **Services:** **Leisure:** L **Off-site:** P

GERMANY

MÖRSLINGEN BAYERN

Mörslingen

89435
☎ 09074 4024
e-mail: mail@camping-moerslingen.de
web: www.camping-moerslingen.de
Attractive well equipped site close to LEGOLAND® Günzburg.
dir: *6km N of Dillengen.*
Open: All Year. **Site:** 1HEC **Facilities:** **Services:** **Leisure:** L P **Off-site:**

MÜHLHAUSEN BEI AUGSBURG BAYERN

Lech Camping

Seeweg 6, 86444
☎ 08207 2200 08207 2202
e-mail: info@lech-camping.de
web: www.lech-camping.de
Level grassland with swimming facilities beside lake. Close to LEGOLAND® Munich and Augsburg.
dir: *4km N towards Neuburg. A8 exit 73.*
GPS: 48.4375, 10.9291
Open: Apr-Oct **Site:** 3HEC **Prices:** 22.50-24.90 **Facilities:** Wi-fi (charged) Play Area **Services:** **Leisure:** L **Off-site:** P

Ludwigshof am See

Augsburger Str 36, 86444
☎ 08207 96170 08207 961770
e-mail: info@bauer-caravan.de
web: www.bauer-caravan.de
Clean site with small lake away from motorway, near restaurant of the same name.
dir: *Motorway exit 73 Augsburg Ost, 1.5km N towards Neuburg.*
Open: Apr-Oct **Site:** 12HEC **Facilities:** **Services:** **Leisure:** L **Off-site:** P R

MÜNCHEN (MUNICH) BAYERN

München-Obermenzing

Lochhausener Str 59, Obermenzing, 81247
☎ 089 8112235 089 8144807
e-mail: campingplatz-obermenzing@t-online.de
web: www.campingplatz-muenchen.de
Park-like site near motorway.
dir: *1km from end of Stuttgart-München motorway.*
GPS: 48.1747, 11.4469
Open: 15 Mar-Oct **Site:** 5.5HEC **Facilities:** Wi-fi (charged) Play Area **Services:** **Off-site:** L P R

NEUBÄU BAYERN

Seecamping

Seestr 4, 93426
☎ 09469 331 09469 397
e-mail: r.notka@see-campingpark.de
web: www.see-campingpark.de
Meadowland site along lakeshore.
dir: *B85 from Schwandorf towards Cham.*
Open: All Year. **Site:** 5HEC **Facilities:** **Services:** **Leisure:** L

NEUKIRCHEN VORM WALD BAYERN

Rotbrunn

Pilling 22, 94154
☎ 08504 920260 08504 920265
e-mail: camping.rotbrunn@vr-web.de
Terraced and partially shaded site on edge of small town with shops and services.
dir: *A3 exit Aicha W, 6km to Neukirchen.*
Open: All Year. **Site:** **Facilities:** **Services:** **Leisure:** L **Off-site:**

NEUSTADT BAYERN

Main-Spessart-Camping-International

97845
☎ 09393 639 09393 1607
e-mail: info@camping-neustadt-main.de
web: www.camping-neustadt-main.de
Beautiful location alongside the River Main. Water sports include water skiing.
dir: *A3 exit Marktheidenfeld towards Lohr.*
GPS: 49.9117, 9.5833
Open: Apr-Sep **Site:** 5.6HEC **Prices:** 19 **Facilities:** Wi-fi (charged) Play Area **Services:** **Leisure:** P R

NÜRNBERG (NUREMBERG) BAYERN

Knaus Campingpark Nürnberg

Hans-Kalb-Str 56, 90471
☎ 0911 9812717 0911 9812718
e-mail: nuernberg@knauscamp.de
web: www.knauscamp.de
Well-kept site in beautiful location in a forest between a stadium with a swimming pool and the Trade Fair Centre.
dir: *A9 exit Nürnberg-Fischbach towards stadium.*
Open: All Year. **Site:** 2.7HEC **Facilities:** **Services:** **Off-site:** L P

GERMANY

BERAMMERGAU BAYERN

Oberammergau

ttaler Str 56, 82487
08822 94105 08822 94197
-mail: service@camping-oberammergau.de
veb: www.campingpark-oberammergau.de
year-round site with modern facilities and fine views of the avarian Alps.

ir: *Signed from town.*

pen: All Year. **Site:** 2HEC **Facilities:**
ervices: **Leisure:** R **Off-site:** P

BERSTDORF BAYERN

Oberstdorf

ubinger Str 16, 87561
08322 6525 08322 809760
-mail: camping-oberstdorf@t-online.de
veb: www.camping-oberstdorf.de
evel grassland site with fine mountain views.

ir: *0.8km N of town centre near railway line.*

pen: All Year. **Site:** 16HEC **Facilities:**
ervices: **Off-site:** L P R

BERWÖSSEN BAYERN

itzelau

3246
08640 8704 08640 5265
-mail: camping-litzelau@t-online.de
eb: www.camping-litzelau.de
most level meadowland surrounded by forested slopes.

ir: *A8 exit 106 Bernau, B305 S through Marquartstein & nterwössen.*

pen: All Year. **Site:** 4.5HEC **Prices:** 17-24.80
acilities: Wi-fi (charged) Kids' Club Play Area
ervices: **Leisure:** R **Off-site:** L P

ASSAU BAYERN

reiflüsse

m Sonnenhang 8, 94113
08546 633 08546 2686
-mail: dreifluessecamping@t-online.de
eb: www.dreifluessecamping.privat.t-online.de
well-equipped site in pleasant wooded surroundings. Close to e city of Passau in the upper Danube valley.

r: *A3 exit Passau-Nord, site signed.*

pen: Apr-Oct **Site:** 5HEC **Prices:** 22
acilities: Wi-fi **Services:**
isure: P

PFRAUNDORF BAYERN

Kratzmühle

85125
08461 64170 08461 641717
e-mail: info@kratzmuehle.de
web: www.kratzmuehle.de
Terraced site, divided into pitches, on a wooded hillside overlooking the River Altmühl.

dir: *From village turn to Kratzmühle.*

GPS: 49.0033, 11.4519

Open: All Year. **Site:** 9.6HEC
Prices: 17.50-23.50 **Facilities:** Wi-fi Play Area
Services: **Leisure:** L R

PIDING BAYERN

Staufeneck

83451
08651 2134 08651 710450
e-mail: camping-staufeneck@t-online.de
web: www.camping-berchtesgadener-land.de
Beautiful and quiet location beside the River Saalach.

dir: *A8 exit Bad Reichenall for 2.5km & turn right.*

Open: Apr-Oct **Site:** 2.7HEC **Facilities:**
Services: **Leisure:** R **Off-site:**

PIELENHOFEN BAYERN

Naabtal-Pielenhofen

The Camping and Caravanning Club The Friendly Club

93188
09409 373 09409 723
e-mail: camping.pielenhofen@t-online.de
web: www.camping-pielenhofen.de
The site is well-situated beside the River Nab, and has a special section for overnight visitors.

C&CC Report *This well-established, family-run, friendly and traditional site is constantly improving, with the main washblock in particular recently renovated to a very high standard, and the play area also renewed. The very good touring pitches are mainly on or near the riverside, while the site is bordered by the Bachs' own peaceful farmland. This is a perfect base for visiting enchanting Regensburg, but the area's wooded valleys are great for walking or cycling year round and dotted with lovely castles and other stately buildings. Alternatively, you can always relax with a meal in the site's traditional biergarten.*

dir: *A3 exit Nittendorf, via Etterzhausen.*

Open: All Year. **Site:** 6HEC **Prices:** 17.60
Facilities: Play Area **Services:**
Leisure: R

GERMANY

PRIEN AM CHIEMSEE BAYERN

Hofbauer

Bernauerstr 110, 83209
☎ 08051 4136 🖷 08051 62657
e-mail: ferienhaus-campingpl.hofbauer@t-online.de
web: www.camping-prien-chiemsee.de

A peaceful location among the Bavarian foothills of the Alps with fine views of the mountains. Site divided into separate plots.

dir: *A8 exit 106 for Bernau, right for Prien, site 3km on left.*

Open: Apr-Oct **Site:** 2HEC **Prices:** 22.50 **Facilities:** Play Area **Services:** **Leisure:** P **Off-site:** L

ROTHENBURG OB DER TAUBER BAYERN

Tauber-Idyll

Detwang 28A, 91541
☎ 09861 3177 🖷 09861 92848
e-mail: camping-tauber-idyll@t-online.de
web: www.rothenburg.de/tauber-idyll

The well-kept site lies on a meadow scattered with trees and bushes, on the outskirts of the northern suburb of Detwang and next to the River Tauber.

dir: *B25 from Nordinger Str W along River Tauber towards Bad Mergentheim. Signed from main roads.*

Open: 1wk before Etr-1 Nov **Site:** 0.5HEC **Prices:** 16 **Facilities:** Wi-fi **Services:** **Off-site:** P R

Tauber-Romantik

Detwang 39, 91541
☎ 09861 6191 🖷 09861 9368889
e-mail: info@camping-tauberromantik.de
web: www.camping-tauberromantik.de

Modern campsite in the pleasant Tauber valley.

GPS: 49.3878, 10.1678

Open: 15 Mar-4 Nov **Site:** 1.2HEC **Prices:** 17-21 Mobile home hire 238-252 **Facilities:** Play Area **Services:** **Off-site:** R

ROTTENBUCH BAYERN

Terrassen-Camping am Richterbichl

82401
☎ 08867 1500 🖷 08867 8300
e-mail: info@camping-rottenbuch.de
web: www.camping-rottenbuch.de

Several pleasant terraces with good views.

dir: *On S outskirts on B23.*

Open: All Year. **Site:** 1.2HEC **Prices:** 19 **Facilities:** Wi-fi Play Area **Services:** **Leisure:** L **Off-site:** P R

RUHPOLDING BAYERN

Ortnerhof

Ort 5, 83324
☎ 08663 1764 🖷 08663 5073
e-mail: camping-ortnerhof@t-online.de
web: www.ruhpolding.de/camping

Well-kept site on a meadow at the foot of the Rauschberg Mountain, opposite the cable-car station.

dir: *Off Deutsche Alpenstr.*

Open: All Year. **Site:** 3HEC **Facilities:** **Services:** **Off-site:**

SCHECHEN BAYERN

Erlensee

Rosenheimer Str 63, 83135
☎ 08039 1695 🖷 08039 9416

The site lies on the shores of an artificial lake.

dir: *From Rosenheim, 10km N onto B15 towards Wasserburg, turn right entering Schechen.*

Open: All Year. **Site:** 6HEC **Prices:** 19.50 **Facilities:** **Services:** **Leisure:** L **Off-site:**

SEEFELD BAYERN

Strandbad Pilsensee

Graf Toerringstr 11, 82229
☎ 08152 7232 🖷 08152 78473
e-mail: campingplatz@toerring-seefeld.de
web: www.schloss-seefeld.de

Within easy reach of the A8 and A96 at the centre of the Bavarian five lake area.

dir: *S towards Pilsensee.*

Open: All Year. **Site:** 10HEC **Prices:** 18.45-19.89 **Facilities:** Wi-fi Play Area **Services:** **Leisure:** L **Off-site:**

SOMMERACH AM MAIN BAYERN

Katzenkopf am See

97334
☎ 09381 9215 🖷 09381 6028
web: www.camping-katzenkopf.de

On level ground beside the river Main. Pitches divided by bushes and good recreational facilities.

dir: *A3 exit Kitzingen-Schwarzach-Volkach for Volkach after 4km follow signs to Sommerach, then follow camping signs.*

GPS: 49.8258, 10.2005

Open: Apr-23 Oct **Site:** 7HEC **Facilities:** Play Area **Services:** **Leisure:** L R **Off-site:** P

GERMANY

TADTSTEINACH BAYERN

Stadtsteinach

adstr 5, 95346
☎ 09225 800394
-mail: info@camping-stadtsteinach.de
eb: www.camping-stadtsteinach.de
erraced site on south-eastern facing slope with a view over the own and surrounding hills.
ir: *Via Badstr.*
pen: All Year. Site: 3.8HEC Facilities: ervices: Off-site: P

ETTENHAUSEN BAYERN

ut Horn

3329
☎ 08681 227 08681 4282
-mail: info@gut-horn.de
eb: www.gut-horn.de
uiet site sheltered by forest in a central location, divided into itches on lake shore.
ir: *SE on Wagingersee.*
pen: Mar-Nov Site: 5HEC Prices: 20.30-21.80
acilities: Wi-fi (charged) Services:
isure: L Off-site:

TTMONING BAYERN

eebauer

urth 9, 84529
☎ 08683 1216 08683 7175
mail: info@camping-seebauer.de
eb: www.camping-seebauer.de
n meadow with a few terraces. In a quiet situation near a farm, side a lake overlooking the Bavarian and Austrian Alps.
r: *3km NW towards Burghausen.*
PS: 48.0727, 12.7394
en: 15 Apr-Sep Site: 2.3HEC Prices: 18 Facilities: Wi-fi (charged) Play Area Services:
Leisure: L P Off-site: L R

RAUSNITZ BAYERN

rausnitz

2555
☎ 09655 1304 09655 1304
eb: www.camping-trausnitz.de
oded surroundings on the shores of a lake with modern cilities.
r: *A93 exit Pfreimd.*
en: All Year. Site: 3.5HEC Facilities:
rvices: Leisure: L R

TÜCHERSFELD BAYERN

Fränkische Schweiz

Tüchersfeld, 91278
☎ 09242 1788 09242 1040
e-mail: info@campingplatz-fraenkische-schweiz.info
web: www.campingplatz-fraenkische-schweiz.info
dir: *A9 exit Pegnitz, 12km W on B470 towards Forchheim.*
Open: 20 Mar-9 Oct Site: 2HEC Facilities:
Services: Leisure: R

VELBURG BAYERN

Am Hauenstein

Seestr 9-11, 92355
☎ 09182 454 09182 902251
e-mail: campingamhauenstein@t-online.de
web: www.campingamhauenstein.de
A well-appointed site, lies on several terraces with generous spaces enjoying the Jura scenery.
dir: *A3 exit Velburg, S through village signed Naturbad.*
GPS: 49.2172, 11.6686
Open: All Year. Site: 5HEC Prices: 18.40-19.40
Facilities: Play Area Services:
Off-site: L

VIECHTACH BAYERN

Knaus Campingpark Viechtach

Waldfrieden 22, 94234
☎ 09942 1095 09942 902222
e-mail: viechtach@knauscamp.de
web: www.knauscamp.de
Site on slightly undulating meadow, divided by rows of trees. The site has modern installations.
dir: *Off Freibad Viechtach onto B85, signed.*
Open: 16 Dec-3 Nov Site: 5.7HEC Facilities:
Services: Leisure: P

WAGING BAYERN

Strandcamping

Am See 1, 83329
☎ 08681 552 08681 45010
e-mail: info@strandcamp.de
web: www.strandcamp.de
Extensive, level grassland site divided in two by access road to neighbouring sailing club. The site lies near the Strandbad and Kurhaus bathing area and spa, and the Casino. There is a Kneipp (hydrotherapeutic) pool in the camp.
dir: *Signed to Strandbad bathing area.*
Open: Mar-Oct Site: 34HEC Prices: 26.80-39.70
Mobile home hire 316 Facilities: Wi-fi (charged) Kids' Club Play Area Services: Leisure: L

GERMANY

WALTENHOFEN BAYERN

Insel-Camping

87448
08379 881 08379 7308
e-mail: info@insel-camping.de
web: www.insel-camping.de

A well-equipped site beside the lake with access to ski slopes.

dir: *Off B19, S of Memhölz.*

GPS: 47.6404, 10.2786

Open: All Year. **Site:** 1.6HEC **Prices:** 17.50-20 **Facilities:** Wi-fi (charged) Play Area **Services:** **Leisure:** L **Off-site:** P R

WEISSACH BAYERN

Wallberg

Rainerweg 10, 83700
08022 5371 08022 670274
e-mail: campingplatz-wallberg@web.de
web: www.campingplatz-wallberg.de

This well-kept site lies on a level meadow with a few trees beside a stream.

dir: *B318 from Gmund to Tegernsee, Bad Wiessee to Weissach, continue 9km.*

Open: All Year. **Site:** 3HEC **Facilities:** **Services:** **Leisure:** R **Off-site:** L P

WEISSENSTADT BAYERN

Weissenstadt

Badstr 91, 95163
09253 288 09253 8507
e-mail: whuettel-stadtbad@t-online.de
web: www.campingplatz-weissenstadt.de

This municipal site is in close proximity to a swimming pool and a lake, so offering numerous sports facilities.

dir: *1km NW of town.*

Open: All Year. **Site:** 1.7HEC **Facilities:** **Services:** **Leisure:** L P **Off-site:**

WEMDING BAYERN

AZUR Waldsee Wemding

Wolferstadter Str 100, 86650
09092 90101 09092 90100
e-mail: info@campingpark-waldsee.de
web: www.campingpark-waldsee.de

A wooded lakeside setting with excellent recreational facilities.

Open: 15 Mar-Oct **Site:** 9HEC **Facilities:** **Services:** **Leisure:** L **Off-site:** P R

WERTACH BAYERN

Grüntensee-International

Grüntenseestr 41, 87497
08365 375 08365 1221
e-mail: info@camping-grueutensee.de
web: www.camping-gruentensee.de

A modern site beside Lake Grünten in the middle of the lovely Allgäuer mountain landscape.

dir: *From Kempten, turn right entering Nesselwang-Werlach & signed.*

Open: All Year. **Site:** 5HEC **Facilities:** Play Area **Services:** **Leisure:** L

ZWIESEL BAYERN

AZUR-Ferienzentrum Bayerischer Wald

Waldesruhweg 34, 94227
09922 802595 09922 802594
e-mail: zwiesel@azur-camping.de
web: www.azur-camping.de

A modern family site. In the middle of a nature reserve in the Bavarian forest.

Open: Apr-Sep and 15 Dec-Feb **Site:** 16HEC **Facilities:** **Services:** **Off-site:** P

SOUTH WEST

ABTSGMÜND BADEN-WÜRTTEMBERG

Hammerschmiede-See

Hammerschmiede 2, Pommertsweiler, 73453
07963 369 07963 840032
e-mail: hug.hammerschmiede@t-online.de
web: www.hug-hammerschmiede.de

A terraced site in a wooded setting beside the lake. Partly divided into pitches with concrete paths.

dir: *From Abtsgmünd for 3km then N to Pommertsweiler, signed.*

Open: May-Sep **Site:** 5HEC **Facilities:** **Services:** **Leisure:** L

ACHERN BADEN-WÜRTTEMBERG

Staedtischer Campingplatz am Achernsee

Am Achernsee 8, 77855
07841 25253 07841 508835
e-mail: camping@achern.de
web: www.achern.de

A family site close to attractive lake with bathing.

Open: All Year. **Site:** 6.5HEC **Prices:** 16-19 **Facilities:** Play Area **Services:** **Leisure:** L **Off-site:** P

LPIRSBACH — BADEN-WÜRTTEMBERG

amping Alpirsbach

rezenbühler Weg 18, 72275
07444 6313 07444 917815
-mail: info@camping-alpirsbach.de
eb: www.camping-alpirsbach.de
uiet, family friendly site, ideal for hiking and cycling in the urrounding countryside. Fishing is available on site, along with able tennis and cycle hire.
pen: All Year. Site: 1.2HEC Prices: 20-22 Mobile ome hire 175 Facilities: Wi-fi Play Area
ervices:

LTNEUDORF — BADEN-WÜRTTEMBERG

teinachperle

9250
06228 467 06228 8568
mail: campingplatz-steinachperle@t-online.de
e site lies in the narrow shady valley of the River Steinach.
r: *Next to Gasthaus zum Pflug on outskirts of Altneudorf.*
en: Apr-Sep Site: 3.5HEC Facilities:
rvices: Leisure: R

ADENWEILER — BADEN-WÜRTTEMBERG

adenweiler

eilertalstr 73, 79410
07632 1550 07632 5268
mail: info@camping-badenweiler.de
b: www.camping-badenweiler.de
vel meadowland site surrounded by beautiful Black Forest enery. Good facilities for local walking.
: *A5 exit Neuenburg.*
en: 16 Jan-14 Dec Site: 1.6HEC Facilities:
Services: Leisure: P

CHHORN BEI ÖHRINGEN — BADEN-WÜRTTEMBERG

eewiese

estr 11, 74629
07941 61568 07941 38527
nail: campingseewiese@t-online.de
b: www.camping-seewiese.de
vell-equipped site on a meadow beside a lake with fine views of surrounding mountains. Good recreational facilities.
: *7km S of Öhringen via Pfedelbach.*
en: All Year. Site: 5.5HEC Prices: 17-19 Facilities:
Play Area Services:
sure: L P

BÜHL — BADEN-WÜRTTEMBERG

Adam

Campingstr 1, 77185
07223 23194 07223 8982
e-mail: webmaster@campingplatz-adam.de
web: www.campingplatz-adam.de
On level grassland, by lake.
dir: *A5 exit Bühl, 1km towards Lichtenau.*
Open: All Year. Site: 15HEC Facilities:
Services: Leisure: L Off-site: P

CREGLINGEN — BADEN-WÜRTTEMBERG

Camping Romantische Strasse

97993
07933 20289 07933 990019
e-mail: camping.hausotter@web.de
web: www.camping-romantische-strasse.de
The site lies on the southern outskirts of Münster and is divided into pitches. Sanitary facilities include individual washing cubicles.
dir: *From Bad Mergentheim or Rothenburg/Tauber onto Romantic road to Creglingen, turn S for 3km to Münster.*
Open: 15 Mar-15 Nov Site: 6HEC
Prices: 17.50-20.70 Facilities: Wi-fi (charged) Play Area Services: Leisure: P R Off-site: L

DINGELSDORF — BADEN-WÜRTTEMBERG

Fliesshorn

78465
07533 5262
e-mail: info@fliesshorn.de
web: www.fliesshorn.de
At a farm, on meadowland with fine trees.
dir: *In town turn off Stadd-Dettingen road & signed NW for 1.3km.*
Open: Apr-3 Oct Site: 5HEC Facilities:
Services: Off-site: L S

DONAUESCHINGEN — BADEN-WÜRTTEMBERG

Riedsee Camping

78166
0771 5511 0771 15138
e-mail: info@riedsee-camping.de
web: www.riedsee-camping.de
Level meadow on lakeside. Kids' club available in July and August.
dir: *A81 exit Geisingen, B31 towards Pfohren, 13km left, continue 1km.*
Open: All Year. Site: 8HEC Prices: 16.50-21.50
Facilities: Wi-fi (charged) Kids' Club Play Area
Services: Leisure: L

GERMANY

DÜRRHEIM, BAD — BADEN-WÜRTTEMBERG

Naturcamping Bad Dürrheim

Am Steigle 1, 78073
☎ 07706 712 🖷 07706 922906
e-mail: info@naturcamping-badduerrheim.info
web: www.naturcamping-badduerrheim.info
Open: All Year. **Site:** 8HEC **Facilities:** **Services:** **Off-site:** P

ELLWANGEN-JAGST — BADEN-WÜRTTEMBERG

AZUR Ellwangen

Rotenbacherstr 45, 73479
☎ 07961 7921 🖷 07961 562330
e-mail: ellwangen@azur-camping.de
web: www.azur-camping.de/ellwangen
A modern site with good facilities in a wooded loaction on the banks of the River Jagst.
Open: Apr-Oct **Site:** 3.5HEC **Facilities:** **Services:** **Leisure:** R **Off-site:** L P

ERPFINGEN — BADEN-WÜRTTEMBERG

AZUR Rosencamping Schwäbische Alb

72820
☎ 07128 466 🖷 07128 30137
e-mail: info@azur-camping.de
web: www.azur-camping.de
Extensive site on a hill.
dir: *From Reutlingen on B312 SE to Grooengstingen, then S on Schwabische Albstr (B313) for 3.5km to Haid, right to Erpfingen, site on W outskirts.*
Open: All Year. **Site:** 9HEC **Facilities:** **Services:** **Leisure:** P **Off-site:** L

ETTENHEIM — BADEN-WÜRTTEMBERG

Oase

77955
☎ 07822 445918 🖷 07822 445919
e-mail: info@campingpark-oase.de
web: www.campingpark-oase.de
Wooded location with modern facilities close to the Black Forest.
dir: *A5 exit Ettenheim.*
Open: 16 Apr-5 Oct **Site:** 5HEC **Prices:** 20.50
Facilities: Wi-fi (charged) Play Area **Services:** **Off-site:** P

FREIBURG IM BREISGAU — BADEN-WÜRTTEMBERG

Breisgau-Silbersee

Seestr 20, 79108
☎ 07665 2346 🖷 07665 2346
Extensive level grassland site on outskirts of town. Section reserved for campers with dogs.
dir: *Autobahn exit Freiburg Nord, site 0.5km E.*
Open: All Year. **Site:** 18HEC **Facilities:** **Services:** **Leisure:** L

Camping am Möslepark

Waldseestr 77, 79117
☎ 0761 7679333 🖷 0761 7679336
e-mail: information@camping-freiburg.com
web: www.camping-freiburg.com
On outskirts of town near Busse's Waldschänke inn.
dir: *Right after town hall over railway & Waldseestr towards Littenweiler.*
Open: 20 Mar-28 Oct **Site:** 0.7HEC **Prices:** 20.1
Facilities: Wi-fi Play Area **Services:** **Off-site:** L P R

FREUDENSTADT — BADEN-WÜRTTEMBER

Langenwald

Strassburgerstr 167, 72250
☎ 07441 2862 🖷 07441 2893
e-mail: info@camping-langenwald.de
web: www.camping-langenwald.de
The site consists of several sections and lies next to a former m beside the River Forbach.
dir: *4km W of Freudenstadt below B28.*
Open: Apr-Nov **Site:** 2HEC **Prices:** 24.50 **Facilities:** Wi-fi Play Area **Services:**
Leisure: P R

HALLWANGEN — BADEN-WÜRTTEMBE

Königskanzel

72280
☎ 07443 6730 🖷 07443 4574
e-mail: info@camping-koenigskanzel.de
web: www.camping-koenigskanzel.de
Set on an elevated position in the centre of the Black Forest.
dir: *B28 from Freudenstadt towards Altensteig, past Hallwang junct, signed on right.*
GPS: 48.4808, 8.5005
Open: All Year. **Site:** 6HEC **Prices:** 18.50-23.30
Facilities: Play Area **Services:** **Leisure:** P **Off-site:**

GERMANY

AUSEN BADEN-WÜRTTEMBERG

'agenburg

rchstr 24, 88637
07579 559
mail: info@camping-wagenburg.de
b: www.camping-wagenburg.de

meadowland between the railway bank and the Danube. Site s spectacular view of surrounding landscape. Entrance through bway.

en: 16 Apr-3 Oct **Site:** 1.2HEC **Facilities:**
rvices: **Leisure:** R

IDELBERG BADEN-WÜRTTEMBERG

eidelberg-Neckartal

hlierbacher Landstr 151, 69118
06221 802506 06221 802506
mail: mail@camping-heidelberg.de
b: www.camping-heidelberg.de

en: 15 Mar-30 Oct **Site:** 3HEC **Facilities:** **Services:** **Leisure:** R

RBOLZHEIM BADEN-WÜRTTEMBERG

rbolzheim

Laue 1, 79336
07643 1460 07643 913382
mail: s.hugoschmidt@t-online.de
b: www.laue-camp.de

leasant rural setting with good facilities, a short distance m the Europa-Park Rust amusement park.

: *On A5 between Freiburg & Offenburg.*

en: 15 Apr-3 Oct **Site:** 3.8HEC **Prices:** 20-23
cilities: Wi-fi (charged) Play Area **Services:** **Off-site:** L P

FEN AN DER ENZ BADEN-WÜRTTEMBERG

ellgrund

339
07081 6984 07081 6984

l-maintained municipal site on grassland between the B294 d the River Enz.

: *B294 SW from Pforzheim to Quelle inn/fuel station at rance to Höfen, turn right.*

en: Nov-Sep **Site:** 3.6HEC **Prices:** 19.50-21
cilities: Play Area **Services:**
sure: R **Off-site:** P

HORB BADEN-WÜRTTEMBERG

Schüttehof

72160
07451 3951 07451 623215
e-mail: camping-schuettehof@t-online.de
web: www.camping-schuettehof.de

Situated on a flat mountain top at the forest edge and 100m from the historic village of Horb on Neckar – the Gate to the Black Forest.

dir: *From Horb towards Freudenstadt, 1.5km after town boundary turn towards stables & site, continue 1km.*

Open: All Year. **Site:** 6HEC **Facilities:** **Services:** **Leisure:** P R

ISNY BADEN-WÜRTTEMBERG

Isny

Lohbauerstr 59-69, 88316
07562 2389 07562 2004
e-mail: info@isny-camping.de
web: www.isny-camping.de

Attractive wooded surroundings beside a lake.

dir: *Lindau-Kempten B12, exit Isny-Mitte.*

Open: Jan-Oct **Site:** 3HEC **Prices:** 20-25.50
Facilities: **Services:** **Leisure:** L P
Off-site:

KEHL BADEN-WÜRTTEMBERG

Kehl-Strassburg

77694
07851 2603 07851 73076

Park-like site divided into separate sections for young campers, transit and holiday campers.

dir: *Turn left at Rhine dam on outskirts of town.*

Open: 15 Mar-Oct **Site:** 2.3HEC **Facilities:**
Services: **Off-site:** P R

KIRCHBERG BADEN-WÜRTTEMBERG

Christophorus

Werte 61, 88486
07354 663 07354 91314
e-mail: info@camping-christophorus.de
web: www.camping-christophorus.de

Completely enclosed, clean site.

dir: *A7 exit Illereichen Allenstadt to town centre & towards railway station.*

Open: All Year. **Site:** 9.2HEC **Facilities:**
Services: **Leisure:** L P

GERMANY

Facilities shop shower electric points for razors electric points for caravans parking by tents permitted pulsory separate car park **Services** café/restaurant bar Camping Gaz International gas other than Camping Gaz first aid facilities laundry **Leisure** swimming L-Lake P-Pool R-River S-Sea **Off-site** All facilities within 5km

KIRCHZARTEN BADEN-WÜRTTEMBERG

Camping Kirchzarten

Diefenbacher Str 17, 79199
☎ 07661 9040910 07661 61624
e-mail: info@camping-kirchzarten.de
web: www.camping-kirchzarten.de

Extensive site with trees providing shade, at the entrance to Freiburg, in the heart of the Southern Black Forest.

dir: *8km E of Freiburg im Breisgau off B31.*

Open: All Year. **Site:** 5.9HEC **Prices:** 21.10-29.30 **Facilities:** **Services:** **Leisure:** P

KRESSBRONN BADEN-WÜRTTEMBERG

Gohren am See

88079
☎ 07543 60590 07543 605929
e-mail: info@campingplatz-gohren.de
web: www.campingplatz-gohren.de

A large site beside the lake. Older parts of the site are divided by hedges and reserved for residential campers. The newer section has fewer bushes.

dir: *3km from Kressbronn, signed from B31.*

Open: 14 Mar-15 Oct **Site:** 38HEC **Facilities:** **Services:** **Leisure:** L
Off-site: P

LAICHINGEN BADEN-WÜRTTEMBERG

Heidehof

Heidehofstr 50, 89150
☎ 07333 6408 07333 21463
e-mail: info@heidehof.info
web: www.camping-heidehof.de

Well-cared for site on hillside with some tall firs. Divided by asphalt roads with a separate section for overnight campers.

dir: *A8 exit Merkingen, site 2km S via Machtolsheim.*

Open: All Year. **Site:** 25HEC **Facilities:** **Services:** **Leisure:** P

LAUTERBURG BADEN-WÜRTTEMBERG

Hirtenteich

Hasenweide 2, 73457
☎ 07365 296 07365 251
e-mail: camphirtenteich@aol.com
web: www.campingplatz-hirtenteich.de

This site lies on gently sloping terrain, near the Hirtenteich recreation area.

dir: *Off B29 in Essingen S for 5km.*

Open: All Year. **Site:** 4HEC **Prices:** 17-17.50 **Facilities:** Wi-fi (charged) **Services:** **Leisure:** P

LENZKIRCH BADEN-WÜRTTEMBERG

Kreuzhof

Bonndorfer Str 65, 79853
☎ 07653 700 07653 6623
e-mail: info@brauerei-rogg.de
web: www.brauerei-rogg.de

Grassland near former farm below the Rogg Brewery.

dir: *B317 from Titisee towards Schaffhausen, onto B315 to Lenzkirch, site 2km from centre.*

Open: All Year. **Site:** 2HEC **Prices:** 20.20 **Facilities:** Wi-fi (charged) Play Area **Services:** **Leisure:** L P

LIEBELSBERG BADEN-WÜRTTEMBERG

Erbenwald

75387
☎ 07053 7382 07053 3274
e-mail: info@camping-erbenwald.de
web: www.camping-erbenwald.de

Pleasant site on edge of wood.

dir: *B463 S from Calw, 6km turn right just before Neubulach, continue N for 2km.*

GPS: 48.6772, 8.6891

Open: All Year. **Site:** 7.2HEC **Prices:** 20 **Facilities:** Wi-fi (charged) Play Area **Services:** **Leisure:** P

GERMANY

LIEBENZELL, BAD — BADEN-WÜRTTEMBERG

Bad-Liebenzell

Pforzheimerstr 34, 75378
07052 935680 07052 935681
e-mail: campingpark@abelundneff.de
web: www.campingpark-badliebenzell.de

Municipal site with trees near tennis courts. Divided by hedges and asphalt roads.

dir: *B463 S from Pforzheim for 19km, left 500m before Bad Liebenzell to site beside River Nagold.*

Open: All Year. **Site:** 3HEC **Facilities:** **Services:** **Leisure:** P R **Off-site:**

MARKDORF — BADEN-WÜRTTEMBERG

Wirthshof

88677
07544 96270 07544 962727
e-mail: info@wirthshof.de
web: www.wirthshof.de

Family friendly site offering a high standard of comfort and lots of activities.

Open: 15 Mar-30 Oct **Site:** 10HEC **Facilities:** **Services:** **Leisure:** P **Off-site:** L

MÖRTELSTEIN — BADEN-WÜRTTEMBERG

Germania

Mühlwiese 1, 06951
06262 1795 06262 1795

The site lies between the River Neckar and a wooded hillside.

dir: *B292 W towards Sinsheim, just after Oberigheim N onto narrow steep road into Neckar Valley.*

Open: 2 Apr-2 Oct **Site:** 0.8HEC **Facilities:** **Services:** **Leisure:** R **Off-site:**

MÜNSTERTAL — BADEN-WÜRTTEMBERG

Münstertal

Dietzelbachstr 6, 79244
07636 7080 07636 7448
e-mail: info@camping-muenstertal.de
web: www.camping-muenstertal.de

Well equipped level, grassy site in pleasant location with fine views.

dir: *Motorway exit Bad Kroningen, SE via Stauffen to W outskirts.*

Open: All Year. **Site:** 7HEC
Prices: 25.20-27.55 **Facilities:** **Services:** **Leisure:** P

MURRHARDT — BADEN-WÜRTTEMBERG

Waldsee

Fornsbach, 71540
07192 6436 07192 935717
e-mail: camping-waldsee@t-online.de
web: www.campingplatz-waldsee-murrhardt.de

The site lies near Lake Waldsee. Asphalt paths and pitches, with gravel surface.

dir: *Murrhardt towards Fornsbach, site on E shore of lake.*

Open: All Year. **Site:** 2HEC **Facilities:** **Services:** **Leisure:** L

NECKARGEMÜND — BADEN-WÜRTTEMBERG

Haide

Ziegelhäuserstr 91, 69151
06223 2111 06223 71959
e-mail: camping-haide@a-mail.eu

A well-appointed site in the picturesque Neckar valley, directly on the river on the outskirts of Heidelberg.

dir: *Follow river towards castle & Neckarsteinach.*

Open: Apr-Oct **Site:** 3.6HEC **Facilities:** **Services:** **Leisure:** R **Off-site:** P

NEUENBURG — BADEN-WÜRTTEMBERG

Gugel

Oberer Wald, 79395
07631 7719 07631 7719
e-mail: info@camping-gugel.de
web: www.camping-gugel.de

An extensive site with many entirely separate pitches. There is a new reception and restaurant, as well as an attractive swimming pool and beach bar. Kids' club at Easter and during summer holidays.

dir: *A5 exit Müllheim/Neuenburg, 3km to site.*

Open: All Year. **Site:** 12.8HEC **Facilities:** Wi-fi Kids' Club Play Area **Services:** **Leisure:** P **Off-site:** L R

NUSSDORF — BADEN-WÜRTTEMBERG

Nell

Zur Barbe 5, Bodensee, 88662
07551 4254 07551 944458
e-mail: info@campingplatz-nell.de
web: www.camping-nell.de

Located within an orchard between a farm and lakeside promenade. Small private beach.

dir: *Off B31.*

GPS: 47.7516, 9.1905

Open: Apr-20 Oct **Site:** 0.6HEC **Prices:** 19.60-21.20 **Facilities:** **Services:** **Leisure:** L **Off-site:** P

GERMANY

ÖSTRINGEN — BADEN-WÜRTTEMBERG

Kraichgau Camping Wackerhof

76684
☎ 07259 361 📠 07259 2431
e-mail: info@wackerhof.de
web: www.wackerhof.de
Between the Black Forest and Odenwald, a peaceful modern terraced site.
dir: *A5 exit Kronau/Bad Schönborn, B292 to Östringen. Campsite in 5km, follow signs.*
GPS: 49.2005, 8.7602
Open: 25 Mar-15 Oct **Site:** 3HEC **Prices:** 10 **Facilities:** **Services:**

PFORZHEIM — BADEN-WÜRTTEMBERG

International Schwarzwald

Freibadweg 4, 75242
☎ 07234 6517 📠 07234 5180
e-mail: fam.frech@t-online.de
web: www.camping-schwarzwald.de
Site on edge of wood with southerly aspect. Separate fields for residential, overnight and holiday campers.
dir: *S through Huchenfeld from Pforzheim to Schellbron (15km).*
Open: All Year. **Site:** 4.5HEC **Prices:** 18 **Facilities:** Play Area **Services:** **Leisure:** P **Off-site:** R

RHEINMÜNSTER — BADEN-WÜRTTEMBERG

Freizeitcenter-Oberrhein

Stollhofen, 77836
☎ 07227 2500 📠 07227 2400
e-mail: info@freizeitcenter-oberrhein.de
web: www.freizeitcenter-oberrhein.de
Modern leisure complex next to the Rhine.
dir: *10km from A5 Baden-Baden/Iffezheim exit from north or Bühl from south.*
GPS: 48.7736, 8.0402
Open: All Year. **Site:** 36HEC **Prices:** 15-25.50 Mobile home hire 343-483 **Facilities:** Wi-fi (charged) Kids' Club Play Area **Services:** **Leisure:** L

ROSENBERG — BADEN-WÜRTTEMBERG

Hüttenhof

Hüttenhof 1, 73494
☎ 07963 203 📠 07963 8418894
e-mail: info@waldcamp.de
Flat meadow on incline in quiet woodland area, next to large farm.
dir: *From Ellwangen N towards Crailsheim for 3km, turn W towards Adelmannsfelden & 8km turn N at Gaishardt.*
Open: 15 Apr-Oct **Site:** 4HEC **Facilities:** **Services:** **Leisure:** L

ST PETER — BADEN-WÜRTTEMBERG

Steingrübenhof

79271
☎ 07660 210 📠 07660 1604
e-mail: info@camping-steingrubenhof.de
web: www.camping-steingrubenhof.de
On a level plateau, surrounded by delightful mountain scenery.
dir: *Via A5 & B294.*
Open: All Year. **Site:** 2HEC **Prices:** 17.70 **Facilities:** Wi-fi (charged) **Services:** **Off-site:** P

SCHAPBACH — BADEN-WÜRTTEMBERG

Alisehof

77776
☎ 07839 203 📠 07839 1263
e-mail: info@camping-online.de
web: www.camping-online.de
The site lies on well-kept ground with several terraces and is separated from the road by the River Wolfach.
dir: *Off B924 in Wolfach at Kinzighbrücke, then 8km N to Schapbach, site 1km N of village.*
GPS: 48.3833, 8.2997
Open: All Year. **Site:** 3HEC **Prices:** 17.20-22.50 Mobile home hire 270-295 **Facilities:** Wi-fi (charged) Play Area **Services:** **Leisure:** R **Off-site:** L P

SCHILTACH — BADEN-WÜRTTEMBERG

Schiltach

77761
☎ 07836 7289 📠 07836 7466
e-mail: info@campingplatz-schiltach.de
web: www.campingplatz-schiltach.de
The site lies on meadowland on the banks of the River Kinzig and is well-placed for excursions.
Open: Apr-3 Oct **Site:** 3.6HEC **Facilities:** **Services:** **Leisure:** R **Off-site:** P

Site 6HEC (site size) grass sand stone little shade partly shaded mainly shaded bungalows for hire (static) caravans for hire tents for hire no dogs site fully accessible for wheelchairs
Prices amount quoted is per night, for 2 adults and car, plus tent or caravan. Mobile home hire is a weekly rate.

GERMANY

SCHÖMBERG — BADEN-WÜRTTEMBERG

Höhen-Camping-Langenbrand

Schömberger Str 32, 75328
07084 6131 07084 931435
e-mail: info@hoehencamping.de
web: www.hoehencamping.de
Open: All Year. **Site:** 1.6HEC **Facilities:** **Services:** **Off-site:**

SCHUSSENRIED, BAD — BADEN-WÜRTTEMBERG

Reiterhof von Steinhausen

Reiterhof, 88427
07583 3060 07583 1004
e-mail: heikeschmid@web.de
A pleasant rural setting.
dir: *Via B30 Ulm-Bad Waldsee.*
Open: All Year. **Site:** 1HEC **Prices:** 11.50-19.70
Facilities: **Services:**
Off-site: L P R

SCHWÄBISCH GMÜND — BADEN-WÜRTTEMBERG

Schurrenhof

Rechberg, 73072
07165 8190 07165 1625
e-mail: info@schurrenhof.de
web: www.schurrenhof.de
The site lies in a beautiful setting on the edge of a forest, and has a lovely view of the surrounding countryside.
dir: *B29 S from Schwäbisch Gmünd, through Strassdorf & Rechberg towards Reichenbach on B10, turn towards Schurrenhof.*
Open: All Year. **Site:** 3HEC **Facilities:**
Services: **Leisure:** P

SCHWÄBISCH HALL — BADEN-WÜRTTEMBERG

Steinbacher See

Mühlsteige 26, 74523
0791 2984 0791 9462758
e-mail: thomas.seitel@t-online.de
web: www.camping-schwaebisch-hall.de
A modern site in the beautiful Kocher Valley. There are good sports facilities and many places of interest nearby, in the medieval town.
dir: *Via B14/19 to Steinbach.*
Open: Feb-Nov **Site:** 1.4HEC **Prices:** 17.90-20.60
Facilities: Wi-fi Play Area **Services:**
Off-site:

STAUFEN — BADEN-WÜRTTEMBERG

Belchenblick

The Camping and Caravanning Club — The Friendly Club

Münstertaler Str 43, 79219
07633 7045 07633 7908
e-mail: info@camping-belchenblick.de
web: www.camping-belchenblick.de
Well-kept site on level ground.
C&CC Report *With a range of excellent facilities, plus the traditional buildings hung with flowers, this is a great base for visiting the Black Forest and for making day trips to Switzerland. Staufen and its castle are very pretty, but picturesque Freiburg is nearby too – if you brave the spiral steps up into the tower of its beautiful minster, the effort is well rewarded.*
dir: *Motorway exit Bad Krozingen/Staufen, site 4km SE.*
GPS: 47.8725, 7.7352
Open: All Year. **Site:** 2.4HEC **Prices:** 23.80-26.80
Facilities: Wi-fi (charged) Kids' Club Play Area **Services:** **Leisure:** P R

STEINACH — BADEN-WÜRTTEMBERG

Kinzigtal

77790
07832 8122 07832 6619
e-mail: webmaster@campingplatz-kinzigtal.de
web: www.campingplatz-kinzigtal.de
Site on level meadowland with tall trees, situated next to the municipal heated swimming pool.
dir: *Signed from Steinach.*
Open: All Year. **Site:** 2.6HEC **Facilities:** Wi-fi Kids' Club Play Area **Services:**
Off-site: P R

STUTTGART — BADEN-WÜRTTEMBERG

Canstatter Wasen

Mercedesstr 40, 70372
0711 556696 0711 557554
e-mail: info@campingplatz-stuttgart.de
web: www.campingplatz-stuttgart.de
Level site with tall poplar trees alongside the River Neckar.
dir: *Via Bad Cannstatt near sports stadium.*
GPS: 48.7938, 9.2186
Open: All Year. **Site:** 1.7HEC **Facilities:** Play Area **Services:** **Off-site:** P R

TENGEN BADEN-WÜRTTEMBERG

Hegau-Familien-Camping

An der Sonnenhalde 1, 78250
☎ 07736 92470 🖹 07736 9247124
e-mail: info@hegau-camping.de
web: www.hegau-camping.de

Quiet, peaceful location close to the Swiss border and with panoramic views. Large pitches. Facilities include an indoor swimming pool with steam bath, whirlpool and sauna.

dir: *10km from A81.*

GPS: 47.8236, 8.6536

Open: All Year. **Site:** 8.5HEC **Prices:** 35 **Facilities:** Wi-fi Kids' Club Play Area **Services:** **Leisure:** L P

TITISEE-NEUSTADT BADEN-WÜRTTEMBERG

Bankenhof

Bruderhalde 31a, 79822
☎ 07652 1351
e-mail: info@camping-bankenhof.de
web: www.camping-bankenhof.de

A family site in a wooded location close to the lake. Access road closed 22.00-06.00 hrs.

dir: *From Titisee signed Camping Platz.*

Open: All Year. **Site:** 3.5HEC **Facilities:** **Services:** **Leisure:** R **Off-site:** L

Bühlhof

Bühlhofweg 13, 79822
☎ 07652 1606 🖹 07652 1827
e-mail: hertha-jaeger@t-online.de
web: www.camping-buehlhof.de

Pleasant location on a hillside above a lake.

dir: *Signed from Titisee.*

Open: 15 Dec-Oct **Site:** 10HEC **Prices:** 16-18 **Facilities:** **Services:** **Off-site:** L P

Sandbank

79822
☎ 07651 8243 🖹 07651 8286
e-mail: info@camping-sandbank.com
web: www.camping-sandbank.com

Lakeside terrain landscaped with trees, upper part terraced.

dir: *From Titisee, N bank of lake, turn into old Feldbergstr, left at SW end of lake onto private road through Camping Bankenhof (closed 22.00-06.00 hrs) to site, 0.7km on SE bank of lake.*

Open: Apr-20 Oct **Site:** 3HEC **Facilities:** **Services:** **Leisure:** L **Off-site:** P

Weiherhof am Titiseeufer

Bruderhalde 26, 79822
☎ 07652 1468 🖹 07652 1478
e-mail: kontakt@camping-titisee.de
web: www.camping-titisee.de

Mainly level site with trees, bordering on lake shore for some 400m.

dir: *Signed from Titisee.*

Open: May-Oct **Site:** 2HEC **Prices:** 21.50 **Facilities:** Kids' Club Play Area **Services:** **Leisure:** L **Off-site:** P

TODTNAU BADEN-WÜRTTEMBERG

Hochschwarzwald

79674
☎ 07671 1288 🖹 07671 9999943
e-mail: camping.hochschwarzwald@web.de
web: www.camping-hochschwarzwald.de

Terraced site, partially grassland, by ski-lift.

dir: *6km NW of Todtnau.*

Open: All Year. **Site:** 2.5HEC **Prices:** 12 **Facilities:** Play Area **Services:** **Leisure:** R

TÜBINGEN BADEN-WÜRTTEMBERG

Tübingen

Rappenberghalde 61, 72070
☎ 07071 43145 🖹 07071 793391
e-mail: mail@neckarcamping.de
web: www.neckarcamping.de

A quiet site on the banks of the River Neckar.

dir: *From town centre over Neckar bridge, turn right, S through Uhlandstr or Bahnhofstr to next bridge, over bridge & upstream to Rappenberghalde hill.*

GPS: 48.51, 9,0352

Open: Apr-Oct **Site:** 1HEC **Prices:** 21.50-22.90 **Facilities:** Wi-fi Play Area **Services:** **Leisure:** R **Off-site:** L P

GERMANY

ÜBERLINGEN BADEN-WÜRTTEMBERG

Überlingen

Bahnhofstr 57, 88662
07551 64583 07551 945895
e-mail: info@campingpark-ueberlingen.de
web: www.campingpark-ueberlingen.de

The site lies on the western outskirts of the town, between the railway line and the road on one side, and the concrete shore wall on the other. It is divided into several sections by low wooden barriers and has a very small beach.

dir: *Off B31 towards lake.*

Open: Apr-10 Oct **Site:** 3HEC **Facilities:** **Services:** **Leisure:** L **Off-site:** P

UHLDINGEN BADEN-WÜRTTEMBERG

Seeperle

Seefelden Hausnr 6, 88690
07556 5454 07556 966221
e-mail: info@camping-seeperle.de
web: www.camping-seeperle.de

This site has some large trees along the shore of the lake and a landing stage.

dir: *Off B31 at Oberuhldingen towards Seefelden, site 1km.*

Open: 15 Apr-15 Sep **Site:** 0.7HEC **Facilities:** **Services:** **Leisure:** L **Off-site:** P

WALDKIRCH BADEN-WÜRTTEMBERG

Elztalblick

79183
07681 4212 07681 4213
e-mail: eltztalblick@t-online.de
web: www.camping-elztalblick.de

A small site with terraced pitches in the heart of the Black Forest.

dir: *Autobahn exit Waldkirch Ost, signed for 3km.*

Open: 15 Apr-20 Oct **Site:** 2HEC **Prices:** 22.80 **Facilities:** Wi-fi Play Area **Services:** **Off-site:** P

WALDSHUT BADEN-WÜRTTEMBERG

Rhein-Camping

ahnweg 22, 79761
07751 3152 07751 3252
e-mail: rheincamping@t-online.de
web: www.rheincamping.de

Wooded surroundings beside the River Rhine.

dir: *1km from Waldshut towards Swiss border.*

Open: All Year. **Site:** 8HEC **Facilities:** **Services:** **Leisure:** R **Off-site:** P

WERTHEIM BADEN-WÜRTTEMBERG

AZUR Wertheim

An den Christwiesen 35, 97877
09342 83111 09342 83171
e-mail: wertheim@azur-camping.de
web: www.azur-camping.de/wertheim

Site lies on a level, long stretch of meadowland on the banks of the River Main next to a swimming pool.

dir: *Towards Miltenberg, 1km right at fuel station towards site.*

Open: Apr-25 Oct **Site:** 7HEC **Facilities:** **Services:** **Leisure:** R **Off-site:** P

Wertheim-Bettingen

Geiselbrunnweg 31, Bettingen, 97877
09342 7077 09342 913077

Peaceful wooded area beside a river.

dir: *A3 exit 66 Wertheim/Lengfurt, site 1km.*

Open: Apr-Oct **Site:** 7.5HEC **Prices:** 15-20 **Facilities:** Wi-fi Play Area **Services:** **Leisure:** R

WILDBAD IM SCHWARZWALD BADEN-WÜRTTEMBERG

AZUR-Camping Schwarzwald

75323
07055 1320 07055 929081
e-mail: wildbad@azur-camping.de
web: www.azur-camping.de/schwarzwald/wildbad.html

Long narrow site with some terraces, set between the River Enz and the wooded hillside. Separate section for young campers.

dir: *From Pforzheim B294 S via Calmbach.*

Open: All Year. **Site:** 2.5HEC **Facilities:** **Services:** **Leisure:** R

Kleinenzhof

75323
07081 3435 07081 3770
e-mail: info@kleinenzhof.de
web: www.kleinenzhof.de

A family site with modern facilities.

dir: *Via B294 3km S of Calmbach.*

GPS: 48.7378, 8.5764

Open: All Year. **Site:** 8HEC **Prices:** 23.30-24.40 **Facilities:** Wi-fi Play Area **Services:** **Leisure:** P R **Off-site:**

GERMANY

BERLIN AND EASTERN PROVINCES

ALT SCHWERIN MEKLENBURG-VORPOMMERN

See

An der Schaftannen Nr 1, 17214
☎ 039932 42073 📠 039932 42072
e-mail: info@camping-alt-schwerin.de
web: www.camping-alt-schwerin.de
A pleasant lakeside site with modern facilities situated north of the lake.
dir: *Via B192.*
GPS: 53.5229, 12.3184
Open: Apr-Oct **Site:** 3.6HEC **Prices:** 20.50-26.50 **Facilities:** Wi-fi Kids' Club Play Area **Services:** **Leisure:** L

BODSTEDT MECKLENBURG-VORPOMMERN

Bodstedt

Damm 43, 18356
☎ 038231 4226 📠 038231 4820
A pleasant site on the shore of the Saaler Bodden with good boating facilities.
dir: *B105 exit Zingst/Barth.*
Site: 3.5HEC **Prices:** 15-17.50 **Facilities:** Wi-fi Play Area **Off-site:** L R

CAPUTH BRANDENBURG

Himmelreich

Wentorfinsel, Geltow, 14542
☎ 033209 70475 📠 033209 20100
e-mail: himmelreich@campingplatz-caputh.de
web: www.campingplatz-caputh.de
Open: All Year. **Site:** 7.5HEC **Facilities:** **Services:** **Leisure:** L R

COLDITZ SACHSEN

Waldbad

04680
☎ 034381 43122 📠 034381 43122
e-mail: info@campingplatz.colditz.de
web: www.campingplatz-colditz.de
Wooded surroundings with some shaded pitches.
dir: *E176 exit Zschadras.*
Open: Apr-Sep **Site:** 2HEC **Facilities:** **Services:** **Leisure:** L P R **Off-site:**

DRESDEN SACHSEN

Wostra

An der Wostra 7, 01259
☎ 0351 2013254 📠 0351 2025448
e-mail: cp-wostra@freenet.de
web: www.dresden.de
dir: *B172 towards Heidenau, site signed.*
Open: Apr-Oct **Site:** 1.8HEC **Facilities:** **Services:** **Off-site:** L P

FALKENBERG BRANDENBURG

Erholungsgebiet Kiebitz

Hörsteweg 2, 04895
☎ 035365 2135 📠 035365 38533
e-mail: info@erholungsgebiet-kiebitz.de
web: www.erholungsgebiet-kiebitz.de
dir: *E55 exit Duben, B87/B101 for Herzberg.*
Open: Apr-Oct **Site:** 5.2HEC **Facilities:** **Services:** **Leisure:** L **Off-site:**

GROSS-LEUTHEN BRANDENBURG

Spreewaldtor

Neue Str 1, Mürkische Heide, 15913
☎ 035471 303 📠 035471 310
e-mail: info@eurocamp-spreewaldtor.de
web: www.eurocamp-spreewaldtor.de
On a level meadow beside the Gross Leuthener See.
dir: *N of town off B179.*
GPS: 52.0481, 14.0392
Open: All Year. **Site:** 9HEC **Facilities:** Wi-fi (charged) Play Area **Services:** **Off-site:** L

GROSS-QUASSOW MECKLENBURG-VORPOMMERN

Camping-und Ferienpark Havelberge

17237
☎ 03981 24790 📠 03981 247999
e-mail: info@haveltourist.de
web: www.haveltourist.de
A rural setting on the lake shore with wooded, hilly terraces.
dir: *1.5km S of town, signed.*
Open: All Year. **Site:** 24HEC **Prices:** 14.20-30.40 **Facilities:** Wi-fi (charged) Kids' Club Play Area **Services:** **Leisure:** L

GERMANY

KELBRA THÜRINGEN

Kelbra

Lange Str 150, 06537
☎ 034651 45290 📠 034651 45292
e-mail: info@seecampingkelbra.de
web: www.seecampingkelbra.de
Open: All Year. Site: 6.5HEC Facilities: Services: Leisure: L P Off-site:

KLADOW THÜRINGEN

DCC Else-Eckert-Platz

Krampnitzer Weg 111-117, 14089
☎ 030 3652797 📠 030 3651245
e-mail: info@dccberlin.de
web: www.dccberlin.de
Large site in woodland close to the lake. Modern facilities.
dir: *B5 & B2 exit Berlin Spandau.*
GPS: 52.455, 13.1133
Open: All Year. Site: 7HEC Prices: 21.50 Facilities: Play Area Services: Off-site: L R

KLEINMACHNOW BRANDENBURG

Yacht-Caravan-Club

Säkehang 9a, 14532
☎ 033203 79684 📠 033203 77913
e-mail: spandau@city-camping-berlin.de
web: www.city-camping-berlin.de
A riverside site with an hotel south west of town off A115.
Open: All Year. Site: 2.2HEC Facilities: Services: Leisure: R

KLEINRÖHRSDORF SACHSEN

LuxOase

The Camping and Caravanning Club The Friendly Club

Arnsdorfer Str 1, 01900
☎ 035952 56666 📠 035952 56024
e-mail: info@luxoase.de
web: www.luxoase.de
A beautiful, peaceful location among meadows and woods, bordering a lake. Situated in the centre of the attraction of Dresden, Saxon, Switzerland, Meissen and Upper Lusatia. New sanitary building and four modern apartments to rent. Dogs must be kept on a lead.

C&CC Report *Few sites are so peaceful, homely, well-equipped, friendly or better at helping you get the most out of your stay. Thomas and Dagmar provide copious information, then take you step-by-step through the details, right down to roads, bus numbers, train stops and times. Yet more services will be offered in a major new facilities building soon, and the site has a special rating for being child-friendly. The excursions programme includes coach trips to Prague and Dresden, while Saxony itself offers the fantastic rock formations and forests of Saxon Switzerland, beautifully restored Dresden and Colditz Castle's escape museum.*

dir: *A4 exit Pulsnitz for Radeberg, 4km through Leppersdorf, 1km turn left.*
GPS: 51.1205, 13.9808
Open: Mar-Dec Site: 7.2HEC Prices: 17-26.20 Mobile home hire 343-483 Facilities: Wi-fi (charged) Kids' Club Play Area Services: Leisure: L P Off-site: L

KLEINSAUBERNITZ SACHSEN

Olbasee

Olbaweg 16, 02694
☎ 035932 30232 📠 035932 30886
e-mail: natur@campingplatz-olbasee.de
web: www.campingplatz-olbasee.de
A rural location on the Olbasee.
dir: *Via S109.*
Open: 16 Apr-17 Oct Site: 7HEC Facilities: Services: Leisure: L Off-site:

KÖNIGSTEIN SACHSEN

Königstein

Schandauer Str 25e, 01822
☎ 035021 68224
e-mail: camp.koenigstein@t-online.de
web: www.camping-koenigstein.de
On level ground in a wooded location with fine views of the surrounding mountains.
dir: *B172 within Königstein near Dresden.*
Open: Apr-Oct Site: 2.4HEC Prices: 16.40-19 Facilities: Services: Leisure: R Off-site: P

GERMANY

LASSAN MEKLENBURG-VORPOMMERN

Lassan

Garthof 5-6, 17440
☎ 038374 80373 🖷 038374 80373
e-mail: naturcampingplatzlassan@gmx.de
web: www.campingplatz-lassan.de
A pleasant site on the Achterwasser.
dir: *Via B110.*
Open: Apr-Sep **Site:** 1.8HEC **Facilities:** Play Area **Services:** **Leisure:** L R S **Off-site:** P

MÜHLBERG THÜRINGEN

Drei Gleichen

99869
☎ 036256 22715 🖷 036256 86801
e-mail: service@campingplatz-muehlberg.de
web: www.campingplatz-muehlberg.de
Pleasant wooded surroundings.
dir: *A4 exit Wandersleben, Mühlberg signed.*
GPS: 50.8747, 10.8088
Open: Apr-Oct **Site:** 2.8HEC **Prices:** 15-20 **Facilities:** **Services:** **Off-site:** L P

NIESKY SACHSEN

Tonschächte

02902
☎ 03588 205771 🖷 03588 259315
Open: 15 Apr-15 Oct **Site:** 15HEC **Facilities:** **Services:** **Leisure:** L **Off-site:**

NIEWISCH BRANDENBURG

Schwielochsee-Camping Niewisch

Uferweg Nord 16, 15848
☎ 033676 5186 🖷 033676 5226
e-mail: camping.niewisch@freenet.de
web: www.camping-niewisch.de
A family site in pleasant wooded surroundings on the banks of the Schwielochsee.
Open: All Year. **Site:** 4.2HEC **Facilities:** Play Area **Services:** **Leisure:** L

PLÖTZKY SACHSEN

Ferienpark Plötzky

Campingplatz Kleiner Waldsee, 39245
☎ 039200 50155 🖷 039200 76082
e-mail: info@ferienpark-ploetzky.de
web: www.ferienpark-ploetzky.de
Set in a wooded location beside a small lake with well-defined pitches.
dir: *Access via A2 & B246.*
Open: All Year. **Site:** 12HEC **Facilities:** **Services:** **Leisure:** L

POTSDAM BRANDENBURG

Sanssouci zu Potsdam/Berlin

An der Pirscheide, Templiner See 41, 14471
☎ 0331 9510988 🖷 0331 9510988
e-mail: info@camping-potsdam.de
web: www.camping-potsdam.de
Wooded surroundings close to Templiner See.
dir: *Signed from B1.*
GPS: 52.3617, 13.0069
Open: Apr-1 Nov **Site:** 6HEC **Prices:** 32.90 **Facilities:** Wi-fi Play Area **Services:** **Leisure:** L R **Off-site:** P

REICHENBERG SACHSEN

Bad Sonnenland

Dresdner Str 115, 01468
☎ 0351 8305495 🖷 0351 8305494
e-mail: info@bad-sonnenland.de
web: www.bad-sonnenland.de
A pleasant location beside the lake with modern facilities.
dir: *A4 exit Wilder Mann. 3km S of Moritzburg.*
Open: Apr-Oct **Site:** 18HEC **Prices:** 19-22.50 **Facilities:** Play Area **Services:** **Leisure:** L **Off-site:** P

SCHMÖCKWITZ BERLIN

Campingplatz Krossinsee

Wernsdorfer Str 38, 12527
☎ 030 6758687 🖷 030 70761058
e-mail: info@campingplatz-krossinsee.de
web: www.campingplatz-krossinsee.de
Quiet grassy site on city outskirts.
dir: *27km SE of Berlin centre. From A10 W ring road exit 9 Niederlehme, in direction of Erkner (Wernsdorf), follow camping signs.*
Open: All Year. **Site:** **Prices:** 21.50 **Facilities:** **Services:** **Leisure:** L **Off-site:**

GERMANY

INNOWITZ MECKLENBURG-VORPOMMERN

Pommernland

Dr Wachsmann-Str 40, 17454
☎ 038377 40348 🖷 038377 40349
-mail: camping-pommernland@m-vp.de
web: www.camping-pommernland.m-vp.de
Wooded surroundings on the coast.

dir: *Via B111.*

Open: All Year. Site: 7.7HEC Facilities: Services: Leisure: S Off-site: P

CENTRAL

SBACHERHÜTTE RHEINLAND-PFALZ

Harfenmühle

Harfenmühle 2, 55758
☎ 06786 7076 🖷 06786 7570
-mail: mail@harfenmuehle.de
web: www.harfenmuehle.net
 quiet site, beautifully situated in the Fischbach Valley. Level grassland, partly terraced. Activities for children include gold digging and looking for gemstones, as well as a sports ground and three playgrounds.

dir: *3km NW of B327 towards Kempfeld.*

GPS: 49.8036, 7.2694

Open: All Year. Site: 6.2HEC Prices: 19
Facilities: Wi-fi (charged) Play Area
Services: Leisure: L

TTENDORN NORDRHEIN-WESTFALEN

Biggesee-Waldenburg

57439
☎ 02722 95500 🖷 02722 955099
-mail: info@camping-waldenburg.de
web: www.biggesee.com
Generously terraced recreational site on the northern shore of the Bigge reservoir, with adjoining public bathing area. Private sunbathing area.

dir: *Via A45/A4.*

Open: Apr-Oct Site: 6.5HEC Facilities:
Services: Leisure: L Off-site: P

Hof Biggen

Finnentroper Str 131, 57439
☎ 02722 95530 🖷 02722 955366
e-mail: info@biggen.de
web: www.biggen.de
Well-equipped terraced site, surrounded by woodlands. Kids' club during regional holidays.

dir: *Atterdorn road to Ahauser reservoir, entrance near Haus am See inn.*

Open: All Year. Site: 18HEC Prices: 19.25 Mobile home hire 175-273 Facilities: Kids' Club Play Area Services: Off-site: L R

BALHORN HESSEN

Erzeberg

34308
☎ 05625 5274 🖷 05625 7116
e-mail: info@campingplatz-erzeberg.de
web: www.campingplatz-erzeberg.de
Site lies on meadowland on slightly sloping ground above the village.

dir: *On B450 between Istha & Fritzlar.*

Open: All Year. Site: 5HEC Facilities:
Services: Leisure: P Off-site:

BARNTRUP NORDRHEIN-WESTFALEN

Ferienpark Teutoburger Wald

Badeanstaltsweg 4, 32683
☎ 05263 2221 🖷 05263 956991
e-mail: info@ferienparkteutoburgerwald.de
web: www.ferienparkteutoburgerwald.de
A well-kept site next to an open-air swimming pool and kids' club available in summer months.

dir: *Signed from Barntrup on B66.*

Open: Apr-Oct Site: 2.4HEC Prices: 10-17
Facilities: Wi-fi Kids' Club Play Area
Services: Leisure: P Off-site:

BERNKASTEL-KUES RHEINLAND-PFALZ

Kueser Werth

Am Hafen 2, 54470
☎ 06531 8200 🖷 06531 8282
web: www.camping-kueser-werth.de
Grassy site near Mosel and boating marina, with view of Landshut castle.

dir: *On S outskirts of town.*

Open: Apr-Oct Site: 2.2HEC Facilities:
Services:

GERMANY

BIRKENFELD — RHEINLAND-PFALZ

Waldwiesen

55765
06782 5215 06782 5219
e-mail: info@waldwiesen.de
web: www.waldwiesen.de
A wooded location close to the lake. A quiet natural campsite close to the lake.
dir: *Off B41 E of Birkenfeld, signed.*
GPS: 49.655, 7.1819
Open: Etr-15 Oct **Site:** 9.5HEC **Prices:** 16.75-20.25 **Facilities:** Play Area **Services:** **Leisure:** L **Off-site:** P R

BÖMIGHAUSEN — HESSEN

Barenberg

34508
05632 1044 05632 1044
e-mail: berthold.trachte@t-online.de
Beautifully terraced site at Neerdar reservoir.
dir: *Via B251 between Korbach & Brilon.*
Open: All Year. **Site:** 0.5HEC **Facilities:** **Services:** **Leisure:** L R

BRAUNFELS — HESSEN

Braunfels

Am Weiherstieg 2, 35619
06442 4366 06442 6895
A terraced site surrounded by a pine forest and deciduous trees. Separate meadow for touring campers.
dir: *A45 exit Limburg, B49 towards town.*
Open: All Year. **Site:** 5.2HEC **Facilities:** **Services:** **Off-site:** P

BREISIG, BAD — RHEINLAND-PFALZ

Rheineck

53498
02633 95645 02633 472008
e-mail: info@camping-rheineck.de
web: www.camping-rheineck.de
A quiet, well-kept site on a level meadow in Vinxtbach Valley.
dir: *B9 NW from Koblenz to Bad Breisig, turn left, over railway & continue 400m.*
Open: All Year. **Site:** 6HEC **Prices:** 17 **Facilities:** **Services:** **Leisure:** R **Off-site:** P

BRUNGERSHAUSEN — HESSEN

Auenland

Zum Dammhammer, 35094
06420 7172 06420 822846
e-mail: info@campingplatz-auenland.de
web: www.campingplatz-auenland.de
Attractive location in a protected area at the foot of the Rimberg mountains. Variety of bird and plant life.
dir: *A2/A3 from N to A45 exit Dillenburg towards Biedenkopf on B62. Exit Brungershausen, site signed.*
Open: All Year. **Site:** 2.4HEC **Facilities:** **Services:** **Leisure:** P R **Off-site:**

BULLAY — RHEINLAND-PFALZ

Bären-Camp

Am Moselufer 1/3, 56859
06542 900097 06542 900098
e-mail: info@baeren-camp.de
web: www.baeren-camp.de
On a level meadow beside the Mosel, next to the football ground with good views.
dir: *Via B49 Cochem-Alf, over bridge, through village, signed.*
Open: Etr-1 Nov **Site:** 1.8HEC **Prices:** 20.20-20.60 **Facilities:** **Services:** **Leisure:** R **Off-site:** P

COCHEM — RHEINLAND-PFALZ

Altes Forsthaus

Haupstr 2, Landkern, 56814
02671 8701 02671 8722
e-mail: info@landkern.com
web: www.landkern.com
The partly terraced site lies near woodland in the valley below Landkern.
dir: *A48 exit Kaisersesch, S to Landkern, site signed.*
Open: All Year. **Site:** 10HEC **Facilities:** **Services:** **Leisure:** P **Off-site:**

Mosel-Camping-Cochem

Stadionstr, 56812
02671 4409 02671 910719
e-mail: info@campingplatz-cochem.de
web: www.campingplatz-cochem.de
Level meadowland with trees beside the Mosel, downstream from the swimming pool and sports ground.
dir: *From B49 in Cochem follow Freizeitzentrum signs, over downstream bridge, left after swimming pool.*
Open: Etr-Oct **Site:** 2.8HEC **Facilities:** **Services:** **Leisure:** R **Off-site:** P

AHN RHEINLAND-PFALZ

üttelwoog

6994
☎ 06391 5622 🖷 06391 5326
mail: buettelwoog@t-online.de
eb: www.camping-buettelwoog.de
te lies in a magnificent pine forest, partly surrounded by steep lls and rocks. Section reserved for young people with tents.
r: *B10 from Pirmasens to Hinterweidenthal then B427 S to ahn.*
pen: Mar-10 Nov **Site:** 6HEC **Prices:** 18-20.90 **acilities:** Wi-fi Play Area **Services:** **Leisure:** P **Off-site:** P

AUSENAU RHEINLAND-PFALZ

ahn-Beach

allgarten 16, 56132
☎ 02603 13964 🖷 02603 919935
mail: info@canutours.de
eb: www.campingplatz-dausenau.de
riverside site in a wooded setting.
PS: 50.3277, 7.7552
pen: Apr-Oct **Site:** 3HEC **Prices:** 16 **Facilities:** ay Area **Services:** **Leisure:** R **Off-site:**

IEZ RHEINLAND-PFALZ

ranienstein

5582
☎ 06432 2122 🖷 06432 924193
mail: info@camping-diez.de
eb: www.camping-diez.de
a meadow beside the River Lahn, below Schloss Oranienstein.
r: *From N A3 exit Diez (from S exit Limburg-Nord), onto B54 for km.*
pen: Apr-Oct **Site:** 7HEC **Facilities:** **rvices:** **Leisure:** R **Off-site:** L

ORSEL AN DER AHR RHEINLAND-PFALZ

tahlhütte

3533
☎ 02693 438 🖷 02693 511
eb: www.campingplatz-stahlhuette.de
te with individual pitches, on meadowland with trees near ver Ahr.
r: *Off B258 Aachen-Koblenz road.*
pen: All Year. **Site:** 7HEC **Prices:** 19.50 **Facilities:** **Services:** **Leisure:** R

DORTMUND NORDRHEIN-WESTFALEN

Hohensyburg

Syburger Dorfstr 69, 44265
☎ 0231 774374 🖷 0231 7749554
e-mail: info@camping-hohensyburg.de
web: www.camping-hohensyburg.de
Terraced site on hilly grassland near Weitkamp inn.
dir: *Via B54.*
Open: All Year. **Site:** 10HEC **Facilities:** **Services:** **Leisure:** L R

DREIEICH-OFFENTHAL HESSEN

Offenthal

Bahnhofstr 77, 63303
☎ 06074 5629 🖷 06074 629133
e-mail: schoenweitz@t-online.de
web: www.campingplatz-dreieich.de
A well-equipped site in wooded surroundings.
dir: *Off B486 at Dreieich-Offenthal towards Dietzenbach.*
GPS: 49.9858, 8.7572
Open: All Year. **Site:** 3.2HEC **Prices:** 14 **Facilities:** Play Area **Services:** **Leisure:** P **Off-site:**

DROLSHAGEN NORDRHEIN-WESTFALEN

Gut Kalberschnacke

57489
☎ 02763 7501 🖷 02763 7879
e-mail: camping-kalberschnacke@t-online.de
web: www.camping-kalberschnacke.de
Terraced site above the Bigge-Lister reservoir in wooded area.
dir: *A45 exit Wegringhausen, site 4km NE.*
Open: All Year. **Site:** 13.5HEC **Facilities:** **Services:** **Off-site:** L

DÜLMEN NORDRHEIN-WESTFALEN

Tannenwiese

Borkenbergestr 217, 48249
☎ 02594 991759
web: www.camping-tannenwiese.de
The site lies on meadowland in a well-wooded area, near the gliderdrome.
dir: *B51 from Recklinghausen to Hausdülmen, follow sign Segelflügplatz Borkenberge.*
Open: Mar-30 Oct **Site:** 3.7HEC **Prices:** 13.20 **Facilities:** Play Area **Services:** **Off-site:**

GERMANY

DÜRKHEIM, BAD RHEINLAND-PFALZ

Knaus Bad Dürkheim

In den Almen 3, 67098
06322 61356 06322 8161
e-mail: badduerkheim@knauscamp.de
web: www.knauscamp.de
Lakeside site on level meadow between vineyards, adjoining a sportsfield.
dir: *Access from E outskirts of town. Turn N at railway viaduct, near fuel station.*
Open: Dec-Oct **Site:** 16.4HEC **Facilities:** **Services:** **Leisure:** L **Off-site:** P

DÜSSELDORF NORDRHEIN-WESTFALEN

Unterbacher See

Kleiner Torfbruch 31, 40627
0211 8992038 0211 8929132
e-mail: service@unterbachersee.de
web: www.unterbachersee.de
Site on sloping grassland.
dir: *From Düsseldorf B326 to Erkrath exit, left by Unterbacher lake.*
Open: Apr-Oct **Site:** 6.5HEC **Facilities:** Play Area **Services:** **Leisure:** L
Off-site:

EPPSTEIN HESSEN

TaunusCamp

Bezirksstr 2, 65817
06198 7000 06198 7002
e-mail: info@taunuscamp.de
web: www.taunuscamp.de
Relaxing terraced site located in Taunus countryside, ideal for cycling and hiking.
dir: *E35 exit 46 onto B455.*
GPS: 50.1475, 8.3619
Open: All Year. **Site:** 7HEC **Prices:** 20-23 Mobile home hire 149-279 **Facilities:** Play Area **Services:** **Off-site:** P

ESCHWEGE HESSEN

Knaus Campingpark Eschwege

Am Werratalsee 2, 37269
05651 338883 05651 338884
e-mail: eschwege@knauscamp.de
web: www.knauscamp.de
Site beside the Werratalsee.
dir: *A7 exit Eschwege, signed.*
Open: 26 Mar-2 Nov **Site:** 6.8HEC **Facilities:** **Services:** **Leisure:** L **Off-site:**

ESSEN NORDRHEIN-WESTFALE

Essen-Werden

Im Lowental 67, Werden, 45239
0201 492978 0201 8496132
e-mail: stadtcamping-essen@t-online.de
web: www.dcc-stadtcamping-essen-werden.de
Several fields divided by bushes and surrounded by thick hedges
dir: *From Essen centre towards Werden, turn towards railway station & signed.*
Open: All Year. **Site:** 6HEC **Prices:** 14.35-16.90 **Facilities:** **Services:** **Leisure:** R **Off-site:** P

FÜRTH IM ODENWALD HESSE

Nibelungen-Camping am Schwimmbad

Tiefertswinkel 20, 64658
06253 5804 06253 3717
e-mail: info@camping-fuerth.de
web: www.camping-fuerth.de
Pleasantly landscaped modern site in beautiful setting next to t municipal open-air swimming pool.
dir: *A5 Darmstadt-Heidelberg.*
Open: 15 Mar-15 Oct **Site:** 4.2HEC **Prices:** 20 **Facilities:** Wi-fi (charged) Play Area **Services:** **Off-site:** P

GAMMELSBACH HESSE

Freienstein

Neckartalstr 172, 64743
06068 912122 06068 912121
e-mail: sabinesiefeit@freenet.de
The site lies just off the B45 in a landscaped preservation area. is terraced and divided into pitches.
Open: All Year. **Site:** 5HEC **Facilities:** **Services:** **Off-site:** L

GEISENHEIM HESSE

Geisenheim

Postfach 1323, 65366
06722 75600 06722 406655
e-mail: info@rheingaucamping.de
web: www.rheingaucamping.de
Pleasant level grassland waterside site.
dir: *Between B42 road & River Rhine.*
Open: Mar-Oct **Site:** 5HEC **Prices:** 23 **Facilities:** **Services:** **Leisure:** R **Off-site:** P

GERMANY

Site 6HEC (site size) grass sand stone little shade partly shaded mainly shaded bungalows for hire (static) caravans for hire tents for hire no dogs site fully accessible for wheelchairs
Prices amount quoted is per night, for 2 adults and car, plus tent or caravan. Mobile home hire is a weekly rate.

GERBACH — RHEINLAND-PFALZ

AZUR-Camping Pfalz

Kahlenbergweiher 1, 67813
06361 8287 06361 22523
e-mail: gerbach@azur-camping.de
web: www.azur-camping.de/gerbach

A site for nature lovers to enjoy also a good location for exploring the well known surrounding cities.

dir: *A8 junct Enkenbach-Hochspeyer, N on B48 via Rockenhausen, at Dielkirchen 4.5km E to Gerbach.*

Open: Apr-Oct **Site:** 8.8HEC **Facilities:** Play Area **Services:** **Leisure:** P

GILLENFELD — RHEINLAND-PFALZ

Feriendorf Pulvermaar

54558
06573 287 06592 982662
e-mail: info@feriendorf-pulvermaar.de
web: www.feriendorf-pulvermaar.de

Partly terraced private site on a slightly sloping meadow above the volcanic lake of Pulvermaar, surrounded by woods on one side.

dir: *A48 exit Mehren/Daun, B421 to the right in the direction of Zell, 2nd turning to Gillenfeld, 200m on right.*

GPS: 50.1301, 6.9319

Open: All Year. **Site:** 4HEC **Prices:** 11-17 **Facilities:** Play Area **Services:** **Off-site:** L P

GIROD — RHEINLAND-PFALZ

Eisenbachtal

56412
06485 766 06485 4938

Close to an old volcano situated in the Nassau nature reserve, an ideal area for walking, rare plants and bird watching.

dir: *A3 exit 41 follow signs for Montabaur, before town left towards Limburg for 5km.*

Open: All Year. **Site:** 3HEC **Prices:** 16 **Facilities:** Play Area **Services:** **Off-site:** P

GLÜDER — NORDRHEIN-WESTFALEN

Waldcamping Glüder

Balkhauser Weg 240, 42659
0212 242120 0212 2421234
e-mail: info@camping-solingen.de
web: www.camping-solingen.de

Site on level terrain surrounded by woodland on banks of the River Wupper.

dir: *B299/B224 from Solingen towards Witzhelden via Burg Hohenscheid.*

Open: All Year. **Site:** 2HEC **Prices:** 14.40-16.40 **Facilities:** Play Area **Services:** **Leisure:** R **Off-site:** P

GRÜNBERG — HESSEN

Spitzer Stein

Alsfelderstr 57, 35305
06401 804117 06401 804103
e-mail: s.moebus@gruenberg.de
web: www.gruenberg.de

Beautiful location at a forest swimming pool.

dir: *A5 exit Grünberg.*

Open: Mar-Oct **Site:** 4HEC **Facilities:** Play Area **Services:** **Leisure:** P **Off-site:**

GRUNDMÜHLE BEI QUENTEL — HESSEN

Grundmühle Quentel

37235
05602 3659 05602 915811
e-mail: info@grundmühle-quentel.de
web: www.grundmühle-quentel.de

Set in a beautiful landscape, this sunny site enjoys the nature of the Meissner Forest.

dir: *B83 from Melsungen to Röhrenfurth, right towards Furstenhagen & via Eiterhagen to Quentel.*

Open: All Year. **Site:** 1.8HEC **Facilities:** **Services:** **Leisure:** P **Off-site:**

HALDERN — NORDRHEIN-WESTFALEN

Strandhaus Sonsfeld

46459
02857 2247 02857 7171

On meadowland at the Hagener-Meer next to B8 and railway line.

Open: All Year. **Site:** 15HEC **Facilities:** **Services:** **Leisure:** L

GERMANY

HAUSBAY RHEINLAND-PFALZ

Schinderhannes

56291
☎ 06746 80280 06746 802814
e-mail: info@countrycamping.de
web: www.countrycamping.de
Terraced site on south facing slope, interspersed by trees and shrubs beside a small lake. Separate section for young people. Ideal to use as a stop over point, as caravans can stay hooked up on certain pitches.

dir: *E of B327. 29km S of Koblenz.*

GPS: 50.1060, 7.5675

Open: All Year. **Site:** 30HEC **Prices:** 16-23 **Facilities:** Wi-fi (charged) Play Area **Services:** **Leisure:** L **Off-site:**

HEIDENBURG RHEINLAND-PFALZ

Moselhöhe

54426
☎ 06509 99016 06509 99017
e-mail: info@cpmh.de
web: www.cpmh.de
A small quiet, well-appointed site on terraces in open meadow.

dir: *A1 exit Mehring towards Thalfang am Erbeskopf.*

Open: All Year. **Site:** 3HEC **Prices:** 16.10-17.70 **Facilities:** Wi-fi Play Area **Services:** **Leisure:** P **Off-site:** R

HEIMBACH NORDRHEIN-WESTFALEN

Rurthal

52396
☎ 02446 3377 02446 911126
e-mail: info@campingplatz-rurthal.de
web: www.campingplatz-rurthal.de
Site with individual pitches on meadowland beside the River Ruhr.

dir: *From Düren S via Nideggen & Abenden to Blens, over bridge & left.*

Open: All Year. **Site:** 7HEC **Facilities:** Play Area **Services:** **Leisure:** P **Off-site:** R

HEIMERTSHAUSEN HESSEN

Heimertshausen

Ehringshauser Str, 36320
☎ 06635 206
e-mail: info@campingplatz-heimertshausen.de
web: www.campingplatz-heimertshausen.de
Near swimming pool in extensive, grassy, wooded valley.

dir: *A5 exit Alsfeld west, continue via Romrod & Zell.*

GPS: 50.7362, 9.1526

Open: Apr-Sep **Site:** 3.6HEC **Facilities:** Play Area **Services:** **Off-site:** P

HELLENTHAL NORDRHEIN-WESTFALEN

Hellenthal

Platiss 1, 53940
☎ 02482 1500 02482 2171
e-mail: info@camphellenthal.de
web: www.camphellenthal.de
On extensive meadowland.

dir: *0.5km S of town.*

Open: All Year. **Site:** 6HEC **Prices:** 17 **Facilities:** Play Area **Services:** **Leisure:** P **Off-site:**

HIRSCHHORN AM NECKAR HESSEN

Odenwald

Langenthalerstr 80, 69430
☎ 06272 809 06272 3658
e-mail: odenwald-camping-park@t-online.de
web: www.odenwald-camping-park.de
Extensive site in wooded valley. Divided by River Ülfenbach and hedges.

dir: *Off B37 towards Wald-Michelbach & continue 1.5km.*

Open: Apr-4 Oct **Site:** 8HEC **Facilities:** **Services:** **Leisure:** P R

HONNEF, BAD NORDRHEIN-WESTFALEN

Jillieshof

Ginsterbergweg 6, 53604
☎ 02224 972066 02224 972067
e-mail: information@camping-jillieshof.de
web: www.camping-jillieshof.de
A quiet, family site at the edge of Aegidienberg, conveniently close to the motorway.

dir: *Via A3 2km.*

GPS: 50.6491, 7.3002

Open: All Year. **Site:** 4HEC **Prices:** 17.50-19.50 Mobile home hire 190-250 **Facilities:** Play Area **Services:** **Off-site:**

GERMANY

HORN-BAD MEINBERG — NORDRHEIN-WESTFALEN

Eggewald

Kempener Str 33, 32805
05255 236 05255 1375
e-mail: j.glitz@traktoren-museum.de
web: www.traktoren-museum.de
Site lies in well-wooded countryside.
dir: *Off B1 in Horn-Bad Meinberg at Waldschlosschen onto Altenbeken road for 8km to Kempen.*
Open: All Year. **Site:** 2HEC **Facilities:** **Services:** **Leisure:** P

HÜNFELD — HESSEN

Knaus Campingpark Praforst

Dr Detlev-Rudelsdorff-Allee 6, 36088
06652 749090 06652 749091
e-mail: huenfeld@knauscamp.dei
web: www.knauscamp.de
Site in mixed woodland with good amenities.
dir: *For access follow B27 from Hünfeld to Shlitz, turn right, 2km to site.*
Open: Jan-Oct **Site:** 3HEC **Facilities:** **Services:**

HUTTEN — HESSEN

Camping Hutten Heiligenborn

Am Heiligenborn 6, 36381
06661 2424 06661 917581
e-mail: helga.herzog-gericke@t-online.de
Site lies at Heiligenborn and has a pleasant southerly aspect.
dir: *B40 from Fulda towards Frankfurt to Flieden for 19km, turn left via Rückers to Hutten (8km).*
Open: All Year. **Site:** 3.5HEC **Prices:** 12-14 **Facilities:** **Services:** **Off-site:** P

INGENHEIM — RHEINLAND-PFALZ

SC Klingbachtal

76831
06349 6278
web: www.klingbachtal.de
Municipal site lies on level meadowland at the edge of the village, next to the sports ground.
dir: *8km S of Landau via B38, signed.*
Open: Apr-Oct **Site:** 1.5HEC **Facilities:** **Services:** **Off-site:** P

IRREL — RHEINLAND-PFALZ

Nimseck

54666
06525 314 06525 1299
e-mail: info@camping-nimseck.de
web: www.camping-nimseck.de
Site on long grassy strip in wooded valley on the bank of River Nims.
dir: *B257 SW from Bitburg, at turning from bypass to Irrel turn left.*
Open: 15 Mar-2 Nov **Site:** 7HEC **Prices:** 10-28 **Facilities:** Wi-fi (charged) Kids' Club Play Area **Services:** **Leisure:** P R **Off-site:**

KELL — RHEINLAND-PFALZ

Freibad Hochwald

54427
06589 1695
On meadow on slightly sloping wooded hillside, near a public open-air swimming pool.
dir: *2km from B407 towards Trier.*
Open: Jun-Aug **Site:** 2HEC **Prices:** 21 **Facilities:** **Services:** **Leisure:** P

KIRCHHEIM — HESSEN

Seepark Kirchheim

36275
06628 1525 06628 8664
e-mail: info@campseepark.de
web: www.campseepark.de
This terraced site, with individual pitches, is part of an extensive and well-equipped leisure and recreation centre.
Open: All Year. **Site:** 10HEC **Facilities:** **Services:** **Leisure:** L P

KIRN — RHEINLAND-PFALZ

Papiermühle

Krebsweilererstr 8, 55606
06752 2267
e-mail: infos@papiermuehle-campingplatz.de
web: www.papiermuehle-campingplatz.de
Quiet terraced site in attractive valley.
dir: *B41 exit Kirn-west, then Meisenheim.*
Open: 15 Mar-15 Nov **Site:** 6HEC **Prices:** 14 **Facilities:** **Services:**

GERMANY

KOBLENZ (COBLENCE) — RHEINLAND-PFALZ

Ziehfurt

Raiffeisen Str 16, 56333
☎ 02606 1800 & 357 🖷 02606 2566
e-mail: ferieninsel-winningen@t-online.de
web: www.mosel-camping.com

Site lies on level wooded meadowland.

dir: *From Koblenz B416 towards Trièr for 11km, access to site at Schwimmbad (swimming pool).*

GPS: 50.3113, 7.4997

Open: Etr-Sep **Site:** 7HEC **Prices:** 20.50 **Facilities:** Wi-fi Play Area **Services:** **Leisure:** R **Off-site:** P

KÖLN (COLOGNE) — NORDRHEIN-WESTFALEN

Berger

Uferstr 71, Rodenkirchen, 50996
☎ 0221 9355240 🖷 0221 9355246
e-mail: camping.berger@t-online.de
web: www.camping-berger-koeln.de

Situated on a meadow beside the River Rhine. Beautiful surrounding area and modern facilities.

Open: All Year. **Site:** 6HEC **Prices:** 22.50 **Facilities:** Play Area **Services:** **Leisure:** R

KÖNEN — RHEINLAND-PFALZ

Horsch

Könenerstr 36, 54329
☎ 06501 17571

Open: Apr-14 Oct **Site:** **Prices:** 16 **Facilities:** **Services:** **Leisure:** R **Off-site:** P

KREUZBERG — RHEINLAND-PFALZ

Viktoria Station

53505
☎ 02643 8338 🖷 02643 3391
e-mail: mail@viktoria-station.de
web: www.viktoria-staion.de

Shady site on meadows by the River Ahr, close to a forest, vineyards and castles.

dir: *A61 exit Meckenheim for Altenahr, site 7km.*

Open: Apr-Oct **Site:** 5.5HEC **Prices:** 17.10-20.60 **Facilities:** Wi-fi (charged) Play Area **Services:** **Leisure:** R **Off-site:** P

KRÖV — RHEINLAND-PFALZ

Kröver-Berg

54536
☎ 06541 70040 🖷 06541 700444
e-mail: info@erlebnis-laendchen.de
web: www.erlebnis-laendchen.de

In a forest setting, family friendly site with leisure activities.

Open: All Year. **Site:** 2.6HEC **Facilities:** Play Area **Services:** **Off-site:** P R

LADBERGEN — NORDRHEIN-WESTFALEN

Waldsee

Waldseestr 81, 49549
☎ 05485 1816 🖷 05485 3560
e-mail: info@waldsee-camping.de
web: www.waldsee-camping.de

Site lies at the inn, near the bathing area of the lake.

dir: *2km N. A1 exit Ladbergen for Saerbeck/Emsdetten, 100m turn right.*

GPS: 52.15, 7.7283

Open: All Year. **Site:** 10.5HEC **Prices:** 17.10 Mobile home hire 210 **Facilities:** Kids' Club Play Area **Services:** **Leisure:** L P **Off-site:** R

LAHNSTEIN — RHEINLAND-PFALZ

Burg Lahneck

The Camping and Caravanning Club — The Friendly Club

Am Burgweg, 56112
☎ 02621 2765 🖷 02621 18290
web: www.camping-burg-lahneck.de

Level grassland site with a sunny aspect and terraces that provide shade. Situated next to Lahneck castle with a pleasant view of the Rhine Valley.

C&CC Report *Few sites enjoy a setting as good as this, overlooking the Rhine valley, with a range of public facilities next door at discount prices for campers. Run with friendly efficiency by Frau Mischke, this is an excellent base for visiting the "Romantic Rhine" area, with its ancient ruins, vine-clad valleys and walking and cycling routes – or the owner's castle, next door. In addition, Germany's Federal Horticultural Show will be held in Koblenz in 2011, with new floral displays throughout the city and 3,000 events between 15 April and 16 October.*

dir: *B42 from Koblenz to Lahnstein, follow signs Burg Lahneck, 1.5km to site.*

Open: Apr-Oct **Site:** 1.8HEC **Facilities:** **Services:** **Off-site:** P

GERMANY

EIWEN RHEINLAND-PFALZ

EGON-Ferienpark Sonnenberg

4340
☎ 06507 93690
-mail: sonnenberg@landal.de
eb: www.landal.de

xtensive terraced site in one of the largest wine growing areas of his district. Lies above the River Mosel.

ir: *Off B53 (Mosel Valley road) over River Mosel at Thornich then ia Leiwen to site.*

pen: 4 Feb-22 Jan **Site:** 25HEC **Facilities:** **Services:** **Leisure:** P R **Off-site:**

EMGO NORDRHEIN-WESTFALEN

emgo

egenstorstr 10, 32657
☎ 05261 14858 0521 459017
-mail: lemgo@meyer-zu-bentrup.de
eb: www.camping-lemgo.de

he site lies by the swimming pool directly on the river.

pen: Mar-30 Dec **Site:** 2.5HEC **Prices:** 17-20.50 obile home hire 242.55-269.50 **Facilities:** Wi-fi harged) Play Area **Services:** **Off-site:** P

IBLAR NORDRHEIN-WESTFALEN

iblarer See

0374
☎ 02235 3899
eb: camping-liblar.de

his site lies at Lake Liblar, with its own bathing area.

ir: *SW from Köln (Cologne) on B265 for 15km, 1km before Liblar eft towards lake.*

pen: All Year. **Site:** 10HEC **Prices:** 14 **Facilities:** Play Area **Services:** **Leisure:** L

IEBENAU-ZWERGEN HESSEN

onyhof Camping Club

eichweg 1, 34396
☎ 05676 1509 05676 8880
-mail: info@ponyhofcamping.de
eb: www.ponyhofcamping.de

south-facing terraced site among magnificent scenery, 300m om a swimming pool.

ir: *Off B83 at Hofgeismar W towards Liebenau. Or off B7 at bemeiser N towards Liebenau.*

pen: 20 Mar-10 Nov **Site:** 7HEC **Facilities:** **Services:** **Leisure:** R **Off-site:** L P

LINDENFELS HESSEN

Terrassencamping Schlierbach

Am Zentbuckel 11, 64678
☎ 06255 630 06255 3526
e-mail: info@terrassencamping-schlierbach.de
web: www.terrassencamping-schlierbach.de

Site is fenced and lies on sloping terrain.

dir: *B47 Bensheim-Michelstadt, turn off in Lindenfels SW to Schlierbach.*

Open: Apr-Oct **Site:** 3.2HEC **Prices:** 13.90-27 **Facilities:** Wi-fi Play Area **Services:** **Off-site:** P

LINGERHAHN RHEINLAND-PFALZ

Mühlenteich

56291
☎ 06746 533 06746 1566
e-mail: info@muehlenteich.de
web: www.muehlenteich.de

Site lies on slightly sloping meadowland, divided into sections by trees. Isolated location at the edge of woodland and adjoining the forest swimming pool (free entry for campers). Trout fishing.

dir: *A61 exit Pfalzfeld. Easier approach for caravans A61 exit Laudert.*

Open: All Year. **Site:** 15HEC **Prices:** 18.50-24 **Facilities:** **Services:** **Leisure:** P **Off-site:** R

LORCH HESSEN

Suleika

Im Bodenthal 2, 65391
☎ 06726 9464 06726 9440
e-mail: suleika-camping@t-online.de
web: www.suleika-camping.de

Well laid-out terraced site in an ideal location for exploring the Rhine Valley. Separate car park for users of the smaller pitches.

dir: *B42 from Assmannshausen towards Lorch for 3km, turn right to site through railway underpass. Larger and higher caravans turn right 1km before Lorch.*

Open: 15 Mar-1 Nov **Site:** 4HEC **Prices:** 19.20-23.20 **Facilities:** **Services:** **Off-site:** L R

GERMANY

LOSHEIM — SAARLAND

AZUR-Camping Girtenmühle

Girtenmühle, 66679
06872 90240 06872 902411
e-mail: info@girtenmuehle.de
web: www.girtenmuehle.de
Quiet forest location.
dir: *Via B268 Trier-Losheim.*
Open: Mar-Oct **Site:** 5HEC **Prices:** 12-19.50 **Facilities:** Play Area **Services:** **Off-site:** L P

MARBURG AN DER LAHN — HESSEN

GC Lahnaue

Trojedamm 47, 35037
06421 21331 06421 175882
e-mail: info@lahnaue.de
web: www.lahnaue.de
Situated on the River Lahn, a municipal site on level meadowland next to the Sommerbad (swimming pool).
dir: *W of town.*
Open: Apr-30 Oct **Site:** 1HEC **Facilities:** **Services:** **Leisure:** R **Off-site:** P

MEERBUSCH — NORDRHEIN-WESTFALEN

Rheincamping Meerbusch

Zur Rheinfähre 21, 40668
02150 707571 02150 912289
e-mail: info@rheincamping.com
web: www.rheincamping.com
A peaceful location on the Rhine within easy reach of Düsseldorf.
dir: *Via A57 Neuss-Krefeld.*
Open: Apr-15 Oct **Site:** 3.8HEC **Prices:** 16.50-23.50 **Facilities:** Wi-fi (charged) Play Area **Services:** **Leisure:** R **Off-site:** P

MEHLEM — NORDRHEIN-WESTFALEN

Genienau

53179
0228 344949 0228 3294989
e-mail: genienau@freenet.de
The site lies opposite the Drachenfels.
Open: All Year. **Site:** 1.8HEC **Prices:** 19-25 **Facilities:** **Services:** **Leisure:** R **Off-site:** P

MEINHARD — HESSEN

Meinhardsee

37276
05651 6200 05651 992301
e-mail: info@werra-meissner-camping.de
web: www.werra-meissner-camping.de
A lakeside site with facilities for water sports.
dir: *Via B27 & B249.*
Open: Apr-Oct **Site:** 7HEC **Facilities:** **Services:** **Leisure:** L **Off-site:** P

MESCHEDE — NORDRHEIN-WESTFALEN

Knaus Campingpark Hennesee

Mielinghausen 7, 59872
0291 952720 0291 9527229
e-mail: hennesee@knauscamp.de
web: www.knauscamp.de
Terraced site on the eastern side of a lake in an attractive location of mountains and forests.
Open: 16 Dec-3 Nov **Site:** 17HEC **Facilities:** **Services:** **Leisure:** L P

MESENICH — RHEINLAND-PFALZ

Family Camping Club

56820
02673 4556
e-mail: info@family-camping.de
web: www.family-camping.de
A family site with plenty of recreational facilities beside the River Moselle. Pitches are divided by trees and hedges.
Open: May-Sep **Site:** 3HEC **Facilities:** **Services:** **Leisure:** P R

MITTELHOF — RHEINLAND-PFALZ

Eichenwald

57537
02742 910643 02742 910645
e-mail: camping@hatzfeldt.de
web: www.camping-im-eichenwald.de
Set in an oak wood, mainly divided into pitches.
dir: *B62 from Siegen towards Wissen, turn to site 4km NE of Wissen.*
Open: All Year. **Site:** 10HEC **Prices:** 13-14 **Facilities:** **Services:** **Leisure:** P **Off-site:** P R

GERMANY

MONSCHAU NORDRHEIN-WESTFALEN

Perlenau

Eifel, 52156
☎ 02472 4136 🖷 02472 4493
e-mail: familie.rasch@monschau-perlenau.de
web: www.monschau-perlenau.de
Open: Apr-Oct **Site:** 2HEC **Facilities:** **Services:** **Leisure:** P R **Off-site:**

MÖRFELDEN-WALLDORF HESSEN

Arndt Mörfelden

Am Zeltplatz 5, 64546
☎ 06105 22289 🖷 06105 277459
e-mail: campingplatz.moerfelden@t-online.de
web: www.campingplatz-moerfelden.de
Well laid-out site in two sections near the motorway.
dir: *A5 exit Langen/Mörfelden, site 0.3km, signed.*
Open: All Year. **Site:** 6HEC **Facilities:** **Services:** **Off-site:** L P

MÜLHEIM RHEINLAND-PFALZ

Mülheim

Moselstr 9, 54486
☎ 06534 940157
e-mail: info@campingmuelheim.nl
web: www.campingmuelheim.nl
Near Mülheim-Lieser bridge over the Mosel.
dir: *B53 from Bernkastel towards Trier for 5.5km.*
Open: Etr-Oct **Site:** 1.5HEC **Facilities:** **Services:** **Leisure:** R **Off-site:**

MÜLHEIM AN DER RUHR NORDRHEIN-WESTFALEN

Entenfangsee

45481
☎ 0203 760111 🖷 0203 765162
Extensive site near a lake. Touring pitches near railway line. Adventure playground.
dir: *Motorway exit Duisburg-Wedau for Bissingheim & lake.*
Open: All Year. **Site:** 12.5HEC **Facilities:** **Services:** **Leisure:** L **Off-site:** P

MÜLLENBACH RHEINLAND-PFALZ

Nürburgring

53520
☎ 02692 224 🖷 02692 1020
e-mail: rezeption@camping-am-nuerburgring.de
web: www.camping-am-nuerburgring.de
A large, well-equipped site in a wooded location with direct access to the Nürburgring Grand-Prix circuit.
dir: *Via A61/A48 & B412.*
Open: All Year. **Site:** 30HEC **Facilities:** **Services:**

NEHREN RHEINLAND-PFALZ

Nehren

56820
☎ 02673 4612 🖷 02671 910754
e-mail: info@campingplatz-nehren.de
web: www.campingplatz-nehren.de
On level terrain beside the River Mosel. Separate section for teenagers. Liable to flood at certain times of the year.
dir: *Off B49 in Nehren.*
Open: Apr-15 Oct **Site:** 5HEC **Prices:** 18 **Facilities:** Wi-fi **Services:** **Leisure:** R

NEUERBURG RHEINLAND-PFALZ

In der Enz

In der Enz 25, 54673
☎ 06564 2660 🖷 06564 2979
e-mail: camping@basse.de
web: www.camping-neuerburg.de
2km outside the historic town of Neuerburg, the site is surrounded by wooded hills and crossed by the River Enz. It offers a peaceful, rural location.
dir: *Access via the B50 (Bitburg-Vianden). At Sinspett turn N, continue to site on N outskirts (7km).*
Open: Mar-Oct & Dec-Jan **Site:** 2HEC **Facilities:** **Services:** **Leisure:** R **Off-site:**

NIEDERKRÜCHTEN NORDRHEIN-WESTFALEN

Lelefeld

Lelefeld 4, 41372
☎ 02163 81203 🖷 02163 81203
e-mail: info@camping-lelefeld.com
web: www.camping-lelefeld.com
A quiet wooded location on the outskirts of the village.
dir: *Signed from Elmpt.*
Open: All Year. **Site:** 1.5HEC **Prices:** 12 Mobile home hire 175 **Facilities:** **Services:** **Off-site:** L P R

GERMANY

NIEDERSFELD NORDRHEIN-WESTFALEN

Vossmecke

59955
02985 8418 02985 553
e-mail: info@camping-vossmecke.de
web: www.camping-vossmecke.de
A pleasant wooded location with facilities for winter camping.
dir: *Off B480 towards Winterberg.*
Open: All Year. **Site:** 4HEC **Facilities:**
Services: **Off-site:** L P

OBERSGEGEN RHEINLAND-PFALZ

Reles-Mühle

Kapellenweg 3, 54675
06566 8741 06566 931064
e-mail: info@eifelcamping.com
web: www.eifelcamping.com
Set in rural surroundings next to a farmhouse, on a level meadow by a brook with trees and bushes.
dir: *B50 from Bitburg towards Vianden, site near Luxembourg frontier.*
Open: All Year. **Site:** 2HEC **Facilities:**
Services: **Leisure:** R **Off-site:** P

OBERWEIS RHEINLAND-PFALZ

Prümtal-Camping

In der Klaus 17, 54636
06527 92920 06527 929232
e-mail: info@pruemtal.de
web: www.pruemtal.de
A family site in pleasant wooded surroundings with good sports and camping facilities. Kids' club available during July and August.
dir: *B50 from Bitburg towards B51 Vianden Luxembourg border.*
Open: All Year. **Site:** 3.8HEC **Prices:** 14-22.70
Facilities: Wi-fi (charged) Kids' Club Play Area
Services: **Leisure:** P R

ODERSBACH HESSEN

Odersbach

Runkler Str 5A, 35781
06471 7620 06471 379603
e-mail: info@camping-odersbach.de
web: www.camping-odersbach.de
A modern and quiet camp site in attractive setting beside the River Lahn.
dir: *On S outskirts of town.*
GPS: 50.4758, 8.2411
Open: Apr-Oct **Site:** 6HEC **Prices:** 14.60
Mobile home hire 455 **Facilities:** Wi-fi Play Area
Services: **Leisure:** P R **Off-site:**

OLPE-SONDERN NORDRHEIN-WESTFALEN

Biggesee-Vier Jahreszeiten

Sonderner Kopf 3, 57462
02761 944111 02761 944122
e-mail: info@camping-sonderner.de
web: www.biggesee.com
A popular site in wooded surroundings on the shore of the Biggesee.
dir: *A45 exit Olpe for Attendorn, 6km turn for Erholungsanlage Biggesee-Sondern.*
GPS: 51.0736, 7.8564
Open: All Year. **Site:** 6HEC **Prices:** 20.70-24
Facilities: Play Area **Services:**
Leisure: L **Off-site:**

PORTA WESTFALICA NORDRHEIN-WESTFALEN

Grosser Weserbogen

32457
05731 6188 05731 6601
e-mail: info@grosserweserbogen.de
web: www.grosserweserbogen.de
dir: *A2 towards Dortmund, exit Porta Westfalica-Minden.*
Open: All Year. **Site:** 9HEC **Facilities:** Play Area
Services: **Leisure:** L

PRÜM RHEINLAND-PFALZ

Waldcampingplatz

54591
06551 2481 06551 6555
e-mail: info@waldcamping-pruem.de
web: www.waldcamping-pruem.de
Site lies on both sides of the River Prüm and is surrounded by woods. Divided into three sections of level meadowland.
dir: *On NW edge of Prüm.*
Open: All Year. **Site:** 3.5HEC **Facilities:**
Services: **Leisure:** R **Off-site:** P

GERMANY

EINSFELD RHEINLAND-PFALZ

ZUR Camping Hunsrück

arkstr 1, 54421
06503 95123 06503 95124
-mail: reinsfeld@azur-camping.de
eb: www.azur-camping.de/reinsfeld
peaceful location close to Trier on the Luxembourg border, urrounded by hills.
ir: *Via B52 or B407.*
pen: All Year. Site: 20HEC Facilities: ervices: Leisure: P

OTHEMANN HESSEN

Rothemann

laulkuppenstr 17, 36124
06659 2285
small, well-kept site surrounded by a hedge, next to the main ulda road.
ir: *A7 onto A66 exit Fulda Süd, 3km S on B27 towards Bad rükenau.*
pen: Apr-Oct Site: 5.4HEC Facilities: ervices: Off-site:

ÜDESHEIM HESSEN

hein

astanienallee, 65385
06722 2528 06722 406783
-mail: mail@campingplatz-ruedesheim.de
eb: www.campingplatz-ruedesheim.de
ear the open-air swimming pool, town centre and the River hine.
PS: 49.9777, 7.9408
pen: May-3 Oct Site: 3HEC Prices: 20.60-25.60
acilities: Play Area Services:
ff-site: P

AARBURG RHEINLAND-PFALZ

andal Greenpark Warsberg

4439
06581 91460 06581 914646
mail: warsberg@landal.de
eb: www.landal.com
en site in a quiet hilltop location. A chairlift (700m) goes down the town.
r: *Signed at N end of town off B51 Trier road, 3km uphill.*
en: 31 Mar-Oct Site: 11HEC Facilities:
Services: Leisure: P

Leukbachtal

54439
06581 2228 06581 5008
e-mail: service@campingleukbachtal.de
web: www.campingleukbachtal.de
Municipal site on level meadows on both sides of the Leuk-Bach (brook).
dir: *B51 from Saarburg towards Trassen, turn left after x-rds.*
GPS: 49.5991, 6.5413
Open: Mar-3 Nov Site: 2.5HEC Prices: 18.50
Facilities: Services: Off-site: P R

Waldfrieden

Im Fichtenhain 4, 54439
06581 2255 06581 5908
e-mail: info@campingwaldfrieden.de
web: www.campingwaldfrieden.de
Site lies next to the Café Waldfrieden on unspoiled, slightly rising meadowland in woods.
dir: *S of town off B51 or B407 towards Nennig (Luxembourg), 200m to site.*
GPS: 49.6008, 6.5283
Open: All Year. Site: 6.5HEC Prices: 18.50 Facilities: Wi-fi (charged) Services:
Leisure: P Off-site:

SAARLOUIS SAARLAND

AZUR-Camping Saarlouis

Marschall-Ney-Weg 2, 66740
06831 3691 06831 122970
e-mail: campsls@aol.com
web: www.camping-saarlouis.de
A municipal site, divided into pitches, and set on level meadowland with tall trees.
dir: *Off B51 in suburb of Roden, over new bridge over River Saar to site beyond sports hall.*
Open: 15 Mar-Oct Site: 2HEC Facilities:
Services: Off-site: P R

GERMANY

ST GOAR — RHEINLAND-PFALZ

Friedenau

Gruendelbach 103, 56329
☎ 06741 368 📠 06741 368
e-mail: info@camping-friedenau.de
web: www.camping-friedenau.de

On level, narrow stretch of meadowland at Gasthaus Friedenau.

dir: *Off B9 in St-Goar, through railway underpass towards Emmelshausen for 1km.*

Open: Mar-1 Dec **Site:** 2HEC **Prices:** 17-19 **Facilities:** **Services:** **Leisure:** R **Off-site:** P

ST GOARSHAUSEN — RHEINLAND-PFALZ

Loreleystadt

56346
☎ 06771 2592 📠 02137 929641

Municipal site on level meadow beside the Rhine. Near a sports field and opposite Rheinfels castle.

dir: *Via B42.*

Open: 15 Mar-Oct **Site:** 1.5HEC **Facilities:** **Services:** **Leisure:** R

SCHACHEN — HESSEN

Hochrhön

36129
☎ 06654 7836 📠 06654 7836
e-mail: campinghochrhoen@aol.com
web: www.rhoenline.de/camping-hochrhoen

Site lies 1.5km from the Kneipp (hydrotherapeutic) Spa area of Gersfeld.

dir: *2km N of Gersfeld.*

Open: All Year. **Site:** 3HEC **Prices:** 13 **Facilities:** Play Area **Services:** **Off-site:** L P

SCHALKENMEHREN — RHEINLAND-PFALZ

Camp am Maar

Maarstr 22, 54552
☎ 06592 95510 📠 06592 955140
e-mail: info@hotelschneider.de
web: www.hotelschneider.de

Terraced lakeside site on meadowland at the Schalkenmehrener Maar (water-filled crater). Towing help for caravans.

dir: *A48 exit Mehren/Daun, B42 to Mehren, turn SW.*

GPS: 50.1663, 6.8572

Open: All Year. **Site:** 1HEC **Prices:** 13-19 **Facilities:** **Services:** **Leisure:** L P **Off-site:**

SCHLEIDEN — NORDRHEIN-WESTFALEN

Schleiden

Im Wiesengrund 39, 53937
☎ 02445 7030 📠 02445 5980

Site lies on hilly, well-wooded country.

dir: *On B258 to Monschau, 1km to site.*

Open: All Year. **Site:** 5HEC **Facilities:** **Services:** **Off-site:** P

SCHÖNENBERG — SAARLAND

Ohmbachsee

66901
☎ 06373 4001 📠 06373 4002
e-mail: ohmbachsee@profimail.de
web: www.campingpark-ohmbachsee.de

Terraced site on sloping ground above east bank of the Ohmbachsee. Separate field for young people.

dir: *Signed.*

Open: All Year. **Site:** 7.8HEC **Facilities:** **Services:** **Leisure:** P **Off-site:** L

SCHOTTEN — HESSEN

Nidda-Stausee

Vogelsbergstr 184, 63679
☎ 06044 1418 📠 06044 987995
e-mail: campingplatz@schotten.de
web: www.schotten.de

A pleasant family site on the shore of a lake.

dir: *Via B455.*

Open: All Year. **Site:** 3.2HEC **Facilities:** **Services:** **Off-site:** L P

SECK — RHEINLAND-PFALZ

Weiherhof

56479
☎ 02664 8555 📠 02664 6388
e-mail: info@camping-park-weiherhof.de
web: www.camping-park-weiherhof.de

Site lies on level meadowland next to a small lake in a wooded nature reserve. Special section reserved for young people. Many bathers at weekends.

dir: *B255 from Rennerod to Hellenbahn-Schellenberg, turn S for 2km.*

Open: All Year. **Site:** 10HEC **Facilities:** **Services:** **Leisure:** L

GERMANY

ENHEIM — RHEINLAND-PFALZ

nternationaler Holländischer Hof

6820
02673 4660 02673 4100
-mail: holl.hof@t-online.de
eb: www.moselcamping.com

n level meadowland, divided into pitches beside the River osel. There are mooring facilities, and a kids' club in July and ugust.

ir: *B49 from Cochem towards Zell, at Senhals over bridge & left.*

pen: 11 Apr-1 Nov **Site:** 4HEC
rices: 14.58-16.20 Mobile home hire 205-425
acilities: Wi-fi Kids' Club Play Area
ervices: **Leisure:** R

ENSWEILER MÜHLE — RHEINLAND-PFALZ

beres Idartal

5758
06786 2114 06786 2222
-mail: cpoberesidartal@aol.com
eb: www.oberes-idartal.de

te surrounded by forest lies on a farm by the Idar, set on several nall meadows and partly on terraced terrain next to Camping ensweiler-Mühle.

r: *B422 from Idar-Oberstein for 10km NW, site between atzenloch & Allenbach.*

PS: 49.7691, 7.2073

pen: All Year. **Site:** 2HEC **Prices:** 14.30 Mobile ome hire 175 **Facilities:** Play Area **Services:** **Leisure:** R **Off-site:** P

ensweiler-Mühle

undestr 422, 55758
06786 2395 06781 35147
mail: info@sensweiler-muehle.de
eb: www.sensweiler-muehle.de

extensive grassland beside the Idar, partially terraced, in ral area near a farm. Views of wooded range of hills. Next to amping Oberes Idartal. Separate section for young groups.

r: *B422 from Idar-Oberstein for 10km NW, site between atzenloch & Allenbach.*

en: Mar-Oct **Site:** 3HEC **Prices:** 13-16.50
cilities: **Services:** **Leisure:** R
-site: L

STADTKYLL — RHEINLAND-PFALZ

Landal Wirfttal

54589
06597 92920 06597 929250
e-mail: wirfttal@landal.de
web: www.landal.com

Extensive, level grassland beside the upper of two small reservoirs, 1km outside the town.

dir: *A1 S from Euskirchen, through Blankenheim towards Stadtkyll.*

Open: All Year. **Site:** 6.4HEC **Facilities:**
Services: **Leisure:** P

STEINEN — RHEINLAND-PFALZ

Hofgut Schönerlen

56244
02666 207 02666 8429
e-mail: camping-kopper@t-online.de
web: www.camping-westerwald.de

Beautiful and quiet site at Lake Hausweiher. Young campers under 18 years old not accepted unless with adults. Dogs are permitted in a separate area.

dir: *B8 to Steinen & left to site.*

GPS: 50.5644, 7.8125

Open: Dec-Oct **Site:** 15HEC **Prices:** 17 **Facilities:** (charged) Play Area **Services:**
Leisure: L **Off-site:**

STUKENBROCK — NORDRHEIN-WESTFALEN

Campingplatz Am Furlbach

Am Furlbach 33, 33758
05257 3373 05257 940373
e-mail: info@campingplatzamfurlbach.de
web: www.campingplatzamfurlbach.de

Extensive site, partly on level, open meadow and partly in woodland.

dir: *A33 Osnabrück-Paderborn exit 23, Hollywood Safari park.*

Open: 15 Mar-1 Nov **Site:** 9HEC **Prices:** 15.50-16
Facilities: Play Area **Services:**
Off-site:

TANN — HESSEN

Ulstertal

Dippach 4, 36142
06682 8292 06682 10086

Terraced site on slightly sloping meadowland.

dir: *Off B278 Bischofsheim-Tann in Wendershausen SE to Dippach.*

Open: All Year. **Site:** 2.4HEC **Facilities:**
Services:

GERMANY

TREIS-KARDEN — RHEINLAND-PFALZ

Mosel-Islands

56253
02672 2613 02672 912102
e-mail: info@mosel-islands.de
web: www.mosel-islands.de

An extensive, level site on a grassy island in the Mosel next to a yacht marina.

dir: *Off B49 in Treis onto S coast road.*

Open: Apr-Oct **Site:** 4.5HEC **Prices:** 18 **Facilities:** **Services:** **Leisure:** R **Off-site:** P

TRENDELBURG — HESSEN

Trendelburg

34388
05675 301 05675 5888
e-mail: conradi-camping@t-online.de
web: www.campingplatz-trendelburg.de

Site located at the foot of the castle, subdivided on the banks of the River Diemel. Covered tennis court. Dogs permitted except in restaurant.

dir: *B83 N from Kessel via Hofgeismar to Trendelburg, over bridge & sharp left to site.*

Open: All Year. **Site:** 2.7HEC **Facilities:** Wi-fi (charged) **Services:** **Leisure:** R **Off-site:** P

TRIER — RHEINLAND-PFALZ

Treviris

Luxemburger Str 81, 54294
0651 8200911 0651 8200567
e-mail: info@camping-treviris.de

Level site owned by the Rowing Club Treviris, beside the Mosel 1.6km from the city centre.

dir: *On Luxembourg road between Romer bridge & Adenauer bridge.*

Open: Apr-19 Dec **Site:** 1.5HEC **Facilities:** **Services:** **Leisure:** R **Off-site:** P

TRIPPSTADT — RHEINLAND-PFALZ

Sägmühle

Sägmühle 1, 67705
06306 92190 06306 2000
e-mail: info@saegmuehle.de
web: www.saegmuehle.de

The site lies in a wooded valley beside Sägmühle (Saw Mill) lake. It consists of several unconnected sections, some of them terraced. Kids' club open during July and August.

dir: *16km S of Kaiserslautern.*

Open: 16 Dec-Oct **Site:** 10HEC **Prices:** 21.40-28 **Facilities:** Wi-fi (charged) Kids' Club Play Area **Services:** **Leisure:** L **Off-site:** P

VINKRATH BEI GREFRATH — NORDRHEIN-WESTFALEN

Ferienpark Waldfrieden

An der Paas 13, 47929
02158 3855 02158 3685
e-mail: ferienpark-waldfrieden@t-online.de
web: www.ferienpark-waldfrieden.de

Site within a nature reserve.

dir: *Off B509 at Grefrath N towards Wankum, 3km turn right.*

Open: All Year. **Site:** 4.5HEC **Prices:** 17.50 **Facilities:** **Services:** **Leisure:** L **Off-site:** L P R

VLOTHO — NORDRHEIN-WESTFALEN

Borlefzen

Borlefzen 2, 32602
05733 80008 05733 89728
e-mail: info@borlefzen.de
web: www.borlefzen.de

Open: Apr-Oct **Site:** 40HEC **Facilities:** **Services:** **Leisure:** L R

WARBURG — NORDRHEIN-WESTFALEN

Eversburg

34414
05641 8668

Site lies next to restaurant of the same name on the south-east outskirts of the town.

Open: All Year. **Site:** 4.5HEC **Prices:** 21 **Facilities:** **Services:** **Leisure:** R **Off-site:** P

GERMANY

WASSERFALL NORDRHEIN-WESTFALEN

Aurora

Aurorastr 9, 59909
☎ 02905 332

Terraced site surrounded by woodland, next to Fort Fun leisure centre. Little room for touring campers during the winter.

dir: *Turn S off B7 10km E of Meschedes, pass Gevelinghausen to Wasserfall.*

Open: All Year. **Site:** 0.7HEC **Facilities:** **Services:** **Off-site:** P R

WAXWEILER RHEINLAND-PFALZ

Eifel Ferienpark Prümtal

Schwimmbadstr 7, 54649
☎ 06554 92000 06554 920029
e-mail: info@ferienpark-waxweiler.de
web: www.ferienpark-waxweiler.de

Site lies on level terrain and is divided into pitches, with a separate field on the opposite side of the River Prüm. There is a kids' club during peak season.

dir: *From N end of Waxweiler turn towards River Prüm.*

Open: Apr-Oct **Site:** 3HEC **Facilities:** Wi-fi (charged) Kids' Club Play Area **Services:** **Leisure:** P R **Off-site:**

WISSEL NORDRHEIN-WESTFALEN

Wisseler See

Zum Wisseler See 15, 47546
☎ 02824 96310 02824 963131
e-mail: info@wisseler-see.de
web: www.wisseler-see.de

Well-kept municipal site with modern equipment beside Lake Wissel. There is a separate car park next to the open-air swimming pool. The pool belongs to the camp. The washrooms are closed lunchtimes and at night.

dir: *B57 from Kieve towards Xanten, 9km turn left, continue 3km towards Wissel.*

Open: All Year. **Site:** 35HEC **Facilities:** **Services:** **Leisure:** L

WITZENHAUSEN HESSEN

Camping Platz Werratal

Am Sande 11, 37213
☎ 05542 1465
e-mail: info@campingplatz-werratal.de
web: www.campingplatz-werratal.de

The site lies on meadow between the outskirts of Witzenhausen and the banks of the Werra.

dir: *Hannover-Kassel motorway exit Werratal, onto B80 to Witzenhausen, signed from market place.*

GPS: 51.3474, 9.8687

Open: All Year. **Site:** 3HEC **Prices:** 15-18.10 Mobile home hire 161-273 **Facilities:** Play Area **Services:** **Leisure:** R **Off-site:** L P

WOLFSTEIN RHEINLAND-PFALZ

Camping am Königsberg

Am Schwimmbad 1, 67752
☎ 06304 4143 06304 7543
e-mail: info@campingwolfstein.de
web: www.campingwolfstein.de

In the middle of an attractive nature zone at the foot of a mountain. The site has an informal atmosphere and good equipment, beside River Lauter.

dir: *Site at S end of Wolfstein on right of B270 from Kaiserslautern.*

Open: All Year. **Site:** 3.8HEC **Prices:** 18-22 **Facilities:** Wi-fi (charged) Kids' Club Play Area **Services:** **Leisure:** P R **Off-site:** L P R

ZERF RHEINLAND-PFALZ

Rübezahl

54314
☎ 06587 814 06587 814
e-mail: seyffardt-zerf@t-online.de

Meadowland site in natural grounds on wooded hillside.

dir: *B268 from Zerf S towards Saarbrücken & turn towards Oberzerf, site 2.5km. Or B407 from Saarburg, turn right after Vierherrenhorn onto track for 60m.*

Open: Apr-Oct **Site:** 2.5HEC **Prices:** 14 **Facilities:** Play Area **Services:** **Leisure:** P

GERMANY

ZWESTEN, BAD — HESSEN

Waldcamping

34596
05626 379 06695 1320
e-mail: info@doering-jesberg.de
web: www.waldcamping.de

Site in bend of River Schwalm. For touring campers there is an overflow site.

dir: *Access from Kassel in SW direction via Fritzlar to Zwesten.*

Open: All Year. **Site:** 5HEC **Facilities:** **Services:** **Leisure:** P R **Off-site:**

NORTH

ALTENAU — NIEDERSACHSEN

Okertalsperre

Kornhardtweg 2, 38707
05328 702 05328 911708
e-mail: info@campingokertal.de
web: www.campingokertal.de

On a long stretch of grassland at the southern end of the Oker reservoir.

dir: *Signed from B498 Oker-Altenau.*

Open: All Year. **Site:** 3HEC **Facilities:** **Services:** **Leisure:** L **Off-site:** P

BLECKEDE — NIEDERSACHSEN

Alt-Garge (ADAC)

Am Waldbad 23, 21354
05854 311 05854 1640
e-mail: adac-camping-altgarge@t-online.de
web: www.camping-altgarge.de

A modern site at the south-eastern end of Alt-Garge, next to a heated swimming pool in the woods.

dir: *5km SE of Bleckede.*

GPS: 53.2592, 10.8053

Open: All Year. **Site:** 6.6HEC **Prices:** 22.50-24.50 **Facilities:** (charged) Play Area **Services:** **Off-site:** L P R

BODENWERDER — NIEDERSACHSEN

Himmelspforte

Ziegeleiweg 1, 37619
05533 4938 05533 4432
e-mail: himmelspforte01@yahoo.de
web: www.camping-weserbergland.de

Site on grassland, with a fruit orchard, next to River Weser. Watersports available. Separate section and common room for young campers.

dir: *Cross River Weser & right towards Rühle, site 2km.*

Open: All Year. **Site:** 11HEC **Facilities:** **Services:** **Leisure:** R **Off-site:** P

Rühler Schweiz

Grosses Tal, 37619
05533 2486 05533 5882
e-mail: info@brader-ruehler-schweiz.de
web: www.brader-ruehler-schweiz.de

This site lies on well-kept meadowland by the River Weser.

dir: *4km from Weser bridge in Bodenwerder towards Rühle.*

Open: Mar-Oct **Site:** 7HEC **Prices:** 12-15.50 **Facilities:** **Services:** **Leisure:** P R

BOTHEL — NIEDERSACHSEN

Hanseat

27384
04266 355 04266 355
e-mail: info@campingpark-hanseat.de

Small quality site on the edge of the town.

Open: All Year. **Site:** 4.5HEC **Facilities:** **Services:** **Off-site:** P

BREMEN — BREMEN

Stadtwaldsee

Hochschulring 1, 28359
0421 8410748 0421 8410749
e-mail: contact@camping-stadtwaldsee.de
web: www.camping-stadtwaldsee.de

Situated near a lake in forest close to the city.

dir: *A27 exit 18.*

Open: All Year. **Site:** 5.8HEC **Facilities:** **Services:** **Off-site:** L P

BRIETLINGEN-REIHERSEE NIEDERSACHSEN

Reihersee 1

Alte Salzstr 8, 21382
☎ 04133 3671 & 3577 🖷 04133 3577

Divided into pitches by hedges and pine trees. Private bathing area.

dir: *Turn E at car park 2km beyond Brietlingen towards Reihersee for 0.8km.*

Open: All Year. **Site:** 6.2HEC **Prices:** 8-11 **Facilities:** **Services:** **Leisure:** L R **Off-site:**

BÜCHEN SCHLESWIG-HOLSTEIN

Waldschwimmbad

21514
☎ 04155 5360 🖷 04155 499140
e-mail: camping-hintz@t-online.de
web: www.camping-buechen.de

On gently sloping grassland.

dir: *From Lauenburg or Mölln to Büchen then signed.*

Open: All Year. **Site:** 1.6HEC **Prices:** 14-17 Mobile home hire 175-230 **Facilities:** **Services:** **Off-site:** P R

BURGWEDEL NIEDERSACHSEN

Erholungsgebiet Springhorstsee

30938
☎ 05139 3232 🖷 05139 27070
e-mail: springhorstsee@aol.com
web: www.springhorstsee.de

On level ground beside a lake with well-defined pitches and modern facilities.

dir: *A7 exit 54, site 2km.*

Open: All Year. **Site:** 29HEC **Facilities:** Play Area **Services:** **Leisure:** L P **Off-site:**

BUTJADINGEN NIEDERSACHSEN

Knaus Campingpark Burhave

Burhave Strand, 26969
☎ 04733 1683 🖷 04733 173206
e-mail: burhave@knauscamp.de
web: www.knauscamp.de

Situated next to a national park with access to fine beaches.

Open: 14 Apr-20 Oct **Site:** 10HEC **Facilities:** **Services:** **Leisure:** S

CLAUSTHAL-ZELLERFELD NIEDERSACHSEN

Prahljust

An den langen Bruchen 4, 38678
☎ 05323 1300 🖷 05323 78393
e-mail: camping@prahljust.de
web: www.prahljust.de

The site lies on slightly sloping grassland in an area of woodland and lakes.

dir: *B242 SE from outskirts towards Braunlage, 2km turn right, site 1.5km.*

Open: All Year. **Site:** 13HEC **Facilities:** Play Area **Services:** **Leisure:** L P **Off-site:** R

Waldweben

Spiegelthalerstr 31, 38678
☎ 05323 81712 🖷 05323 962134
e-mail: waldweben@t-online.de
web: www.campingplatz-waldweben.de

Holiday village with individual pitches in open meadow and coniferous woodland by three small lakes.

dir: *Signed from B241 towards Goslar.*

GPS: 51.8231, 10.3166

Open: All Year. **Site:** 4.5HEC **Prices:** 15.60 **Facilities:** Wi-fi Play Area **Services:** **Off-site:** L P

DAHRENHORST NIEDERSACHSEN

Irenensee

31311
☎ 05173 98120 🖷 05173 981213
e-mail: info@irenensee.de
web: www.irenensee.de

A lakeside site on meadowland, partly surrounded by woods, with separate section for tourers, statics and residentials.

dir: *B188 from Burgdorf towards Uetze for 15km.*

Open: Apr-Oct **Site:** 120HEC **Facilities:** **Services:** **Leisure:** L

DETERN NIEDERSACHSEN

Jümmesee

26847
☎ 04957 1808 🖷 04957 8112
e-mail: info@detern.de
web: www.detern.de

Family site with leisure complex and a central lake.

dir: *Via B72 Aurich-Cloppenburg.*

Open: All Year. **Site:** 11.5HEC **Facilities:** Play Area **Services:** **Leisure:** L R **Off-site:**

GERMANY

DORUM — NIEDERSACHSEN

AZUR Nordseecamp Dorumer Tief

Am Kutterhafen, 27632
☎ 04741 5020 📠 04741 914061
e-mail: dorum@azur-camping.de
web: www.azur-camping.de/dorum
Next to a small harbour. Separated from the beach by a dyke.
dir: *Via A27 Bremerhaven-Cuxhaven.*
Open: Apr-Sep **Site:** 7HEC **Facilities:** **Services:** **Leisure:** P S

ECKWARDERHÖRNE — NIEDERSACHSEN

Knaus Camping Park Eckwarderhörne

Butjadinger Str 116, 26969
☎ 04736 1300 📠 04736 102593
e-mail: eckwarderhoerne@knauscamp.de
web: www.knauscamp.de
Parkland site adjoining the North Sea.
Open: 30 Mar-5 Nov **Site:** 7.7HEC **Facilities:** **Services:** **Leisure:** S

EGESTORF — NIEDERSACHSEN

Regenbogen Camp Egestorf

Alte Dorfstr 1, 21272
☎ 04175 661 📠 04175 8383
e-mail: egestorf@regenbogen-camp.de
Modern site on wooded heathland on the edge of the Lüneburg Heath nature reserve, 2km south of town on slightly sloping terrain with asphalt internal roads.
dir: *A7 exit Egestorf or Evendorf.*
Open: Apr-Oct **Site:** 22HEC **Facilities:** **Services:** **Leisure:** P **Off-site:**

EIMKE — NIEDERSACHSEN

Extertal

1 Beurteilung, Eimke 4, 32699
☎ 05262 3307 📠 05262 992404
e-mail: info@campingpark-extertal.de
web: www.campingpark-extertal.de
Extensive, partly terraced site on slightly sloping meadowland with two ponds.
dir: *A2 exit 35, B238 past Rinteln, left onto Extertal-Barntrup road for 18km.*
Open: All Year. **Site:** 20HEC **Prices:** 14 **Facilities:** Wi-fi (charged) Play Area **Services:** **Leisure:** L **Off-site:** P

ELISABETH SOPHIENKOOG (ISLAND OF NORDSTRAND) — SCHLESWIG-HOLSTEIN

Elisabeth-Sophienkoog

Nordstrand, 25845
☎ 04842 8534 📠 04842 8306
e-mail: camping-nordstrand@t-online.de
web: www.nordstrandcamping.de
On meadowland behind the sea dyke with bathing beach. A quiet site with good facilities for campers.
dir: *Via Husum to Island of Nordstrand.*
Open: Apr-Oct **Site:** 1.7HEC **Facilities:** Wi-fi (charged) Play Area **Services:** **Leisure:** S **Off-site:** P

ESENS-BENSERSIEL — NIEDERSACHSEN

Bensersiel

Am Strand 8, 26427
☎ 04971 917121 📠 04971 917190
e-mail: camping@bensersiel.de
web: www.camping-bensersiel.de
Well-managed, extensive leisure centre with harbour, good fish restaurant and reading room. Swimming pools have sea water and artificial waves.
dir: *B210 NE from Aurich to Ogenbargenn then via Esens.*
GPS: 53.6752, 7.5699
Open: Apr-15 Oct **Site:** 10HEC **Prices:** 25-26.50 **Facilities:** Wi-fi (charged) Kids' Club Play Area **Services:** **Leisure:** P S **Off-site:** L R

EUTIN-FISSAU — SCHLESWIG-HOLSTEIN

Prinzenholz

Prinzenholzweg 20, 23701
☎ 04521 5281 📠 04521 790693
e-mail: info@nc-prinzenholz.de
web: www.nc-prinzenholz.de
Terraced lakeside site divided by trees and bushes.
dir: *N of town onto Malente road, 2km turn right.*
Open: Apr-Oct **Site:** 2HEC **Prices:** 23.50-25.50 **Facilities:** Wi-fi Play Area **Services:** **Leisure:** L **Off-site:** P

GERMANY

FALLINGBOSTEL NIEDERSACHSEN

Böhmeschlucht

Vierde 22, 29683
05162 5604 05162 5160
e-mail: campingplatz-boehmeschlucht@t-online.de
web: www.boehmeschlucht.de
Site located in a nature reserve beside the river Böhme.
dir: *A7 exit 46/47, site signed 3km N.*
Open: All Year. Site: 4HEC Prices: 17.70-19.50 Facilities: Play Area Services: Leisure: R Off-site: P

FEHMARNSUND SCHLESWIG-HOLSTEIN

Miramar

23769
04371 3220 04371 868044
e-mail: campingmiramar@t-online.de
web: www.camping-miramar.de
A family site on meadowland at the southern end of the island.
dir: *Off B207 at 1st turn after Sundbrücke (bridge) towards Svendorf.*
Open: All Year. Site: 13HEC Prices: 26 Mobile home hire 504 Facilities: Kids' Club Play Area Services: Leisure: L S

GANDERSHEIM, BAD NIEDERSACHSEN

DCC Kur-Campingpark

Braunschweiger Str 12, 37581
05382 1595 05382 1599
e-mail: info@camping-bad-gandersheim.de
web: www.camping-bad-gandersheim.de
On a level meadow, divided in two by a brook beside a public park. Good sports facilities. Separate section for young people.
dir: *A7 exit 67 Soesen onto B64 W.*
Open: All Year. Site: 9HEC Facilities: Services:

GARBSEN NIEDERSACHSEN

Blauer See

30823
05137 89960 05137 899677
e-mail: info@camping-blauer-see.de
web: www.camping-blauer-see.de
On a small lake beside the Garbsen service area on the A2 motorway.
Open: All Year. Site: 22HEC Facilities: Services: Leisure: L

GLÜCKSBURG SCHLESWIG-HOLSTEIN

Ostseecamp Glücksburg-Holnis

An der Promenade 1, 24960
04631 622071 04631 622072
e-mail: info@ostseecamp-holnis.de
web: www.ostseecamp-holnis.de
Open: Apr-Oct Site: 6HEC Prices: 18.80-20.30 Mobile home hire 315-343 Facilities: Wi-fi Play Area Services: Off-site: S

GRUBE SCHLESWIG-HOLSTEIN

Rosenfelder Strand Ostsee Camping

Rosenfelder Strand 1, 23749
04365 979722 04365 979594
e-mail: info@rosenfelder-strand.de
web: www.rosenfelder-strand.de
Excellently managed family site beside the sea with a 1km-long beach. Divided into separate fields by rows of bushes. Children's playground in woodland between site and sea.
dir: *E47/A1 Hamburg/Lübeck/Oldenburg-H exit 12 towards Grube then left onto B501 towards Heiligenhafen. After 4km turn right toward Rosenfelde; pass farm then left at sign.*
GPS: 54.2651, 11.0776
Open: 25 Mar-16 Oct Site: 24HEC Prices: 16.60-25.10 Facilities: Wi-fi (charged) Kids' Club Play Area Services: Leisure: S

HADDEBY SCHLESWIG-HOLSTEIN

Haithabu

Haddebyer Chaussee 15, 24866
04621 32450 04621 33122
e-mail: info@campingplatz-haithabu.de
web: www.campingplatz-haithabu.de
Clean, tidy site beside the River Schlei.
dir: *B76 from Schleswig towards Eckernförde.*
Open: Apr-Oct Site: 5HEC Facilities: Play Area Services: Leisure: R

HAHNENKLEE NIEDERSACHSEN

Kreuzeck

38644
05325 2570 05325 3392
e-mail: kreuzeck@aol.com
web: www.kreuzeck.de
Terraced site in a forest beside a lake. Separate section for dog owners.
dir: *Beside Café am Kreuzeck at junct B241 & road to Hahnenklee.*
Open: All Year. Site: 5HEC Facilities: Services: Leisure: L P Off-site:

HARDEGSEN — NIEDERSACHSEN

Ferienpark Solling

Auf dem Gladeberg 1, 37181
☎ 05505 2272 📠 05505 5585
e-mail: ferienparksolling@web.de
Terraced site in forested area. Separate field for touring pitches.
dir: *In town onto Waldgebiet Gladeberg road.*
GPS: 51.6405, 9.831
Open: All Year. **Site:** 2.4HEC **Prices:** 14-15 **Facilities:** **Services:** **Off-site:** P

HASSENDORF — NIEDERSACHSEN

Stürberg

27367
☎ 04264 9124 📠 04264 821440
e-mail: campingpark-stuerberg@gmx.de
web: www.stuerberg.de
Pleasant wooded surroundings beside a lake.
dir: *A1 exit 50 Stuckenborstel, B75 for Rotenburg for 5km.*
GPS: 53.1202, 9.2783
Open: 15 Mar-Oct **Site:** 2HEC **Prices:** 15 **Facilities:** Play Area **Services:** **Leisure:** L **Off-site:** P

HATTEN — NIEDERSACHSEN

Freizeitzentrum Hatten

Kreyenweg 8, 26209
☎ 04482 677 📠 04482 928027
e-mail: info@fzz.hatten.de
web: www.fzz-hatten.de
Well equipped site at the edge of Kirchhatten.
Open: All Year. **Site:** 2HEC **Prices:** 14.10-18.10 **Facilities:** **Services:** **Leisure:** P

HATTORF — NIEDERSACHSEN

Oderbrücke

37197
☎ 05521 4359 📠 05521 4360
e-mail: info@oderbruecke.info
web: www.oderbruecke.info
A pleasant wooded location with good recreational and sanitary facilities.
dir: *On B27 towards Herzberg.*
GPS: 51.6280, 10.2708
Open: All Year. **Site:** 2.5HEC **Prices:** 12.20 **Facilities:** Play Area **Services:** **Leisure:** R **Off-site:**

HEIKENDORF — SCHLESWIG-HOLSTEIN

Möltenort

24226
☎ 0431 241316 📠 0431 2379920
e-mail: gronau.heikendorf@freenet.de
web: www.camping-ostsee-online.de
Terraced site by the Kieler Förde.
dir: *15km NE of Kiel to W of road B502. Access via narrow, winding road.*
Open: Apr-1 Oct **Site:** 2HEC **Facilities:** **Services:** **Leisure:** S **Off-site:** P

HEMELN — NIEDERSACHSEN

Wesercamping Hemeln

Unterdorf 34, 34346
☎ 05544 1414 📠 05544 1439
e-mail: info@wesercamping.de
web: www.wesercamping.de
Well-kept site on northern outskirts of village, beside the River Weser and close to Hann Münden Naturpark.
dir: *A7 exit Göttingen, B3 to Dransfeld & signed.*
GPS: 51.5041, 9.6027
Open: All Year. **Site:** 2.4HEC **Prices:** 17 Mobile home hire 202 **Facilities:** Wi-fi Play Area **Services:** **Leisure:** R **Off-site:** P

HERMANNSBURG — NIEDERSACHSEN

Örtzetal

Dicksbarg 46, 29320
☎ 05052 3072 & 1555
web: www.campingplatz-oldendorf.de
Site lies on meadows on the eastern bank of the River Örtze, set in unspoiled woodlands on Lüneburg Heath. Boat landing stage.
dir: *Off B3 in Bergen NE towards Hermannsburg & Eschwege.*
Open: 15 Mar-Oct **Site:** 6HEC **Facilities:** **Services:** **Leisure:** R **Off-site:** P

HOHEGEISS — NIEDERSACHSEN

Bärenbache

Barenbachweg 10, 38700
☎ 05583 1306 📠 05583 1300
e-mail: info@campingplatz-hohegeiss.de
web: www.campingplatz-hohegeiss.de
Terraced site, divided by hedges on south-facing slope. A short walk from the town centre.
Open: All Year. **Site:** 3HEC **Facilities:** **Services:** **Off-site:** P

GERMANY

Site 6HEC (site size) grass sand stone little shade partly shaded mainly shaded bungalows for hire (static) caravans for hire tents for hire no dogs site fully accessible for wheelchairs
Prices amount quoted is per night, for 2 adults and car, plus tent or caravan. Mobile home hire is a weekly rate.

HOLLE — NIEDERSACHSEN

Seecamp-Derneburg

An der B6, Derneburg, 31188
☎ 05062 565
e-mail: info@seecamp-derneburg.de
web: www.seecamp-derneburg.de

A terraced lakeside site on a hill slope with a southerly aspect. Separate towing field. Useful stopover site near autobahn.

dir: *Motorway exit Derneburg onto B6.*

Open: Apr-15 Sep **Site:** 7.8HEC **Facilities:** **Services:** **Leisure:** L **Off-site:** R

HÖSSERINGEN — NIEDERSACHSEN

Hardausee

29556
☎ 05826 7676 05826 8303
e-mail: info@camping-hardausee.de
web: www.camping-hardausee.de

Grassland site without firm internal roads. Statics have individual pitches and outbuildings. Separate fields for tourers.

dir: *From Uelzen S on B4, 9km turn right, continue via Suderburg to site on right before Hösseringen.*

Open: Mar-Oct **Site:** 12HEC **Prices:** 15-19 **Facilities:** Play Area **Services:** **Off-site:** L

ISERNHAGEN — NIEDERSACHSEN

Parksee Lohne

Alter Postweg 12, 30916
☎ 05139 88260 05139 891665
e-mail: parksee-lohne@t-online.de
web: www.parksee-lohne.de

Recreation area by a lake. On the flight approach path for Hannover Langenhagen airport. Separate section for tourers.

dir: *Motorway exit Kirchorst, Altwarmbüchen road to Isernhagen.*

Open: Apr-15 Oct **Site:** 13HEC **Facilities:** **Services:** **Leisure:** L

KLAUSDORF (ISLAND OF FEHMARN) — SCHLESWIG-HOLSTEIN

Klausdorfer Strand

23769
☎ 04371 2549 04371 2481
e-mail: info@camping-klausdorferstrand.de
web: www.camping-klausdorferstrand.de

A grassy site with sea views. Divided into pitches. Sandy beach.

dir: *From Burg turn off main road 2.5km before Klausdorf onto narrow asphalt road.*

GPS: 54.4572, 11.2719

Open: Apr-15 Oct **Site:** 12HEC **Prices:** 14-24 **Facilities:** Wi-fi (charged) Kids' Club Play Area **Services:** **Leisure:** S **Off-site:** L P

KLEINWAABS — SCHLESWIG-HOLSTEIN

Ostsee Heide

24369
☎ 04352 2530 04352 1398
e-mail: info@waabs.de
web: www.waabs.de

Divided into pitches and pleasantly landscaped. Large games room for teenagers.

Open: Mar-Oct **Site:** 22HEC **Facilities:** **Services:** **Leisure:** P S

KLINT-BEI-HECHTHAUSEN — NIEDERSACHSEN

Geesthof

Am Ferienpark 1, 21755
☎ 04774 512 04774 9178
e-mail: info@geesthof.de
web: www.geesthof.de

On dry meadowland next to the River Oste, in quiet setting with trees.

dir: *Off B73 in Hechthausen W towards Lamstedt for 3km.*

Open: All Year. **Site:** 15HEC **Prices:** 11-19 **Facilities:** **Services:** **Leisure:** P S

GERMANY

LOOSE — SCHLESWIG-HOLSTEIN

Gut Ludwigsburg

24369
04358 370 04358 460
e-mail: info@ostseecamping-ludwigsburg.de
web: www.ostseecamping-ludwigsburg.de

A well presented site with good amenities and recreational facilities between the old Hanseatic cities of Lübeck and Wismar. Kids' club in July and August.

dir: *From Eckernförde towards Klein-Wabbs, at Gut Ludwigsburg onto track for 2km.*

GPS: 54.5031, 9.9577

Open: Apr-Sep **Site:** 10HEC **Prices:** 14-20 **Facilities:** Wi-fi Kids' Club Play Area **Services:** **Leisure:** L S

LÜGDE — NIEDERSACHSEN

Eichwald

Obere Dorfstr 80, 32676
05283 335 05283 640
e-mail: info@camping-eichwald.de
web: www.camping-eichwald.de

Pleasant grassy site near woodland and a pool.

dir: *S of Lüdge towards Rischenau to Elbrinxen.*

Open: All Year. **Site:** 10HEC **Facilities:** **Services:** **Off-site:** P

MALENTE-GREMSMÜHLEN — SCHLESWIG-HOLSTEIN

Schwentine

Wiesenweg 14, 23714
04523 4327 04523 207602
e-mail: info@camping-bad-malente.de
web: www.camping-bad-malente.de

A park-like setting with trees and bushes, at a river within the village of Malente.

dir: *A1 Hamburg/Lübeck/Puttgarden, then Eutin B76 in direction of Süseler and Eutin. A7 Hamburg/Flensburg.*

Open: Apr-Oct **Site:** 2.5HEC **Prices:** 15.20-19 **Facilities:** Wi-fi Play Area **Services:** **Leisure:** R **Off-site:** L P

NEUSTADT — SCHLESWIG-HOLSTEIN

Strande

Sandberger Weg 94, 23730
04561 4188 04361 7125
e-mail: info@amstrande.de
web: www.amstrande.de

The site is divided into small sections and slopes down to the sea. Narrow sandy beach.

dir: *From Neustadt towards Schön Klinik, 1st site on right.*

Open: Apr-Sep **Site:** 4.7HEC **Prices:** 18-22 **Facilities:** Wi-fi (charged) **Services:** **Leisure:** S **Off-site:**

NORTHEIM — NIEDERSACHSEN

Sultmer Berg

Sultmerberg 3, 37154
05551 51559 05551 5656
e-mail: campingplatzmajora@web.de
web: www.campingplatzsultmerberg.de

Grassland site with views of surrounding hills.

dir: *B3 from town centre.*

Open: 15 Jan-Dec **Site:** 2.7HEC **Facilities:** **Services:** **Leisure:** P **Off-site:** L R

ORTSTEIL GÖTTINGERODE — NIEDERSACHSEN

Harz-Camp Göttingerode

Kreisstr 66, 38667
05322 81215 05322 877533
e-mail: harz-camp@t-online.de
web: www.harz-camp.de

On outskirts of village next to main road. Terraced site with separate touring field.

dir: *On L501 between Bad Harzburg & Goslar.*

Open: All Year. **Site:** 6.5HEC **Prices:** 22.70 Mobile home hire 263.20-284.20 **Facilities:** Wi-fi (charged) Play Area **Services:** **Leisure:** P **Off-site:**

OSNABRÜCK — NIEDERSACHSEN

Niedersachsenhof

Nordstr 109, 49084
0541 77226 0541 70627
e-mail: osnacamp@aol.com
web: www.osnacamp.de

The site lies on a gently sloping meadow bordering a forest, near a converted farmhouse with an inn.

dir: *5km NW from town centre on B51/65 towards Bremen, turn right, site 300m.*

Open: All Year. **Site:** 3HEC **Prices:** 18.50 **Facilities:** Play Area **Services:** **Off-site:** P R

GERMANY

OSTRHAUDERFEHN NIEDERSACHSEN

Frieizeitanlage Idasee

Idafehn-Nord 77 B, 26842
☎ 04952 994297 🖹 04952 808628
e-mail: info@camping-idasee.de
web: www.camping-idasee.de
A lakeside site between Oldenburg and the Dutch border with good water sports.
dir: *Via B27 Cloppenburg-Aurich.*
Open: All Year. **Site:** 11HEC **Facilities:** **Services:** **Leisure:** L

OTTERNDORF NIEDERSACHSEN

See Achtern Diek

Am Campingplatz 3, 21762
☎ 04751 2933 🖹 04751 3016
e-mail: campingplatz.otterndorf@ewetel.net
web: www.otterndorf.de
A family site with good facilities close to the coast.
dir: *Via B73 Cuxhaven-Hamburg.*
Open: Apr-Oct **Site:** 15HEC **Prices:** 18-20 **Facilities:** Kids' Club Play Area **Services:** **Leisure:** L **Off-site:** P R S

OYTEN NIEDERSACHSEN

Knaus Campingplatz Oyten

Erholungsgebiet Oyter See, 28876
☎ 04207 2878 🖹 04207 909005
e-mail: oyten@knauscamp.de
web: www.knauscamp.de
Parkland site next to a lake on the outskirts of Bremen.
Open: 14 Mar-3 Nov **Site:** 15.6HEC **Facilities:** **Services:** **Leisure:** L

PLÖN SCHLESWIG-HOLSTEIN

Spitzenort

Ascheberger Str 76, 24306
☎ 04522 2769 🖹 04522 4574
A pleasant site with hedges surrounded by Plön lake on three sides. Ideal for water sports.
dir: *B430 from Plön towards Neumünster.*
Open: Apr-15 Oct **Site:** 4.5HEC **Facilities:** **Services:** **Leisure:** L **Off-site:** P

RIESTE NIEDERSACHSEN

Alfsee

Am Campingpark 10, 49597
☎ 05464 92120 🖹 05464 5837
e-mail: info@alfsee.de
web: www.alfsee.com
Open: All Year. **Site:** 16HEC **Facilities:** **Services:** **Leisure:** L

RINTELN NIEDERSACHSEN

Doktor-See

am Doktorsee 8, 31722
☎ 05751 964860 🖹 05751 964888
e-mail: info@doktorsee.de
web: www.doktorsee.de
A beautiful location beside a recreation area and the Doktor-See bathing beach. Section for touring campers.
dir: *In town turn downstream at River Weser bridge along left bank for 1.5km.*
GPS: 52.1864, 9.0597
Open: All Year. **Site:** 152HEC **Facilities:** Play Area **Services:** **Leisure:** L **Off-site:** P R

RÖTGESBÜTTEL NIEDERSACHSEN

Glockenheide

38531
☎ 05304 1581 🖹 05304 1581
e-mail: camping-glockenheide@t-online.de
web: www.glockenheide.de
Tranquil site in heathland.
dir: *In Rötgesbüttel turn left & left again after level crossing.*
Open: All Year. **Site:** 5HEC **Facilities:** **Services:** **Off-site:**

ST ANDREASBERG NIEDERSACHSEN

Erikabrücke

37444
☎ 05582 1431 🖹 05582 923056
dir: *Off B27 from Bad Lauterberg towards Braunlage*
Open: All Year. **Site:** 5.5HEC **Facilities:** **Services:** **Leisure:** L R

GERMANY

SCHOBÜLL — SCHLESWIG-HOLSTEIN

Seeblick

Nordseestr 39, 25813
04841 3321 04841 5773
e-mail: info@camping-seeblick.de
web: www.camping-seeblick.de
Beautiful location beside the sea. Site divided into two sections.

dir: *Off B5 on N outskirts of Husum towards Insel Nordstrand for 4km to Schobüll.*

Open: 18 Mar-23 Oct **Site:** 3.4HEC **Prices:** 14.50-19 Mobile home hire 84-175 **Facilities:** Wi-fi Play Area **Services:** **Leisure:** S **Off-site:** P

STRUKKAMPHUK (ISLAND OF FEHMARN) — SCHLESWIG-HOLSTEIN

Strukkamphuk

23769
04371 2194 04371 87178
e-mail: camping@strukkamphuk.de
web: www.strukkamphuk.de
Site in the south of the island of Fehmarn, situated behind the dyke, directly on the Baltic Sea.

GPS: 54.4105, 11.1005

Open: All Year. **Site:** 20HEC **Prices:** 13.10-34.30 **Facilities:** Kids' Club Play Area **Services:** **Leisure:** L P S

STUHR — NIEDERSACHSEN

Steller See

Zum Steller See 15, 28816
04206 6490 04206 6668
e-mail: steller.see@t-online.de
web: www.steller-see.de
Located on a nature reserve with good access to the motorway. On-site lake where water sports are available.

dir: *Dreieck Stuhr exit off motorway A1.*

GPS: 53.0075, 8.6925

Open: Apr-Sep **Site:** 16HEC **Prices:** 15.50-16.50 **Facilities:** Play Area **Services:** **Leisure:** L

TARMSTEDT — NIEDERSACHSEN

Rethbergsee

27412
04283 422 04283 980139
e-mail: camping-rethbergsee@t-online.de
web: www.rethbergsee-wochenendpark.de
Level site on a grand scale.

dir: *Halfway between Bremen-Lilienthal & Zeven.*

Open: All Year. **Site:** 10HEC **Prices:** 16 **Facilities:** **Services:** **Leisure:** L **Off-site:**

TELLINGSTEDT — SCHLESWIG-HOLSTEIN

Tellingstedt

Teichstr, 25782
04838 657 04836 99060
e-mail: info@amt-eider.de
Divided by a row of high shrubs.

dir: *Off B203 towards swimming pool.*

Open: May-15 Sep **Site:** 1.2HEC **Prices:** 10-13 **Facilities:** **Services:** **Leisure:** P **Off-site:**

TÖNNING — SCHLESWIG-HOLSTEIN

Lilienhof

Katinger Landstr 5, 25832
04861 439 04861 610159
e-mail: info@camping-lilienhof.de
web: www.camping-lilienhof.de
Well-maintained site in the woodland grounds of an old manor house next to a quiet country road.

dir: *Off B202 at end of Tönning & 2km W towards Welt.*

GPS: 54.3119, 8.9036

Open: All Year. **Site:** 2HEC **Prices:** 18.50 Mobile home hire 296 **Facilities:** Play Area **Services:** **Off-site:** P R

TOSSENS — NIEDERSACHSEN

Knaus Campingpark Tossens

Tossener Deich, 26969
04736 219 04736 102168
e-mail: tossens@knauscamp.de
web: www.knauscamp.de
Situated next to the beach facing the North Sea.

Open: 14 Apr-20 Oct **Site:** 8HEC **Facilities:** **Services:** **Leisure:** S **Off-site:** P

GERMANY

WALKENRIED — NIEDERSACHSEN

Knaus Campingpark Walkenried

Ellricher Str 7, 37445
☎ 05525 778 🖷 05525 2332
e-mail: walkenreid@knauscamp.de
web: www.knauscamp.de

An attractive location in the southern Harz area.

dir: *A7 exit Seesen, B243 via Herzberg & Bad Sachsa.*

Open: 16 Dec-3 Nov **Site:** 5.5HEC **Facilities:** **Services:** **Off-site:**

WALLENSEN — NIEDERSACHSEN

Humboldt See

31020
☎ 05186 957140 🖷 05186 957139
web: www.campingpark-humboldtsee.de

Close to Humboldt Lake, the site is ideally located for hiking and walking holidays in mountainous country surrounding the River Weser and the town of Hameln.

Open: All Year. **Site:** 6.5HEC **Facilities:** **Services:** **Off-site:** L

WEISSENHAUS — SCHLESWIG-HOLSTEIN

Triangel

23758
☎ 04361 507890 🖷 04361 5078969
e-mail: info@campingplatz-triangel.de
web: www.campingplatz-triangel.de

Eco-friendly campsite set in attractive countryside close to the dunes and a Baltic Sea beach.

dir: *E47/E22 Hamburg-Puttgarden, exit Oldenburg in Holstein. Direction towards Kiel, exit Weissenhäuser Strand.*

Open: 26 Mar-3 Oct **Site:** 12HEC **Prices:** 19-25.50 **Facilities:** Play Area **Services:** **Leisure:** S

WIETZENDORF — NIEDERSACHSEN

Südsee

Südsee-Camp 1, 29649
☎ 05196 980116 🖷 05196 980299
e-mail: info64@suedseecamp.de
web: www.5-sterne-camping.de

Beautiful location in a forest beside a lake in the middle of the Lünerburger Heide.

dir: *A7 exit 45 Soltau-Süd, B3 S towards Bergen for 2km, at underpass in Bokel left for Wietzendorf for 4km.*

Open: All Year. **Site:** 80HEC **Prices:** 17.50-37 Mobile home hire 364-637 **Facilities:** Wi-fi (charged) Kids' Club Play Area **Services:** **Leisure:** L P

WILSUM — NIEDERSACHSEN

AZUR-Ferienpark Wilsumer Berge

Zum Feriengebiet 1, 49849
☎ 05945 995580 🖷 05945 995599
e-mail: info@wilsumerberge.nl
web: www.wilsumerberge.nl

Parts of the site adjoin a large lake. The separate section for touring campers has its own sanitary building.

dir: *B403 from Nordhorn via Uelsen to Wilsum, turn right near Wilsum.*

Open: All Year. **Site:** 88HEC **Facilities:** **Services:** **Leisure:** L

WINGST — NIEDERSACHSEN

Knaus Campingpark Wingst

Schwimmbadallee 13, 21789
☎ 04778 7604 🖷 04778 7608
e-mail: wingst@knauscamp.de
web: www.knauscamp.de

This modern comfortable site extends over several terraces, above a small artificial lake on the northern edge of an extensive forested area. Municipal recreation centre across the road.

dir: *Off B73 between Stade & Cuxhaven, 3km S of Cadenberge.*

Open: 14 Mar-3 Nov **Site:** 11.6HEC **Facilities:** Wi-fi (charged) Play Area **Services:** **Off-site:** P R

WINSEN — NIEDERSACHSEN

Hüttensee

29308
☎ 05056 941880 🖷 05056 941881
e-mail: info@campingpark-huettensee.de
web: www.campingpark-huettensee.de

Site beside a large stretch of water on Lüneburg Heath, suitable for swimming and water sports. Fine sandy beach. The area is rich in wildlife.

Open: All Year. **Site:** 17HEC **Facilities:** **Services:** **Leisure:** L P

GERMANY

Facilities shop shower electric points for razors electric points for caravans parking by tents permitted compulsory separate car park **Services** café/restaurant bar Camping Gaz International gas other than Camping Gaz first aid facilities laundry **Leisure** swimming L-Lake P-Pool R-River S-Sea **Off-site** All facilities within 5km

WINSEN-ALLER NIEDERSACHSEN

Winsen

29308
☎ 05143 93199 📠 05143 93144
e-mail: info@camping-winsen.de
web: www.camping-winsen.de
Site lies on meadowland at the River Aller. Water sports available.
dir: *NW from Celle to Winsen.*
Open: All Year. **Site:** 12HEC **Facilities:** **Services:** **Leisure:** R **Off-site:** P

WITTENBORN SCHLESWIG-HOLSTEIN

Weisser Brunnen

23829
☎ 04554 1757 & 1413 📠 04554 4833
e-mail: gert.petzold@t-online.de
web: www.naturcamping-weisser-brunnen.de
A lakeside site consisting of several sections, hilly in parts, next to Lake Mözen. A public road, leading to the lake, passes through part of the site.
dir: *Off B206 at Km23.6 towards lake.*
Open: Apr-Oct **Site:** 7HEC **Prices:** 14-19 Mobile home hire 280 **Facilities:** Play Area **Services:** **Leisure:** L

WULFEN (ISLAND OF FEHMARN) SCHLESWIG-HOLSTEIN

Wulfener Hals

23769
☎ 04371 86280 📠 04371 3723
e-mail: camping@wulfenerhals.de
web: www.wulfenerhals.de
A meadowland site beside the Baltic Sea and an inland lake (Burger Binnensee), with a 1.7km long private beach.
dir: *Off B20 (Vogelfluglinie) after Sundbrücke towards Avendorf, then Wulfen & Wulfener Hals.*
Open: All Year. **Site:** 34HEC **Prices:** 14.71-42.50 Mobile home hire 203-889 **Facilities:** Kids' Club Play Area **Services:** **Leisure:** P S

ZORGE NIEDERSACHSEN

Harz Camping Im Waldwinkel

37449
☎ 05586 1048 📠 05586 8113
A site on different levels, surrounded by high trees, 200m from an open-air woodland pool in Kunzen Valley.
Open: All Year. **Site:** 1.5HEC **Prices:** 16.70 Mobile home hire 245 **Facilities:** Wi-fi (charged) Play Area **Services:** **Off-site:** P

GERMANY

Drinking & Driving

If the level of alcohol in the bloodstream is 0.05 per cent or more it is a criminal offence. A lower unit of 0.02 per cent applies to drivers who have held a licence for less than two years, and to motorcyclists.

Driving Licence

Minimum age at which a UK licence holder may drive temporarily imported car and/or motorcycle (over 50cc): 17.

Fines

Police can impose fines but not collect them on the spot. The fine must be paid at a Public Treasury office within 10 days. You can be fined for the unnecessary use of a car horn. Vehicles may be towed away if parked illegally, or if violating traffic regulations.

Lights

Dipped headlights should be used in poor daytime visibility. The use of undipped headlights in towns is strictly prohibited.

Motorcycles

Use of dipped headlights during the day compulsory. The wearing of crash helmets is compulsory.

Motor Insurance

Third-party compulsory.

Passengers & Children

Children under 3 years must be placed in a suitable child restraint. Approved child restraints are those conforming with standard ECE R44/03 (or later). Children between 3 and 11 years, measuring less than 1.35m must be seated in an appropriate child restraint for their size.
From the age of 12, children measuring over 1.35m can wear an adult seat belt. Placing a rear-facing child restraint in the front passenger seat is allowed only on condition that the passenger airbag is deactivated.

Seat Belts

Compulsory for front-seat occupants to wear seat belts.

Speed Limits:

Unless signed otherwise

Built-up areas (cars)	50km/h
Built-up areas (motorcycles)	40km/h
Outside built-up areas (cars)	90km/h or 110km/h
Outside built-up areas (motorcycles)	70km/h
Motorways (cars)	130km/h
Motorways (motorcycles)	90km/h
Cars towing a light trailer	
Motorways	90km/h
Built up areas	50km/h
Cars towing a trailer	
Motorways	80km/h
Built-up areas	50km/h
Motorhomes	
Motorways	90km/h
Built-up areas	50km/h
Motorhomes towing a trailer	
Motorways	80km/h
Built-up areas	50km/h

Additional Information

Compulsory equipment in Greece:

- Fire extinguisher
- First-aid kit
- Warning triangle

Other rules/regulations in Greece:
The police are empowered to confiscate the number plates of illegally parked vehicles throughout Greece. Generally this only applies to Greek-registered vehicles, but the drivers of foreign registered vehicles should beware of parking illegally.

Tolls Currency Euro (€)	Car
1/E75 - Afidnes - Athina	€1.90
1/E75 - Thessaloniki - Katerini	€2.00
1/E75 - Lamia - Thiva	€2.25
1/E75 - Thiva - Afidnes	€2.35
1/E75 - Katerini - Larisa	€5.10
1/E75 - Larisa - Lamia	€5.20
7/E65 - Korinthos - Tripoli	€2.80
8A/E65-E55 - Korinthos - Patra	€2.90
8A/E94 - Attiki Odos	€2.80
8A/E94 - Athina - Korinthos	€4.00

Bridges/Tunnels Currency Euro (€)	Car
8A/E65-E55 - The Rion-Antirio Bridge	€12.20
E55 - Aktion Tunnel	€3.00

AGIÓKAMBOS — THESSALY

Aegeas

40003
☎ 24940 51580 🖷 24940 51581

Shady site with marked pitches situated on the coast by a sandy beach.

Open: May-Sep **Site:** 1.2HEC **Facilities:** **Services:** **Off-site:** P S

ALEXANDROÚPOLI — THRACE

Alexandroúpolis

Makris Av, 68100
☎ 25510 28735 🖷 25510 28735
e-mail: camping@ditea.gr
web: www.ditea.gr

A large site on a meadow near the waterfront with concrete pitches.

dir: *Between Thessaloniki-Istanbul road & beach to W of town.*

Open: All Year. **Site:** 7HEC **Facilities:** **Services:** **Leisure:** S

ATHÍNAI (ATHENS) — ATTICA

Athens

Leoforos Athinon 198, Peristeri, 12136
☎ 210 5814114 🖷 210 5820353
e-mail: info@campingathens.com.gr
web: www.campingathens.com.gr

Pitches of a reasonable size and generally well-shaded, although some are near a busy road. Convenient for visiting the city.

dir: *Take Athens-Pireas road to Peiraias, 2nd exit to Korinthos E94. Site 2km on right.*

Open: All Year. **Site:** **Prices:** 27 **Facilities:** Wi-fi **Services:**

Nea Kifissia

60 Potamou & Dimitsanas Adames, Nea Kifissia, 14564
☎ 210 8075579 🖷 210 8075579
e-mail: camping@hol.gr

A small family run site with level pitches, some shady. Quiet location but very convenient for visiting the sites of the city.

dir: *16km N of Athens. Signed from Aharnes exit on Athens-Lamia motorway.*

Open: All Year. **Site:** 2.2HEC **Facilities:** **Services:** **Leisure:** P

DELFOÍ (DELPHI) — CENTRAL GREECE

Camping Apollon

Old National Rd, 33054
☎ 22650 82762 🖷 22650 82888
e-mail: apollon4@otenet.gr
web: www.apolloncamping.gr

Located within easy reach of the ancient site of Delphi, the site offers take away meals and an internet café.

Open: All Year. **Site:** **Prices:** 25.50-29 Mobile home hire 350 **Facilities:** Wi-fi (charged) Play Area **Services:** **Leisure:** P **Off-site:**

Chrissa

33054
☎ 22650 82050 🖷 22650 83148
e-mail: info@chrissacamping.gr
web: www.chrissacamping.gr

Terraced site on a hill overlooking the sea with fine views of Delphi and the Corinth Bay. Leisure facilities available and a tavern with take-away meals.

dir: *6km on Delphi-Itea-Amfissa highway near village of Chrisso.*

Open: All Year. **Site:** 1.6HEC **Prices:** 18-22 Mobile home hire 280-420 **Facilities:** Wi-fi (charged) Play Area **Services:** **Leisure:** P **Off-site:** S

EPIDAVROS — PELOPONNESE

Camping Bekas

Gialasi Beach, 21059
☎ 27530 99930 🖷 27530 99931
e-mail: info@bekas.gr
web: www.bekas.gr

Quiet site next to the beach with green surroundings.

Open: Apr-25 Oct **Site:** 2.8HEC **Prices:** 20-29 **Facilities:** Wi-fi **Services:** **Leisure:** S **Off-site:** P

EVIA, ISLAND OF — CENTRAL GREECE

Milos

Lepira, 34008
☎ 22290 60420 🖷 22290 60360
e-mail: info@camping-in-evia.gr
web: www.camping-in-evia.gr

A site with modern facilities set in a background of mountains close to the sea. Convenient for visiting Athens.

dir: *On island of Evia route 44. Campsite 1.5km before Eretria on right. Signed.*

Open: Apr-Sep **Site:** 1.8HEC **Prices:** 19.30-22.30 **Facilities:** Wi-fi **Services:** **Leisure:** P S

GREECE

'INIKOUNDA — PELOPONNESE

.outsa

!4006

27230 71169 27230 71445

-mail: campingloutsa@hol.gr

'icturesque site in shady natural surroundings next to a fine ›each.

ir: *National road Methoni-Koroni.*

pen: May-Oct **Site:** 0.8HEC **Facilities:** **ervices:** **Leisure:** S **Off-site:** P

;IALOVA — PELOPONNESE

Vavarino Beach

!4001

27230 22973 27230 23512

-mail: info@navarino-beach.gr

veb: www.navarino-beach.gr

Aost pitches face the sea and are shaded by trees. The shallow ;andy beach is ideal for children.

)pen: All Year. **Site:** 2.4HEC **Facilities:** **ervices:** **Leisure:** S

;LIFA — PELOPONNESE

onion Beach

'7050

26230 96395 26230 96425

-mail: ioniongr@otenet.gr

veb: www.ionion-beach.gr

amily run site in a shady location by the sea.

ir: *From national road Patras-Pyrgos turn right via Gatsouni ؛ Vartalomia at 67km sign towards Loutra Killini. Left at fork owards Glifa Beach. Follow signs.*

pen: All Year. **Site:** **Prices:** 19.80-25 **Facilities:** Wi-fi (charged) Play Area **Services:** **eisure:** P S

;YTHEIO — PELOPONNESE

Aani Beach

3200

27330 23450 27330 25400

-mail: info@manibeach.gr

eb: www.manibeach.gr

ite with many facilities close to a fine sandy beach with clear 'ater. Several interesting tourist sites nearby.

ir: *4 km S of Gythion on Aeropolis road.*

pen: All Year. **Site:** 3.5HEC **Facilities:** **ervices:** **Off-site:** S

ITÉA — CENTRAL GREECE

Ayannis

33200

22650 32555 22650 33870

The site stretches over several terraces and is scattered with small olive trees and strengthened by stone walls. There are fine views over the Gulf of Corinth.

Open: Apr-Oct **Site:** 2HEC **Facilities:** **Services:** **Leisure:** S

KATO ALISSOS — PELOPONNESE

Kato Alissos

25002

26930 71249 26930 71150

e-mail: demiris-cmp@otenet.gr

web: www.camping-kato-alissos.gr

Shady site located in an olive grove.

dir: *Take National Road from Patras to Pyrgos for 21km, turn right following signs for 500m.*

Open: Apr-25 Oct **Site:** 1.2HEC **Facilities:** **Services:** **Leisure:** S **Off-site:** R

KATO GATZEA — THESSALY

Hellas

Volos, 38500

24230 22267 24230 22492

e-mail: info@campinghellas.gr

web: www.campinghellas.gr

The site lies in an olive grove on sloping ground between the road and the beach.

dir: *10km W of Volos, take route Pilio-Argalasti for 18 km, site signposted.*

Open: Apr-Oct **Site:** 2.8HEC **Facilities:** Wi-fi **Services:** **Leisure:** S

Sikia

38500

24230 22279 24230 22720

e-mail: info@camping-sikia.gr

web: www.camping-sikia.gr

Family run terraced site by the seashore.

dir: *From Volos follow coastal road towards Argalasti. Site 18km on right after Kato Gatzea.*

Open: Apr-Oct **Site:** 3HEC **Prices:** 17-25 **Facilities:** Wi-fi (charged) **Services:** **Leisure:** S **Off-site:**

GREECE

KAVALA — MACEDONIA

Batis Multiplex

65500
☎ 2510 245918 2510 245690
e-mail: info@batis-sa.gr
web: www.batis-sa.gr

Secure site with trees providing natural shade, located next to a beach 4km west of Kavala. Swimming pool and first aid facilities available in high season only.

Open: All Year. **Site:** 3.3HEC **Prices:** 18-26 **Facilities:** Wi-fi Play Area **Services:** **Leisure:** P S **Off-site:**

KÉRKIRA (CORFU)

DASSIA

Karda Beach

49083
☎ 26610 93595 26610 93595
e-mail: campco@otenet.gr
web: www.kardacamp.gr

Situated in an olive grove, 100m from a good clean beach.

dir: *12km N of Kerkira, on right of main road from Kerkira-Kassiopi.*

Open: 9 Apr-30 Oct **Site:** 2.6HEC **Facilities:** **Services:** **Leisure:** P **Off-site:** S

KRÍTI (CRETE)

RÉTHYMNO

Elizabeth

Ionias 84, Misiria, 74100
☎ 28310 28694 28310 28694
e-mail: info@camping-elizabeth.com
web: www.camping-elizabeth.com

A quiet family site with spacious pitches under shady trees. Please check for winter opening.

dir: *3km E. From Heraklion, before Réthymon, exit Platanes/Arkadi. Follow road, camp site 1km before Platanes, on the right along short, unsurfaced road.*

Open: All Year. **Site:** 25HEC **Prices:** 19.80-25.50 **Facilities:** Wi-fi **Services:** **Leisure:** S **Off-site:** P

LECHEON — PELOPONNESE

Blue Dolphin

20011
☎ 27410 25766 27410 85959
e-mail: skouspos@otenet.gr
web: www.camping-blue-dolphin.gr

Situated adjacent to the beach on the Corinthian Gulf. There is an abundance of shade, which is created by the trees and roofing made from bamboo sticks.

dir: *6km W of Corinth off Athens-Patras road.*

Open: Apr-Oct **Site:** 4HEC **Prices:** 21.50-26.50 **Facilities:** Wi-fi Play Area **Services:** **Leisure:** S **Off-site:** P

LITÓCHORO — MACEDONIA

Mytikas

60200
☎ 23520 61275 23520 61276
e-mail: camp.mitikas@gmail.com
web: www.campingmitikas.com

A family run camping located 100m from a fine beach with a magnificent view of Mount Olympus.

dir: *Approx 15km S of Katerini, turn towards Gritsa Beach. Site on right beyond railway line.*

Open: Apr-15 Oct **Site:** 8.5HEC **Prices:** 16-18.50 **Facilities:** **Services:** **Leisure:** P S

MARATHONAS — ATTICA

Ramnous

Posidonos 174, 19007
☎ 22940 55855 22940 55244
e-mail: campingramnous@otenet.com

Peaceful site in a beach location with a regular bus to Athens.

dir: *Athens-Marathon road, right at lights about 6km past Nea Makri, right at Kato Souli Schinias sign, then follow signs for 4.5km.*

Open: Apr-Oct **Site:** 20HEC **Facilities:** **Services:** **Leisure:** S **Off-site:** L

’LATARIÁ — MACEDONIA

(alami Beach

ɪ6100
26650 71211 26650 71245
ɪ-mail: info@campingkalamibeach.gr
ɹeb: www.campingkalamibeach.gr
;ite close to Corfu in green surroundings with views of a fine lean beach.
lir: *Igoumenitsa to Plataria road, after 7km 1st campsite on ight, signed*
ɪpen: Apr-Oct **Site:** 1.2HEC **Facilities:**
ervices:

’YLOS — PELOPONNESE

;amping Erodios

;ialova, 24001
27230 28240 27230 28241
-mail: erodioss@otenet.gr
eb: www.erodioss.gr
ɪose to Gialova and 15 minutes from Pylos, the site is set in olive ees by the sea.
PS: 36.9508, 21.7008
ɔen: 15 Apr-15 Oct **Site:** 4.3HEC
rices: 20-30 Mobile home hire 160.65-359.10 **Facilities:**
Wi-fi Play Area **Services:**
ɜisure: S

ɪO — PELOPONNESE

’ion

6500
26109 91585 26109 93388
te beside the sea on level ground with asphalt roads and ɪncrete pitches for caravans. Pines and poplar trees offer shade.
r: *9km E of Patras on Rion Beach.*
ɔen: Feb-1 Dec **Site:** 5HEC **Facilities:**
ɪrvices: **Leisure:** S

SÉRIFOS

LIVADAKIA

Coralli Camping Bungalows

84005
22810 51500 22810 51073
e-mail: info@coralli.gr
web: www.coralli.gr
Located on the Island of Sérifos next to a sandy beach.
Site: **Facilities:** Wi-fi **Services:**
Leisure: P S

STYLIDA — CENTRAL GREECE

Interstation

230km National Rd, Athens-Thessaloniki, 35300
22380 23827/8 22380 23828
web: www.campinginterstation.com
Site located among hills and national parks with good facilities.
Open: All Year. **Site:** 8HEC **Facilities:**
Services: **Leisure:** S

Hungary

Drinking & Driving

Nil percentage of alcohol allowed in drivers' blood; amounts of less than 0.08 per cent incur a fine, more than 0.08 per cent, legal proceedings.

Driving Licence

Minimum age at which a UK driving licence holder may drive a temporarily imported car and/or motorcycle 17. All valid UK driving licences should be accepted in Hungary. This includes the older all-green style UK licences (in Northern Ireland older paper style with photographic counterpart). Older licences may be accompanied by an International Driving Permit (IDP).

Fines

On-the-spot. Police must hand over the payment order to transfer the amount of the fine within 30 days. The fine is only payable in HUF, credit cards are not accepted. Cash should not be given to a policeman at the roadside. Wheel clamps are in use.

Lights

Use of dipped headlights compulsory at all times outside built-up areas. At night the use of full beam, in built up areas, is prohibited.

Motorcycles

Use of dipped headlights compulsory at all times as is wearing of crash helmets for both driver and passenger.

Motor Insurance

Third-party compulsory. Should a visitor cause an accident with a Hungarian citizen they must report it to the Association of Hungarian Insurance Companies.

Passengers & Children

A child under 3 years of age may only travel in a vehicle if using a suitable child restraint system appropriate for their weight. They are permitted to travel in the front of the vehicle using this restraint if it is rear facing and there is no airbag, or it has been deactivated. Children under 1.5m and over 3 years of age must use a suitable child restraint system and sit in the rear of the vehicle.

Seat Belts

Compulsory for all occupants, where fitted.

Speed Limits

Unless signed otherwise

Private vehicles without trailers

Built-up areas	50km/h
Outside built-up areas	90km/h
Semi-motorways	110km/h
Motorways	130km/

Lower speed limits may apply on the approach to level crossings.

Vehicle towing a caravan or trailer

Built-up areas	50km/
Outside built-up areas	70km/
Motorways	80km/
Semi-motorway	70km/

Vehicles with snow chains must not exceed 50km/h.

In city centres, areas with a 30km/h speed limit are increasingly common.

Additional Information

Compulsory equipment in Hungary: First-aid kit; Warning triangle; Reflective Jacket - Anyone walking on a road, or road shoulder outside a built up area must wear a reflective jacket at night and in case of bad visibility; Snow chains - The use of or their presence in a car can be made compulsory on some roads when weather conditions require.

Other rules/regulations in Hungary:

Spare bulb kit recommended as its carriage is compulso for Hungarian registered vehicles; Recommended that the driver of a conspicuously damaged vehicle entering Hungary obtain a police report confirming the damage at the time of entry, otherwise lengthy delays may be encountered at the frontier when leaving Hungary. This report should be obtained from the police of the country where the car was damaged.

Motorists should be wary of contrived incidents, particularly on the Vienna – Budapest motorway, designed to stop motorists and expose them to robbery.

A new directive by the Hungarian authorities means tha traffic will be restricted from entering Budapest when th dust in the air exceeds a fixed level on two consecutive days. The restriction depends upon the number on whic a registration plate ends, licence plates ending in odd numbers will be permitted to enter Budapest on odd numbered days, even number on even days.

The restriction also applies to UK registered vehicles, however as UK registration plates tend to end in a lette rather than a number we are waiting for confirmation as to how the restriction will apply. The restriction will be applicable from 0600 to 2200 with a fine imposed for nc compliance.

Spiked tyres are prohibited.

The use of the horn is prohibited in built-up areas, exce in the case of danger.

otorway tax payable for use of:
1 (Budapest - Hegyeshalom)
3 (Budapest - Gorbehaza - Nyiregyhaza)
5 (Budapest - Kiskunfelegyhaza - Szeged - Roszke/ order with Serbia)
6 (M0- Erd - Dunaujvaros)
7 (Budapest - Lake Balaton - Letenye, border with oatia)
30 (Emod - Miskolc)
35 (Gorbehaza - Debrecen)
e electronic vignette and any toll charges must be id in Forints. Credit cards accepted: Visa, Eurocard/ astercard, DKV and UTA. The vignette can be purchased person, online, or by telephone (land line or mobile). hen a motorist has purchased an e-vignette, a nfirmation message will be sent or a coupon issued. is document must be kept for one year after the expiry validity. The motorway authorities check all vehicles ectronically, and verify the registration number, the tegory of toll paid and the validity of the e-vignette. rther information: www.motorway.hu – available for days (vehicles up to 3.5t only), 1 week, 1 month or 13 months. Fines imposed for non-display. The Hungarian Motoring Association recommend foreign motorists wishing to purchase a vignette at the border have cash in Hungarian Forints. Vignettes should only be purchased from outlets where the prices are clearly displayed at the set rate.

Tolls Currency Forints (HUF)	Car	Car Towing Caravan/Trailer
M1/M3/M5/M7 4 Day Vignette (September to May)	1170HUF	1170HUF
M1/M3/M5/M7 4 Day Vignette (May to September)	1530HUF	1530HUF
M1/M3/M5/M7 Weekly Vignette	2550HUF	2550HUF
M1/M3/M5/M7 Monthly Vignette	4200HUF	4200HUF
M1/M3/M5/M7 1 year	37200HUF	37200HUF

SÓÖRS — VESZPRÉM

alatontourist Camping Európa

redi u 1, 8226
87 555021 87 555022
mail: europa@balatontourist.hu
b: www.balatontourist.hu

rge site with neat pitches on the lake shore. Entertainment ailable with a choice of restaurants nearby. Dogs allowed in tain areas of the site only.

S: 46.9755, 17.9569

en: 13 May-11 Sep **Site:** 20HEC **Facilities:** Wi-fi (charged) Play Area **Services:** sure: L P

LATONAKALI — VESZPRÉM

alatontourist Camping Naturist Levendula

kuli u 25, 8243
87 544011 87 544012
nail: levendula@balatontourist.hu
b: www.balatontourist.hu

ferent-sized pitches divided by hedges are available at this turist campsite on the shores of Lake Balaton.

en: 6 May-11 Sep **Site:** 2.2HEC **Facilities:** Wi-fi (charged) Play Area **Services:** **Leisure:** L
-site:

Balatontourist Camping Strand-Holiday

Strand u 2, 8243
87 544021 87 544022
e-mail: strand@balatontourist.hu
web: www.balatontourist.hu

On the shores of Lake Balaton with facilities including sunbathing platforms, children's beach and an outdoor theatre. Ideal for families.

GPS: 46.8811, 17.7452

Open: 15 Apr-25 Sep **Site:** 9HEC **Facilities:** Wi-fi (charged) Play Area **Services:** **Leisure:** L

BALATONALMÁDI — VESZPRÉM

Balatontourist Camping Yacht

Véghely D u 18, 8220
87 584101 87 584102
e-mail: yacht@balatontourist.hu
web: www.balatontourist.hu

A short walk from the town centre, a well-equipped site with a beach on Lake Balaton. Swimming pool available for children.

Open: 27 Apr-18 Sep **Site:** 2.7HEC **Facilities:** Wi-fi (charged) Play Area **Services:** **Leisure:** L

BALATONBERÉNY — SOMOGY

Balatontourist Camping Naturist Berény

Hétvezér u 2, 8649
☎ 85 377299 🖷 85 377715
e-mail: bereny@balatontourist.hu
web: www.balatontourist.hu

Biggest naturist site on the shores of Lake Balaton with a motel and apartments also available. Sporting facilities.

GPS: 46.7131, 17.3106

Open: 13 May-11 Sep **Site:** 5.5HEC **Facilities:** Wi-fi (charged) Play Area **Services:** **Leisure:** L

BALATONFÜRED — VESZPRÉM

Balatontourist Camping & Bungalows Füred

Széchenyi u 24, 8230
☎ 87 580241 🖷 87 342341
e-mail: fured@balatontourist.hu
web: www.balatontourist.hu

Largest campsite on Lake Balaton with sunny and shaded pitches. Daily programmes (including sports) for both adults and children.

GPS: 46.9457, 17.8771

Open: 22 Apr-2 Oct **Site:** 21HEC **Facilities:** Play Area **Services:** **Leisure:** L P

BALATONSZEMES — SOMOGY

Balatontourist Camping & Bungalows Vadvirág

Lellei u 1-2, 8636
☎ 84 360114 🖷 84 360115
e-mail: vadvirag@balatontourist.hu
web: www.balatontourist.hu

Directly on the shore of Lake Balaton, with a good range of sporting facilities including a children's swimming pool. Paddle boats, cycles, scooters etc can be hired.

GPS: 46.8009, 17.7402

Open: 22 Apr-11 Sep **Site:** 20HEC **Facilities:** Wi-fi (charged) Play Area **Services:** **Leisure:** L P **Off-site:**

Balatontourist Camping Lidó

Ady Endre u 8, 8636
☎ 84 360112 🖷 84 360112
e-mail: lido@balatontourist.hu
web: www.balatontourist.hu

Directly on the shore of Lake Balaton, with shallow water and a beach suitable for families with small children. Leisure facilities include table tennis and tennis court.

Open: 6 May-4 Sep **Site:** 1.8HEC **Facilities:** Wi-fi (charged) **Services:** **Leisure:** L **Off-site:**

BALATONSZEPEZD — VESZPRÉM

Balatontourist Camping Venus

Halász u 1, 8252
☎ 87 568061 🖷 87 568062
e-mail: venus@balatontourist.hu
web: www.balatontourist.hu

A family friendly site and popular with fishermen, located on the shores of Lake Balaton. Cycles can be rented to explore the surrounding national park.

Open: 13 May-11 Sep **Site:** 2.8HEC **Facilities:** Wi-fi (charged) **Services:** **Leisure:** L **Off-site:**

BUDAPEST — BUDAPEST

Camping Haller

Haller Utca 27, 1096
☎ 1 476 3418
e-mail: info@hallercamping.hu
web: www.hallercamping.hu

Centrally located with 24-hour reception. Discounts are available for stays over four nights.

GPS: 47.4758, 19.0829

Open: 10 May-20 Sep **Site:** 1.5HEC **Prices:** 4770-640 **Facilities:** Wi-fi Play Area **Services:** **Off-site:**

BÜKFÜRDŐ — VA

Romantik

Thermal Krt 12, 9740
☎ 94 558050 🖷 94 558051
e-mail: info@romantikcamping.com
web: www.romantikcamping.com

Flat wooded site with unmarked pitches 2km from the spa town of Buk.

Open: All Year. **Site:** 6HEC **Facilities:** Wi-fi Play Area **Services:** **Leisure:** P **Off-site:**

ÉRD — PE

Flamingo

Furdo u 4, 2030
☎ 23 375328 🖷 23 375328
e-mail: flamingocamp@t-online.hu

Good transport links to the centre of Budapest, sightseeing trip can be arranged. Camping field with bordered pitches.

dir: *On Highway 7.*

Open: Apr-Oct **Site:** 1HEC **Facilities:** Wi-fi Play Area **Services:** **Leisure:** P **Off-site:**

SZTERGOM KOMÁRON-ESZTERGOM

ran Camping, Bungalow & Youth Hostel

agy Duna Setany 3, 2500
☎ 33 402513 🖷 33 411953
-mail: fortanex@t-online.hu
eb: www.grancamping-fortanex.hu

cenic site on the island of Primas by the river Danube. Short alk to the town centre and to the bridge across the Danube to ovakia.

r: *From Tat via route 11 to Esztergom. In Esztergom, at rdbt wards Parkany/Sturovo. Campsite over bridge, beyond bend.*

pen: May-Sep **Site:** 4HEC **Facilities:** Wi-fi harged) **Services:** **Leisure:** P **Off-site:**

ELSÖPAHOK ZALA

ortuna Camping

zent Istvan u 89, 8395
☎ 83 344630 🖷 83 340363
-mail: fortuna.camping@gmail.com
eb: www.fortuna-camping.hu

uiet site very close to the natural thermal lake of Spa Heviz.

pen: Apr-20 Oct **Site:** 0.8HEC **Facilities:** **rvices:** **Off-site:** L

ONYÓD-BÉLATELEP SOMOGY

alatontourist Camping & Bungalows Napsugár

ekerle u 5, 8640
☎ 85 361211 🖷 85 361024
mail: napsugar@balatontourist.hu
eb: www.balatontourist.hu

cated in a shady, wooded area, the grassy beach on Lake laton is separated from the pitches by a railway.

'S: 46.7327, 17.5326

en: 6 May-4 Sep **Site:** 9.5HEC **Facilities:** Wi-fi (charged) Play Area **Services:** **Leisure:** L **-site:**

ENESDIÁS ZALA

ellness Park Pension & Camping

pfény u 6, 8315
☎ 83 316483 🖷 83 316483
mail: info@wellness-park.hu
b: www.wellness-park.hu

se to Lake Balaton, part of a complex that includes a guest use and spa, with tennis and petanque courts. Charge made dogs.

en: All Year. **Site:** 2HEC **Facilities:** Wi-fi Play Area **Services:** **Leisure:** P **-site:** L

KEMENESKÁPOLNA VAS

Vulkán Resort

Szabadság u 02, 9553
☎ 95 466060 🖷 95 466056
e-mail: info@vulkanresort.com
web: www.vulkanresort.com

A site based on the principles of Feng Shui. A small health spa includes an indoor swimming pool and massage room.

GPS: 47.2147, 17.1004

Open: Apr-Oct **Site:** 5HEC **Facilities:** Wi-fi (charged) Play Area **Services:** **Leisure:** P **Off-site:**

KESZTHELY ZALA

Balatontourist Camping & Bungalows Zala

Entz Géza sétány 1, 8360
☎ 83 312782 🖷 83 312782
e-mail: zala@balatontourist.hu
web: www.balatontourist.hu

Quiet site to the south of the town on the shore of Lake Balaton, with its own beach. Cycle route runs adjacent to the site and bikes are available to rent.

GPS: 46.7467, 17.2442

Open: 15 Apr-2 Oct **Site:** 7.2HEC **Facilities:** Wi-fi (charged) Play Area **Services:** **Leisure:** L P **Off-site:**

NESZMÉLY KOMÁROM-ESZTERGOM

Eden

Dunapart, 2544
☎ 33 474183 🖷 33 474327
e-mail: eden@mail.holop.hu
web: www.edencamping.com

Site on the banks of the Danube next to a nature conservation area.

dir: *Main route 10 from Gyor-Budapest, campsite between villages of Neszmély & Sutto*

Open: Apr-Sep **Site:** 4HEC **Facilities:** **Services:** **Leisure:** P R

RÉVFÜLÖP — VESZPRÉM

Balatontourist Camping Napfény

Halász u 5, 8253
☎ 87 563031 87 464309
e-mail: napfeny@balatontourist.hu
web: www.balatontourist.hu

Site with grassy area on the shores of Lake Balaton, ideal for bathing and windsurfing. Friendly atmosphere with neat pitches. Swimming pool available for children.

GPS: 46.8292, 17.64

Open: 29 Apr-2 Oct **Site:** 7.2HEC **Facilities:** Wi-fi (charged) Play Area **Services:** **Leisure:** L **Off-site:**

SIÓFOK — SOMOGY

Balatontourist Camping & Bungalows Aranypart

Szent Lászlo u 183-185, 8600
☎ 84 353399 84 352801
e-mail: aranypart@balatontourist.hu
web: www.balatontourist.hu

5km from the centre of town directly on the lake shore. Entertainment for children in high season and water-skiing nearby.

GPS: 46.9281, 18.1032

Open: 22 Apr-11 Sep **Site:** 9.1HEC **Facilities:** Wi-fi (charged) Play Area **Services:** **Leisure:** L **Off-site:** P

Balatontourist Camping Ifjúság

Pusztatorony tér, 8604
☎ 84 352851 84 352571
e-mail: ifjusag@balatontourist.hu
web: www.balatontourist.hu

Peaceful setting, 9km from city centre and 150m from Lake Balaton.

GPS: 46.9375, 18.1290

Open: 20 May-4 Sep **Site:** 8.2HEC **Facilities:** Wi-fi (charged) Play Area **Services:** **Off-site:** L

ÜRÖM — PEST

Jumbo Camping

Budakalászi út 23-25, 2096
☎ 26 351251 26 351251
e-mail: jumbo@campingbudapest.com
web: www.campingbudapest.com

Family-run site on a south facing hillside with terraced pitches.

GPS: 47.6014, 19.0194

Open: Apr-Oct **Site:** 1HEC **Prices:** 4300-5200 **Facilities:** Wi-fi Play Area **Services:** **Leisure:** P **Off-site:**

VONYARCVASHEGY — ZAL

Balatontourist Camping & Bungalows Park

Szent Mihály-domb, 8314
☎ 83 348044 83 348044
e-mail: park@balatontourist.hu
web: www.balatontourist.hu

In a sheltered and quiet position at the foot of St Michael Hill. Leisure facilities include a beach, volleyball and fishing.

Open: 15 Apr-2 Oct **Site:** 4.7HEC **Facilities:** Wi-fi (charged) Play Area **Services:** **Leisure:** L

ZALAKAROS — ZAL

Balatontourist Camping Termál

Gyógyfürdõ tér 6, 8749
☎ 93 340105 93 340105
e-mail: termal@balatontourist.hu
web: www.balatontourist.hu

Located in a spa town known for its thermal pools, a relaxing sit with shop nearby.

GPS: 46.7511, 17.3333

Open: Apr-Oct **Site:** 4HEC **Facilities:** Wi-fi (charged) **Services:** **Off-site:** P

ZAMÁRDI — SOMOG

Balatontourist Camping Autós

Szent István út hrsz 3512, 8621
☎ 84 348931 84 348931
e-mail: autos@balatontourist.hu
web: www.balatontourist.hu

Picturesque views from this peaceful site, ideal for families with children. Some pitches are located next to Lake Balaton.

GPS: 46.8807, 17.9156

Open: 29 Apr-11 Sep **Site:** 6.7HEC **Facilities:** Wi-fi (charged) **Services:** **Leisure:** L **Off-site:**

Italy

Drinking and Driving

If the level of alcohol in the bloodstream is 0.051 per cent or more, penalties include fines, confiscation of vehicle and imprisonment.

Driving Licence

Minimum age at which a UK licence holder may drive temporarily imported car and/or motorcycle (over 125cc or with passenger) 18. All valid UK driving licences should be accepted in Italy. Older licences may be accompanied by an International Driving Permit (IDP).

Fines

On-the-spot. Fines are particularly heavy for speeding offences. The police can impose the fine and collect 25% of the maximum fine, and must give a receipt paid. Fines for serious offences committed between 2200 and 0700 hours increase by a third. Illegally parked vehicles can be clamped or towed away and a fine imposed.

Lights

Use of dipped headlights during the day compulsory outside built-up areas and during snow and rain/poor visibility. Rear fog lights may only be used when visibility is less than 50 metres, or in case of strong rain or heavy snow. Lights must be switched on in tunnels.

Motorcycles

Use of dipped headlights during the day compulsory on all roads. The wearing of crash helmets is compulsory for both driver and passenger. The vehicle can be seized for non-compliance. It is prohibited to carry a child less than 5 years on a moped or motorcycle. The registration certificate must state that the moped/motorcycle is designed to carry a passenger. Motorcycles under 150cc are not allowed on motorways.

Motor Insurance

Third-party compulsory.

Passengers & Children

Children travelling in a UK registered vehicle must be secured according to UK legislation.

Seat Belts

Compulsory for all occupants, if fitted.

Speed Limits

Unless signed otherwise

Private vehicles without trailers

Built-up areas	50km/h
Outside built-up areas	90km/h
Dual carriageways	110km/h
Motorways	130km/h

In wet weather lower speed limits of 90km/h apply on dual carriageways and 110km/h on motorways.

Car towing a caravan or trailer

Built-up areas	50km/h
Outside built up areas	70km/h
Motorways	80km/h

Camper Vans up to 3.5t

Built-up areas	50km/h
Outside built up areas	90km/h
Dual carriageways	110km/h
Motorways	130km/h

Camper Vans 3.5t to 12t

Built-up areas	50km/h
Outside built up areas	80km/h
Motorways	100km/h

Restrictions apply if vehicles are using spiked tyres.

Additional Information

Compulsory equipment: Warning triangle; Reflective jacket (wearing of reflective jacket/waistcoat compulsory if driver and/or passenger(s) exits vehicle which is immobilised on the carriageway at night or in poor visibility; Snow chains (between the 15 Oct and 15 Apr, or at other times if conditions dictate. Provinces can introduce their own legislation making the use of winter tyres or snow chains compulsory.)

Other rules/requirements in Italy and San Marino:

It is recommended that visitors equip their vehicles with a set of replacement bulbs. Any vehicle with an overhanging load (e.g. carrying bicycle at rear) must display a fully reflectorised square panel 50cm x 50cm which is red and white diagonally striped, a fine may be imposed if the sign is not displayed. This also applies to vehicles carrying bicycles at the rear.

Tolls are levied on the majority of motorways.

In built up areas the use of the horn is prohibited except in cases of immediate danger. The transportation or use of radar detectors is prohibited. Violation of this regulation will result in a fine between 708 and 2834 Euros and confiscation of the device.

Eco-pass:- An experimental pollution charge is levied in the centre of Milan. Charges apply Mon-Fri and generally from 7.30am to 7.30pm. Drivers must purchase an eco-pass before entering the restricted zone. Tariffs vary according to the emissions of the vehicle. Full information can be found by going to this website (Italian only) www.comune.milano.it/dseserver/ecopass/richiedere.html

Traffic is restricted in many historical centres/major towns known as 'Zone a Traffico Limitato' or ZTL's, circulation is only permitted for residents. Entering such areas normally results in a fine by post.

Italy

Tolls & Tunnels

Tolls Currency Euro (€)	Car	Car Towing Caravan/Trailer
A1 - Bologna - Firenze	€6.50	€8.30
A1 - Roma - Napoli	€11.60	€15.00
A1 - Milano - Bologna	€12.00	€15.50
A1 - Firenze - Roma	€14.60	€18.80
A1 - Milano - Napoli	€45.10	€58.30
A10 - Genova - Savona	€2.40	€3.00
A10 - Savona - Ventimiglia - (French Border)	€11.50	€21.70
A11 - Firenze - Pisa	€5.90	€7.80
A12 - La Spezia - Livorno	€6.60	€9.30
A12 - Livorno - Roma	€8.30	€11.00
A12 - Genova - La Spezia	€9.20	€12.40
A12 - Genova - Viareggio	€11.40	€15.60
A12 - Genova - Livorno	€14.00	€19.30
A13 - Bologna - Ferrara	€1.90	€2.40
A13 - Ferrara - Pádova	€4.50	€5.80
A13 - Bologna - Pádova	€5.60	€7.20
A14 - Bari - Taranto	€3.80	€5.00
A14 - Ancona - Pescara	€8.70	€11.20
A14 - Bologna - Ancona	€11.40	€14.70
A14 - Pescara - Bari	€17.80	€23.00
A14 - Pescara - Taranto	€21.60	€23.20
A14 - Bologna - Taranto	€42.50	€54.90
A14/A14 Dir - Bologna - Ravenna	€4.10	€5.30
A15 - Parma - La Spezia	€10.90	€15.20
A16 - Napoli - Bari	€15.70	€20.20
A18 - Messina - Catania	€3.30	€14.80
A20 - Messina - Caccamo	€10.40	€30.60
A21 - Piacenza - Brescia	€3.80	€5.00
A21 - Alessandria - Piacenza	€4.90	€6.40
A21 - Torino - Alessandria	€5.90	€7.70
A21 - Torino - Piacenza	€11.30	€14.80
A22 - Verona - Modena	€5.30	€6.90
A22 - Trento - Verona	€5.50	€7.10

Tolls Currency Euro (€)	Car	Car Towing Caravan/Trailer
A22 - Brenner Pass - Trento	€8.00	€10.30
A22 - Brenner Pass (Austrian Border) - Modena	€18.80	€24.20
A23 - Udine - Tarvisio (Austria)	€6.00	€7.70
A24 - Roma - Teramo	€11.60	€14.80
A25 - Roma - Pescara	€13.60	€17.60
A26 - Genova - Alessandria	€4.30	€5.50
A26 - Genova - Iselle (Swiss Frontier)	€12.50	€16.00
A27 - Venezia - Belluno	€6.60	€8.40
A3 - Napoli - Salerno	€1.60	€3.50
A30 - Caserta - Salerno	€3.30	€4.30
A31 - Vicenza - Trento	€1.50	€2.00
A32 - Torino - Tunnel du Frejus (France)	€9.80	€17.60
A4 - Padova - Venezia	€2.70	€3.60
A4 - Brescia - Verona	€2.90	€3.80
A4 - Verona - Padova	€3.70	€4.90
A4 - Milano - Brescia	€5.60	€7.10
A4 - Venezia - Trieste	€7.00	€9.20
A4 - Torino - Milano	€9.60	€12.10
A4 - Milano - Venezia	€15.70	€20.40
A5 - Santhia - Aosta	€11.30	€17.00
A5 - Torino - Aosta	€12.90	€19.30
A6 - Torino - Savona	€10.90	€14.70
A7 - Milano - Tortona	€3.60	€4.70
A7 - Milano - Génova	€7.50	€9.80
A8 - Milano - Varese	€2.60	€3.40
A8/A9 - Milano - Chiasso (Swiss Frontier)	€3.20	€4.10
Tunnels Currency Euro (€)	**Car**	**Car Towing Caravan/Trailer**
On A32 (E70) -Tunnel del Frejus	€35.10	€46.40
T2 - Grand St Bernard Tunnel	€23.60	€36.50
On A5 (E25) -Mont Blanc Tunnel	€35.10	€46.40
Munt La Schera Tunnel - Livigno	€10.00	€20.00

NORTH WEST/ALPS & LAKES

ANFO — BRESCIA

Pilù

via Venturi 4, 25070
☎ 0365 809037 🖷 0365 809207
e-mail: info@pilu.it
web: www.pilu.it

A well-maintained, slightly sloping site subdivided by trees and rows of shrubs. Separated from the pebble beach by a public footpath.

dir: *Signed on S outskirts.*

Open: Apr-Sep **Site:** 2HEC **Prices:** 23.50-31.50 **Facilities:** Wi-fi (charged) Play Area **Services:** **Leisure:** L P R **Off-site:**

ANGERA — VARESE

Città di Angera

via Bruschera 99, 21021
☎ 0331 930736 🖷 0331 960367
e-mail: info@campingcittadiangera.it
web: www.campingcittadiangera.it

Large family site with plenty of recreational facilities.

dir: *Signed.*

Open: 15 Feb-14 Nov **Site:** 10HEC **Prices:** 32-34 **Facilities:** Kids' Club Play Area **Services:** **Leisure:** L P **Off-site:**

ARVIER — AOSTA

Arvier

via Chaussa 17, 11011
☎ 0165 069006 🖷 0165 99045
e-mail: campingarvier@yahoo.it
web: www.campingarvier.com

Quiet wooded site close to mountains and a peaceful village.

Open: Jun-Aug **Site:** 1HEC **Prices:** 24.60 Mobile home hire 280 **Facilities:** Wi-fi Play Area **Services:** **Leisure:** P **Off-site:** R

BASTIA MONDOVI — CUNEO

Cascina

loc Pieve 23, 12060
☎ 0174 60181 🖷 0174 60181
e-mail: info@campinglacascina.it
web: www.campinglacascina.it

A peaceful site on level land surrounded by mountains.

dir: *Towards Bastia.*

Open: Jan-30 Aug & Oct-Dec **Site:** 4HEC **Facilities:** **Services:** **Leisure:** P R

BAVENO — NOVARA

Tranquilla

via Cave-Oltrefiume 02, 28831
☎ 0323 923452 🖷 0323 923452
e-mail: info@tranquilla.com
web: www.tranquilla.com

A peaceful location with panoramic views of the surrounding mountains and Lake Maggiore. Modern facilities with trekking opportunities nearby.

dir: *4km from Stresa. 1km from Baveno.*

GPS: 45.9124, 8.4886

Open: 15 Mar-15 Oct **Site:** 1.8HEC **Prices:** 12.20-26 **Facilities:** Wi-fi Play Area **Services:** **Leisure:** P **Off-site:** L R

BELLAGIO — COMO

Azienda Agricola Clarke

via Valassina 170/c, 22021
☎ 031 951325
e-mail: elizabethclarke@tin.it
web: www.bellagio-camping.com

A small, secluded site on a horsebreeding farm close to Lake Bellagio, up towards the mountains with fine views. No dogs allowed.

Open: Jun-Sep **Site:** 0.5HEC **Facilities:** **Services:** **Off-site:** L P

BOLZANO-BOZEN — BOLZANO

Moosbauer

Moritzingerweg 83, 39100
☎ 0471 918492 🖷 0471 204894
e-mail: info@moosbauer.com
web: www.moosbauer.com

Small site in attractive valley at the Gateway to the Dolomites.

Open: All Year. **Site:** 1.2HEC **Facilities:** **Services:** **Leisure:** P **Off-site:**

BRÉCCIA — COMO

International

via Cecilio, 22100
☎ 031 521435 🖷 031 521435
e-mail: campingint@hotmail.com
web: www.camping-internazionale.it

On a level meadow near the motorway.

dir: *Off A9 Como-Milan.*

Open: 28 Mar-30 Oct **Site:** 1.3HEC **Prices:** 23.50 Mobile home hire 310 **Facilities:** Play Area **Services:** **Leisure:** P

BRESSANONE-BRIXEN BOLZANO

Löwenhof-Leone

via Brennero 60 - quartiere Leone, 39040
0472 836216 0472 801337
e-mail: info@loewenhof.it
web: www.loewenhof.it
Site offers rafting and canoeing school as well as a sauna and pool, which are avaliable in the Dolomiti resort 8km away.
dir: *Bolzano-Brenner motorway exit Varna, site just before Brixen.*
GPS: 46.7344, 11.6472
Open: Mar-26 Oct **Site:** 0.5HEC **Prices:** 26-36 **Facilities:** Wi-fi (charged) **Services:** **Leisure:** P R **Off-site:** L

CALCERANICA TRENTO

Al Pescatore

via dei Pescatori 1, 38050
0461 723062 0461 724212
e-mail: trentino@campingpescatore.it
web: www.campingpescatore.it
The site consists of several sections of meadowland, inland from the lake shore road to Lago di Caldonazzo. Well maintained with private beach.
Open: 22 May-15 Sep **Site:** 3.8HEC **Facilities:** **Services:** **Leisure:** L P **Off-site:**

Fleiola

via Trento 42, 38050
0461 723153 0461 724386
e-mail: info@campingfleiola.it
web: www.campingfleiola.it
Site is divided into sectors beside lake.
dir: *Verona-Brenner motorway exit Trento, signs for Pergine & Caldonazzo.*
Open: Apr-5 Oct **Site:** 1.2HEC **Prices:** 18-38 **Facilities:** Wi-fi Kids' Club Play Area **Services:** **Leisure:** L **Off-site:**

Riviera

viale Venezia 10, 38050
0461 724464 0461 718689
e-mail: riviera@dnet.it
web: www.campingriviera.net
Open: Etr-15 Sep **Site:** 1.5HEC **Facilities:** **Services:** **Leisure:** L **Off-site:**

CAMPITELLO DI FASSA TRENTO

Miravalle

vicolo camping 15, 38031
0462 750502 0462 751563
e-mail: info@campingmiravalle.it
web: www.campingmiravalle.it
Wooded mountain setting beside the River Avisio and close to the town centre.
dir: *Signed.*
Open: Jun-Sep & Dec-Apr **Site:** 3HEC **Facilities:** **Services:** **Leisure:** R **Off-site:** P

CANAZEI TRENTO

Marmolada

via Pareda 60, 38032
0462 601660 0462 601722
e-mail: campingmarmolada@virgilio.it
Grassland site extending to the river, part of it in spruce woodland.
dir: *On S outskirts on right of road to Alba Penia.*
Open: All Year. **Site:** 3HEC **Facilities:** **Services:** **Leisure:** R **Off-site:** P

CANNOBIO NOVARA

International Paradis

via Casali Darbedo 12, 28052
0323 71227 0323 72591
e-mail: info@campinglagomaggiore.it
web: www.campinglagomaggiore.it
A level site on the bank of a lake.
dir: *Off SS34 at Km35/V.*
Open: 20 Mar-15 Oct **Site:** 1.2HEC **Facilities:** **Services:** **Leisure:** L **Off-site:** R

Residence Campagna

via Casali Darbedo 20/22, 28822
0323 70100 0323 71190
e-mail: info@campingcampagna.it
web: www.campingcampagna.it
A well-equipped site in a pleasant lakeside location.
dir: *Off SS34 to Locarno at Km35/V on N outskirts of village. W of lake on road 21.*
GPS: 46.0711, 8.6936
Open: 20 Mar-23 Oct **Site:** 1.2HEC **Prices:** 23-32 Mobile home hire 350-630 **Facilities:** Wi-fi (charged) Play Area **Services:** **Leisure:** L **Off-site:** R

Valle Romantica

via Valle Cannobina, 28822
☎ 0323 71249 🖷 0323 71249
e-mail: valleromantica@riviera-valleromantica.com
web: www.riviera-valleromantica.com

A pleasant site with trees, shrubs and flowers. Internal roads are asphalted and a mountain stream provides bathing facilities as well as a swimming pool.

dir: *1.5km W off road to Malesco.*

Open: Apr-12 Sep **Site:** 30HEC **Prices:** 23-32 Mobile home hire 370-545 **Facilities:** Wi-fi (charged) Play Area **Services:** **Leisure:** P R **Off-site:** L

CASTELLETTO TICINO — NOVARA

Italia Lido

via Cicognola 104, 28053
☎ 0331 923032 🖷 0331 923032
e-mail: info@campingitalialido.it
web: www.campingitalialido.it

A large family site with its own private beach on Lake Maggiore. The site is popular with families and there are good recreational facilities.

dir: *A8 onto A26 & signed.*

Open: Mar-30 Oct **Site:** 3HEC **Prices:** 15.50-23 **Facilities:** Play Area **Services:** **Leisure:** L **Off-site:**

CHIUSA-KLAUSEN — BOLZANO

Gamp

Griesbruck 10, 39043
☎ 0472 847425 🖷 0472 845067
e-mail: info@camping-gamp.com
web: www.camping-gamp.com

The site lies next to the Gasthof Gamp, between the Brenner railway line and the motorway bridge, which passes high above the site.

dir: *Motorway exit onto SS12, signed.*

Open: All Year. **Site:** 0.6HEC **Facilities:** **Services:** **Leisure:** P **Off-site:** P

CHIUSI DELLA VERNA — TRENTO

La Verna

Vezzano, 52010
☎ 0575 532121 🖷 0575 532041
e-mail: info@campinglaverna.it
web: www.campinglaverna.it

On the borders of the Casentino Forest Park in attractive Tuscan scenery. Pitches are of varying sizes and levels of shade.

Open: 11 Apr-4 Oct **Site:** 2.2HEC **Facilities:** **Services:** **Leisure:** P **Off-site:** R

COLFOSCO — BOLZANO

Colfosco

via Sorega 15, 39030
☎ 0471 836515 🖷 0471 830801
e-mail: info@campingcolfosco.org
web: www.campingcolfosco.org

A beautiful setting at the foot of the Sella mountains.

Open: Dec-10 Apr & Jun-Sep **Site:** 2.5HEC **Prices:** 23-35.70 **Facilities:** Wi-fi (charged) Play Area **Services:** **Leisure:** R **Off-site:** L

COLOMBARE — BRESCIA

Sirmione

via Sirmioncino 9, 25019
☎ 030 919045 🖷 030 919045
e-mail: info@camping-sirmione.it
web: www.camping-sirmione.it

A well-equipped site in a beautiful location on the Sirmione peninsula, with direct access to Lake Garda.

dir: *SS11 towards Sirmione, 0.4km turn right.*

Open: 25 Mar-5 Oct **Site:** 3.5HEC **Facilities:** Play Area **Services:** **Leisure:** L P **Off-site:**

DESENZANO DEL GARDA — BRESCIA

Vò

via Vò 9, 25015
☎ 030 9121325 🖷 030 9120773
e-mail: vo@voit.it
web: www.voit.it

Situated on Lake Garda, 1.5km from Desenzano, surrounded by meadows and woods.

dir: *Between Padenghe & Sirmione on Lake Garda, 2km from Desenzano.*

Open: Apr-Sep **Site:** 5HEC **Prices:** 24-33 **Facilities:** **Services:** **Leisure:** L P **Off-site:**

DIMARO — TRENTO

Dolomiti Camping Village
via Gole 105, 38025
0463 974332 0463 973200
e-mail: info@campingdolomiti.com
web: www.campingdolomiti.com
The site has large flat plots surrounded by tall pines. Good sports facilities and tuition for canoeing and white-water rafting. There is a spa available and a kids' club in July and August.
dir: *Off SS42 at Km173.5.*
GPS: 46.3253, 10.8631
Open: 20 May-26 Sep & 5 Dec-10 Apr **Site:** 4HEC **Facilities:** Wi-fi (charged) Kids' Club Play Area **Services:** **Leisure:** P **Off-site:** R

DOMASO — COMO

Gardenia
via Case Sparse 164, 22013
0344 96262 0344 83381
e-mail: info@domaso.biz
web: www.domaso.biz
A family-run site on the west bank of Lake Como, ideally located for sports and relaxation.
dir: *N at Case Sparse.*
GPS: 46.1528, 9.3344
Open: Apr-Sep **Site:** 18.5HEC **Prices:** 20.30-22.60 **Facilities:** Wi-fi (charged) Play Area **Services:** **Leisure:** L **Off-site:** P R

DORMELLETTO — NOVARA

Lago Azzurro
via E-Fermi 2, 28040
0322 497197 0322 497197
e-mail: info@campinglagoazzurro.it
web: www.campinglagoazzurro.it
A lakeside site in beautiful surroundings with fine sports facilities.
dir: *S of Arona off SS Sempione 33.*
GPS: 45.7374, 8.5765
Open: All Year. **Site:** 2.5HEC **Prices:** 21.50-32 **Facilities:** **Services:** **Leisure:** L P

Lago Maggiore
via L-da-Vinci 7, 28040
0322 497193 0322 498600
e-mail: info@lagomag.com
web: www.lagomag.com
Well-maintained site divided into plots, pleasantly landscaped by the lakeside.
dir: *Off SS33, signed.*
Open: Apr-Sep **Site:** 7HEC **Prices:** 18-36 Mobile home hire 348-1250 **Facilities:** Wi-fi (charged) Kids' Club Play Area **Services:** **Leisure:** L P **Off-site:**

Lido Holiday Inn
via M-Polo 1, 28040
0322 497047 0322 497047
e-mail: info@campingholidayinn.com
web: www.campingholidayinn.com
Site on bank of the lake, with some trees.
dir: *A8/A26, exit for Castelletto Ticino, site 2km.*
Open: All Year. **Site:** 3.5HEC **Facilities:** **Services:** **Leisure:** L P **Off-site:**

Smeraldo
via Cavour 131, 28040
0322 497031 0322 498789
e-mail: info@camping-smeraldo.com
web: www.camping-smeraldo.com
Well-landscaped site in woodland beside a lake. Divided into plots.
dir: *Off SS33.*
Open: Mar-Oct **Site:** 24HEC **Facilities:** **Services:** **Leisure:** L P **Off-site:**

EDOLO — BRESCIA

Adamello
via Campeggio 10, 25048
0364 71694 0364 71694
e-mail: info@campingadamello.com
web: www.campingadamello.com
A terraced site in wooded surroundings, 1km from the lake.
dir: *1.5km W of SS39.*
Open: Dec-10 Jan & Apr-15 Oct **Site:** 1.2HEC **Facilities:** **Services:** **Off-site:** L P R

FERIOLO NOVARA

Orchidea

via 42 Martiri 20, 28831
☎ 0323 28257 📠 0323 28573
e-mail: info@campingorchidea.it
web: www.campingorchidea.it

A modern family site on Lake Maggiore with good sports and entertainment facilities.

dir: *Via SS33.*

Open: 21 Mar-10 Oct **Site:** 4HEC **Prices:** 21-41 Mobile home hire 350-840 **Facilities:** Wi-fi (charged) Kids' Club Play Area **Services:** **Leisure:** L **Off-site:** P R

FONDOTOCE NOVARA

Camping Village Continental

via 42 Martiri 156, 28924
☎ 0323 496300 📠 0323 496218
e-mail: info@campingcontinental.com
web: www.campingcontinental.com

By Lake Mergozzo and 1km from Lake Maggiore. Dogs not permitted in accommodation.

dir: *On right of road Verbania Fondotoce-Gravellona.*

Open: 15 Apr-26 Sep **Site:** 10HEC **Prices:** 18.80-42.60 Mobile home hire 258.14-794.94 **Facilities:** Wi-fi (charged) Kids' Club Play Area **Services:** **Leisure:** L P **Off-site:** R

Lido Toce Camping

via per Feriolo 41, 28924
☎ 0323 496298 📠 0323 496220
e-mail: info@campinglidotoce.eu
web: www.campinglidotoce.eu

A beautiful location with spectacular views on the eastern shore of the lake. Good recreational facilities.

Open: Apr-Sep **Site:** 2HEC **Facilities:** Play Area **Services:** **Leisure:** L R **Off-site:** P

Village Isolino

via Per Feriolo 25, 28924
☎ 0323 496080 📠 0323 496414
e-mail: info@isolino.com
web: www.isolino.it

Peaceful site with panoramic views and large pitches. Swimming pool complex. Kids' club available 21 April to 11 September. Dogs accepted but restrictions apply.

Open: 15 Apr-26 Sep **Site:** 12HEC **Prices:** 18.80-48.40 **Facilities:** Wi-fi (charged) Kids' Club Play Area **Services:** **Leisure:** L P **Off-site:** R

FUCINE DI OSSANA TRENTO

Cevedale

via di Sotto Pila 4, 38026
☎ 0463 751630 📠 0463 751630
e-mail: info@campingcevedale.it
web: www.campingcevedale.it

A well-equipped site in a peaceful location at an altitude of 900m, close to the local ski resorts. Kids' club available during June and July.

dir: *A22 exit San Michele direction Tonale.*

GPS: 46.3083, 10.7336

Open: All Year. **Site:** 3.7HEC **Prices:** 25-32 **Facilities:** Wi-fi Kids' Club Play Area **Services:** **Leisure:** R **Off-site:** L P

GHIRLA VARESE

Trelago

via Trelago 20, 21030
☎ 0332 716583 📠 0332 719650
e-mail: info@3lagocamping.com
web: www.3lagocamping.com

Lakeside site with grassy pitches shaded by tall trees.

dir: *Signs from Milan to Varese & Ghirla, site 15km from Varese.*

Open: Apr-Sep **Site:** 3.3HEC **Prices:** 19 **Facilities:** Wi-fi Play Area **Services:** **Leisure:** L P **Off-site:** R

IDRO BRESCIA

AZUR Rio Vantone

25074
☎ 0365 83125 📠 0365 823663
e-mail: idro@azur-freizeit.de
web: www.azur-camping.de/idro

The site lies at the mouth of the river of same name beside Lake Idro. Subdivided into pitches (separate pitches for youths) on grass and woodland at the foot of distinctive rock formations.

dir: *Approach from Idro towards Vantone & signed.*

Open: Apr-Oct **Site:** 4.5HEC **Facilities:** **Services:** **Leisure:** L P R

Vantone Pineta

via Capovalle 11, 25074
☎ 0365 823385
e-mail: info@vantonepineta.it
web: www.vantonepineta.it

On eastern shore of lake. Grassland enclosed by rush and willow fencing. Part of the site is in a small wood on the bank of a stream.

dir: *Approach from Idro & signs for Camping Idro Rio Vantone.*

Open: 31 Mar-Sep **Site:** 2HEC **Prices:** 23.50-31.50 **Facilities:** Wi-fi (charged) Play Area **Services:** **Leisure:** L P **Off-site:**

ISEO — BRESCIA

Punta d'Oro

via Antonioli 51/53, 25049
☎ 030 980084 🖷 030 980084
e-mail: info@camping-puntadoro.com
web: www.camping-puntadoro.com

A well-set out site with roads and paths to every pitch.

dir: *A4 exit Rovato, signs for Iseo.*

Open: Apr-Oct **Site:** 0.6HEC **Prices:** Mobile home hire 259-574 **Facilities:** Wi-fi Play Area **Services:** **Leisure:** L **Off-site:** P

Quai

via Antonioli 73, 25049
☎ 0309 821610 🖷 0309 981161
e-mail: info@campingquai.it
web: www.campingquai.it

Shady site close to the edge of Lake Iseo.

dir: *W of town, signed.*

GPS: 45.6661, 10.0628

Open: 8 Apr-26 Sep **Site:** 1.3HEC **Prices:** 23-26 **Facilities:** Wi-fi (charged) **Services:** **Leisure:** L **Off-site:** P

Sassabanek

via Colombera 2, 25049
☎ 030 980300 🖷 030 9821360
e-mail: sassabanek@sassabanek.it
web: www.sassabanek.it

A pleasant wooded location on the shore of Lake Iseo with good recreational facilities.

Open: Apr-Sep **Site:** 3.5HEC **Facilities:** **Services:** **Leisure:** L P **Off-site:**

LAIVES-LEIFERS — BOLZANO

Steiner

Kennedystr 34, 39055
☎ 0471 950105 🖷 0471 593141
e-mail: info@campingsteiner.com
web: www.campingsteiner.com

The site lies in the Etsch valley, only 8km from Bolzano. There are 140 pitches set amongst apple and elm trees. Facilities include swimming pools, a TV room and a shop.

dir: *Off SS12 on N outskirts of village.*

Open: 10 Apr-7 Nov **Site:** 2.5HEC **Prices:** 26-32 **Facilities:** Wi-fi (charged) Play Area **Services:** **Leisure:** P **Off-site:**

LATSCH — BOLZANO

Latsch an der Etsch

Reichstr 4, 39021
☎ 0473 623217 🖷 0473 622333
e-mail: info@camping-latsch.com
web: www.camping-latsch.com

A terraced site beside the river.

dir: *Signed on SS38.*

Open: 11 Dec-10 Nov **Site:** 2.2HEC **Prices:** 27-30.80 Mobile home hire 508.20-613.80 **Facilities:** Wi-fi (charged) Play Area **Services:** **Leisure:** P R **Off-site:** L

LECCO — COMO

Rivabella

via Alla Spiaggia 35, 23900
☎ 0341 421143 🖷 0341 421143
e-mail: rivabellalecco@libero.it
web: www.rivabellalecco.it

On a private, guarded beach on the shore of Lake Como.

dir: *3km S towards Bergamo.*

Open: 25 Apr-Sep **Site:** 2HEC **Prices:** 25 **Facilities:** Wi-fi Play Area **Services:** **Leisure:** L **Off-site:** P

LEVICO TERME — TRENTO

Due Laghi

Loc Costa 3, 38056
☎ 0461 706290 🖷 0461 707381
e-mail: info@campingclub.it
web: www.campingclub.it

Mainly family site with 400 large, flat, grass pitches.

dir: *From Trento signs for Pergine & Lake Caldonazza.*

Open: 14 Apr-11 Sep **Site:** 12HEC **Prices:** 19-40 **Facilities:** Wi-fi (charged) Kids' Club Play Area **Services:** **Leisure:** L P

Jolly

Loc Pleina, 38056
☎ 0461 706934 🖷 0461 700227
e-mail: info@lagolevico.com
web: www.lagolevico.com

The site is divided into plots and lies 200m from the lake. Three indoor swimming pools.

Open: Apr-19 Sep **Site:** 3.5HEC **Facilities:** Wi-fi (charged) Kids' Club Play Area **Services:** **Leisure:** L P **Off-site:** R

Site 6HEC (site size) grass sand stone little shade partly shaded mainly shaded bungalows for hire (static) caravans for hire tents for hire no dogs site fully accessible for wheelchairs
Prices amount quoted is per night, for 2 adults and car, plus tent or caravan. Mobile home hire is a weekly rate.

ITALY

Levico

38056
☎ 0461 706491 0461 707735
e-mail: info@lagolevico.com
web: www.lagolevico.com
Site is by Lake Levico with a private beach.
dir: *SS47 exit Levico/Caldonazzo, site signed.*
Open: 15 Apr-10 Oct **Site:** 5HEC **Prices:** 35.30-41.80 **Facilities:** Wi-fi (charged) Kids' Club Play Area **Services:** **Leisure:** L P R

LIMONE PIEMONTE CUNEO

Luis Matlas

12015
☎ 0171 927565 0171 927565
This tidy site offers winter facilities and skiing lessons are provided by the owner. Fishing is also available.
dir: *N of town off Limone-Nice road.*
Open: Jan-7 May & 20 May-Sep & Nov-Dec **Site:** 1.5HEC **Prices:** 21.50 **Facilities:** Play Area **Services:** **Leisure:** R **Off-site:**

LIMONE SUL GARDA BRESCIA

Nanzel

via 4 Novembre 3, 25010
☎ 0365 954155 0365 954468
e-mail: campingnanzel@libero.it
web: www.campingnanzel.it
Well-managed site, with low terraces in olive grove.
dir: *Access from Km101.2 (Hotel Giorgiol).*
Open: 14 Apr-23 Oct **Site:** 0.7HEC **Prices:** 23.50-30.80 **Facilities:** **Services:** **Leisure:** L **Off-site:**

MACCAGNO VARESE

AZUR-Lago Maggiore

21010
☎ 0332 560203 0332 561263
e-mail: maccagno@azur-camping.de
web: www.azur-camping.de/maccagno
A popular site on the shore of the lake.
dir: *Off SS394 in village at Km43/III towards lake, 0.5km turn right.*
Open: 15 Mar-15 Nov **Site:** 1.5HEC **Facilities:** **Services:** **Leisure:** L R

Lido

via Pietraperzia 13, 21010
☎ 0332 560250 0332 560250
e-mail: lido@boschettoholiday.it
web: www.boschettoholiday.it/lido
Lakeside site with good facilities, 200m from the river.
Open: Apr-Sep **Site:** 0.8HEC **Facilities:** **Services:** **Leisure:** L **Off-site:** R

MANERBA DEL GARDA BRESCIA

Belvedere

via Cavalle 5, 25080
☎ 0365 551175 0365 552350
e-mail: info@camping-belvedere.it
web: www.camping-belvedere.it
Terraced site by Lake Garda.
dir: *Signed from SS572.*
Open: 15 Mar-5 Oct **Site:** 2.1HEC **Facilities:** **Services:** **Leisure:** L P **Off-site:**

Rio Ferienglück

via del Rio 37, 25080
☎ 0365 551075 0365 551044
A quiet site on the banks of Lake Garda.
dir: *Off SS572 Desenzano-Salò between Km8 & Km9, site 4km N.*
Open: Apr-Sep **Site:** 5HEC **Prices:** 19-26.50 **Facilities:** Wi-fi (charged) Play Area **Services:** **Leisure:** L P R

Rocca

via Cavalle 22, 25080
☎ 0365 551738 0365 552045
e-mail: info@laroccacamp.it
web: www.laroccacamp.it
A picturesque location with fine views over the gulf of Manerba.
Open: 31 Mar-Sep **Site:** 5HEC **Facilities:** **Services:** **Leisure:** L P

ITALY

ITALY

Zocco

via del Zocco 43, 25080
☎ 0365 551605 0365 552053
e-mail: info@campingzocco.it
web: www.campingzocco.it
On the banks of Lake Garda with direct access to a beach and private landing stage. Leisure facilities include tennis courts and a football pitch.

dir: *0.5km S of Gardonicino di Manerba.*

GPS: 45.5397, 10.5560

Open: 16 Apr-25 Sep **Site:** 5HEC **Prices:** 15-31.80 **Facilities:** Wi-fi **Services:** **Leisure:** L P

MARONE — BRESCIA

Riva di San Pietro

via Cristini 9, 25054
☎ 030 9827129 030 9827129
e-mail: info@rivasanpietro.it
web: www.rivasanpietro.it
A modern site on the eastern side of Lake Iseo. Plenty of recreational facilities.

dir: *Milano-Venezia road exit Rovato or Palazzolo for Iseo, Marone 10km N.*

Open: May-Sep **Site:** 2HEC **Facilities:** Wi-fi (charged) **Services:** **Leisure:** L P **Off-site:**

MOLVENO — TRENTO

Spiaggia-Lago di Molveno

via Lungolago 27, 38018
☎ 0461 586978 0461 586330
e-mail: camping@molveno.it
web: www.campingmolveno.it
A picturesque setting by the lake, at the foot of the Brenta Dolomites.

dir: *Signed from SS421.*

Open: All Year. **Site:** 4HEC **Facilities:** **Services:** **Off-site:** L P

MONIGA DEL GARDA — BRESCIA

Fontanelle

via Magone 13, 25080
☎ 0365 502079 0365 503324
e-mail: info@campingfontanelle.it
web: www.campingfontanelle.it
Peaceful site on the shores of Lake Garda shaded by olive trees. A kids' club is available in high season.

Open: 20 Apr-17 Sep **Site:** 45HEC **Prices:** 23-35 **Facilities:** Wi-fi (charged) Kids' Club Play Area **Services:** **Leisure:** L P **Off-site:**

San Michele

via San Michele 8, 25080
☎ 0365 502026 0365 503443
e-mail: info@campingsanmichele.it
web: www.campingsanmichele.it
A family site with good facilities and direct access to the lake via a private beach.

dir: *A4 exit Desenzano, site 8km towards Salò.*

Open: 10 Mar-2 Nov **Site:** 3HEC **Facilities:** **Services:** **Leisure:** L P **Off-site:**

NOVATE MEZZOLA — SONDRIO

El Ranchero

via Nazionale 3, 23025
☎ 0343 44169 0343 44169
e-mail: info@elranchero.it
web: www.elranchero.it
Located on the edge of the Mezzola Lake in front of a spectacular view of the mountains.

Open: May-15 Oct **Site:** 1HEC **Prices:** 25 **Facilities:** Wi-fi (charged) Play Area **Services:** **Leisure:** L **Off-site:** P R

ORTA SAN GIULIO — NOVARA

Camping Cusio

Lago d'Orta, via Don Boslo, 5, 28016
☎ 0322 90290 0322 90290
e-mail: cusio@tin.it
web: www.campingcusio.it
Site surrounded by woodland on Lake Orta in a picturesque alpine valley. Good facilities.

dir: *S of Omegna towards Borgomanero.*

Open: Apr-Nov **Site:** 2HEC **Facilities:** Wi-fi (charged) Play Area **Services:** **Leisure:** P **Off-site:** L

PADENGHE — BRESCIA

La Cá

via della Colombaia 6, 25080
☎ 030 9907006 030 9907693
e-mail: info@campinglaca.it
web: www.campinglaca.it
A park-like setting on terraced ground.

dir: *Off road along Lake Garda, 1.5km N turn for Padenghe & down steep road towards lake.*

Open: Mar-30 Oct **Site:** 2HEC **Prices:** 12.40-30.50 Mobile home hire 154-322 **Facilities:** Wi-fi (charged) **Services:** **Leisure:** L P

Villa Garuti

via del Porto 5, 25080
030 9907134 030 9907817
e-mail: info@villagaruti.it
web: www.villagaruti.it

A campsite and holiday village in the garden of the old Villa Garuti, beside the lake with its own beach.

dir: *A4 exit Desenzano, SS572 to Padenghe.*

Open: Apr-10 Oct **Site:** 1.5HEC **Prices:** 20-40 **Facilities:** Wi-fi Play Area **Services:** **Leisure:** L P **Off-site:**

PEIO TRENTO

Val di Sole

Loc Dossi di Cavia, 38024
0463 753177 0463 753176
e-mail: valdisole@camping.it
web: www.valdisolecamping.it

The site lies on terraced slopes at the foot of the Ortier mountain range.

dir: *400m off SP87.*

Open: Jun-5 Nov & Dec-5 May **Site:** 2.3HEC **Facilities:** **Services:** **Off-site:** P

PERA DI FASSA TRENTO

Soal

Strada Dolomites 190, 38036
0462 764519 0462 764519
e-mail: info@campingsoal.com
web: www.campingsoal.com

Breath-taking location among the Dolomites, ideal for skiing and walking.

Open: All Year. **Site:** 30HEC **Prices:** 19-25 **Facilities:** Play Area **Services:** **Leisure:** R

PÉRGINE TRENTO

Punta Indiani

Lago di Caldonazzo, 38058
0461 548062 0461 548607
e-mail: info@campingpuntaindiani.it
web: www.campingpuntaindiani.it

On level ground surrounded by trees with direct access to 400m of private beach on the banks of the lake.

dir: *A22 exit Trento, signs for Pergine, S Cristoforo & Caldonazzo.*

GPS: 46.0267, 11.2303

Open: 22 Apr-3 Oct **Site:** 1.5HEC **Prices:** 20-36 **Facilities:** Wi-fi (charged) **Services:** **Leisure:** L **Off-site:**

San Cristoforo

via dei Pescatori, 38057
0461 512707 0461 707381
e-mail: info@campingclub.it
web: www.campingclub.it

A family-run site in a prime position on the sunniest side of lake.

dir: *SS47 from Trento towards Venice for 14km, site in centre of San Cristoforo.*

Open: 20 May-12 Sep **Site:** 2.5HEC **Facilities:** **Services:** **Leisure:** L P **Off-site:**

PIEVE DI MANERBA BRESCIA

Faro

via Repubblica 52, 25080
0365 651704 0365 651704
e-mail: campeggioilfaro@virgilio.it
web: www.campingilfaro.it

Set in a peaceful rural area close to the sea.

dir: *Off A4 at Desenzano onto N572 to Manerba del Garda.*

Open: 15 Apr-15 Sep **Site:** 1HEC **Facilities:** **Services:** **Leisure:** P **Off-site:** L

PISOGNE BRESCIA

Eden

via Piangrande 3, 25055
0364 880500 0364 880500
e-mail: info@campeggioeden.com
web: www.campeggioeden.com

The site lies on the eastern shore of the lake with tall trees and a level beach.

dir: *Off SS510 at Km37/VII, over railway towards lake.*

Open: May-15 Sep **Site:** 2.5HEC **Facilities:** **Services:** **Leisure:** L **Off-site:** P R

PORLEZZA COMO

OK La Rivetta

via Calbiga,30, 22018
0344 70393 0344 70715
e-mail: info@campingoklarivetta.com
web: www.campingoklarivetta.com

The site lies in meadowland on the north eastern lake shore.

dir: *S from SS340.*

Open: 15 Mar-15 Nov **Site:** 5HEC **Facilities:** **Services:** **Leisure:** L P **Off-site:** R

POZZA DI FASSA — TRENTO

Rosengarten

Srada de Pucia, 4, Loc Puccia, 38036
☎ 0462 763305 🖹 0462 762247
e-mail: info@catinacciorosengarten.com
web: www.catinacciorosengarten.com

A well-tended site in the heart of the Dolomites, only 200m from the town of Pozza Di Fassa. A good base for a skiing or walking holiday, there is a free bus to the ski slopes.

dir: *Signed from SS48.*

Open: 10 Jun-Sep & Dec-25 Apr **Site:** 3HEC
Facilities: Wi-fi (charged) Kids' Club Play Area
Services: **Leisure:** R
Off-site: P

Vidor Family & Wellness Resort

Strada de Ruf de Ruacia 15, 38036
☎ 0462 760022 🖹 0462 762007
e-mail: info@campingvidor.it
web: www.campingvidor.it

A traditional family-run site in a pine forest. Ideal for skiers, nature lovers and families. Health and beauty spa on site.

dir: *Signed from SS48.*

Open: 27 Nov-2 Nov **Site:** 2.8HEC **Prices:** 20-35
Facilities: Wi-fi (charged) Kids' Club Play Area
Services: **Leisure:** P **Off-site:** R

RASUN — BOLZANO

Corones

39030
☎ 0474 496490 🖹 0474 498250
e-mail: info@corones.com
web: www.corones.com

A modern site in an ideal mountain location with good sports facilities.

dir: *Milan-Brenner motorway exit Val Pusteria, through Brunico & Valdaora to Rasun.*

Open: May-Oct & Dec-Mar **Site:** 2.7HEC **Prices:** 16-29
Facilities: Wi-fi (charged) Kids' Club Play Area
Services: **Leisure:** P

RIVA DEL GARDA — TRENTO

Bavaria

viale Rovereto 100, 38066
☎ 0464 552524 🖹 0464 559126
e-mail: info@bavarianet.it
web: www.bavarianet.it

Site faces directly onto a lake, ideal for watersports enthusiasts.

dir: *On SS240 towards Rovereto.*

Open: Apr-Oct **Site:** 0.6HEC **Prices:** 28 **Facilities:** Wi-fi **Services:** **Leisure:** L
Off-site:

Brione

via Brione 32, 38066
☎ 0464 520885 🖹 0464 520890
e-mail: info@campingbrione.com
web: www.campingbrione.com

This quiet site is at the foot of a hill covered with olive trees, ideally located near Lake Garda.

Open: Apr-Oct **Site:** 3.3HEC **Prices:** 27-30.50
Facilities: Wi-fi (charged) Play Area
Services: **Leisure:** P **Off-site:** L

RIVOLTELLA — BRESCIA

San Francesco

strada Vicinale San Francesco, 25010
☎ 030 9110245 🖹 030 9119464
e-mail: moreinfo@campingsanfrancesco.com
web: www.campingsanfrancesco.com

This well-kept site is divided into many sections by drives, vineyards and orchards and has a private gravel beach.

dir: *At Km268 on SSN11.*

Open: Apr-Sep **Site:** 10.4HEC **Facilities:** **Services:** **Leisure:** L P

SAN ANTONIO DI MAVIGNOLA — TRENTO

Fae

38086
☎ 0465 507178 🖹 0465 507178
e-mail: info@campingfae.it
web: www.campingfae.it

Situated in the winter skiing region of Madonna di Campiglio. Good base for climbing in the Brenta range. Set on on four gravel terraces, and an alpine meadow in a hollow.

dir: *Off SS239.*

Open: Jun-Sep & Dec-Apr **Site:** 2.1HEC **Prices:** 27-32
Facilities: Play Area **Services:**
Off-site: L P R

AN FELICE DEL BENACO BRESCIA

Camping Europa-Silvella

ia Silvella 10, 25010
0365 651095 0365 654395
-mail: info@europasilvella.it
eb: www.europasilvella.it
ite separated in two by the approach road. The beach is 80m elow.
ir: *Signed.*
pen: 25 Apr-20 Sep **Site:** 7.5HEC **Facilities:** **Services:** **Leisure:** L P

ornella

ia Fornella 1, 25010
0365 62294 0365 559418
-mail: fornella@fornella.it
eb: www.fornella.it
quiet site in an ideal location on the shore of Lake Garda. Kids' ub in high season.
ir: *Signed from SS572 Salò-Desenzano.*
pen: 22 Apr-25 Sep **Site:** 9.2HEC **Facilities:** Wi-fi (charged) Kids' Club Play Area **Services:** **Leisure:** L P

ardiola

ia Gardiola 36, 25010
0365 559240 0365 690724
-mail: info@lagardiola.com
eb: www.baiaholiday.com
terraced site with a variety of good facilities on the shore of ake Garda.
ir: *S of San Felice del Benaco off SS572.*
pen: Apr-22 Oct **Site:** 0.37HEC **Prices:** 20-42
acilities: Wi-fi (charged) **Services:**
eisure: L **Off-site:** P R

deal Molino

5010
0365 62023 0365 559395
-mail: info@campingmolino.it
eb: www.campingmolino.it
harming and quiet site beside Lake Garda, set among beautiful enery 1km from San Felice. On the beach there is a pier and at moorings. Pedal boats can be hired for lake trips.
PS: 45.5786, 10.5547
pen: Apr-4 Oct **Site:** 2HEC **Prices:** 25-41
obile home hire 455-1050 **Facilities:** Kids' Club
ervices: **Leisure:** L **Off-site:**

Weekend

The Camping and Caravanning Club — The Friendly Club

via Vallone della Selva 2, 25010
0365 43712 0365 42196
e-mail: info@weekend.it
web: www.weekend.it
A quiet family site with modern facilities, situated in an olive grove overlooking Lake Garda.

C&CC Report *A lovely site in a really spectacular setting. The views from the pool and from the bar's garden terrace are truly exceptional. Boat trips run from nearby Portese, and a visit to any of the towns around the lake, from Riva del Garda in the north to the beautiful fortified lake town of Sirmione in the south, is really rewarding. Just a short walk away you can go wine-tasting at Portese, while back on site, the weekly Italian buffet is very popular with the visiting campers from all over Europe and one of the highlights of the site's popular activities programme.*

dir: *A4 exit Desenzano, to Cisano, signed San Felice D-B.*
Open: 20 Apr-20 Sep **Site:** 9HEC **Facilities:** Wi-fi (charged) Kids' Club Play Area **Services:** **Leisure:** P **Off-site:** L

SAN MARTINO DI CASTROZZA TRENTO

Sass Maor

via Laghetto 48, 38058
0439 68347 0439 68347
e-mail: info@campingsassmaor.it
web: www.campingsassmaor.it
A winter sports site in a beautiful mountain setting.
dir: *From Trento to Ora, Cavalese & S Martino di Castrozza.*
Open: All Year. **Site:** 0.19HEC **Facilities:** **Services:** **Off-site:**

SAN PIETRO DI CORTENO GOLGI BRESCIA

Camping Villaggio Aprica

via Nazionale 507, 25040
0342 710001
e-mail: info@campingaprica.it
web: www.campingaprica.it
A small natural park ideal for winter skiing and summer walking or cycling.
dir: *On SS39 Aprica-Edolo.*
Open: All Year. **Site:** 2.1HEC **Facilities:** **Services:** **Leisure:** R **Off-site:** L P

Facilities shop shower electric points for razors electric points for caravans parking by tents permitted mpulsory separate car park **Services** café/restaurant bar Camping Gaz International gas other than Camping Gaz first aid facilities laundry **Leisure** swimming L-Lake P-Pool R-River S-Sea **Off-site** All facilities within 5km

SAN VIGILIO DI MAREBBE BOLZANO

Al Plan

39030
☎ 0474 501694 🖷 0474 506550
e-mail: camping.alplan@rolmail.net
web: www.campingalplan.com

Surrounded by the Dolomites, at an altitude of 1200m, this quiet site offers plenty of summer and winter activities.

dir: *Off A22.*

Open: 5 Dec-29 Apr & 11 Jun-18 Oct **Site:** 1.2HEC **Prices:** 22-29 **Facilities:** Play Area **Services:** **Off-site:** R

SARRE AOSTA

Monte Bianco

Fraz St Maurice 15, 11010
☎ 0165 257523 🖷 0165 257275
e-mail: info@campingmontebianco.it
web: www.campingmontebianco.it

Wooded surroundings close to the town centre.

dir: *SS26 towards Aosta & Courmayer.*

GPS: 45.7171, 7.2612

Open: May-Sep **Site:** 7.5HEC **Prices:** 17.50-19.10 **Facilities:** Wi-fi Play Area **Services:** **Leisure:** R **Off-site:** P

SEXTEN BOLZANO

Sexten

St-Josefstr 54, 39030
☎ 0474 710444 🖷 0474 710053
e-mail: info@patzenfeld.com
web: www.patzenfeld.com

This family-run site, located in the Dolomite mountain region, has modern facilities. The site offers swimming pools, a spa and plenty of activities, including skiing in winter. A kids' club is available in high season.

GPS: 46.6678, 13.3991

Open: All Year. **Site:** 6.5HEC **Prices:** 40.50 **Facilities:** Wi-fi (charged) Kids' Club Play Area **Services:** **Leisure:** P R

SORICO COMO

La Riva

via Pomciome 3, 22010
☎ 0344 94571 🖷 0344 94571
e-mail: info@campinglariva.com
web: www.campinglariva.com

Set in stunning countryside in the Italian Lakes area.

Open: Apr-3 Nov **Site:** 1.4HEC **Prices:** 23-35 **Facilities:** Wi-fi Play Area **Services:** **Leisure:** L P **Off-site:**

TORBOLE TRENTO

Camping Al Porto

38069
☎ 0464 505891 🖷 0464 505891
e-mail: info@campingalporto.it
web: www.campingalporto.it

A site with modern facilities, situated in a quiet position near the lake. Ideal for sports and families.

dir: *From Torbole onto SS240, signed.*

Open: 9 Apr-10 Oct **Site:** 1.1HEC **Prices:** 20-28.50 **Facilities:** Wi-fi (charged) Play Area **Services:** **Off-site:** L R

TORRE DANIELE TORINO

Mombarone

via Nazionale 54, 10010
☎ 0125 757907 🖷 0125 757396
e-mail: info@campingmombarone.it
web: www.campingmombarone.it

dir: *13km N of Ivrea on SS26. Close to river.*

Open: All Year. **Site:** 2HEC **Prices:** 20.50 **Facilities:** Wi-fi Play Area **Services:** **Leisure:** P R **Off-site:**

VALNONTEY AOSTA

Lo Stambecco

11012
☎ 0165 74152
e-mail: infotiscali@campeggiolostambecco.it
web: www.campeggiolostambecco.it

Site with terraced pitches, ideal for hiking in surrounding mountains.

Open: 15 May-25 Sep **Site:** 1.6HEC **Facilities:** **Services:** **Leisure:** R **Off-site:**

VENICE/NORTH

ARSIE BELLUNO

Gajole

Loc Soravigo, 32030
0439 58505 0439 58505
e-mail: info@campinggajole.it
web: www.campinggajole.it
delightful, peaceful setting on the shore of Lake Corlo.
ir: *Off SS50 bis.*
pen: Apr-Sep **Site:** 1.8HEC **Prices:** 20-23 **Facilities:** Wi-fi (charged) Play Area **Services:** **eisure:** L **Off-site:**

SIAGO VICENZA

kar

oc Ekar, 36012
0424 455157 0424 455161
-mail: info@campingasiagoekar.com
eb: www.campingasiagoekar.com
n a level meadow in a striking setting among wooded hills in a opular skiing region.
pen: 5 May-Sep & 15 Nov-6 Apr **Site:** 3.5HEC
acilities: **Services:**

URISINA TRIESTE

grituristico Imperial

urisina Cave 55, 34011
040 200459 040 200459
-mail: campimperial@libero.it
eb: www.campingimperialcarso.it
well-maintained site in a secluded, wooded location.
r: *Via SS14 Sistiana-Aurisina.*
pen: 20 May-20 Sep **Site:** 1.2HEC **Prices:** 17.50-26.50
acilities: **Services:** **Leisure:** P
ff-site: S

ARDOLINO VERONA

ontinental

oc Reboin, 37011
045 7210192 045 7211756
mail: continental@campingarda.it
eb: www.campingarda.it
pleasant site directly on the lake with modern facilities.
en: Apr-10 Oct **Site:** 3.5HEC **Facilities:**
Services: **Leisure:** L

Rocca

Loc S Pietro, 37011
045 7211111 045 7211300
e-mail: info@campinglarocca.com
web: www.campinglarocca.com
Slightly sloping grassland broken by rows of trees, separated from the lake by a public path (no cars). Part of site is on the other side of the main road, terraced among vines and olives with lovely view of lake.
dir: *Below SS249 at Km40/IV.*
Open: 26 Mar-4 Oct **Site:** 8HEC **Facilities:** **Services:** **Leisure:** L P **Off-site:**

BIBIONE VENEZIA

Villagio Turistico Internazionale

via Colonie 2, 30020
0431 442611 0431 442699
e-mail: info@vti.it
web: www.vti.it
Mostly sandy terrain under pine trees. Some meadowland with a few deciduous trees. Wide sandy beach. Leisure facilities include tennis court, swimming pool complex and direct access to a private beach.
dir: *Signed along approach road.*
GPS: 45.635, 13.0375
Open: 16 Apr-24 Sep **Site:** 15HEC
Prices: 19-59 **Facilities:** Wi-fi (charged) Kids' Club Play Area **Services:** **Leisure:** P S

CA'NOGHERA VENEZIA

Alba d'Oro

via Triestina 214G, 30030
041 5415102 041 5415971
e-mail: albadoro@ecvacanze.it
web: www.ecvacanze.it
On level ground directly on the lagoon with modern facilities including moorings for small boats. Regular bus service to Venice.
dir: *Off SS14.*
Open: 15 Apr-14 Nov **Site:** 7HEC **Facilities:** **Services:** **Leisure:** P R
Off-site: L S

ITALY

CAORLE — VENEZIA

Pra'delle Torri

viale Altanea 201, 30021
0421 299063 0421 299035
e-mail: info@pradelletorri.it
web: www.pradelletorri.it

Extensive site on flat ground.

dir: *3km W by beach.*

Site: 120HEC **Prices:** 16.40-43.80 Mobile home hire 404.60-1047.20 **Facilities:** Kids' Club Play Area **Services:** **Leisure:** P S

CA'SAVIO — VENEZIA

Ca'Savio

The Camping and Caravanning Club The Friendly Club

via di Ca'Savio 77, 30013
041 966017 041 5300707
e-mail: fuin@casavio.it
web: www.casavio.it

Flat site among trees next to beach.

C&CC Report *A large, well-equipped and very well run site, great for combining a lively beach holiday in a popular tourist area with visits to the marvel that is Venice, the famous glass-making island of Murano, or beyond. From here you arrive in Venice in best Marco Polo fashion – by sea, taking a ferry across the lagoon to St. Mark's Square.*

dir: *Jesolo-Punta Sabbione road, on left.*

Open: May-Sep **Site:** 26.8HEC **Prices:** 19.10-37.50 **Facilities:** Wi-fi Kids' Club Play Area **Services:** **Leisure:** P S **Off-site:**

CASSONE — VERONA

Bellavista

via Gardesana, 37018
045 7420244 045 7420244
e-mail: info@campingbellavistamalcesine.com
web: www.campingbellavistamalcesine.com

A fine position in an olive grove overlooking Lake Garda with modern sanitary installations. Access to the lake is by an underpass and water sports are available.

Open: All Year. **Site:** 27HEC **Facilities:** **Services:** **Leisure:** L **Off-site:** P R

CASTELLETTO DI BRENZONE — VERONA

Le Maior

via Croce N.10, 37010
045 7430333 045 7430333
e-mail: camplemaior@brenzone.com
web: www.campinglemaior.it

A comfortable, modern site in a pleasant, quiet location.

Open: Etr-29 Sep **Site:** 8HEC **Prices:** 26-31 **Facilities:** Wi-fi **Services:** **Off-site:** L

San Zeno

via A Vespucci 97, 37010
045 7430231 045 4430171
e-mail: info@campingsanzeno.it
web: www.campingsanzeno.it

Situated close to the lake and surrounded by hundred-year old olive groves.

dir: *Motorway exit Rovereto/Trento, continue S, site 10km S of Malcesine.*

Open: May-Sep **Site:** 1.4HEC **Prices:** 25-32 Mobile home hire 280-315 **Facilities:** **Services:** **Off-site:** L

CAVALLINO — VENEZIA

Cavallino

via delle Batterie 164, 30013
041 966133 041 5300827
e-mail: info@campingcavallino.com
web: www.baiaholiday.com

Set in a pine wood close to the sea with plenty of recreational facilities.

Open: Apr-22 Oct **Site:** 10.2HEC **Prices:** 19-44 Mobile home hire 252-693 **Facilities:** Wi-fi (charged) Kids' Club Play Area **Services:** **Leisure:** P S

Europa Camping Village

via Fausta 332, 30013
041 968069 041 5370150
e-mail: info@campingeuropa.com
web: www.campingeuropa.com

Located on the Cavallino coast, this family site has modern facilities. A kids' club is available from mid May to mid September.

dir: *Signed on Punta Sabbioni road.*

Open: 2 Apr-Sep **Site:** 11HEC **Prices:** 19.85-44.60 Mobile home hire 321.30-660.80 **Facilities:** Wi-fi (charged) Kids' Club Play Area **Services:** **Leisure:** P S **Off-site:**

Site 6HEC (site size) grass sand stone little shade partly shaded mainly shaded bungalows for hire (static) caravans for hire tents for hire no dogs site fully accessible for wheelchairs
Prices amount quoted is per night, for 2 adults and car, plus tent or caravan. Mobile home hire is a weekly rate.

taly

/ia Fausta 272, 30013
☎ 041 968090 🖷 041 5370076
-mail: info@campingitaly.it
veb: www.campingitaly.it
Small family site on a peninsula 6km from Lido di Jesolo. Venice an be reached by public ferry.
ir: *Brenner-Venezia motorway exit signs for Jesolo-Cavallino.*
pen: 21 Apr-18 Sep **Site:** 3.9HEC **acilities:** **Services:** **eisure:** P S **Off-site:**

Residence Village

via F-Baracca 47, 30013
☎ 041 968027 🖷 041 5370340
-mail: info@residencevillage.com
eb: www.residencevillage.com
Vell-laid out family site on level, wooded grassland. Located by a andy beach between Jesolo and Cavallino.
ir: *Signed.*
PS: 45.4805, 12.5744
pen: 14 May-18 Sep **Site:** 8.5HEC
rices: 19.10-40 **Facilities:** Wi-fi (charged) Kids' lub Play Area **Services:** **Leisure:** P S
ff-site: R

ant' Angelo

ia F-Baracca 63, 30013
☎ 041 968882 🖷 041 5370242
mail: info@santangelo.it
eb: www.santangelo.it
large beach site decorated by trees and flower beds. Good tertainment, sports and eating facilities.
r: *Outside Venice signs for Caposile & Jesolo, cross bridge just fter Lido di Jesolo & right to coast.*
pen: 6 May-24 Sep **Site:** 20HEC **Facilities:** **Services:** **Leisure:** P S

carpiland

a A-Poerio 14, 30013
☎ 041 966488 🖷 041 966488
mail: info@scarpiland.com
eb: www.scarpiland.com
beautiful location surrounded by a pine wood with sea views d direct access to the beach.
en: 24 Apr-18 Sep **Site:** 4.5HEC **Facilities:** **Services:** **Leisure:** S

Silva

via F-Baracca 53, 30013
☎ 041 968087 🖷 041 968087
e-mail: info@campingsilva.it
web: www.campingsilva.it
The site lies on sand and grassland and is located between road and beach, divided by a vineyard. The section of site near the beach is quiet.
Open: 6 May-19 Sep **Site:** 3.3HEC **Prices:** 16-33 Mobile home hire 175-455 **Facilities:** Play Area **Services:** **Leisure:** S **Off-site:** R

Union-Lido

via Fausta 258, 30013
☎ 041 2575111 🖷 041 5370355
e-mail: info@unionlido.com
web: www.unionlido.com
This large site lies on a long stretch of land next to a 1km-long beach. Separate section for tents and caravans. Ideal for families.
dir: *Motorway from Tarvisio via Udine, San Dona di Piave then signed to Jesolo & Cavallino.*
GPS: 45.4675, 12.5314
Open: 22 Apr-25 Sep **Site:** 60HEC **Prices:** 25.40-63.90 **Facilities:** Wi-fi (charged) Kids' Club Play Area **Services:** **Leisure:** P S

Villa al Mare

via del Faro 12, 30013
☎ 041 968066 🖷 041 5370576
e-mail: info@villaalmare.com
web: www.villaalmare.com
Level site divided into plots on a peninsula behind the lighthouse. Direct access to a long, sandy beach.
Open: Apr-Sep **Site:** 2.02HEC **Facilities:** **Services:** **Leisure:** P R S

CHIOGGIA **VENEZIA**

Miramare

via A-Barbarigo 103, 30015
☎ 041 490610 🖷 041 490610
e-mail: campmir@tin.it
web: www.miramarecamping.com
A peaceful site, divided into two parts, with a private beach. Sports facilities and entertainment for children in high season.
dir: *SS309 Strada Romeo towards Chioggia Sottomarina, turn right at beach, site 0.5km.*
GPS: 45.1903, 12.3033
Open: 20 Apr-19 Sep **Site:** 6HEC
Prices: 19.50-33.30 Mobile home hire 300-900 **Facilities:** Wi-fi (charged) Kids' Club Play Area **Services:** **Leisure:** P S **Off-site:**

Villaggio Turistico Isamar

via Isamar 9, Isolaverde, 30015
041 5535811 041 490440
e-mail: info@villaggioisamar.com
web: www.villaggioisamar.com

The site lies on level grassland at the mouth of the River Etsch. Shade is provided by high poplars. Good beach.

dir: *Off SS309. NB Caravans are advised to approach via Km84/VII near Brenta.*

Open: 15 May-10 Sep **Site:** 33HEC **Prices:** 15-45 Mobile home hire 350-1330 **Facilities:** Wi-fi (charged) Kids' Club Play Area **Services:** **Leisure:** P R S

CHIOGGIA SOTTOMARINA — VENEZIA

Oasi

via A-Barbarigo 147, 30019
041 5541145 041 490801
e-mail: info@campingoasi.com
web: www.campingoasi.com

A well-equipped site on a wooded peninsula near the mouth of the Brenta River with a wide private beach.

dir: *W of town centre towards river & beach.*

Open: 30 Mar-Sep **Site:** 3HEC **Prices:** 20.10-35.10 **Facilities:** Wi-fi Kids' Club Play Area **Services:** **Leisure:** P R S **Off-site:**

CISANO — VERONA

Camping Cisano

via Peschiera 52 CP 126, 37011
045 6229098 045 6229059
e-mail: cisano@camping-cisano.it
web: www.camping-cisano.it

Quiet, partly terraced site beside Lake Garda with good water sports and entertainment.

dir: *Brenner-Verona motorway exit AFFI, site 8km.*

Open: 26 Mar-8 Oct **Site:** 14HEC **Prices:** 18.10-41.10 Mobile home hire 280-770 **Facilities:** Kids' Club Play Area **Services:** **Leisure:** L P

San Vito

via Pralesi 3, 37011
045 6229026 045 6229059
e-mail: cisano@camping-cisano.it
web: www.camping-cisano.it

A tranquil and shady site with many modern facilities.

dir: *8km from Brenner motorway, exit signed AFFI.*

Open: 26 Mar-8 Oct **Site:** 5HEC **Prices:** 18.10-41.10 Mobile home hire 280-735 **Facilities:** Kids' Club Play Area **Services:** **Leisure:** L P

CORTINA D'AMPEZZO — BELLUNO

Cortina

via Campo 2, 32043
0436 867575 0436 867917
e-mail: campcortina@tin.it
web: www.campingcortina.it

This site lies among pine trees several hundred metres from the edge of town.

dir: *Off Dolomite road towards Belluno, site 1km by small river.*

Open: All Year. **Site:** 4.6HEC **Prices:** 18-25 **Facilities:** Wi-fi (charged) **Services:** **Leisure:** P R **Off-site:**

Dolomiti

via Campo di Sotto, 32043
0436 2485 0436 5403
e-mail: campeggiodolomiti@tin.it
web: www.campeggiodolomiti.it

The site is beautifully situated on grassland with pine trees in a hollow, not far from the Olympic ski jump.

dir: *2.7km S of Cortina. Off Dolomite road towards Belluno, site 1.5km.*

Open: Jun-19 Sep **Site:** 5.4HEC **Prices:** 18-24 **Facilities:** Play Area **Services:** **Leisure:** P R **Off-site:** L

Olympia

Fiames 1, 32043
0436 5057 0436 5057
e-mail: info@campingolympiacortina.it
web: www.campingolympiacortina.it

A very beautiful site set in the centre of the magnificent Dolomite landscape.

dir: *N of town off SS51.*

Open: 5 Dec-5 Nov **Site:** 4HEC **Facilities:** **Services:** **Leisure:** R **Off-site:** L P

Rocchetta

via Campo 1, 32043
0436 5063 0436 5063
e-mail: camping@sunrise.it
web: www.campingrocchetta.it

Set in beautiful wooded surroundings.

dir: *S from Cortina via SS51.*

GPS: 46.5225, 12.1342

Open: Jun-20 Sep & Dec-10 Apr **Site:** 2.5HEC **Prices:** 18-26 **Facilities:** Wi-fi (charged) Play Area **Services:** **Leisure:** R **Off-site:** L

ERACLEA MARE — VENEZIA

Portofelice

viale dei Fiori 15, 30020
0421 66411 0421 66021
-mail: info@portofelice.it
veb: www.portofelice.it

well-equipped family village site separated from the beach by a ine wood. A variety of recreational facilities is available.

ir: *A4 exit Venice/Mestre or San Donà di Piave, signs for Caorle & Eraclea Mare.*

PS: 45.5536, 12.7664

pen: 7 May-15 Sep **Site:** 17.5HEC **rices:** 15-44 **Facilities:** Wi-fi (charged) Kids' Club lay Area **Services:** **eisure:** P S **Off-site:** R

USINA VENEZIA — VENEZIA

'usina

ia Moranzani 79, 30030
041 5470055 041 5470050
-mail: info@campingfusina.com
eb: www.campingfusina.com

nis well-equipped site is ideal for those visiting Venice and the agoon.

PS: 45.4194, 12.2561

pen: All Year. **Site:** 5.5HEC **Prices:** 30.50-33 **acilities:** Wi-fi (charged) **Services:** **Leisure:** S

EMONA DEL FRIÚLI — UDINE

i Pioppi

a del Bersaglio 118, 33013
0432 980358
mail: bar-camping-taxi@aipioppi.it
eb: www.aipioppi.it

uiet, well-equipped site in a pleasant mountain setting.

r: *1km from town centre via N13.*

en: 15 Mar-30 Oct **Site:** 11HEC **Prices:** 17-22 **cilities:** Wi-fi (charged) **Services:** **f-site:** P R

GRADO — GORIZIA

Europa

34073
0431 80877 0431 82284
e-mail: info@villaggioeuropa.com
web: www.villaggioeuropa.com

Level terrain under half-grown poplars, and partly in pine forest.

dir: *On road to Monfalcone, 20km from Palmanova via Aquileia.*

GPS: 45.6967, 13.4550

Open: 22 Apr-25 Sep **Site:** 22HEC **Prices:** 21-40.50 **Facilities:** Kids' Club Play Area **Services:** **Leisure:** P S

Tenuta Primero

via Monfalcone 14, 34073
0431 896900 0431 896901
e-mail: info@tenuta-primero.com
web: www.tenuta-primero.com

The site lies in extensive level grassland between the road and the dam, which is 2m high along the narrow and level beach. Signed off Monfalcone road.

Open: 14 Apr-3 Oct **Site:** 20HEC **Prices:** 19-49 **Facilities:** Wi-fi (charged) Kids' Club Play Area **Services:** **Leisure:** P S

JÉSOLO, LIDO DI — VENEZIA

Malibu Beach

viale Oriente 78, 30017
0421 362212 0421 961338
e-mail: info@campingmalibubeach.com
web: www.campingmalibubeach.com

Set in a pine wood facing the sea and a fine sandy beach.

dir: *From Venezia via Cavallino on coast road to Cortellazzo.*

Open: 12 May-15 Sep **Site:** 10HEC **Facilities:** **Services:** **Leisure:** P S

Waikiki

viale Oriente 144, 30016
0421 980186 0421 378040
e-mail: info@campingwaikiki.com
web: www.campingwaikiki.com

A family site in a pine wood with direct access to the beach. Regular bus service to Venice passes the site.

Open: 14 May-18 Sep **Site:** 5.2HEC **Prices:** 17.95-34.90 Mobile home hire 41.50-80 **Facilities:** Wi-fi (charged) Kids' Club Play Area **Services:** **Leisure:** P S **Off-site:** R

Site 6HEC (site size) grass sand stone little shade partly shaded mainly shaded bungalows for hire (static) caravans for hire tents for hire no dogs site fully accessible for wheelchairs

Prices amount quoted is per night, for 2 adults and car, plus tent or caravan. Mobile home hire is a weekly rate.

AZISE VERONA

Camping La Quercia

7017
045 6470577 045 6470243
-mail: laquercia@laquercia.it
veb: www.laquercia.it
he site is divided into many large sections by tarred drives and es on terraced ground, sloping gently down to a lake. There is a arge private beach.
ir: *Off SS49 at Km31/8 & site 400m.*
pen: Apr-Sep **Site:** 20HEC **Facilities:** Vi-fi (charged) Kids' Club Play Area **Services:** eisure: L P **Off-site:**

see advert on opposite page

Parc

ia Gardesana 110, 37017
045 7580127 045 6470150
-mail: duparc@camping.it
veb: www.campingduparc.com
Vell-kept, lakeside site off main road.
ir: *From Garda, site on S side of Lazise just after turning for Verona.*
pen: 15 Mar-30 Oct **Site:** 6HEC **Facilities:** **Services:** **Leisure:** L P **Off-site:**

IGNANO SABBIADORO UDINE

Camping Sabbiadoro

ia Sabbiadoro 8, 33054
0431 71455 0431 721355
-mail: campsab@lignano.it
veb: www.campingsabbiadoro.it
tranquil site in a pine grove near the beach and the centre of ignano.
ir: *Via A4 Venice-Trieste (exit Latisana) onto S354.*
pen: 16 Apr-9 Oct **Site:** 13HEC **rices:** 21.60-39.10 **Facilities:** Wi-fi (charged) Kids' lub Play Area **Services:** **Leisure:** P **ff-site:** S

ALCESINE VERONA

Claudia

ardesana 394, 37018
045 7400786 045 7400786
-mail: info@campingclaudia.it
eb: www.campingclaudia.it
at grassy site only 30m from the lake. Excellent facilities, specially for water sports.
ir: *From Rome/Brenner motorway, continue via Trento, Arco & orbole, site on outskirts of Malcesine.*
pen: Apr-20 Oct **Site:** 1HEC **Facilities:** **ervices:** **Off-site:** L

MALGA CIAPELA BELLUNO

Malga Ciapela Marmolada

32020
0437 722064 0437 722064
e-mail: camping.mc.marmolada@dolomiti.com
A terraced site in tranquil wooded surroundings at the foot of Monte Marmolada.
dir: *Brenner-Verona motorway exit Bozen, signs for Canazei, Malga Ciapela & site at Marmolada.*
Open: Dec-25 Apr & Jun-20 Sep **Site:** 3HEC **Facilities:** **Services:** **Leisure:** R **Off-site:**

MASARÈ BELLUNO

Alleghe

32022
0437 723737 0437 723874
e-mail: alleghecamp@dolomites.com
web: www.camping.dolomiti.com/alleghe
Several terraces on a wooded incline below a road.
Open: 6 Dec-Apr & 14 Jun-29 Sep **Site:** 2HEC **Facilities:** **Services:** **Off-site:** L P

MONTEGROTTO TERME PADOVA

Sporting Center

35036
049 793400 049 8911551
e-mail: sporting@sportingcenter.it
web: www.sportingcenter.it
A peaceful site in a pleasant setting in the Euganean hills with good facilities including a thermal treatment centre.
Open: Mar-12 Nov **Site:** 6.5HEC **Facilities:** **Services:** **Leisure:** P **Off-site:**

ORIAGO VENEZIA

Serenissima

via Padana 334, 30034
041 920286 041 920286
e-mail: info@campingserenissima.it
web: www.campingserenissima.com
A well-looked after site with shade provided by the local woodland. Local bus service every 20 minutes to Venice.
dir: *A4 to Venice, SS11 at Oriago.*
Open: Etr-10 Nov **Site:** 2HEC **Prices:** 27-32 **Facilities:** Play Area **Services:** **Leisure:** R

ITALY

PACENGO VERONA

Camping Lido

via Peschiera 2, 37017
045 7590030 045 7590611
e-mail: info@campinglido.it
web: www.campinglido.it

Open: Apr-Oct **Site:** 10HEC **Facilities:** Wi-fi (charged) Kids' Club Play Area **Services:** **Leisure:** L P

PALAFAVERA BELLUNO

Palafavera

32010
0437 788506 0437 788857
e-mail: palafavera@sunrise.it
web: www.camping.dolomiti.com/palafavera

A beautiful location in the heart of the Dolomites at an altitude of 1514m. Modern sanitary installations and plenty of recreational facilities.

Open: Dec-Apr & Jun-Sep **Site:** 5HEC **Prices:** 16.50-24 **Facilities:** Play Area **Services:** **Leisure:** L P R **Off-site:** P

PESCHIERA DEL GARDA VERONA

Bella Italia

via Bella Italia 2, 37019
045 6400688 045 6401410
e-mail: info@camping-bellaitalia.it
web: www.camping-bellaitalia.it

Extensive lakeside site. No animals or motorcycles allowed. No credit cards accepted. Kids' club available for 4-10 year olds.

dir: *Off Brescia road between Km276.2 & Km275.8 towards lake.*

Open: 26 Mar-23 Oct **Site:** 30HEC **Facilities:** Kids' Club Play Area **Services:** **Leisure:** P **Off-site:** L R

Bergamini

Str Bergamini 51, Porto Bergamini, 37019
045 7550283 045 7550283
e-mail: info@campingbergamini.it
web: www.campingbergamini.it

Ideal for young families as site has two children's pools and extensive play areas.

dir: *Signs for Porto Bergamini.*

GPS: 45.4503, 10.6706

Open: May-20 Sep **Site:** 1.4HEC **Prices:** 30-42 **Facilities:** Kids' Club Play Area **Services:** **Leisure:** L P **Off-site:** R

San Benedetto

Str Bergamini 14, 37019
045 7550544 045 7551512
e-mail: info@campingsanbenedetto.it
web: www.campingsanbenedetto.it

A family site in a fine position overlooking the lake.

Open: 15 Mar-Sep **Site:** 22HEC **Facilities:** **Services:** **Leisure:** L P **Off-site:** R

PUNTA SABBIONI VENEZIA

Marina di Venezia

via Montello 6, 30013
041 5302511 041 966036
e-mail: camping@marinadivenezia.it
web: www.marinadivenezia.it

Extensive, well-organised and well-maintained holiday centre, extremely well-appointed, with ample shade by trees. A section of the site is designated for dog owners, caravans and tents.

dir: *Along coast road, 0.5km before end turn onto narrow asphalt road towards sea, signed.*

GPS: 45.4375, 12.4381

Open: 16 Apr-Sep **Site:** 70HEC **Prices:** 19.80-42.90 **Facilities:** Wi-fi (charged) Kids' Club Play Area **Services:** **Leisure:** P S

Miramare

Lungomare D-Alighieri 29, 30013
041 966150 041 5301150
e-mail: info@camping-miramare.it
web: www.camping-miramare.it

A magnificent location overlooking the lagoon.

Open: Apr-Nov **Site:** 1.8HEC **Facilities:** **Services:** **Off-site:** S

ROSOLINA MARE ROVIGO

Margherita

via Foci Adige 10, 45010
0426 68212 0426 329016

A well-equipped family site situated between the sea and a pine wood in the Po Delta Park.

Open: May-25 Sep **Site:** 6.4HEC **Facilities:** **Services:** **Leisure:** P R S

Rosapineta

Strada Nord 24, 45010
0426 68033 0426 68105
e-mail: info@rosapineta.it
web: www.rosapineta.com

The site lies in the grounds of an extensive holiday camp. Pitches for caravans and tents are separate. Dogs are accepted but restrictions apply.

dir: *Strada Romea towards Ravenna & over River Adige, 0.8km turn off, over bridge towards Rosolina Mare & Rosapineta (8km).*

GPS: 45.1389, 12.3236

Open: 12 May-17 Sep **Site:** 47HEC **Prices:** 23.20-34.70 Mobile home hire 115-462 **Facilities:** Wi-fi (charged) Kids' Club Play Area **Services:** **Leisure:** P S **Off-site:** R

SISTIANA — TRIESTE

Marepinetá

34019
040 299264 040 299265
e-mail: info@marepineta.com
web: www.baiaholiday.com

A modern site in a pleasant wooded location near the harbour and beach with a range of recreational facilities. Free bus service to the beach.

dir: *A4 exit Duino, 1km on SS14.*

Open: Apr-18 Oct **Site:** 10.8HEC **Facilities:** **Services:** **Leisure:** P **Off-site:** S

TREPORTI — VENEZIA

Camping Village Mediterráneo

via delle Batterie 38, Ca'Vio, 30013
041 966721 041 966944
e-mail: mediterraneo@vacanze-natura.it
web: www.campingmediterraneo.it

A family site with pitches near the beach or surrounded by pine trees.

dir: *Signed from Jesolo.*

GPS: 45.4542, 12.4814

Open: 18 Apr-28 Sep **Site:** 17HEC **Facilities:** Wi-fi (charged) Kids' Club Play Area **Services:** **Leisure:** P S **Off-site:** R

Ca' Pasquali Village

via Poerio 33, 30013
041 966110 041 5300797
e-mail: info@capasquali.it
web: www.capasquali.it

Sandy, meadowland site with poplar and pine trees.

dir: *Off Cavallino-Punta Sabbioni coast road onto asphalt road for 400m.*

GPS: 45.4525, 12.4901

Open: 21 Apr-24 Sep **Site:** 9.8HEC **Prices:** 16.90-48.40 Mobile home hire 127.50-940.80 **Facilities:** Wi-fi (charged) Kids' Club Play Area **Services:** **Leisure:** P S **Off-site:**

Fiori

via Vettor Pisani 52, 30013
041 966448 041 966724
e-mail: fiori@vacanze-natura.it
web: www.deifiori.it

The site stretches over a wide area of dunes and pine trees with separate sections for caravans and tents.

dir: *A4 from Venice onto coast road via Jesolo to Lido del Cavallino.*

GPS: 45.4494, 14.4494

Open: 21 Apr-Sep **Site:** 11HEC **Facilities:** Wi-fi (charged) **Services:** **Leisure:** P S

VICENZA — VICENZA

Vicenza

via U Scarpelli 35, 36100
0444 582311 0444 582434
e-mail: info@campingvicenza.it
web: www.ascom.vi.it/camping

A modern, well-equipped site.

dir: *A4 exit Vicenza-Est.*

Open: Apr-Sep **Site:** 3HEC **Prices:** 25.60-33.30 **Facilities:** Play Area **Services:** **Off-site:** R

ZOLDO ALTO — BELLUNO

Pala Favera

32010
0437 788506 0437 788857
e-mail: palafavera@sunrise.it
web: www.campingpalafavera.com

Site with some woodland, at the foot of Monte Pelmo.

Open: Dec-Apr & Jun-Sep **Site:** 5HEC **Prices:** 16.50-24 **Facilities:** Play Area **Services:** **Leisure:** R **Off-site:** P

Facilities shop shower electric points for razors electric points for caravans parking by tents permitted [illegible]…mpulsory separate car park **Services** café/restaurant bar Camping Gaz International gas other than Camping Gaz first aid facilities laundry **Leisure** swimming L-Lake P-Pool R-River S-Sea **Off-site** All facilities within 5km

NORTH WEST/MED COAST

ALBENGA — SAVONA

Bella Vista

Campochiesa, Reg Campore 23, 17031
☎ 0182 540213 🖷 0182 554925
e-mail: info@campingbellavista.it
web: www.campingbellavista.it
A friendly, family orientated site with good facilities. Pitches are divided by bushes and flowerbeds.
dir: *1km from Km613.5 on SS1.*
Open: 15 Mar-15 Oct **Site:** 1.4HEC **Facilities:** **Services:** **Leisure:** P **Off-site:** S

Roma

Regione Foce, 17031
☎ 0182 52317 🖷 0182 555075
e-mail: info@campingroma.com
web: www.campingroma.com
The site is divided into pitches and laid out with many flower beds.
dir: *N of bridge over Centa, turn left.*
Open: Apr-29 Sep **Site:** 1HEC **Prices:** 22-35 **Facilities:** Play Area **Services:** **Leisure:** R S **Off-site:** P

ALBINIA — GROSSETO

Acapulco

via Aurelia Km155, 58010
☎ 0564 870165 🖷 0564 870165
e-mail: info@campeggioacapulco.com
web: www.campeggioacapulco.com
Set on hilly terrain in pine woodland.
dir: *Off via Aurelia at Km155 onto coast road.*
Open: May-14 Sep **Site:** 2HEC **Facilities:** **Services:** **Leisure:** S

Hawaii

58010
☎ 0564 870164
e-mail: info@campinghawaii.it
web: www.campinghawaii.it
The site lies in a pine forest on rather hilly ground.
dir: *Off via Aurelia at Km154/V towards sea.*
Open: 16 Apr-27 Sep **Site:** 4HEC **Facilities:** **Services:** **Leisure:** S

BIBBONA, MARINA DI — LIVORNO

Camping Casa di Caccia

via del Mare 40, 57020
☎ 0586 600000 🖷 0586 600000
e-mail: info@campingcasadicaccia.com
web: www.campingcasadicaccia.com
A tranquil site by the sea, with direct access to a private beach and pitches nestled amongst pine trees. A kids' club is available in high season.
dir: *A12 exit Rosignano, SS1 direction Grosseto, exit La California, site 4km; From Rome SS1 direction Livorno, exit Donoratico, site 8km.*
Open: 2 Apr-Oct **Site:** 3.5HEC **Prices:** 19.50-43.50 Mobile home hire 210-1200 **Facilities:** Wi-fi (charged) Kids' Club Play Area **Services:** **Leisure:** S

Capanne

via Aurelia KM.273, 57020
☎ 0586 600064 🖷 0586 600198
e-mail: info@campinglecapanne.it
web: www.campinglecapanne.it
A pleasant family site set in a spacious wooded park in magnificent Tuscan scenery. Defined pitches and a variety of recreational facilities.
dir: *Access from Km273 via Aurelia travelling inland.*
Open: 22 Apr-25 Sep **Site:** 6HEC **Prices:** 21.60-43 **Facilities:** Kids' Club Play Area **Services:** **Leisure:** P **Off-site:** L S

Capannino

via Cavalleggeri Sud 26, 57020
☎ 0586 600252 🖷 0586 600720
e-mail: capannino@capannino.it
web: www.capannino.it
Well-tended park site in pine woodland with private beach.
dir: *Off via Aurelia at Km272/VII towards sea.*
Open: 22 Apr-18 Sep **Site:** 3HEC **Prices:** 28.50-47 **Facilities:** Wi-fi (charged) Play Area **Services:** **Leisure:** S **Off-site:** P

Forte

via dei Platani 58, 57020
☎ 0586 600155 🖷 0586 600123
e-mail: campeggiodelforte@campeggiodelforte.it
web: www.campeggiodelforte.it
Level site, grassy, sandy terrain.
dir: *SS1 direction Grosseto, exit La California, take SS Aurelia direction San Vicenzo, after 2km right to Marina di Bibbona.*
GPS: 43.2344, 10.5349
Open: 23 Apr-18 Sep **Site:** 8HEC **Facilities:** Kids' Club Play Area **Services:** **Leisure:** P **Off-site:** S

Site 6HEC (site size) grass sand stone little shade partly shaded mainly shaded bungalows for hire (static) caravans for hire tents for hire no dogs site fully accessible for wheelchairs
Prices amount quoted is per night, for 2 adults and car, plus tent or caravan. Mobile home hire is a weekly rate.

Free Beach

via Cavalleggeri Nord 88, 57020
0586 600388 0586 602984
e-mail: info@campingfreebeach.it
web: www.campingfreebeach.it
Situated 300m from the sea through pine woods.

dir: *From SS206 at Cecina signs to S Guido.*

Open: 22 Apr-19 Sep **Site:** 9HEC **Prices:** 24-40 **Facilities:** Wi-fi Play Area **Services:** **Leisure:** P **Off-site:** S

Il Gineprino

via dei Platani,56a, 57020
0586 600550 0586 636866
e-mail: info@ilgineprino.it
web: www.ilgineprino.it
A modern site situated on the Tuscany coast and shaded by a pine wood. There are good recreational facilities and the beach is within 700m. Cars parked by tents in low season. A kids' club is available during high season.

dir: *Motorway exit La California for Marina di Bibbona.*

Open: Apr-Sep **Site:** 1.5HEC **Prices:** 22-34.50 Mobile home hire 170-600 **Facilities:** Kids' Club Play Area **Services:** **Leisure:** P **Off-site:** S

BOGLIASCO — GENOVA

Genova Est

via Marconi, Cassa, 16031
010 3472053 010 3472053
e-mail: info@camping-genova-est.it
web: www.camping-genova-est.it
Quiet and shady site 1km from the sea. A free bus service operates from the site to the railway station for links to Genoa and Portofino.

dir: *A12 exit Nervi, 8km E.*

GPS: 44.3807, 9.0723

Open: 15 Mar-20 Oct **Site:** 1.2HEC **Prices:** 20.50-23.20 Mobile home hire 224-252 **Facilities:** Wi-fi **Services:** **Off-site:** P S

BOTTAI — FIRENZE

Internazionale Firenze

via S Cristoforo 2, 50029
055 2374704 055 2373412
e-mail: internazionale@florencecamping.it
web: www.campingflorence.com
Situated on the Florentine hills, the site offers a restful atmosphere close to many historic places.

Open: Apr-29 Oct **Site:** 6HEC **Facilities:** **Services:** **Leisure:** P **Off-site:** L R

CAPANNOLE — AREZZO

Chiocciola

via G-Cesare 14, 52020
055 995776 055 995776
web: www.campinglachiocciola.com
A modern site in a rural setting among chestnut trees at an altitude of 250m.

Open: Mar-1 Nov **Site:** 3HEC **Facilities:** **Services:** **Leisure:** P **Off-site:** L R

CASALE MARITTIMO — PISA

Valle Gaia

via Cecinese 87, 56040
0586 681236 0586 683551
e-mail: info@vallegaia.it
web: www.vallegaia.it
Site among pines and olive trees in a quiet rural location.

dir: *Autostrada/superstrada exit Casale Marittimo for Cecina, site signed.*

Open: 27 Mar-9 Oct **Site:** 4HEC **Facilities:** **Services:** **Leisure:** P **Off-site:**

CASTAGNETO CARDUCCI — LIVORNO

Climatico Le Pianacce

via Bolgherese, 57022
0565 763667 0565 766085
e-mail: info@campinglepianacce.it
web: www.campinglepianacce.it
Terraced site on slopes of mountain in typical Tuscany landscape, enhanced by site landscaping. Pleasant climate due to height.

dir: *Off via Aurelia at Km344/VIII towards Castagneto Carducci/ Sassetta, 3.2km left for Bolgheri, 0.5km right towards mountains.*

Open: 23 Apr-26 Sep **Site:** 9HEC **Facilities:** **Services:** **Leisure:** P

CASTEL DEL PIANO — GROSSETO

Amiata

via Roma 15, 58033
0564 955107 0564 955107
e-mail: info@amiata.org
web: www.amiata.org
A grassland site with a separate section for dog owners.

Open: All Year. **Site:** 4.2HEC **Prices:** 16.50-22.80 **Facilities:** Play Area **Services:** **Off-site:** P

ITALY

CASTIGLIONE DELLA PESCAIA — GROSSETO

Santa Pomata

Strada della Rocchette, 58043
0564 941037 0564 941221
e-mail: info@campingsantapomata.it
web: www.campingsantapomata.it
Site in hilly woodland terrain with some pitches among bushes. Flat clean sandy beach.
dir: *Off SS322 at Km20 towards Le Rocchette 4.5km NW, continue to sea, site 1km on left.*
Open: 20 Apr-20 Oct **Site:** 6HEC **Facilities:** **Services:** **Leisure:** S

CERIALE — SAVONA

Baciccia

via Torino 19, 17023
0182 990743 0182 993839
e-mail: info@campingbaciccia.it
web: www.campingbaciccia.it
An orderly site, lying inland off the via Aurelia, 0.5km from the sea.
dir: *Entrance 100m W of Km612/V.*
Open: 20 Mar-5 Nov & Dec-10 Jan **Site:** 1.5HEC **Facilities:** **Services:** **Leisure:** P
Off-site: S

CERVO — IMPERIA

Lino

via N Sauro 4, 18010
0183 400087 0183 400089
e-mail: info@campinglino.it
web: www.campinglino.com
A clean, well-managed seaside site shaded by grape vines. There is a knee-deep lagoon suitable for children.
dir: *Off via Aurelia at Km637/V near railway underpass onto via Nazionale Sauro towards sea.*
GPS: 43.9239, 8.1081
Open: All Year. **Site:** 1.1HEC **Facilities:** Wi-fi (charged) Play Area **Services:**
Leisure: P S **Off-site:**

CUTIGLIANO — PISTOIA

Betulle

via Cantamaggio 6, 51024
0573 68004 0573 68004
e-mail: info@campeggiolebetulle.it
web: www.campeggiolebetulle.it
A pleasant year-round site with good facilities in a central location with access to three popular ski stations.
Open: All Year. **Site:** 4HEC **Prices:** 20.50
Facilities: **Services:**
Leisure: L R **Off-site:** P

DEIVA MARINA — LA SPEZIA

La Sfinge

Gea 5, 19013
0187 825464 0187 825464
e-mail: lasfinge@camping.it
web: www.campinglasfinge.com
Partly terraced site in pleasant wooded surroundings. Ideal for both nature lovers and families.
dir: *Via A12 Genova-La Spezia.*
Open: All Year. **Site:** 1.8HEC **Facilities:** **Services:** **Leisure:** R S

Villaggio Turistico Arenella

Arenella, 19013
0187 825259 0187 826884
e-mail: info@campingarenella.it
web: www.campingarenella.it
Set in a beautiful quiet valley 1.5km from the sea with good facilities.
dir: *Via A12 Genoa-La Spezia.*
Open: Dec-Oct **Site:** 16.2HEC **Prices:** 22-33
Facilities: Wi-fi (charged) **Services:**
Off-site: S

DONORATICO — LIVORNO

Continental

via I Maggio, Marina di Castagneto, 57024
0565 744014 0565 744168
e-mail: info@campingcontinental.it
web: www.campingcontinental.it
Situated directly on a blue flag beach within an ancient pine forest.
Open: Apr-Sep **Site:** 6.5HEC **Facilities:**
Services: **Leisure:** S

LACONA ELBA, ISOLA D'

Lacona Pineta

Lacona CP 186, 57037
0565 964322 0565 964087
e-mail: info@campinglaconapineta.com
web: www.campinglaconapineta.com

A picturesque location on a thickly wooded hillside sloping gently towards a sandy beach, with plenty of recreational facilities.

Open: Apr-Oct **Site:** 4HEC **Facilities:** **Services:** **Leisure:** P S

NISPORTO ELBA, ISOLA D'

Sole e Mare

57039
0565 934907 0565 961180
e-mail: info@soleemare.it
web: www.soleemare.it

A well-equipped, modern site in pleasant wooded surroundings close to the beach. A variety of recreational facilities is available.

Open: Apr-15 Oct **Site:** 2HEC **Facilities:** Wi-fi (charged) Kids' Club Play Area **Services:** **Leisure:** S

OTTONE ELBA, ISOLA D'

Rosselba le Palme

Loc Ottone 3, 57037
0565 933101 0565 933041
e-mail: info@rosselbalepalme.it
web: www.rosselbalepalme.it

Pitches are on varying heights up from the beach. Shade is provided by large palm trees.

dir: *8km from Portoferraio around bay via Bivo Bagnaia.*

Open: 25 Apr-18 Oct **Site:** 30HEC **Facilities:** **Services:** **Leisure:** P S

PORTO AZZURRO ELBA, ISOLA D'

Reale

57036
0565 95678 0565 920127
e-mail: campingreale@tin.it
web: www.isolaelbacampingreale.com

A well-equipped site in a wooded location with direct access to the beach.

dir: *From Portoferraio towards Porto Azzurro for 13km, towards Rio Marina for 2km & signed.*

Open: Apr-30 Oct **Site:** 2HEC **Prices:** 26.50-43 **Facilities:** Play Area **Services:** **Leisure:** S **Off-site:** P

PORTOFERRAIO ELBA, ISOLA D'

Acquaviva

Acquaviva, 57037
0565 919103 0565 915592
e-mail: campingacquaviva@elbalink.it
web: www.campingacquaviva.it

This seafront site is surrounded by trees and has excellent facilities for scuba diving and water sports. Cars may be parked by tents in low season only.

dir: *3km W of town.*

Open: Etr-Oct **Site:** 2HEC **Prices:** 24.50-51 Mobile home hire 189-805 **Facilities:** (charged) Play Area **Services:** **Leisure:** S **Off-site:**

Enfola

Enfola, Casella Postale 147, 57037
0565 939001 0565 918613
e-mail: info@campingenfola.it
web: www.campingenfola.it

Located on the Isle of Elba, ideal for scuba-diving and sailing.

Open: Etr-Oct **Site:** 0.8HEC **Facilities:** **Services:** **Off-site:** S

Scaglieri

via Biodola 1, 57037
0565 969940 0565 969834
e-mail: info@campingscaglieri.it
web: www.campingscaglieri.it

Sloping terraces 10m from the sea make up this site. Facilities such as tennis and golf are avaliable at the nearby Hotel Hermitage.

dir: *Island accessable by plane & ferry. Site on N coast 7km from Portoferraio.*

Open: 10 Apr-20 Oct **Site:** 1.7HEC **Prices:** 27-63 **Facilities:** Wi-fi (charged) Kids' Club Play Area **Services:** **Leisure:** P **Off-site:** S

FIÉSOLE FIRENZE

Panoramico

via Peramonda 1, 50014
055 599069 055 59186
e-mail: panoramico@florencecamping.com
web: www.florencecamping.com

Site stretches over wide terraces on the Fiésole hillside surrounded by tall evergreens. There is a free shuttle bus to Fiésole.

dir: *A1 exit Firenze Sud, signs through city to Fiésole, site on SS Bolognese.*

Open: All Year. **Site:** 5HEC **Prices:** 30-35 **Facilities:** Wi-fi (charged) **Services:** **Leisure:** P **Off-site:**

ITALY

FIGLINE VALDARNO FIRENZE

Norcenni Girasole Club

The Camping and Caravanning Club The Friendly Club

via Norcenni 7, 50063
☎ 055 915141 🖷 055 9151402
e-mail: girasole@ecvacanze.it
web: www.ecvacanze.it

Terraced site on partial slope. Kids' club available in high season.

C&CC Report *Large, lively, popular site with superb facilities, excursions and activities, yet a family atmosphere and traditional style still permeate this beautiful Tuscan hillside location. You can count on terrific holidays for families of all ages, but this is also a wonderful low season base for discovering the real Tuscany.*

dir: *A1 exit onto road 69 for Figline, right for Greve & signed.*

GPS: 43.6133, 11.4494

Open: 16 Apr-9 Oct **Site:** 15HEC **Facilities:** Wi-fi (charged) Kids' Club Play Area **Services:** **Leisure:** P **Off-site:**

FIRENZE (FLORENCE)

See **TROGHI**

GROSSETO, MARINA DI GROSSETO

Le Marze

Strada Provinciale 158, 58046
☎ 0564 35501 🖷 0564 744503
e-mail: lemarze@boschettoholiday.it
web: www.boschettoholiday.it/lemarze
dir: *Via SS322.*

Open: Apr-3 Sep **Site:** 20HEC **Prices:** 21.60-42.10 **Facilities:** Wi-fi (charged) Kids' Club Play Area **Services:** **Leisure:** P R S

Rosmarina

via delle Colonie 37, 58100
☎ 0564 36319 🖷 0564 34758
e-mail: info@campingrosmarina.it
web: www.campingrosmarina.it

A modern site in a pine wood close to the sea. Beautiful views, and various sports and entertainment for everyone.

Open: Apr-Sep **Site:** 1.4HEC **Prices:** 19-42 **Facilities:** **Services:** **Leisure:** S

LERICI LA SPEZIA

Maralunga

via Carpanini 61, Maralunga, 19032
☎ 0187 966589 🖷 0187 966589
e-mail: info@campeggiomaralunga.it

This terraced site is directly on the seafront and surrounded by olive groves.

dir: *Access from Sarzana-La Spezia motorway.*

Open: Jun-Sep **Site:** 1HEC **Facilities:** **Services:** **Leisure:** S **Off-site:** P

LIMITE FIRENZE

San Giusto

via Castra 71, 50050
☎ 055 8712304 🖷 055 8711856
e-mail: info@campingsangiusto.it
web: www.campingsangiusto.it

A useful site on slightly sloping ground within easy reach of Florence, Pisa, Siena and Lucca by car or public transport.

Open: Etr-Oct **Site:** 7.3HEC **Prices:** 20.50-28 Mobile home hire 143.50-238 **Facilities:** Wi-fi (charged) Play Area **Services:** **Leisure:** P **Off-site:** L R

MARCIALLA FIRENZE

Panorama del Chianti

via Marcialla 349, Certaldo, 50020
☎ 0571 669334 🖷 0571 669334
e-mail: info@campingchianti.it
web: www.campingchianti.it

A sloping, terraced site with good facilities, surrounded by vineyards and olive groves. There is a charge for wi-fi from 10 July to 20 August.

dir: *Autostrada del Sole exit Firenze-Certosa. Or Autostrada del Palio exit Tavarnelle Valpesa.*

Open: 15 Mar-15 Oct **Site:** 2.17HEC **Prices:** 25.50-29.50 Mobile home hire 270-300 **Facilities:** Wi-fi Play Area **Services:** **Leisure:** P **Off-site:** L

MASSA, MARINA DI MASSA CARRARA

Giardino

viale delle Pinete 382, 54100
☎ 0585 869291 🖷 0585 240781
e-mail: info@campinggiardino.it
web: www.campinggiardino.com

Site in pine woodland and on two meadows, shade provided by roof matting.

dir: *On island side of SS328 to Pisa.*

Open: Apr-Sep **Site:** 3.2HEC **Facilities:** **Services:** **Leisure:** P **Off-site:** S

IONÉGLIA GENOVA

'illaggio Smeraldo

'reata, 16030
☎ 0185 49375 🖷 0185 490484
-mail: info@villaggiosmeraldo.it
'eb: www.villaggiosmeraldo.it

pleasant site in a pine wood overlooking the sea with modern acilities and direct access to the beach.

ir: *Via A12/SS1.*

pen: All Year. **Site:** 1.5HEC **Facilities:** **ervices:** **Leisure:** S

IONTECATINI TERME PISTOIA

elsito

ia delle Vigne 1/A, Vico, 51016
☎ 0572 67373 🖷 0572 67373
-mail: info@campingbelsito.it
eb: www.campingbelsito.it

quiet site at an altitude of 250m with good sized pitches.

pen: Apr-Sep **Site:** 6HEC **Prices:** 24.50-34.50 **acilities:** Wi-fi (charged) Play Area **ervices:** **Leisure:** P

IONTERIGGIONI SIENA

uxor Quies

oc Trasqua, 53032
☎ 0577 743047 🖷 0577 743131
mail: info@luxorcamping.com
eb: www.luxorcamping.com

es on a flat-topped hill, partly in an oak wood, partly in eadowland.

r: *Off SS2 at Km239/II or Km238/IX, site 2.5km over railway ne. Very steep & winding road to site.*

PS: 43.3997, 11.2484

en: 21 May-11 Sep **Site:** 1.5HEC **Prices:** 27.90 **cilities:** Play Area **Services:** **isure:** P

MONTESCUDÁIO LIVORNO

Montescudáio

via del Poggetto, 56040
☎ 0586 683477 🖷 0586 630932
e-mail: info@camping-montescudaio.it
web: www.camping-montescudaio.it

This modern site on a hill is divided into individual pitches, some of which are naturally screened.

dir: *From SS1 via Aurelia at Cecinia towards Guardistallo for 2.5km.*

Open: 13 May-15 Sep **Site:** 25HEC **Prices:** 23.50-40 Mobile home hire 321-987 **Facilities:** Wi-fi **Services:** **Leisure:** P S **Off-site:**

MONTICELLO AMIATA GROSSETO

Lucherino

Lucherino, 58044
☎ 0564 992975 🖷 0564 992975
e-mail: info@campinglucherino.net
web: www.campinglucherino.net

A peaceful site 735m above sea level on the slopes of Monte Amiata. The shady but sloping site is ideal for walkers and historians.

dir: *SS223 to Paganico then signs to Monte Amiata.*

Open: May-Sep **Site:** 2HEC **Prices:** 18-33 Mobile home hire 294-420 **Facilities:** Wi-fi (charged) Play Area **Services:** **Leisure:** P **Off-site:** R

PEGLI GENOVA

Villa Doria

via al Campeggio 15n, 16156
☎ 010 6969600 🖷 010 6969600
e-mail: villadoria@camping.it
web: www.camping.it/liguria/villadoria

Quiet site in pleasant wooded surroundings.

dir: *Signed via SS1.*

Open: 7 Feb-7 Jan **Site:** 0.45HEC **Prices:** 31 **Facilities:** Wi-fi (charged) **Services:** **Off-site:** S

ITALY

PISA — PISA

Camping Village Torre Pendente

viale della Cascine 86, 56122
050 561704 050 561734
e-mail: info@campingtorrependente.it
web: www.campingtorrependente.it

Pleasant, modern site with spacious pitches on level ground in a rural setting. 1km walk to the Leaning Tower and ideal for visiting the ancient city centre. Kids' club in high season.

dir: *SS12 from Lucca to Pisa, continue N with town on left for 1km, site on right.*

GPS: 43.7242, 10.3831

Open: Apr-15 Oct **Site:** 2.5HEC **Prices:** 29-33.50 **Facilities:** Wi-fi (charged) Kids' Club Play Area **Services:** **Leisure:** P **Off-site:** R

SAN BARONTO — FIRENZE

Barco Reale

via Nardini 11, San Baronto, 51035
0573 88332 0573 856003
e-mail: info@barcoreale.com
web: www.barcoreale.com

A well-equipped site in a hilly, wooded location.

dir: *Signed from Lamporecchio.*

Open: Apr-Sep **Site:** 10HEC **Facilities:** Wi-fi (charged) Kids' Club Play Area **Services:** **Leisure:** P

SAN GIMIGNANO — SIENA

Boschetto di Piemma

Santa Lucia, 53037
0577 940352 0577 907453
e-mail: info@boschettodipiemma.it
web: www.boschettodipiemma.it

This small grassy site is well-equipped and has many facilities for both families and individuals. Kids' club available in July and August.

Open: Apr-Oct **Site:** 6HEC **Facilities:** Kids' Club Play Area **Services:** **Leisure:** P **Off-site:**

SAN GIOVANNI D'ASSO — SIENA

San Giovanni D'Asso

SP14 Traversa dei Monti, 53020
0340 3664359
e-mail: enquiries@camptuscany.co.uk
web: www.camptuscany.co.uk

Small, quiet site with level pitches among attractive hills and surrounded by tall trees which offer some shade. Individual pitches marked out by potted flowers and shrubs.

Open: 26 Apr-26 Sep **Site:** 0.65HEC **Facilities:** **Services:** **Off-site:**

SAN PIERO A SIEVE — FIRENZE

Village Mugello Verde

via Massorondinaio 39, 50037
055 848511 055 8486910
e-mail: mugelloverde@florencecamping.com
web: www.florencecamping.com

Terraced site in wooded surroundings.

dir: *Motorway exit 18 & signed.*

Open: All Year. **Site:** 12HEC **Prices:** 21-29 **Facilities:** Wi-fi (charged) Play Area **Services:** **Leisure:** P **Off-site:** L R

SAN VINCENZO — LIVORNO

Park Albatros

The Camping and Caravanning Club — The Friendly Club

Pineta di Torre Nuova, 57027
0565 701018 0565 701400
e-mail: parkalbatros@ecvacanze.it
web: www.ecvacanze.it

The site lies among beautiful tall pine trees, 1km from the sea. Kids' club available for 4-11 year olds.

C&CC Report *An ideal site for those who like to combine lazy days on the beach with visits to the fascinating towns and cities of Tuscany. The great range of facilities, including the extensive pool complex, makes it difficult to leave the site. For the more adventurous why not try a day trip to the beautiful island of Elba, last home of the exiled Napoleon Bonaparte.*

dir: *Off SP23 beyond San Vincenzo at Km7/III & continue 0.6km inland.*

Open: 22 Apr-18 Sep **Site:** 30HEC **Prices:** 11.50-20.90 **Facilities:** (charged) Kids' Club Play Area **Services:** **Leisure:** P **Off-site:** S

Site 6HEC (site size) grass sand stone little shade partly shaded mainly shaded bungalows for hire (static) caravans for hire tents for hire no dogs site fully accessible for wheelchairs
Prices amount quoted is per night, for 2 adults and car, plus tent or caravan. Mobile home hire is a weekly rate.

SARTEANO — SIENA

Parco delle Piscine

via del Bagno Santo 29, 53047
☎ 0578 26971 📠 0578 265889
e-mail: info@parcodellepiscine.it
web: www.parcodellepiscine.it

A well shaded location on a plateau surrounded by hills. The three pools on the site are fed by mineral rich spring water. A kids' club is available in July and August.

dir: *A1 exit 29 Chiusi-Chianciano terme. Follow signs to Sarteano for 5km. Cross main square, follow main road, site on left.*

Open: Apr-Sep **Site:** 15HEC **Prices:** 34-55 **Facilities:** Wi-fi (charged) Kids' Club Play Area **Services:** **Leisure:** P

SARZANA — LA SPEZIA

Iron Gate

Via XXV Aprile 54, 19038
☎ 0187 676370 📠 0187 675014
e-mail: info@marina3b.it

A modern site with good facilities attached to the Iron Gate marina.

Open: All Year. **Site:** 2HEC **Facilities:** **Services:** **Leisure:** P R **Off-site:**

SAVIGNANO MARE — FORLI

Camping Village Rubicone

Via Matrice Destra 1, 47039
☎ 0541 346377 📠 0541 346999
e-mail: info@campingrubicone.com
web: www.campingrubicone.com

Located on the sea front, this large site has direct access to a sandy beach.

dir: *A14 from Bologna, exit Rimini Nord, then SS16 direction Ravenna, exit Savignano Mare.*

GPS: 43.1630, 12.4433

Open: 21 May-18 Sep **Site:** 13HEC **Prices:** 21.60-37.80 **Facilities:** Wi-fi (charged) Kids' Club Play Area **Services:** **Leisure:** P R S **Off-site:**

SIENA — SIENA

Camping Siena Colleverde

Strada di Scacciapensieri 47, 53100
☎ 0577 334080 📠 0577 334005
e-mail: info@sienacamping.com
web: www.sienacamping.com

The site offers both large areas for caravans and mobile homes and a large grassy area for tents. There is a local bus service to the centre of Siena.

GPS: 43.3375, 11.3306

Open: Mar-Dec **Site:** 5HEC **Prices:** 33.70-35 Mobile home hire 315-805 **Facilities:** Wi-fi (charged) Play Area **Services:** **Leisure:** P **Off-site:**

Montagnola

Sovicille, 53018
☎ 0577 314473 📠 0577 314473
e-mail: montagnolacamping@libero.it

Quiet site in an oak wood with individual plots separated by hedges. Facilities are modern and extensive.

dir: *A1 W exit Siena, site signed towards Sovicille.*

Open: Etr-29 Sep **Site:** 2.5HEC **Facilities:** **Services:** **Off-site:**

Le Soline

Casciano di Murlo, 53016
☎ 0577 817410 📠 0577 817415
e-mail: camping@lesoline.it
web: www.camping.it/toscana/lesoline

Terraced hilly site surrounded by woodland with a variety of sports facilities and family entertainment.

dir: *Via SS223.*

GPS: 43.1552, 11.3323

Open: All Year. **Site:** 6HEC **Prices:** 15-23.50 **Facilities:** Wi-fi Play Area **Services:** **Leisure:** P

STELLA SAN GIOVANNI — SAVONA

Dolce Vita

via Rio Basco 62, 17044
☎ 019 703269 📠 019 703269
e-mail: campingdolcevita@libero.it
web: www.campingdolcevita.it

Wooded surroundings with well-defined pitches, 5.5km from the coast.

dir: *Via SS334.*

GPS: 44.3856, 8.5022

Open: All Year. **Site:** 10HEC **Prices:** 26-31 **Facilities:** Wi-fi Play Area **Services:** **Leisure:** P **Off-site:** S

ITALY

ITALY

TORRE DEL LAGO PUCCINI LUCCA

Burlamacco

viale G-Marconi Int, 55048
0584 359544 0584 359387
e-mail: info@campingburlamacco.com
web: www.campingburlamacco.com

A beautiful wooded location 1km from the sea on the Versilia Riviera, close to the former home of Puccini. A variety of facilities are available.

Open: Apr-Sep **Site:** 4.5HEC **Prices:** 19.30-30.30 Mobile home hire 210-280 **Facilities:** Play Area **Services:** **Leisure:** P **Off-site:** L S

Camping Italia

52 viale dei Tigli, 55048
0584 359828 0584 341504
e-mail: info@campingitalia.net
web: www.campingitalia.net

This site is divided into pitches and lies in meadowland planted with poplar trees. A kids' club is available during July and August.

dir: *Inland off Viareggio road (viale dei Tigli).*

Open: 20 Apr-23 Sep **Site:** 9HEC **Prices:** 15.50-30.50 **Facilities:** Wi-fi (charged) Kids' Club Play Area **Services:** **Leisure:** P **Off-site:** L S

Europa

viale dei Tigli, 55049
0584 350707 0584 342592
e-mail: info@europacamp.it
web: www.europacamp.it

Site in pine and poplar woodland. A kids' club is available in June, July and August.

dir: *From Viareggio, on land side of Viale dei Tigli.*

Open: 9 Apr-15 Oct **Site:** 60HEC **Prices:** 17-39 **Facilities:** Wi-fi (charged) Kids' Club Play Area **Services:** **Leisure:** P **Off-site:** R S

Tigli

viale dei Tigli, 54, 55049
0584 341278 0584 341278
e-mail: info@campingdeitigli.com
web: www.campingdeitigli.com

Shady site close to a Regional Park, Lake Massaciuccoli, and the villa where Puccini wrote much of his music.

Open: Apr-Sep **Site:** 9HEC **Prices:** 20-35 **Facilities:** **Services:** **Leisure:** P **Off-site:** L S

TROGHI FIRENZE

Camping Village "Il Poggetto"

Strada Provinciale 1, 50067
055 8307323 055 8307323
e-mail: info@campingilpoggetto.com
web: www.campingilpoggetto.com

A modern site with good facilities. Large, level, grassy pitches.

dir: *A1 exit Incisa Valdarno, site 5km.*

Open: Apr-15 Oct **Site:** 4.5HEC **Prices:** 28-34 **Facilities:** Wi-fi (charged) **Services:** **Leisure:** P **Off-site:** L

VADA LIVORN

Fiori

Loc Campo di Fiori 4, 57018
0586 770096 0586 770323
e-mail: campofiori@multinet.it
web: www.campingcampodeifiori.it

Level grassland surrounded by fields, with trees providing a good deal of shade.

dir: *A12 to Rosignano.*

Open: 23 Apr-25 Sep **Site:** 15HEC **Prices:** 19.50-36 **Facilities:** Play Area **Services:** **Leisure:** P **Off-site:** S

VIAREGGIO LUCC

Camping Pineta SRL

via dei Lecci 107, 55049
0584 383397
e-mail: campinglapineta@interfree.it
web: www.campinglapineta.com

A well-organised site in a wooded location, 1km from a private beach. Dogs not permitted in July and August.

dir: *Via SSN1 between Km354 & Km355.*

Open: Apr-25 Sep **Site:** 3.2HEC **Prices:** 16.50-34.50 **Facilities:** **Services:** **Leisure:** P **Off-site:** S

Viareggio

via Comparini 1, 55049
0584 391012 0584 391012
e-mail: info@campingviareggio.it
web: www.campingviareggio.it

The site lies in a poplar wood 0.7km from the beach.

dir: *1.5km S of town. From Km354/V towards coast.*

Open: Apr-Sep **Site:** 3HEC **Prices:** 18-33 **Facilities:** Wi-fi (charged) Play Area **Services:** **Leisure:** P **Off-site:** S

Site 6HEC (site size) grass sand stone little shade partly shaded mainly shaded bungalows for hire (static) caravans for hire tents for hire no dogs site fully accessible for wheelchairs
Prices amount quoted is per night, for 2 adults and car, plus tent or caravan. Mobile home hire is a weekly rate.

ZINOLA SAVONA

Buggi International

via N S del Monte 15, 17049
019 860120 019 804573

A well-equipped site with plenty of space for tents, 0.9km from the sea.

dir: *4km W of Savona*

Open: All Year. **Site:** 2HEC **Prices:** 26 Mobile home hire 420 **Facilities:** (charged) **Services:** **Off-site:** S

NORTH EAST/ADRIATIC

ASSISI PERUGIA

Village Assisi

Campiglione No 110, 06081
075 813710 075 812335
e-mail: info@campingassisi.it
web: www.campingassisi.it

Set at the foot of the hill on which Assisi stands, this modern, well-equipped site is a good touring base.

dir: *W via SS147.*

GPS: 43.5744, 12.0755

Open: Apr-Oct **Site:** 3HEC **Prices:** 22-34 **Facilities:** Wi-fi (charged) Play Area **Services:** **Leisure:** P **Off-site:** R

BARREA L'AQUILA

Genziana

Parco Nazionale d'Abruzzo, Tre Croci, 67030
0864 88101 0864 88101
e-mail: pasettanet@tiscali.it
web: www.campinglagenzianapasetta.it

Located in the Parco Nazionale d'Abruzzo with views over Barrea lakes. The owner is an expert in alpine walking and can provide information about local walks.

Open: All Year. **Site:** 2HEC **Prices:** 28.90-31.50 **Facilities:** Play Area **Services:** **Off-site:** L

BASCHI TERNI

Camping Gole del Forello

SS448, 05023
0335 8171500 0763 300182
e-mail: info@goledelforello.it
web: www.goledelforello.it

In a quiet countryside location and close to Orvieto and Todi, the site has two swimming pools, football and tennis courts.

Open: 22 Apr-Sep **Site:** 4.5HEC **Prices:** 17.50-23.20 **Facilities:** Wi-fi **Services:** **Leisure:** L P **Off-site:** R

BELLARIA FORLI

Happy

via Panzini 228, 47814
0541 346102 0541 346408
e-mail: info@happycamping.it
web: www.happycamping.it

The site is in a quiet position on the sea shore close to the centre of town.

dir: *A14/SS16 exit Bellaria Cagnona S Mauro Mare, signs for Acquabell, over level crossing, site on right.*

Open: All Year. **Site:** 4HEC **Prices:** 23-39 **Facilities:** Wi-fi (charged) Kids' Club Play Area **Services:** **Leisure:** P S **Off-site:** R

BEVAGNA PERUGIA

Pian di Boccio

Pian di Boccio 10, 06031
0742 360164 0742 360391
e-mail: info@piandiboccio.com
web: www.piandiboccio.com

In wooded surroundings in the centre of the Umbria region with modern facilities. Popular with families.

Open: Apr-Sep **Site:** 8.5HEC **Facilities:** **Services:** **Leisure:** L P

BOLOGNA BOLOGNA

Citta di Bologna

via Romita 12/IVA, 40127
051 325016 051 325318
e-mail: info@hotelcamping.com
web: www.hotelcamping.com

Situated close to the centre of Bologna with good transport links to the city. Facilities include a fitness gym.

Open: 10 Jan-20 Dec **Site:** 6.3HEC **Prices:** 20-32 **Facilities:** Wi-fi (charged) Play Area **Services:** **Leisure:** P **Off-site:**

ITALY

BORGHETTO — PERUGIA

Badiaccia

via Pratovecchio 1, 06061
☎ 075 9659097 📠 075 9659019
e-mail: info@badiaccia.com
web: www.badiaccia.com

A well-equipped site with large grassy pitches and direct access to the lake.

dir: *A1 exit Valdichiana for Perugia & signs for Lake Trasimeno.*

GPS: 43.1803, 12.0161

Open: Apr-Sep **Site:** 5.5HEC **Prices:** 15-25 Mobile home hire 228-504 **Facilities:** Wi-fi (charged) Kids' Club Play Area **Services:** **Leisure:** L P **Off-site:**

CASAL BORSETTI — RAVENNA

Reno

via Spallazzi 11, 48123
☎ 0544 445020 📠 0544 442056
e-mail: info@campingreno.it
web: www.campingreno.it

Meadowland in sparse pine woodland and separated from the sea by dunes.

dir: *Off SS309 at Km8 or Km14.*

Open: Apr-Oct **Site:** 3.3HEC **Prices:** 18.80-28.60 Mobile home hire 236-480.50 **Facilities:** Play Area **Services:** **Off-site:** S

CASTIGLIONE DEL LAGO — PERUGIA

Listro

via Lungolago, 06061
☎ 075 951193 📠 075 951193
e-mail: listro@listro.it
web: www.listro.it

Attractive site on a peninsula in Lake Trasimeno.

Open: Apr-Sep **Site:** 1HEC **Facilities:** **Services:** **Leisure:** L **Off-site:** P

CERVIA — RAVENNA

Adriatico

via Pinarella 90, 48015
☎ 0544 71537 📠 0544 72346
e-mail: info@campingadriatico.net
web: www.campingadriatico.net

Level meadowland site with plenty of shade, pleasantly landscaped with olives, willows, elms and maples.

dir: *Site before Pinarella di Cervia off SS16 Cadulti per le Liberta 0.6km from sea.*

Open: 22 Apr-12 Sep **Site:** 3.4HEC **Facilities:** **Services:** **Leisure:** P S **Off-site:** L

CESENATICO — FORLI

Cesenatico

via Mazzini 182, 47042
☎ 0547 81344 📠 0547 672452
e-mail: info@campingcesenatico.it
web: www.campingcesenatico.com

200m from the beach and close to the city centre. Facilities include two swimming pools and a jacuzzi.

dir: *1.5km N, off the SS16 at Km178 towards sea.*

Open: All Year. **Site:** 18HEC **Facilities:** **Services:** **Leisure:** P S **Off-site:**

Zadina

via Mazzini 184, 47042
☎ 0547 82310 📠 0547 702381
e-mail: info@campingzadina.it

Very pleasant terrain in dunes on two sides of a canal.

Open: 23 Apr-16 Sep **Site:** 6HEC **Facilities:** **Services:** **Leisure:** S

CITTA DI CASTELLO — PERUGIA

La Montesca

06012
☎ 075 8558566 📠 075 852018
e-mail: info@lamontesca.it
web: www.lamontesca.it

Set in a large wooded park with excellent facilities. A good base for exploring the area.

dir: *3km from town beside River Tiber.*

Open: 15 May-15 Sep **Site:** 5HEC **Facilities:** **Services:** **Leisure:** P **Off-site:** R

COSTACCIARO PERUGIA

Villaggio Rio Verde

Loc Fornace 1, 06021
☎ 075 9170138 ▤ 075 9170181
e-mail: info@campingrioverde.it
web: www.campingrioverde.it

Located in a pine wood in the grounds of a country house, with an abundance of wildlife.

GPS: 43.3508, 12.6845

Open: 20 Apr-Sep **Site:** 5HEC **Prices:** 25-27
Facilities: Wi-fi Play Area **Services:**
Leisure: P R **Off-site:**

CUPRA MARITTIMA ASCOLI PICENO

Calypso

via Boccabianca 8, 63012
☎ 0735 778686 ▤ 0735 778106
e-mail: calypso@camping.it
web: www.campingcalypso.it
Open: Apr-29 Sep **Site:** 26HEC **Facilities:** **Services:** **Leisure:** P S

DANTE, LIDO DI RAVENNA

Classe

viale Catone, 48100
☎ 0544 492005 ▤ 0544 492058
e-mail: info@campingclasse.it
web: www.campingclasse.it

Level meadowland in grounds of former farm.

dir: *Off SS16 at Km154/V towards sea, 9km to site.*

Open: 28 Mar-10 Oct **Site:** 7HEC **Facilities:** **Services:** **Leisure:** P S **Off-site:** L R

FANO PESARO & URBINO

Mare Blu

61032
☎ 0721 884201 ▤ 0721 884389
e-mail: info@campingmareblu.net
web: www.campingmareblu.net

The site is surrounded by tall poplars with direct access to a sandy beach. Facilities for most water sports, and entertainment for children and families.

dir: *A14 exit Fano, site 3km S.*

Open: Apr-Sep **Site:** 3HEC **Facilities:**
Services: **Leisure:** P S **Off-site:** R

FERRARA FERRARA

Estense

via Gramicia 76, 44100
☎ 0532 752396 ▤ 0532 752396
e-mail: camping.estense@libero.it

A good overnight stop on the way south.

dir: *NE outskirts of Ferrara.*

Open: 27 Feb-9 Jan **Site:** 3.3HEC **Prices:** 16.50-21.50
Facilities: **Off-site:** P R

FIORENZUOLA DI FOCARA PESARO & URBINO

Panorama

Strada Panoramica, 61121
☎ 0721 208145 ▤ 0721 209799
e-mail: info@campingpanorama.it
web: www.campingpanorama.it

Located in a park 100m above sea level this site welcomes families, animals, cyclists and those wishing to relax.

dir: *Signed off SS16. 10km from Gabicce, 7km from Pesaro.*

Open: 15 Apr-Sep **Site:** 2.2HEC **Facilities:** Wi-fi (charged) Play Area **Services:**
Leisure: P S

GATTEO MARE FORLI

Delle Rose

via Adriatica 29, 47043
☎ 0547 86213 ▤ 0547 87583
e-mail: info@villaggiorose.com
web: www.villaggiorose.com

A peaceful setting close to the sea and the town centre.

dir: *Off SS16 at Km186.*

Open: 20 Mar-20 Sep **Site:** 4HEC **Prices:** 24-40
Mobile home hire 175-600 **Facilities:** Kids' Club Play Area **Services:** **Leisure:** P S
Off-site: R

GIULIANOVA LIDO TERAMO

Don Antonio

via Padova, 64021
☎ 085 8008928 ▤ 085 8006172
e-mail: info@campingdonantonio.it
web: www.campingdonantonio.it

A family site in a wooded location with direct access to a private beach. A variety of sports and entertainment facilities are available, particularly in July and August, when all cars must use the designated car park. Dogs allowed during low season.

dir: *Access via A14 & SS80.*

GPS: 42.7781, 13.9556

Open: 14 May-11 Sep **Site:** 5HEC **Prices:** 19-44
Facilities: Wi-fi (charged) Kids' Club Play Area
Services: **Leisure:** P S **Off-site:** R

Facilities shop shower electric points for razors electric points for caravans parking by tents permitted compulsory separate car park **Services** café/restaurant bar Camping Gaz International gas other than Camping Gaz first aid facilities laundry **Leisure** swimming L-Lake P-Pool R-River S-Sea **Off-site** All facilities within 5km

GUBBIO — PERUGIA

Villa Ortoguidone

Fraz. Cipolleto 49, Ortoguidone, 06024
☎ 075 9272037 075 9276620
e-mail: info@gubbiocamping.com
web: www.gubbiocamping.com

One of two well-equipped sites in the same location. Plenty of space for tents. Dogs accepted, restrictions apply.

dir: *Via SS298 Gubbio-Perugia.*

GPS: 43.3217, 12.5687

Open: 20 Apr-18 Sep **Site:** 0.5HEC **Prices:** 24-31 Mobile home hire 252-770 **Facilities:** Play Area **Services:** **Leisure:** P **Off-site:**

MARCELLI DI NUMANA — ANCONA

Conero Azzurro

via Litoranea, 60026
☎ 071 7390507 071 7390986
e-mail: info@coneroazzurro.it

Well-equipped site between the Adriatic and Monte Conero.

Open: Jun-15 Sep **Site:** 5HEC **Facilities:** **Services:** **Leisure:** P S **Off-site:**

MAROTTA — PESARO & URBINO

Gabbiano

via Faa' di Bruno 95, 61035
☎ 0721 96691 0721 96691
e-mail: info@campingdelgabbiano.it
web: www.campingdelgabbiano.it

Quiet location surrounded by trees overlooking the sea.

dir: *A14 exit Marotta, SS16 for Fano for 2.5km.*

Open: May-Sep **Site:** 1.9HEC **Facilities:** **Services:** **Leisure:** P S

MARTINSICURO — TERAMO

Duca Amedeo

Lungomare Europa 158, 64014
☎ 0861 797376 0861 797264
e-mail: ducaamedeo@camping.it
web: www.ducaamedeo.it

A pleasant location close to the sea, surrounded by trees and lush vegetation.

dir: *A14 exit Martinsicuro.*

GPS: 42.8811, 13.9206

Open: 30 Apr-27 Sep **Site:** 3.7HEC **Prices:** 15-45 Mobile home hire 100-140 **Facilities:** Wi-fi (charged) Kids' Club Play Area **Services:** **Leisure:** P S **Off-site:**

MARZABOTTO — BOLOGNA

Piccolo Paradiso

via Ca' Bianca, 40043
☎ 051 842680 051 6756581
e-mail: piccoloparadiso@aruba.it
web: www.campingpiccoloparadiso.eu

Pleasant site with plenty of trees. A sports centre less than 100m from the site provides excellent facilities for sports and recreation.

dir: *A1 exit for town, towards Vado for 2km, signed.*

Open: 15 Mar-15 Oct **Site:** 6.5HEC **Facilities:** **Services:** **Leisure:** L P **Off-site:** R

MILANO MARITTIMA — RAVENNA

Romagna

viale Matteotti 190, 48016
☎ 0544 949326 0544 949345
e-mail: info@campeggioromagna.it
web: www.campeggioromagna.it

This site lies beside a pine forest on the Adriatic coast and has direct access to the beach.

dir: *SS16 Strada Adriatica, turn off after Milano Marittima & signed.*

Open: 12 Apr-10 Sep **Site:** 40HEC **Prices:** 18-35 **Facilities:** Play Area **Services:** **Leisure:** P S **Off-site:**

MODENA — MODENA

International Camping

Strada Cave di Ramo 111, 41123
☎ 059 332252 059 823235
e-mail: internationalcamping.int@tin.it
web: www.internationalcamping.org

5km from Modena and close to the motorway. Pitches vary in terrain and are shaded.

GPS: 44.6544, 10.8675

Open: All Year. **Site:** 2.3HEC **Prices:** 28 **Facilities:** Wi-fi Play Area **Services:** **Leisure:** P **Off-site:**

MONTECRETO — MODENA

Parcodei Castagni SRL

via del Parco 5, 41025
☎ 0536 63595 🖹 0536 63630
e-mail: camping@parcodeicastagni.it
web: www.parcodeicastagni.it

Site set among mature chestnut trees in an environmentally friendly location, with pitches separated by small trees. A chair lift provides access to the surrounding high mountains.

GPS: 44.2467, 10.7119

Open: All Year. **Site:** 0.9HEC **Prices:** 24-27 **Facilities:** Play Area **Services:** **Leisure:** P **Off-site:** R

MONTENERO, MARINA DI — CAMPOBASSO

Costa Verde

86036
☎ 0873 803144 🖹 0873 9931179
e-mail: info@costaverde.it
web: www.costaverde.it

A level site with good facilities and direct access to the beach east of San Salvo Marino.

dir: *Off SS16 coast road at Km525/VII onto farm road for 300m.*

Open: 15 May-15 Sep **Site:** 1HEC **Prices:** 17.50-31.50 **Facilities:** Wi-fi (charged) Kids' Club Play Area **Services:** **Leisure:** P R S

NARNI — TERNI

Monti del Sole

strada di Borgheria 22, 05035
☎ 0744 796336 🖹 0744 796336
e-mail: info@campingmontidelsole.it
web: www.campingmontidelsole.it

A spacious wooded site, shaded and flat. All plots are grassed and easily reached by firm lanes.

dir: *A1 exit Magliano Sabina for Terni, signs for Narni.*

Open: Apr-Sep **Site:** 8HEC **Prices:** 22.50-25.50 **Facilities:** Play Area **Services:** **Leisure:** P

NAZIONI, LIDO DELLE — FERRARA

Tahiti Village

viale Libia 133, 44020
☎ 0533 379500 🖹 0533 379700
e-mail: info@campingtahiti.com
web: www.campingtahiti.com

Attractively planned site, 0.65km from the sea. The site's private beach is accessible via a miniature railway.

dir: *Off SS309 near Km32.5 & 2km to site, signed.*

Open: 26 May-19 Sep **Site:** 12HEC **Prices:** 24.10-39.70 **Facilities:** Wi-fi (charged) Kids' Club Play Area **Services:** **Leisure:** P **Off-site:** L S

PASSIGNANO — PERUGIA

Europa

Loc San Donato, 06065
☎ 075 827405 🖹 075 829200
e-mail: info@camping-europa.it
web: www.camping-europa.it

Situated by Lake Trasimeno with a private beach.

dir: *Motorway exit Passignano Est, site signed.*

Open: Etr-Oct **Site:** 3HEC **Facilities:** Wi-fi (charged) Play Area **Services:** **Leisure:** L P

Kursaal

viale Europa 24, 06065
☎ 075 828085 🖹 075 827182
e-mail: info@campingkursaal.it
web: www.campingkursaal.it

The site lies on the banks of Lake Trasimeno, between Umbria and Tuscany.

dir: *Off SS75 at Km35.2.*

GPS: 43.1826, 12.1508

Open: Apr-Oct **Site:** 1HEC **Prices:** 24-30 **Facilities:** Wi-fi (charged) **Services:** **Leisure:** L P **Off-site:**

La Spiaggia

viale Europa 22, 06065
☎ 075 827246 🖹 075 827276
e-mail: info@campinglaspiaggia.it
web: www.campinglaspiaggia.it

On the northern shore of Lake Trasimeno in a tranquil wooded location. Large grassy pitches.

GPS: 43.1839, 12.1486

Open: 31 Mar-9 Oct **Site:** 1.8HEC **Prices:** 21.50-27 **Facilities:** Wi-fi Play Area **Services:** **Leisure:** L P **Off-site:**

ITALY

ITALY

PERUGIA — PERUGIA

Rocolo

strada Fontana la Trinita 1/N, 06132
075 5181635 075 5181635
e-mail: giaco86@hotmail.it
web: www.ilrocolo.it
A quiet site with good facilities and pitches surrounded by oak and cypress trees.
GPS: 43.1100, 12.3272
Open: 15 Apr-Oct **Site:** 2.4HEC **Facilities:** Wi-fi Play Area **Services:** **Off-site:** P

PIEVEPELAGO — MODENA

Rio Verde

via M di Canossa 34, 41027
0536 72204 0536 72204
e-mail: campingrioverde@alice.it
web: www.camping-rioverde.it
Wooded mountain setting close to the river with modern facilities.
dir: *SS12 from Modena.*
Open: All Year. **Site:** 1.8HEC **Prices:** 19-25
Facilities: Play Area **Services:**
Leisure: R **Off-site:** L P

PINARELLA — RAVENNA

Safari

viale Titano 130, 48015
0544 987356 0544 987356
e-mail: csafari@cervia.com
web: www.campingsafari.it
The site is divided into several sections. Only families are accepted.
Open: 22 Apr-13 Sep **Site:** 3.1HEC **Facilities:** **Services:** **Off-site:** S

PINETO — TERAMO

International Torre Cerrano

Loc Torre Cerrano, 64025
085 930639 085 930639
e-mail: info@internationalcamping.it
web: www.internationalcamping.it
Site on level terrain with young poplars. Sunshade roofing on the beach.
dir: *Off SS16 at Km431.2 & under railway underpass, site next to railway line.*
GPS: 42.5814, 14.0929
Open: May-Sep **Site:** 1.5HEC **Prices:** 18.50-41
Facilities: Wi-fi Play Area **Services:**
Leisure: S

POMPOSA — FERRARA

International I Tre Moschettieri

via Capanno Garibaldi 22, 44020
0533 380376 0533 380377
e-mail: info@tremoschettieri.com
web: www.tremoschettieri.com
Site set beneath pine trees next to sea.
dir: *Signed from SS309.*
GPS: 44.7267, 12.2361
Open: 20 Apr-18 Sep **Site:** 11HEC
Prices: 20-34 **Facilities:** Wi-fi (charged) Play Area
Services: **Leisure:** P S **Off-site:** L

PORTO SANT'ELPÍDIO — ASCOLI PICENO

Risacca

via Europa 100, 63018
0734 991423 0734 997276
e-mail: info@larisacca.it
web: www.larisacca.it
Clean, well-kept site on level meadowland, with some trees surrounded by fields.
dir: *Off SS16 N of village, towards sea under railway (narrow underpass maximum height 3m) & 1.2km along field paths to site. Caravan access 400m further S along SS16, under railway & along field paths to site.*
Open: 21 May-9 Sep **Site:** 8HEC
Prices: 16-36 Mobile home hire 182-441
Facilities: Wi-fi (charged) Kids' Club Play Area
Services: **Leisure:** P S **Off-site:** R

PRECI — PERUGIA

Il Collaccio

Castelvecchio di Preci, 06047
0743 939005 0743 939094
e-mail: info@ilcollaccio.com
web: www.ilcollaccio.com
Beautiful natural surroundings with plenty of roomy pitches and good recreational facilities.
dir: *Via SS209.*
Open: Apr-Sep **Site:** 10HEC **Prices:** 21-35
Facilities: Wi-fi (charged) **Services:**
Leisure: P **Off-site:** R

PUNTA MARINA TERME — RAVENNA

Adriano Camping Village

via dei Campeggi 7, 48122
0544 437230 0544 438510
e-mail: info@adrianocampingvillage.com
web: www.adrianocampingvillage.com

A landscaped site among the dunes of the Punta Marina, 300m from the sea.

dir: *On SS309 via Lido Adriano to Punta Marina.*

Open: 21 Apr-18 Sep **Site:** 14HEC **Prices:** 20.50-41.50 **Facilities:** Wi-fi (charged) Kids' Club Play Area **Services:** **Leisure:** P S **Off-site:**

Coop 3

via dei Campeggi 8, 48100
0544 437353 0544 438144
e-mail: info@campingcoop3.it
web: www.campingcoop3.it

Level site with some high pines and poplars. Beach 300m away across flat dunes.

dir: *Signed.*

Open: 21 Apr-10 Sep **Site:** 7HEC **Facilities:** **Services:** **Off-site:** P S

RAVENNA, MARINA DI — RAVENNA

Piomboni Camping Village

viale Della Pace 421, 48122
0544 530230 0544 538618
e-mail: info@campingpiomboni.it
web: www.campingpiomboni.it

Site on slightly undulating mainly grassy terrain with pines and poplars. Separate section for tents and a kids' club from mid June to August.

dir: *Access from SS309 or A14.*

GPS: 44.4664, 12.2853

Open: 22 Apr-12 Sep **Site:** 5HEC **Prices:** 17.40-29.10 Mobile home hire 217-392 **Facilities:** Kids' Club Play Area **Services:** **Leisure:** S **Off-site:** P

RICCIONE — FORLI

Alberello

via Torino 80, 47036
0541 615402 0541 615248
e-mail: direzione@alberello.it
web: www.alberello.it

On the seafront connected to the beach by a private subway. Popular with families, with a range of recreational facilities.

dir: *Via A14 & SS16.*

GPS: 43.9872, 12.6883

Open: 21 Apr-19 Sep **Site:** 4HEC **Prices:** 18.90-38 **Facilities:** Kids' Club Play Area **Services:** **Off-site:** L P R S

Fontanelle

via Torino 56, 47838
0541 615449 0541 610193
e-mail: info@campingfontanelle.com
web: www.campingfontanelle.com

On southern outskirts, separated from the beach by the coast road. The public beach is reached by an underpass.

dir: *Off SS16 between Km216 & Km217.*

Open: 21 Apr-22 Sep **Site:** 6HEC **Facilities:** **Services:** **Leisure:** S **Off-site:** P R

Riccione

via Marsala N10, 47838
0541 690160 0541 690044
e-mail: info@campingriccione.it
web: www.campingriccione.it

Extensive flat meadowland with poplars, 400m from the sea.

dir: *Off SS16 on S outskirts of town towards sea for 200m.*

GPS: 43.9853, 12.6786

Open: 20 Apr-18 Sep **Site:** 6.5HEC **Prices:** 22.70-37.80 **Facilities:** Wi-fi (charged) Kids' Club Play Area **Services:** **Leisure:** P S

ROSETO DEGLI ABRUZZI — TERAMO

Eurcamping

Lungomare Trieste Sud 90, 64026
085 8993179 085 8930552
e-mail: eurcamping@camping.it
web: www.eurcamping.it

A quiet site, near to the beach, offering pitches shaded by trees.

dir: *Off SS16 in town, site 0.5km.*

Open: May-Sep **Site:** 5HEC **Prices:** 14.50-40.50 **Facilities:** Wi-fi (charged) Kids' Club Play Area **Services:** **Leisure:** P S **Off-site:** R

ITALY

SALSOMAGGIORE TERME PARMA

Arizona

via Tabiano 42 A, 43039
☎ 0524 565648 🖷 0524 567589
e-mail: info@camping-arizona.it
web: www.camping-arizona.it

Family site with plenty of activities, and close to two thermal cure establishments.

dir: *Off A1 to Tabiano.*

Open: Apr-15 Oct **Site:** 13HEC **Prices:** 20-31.50
Facilities: Wi-fi (charged) Play Area
Services: **Leisure:** P **Off-site:**

S ARCANGELO SUL TRASIMENO PERUGIA

Polvese

via Montivalle, 06063
☎ 075 848078 🖷 075 848050
e-mail: polvese@polvese.com
web: www.polvese.com

A peaceful location beside Lake Trasimeno with plenty of recreational facilities.

Open: 2 Apr-Sep **Site:** 5HEC **Prices:** 18-22
Facilities: Wi-fi (charged) Kids' Club Play Area
Services: **Leisure:** L P

Villaggio Italgest

via Martiri di Cefalonia, 06063
☎ 075 848238 🖷 075 848085
e-mail: camping@italgest.com
web: www.italgest.com

On the border between Umbria and Tuscany, the site is situated on the banks of a lake and surrounded by woodland. There are modern facilities and various activities are available.

GPS: 43.0881, 12.1564

Open: 20 Apr-Sep **Site:** 5.5HEC **Prices:** 20.50-28.50
Mobile home hire 282-875 **Facilities:** Wi-fi (charged) Kids' Club Play Area **Services:**
Leisure: L P

SAN MARINO

Centro Vacanze San Marino

Strada San Michele 50, 47893
☎ 0549 903964 🖷 0549 907120
e-mail: info@centrovacanzesanmarino.com
web: www.centrovacanzesanmarino.com

A quiet wooded location close to the centre of the Republic of San Marino.

dir: *A14 exit Rimini Sud.*

Open: All Year. **Site:** 10HEC **Prices:** 20-35
Facilities: Wi-fi Kids' Club Play Area
Services: **Leisure:** P **Off-site:**

SCACCHI, LIDO DEGLI FERRARA

Florenz

via Alpi Centrali 199, 44020
☎ 0533 380193 🖷 0533 381456
e-mail: info@campingflorenz.com
web: www.campingflorenz.com

Site with dunes extending to the sea.

dir: *Off Strada Romea for Lido Degli Scacchi, continue on asphalt road to beach.*

Open: 15 Mar-28 Sep **Site:** 8HEC **Facilities:**
Services: **Leisure:** P S

SENIGALLIA ANCONA

Summerland

via Podesti 236, 60019
☎ 071 7926816 🖷 071 7927758
e-mail: info@campingsummerland.it
web: www.campingsummerland.it

A pleasant site with good facilities, 150m from the sea.

dir: *SS16 exit Senigallia, site 3km.*

Open: Jun-15 Sep **Site:** 4.5HEC **Prices:** 25-39
Facilities: Wi-fi Kids' Club Play Area
Services: **Off-site:** P S

SILVI TERAMO

Centro Vacanze Europe Garden

Contrada Vallescura 10, 64028
☎ 085 930137 🖷 085 932846
e-mail: info@europegarden.it
web: www.europegarden.it

Set in the shade of olive trees with panoramic views over the Adriatic. Extensive leisure facilities include access to a large private beach with a shuttle bus service, two swimming pools, volleyball, archery and 5-a-side football.

GPS: 42.5678, 14.0925

Open: 23 Apr-17 Sep **Site:** 5HEC **Prices:** 22.50-39
Facilities: Wi-fi Kids' Club Play Area
Services: **Leisure:** P S **Off-site:**

SPINA, LIDO DI — FERRARA

International Camping Mare e Pineta

via delle Acacie 67, 44029
☎ 0533 330110 🖷 0533 330052
e-mail: info@campingmarepineta.com
web: www.campingmarepineta.com
Located in the middle of a pinewood, with direct acess to a sandy beach, this site has touring pitches, mobile homes and bungalows
dir: *2km SE of Port Garibaldi.*
GPS: 44.6558, 12.2453
Open: 20 Apr-19 Sep **Site:** 16HEC **Prices:** 17.80-35.85 Mobile home hire 329-966 **Facilities:** Wi-fi (charged) Kids' Club **Services:** **Leisure:** P S **Off-site:**

Spina Camping Village

via del Campeggio 99, 44024
☎ 0533 330179 🖷 0533 333566
e-mail: info@spinacampingvillage.com
web: www.spinacampingvillage.com
Extensive site on level meadowland and slightly hilly dune terrain. Separate section for dog owners.
dir: *Signed off SS309.*
Open: Apr-Sep **Site:** 24HEC **Facilities:** **Services:** **Leisure:** P S **Off-site:**

TORINO DI SANGRO MARINA — CHIETI

Belvedere

66020
☎ 0873 911381 🖷 0873 911122
e-mail: campingbelvedere@hotmail.it
Open: Jun-6 Sep **Site:** 1.5HEC **Prices:** 25-30 Mobile home hire 400-450 **Facilities:** Play Area **Services:** **Leisure:** S **Off-site:** P

VALLICELLA DI MONZUNO — BOLOGNA

Le Querce

Strada Prov 61, 40036
☎ 051 6770394 🖷 051 6770394
e-mail: contatti@campinglequerce.com
web: www.campinglequerce.com
A well-equipped site in a wooded mountain setting.
dir: *Access via Autostrada del Sole.*
Open: May-Sep **Site:** 12HEC **Prices:** 22-25 **Facilities:** Play Area **Services:** **Leisure:** L P R

VASTO — CHIETI

Europa

66055
☎ 0873 801988 🖷 0873 802553
e-mail: info@campingeuropasrl.it
web: www.campingeuropasrl.it
Site on level terrain by the road with poplars.
dir: *On SS16 at Km522.*
Open: Apr-Sep **Site:** 2.3HEC **Facilities:** **Services:** **Leisure:** S **Off-site:**

Grotta del Saraceno

via Osca 6, 66054
☎ 0873 310213 🖷 0873 310295
e-mail: info@grottadelsaraceno.it
web: www.grottadelsaraceno.it
Site in olive grove on steep coastal cliffs with lovely views. Steep path to beach.
dir: *Off SS16 at Km512.2.*
Open: 15 Jun-12 Sep **Site:** 14HEC **Facilities:** Kids' Club Play Area **Services:** **Leisure:** S **Off-site:**

Pioppeto

66055
☎ 0873 801466 🖷 0873 801466
e-mail: infocampeggio@ilpioppeto.it
web: www.ilpioppeto.it
Open: 15 May-14 Sep **Site:** 1.7HEC **Facilities:** **Services:** **Leisure:** S **Off-site:** P R

ZOCCA — MODENA

Montequestiolo

via Montequestiolo 184, 41059
☎ 059 986800 🖷 059 986800
e-mail: jagat22@libero.it
web: www.campeggiomontequestiolo.it
Open: Mar-Oct **Site:** 1.8HEC **Facilities:** **Services:** **Off-site:** P

ROME

BOLSENA — VITERBO

Blu International

via Cassia km 111.650, 01023
0761 798855 0761 798855
e-mail: info@blucamping.it
web: www.blucamping.it

A modern site with good facilities in a wooded location on the shore of Lake Bolsena.

dir: *A1 exit Orvieto.*

GPS: 42.6311, 11.9944

Open: 18 Apr-Sep **Site:** 3HEC **Prices:** 18-24 **Facilities:** Play Area **Services:** **Leisure:** L P **Off-site:**

Lido

via Cassia km111, 01023
0761 799258 0761 796105
e-mail: lidocamping@bolsenahotel.it
web: www.bolsenacamping.it

A lakeside family site with modern facilities including supermarket and restaurant/pizzeria. Kids' club available in July and August.

dir: *Motorway exit Orvieto.*

Open: 21 Apr-Sep **Site:** 10HEC **Prices:** 23.50-33.50 **Facilities:** Kids' Club Play Area **Services:** **Leisure:** L P

BRACCIANO — ROMA

Porticciolo

via Porticciolo, 00062
06 99803060 06 99803030
e-mail: info@porticciolo.it
web: www.porticciolo.it

A family site in a pleasant location on the shore of a lake.

dir: *SS493 to Bracciano.*

Open: Apr-Sep **Site:** 3.2HEC **Facilities:** **Services:** **Leisure:** L **Off-site:**

FIANO ROMANO — ROMA

Family Park I Pini

The Camping and Caravanning Club The Friendly Club

via delle Sassete 1A, 00065
0765 453349 0765 453057
e-mail: ipini@camping.it
web: www.ecvacanze.it

A modern, well-equipped site within easy reach of the centre of Rome. A good base for excursions. Kids' club in high season.

C&CC Report *A superbly located campsite that allows you to explore Rome without hassle, as well as providing easy access to all the attractions of the region of Lazio. This great site caters for families and couples alike. Children are kept busy with the animation programme and great swimming pools, and the surrounding woodland area is ready to be explored by foot or by bike. The shuttle service to Rome directly from the site makes it so easy to explore the history and culture of this fascinating city, before returning back to the site to relax for the evening.*

dir: *A1 exit Roma Nord-Fiano Romano, follow signs for Fiano Romano. At 1st rdbt after Palace Inn, turn right. After 2km, at 2nd rdbt straight on to lights. Take left, follow signs for Park I Pini.*

Open: 20 Apr-25 Sep **Site:** 5HEC **Prices:** 28.50-36 **Facilities:** Wi-fi Kids' Club Play Area **Services:** **Leisure:** P

FORMIA — LATINA

Gianola

via delle Vigne, 04023
0771 720223 0771 720223
e-mail: gianolacamping@tiscali.it
web: www.gianolacamping.it

A narrow grassland area near a stream and trees amid agricultural land. Pleasant sandy beach edged by rocks.

dir: *Off Roma-Napoli road, 0.8km from S Croce.*

Open: Apr-Sep **Site:** 4HEC **Prices:** 14.40-35.90 **Facilities:** Play Area **Services:** **Leisure:** R S **Off-site:** L P

MINTURNO, MARINA DI — LATINA

Golden Garden

via Dunale 74, 04020
0771 681425 0771 614059
e-mail: servizio.clienti@goldengarden.it
web: www.goldengarden.it

Secluded quiet site within agricultural area by the sea.

dir: *SS7 over river bridge (Garigliano), continue 4.6km (last 1km sandy track).*

Open: 30 May-Aug **Site:** 2.3HEC **Facilities:** **Services:** **Leisure:** S **Off-site:** P R

MONTALTO DI CASTRO, MARINA DI — VITERBO

California

01014
☎ 0766 802848 ▤ 0766 801210
e-mail: info@californiacampingvillage.com
web: www.californiacampingvillage.com

Situated on the coast below an ancient pine grove with good facilities for sports and leisure.

Open: May-14 Sep **Site:** 14HEC **Facilities:** **Services:** **Leisure:** P S

Internazionale Pionier Etrusco

via Vulsinia, 01014
☎ 0766 802199 ▤ 0766 801214
e-mail: info@campingpionieretrusco.it
web: www.campingpionieretrusco.eu

Situated in a pine forest close to the beach. Various leisure and sports activities, and a relaxing atmosphere.

Open: Mar-15 Oct **Site:** 8HEC **Facilities:** **Services:** **Off-site:** R S

ROMA (ROME) — ROMA

Flaminio Village

via Flaminia Nuova 821, 00189
☎ 06 3332604 ▤ 06 3330653
e-mail: info@villageflaminio.com
web: www.villageflaminio.com

An extensive site with good facilities, set on narrow hill terraces in a quiet valley.

dir: *Off ring road onto SS3 (via Flaminia) for 2.5km towards city centre.*

GPS: 41.9562, 12.4824

Open: All Year. **Site:** 10HEC **Facilities:** Wi-fi (charged) Play Area **Services:** **Leisure:** P **Off-site:** R

Happy

via Prato della Corte 1915, 00123
☎ 06 33626401 ▤ 06 33613800
e-mail: info@happycamping.net
web: www.happycamping.net

Convenient location in the north of the town. Modern installations.

dir: *Grande Raccordo Anulare (ring road) exit 5.*

Open: Mar-6 Nov **Site:** 3.6HEC **Facilities:** **Services:** **Leisure:** P

Roma

via Aurelia 831, 00165
☎ 06 6623018 ▤ 06 66418147
e-mail: campingroma@ecvacanze.it
web: www.ecvacanze.it

The site lies on terraces on a hill near the AGIP Motel. Various excursions can be arranged.

dir: *From ring road onto SS1 (via Aurelia) for 1.5km towards town centre, turn to site at Km8/11.*

Open: All Year. **Site:** 3HEC **Facilities:** Wi-fi Play Area **Services:** **Leisure:** P **Off-site:**

Seven Hills

via Cassia 1216, 00189
☎ 06 30310826 ▤ 06 30310039
e-mail: info@sevenhills.it
web: www.sevenhillscamping.com

A fine, partly terraced site in beautiful rural surroundings. Well placed for access to the city by bus or underground.

dir: *Outer ring road exit 3, site 2.5km NE.*

Open: Mar-1 Nov **Site:** 5HEC **Facilities:** **Services:** **Leisure:** P

Tiber

via Tiberina Km1400, 00188
☎ 06 33610733 ▤ 06 33612314
e-mail: info@campingtiber.com
web: www.campingtiber.com

On level grassland, shaded by poplars beside the Tiber.

dir: *Ring road exit 3, site signed N of city. From S signs for Prima Porta.*

Open: 15 Mar-Oct **Site:** 5HEC **Facilities:** **Services:** **Leisure:** P R

SALTO DI FONDI — LATINA

Holiday Village

via Flacca Km 6800, 04020
☎ 0771 555009 ▤ 0771 555009
e-mail: info@holidayvillage.it
web: www.holidayvillage.it

A well-shaded and well-equipped site beside the Mediterranean.

Open: Jan-Sep **Site:** 4HEC **Prices:** 22-58 **Facilities:** Kids' Club Play Area **Services:** **Leisure:** P S

ITALY

TERRACINA — LATINA

Badino

Porto Badino, 04019
0773 764430 0773 764430

Wooded surroundings with direct access to the beach.

dir: *Off Roma-Napoli road towards canal (Porto Canale Badino) & sea.*

Open: Apr-15 Oct **Site:** 1.8HEC **Prices:** 23-47 **Facilities:** Play Area **Services:** **Leisure:** S **Off-site:**

SOUTH

BAIA DOMIZIA — CASERTA

Baia Domizia Villaggio Camping

81030
0823 930164 0823 930375
e-mail: info@baiadomizia.it
web: www.baiadomizia.it

Part of this extensive seaside site is laid out with flower beds. Good sports and leisure facilities. Ideal for families.

dir: *Off SS7 at Km6/V & 3km towards sea.*

Open: 6 May-17 Sep **Site:** 30HEC **Prices:** 22.50-46 **Facilities:** **Services:** **Leisure:** P S

BRIATICO — CATANZARO

Dolomiti

89817
0963 391355 0963 393009
e-mail: info@dolomitisulmare.com
web: www.dolomitisulmare.com

The site is in a delightful setting on two terraces planted with olive trees. It lies by the road and 150m from the railway.

dir: *Off road SS522 between Km17 & Km18 towards sea.*

Open: 24 Jun-10 Sep **Site:** 5HEC **Facilities:** **Services:** **Leisure:** P S **Off-site:**

CAMEROTA, MARINA DI — SALERNO

Risacca

via delle Barche 11, Lentiscella, 84059
0974 932415 0974 932415
e-mail: info@larisacca.eu
web: www.larisacca.eu

On level ground, shaded by olive trees, with direct access to a sandy beach.

dir: *Approach via SS18.*

Open: 20 May-20 Sep **Site:** 2HEC **Facilities:** **Services:** **Leisure:** S **Off-site:**

CAPO VATICANO — CATANZARO

Gabbiano

San Nicolo di Ricadi, 89865
0963 663384 0963 665442
e-mail: info@villaggioilgabbiano.com
web: www.villaggioilgabbiano.com

Open: Apr-Oct **Site:** **Facilities:** **Services:** **Leisure:** P S

CIRÒ MARINA — CATANZARO

Punta Alice

88811
0962 31160 0962 373823
e-mail: info@puntalice.it
web: www.puntalice.it

Meadowland among lush Mediterranean vegetation, bordering a fine gravel beach 50m wide.

dir: *2km from town. Off SS106 Strada Ionica at Km290 to Cirò Marina, through village & beach road towards lighthouse for 1.5m.*

Open: Apr-Sep **Site:** 5.5HEC **Facilities:** **Services:** **Leisure:** P S

CORIGLIANO CÁLABRO — COSENZA

Thurium

Contrada Ricota Grande, 87060
0983 851101 0983 851955
e-mail: info@campingthurium.com
web: www.campingthurium.com

Situated close to the beach, the site has leisure facilities including football, evening entertainment and guided tours. Dogs accepted but restrictions apply.

Open: 20 Mar-27 Nov **Site:** 16HEC **Prices:** 13.40-46.50 **Facilities:** **Services:** **Leisure:** P S

EBOLI — SALERNO

Paestum

Foce Sele, 84020
0828 691003 0828 691003
e-mail: info@campingpaestum.it
web: www.campingpaestum.it

Sandy, meadowland site in tall poplar wood by the mouth of a river. Steps and bus service to private beach, 0.6km from site.

dir: *Off Litoranea at Km20 at fork to Santa Cecilia, continue 300m, signed.*

Open: 15 May-15 Sep **Site:** 8HEC **Facilities:** **Services:** **Leisure:** P **Off-site:** R S

Site 6HEC (site size) grass sand stone little shade partly shaded mainly shaded bungalows for hire (static) caravans for hire tents for hire no dogs site fully accessible for wheelchairs
Prices amount quoted is per night, for 2 adults and car, plus tent or caravan. Mobile home hire is a weekly rate.

GALLIPOLI — LECCE

Baia di Gallipoli

73014
☎ 0833 273210
e-mail: info@baiadigallipoli.com
web: www.baiadigallipoli.com

A holiday village set amid pine woods close to the sea with good facilities.

dir: *5km SE of Gallipoli.*

Open: Etr-Sep **Site:** 14HEC **Facilities:** **Services:** **Leisure:** P **Off-site:** S

LEPORANO, MARINA DI — TARANTO

Porto Pirrone

Litoranea Salentina, 74020
☎ 099 5315184 099 5315184
e-mail: info@portopirronecamping.it
web: www.portopirronecamping.it

Set in a pine wood offering flat large plots for both tents and caravans. Good sports and entertainment.

dir: *A14 from Massafra towards Taranto & Leporano, site near marina.*

Open: Mar-Oct **Site:** 3.2HEC **Prices:** 22-31 **Facilities:** Kids' Club **Services:** **Leisure:** S **Off-site:**

MÁCCHIA — FOGGIA

Monaco

71030
☎ 0884 530280 0884 565737
e-mail: info@baiadelmonaco.it
web: www.baiadelmonaco.it

A pleasant location with good facilities and direct access to the beach.

Open: Jun-15 Sep **Site:** 5.3HEC **Facilities:** **Services:** **Leisure:** P S

MANFREDONIA — FOGGIA

Ippocampo

SS159, 71043
☎ 0884 571121
e-mail: campingippocampo@email.it
web: www.campingippocampo.it

Set in the grounds of a holiday village.

Open: May-Sep **Site:** 8HEC **Facilities:** **Services:** **Leisure:** S **Off-site:** P

OTRANTO — LECCE

Mulino d'Acqua

via S Stefano, 73028
☎ 0836 802191 0836 802196
e-mail: mulino.camping@anet.it
web: www.mulinodacqua.it

Shaded by olive trees, close to the beach and with plenty of organised activities. Only small dogs allowed.

Open: end May-mid Sep **Site:** 10HEC **Facilities:** Wi-fi (charged) Play Area **Services:** **Leisure:** P S **Off-site:**

PESCHICI — FOGGIA

Centro Turistico San Nicola

Loc San Nicola, 71010
☎ 0884 964024

Terraced site in lovely location by the sea, in a bay enclosed by rocks.

dir: *Off Peschici-Vieste coast road, signed along winding road to site in 1km.*

Open: Apr-15 Oct **Site:** 14HEC **Facilities:** **Services:** **Leisure:** S

Internazionale Manacore

71010
☎ 0884 911020 0884 911049
e-mail: manacore@grupposaccia.it
web: www.grupposaccia.it

Meadowland with a few terraces in attractive bay, surrounded by wooded hills.

dir: *Off Peschici-Vieste coast road towards sea on wide U bend.*

Open: 15 May-Sep **Site:** 22HEC **Facilities:** **Services:** **Leisure:** S

PIZZO — CATANZARO

Pinetamare

89812
☎ 0963 534871 0963 534871
e-mail: info@villaggiopinetamare.com

A sandy site surrounded by tall pine trees. Most water sports are available along the private beach and families are welcome.

dir: *Salerno-Reggio motorway exit Pizzo, site N of town.*

Open: Jun-15 Sep **Site:** 10HEC **Facilities:** **Services:** **Leisure:** P S **Off-site:** L

ITALY

Facilities shop shower electric points for razors electric points for caravans parking by tents permitted mpulsory separate car park **Services** café/restaurant bar Camping Gaz International gas other than Camping Gaz first aid facilities laundry **Leisure** swimming L-Lake P-Pool R-River S-Sea **Off-site** All facilities within 5km

POMPEI — NAPOLI

Spartacus

via Plinio 127, 80045
081 8624078 081 8624078
e-mail: campingspartacus@tin.it
web: www.campingspartacus.it
Site on a level meadow with orange trees. Located near the main entrance for the Pompeii ruins.

dir: *Motorway exit Pompei, off Napoli road, opposite Scavi di Pompei, near fuel station.*

GPS: 40.7456, 14.4839

Open: All Year. **Site:** 9HEC **Prices:** 12-25 **Facilities:** Play Area **Services:** **Leisure:** P

POZZUOLI — NAPOLI

Vulcano Solfatara

via Solfatara 161, 80078
081 5267413 081 5263482
e-mail: info@solfatara.it
web: www.solfatara.it
Clean and orderly site in a forest near the crater of the extinct Solfatara Volcano.

dir: *From Nuova via Domiziana (SS7) at Km60/1 (6km before Napoli) turn inland through stone gate.*

Open: All Year. **Site:** 3HEC **Prices:** 25.30-30.80 Mobile home hire 98-176 **Facilities:** Wi-fi (charged) **Services:** **Leisure:** P **Off-site:** S

PRÁIA A MARE — COSENZA

International Camping Village

Lungomare Sirimarco, 87028
0985 72211 0985 72211
e-mail: reception@campinginternational.it
web: www.campinginternational.it
A beautiful location on the gulf of Policastro with fine recreational facilities.

dir: *A3 to Falerna, onto SS18 (south); A3 Logonegro (north).*

Open: May-Sep **Site:** 5.5HEC **Prices:** 13-40.50 **Facilities:** Play Area **Services:** **Leisure:** S

RODI GARGANICO — FOGGIA

Ripa

Contrada Ripa, 71012
0884 965367 0884 965695
e-mail: info@villaggioripa.it
web: www.villaggioripa.it
Well-equipped and attractive site close to the beach.

Open: 15 Jun-15 Sep **Site:** 6HEC **Facilities:** Wi-fi Play Area **Services:** **Leisure:** P S **Off-site:** L

ROSSANO SCALO — COSENZA

Marina di Rossano

Contrada Leuca, 87068
0983 516054 0983 514106
e-mail: marina.club@tiscalinet.it
web: www.marinadirossano.it
Wooded surroundings close to the beach with modern facilities.

dir: *Via N106.*

Open: 15 May-29 Sep **Site:** 7HEC **Prices:** 12-39 **Facilities:** Wi-fi Kids' Club Play Area **Services:** **Leisure:** P S **Off-site:**

SAN MENÁIO — FOGGIA

Valle d'Oro

Loc Aia del Cervone, 71010
0884 991580 0884 991580
e-mail: info@campingvalledoro.it
web: www.campingvalledoro.it
Site in an olive grove with some terraces and surrounded by wooded hills, 2km from the sea.

dir: *Off SS89 onto SS528 to site at Km1.800.*

Open: 15 Jun-15 Sep **Site:** 3HEC **Facilities:** **Services:** **Off-site:** P S

SANTA CESÁREA TERME — LECCE

Scogliera

73020
0836 949802 0836 949802
e-mail: info@campinglascogliera.it
Attractive site close to the sea.

dir: *1km S on SS173.*

Open: All Year. **Site:** 8HEC **Prices:** 14-34 **Facilities:** **Services:** **Leisure:** P **Off-site:** S

SANTA MARIA DI CASTELLABATE — SALERNO

Trezene

84072
0974 965027 0974 965013
e-mail: info@trezene.com
web: www.trezene.com

The site is partly divided into pitches and consists of two sections lying either side of the access road. Pitches between road and fine sandy beach are reserved for touring campers.

Open: Apr-Oct **Site:** 2.5HEC **Facilities:** **Services:** **Leisure:** S **Off-site:**

SORRENTO — NAPOLI

International Camping Nube d'Argento

via Capo 21, 80067
081 8781344 081 8073450
e-mail: info@nubedargento.com
web: www.nubedargento.com

The site lies on narrow terraces just off a steep concrete road between the beach and the outskirts of the town.

dir: *Access difficult for caravans.*

Open: 15 Mar-10 Jan **Site:** 1.5HEC **Facilities:** **Services:** **Leisure:** P S

Santa Fortunata Campogaio

via Capo 39, 80067
081 8073579 081 8073590
e-mail: info@santafortunata.eu
web: www.santafortunata.eu

A well-appointed, terraced site shaded by olive trees and with direct access to the sea (50m).

dir: *2km from town centre. 400m after exit from SS145 on road towards Massa Lubrense.*

GPS: 40.6274, 14.3374

Open: 7 Apr-17 Oct **Site:** 20HEC **Prices:** 23.50-38.50 **Facilities:** Wi-fi (charged) **Services:** **Leisure:** P S

SPECCHIOLLA, LIDO DI — BRINDISI

Pineta al Mare

72012
0831 987024 0831 994057
e-mail: info@campingpinetamare.com
web: www.campingpinetamare.com

Site in pine woodland with sandy beach and some rocks.

dir: *E of Bari-Brindisi road at Km21.5.*

Open: Apr-20 Sep **Site:** 5.5HEC **Prices:** 23-42 **Facilities:** Wi-fi (charged) Kids' Club Play Area **Services:** **Leisure:** P S **Off-site:**

TORRE RINALDA — LECCE

Torre Rinalda Camping Village

Litoranea Salentina CP152, 73100
0832 382161 0832 372303
e-mail: info@torrerinalda.it
web: www.torrerinalda.it

An extensive level meadow separated from the sea by dunes. There is a disco and a kids' club in high season.

dir: *SS613 Brindisi-Lecce exit Trepuzzi, coast road for 1.5km.*

Open: 4 Jun-11 Sep **Site:** 15HEC **Prices:** 14-34.40 Mobile home hire 245-840 **Facilities:** Wi-fi (charged) Kids' Club Play Area **Services:** **Leisure:** P S

UGENTO — LECCE

Riva di Ugento

Litoranea Gallipoli-SM di Leuca, 73059
0833 933600 0833 933601
web: www.rivadiugento.it

A well-equipped site in wooded surroundings close to the beach.

Open: 14 May-Sep **Site:** 32HEC **Prices:** 19-43 Mobile home hire 245-560 **Facilities:** Wi-fi Play Area **Services:** **Leisure:** P S

VARCATURO, MARINA DI — NAPOLI

Partenope

80014
081 5091076 081 5096767
e-mail: info@campingpartenope.it
web: www.campingpartenope.it

Partially undulating terrain in woodland with access to a private beach. Leisure facilities include tennis, football and evening entertainment.

dir: *Off SS7 (via Domiziana) at Km45/II towards sea for 300m.*

Open: Jun-8 Sep **Site:** 6HEC **Facilities:** **Services:** **Leisure:** R S

VICO EQUENSE — NAPOLI

Sant' Antonio

Marina d'Equa, 80069
081 8028570 081 8028570
e-mail: info@campingsantantonio.it
web: www.campingsantantonio.it

A modern site set among fruit trees, close to the beach with fine views over the Bay of Naples.

Open: 15 Mar-Oct **Site:** 1HEC **Prices:** 25-33 **Facilities:** Wi-fi (charged) **Services:** **Leisure:** S **Off-site:** P

Facilities shop shower electric points for razors electric points for caravans parking by tents permitted ompulsory separate car park **Services** café/restaurant bar Camping Gaz International gas other than Camping Gaz first aid facilities laundry **Leisure** swimming L-Lake P-Pool R-River S-Sea **Off-site** All facilities within 5km

ITALY

Seiano Spiaggia

Marina Aequa, via Murrano 15, 80069
☎ 081 8028560 Fax 081 8028560
e-mail: info@campingseiano.it
web: www.campingseiano.it

Set in a plantation of evergreen and orange trees close to the sea. There are good facilities and the site is well situated for Pompeii, Naples and Vesuvius.

dir: *A3 exit Castellammare di Stabia, highway 145, after Seiano tunnel & bridge right to Marina Aequa. By train Naples-Sorrento line to Seiano.*

GPS: 40.6602, 14.4203

Open: Apr-Sep **Site:** 1HEC grass, mainly shaded, bungalows for hire **Prices:** 22.50-26 **Facilities:** **Services:** **Off-site:** P S

Villaggio Turistico Azzurro

via Murrano 9, 80066
☎ 081 8029984 Fax 081 8029176
e-mail: info@villaggioazzurro.net
web: www.villaggioazzurro.net

Shaded site among ancient olive groves, by the sea and in close proximity to the Isle of Capri.

dir: *A3 exit Castellammare, signs for Vico Equense, after 3rd tunnel & bridge right to Marina Aequa.*

Open: Mar-1 Dec **Site:** 11HEC grass, mainly shaded, bungalows for hire, (static) caravans for hire, tents for hire **Prices:** 22.50-29 Mobile home hire 266-336 **Facilities:** Play Area **Services:** **Leisure:** S **Off-site:**

VIESTE **FOGGIA**

Capo Vieste

71019
☎ 0884 706326 Fax 0884 705993
e-mail: info@capovieste.it
web: www.capovieste.it

The site lies on a large area of unspoiled land, planted with a few rows of poplar and pine trees. It is by the sea and has a large bathing area.

dir: *Off coast road to Peschici, 7km beyond Vieste.*

Open: 20 Apr-15 Oct **Site:** 6HEC grass, sand, partly shaded, mainly shaded, bungalows for hire, (static) caravans for hire **Facilities:** **Services:** **Leisure:** P S

Umbramare

Santa Maria di Merino, 71019
☎ 0884 706174 Fax 0884 706174
e-mail: umbramarevieste@tiscali.it
web: www.umbramarevieste.it

Site with access to a private beach and a small children's play park.

dir: *Off A14 at Poggio Imperiale onto route via Rodi Gargánico & Peschici.*

Open: Apr-Oct **Site:** 10.5HEC grass, sand, mainly shaded, bungalows for hire, no dogs **Prices:** 15-36 **Facilities:** Play Area **Services:** **Leisure:** S **Off-site:**

Vieste Marina

Litoranea Vieste-Peschici Km 5, 71019
☎ 0884 706471 Fax 0884 706471
e-mail: viestemarina@tiscali.it
web: www.garganovacanze.it

Tree-lined level site adjacent to the coast road in a quiet location with good facilities.

dir: *5km N of Vieste, signed.*

Open: May-Sep **Site:** 5HEC grass, mainly shaded, bungalows for hire **Facilities:** **Services:** **Leisure:** P S **Off-site:**

Village Punta Lunga

Defensola, CP 339, 71019
☎ 0884 706031 Fax 0884 706910
e-mail: info@puntalunga.it
web: www.puntalunga.it

A terraced site in wooded surroundings encompassing two sandy bathing bays and a rocky peninsula.

dir: *2km N of Vieste, signed from coast road.*

Open: 28 Apr-1 Oct **Site:** 6HEC sand, mainly shaded, bungalows for hire, no dogs **Facilities:** **Services:** **Leisure:** S

THE ISLANDS

SARDEGNA (SARDINIA)

AGLIENTU SASSARI

Baia Blu la Tortuga

Pineta di Vignola Mare, 07020
☎ 079 602200 📠 079 602040
e-mail: info@baiablu.com
web: www.baiaholiday.com
Site in pine forest by the sea.
Open: Apr-22 Oct **Site:** 17HEC **Prices:** 19-51 Mobile home hire 200-805 **Facilities:** Wi-fi (charged) Kids' Club Play Area **Services:** **Leisure:** S

ARBATAX NUORO

Telis

Porto Frailis, 08041
☎ 0782 667261 📠 0782 667140
e-mail: telisca@tiscali.it
web: www.campingtelis.com
Located in the bay of Porto Frailis, this terraced site is surrounded by beautiful scenery. There are good facilities and pitches surrounded by eucalyptus and mimosa trees.
dir: *SS125 between Cagliari & Olbia.*
Open: All Year. **Site:** 3HEC **Prices:** 20-41 **Facilities:** Wi-fi Kids' Club Play Area **Services:** **Leisure:** P S **Off-site:**

CALASETTA CAGLIARI

Le Saline

09011
☎ 0781 88615 📠 0781 435510
e-mail: info@campinglesaline.com
web: www.campinglesaline.com
Wooded surroundings close to the beach, 0.5km from the village with good recreational facilities.
Open: May-Oct **Site:** 7HEC **Prices:** 20-41 **Facilities:** Play Area **Services:** **Leisure:** S **Off-site:**

CANNIGIONE-ARZACHENA SASSARI

Isuledda

07021
☎ 0789 86003 📠 0789 86089
e-mail: info@isuledda.it
web: www.isuledda.it
Near the sea on the beautiful Costa Smeralda with modern sanitary installations and plentiful sports and entertainment facilities.
Open: Apr-Oct **Site:** 15HEC **Facilities:** **Services:** **Leisure:** S

LOTZORAI NUORO

Cernie

via Case Sparse 17, 08040
☎ 0782 669472 📠 06 91659297
e-mail: info@campinglecernie.it
web: www.campinglecernie.com
Close to the beach with beautiful views on all sides. Varied sports and leisure activities.
Open: May-Oct **Site:** 1.5HEC **Prices:** 14-50 Mobile home hire 189-560 **Facilities:** Play Area **Services:** **Leisure:** S **Off-site:**

PORTO ROTONDO SASSARI

Cugnana

Loc Cugnana, 07026
☎ 0789 33184 📠 0789 33398
e-mail: info@campingcugnana.it
web: www.campingcugnana.it
A well-appointed family site with good recreational facilities and offering free transport to the local beaches.
Open: Apr-10 Oct **Site:** 5HEC **Facilities:** **Services:** **Leisure:** P **Off-site:** S

PORTO TRAMATZU CAGLIARI

Porto Tramatzu

09019
☎ 070 9283027 📠 070 9283028
e-mail: coop.proturismo@libero.it
web: www.camping.it
With extensive facilities and large individual plots. The site is less than 100m from the beautiful Porto Tramatzu.
dir: *SS195 from Cagliari.*
Open: Etr-Oct **Site:** 3.5HEC **Facilities:** **Services:** **Leisure:** S

ITALY

SANTA LUCIA — NUORO

Calapineta

SS Orientale Sarda 125, 08029
☎ 0784 819184 🖷 0784 818128
e-mail: info@calapineta.it
web: www.calapineta.it

Well-equipped site 1.5km from a white sand beach.

Open: Jun-15 Sep **Site:** 10HEC **Prices:** 18.50-33 Mobile home hire 210-420 **Facilities:** Play Area **Services:** **Leisure:** S

Selema

08029
☎ 0784 37349
e-mail: info@selemacamping.com
web: www.selemacamping.com

Wooded beach site.

Open: Apr-Oct **Site:** 7.5HEC **Facilities:** **Services:** **Leisure:** R S **Off-site:**

SANT'ANTIOCO — CAGLIARI

Tonnara

Loc Calasapone, 09017
☎ 0781 809058 🖷 0781 809036
e-mail: mail@camping-tonnara.it
web: www.campingtonnara.it

Situated in the centre of Cala Sapone Bay with enclosed plots, good sports facilities and access to a sandy beach.

dir: *S of Carbonia, road to island of St Antioco.*

Open: Apr-Oct **Site:** 7HEC **Facilities:** **Services:** **Leisure:** P S

TORRE SALINAS — CAGLIARI

Torre Salinas

09043
☎ 070 999032 🖷 070 999001
e-mail: information@camping-torre-salinas.de
web: www.camping-torre-salinas.de

On south-eastern coast of Sardinia, close to a lagoon.

Open: Apr-14 Oct **Site:** 1.5HEC **Facilities:** **Services:** **Leisure:** S

VALLEDORIA — SASSARI

Foce

via Ampurias 110, 07039
☎ 079 582109 🖷 079 582191
e-mail: info@lafoce.eu
web: www.lafoce.eu

A delightful wooded setting separated from the beach by the River Coghinas, which can be crossed by ferry. Modern sanitary installations and plenty of recreational facilities, including a kids' club in July and August.

GPS: 40.9336, 8.8172

Open: 25 Apr-29 Sep **Site:** 20HEC **Prices:** 17.50-35 **Facilities:** Wi-fi Kids' Club Play Area **Services:** **Leisure:** P R S **Off-site:** L

Valledoria International Camping

07039
☎ 079 584070 🖷 079 584058
e-mail: info@campingvalledoria.com
web: www.campingvalledoria.com

Located in a pine wood, this site has both white sand beaches and rocky cliffs.

Open: 15 May-29 Sep **Site:** 10HEC **Prices:** 15-28.50 **Facilities:** Wi-fi (charged) Play Area **Services:** **Leisure:** S **Off-site:**

SICILIA (SICILY)
AVOLA — SIRACUSA

Sabbia d'Oro

via Chiusa di Carlo, 96012
☎ 0931 822415 🖷 0931 822415 & 560000
e-mail: info@campeggiosabbiadoro.com
web: www.campeggiosabbiadoro.com

Situated close to the beach in a picturesque area surrounded by trees with magnificient views.

Open: All Year. **Site:** 2.2HEC **Facilities:** **Services:** **Leisure:** S **Off-site:** P R

CASTEL DI TUSA — MESSINA

Scoglio

98079
☎ 0921 334345 🖷 0921 334345
e-mail: loscoglio@loscoglio.net
web: www.loscoglio.net

A terraced site. No shade on the gravel beach.

dir: *A20 from Uscita, off SS113 Km 164.*

GPS: 38.0100, 14.2307

Open: Apr-Sep **Site:** 1.5HEC **Prices:** 15-38 **Facilities:** Wi-fi (charged) Play Area **Services:** **Leisure:** P S

CATÁNIA — CATANIA

Jonio

via Villini a Mare 2, 95126
095 491139 095 492277
e-mail: info@campingjonio.com
web: www.jonioeventi.it
On a clifftop plateau. Access to beach via steps.
dir: *Off SS14 N of town towards sea.*
Open: All Year. **Site:** 1.2HEC **Facilities:** **Services:** **Leisure:** S

FINALE DI POLLINA — PALERMO

Rais Gerbi

90010
0921 426570 0921 426577
e-mail: camping@raisgerbi.it
web: www.raisgerbi.it
A well-equipped, modern site with its own private beach in picturesque wooded surroundings.
dir: *Off SS113 at Km172.9.*
Open: All Year. **Site:** 5HEC **Facilities:** **Services:** **Leisure:** P S **Off-site:**

FÚRNARI MARINA — MESSINA

Village Bazia

Contrada Bazia, 98054
0941 800130 0941 81006
e-mail: info@bazia.it
web: www.bazia.it
A pleasant seaside site with plenty of recreational facilities.
Open: Jun-10 Sep **Site:** 4HEC **Facilities:** **Services:** **Leisure:** P S **Off-site:**

ÍSOLA DELLE FÉMMINE — PALERMO

La Playa

viale Marino 55, 90040
091 8677001 091 8677001
e-mail: campinglaplaya@virglio.it
web: www.laplayacamping.it
A ideal site for a relaxing holiday with beautiful views and quiet woodland walks. Beach lies in front of the campsite.
dir: *A29 Palermo to Trapani & SS113.*
Open: 15 Mar-15 Oct **Site:** 2.2HEC **Prices:** 20.50-31 **Facilities:** Wi-fi (charged) Play Area **Services:** **Leisure:** S **Off-site:**

MENFI — AGRIGENTO

Palma

via delle Palme n 29, 92013
0925 78392 0925 78392
e-mail: campinglapalma@libero.it
web: www.campinglapalma.com
dir: *6km S.*
Open: All Year. **Site:** 1HEC **Facilities:** **Services:** **Leisure:** S

NICOLOSI — CATANIA

Etna

via Goethe, 95030
095 914309 095 914309
e-mail: camping.etna@tiscali.it
Open: All Year. **Site:** 2.9HEC **Facilities:** **Services:** **Leisure:** P **Off-site:**

OLIVERI — MESSINA

Marinello

Contrada Marinello, 98060
0941 313000 0941 313702
e-mail: marinello@camping.it
web: www.villaggiomarinello.it
Site consists of small pitches set in a woodland area 100m from the sea. Dogs not permitted in July and August.
dir: *A20 exit Falcone.*
Open: All Year. **Site:** 3.2HEC **Facilities:** **Services:** **Leisure:** S **Off-site:**

PORTOPALO — SIRACUSA

Capo Passero

96010
0931 842333
Slightly sloping site towards the sea with view of fishing harbour of Portopalo.
dir: *Turn S on 115 in Noto or Iolspica towards Pachino.*
Open: 30 Mar-10 Oct **Site:** 3.5HEC **Facilities:** **Services:** **Leisure:** P S **Off-site:**

ITALY

PUNTA BRACCETTO RAGUSA

Camping Luminoso

viale dei Canalotti sn, 97017
☎ 0932 918401 🖷 0932 918455
e-mail: info@campingluminoso.com
web: www.campingluminoso.com

Relaxing site, ideal for families, with direct access to a sandy beach. Kids' club in July and August. Cars can be parked by tents except July and August.

GPS: 36.8172, 14.4658

Open: All Year. **Site:** 15HEC **Facilities:** Wi-fi (charged) Kids' Club Play Area **Services:** **Leisure:** S **Off-site:**

Rocca dei Tramonti

97017
☎ 0932 863208 🖷 0932 918054

The site lies in a quiet setting on rather barren land near a beautiful sandy bay surrounded by cliffs.

dir: *From Marina di Ragusa 10km W on coast road to Punta Braccetto.*

Open: May-Sep **Site:** 3HEC **Facilities:** **Leisure:** S **Off-site:**

SANT' ALESSIO SICULO MESSINA

Focetta Sicula

Contrada Siena 40, 98030
☎ 0942 751657 🖷 0942 756708
e-mail: lafocetta@camping.it
web: www.lafocetta.it

A well-equipped site with a private beach in a quiet beautiful location.

GPS: 37.9314, 15.3556

Open: All Year. **Site:** 1.2HEC **Prices:** 17-30 Mobile home hire 350-910 **Facilities:** Wi-fi (charged) Play Area **Services:** **Leisure:** S **Off-site:**

SECCAGRANDE AGRIGENTO

Kamemi Camping Village

92016
☎ 0925 69212 🖷 0925 69212
e-mail: info@kamemicamping.com
web: www.kamemivillage.com

Wooded surroundings close to the beach with good recreational facilities.

Open: All Year. **Site:** 5HEC **Prices:** 15-43 **Facilities:** Kids' Club **Services:** **Leisure:** P S **Off-site:**

Luxembourg

Drinking and Driving
If the level of alcohol in the bloodstream is 0.05 per cent or more severe penalties include fines and / or prison. Young driver's blood alcohol level is 0.019 per cent.

Driving Licence
Minimum age at which a UK licence holder may drive temporarily imported car and / or motorcycle 18.

Fines
On-the-spot. Unauthorised and dangerous parking can result in the car being impounded or removed.

Lights
Sidelights required when parking where there isn't any public lighting. When visibility is reduced to fewer than 100 metres due to fog, snow, heavy rain etc, dipped headlights must be used. It is compulsory to flash headlights at night when overtaking outside built-up areas. In tunnels indicated by a sign, drivers must use their passing lights.

Motorcycles
Use of dipped headlights during the day compulsory. The wearing of crash helmets is compulsory for both driver and passenger. Child under 12 not permitted as a passenger.

Motor Insurance
Third-party compulsory.

Passengers & Children
Children under 3 years of age must be seated in an approved restraint system. Children aged 3 to 18 years and / or under 1.5m must be seated in an appropriate restraint system. If their weight is over 36kg a seatbelt can be used but only on the rear seat of the vehicle. Rearward facing child restraint systems are prohibited on seats with frontal airbags unless the airbag is disabled.

Seat Belts
Compulsory for front / rear seat occupants to wear seat belts, if fitted.

Speed Limits
Unless signed otherwise

Private vehicles without trailers	
Built-up areas	50km/h
Outside built-up areas	90km/h
Motorways	130km/h
(in case of rain or snow)	110km/h
vehicles with spiked tyres	70km/h
Vehicle with trailer	
Built-up areas	50km/h
Outside built-up areas	75km/h
Motorways	90km/h

CLERVAUX

Official de Clervaux

33 r Klatzewee, 9714
☎ 920042 🖹 929728
e-mail: info@camping-clervaux.lu
web: www.camping-clervaux.lu

Situated next to the sports stadium, between the La Clerve stream and the railway, in a forested area. Trains only run during the day and there is little noise. Separate field for tents.

Dir: *0.5km SW from village.*

Open: 15 Mar-30 Oct **Site:** 3HEC **Facilities:** **Services:** **Leisure:** P R **Off-site:**

DIEKIRCH

Bleesbruck

9359
☎ 803134 🖹 802718
e-mail: info@camping-bleesbruck.lu
web: www.camping-bleesbruck.lu

A modern site in tranquil wooded surroundings, with a separate naturist area.

Open: Apr-Oct **Site:** 4HEC **Facilities:** Play Area **Services:** **Leisure:** R **Off-site:** P

Facilities shop shower electric points for razors electric points for caravans parking by tents permitted compulsory separate car park **Services** café/restaurant bar Camping Gaz International gas other than Camping Gaz first aid facilities laundry **Leisure** swimming L-Lake P-Pool R-River S-Sea **Off-site** All facilities within 5km

Op der Sauer

rte de Gilsdorf, 9201
☎ 808590 🖷 809470
web: www.campsauer.lu
All necessary ingredients for a good camping experience. Spacious pitches and many facilities around the park. Younger guests are provided for as well.
dir: *0.5km from town centre on road to Gilsdorf, near stadium.*
Open: All Year. **Site:** 5HEC **Facilities:** **Services:** **Leisure:** P

DILLINGEN

Wies-Neu

12 r de la Sûre, 6350
☎ 836110 🖷 26876438
web: www.camping-wies-neu.lu
A comfortable family site on the bank of the River Sûre.
dir: *Between Diekirch & Echternacht.*
Open: Apr-30 Oct **Site:** 45HEC **Facilities:** **Services:** **Leisure:** R **Off-site:**

ECHTERNACH

Official

17 rte de Diekirch, 6430
☎ 720272 🖷 26720847
e-mail: info@camping-echternach.lu
web: www.camping-echternach.lu
Just 10 minutes from the centre of Echternach, this terraced site is divided into three areas. A kids' club is available from mid July to mid August.
dir: *E42 to Echternach.*
Open: 15 Mar-1 Nov **Site:** 7HEC **Prices:** 17.10 Mobile home hire 250-300 **Facilities:** Kids' Club Play Area **Services:** **Leisure:** P **Off-site:** L P R

ENSCHERANGE

Val d'Or

9747
☎ 920691 🖷 929725
e-mail: valdor@pt.lu
web: www.valdor.lu
Quiet family site in a beautiful natural setting beside the River Clerve. Wi-fi available free of charge for one hour daily.
dir: *8km S of Clervaux between Drauffelt & Wilwerwiltz.*
GPS: 50.0001, 5.9910
Open: Apr-1 Nov **Site:** 4HEC **Prices:** 14-20 Mobile home hire 210-650 **Facilities:** Wi-fi Kids' Club Play Area **Services:** **Leisure:** R **Off-site:**

ESCH-SUR-ALZETTE

Gaalgebierg

4001
☎ 541069 🖷 549630
web: www.gaalgebierg.lu
A level park-like site with lovely trees on a hillock.
dir: *N6 SE from town centre towards Dudelange, right at motorway underpass, steep climb uphill.*
Open: All Year. **Site:** 2.5HEC **Facilities:** **Services:** **Off-site:** P

HEIDERSCHEID

Fuussekaul

4 Fuussekaul, 9156
☎ 2688881 🖷 26888828
e-mail: info@fuussekaul.lu
web: www.fuussekaul.lu
A level grassland family site adjoining a woodland area. Good recreational facilities.
dir: *Off N15 Bastogne-Diekirch.*
Open: All Year. **Site:** 18HEC **Prices:** 18.50-38 **Facilities:** Wi-fi (charged) Kids' Club Play Area **Services:** **Leisure:** P **Off-site:** L R

INGLEDORF

Gritt

r du Pont, 9161
☎ 802018 🖷 802019
Set on the southern bank of the Sûre between Ettelbruck and Diekirch. A beautiful country setting ideal for fishing.
Open: Apr-Oct **Site:** 5HEC **Prices:** 16.60-21.50 **Facilities:** **Services:** **Leisure:** P R **Off-site:** L

KOCKELSCHEUER

Kockelscheuer

22 rte de Bettembourg, 1899
☎ 471815 🖷 401243
e-mail: caravani@pt.lu
web: www.camp-kockelscheuer.lu
A modern site on the edge of a forest.
dir: *4km from Luxembourg off N31.*
GPS: 49.5722, 6.1083
Open: Etr-Oct **Site:** 3.8HEC **Prices:** 13 **Facilities:** **Services:** **Off-site:**

LAROCHETTE

Kengert

7633
☎ 837186 878323
e-mail: info@kengert.lu
web: www.kengert.lu

On gently sloping meadow in a pleasant rural location.

C&CC Report *The Ardennes is a gorgeous region in which to unwind, with its beautiful, unspoiled, uncrowded countryside of high, forested, rolling hills and deep, lush valleys peppered with striking rock formations. Popular for short and long stays alike, Auf Kengert is a particularly welcoming and homely site, while the free local transport and entry to attractions throughout the Grand Duchy, with the special Luxembourg Card, are a major bonus.*

dir: *N8 towards Mersch, CR119 towards Nommern, 2km turn right.*

GPS: 49.8003, 6.1985

Open: Mar-7 Nov **Site:** 4HEC **Prices:** 20-30 **Facilities:** Wi-fi Play Area **Services:** **Leisure:** P

MAULUSMÜHLE

Woltzdal

Maison 12, 9974
☎ 998938 979739
e-mail: info@woltzdal-camping.lu
web: www.campingwoltzdal.com

Quiet family site in the deep Woltz Valley.

dir: *N30 from Liège to Bastogne, N874 to Clervaux & onto N12.*

Open: Apr-Oct **Site:** 1.5HEC **Prices:** 20-21 Mobile home hire 475-670 **Facilities:** Wi-fi (charged) Play Area **Services:** **Leisure:** R

MERSCH

Krounebierg

r du camping, 7572
☎ 329756 327987
e-mail: contact@campingkrounebierg.lu
web: www.campingkrounebierg.lu

A clean, well-kept site on five terraces, split into sections by hedges.

dir: *0.5km W of village church.*

Open: Apr-Oct **Site:** 5.5HEC **Prices:** 19.80-30.90 Mobile home hire 385-595 **Facilities:** Wi-fi Kids' Club Play Area **Services:** **Leisure:** P

NOMMERN

Europacamping Nommerlayen

r Nommerlayen, 7465
☎ 878078 879678
e-mail: nommerlayen@vo.lu
web: www.nommerlayen-ec.lu

A terraced site in wooded surroundings with plenty of recreational facilities. A kid's club is available during the school holidays.

Open: Feb-Nov **Site:** 15HEC **Prices:** 26-43 Mobile home hire 365-880 **Facilities:** Wi-fi (charged) Kids' Club Play Area **Services:** **Leisure:** P

OBEREISENBACH

Kohnenhof

1 Kounenhaff, 9838
☎ 929464 929690
e-mail: kohnenhof@pt.lu
web: www.campingkohnenhof.lu

Quiet site in a rural setting in the River Our valley. The site has a restaurant in an old farmhouse.

Open: All Year. **Site:** 6HEC **Prices:** 20.90-29 Mobile home hire 350-770 **Facilities:** Wi-fi Kids' Club Play Area **Services:** **Leisure:** R

ROSPORT

Barrage

rte d'Echternach, 6580
☎ 730160 735155
e-mail: campingrosport@pt.lu
web: www.campingrosport.com

Situated by Lake Sûre on the German border at the entrance to Luxembourg's Little Switzerland.

dir: *Main road from Echternach to Wasserbillig.*

Open: 15 Mar-Oct **Site:** 3.2HEC **Facilities:** Wi-fi (charged) Play Area **Services:** **Leisure:** L P R **Off-site:**

STEINFORT

Steinfort

72 rte de Luxembourg, 8440
☎ 398827 397410
e-mail: campstei@pt.lu
web: www.camping-steinfort.lu

A small family site with good recreational and entertainment facilities, well situated for exploring the Seven Castles area.

dir: *E25 exit Steinfort.*

Open: All Year. **Site:** 3.5HEC **Prices:** 11.70-23 **Facilities:** Kids' Club **Services:** **Leisure:** P **Off-site:**

LUXEMBOURG

Netherlands

Drinking & Driving
If the level of alcohol in the bloodstream is over 0.05 per cent, severe penalties include fine, withdrawal of driving licence, fine and imprisonment. The lower limit of 0.02 per cent applies to new drivers for the first five years and moped riders up to the age of 24.

Driving Licence
Minimum age at which a UK licence holder may drive a temporarily imported car and/or motorcycle 18.

Fines
On-the-spot. In the case of illegal parking the police can impose on-the-spot fines or tow the vehicle away. Vehicles can be confiscated in cases of heavy excess of speed and drink driving.

Lights
The use of dipped headlights during the day is recommended. At night it is prohibited to drive with only sidelights.

Motorcycles
The use of dipped headlights during the day is recommended. The wearing of crash helmets is compulsory for all motorcycles which are capable of exceeding 25 km/h this is also applicable to drivers and passengers of open micro-cars without seatbelts.

Motor Insurance
Third-party compulsory.

Passengers & Children
Children up to the age of 18 and less than 1.35m in height cannot travel as a front or rear seat passenger unless using a suitable restraint system adapted to their size. Suitable child restraint systems must meet the safety approval of ECE 44/03 or 44/04. If the vehicle is not fitted with rear seat belts children under 3 are not permitted to travel in the vehicle. Children under 3 are permitted to travel in the front seats if using a rear facing child seat with the airbag deactivated (if fitted). If the vehicle's front seats are not fitted with seat belts only passengers measuring 1.35m or more may travel in the front seat.

Seat Belts
Compulsory for front and rear seat occupants to wear seat belts, if fitted.

Speed Limits
Unless signed otherwise

private vehicles without trailers

Built-up areas	50km/h
Outside built-up areas	80km/h or 100km/h
Motorways	120km/h

Campervan/Vehicle with trailer (Under 3.5 tonnes)

Inside built-up areas	50km/h
Motorways	90km/h
Main roads	90km/h
Other roads	80km/h

Campervan/Vehicle with trailer (Over 3.5 tonnes)

Inside built-up areas	50km/h
Motorways	80km/h
Main roads	80km/h
Other roads	80km/h

No minimum speed on motorways.

Additional Information
Warning triangle or hazard warning lights must be used in case of accident or breakdown (recommended that warning triangle always be carried).

Buses have right of way when leaving bus stops in built-up areas.

Trams have right of way except when crossing a priority road. Beware of large numbers of cyclists and skaters.

Spiked tyres are prohibited.

The use of a radar detector is prohibited, if a person is caught using such a device by the police the radar detector will be confiscated and you will be fined €250.

Horns should not be used at night and only used in moderation during the day.

Parking discs can be obtained from local stores.

Tolls Vignette Currency Euro (€)	Car	Car Towing Caravan/Trailer
Bridges and Tunnels		
Westerschelde Tunnel	€4.70	€7.00

NORTH

AMEN DRENTHE

Vakantiepark Diana Heide

53 Amen, 9446
☎ 0592 389297 🖷 0592 389432
e-mail: info@dianaheide.nl
web: www.dianaheide.nl

An ideal site for relaxation, set away from traffic among forest and heathland.

dir: *E35 from Assen, through Amen towards Hooghalen.*

Open: Apr-Oct **Site:** 30HEC **Prices:** 20.10-27.10 **Facilities:** Wi-fi (charged) Kids' Club Play Area **Services:** **Leisure:** L P **Off-site:** R

ANNEN DRENTHE

Hondsrug

Annerweg 3, 9463
☎ 0592 271292 🖷 0592 271440
e-mail: info@hondsrug.nl
web: www.hondsrug.nl

A family site in a pleasant rural setting with good recreational facilities.

dir: *On N34 SE of Annen.*

GPS: 53.0361, 6.7392

Open: Apr-1 Oct **Site:** 18HEC **Prices:** 21-27.90 Mobile home hire 300-540 **Facilities:** Wi-fi (charged) Kids' Club **Services:** **Leisure:** P

ASSEN DRENTHE

Valiantiepark Witterzomer

Witterzomer 7, 9405
☎ 0592 393535 🖷 0592 393530
e-mail: info@witterzomer.nl
web: www.witterzomer.nl

A large site with internal asphalt roads, lying in mixed woodland near a nature reserve. Separate sections for dog owners. Individual washing facilities for disabled people.

dir: *Off A28.*

Open: All Year. **Site:** 75HEC **Prices:** 18-26 Mobile home hire 225-725 **Facilities:** Wi-fi (charged) **Services:** **Leisure:** L P

BERGUM FRIESLAND

Bergumermeer

Solcamastr 30, 9262
☎ 0511 461385 🖷 0511 463955
e-mail: info@bergumermeer.nl
web: www.bergumermeer.nl

Pleasant wooded surroundings with good recreational facilities, close to the marina on Bergumermeer. Kids' club available in July to August.

dir: *N355 onto N356 S, exit E to Sumar towards Oostermeer.*

Open: 27 Mar-Oct **Site:** 29HEC **Prices:** 22-30 **Facilities:** Wi-fi (charged) Kids' Club **Services:** **Leisure:** L P

BORGER DRENTHE

Hunzedal

De Drift 3, 9531
☎ 0599 234698 🖷 0599 235183
e-mail: info@hunzedal.nl
web: www.vakantiegevoel.nl

The site is clean, well-kept and lies north east of the village.

dir: *Off road towards Buinen, over Buinen-Schoondoord canal, 200m E turn S for 1km.*

Open: 29 Mar-1 Nov **Site:** 30HEC **Facilities:** **Services:** **Leisure:** L P

DIEVER DRENTHE

Hoeve aan den Weg

Bosweg 12, 8439
☎ 0521 387269 🖷 0521 387413
e-mail: camping@hoeveaandenweg.nl
web: www.hoeveaandenweg.nl

Pleasant wooded surroundings with good recreational facilities.

dir: *Off A32.*

Open: Apr-Oct **Site:** 9HEC **Facilities:** **Services:** **Leisure:** P

DWINGELOO DRENTHE

Noordster

Noordster 105, 7991
☎ 0521 597238 🖷 0521 597589
e-mail: noordster@rcn.nl
web: www.rcn.nl

A large family site with static and touring pitches, surrounded by woodland.

dir: *3km S on E35.*

Open: All Year. **Site:** 42HEC **Prices:** 25-38 Mobile home hire 300-670 **Facilities:** **Services:** **Leisure:** P

FRANEKER — FRIESLAND

Bloemketerp

Burg J Dykstraweg 3, 8801
☎ 0517 395099 🖹 0517 395150
e-mail: info@bloemketerp.nl
web: www.bloemketerp.nl

Set in a well-equipped leisure centre near the historic city centre of Franeker.

Open: All Year. **Site:** 5HEC **Facilities:** **Services:** **Off-site:** L P R S

GRONINGEN — GRONINGEN

Stadspark

Campinglaan 6, 9727
☎ 050 5251624 🖹 050 5250099
e-mail: info@campingstadspark.nl
web: www.campingstadspark.nl

A well-kept site on patches of grass between rows of bushes and groups of pine and deciduous trees. Some of its pitches are naturally screened.

dir: *From SW outskirts of town towards Peize & Roden.*

Open: 15 Mar-15 Oct **Site:** 6HEC **Prices:** 16.20-23.70 **Facilities:** **Services:** **Off-site:** L P

HARLINGEN — FRIESLAND

Zeehoeve

8862
☎ 0517 413465 🖹 0517 416971
e-mail: info@zeehoeve.nl
web: www.zeehoeve.nl

A well-kept meadowland site divided into large sections by rows of bushes.

dir: *1km S of Harlingen near a dyke.*

Open: Apr-Sep **Site:** 10HEC **Facilities:** **Services:** **Leisure:** S **Off-site:**

HEE (ISLAND OF TERSCHELLING) — FRIESLAND

Camping de Kooi

Heester Kooiweg 20, 8882
☎ 0562 442743 🖹 0562 442835
e-mail: info@campingdekooi.nl
web: www.campingdekooi.nl

Quiet and spacious site surrounded by woodland and dunes.

dir: *5km from harbour.*

Open: 15 Apr-15 Sep **Site:** 8.5HEC **Prices:** 20.60-23.60 **Facilities:** **Services:** **Leisure:** L **Off-site:** S

HINDELOOPEN — FRIESLAND

Hindeloopen

Westerdijk 9, 8713
☎ 0514 521452 🖹 0514 523221
e-mail: info@campinghindeloopen.nl
web: www.campinghindeloopen.nl

A peaceful site on the Ijsselmeer with fishing and water sports.

dir: *Via N359.*

Open: Apr-Oct **Site:** 16HEC **Facilities:** **Services:** **Leisure:** L

KOUDUM — FRIESLAND

De Kuilart

Kuilart 1, 8723
☎ 0514 522221 🖹 0514 523010
e-mail: info@kuilart.nl
web: www.kuilart.nl

A camping and water-sports centre on the shores of De Fluessen lake.

dir: *Via N359.*

Open: All Year. **Site:** 37HEC **Facilities:** **Services:** **Leisure:** L P **Off-site:** S

LAUWERSOOG — GRONINGEN

Lauwersoog

Strandweg 5, 9976
☎ 0519 349133 🖹 0519 349195
e-mail: info@lauwersoog.nl
web: www.lauwersoog.nl

A pleasant location on the shores of Lauwersmeer. A good excursion centre with water sports.

Open: All Year. **Site:** 35HEC **Facilities:** **Services:** **Leisure:** L S

MAKKUM — FRIESLAND

Holle Poarte

Holle Poarte 2, 8754
☎ 0515 231344 🖹 0515 231339
e-mail: info@hollepoarte.nl
web: www.hollepoarte.nl

A modern site with water sports on the Ijsselmeer.

Open: All Year. **Site:** 32HEC **Facilities:** **Services:** **Leisure:** L

NETHERLANDS

OPENDE FRIESLAND

Strandheem

Parkweg 2, 9865
☎ 0594 659555 🖹 0594 658592
e-mail: info@strandheem.nl
web: www.strandheem.nl

A family site with modern sanitary blocks and a variety of recreational facilities.

dir: *A7 exit 31.*

Open: Apr-1 Oct **Site:** 15HEC **Prices:** 17.50-25.50 Mobile home hire 195-700 **Facilities:** **Services:** **Leisure:** L P

RUINEN DRENTHE

Wiltzangh

Witteveen 2, 7963
☎ 0522 471227 🖹 0522 472178
e-mail: info@dewiltzangh.ruinen.nl
web: www.dewiltzangh.com

Set in the middle of a coniferous and deciduous forest, and within the grounds of a big holiday village.

dir: *From Ruinen towards Ansen, 3km turn N.*

Open: Apr-Oct **Site:** 13HEC **Facilities:** **Services:** **Leisure:** P

TERMUNTERZIJL GRONINGEN

Zeestrand Eems-Dollard

Schepperbuurt 4a, 9948
☎ 0596 601443 🖹 0596 601209
e-mail: campingzeestrand@online.nl
web: www.campingzeestrand.nl

Situated on a tongue of land in the Wadden See with views of Germany. Close to a beach.

dir: *A7 exit 45 for Delfzijl, site signed.*

Open: Apr-1 Nov **Site:** 6.5HEC **Facilities:** **Services:** **Leisure:** L P R S **Off-site:**

WEDDE GRONINGEN

Wedderbergen

Molenweg 2, 9698
☎ 0597 561673
e-mail: info@wedderbergen.nl
web: www.wedderbergen.nl

Meadowland site divided by deciduous trees and hedges.

dir: *From E outskirts of village onto narrow asphalt road N, 3.2km onto Spanjaardsweg & Molenweg to site.*

GPS: 53.0861, 7.0819

Open: Apr-Sep **Site:** 40HEC **Prices:** 19.50-27.50 Mobile home hire 250-425 **Facilities:** Wi-fi (charged) Kids' Club Play Area **Services:** **Leisure:** L R **Off-site:** P

CENTRAL

ALKMAAR NOORD-HOLLAND

Alkmaar

Bergerweg 201, 1817
☎ 072 5116924
e-mail: info@campingalkmaar.nl
web: www.campingalkmaar.nl

The site is well-kept and divided into many sections by rows of trees and bushes.

dir: *On NW outskirts of town, off Bergen road.*

Open: Mar-Oct **Site:** 3HEC **Facilities:** **Services:** **Off-site:** P

AMSTELVEEN NOORD-HOLLAND

Het Amsterdam Bos

Kleine Noorddijk 1, 1432
☎ 020 6416868 🖹 020 6402378
e-mail: info@campingamsterdam.com
web: www.campingamsterdam.com

The site is in a park-like setting in the Amsterdam wood. The camp is near the airport flight path and is subject to noise depending on the wind direction.

dir: *From The Hague along motorway, turn at N edge of airport towards Amstelveen, signs for Aalsmeer. From Utrecht, motorway exit Amstelveen for Aalsmeer, through Bovenkerk.*

Open: Apr-Oct **Site:** 6.8HEC **Facilities:** **Services:** **Off-site:** L P R

NETHERLANDS

AMSTERDAM — NOORD-HOLLAND

Gaasper Camping Amsterdam

Loosdrechtdreef 7, 1108
☎ 020 6967326 🖹 020 6969369
web: www.gaaspercamping.nl

Situated on the edge of the beautiful Gaasperpark within easy reach, by metro, to the centre of Amsterdam.

dir: *A9 exit Gaasperplas/Weesp (S113), campsite signed.*

GPS: 52.3128, 4.9906

Open: 15 Mar-1 Nov **Site:** 5.5HEC **Prices:** 22 **Facilities:** Play Area **Services:** **Off-site:** L

Zeeburg

Zuider Ijdijk 20, 1095
☎ 020 6944430 🖹 020 6946238
e-mail: info@campingzeeburg.nl
web: www.campingzeeburg.nl

On an island in the Ijmeer, 15 minutes from the city centre, with good facilities. Popular with backpackers and holidaymakers alike.

dir: *A10 exit S114 for Zeeberg*

Open: All Year. **Site:** 4HEC **Prices:** 21-26 **Facilities:** Wi-fi **Services:** **Leisure:** L **Off-site:** P

ANDIJK — NOORD-HOLLAND

Vakantiedorp Het Grootslag

Proefpolder 4, 1619
☎ 0228 592944 🖹 0228 592457
e-mail: info@andijkvakanties.nl
web: www.andijkvakanties.nl

A well-equipped site situated on the Ijsselmeer. Individual bathrooms are allocated to some of the pitches and a range of recreational facilities are available.

dir: *A7 exit Hoorn-Noord/Enkhuizen/Lelystad, left for Andijk, signs for Het Grootslag & Dijkweg.*

Open: Apr-30 Oct **Site:** 40HEC **Facilities:** **Services:** **Leisure:** L P

APPELTERN — GELDERLAND

Het Groene Eiland

Lutenkampstr 2, 6629
☎ 0487 562130 🖹 0487 561540
e-mail: info@hetgroeneeiland.nl
web: www.hetgroeneeiland.nl

Set in a water recreation park with plenty of sports facilities and sauna.

dir: *A15 exit Leeuwen & signed.*

Open: 20 Feb-9 Jan **Site:** 16HEC **Prices:** 17.85-22.30 Mobile home hire 271-824 **Facilities:** Wi-fi (charged) Kids' Club Play Area **Services:** **Leisure:** L R

ARNHEM — GELDERLAND

Arnhem

Kemperbergerweg 771, 6816
☎ 026 4431600 🖹 026 4457705
e-mail: info@recreatieparkarnhem.nl
web: www.recreatieparkarnhem.nl

The site lies on grassland and is surrounded by trees.

dir: *NW of town & S of E36.*

Open: Apr-Oct **Site:** 36HEC **Facilities:** **Services:** **Leisure:** P

Buitengoed Hooge Veluwe

Koningsweg 14, 6816
☎ 026 4432272 🖹 026 4436809
e-mail: info@hoogeveluwe.nl
web: www.hoogeveluwe.nl

Situated in a pleasant natural park with good facilities.

dir: *E36 exit Apeldoorn, NW towards Hooge Veluwe.*

Open: 31 Mar-28 Oct **Site:** 18HEC **Facilities:** **Services:** **Leisure:** P

Warnsborn

Bakenbergseweg 257, 6816
☎ 026 4423469 🖹 026 4421095
e-mail: info@campingwarnsborn.nl
web: www.campingwarnsborn.nl

The site is surrounded by woodland and lies on slightly sloping meadowland. Near zoo and open-air museum.

dir: *Near E36 NW of town towards Utrecht. 200m S of fuel station, continue W for 0.7km.*

Open: Apr-Oct **Site:** 3.5HEC **Prices:** 18.50-20.50 Mobile home hire 280-400 **Facilities:** Wi-fi (charged) **Services:** **Off-site:** P

BABBERICH — GELDERLAND

Rivo Torto

Beekseweg 8, 6909
☎ 0316 247332 🖷 0316 246628
e-mail: info@rivotorto.nl
web: www.rivotorto.nl
A riverside site with good recreational facilities.
dir: *3km W on E36.*
Open: 15 Mar-Oct **Site:** 8.5HEC **Prices:** 15-18.50 **Facilities:** **Services:** **Off-site:**

BERKHOUT — NOORD-HOLLAND

Westerkogge

Kerkebuurt 202, 1647
☎ 0229 551208 🖷 0229 551390
e-mail: info@westerkogge.nl
A fine location with sheltered pitches and a good range of recreational facilities.
dir: *A7 exit Hoorn-Berkhout or Berkhout-Avenhorn.*
Open: Apr-Oct **Site:** 11HEC **Facilities:** **Services:** **Leisure:** P

BIDDINGHUIZEN — GELDERLAND

Riviera Park

Spijkweg 15, 8256
☎ 0321 331344 🖷 0321 331402
e-mail: info@riviera.nl
web: www.riviera.nl
Grassland site surrounded by shrubs near a deciduous forest.
dir: *On Polder beside Veluwemeer, 5km S of Biddinghuizen turn left.*
Open: Apr-30 Oct **Site:** 60HEC **Facilities:** **Services:** **Leisure:** L P

BILTHOVEN — UTRECHT

Bospark Bilthoven

Burg v.d Borchlaan 7, 3722
☎ 030 2286777 🖷 030 2293888
e-mail: info@bosparkbilthoven.nl
web: www.bosparkbilthoven.nl
Family site in wooded surroundings with asphalt drives.
dir: *Signed from town centre.*
Open: Apr-Oct **Site:** 20HEC **Facilities:** **Services:** **Leisure:** P **Off-site:**

BLOKZIJL — OVERIJSSEL

Tussen de Diepen

Duinigermeerweg 1A, 8356
☎ 0527 291565 🖷 0527 292203
e-mail: camping@tussendediepen.nl
web: www.tussendediepen.nl
Secluded site surrounded by water. Fishing, water sports and sailing.
Open: Apr-Oct **Site:** 5.2HEC **Facilities:** **Services:** **Leisure:** L R **Off-site:** P

BUURSE — OVERIJSSEL

't Hazenbos

Oude Buurserdijk 1, 7481
☎ 053 5696338
e-mail: info@hazenbos.nl
web: www.hazenbos.nl
On several meadows, partially surrounded by trees.
dir: *7km from German border.*
Open: 15 Mar-Oct **Site:** 6HEC **Prices:** 14.20-16.50 **Facilities:** **Services:** **Off-site:** L

CALLANTSOOG — NOORD-HOLLAND

Recreatiecentrum de Nollen

Westerweg 8, 1759
☎ 0224 581281 🖷 0224 582098
e-mail: info@denollen.nl
web: www.denollen.nl
A modern family site with plenty of facilities, less than 1.6km from the beach.
dir: *E of town towards N9.*
Open: 28 Mar-1 Nov **Site:** 9HEC **Facilities:** **Services:** **Off-site:** P S

Tempelhof

Westerweg 2, 1759
☎ 0224 581522 🖷 0224 582133
e-mail: info@tempelhof.nl
web: www.tempelhof.nl
Well-equipped site on level meadowland.
dir: *N9 5km.*
GPS: 52.8472, 4.7153
Open: All Year. **Site:** 12.7HEC **Prices:** 17-37 Mobile home hire 385-609 **Facilities:** Wi-fi (charged) Kids' Club Play Area **Services:** **Leisure:** P **Off-site:** S

NETHERLANDS

DENEKAMP — OVERIJSSEL

Papillon

Kanaalweg 30, 7591
05413 51670 05413 55217
e-mail: info@depapillon.nl
web: www.depapillon.nl

Mostly a chalet site on meadowland in a coniferous and deciduous forest, 2km north of Denekamp. There are a few naturally screened pitches.

dir: *Off E72 towards Nordhorn (Germany) 300m N of sign for Almelo-Nordhorn canal, continue NE 1.5km.*

Open: Apr-1 Oct **Site:** 16.5HEC **Prices:** 12.90-27 Mobile home hire 240-695 **Facilities:** Wi-fi Kids' Club Play Area **Services:** **Leisure:** L P

DIEPENHEIM — OVERIJSSEL

Molnhofte

Nyhofweg 5, 7478
0547 351514 0547 351641
e-mail: info@molnhofte.nl
web: www.molnhofte.nl

A family site in a rural setting with modern bungalows for hire.

dir: *E of town.*

Open: All Year. **Site:** 6HEC **Prices:** 14.80-20.80 **Facilities:** Wi-fi (charged) **Services:** **Leisure:** P

DOETINCHEM — GELDERLAND

Wrange

Rekhemseweg 144, 7004
0314 324852 0314 378470
e-mail: info@dewrange.nl
web: www.dewrange.nl

On the eastern outskirts of the town, set in meadowland and surrounded by bushes and deciduous trees.

dir: *200m E of link road between roads to Varsseveld & Terborg.*

Open: All Year. **Site:** 12HEC **Facilities:** **Services:** **Leisure:** P

DOORN — UTRECHT

Het Grote Bos

Hydeparklaan 24, 3941
0343 513644 0343 512324
e-mail: het-grote-bos@rcn.nl
web: www.rcn.nl

Well laid-out site on wooded grassland. Varied leisure activities for children and adults.

dir: *1km NW of Doorn.*

Open: All Year. **Site:** 80HEC **Facilities:** **Services:** **Leisure:** P

EDAM — NOORD-HOLLAND

Strandbad-Edam

Zeevangszeedijk 7a, 1135
0299 371994 0299 371510
e-mail: info@campingstrandbad.nl
web: www.campingstrandbad.nl

A friendly family site on Ijssel Lake with plenty of facilities and close to the historical town of Edam.

dir: *N247 exit signed Edam North.*

Open: Apr-Sep **Site:** 5HEC **Prices:** 15.60-20.45 **Facilities:** Wi-fi (charged) Play Area **Services:** **Leisure:** L **Off-site:** P

EERBEEK — GELDERLAND

Landal Greenparks Coldenhove

Boshoffweg 6, 6961
0313 659101 0313 654776
e-mail: coldenhove@landal.nl
web: www.landal.com

Set in woodland.

dir: *From Apeldoorn-Dieren road 2km SW, then NW for 1km.*

Open: 18 Mar-1 Nov **Site:** 74HEC **Facilities:** **Services:** **Leisure:** P

Robertsoord

Doonweg 4, 6961
0313 651346 0313 655751
e-mail: info@robertsoord.nl
web: www.robertsoord.nl

Wooded location with good recreational facilities.

dir: *1km SE.*

Open: Apr-Oct **Site:** 2.5HEC **Prices:** 15-20 **Facilities:** Wi-fi **Services:** **Off-site:** P

ENSCHEDE — OVERIJSSEL

De Twentse Es

Keppelerdijk 200, 7534
☎ 053 4611372 Fax 053 4618558
e-mail: info@twentse-es.nl
web: www.twentse-es.nl
Wooded location with good recreational facilities.
dir: *Signed on A35.*
Open: All Year. **Site:** 10HEC **Prices:** 21.90-25.75 **Facilities:** Wi-fi Kids' Club Play Area **Services:** **Leisure:** P

ERMELO — GELDERLAND

Haeghehorst

Fazantlaan 4, 3852
☎ 0341 553185 Fax 0341 562751
e-mail: info@haeghehorst.nl
web: www.haeghehorst.nl
Well-equipped site in pleasant wooded surroundings.
dir: *A28 towards Amersfoort, onto N303.*
Open: All Year. **Site:** 10HEC **Facilities:** **Services:** **Leisure:** P

GROOTE KEETEN — NOORD-HOLLAND

Callassande

Voorweg 5A, 1759
☎ 0224 581663 Fax 0224 582588
e-mail: info@callassande.nl
web: www.callassande.nl
A large site with fine facilities close to the sea.
Open: Apr-Oct **Site:** 12HEC **Prices:** 24-32 Mobile home hire 500-650 **Facilities:** Wi-fi (charged) **Services:** **Leisure:** P **Off-site:** S

HAAKSBERGEN — OVERIJSSEL

't Stien'n Boer

Scholtenhagenweg 42, 7481
☎ 053 5722610 Fax 053 5729394
e-mail: info@stien-nboer.nl
web: www.stien-nboer.nl
A family site with good recreational facilities, including indoor swimming pool with separate pool for children, near the town.
Open: Apr-Oct **Site:** 10.5HEC **Facilities:** **Services:** **Leisure:** P

HALFWEG — NOORD-HOLLAND

Droompark Spaarnwoude

Zuiderweg 2, 1165
☎ 020 4972796 Fax 020 4975887
e-mail: info@droomparkspaarnwoude.nl
web: www.droomparkspaarnwoude.nl
Grassy site on several levels subdivided by trees, hedges and shrubs. Separate section for young campers and hiker cabins are rentable. Kids' club available in school holidays.
dir: *A5 exit Spaarnwoude, site signed.*
Open: Apr-Oct **Site:** 13HEC **Prices:** 15-24 Mobile home hire 180-475 **Facilities:** Wi-fi (charged) Kids' Club Play Area **Services:** **Leisure:** L **Off-site:** P

HATTEM — GELDERLAND

Molecaten Park de Leemkule

Leemkuilen 6, 8051
☎ 038 4441945 Fax 038 4446280
e-mail: info@leemkule.nl
web: www.leemkule.nl
The holiday centre is in one of the largest nature reserves in the country. Kids' club available during Dutch school holidays.
dir: *2.5km SW.*
Open: Apr-Oct **Site:** 16HEC **Prices:** 20.10-24.60 **Facilities:** Wi-fi (charged) Kids' Club **Services:** **Leisure:** P **Off-site:**

HEILOO — NOORD-HOLLAND

Heiloo

De Omloop 24, 1852
☎ 072 5355555 Fax 072 5355551
e-mail: info@campingheiloo.nl
web: www.campingheiloo.nl
One of the best sites in the area. It is divided into many large squares by hedges.
Open: Apr-Oct **Site:** 4HEC **Facilities:** Wi-fi **Services:** **Off-site:** L P

Klein Varnebroek

De Omloop 22, 1852
☎ 072 5331627 Fax 072 5331620
e-mail: info@kleinvarnebroek.nl
web: www.kleinvarnebroek.nl
A grassy, family site surrounded by trees.
dir: *Off Alkmaar road towards swimming pool.*
Open: 31 Mar-25 Sep **Site:** 4.86HEC **Prices:** 15.50-24.50 **Facilities:** **Services:** **Off-site:** L P S

NETHERLANDS

Facilities shop · shower · electric points for razors · electric points for caravans · parking by tents permitted · compulsory separate car park **Services** café/restaurant · bar · Camping Gaz International · gas other than Camping Gaz · first aid facilities · laundry **Leisure** swimming L-Lake P-Pool R-River S-Sea **Off-site** All facilities within 5km

HELDER, DEN — NOORD-HOLLAND

Donkere Duinen

Jan Verfailleweg 616, 1783
☎ 0223 614731
e-mail: info@donkereduinen.nl
web: www.donkereduinen.nl

A quiet, pleasant site with good facilities.

dir: *Signs for Nieuw-Den Helder Strand, 0.8km towards beach.*

Open: 23 Apr-30 Aug **Site:** 7HEC **Facilities:** **Services:** **Leisure:** S **Off-site:** P

't Noorder Sandt

Noorder Sandt 2, Julianadorp aan Zee, 1787
☎ 0223 641266 0223 645600
e-mail: noordersandt@ardoer.com
web: www.ardoer.com/noordersandt

A flat, well-maintained site on meadowland, with good sanitary blocks. Kids' club during July and August.

dir: *Access from Den Helder to Callantsoog coast road.*

Open: 26 Mar-26 Oct **Site:** 11HEC **Prices:** 21-36 **Facilities:** Wi-fi Kids' Club Play Area **Services:** **Leisure:** P **Off-site:** S

HENGELO — OVERIJSSEL

Zwaaikom

Kettingbrugweg 60, 7552
☎ 074 2916560 074 2916785
e-mail: smink_zwaaikom@planet.nl
web: www.dezwaaikom.tk

A family site on the Twente canal, with good facilities.

dir: *SE towards Enschede between canal & road.*

Open: 15 Apr-15 Sep **Site:** 4HEC **Prices:** 15.85 **Facilities:** Wi-fi (charged) **Services:** **Leisure:** P

HEUMEN — GELDERLAND

Heumens Bos

Vosseneindseweg 46, 6582
☎ 024 3581481 024 3583862
e-mail: info@heumensbos.nl
web: www.heumensbos.nl

One of the best sites in the area with modern facilities and spacious pitches.

dir: *NW of village, 100m N of Wijchen road.*

Open: All Year. **Site:** 16HEC **Prices:** 16-28 Mobile home hire 300-600 **Facilities:** Wi-fi Play Area **Services:** **Leisure:** P **Off-site:** L R

HOENDERLOO — GELDERLAND

Pampel

Woeste Hoefweg 35, 7351
☎ 055 3781760 055 3781992
e-mail: info@pampel.nl
web: www.pampel.nl

A most attractive site in pleasant wooded surroundings with good facilities for families, including a kids' club and indoor play area in high season.

Open: All Year. **Site:** 14.5HEC **Prices:** 18.50-20 **Facilities:** Wi-fi (charged) Kids' Club Play Area **Services:** **Leisure:** P **Off-site:**

HOORN, DEN (ISLAND OF TEXEL) — NOORD-HOLLAND

Kogerstrand

Badweg 33, 1796
☎ 0222 327806 0222 317018
e-mail: info@texelcampings.nl
web: www.texelcampings.nl

Located in the National Park of the Dunes of Texel, next to the sea. There is a separate area for young people aged 15-25 and dogs are only allowed on the southside. There is a restricted traffic policy and cars are parked in a central car park.

dir: *From ferry proceed to De Koog, continue along road (Nikadel). Pass Catholic church, continue along Badweg to end of road. Located behind the big hill/dune.*

Open: Apr-Oct **Site:** 52HEC **Prices:** 9.50-29 **Facilities:** Wi-fi (charged) Kids' Club Play Area **Services:** **Leisure:** S **Off-site:** P

Texelcamping Loodsmansduin

Rommelpot 19, 1797
☎ 0222 317208 0222 317018
e-mail: info@texelcampings.nl
web: www.texelcampings.nl

Close to Den Hoorn in the middle of the National Park of the Dunes of Texel. A section of the site is reserved for naturists and there is a naturist beach 1.5km away.

dir: *N501 follow signs for Den Hoorn, then small green signs.*

Open: All Year. **Site:** 38HEC **Prices:** 9.50-29 **Facilities:** Wi-fi (charged) Kids' Club Play Area **Services:** **Leisure:** P **Off-site:** S

NETHERLANDS

KESTEREN — GELDERLAND

Camping Betuwe

Hogedijkseweg 40, 4041
☎ 0488 481477 📠 0488 482599
e-mail: info@campingbetuwe.nl
web: www.campingbetuwe.nl

On level meadowland surrounded by bushy hedges and divided into individual pitches. 100m from private beach and pool.

dir: *2km N of village, turn W off main Rhenen-Kesteren road, continue 2.7km.*

Open: All Year. **Site:** 30HEC **Facilities:** **Services:** **Leisure:** L

KOOG, DE (ISLAND OF TEXEL) — NOORD-HOLLAND

Om de Noord

Boodtlaan 80, 1796
☎ 0222 317208 📠 0222 317018
e-mail: info@texelcampings.nl
web: www.rsttexel.nl

Site with spacious pitches located close to woodlands, dunes and the beach.

dir: *From ferry to De Koog, continue along road (Nikadel), pass Catholic church on right, turn right at junct with Boodtlaan, continue to football pitch, driveway on left.*

Open: Apr-Oct **Site:** 3.3HEC **Prices:** 20.45-44.60 **Facilities:** Wi-fi (charged) Kids' Club Play Area **Services:** **Off-site:** P S

Shelter

Boodtlaan 43, 1796
☎ 0222 317208 📠 0222 317018
e-mail: info@texelcampings.nl
web: www.texelcampings.nl

Small family camping site close to a forest, the beach and national parks.

dir: *N501 to De Koog. Follow road to Motel Texel, turn left, 500m on left.*

Open: All Year. **Site:** 1.1HEC **Prices:** 20.45-38.60 **Facilities:** Wi-fi (charged) Kids' Club Play Area **Services:** **Off-site:** P S

LATHUM — GELDERLAND

De Mars

Marsweg 6, 6988
☎ 0313 631131 📠 0313 631435
e-mail: info@campingdemars.nl
web: www.campingdemars.nl

Divided into pitches on level meadowland beside a dammed tributary of River Ijssel.

dir: *Off Arnhem-Doesburg road N of village & W for 1.7km.*

Open: Apr-Oct **Site:** 10HEC **Prices:** 17 **Facilities:** **Services:** **Leisure:** L

LUTTENBERG — OVERIJSSEL

Luttenberg

Heuvelweg 9, 8105
☎ 0572 301405 📠 0572 301757
e-mail: info@luttenberg.nl
web: www.luttenberg.nl

A large holiday park with spacious, well-defined pitches separated by bushes. Variety of recreational facilities.

Open: Apr-Sep **Site:** 9HEC **Facilities:** **Services:** **Leisure:** P

MAARN — UTRECHT

Laag-Kanje

Laan van Laag-Kanje 1, 3951
☎ 0343 441348 📠 0343 443295
e-mail: allurepark@laagkanje.nl
web: www.laagkanje.nl

Pleasant site with good facilities situated 0.5km from the lake.

dir: *2km NE.*

Open: Apr-Sep **Site:** 28HEC **Prices:** 22 **Facilities:** Wi-fi (charged) Kids' Club **Services:** **Off-site:** L

MIJNDEN — UTRECHT

Mijnden

Bloklaan 22a, 1231
☎ 0294 233165 📠 0294 233402
e-mail: info@mijnden.nl
web: www.mijnden.nl

Situated on Loosdrechtse Plassen lake with good sports facilities. Kids' club available during high season.

dir: *A2 exit Hilversum, after bridge turn right, through Loenen & left.*

Open: 15 Apr-25 Sep **Site:** 25HEC **Prices:** 15.50-25 **Facilities:** Wi-fi (charged) Kids' Club **Services:** **Leisure:** L **Off-site:**

NETHERLANDS

NOORD SCHARWOUDE — NOORD-HOLLAND

Molengroet Droompark

Molengroet 1, 1723
☎ 0226 393444 📠 0226 391426
e-mail: info@molengroet.nl
web: www.molengroet.nl

Site with modern facilities within easy reach of the beach and the Geestmerambacht water park. Kids' club available in high season.

dir: *Signed on N245.*

Open: Apr-Oct **Site:** 11HEC **Prices:** 19.50-30 **Facilities:** Wi-fi (charged) Kids' Club **Services:** **Leisure:** L P **Off-site:** S

NUNSPEET — GELDERLAND

Vossenberg

Groenlaantje 25, 8071
☎ 0341 252458 📠 0341 279500
e-mail: info@vrijetijdspark.nl
web: www.campingdevossenberg.nl

Open: Apr-1 Nov **Site:** 3.6HEC **Facilities:** **Services:** **Off-site:** L P

PUTTEN — GELDERLAND

Strandpark Putten

Strandboulevard 27, 3882
☎ 0341 361304 📠 0341 361210

Campsite is by a lake and has a private beach. Excellent facilities for windsurfing and yachting.

dir: *Off A28*

Open: Apr-Oct **Site:** 8HEC **Facilities:** **Services:** **Leisure:** L **Off-site:** P

REUTUM — OVERIJSSEL

De Molenhof

Kleijsenweg 7, 7667
☎ 0541 661165 📠 0541 662032
e-mail: info@demolenhof.nl
web: www.demolenhof.nl

A large family site in wooded surroundings with plenty of modern facilities.

dir: *Via A1.*

Open: 4 Apr-27 Sep **Site:** 16HEC **Facilities:** **Services:** **Leisure:** P

RHENEN — UTRECHT

Thymse Berg

Nieuwe Veenendaalseweg 229, 3911
☎ 0317 612384 📠 0317 618119
e-mail: allurepark@thijmseberg.nl
web: www.thijmseberg.nl

dir: *N of town.*

Open: Apr-Oct **Site:** 10HEC **Prices:** 20-30 Mobile home hire 275-375 **Facilities:** Wi-fi Kids' Club Play Area **Services:** **Leisure:** P **Off-site:** L R

ST MAARTENSZEE — NOORD-HOLLAND

St Maartenszee

Westerduinweg 30, 1753
☎ 0224 561401 📠 0224 561901
e-mail: info@campingsintmaartenszee.nl
web: www.campingsintmaartenszee.nl

Completely surrounded and divided into pitches by hedges, lying on meadowland beside a wide belt of dunes.

dir: *Via N9 towards Den Helder, signed in village St Maartensvlotbrug.*

Open: 30 Mar-Oct **Site:** 5HEC **Prices:** 27-36 **Facilities:** Wi-fi (charged) Kids' Club **Services:** **Off-site:** L P S

STEENWIJK — OVERIJSSEL

Kom

Bultweg 25, 8346
☎ 0521 513736 📠 0521 518736
e-mail: info@campingdekom.nl
web: www.campingdekom.nl

Split into two sections, lying near a country house, and surrounded by a beautiful oak forest.

dir: *Off Steenwijk-Frederiksoord road (NB easy to miss).*

Open: All Year. **Site:** 12.5HEC **Facilities:** **Services:** **Leisure:** P

UITDAM — NOORD-HOLLAND

Uitdam

Zeedijk 2, 1154
☎ 020 4031433 📠 020 4033692
e-mail: info@campinguitdam.nl
web: www.campinguitdam.nl

A well-maintained site on the Markermeer adjoining the marina.

dir: *Via N247 Amsterdam-Monnickendam.*

Open: Mar-Oct **Site:** 21HEC **Prices:** 16-23 **Facilities:** **Services:** **Leisure:** L

VOGELENZANG — NOORD-HOLLAND

Vogelenzang

Doodweg Tweede 17, 2114
023 5847014 023 5849249
e-mail: camping@vogelenzang.nl
web: www.vogelenzang.nl

Quiet, family site.

dir: *1km W.*

Open: Etr-15 Sep **Site:** 16HEC **Prices:** 23.50 **Facilities:** Kids' Club Play Area **Services:** **Leisure:** P **Off-site:** S

WIJDENES — NOORD-HOLLAND

Het Hof

Zuideruitweg 64, 1608
0229 501435 0229 503244
e-mail: info@campinghethof.nl
web: www.campinghethof.nl

A series of fields in a sheltered position on the shore of the Ijsselmeer.

dir: *A7 exit 8 Hoorn, onto N506 for Enkhuizen, right to Wijdenes & signed.*

Open: 30 Mar-Sep **Site:** 3.9HEC **Facilities:** **Services:** **Leisure:** L P

WINTERSWIJK — GELDERLAND

Twee Bruggen

Meenkmolenweg 11, 7109
0543 565366 0543 565222
e-mail: info@detweebruggen.nl
web: www.detweebruggen.nl

A family site in pleasant wooded surroundings with modern facilities.

Open: All Year. **Site:** 34HEC **Facilities:** **Services:** **Leisure:** L P

SOUTH

AFFERDEN — LIMBURG

Klein Canada

Dorpsstr 1, 5851
0485 531223 0485 532218
e-mail: info@kleincanada.nl
web: www.kleincanada.nl

Situated among heath and woodland close to the River Meuse.

Open: All Year. **Site:** 12.5HEC **Facilities:** **Services:** **Leisure:** P

BAARLAND — ZEELAND

Comfort Camping Scheldeoord

Landingsweg 1, 4435
0113 639900 0113 639500
e-mail: info@scheldeoord.nl
web: www.scheldeoord.nl

A popular family site in a beautiful location by the River Westerschelde.

dir: *S of town on coast.*

Open: Apr-Oct **Site:** 16HEC **Prices:** 19-37 **Facilities:** Wi-fi (charged) Kids' Club **Services:** **Leisure:** P S

BERG EN TERBLIJT — LIMBURG

Oriëntal

Rijksweg 6, 6325
043 6040075 043 6042912
e-mail: info@campingoriental.nl
web: www.campingoriental.nl

Quietly situated in an outstanding spot on the Mergelland, close to the city of Maastricht. The site sits concealed among the greenery of a former orchard.

dir: *On Maastricht-Valkenburg road, 3km from Maastricht.*

Open: Apr-Oct **Site:** 5.5HEC **Facilities:** **Services:** **Leisure:** P

BERGEYK — NOORD-BRABANT

Paal

De Paaldreef 14, 5571
0497 571977 0497 577164
e-mail: info@depaal.nl
web: www.depaal.nl

Site catering especially for families.

dir: *Signed.*

Open: Apr-Oct **Site:** 41HEC **Facilities:** **Services:** **Leisure:** P **Off-site:** L

BOSSCHENHOOFD — NOORD-BRABANT

Langoed de Wildert

Pagnevaartdreef 3, 4744
0165 312582
web: www.landgoeddewildert.nl

Peaceful location in woodland.

dir: *A58 exit 21 to Bosschenhoofd, pass church on right, site 0.5km on left.*

Open: Apr-Sep **Site:** 15HEC **Prices:** 22 **Facilities:** **Services:** **Off-site:** P

NETHERLANDS

Facilities shop shower electric points for razors electric points for caravans parking by tents permitted ompulsory separate car park **Services** café/restaurant bar Camping Gaz International gas other than Camping Gaz first aid facilities laundry **Leisure** swimming L-Lake P-Pool R-River S-Sea **Off-site** All facilities within 5km

BRESKENS — ZEELAND

Napoleon Hoeve

Zandertje 30, 4511
☎ 0117 383838 0117 383550
e-mail: info@napoleonhoeve.nl
web: www.napoleonhoeve.nl
A family site with access to the beach.

Open: All Year. **Site:** 13HEC **Prices:** 15-37 **Facilities:** Wi-fi (charged) Play Area **Services:** **Leisure:** P S

Schoneveld

Schoneveld 1, 4511
☎ 0117 383220 0117 383650
e-mail: info@droomparkschoneveld.nl
web: www.beachparcschoneveld.nl
dir: *3km S at beach.*

Open: All Year. **Site:** 14HEC **Facilities:** **Services:** **Leisure:** P S

BRIELLE — ZUID-HOLLAND

Krabbeplaat

Oude Veerdam 4, 3231
☎ 0181 412363 0181 412093
e-mail: info@krabbeplaat.nl
web: www.krabbeplaat.com
On level ground scattered with trees and groups of bushes. It has asphalt drives. Nearest site to the coast and ferries.
dir: *Signed.*

Open: Apr-Oct **Site:** 18HEC **Facilities:** **Services:** **Leisure:** L

BROEKHUIZENVORST — LIMBURG

Kasteel Ooyen

Blitterswijkseweg 2, 5871
☎ 077 4631307 077 4632765
e-mail: info@kasteelooijen.nl
web: www.kasteelooijen.nl
dir: *Off A73.*

Open: Apr-Oct **Site:** 16HEC **Facilities:** **Services:** **Leisure:** P **Off-site:**

BROUWERSHAVEN — ZEELAND

Osse

Blankersweg 4, 4318
☎ 0111 691513 0111 691058
e-mail: denosse@zeelandnet.nl
web: www.campingdenosse.nl
An attractive site with good water sports.

Open: Apr-6 Nov **Site:** 8.3HEC **Prices:** 11.25-27 Mobile home hire 270-615 **Facilities:** Wi-fi (charged) Kids' Club Play Area **Services:** **Leisure:** P S **Off-site:** L

BURGH-HAAMSTEDE — ZEELAND

Camping Ginsterveld

Maireweg 10, 4328
☎ 0111 651590 0111 653040
e-mail: info@ginsterveld.nl
web: www.ginsterveld.nl
A family holiday centre with well-defined pitches on level ground and plenty of recreational facilities.
dir: *NW of town, signed from R107.*

Open: Apr-Oct **Site:** 14HEC **Prices:** 18.50-35.50 **Facilities:** Wi-fi Kids' Club Play Area **Services:** **Leisure:** P **Off-site:** S

DELFT — ZUID-HOLLAND

Delftse Hout

The Camping and Caravanning Club The Friendly Club

Korftlaan 5, 2616
☎ 015 2130040 015 2131293
e-mail: info@delftsehout.nl
web: www.delftsehout.nl
On a level meadow surrounded by woodland close to the lake.

C&CC Report *A great site for all ages wanting a well-placed, comfortable base to explore picturesque Delft, The Hague, Rotterdam, Amsterdam and the coastal resorts and other attractions of central Holland. Many destinations are accessible by public transport, including Delft city centre itself, but it's also a great area for the classic Dutch mode of transport – the bike.*

dir: *1.6km E of A13, signed.*

Open: Apr-1 Nov **Site:** 5.5HEC **Facilities:** **Services:** **Leisure:** P **Off-site:** L

ECHT — LIMBURG

Marisheem

Brugweg 89, 6102
0475 481458 0475 488018
e-mail: info@marisheem.nl
web: www.marisheem.nl
The site is well-kept and lies east of the village.
dir: *From town towards Echterbosch & border, 2.2km turn left.*
Open: Apr-Oct **Site:** 12HEC **Facilities:** **Services:** **Leisure:** P

EERSEL — NOORD-BRABANT

Ter Spegelt

Postelseweg 88, 5521
0497 512016 0497 514162
e-mail: info@terspegelt.nl
web: www.terspegelt.nl
A large family-orientated site with good recreational facilities.
Open: Apr-30 Oct **Site:** 63HEC **Facilities:** **Services:** **Leisure:** L P

GROEDE — ZEELAND

Groede

Zeeweg 1, 4503
0117 371384 0117 372277
e-mail: info@strandcampinggroede.nl
web: www.strandcampinggroede.nl
A large family site with a variety of leisure facilities and close to the beach.
Open: Apr-Oct **Site:** 20HEC **Facilities:** **Services:** **Leisure:** S

HELLEVOETSLUIS — ZUID-HOLLAND

'T Weergors

Zuiddyk 2, 3221
0181 312430 0181 311010
e-mail: weergors@pn.nl
web: www.weergors.nl
A pleasant, peaceful site on a level meadow close to the beach. A good overnight stopping place or holiday site. Kids' club available during summer holiday.
Open: Apr-Oct **Site:** 9.7HEC **Prices:** 19 Mobile home hire 250-450 **Facilities:** Wi-fi (charged) Kids' Club Play Area **Services:** **Leisure:** S
Off-site: L P R

HERPEN — NOORD-BRABANT

Herperduin

Schaijkseweg 12, 5373
0486 411383 0486 416171
e-mail: info@herperduin.nl
web: www.herperduin.nl
Situated in extensive woodland.
Open: Apr-20 Oct **Site:** 7HEC **Prices:** 18-24
Facilities: **Services:**
Leisure: P

HOEK — ZEELAND

Braakman Holiday Park

Middenweg 1, 4542
0115 481730 0115 482077
e-mail: info@braakman.co.uk
web: www.braakman.co.uk
A large family site on the edge of extensive nature reserves. The pitches are shaded by woodland and there is direct access to Braakman lake. Plenty of recreational facilities.
dir: *4km W of town, signed from N61.*
Open: All Year. **Site:** 80HEC **Facilities:** **Services:** **Leisure:** L P

HOEK VAN HOLLAND — ZUID-HOLLAND

Hoek van Holland

Wierstr 100, 3151
0174 382550 0174 310210
e-mail: camping.hvh@hetnet.nl
web: www.campinghoekvanholland.nl
On grass, surrounded by bushes and paved drives.
dir: *From N, off E36 to beach.*
Open: 14 Mar-24 Oct **Site:** 5.5HEC **Prices:** 17.50-26.35
Facilities: **Services:**
Off-site: S

HOEVEN — NOORD-BRABANT

Molecaten Park Bosbad Hoeven

Oude Antwerpse Postbaan 81b, 4741
0165 502570 0165 504254
e-mail: info@bosbadhoeven.nl
web: www.bosbadhoeven.nl
Extensive site with modern facilities including a waterpark.
dir: *A58 exit 20 St Willebrord, follow signs for Hoeven.*
Open: Apr-Oct **Site:** 35HEC **Prices:** 18-30 Mobile home hire 195-690 **Facilities:** Wi-fi (charged) Kids' Club Play Area **Services:** **Leisure:** P

NETHERLANDS

Facilities shop shower electric points for razors electric points for caravans parking by tents permitted compulsory separate car park **Services** café/restaurant bar Camping Gaz International gas other than Camping Gaz first aid facilities laundry **Leisure** swimming L-Lake P-Pool R-River S-Sea **Off-site** All facilities within 5km

KAMPERLAND ZEELAND

Roompot

Mariapolderseweg 1, 4493
0113 374000 0113 374170
e-mail: info@roompot.nl
web: www.roompot.nl
A level, well-maintained site with a private beach.
dir: *Off Kamperland-Wissenkerke road & N for 0.5km.*
Open: All Year. **Site:** 33HEC **Facilities:** Wi-fi (charged) Kids' Club Play Area **Services:** **Leisure:** P S

KATWIJK AAN ZEE ZUID-HOLLAND

Recreatiecentrum De Noordduinen

Campingweg 1, 2221
071 4025295 071 4033977
e-mail: info@noordduinen.nl
web: www.noordduinen.nl
Family site among dunes close to the sea.
dir: *Via Hoorneslaan.*
Open: All Year. **Site:** 11HEC **Prices:** 23.50-31.50 Mobile home hire 340-800 **Facilities:** Wi-fi Kids' Club Play Area **Services:** **Leisure:** P S

KORTGENE ZEELAND

De Paardekreek

Havenweg 1, 4484
0113 302051 0113 302280
e-mail: paardekreek@ardoer.com
web: www.ardoer.com/paardekreek
A municipal site next to the Veerse Meer canal.
dir: *Off Zierikzee-Goes road at fuel station towards Kortgene, through village & continue SW.*
Open: Apr-Oct **Site:** 10HEC **Facilities:** **Services:** **Leisure:** L P

KOUDEKERKE ZEELAND

Dishoek

Dishoek 2, 4371
0118 551348 0118 552990
e-mail: info@campingdishoek.nl
web: www.roompot.nl
dir: *W on Vlissingen-Dibhoek road*
Open: 18 Mar-23 Oct **Site:** 6HEC **Facilities:** **Services:** **Off-site:** S

Duinzicht

Strandweg 7, 4371
0118 551397 0118 553222
e-mail: info@campingduinzicht.nl
web: www.campingduinzicht.nl
A small family site with good facilities.
dir: *1.5km SW of Koudekerke.*
Open: Apr-Oct **Site:** 6.5HEC **Facilities:** **Services:** **Off-site:** S

LAGE MIERDE NOORD-BRABANT

Vakantiecentrum de Hertenwei

Wellenseind 7-9, 5094
013 5091295
e-mail: reception@hertenwei.nl
web: www.hertenwei.nl
Pleasant wooded site with modern facilities. A kids' club is available during school holidays.
dir: *2km N on N269 (Tilburg-Reusel).*
Open: All Year. **Site:** 20HEC **Prices:** 17.75-29 Mobile home hire 260-490 **Facilities:** Wi-fi Kids' Club Play Area **Services:** **Leisure:** P

LUYKSGESTEL NOORD-BRABANT

Zwarte Bergen

Zwarte Bergen Dreef 1, 5575
0497 541373 0497 542673
e-mail: info@zwartebergen.nl
web: www.zwartebergen.nl
Isolated and very quiet site in a pine forest.
dir: *From Eindhoven through Valkenswaard & Bergiejkl, signed.*
Open: 2 Apr-2 Oct **Site:** 25.5HEC **Facilities:** **Services:** **Leisure:** P

MAASBREE LIMBURG

BreeBronne

Lange Heide 9, 5993
077 4652360 077 4652095
e-mail: info@breebronne.nl
web: www.breebronne.nl
A family site in quiet surroundings with good facilities.
dir: *On E3 just before Venlo, on German border.*
Open: Mar-Oct **Site:** 23HEC **Prices:** 21.40-48.80 **Facilities:** Wi-fi Kids' Club Play Area **Services:** **Leisure:** L P **Off-site:** R

NETHERLANDS

MIDDELBURG ZEELAND

Middelburg

Koninginnelaan 55, 4335
☎ 0118 625395
web: www.campingmiddelburg.nl
On meadowlands surrounded by trees and bushes.
dir: *On W outskirts of town.*
Open: Etr-15 Oct **Site:** 3.4HEC **Facilities:** **Services:** **Off-site:** P S

MIERLO NOORD-BRABANT

Wolfsven

Patrijslaan 4, 5731
☎ 0492 661661 0492 663895
e-mail: info.wolfsven@rpholidays.nl
web: www.roompot.nl
Large site with wooded areas and several lakes. Asphalt drives.
Open: 3 Apr-1 Nov **Site:** 67HEC **Facilities:** **Services:** **Leisure:** L P **Off-site:**

NIEUWVLIET ZEELAND

Pannenschuur

Zeedijk 19, 4504
☎ 0117 372300 0117 371415
e-mail: info@pannenschuur.nl
web: www.pannenschuur.nl
A modern site with good facilities. Close to the beach.
dir: *NW of town, signed.*
Open: All Year. **Site:** 14HEC **Facilities:** **Services:** **Leisure:** P S

NOORDWIJK AAN ZEE ZUID-HOLLAND

Noordwijkse Duinen

Kapelleboslaan 10, 2204
☎ 0252 372485 0252 340140
e-mail: info@noordwijkseduinen.nl
web: www.noordwijkseduinen.nl
A well-equipped family site in a wooded location 2km from the beach.
dir: *A44 - N206.*
Open: All Year. **Site:** 6HEC **Prices:** 16.50-30.50 **Facilities:** Wi-fi (charged) Kids' Club Play Area **Services:** **Leisure:** P **Off-site:** L S

Parc du Soleil

Kraaierslaan 7, 2204
☎ 0252 374225 0252 376450
e-mail: info@parcdusoleil.nl
web: www.parcdusoleil.nl
A pleasant location near the bulb fields and the sea.
dir: *Signed.*
Open: Apr-Nov **Site:** 5.5HEC **Prices:** 15-36 Mobile home hire 267-749 **Facilities:** Play Area **Services:** **Leisure:** P **Off-site:** L S

OISTERWIJK NOORD-BRABANT

Reebok

Duinenweg 4, 5062
☎ 013 5282309 013 5217592
e-mail: info@dereebok.nl
web: www.dereebok.nl
Situated in a large pine forest within attractive surroundings with numerous small lakes. There is a kids' club available in high season.
dir: *SE of town.*
GPS: 51.5733, 5.2322
Open: All Year. **Site:** 8HEC **Prices:** 20.50-26 **Facilities:** Wi-fi (charged) Kids' Club Play Area **Services:** **Off-site:** L P

OOSTERHOUT NOORD-BRABANT

Katjeskelder

Katjeskelder 1, 4904
☎ 0162 453539 0162 454090
e-mail: kkinfo@katjeskelder.nl
web: www.katjeskelder.nl
A large, modern family site with good sanitary and recreational facilities.
dir: *A27 exit 17 & signed.*
Open: All Year. **Site:** 25HEC **Facilities:** **Services:** **Leisure:** P **Off-site:**

OOSTKAPELLE ZEELAND

Dennenbos

Duinweg 64, 4356
☎ 0118 581310 0118 583773
e-mail: dennenbos@zeelandnet.nl
web: www.dennenbos.nl
A well-maintained family site in a wooded location, 0.5km from the beach.
Open: Mar-Nov **Site:** 3HEC **Facilities:** **Services:** **Leisure:** P S

NETHERLANDS

In de Bongerd

Brouwerijstr 13, 4356
☎ 0118 581510 📠 0118 581510
e-mail: info@campingindebongerd.nl
web: www.campingindebongerd.nl

A well-kept family site, set in a meadow with hedges and apple trees. There are fine recreational facilities and the beach is within easy reach.

dir: *0.5km S.*

Open: 30 Mar-28 Oct **Site:** 7.4HEC **Facilities:** **Services:** **Leisure:** P S

Ons Buiten

Aagtekerkseweg 2a, 4356
☎ 0118 581813 📠 0118 583771
e-mail: onsbuiten@ardoer.com
web: www.ardoer.com/onsbuiten

A beautiful location with a choice of recreational activities.

dir: *From church S towards Grijpskerke, turn W for 400m.*

Open: 31 Mar-Oct **Site:** 11.5HEC **Facilities:** **Services:** **Leisure:** P S

Pekelinge

Landmetersweg 1, 4356
☎ 0118 582820 📠 0118 583782
e-mail: pekelinge@ardoer.com
web: www.ardoer.com/pekelinge

A spacious site for families, with pitches also available for the less able-bodied. Kids' club available during weekends and holidays.

Open: Apr-Oct **Site:** 18HEC **Prices:** 18.50-44.50 Mobile home hire 308-833 **Facilities:** Kids' Club Play Area **Services:** **Leisure:** P
Off-site: S

OOSTVOORNE ZUID-HOLLAND

Kruininger Gors

Gorspl 2, 3233
☎ 0181 482711 📠 0181 485957
e-mail: info@kruiningergors.nl
web: www.kruiningergors.nl

Located on the shores of Lake Brielle, a lively site with private sandy beaches and moorings for boats.

dir: *Via A15/N218.*

Open: Apr-Sep **Site:** 108HEC **Prices:** 16.90-19.90 **Facilities:** Wi-fi (charged) Kids' Club Play Area **Services:** **Leisure:** L **Off-site:** S

OUDDORP ZUID-HOLLAND

Klepperstee

Vrijheidsweg 1, 3253
☎ 0187 681511 📠 0187 683060
e-mail: info@klepperstee.com
web: www.klepperstee.com

On level meadow divided by hedges and trees.

dir: *N57 exit Ouddorp.*

Open: Apr-Oct **Site:** 40HEC **Facilities:** **Services:** **Leisure:** P **Off-site:** L S

PLASMOLEN LIMBURG

Eldorado

Witteweg 18, 6586
☎ 024 6961914 📠 024 6963017
e-mail: info@eldorado-mook.nl
web: www.eldorado-mook.nl

Well-equipped site in wooded surroundings on the Mooker See.

dir: *S of N271.*

Open: Apr-1 Oct **Site:** 6HEC **Facilities:** **Services:** **Leisure:** L

RENESSE ZEELAND

International

Scharendijkseweg 8, 4325
☎ 0111 461391 📠 0111 462571
e-mail: info@camping-international.net
web: www.camping-international.net

On grassland, between rows of tall shrubs and trees. Between dyke road and main road to Scharendijk on eastern outskirts of village.

Open: Mar-Nov **Site:** 3HEC **Prices:** 16.95-29.55 **Facilities:** Wi-fi (charged) **Services:** **Leisure:** S **Off-site:** P

Wijde Blick

Lagezoom 23, 4325
☎ 0111 468888 📠 0111 468889
e-mail: wijdeblick@ardoer.com
web: www.ardoer.com

A family site with good facilities.

dir: *Signed.*

Open: All Year. **Site:** 10HEC **Facilities:** **Services:** **Leisure:** P **Off-site:** S

NETHERLANDS

RETRANCHEMENT ZEELAND

De Zwinhoeve

Duinweg 1, 4525
☎ 0117 392120 🖷 0117 392248
e-mail: info@zwinhoeve.nl
web: www.zwinhoeve.nl

A beautiful position backed by dunes with easy access to the fine beaches of the Zeeuws-Vlaanderen coast.

Open: 19 Mar-26 Oct **Site:** 9HEC **Facilities:** **Services:** **Leisure:** S **Off-site:** P

RIJNSBURG ZUID-HOLLAND

Koningshof

Elsgeesterweg 8, 2231
☎ 071 4026051 🖷 071 4021336
e-mail: info@koningshofholland.nl
web: www.koningshofholland.nl

Modern site on level meadow near the flower fields.

C&CC Report *A friendly site with very good facilities, close to many attractions. A great site for younger children. Beaches, cities and countryside are all in easy driving distance. Keukenhof gardens and the bulb fields are a particular delight in spring. Cycling on the excellent cycle path network is highly recommended for getting around, too.*

dir: *A44 exit 7 to Rijnsburg, site 1km N, signed.*

Open: Apr-Nov **Site:** 7.5HEC **Prices:** 25.50-29 Mobile home hire 500-900 **Facilities:** **Services:** **Leisure:** P **Off-site:** S

ROCKANJE ZUID-HOLLAND

Waterboscamping

Duinrand 11, 3235
☎ 0181 401900 🖷 0181 404233
e-mail: info@waterboscamping.nl
web: www.waterboscamping.nl

A small, pleasant site near the beach. The large trees, pond and playground at the central site Waterbos determine its atmosphere. They give this site the seaside fun and charming character.

dir: *Via N15.*

Open: Apr-Sep **Site:** 7HEC **Prices:** 17-30 Mobile home hire 195-575 **Facilities:** Wi-fi (charged) Kids' Club Play Area **Services:** **Off-site:** S

ROERMOND LIMBURG

Resort Marina Oolderhuuske

Oolderhuuske 1, 6041
☎ 0475 588686 🖷 0475 582652
e-mail: info@oolderhuuske.nl
web: www.oolderhuuske.nl

A well-equipped site within the marina area on the Maasplassen. A kids' club is available during the holidays.

Open: Apr-Oct **Site:** 22HEC **Prices:** 25.50-34.50 Mobile home hire 275-555 **Facilities:** Wi-fi Kids' Club **Services:** **Leisure:** L P R

ROOSENDAAL NOORD-BRABANT

Zonneland

Turfvaartsestr 6, 4709
☎ 0165 365429
e-mail: info@zonneland.nl
web: www.zonneland.nl
dir: *S of town towards Belgian border.*

Open: Mar-1 Oct **Site:** 14HEC **Facilities:** **Services:** **Leisure:** P

SCHIN OP GEUL LIMBURG

Vinkenhof

Engwegen 2a, 6305
☎ 043 4591389 🖷 043 4591780
e-mail: info@campingvinkenhof.nl
web: www.campingvinkenhof.nl

Small, friendly site on flat ground at foot of hill and on edge of village.

C&CC Report *Woods, farms and rolling hills, full of wildlife, provide the backdrop for this lovely, village site, that continues to improve each year. The Weijts family continue to offer a warm welcome at Vinkenhof, with the attractive bar terrace and cosy restaurant adding to the homely feel. Pretty Valkenburg with its Roman catacombs is a must to visit, while Belgium, Germany and Maastricht, are all within easy reach, as are the Dutch hills fringing the atmospheric Ardennes.*

dir: *A76, exit at Nuth for Schin op Geul.*

Open: Mar-3 Jan **Site:** 2.2HEC **Prices:** 20.55-27.55 **Facilities:** **Services:** **Leisure:** P **Off-site:**

NETHERLANDS

SEVENUM LIMBURG

Schatberg

Midden Peelweg 5, 5975
077 4677777 077 4677799
e-mail: receptie@schatberg.nl
web: www.schatberg.nl

A well-appointed family site in wooded surroundings with plenty of leisure facilities.

dir: *A67 exit 38 for Schatberg & SW towards Eindhoven.*

Open: All Year. **Site:** 86HEC **Prices:** 18.60-29.76 **Facilities:** Play Area **Services:** **Leisure:** L P

'S-GRAVENZANDE ZUID-HOLLAND

Jagtveld

Nieuwlandsedijk 41, 2691
0174 413479 0174 422127
e-mail: info@jagtveld.nl
web: www.jagtveld.nl

A quiet family site on level meadowland with good facilities.

dir: *Via N220.*

Open: Apr-Sep **Site:** 3.3HEC **Facilities:** **Services:** **Off-site:** S

SLUIS ZEELAND

Meidoorn

Hoogstr 68, 4524
0117 461662 0117 461662
e-mail: meidoorn@zeelandnet.nl
web: www.campingdemeidoorn.nl

A meadowland site surrounded by rows of deciduous trees.

dir: *N on road to Zuidzande.*

Open: Apr-22 Oct **Site:** 6.5HEC **Facilities:** **Services:** **Off-site:**

VENRAY LIMBURG

de Oude Barrier

Maasheseweg 93, 5817
0478 582305
e-mail: info@deoudebarrier.nl
web: www.deoudebarrier.nl

A quiet site recommended for young children.

dir: *NE of town.*

Open: Apr-Sep **Site:** 14HEC **Prices:** 13.50 **Facilities:** Wi-fi Play Area **Services:** **Leisure:** P **Off-site:** R

VROUWENPOLDER ZEELAND

Oranjezon

Koningin Emmaweg 16a, 4354
0118 591549 0118 591920
e-mail: oranjezon@oranjezon.nl
web: www.oranjezon.nl

Situated to the west of the village, a well-kept site with pitches between tall, thick hedges and bushes. Kids' club available in high season.

dir: *Towards Oostkapelle, 2.5km turn N for 300m.*

Open: Apr-Oct **Site:** 9.75HEC **Prices:** 24.50-44 Mobile home hire 340-665 **Facilities:** Wi-fi (charged) Kids' Club **Services:** **Leisure:** P S

Zandput

Vroondijk 9, 4354
0118 597210 0118 591954
e-mail: info.zandput@rphdidays.nl
web: www.roompot.nl

On level ground behind dunes and close to the beach.

dir: *2km N.*

Open: 3 Apr-1 Nov **Site:** 12HEC **Facilities:** **Services:** **Off-site:** L S

WASSENAAR ZUID-HOLLAND

Duinhorst

Buurtweg 135, 2244
070 3242270 070 3246053
e-mail: info@duinhorst.nl
web: www.duinhorst.nl

A peaceful site in wooded surroundings with modern facilities and fine opportunities for sports and entertainment.

Open: Apr-Sep **Site:** 11HEC **Prices:** 20-24 **Facilities:** Kids' Club **Services:** **Leisure:** P

Duinrell

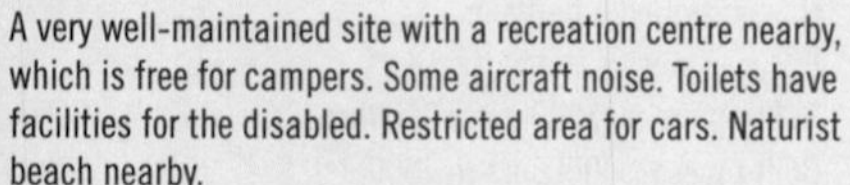

Duinrell 1, 2242
☎ 070 5155255 🖷 070 5155371
e-mail: info@duinrell.nl
web: www.duinrell.nl

A very well-maintained site with a recreation centre nearby, which is free for campers. Some aircraft noise. Toilets have facilities for the disabled. Restricted area for cars. Naturist beach nearby.

C&CC Report *Duinrell is much, much more than just a campsite – with its own amusement park (free to campers), fantastic Tiki Pool complex (payable on site), and themed restaurants, children of all ages will find plenty to do. The site's location in the beautiful woodland and dune area on the coast of South Holland, next to the beach and within walking distance of the attractive village of Wassenaar, makes Duinrell the perfect place to visit, all year round.*

dir: *Off A44 at lights in Wassenaar, signed.*

Open: All Year. **Site:** 110HEC **Prices:** 40.24-50.24 Mobile home hire 275-1130 **Facilities:** Kids' Club **Services:** **Leisure:** P **Off-site:** L S

WEERT — LIMBURG

De Yzeren Man

Heerenvennenweg 60, 6006
☎ 0495 533202 🖷 0495 546812
e-mail: info@resortdeyzerenman.nl
web: www.resortdeyzerenman.nl

Well-kept site with asphalt drives, set in a big nature reserve with zoo, heath and forest.

dir: *A2 Eindhoven-Maastricht.*

Open: Apr-1 Nov **Site:** 8.5HEC **Facilities:** **Services:** **Leisure:** P **Off-site:**

WELL — LIMBURG

Vakantiepark Leukermeer

De Kamp 5, 5855
☎ 0478 502444 🖷 0478 501260
e-mail: vakantie@leukermeer.nl
web: www.leukermeer.nl

Beautiful surroundings on Leukermeer with modern installations and plenty of leisure facilities.

dir: *Signed from N271.*

GPS: 51.5669, 6.0594

Open: Apr-1 Nov **Site:** 14HEC **Prices:** 22.90-41.40 Mobile home hire 199-649 **Facilities:** Wi-fi (charged) Kids' Club Play Area **Services:** **Leisure:** L P **Off-site:**

WEMELDINGE — ZEELAND

Linda

Oostkanaalweg 4, 4424
☎ 0113 621259 🖷 0113 622638
e-mail: info@campinglinda.nl
web: www.campinglinda.nl

On meadowland surrounded by rows of tall shrubs. At the Eastern National Park and a short walk from the historic village Wemeldinge.

dir: *Turn opposite bridge in town for 100m, over bridge to site.*

Open: Apr-Nov **Site:** 8HEC **Prices:** 15-21 Mobile home hire 255-525 **Facilities:** Wi-fi Kids' Club Play Area **Services:** **Leisure:** S

WESTKAPELLE — ZEELAND

Boomgaard

Domineeshofweg 1, 4361
☎ 0118 571377 🖷 0118 572383
e-mail: info@deboomgaard.info
web: www.deboomgaard.info

A flat grassy site.

dir: *Signed off Middleburg road on S outskirts of town.*

Open: 27 Mar-24 Oct **Site:** 8HEC **Facilities:** **Services:** **Leisure:** P **Off-site:** S

NETHERLANDS

Facilities shop, shower, electric points for razors, electric points for caravans, parking by tents permitted, compulsory separate car park **Services** café/restaurant, bar, Camping Gaz International, gas other than Camping Gaz, first aid facilities, laundry **Leisure** swimming L-Lake P-Pool R-River S-Sea **Off-site** All facilities within 5km

Poland

Drinking & Driving
The maximum level of alcohol in the bloodstream is 0.02 per cent. Between 0.021% and 0.05% per cent a heavy fine imposed and suspension of licence. Over 0.05% the fine is determined by a tribunal along with the prison sentence and suspension of licence.

Driving Licence
Minimum age at which a UK licence holder may drive a temporarily imported car and / or motorcycle (over 125cc) 18. All valid UK driving licences should be accepted in Poland.

Fines
On-the-spot. An official receipt should be obtained. The Police are authorised to request foreign motorists pay their fines in cash. Wheel clamps are in use. Illegally parked cars causing an obstruction may be towed away and impounded.

Lights
Dipped headlights or daytime running lights are compulsory for all vehicles at all times. Fine imposed for non-compliance.

Motorcycles
Dipped headlights or daytime running lights are compulsory for all vehicles at all times. The wearing of crash helmets is compulsory for both driver and passenger.

Motor Insurance
Third-party compulsory.

Passengers & Children
Children under 12 and 1.5 metres in height cannot travel as front or a rear seat passenger unless using a suitable restraint system adapted to their size. If a car is equipped with front seat airbags it is prohibited to place a child in a rear facing seat.

Seat Belts
Compulsory for front / rear seat occupants to wear seat belts, if fitted.

Speed Limits
Unless signed otherwise

Private vehicles without trailers	
Built-up areas (2300hrs to 0500hrs)	60km/h
Built-up areas (0500hrs to 2300hrs)	50km/h
Outside built-up areas	90km/h
Express roads (2 x 1 lanes)	100km/h
Express roads (2 x 2 lanes)	110km/h
Motorways	130km/h
Minimum speed on motorways	40km/h
Some residential zones	20km/h
Car towing a trailer or caravan	
In built-up areas	30km/h
Motorways	80km/h
Express roads & dual carriageways	80km/h
Other roads	70km/h

Additional Information
Compulsory equipment in Poland: Warning triangle (compulsory for all vehicles with more than two wheels).
It is recommended that visitors equip their vehicle with a first aid kit and a set of replacement bulbs. It is also recommended that a fire extinguisher be carried as its carriage is compulsory for Polish registered vehicles.
The use of spiked tyres is prohibited. Snow chains may be used only on roads covered with snow.
It is prohibited to carry and/or use a radar detector.
The use of the horn is prohibited in built-up areas except to avoid an accident.

Tolls Currency Zlotys (PLN)	Car	Car Towing Caravan/Trailer
A2 Wrzesnia - Konin	11PLN	18PLN
A2 Komoraiki - Now/Tomysl	11PLN	18PLN
A2 Krzesiny - Wrzesia	11PLN	18PLN
A4 Katowice - Krakow	11PLN	15PLN

:HMIELNO ZACHODNIOPOMORSKIE

amowa

'awory 47, 83-333
☎ 058 6842535 🖷 058 6842535
-mail: camping@tamowa.pl
'eb: www.tamowa.pl

ite on the shore of Lake Klodno with private beach. Good for oating and water sports. Walking and bike routes available. ossibility of fishing too.

ir: *Route 211 Stupsk-Gdansk.*

pen: All Year. Site: 2HEC Prices: 35-55 Facilities: Play Area Services: Leisure: L ff-site:

ZIWNÓWEK ZACHODNIOPOMORSKIE

Bialy Dom

l Kamienska 11-12, 72-420
☎ 091 3811171 🖷 091 3811446
'eb: www.campingbialydom.com

ite located 50m from the beach.

PS: 54.0352, 14.8036

pen: Mar-Oct Site: 2.5HEC Prices: 47-85 acilities: Wi-fi Play Area Services: ff-site: L P S

IZYCKO WARMIŃSKO-MAZURSKIE

lixir Hotelik Caravan Camping

uty 9, 11-500
☎ 087 4282826
-mail: office@elixirhotel.com
eb: www.elixirhotel.com

'ith lake shoreline and jetties for fishing, this site offers peace nd quiet to visitors. Children are well catered for with scooters, cycles and go-karts available.

pen: May-Oct Site: 3.5HEC Prices: 65-85 acilities: Wi-fi Kids' Club Play Area ervices: Leisure: L Off-site:

JELENIA GÓRA DOLNOSLASKIE

Camping Sloneczna Polana

ul M Rataja 9, 58-560
☎ 075 7552566
e-mail: info@campingpolen.com
web: www.campingpolen.com

A quiet, family site with spacious plots. Facilities include satellite TV, safe rental and sports.

dir: *On route from Jelenia Góra to the Czech Republic border (E3).*

Open: May-Sep Site: 2.5HEC Prices: 62.20 Facilities: Wi-fi Play Area Services: Leisure: P R Off-site:

KRAKÓW MALOPOLSKIE

Krakowianka

ul Zywiecka Boczna 2, 30-427
☎ 012 2681135 🖷 012 2681417
e-mail: noclegi@krakowianka.info
web: www.krakowianka.info

Located on the outskirts of Kraków in a park complex with good recreational facilities.

GPS: 50.0146, 19.9247

Open: May-Sep Site: 3.8HEC Prices: 50-80 Facilities: Wi-fi Services: Off-site: L

MIELNO ZACHODNIOPOMORSKE

Rodzinny

ul Chrobrego 51, 76-032
☎ 094 3189385 🖷 094 3475008
e-mail: recepcja@campingrodzinny.pl
web: www.campingrodzinny.pl

Family run campsite close to the sea and a marina.

GPS: 54.2627, 16.0722

Open: 15 Apr-15 Nov Site: 0.5HEC Prices: 46-55 Facilities: Wi-fi (charged) Play Area Services: Off-site: L P S

MIKOLAJKI WARMIŃSKO-MAZURSKIE

Kama

Talty 36, 11-730
☎ 087 4216575 🖷 087 4216575
e-mail: camping@kama.mazury.pl
web: www.kama.mazury.pl

Situated on the bank of Lake Talty. Excellent for fishing and water sports.

Open: May-15 Oct Site: 2HEC Prices: 49-75 Facilities: Wi-fi (charged) Play Area Services: Leisure: L Off-site: P R S

POLAND

PRZEWORSK PODKARPACKIE

Pastewnik

ul Lancucka 2, 37-200
☎ 016 6492300 📠 016 6492301
e-mail: zajazdpastewnik@hot.pl
web: www.pastewnik.pl

A unique place which functions as an inn, camping site, and open-air museum.

dir: *From Przeworsk on A4 (E40) towards Rzeszow, campsite on right after bridge.*

Open: May-Sep **Site:** 2HEC **Prices:** 46 **Facilities:** Wi-fi Play Area **Services:** **Off-site:** P

SOPOT POMORSKIE

Przy Plazy

Bitwy pod Plowcami 73, 81-831
☎ 058 5516523
e-mail: camping67@sopot.pl
web: www.camping67.sopot.pl

Next to a beach in a shaded woody location.

Open: 15 Jun-Aug **Site:** 3HEC **Facilities:** **Services:** **Off-site:**

WOLIBÓRZ DOLNOSLASKIE

Lesny Dwor-Waldgut

Woliborz 12b, 57-431
☎ 074 8724590
e-mail: waldgut@waldgut.de
web: www.waldgut.de

Campsite in grounds of a manor house in attractive mountainous location.

dir: *On Wat Brzych-Ktodzko route 381: near Nowa Rudna follow signs towards Wolibórz. Campsite signed.*

Open: All Year. **Site:** 2HEC **Facilities:** **Services:** **Leisure:** P **Off-site:**

WROCLAW DOLNOSLASKIE

Stadion Olimpijski

ul Paderewskieg 35, 51-612
☎ 071 3484651 📠 071 3483928

Site close to the Stadium. Convenient for short breaks to the city.

Open: May-15 Oct **Site:** 2HEC **Prices:** 20-70 **Facilities:** **Services:** **Off-site:** L

ZAKOPANE MALOPOLSKIE

Pod Krokwia

ul Zeromskiego, 34-500
☎ 018 2012256 📠 018 2012256
e-mail: camp@podkrokwia.pl
web: www.podkrokwia.pl

Close to a national park area with mountain views.

dir: *In Zakopane turn left at 1st rdbt, straight over next rdbt, right at 3rd rdbt, campsite 150mtrs on right.*

Open: All Year. **Site:** 4HEC **Facilities:** **Services:** **Off-site:** P R

Ustup

Ustup 5B, 34-500
☎ 060 5950007
e-mail: camping.ustup@gmail.com
web: www.camping-ustup.pl

On the rivers Zakopianka and Olczyski Potok with fine views of Tatry Mountains.

dir: *Route DK7-DK47 Kraków - Zakopane.*

GPS: 49.3220, 19.9856

Open: May-Sep **Site:** 0.8HEC **Prices:** 46-50 **Facilities:** Wi-fi **Services:** **Off-site:** L P R

POLAND

Portugal

Drinking and driving

If the level of alcohol in the bloodstream is 0.05% to 0.08%, fine and withdrawal of the driving licence for a minimum of one month to a maximum of one year; more than 0.08%, fine and withdrawal of driving licence for a minimum of two months up to a maximum of two years. The police are also empowered to carry out testing on drivers for narcotics.

Driving licence

Minimum age at which a UK licence holder may drive a temporarily imported car and/or motorcycle (over 50cc) 17; however visitors under the age of 18 years may encounter problems even though they hold a valid UK licence. All valid UK driving licences should be accepted in Portugal. This includes the older all-green style UK licences (in Northern Ireland older paper style with photographic counterpart). Older licences may be accompanied by an International Driving Permit (IDP).

Fines

On-the-spot and must be paid in Euros. Most police vehicles are equipped with portable ATM machines or immediate payment of the fines. An official receipt howing the maximum fine amount should be obtained. Note: foreign motorists refusing to pay an on-the-spot ne will be asked for a deposit to cover the maximum ne for the offence committed. If a motorist refuses to do his, the police can take the driving licence, registration ocument or failing that they can confiscate the vehicle. Wheel-clamping and towing are in operation for illegally arked vehicles.

Lights

Dipped headlights are compulsory in poor daytime visibility and in tunnels.

Motorcycles

Use of dipped headlights during the day is compulsory. The wearing of crash helmets is compulsory. Child under not permitted as passenger.

Motor insurance

Third-party compulsory.

Passengers/children in cars

Children under 12 and less than 1.50 metres in height cannot travel as front seat passengers. They must travel the rear in a special restraint system adapted to their ze, unless the vehicle has only two seats, or is not fitted with seat belts.

Children under 3 can be seated in the front passenger seat if using a suitable child restraint however, the airbag must be switched off if using a rear-facing child restraint system.

Seat belts

Compulsory for front/rear seat occupants to wear seat belts, if fitted.

Speed limits

Unless signed otherwise

Private vehicles without trailers

Built-up areas	50km/h
Outside built-up areas	90km/h or 100km/h
Motorways	120km/h
The minimum speed on motorways	50km/h

(Motorists who have held a driving licence for less than one year must not exceed 90 km/h or any lower speed limit).

Car towing a trailer or caravan

Built-up areas	50km/h
Outside built up areas	70-80km/h
Motorways	100km/h

Additional information

Compulsory equipment in Portugal: Photographic proof of identity (a legal requirement for everyone in Portugal); Reflective jacket (compulsory for residents, recommended for visitors); Other rules/requirements in Portugal: Carrying a warning triangle recommended as the use of hazard warning lights or a warning triangle is compulsory in an accident/breakdown situation. It is prohibited to carry and/or use a radar detector. Spiked tyres and winter tyres are prohibited. Snow chains may be used, where the weather conditions require. It is illegal to carry bicycles on the back of a passenger car.

The wearing of reflective jacket/waistcoat is recommended if the driver and/or passenger(s) exits a vehicle which is immobilised on the carriageway of all motorways and main or busy roads. We recommend the jacket be carried in the passenger compartment of the vehicle (not the boot). This is a compulsory requirement for residents.

In built-up areas the use of the horn is prohibited during the hours of darkness except in the case of immediate danger.

Portugal

Tolls & Bridges

Tolls Currency Euro (€)	Car with or without Caravan/Trailer
A1 Lisboa - Porto	€19.55
A10 A9 - Arruda dos Vinhos - A13	€2.10
A11 A28/Braga (A3) - Guimaraes (A7) - A4	€0.80
A12 Setubal - Pte Vasco de Gama	€1.95
A13 Santo Estevao - Marateca (A2/A6)	€8.90
A14 Figueira da Foz - Coimbra Nord	€2.20
A15 Caldas da Rainha - Santarem	€3.55
A2 Lisboa - VLA (Algarve)	€18.40
A21 Malveria (A8) - Ericeira	€1.80
A3 Porto - Valença do Minho (Spain/Vigo)	€7.85

Tolls Currency Euro (€)	Car Towing Caravan/Trailer
A4 Porto - Amarante	€3.65
A5 Lisboa - Cascais	€1.25
A6/A2 A2/Marateca - Elvas (Spanish border)	€11.90
A7 Vila Nova de Famalicao - Guimaraes	€1.55
A8 Lisboa - Leiria	€10.20
A9 Alverca - Oeiras	€2.95
Bridges and Tunnels	
25 de Abril Bridge (Ponte 25 de Abril) On A2 (payable in one direction - north into Lisboa - only. No toll in August)	€1.35
Vasco da Gama Bridge On A12 (North only) (Ponte Vasco da Gama)	€2.35

SOUTH

ALBUFEIRA — ALGARVE

Albufeira

The Camping and Caravanning Club — The Friendly Club

8200-555
☎ 289587629 📠 289587633
e-mail: campingalbufeira@mail.telepac.pt
web: www.campingalbufeira.net

A modern, purpose-built site with excellent sanitary blocks and a variety of sports and entertainment facilities.

C&CC Report *Albufeira is in an area renowned among golfers and sunseekers throughout Europe and is a firm perennial favourite. The town centre, a few kiolmetres away, is easily accessible, as are the many good quality restaurants, beaches and other local towns and attractions. For trips further afield, you are only 5km from the motorway, which travels the length of the Algarve, giving you the opportunity to visit many of the towns and attractions that the Algarve has to offer.*

dir: *1.5km from Albufeira, signed from N125.*

Open: All Year. **Site:** 19HEC **Facilities:** **Services:** **Leisure:** P **Off-site:** S

ALVITO — BAIXO ALENTEJO

Markádia

Barragem de Odivelas, Apartado 17, 7920-999
☎ 284763141 📠 284763102
e-mail: markadia@hotmail.com
web: www.markadia.net

Open savannah terrain beside a lake with modern facilities. No dogs July and August.

dir: *Via N257.*

Open: All Year. **Site:** 10HEC **Prices:** 11.60-23.20 **Facilities:** Play Area **Services:** **Leisure:** L **Off-site:** P

BEJA — BAIXO ALENTEJO

CM de Beja

av Vasco da Gama, 7800-397
☎ 284311911 📠 284311911
e-mail: campismo@cm-beja.pt
web: www.cm-beja.pt

dir: *AZ-IP8-Bejz.*

Open: All Year. **Site:** 1HEC **Facilities:** **Services:** **Off-site:** L P R S

Site 6HEC (site size) grass sand stone little shade partly shaded mainly shaded bungalows for hire (static) caravans for hire tents for hire no dogs site fully accessible for wheelchairs
Prices amount quoted is per night, for 2 adults and car, plus tent or caravan. Mobile home hire is a weekly rate.

LAGOS — ALGARVE

Turiscampo

E N125, 8600-109
282789265 282788578
e-mail: reservas@turiscampo.com
web: www.turiscampo.com

Site with large shaded pitches offering extensive leisure facilities and entertainment.

C&CC Report *This high quality modern camp site, in the western Algarve, is known for its very friendly welcome and for the quality of its facilities. The Coll family are carefully redeveloping the site with priority being given to good-sized pitches and facilities for campers. Within easy reach are white sandy beaches and a picturesque rocky coastline, with the most south-westerly point of Europe, Cape St. Vincent, and its famous lighthouse, about 20km away. The nearby town of Lagos is steeped in history from Roman times, the occupation by the Moors to more recent Portuguese explorers.*

dir: *From A22/IC4 exit 1, Lagos-Vila do Bispo, towards Lagos, then N125 towards Sagres until approaching Espiche.*

Open: All Year. **Site:** 7.5HEC
Prices: 16.50-31.50 Mobile home hire 182-714
Facilities: Wi-fi (charged) Kids' Club Play Area **Services:** **Leisure:** P
Off-site: S

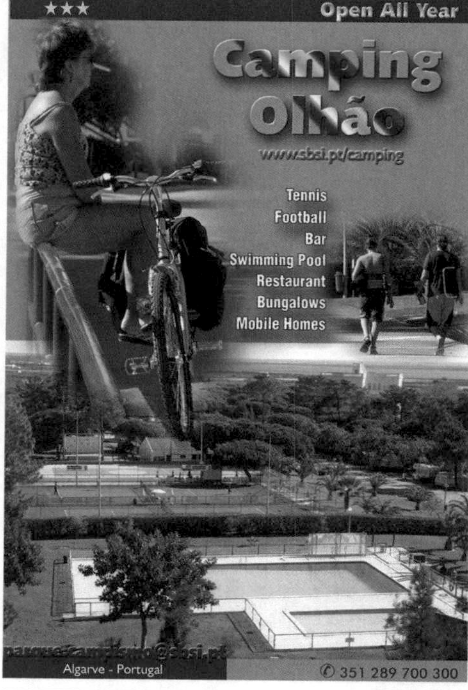

★★★
Open All Year
Camping
Olhão
www.sbsi.pt/camping
Tennis
Football
Bar
Swimming Pool
Restaurant
Bungalows
Mobile Homes
Algarve - Portugal
© 351 289 700 300

DEMIRA — BAIXO ALENTEJO

Zmar

7630-011
707200626
e-mail: info@zmar.eu
web: www.zmar.eu

Dogs allowed at an extra charge, no dangerous dogs.

C&CC Report *Zmar is the first Eco Camping Resort in Portugal. It is a very spacious site with permanent accommodation, which does not impact on the camping areas, as the wooden chalets are spread out in separate areas and make a minimal impact on the environment. The main facilities have to be seen to be believed. This is a campsite where you can either pamper yourself in the spa or simply enjoy all the inclusive facilities. The south west corner of the Alentejo district of Portugal is completely unspoilt by tourist development and is an easily accessible area with gently rolling hills, a national park and beautiful beaches. If all you know of Portugal is the Algarve, you are in for a surprise.*

dir: *From the N393 take the N393/1 heading for Cabo Sardao/Zambujeira.*

Site: **Facilities:** Play Area
Services: **Leisure:** P

OLHÃO — ALGARVE

Olhão

Pinheiros de Marim, 8700-914
289700300 289700390
e-mail: parque.campismo@sbsi.pt

C&CC Report *An excellent location for exploring the less developed eastern Algarve. Camping Olhão offers an easy-going environment with good on-site facilities. Olhão itself is a working fishing port, renowned for its shellfish and little touched by tourism. You'll still see traditional buildings and traditionally dressed locals.*

GPS: 37.0352, -7.8225

Open: All Year. **Site:** 10HEC **Facilities:** Wi-fi (charged) **Services:** **Leisure:** P **Off-site:** S

see advert on this page

PORTUGAL

Facilities shop shower electric points for razors electric points for caravans parking by tents permitted
npulsory separate car park **Services** café/restaurant bar Camping Gaz International gas other than Camping Gaz
first aid facilities laundry **Leisure** swimming L-Lake P-Pool R-River S-Sea **Off-site** All facilities within 5km

PORTIMÃO — ALGARVE

Da Dourada

Alvor, 8500-053
☎ 282459178 🖷 282459178
e-mail: campingdourada@hotmail.com

Set in a park-like area close to the beach with good facilities.

dir: *N off Portimão-Lagos road.*

Open: All Year. **Site:** 4HEC **Prices:** 8-19 Mobile home hire 260-520 **Facilities:** **Services:** **Leisure:** P R S

PRAIA DA LUZ — ALGARVE

Orbitur

Estrada da Praia da Luz, Valverde, 8600-148
☎ 282789211 🖷 282789213
e-mail: valverde@orbitur.pt
web: www.orbitur.pt

Well-equipped site with children's playground and tennis courts.

dir: *Off N125 Lagos-Cape St Vincent road. 4km from Lagos.*

Open: All Year. **Site:** 9.1HEC **Facilities:** **Services:** **Leisure:** P **Off-site:** S

PRAIA DE SALEMA — ALGARVE

Quinta dos Carriços

Praia da Salema, 8650-196
☎ 282695201 🖷 28265122
e-mail: quintacarrico@oninet.pt
web: www.quintadoscarricos.com

A well-equipped site with good facilities. There is a naturist section in a separate valley with its own facilities.

GPS: 37.0752, -8.8311

Open: All Year. **Site:** 20HEC **Prices:** 22.60-38.80 **Facilities:** **Services:** **Off-site:** S

QUARTEIRA — ALGARVE

Orbitur

The Camping and Caravanning Club — The Friendly Club

Estrada da Forte Santa,
av Sá Carneiro, 8125-618
☎ 289302826 🖷 289302822
e-mail: quarteira@orbitur.pt
web: www.orbitur.pt

A terraced site at the top of a hill.

C&CC Report *This extremely well-located site on the popular Algarve coast is particularly well suited to those who like the local facilities such as shops, restaurants and buses to be within reasonable walking distance. This site is great for, and much appreciated by, those who prefer quieter sites. Quarteira is one of the smaller modern resorts of this much-loved coastal region and is well placed for day trips to many of the Algarve's places of interest. Vilamoura and Val de Lobo are both within a good walking distance – well worth visiting for golfers and non-golfers alike.*

dir: *Off M125 in Almoncil, signs to Quarteira, left 0.5km before sea.*

Open: All Year. **Site:** 9.7HEC **Facilities:** **Services:** **Leisure:** P **Off-site:** S

SAGRES — ALGARVE

Orbitur

Cerro das Moitas, 8650-998
☎ 282624371 🖷 282624445
e-mail: sagres@orbitur.pt
web: www.orbitur.pt

Situated in a dune and forest area.

dir: *1.5km W of N268.*

Open: All Year. **Site:** 6.7HEC **Facilities:** **Services:** **Off-site:** S

VILA NOVA DE MILFONTES — BAIXO ALENTEJO

Milfontes

7645-300
☎ 283996104 🖷 283996104
e-mail: geral@campingmilfontes.com
web: www.campingmilfontes.com

Open: All Year. **Site:** 6.5HEC **Facilities:** **Services:** **Off-site:** R S

PORTUGAL

NORTH

ANGEIRAS DOURO LITORAL

Orbitur

4455-039
☎ 229270571 🖹 229271178
e-mail: angeiras@orbitur.pt
web: www.orbitur.pt
A modern, well-kept site in a pine wood on a hill overlooking the sea.
dir: *W of N13 x-rds at Km12.1. E of Vila do Pinheiro towards sea for 5km.*
Open: All Year. **Site:** 7HEC **Facilities:** **Services:** **Leisure:** P **Off-site:** S

CAMINHA MINHO

Orbitur

Mata do Camarido, E N13, Km 90, 4910-180
☎ 258921295 🖹 258921473
e-mail: caminha@orbitur.pt
web: www.orbitur.pt
On undulating sandy ground with trees.
dir: *Off N13 at Km89.7, W along Rio Minho for 0.8km & left.*
Open: Jan-Nov **Site:** 2.1HEC **Facilities:** **Services:** **Off-site:** S

CAMPO DO GERES MINHO

Cerdeira

4840-030
☎ 253351005 🖹 253353315
e-mail: info@parquecerdeira.com
web: www.parquecerdeira.com
A picturesque wooded location with mature oak trees surrounding the pitches.
Open: All Year. **Site:** 7HEC **Facilities:** Wi-fi **Services:** **Leisure:** P **Off-site:** L R

PÓVOA DE VARZIM DOURO LITORAL

Rio Alto

E N13 - Km 13, Estela-Rio Alto, 4570-275
☎ 252615699 🖹 252615599
e-mail: rioalto@orbitur.pt
web: www.orbitur.pt
Situated near dunes, 150m from the sea.
dir: *Off N13 towards Viana.*
Open: All Year. **Site:** 7.9HEC **Facilities:** **Services:** **Leisure:** P S

VIANA DO CASTELO MINHO

Orbitur

Rua Diogo Álvares, Cabedelo, 4900-161
☎ 258322167 🖹 258321946
e-mail: viana@orbitur.pt
web: www.orbitur.pt
A well-equipped site with direct access to a sandy beach.
dir: *Approach via N13 Porto-Viana do Castelo.*
Open: All Year. **Site:** 3HEC **Facilities:** **Services:** **Leisure:** P S

VILA NOVA DE GAIA DOURO LITORAL

Orbitur

Rua do Cerro, 608, Praia da Madalena, 4405-736
☎ 227122520 🖹 227122534
e-mail: madalena@orbitur.pt
web: www.orbitur.pt
Well-equipped site in a pine wood 0.5km from Madalena beach.
Open: All Year. **Site:** 2.4HEC **Facilities:** **Services:** **Leisure:** P **Off-site:** R S

VILA REAL TRAS-OS-MONTES ALTO DOURO

Parque Campismo de Vila Real

Rua Dr-Manuel Cardona, 5000-558
☎ 259324724
dir: *In E part of town off N2 by fuel station.*
Open: Mar-Nov **Site:** 4HEC **Facilities:** **Services:** **Off-site:** P R

CENTRAL

ALENQUER ESTREMADURA

Alenquer

E N9-KM94, 2580-330
☎ 263710375 🖹 263710375
e-mail: camping@dosdin.pt
web: www.dosdin.pt/camping
A modern well-equipped terraced site surrounded by walnut trees.
dir: *Via A1.*
Open: All Year. **Site:** 1.5HEC **Prices:** 15.50-18 Mobile home hire 350-455 **Facilities:** Wi-fi (charged) Play Area **Services:** **Leisure:** P **Off-site:** R

PORTUGAL

Facilities shop shower electric points for razors electric points for caravans parking by tents permitted compulsory separate car park **Services** café/restaurant bar Camping Gaz International gas other than Camping Gaz first aid facilities laundry **Leisure** swimming L-Lake P-Pool R-River S-Sea **Off-site** All facilities within 5km

ARGANIL — BEIRA LITORAL

Arganil

Sarzedo, 3300-432
235200133 235200134
e-mail: camping@mail.telepac.pt
web: www.cm-arganil.pt
A pleasant location among pine trees, close to the River Alva.
dir: *On N342-4.*
Open: All Year. **Site:** 3HEC **Facilities:** **Services:** **Leisure:** R **Off-site:**

CALDAS DA RAINHA — ESTREMADURA

Orbitur Foz do Arelho

Rua Maldonado Freitas, Foz do Arelho, 2500-516
262978683 262978685
e-mail: fozarelho@orbitur.pt
web: www.orbitur.pt
Situated in a fine lagoon on the Arelho estuary.
dir: *3km SE of Foz do Arelho.*
Open: All Year. **Site:** 6HEC **Facilities:** **Services:** **Leisure:** P **Off-site:** L S

CASFREIRES — BEIRA LITORAL

Quinta Chave Grande

Ferreira d'aves, 3560-043
232665552 232665552
e-mail: chave-grande@sapo.pt
web: www.chavegrande.com
A terraced site overlooking a beautiful valley. There are modern installations and leisure facilities.
Open: 15 Mar-Oct **Site:** 10HEC **Prices:** 19-27
Facilities: **Services:** **Leisure:** P
Off-site: L R

COSTA DA CAPARICA — ESTREMADURA

Orbitur

Av Afonso de Albuquerque, Quinta de St. António, 2825-450
212901366 212900661
e-mail: caparica@orbitur.pt
web: www.orbitur.pt
This site has a small touring section and is 200m from a fine sandy beach.
dir: *After crossing Ponte Sul on road to Caparica, turn right at lights, site 1km on left.*
Open: All Year. **Site:** 5.7HEC **Facilities:** **Services:** **Off-site:** S

ÉVORA — ALTO ALENTEJO

Orbitur

The Camping and Caravanning Club — The Friendly Club

Estrada de Alcacovas,
Herdade Esparragosa, 7005-206
266705190 266709830
e-mail: evora@orbitur.pt
web: www.orbitur.pt
Wooded surroundings with modern facilities.
C&CC Report *Located about a mile from the Lisbon to Beja road in the southern suburbs of Évora, just over 1km from the city walls of this UNESCO World Heritage city.*
dir: *2km S near Km94.5.*
Open: All Year. **Site:** 3.3HEC **Facilities:** **Services:** **Leisure:** P

ÉVORA DE ALCOBAÇA — ESTREMADURA

Rural de Silveira

Capuchos, 2460-479
262509573
e-mail: silveira.capuchos@gmail.com
web: www.campingsilveira.com
Set in a rural wooded location.
dir: *3km from Alcobaça on N86.*
Open: 15 May-15 Sep **Site:** 0.5HEC **Prices:** 12-14
Facilities: Play Area **Services:** **Off-site:** R

FIGUEIRA DA FOZ — BEIRA LITORAL

Orbitur

E N109 - Km 4, Gala, 3080-458
233431492 233431231
e-mail: info@orbitur.pt
web: www.orbitur.pt
An enclosed area set within a municipal park on top of Guarda hill.
dir: *On NW outskirts of town. Turn left off N16 Porto road at Km177, uphill for 0.5km.*
Open: All Year. **Site:** 6HEC **Facilities:** **Services:** **Leisure:** P **Off-site:** S

Site 6HEC (site size) grass sand stone little shade partly shaded mainly shaded bungalows for hire (static) caravans for hire tents for hire no dogs site fully accessible for wheelchairs
Prices amount quoted is per night, for 2 adults and car, plus tent or caravan. Mobile home hire is a weekly rate.

GOUVEIA — BEIRA LITORAL

Curral do Negro

6290-528
☎ 961350810 📠 238458041
e-mail: info@curraldonegro.com
web: www.curraldonegro.com
A mountain setting surrounded by woodland.
dir: *Signed.*
Open: 18 Jan-30 Oct **Site:** 2HEC **Facilities:** **Services:** **Leisure:** P

GUINCHO — ESTREMADURA

Orbitur

The Camping and Caravanning Club The Friendly Club

E N247-6, Lugar de Areia, Guincho, 2750-053
☎ 214870450 📠 214857413
e-mail: guincho@orbitur.pt
web: www.orbitur.pt
On hilly ground in a pine wood in the Parque du Guincho, near the Boca do Inferno.
C&CC Report *Very convenient for Lisbon, with regular bus services from the site to Cascais and a good train connection from there to the capital.*
dir: *5km NW of Cascais, off road 247-7.*
Open: All Year. **Site:** 7.7HEC **Facilities:** **Services:** **Off-site:** S

DANHA-A-NOVA — BEIRA BAIZE

rbitur Idanha-a-Nova

N354 - Km 8, Barragem de Idanha-a-Nova, 060-166
277202793 📠 277202945
-mail: info@orbitur.pt
eb: www.orbitur.pt
he campsite is near the Marechal Carmona Dam and near e Monfortinho hot springs in an area rich in history and rchitectural heritage. Individual marked pitches. Good for milies and outdoor sports.
r: *Off E N353, S from Fundão.*
pen: All Year. **Site:** 8HEC **Facilities:** **ervices:** **Leisure:** P **Off-site:** L R

LUSO — BEIRA LITORAL

Luso

E N336, Pampilhosa, Quinta Do Vale Do Jorge, 3050-246
☎ 231107551
e-mail: parquecampismoluso@gmail.com
Open: All Year. **Site:** 3HEC **Facilities:** **Services:** **Off-site:** L P

MONTARGIL — ALTO ALENTEJO

Orbitur

E N2, 7425-017
☎ 242901207 📠 242901220
e-mail: montargil@orbitur.pt
web: www.orbitur.pt
A beautiful wooded location with good recreational facilities close to the River Alva.
dir: *N off N2.*
Open: All Year. **Site:** 6HEC **Facilities:** **Services:** **Off-site:** L

NAZARÉ — ESTREMADURA

Orbitur Valado

Rua dos Combatentes do Ultramar 2, 2450-148
☎ 262561111 📠 262561137
e-mail: valado@orbitur.pt
web: www.orbitur.pt
Set in a pine wood 2km from the village with good facilities.
dir: *300m E of village, S of road E N8-5 Nazaré-Alcobaça.*
Open: Feb-Oct **Site:** 6.3HEC **Facilities:** **Services:** **Off-site:** S

Vale Paraiso

E N242, 2450-138
☎ 262561800 📠 262561900
e-mail: info@valeparaiso.com
web: www.valeparaiso.com
Situated in a beautiful natural park among tall pines. The site is well appointed with high standards of hygiene and varied recreational facilities.
GPS: 39.6203, -9.0564
Open: Jan-18 Dec, 27-31 Dec **Site:** 8.3HEC **Prices:** 12.60-17.80 **Facilities:** Wi-fi Kids' Club Play Area **Services:** **Leisure:** P **Off-site:** S

PORTUGAL

OUTEIRO DE LOURIÇAL BEIRA LITORAL

Tamanco

Rua do Lourical 11, Casas Brancas, 3105-158
☎ 236952551 🖹 236952551
e-mail: tamanco@mac.com
web: www.campismo-o-tamanco.com
Pleasant wooded surroundings.
dir: *Via N109 or A1.*
Open: All Year. **Site:** 1.5HEC **Prices:** 8-15 **Facilities:** **Services:** **Leisure:** P **Off-site:**

PALHEIROS DE MIRA BEIRA LITORAL

Orbitur

Estrada Florestal 1 - km 2, Dunas de Mira, 3070-792
☎ 231471234 🖹 231472047
e-mail: mira@orbitur.pt
web: www.orbitur.pt
Site lies in a dense forest.
dir: *N off N334 at Km2 towards Videira, opposite road fork.*
Open: Jan-Nov **Site:** 3HEC **Facilities:** **Services:** **Leisure:** S **Off-site:** L

PENICHE ESTREMADURA

CM

Av Monsenhor Bastos, 2520-206
☎ 262789529 🖹 262789529
e-mail: campismo-peniche@sapo.pt
web: www.cm-peniche.pt
On a sandy hillock, partly wooded, 0.5km from sea.
dir: *2km E.*
Open: All Year. **Site:** 12.6HEC **Facilities:** **Services:** **Off-site:** P S

Peniche Praia

Estrada Marginal Norte, 2520-605
☎ 262783460 🖹 262785334
e-mail: geral@penichepraia.pt
web: www.penichepraia.pt
On level ground 0.5km from the sea.
dir: *N towards Cabo Carudeiro.*
Open: All Year. **Site:** 1.5HEC **Facilities:** **Services:** **Off-site:** P S

QUIAIOS BEIRA LITORAL

Orbitur Quiaios

Praia de Quiaios, 3080-515
☎ 233919995 🖹 233919996
e-mail: info@orbitur.pt
web: www.orbitur.pt
Situated adjacent to the beach in an area abounding in architectural heritage. The surrounding pine wood adds to the peaceful and relaxing environment.
dir: *8km from Figueira da Foz.*
Open: All Year. **Site:** **Facilities:** **Services:** **Leisure:** S **Off-site:** L

SÃO JACINTO BEIRA LITORAL

Orbitur

E N327 - Km 20, 3800-901
☎ 234838284 🖹 234838122
e-mail: sjacinto@orbitur.pt
web: www.orbitur.pt
Set in a dense pine wood, towards the sea from the uneven pavec Ovar road that runs alongside the lagoon.
dir: *1.5km from sea.*
Open: Feb-Oct **Site:** 2.25HEC **Facilities:** **Services:** **Leisure:** R **Off-site:** S

SÃO PEDRO DE MOEL ESTREMADURA

Orbitur

Rua Volta do Sete, 2430-440
☎ 244599168 🖹 244599148
e-mail: spedro@orbitur.pt
web: www.orbitur.pt
On a hill among pine trees.
dir: *Off road 242-2 from Marinha Grande at rdbt near fuel static on E outskirts of village, N for 100m.*
Open: All Year. **Site:** 7HEC **Facilities:** **Services:** **Leisure:** P **Off-site:** P S

PORTUGAL

Romania

Drinking & Driving

Strictly forbidden. 0% of alcohol allowed in drivers' blood. Driving licence can be suspended for a maximum of 90 days, or a prison sentence may be imposed.

Driving Licence

Minimum age at which a UK licence holder may drive a temporarily imported car and / or motorcycle (for up to 90 days) 18.

Driving licences issued in the UK that do not incorporate a photograph must be accompanied by an International Driving Permit (IDP).

Fines

Police can impose fines and collect them on-the-spot, a receipt must be obtained. A vehicle which is illegally parked may be clamped and removed. If a fine is paid within 48 hours, the fine amount is halved.

Lights

Forbidden to drive at night if vehicle lighting faulty. Additional headlamps prohibited. Dipped headlights must be used outside built-up areas during the day.

Motorcycles

Use of dipped headlights during the day compulsory. Wearing of crash helmets is compulsory for driver and passenger of machines 50cc and over.

Motor Insurance

Green Card / third party insurance compulsory. Drivers of vehicles registered abroad who are not in possession of a valid green card must take out short term insurance at the frontier.

Passengers & Children

Child under 12 cannot travel as a front seat passenger.

Seat belts

Compulsory for front/rear seat occupants to wear seat belts, if fitted.

Speed limits

Unless signed otherwise

Private vehicles without trailers

Built-up areas	50km/h
Outside built-up areas	90km/h
Dual carriageways	100km/h
Motorways	130km/h

No minimum speed on motorways.

Private vehicle towing a caravan or trailer; Motorhomes (camper vans) with or without a trailer or car

Inside built up areas	50km/h
Motorways	110km/h
Main roads	90km/h
Other roads	80km/h

A driver who has held a licence for less than 1 year is restricted to a speed limit of 20km/h below the indicated speed.

Mopeds

Inside and outside built-up areas	45km/h

Additional information

Compulsory equipment:

- First aid kit
- Fire extinguisher
- Red warning triangle - not required for two wheeled vehicles.

Other rules/requirements:

It is against the law to drive a dirty car.

If a temporarily imported vehicle is damaged before arrival in Romania, the importer must ask a Romanian Customs or Police Officer to write a report on the damage so that he can export the vehicle without problems. If any damage occurs inside the country a report must be obtained at the scene of the accident. Damaged vehicles may only be taken out of the country on production of this evidence.

"Claxonarea interzisa" – use of horn prohibited. The use of the horn is prohibited between 2200hrs and 0600hrs in built-up areas.

Spiked tyres prohibited.

The use of snow chains is recommended for winter journeys to the mountains and may be compulsory in case of heavy snow.

"Rovinieta" - a road tax is levied on all motor vehicles both residents and visitors. Road tax 'stickers' known as "rovinieta" are available from border crossing points, petrol stations and post offices in Romania. The cost depends on the vehicle emissions category and period of use in Romania.

Foreign drivers failing to purchase a "rovinieta" during their stay may incur a fine between €3000 and €4000 when leaving the country. Proof of insurance and the car's registration document is required when purchasing the "rovinieta".

Bulgaria

Drinking & Driving

If the level of alcohol in the bloodstream is 0.05 per cent or more the driver will be prosecuted and receive a fine and driving suspension. The police carry out random breath tests. If the test is positive, the driver will be required to undergo a blood test carried out by a hospital doctor.

Driving Licence

Minimum age at which a UK driving licence holder may drive a temporarily imported car and / or motorcycle 18. It is recommended that an International Driving Permit (IDP) accompanies older licences.

Fines

On-the-spot. An official receipt should be obtained. Wheel clamps are in use for illegally parked cars. Vehicles causing an obstruction will be towed away.

Lights

The use of dipped headlights during daylight hours throughout the year is recommended, however their use is compulsory from the 1 Nov to 1 Mar.

Motorcycles

Wearing of crash helmets compulsory for both driver and passenger. Motorcyclists must have their lights on at all times.

Motor insurance

Third party insurance compulsory. Green Cards are recognised.

Passengers & Children

Children under 12 cannot travel as a front seat passenger. Children must be placed in special restraints suitable for their size.

Seat Belts

Compulsory for front and rear seat occupants to wear seat belts, if fitted.

Speed Limits

Unless signed otherwise

Private vehicles without trailers	
Built-up areas	50km/h
Outside built-up areas	90km/h
Motorways	130km/h
Cars with caravan/trailer	
Inside built-up areas	50km/h
Outside built-up areas	70km/h
Motorways	100km/h

Additional Information

Compulsory equipment in Bulgaria:

- Fire extinguisher – Not required for two wheeled vehicles
- First-aid kit
- Warning triangle - not required for two wheeled vehicles
- Reflective jackets - The wearing of a reflective jacket is compulsory for any person who has to step out of their car, day or night in case of breakdown or emergency on a motorway. This regulation also applies to motorcyclists.

Other rules/requirements Bulgaria:

In built-up areas it is prohibited to use the horn between 2200hrs and 0600hrs (0900hrs on public holidays), and between 1200hrs and 1600hrs.

Visiting motorists are required to drive through a liquid disinfectant on entry for which the charge is (approx) €4, and also purchase a 'vignette' (road tax). The vignette is available at the border, UAB offices, most petrol stations and offices of the CI and DZI Bank, weekly, monthly or annually. Heavy fines are imposed for non-compliance.

Snow chains are permitted. Their use can become compulsory according to road conditions, in which case this is indicated by the international road sign. Spiked tyres are forbidden.

Drivers of luxury or 4 x 4 vehicles are advised to use guarded car parks.

A GPS based navigation system which has maps indicating the location of fixed speed cameras must have the 'fixed speed camera POI (Points Of Interest)' function deactivated. The use of radar detectors is prohibited.

In one way streets parking is on the left only.

BULGARIA

DRYANOVO — GABROVO

Strinava

Dryanovo Monastery, 5370
☎ 0676 72332
e-mail: bacho_kiro2@abv.bg
web: www.dryanovo.com

Site situated near the outskirts of Dryanovo Monastery, by the banks of the river Dryanovska in an attractive location with much natural wildlife. Booking required Apr, Oct & Nov.

dir: *1km from the main road Veliko Tarnovo - Gabrovo.*

Open: Apr-Nov **Site:** **Prices:** 10 **Facilities:** **Leisure:** R **Off-site:** P

HARMANLI — HASKOVO

Sakar Hills Camping

? Georgi Rakovski St, Biser, 6470
☎ 0885 504338
e-mail: mail@sakar-hills.com
web: www.sakar-hills.com

Located close to the Greek and Turkish borders, large pitches and covered outdoor seating area for campers use.

dir: *1km from E85 Sofia-Istanbul road.*

GPS: 41.8703, 25.9913

Open: Apr-Oct **Site:** 0.5HEC **Prices:** 8-12 **Facilities:** Wi-fi **Services:** **Off-site:** L P R

YASKOVETS — VELIKO TARNOVO

Camping Veliko Tarnovo

0 Vail Levski St, Dragizhevo Village, 5145
☎ 0619 42777
e-mail: office@campingvelikotarnovo.com
web: www.campingvelikotarnovo.com

Set in a rural, picturesque valley and close to tourist attractions. Fully serviced pitches and family bathroom available. Swimming pool due for completion in 2011.

dir: *A4/E772 Veliko Tarnovo - Varna.*

Open: Mar-Oct **Site:** 1.5HEC **Prices:** 18-26 **Facilities:** Wi-fi Play Area **Services:** **Leisure:** R **Off-site:** L

ROMANIA

Please note: Although the official currency of Romania is the Romanian leu, the campsites featured in this guide have quoted their prices in Euros.

AUREL VLAICU — ARAD

Aurel Vlaicu

str Principale 155, 335401
☎ 0254 245541
e-mail: zeerom@zeelandnet.nl
web: www.campingaurelvlaicu.ro

Situated in a quiet village with fine views of the mountains.

Open: 15 Apr-Sep **Site:** 0.7HEC **Facilities:** **Services:** **Leisure:** P **Off-site:** R

BLAJEL — SIBIU

Doua Lumi

str Tudor Vladimirescu 87-89, 557050
☎ 0269 851079
e-mail: info@doualumi.com
web: www.doualumi.com

Small site in the heart of Transylvania.

dir: *6km N of Medias, off DN14a Medias-Tarnaveni.*

GPS: 46.2114, 24.3242

Open: Apr-Oct **Site:** 0.5HEC **Prices:** 13-16 **Facilities:** Wi-fi Play Area **Services:** **Leisure:** P **Off-site:**

BRAN — BRASOV

Vampire Camping

str Principala 77C, 507025
☎ 0625 083909
e-mail: info@vampirecamping.com
web: www.vampirecamping.com

Peaceful location bordered by hills and mountains. Ideally located for visiting Bran Castle, most commonly known as Dracula's Castle, home of the famous fictional vampire.

dir: *On DN73 Brasov-Pitesti.*

Open: Apr-1 Nov **Site:** 3.5HEC **Facilities:** **Services:** **Leisure:** R

ROMANIA

CÂRTA — SIBIU

De Oude Wilg

str Prundului 311, 557070
0269 521347
e-mail: de_oude_wilg@yahoo.com
web: www.campingdeoudewilg.nl

Centrally located, north of the Fagaras mountains in a broad valley. Small site with level pitches reached by a bridge, so not suitable for very large vehicles.

Open: All Year. **Site:** 1HEC **Facilities:** **Services:** **Leisure:** R **Off-site:**

CISNADIOARA — SIBIU

Ananas

str Cimitirului 32, 555301
0269 566066
e-mail: m.benoehr@ananas7b.de
web: www.ananas7b.de

Situated in the heart of Transylvania with a mountain landscape, forests and meadows.

dir: *10km S of Sibiu.*

Open: May-Sep **Site:** **Facilities:** **Leisure:** P **Off-site:**

DARMANESTI — SUCEAVA

Trotus Valley

Calea Trotusului 272, 605300
0234 374705 0234 374705
e-mail: info@camperland.ro
web: www.camperland.ro

Site located in mountainous region in east of country between the Black Sea and the monasteries in Northern Moldova. Trips can be arranged for small groups.

dir: *Off DN12A (Adjud-Mercuiri).*

Open: 15 Apr-15 Oct **Site:** 1.5HEC **Facilities:** **Services:** **Off-site:** R

EFORIE — CONSTANTA

Meduza

str Sportului, 905350
0767 707122
e-mail: n_t_sco@yahoo.com

Site located near 4km of beaches and Lake Techirghiol with its spa properties.

Open: Jun-15 Sep **Site:** 2.2HEC **Facilities:** **Services:** **Off-site:** S

GILAU — CLU

Eldorado

DN1-E60, 407310
0264 371688 0264 371688
e-mail: info@campingeldorado.com
web: www.campingeldorado.com

Situated in the tourist area of Transylvania at the foot of the Apuseni Mountains. Tents are available for hire for groups.

dir: *Off E60.*

GPS: 46.7669, 23.3530

Open: 15 Apr-15 Oct **Site:** 3.8HEC **Facilities:** Wi-fi Play Area **Services:** **Leisure:** L P **Off-site:**

MINIŞ — ARA

Camping Route Roemenië

317137
0742 678111 0742 540620
e-mail: camping.route.roemenie@gmail.com
web: www.routeroemenie.nl

Small, relaxing site surrounded by mountains, 3km from a lake where fishing and swimming are available. Restrictions apply as to when cars can be parked by tents.

GPS: 46.1336, 21.5983

Open: Apr-Sep **Site:** 0.5HEC **Prices:** 12.50-15.50 Mobile home hire 150-160 **Facilities:** Wi-fi Play Area **Services:** **Leisure:** P **Off-site:** L

Site 6HEC (site size) grass sand stone little shade partly shaded mainly shaded bungalows for hire (static) caravans for hire tents for hire no dogs site fully accessible for wheelchairs
Prices amount quoted is per night, for 2 adults and car, plus tent or caravan. Mobile home hire is a weekly rate.

MURIGHIOL TULCEA

Camping Lac Murighiol

827150
☎ 0740 501297
e-mail: contact@campinglacmurighiol.ro
web: www.campinglacmurighiol.ro

Peaceful site situated near the Danube Delta. Organised trips are available for campers to experience the wildlife and ecology of the area. Charge made for dogs.

dir: *On Main St.*

GPS: 45.0464, 29.1606

Open: All Year. **Site:** 0.25HEC **Prices:** 10.50-13.50 **Facilities:** Play Area **Services:** **Off-site:** L R

RUCAR ARGES

Panorama

str Brasovului 219, 117630
☎ 0740 666279
e-mail: campingpanorama@hotmail.com

Situated in the spectacular Carpathian mountain area.

dir: *Route E574 Brasov-Pitesti.*

Open: May-Sep **Site:** 1.1HEC **Facilities:** **Services:** **Off-site:**

SÓVATA MURES

Vasskert

str Prinzipala 129/A, 545500
☎ 0265 570902 0265 570902
e-mail: vasskert@szovata.hu
web: www.szovata.hu

Unspoilt location with mountain streams and forests, close to the famous Bear Lake with its spa properties.

Open: May-Sep **Site:** 0.8HEC **Prices:** 14
Facilities: Wi-fi Play Area **Services:**
Leisure: R **Off-site:** L P

ROMANIA

Slovenia

Drinking & Driving

If the level of alcohol in the bloodstream is 0.05% or more, severe penalties include fine or suspension of driving licence. 0% of alcohol is permitted in the drivers' blood if the licence has been held for less than 3 years, the person is under 21 or is a professional driver. A driver can still be fined for levels under 0.05% if they are unable to drive safely. These rules also apply to narcotics.

Driving Licence

Minimum age at which a UK licence holder may drive a temporarily imported car and / or motorcycle (exceeding 125cc) 18. An International Driving Permit (IDP) is compulsory for holders of driving licences not incorporating a photograph.

Fines

On-the-spot, they must be paid in local currency. Refusal to pay could result in your passport being held. Illegally parked vehicles will be towed away or clamped.

Lights

Use of dipped headlights during the day compulsory.

Motorcycles

Use of dipped headlights during the day compulsory. Wearing of crash helmets is compulsory for both driver and passenger. Children under 12 not permitted as a passenger.

Motor Insurance

Third-party compulsory.

Passengers & Children

Child under 12 and smaller than 1.5 metres must use suitable restraint system for their age and size and they are only permitted to travel in the rear seats. Children over 12 may wear normal seat belts.

Seat Belts

Compulsory for all occupants to wear seat belts, if fitted.

Speed Limits

Unless signed otherwise

private vehicles without trailers

Built-up areas	50km/h
Outside built-up areas	90km/h
Dual carriageways	100km/h
Motorways	130km/h

private vehicle towing a trailer or caravan

Built-up areas	50km/h
Motorways	80km/h
Fast roads	80km/h
Other roads	80km/h

Some areas have a restricted speed limit of 30km/h. Minimum speed on motorways is 60km/h. Vehicles equipped with snow chains must not exceed 50km/h. In bad weather and when visibility is reduced to less than 50mtrs, the maximum speed limit is 50km/h.

Additional Information

Compulsory equipment: Reflective jacket – (not motorcycles); Reflective waistcoat/s should be kept in the vehicle and not in the boot as any person exiting a vehicle must wear one in an accident/breakdown situation. Fine for non-compliance; Warning triangle – two if towing a trailer. Not required for two wheeled vehicles; Snow chains – must be carried between 15 Nov and 15 Mar (and at other times in winter weather conditions) by private cars and vehicles up to 3.5tonnes unless vehicle fitted with 4 winter tyres. Minimum tread depth is 3mm.

Other rules/requirements in Slovenia:

At night if hazard lights fail, in addition to a warning triangle a yellow flashing light or position lights must mark the vehicle. Fire extinguisher, first-aid kit and set of replacement bulbs recommended.

Foreign drivers involved in an accident must call the police and obtain a written report. On leaving the country, damaged vehicles must be accompanied by this report, as Customs will ask to see it, to allow exit.

It is prohibited to overtake a bus transporting children when passengers are getting on or off. Use of the horn is prohibited in built-up areas or at night, except in emergencies.

A vignette system has been introduced which replaces tolls. The vignette will have to be displayed when travelling on motorways and expressways and will be available to purchase from filling stations in Slovenia and in neighbouring countries. The vignettes are available with validities of 1 year (vehicle up to 3.5t €95), per month (vehicle up to 3.5t €30) and for 7 days (vehicle up to 3.5t €15), with the yearly one being valid from 1 Dec to 31 Jan the following year, fine for non-display €300 minimum.

Further information can be found on www.dars.si

The use of spiked tyres is prohibited. Hazard warning lights must be used when reversing.

Vignettes Currency Euro (€)	Car	Car Towing Caravan/Trailer
weekly vignette	€15.00	€15.00
monthly vignette	€30.00	€30.00
annual vignette	€95.00	€95.00

ANKARAN — PRIMORSKA

Adria Ankaran

Jadranska cesta 25, 6280
05 663 7350 05 663 7360
e-mail: camp@adria-ankaran.si
web: www.adria-ankaran.si

Shady campsite on hills overlooking the sea. Water slide, an Olympic size swimming pool and a spa centre on site.

dir: *From border at Skofije. 4km to Koper, exit for Ankaran, campsite 5km on left.*

Open: 25 Apr-Sep **Site:** 7HEC **Facilities:** **Services:** **Leisure:** P S **Off-site:**

BANOVCI — POMURJE

Banovci

Banovci 1a, 9241
02 513 1400 02 587 1703
e-mail: terme@terme-banovci.si
web: www.terme-banovci.si

Site in a thermal spa location with pool complex featuring whirlpools, fountains and water slides. Separate naturist section.

dir: *On Ormoz-Radenci road, past Ljutomer & right after level crossing, campsite signed.*

Open: All Year. **Site:** 8HEC **Facilities:** **Services:** **Leisure:** P **Off-site:** R

BLED — GORENJSKA

Bled

The Camping and Caravanning Club The Friendly Club

Kidriceva 10c, 4260
04 575 2000 04 575 2002
e-mail: info@camping.bled.si

Well-run site in stunning location with many activities.

C&CC Report *The Julian Alps are an especially beautiful part of Europe's greatest mountain range, with vast limestone crags topping steep and densely wooded slopes. Friendly, well run and with very good facilities, Camping Bled is in a stunning location by the unspoilt lake. Gems to visit include Slovenia's only island, on Lake Bled; lovely Lake Bohinj; Europe's largest show caves at Postojna; Pokljuka plateau, with its soaring pine forests, wild flowers and tiny farming villages; and General Tito's former residence. The Bled Days festival is held on the fourth weekend in July each year and includes Bled Night, with thousands of candles adrift on the lake.*

dir: *Drive from Bled along the lake in direction of Bohinjska Bistrica. Turn right after 1.5 km, campsite 1km.*

Open: 20 Mar-15 Oct **Site:** 6.5HEC **Facilities:** **Services:** **Leisure:** L **Off-site:** P

BOHINJSKA BISTRICA — GORISKA

Danica

Triglavska 60, 4264
04 572 1702 04 572 3330
e-mail: info@camp-danica.si
web: www.camp-danica.si

Site ringed by the Julian Alps and in a pleasant location by the River Sava and Lake Bohinj.

Open: May-Oct **Site:** 4.5HEC **Facilities:** **Services:** **Leisure:** R **Off-site:** L P

BOVEC — GORISKA

Polovnik

Ledina 8, 5230
05 389 6007 05 389 6006
e-mail: kamp.polovnik@siol.net
web: www.kamp-polovnik.com

Located in a beautiful park in the Soea Valley and a short walk from the centre of Bovec. The layout of the campsite enables guests to reach all the local attractions by foot.

dir: *N side of Bovec, follow camping signs. Approach via Passo de Predil not recommended for large caravans.*

Open: Apr-15 Oct **Site:** 1.2HEC **Prices:** 16.02-18.02 **Facilities:** Wi-fi **Services:** **Off-site:** R

IZOLA — PRIMORSKA

Belvedere

Dobrava 1a, 6310
05 660 5100 05 660 5182
e-mail: belvedere@belvedere.si
web: www.belvedere.si

On a hill, near the coast overlooking the Bay of Trieste.

dir: *From Koper, campsite 1km after Izola. NB Do not take Izola exit but drive towards Portoroz & follow campsite signs.*

Open: Apr-Sep **Site:** 3HEC **Facilities:** **Services:** **Leisure:** P S **Off-site:**

KOBARID — GORISKA

Kamp Nadiža Podbela

5223
04 144 3535
e-mail: info@kamp-nadiza.com
web: www.kamp-nadiza.com

Suitable for families with small children and on the banks of Nadiža river.

Open: 15 Mar-Oct **Site:** 3HEC **Prices:** 20-27 Mobile home hire 420-490 **Facilities:** Wi-fi Kids' Club Play Area **Services:** **Leisure:** R **Off-site:** R

Koren

Drezniske Ravne 33, 5222
05 389 1311 05 389 1310
e-mail: info@kamp-koren.si
web: www.kamp-koren.si

In a picturesque location by the Soca river and under Mount Krn. Good facilities for water sports, hiking and mountaineering.

dir: *At Dreznica, 5km E of Kobarid (Bovec-Tolmin road).*

GPS: 46.2508, 13.5867

Open: All Year. **Site:** 2HEC **Prices:** 20-23 **Facilities:** Wi-fi (charged) Play Area **Services:** **Leisure:** R **Off-site:**

LESCE — GORENJSKA

Camping Šobec

Šobčeva resta 25, 4248
04 535 3700 04 535 3701
e-mail: sobec@siol.net
web: www.sobec.si

In a wooded area on lake shore.

Open: 16 Apr-2 Oct **Site:** 16HEC **Prices:** 21.40-25.60 **Facilities:** Wi-fi Kids' Club Play Area **Services:** **Leisure:** L R **Off-site:** P

LJUBLJANA — GORENJSKA

Ljubljana Resort

Dunadska cesta 270, 1000
01 568 3913 01 568 3912
e-mail: ljubljana.resort@gpl.si
web: www.ljubljanaresort.si

A shaded site by the Sava river, part of larger complex which includes a hotel.

GPS: 46.0978, 14.5189

Open: 14 Mar-Dec **Site:** 3HEC **Prices:** 22.50-23.50 Mobile home hire 476-770 **Facilities:** Wi-fi (charged) Kids' Club Play Area **Services:** **Leisure:** P R **Off-site:**

MOJSTRANA — GORENJSKA

Kamne

Dovje 9, 4281
04 589 1105 04 589 1105
e-mail: campingkamne@telemach.net
web: www.campingkamne.com

In the immediate vicinity of Triglav National park, an area of mountains and scenic valleys.

dir: *E of Dovje, off Kranjska Gora-Jesenice road.*

Open: All Year. **Site:** 1.5HEC **Prices:** 15.42-17.62 **Facilities:** **Services:** **Leisure:** P **Off-site:**

MORAVSKE TOPLICE — POMURJE

Camping Terme 3000

Kranjčeva 12, 9226
02 512 1200 02 512 1148
e-mail: recepcija.camp2@terme3000.si
web: www.sava-hotels-resorts.com

Shaded by trees, this site has modern facilities and access is available to the Terme 3000 waterpark.

GPS: 46.6801, 16.2206

Open: All Year. **Site:** 7HEC **Prices:** 32-36 **Facilities:** Wi-fi (charged) Kids' Club Play Area **Services:** **Off-site:** P

PORTOROZ — PRIMORSKA

Lucija

Seca 204, 6320
05 690 6000 05 690 6900
e-mail: camp@metropolgroup.si
web: www.metropol-hotels.com

Close to the Adriatic seaside resort of Portoroz with its many attractions. Dance and music evenings organised on the site.

Open: 10 Apr-4 Oct **Site:** 5.5HEC **Facilities:** **Services:** **Leisure:** S **Off-site:** P

RECICA OB SAVINJI — SAVINJSKO

Menina

Varpolje 105, 3332
04 052 5266
e-mail: info@campingmenina.com
web: www.campingmenina.com

Peaceful site set in a scenic location by the Savinja River and the Kamnik-Savinja Alps.

dir: *800m off main Mozirje - Ljubno road.*

Open: All Year. **Site:** 8.5HEC **Prices:** 25 **Facilities:** Wi-fi Kids' Club Play Area **Services:** **Leisure:** L R **Off-site:**

Spain

Drinking and driving

If the level of alcohol in the bloodstream is 0.05% or more, severe penalties include fines and withdrawal of visitor's driving licence. Drivers with less than 2 years experience, 0.03%. Severe penalties include imprisonment for non compliance

Driving licence

Minimum age at which a UK licence holder may drive a temporarily imported car 18. Motorcycles up to 125cc 16 years, over125cc 18 years. All valid UK driving licences should be accepted in Spain. This includes the older all-green style UK licences (in Northern Ireland older paper style with photographic counterpart). Older licences may be accompanied by an International Driving Permit (IDP).

Fines

On-the-spot. An official receipt should be obtained. Illegally parked vehicles can be towed away. Wheel clamps are also in use.

Lights

Use of full headlights in built-up areas is prohibited; use sidelights or dipped headlights depending on how well lit the roads are. Dipped headlights must be used in tunnels.

Motorcycles

Dipped headlights during the day compulsory. Wearing of crash helmets compulsory, this includes trikes and quads unless they are equipped with seat belts. It is prohibited to transport a passenger under 18 years of age on a moped. A child over 7 years old may be transported as a passenger on a motorcycle driven by parent or authorised person. Child must wear a helmet suitable for their size.

Motor Insurance

Third-party compulsory.

Passengers/Children in cars

Children measuring less than 1.35m must be seated in a child restraint system adapted to their size and weight, except when travelling in a taxi in an urban area. Children measuring more than 1.35m may use an adult seatbelt.

Seat belts

Compulsory for occupants to wear seat belts, if fitted.

Speed limits

Unless signed otherwise

Private vehicles without trailers	
Built-up areas	50km/h
Outside built-up areas (2nd category)	90km/h
(1st category)	100km/h
Motorways	120km/h
Motorways/dual carriageways in built-up areas	80km/h
Minimum speed motorways/dual carriageways	60km/h
Some residential zones	20km/h
Motor home or car towing a trailer	
Built up areas	50km/h
Motorways & dual carriageways in built-up areas	80km/h
Motor home or car towing trailer up to 750kg	
Motorways and dual carriageways	90km/h
1st category roads	80km/h
2nd category roads	70km/h
Vehicle towing a trailer over 750kg	
Motorways and dual carriageways	80km/h
1st category roads	80km/h
2nd category roads	70km/h

Additional information

Compulsory equipment: Spare tyre (or tyre repair kit and equipment to change the tyre); Warning triangle (one triangle is compulsory but carrying two is recommended as, in an accident/breakdown situation; local officials may impose a fine if only one is produced. Not required for motorcycles); Reflective jacket (wearing of this is compulsory if driver and/or passenger(s) exits vehicle immobilised on the carriageway of any motorway, main or busy road. It is not mandatory to carry a reflective jacket in the vehicle but it is recommended. Car Hire Companies are not under legal obligation to supply them to persons hiring vehicles, so often don't).

Other rules/requirements: Drivers who wears glasses should carry a spare pair with them if this is noted on their driving licence. Apparatus with a screen which can distract a driver (TV, video, DVD etc) should be positioned where the driver cannot see them. This excludes GPS systems. It is prohibited to touch or program the device unless parked in a safe place. The use of radar detectors is prohibited. In urban areas it is prohibited to sound the horn except in an emergency. Lights may be flashed instead. Snow chains are recommended in snowy conditions, police can stop vehicles without snow chains. In winter, spikes on spiked tyres must not exceed 2mm in length and must only be used on snow or ice-covered roads. In case of a car towing a caravan/trailer exceeding 12m, there must be two yellow reflectors at the rear of the caravan or trailer. A load may exceed the length of a private vehicle at the rear by up to 10% of its length. The load must be indicated by a panel with diagonal red and white stripes. If you wish to carry bicycles on the rear of your vehicle, you will need a 50x50cm reflectorised panel, which can be bought from most caravan/motor home accessory shops or from www.fiamma.com.

Spain

Tolls (Private car, with or without trailer)	
A1 Burgos - A68 (near Miranda de Ebro)	€8.75
A12 Leon - Astorga	€3.85
A15/A68 Pamplona (Irunea) - Tudela	€12.05
A19 Barcelona - Blanes	€3.97
A2 Zaragoza - Tarragona	€16.25
A3 Madrid - Casa de la Moraleja	€3.40
A4 Cadiz - Dos Hermanas (Sevilla)	€5.90
A41 Madrid - Toledo	€2.20
A51 Madrid - Avila	€8.10
A55 La Coruna - Carballo	€2.30
A57 Vigo - Baiona	€1.45
A6 Villalba - Adanero	€9.35
A61 Madrid - Segovia	€7.35
A66 Leon - Oviado	€10.60
A68 Miranda de Ebro - Bilbao (Bilbo)	€8.80
A68 Zaragoza - Miranda de Ebro	€17.65
A7 Alicante (Alacant) - Cartagena	€3.15
A7 Barcelona - Tarragona	€11.26
A7 La Jonquera (French Frontier) - Barcelona	€12.56
A7 Malaga - Gibraltar	€13.15
A7 Valencia - Alicante (Alacant)	€13.90
A7 Tarragona - Valencia	€22.00
A8 Bilbao (Bilbo) - Irun (French Frontier)	€8.59
A9 Ferrol - La Coruna	€3.60
A9 La Coruna - Santiago de Compostela	€5.15
A9 Santiago de Compostela - Vigo	€7.35
AP53 Santiago de Compostela - Ourense	€5.15
C16 Barcelona - Puigcerda (Tunel del Cadi)	€20.83
C32 Barcelona - Tarragona	€11.26
E9 Barcelona - Tunel de Vallviderol	€3.52
M12 Madrid (Barajas) Airport - Alcobendas (E5/A1)	€1.75
R2 Madrid - Guadalajara	€6.85
R5 Madrid - Navadcarnero	€3.50
Tunnels	
Tunel del Cadi (Spanish/French border)	€11.00
Tunels de Vallvidrera - Barcelona	€3.52

Andorra

Drinking and driving
Permitted level of alcohol in the bloodstream is 0.05%.

Driving licence
Minimum age at which a UK licence holder may drive temporarily imported car and/or motorcycle 18.

Fines
On-the-spot.

Lights
Dipped headlights should be used in poor daytime visibility.

Motorcycles
Use of dipped headlights during the day compulsory. The wearing of a crash helmet is compulsory.

Motor Insurance
Third party insurance is compulsory.

Passengers/Children in cars
Child under 10 cannot travel as a front seat passenger.

Seat belts
Compulsory for front seat occupants to wear seat belts, if fitted.

Speed limits
Unless otherwise signed

Private vehicles with or without trailers

Built-up areas	50km/h
Outside built-up areas	between 60 and 90 km/h

Additional information
Compulsory equipment in Andorra:

- Spare bulbs
- Warning triangle
- Reflective yellow waistcoat

Other rules/requirements in Andorra:

Winter tyres are recommended.

Snow chains must be used when road conditions or signs indicate.

NORTH EAST COAST

BEGUR — GIRONA

Begur

ctra D'Esclanya km2, 17255
972 623201 972 624566
e-mail: info@campingbegur.com
web: www.campingbegur.com

A terraced site in a wooded valley.

dir: *1.4km SE of town. Right of road to Palafrugell, 400m after turning for Fornells & Aiguablava.*

Open: 15 Apr-25 Sep **Site:** 8HEC **Prices:** 26-45.40 **Facilities:** Play Area **Services:** **Leisure:** P **Off-site:** S

Maset

Playa de sa Riera, 17255
972 623023 972 623901
e-mail: info@campingelmaset.com
web: www.campingelmaset.com

A well-kept terraced site, divided into pitches in a beautiful valley, 300m from the sea.

dir: *2km N of Begur. If entering from W, turn left just before town.*

Open: 18 Apr-24 Sep **Site:** 1.2HEC **Prices:** 23.30-33.60 Mobile home hire 364-749 **Facilities:** Wi-fi Play Area **Services:** **Leisure:** P **Off-site:** S

BLANES — GIRONA

Bella Terra

av Villa de Madrid, 17300
972 348017 972 348275
e-mail: info@campingbellaterra.com
web: www.campingbellaterra.com

A large family site in a lovely pine wood beside the beach with modern facilities.

dir: *Via N11.*

Open: Apr-Sep **Site:** 10.5HEC **Facilities:** **Services:** **Leisure:** P S

Blanes

av Villa de Madrid 33, 17300
972 331591 972 337063
-mail: info@campingblanes.com
veb: www.campingblanes.com

Set in a pine forest with direct path to the beach, 1km from the own centre reached along a sea promenade.

ir: *On left of Paseo Villa de Madrid coast road towards town.*

PS: 41.6591, 2.7795

pen: All Year. **Site:** 2HEC **Prices:** 25.20-35.90 **acilities:** Wi-fi (charged) Play Area **ervices:** **Leisure:** P S **Off-site:** R

Masia

c Colon 44, Los Pinos, 17300
972 331013 972 333128
e-mail: info@campinglamasia.com
web: www.campinglamasia.com

A pleasant family site on level ground with shady pitches, 150m from the sea.

dir: *50m inland from Paseo Villa de Madrid coast road.*

Open: May-Sep **Site:** 9HEC **Facilities:** Wi-fi (charged) Kids' Club Play Area **Services:** **Leisure:** P R S

Pinar

av Villa de Madrid, 17300
972 331083 972 331100
e-mail: camping@elpinarbeach.com
web: www.elpinarbeach.com

Divided into two by the coastal road. Partially meadow under poplars.

dir: *1km on Paseo Villa de Madrid coast road.*

Open: Apr-Sep **Site:** 5HEC **Facilities:** **Services:** **Leisure:** P S

S'Abanell

av Villa de Madrid 7-9, 17300
972 331809 972 350506
e-mail: info@sabanell.com
web: www.sabanell.com

Set within a pine wood, part of which is inland and open to the public.

dir: *On either side of Avenida Villa de Madrid road. Off coast road S of Blanes.*

Open: 8 Jan-23 Dec **Site:** 3.3HEC **Prices:** 14-35.90 Mobile home hire 298-793 **Facilities:** Wi-fi (charged) **Services:** **Leisure:** S

CALELLA DE LA COSTA — BARCELONA

Botanic Bona Vista

08370
93 7692488 93 7695804
e-mail: info@botanic-bonavista.net
web: www.botanic-bonavista.net

Subdivided and well-tended terraced site on a hillside, beautifully landscaped. Steep internal roads. Access to the beach via a pedestrian underpass.

dir: *Off NII at Km665, site round blind corner.*

Open: All Year. **Site:** 2.85HEC **Facilities:** **Services:** **Leisure:** P S

Facilities shop shower electric points for razors electric points for caravans parking by tents permitted mpulsory separate car park **Services** café/restaurant bar Camping Gaz International gas other than Camping Gaz first aid facilities laundry **Leisure** swimming L-Lake P-Pool R-River S-Sea **Off-site** All facilities within 5km

Far

08370
93 7690967 93 7693197
e-mail: info@campingelfar.com
web: www.campingelfar.com
Terraced site on a hillock under deciduous trees with lovely view of Calella and out to sea. Steep internal roads.
dir: *S on NII, site before left bend at Km 666.*
Open: Apr-Sep **Site:** 2.5HEC **Facilities:** **Services:** **Leisure:** P **Off-site:** S

CASTELL D'ARO GIRONA

Castell d'Aro

crta S'Agaro, 17249
972 819699 972 819699
e-mail: campingcastelldaro@gmail.com
web: www.campingcastelldaro.com
A quiet family site, 2km from the beach, with good recreational facilities.
Open: Apr-Sep **Site:** 8HEC **Facilities:** Play Area **Services:** **Leisure:** P
Off-site: S

CASTELLÓ D'EMPURIES GIRONA

Castell-Mar

Platja de la Rubina, 17486
972 450822 972 452330
e-mail: cmar@campingparks.com
web: www.campingparks.com
A modern family site close to the beach on the edge of a national park. Entertainment nightly during July and August.
Open: 21 May-18 Sep **Site:** 5HEC **Prices:** 18-48
Facilities: Wi-fi (charged) Kids' Club Play Area
Services: **Leisure:** P S

Mas-Nou

C/ Mas Nou No 7, 17486
972 454175 972 454358
e-mail: info@campingmasnou.com
web: www.campingmasnou.com
A family site with good recreational facilities, 2.5km from the coast.
dir: *Off A7 onto Figueres-Roses road.*
Open: 16 Apr-25 Sep **Site:** 7.8HEC **Prices:** 20.10-38.70
Facilities: Wi-fi **Services:** **Leisure:** P
Off-site: R S

Nautic Almata

17486
972 454477 972 454686
e-mail: info@almata.com
web: www.almata.com
A level meadowland site reaching as far as the sea and bordering the River Fluvia, which has been made into a canal. Shade, good facilities. Boating is possible in the canal, which flows into the sea.
dir: *Turn S off C260 at Km11, E onto track for 2.2km.*
Open: 14 May-18 Sep **Site:** 22HEC
Prices: 28.30-56.60 **Facilities:** Wi-fi (charged) Kids' Club Play Area **Services:** **Leisure:** P R S

CUBELLES BARCELONA

La Rueda

08880
938 950207 938 950347
e-mail: larueda@la-rueda.com
web: www.la-rueda.com
Level terrain between road and railway. Access to beach by means of an underpass.
dir: *1km N of Cunit near C31 Km146.2.*
GPS: 41.1998, 1.6433
Open: 16 Apr-1 Sep **Site:** 6HEC **Prices:** 20.70-34.50
Facilities: Wi-fi (charged) **Services:**
Leisure: P **Off-site:** S

ESCALA, L' GIRONA

Maite

Playa Riells, 17310
972 770544 972 770599
e-mail: maite@campings.net
web: www.campings.net/maite
An extensive site, lying inland, but near the sea, at a small lake. Partly on a hillock under pine trees.
Open: Jun-15 Sep **Site:** 6HEC **Facilities:**
Services: **Leisure:** L S

Neus

Cala Montgó, 17130
972 770403 972 222409
e-mail: info@campingneus.cat
web: www.campingneus.cat
Peaceful location among pine trees, 0.8km from the beach.
dir: *A7 exit 5.*
GPS: 42.1050, 3.1572
Open: 20 May-18 Sep **Site:** 4HEC **Prices:** 18-40
Facilities: Wi-fi Kids' Club Play Area **Services:**
Leisure: P **Off-site:** S

ESTARTIT, L' — **GIRONA**

Castell Montgri

17258

972 751630 972 750906

e-mail: cmontgri@campingparks.com

web: www.campingparks.com

On a large terraced meadow in pine woodlands. The site is at the foot of the Rocamaura mountain, set in a 230,000m2 plot of land, at the entrance to the coastal village of l'Estartit. Integrated into the natural surroundings and not far from the village.

Open: 14 May-25 Sep **Site:** 25HEC **Prices:** 19-50 Mobile home hire 306-1092 **Facilities:** Wi-fi (charged) Play Area **Services:** **Leisure:** P **Off-site:** S

see advert on this page

Estartit

Cap Villa Primavera 12, 17258

972 751909 972 750991

e-mail: campingestartit@hotmail.com

web: www.campingestartit.com

Set in a valley on sloping ground, which can be steep in places. Some terraces, shaded by pines. Dogs are not permitted during July and August.

dir: *200m from church & road from Torroella de Montgri.*

GPS: 42.0568, 3.1974

Open: Apr-Sep **Site:** 2.5HEC **Prices:** 24.56 Mobile home hire 420 **Facilities:** Wi-fi (charged) **Services:** **Leisure:** L P R S **Off-site:**

Medes

17258

972 751805 972 750413

e-mail: info@campinglesmedes.com

web: www.campinglesmedes.com

Quiet holiday site in rural surroundings with clearly marked pitches and modern facilities.

Open: Dec-Oct **Site:** 2.6HEC **Prices:** 17.70-35.90 **Facilities:** Wi-fi (charged) Kids' Club Play Area **Services:** **Leisure:** P **Off-site:** S

Facilities shop shower electric points for razors electric points for caravans parking by tents permitted compulsory separate car park **Services** café/restaurant bar Camping Gaz International gas other than Camping Gaz first aid facilities laundry **Leisure** swimming L-Lake P-Pool R-River S-Sea **Off-site** All facilities within 5km

GUARDIOLA DE BERGUEDA BARCELONA

El Bergueda

08694
☎ 93 8227432 Fax 93 8227432
e-mail: info@campingbergueda.com
web: www.campingbergueda.com

Located next to the Cadí-Moixeró natural park this peaceful site is in the middle of a forest at an altitude of 900m. There is a variety of sports facilities and tourist attractions nearby.

dir: *On B400.*

GPS: 42.2166, 1.8375

Open: 24 Jun-1 Sep **Site:** 3HEC
Prices: 20.16-22.40 **Facilities:** Wi-fi
Services: **Leisure:** P **Off-site:** R

GUILS DE CERDANYA GIRONA

Pirineus

17528
☎ 972 881062 Fax 972 882471
e-mail: guils@stel.es
web: www.stel.es

A fine level location at an altitude of 1200m with views over the Cerdanya Valley.

dir: *On Puigcerda-Guils de Cerdanya road.*

Open: 18 Jun-12 Sep **Site:** 5HEC
Prices: 29.70-37.20 **Facilities:** Wi-fi
Services: **Leisure:** P

LLORET DE MAR GIRONA

Tucan

ctra de Lloret a Blanes, 17310
☎ 972 369965 Fax 972 360079
e-mail: info@campingtucan.com
web: www.campingtucan.com

A modern family site, close to the sea, with plenty of recreational facilities.

dir: *A7 exit 9 to Lloret de Mar.*

Open: Apr-25 Sep **Site:** 4HEC **Prices:** 20.40-64 Mobile home hire 278.60-1064 **Facilities:** Wi-fi (charged) Kids' Club Play Area **Services:**
Leisure: P **Off-site:** S

PALAFRUGELL GIRONA

Kim's Camping SL

Font d'En Xeco 1, 17211
☎ 972 301156 Fax 972 610894
e-mail: info@campingkims.com
web: www.campingkims.com

Terraced site with large flat areas, lying on the wooded slopes of a beautiful valley leading to the sea.

dir: *Turn right off Palafrugell-Tamariu road for 1km, pass Club Tennis Llafranc, 400m from sea.*

GPS: 41.8989, 3.1864

Open: 15 Apr-16 Oct **Site:** 5.8HEC **Prices:** 16-41.75
Facilities: Wi-fi (charged) Kids' Club Play Area
Services: **Leisure:** P **Off-site:** S

Relax-Ge

ctra Girona-Palamós, C-31 km 329, 17253
☎ 972 301549 Fax 972 601100
e-mail: info@campingrelaxge.com
web: www.campingrelaxge.com

Level meadow under poplars and olive trees.

dir: *Off C255 at Km38.7 & 4km towards sea.*

Open: Apr-Sep **Site:** 3HEC **Prices:** 23.50-32.50
Facilities: **Services:**
Leisure: P **Off-site:** S

PALAMÓS GIRONA

Cala Gogo

Calonge, 17251
☎ 972 651564 Fax 972 650553
e-mail: calagogo@calagogo.es
web: www.calagogo.es

Terraced site in tall pine woodland and poplars with some good views of the sea. Underpass across to section of site with private beach. Some internal dusty roads.

dir: *From Palamós 4km S on C253 coast road, site on right after Km47.*

GPS: 41.8312, 3.0837

Open: 18 Apr-18 Sep **Site:** 20HEC
Prices: 19.90-50.20 Mobile home hire 288-1176 **Facilities:** Wi-fi Kids' Club Play Area **Services:**
Leisure: P S

Castell Park

17230
☎ 972 315263 🖷 972 315263
e-mail: info@campingcastellpark.com
web: www.campingcastellpark.com

Level and gently sloping meadow with poplars and pine woodland on a hill. Quiet, family campsite.

dir: *At Km328 to right of C31 to Palamós, 3km S of Montras.*

GPS: 41.8819, 3.1408

Open: 16 Apr-11 Sep **Site:** 4.5HEC **Prices:** 16.70-35 **Facilities:** Play Area **Services:** **Leisure:** P **Off-site:** S

Internacional de Calonge

Calonge, 17250
☎ 972 651233 🖷 972 652507
e-mail: info@intercalonge.com
web: www.intercalonge.com

Set on a pine covered hill overlooking the sea within easy reach of a sandy beach.

Open: Apr-Oct **Site:** 13HEC **Facilities:** **Services:** **Leisure:** P S

Internacional Palamós

Cami Cap de Planes s/n, 17230
☎ 972 314736 🖷 972 317626
e-mail: info@internacionalpalamos.com
web: www.internacionalpalamos.com

A family site in a picturesque wooded location close to the beach and the town centre. Well equipped with good facilities and larger pitches for families.

GPS: 41.8572, 3.1381

Open: Apr-Sep **Site:** 5.2HEC **Prices:** 24.30-53.55 Mobile home hire 385-840 **Facilities:** Wi-fi (charged) Play Area **Services:** **Leisure:** P S **Off-site:**

see advert on this page

Palamós

ctra la Fosca 12, 17230
☎ 972 314296 🖷 972 601100
e-mail: campingpal@grn.es
web: www.campingpalamos.com

A picturesque location on a wooded headland overlooking the sea.

Open: 2 Apr-25 Sep **Site:** 5.5HEC **Prices:** 26.55-40.45 Mobile home hire 280-693 **Facilities:** Wi-fi Play Area **Services:** **Leisure:** P S **Off-site:**

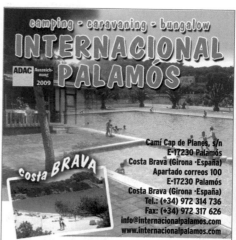

PALS — GIRONA

Cypsela

C/Rodors, 7, 17256
☎ 972 667696 🖷 972 667300
e-mail: info@cypsela.com
web: www.cypsela.com

Well-kept grassy site in a pine wood.

dir: *Turn towards sea N of Pals towards Playa de Pals, turn left after Km3.*

GPS: 41.9861, 3.1809

Open: 15 May-14 Sep **Site:** 20HEC **Prices:** 35.10-78.40 **Facilities:** Wi-fi (charged) Kids' Club Play Area **Services:** **Leisure:** P **Off-site:** R S

Mas Patoxas

crta C31, Palafrugell-Pals Km 339, 17256
☎ 972 636928 🖷 972 667349
e-mail: info@campingmaspatoxas.com
web: www.campingmaspatoxas.com

A family site in a quiet location close to the sea. Modern sanitary blocks and plenty of recreational facilities.

dir: *At Km5 on Palafrugell to Torroella.*

Open: 15 Jan-19 Dec **Site:** 5.5HEC **Facilities:** **Services:** **Leisure:** P

SPAIN

Playa Brava

av del Grau, 1, 17256
☎ 972 636894 🖷 972 636952
e-mail: info@playabrava.com
web: www.playabrava.com
On level terrain adjoining pine woodlands, golf course, lake and sea. Direct access to the beach of Pals.
dir: *From N end of Pals turn towards sea & Playa de Pals. From AP7/E15 Girona, exit 6 towards Palamos on C-66, 7.5km past La Bisbal, exit to Pals on GIV-6502 & follow signs for Platzare Pals.*
GPS: 42.0011, 3.1938
Open: 14 May-11 Sep **Site:** 11HEC **Prices:** 32.10-53.80 **Facilities:** Wi-fi (charged) Kids' Club Play Area **Services:** **Leisure:** L P R S

PINEDA DE MAR — BARCELONA

Camell

av de los Naranjos 12, 08397
☎ 93 7671520 🖷 93 7629181
e-mail: campingcamell@yahoo.es
Surrounded by deciduous trees next to a small wood owned by the Taurus Hotel.
dir: *Off NII at Km670 onto av de los Naranjos towards sea.*
Open: May-Sep **Site:** 2.2HEC **Facilities:** **Services:** **Leisure:** P S **Off-site:**

PLATJA D'ARO, LA — GIRONA

Valldaro

Cami Vell 63, 17250
☎ 972 817515 🖷 972 816662
e-mail: info@valldaro.com
web: www.valldaro.com
Extensive level meadowland under poplars, pines and eucalyptus trees. Kids' club in July and August.
GPS: 41.8238, 3.0522
Open: Apr-25 Sep **Site:** 18HEC **Prices:** 20.50-48 **Facilities:** Wi-fi (charged) Kids' Club Play Area **Services:** **Leisure:** P **Off-site:** S

PUIGCERDÀ — GIRONA

Stel

ctra Llivia, 17520
☎ 972 882361 🖷 972 140419
e-mail: puigcerda@stel.es
web: www.stel.es
Modern site in the Pyrénées on level land. Has wonderful views of the mountains and surrounding area. Good sanitary installations.
dir: *Via N340 between Comarruga & Tarragona.*
Open: 4 Jun-12 Sep **Site:** 7HEC **Facilities:** **Services:** **Leisure:** P

SALDES — BARCELONA

Repos del Pedraforca

08697
☎ 93 8258044 🖷 93 8258061
e-mail: pedra@campingpedraforca.com
web: www.campingpedraforca.com
A well-equipped site situated in an area of natural beauty. Activities for children in summer.
dir: *C-17/E9 exit Guardiola de Berguedà, then B-400 direction Saldes*
GPS: 42.2275, 1.7597
Open: 24 Jun-11 Sep **Site:** 4HEC **Prices:** 23.75-29.30 **Facilities:** Wi-fi Play Area **Services:** **Leisure:** P **Off-site:** R

SANTA CRISTINA D'ARO — GIRONA

Mas St Josep

ctra Sta Cristina, a Playa de Aro, 17246
☎ 972 835108 🖷 972 837018
e-mail: info@campingmassantjosep.com
web: www.campingmassantjosep.com
A family site with plenty of recreational facilities.
GPS: 41.8116, 3.0182
Open: 15 Apr-11 Sep **Site:** 35HEC **Prices:** 15-52 **Facilities:** Wi-fi (charged) Kids' Club Play Area **Services:** **Leisure:** P **Off-site:** S

SANT ANTONI DE CALONGE — GIRONA

Eurocamping

av Catalunya 15, 17252
☎ 972 650879 🖷 972 661987
e-mail: info@euro-camping.com
web: www.euro-camping.com
A family site in a peaceful location close to the sea with fine recreational facilities.
dir: *A7 exit 6.*
Open: 16 Apr-18 Sep **Site:** 13HEC **Prices:** 26-48.25 **Facilities:** Kids' Club Play Area **Services:** **Leisure:** P **Off-site:** S

Treumal

San Feliu Quixols a Palamos, Km 47.5, 17251
☎ 972 651095 🖷 972 651671
e-mail: info@campingtreumal.com
web: www.campingtreumal.com
A peaceful family site in a beautiful location between a pine wood and the beach.
GPS: 41.8364, 3.0872
Open: Apr-Sep **Site:** 8HEC **Prices:** 23.70-47.40 **Facilities:** Wi-fi (charged) Play Area **Services:** **Leisure:** P S

see advert on opposite page

SANT CEBRIÁ DE VALLALTA — BARCELONA

La Verneda

av Maresme 35, 08396
☎ 93 7631185 📠 93 7631185
e-mail: verneda50@hotmail.com
web: www.campinglaverneda.com

A level family site with 150 shady pitches. Located 3km from the fishing village of Sant Pol de Mar, 40km from Girona and 50km from Barcelona, the site is an ideal base.

dir: *Off NII Girona-Barcelona at end of Sant Pol de Mar, turn inland at Km670, 2km to edge of village & right before bridge over river.*

Open: Apr-Sep **Site:** 1.6HEC **Prices:** 23 **Facilities:** Wi-fi (charged) **Services:** **Leisure:** P **Off-site:** S

SANT FELIU DE GUIXOLS — GIRONA

Sant Pol

Doctor Fleming 1, 17220
☎ 972 327269 📠 972 222409
e-mail: info@campingsantpol.cat
web: www.campingsantpol.cat

Wooded surroundings near the beach with good facilities.

dir: *0.8km from town centre towards Palamos.*

Open: Apr-1 Nov & 2-11 Dec **Site:** 1.17HEC **Prices:** 14-41 **Facilities:** Wi-fi (charged) Kids' Club Play Area **Services:** **Leisure:** P **Off-site:** S

SANT PERE PESCADOR — GIRONA

Amfora

av J-Terradellas 2, 17470
☎ 972 520540 📠 972 520539
e-mail: info@campingamfora.com
web: www.campingamfora.com

A pleasant site, directly on the beach, with modern sanitary facilities. There are plentiful leisure facilities. Bungalows and mobile homes to hire.

Open: 15 Apr-Sep **Site:** 12HEC **Prices:** 25-53 **Facilities:** Wi-fi (charged) Kids' Club Play Area **Services:** **Leisure:** P R S **Off-site:** L

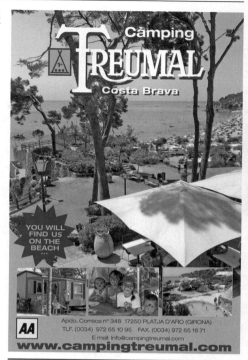

Aquarius

The Camping and Caravanning Club — The Friendly Club

17470
☎ 972 520003 📠 972 550216
e-mail: camping@aquarius.es
web: www.aquarius.es

Level grassy location, near fields and fruit plantations. Partially in shade, quiet well-organised Site, with plenty to do, by the lovely sandy beach of Bahia de Rosas.

C&CC Report *Popular with campers from all over Europe, the relaxed atmosphere of this friendly and attractive site adds to its appeal for families who love the beach. Musical and other events, set around a beautiful flower-filled courtyard on site, are complemented by local beauty spots, such as the traditional fishing village of Cadaqués, where you can also visit the house of Salvador Dalí. Meanwhile in Figueres, the surrealist master's museum features some of his more bizarre works and offers an interesting day out.*

dir: *Towards l'Escala & signed towards beach.*

Open: 15 Mar-5 Nov **Site:** 8HEC **Prices:** 20-45.40 **Facilities:** **Services:** **Leisure:** S

Site 6HEC (site size) grass sand stone little shade partly shaded mainly shaded bungalows for hire (static) caravans for hire tents for hire no dogs site fully accessible for wheelchairs

Prices amount quoted is per night, for 2 adults and car, plus tent or caravan. Mobile home hire is a weekly rate.

Ballena Alegre

17470
☎ 902 510520 📠 902 510521
e-mail: info2@ballena-alegre.com
web: www.ballena-alegre.com

Extensive site near wide sandy beach with dunes. Large shopping complex. Modern washing and sanitary facilities.

dir: *Travelling with caravan or camper exit 5 AP-7 (E-15) L'Escala/Empuries. Then GI-623, after 18.5 km at rdbt turn left to San Martí D'Empuries, 1 km to site.*

GPS: 42.1522, 3.1117

Open: 14 May-26 Sep **Site:** 24HEC **Prices:** 25.60-55.90 **Facilities:** Wi-fi (charged) Kids' Club Play Area **Services:** **Leisure:** P S **Off-site:** L R

Dunas

17470
☎ 972 521717 📠 972 550046
e-mail: info@campinglasdunas.com
web: www.campinglasdunas.com

Level extensive grassland site with young poplars, some of medium height, on the beach, totally subdivided.

Open: May-Sep **Site:** 30HEC **Facilities:** **Services:** **Leisure:** P S

see advert on opposite page

Palmeras

ctra de la Platja, 17470
☎ 972 520506 📠 972 550285
e-mail: info@campinglaspalmeras.com
web: www.campinglaspalmeras.com

On level grassland with plenty of shade. Family friendly facilities close to the beach.

dir: *From Sant Pere Pescador to beach, 200m from sea.*

Open: 15 Apr-5 Nov **Site:** 5HEC **Prices:** 20.40-47.70 **Facilities:** Wi-fi (charged) Kids' Club **Services:** **Leisure:** P S **Off-site:** R

SITGES BARCELONA

El Garrofer

ctra C 246A Km 39, 08870
☎ 93 8941780 📠 93 8110623
e-mail: info@garroferpark.com
web: www.garroferpark.com

An area close to the beach with many pine trees, surrounded by a golf course and the Garraf nature reserve.

Open: 28 Jan-18 Dec **Site:** 8HEC **Prices:** 23.75-35.40 **Facilities:** Wi-fi (charged) **Services:** **Leisure:** P **Off-site:** S

TAMARIU — GIRONA

Tamariu

17212

☎ 972 620422

e-mail: info@campingtamariu.com

web: www.campingtamariu.com

Terraced site with mixture of high young pines. Direct access to the beach.

dir: *Turning to site at beach parking area, continue 300m.*

Open: May-Sep **Site:** 2HEC **Prices:** 16.50-25 Mobile home hire 300-450 **Facilities:** **Services:** **Leisure:** P **Off-site:** S

TARADELL — BARCELONA

La Vall

Cami de la Vallmitjana, 08552

☎ 93 8126336 93 8126027

e-mail: lavallpark@campinglavallpark.cat

web: www.campinglavall.com

Set in the mountains on the outskirts of Taradell near the Guilleries-Montseny, with good recreational facilities.

Open: 7 Jan-16 Dec **Site:** 8HEC **Prices:** 21.60-36.95 **Facilities:** Wi-fi **Services:** **Leisure:** P

TORROELLA DE MONTGRI — GIRONA

Delfin Verde

17257

☎ 972 758450 972 760070

e-mail: info@eldelfinverde.com

web: www.eldelfinverde.com

On undulating ground with some pine trees, and an open meadow beside the long sandy beach.

dir: *2km S of Torroella de Montgri towards Begur, left towards Maspinell & sea for 4.8km.*

Open: Apr-Sep **Site:** 35HEC **Facilities:** **Services:** **Leisure:** P R S

see advert on page 445

TOSSA DE MAR — GIRONA

Cala Llevadó

17320

☎ 972 340314 972 341187

e-mail: info@calallevado.com

web: www.calallevado.com

Magnificent terraced site with hairpin roads overlooking three bays, all suitable for bathing. The narrow, winding drives are quite steep in parts. Separate section for caravans.

dir: *Coast road towards Lloret de Mar, 4km turn towards sea.*

Open: May-Sep **Site:** 17HEC **Facilities:** **Services:** **Leisure:** P S

Can Marti

17320

☎ 972 340851 972 342461

e-mail: info@campingcanmarti.com

web: www.campingcanmarti.com

Pleasant, unspoiled site in a partly wooded location. Good modern facilities.

dir: *1km from sea.*

Open: Jun-Aug **Site:** 10HEC **Prices:** 22-32 **Facilities:** Play Area **Services:** **Leisure:** P **Off-site:** L R S

Site 6HEC (site size) grass sand stone little shade partly shaded mainly shaded bungalows for hire (static) caravans for hire tents for hire no dogs site fully accessible for wheelchairs
Prices amount quoted is per night, for 2 adults and car, plus tent or caravan. Mobile home hire is a weekly rate.

VALLROMANES — BARCELONA

El Vedado

08188
☎ 93 5729026 🖷 93 5729621
e-mail: info@campingelvedado.com
web: www.campingelvedado.com

A valley site surrounded by wooded mountains with the beach only a short drive away. Ideal for visiting Barcelona, there is a bus from the site.

dir: *AP7 exit 13 for Masnou, C32 exit 86 for Granollers.*

GPS: 41.5236, 2.2936

Open: Mar-2 Nov **Site:** 100HEC **Prices:** 22-32
Facilities: **Services:**
Leisure: P **Off-site:** S

VILALLONGA DE TER — GIRONA

Conca de Ter

ctra Camprodon-Setcases s/n, 17869
☎ 972 740629 🖷 972 130171
e-mail: concater@concater.com
web: www.concater.com

A pleasant family site in wooded surroundings with a variety of recreational facilities.

dir: *Between Camprodón & Setcases, 20km from French border.*

Open: All Year. **Site:** 3.2HEC **Facilities:**
Services: **Leisure:** P R **Off-site:** R

VILANOVA I LA GELTRÚ — BARCELONA

Vilanova Park

The Camping and Caravanning Club The Friendly Club

08800
☎ 93 8933402 🖷 93 8935528
e-mail: info@vilanovapark.es
web: www.vilanovapark.es

A well-equipped family site on the edge of a densely wooded area close to the coast in the Catalonian wine-producing area. Modern sanitary block.

C&CC Report *Whatever the time of year you go, Vilanova Park takes some beating, with its pleasant climate and its high quality facilities open all year. Within easy reach are Barcelona, some of Europe's best beaches, Sitges' old-world charm, Vilafranca's wine cellars to which the site runs excursions, and Montserrat's mountain monastery.*

dir: *A7 exit 29.*

Open: All Year. **Site:** 51HEC **Prices:** 27.20-46.70
Facilities: Wi-fi (charged) Kids' Club Play Area
Services: **Leisure:** P **Off-site:** L S

see advert on opposite page

CENTRAL

ALBARRACIN — TERUEL

Ciudad de Albarracin

Camino de Gea, Arrabal, 44100
☎ 978 710197 🖷 978 710197
e-mail: campingalbarracin5@hotmail.com
web: www.campingalbarracin.com

A modern site on mainly level ground with good facilities.

dir: *Signed from A1512.*

GPS: 40.4116, -1.4272

Open: Mar-3 Nov **Site:** 2.5HEC **Prices:** 15.75
Facilities: Wi-fi Play Area **Services:**
Off-site: L P R

ARANJUEZ — MADRID

Internacional de Aranjuez

The Camping and Caravanning Club The Friendly Club

Soto Del Rebollo S/N, 28300
☎ 91 8911395 🖷 91 8920406
e-mail: info@campingaranjuez.com
web: www.campingaranjuez.com

Site divided in two parts with trees and lawns in a large castle park.

C&CC Report *Located in the town of Aranjuez in the former grounds of the castle, convenient for visiting Madrid by train.*

dir: *Off NIV at Km46 into village, 200m beyond fuel station turn sharp NE for 1km.*

GPS: 40.0419, -3.5991

Open: All Year. **Site:** 3.3HEC **Facilities:**
Wi-fi (charged) **Services:** **Leisure:** P R

see advert on page 448

CABRERA, LA — MADRID

Pico de la Miel

The Camping and Caravanning Club The Friendly Club

ctra A-1, Salida 57, 28751
☎ 91 8688082 🖷 91 8688541
e-mail: info@picodelamiel.com
web: www.picodelamiel.com

Good quality camping just forty minutes from Madrid with regular bus service available. Attractive location with access to arts and culture.

C&CC Report *Just off the A1 Madrid to Burgos motorway, at the foot of the Sierra de Guadarrama and the honey-coloured peak from which the site takes its name. Shops and local village services 500m.*

dir: *A1 exit Km57 or Km60.*

Open: All Year. **Site:** 10.5HEC **Prices:** 18-25
Facilities: Wi-fi (charged) Play Area
Services: **Leisure:** P **Off-site:**

CÁCERES — CÁCERES

Cáceres

The Camping and Caravanning Club — The Friendly Club

ctra N-630, km. 549.5, 10005
☎ 927 233100 🖷 927 235896
e-mail: info@campingcaceres.com
web: www.campingcaceres.com
C&CC Report *Less than a mile from Cáceres with bus services into town. Cáceres is a UNESCO World Heritage site with a wide range of architecture, cobbled streets and medieval fortified homes. Each pitch has its own sanitation block which is popular with campers.*
dir: *A66 exit 545.*
Open: All Year. **Site:** **Facilities:** **Services:** **Leisure:** P

CUENCA — CUENCA

Cuenca

ctra Cuenca-Tragacete KM7, 16147
☎ 969 231656 🖷 969 231656
e-mail: info@campingcuenca.com
web: www.campingcuenca.com
A modern site in a peaceful wooded location.
dir: *N towards Mariana.*
Open: 15 Apr-16 Oct **Site:** 23HEC **Prices:** 19-21
Facilities: **Services:**
Leisure: P **Off-site:** L R

ESCORIAL, EL — MADRID

El Escorial

ctra Guadarrama, km 3500, 28280
☎ 918 902412 🖷 918 961062
e-mail: info@campingelescorial.com
web: www.campingelescorial.com
Pleasant wooded surroundings with good recreational facilities.
Open: All Year. **Site:** 40HEC **Facilities:**
Services: **Leisure:** P

FUENTE DE SAN ESTEBAN, LA — SALAMANCA

Cruce

37200
☎ 923 440130
e-mail: campingelcruce@yahoo.es
Useful stopover site in a quiet location in the Castillian countryside.
dir: *50m from N620 at Km291. 400m A-62 exit 293.*
Open: May-Sep **Site:** 0.5HEC **Prices:** 13.50
Facilities: Wi-fi **Services:**
Off-site: P R

GARGANTILLA DE LOZOYA — MADRID

Monte Holiday

28739
☎ 91 8695278 🖷 91 8695278
e-mail: monteholiday@monteholiday.com
web: www.monteholiday.com
A terraced site with modern facilities in a beautiful mountain setting and near a large nature reserve. The area is ideal for anglers and walkers and many outdoor sports enthusiasts. Mainly flat pitches with grass or gravel surfaces and shade from mature trees. Children's activities in high season.
dir: *Off N1 at Km69 towards Cobos for 10km.*
Open: All Year. **Site:** 30HEC **Prices:** 25.60
Facilities: Wi-fi (charged) **Services:**
Leisure: P **Off-site:** L R

Site 6HEC (site size) grass sand stone little shade partly shaded mainly shaded bungalows for hire (static) caravans for hire tents for hire no dogs site fully accessible for wheelchairs
Prices amount quoted is per night, for 2 adults and car, plus tent or caravan. Mobile home hire is a weekly rate.

GETAFE — MADRID

Alpha

C/Calidad 1, 28906
☎ 91 6958069 🖷 91 6831659
e-mail: info@campingalpha.com
web: www.campingalpha.com

Surrounded by pine woods at roughly the geographical centre of Spain with well-defined pitches and modern facilities. Direct bus service to Madrid.

dir: *Via NIV at Km12.4.*

GPS: 40.3172, -3.6889

Open: All Year. **Site:** 4.8HEC **Prices:** 27.95-33.85 **Facilities:** Wi-fi (charged) **Services:** **Leisure:** P

MADRID — MADRID

Arco Iris

28670
☎ 91 6160387 🖷 91 6160059
e-mail: madrid@bungalowsarcoiris.com
web: www.bungalowsarcoiris.com

A family site in a peaceful location, yet with easy access to Madrid. Dogs not permitted in bungalows.

dir: *M40 ring road exit 36, then M501, continue up to KM7100.*

GPS: 40.3818, -3.9080

Open: All Year. **Site:** 4HEC **Prices:** 20.85-27.80 **Facilities:** Wi-fi **Services:** **Leisure:** P **Off-site:** R

Osuna

Av de Logrono, 28042
☎ 91 7410510 🖷 91 3206365

On long stretch of land, shade being provided by pines, acacias and maple. Some noise from airfield, road and railway.

dir: *M11 from town centre towards Barajas, 7.5km turn right at Km1 after railway underpass.*

Open: All Year. **Site:** 2.3HEC **Facilities:** **Services:** **Off-site:** L P R

MALPARTIDA DE PLASENCIA — CÁCERES

Parque Natural de Monfrague

Ctra Plasencia-Trujillo km-10, 10680
☎ 927 459220 🖷 927 459233
e-mail: contacto@campingmonfrague.com
web: www.campingmonfrague.com

A modern site with well-defined pitches and good facilities.

dir: *9km from EX208.*

Open: All Year. **Site:** 7HEC **Prices:** 16.40 **Facilities:** Wi-fi Kids' Club Play Area **Services:** **Leisure:** P **Off-site:**

MÉRIDA — BADAJOZ

Mérida

Apto. 465, 06800
☎ 924 303453
dir: *3km off A5.*

Open: All Year. **Site:** **Facilities:** **Services:**

MIRANDA DEL CASTAÑAR — SALAMANCA

El Burro Blanco

37660
☎ 923 161100
e-mail: camping.elburroblanco@gmail.com
web: www.elburroblanco.net

A well-equipped site in an area of woodland overlooking the village.

dir: *1km from village centre.*

Open: Apr-Sep **Site:** 3.5HEC **Prices:** 19 **Facilities:** **Services:** **Off-site:** P R

NAVALAFUENTE — MADRID

Camping Piscis

ctra Guadalix a Navalafuente, km3, 28729
☎ 91 8432253 🖷 91 8432253
e-mail: campiscis@campiscis.com
web: www.campiscis.com

Spacious pitches surrounded by oak trees.

dir: *N1 exit 50 towards Guadalix de la Sierra.*

Open: All Year. **Site:** 23HEC **Prices:** 24.20 Mobile home hire 346-360 **Facilities:** Wi-fi (charged) **Services:** **Leisure:** P

RIAZA — SEGOVIA

Riaza

ctra de la Estacion s/n, 40500
☎ 921 550580 🖷 921 550580
e-mail: info@camping-riaza.com
web: www.camping-riaza.com

Spectacular location with mountains, rivers and forests. Excellent sanitation facilities.

dir: *From Burgos A1 exit 104. From Madrid A1 exit 103 direction Riaza and Soria (N110). Right at rdbt after 12km. Camp site on left.*

GPS: 41.2830, -3.4666

Open: All Year. **Site:** 12HEC **Prices:** 17-24 **Facilities:** Wi-fi (charged) Kids' Club Play Area **Services:** **Leisure:** P **Off-site:** L R

SPAIN

SPAIN

SALAMANCA — SALAMANCA

Don Quijote

ctra Aldealengua km 4, Cabrerizos, 37193
☎ 923 209052 923 209052
e-mail: info@campingdonquijote.com
web: www.campingdonquijote.com
Near to the town centre, quiet, family campsite.

dir: *NE of town towards Aldealengua.*

GPS: 40.975, -5.6030

Open: Mar-Oct **Site:** 6.5HEC **Prices:** 16.40-19
Facilities: Wi-fi (charged) Play Area
Services: **Leisure:** P R

SANTA MARTA DE TORMES — SALAMANCA

Regio

The Camping and Caravanning Club The Friendly Club

ctra Salamanca/Madrid Km4, 37900
☎ 923 138888 923 138044
e-mail: recepcion@campingregio.com
web: www.campingregio.com
A pleasant site, divided into several fields.

C&CC Report *Set among trees next to the hotel to which the site belongs and located about 500m from the N501 Salamanca to Ávila road, in the southern suburbs of Salamanca, about 1.5km from the city centre, which is accessible by bus from the site.*

dir: *100m from N501 Salamanca-Ávila, behind Hotel Jardin-Regio.*

Open: All Year. **Site:** 3HEC **Prices:** 19.40-21.70
Facilities: **Services:**
Leisure: P R

SEGOVIA — SEGOVIA

Acueducto

ctra de la Granja, 40004
☎ 921 425000 921 425000
e-mail: informacion@campingacueducto.com
web: www.campingacueducto.com
Located 3km from Segovia city, in a characteristic Castilian landscape with magnificent views to the mountain range. A well equipped site offering many facilities.

dir: *SE next to N601 at Km112.*

Open: Apr-Sep **Site:** 3HEC **Facilities:**
Services: **Leisure:** P **Off-site:** L

TOLEDO — TOLEDO

Greco

45004
☎ 925 220090 925 220090
e-mail: campingelgreco@telefonica.net
web: www.campingelgreco.es
Few shady terraces on slope leading down to the River Tajo. On south-western outskirts of town.

dir: *From town centre C401 Carretera Comarcal SW for 2km, right at Km28, 300m towards Puebla de Montalban.*

Open: All Year. **Site:** 2.5HEC **Facilities:**
Services: **Leisure:** P R **Off-site:**

VALDEMAQUEDA — MADRID

El Canto la Gallina

28295
☎ 091 8984820 091 8984823
e-mail: camping@elcantolagallina.com
web: www.elcantolagallina.com
Wooded location at the foot of a mountain.

Open: All Year. **Site:** 12.5HEC **Facilities:**
Services: **Leisure:** P **Off-site:** R

SOUTH EAST COAST

ALCOSSEBRE — CASTELLÓN

Playa Tropicana

The Camping and Caravanning Club The Friendly Club

12579
☎ 964 412463 964 412805
e-mail: info@playatropicana.com
web: www.playatropicana.com
On a 0.5km long sandy beach 3km from the village.

C&CC Report *Playa Tropicana is a top quality site opposite a long sandy beach on this tranquil part of the coastline, with high quality facilities in lovely surroundings. The site lives up to its name with exotic plants, palm trees and classical statues lining the roads. Tourist information is available from reception with ideas for local visits, walking and cycling routes and local festivals. Local fishing clubs welcome visitors and if you are interested in diving then speak with the site owner, Vera, about visiting the protected Columbretes isles.*

dir: *Motorway exit 44, onto N340 N for 3km, turn towards sea at Km1018.*

Open: All Year. **Site:** 3HEC **Prices:** 11-49
Facilities: Wi-fi (charged) Kids' Club Play Area
Services: **Leisure:** P S

Ribamar

Partida Ribamar s/n, 12579
964 761163 964 767231
e-mail: info@campingribamar.com
web: www.campingribamar.com
Quiet wooded site with individual pitches, set between the sea and mountains.
dir: *AP7 exit 44 (Torreblanca-Alcossebre) onto N340.*
Open: All Year. **Site:** 2.2HEC **Prices:** 17.40-41.50 **Facilities:** Wi-fi (charged) Play Area **Services:** **Leisure:** P **Off-site:** S

ALTEA — ALICANTE

Cap Blanch

Playa del Cap-Blanch, 03590
96 5845946 96 5844556
e-mail: capblanch@ctv.es
web: www.camping-capblanch.com
A well-equipped site on Albir beach backed by imposing mountains. Good sports and recreational facilities.
dir: *A7 exit 65.*
Open: All Year. **Site:** 4HEC **Facilities:** **Services:** **Leisure:** S **Off-site:**

AMETLLA DE MAR, L' — TARRAGONA

L'Ametlla Village Platja

Paratge Santes Creus, 43860
977 267784 977 267868
e-mail: info@campingametlla.com
web: www.campingametlla.com
A modern site with good facilities and direct access to two beaches. Improved access road.
dir: *2km W, S of A7.*
Open: 9 Apr-Sep **Site:** 8HEC **Facilities:** **Services:** **Leisure:** P S

BENICARLÓ — CASTELLÓN

Alegria del Mar

Playa Norte, 12580
964 470871 964 470871
e-mail: info@campingalegria.com
web: www.campingalegria.com
Small British owned and managed. Suitable for long and short term camping close to the beach and Benicarlo.
dir: *Via N340, 1046km.*
GPS: 40.4263, 0.4374
Open: All Year. **Site:** 10HEC **Prices:** 5.47-22 **Facilities:** Wi-fi (charged) Play Area **Services:** **Leisure:** P S

BENICASIM — CASTELLÓN

Bonterra Park

The Camping and Caravanning Club — The Friendly Club

av Barcelona 47, 12560
964 300007 964 300008
e-mail: info@bonterrapark.com
web: www.bonterrapark.com
Site of clean and neat appearance with tarmac roads, gravel covered pitches, palms, grass and a number of trees which give good shade. Overhead sunshades are provided for the more open pitches in summer and there is also a cycle path nearby.
C&CC Report *Bonterra Park is a high quality site, with covered heated pool, bar and restaurant facilities. There is a lot to do in the area, both on the coast and inland. An ideal site for motorhome owners and cyclists alike, being within walking distance of the town with a lovely beach, and with convenient public transport near the site entrance.*
dir: *300m N towards Las Villas de Benicasim.*
Open: All Year. **Site:** 5HEC **Prices:** 15-54.36 **Facilities:** Wi-fi (charged) Kids' Club Play Area **Services:** **Leisure:** P
Off-site: S

BENIDORM — ALICANTE

Arena Blanca

av Dr Severo Ochoa 44, 03503
96 5861889 96 5861107
e-mail: info@camping-arenablanca.es
web: www.camping-arenablanca.es
A modern family site not far from a sandy beach.
dir: *Via N332 Benidorm-Altea.*
Open: All Year. **Site:** 2.2HEC **Prices:** 23.54 **Facilities:** Wi-fi **Services:** **Leisure:** P S

Armanello

av Comunidad Valenciana S/N, 03503
96 5853190 96 5853100
e-mail: info@campingarmanello.com
web: www.campingarmanello.com
Divided by bushes with large pitches on terraces under olive and palm trees next to a small orange grove.
dir: *N of town off N332 at Km123.1.*
Open: All Year. **Site:** 1.6HEC **Facilities:** **Services:** **Leisure:** P S

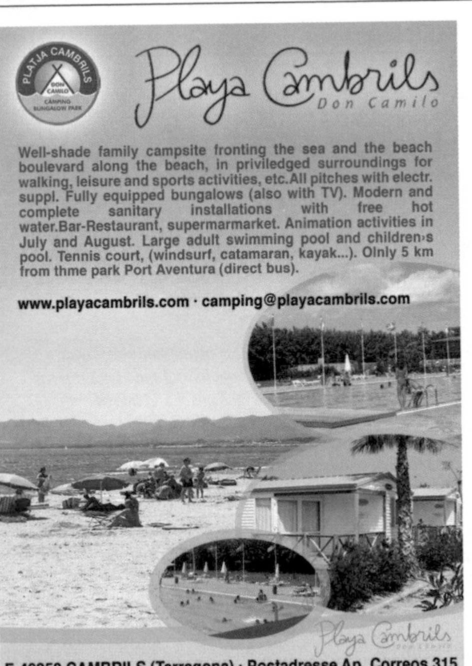

Playa Cambrils
Don Camilo
Well-shade family campsite fronting the sea and the beach boulevard along the beach, in priviledged surroundings for walking, leisure and sports activities, etc.All pitches with electr. suppl. Fully equipped bungalows (also with TV). Modern and complete sanitary installations with free hot water.Bar-Restaurant, supermarmarket. Animation activities in July and August. Large adult swimming pool and children›s pool. Tennis court, (windsurf, catamaran, kayak...). Olnly 5 km from thme park Port Aventura (direct bus).
www.playacambrils.com · camping@playacambrils.com
E-43850 CAMBRILS (Tarragona) · Postadresse Ap. Correos 315
tel.: (34) 977 361 490 · Fax (34) 977 364 988

CAMBRILS — TARRAGONA

Playa Cambrils-Don Camilo

av Oleastrum 2, 43850
☎ 977 361490 ▤ 977 364988
e-mail: camping@playacambrils.com
web: www.playacambrils.com

Divided into pitches, lying on both sides of the coast road in a wooded location.

dir: *2km N of town towards Salou & W of bridge over river.*

Open: 15 Mar-12 Oct **Site:** 9HEC **Prices:** 18.55-42.10
Facilities: Wi-fi **Services:**
Leisure: P **Off-site:** S

see advert on this page

CAMPELLO — ALICANTE

Costa Blanca

c Convento 143, 03560
☎ 965 630670 ▤ 965 630670
e-mail: info@campingcostablanca.com
web: www.campingcostablanca.com

On mostly level ground scattered with old olive and eucalyptus trees. The Alicante-Denia railway line runs behind the camp.

dir: *Off N332 at Km94.2 & fuel station onto narrow gravel track towards sea for 0.5km.*

Open: All Year. **Site:** 1.1HEC **Prices:** 15-29.82
Facilities: Wi-fi (charged) Play Area **Services:**
Leisure: P **Off-site:** S

CUNIT — TARRAGONA

Mar de Cunit

Playa Cunit, 43881
977 674058 977 675006
e-mail: mardecunit@seker.es
web: www.mardecunit.com

A friendly site on level ground overlooking the beach.

Open: 15 May-15 Sep **Site:** 1.2HEC **Prices:** 32.40 **Facilities:** **Services:** **Leisure:** L S **Off-site:**

GUARDAMAR DEL SEGURA — ALICANTE

Marjal

The Camping and Caravanning Club The Friendly Club

Cartagena-Alicante Rd (N 332), 03140
966 725022 966 726695
e-mail: camping@marjal.com
web: www.campingmarjal.com

Located in Dunas de Guardamar national park next to the Segura estuary, alongside pine and eucalyptus forests with access to fine sandy beaches.

C&CC Report *Popular Marjal is one of the most modern camp sites on the Mediterranean. In an excellent location on the Costa Blanca, with high quality facilities, including the very well-equipped sports complex where you can keep fit or simply unwind. The site's restaurant offers ample opportunity for any cook in your party to take a break, with reasonably priced menus catering for all tastes.*

GPS: 38.1092, -0.6547

dir: *A7 exit 72, then N332.*

Open: All Year. **Site:** 3.5HEC **Facilities:** **Services:** **Leisure:** P **Off-site:** S

see advert on opposite page

Palm Mar

03140
96 5728856 96 5728856
e-mail: campingpalmmar@hotmail.com
web: www.campingpalmmar.es

Open: Jun-Sep **Site:** 2HEC **Facilities:** **Services:** **Leisure:** S **Off-site:** P

HOSPITALET DE L'INFANT, L' — TARRAGONA

El Templo del Sol

Platja del Torn, 43890
977 823434 977 823464
e-mail: info@eltemplodelsol.com
web: www.eltemplodelsol.com

Site with modern sanitary installations and good recreational facilities on a 1.5km-long beach. This is a naturist site. Only families or holders of an International Naturism Carnet are allowed.

dir: *A3 exit 38, 4km towards sea.*

Open: 29 Mar-22 Oct **Site:** 14HEC **Prices:** 19.25-53.55 **Facilities:** Wi-fi (charged) **Services:** **Leisure:** P S

JARACO — VALENCIA

San Vincente

Playa Xeraco, 46770
96 2888188 96 2888147
e-mail: consultas@campingsanvincente.com

Level subdivided site with some trees.

dir: *Off N332 Jaraco at Km332 towards Playa, off at Km304 & site 3.5km.*

Open: All Year. **Site:** 5HEC **Facilities:** **Services:** **Leisure:** S **Off-site:** P R

MARINA, LA — ALICANTE

International la Marina

03194
96 5419200 96 5419110
e-mail: info@campinglamarina.com
web: www.campinglamarina.com

A large modern site in a wooded setting, 0.5km from a sandy beach.

dir: *A7 exit 72 junct with N332 in direction of Cartagena. Continue until the village of La Marina & 2km S on the old highway. Site entrance at KM76.*

GPS: 38.1297, -0.6497

Open: All Year. **Site:** 6.3HEC **Facilities:** Wi-fi (charged) Kids' Club Play Area **Services:** **Leisure:** P **Off-site:** S

see advert on page 454

MIRAMAR PLAYA VALENCIA

Coelius

av del Mar, 46711
☎ 96 2819574 📠 96 2818897
e-mail: camping@coelius.com
web: www.coelius.com

A site with modern facilities, 0.5km from Miramar beach.

dir: *A7 exit 61 then N332 in direction of Gandia and then Bellereguard-Miramar.*

Open: All Year. **Site:** 2HEC **Prices:** 16.90-32.90 Mobile home hire 145.70-374.50 **Facilities:** Wi-fi Play Area **Services:** **Leisure:** P **Off-site:** S

SPAIN

MONCOFA CASTELLÓN

Monmar

The Camping and Caravanning Club The Friendly Club

c/ Serratelles, s/n, 12593
☎ 964 588592 📠 964 588592
e-mail: campingmonmar@terra.es
web: www.campingmonmar.blogspot.com

Close to road network, beach and town.

C&CC Report *A site with top quality facilities in an expanding town with owners and staff who look after campers exceptionally well. The surrounding region is fascinating. Nearby Vall d'Uixo has a street market and the longest underground river in Europe, while the area is also well-known for its ceramics. Valencia with its historic centre, the modern "City of Arts and Sciences" and the world-famous Lladró porcelain, is just a short drive away. The regional coastline has abundant sandy beaches sometimes separated from the sea by wetlands, including lagoons, marshes and salt flats.*

dir: *23km S of Castellon city.*

GPS: 39.8083, -0.1272

Open: All Year. **Site:** 3HEC **Facilities:** Play Area **Services:** **Leisure:** L P S

Site 6HEC (site size) grass sand stone little shade partly shaded mainly shaded bungalows for hire (static) caravans for hire tents for hire no dogs site fully accessible for wheelchairs
Prices amount quoted is per night, for 2 adults and car, plus tent or caravan. Mobile home hire is a weekly rate.

MONT-ROIG DEL CAMP — TARRAGONA

Marius

43892

☎ 977 810684 🖷 977 179658

e-mail: info@campingmarius.com

web: www.campingmarius.com

Pitches are planted with flowers and shrubs. Separate section for dog owners.

dir: *Off N340 Tarragona-Valencia at Km1137, through 4.9m-wide railway underpass (height 3.65m) towards beach.*

Open: 7 Mar-12 Oct **Site:** 4.5HEC **Facilities:** **Services:** **Leisure:** P S

Playa Montroig

43300

☎ 977 810637 🖷 977 811411

e-mail: info@playamontroig.com

web: www.playamontroig.com

An ideal holiday centre for the whole family with sanitary installations of the highest quality. Situated on a fine sandy beach and surrounded by tropical gardens, this site offers a range of sports and recreational facilities and is noted for its helpful and friendly staff.

dir: *AP7 exit 37 or 38, onto N340, left at Km1136.*

Open: 14 Mar-2 Nov **Site:** 35HEC
Prices: 65 **Facilities:** Wi-fi Play Area
Services: **Leisure:** P S

Torre Del Sol

43892

☎ 977 810486 🖷 977 811306

e-mail: info@latorredelsol.com

web: www.latorredelsol.com

A level tidy grassland site on two levels, with young poplars and some of medium height between a long stretch of beach and the railway.

dir: *Off N340 at Km224.1 towards sea.*

Open: 15 Mar-Oct **Site:** 24HEC
Prices: 20.30-53.05 **Facilities:** Wi-fi Kids' Club Play Area **Services:** **Leisure:** P S

see advert on this page

SPAIN

NAVAJAS CASTELLÓN

Altomira

12470
964 713211 964 713512
e-mail: reservas@campingaltomira.com
web: www.campingaltomira.com

Terraced site in the Pàlancia Valley, with touring pitches on the higher levels.

C&CC Report *Conveniently located just outside the town of Navajas, with easy acess to the A23 motorway.*

dir: *A23 Sagunto to Teruel exit 33 Navajas.*

Open: All Year. **Site:** 2.5HEC **Prices:** 17.68-22.10
Facilities: Wi-fi (charged) Play Area
Services: **Leisure:** P **Off-site:** L R

OLIVA VALENCIA

Azul

Apartado de Correos 96, 46780
96 2854106 96 2854096
e-mail: campingazul@ctv.es
web: www.campingazul.com

A well-equipped site with spacious individual plots and direct access to the beach.

GPS: 38.9069, -0.0686

Open: Mar-1 Nov **Site:** 2.5HEC **Prices:** 10.62-25.60
Facilities: Wi-fi (charged) Kids' Club Play Area
Services: **Leisure:** S **Off-site:** R

Euro Camping

46780 96 2854098 96 2851753
e-mail: info@eurocamping-es.com
web: www.eurocamping-es.com

On a wide sandy beach between orange groves and well-shaded with poplar and eucalyptus trees.

dir: *Off N332 at Km184.9, 0.6km from Oliva, towards sea for 3.3km, site signed. Narrow access road & blind corners.*

GPS: 38.9053, -0.0665

Open: All Year. **Site:** 4.5HEC **Prices:** 16.78-44.39
Facilities: Wi-fi (charged) Play Area
Services: **Leisure:** S **Off-site:** L R

Ferienplatz Olé

46780 96 2857517 96 2857517
e-mail: camping-ole@hotmail.com
web: www.camping-ole.com

An extensive site with some pitches among dunes.

dir: *Off N332 at Km209.9 5km S of Oliva, 3km onto part asphalt road through orchard.*

Open: All Year. **Site:** 46HEC **Prices:** 19.62-32.72
Facilities: **Services:**
Leisure: P S

Kiko Park

Playa de Oliva, 46780
96 2850905 96 2854320
e-mail: kikopark@kikopark.com
web: www.kikopark.com

Family holiday camp, divided into pitches, lying between marshland and vineyard. The sea can be reached by crossing a dyke and there are sunshade roofs.

C&CC Report *Camping Kiko Park is in an excellent location, offering very good on-site facilities and the opportunity to explore both the coastal region as well as the inland Valèncian region. Site facilities include an outdoor pool and indoor spa area. The popular camp site bar/restaurant offers high-quality local Valèncian and international dishes, with light meals also available, or you can just enjoy a drink at the bar. The site overlooks the fine, sandy, Blue Flag beach across the recently re-naturalised dunes, and the small yachting harbour.*

dir: *A7 exit 61, onto N332 towards Oliva.*

Open: All Year. **Site:** 4HEC **Prices:** 13.50-53.60
Facilities: Wi-fi (charged)
Services: **Leisure:** P S
Off-site: P

OROPESA DEL MAR CASTELLÓN

Didota

av de la Didota, 12594
964 319551 964 319568

Family campsite with good facilities and close to the sea.

Open: All Year. **Site:** 1.7HEC **Facilities:** (charged) **Services:** **Leisure:** P
Off-site: S

PEÑISCOLA CASTELLÓN

Eden

av Papa Luna, KM6, 12598
964 480562 964 489828
e-mail: camping@camping-eden.com
web: www.camping-eden.com

A modern, well-appointed site on level ground close to the seafront.

dir: *Off A7 for Peñiscola, turn towards Benicarlo.*

Open: All Year. **Site:** 4HEC **Facilities:**
Services: **Leisure:** P **Off-site:** S

SPAIN

Spa Natura Resort

The Camping and Caravanning Club — The Friendly Club

Ptda Villarroyos s/n, 12598
☎ 964 475480 🖷 964 465121
e-mail: info@campingazahar.com
web: www.campingazahar.com

Family friendly site, close to sandy beaches with extensive leisure facilities including a spa and mini-golf. Ideal for hiking and horse riding in the surrounding countryside.

C&CC Report *Spa Natura Resort is in a convenient location on the edge of Peñiscola, among orange and olive groves, close to junction 43 of the A7 motorway. The campsite has developed a new area to provide more touring pitches as well as high quality permanent accommodation and more recreational facilities. There is a covered swimming pool and a Wellness centre and spa (charge applies), where a range of treatments are available, while the bar/restaurant offers a wide range of cuisine. Other amenities available locally, making this a good place for long or short stays.*

dir: *A7 exit 43.*

GPS: 40.4016, 0.3811

Open: All Year. **Site:** 3HEC **Prices:** 15-45 **Facilities:** Wi-fi (charged) Play Area **Services:** **Leisure:** P **Off-site:** S

SALOU — TARRAGONA

Sanguli-Salou

43840
☎ 977 381641 🖷 977 384616
e-mail: mail@sanguli.es
web: www.sanguli.es

A large, family site in pleasant wooded surroundings, 50m from the beach, with extensive sports and entertainment facilities.

dir: *3km SW from Port Aventura, 50m inland from coast road to Cambrils.*

Open: 14 Mar-2 Nov **Site:** 24HEC **Facilities:** **Services:** **Leisure:** P S

see advert on page 457

Union

c Pompeu Fabra 37, 43840
☎ 977 384816 🖷 977 351444
e-mail: reservas@campinglaunion.com
web: www.campinglaunion.com

A well-equipped site in wooded surroundings, 350m from the sea.

dir: *On S outskirts, 1km from Port Aventura theme park.*

Open: Apr-Sep **Site:** 3.84HEC **Facilities:** **Services:** **Leisure:** P S

TAMARIT — TARRAGONA

Caledonia

43008
☎ 977 650098 🖷 977 652867
e-mail: caledonia@campingcaledonia.com
web: www.campingcaledonia.com

A well-appointed site in wooded surroundings, 0.8km from the sea. Kids' club open from July to August.

dir: *On N340 at Km1172.*

Open: 15 May-20 Sep **Site:** 3.5HEC **Facilities:** Wi-fi (charged) Kids' Club **Services:** **Leisure:** P **Off-site:** S

Trillas Platja Tamarit

43008
☎ 977 650249 🖷 977 650926
e-mail: info@campingtrillas.com
web: www.campingtrillas.com

On several terraces planted with olive trees next to a farm, 50m from the sea.

dir: *Off N340 at Km1.172 8km N of Tarragona, over narrow railway bridge (beware oncoming traffic).*

Open: Apr-2 Oct **Site:** 4HEC **Facilities:** **Services:** **Leisure:** P R S

TARRAGONA — TARRAGONA

Tamarit-Park

Platja Tamarit, 43008
☎ 977 650128 🖷 977 650451
e-mail: resort@tamarit.com
web: www.tamarit.com

Well-kept site at the sea beneath Tamarit castle. One section lies under tall shady trees, and another lies in a meadow with some trees.

dir: *Off N340 at Km1171.5 towards beach, left at end of road.*

Open: 7 Apr-Oct **Site:** 17HEC **Facilities:** **Services:** **Leisure:** P R S

VILANOVA DE PRADES — TARRAGONA

Serra de Prades

Sant Antoni, 43439
☎ 977 869050 🖷 977 869050
e-mail: info@serradeprades.com
web: www.serradeprades.com

A fine site close to the beach and within easy reach of Barcelona and the Port Aventura theme park.

dir: *Via N240.*

Open: All Year. **Site:** 5HEC **Facilities:** **Services:** **Leisure:** P **Off-site:** R

VILLARGORDO DEL CABRIEL — VALENCIA

Kiko Park Rural

ctra Embalse Contreras km3, 46317
96 2139082 96 2139337
e-mail: kikoparkrural@kikopark.com
web: www.kikopark.com/rural

Campsite built on site of a small village and farm with former buildings used for amenities and many young trees planted for shade. Pitches divided by hedges and all have fine views.

dir: *A3 (Madrid-Valencia), exit 255 towards Villargordo Cabriel. Signed.*

Open: All Year. **Site:** 2.2HEC **Prices:** 22-32.30 **Facilities:** **Services:** **Leisure:** P **Off-site:** L R

NORTH COAST

AJO-BAREYO — CANTABRIA

Cabo de Ajo

ctra al Faro, 39170
942 670624 942 630725

On level ground 2km from the coast.

dir: *A8 exit Beranga Km185.*

Open: Jun-Sep & Etr **Site:** **Facilities:** **Services:** **Leisure:** P **Off-site:** S

BAREYO — CANTABRIA

Los Molinos de Bareyo

ctra Bareyo-Güemes, 39190
942 670569 942 670569
e-mail: losmolinosdebareyo@ceoecant.es
web: www.campinglosmolinos.com

A quiet location with fine views.

Open: Jun-Sep & Etr **Site:** 12HEC **Prices:** 15.50-22.50 **Facilities:** **Services:** **Leisure:** P **Off-site:** R

BARREIROS — LUGO

Camping Poblado Gaivota

Playa de Barreiros, 27790
982 124451
web: www.campingpobladogaivota.com

Site leads down to a sandy beach with windsurfing. The main buildings have been designed and built by the owner, who is a painter.

GPS: 43.5622, -7.2075

Open: Etr-Sep **Site:** 1HEC **Prices:** 20.84 **Facilities:** Wi-fi Play Area **Services:** **Leisure:** S **Off-site:** P R

CADAVEDO — ASTURIAS

Regalina

ctra de la Playa, 33788
98 5645056
e-mail: info@laregalina.com
web: www.laregalina.com

A modern site with good facilities noted for its mountain and sea views.

dir: *On N632 between Luarca & Avilés.*

Open: Jul-Aug **Site:** 1HEC **Facilities:** **Services:** **Leisure:** P **Off-site:** S

COMILLAS — CANTABRIA

Comillas

ctra M-Noriga, 39520
942 720074 942 215206
e-mail: info@campingcomillas.com
web: www.campingcomillas.com

Level grassland site to the right of the road to the beach.

dir: *E on C6316 at Km23.*

Open: Jun-Sep **Site:** 3HEC **Facilities:** **Services:** **Leisure:** S **Off-site:** P

FRANCA, LA — ASTURIAS

Las Hortensias

Playa de la Franca, 33590
985 412442 985 5412153
e-mail: lashortensias@campinglashortensias.com
web: www.campinglashortensias.com

A well-maintained site with good facilities beside the La Franca beach.

Open: Jun-Sep **Site:** 2.8HEC **Facilities:** **Services:** **Leisure:** R S **Off-site:**

ISLARES — CANTABRIA

Playa Arenillas

39798
942 863152 942 863152
e-mail: cueva@mundivia.es
web: www.campingplayaarenillas.com

Well-equipped site in meadowland with some pine trees, 100m from the beach.

dir: *N off N634 at Km155.8 for 100m. Steep entrance.*

Open: Apr-Sep **Site:** 2HEC **Prices:** 23.50 **Facilities:** Wi-fi **Services:** **Leisure:** S

SPAIN

SPAIN

LLANES ASTURIAS

Palacio de Garaña

33591

98 5410075 98 5410298

e-mail: info@campingpalacio.com

web: www.campingpalacio.com

Situated in the grounds of the former Palace of the Marquis of Argüelles, the site is enclosed by stone walls and has good facilities.

Open: 20 Jun-15 Sep **Site:** 2.8HEC **Prices:** 26.03-28.19 **Facilities:** Wi-fi (charged) Play Area **Services:** **Leisure:** P **Off-site:** R S

La Paz

The Camping and Caravanning Club The Friendly Club

Playa de Vidiago, 33597

98 5411012 98 5411235

e-mail: delfin@campinglapaz.com

web: www.campinglapaz.com

C&CC Report *It's hard to overstate just how special La Paz's location is. Many pitches have breathtaking views – with the Picos de Europa behind and a superb beach below. This is Green Spain at its absolute best. An ideal site for active and adventurous couples and families. There is even help siting units on the terraces for those who want it.*

dir: *Access to site at km292 from town centre on N634.*

Open: Apr-Sep **Site:** **Facilities:** **Services:** **Leisure:** S

LUARCA ASTURIAS

Cantiles

33700

98 5640938 98 5640938

e-mail: cantiles@campingloscantiles.com

web: www.campingloscantiles.com

Meadowland site beautifully situated high above the cliffs. Limited shade from bushes. Footpath to the bay 70m below.

dir: *N634 from Oviedo, turn at Km308.5 towards Faro de Luarca after fuel station, in Villar de Luarca turn right & 1km to site.*

Open: Jul-15 Sep **Site:** 2.3HEC **Facilities:** Wi-fi (charged) **Services:** **Off-site:** P R S

MOTRICO (MUTRIKU) GUIPÚZCOA

Aitzeta

20830

943 603356 943 603106

On two sloping meadows, partially terraced. Lovely view of the sea 1km away.

dir: *0.5km NE on C6212 turn at KmSS56.1.*

GPS: 43.3055, -2.3780

Open: May-Sep **Site:** 1.5HEC **Prices:** 20-21 **Facilities:** Play Area **Services:** **Leisure:** S **Off-site:**

NOJA CANTABRIA

Los Molinos

av Ris s/n, 39180

942 630426 942 630725

e-mail: losmolinos@ceoecant.es

web: www.campinglosmolinos.com

Pleasant surroundings close to the Emerald coast and fine beaches. Various leisure and sports activities.

Open: Etr & Jun-Sep **Site:** 18HEC **Prices:** 19-27 **Facilities:** **Services:** **Leisure:** P **Off-site:** S

Playa Joyel

The Camping and Caravanning Club The Friendly Club

Playa de Ris, 39180

942 630081 942 631294

e-mail: playajoyel@telefonica.net

web: www.playajoyel.com

Set in a level meadow on a peninsula with direct access to the beach.

C&CC Report *A wide range of high quality facilities, set among mature trees and next to the beach, make this an outstanding high or low season site. Ideal for those who like lots going on. Close by is the excellent municipal sports centre. The Guggenheim museum in Bilbao, and the Costa Verde's stunning mountains, are among other attractions close to hand.*

dir: *Between Laredo & Solares via A8, exit 185.*

Open: 15 Apr-2 Oct **Site:** 24HEC **Prices:** 28.20-47.40 **Facilities:** Wi-fi (charged) **Services:** **Leisure:** P S

ORIO — GUIPÚZCOA

CM Playa de Orio

20810
☎ 943 834801 943 133433
e-mail: kanpina@terra.es
web: www.oriora.com

On two flat terraces along cliffs and surrounded by hedges. Wheelchair accessible everywhere except swimming pool.

dir: *Off N634 near Km12.5 in Orio, before bridge over River Orio turn towards sea for 1.5km.*

Open: Mar-1 Nov **Site:** 3HEC **Prices:** 18.45-29.80 **Facilities:** Wi-fi **Services:** **Leisure:** P **Off-site:** R S

PECHÓN — CANTABRIA

Arenas

39594
☎ 942 717188 942 717188
e-mail: info@campinglasarenas.com
web: www.campinglasarenas.com

On terraces between rocks, reaching down to the sea.

dir: *Off N634 E of Unquera at Km74 towards sea & onto road S.*

Open: 2 Jun-29 Sep **Site:** 12HEC **Prices:** 32.80 **Facilities:** Wi-fi Play Area **Services:** **Leisure:** P R S

PERLORA-CANDAS — ASTURIAS

Perlora

33491
☎ 98 5870048 98 5870048
e-mail: recepcion@campingperlora.com
web: www.campingperlora.com

On top of a large hill on a peninsula with a few terraced pitches.

dir: *7km W of Gijon. Off N632 towards Luanco for 5km.*

GPS: 43.5838, -5.7560

Open: All Year. **Site:** 1.4HEC **Prices:** 18.85-19.55 **Facilities:** **Services:** **Leisure:** S **Off-site:**

REINANTE — LUGO

Reinante

27279
☎ 982 134005 982 134005

Longish site beyond a range of dunes on a lovely sandy beach.

dir: *On N634 at Km391.7.*

Open: All Year. **Site:** 32HEC **Facilities:** **Services:** **Leisure:** L R S

SAN SEBASTIÁN (DONOSTIA) — GUIPÚZCOA

Camping Bungalows Igueldo

Aita Orkolaga Pasealekua 69, Igueldo, 20008
☎ 943 214502 943 280411
e-mail: info@campingigueldo.com
web: www.campingigueldo.com

5km from San Sebastián, terraced site on Monte Igueldo divided by hedges. Good public transport links.

dir: *From town signs for Monte Igueldo & beach road for 4.5km.*

GPS: 43.3046, -2.0459

Open: All Year. **Site:** 5HEC **Prices:** 17-32.20 **Facilities:** Wi-fi Play Area **Services:** **Off-site:** P S

SANTIAGO DE COMPOSTELA — LA CORUÑA

As Cancelas

r do 25 de Xullo 35, 15704
☎ 981 580266 981 575553
web: www.campingascancelas.com

Quiet site located 2km from the city centre.

Open: All Year. **Site:** 1.8HEC **Facilities:** **Services:** **Leisure:** P

VALDOVIÑO — LA CORUÑA

Valdoviño

ctra de la Playa, 15552
☎ 981 487076 981 486131
e-mail: campingvaldovino@yahoo.com
web: www.turvaldovino.com

Six gently sloping fields partly in shade. Located behind Cafeteria Andy and block of flats with several villas beyond.

dir: *Off C646 towards Cedeira & sea, 0.7km to site.*

Open: Jun-Sep **Site:** 2HEC **Prices:** 26.60 **Facilities:** Wi-fi **Services:** **Off-site:** L P R S

VIVEIRO — LUGO

Vivero

27850
☎ 982 560004
e-mail: campingvivero@gmail.com

Set in tall woodland near the beach road and sea.

dir: *Off C642 Barreois-Ortueire at Km443.1 & signed.*

Open: Jun-Sep **Site:** 1.2HEC **Facilities:** **Services:** **Off-site:** R S

SPAIN

SPAIN

ZARAUZ (ZARAUTZ) GUIPÚZCOA

Talai Mendi

20800

☎ 943 830042 🖷 943 830042

A meadowland site on a hillside with shade, 0.5km from the sea. Divided by internal roads.

dir: *On outskirts of town, off N634 at Km17.5 by fuel station towards sea for 350m (narrow asphalt road).*

Open: Jul-Aug **Site:** 3.8HEC **Facilities:** **Services:** **Leisure:** S **Off-site:** R

Zarautz

Monte Talai-Mendi, 20800

☎ 943 831238 🖷 943 132486

e-mail: info@grancampingzarautz.com

web: www.grancampingzarautz.com

Site with terraces separated by hedges. At the foot of Monte Talai-Mendi, the eastern end of Zarautz, from here admire the impressive panorama of the beach and surrounding areas. A fully equipped site with modern facilities.

dir: *1.8km from N634 San Sebastian-Bilbao road. Asphalt access road from Km15.5.*

GPS: 43.2894, -2.1466

Open: All Year. **Site:** 5HEC **Prices:** 22.15 **Facilities:** **Services:** **Off-site:** P R S

NORTH EAST

ARANDA DE DUERO BURGOS

Costajàn

09400

☎ 947 502070 🖷 947 511354

e-mail: campingcostajan@camping-costajan.com

Wooded setting with good facilities.

dir: *Off N1 Burgos-Madrid at Km162.1 N of town.*

Open: All Year. **Site:** 1.8HEC **Facilities:** **Services:** **Leisure:** P **Off-site:** L R

BELLVER DE CERDANYA LLEIDA

Solana del Segre

25720

☎ 973 510310

e-mail: info@solanadelsegre.com

web: www.solanadelsegre.com

A well-equipped site on the River Segre, known for its trout fishing.

dir: *Off N260 km198.*

Open: Jul-Aug **Site:** 6.5HEC **Prices:** 37.50 **Facilities:** Wi-fi Play Area **Services:** **Leisure:** P R **Off-site:** L

BONANSA HUESCA

Baliera

22486

☎ 974 554016 🖷 974 554099

e-mail: info@baliera.com

web: www.baliera.com

A well-equipped site in a beautiful Pyrenean location on the bank of a river. Kids' club available during most of July and August.

dir: *At Km365.5 on N260.*

Open: Jan-Oct & Dec **Site:** 5HEC **Prices:** 24-30 **Facilities:** Wi-fi Kids' Club Play Area **Services:** **Leisure:** L P R

BORDETA, LA LLEIDA

Prado Verde

25551

☎ 973 647172 🖷 973 647172

web: www.campingpradoverde.es

Level meadowland on River Garona with sparse trees and sheltered by high hedges from traffic noise.

dir: *On N230 at Km199 behind fuel station.*

Open: All Year. **Site:** 1.7HEC **Facilities:** **Services:** **Leisure:** L P R

BOSSOST LLEIDA

Bedurá-Park

Era Bordeta, 25551

☎ 973 648293 🖷 973 647038

e-mail: info@bedurapark.com

web: www.bedurapark.com

A terraced site in the Aran Valley offering spectacular views over the surrounding mountains. The site, in wooded surroundings, offers all modern facilities and a variety of sports opportunities.

dir: *Via N230 Km174.4.*

Open: Apr-15 Sep **Site:** 5HEC **Prices:** 21.10-24.15 **Facilities:** Wi-fi Play Area **Services:** **Leisure:** P R **Off-site:** L

CALATAYUD ZARAGOZA

Calatayud

ctra Nacional 11 km 239, 50300

☎ 976 880592 🖷 976 360776

e-mail: campingcalatayud@gmail.com

Open: 15 Mar-10 Nov **Site:** 1.7HEC **Facilities:** **Services:** **Leisure:** P **Off-site:**

ESPOT — LLEIDA

Sol I Neu

ctra d'Espot, 25597
☎ 973 624001 🖷 973 624107
e-mail: camping@solineu.com
web: www.solineu.com

A peaceful site in a beautiful mountain setting with modern facilities. Organised excursions available.

Open: Jul-Aug **Site:** 1.5HEC **Prices:** 24.90-27.90
Facilities: Wi-fi Play Area **Services:**
Leisure: P R **Off-site:** L

ESTELLA — NAVARRA

Lizarra

Paraje de Ordoiz, 31200
☎ 948 551733 🖷 948 554755
e-mail: info@campinglizarra.com
web: www.campinglizarra.com
Open: All Year. **Site:** 4HEC **Facilities:**
Services: **Leisure:** P

GAVIN — HUESCA

Gavin

The Camping and Caravanning Club The Friendly Club

ctras N260 km 503, 22639
☎ 974 485090 🖷 974 485017
e-mail: info@campinggavin.com
web: www.campinggavin.com

Located at the mouth of the Tena Valley, a campsite with modern, comfortable installations and a comprehensive range of facilities and services.

C&CC Report *Expect a friendly welcome from the helpful staff at Camping Gavin. The high-quality facilities are in traditional-style buildings and the site enjoys a south-facing location. Camping Gavin offers snow-covered mountains, lakes and rivers, as well as the culture and restaurants of the local towns and villages. The Aragon region is different to any other. Once you have discovered it, you will want to return again.*

GPS: 42.6203, -0.3110

Open: All Year. **Site:** 7.2HEC **Prices:** 23.44-31.42
Facilities: Wi-fi Play Area **Services:**
Leisure: P **Off-site:** L R

HARO — LA RIOJA

Haro

The Camping and Caravanning Club The Friendly Club

av Miranda 1, 26200
☎ 941 312737 🖷 941 312068
e-mail: campingdeharo@fer.es
web: www.campingdeharo.com

On the outskirts of the city on the banks of the river Tirón.

C&CC Report *Conveniently located in the heart of Rioja near to major route, suitable for overnight stops. Local wine bodegas within walking distance, river and town are great for a short break.*

dir: *AP68 exit 9.*

Open: 14 Jan-8 Dec **Site:** 5HEC
Prices: 16.60-20.80 **Facilities:** Wi-fi (charged)
Services: **Leisure:** P **Off-site:**

HUESCA — HUESCA

San Jorge

Ricardo del Arco, 22004
☎ 974 227416 🖷 974 227416
e-mail: contacto@campingsanjorge.com
web: campingsanjorge.com

Site with sports field surrounded by high walls. Subdivided by hedges, sparse woodland.

dir: *M123 from town centre towards Zaragoza for 1.5km & signed.*

Open: 15 Mar-15 Oct **Site:** 0.7HEC **Prices:** 18.16-18.48
Facilities: Wi-fi **Services:** **Leisure:** P
Off-site:

LABUERDA — HUESCA

Peña Montañesa

ctra Aínsa-Francia,KM2, 22360
☎ 974 500032 🖷 974 500991
e-mail: info@penamontanesa.com
web: www.penamontanesa.com

A well-equipped family site in a wooded location near the entrance to the Ordesa and Monte Perdido national park.

Open: All Year. **Site:** 10HEC
Facilities: **Services:**
Leisure: P **Off-site:** L R

MENDIGORRIA — NAVARRA

Errota - El Molino

31150
948 340604 948 340082
e-mail: info@campingelmolino.com
web: www.campingelmolino.com

Site includes both individual plots separated by hedges, and a free area with no division. River on site and canoes and pedal boats for hire.

dir: *Access from the N111 (Pamplona - Logroño). At Puente la Reina, take N6030 to Mendigorría, after 6km, take turn for Larraga by Arga River.*

Open: All Year. **Site:** 15HEC **Facilities:** **Services:** **Leisure:** P R **Off-site:**

NÁJERA — LA RIOJA

Ruedo

ps San Julian 24, 26300
941 360102

Set among poplars but with very little shade.

dir: *Off N120 Logroño-Burgos in Nájera, along river just before stone bridge across River Majerilla & left.*

Open: Etr-10 Sep **Site:** 0.5HEC **Prices:** 20.20 **Facilities:** **Services:** **Off-site:** P R

NUEVALOS — ZARAGOZA

Lago Park

ctra Alhama de Aragón-Nuevalos, 50210
976 849038 976 849038
e-mail: info@campinglago-park.com
web: www.campinglago-park.com

A pleasant location 100m from Laguna de la Tranquera.

dir: *NE towards Alhama de Aragón.*

Open: Apr-Oct **Site:** 3HEC **Prices:** 18.20-27.90 **Facilities:** Wi-fi **Services:** **Leisure:** L P R

ORICAIN — NAVARRA

Ezcaba

ctra Francia-Irun km7, 31194
948 330315 948 331316
e-mail: info@campingezcaba.com
web: www.campingezcaba.com

Gently sloping meadowland and a few terraces on a flat topped hill.

dir: *N of Pamplona. Off N121 at Km7.3 towards Berriosuso, after River Ulzama turn right & uphill.*

GPS: 42.8569, -1.6233

Open: 15 Jun-15 Sep **Site:** 2HEC **Prices:** 22.85-23.50 **Facilities:** Wi-fi (charged) Play Area **Services:** **Leisure:** P **Off-site:** R

PANCORBO — BURGOS

Desfiladero

09280
947 354027
e-mail: campingeldesfiladero@hotmail.com
web: www.eldesfiladero.com

A well-appointed site close to the river.

dir: *Off N1 at Km305.2.*

Open: All Year. **Site:** 13HEC **Facilities:** **Services:** **Leisure:** L **Off-site:** P R

PUEBLA DE CASTRO, LA — HUESCA

Lago Barasona

crta Nacional 123 A km25, 22435
974 545148 974 545148
e-mail: info@lagobarasona.com
web: www.lagobarasona.com

A well-equipped, terraced site in a beautiful setting beside the lake and backed by mountains.

Open: Mar-10 Dec **Site:** 5HEC **Prices:** 23-36.80 **Facilities:** Wi-fi Kids' Club **Services:** **Leisure:** P **Off-site:** L R

RIBERA DE CARDÓS — LLEIDA

Cardós

25570
973 623112 973 623183
web: www.campingdelcardos.com

Long stretch of meadowland divided by four rows of poplars.

dir: *Near electricity plant in Llavorsi turn NE onto Ribera road for 9km, site near hostel Soly Neu.*

Open: Apr-29 Sep **Site:** 3HEC **Facilities:** **Services:** **Leisure:** P R

SANTO DOMINGO DE LA CALZADA — LA RIOJA

Bañares

26250

941 342804 941 340131

web: www.campingbanares.es

Open: All Year. **Site:** 12HEC **Facilities:** **Services:** **Leisure:** P

SOLSONA — LLEIDA

Solsonès

25280

973 482861 973 481300

e-mail: info@campingsolsones.com

web: www.campingsolsones.com

A well-equipped site in a picturesque mountain setting with facilities for both summer and winter holidays.

Open: 10 Jan-10 Dec **Site:** 6.3HEC **Facilities:** Wi-fi Kids' Club Play Area **Services:** **Leisure:** P

TIERMAS — ZARAGOZA

Mar del Pirineo

50682

948 398073 948 871313

On broad terraces sloping down to the banks of the Embalse de Yese. Roofing provides shade for tents and cars.

dir: *On N240 at Km317.7.*

Open: May-Sep **Site:** 2.88HEC **Facilities:** **Services:** **Leisure:** L P

TORLA — HUESCA

Ordesa

ctra de Ordesa s/n, 22376

974 486146 974 486381

e-mail: camping@hotelordesa.com

web: www.hotelordesa.com

On three terraces between well-kept hedges.

dir: *2km N of village at Km96 & N of C138.*

Open: All Year. **Site:** 3.5HEC **Facilities:** **Services:** **Leisure:** P **Off-site:** R

VILLOSLADA DE CAMEROS — LA RIOJA

Los Cameros

ctra La Virgen, 26125

941 747021 941 742091

e-mail: info@camping-loscameros.com

web: www.camping-loscameros.com

Situated in the Sierra Cebollera national park in the Iberian mountain range.

dir: *Off N111 towards Soria & onto Villoslada.*

Open: All Year. **Site:** 4HEC **Facilities:** **Services:** **Leisure:** R

ZARAGOZA — ZARAGOZA

Ciudad de Zaragoza

The Camping and Caravanning Club — The Friendly Club

San Juan Bautista de la Salle, 50012

876 241495

e-mail: info@campingzaragoza.com

web: www.campingzaragoza.com

Surburban campsite, around 3km from the centre of Zaragoza.

C&CC Report *Located in a suburban setting, just over 3km from Zaragoza, the capital of Aragon with its 2,000 years of history.*

dir: *Z40 (Zaragova ring road), exit 33a then NII. Situated off Maurice Ravel Street.*

Open: All Year. **Site:** **Facilities:** **Services:** **Leisure:** P

NORTH WEST

BAYONA — PONTEVEDRA

Bayona Playa

ctra Vigo-Bayona km 19.4, 36393

986 350035 986 352952

e-mail: campingbayona@campingbayona.com

web: www.campingbayona.com

On a long sandy peninsula on the Galicia coast with direct access to the beach. The site has modern facilities and a variety of water sports are available.

dir: *Autopista AP9 Salida No 5 (Baiona Norte).*

Open: All Year. **Site:** 4HEC **Facilities:** **Services:** **Leisure:** P R S

SPAIN

Facilities shop shower electric points for razors electric points for caravans parking by tents permitted ompulsory separate car park **Services** café/restaurant bar Camping Gaz International gas other than Camping Gaz first aid facilities laundry **Leisure** swimming L-Lake P-Pool R-River S-Sea **Off-site** All facilities within 5km

CUBILLAS DE SANTA MARTA — VALLADOLID

Cubillas

47290
983 585002 983 585016
e-mail: info@campingcubillas.com
web: www.campingcubillas.com
Meadowland with young trees, subdivided by hedges. Steep ascent to the site.
dir: *On right of N620 from Burgos between km100 & km101.*
Open: 9 Jan-13 Dec **Site:** 4HEC **Facilities:** Wi-fi (charged) Play Area **Services:** **Leisure:** P **Off-site:** R

PORTONOVO — PONTEVEDRA

Paxariñas

36970
986 723055 986 721356
e-mail: info@campingpaxarinas.com
web: www.campingpaxarinas.com
Slightly sloping site towards a bay, among dunes and tall pines and young deciduous trees. Lovely beach.
Open: Apr-Oct **Site:** 3HEC **Prices:** 28-32
Facilities: Wi-fi **Services:** **Leisure:** S **Off-site:** P

SANTA MARINA DE VALDEON — LÉON

El Cares

24915
987 742676 987 742676
Wooded mountain setting with good facilities.
dir: *N off N621 from Portilla de la Reina.*
Open: Jun-Sep **Site:** 15HEC **Facilities:** **Services:** **Leisure:** R **Off-site:** L

SAN VICENTE DO MAR — PONTEVEDRA

Siglo XXI

36988
986 738100 986 738113
e-mail: info@campingsiglo21.com
web: www.campingsiglo21.com
A popular modern site with individual sanitary facilities attached to each pitch.
Open: Jun-Sep **Site:** 1.5HEC **Prices:** 23-32.50
Facilities: Wi-fi Play Area
Services: **Leisure:** P **Off-site:** S

TORDESILLAS — VALLADOLID

Astral

Camino de Pollos 8, 47100
983 770953 983 770953
e-mail: info@campingelastral.es
web: www.campingelastral.es
A well-equipped site in a pleasant rural location close to the River Duero.
dir: *Motorway exit Tordesillas & signed.*
GPS: 41.4953, -5.0052
Open: Apr-Sep **Site:** 3HEC **Prices:** 17.40-25.85 **Facilities:** Wi-fi (charged) Play Area
Services: **Leisure:** P **Off-site:** R

VALENCIA DE DON JUAN — LÉON

Pico Verde

ctra C621 Mayorga-Astorga, 24200
987 750525 987 750525
e-mail: campingpicoverd@terra.es
web: www.verial.es/campingpicoverde
A green and quiet site, just off A66.
dir: *6km off A66.*
Open: 15 Jun-4 Sep **Site:** 2.7HEC **Facilities:** Play Area **Services:** **Leisure:** P
Off-site: R

SOUTH

ALHAURIN DE LA TORRE — MÁLAGA

Malaga Monte Parc

The Camping and Caravanning Club — The Friendly Club

29130
951 296028 951 296028
e-mail: info@malagamonteparc.com
web: www.malagamonteparc.com
C&CC Report *Located in the hills behind the Costa del Sol, with a restaurant adjacent. About 3km from the centre of Alhaurin de la Torre, where local services can be found.*
Open: All Year. **Site:** **Facilities:**
Services: **Leisure:** P

BAÑOS DE FORTUNA MURCIA

Fuente

30326

☎ 968 685017 968 685125

e-mail: info@campingfuente.com

web: www.campingfuente.com

A camping ground within a hotel complex with individual bathroom facilities attached to each pitch and good recreational facilities.

dir: *C3223 from Fortuna à Pinoso to Balneario de Fortuna, signed.*

Open: All Year. **Site:** 1.9HEC **Prices:** 11.87-18.90
Facilities: Wi-fi **Services:**
Leisure: P

CABO DE GATA ALMERIA

Cabo de Gata

The Camping and Caravanning Club The Friendly Club

04150

☎ 950 160443 950 520003

e-mail: info@campingcabodegata.com

web: www.campingcabodegata.com

Natural parkland site with separate pitches, 1km from the beach.

C&CC Report *Many choose Cabo de Gata for its very peaceful surroundings in the semi-arid Cabo de Gatar-Nijar natural park, on the Gulf of Almería, one of the most southerly and reputedly driest points in Europe. With good modern facilities, the site makes a good base for visiting the natural park with its salinas and their abundant bird life. You can walk out of the camp site entrance straight into the park's famous flat sand dunes.*

dir: *N340 exit 460 or 467.*

GPS: 36.8008, -2.2461

Open: All Year. **Site:** 3.6HEC **Prices:** 10.44-24.85
Facilities: Wi-fi (charged) Play Area
Services: **Leisure:** P S

see advert on this page

CARCHUNA GRANADA

Don Cactus

The Camping and Caravanning Club The Friendly Club

Carchuna-Motril, 18730

☎ 958 623109 958 624294

e-mail: camping@doncactus.com

web: www.doncactus.com

A well established modern site adjoining the beach.

C&CC Report *A good quality, popular site, with good facilities and a warm welcome from the family owners. Lots to see and do in the way of day trips, such as the Sierra Nevada National Park and Granada with its Alhambra Palace. With the exception of the beach and the beach road to Calahonda, the immediate locality is not suited to cycling and walking directly off site. To get the most out of this region you need to use your own vehicle to get out and about, and motor caravanners in particular should note this. The locality around this high quality site is under literally kilometres of plastic due to the intensive greenhouse horticulture of the region. However, this is not obtrusive when on site.*

dir: *On N340 Carchuna-Motril at Km343.*

GPS: 36.6958, -3.4433

Open: All Year. **Site:** 4HEC **Prices:** 8.90-29.65
Facilities: Wi-fi (charged) Play Area
Services: **Leisure:** P S

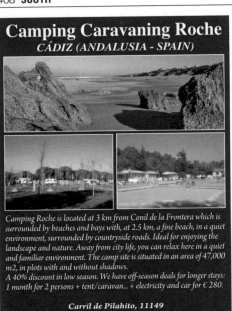

CARLOTA, LA — CORDOBA

Carlos III

ctra N4 km430, 14100
957 300697 957 3000697
e-mail: camping@campingcarlosIII.com
web: www.campingcarlosIII.com

Wooded surroundings with modern facilities.

dir: *NIV exit La Carlota.*

GPS: 37.6825, -4.9180

Open: All Year. **Site:** 7HEC **Prices:** 20.50-20.85
Facilities: Wi-fi (charged) Kids' Club Play Area
Services: **Leisure:** P **Off-site:** P

CASTILLO DE BAÑOS — GRANADA

Castillo de Baños

The Camping and Caravanning Club The Friendly Club

Castillo de Baños, La Mamola, 18750
958 829528 958 829768
e-mail: info@campingcastillo.com
web: www.campingcastillo.com

Well-equipped site next to the beach.

C&CC Report *This is a small site with a relaxing atmosphere, for those who want something a bit different. The site's location also makes it a convenient place to break the journey when travelling between the Mediterranean and Atlantic camp sites. You will get the most out of this area by using your own vehicle to get out and about. Many of the best parts of beautiful Andalucía are within easy day-trip reach. Granada with its historic jewel – the Alhambra Palace – is just one recommendation.*

dir: *At Km360 on N340 Castillo de Baños-La Mamola.*

GPS: 36.7408, -3.3011

Open: All Year. **Site:** 3HEC **Prices:** 7.40-24.61
Facilities: Wi-fi (charged) Play Area
Services: **Leisure:** P S

CONIL DE LA FRONTERA — CÁDIZ

Camping La Rosaleda

The Camping and Caravanning Club The Friendly Club

ctra del Pradillo km1.3, 11140
956 443327 956 443385
e-mail: info@campinglarosaleda.com
web: www.campinglarosaleda.com

Situated on the Costa de la Luz, the site has good sporting facilities and entertainment programme.

C&CC Report *Camping La Rosaleda is a gem of a site. Family owned and run, the care taken in providing high quality facilities for all campers is obvious. Activities, entertainment and excursions are organised regularly, even a trip to Tangiers, in Morocco, subject to minimum numbers. Africa is only 35 minutes by fast craft from Tarifa. This green and verdant region offers several interesting itineraries to follow and the camp site is central to several natural parks, with the coast very good for exploring by bike.*

Open: All Year. **Site:** 5HEC **Prices:** 17-34
Facilities: Wi-fi Kids' Club Play Area
Services: **Leisure:** P **Off-site:** S

Fuente del Gallo

Fuente del Gallo, 11140
956 440137 956 442036
e-mail: camping@campingfuentedelgallo.com
web: www.campingfuentedelgallo.com

A well-equipped site in a wooded location 300m from the beach.

dir: *Signed from N340, Km23.*

Open: Apr-Sep **Site:** 2.5HEC **Prices:** 20-23.50
Facilities: Wi-fi (charged) Play Area
Services: **Leisure:** P **Off-site:** S

Roche

Carril de Pilahito, s/n, 11149
☎ 956 442216 🖹 956 443002
e-mail: info@campingroche.com
web: www.campingroche.com

Spread among pine groves with well-defined pitches close to the beach.

dir: *Via N340 from Cádiz to Algeciras, 19.5km.*

Open: All Year. **Site:** 5HEC **Prices:** 15.97-28
Facilities: **Services:**
Leisure: P **Off-site:** R S

see advert on opposite page

EL ROCÍO — HUELVA

Aldea

The Camping and Caravanning Club The Friendly Club

ctra del Rocío km 25, 21750
☎ 959 442677 🖹 959 442582
e-mail: info@campinglaaldea.com
web: www.campinglaaldea.com

Situated in the village of El Rocío, at the entrance of Doñana, a national and natural park.

C&CC Report *La Aldea is a modern camp site offering a wide range of high quality facilities and services. Located on the edge of the most important protected nature area in Europe – Spain's best kept secret, the unique Doñana natural park – an area with more than 300 bird species, including one of the world's largest colonies of Spanish imperial eagles. The natural areas are accessible through a number of visitor centres, nature trails with guided half-day trips in four-wheel drive vehicles, horse-guided routes and waymarked walks. This site will also appeal to those who want to experience traditional Spanish culture. El Rocio with its sand streets and hitch rails for horses is a popular place of pilgrimage, especially on Sundays.*

dir: *A49/H612, follow directions for Matalascanas.*

Open: All Year. **Site:** 5.8HEC **Prices:** 23.20-26
Facilities: Wi-fi (charged) Play Area
Services: **Leisure:** P

ESTEPONA — MALÁGA

Parque Tropical

ctra A7, 29680
☎ 952 793618 🖹 952 793618
e-mail: parquetropicalcamping@hotmail.com
web: www.parquetropicalcamping.com

A modern site at the foot of the Sierra Bermeja mountains, a short walk from the sea.

dir: *Via N340 at Km162.*

Open: All Year. **Site:** 12.4HEC **Prices:** 9.80-29
Facilities: Wi-fi (charged)
Services: **Leisure:** P **Off-site:** S

FUENTE DE PIEDRA — MALÁGA

Espacious Rurales

Camino de la Rábita s/n, 29520
☎ 952 735294 🖹 952 735461
e-mail: info@camping-rural.com
web: www.camping-rural.com

Situated within a wildlife reserve on the shores of a lagoon.

Open: All Year. **Site:** 2HEC **Facilities:**
Services: **Leisure:** L P **Off-site:**

GALLARDOS, LOS — ALMERIA

Gallardos

04280
☎ 950 528324 🖹 950 469596
e-mail: campinglosgallardos@hotmail.com
web: www.campinglosgallardos.com

Level site with individual pitches, 11km from the sea and 10km from the old Moorish village of Mojácar.

dir: *0.5km from Km525 on N340.*

Open: All Year. **Site:** 3.5HEC **Facilities:**
Services: **Leisure:** P

GRANADA — GRANADA

Sierra Nevada

av Juan Pablo II, 23, 18014
☎ 958 150062 🖹 958 150954
e-mail: campingmotel@terra.es
web: www.campingsierranevada.com

Almost level grassy and shady site, in numerous sections, within a motel complex. Good transport links to the city centre.

Open: Mar-1 Nov **Site:** 3HEC **Prices:** 25.80
Facilities: Wi-fi Play Area **Services:**
Leisure: P **Off-site:** L R

GÜÉJAR-SIERRA — GRANADA

Las Lomas

The Camping and Caravanning Club The Friendly Club

ctra Güéjar-Sierra Km 6.5, 18160
☎ 958 484742 🖹 958 484742
e-mail: laslomas@campings.net
web: www.campingsonline.com/lomas

C&CC Report *Peaceful hillside setting above a reservoir, with modern wash blocks and private bathrooms for hire. Convenient for visiting the Sierra Nevada mountains, Granada and the Alhambra Palace.*

dir: *E902 (Motril-Jaen), exit 132 to Ronda Sur. Follow Sierra Nevada. Take right hand lane 3km past the tunnel then turn left. Follow signs 'Güéjar Sierra' and 'Las Lomas'.*

Open: All Year. **Site:** **Facilities:**
Services: **Leisure:** P

SPAIN

Facilities shop shower electric points for razors electric points for caravans parking by tents permitted Compulsory separate car park **Services** café/restaurant bar Camping Gaz International gas other than Camping Gaz first aid facilities laundry **Leisure** swimming L-Lake P-Pool R-River S-Sea **Off-site** All facilities within 5km

GUIJARROSA, LA — CORDOBA

Campiña

14547
☎ 957 315303 957 315303
e-mail: info@campinglacampina.com
web: www.campinglacampina.com

A quiet rural setting surrounded by olive trees and elms with modern facilities, and a bus from the gate to Cordoba. Breakfast is included in pitch prices.

dir: *Off N4 at Km424 or Km441 & signs to Santaella & site or A45 exit km27 La Rambla.*

GPS: 37.6225, -4.8591

Open: All Year. **Site:** 0.7HEC **Prices:** 18-26.90 **Facilities:** Wi-fi **Services:** **Leisure:** P

HUMILLADERO — MÁLAGA

Sierrecilla

29531
☎ 951 199090
e-mail: info@lasierrecilla.com
web: www.lasierrecilla.com

Modern and luxurious facilities with plots of different sizes. 40 minutes from the beaches of Málaga and 1 hour from Granada, Seville and Cordoba, an ideal place to discover Andalucia. Eagles, vultures and falcons can be seen locally.

C&CC Report *Conveniently located, not far from the A92 Granada-Seville motorway, this newly redeveloped site is on the outskirts of the village of Humilladero with local shops, bars and restaurants within walking distance.*

dir: *A 92 exit 138 at 1st rdbt to Humilladero at town entrance rdbt take 2nd exit, follow to bottom turn right & next corner to left.*

GPS: 37.1081, -4.6871

Site: **Prices:** 17.50-21.50 **Facilities:** Wi-fi **Services:** **Leisure:** P

ISLA CRISTINA — HUELVA

Giralda

21410
☎ 959 343318 959 343318
e-mail: recepcion@campinggiralda.com
web: www.campinggiralda.com

On level ground dotted with trees within easy reach of the beach. Modern facilities and plenty of entertainment.

dir: *On Isla Cristina-La Antilla road.*

Open: All Year. **Site:** 15HEC **Facilities:** **Services:** **Leisure:** P R **Off-site:** S

ISLA PLANA — MURCIA

Madriles

ctra de la Azohia Km45, 30868
☎ 968 152151 968 152092
e-mail: camplosmadriles@terra.es
web: www.campinglosmadriles.com

A large family site with a variety of recreational facilities.

dir: *Via Mazarron-Cartagena road.*

GPS: 37.5780, -1.1963

Open: 15 Jun-15 Sep **Site:** 7.2HEC **Prices:** 15-34.67 **Facilities:** Wi-fi (charged) Play Area **Services:** **Leisure:** P S **Off-site:**

MANGA DEL MAR MENOR, LA — MURCIA

La Manga

Autovia de la Manga, Salida 11, 30386
☎ 968 563014 968 563426
e-mail: lamanga@caravaning.es
web: www.caravaning.es

A large family site on the Mar Menor lagoon. Pitches separated by hedges or trees. Good recreational facilities.

C&CC Report *A great location and a high quality site. La Manga resort, the beautiful coastal area of Calblanque and fishing villages such as Cabo de Palos are all nearby. Several golf courses are close by, too. The area can be bustling with visitors from across Europe and space is usually at a premium. During Semana Sancta (Holy Week) leading up to Easter Sunday, the campsite and the local area are likely to be very busy as the Spanish come to celebrate. During this week local celebrations are liable to last well into the night and provide an insight into how the Spanish love to fiesta.*

dir: *Off Cartagena motorway.*

Open: All Year. **Site:** 32HEC **Facilities:** **Services:** **Leisure:** P S

MARBELLA — MÁLAGA

Buganvilla

29600
☎ 952 831973 952 831974
e-mail: info@campingbuganvilla.com
web: www.campingbuganvilla.com

A well-equipped site in a pine forest close to the beach.

dir: *E of Marbella off N340 coast road towards Mijas.*

Open: All Year. **Site:** 4HEC **Facilities:** **Services:** **Leisure:** P S **Off-site:**

Cabopino

29600
☎ 952 834373 952 834373
e-mail: info@campingcabopino.com
web: www.campinngcabopino.com

The Camping and Caravanning Club The Friendly Club

A well run site in a pleasant location 75m from the beach.

C&CC Report *A well-located site in the heart of the Costa del Sol. Like the surrounding area the site is busy all year round and space is at a premium. Across the road is Puerto Cabopino, a tiny port where convertibles sit beside powerboats and cruisers. Places to visit include Gibraltar, about 80km away, Marbella and the high-life port at Puerto Banús. Inland from Marbella, the stunning, gorge-spanning town of Ronda is a beautiful drive away, while numerous nature reserves and small sierras offer a very peaceful contrast to the non-stop hustle and bustle of the coast.*

dir: *Off N340 (A7) km194.7.*

GPS: 36.4886, -4.7427

Open: All Year. **Site:** 12HEC
Prices: 23.11-34.82 **Facilities:** Wi-fi (charged) Kids' Club Play Area **Services:**
Leisure: P **Off-site:** S

MAZAGÓN — HUELVA

Mazagón

cuesta de la Barca s/n, 21130
☎ 959 376208 959 536256
e-mail: info@campingplayamazagon.com
web: www.campingplayamazagon.com

Undulating terrain among dunes in a sparse pine forest. Long sandy beach.

dir: *Off N431 Sevilla-Huelva before San Juan del Puerto towards Moguer, continue S via Palso de la Frontera.*

Open: All Year. **Site:** 8HEC **Facilities:**
Services: **Leisure:** P **Off-site:** S

MOJÁCAR — ALMERIA

Sopalmo

Sopalmo, 04637
☎ 950 478413
e-mail: macusimon@hotmail.com
web: www.campingsopalmoelcortijillo.com

Open: All Year. **Site:** 1.7HEC **Facilities:**
Services: **Off-site:** S

MORATALLA — MURCIA

La Puerta

ctra del Canal, Paraje La Puerta Km8, 30440
☎ 968 730008 968 706365
e-mail: info@campinglapuerta.com
web: www.campinglapuerta.com

Wooded site alongside the river Alhárabe with big pitches and pleasant views.

dir: *A30 Albacete to Murcia, onto C415 to Moratalla.*

Open: All Year. **Site:** 10HEC **Facilities:**
Services: **Leisure:** P R **Off-site:**

MOTRIL — GRANADA

Playa de Poniente

Playa de Poniente s/n, 18613
☎ 958 820303 958 604191
e-mail: info@campingplayadeponiente.com
web: www.campingplayadeponiente.com

Situated on a magnificent beach in the centre of the tropical coast. Enjoying a privileged environment and a climate that allows all kinds of sports and activities.

GPS: 36.7180, -3.5463

Open: All Year. **Site:** 2.4HEC **Prices:** 12.37-24.75
Facilities: Wi-fi Play Area **Services:**
Leisure: P S

OTURA — GRANADA

Suspiro del Moro

18630
☎ 958 555411 958 555411
e-mail: campingsuspirodelmoro@yahoo.es
web: www.campingsuspirodelmoro.com

A modern site with good facilities close to the town centre.

dir: *10km S of Granada via N323.*

Open: 15 Jun-15 Sep **Site:** 1HEC **Facilities:**
Services: **Leisure:** P **Off-site:** R

PELIGROS — GRANADA

Granada

Aurovía Granada - Jaén, Salida 121, 18210
☎ 958 340548 958 340548
e-mail: pruizlopez1953@yahoo.es
web: www.campinggranada.es

Wooded location with panoramic views.

dir: *N323 exit 123 for Peligros.*

Open: 15 Mar-Sep **Site:** 2.2HEC **Facilities:**
Services: **Leisure:** P

Facilities shop shower electric points for razors electric points for caravans parking by tents permitted
mpulsory separate car park **Services** café/restaurant bar Camping Gaz International gas other than Camping Gaz
first aid facilities laundry **Leisure** swimming L-Lake P-Pool R-River S-Sea **Off-site** All facilities within 5km

PUERTO DE SANTA MARÍA, EL — CÁDIZ

Playa Las Dunas

ps Maritimo de la Puntilla S/N, 11500
956 872210 956 860117
e-mail: info@lasdunascamping.com
web: www.lasdunascamping.com
Large site with good recreational facilities close to the beach.

GPS: 36.5875, -6.2408

Open: All Year. **Site:** 13.2HEC **Prices:** 17.90-21.14
Facilities: Wi-fi (charged) **Services:**
Leisure: P S **Off-site:** R

RONDA — MÁLAGA

El Sur

ctra de Algeciras A369 2.8km, 29400
952 875939 952 877054
e-mail: info@campingelsur.com
web: www.elsur.com
A beautiful location in the heart of the Serrania of Ronda.

Open: All Year. **Site:** 4HEC **Prices:** 18-24 **Facilities:**
Wi-fi (charged) **Services:**
Leisure: P

ROQUETAS-DE-MAR — ALMERIA

Roquetas

Los Parrales, 04740
950 343809 950 342525
e-mail: info@campingroquetas.com
web: www.campingsroquetas.com
A family site on the coast with good facilities. Discounts available in low season.

dir: *Access by road 340. 1.7km from Km428.6*

Open: All Year. **Site:** 8HEC **Prices:** 20.20
Facilities: Wi-fi **Services:**
Leisure: L P S

SANTA ELENA — JAÉN

Despeñaperros

23213
953 664192 953 664192
e-mail: info@campingdespenaperros.com
web: www.campingdespenaperros.com
A clean, restful site in a nature reserve with views of the surrounding mountains.

C&CC Report *Very convenient for routes south and south-west, with views over the Natural Park and villages services within 1km.*

dir: *On A4-E5 at Km257.*

Open: All Year. **Site:** 5HEC **Prices:** 17.80-18.95
Facilities: **Services:**
Leisure: P

TARIFA — CÁDIZ

Paloma

11380
956 684203 956 684233
e-mail: campingpaloma@yahoo.es
web: www.campingpaloma.com
A modern site in a secluded location next to the prehistoric Necropolis de los Algarbes, 400m from the beach and. Fine views of the African coast across the Straits of Gibraltar.

dir: *Via N340 Cádiz-Málaga at Km74.*

Open: All Year. **Site:** 4.9HEC **Facilities:**
Services: **Leisure:** P **Off-site:** R S

Rió Jara

11380
956 680570 956 680570
e-mail: campingriojara@terra.es
web: www.campingriojara.com
Extensive site on meadowland with good tree cover. Long sandy beach.

dir: *Off N340 at Km79.7 towards sea.*

Open: All Year. **Site:** 3HEC **Facilities:**
Services: **Leisure:** R S

Site 6HEC (site size) grass sand stone little shade partly shaded mainly shaded bungalows for hire (static) caravans for hire tents for hire no dogs site fully accessible for wheelchairs
Prices amount quoted is per night, for 2 adults and car, plus tent or caravan. Mobile home hire is a weekly rate.

Tarifa

11380
956 684778 956 684778
e-mail: info@campingtarifa.es
web: www.campingtarifa.es

A terraced site in wooded surroundings, 100m from the sea.

dir: *N340 at Km78 on Málaga-Cádiz road.*

GPS: 36.0548, -5.6494

Open: Mar-Oct **Site:** 3.2HEC **Prices:** 23.50-35.50 **Facilities:** Wi-fi Play Area **Services:** **Leisure:** P **Off-site:** R S

TORROX-COSTA — MÁLAGA

El Pino

Torrox-Park s/n, 29793
952 530006 952 532578
e-mail: info@campingelpino.com
web: www.campingelpino.com

Quiet site with a family atmosphere, situated and surrounded by avocado and tropical trees, offering shade in summer. More sunny sites for winter making a pleasant location all year.

dir: *Autovia del Mediterraneo km 285, 500m from rdbt & bridge access to Torrox Park.*

Open: All Year. **Site:** 50HEC **Prices:** 13-18 **Facilities:** Wi-fi Play Area **Services:** **Leisure:** P **Off-site:** S

see advert on this page

VILLAFRANCA DE CÓRDOBA — CÓRDOBA

Albolafia

Camino de la Vega s/n, 14420
957 190835 957 190835
e-mail: informacion@campingalbolafia.com
web: www.campingalbolafia.com

A site with modern well designed facilities. The entrance buildings are in a semicircular way, with a central fountain built on an ancient well. Cordoba is within easy reach and there are good transport links.

dir: *Autovia A4 at km 377.*

GPS: 38.5933, -4.9283

Open: All Year. **Site:** 3HEC **Prices:** 20 **Facilities:** Wi-fi Play Area **Services:** **Leisure:** P R

ANDORRA

SANT JULIÀ DE LÒRIA

Huguet

ctra de Fontaneda
376843718 376843803

On level strip of meadowland with rows of fruit and deciduous trees.

Open: All Year. **Site:** 1.5HEC **Facilities:** **Services:** **Leisure:** R **Off-site:** L P

Facilities shop shower electric points for razors electric points for caravans parking by tents permitted mpulsory separate car park **Services** café/restaurant bar Camping Gaz International gas other than Camping Gaz first aid facilities laundry **Leisure** swimming L-Lake P-Pool R-River S-Sea **Off-site** All facilities within 5km

Switzerland

Drinking & Driving
If the level of alcohol in the bloodstream is 0.05% or more, penalties may include fine or prison. The police can request any driver to undergo a breath test or drugs test. Visiting motorists may be forbidden from driving in Switzerland for a minimum of one month.

Driving Licence
Minimum age at which a UK licence holder may drive temporarily imported car 18, motorcycle (up to 50cc) 16, motorcycle (50cc or over) 18.

Fines
On-the-spot fines imposed in certain cases. Vehicle clamps are not used in Switzerland but vehicles causing an obstruction can be removed. Fines are severe.

Lights
Use of dipped headlights during the day recommended for all vehicles. Compulsory when passing through tunnels even if they are well lit. Fine for non-compliance.

Motorcycles
Wearing of crash helmets compulsory. Use of dipped headlights during the day recommended.

Motor Insurance
Third-party compulsory.

Passengers & Children
Vehicles registered outside Switzerland must comply with the requirements of their country of registration with regard to child restraint regulations. From 1 Apr 2010 children up to 12 years of age will have to be placed in a child restraint type approved complying with UN ECE regulation 44.03. Children measuring more than 1.50m will not be included. Children less than 7 years old must be in an appropriate child restraint.

Seat Belts
Compulsory for all occupants.

Speed Limits
Unless signed otherwise

Private vehicles without trailers

Built-up areas	50km/h
Outside built-up areas	80km/h
Semi-motorways	100km/h
Motorways	120km/h

Private vehicle with trailer

Semi-motorways and motorways	80 or 60km/h
Minimum speed on motorways	80km/h

NOTE Towing of cars on a motorway is only permitted up to the next exit, at a maximum speed of 40km/h.

Additional Information
Compulsory equipment: Snow chains (in areas indicated by appropriate sign. Must be fitted on at least two drive wheels); warning triangle (each motor vehicle must be equipped with a warning triangle which must be kept within easy reach (not in the boot), to be used in any breakdown/emergency situation. Hitchhiking prohibited on motorways and semi-motorways.

The Swiss authorities levy an annual motorway tax, and a vehicle sticker for vehicles up to 3.5 tonnes maximum total weight (known locally as a 'vignette') must be displayed in the prescribed manner by each vehicle (including motorcycles, trailers and caravans) using Swis motorways and semi-motorways. The fine for non-displa is the cost of vignette(s) plus CHF100. Motorists may purchase the stickers in the UK (telephone the Swiss Centre on free-phone 00800 100 20030 for information) or in Switzerland from customs offices at the frontier, or service stations and garages throughout the country. Vehicles over 3.5 tonnes maximum total weight are taxed on all roads; coaches and caravans pay a fixed tax for periods of one day, 10 days, one month or one year but lorries are taxed on weight and distance travelled. Sat-navs with maps indicating the location of fixed spee cameras must have this function deactivated. Radar detectors are prohibited even if not switched on. All vehicles with spiked tyres are prohibited on motorways and semi-motorways except for parts of the A13 and A2 Snow tyres are not compulsory, but vehicles which are not equipped to travel in snow and impede traffic are liable to a fine. During daylight hours outside built-up areas drivers must sound their horns before sharp bends where visibility is limited, after dark this warning must b given by flashing headlights. In Switzerland, pedestrians generally have right of way and expect vehicles to stop. Some pedestrians may just step in to the road when on crosswalks and will expect your vehicle to stop. Blue zo parking discs are available from many petrol stations, garages, kiosks, restaurants and police stations.

Tolls Currency Swiss Franc (CHF)	Car	Car Towing Caravan/Trailer
Annual vignette (includes use of Gotthard Tunnel and San Bernardino Tunnel)	40CHF	40CHF
Bridges and Tunnels		
Munt La Schera Tunnel	15CHF	20CHF
Grand St Bernard Tunnel	29.80CHF	46.20CHF

NORTH

KÜNTEN — AARGAU

Sulz

5444

056 4964879 & 079 6607426 (mob)

056 4964847

e-mail: info@camping-sulz.ch

web: www.camping-sulz.ch

Situated by a river, with good sized spaces.

dir: *A1 exit Baden towards Bremgarten.*

Open: 15 Mar-Oct **Site:** 3HEC **Prices:** 20-30 **Facilities:** Wi-fi (charged) Play Area **Services:** **Leisure:** P R

MÖHLIN — AARGAU

Bachtalen

4313

061 8515095 & 079 4079971 (mob)

e-mail: info@camping-moehlin.ch

web: www.camping-moehlin.ch

A pleasant site in a wooded rural setting.

dir: *2km N towards the Rhine.*

Open: Apr-Oct **Site:** 1HEC **Facilities:** **Services:** **Off-site:** P R

REINACH — BASEL

Waldhort

Heideweg 16, 4153

061 7116429 061 7139835

e-mail: info@camping-waldhort.ch

web: www.camping-waldhort.ch

Pleasant wooded surroundings close to the Basle-Delémont road.

Open: Mar-25 Oct **Site:** 3.3HEC **Prices:** 38 **Facilities:** Wi-fi Play Area **Services:** **Leisure:** P **Off-site:**

ZURZACH — AARGAU

Oberfeld

5330

056 2492575 056 2492579

e-mail: presi@camping-zurzach.ch

web: www.camping-zurzach.ch

Open: 24 Mar-27 Oct **Site:** 2HEC **Facilities:** **Services:** **Leisure:** P R

NORTH EAST

ALTNAU — THURGAU

Ruderbaum

Ruderbaum 3, 8595

071 6952965 071 6900631

e-mail: camping@ruderbaum.ch

web: www.ruderbaum.ch

A small site with ample facilities.

dir: *Close to railway station by Lake Bodensee between Constance & Romanshorn.*

Open: Apr-Oct **Site:** 7.5HEC **Prices:** 26.50-40 **Facilities:** Play Area **Services:** **Leisure:** L **Off-site:**

APPENZELL — APPENZELL

Eischen

Kaustr 123, 9050

071 7875030 071 7875660

e-mail: info@eischen.ch

web: www.eischen.ch

A woodland site with modern installations.

dir: *S of Appenzell towards Wattwil.*

Open: All Year. **Site:** 2HEC **Facilities:** **Services:**

ESCHENZ — THURGAU

Hüttenberg

Hüttenberg, 8264

052 7412337 052 7415671

e-mail: info@huettenberg.ch

web: www.huettenberg.ch

Terraced site with good facilities lying above village.

dir: *1km SW.*

GPS: 47.6447, 8.8597

Open: 9 Apr-18 Oct **Site:** 6HEC **Prices:** 27-33.50 **Facilities:** Wi-fi (charged) Play Area **Services:** **Leisure:** P **Off-site:** L R

GOLDINGEN — ST-GALLEN

Atzmännig

8638

055 2846434 055 2846435

e-mail: info@atzmaennig.ch

web: www.atzmaennig.ch

Suitable for summer and winter holidays, the site is close to the main cable car and ski-lift stations and giant mountainside slide.

Open: All Year. **Site:** 1.5HEC **Facilities:** **Services:** **Off-site:**

SWITZERLAND

Facilities shop shower electric points for razors electric points for caravans parking by tents permitted ompulsory separate car park **Services** café/restaurant bar Camping Gaz International gas other than Camping Gaz first aid facilities laundry **Leisure** swimming L-Lake P-Pool R-River S-Sea **Off-site** All facilities within 5km

KRUMMENAU ST-GALLEN

Adler

9643
☎ 071 9941030
dir: *On edge of village.*

Open: All Year. **Site:** 0.8HEC **Facilities:** **Services:**

MAMMERN THURGAU

Guldifuss

Guldifusstr 1, 8265
☎ 052 7411320 052 7411342
web: www.guldifuss.ch

A terraced site directly on the Untersee.

Open: Apr-Oct **Site:** 1.6HEC **Prices:** 34 **Facilities:** **Services:** **Leisure:** L **Off-site:**

OTTENBACH ZÜRICH

Reussbrücke

Muristr 32, 8913
☎ 044 7612022 044 7612042
e-mail: reussbruecke@tcs-ccz.ch
web: www.tcs-ccz.ch

By river of same name.

dir: *Access from Zürich via road 126 in SW direction, via Affoltern to Ottenbach.*

Open: Apr-Oct **Site:** 1.8HEC **Facilities:** **Services:** **Leisure:** P R **Off-site:**

SCHÖNENGRUND APPENZELL

Kronenfeld

Hauptstr 43, 9105
☎ 071 3611268 071 3611166
e-mail: camp.schoenengrund@bluewin.ch
web: www.schoenengrund.ch

A comfortable, partly residential site with well-defined touring pitches.

Open: All Year. **Site:** 1HEC **Facilities:** Play Area **Services:** **Off-site:** P

WAGENHAUSEN SCHAFFHAUSEN

Wagenhausen

Hauptstr 82, 8259
☎ 052 7414271 052 7414157
e-mail: campingwagenhausen@bluewin.ch
web: www.campingwagenhausen.ch

A delightful wooded location beside the River Rhine, close to the historic city Stein am Rhein.

Open: Apr-Oct **Site:** 4.5HEC **Prices:** 29-36 **Facilities:** Wi-fi (charged) Play Area **Services:** **Leisure:** P R

WALENSTADT ST-GALLEN

See-Camping

8880
☎ 081 7351896 081 7351841
e-mail: kontakt@see-camping.ch
web: www.see-camping.ch

A well-equipped family site with direct access to the Walensee.

dir: *Motorway Zürich-Chur exit.*

Open: May-Sep **Site:** 1.2HEC **Prices:** 35 **Facilities:** Play Area **Services:** **Leisure:** L **Off-site:** P

WILDBERG ZÜRICH

Weid

8489
☎ 052 3853388 052 3853477
e-mail: campingweid@bluewin.ch

On a terraced meadow in a very peaceful location surrounded by woods.

dir: *From Winterthur signs for Tösstal, right after spinning-mill in Turbenthal.*

Open: All Year. **Site:** 6.1HEC **Prices:** 24-26 **Facilities:** Play Area **Services:** **Off-site:** P R

WINTERTHUR ZÜRICH

Schützenweiher

Eichliwaldstr 4, 8400
☎ 052 2125260 052 2125260
e-mail: campingplatz@win.ch
web: www.campingwinterthur.ch

Site set amongst trees and shrubs and located on a lake.

dir: *To the left of the Schaffhausen road, near Schützenhaus restaurant.*

GPS: 47.5194, 8.7163

Open: All Year. **Site:** 0.8HEC **Prices:** 26.50-37 **Facilities:** Wi-fi Play Area **Services:** **Off-site:** P

NORTH WEST/CENTRAL

AESCHI BERN

Panorama

3703
☎ 033 2233656
e-mail: postmaster@camping-aeschi.ch
web: www.camping-aeschi.ch
A well kept campsite surrounded by trees and mountains, close to Lake Thun.
dir: *400m SE of Camping Club Bern.*
Open: 15 May-15 Oct **Site:** 1HEC **Facilities:** **Services:** **Off-site:** P

BRENZIKOFEN BERN

Wydeli

Wydeli 60, 3671
☎ 031 7711141
e-mail: info@camping-brenzikofen.ch
web: www.camping-brenzikofen.ch
Small site in pleasant countryside.
dir: *8km N of Thun.*
Open: May-Sep **Site:** 1.3HEC **Prices:** 23.60-34.30 Mobile home hire 450 **Facilities:** Play Area **Services:** **Leisure:** P **Off-site:**

BRUNNEN SCHWYZ

Hopfreben

6440
☎ 041 8201873 041 8201873
web: www.camping-brunnen.ch
On the right bank of the Muotta stream, 100m before it flows into the lake.
dir: *1km W.*
GPS: 46.9968, 8.5934
Open: 15 Apr-24 Sep **Site:** 1.5HEC **Prices:** 37-41 **Facilities:** Wi-fi Play Area **Services:** **Leisure:** L P R

COLOMBIER NEUCHÂTEL

Paradis-Plage

allée du Port 8, 2013
☎ 032 8412446 032 8414305
e-mail: info@paradisplage.ch
web: www.paradisplage.ch
A delightful setting beside Lake Neuchâtel with modern facilities.
Open: Mar-Oct **Site:** 4HEC **Prices:** 35-43 Mobile home hire 630-840 **Facilities:** Wi-fi Play Area **Services:** **Leisure:** L

ERLACH BERN

Mon Plaisir

3235
☎ 032 3381358 032 3381305
e-mail: info@camping24.ch
web: www.camping24.ch
Well-equipped site beside the lake.
Open: All Year. **Site:** 0.6HEC **Facilities:** **Services:** **Leisure:** L **Off-site:** P R

EUTHAL SCHWYZ

Euthal

Euthalerstr 10, 8844
☎ 079 5017673 055 4127673
e-mail: info@hotelposteuthal.ch
web: www.hotelposteuthal.ch
On the shore of the Sihlsee in a beautiful mountain setting.
Open: May-Oct **Site:** 1HEC **Prices:** 30.70-36.80 **Facilities:** Wi-fi Play Area **Services:** **Leisure:** L **Off-site:** P R

FLÜELEN URI

Urnersee

6454
☎ 041 8709222 041 8709216
e-mail: info@windsurfing-urnersee.ch
web: www.windsurfing-urnersee.ch
On level ground on the shore of the Vierwaldstättersee with plenty of sports facilities.
Open: 15 Apr-Oct **Site:** 4.5HEC **Facilities:** **Services:** **Leisure:** L R **Off-site:** P

FRUTIGEN BERN

Grassi

3714
☎ 033 6711149 033 6711380
e-mail: campinggrassi@bluewin.ch
web: www.camping-grassi.ch
Site scattered with fruit trees beside a farm on the River Engstilgern.
dir: *From the Haupstr, turn right at Simplon Hotel.*
Open: All Year. **Site:** 1.5HEC **Facilities:** **Services:** **Off-site:** P

GAMPELEN — BERN

Fanel

Seestr 50, 3236
032 3132333 032 3131407
e-mail: camping.gampelen@tcs.ch
web: www.campingtcs.ch
A level site on the shore of Lake Neuchâtel protected by trees and bushes. 2 dogs per pitch.
dir: *On A5 towards Gampelen.*
Open: Apr-2 Oct **Site:** 11.3HEC
Prices: 36.90-49.60 Mobile home hire 490-840
Facilities: Wi-fi (charged) Play Area
Services: **Leisure:** L **Off-site:** R

GISWIL — OBWALDEN

Giswil

Campingstr 11, 6074
041 6752355 041 6752351
e-mail: giswil@camping-international.ch
web: www.camping-international.ch
Open: Apr-20 Oct **Site:** 1.9HEC **Facilities:** **Services:** **Leisure:** L

GOLDAU — SCHWYZ

Bernerhöhe-Ranch

Gotthardstr 107, 6410
041 8551887 041 8554161
On the edge of a forest with a beautiful view of Lake Lauerz. Separate field for tents. Bar, café and restaurant open during summer.
dir: *1.5km SE & turn left.*
Open: All Year. **Site:** 2.5HEC **Facilities:** Play Area **Services:**

GRINDELWALD — BERN

Aspen

3818
033 8544000 033 8544004
e-mail: aspen@grindelwald.ch
web: www.hotel-aspen.ch
Sunny hill terraces.
Open: Jun-15 Oct **Site:** 2.5HEC **Facilities:** **Services:** **Off-site:** P R

GSTAAD — BERN

Bellerive

3780
033 7446330 033 7446345
e-mail: bellerive.camping@bluewin.ch
web: www.bellerivecamping.ch
Open: All Year. **Site:** 0.8HEC **Facilities:** **Services:** **Leisure:** R **Off-site:** P

INNERTKIRCHEN — BERN

Aareschlucht

Hauptstr 34, 3862
033 9715532 033 9715344
e-mail: campaareschlucht@bluewin.ch
web: www.camping-aareschlucht.ch
A beautiful Alpine location with superb mountain views.
Open: May-Oct **Site:** 0.5HEC **Facilities:** **Services:** **Off-site:** R

Grund

3862
033 9714409 033 9714767
e-mail: info@camping-grund.ch
web: www.camping-grund.ch
Next to farm on southern outskirts of village.
dir: *Turn S off main road in village centre at Hotel Urweider, 0.3km turn right.*
Open: All Year. **Site:** 120HEC **Facilities:** **Services:** **Off-site:** R

INTERLAKEN — BERN

Hobby 3

Lehnweg 16, 3800
033 8229652 033 8229657
e-mail: info@campinghobby.ch
web: www.campinghobby.ch
Family site in a quiet location with fine views of the surrounding mountains and within easy walking distance of Interlaken.
dir: *N8 exit 24 for Unterseen, follow camping sign No 3. Or N8 exit 24 (right lane in tunnel), turn right & follow camping sign No 3.*
GPS: 46.6855, 7.8311
Open: Apr-Sep **Site:** 1.5HEC **Prices:** 38.30-54.10
Facilities: Wi-fi Play Area **Services:**
Off-site: L P R

Site 6HEC (site size) grass sand stone little shade partly shaded mainly shaded bungalows for hire (static) caravans for hire tents for hire no dogs site fully accessible for wheelchairs
Prices amount quoted is per night, for 2 adults and car, plus tent or caravan. Mobile home hire is a weekly rate.

Jungfraublick

Gsteigstr 80, 3800
☎ 033 8224414 📠 033 8221619
e-mail: info@jungfraublick.ch
web: www.jungfraublick.ch

A family site with clean, modern facilities in a fine central location.

dir: *A8 exit 25, site 300m on left towards Matteu-Interlaken.*

GPS: 46.673, 7.866

Open: May-20 Sep **Site:** 1.3HEC **Prices:** 30-48
Facilities: Wi-fi **Services:**
Leisure: P **Off-site:** R

Jungfraucamp

Steindlerstr 60, 3800
☎ 033 8227107 📠 033 8225730
e-mail: info@jungfraucamp.ch
web: www.jungfraucamp.ch

Beautiful views of the Eiger, the Mönch and the Jungfrau.

dir: *Turn right at Unterseen, through Schulhaus & Steindlerstr to site.*

Open: 15 May-20 Sep **Site:** 2.5HEC **Prices:** 34.80-48.80
Facilities: **Services:**
Leisure: P **Off-site:** L R

Lazy Rancho 4

The Camping and Caravanning Club — The Friendly Club

Lehnweg 6, 3800
☎ 033 8228716 📠 033 8231920
e-mail: info@lazyrancho.ch
web: www.lazyrancho.ch

A family site in a magnificent position with views of the Eiger, Mönch and Jungfrau with good facilities.

C&CC Report *Dump the car! The great Swiss integrated boat, rail and bus transport system starts five minutes' walk from this quiet family site, with free bus and train transport throughout the Interlaken area. Cycling on Interlaken's speed-restricted roads is a dream. To many of us this region is classic Switzerland, and the camp site owners are a mine of local information, so take your pick of Alpine activities on land or water or in the air – or just look at it all.*

dir: *A8 exit Unterseen for Gunten, 2km turn right, left at Landhotel Golf.*

GPS: 46.6855, 7.8308

Open: 22 Apr-15 Oct **Site:** 16HEC **Facilities:** Wi-fi Play Area **Services:** **Leisure:** P
Off-site: L R

Manor Farm 1

3800
033 8222264 033 8222279
e-mail: manorfarm@swisscamps.ch
web: www.manorfarm.ch

A well-equipped site in a beautiful mountain setting.

dir: *A8 exit Gunten/Beatenberg, signed.*

Open: All Year. **Site:** 7.5HEC **Facilities:** **Services:** **Leisure:** L R **Off-site:** P

KANDERSTEG — BERN

Rendez-Vous

Hubleweg, 3718
033 6751534 033 6751737
e-mail: rendez-vous.camping@bluewin.ch
web: www.camping-kandersteg.ch

A delightful mountain setting with modern facilities.

dir: *0.75km E of town.*

GPS: 46.4967, 7.6836

Open: All Year. **Site:** 1HEC **Prices:** 27.80-39.30 **Facilities:** Wi-fi (charged) **Services:** **Off-site:** L P

KRATTIGEN — BERN

Stuhlegg

3704
033 6542723 033 6546703
e-mail: campstuhlegg@bluewin.ch
web: www.camping-stuhlegg.ch

On a quiet and sunny terrace in Krattigen, above Lake Thun, 5km from the motorway at Spiez. Its central position allows day excursions over the Bernese Oberland.

Open: Jan-Oct & Dec **Site:** 2.4HEC **Prices:** 30-40 **Facilities:** Wi-fi Play Area **Services:** **Leisure:** P **Off-site:** L

LANDERON, LE — NEUCHÂTEL

Peches

2525
032 7512900 032 7516354
e-mail: info@camping-lelanderon.ch
web: www.camping-lelanderon.ch

A small site at the meeting point of the River Thielle and the Lac de Bienne.

Open: Apr-15 Oct **Site:** 2.1HEC **Prices:** 37-41 Mobile home hire 615-790 **Facilities:** Wi-fi Play Area **Services:** **Off-site:** L P R

LAUTERBRUNNEN — BERN

Jungfrau

3822
033 8562010 033 8562020
e-mail: info@camping-jungfrau.ch
web: www.camping-jungfrau.ch

Widespread site in meadowland crossed by a stream. Partly divided into pitches.

dir: *Turn right 100m before church, campsite in 400m.*

Open: All Year. **Site:** 5HEC **Facilities:** **Off-site:** P

see advert on this page

Schützenbach

3822
033 8551268 033 8551275
e-mail: info@schuetzenbach.ch
web: www.schuetzenbach.ch

A fine Alpine location close to the main skiing areas, with a free ski bus in the winter, and 300m from the lake.

dir: *0.8km S of village on left of road to Stechelberg opp B50.*

Open: All Year. **Site:** 3HEC **Prices:** 33.80 **Facilities:** Wi-fi (charged) Play Area **Services:** **Off-site:** P R

Site 6HEC (site size) grass sand stone little shade partly shaded mainly shaded bungalows for hire (static) caravans for hire tents for hire no dogs site fully accessible for wheelchairs
Prices amount quoted is per night, for 2 adults and car, plus tent or caravan. Mobile home hire is a weekly rate.

LIGNIÈRES — NEUCHÂTEL

Fraso-Ranch

2523
032 7514616 032 7514614
e-mail: camping.fraso-ranch@bluewin.ch

A modern family site with good recreational facilities and a separate section for tourers.

dir: *NE of Lignières on Nods road, signed.*

Open: 24 Dec-Oct **Site:** 8.7HEC **Facilities:** **Services:** **Leisure:** P

LOCLE, LE — NEUCHÂTEL

Communal

Mont Pugin 6, 2400
032 9317493 032 9317408
e-mail: camping.lelocle@tcs.ch
web: www.campingtcs.ch

On a level meadow surrounded by woodland. Good recreational facilities.

dir: *S of town off La Sagne road.*

Open: 27 Apr-21 Oct **Site:** 1.2HEC **Facilities:** **Services:** **Leisure:** P **Off-site:**

LUNGERN — OBWALDEN

Obsee

6078
041 6781463 041 6782163
e-mail: camping@obsee.ch
web: www.obsee.ch

A beautiful setting between the lake and the mountains with facilities for water sports.

dir: *1km W.*

Open: All Year. **Site:** 1.5HEC **Prices:** 27.40-35.40 **Facilities:** Wi-fi Play Area **Services:** **Leisure:** L R **Off-site:** P

LUZERN (LUCERNE) — LUZERN

Steinibachried (TCS)

Horw, 6048
041 3403558 041 3403556
e-mail: camping.horw@tcs.ch
web: www.campingtcs.ch

A gently sloping meadow next to the football ground and the beach, separated from the lake by a wide belt of reeds.

dir: *3.2km S of Luzern.*

Open: Apr-2 Oct **Site:** 2HEC **Prices:** 36.70-45.30 Mobile home hire 490-840 **Facilities:** Wi-fi (charged) Play Area **Services:** **Off-site:** L P

MOSEN — LUZERN

Seeblick

6295
041 9171666 041 9171666
e-mail: infos@camping-seeblick.ch
web: www.camping-seeblick.ch

Set on two strips of land on edge of lake, divided by paths into several squares.

dir: *N on A26.*

GPS: 47.2447, 8.2244

Open: Mar-Oct **Site:** 2HEC **Prices:** 30.40 **Facilities:** Wi-fi (charged) Play Area **Services:** **Leisure:** L **Off-site:**

NOTTWIL — LUZERN

St Margrethen

6207
041 9371404
e-mail: st-margrethen@swisscamps.ch
web: www.camping-nottwil.ch

Natural meadowland with fruit trees, with own access to lake.

dir: *Off road to Sursee 400m NW of Nottwil, towards lake for 100m.*

GPS: 47.1429, 8.1239

Open: Apr-Oct **Site:** 1.4HEC **Prices:** 25.80-27.80 **Facilities:** Wi-fi (charged) Play Area **Services:** **Leisure:** L **Off-site:** L P

PRÊLES — BERN

Prêles

2515
032 3151716 032 3155160
e-mail: info@camping-jura.ch
web: www.camping-jura.ch

On a wooded plateau overlooking Lake Biel.

dir: *Off Biel-Neuchâtel road at Twann & signs for Prêles, through village, site on left.*

Open: Apr-Oct **Site:** 6HEC **Facilities:** **Services:** **Leisure:** P

SAANEN — BERN

Saanen beim Kappeli

Campingstr 15, 3792
033 7446191 033 7446184
e-mail: info@camping-saanen.ch
web: www.camping-saanen.ch

Set in a long meadow between the railway and the River Saane.

dir: *1km SE of town.*

Open: Jan-Oct & Dec **Site:** 0.8HEC **Facilities:** Wi-fi Play Area **Services:** **Leisure:** R **Off-site:** P

SACHSELN — OBWALDEN

Ewil

Brünigstr 258, 6072
☎ 041 6663270
e-mail: info@camping-ewil.ch
web: www.camping-ewil.ch

On a level meadow on the south-western shore of the Sarnensee.

dir: *W of Sachseln-Ewil road towards lake.*

Open: Apr-Sep **Site:** 1.5HEC **Prices:** 25.40-29.40 **Facilities:** Wi-fi **Services:** **Leisure:** L **Off-site:** P R

SEMPACH — LUZERN

Seeland

6204
☎ 041 4601466 041 4604766
e-mail: camping.sempach@tcs.ch
web: www.campingtcs.ch

Rectangular, level site on south-western shore of lake. Kids' club available during high season only.

dir: *0.7km S on Luzern road by lake.*

Open: Apr-2 Oct **Site:** 5.2HEC **Prices:** 44.60-57.60 **Facilities:** Wi-fi (charged) Kids' Club Play Area **Services:** **Leisure:** L

STECHELBERG — BERN

Breithorn

3824
☎ 033 8551225 033 8553561
e-mail: breithorn@stechelberg.ch

A beautiful location in the Lauterbrunnen Valley.

dir: *3km S of Lauterbrunnen.*

Open: All Year. **Site:** 1HEC **Prices:** 27.40-31.40 **Facilities:** **Services:**

SURSEE — LUZERN

Camping Sursee

Baselstr, Waldheim, 6210
☎ 041 9211161
e-mail: info@camping-sursee.ch
web: www.camping-sursee.ch

Natural and quiet site, 1.2km away from shopping centre and railway station.

dir: *A2 Basel-Gotthard exit 20 Sursee, direction Sursee, Basel 2 (blue signs at 4 rdbts).*

GPS: 47.175, 8.0869

Open: Apr-Sep **Site:** 1.7HEC **Prices:** 22.60-24.60 Mobile home hire 250-350 **Facilities:** Wi-fi (charged) Play Area **Services:** **Off-site:** L P

VITZNAU — LUZERN

Vitznau

The Camping and Caravanning Club — The Friendly Club

6354
☎ 041 3971280 041 3972457
e-mail: info@camping.vitznau.ch
web: www.camping-vitznau.ch

Well-tended terraced site, in lovely countryside with fine views of lake.

C&CC Report *The wonderful combination of a spectacular setting, a very friendly welcome, superb travel deals and a short hop to Lucerne, constitutes the recipe for a relaxing and invigorating holiday. Miles of walking are possible on Mount Rigi, after the ride up Europe's first rack railway, while the world's steepest cog railway runs up Mount Pilatus.*

dir: *From N turn towards mountain at church & signed.*

Open: Apr-Oct **Site:** 1.8HEC **Facilities:** **Services:** **Leisure:** P **Off-site:** L

WABERN — BERN

SC Eichholz

Strandweg 49, 3084
☎ 031 9612602 031 9613526
e-mail: info@campingeichholz.ch
web: www.campingeichholz.ch

Set in municipal parkland with a separate section for caravans.

dir: *Approach via Gossetstr & track beside river.*

GPS: 46.9330, 7.4558

Open: 20 Apr-Sep **Site:** 2HEC **Prices:** 29.50-40.50 **Facilities:** Wi-fi (charged) Play Area **Services:** **Leisure:** R S **Off-site:** P

WILDERSWIL — BERN

Oberei

Obereigasse 9, 3812
☎ 033 8221335 033 8221335
e-mail: oberei8@swisscamps.ch
web: www.campingwilderswil.ch

A peaceful site in a picturesque village with fine views of the Jungfrau and surrounding mountains. There are good facilities. Well situated for walks and excursions to the mountains by train, 6 minutes away.

Open: May-15 Oct **Site:** 0.55HEC **Prices:** 33.80-37.80 **Facilities:** Play Area **Services:** **Off-site:** L P R

ZUG — ZUG

Zugersee

Chamer Fussweg 36, 6300

041 7418422 041 7418430

e-mail: camping.zug@tcs.ch

web: www.campingtcs.ch

Pleasant location with beautiful view of Lake Zug and the surrounding mountains. Much traffic on the railway that passes the site.

dir: *1km NW by lake.*

Open: Apr-3 Oct **Site:** 1.1HEC **Facilities:** **Services:** **Leisure:** L R **Off-site:**

EAST

ANDEER — GRAUBÜNDEN

Sut Baselgia

7440

081 6611453 081 6307077

e-mail: camping.andeer@bluewin.ch

web: www.campingandeer.ch

A pleasant, peaceful setting north towards Chur.

Open: All Year. **Site:** 1.2HEC **Prices:** 36.20 **Facilities:** Wi-fi **Services:** **Off-site:** P

AROSA — GRAUBÜNDEN

Arosa Tourismus

7050

081 3771745 081 3773005

web: www.arosa.ch

Open: All Year. **Site:** 0.6HEC **Facilities:** **Services:** **Off-site:** L P

LENZ — GRAUBÜNDEN

St Cassian

7083

081 3842472 081 3842489

e-mail: info@st-cassian.ch

web: www.st-cassian.ch

A level, shady site in a beautiful location at an altitude of 1415m above sea level. There are good facilities and the site is 1km from the town.

dir: *Motorway exit Chur-Süd, signs for Lenzerheide/St Moritz, up good mountain road.*

Open: All Year. **Site:** 25HEC **Prices:** 33.60-38.60 **Facilities:** **Services:** **Off-site:**

MÜSTAIR — GRAUBÜNDEN

Clenga

7537

081 8585410 081 8585422

e-mail: clenga@campclenga.ch

web: www.campclenga.ch

Next to small river near the Italian frontier.

Open: May-20 Oct **Site:** 1.5HEC **Facilities:** **Services:** **Leisure:** R

POSCHIAVO — GRAUBÜNDEN

Boomerang

7745

081 8440713 081 8441575

e-mail: info@camping-boomerang.ch

web: www.camping-boomerang.ch

A quiet setting in the heart of green countryside of the Rhaetian Alps. The site is equipped with all modern comforts.

dir: *2km SE.*

GPS: 46.3099, 10.0747

Open: All Year. **Site:** 1.5HEC **Prices:** 32-43 **Facilities:** Wi-fi Play Area **Services:** **Off-site:** L P R

SAMEDAN — GRAUBÜNDEN

Punt Muragl

via da Puntraschigna 56, 7503

081 8428197 081 8428197

e-mail: camping.samedan@tcs.ch

web: www.campingtcs.ch

A summer and winter site in a pleasant alpine setting.

dir: *Near Bernina railway halt, to right of fork of roads Samedan & Celerina/Schlarigna to Pontresina.*

Open: Jun-3 Oct, Dec-15 Apr **Site:** 2HEC **Facilities:** **Services:** **Off-site:** L

SPLÜGEN — GRAUBÜNDEN

Sand

7435

081 6641476 081 6641460

e-mail: camping@splugen.ch

web: www.campingsplugen.ch

On the River Hinterrhein. Ideal starting point for skiing, cross country skiing or, throughout the year, hiking.

dir: *Off main road in village & signed.*

GPS: 46.5491, 9.3141

Open: All Year. **Site:** 0.8HEC **Prices:** 43-48 **Facilities:** Wi-fi Play Area **Services:** **Leisure:** R

SWITZERLAND

Facilities shop shower electric points for razors electric points for caravans parking by tents permitted compulsory separate car park **Services** café/restaurant bar Camping Gaz International gas other than Camping Gaz first aid facilities laundry **Leisure** swimming L-Lake P-Pool R-River S-Sea **Off-site** All facilities within 5km

SUSCH — GRAUBÜNDEN

Muglinas

7542
081 8561927 081 8622860
dir: *200m W of town.*

Open: 15 May-30 Oct **Site:** 1HEC **Facilities:** **Services:** **Leisure:** R **Off-site:**

THUSIS — GRAUBÜNDEN

Viamala

7430
081 6512472 081 6512472
e-mail: info@camping-thusis.ch
web: www.camping-thusis.ch

Pleasant wooded surroundings near the River Hinterrhein and close to the beautiful Viamala gorge.

dir: *NE towards Chur.*

Open: May-Sep **Site:** 4.5HEC **Facilities:** **Services:** **Off-site:** P R

TSCHIERV — GRAUBÜNDEN

Staila

Chasa Maruya, 7532
081 8585628
e-mail: maruya@gmx.net
web: www.muenstertal.ch

Site in the village behind the Sternen Hotel.

dir: *Between Ofen Pass & Santa Maria.*

Open: Jul-Aug **Site:** 1HEC **Prices:** 30 **Facilities:** Play Area **Services:** **Leisure:** P R

SOUTH

AGNO — TICINO

Eurocampo

via Molinazzo 9, 6982
091 6052114 091 6053187
e-mail: eurocampo@ticino.com
web: www.eurocampo.ch

Part of site is near its own sandy beach and is divided by groups of trees.

dir: *0.6km E on Lugano-Ponte Tresa road, opp Aeroport sign & MIGROS building.*

Open: Apr-Oct **Site:** 6.5HEC **Prices:** 30-35 **Facilities:** **Services:** **Leisure:** L R

CUGNASCO — TICINO

Park-Camping Riarena

6516
091 8591688 091 8592885
e-mail: camping.riarena@bluewin.ch
web: www.camping-riarena.ch

Beautiful park-like family site in level, natural woodland. All facilities are well-maintained and Lake Maggiore is within easy reach.

dir: *1.5km NW. Off road 13 at fuel station 9km NE of Locarno & continue 0.5km.*

Open: Mar-20 Oct **Site:** 3.2HEC **Facilities:** **Services:** **Leisure:** P **Off-site:** R

GORDEVIO — TICINO

Bellariva

6672
091 7531444 091 7531764
e-mail: camping.gordevio@tcs.ch
web: www.campingtcs.ch

A quiet location between the road and the River Maggia.

Open: Apr-9 Oct **Site:** 2.5HEC **Prices:** 43.50-55.50 Mobile home hire 595-980 **Facilities:** Wi-fi (charged) Play Area **Services:** **Leisure:** P R

LOCARNO — TICINO

Delta

via Respini 7, 6600
091 7516081 091 7512243
e-mail: info@campingdelta.com
web: www.campingdelta.com

A beautiful, well-equipped and well-organised site at Lake Maggiore.

dir: *2km from city.*

Open: Mar-Oct **Site:** 5.4HEC **Prices:** 49-89 Mobile home hire 588-1036 **Facilities:** Wi-fi (charged) Kids' Club Play Area **Services:** **Leisure:** L R **Off-site:** P

MOLINAZZO DI MONTEGGIO — TICINO

Tresiana

6995

091 6083342 · 091 6083142

e-mail: info@camping-tresiana

web: www.camping-tresiana.ch

A family site on meadowland with trees on riverbank.

dir: *Right after bridge in Ponte Tresa, site 5km.*

Open: 16 Apr-23 Oct **Site:** 1.5HEC **Prices:** 26.50-46.50 Mobile home hire 350-770 **Facilities:** Wi-fi (charged) **Services:** **Leisure:** P R **Off-site:** L

TENERO — TICINO

Campofelice

via alle Brere 7, 6598

091 7451417 · 091 7451888

e-mail: camping@campofelice.ch

web: www.campofelice.ch

A beautifully situated and extensive site, divided into pitches and crossed by asphalt drives.

dir: *1.9km S, signed.*

GPS: 46.1688, 8.8558

Open: 24 Mar-Oct **Site:** 15HEC **Facilities:** Wi-fi (charged) Play Area **Services:** **Leisure:** L R **Off-site:** P

Lido Mappo

via Mappo, 6598

091 7451437 · 091 7454808

e-mail: camping@lidomappo.ch

web: www.lidomappo.ch

A well-appointed site, beautifully situated by a lake. Teenagers not accepted on their own. Minimum stay, one week in July and August.

dir: *A2 exit for Bellinzona Sud, towards Locarno & exit for Tenero, site signed.*

GPS: 46.1769, 8.8419

Open: Apr-Oct **Site:** 6.5HEC **Prices:** 36-93 **Facilities:** Wi-fi Play Area **Services:** **Leisure:** L **Off-site:** P R

Tamaro

via Mappo 32, 6598

091 7452161 · 091 7456636

e-mail: info@campingtamaro.ch

web: www.campingtamaro.ch

Well-equipped site with direct access to the lake. Groups of young persons must be accompanied by adults.

dir: *4km from Locarno, signed from motorway.*

Open: 5 Mar-Oct **Site:** 5HEC **Facilities:** **Services:** **Leisure:** L P

SOUTH WEST

AGARN — VALAIS

Gemmi

Briannenstr 4, 3952

027 4731154 · 027 4734295

e-mail: info@campinggemmi.ch

web: www.campinggemmi.ch

A very pleasant location on the outskirts of the town, with outstanding views of the surrounding mountains. There are clean, modern facilities and individual bathrooms are available for weekly hire.

dir: *A9 exit Agarn, signed.*

Open: 17 Apr-16 Oct **Site:** 0.9HEC **Facilities:** **Services:** **Off-site:** P R

AROLLA — VALAIS

Petit Praz

1986

027 2832295

e-mail: camping@arolla.com

web: www.camping-arolla.com

An imposing mountain setting.

Open: Jun-20 Sep **Site:** 1HEC **Prices:** 25-28 **Facilities:** Wi-fi **Services:** **Off-site:**

BALLENS — VAUD

Bois Gentil

1144

021 8095120 · 021 8095120

e-mail: py30@bluewin.ch

dir: *200m S of station*

Open: Apr-Oct **Site:** 2.5HEC **Prices:** 21 **Facilities:** **Services:** **Leisure:** P

BOUVERET, LE — VALAIS

Rive Bleue Camping

130 rte de la Plage, 1897

024 4812161 · 024 4812108

e-mail: info@camping-rive-bleue.ch

web: www.camping-rive-bleue.ch

Set beside a lake with a natural sandy beach and modern facilities.

dir: *Off A37 to Monthey in SW outskirts of Bouveret & continue NE for 0.8km.*

Open: Apr-17 Oct **Site:** 3HEC **Prices:** 32-39 **Facilities:** **Services:** **Leisure:** L P **Off-site:** R

BULLET — VAUD

Cluds

1453
024 4541440 024 4541440
e-mail: vd28@campings-ccyverdon.ch
web: www.campings-ccyverdon.ch
A beautiful mountain setting among pine trees.

dir: *1.5km NE.*

Open: All Year. **Site:** 1.2HEC **Prices:** 28-30 Mobile home hire 300-490 **Facilities:** Wi-fi (charged) Play Area **Services:** **Off-site:**

CHÂTEAU-D'OEX — VAUD

Berceau

1837
026 9246234 026 9242526
e-mail: info@chateaudoex.ch
web: www.chateau-doex.ch
On level strip of grass between the mountain and the river bank.

dir: *1km SE at junct roads 77 & 76.*

Open: All Year. **Site:** 1HEC **Facilities:** **Services:** **Leisure:** P R **Off-site:**

CHÂTEL-ST-DENIS — FRIBOURG

Bivouac

rte des Paccots, 1618
021 9487849 021 9487849
e-mail: info@le-bivouac.ch
web: www.le-bivouac.ch
Beautiful views of the rolling Swiss countryside. Various sports and leisure activities.

dir: *Turn E in Chatel-St Denis & continue 2km.*

Open: Apr-Sep **Site:** 2HEC **Facilities:** **Services:** **Leisure:** P R

CHESSEL — VAUD

Grand Bois

1846
024 4814225 024 4815113
e-mail: au.grand-bois@bluewin.ch
web: www.augrandbois.ch
On a level meadow close to a canal, only a few kilometres from Lake Geneva.

dir: *N of town towards lake.*

GPS: 46.3561, 6.8991

Open: All Year. **Site:** 4HEC **Prices:** 14-19 Mobile home hire 450-600 **Facilities:** Wi-fi **Services:** **Leisure:** P R **Off-site:** L

CUDREFIN — VAUD

Chablais

1588
026 6773277
e-mail: camping@cudrefin.ch
web: www.cudrefin.ch
Site by the lake, 0.5km from the town centre.

Open: 15 Mar-Oct **Site:** 6HEC **Facilities:** **Services:** **Leisure:** L **Off-site:** R

DÜDINGEN — FRIBOURG

Schiffenensee

3186
026 4931917
e-mail: info@camping-schiffenen.ch
web: www.camping-schiffenen.ch
dir: *A12 exit Düdingen & N towards Murten.*

Open: Apr-Oct **Site:** 9HEC **Facilities:** **Services:** **Leisure:** L P **Off-site:**

EVOLÈNE — VALAIS

Evolène

1983
027 2831144 027 2833255
e-mail: info@camping-evolene.ch
web: www.camping-evolene.ch
On a level meadow with fine views of the surrounding mountains.

dir: *200m from town.*

Open: All Year. **Site:** 10HEC **Facilities:** **Services:** **Leisure:** P **Off-site:** R

FOULY, LA — VALAIS

Glaciers

1944
027 7831826 027 7833605
e-mail: info@camping-glaciers.ch
web: www.camping-glaciers.ch
At end of village in a beautiful Alpine location with fine views of the surrounding mountains.

Open: 15 May-Sep **Site:** 7HEC **Facilities:** **Services:** **Off-site:**

GRANDSON — VAUD

Pécos

VD24, 1422
☎ 024 4454969 🖷 024 4462904
e-mail: vd24@campings-ccyverdon.ch
web: www.campings-ccyverdon.ch

Shaded by trees and with access to a lake, where water sports are available.

dir: *400m SW of railway station between railway & lake.*

Open: Apr-Sep **Site:** 2HEC **Facilities:** **Services:** **Leisure:** L

GUMEFENS — FRIBOURG

Camping du Lac

1643
☎ 026 9152162 🖷 026 9152168
e-mail: info@campingdulac-gruyere.ch
web: www.campingdulac-gruyere.ch

On the borders of the lake.

GPS: 46.6756, 7.085

Open: Jul-Aug & wknds May-Jun & Sep **Site:** 1.5HEC **Prices:** 32.70 **Facilities:** Wi-fi **Services:** **Leisure:** L

LAUSANNE — VAUD

Vidy

chemin du Camping 3, 1007
☎ 021 6225000 🖷 021 6225001
e-mail: info@clv.ch
web: www.clv.ch

A delightful location among trees and flowerbeds overlooking Lac Léman.

GPS: 46.5176, 6.5976

Open: All Year. **Site:** 4.5HEC **Facilities:** Wi-fi (charged) Play Area **Services:** **Leisure:** L P

LEYSIN — VAUD

Soleil

1854
☎ 024 4943939
e-mail: info@camping-leysin.ch
web: www.camping-leysin.ch

A picturesque Alpine setting.

dir: *Enter village & left at fuel station, site 400m.*

Open: Dec-Oct **Site:** 1.1HEC **Facilities:** **Services:** **Off-site:** P

MORGINS — VALAIS

Morgins

1875
☎ 024 4772361 🖷 024 4773708
e-mail: touristoffice@morgins.ch
web: www.morgins.ch

Terraced site below a pine forest.

dir: *Left at end of village towards Pas de Morgins near Swiss customs.*

Open: All Year. **Site:** 1.3HEC **Facilities:** **Services:** **Off-site:** P R

RARON — VALAIS

Santa Monica

Kantonsstr 56, 3942
☎ 027 9342424 🖷 027 9342450
e-mail: info@santa-monica.ch
web: www.santa-monica.ch

Open: Apr-Oct **Site:** 4HEC **Facilities:** **Services:** **Leisure:** P **Off-site:** L R

RECKINGEN — VALAIS

Residence Camping Augenstern

3998
☎ 027 9731395 🖷 027 9732677
e-mail: info@campingaugenstern.ch
web: www.campingaugenstern.ch

On an alpine meadow close to the River Rhône.

dir: *400m S on bank of Rhône.*

GPS: 46.465, 8.245

Site: 3HEC **Prices:** 32.70-36.70 **Facilities:** Wi-fi (charged) **Services:** **Leisure:** R **Off-site:** P R

RIED-BRIG — VALAIS

Tropic

3911
☎ 027 9232537

In the sunny Valais, Brig and surrounding area offers a wide variety of sporting and cultural events, activities and recreational opportunities.

dir: *On left of Simplon road near entrance to village. 3km above Brig.*

Open: Jun-Aug **Site:** 1.5HEC **Facilities:** **Services:** **Off-site:**

SWITZERLAND

SAAS-GRUND VALAIS

Kapellenweg

3910
☎ 027 9574997 027 9573316
e-mail: camping@kapellenweg.ch
web: www.kapellenweg.ch
On a level meadow in a picturesque mountain setting in the Saas Valley. Modern facilities.
dir: *Over bridge & right towards Saas-Almagell.*
Open: 15 May-15 Oct **Site:** 1.46HEC **Prices:** 25 Mobile home hire 252.50 **Facilities:** Wi-fi (charged) **Services:** **Leisure:** R **Off-site:**

SALGESCH VALAIS

Swiss Plage

3970
☎ 027 4816023 027 4813215
e-mail: info@swissplage.ch
web: swissplage.ch
Situated beside a small lake and surrounded by vineyards. Good recreational facilities.
Open: Etr-1 Nov **Site:** 10HEC **Facilities:** **Services:** **Leisure:** L R **Off-site:** P

SATIGNY GENÈVE

Bois-de-Bay

1242
☎ 022 3410505 022 3410606
e-mail: boisdebay@sccv.ch
web: www.sccv.ch
dir: *Off A1 at Bernex & signed.*
Open: 17 Jan-10 Dec **Site:** 2.8HEC **Prices:** 29-37.50 Mobile home hire 315 **Facilities:** Wi-fi (charged) Play Area **Services:**

SIERRE VALAIS

Bois de Finges

3960
☎ 027 4550284 027 4553351
e-mail: camping.sierre@tcs.ch
web: www.campingtcs.ch
Situated in a pine forest with well-defined pitches set on terraces.
dir: *Motorway exit Sierre-Ouest for Sierre.*
Open: 24 Apr-27 Sep **Site:** 5HEC **Facilities:** **Services:** **Leisure:** P **Off-site:** L R

SORENS FRIBOURG

Forêt

rte Principale 271, 1642
☎ 026 9151882 026 9150363
e-mail: info@camping-la-foret.ch
web: www.camping-la-foret.ch
A pleasant site on a level meadow surrounded by woodland.
dir: *Off A12 to village.*
Open: All Year. **Site:** 4HEC **Prices:** 25.70 **Facilities:** Play Area **Services:** **Leisure:** P

SUSTEN VALAIS

Bella-Tola

Waldstr 57, 3952
☎ 027 4731491 027 4733641
e-mail: info@bella-tola.ch
web: www.bella-tola.ch
A peaceful, terraced site at an altitude of 750m, shielded by a belt of woodland. Good, clean modern facilities.
dir: *Off A9, 2km from village.*
Open: 26 Apr-26 Oct **Site:** 3.6HEC **Facilities:** **Services:** **Leisure:** P

ULRICHEN VALAIS

Nufenen

3988
☎ 027 9731437
e-mail: info@camping-nufenen.ch
web: www.camping-nufenen.ch
Family friendly, secluded campsite, 1km south-east of Ulrichen.
dir: *1km SE to right of road to Nufenen Pass.*
Open: Jun-Sep **Site:** 8HEC **Facilities:** **Services:** **Leisure:** R **Off-site:** L

VALLORBE VAUD

Pré sous Ville

1337
☎ 021 8432309
A wooded riverside location. The neighbouring swimming pool is available free to campers.
dir: *On left bank of River Orbe.*
Open: mid Apr-mid Oct **Site:** 1HEC **Facilities:** **Services:** **Leisure:** P **Off-site:** R

VERS-L'ÉGLISE VAUD

Murée

1864
079 4019915
e-mail: dagonch@bluewinch.ch
web: www.camping-caravaningvd.com
Partially terraced site by a stream.

dir: *N9 exit Aigle-Aprés, take direction Aigle-Le Supey. 8km in direction of Les Diablerets/Col du Pillon at entrance to village, site signed on right.*

GPS: 46.3550, 7.1266

Open: All Year. **Site:** 1.1HEC **Prices:** 27.40-28.40 **Facilities:** **Services:** **Leisure:** R **Off-site:**

VÉSENAZ GENÈVE

Pointe á la Bise

1222
022 7521296 022 7523767
e-mail: camping.geneve@tcs.ch
web: www.campingtcs.ch
A pleasant wooded setting on the shore of Lake Léman.

dir: *NE between Vésenaz & Collonge-Bellerive.*

Open: Apr-2 Oct **Site:** 3.2HEC **Prices:** 43-53.70 **Facilities:** Wi-fi (charged) Play Area **Services:** **Leisure:** L P

VÉTROZ VALAIS

Botza

rte du Camping 1, 1963
027 3461940 027 3462535
e-mail: info@botza.ch
web: www.botza.ch
On a level meadow with pitches divided by hedges. Fine panoramic views and good leisure facilities.

GPS: 46.2058, 7.2786

Open: All Year. **Site:** 3HEC **Prices:** 21.40-42.20 **Facilities:** Wi-fi Kids' Club Play Area **Services:** **Leisure:** P

YVONAND VAUD

VD 8 Pointe D'Yvonand

1462
024 4301655 024 4302463
e-mail: vd8@campings-ccyverdon.ch
web: www.campings-ccyverdon.ch
Site borders Lake Neuchâtel with a private beach 1km away. Boat moorings, private jetty and boat hire.

dir: *3km W, signed.*

Open: Apr-Sep **Site:** 5HEC **Facilities:** **Services:** **Leisure:** L

SWITZERLAND

Turkey

Accident & Emergency
Police 155; Medical 112; Fire 110
Gendarmerie 156; Coast Guard 158

Drinking & Driving
If the level of alcohol in the bloodstream is 0.05% or more, penalties are severe. For drivers of cars with caravans or trailers the alcohol level in the bloodstream is 0%.

Driving Licence
The minimum age at which a UK licence holder may drive a temporarily imported car and/or motorcycle 18. UK driving licence valid for 90 days; licences that do not incorporate a photograph must be accompanied by an International Driving Permit (IDP).

Fines
On-the-spot. Vehicles may be towed away if causing an obstruction.

Lights
Dipped headlights should be used in poor daytime visibility, and after sunset in built up areas.

Motorcycles
Wearing of crash helmets compulsory.

Motor Insurance
Third party insurance compulsory. Foreign insurance e.g. UK insurance is recognised in the European part of Turkey, check to ensure your policy covers Turkey.
Visiting motorists driving vehicles registered in the UK may use a valid Green Card when driving in Turkey. The Green Card must cover the whole of Turkey, i.e. both the European Part and the Asian part (Anatolia).
Visiting motorists who are not in possession of a valid Green Card or who are not in possession of a valid UK insurance policy (validated for the whole of Turkey) must take out short term insurance at the border or TTOK offices.

Passengers & Children
Child under 12 cannot travel as a front seat passenger.

Seat Belts
Compulsory for front seat occupants to wear seat belts, if fitted. Compulsory for rear seat passengers to wear seat belts outside built-up areas

Speed Limits
Unless otherwise signed

Private vehicles without trailers	
Built-up areas	50km/h
Outside built-up areas	90km/h
Motorways	120km/h
Minimum speed on motorways	40km/h

Speed limits are 10km/h less if the car has a trailer.

Motorcycles	
Outside built-up	70km/h
Motorways	80km/h
Vehicle with trailers	
Built up areas	40km/h
Outside built-up areas	80km/h
Motorways	110km/h
Motorhome with trailer	
Built up areas	40km/h
Outside built-up areas	70km/h
Motorways	80km/h

Additional Information
Compulsory equipment in Turkey:

- First aid kit – Not required for two wheeled vehicles
- Fire extinguisher – Not required for two wheeled vehicles
- Warning triangle – two required

Other rules/requirements in Turkey:
The use of the horn is generally prohibited in towns between 2200 hours until sunrise.
The use of spiked tyres is prohibited.
It is recommended that winter tyres are used in snowy areas and snow chains are carried.
In the event of an accident it is compulsory for the police to be called and a report obtained.

Tolls Currency Turkish Lire (TRY)	Car	Car Towing Caravan/Trailer
021 (E90) Pozanti - Tarus	3.50TRY	7.75TRY
03 (E80) Edirne - Istanbul	8.50TRY	15.25TRY
031 (E87) Izmir - Aydin	3.50TRY	6.50TRY
032 (E881) Izmir - Cesme	2.25TRY	5.00TRY
04 (E80/E89) Istanbul - Ankara	17.00TRY	30.50TRY
052 (E90) Adana - Sanliurfa	10.50TRY	20.50TRY
053 (E91) Ceyhan - Iskenderun	3.50TRY	7.00TRY
Bridges and Tunnels		
Bosphorus and Fatih Sultan Mehmet Bridge Istanbul on E80 (Eastbound only)	3.75TRY	23.50TRY

Please note: Although the official currency of Turkey is the Turkish lira, the campsites featured in this guide have quoted their prices in Euros.

BODRUM — AEGEAN

Zetas Camping Gumbet

Mahallesi Etem Kaptan 10, 48400
☎ 0252 3192231 🖷 0252 3195741
e-mail: info@zetastourism.com
web: www.zetastourism.com

Located in one of the most picturesque areas of Turkey with a scenic coastline and a picturesque harbour. The campsite is located directly on Gumbet Beach.

dir: *3km from centre of Bodrum.*

Open: All Year. **Site:** 1.2HEC **Prices:** 10 **Facilities:** Wi-fi Play Area **Services:** **Leisure:** S

BOGAZKALE — CENTRAL ANATOLIA

Asikoglu Tourist Camp

Ankara Sungurlu Asfaiti, 19310
☎ 0364 4522004 🖷 0364 4522171
e-mail: info@hattusas.com
web: www.hattusas.com

Site in an historic location dating back to the Bronze Age.

dir: *250km from Ankaran. From Corum towards Bogazkale, campsite on right at 1st crossing in Bogazkale.*

Open: 15 Mar-15 Nov **Site:** **Facilities:** **Services:** **Leisure:** L **Off-site:**

GÖREME — CENTRAL ANATOLIA

Goreme Panorama Teras

50500
☎ 0384 2712352 🖷 0384 2712632
e-mail: panoramacamping@hotmail.com
web: www.goremepanoramacamping.com

A family-owned site with 24hr access in the centre of Cappadocia. All local amenities and sightseeing options may be arranged at preferential rates. Medical assistance on call.

dir: *250km from Ankaran. Nevcehir-Göreme road, campsite on left entering Göreme.*

Open: All Year. **Site:** 1HEC **Facilities:** Wi-fi **Services:** **Leisure:** P **Off-site:**

SELCUK — AEGEAN

Dereli

Pamucak, 35920
☎ 0232 8931205 🖷 0232 8931203
e-mail: derelipamucak@superonline.com
web: www.dereli-ephesus.com

A short distance from Ephesus overlooking a sandy beach and shaded by eucalyptus trees.

dir: *In Selcuk towards Kusadasi, at junct straight ahead to Pamucak, campsite signed before left turn.*

Open: Mar-Oct **Site:** **Prices:** 18 **Facilities:** **Services:** **Leisure:** S

SULTANHANI — CENTRAL ANATOLIA

Kervan

Sultanhani Kasabi, 68190
☎ 0382 2422325 🖷 0382 2422411
e-mail: kervancamping@mynet.com
web: www.kervancamping.com

Family campsite situated in the middle of the flat plain between Konya and Aksaray at a former oasis on the ancient Silk Road.

dir: *Route 300 from Aksaray to Konya. 39km after Aksaray left at exit Sultanhani, follow signs to campsite on right.*

Open: Mar-Nov **Site:** 4.1HEC **Prices:** 12 **Facilities:** **Services:** **Off-site:**

TURKEY

Country Map Section

AUSTRIA

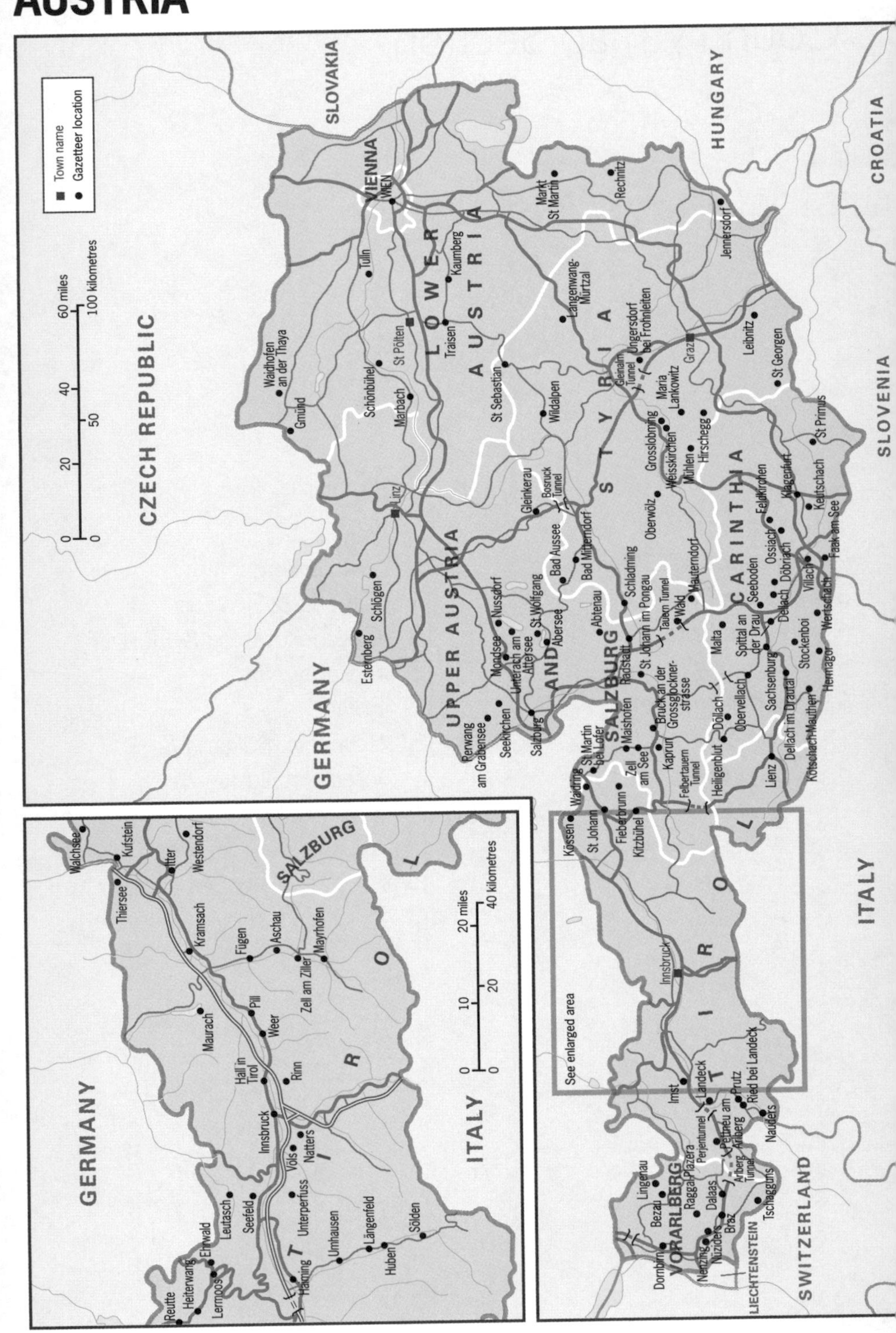

Town name
Gazetteer location
0 20 40 60 miles
0 50 100 kilometres
CZECH REPUBLIC
SLOVAKIA
HUNGARY
CROATIA
SLOVENIA
ITALY
SWITZERLAND
LIECHTENSTEIN
GERMANY
VIENNA
WIEN
LOWER AUSTRIA
UPPER AUSTRIA
STYRIA
CARINTHIA
SALZBURG
LAND
TIROL
VORARLBERG
Waidhofen an der Thaya
Gmünd
Tulln
St Pölten
Schönbühel
Marbach
Traisen
Kaumberg
Markt St Martin
Rechnitz
Jennersdorf
Langenwang-Mürztal
Ungersdorf bei Frohnleiten
Graz
Leibnitz
St Georgen
Gleinalm Tunnel
Maria Lankowitz
Hirschegg
Mühlen
Grosslobming
Weisskirchen
St Sebastian
Wildalpen
Gleinkerau
Bosruck Tunnel
Linz
Schlögen
Esternberg
Nussdorf
Mondsee
Unterach am Attersee
St Wolfgang
Abersee
Bad Aussee
Bad Mitterndorf
Schladming
Oberwölz
Abtenau
St Johann im Pongau
Tauern Tunnel
Wald
Mauterndorf
Radstadt
Perwang am Grabensee
Seekirchen
Salzburg
Maishofen
Zell am See
Bruck an der Grossglockner-strasse
Kaprun
St Martin bei Lofer
Waidring
Kössen
St Johann
Fieberbrunn
Kitzbühel
Felbertauern Tunnel
Heiligenblut
Döllach
Obervellach
Malta
Spittal an der Drau
Seeboden
Dellach
Döbriach
Ossiach
Feldkirchen
Klagenfurt
St Primus
Keutschach
Faak am See
Villach
Wertschach
Stockenboi
Hermagor
Sachsenburg
Dellach im Drautal
Kötschach-Mauthen
Lienz
Innsbruck
See enlarged area
Imst
Landeck
Prutz
Ried bei Landeck
Pettneu am Arlberg
Perjentunnel
Arlberg Tunnel
Nauders
Lingenau
Bezau
Raggal-Plazera
Dalaas
Tschagguns
Bürs
Nüziders
Nenzing
Dornbirn
Walchsee
Kufstein
Thiersee
Itter
Westendorf
Kramsach
Fügen
Aschau
Mayrhofen
Zell am Ziller
Maurach
Pill
Weer
Hall in Tirol
Rinn
Völs
Natters
Unterperfuss
Seefeld
Leutasch
Ehrwald
Heiterwang
Lermoos
Reutte
Haiming
Umhausen
Längenfeld
Huben
Sölden
0 10 20 miles
0 20 40 kilometres

BELGIUM & LUXEMBOURG

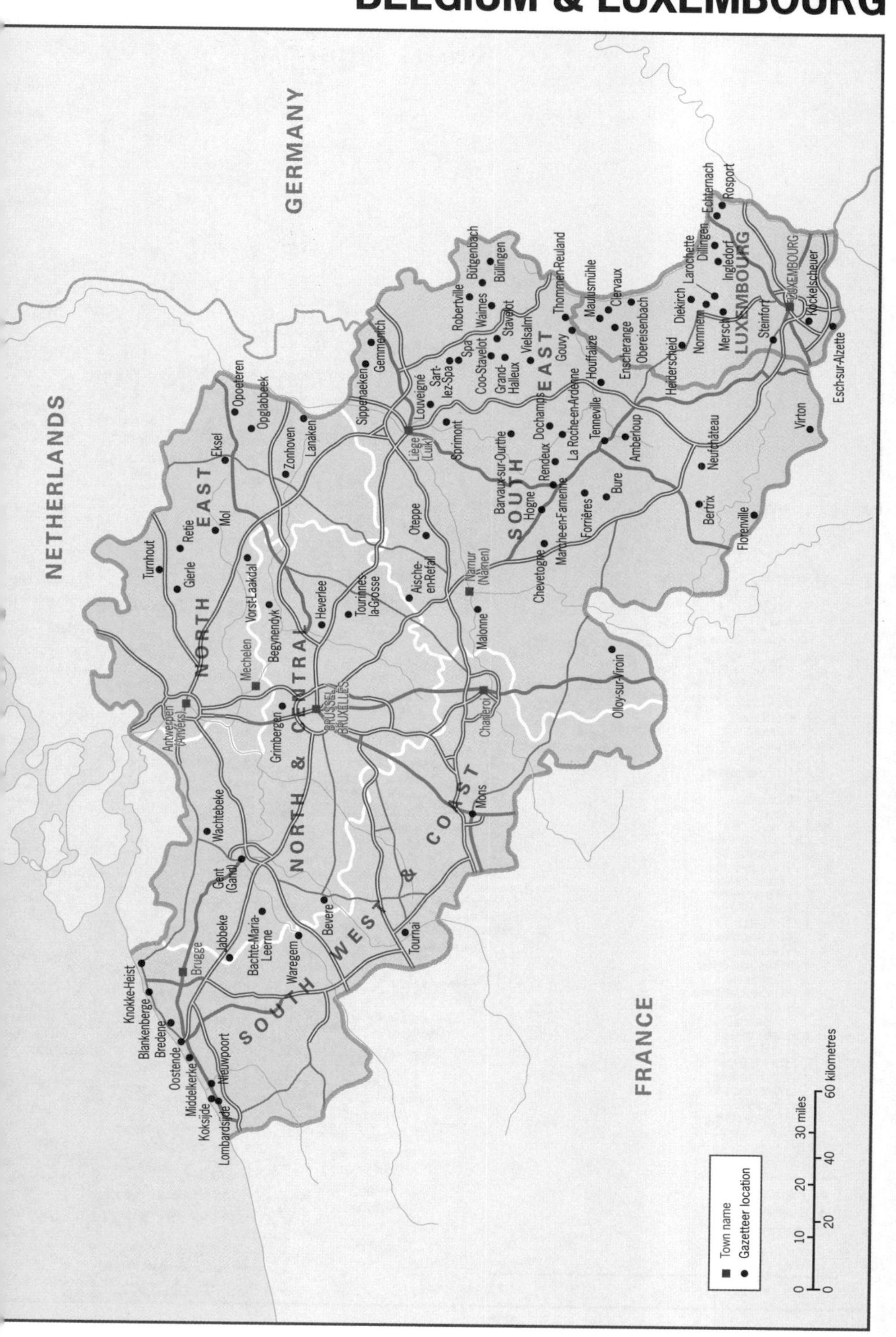

FRANCE

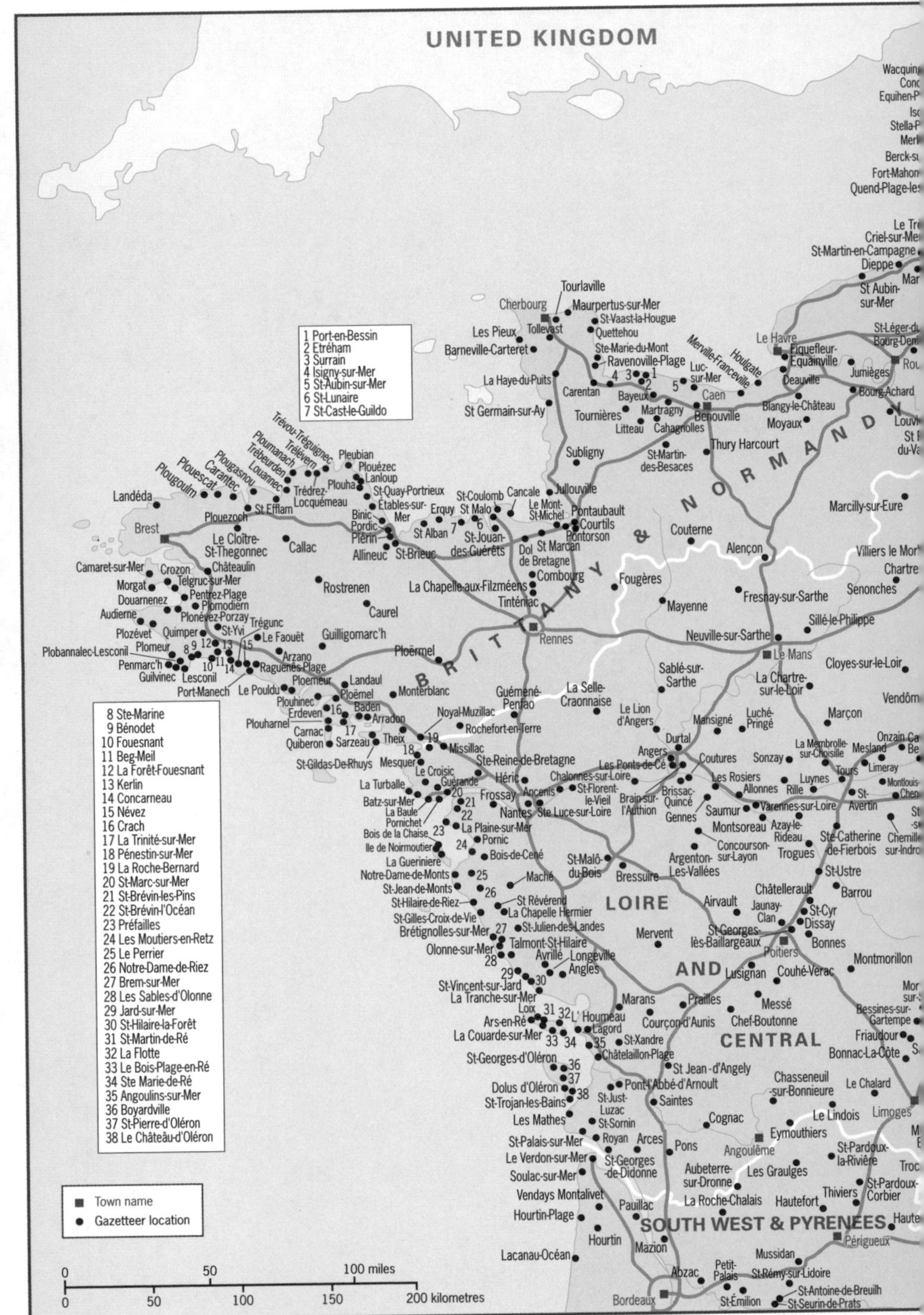
UNITED KINGDOM
1 Port-en-Bessin
2 Etréham
3 Surrain
4 Isigny-sur-Mer
5 St-Aubin-sur-Mer
6 St-Lunaire
7 St-Cast-le-Guildo
8 Ste-Marine
9 Bénodet
10 Fouesnant
11 Beg-Meil
12 La Forêt-Fouesnant
13 Kerlin
14 Concarneau
15 Névez
16 Crach
17 La Trinité-sur-Mer
18 Pénestin-sur-Mer
19 La Roche-Bernard
20 St-Marc-sur-Mer
21 St-Brévin-les-Pins
22 St-Brévin-l'Océan
23 Préfailles
24 Les Moutiers-en-Retz
25 Le Perrier
26 Notre-Dame-de-Riez
27 Brem-sur-Mer
28 Les Sables-d'Olonne
29 Jard-sur-Mer
30 St-Hilaire-la-Forêt
31 St-Martin-de-Ré
32 La Flotte
33 Le Bois-Plage-en-Ré
34 Ste Marie-de-Ré
35 Angoulins-sur-Mer
36 Boyardville
37 St-Pierre-d'Oléron
38 Le Château-d'Oléron
BRITTANY & NORMANDY
LOIRE AND CENTRAL
SOUTH WEST & PYRENEES
Town name
Gazetteer location
0 50 100 miles
0 50 100 150 200 kilometres

4

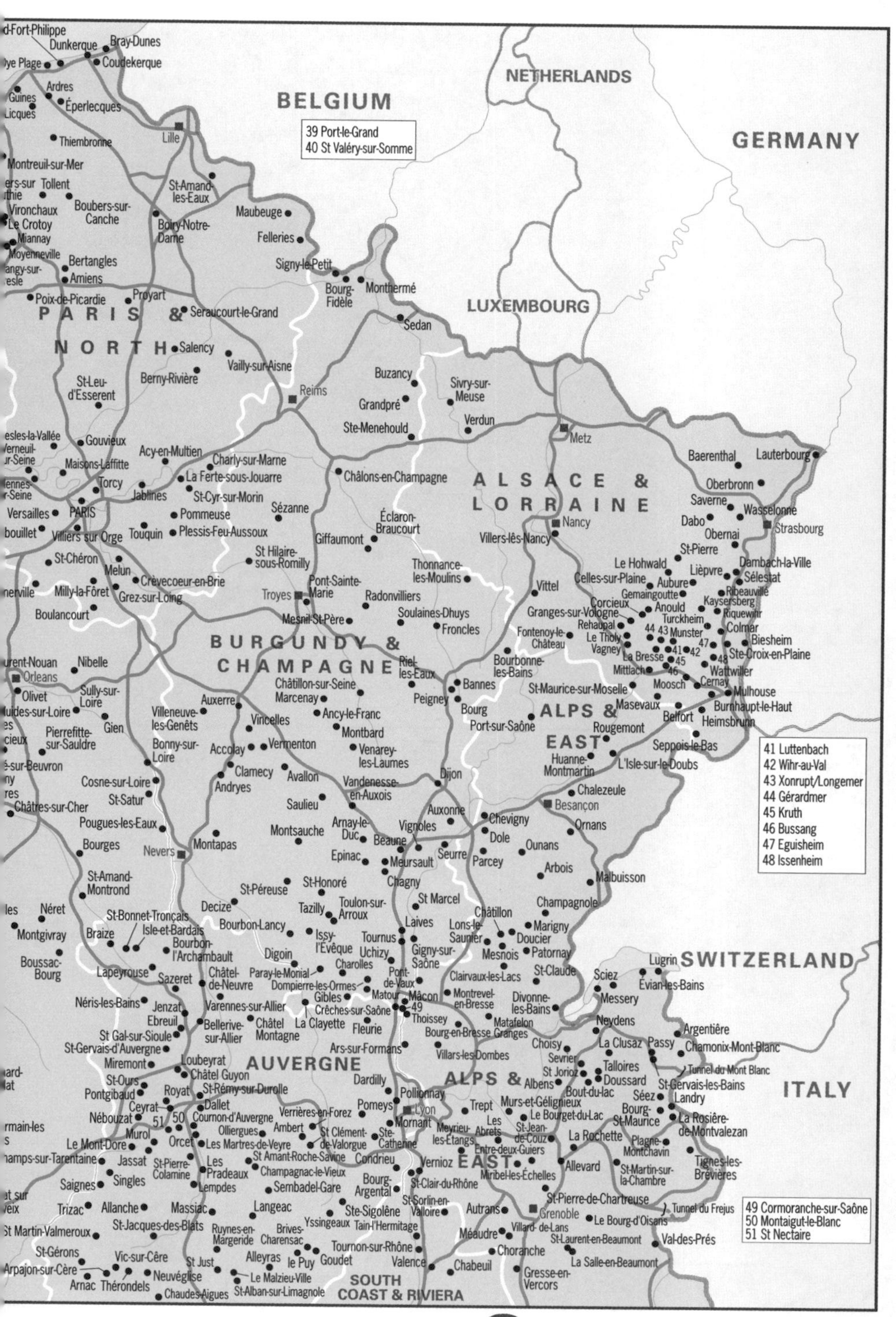

BELGIUM
NETHERLANDS
GERMANY
LUXEMBOURG
SWITZERLAND
ITALY
39 Port-le-Grand
40 St Valéry-sur-Somme
PARIS & NORTH
BURGUNDY & CHAMPAGNE
ALSACE & LORRAINE
ALPS & EAST
AUVERGNE
SOUTH COAST & RIVIERA
Dunkerque
Bray-Dunes
Coudekerque
Ardres
Guînes
Licques
Éperlecques
Thiembronne
Lille
Montreuil-sur-Mer
Tollent
Vironchaux
Boubers-sur-Canche
Le Crotoy
Miannay
Moyenneville
Bertangles
Amiens
Poix-de-Picardie
Proyart
Seraucourt-le-Grand
St-Amand-les-Eaux
Maubeuge
Felleries
Boiry-Notre-Dame
Signy-le-Petit
Bourg-Fidèle
Monthermé
Sedan
Salency
Vailly-sur-Aisne
Berny-Rivière
St-Leu-d'Esserent
Reims
Buzancy
Grandpré
Sivry-sur-Meuse
Verdun
Ste-Menehould
Metz
Gouvieux
Maisons-Laffitte
Acy-en-Multien
Charly-sur-Marne
La Ferte-sous-Jouarre
St-Cyr-sur-Morin
Torcy
Jablines
Versailles
PARIS
Villiers sur Orge
Touquin
Pommeuse
Plessis-Feu-Aussoux
Sézanne
Châlons-en-Champagne
Éclaron-Braucourt
Giffaumont
St-Chéron
Melun
Crèvecoeur-en-Brie
Milly-la-Fôret
Grez-sur-Loing
St Hilaire-sous-Romilly
Troyes
Pont-Sainte-Marie
Radonvilliers
Mesnil-St-Père
Soulaines-Dhuys
Froncles
Thonnance-les-Moulins
Boulancourt
Nibelle
Orleans
Olivet
Sully-sur-Loire
Gien
Pierrefitte-sur-Sauldre
Auxerre
Villeneuve-les-Genêts
Vincelles
Bonny-sur-Loire
Accolay
Vermenton
Clamecy
Andryes
Avallon
Cosne-sur-Loire
St-Satur
Châtres-sur-Cher
Pougues-les-Eaux
Bourges
Nevers
Montapas
Châtillon-sur-Seine
Marcenay
Ancy-le-Franc
Montbard
Venarey-les-Laumes
Vandenesse-en-Auxois
Saulieu
Montsauche
Arnay-le-Duc
Beaune
Epinac
Meursault
Chagny
Riel-les-Eaux
Peigney
Bannes
Bourg
Port-sur-Saône
Dijon
Auxonne
Vignoles
Seurre
Chevigny
Dole
Parcey
Ounans
Arbois
Baerenthal
Lauterbourg
Oberbronn
Saverne
Wasselonne
Dabo
Strasbourg
Obernai
St-Pierre
Nancy
Villers-lès-Nancy
Vittel
Le Hohwald
Celles-sur-Plaine
Lièpvre
Dambach-la-Ville
Sélestat
Aubure
Gemaingoutte
Ribeauvillé
Kaysersberg
Corcieux
Anould
Riquewihr
Granges-sur-Vologne
Turckheim
Colmar
Rehaupal
Munster
Biesheim
Fontenoy-le-Château
Le Tholy
Vagney
La Bresse
Ste-Croix-en-Plaine
Mittlach
Wattwiller
Bourbonne-les-Bains
St-Maurice-sur-Moselle
Moosch
Cernay
Mulhouse
Masevaux
Burnhaupt-le-Haut
Belfort
Heimsbrunn
Rougemont
Seppois-le-Bas
Huanne-Montmartin
L'Isle-sur-le-Doubs
Chalezeule
Besançon
Ornans
Malbuisson
41 Luttenbach
42 Wihr-au-Val
43 Xonrupt/Longemer
44 Gérardmer
45 Kruth
46 Bussang
47 Eguisheim
48 Issenheim
St-Amand-Montrond
St-Péreuse
St-Honoré
Néret
Montgivray
St-Bonnet-Tronçais
Isle-et-Bardais
Braize
Decize
Bourbon-Lancy
Tazilly
Toulon-sur-Arroux
St Marcel
Châtillon
Champagnole
Marigny
Boussac-Bourg
Bourbon-l'Archambault
Lapeyrouse
Sazeret
Issy-l'Évêque
Digoin
Tournus
Uchizy
Gigny-sur-Saône
Lons-le-Saunier
Doucier
Mesnois
Patornay
Paray-le-Monial
Charolles
Châtel-de-Neuvre
Dompierre-les-Ormes
Pont-de-Vaux
Clairvaux-les-Lacs
St-Claude
Lugrin
Évian-les-Bains
Sciez
Messery
Néris-les-Bains
Jenzat
Ebreuil
Varennes-sur-Allier
Gibles
Matour
Mâcon
Montrevel-en-Bresse
Divonne-les-Bains
Bellerive-sur-Allier
Châtel Montagne
La Clayette
Crêches-sur-Saône
Thoissey
Fleurie
Bourg-en-Bresse
Matafelon Granges
Neydens
Argentière
St Gal-sur-Sioule
St-Gervais-d'Auvergne
Ars-sur-Formans
Villars-les-Dombes
Choisy
La Clusaz
Passy
Chamonix-Mont-Blanc
Miremont
Loubeyrat
Châtel Guyon
Sevrier
St Jorioz
Talloires
Doussard
Tunnel du Mont Blanc
St-Ours
Pontgibaud
Royat
St-Rémy-sur-Durolle
Dardilly
Albens
Bout-du-lac
St-Gervais-les-Bains
Ceyrat
Dallet
Pollionnay
Pomeys
Trept
Murs-et-Gélignieux
Sééz
Landry
Nébouzat
51
50
Cournon-d'Auvergne
Verrières-en-Forez
Olliergues
Ambert
Lyon
Le Bourget-du-Lac
Bourg-St-Maurice
La Rosière-de-Montvalezan
Murol
St Clément-de-Valorgue
Ste-Catherine
Mornant
Meyrieu-les-Étangs
Les Abrets
St-Jean-de-Couz
Entre-deux-Guiers
La Rochette
Plagne-Montchavin
Le Mont-Dore
Orcet
Les Martres-de-Veyre
Jassat
St-Pierre-Colamine
St Amant-Roche-Savine
Condrieu
Vernioz
Miribel-les-Échelles
Allevard
St-Martin-sur-la-Chambre
Tignes-les-Brévières
Champs-sur-Tarentaine
Saignes
Singles
Les Pradeaux
Champagnac-le-Vieux
Lempdes
Sembadel-Gare
Bourg-Argental
St-Clair-du-Rhône
St-Sorlin-en-Valloire
St-Pierre-de-Chartreuse
Trizac
Allanche
Massiac
Langeac
Ste-Sigolène
Autrans
Grenoble
Tunnel du Frejus
St Martin-Valmeroux
St-Jacques-des-Blats
Ruynes-en-Margeride
Brives-Charensac
Yssingeaux
Tain-l'Hermitage
Villard-de-Lans
Méaudre
Le Bourg-d'Oisans
St-Laurent-en-Beaumont
Val-des-Prés
49 Cormoranche-sur-Saône
50 Montaigut-le-Blanc
51 St Nectaire
St-Gérons
Vic-sur-Cère
Alleyras
le Puy
Goudet
Tournon-sur-Rhône
Choranche
Arpajon-sur-Cère
Neuvéglise
St Just
Valence
Chabeuil
La Salle-en-Beaumont
Arnac
Thérondels
Le Malzieu-Ville
Gresse-en-Vercors
Chaudes-Aigues
St-Alban-sur-Limagnole
4

FRANCE

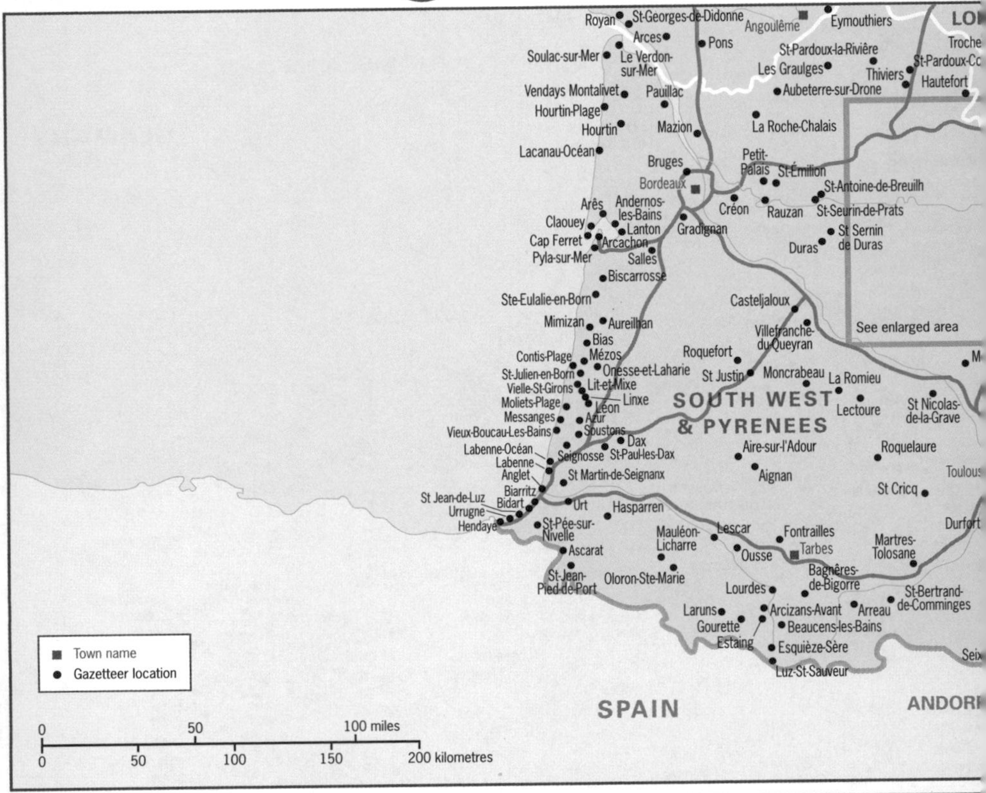

Royan
St-Georges-de-Didonne
Angoulême
Eymouthiers
Arces
Pons
Soulac-sur-Mer
Le Verdon-sur-Mer
St-Pardoux-la-Rivière
Les Graulges
Thiviers
St-Pardoux-Co
Hautefort
Troche
Aubeterre-sur-Drone
Vendays Montalivet
Pauillac
Hourtin-Plage
Hourtin
Mazion
La Roche-Chalais
Lacanau-Océan
Bruges
Petit-Palais
St-Émilion
Bordeaux
St-Antoine-de-Breuilh
Arès
Andernos-les-Bains
Créon
Rauzan
St-Seurin-de-Prats
Claouey
Lanton
Gradignan
Cap Ferret
Arcachon
St Sernin de Duras
Duras
Pyla-sur-Mer
Salles
Biscarrosse
Ste-Eulalie-en-Born
Casteljaloux
Mimizan
Aureilhan
Villefranche-du-Queyran
See enlarged area
Bias
Contis-Plage
Mézos
Roquefort
St-Julien-en-Born
Onesse-et-Laharie
St Justin
Moncrabeau
La Romieu
Vielle-St-Girons
Lit-et-Mixe
Linxe
Moliets-Plage
Léon
SOUTH WEST & PYRENEES
Lectoure
St Nicolas-de-la-Grave
Messanges
Azur
Vieux-Boucau-Les-Bains
Soustons
Dax
Roquelaure
Labenne-Océan
Aire-sur-l'Adour
Seignosse
St-Paul-les-Dax
Labenne
Anglet
St Martin-de-Seignanx
Aignan
Toulous
Biarritz
St Cricq
St Jean-de-Luz
Bidart
Urt
Hasparren
Urrugne
Hendaye
St-Pée-sur-Nivelle
Mauléon-Licharre
Lescar
Fontrailles
Durfort
Tarbes
Martres-Tolosane
Ascarat
Ousse
St-Jean-Pied-de-Port
Oloron-Ste-Marie
Bagnères-de-Bigorre
Lourdes
St-Bertrand-de-Comminges
Laruns
Arcizans-Avant
Arreau
Gourette
Beaucens-les-Bains
Estaing
Esquièze-Sère
Seix
Luz-St-Sauveur
SPAIN
ANDORR

Town name
Gazetteer location

0 50 100 miles
0 50 100 150 200 kilometres

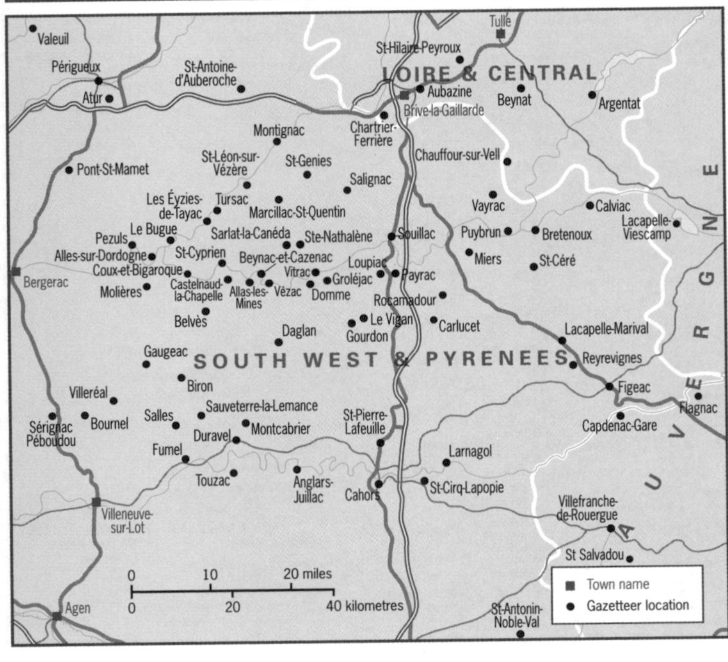

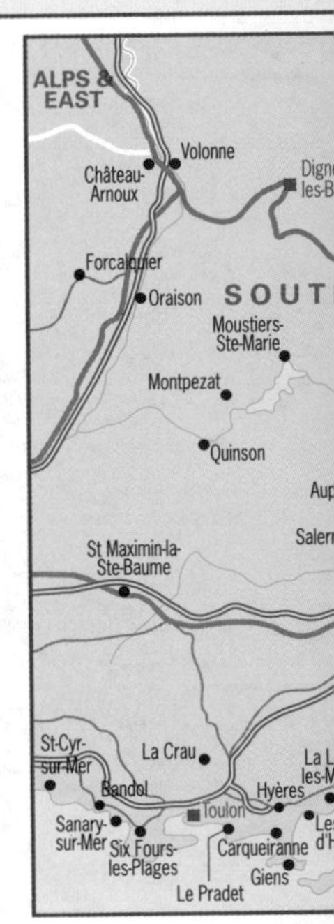

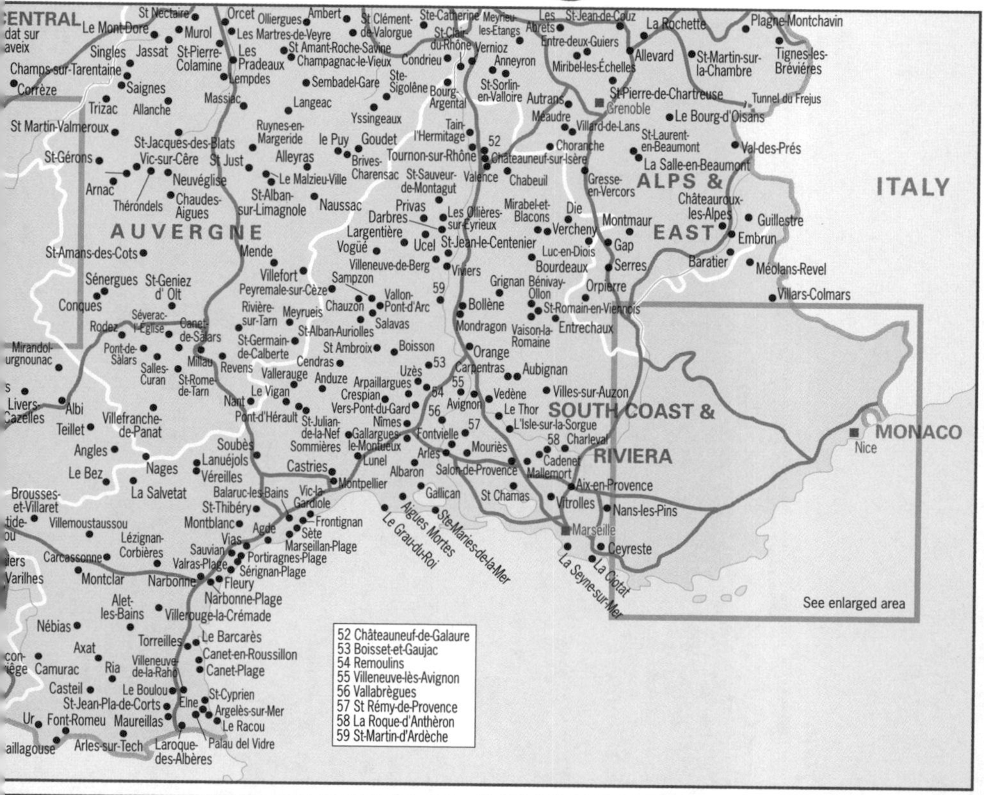

CENTRAL
AUVERGNE
ALPS & EAST
SOUTH COAST & RIVIERA
ITALY
MONACO

St Nectaire, Le Mont-Dore, Murol, Orcet, Olliergues, Ambert, St Clément-de-Valorgue, Ste-Catherine, Meyrieu-les-Etangs, Les Abrets, St-Jean-de-Couz, La Rochette, Plagne-Montchavin, Singles, Jassat, St-Pierre-Colamine, Les Martres-de-Veyre, St Amant-Roche-Savine, St-Clair-du-Rhône, Vernioz, Entre-deux-Guiers, Allevard, St-Martin-sur-la-Chambre, Tignes-les-Brévières, Champs-sur-Tarentaine, Les Pradeaux, Champagnac-le-Vieux, Condrieu, Anneyron, Miribel-les-Echelles, Corrèze, Saignes, Lempdes, Sembadel-Gare, Ste-Sigolène, Bourg-Argental, St-Sorlin-en-Valloire, Autrans, Grenoble, St-Pierre-de-Chartreuse, Tunnel du Frejus, Trizac, Allanche, Massiac, Langeac, Yssingeaux, Tain-l'Hermitage, Méaudre, Villard-de-Lans, Le Bourg-d'Oisans, St Martin-Valmeroux, Ruynes-en-Margeride, le Puy, Goudet, 52, Choranche, St-Laurent-en-Beaumont, Val-des-Prés, St-Jacques-des-Blats, Tournon-sur-Rhône, Châteauneuf-sur-Isère, La Salle-en-Beaumont, St-Gérons, Vic-sur-Cère, St Just, Alleyras, Brives-Charensac, St-Sauveur-de-Montagut, Valence, Chabeuil, Gresse-en-Vercors, Arnac, Neuvéglise, Le Malzieu-Ville, St-Alban-sur-Limagnole, Naussac, Privas, Mirabel-et-Blacons, Die, Châteauroux-les-Alpes, Guillestre, Thérondels, Chaudes-Aigues, Darbres, Les Ollières-sur-Eyrieux, Verchen, Montmaur, Embrun, Largentière, St-Jean-le-Centenier, Luc-en-Diois, Gap, Baratier, St-Amans-des-Cots, Mende, Vogüé, Ucel, Villeneuve-de-Berg, Viviers, Bourdeaux, Serres, Méolans-Revel, Villefort, Sampzon, Grignan, Bénivay-Ollon, Orpierre, Villars-Colmars, Sénergues, St-Geniez d'Olt, Peyremale-sur-Cèze, Vallon-Pont-d'Arc, 59, Bollène, St-Romain-en-Viennois, Conques, Rivière-sur-Tarn, Meyrueis, Chauzon, Salavas, Mondragon, Vaison-la-Romaine, Entrechaux, Sévérac-l'Église, Rodez, Canet-de-Salars, St-Germain-de-Calberte, St-Alban-Auriolles, St Ambroix, Boisson, Orange, Mirandol-Bourgnounac, Pont-de-Salars, Salles-Curan, Millau, Revens, Cendras, Uzès, 53, Carpentras, Aubignan, St-Rome-de-Tarn, Vallerauge, Anduze, Arpaillargues, 55, Villes-sur-Auzon, Livers-Cazelles, Albi, Le Vigan, Crespian, 54, Vedène, Nant, Vers-Pont-du-Gard, 56, Avignon, Le Thor, Teillet, Villefranche-de-Panat, Pont-d'Hérault, St-Julian-de-la-Nef, Nîmes, 57, L'Isle-sur-la-Sorgue, Sommières, Gallargues-le-Montueux, Fontvieille, 58, Charleval, Angles, Soubès, Arles, Mouriès, Nice, Le Bez, Nages, Lanuéjols, Castries, Lunel, Salon-de-Provence, Cadenet, Véreilles, Albaron, Mallemort, La Salvetat, Montpellier, Gallican, St Chamas, Aix-en-Provence, Brousses-et-Villaret, Balaruc-les-Bains, Vic-la-Gardiole, Vitrolles, St-Thibéry, Frontignan, Aigues Mortes, Ste-Maries-de-la-Mer, Nans-les-Pins, Villemoustaussou, Montblanc, Agde, Sète, Le Grau-du-Roi, Marseille, Lézignan-Corbières, Vias, Marseillan-Plage, Ceyreste, Carcassonne, Sauvian, Portiragnes-Plage, La Ciotat, Valras-Plage, Sérignan-Plage, La Seyne-sur-Mer, Varilhes, Montclar, Narbonne, Fleury, Narbonne-Plage, Alet-les-Bains, Villerouge-la-Crémade, Nébias, Torreilles, Le Barcarès, Axat, Villeneuve-de-la-Raho, Canet-en-Roussillon, Camurac, Ria, Canet-Plage, Casteil, Le Boulou, St-Cyprien, St-Jean-Pla-de-Corts, Elne, Argelès-sur-Mer, Ur, Font-Romeu, Maureillas, Le Racou, Arles-sur-Tech, Laroque-des-Albères, Palau del Vidre

See enlarged area

52 Châteauneuf-de-Galaure
53 Boisset-et-Gaujac
54 Remoulins
55 Villeneuve-lès-Avignon
56 Vallabrègues
57 St Rémy-de-Provence
58 La Roque-d'Anthèron
59 St-Martin-d'Ardèche

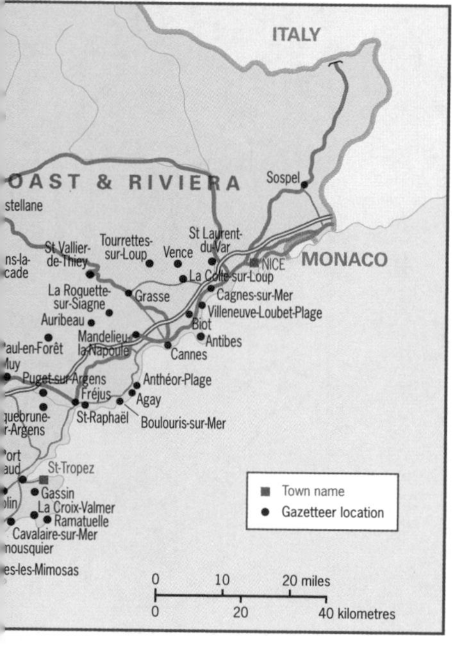

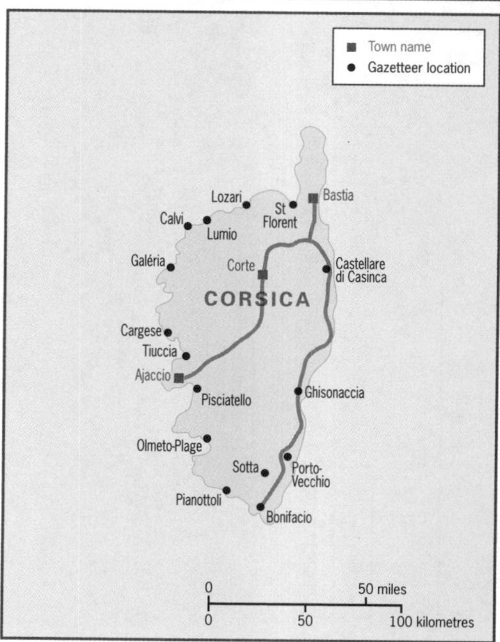

GERMANY

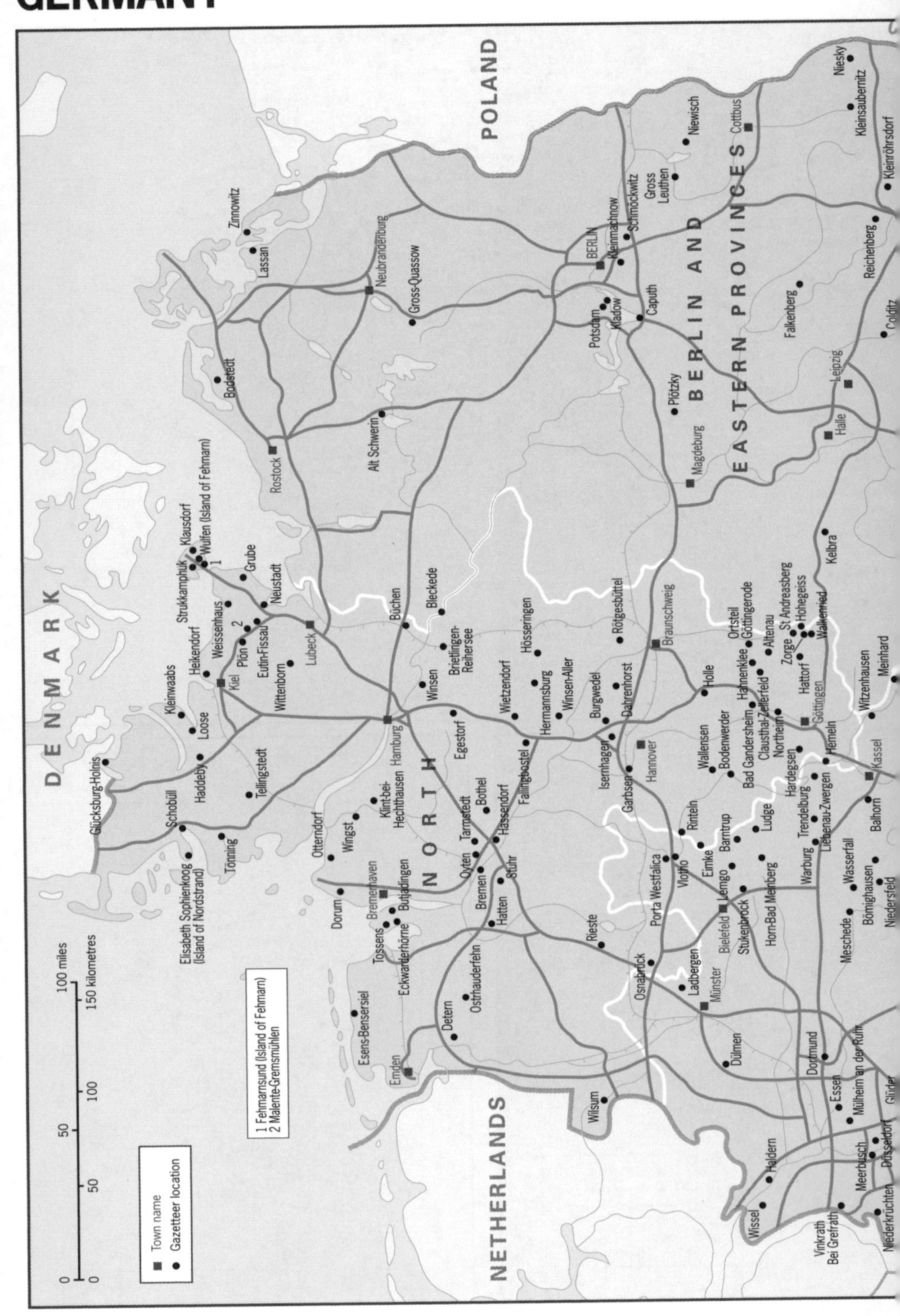

DENMARK
POLAND
NETHERLANDS
NORTH
BERLIN AND EASTERN PROVINCES
Town name
Gazetteer location
0 50 100 miles
0 50 100 150 kilometres
1 Fehmarnsund (Island of Fehmarn)
2 Malente-Gremsmühlen
Glücksburg-Holnis
Schobüll
Elisabeth Sophienkoog (Island of Nordstrand)
Tönning
Haddeby
Tellingstedt
Kleinwaabs
Loose
Kiel
Heikendorf
Weissenhaus
Plön
Eutin-Fissau
Wittenborn
Strukkamphuk
Klausdorf
Wulfen (Island of Fehmarn)
Grube
Neustadt
Lubeck
Rostock
Bodstedt
Zinnowitz
Lassan
Neubrandenburg
Gross-Quassow
Alt Schwerin
Büchen
Bleckede
Winsen
Brietlingen-Reihersee
Hamburg
Egestorf
Otterndorf
Wingst
Klint-bei-Hechthausen
Tarmstedt
Bothel
Hassendorf
Fallingbostel
Wietzendorf
Hermannsburg
Hösseringen
Winsen-Aller
Rötgesbüttel
Braunschweig
Burgwedel
Dahrenhorst
Isernhagen
Hannover
Garbsen
Dorum
Bremerhaven
Butjadingen
Tossens
Eckwarderhörne
Oyten
Bremen
Stuhr
Hatten
Ostrhauderfehn
Esens-Bensersiel
Emden
Detern
Wilsum
Rieste
Osnabrück
Porta Westfalica
Vlotho
Rinteln
Eimke
Barntrup
Lemgo
Bielefeld
Stukenbrock
Horn-Bad Meinberg
Lüdge
Ladbergen
Münster
Dülmen
Dortmund
Essen
Mülheim an der Ruhr
Haldern
Wissel
Meerbusch
Düsseldorf
Vinkrath Bei Grefrath
Niederkrüchten
Wallensen
Bodenwerder
Bad Gandersheim
Holle
Hahnenklee
Clausthal-Zellerfeld
Northeim
Hardegsen
Hemeln
Göttingen
Ortsteil Göttingerode
Altenau
Zorge
St Andreasberg
Hohegeiss
Hattorf
Walkenried
Witzenhausen
Meinhard
Kassel
Trendelburg
Liebenau-Zwergen
Warburg
Balhorn
Wasserfall
Bömighausen
Niedersfeld
Meschede
Kelbra
Magdeburg
Plötzky
Halle
Leipzig
Potsdam
Kladow
Caputh
BERLIN
Kleinmachnow
Schmöckwitz
Gross Leuthen
Niewisch
Cottbus
Niesky
Kleinsaubernitz
Kleinröhrsdorf
Reichenberg
Falkenberg
Colditz

BELGIUM
LUXEMBOURG
Bonn
Frankfurt am Main
Mannheim
Stuttgart
Mühlberg
Joditz
Issigau
Stadtsteinach
Hofheim
Weissenstadt
Bayreuth
Fichtelberg
CZECH REPUBLIC
Estenfeld
Escherndorf
Sommerach am Main
Bamberg
Würzburg
Frickenhausen
Kitzingen
Erlangen
Tüchersfeld
Nürnberg
Trausnitz
Rothenburg ob der Tauber
Langlau
Fürth im Wald
Neubäu
Velburg
Viechtach
Pielenhofen
Regensburg
Zwiesel
Dinkelsbühl
Klingenbrunn
Pfraundorf
Rosenberg
Wemding
Kipfenberg
Finsterau
Abtsgmünd
Lackenhäuser
SOUTH EAST
Ingolstadt
Lauterburg
Neukirchen vorm Wald
Mörslingen
Passau
Bad Griesbach
SOUTH WEST
Ulm
Mühlhausen bei Augsburg
Bad Füssing
FRANCE
Augsburg
München (Munich)
Tittmoning
Schechen
Kirchberg
Seefeld
Tettenhausen
Arlaching
Kühnhausen
Buxheim
Diessen
Bad Endorf
Waging
Gaden
Aitrang
Königsdorf
Rottenbuch
Bad Feilnbach
Prien am Chiemsee
Bergen
Piding
Ruhpolding
Oberammergau
Waltenhofen
Weissach
Oberwössen
Bischofswiesen
Berchtesgaden
Füssen
Brunnen Forggensee
Wertach
AUSTRIA
Königssee
Haslach
Krun
Garmisch-Partenkirchen
See enlarged area
Oberstdorf
SWITZERLAND
LIECHTENSTEIN
ITALY

GERMANY

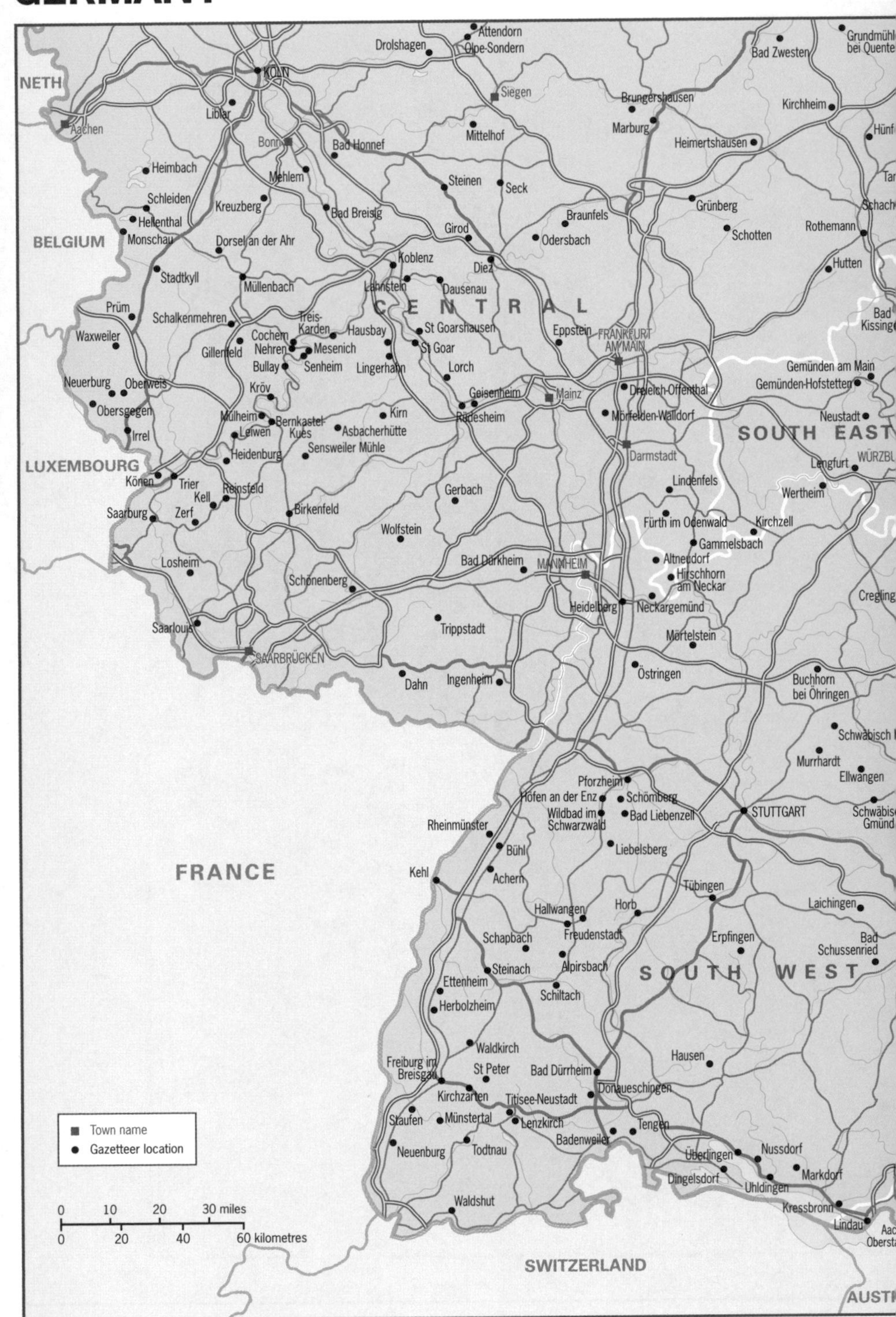

NETH
BELGIUM
LUXEMBOURG
FRANCE
SWITZERLAND
AUSTI
C E N T R A L
SOUTH EAST
SOUTH WEST
Köln
Aachen
Bonn
Siegen
Koblenz
Frankfurt am Main
Mainz
Darmstadt
Mannheim
Saarbrücken
Stuttgart
Würzburg
Attendorn
Olpe-Sondern
Drolshagen
Liblar
Bad Honnef
Mittelhof
Brungershausen
Marburg
Bad Zwesten
Grundmühle bei Quente
Kirchheim
Heimertshausen
Heimbach
Mehlem
Steinen
Seck
Schleiden
Kreuzberg
Bad Breisig
Hellenthal
Monschau
Grünberg
Braunfels
Odersbach
Schotten
Rothemann
Girod
Dorsel an der Ahr
Diez
Hutten
Stadtkyll
Müllenbach
Lahnstein
Dausenau
Prüm
Schalkenmehren
Treis-Karden
Hausbay
St Goarshausen
St Goar
Eppstein
Bad Kissingen
Waxweiler
Cochem
Nehren
Mesenich
Gillenfeld
Bullay
Senheim
Lingerhahn
Lorch
Gemünden am Main
Gemünden-Hofstetten
Neuerburg
Oberweis
Kröv
Geisenheim
Dreieich-Offenthal
Obersgegen
Mülheim
Bernkastel-Kues
Kirn
Rüdesheim
Mörfelden-Walldorf
Neustadt
Irrel
Leiwen
Asbacherhütte
Heidenburg
Sensweiler Mühle
Lengfurt
Könen
Trier
Kell
Reinsfeld
Gerbach
Lindenfels
Wertheim
Saarburg
Zerf
Birkenfeld
Fürth im Odenwald
Kirchzell
Wolfstein
Gammelsbach
Losheim
Bad Dürkheim
Altneudorf
Hirschhorn am Neckar
Schönenberg
Heidelberg
Neckargemünd
Creglingen
Saarlouis
Trippstadt
Mörtelstein
Östringen
Buchhorn bei Öhringen
Dahn
Ingenheim
Schwäbisch Hall
Murrhardt
Ellwangen
Pforzheim
Höfen an der Enz
Schömberg
Wildbad im Schwarzwald
Bad Liebenzell
Schwäbisch Gmünd
Rheinmünster
Bühl
Liebelsberg
Kehl
Achern
Tübingen
Hallwangen
Horb
Laichingen
Freudenstadt
Schapbach
Erpfingen
Bad Schussenried
Steinach
Alpirsbach
Ettenheim
Schiltach
Herbolzheim
Waldkirch
Hausen
Freiburg im Breisgau
St Peter
Bad Dürrheim
Kirchzarten
Titisee-Neustadt
Donaueschingen
Staufen
Münstertal
Lenzkirch
Tengen
Badenweiler
Neuenburg
Todtnau
Überlingen
Nussdorf
Markdorf
Dingelsdorf
Uhldingen
Kressbronn
Waldshut
Lindau
Aach Oberstaufen
Town name
Gazetteer location
0
10
20
30 miles
0
20
40
60 kilometres

NETHERLANDS

SPAIN AND PORTUGAL

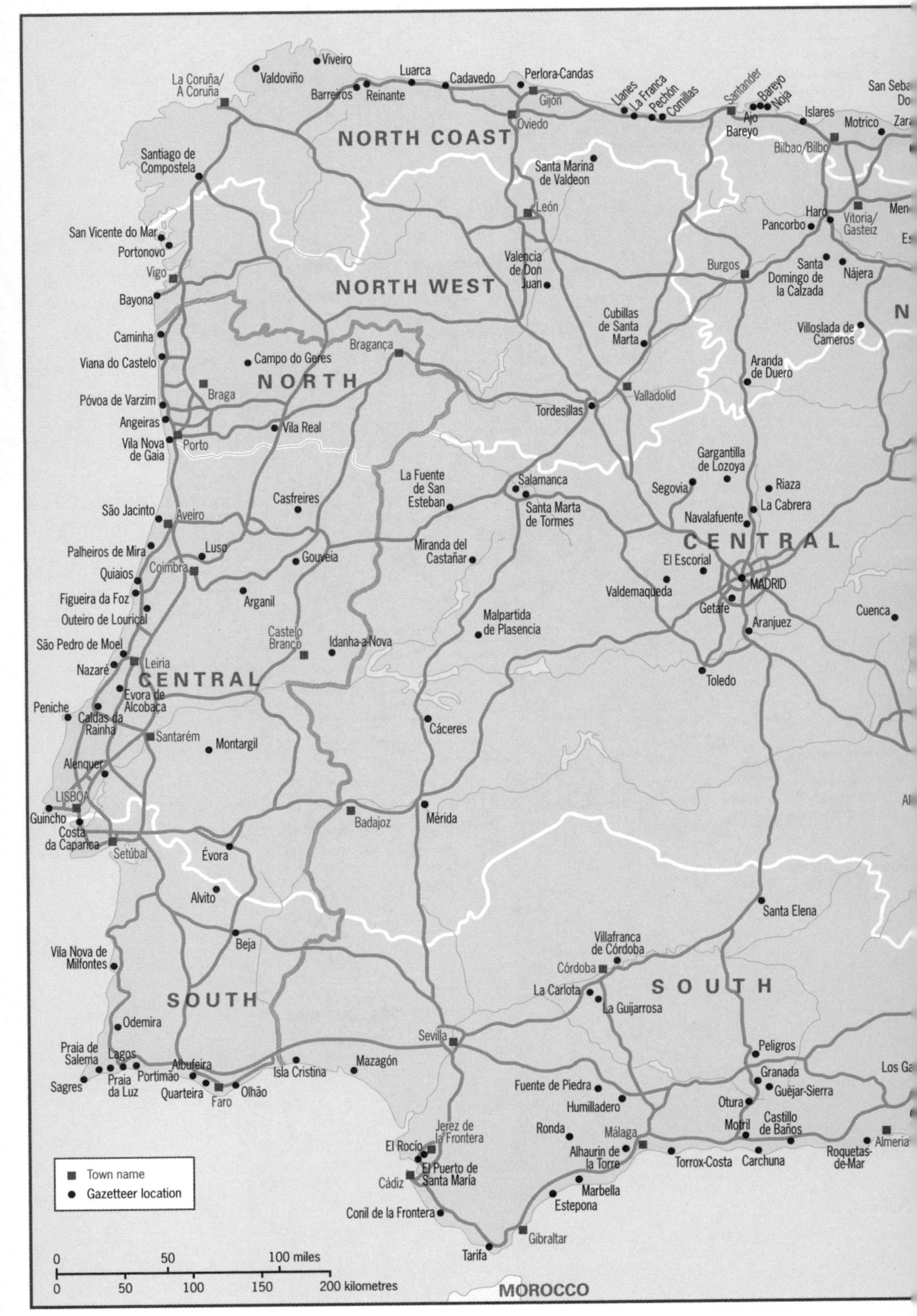

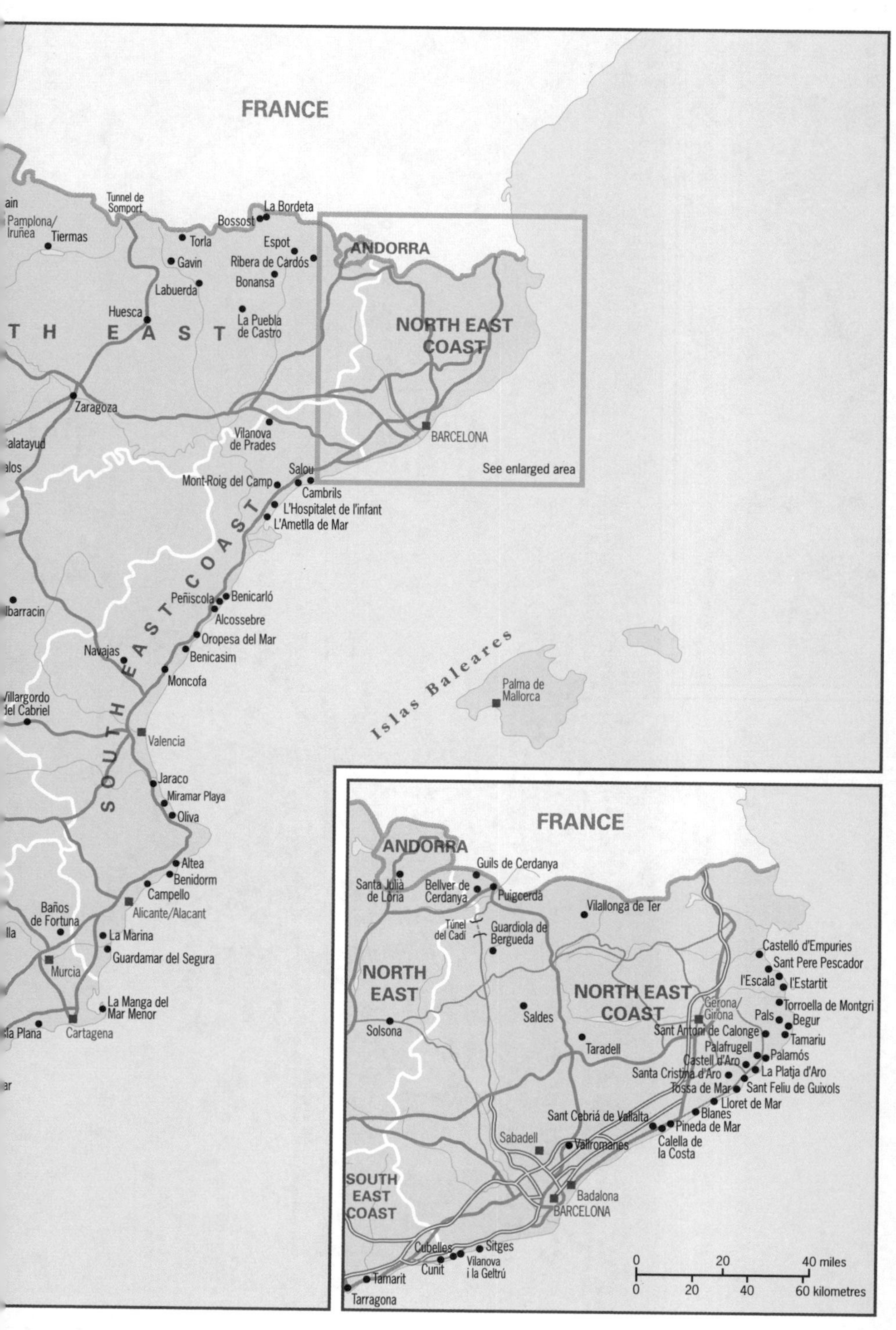
FRANCE
Tunnel de Somport
La Bordeta
Bossost
Pamplona/ Iruñea
Tiermas
Torla
Espot
Gavin
Ribera de Cardós
ANDORRA
Labuerda
Bonansa
Huesca
La Puebla de Castro
NORTH EAST COAST
Zaragoza
Vilanova de Prades
BARCELONA
See enlarged area
Salou
Mont-Roig del Camp
Cambrils
L'Hospitalet de l'infant
L'Ametlla de Mar
Peñiscola
Benicarló
Alcossebre
Oropesa del Mar
Navajas
Benicasim
Moncofa
Palma de Mallorca
Islas Baleares
SOUTH EAST COAST
Valencia
Jaraco
Miramar Playa
Oliva
Altea
Benidorm
Campello
Baños de Fortuna
Alicante/Alacant
La Marina
Guardamar del Segura
Murcia
La Manga del Mar Menor
Cartagena
FRANCE
ANDORRA
Guils de Cerdanya
Santa Julià de Lòria
Bellver de Cerdanya
Puigcerdà
Vilallonga de Ter
Túnel del Cadí
Guardiola de Bergueda
Castelló d'Empuries
Sant Pere Pescador
NORTH EAST
l'Escala
l'Estartit
NORTH EAST COAST
Gerona/ Girona
Torroella de Montgri
Saldes
Solsona
Pals
Begur
Sant Antoni de Calonge
Tamariu
Taradell
Palafrugell
Castell d'Aro
Palamós
Santa Cristina d'Aro
La Platja d'Aro
Tossa de Mar
Sant Feliu de Guixols
Lloret de Mar
Blanes
Sant Cebriá de Vallalta
Pineda de Mar
Sabadell
Vallromanes
Calella de la Costa
SOUTH EAST COAST
Badalona
BARCELONA
Cubelles
Sitges
Cunit
Vilanova i la Geltrú
Tamarit
Tarragona
0
20
40 miles
0
20
40
60 kilometres

ITALY

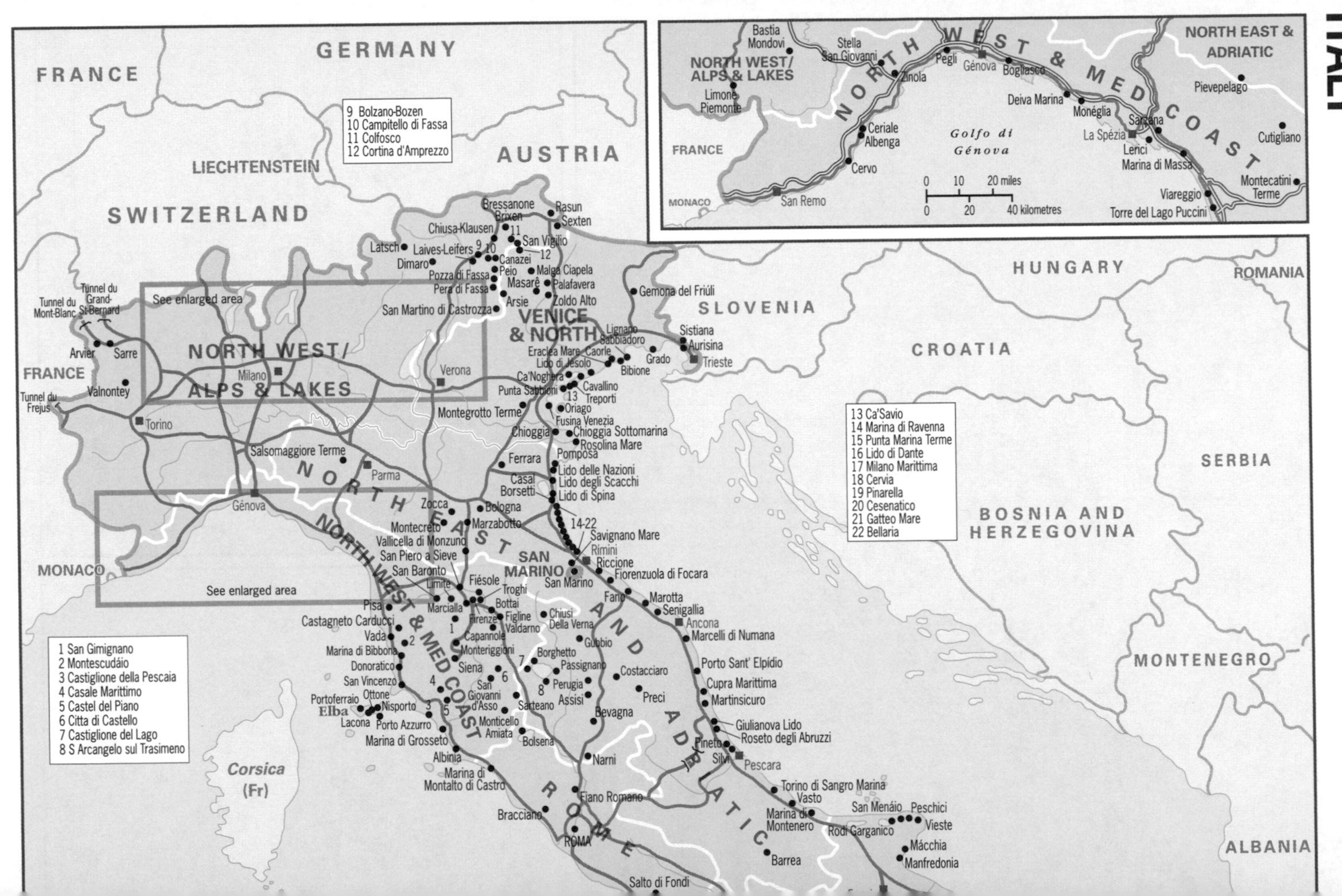
NORTH WEST/ ALPS & LAKES
NORTH WEST & MED COAST
NORTH EAST & ADRIATIC
FRANCE
MONACO
Golfo di Génova
0 10 20 miles
0 20 40 kilometres
GERMANY
FRANCE
AUSTRIA
LIECHTENSTEIN
SWITZERLAND
SLOVENIA
HUNGARY
ROMANIA
CROATIA
SERBIA
BOSNIA AND HERZEGOVINA
MONTENEGRO
ALBANIA
Corsica (Fr)
Elba
VENICE & NORTH
SAN MARINO
ROME
ADRIATIC
See enlarged area
See enlarged area
9 Bolzano-Bozen
10 Campitello di Fassa
11 Colfosco
12 Cortina d'Amprezzo
13 Ca'Savio
14 Marina di Ravenna
15 Punta Marina Terme
16 Lido di Dante
17 Milano Marittima
18 Cervia
19 Pinarella
20 Cesenatico
21 Gatteo Mare
22 Bellaria
1 San Gimignano
2 Montescudáio
3 Castiglione della Pescaia
4 Casale Marittimo
5 Castel del Piano
6 Citta di Castello
7 Castiglione del Lago
8 S Arcangelo sul Trasimeno
Torino
Milano
Génova
Verona
Parma
Bologna
Firenze
Pisa
Siena
Perugia
Rimini
Ancona
Pescara
ROMA
Trieste

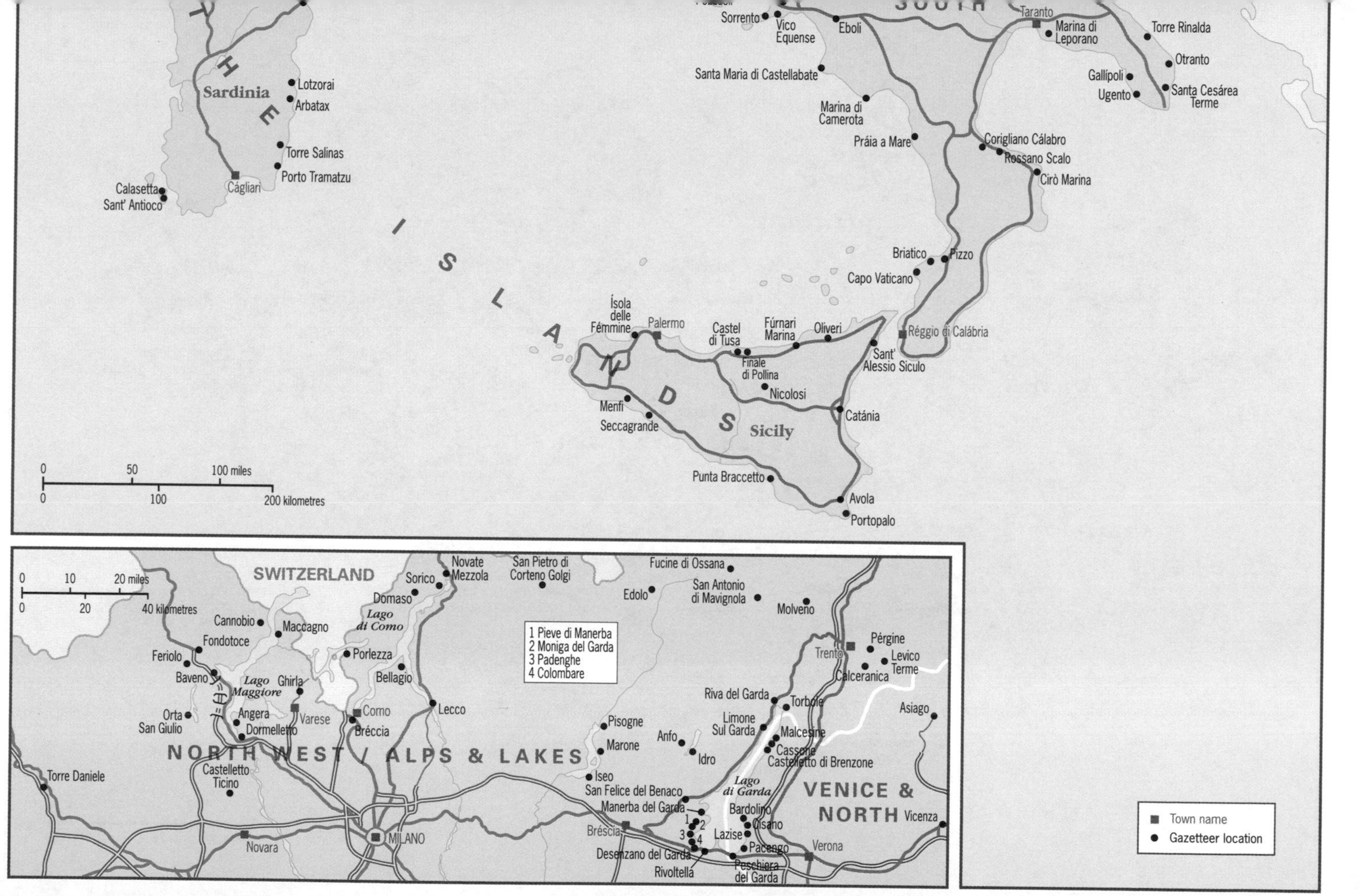

THE ISLANDS
SOUTH
Sardinia
Lotzorai
Arbatax
Torre Salinas
Porto Tramatzu
Cágliari
Calasetta
Sant' Antioco
Sorrento
Vico Equense
Eboli
Santa Maria di Castellabate
Marina di Camerota
Práia a Mare
Taranto
Marina di Leporano
Torre Rinalda
Otranto
Gallipoli
Ugento
Santa Cesárea Terme
Corigliano Cálabro
Rossano Scalo
Cirò Marina
Briatico
Pizzo
Capo Vaticano
Réggio di Calábria
Sicily
Ísola delle Fémmine
Palermo
Castel di Tusa
Fúrnari Marina
Oliveri
Finale di Pollina
Sant' Alessio Siculo
Nicolosi
Catánia
Menfi
Seccagrande
Punta Braccetto
Avola
Portopalo
0 50 100 miles
0 100 200 kilometres
SWITZERLAND
NORTH WEST / ALPS & LAKES
VENICE & NORTH
0 10 20 miles
0 20 40 kilometres
Cannobio
Maccagno
Fondotoce
Feriolo
Baveno
Lago Maggiore
Ghirla
Varese
Orta San Giulio
Angera
Dormelletto
Castelletto Ticino
Torre Daniele
Novara
MILANO
Sorico
Novate Mezzola
Domaso
Lago di Como
Porlezza
Bellagio
Como
Bréccia
Lecco
San Pietro di Corteno Golgi
Fucine di Ossana
Edolo
San Antonio di Mavignola
Molveno
1 Pieve di Manerba
2 Moniga del Garda
3 Padenghe
4 Colombare
Pisogne
Marone
Iseo
Anfo
Idro
San Felice del Benaco
Manerba del Garda
Bréscia
Desenzano del Garda
Rivoltella
Riva del Garda
Torbole
Limone Sul Garda
Malcesine
Cassone
Castelletto di Brenzone
Lago di Garda
Bardolino
Cisano
Lazise
Pacengo
Peschiera del Garda
Verona
Trento
Pérgine
Levico Terme
Calceranica
Asiago
Vicenza
Town name
Gazetteer location

SWITZERLAND

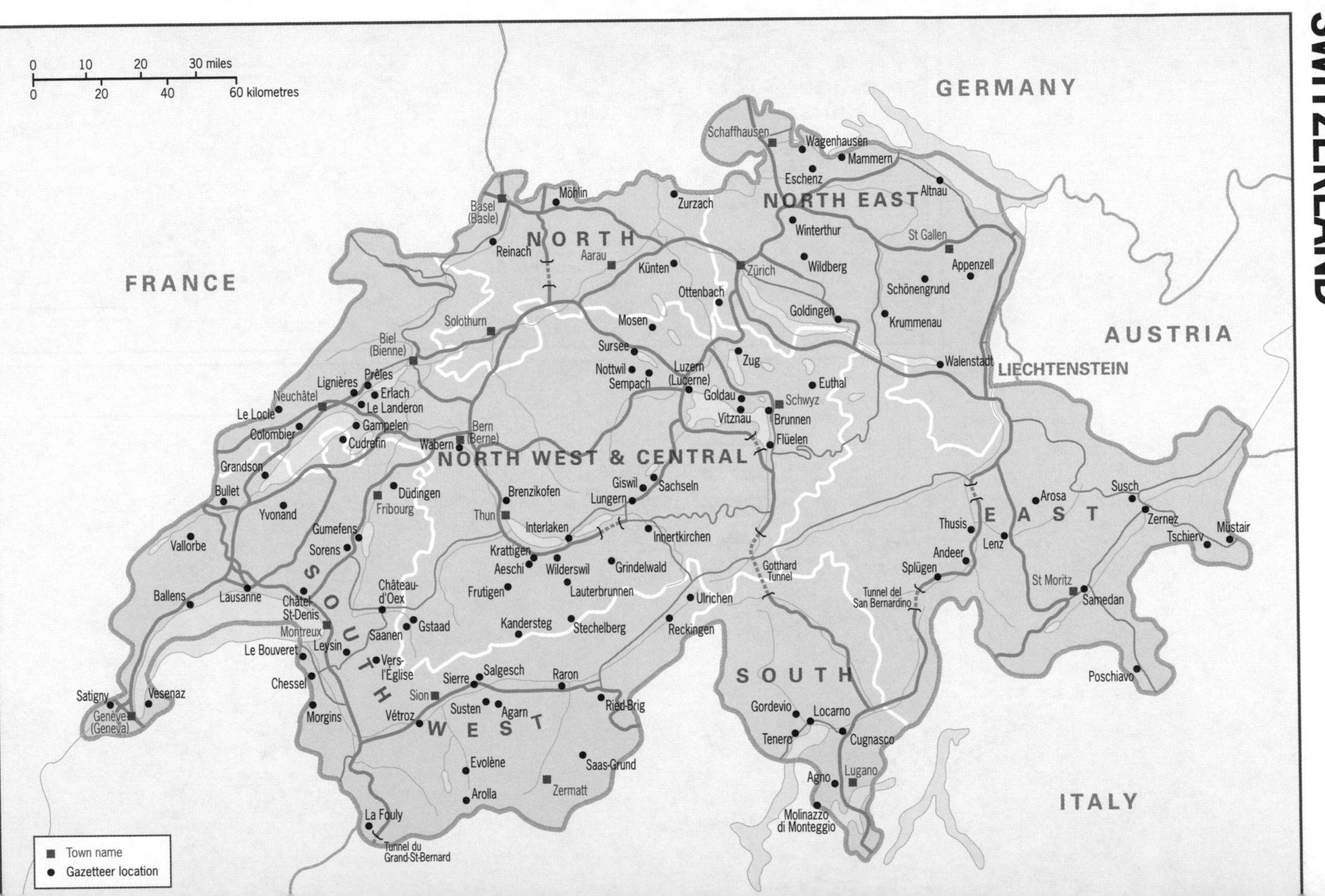

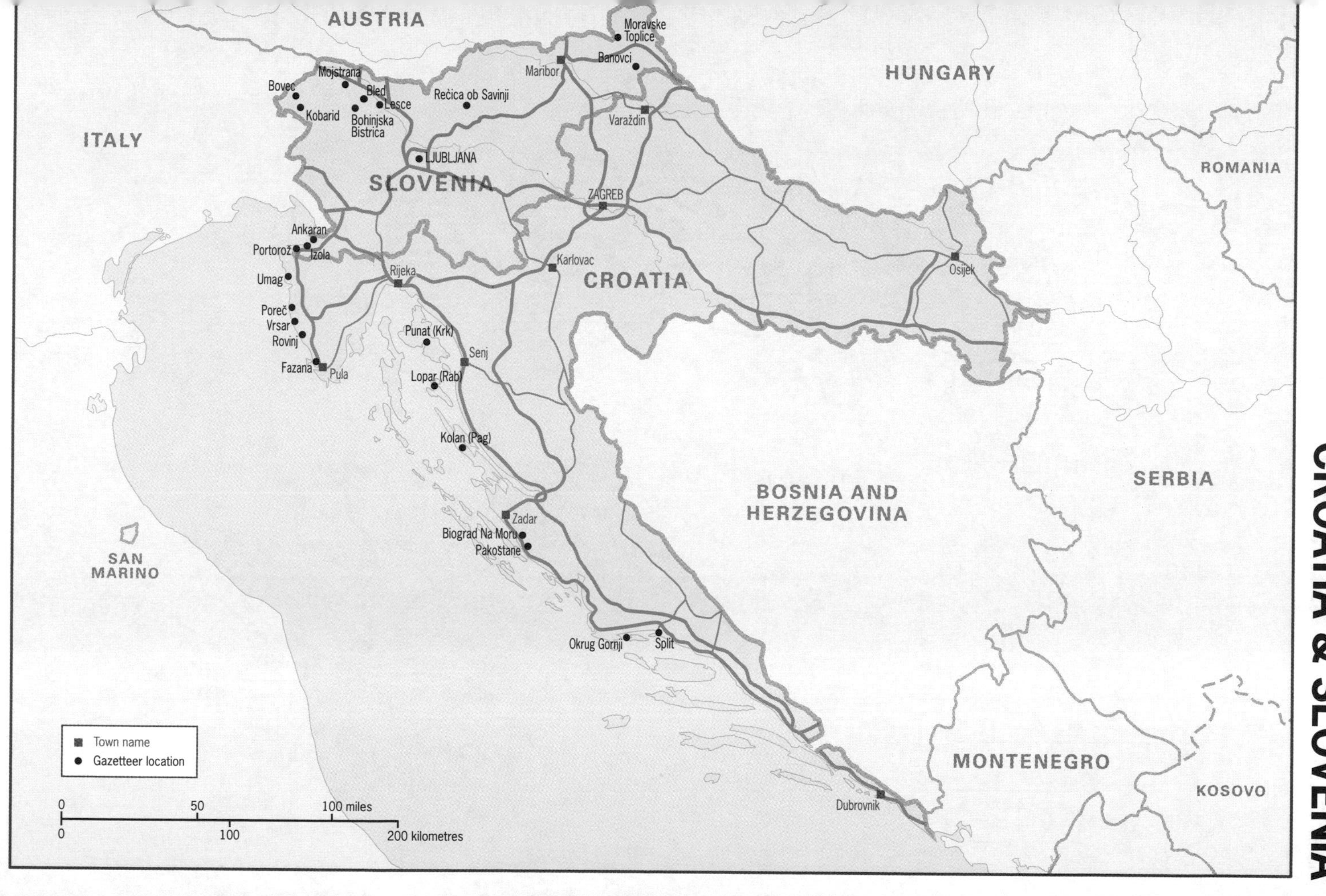
AUSTRIA
HUNGARY
ITALY
ROMANIA
SLOVENIA
CROATIA
BOSNIA AND HERZEGOVINA
SERBIA
SAN MARINO
MONTENEGRO
KOSOVO
Moravske Toplice
Banovci
Maribor
Mojstrana
Bovec
Bled
Lesce
Kobarid
Bohinjska Bistrica
Rečica ob Savinji
Varaždin
LJUBLJANA
ZAGREB
Ankaran
Portorož
Izola
Rijeka
Karlovac
Osijek
Umag
Poreč
Vrsar
Rovinj
Punat (Krk)
Senj
Fazana
Pula
Lopar (Rab)
Kolan (Pag)
Zadar
Biograd Na Moru
Pakoštane
Okrug Gornji
Split
Dubrovnik
Town name
Gazetteer location
0
50
100 miles
0
100
200 kilometres

CZECH REPUBLIC & HUNGARY

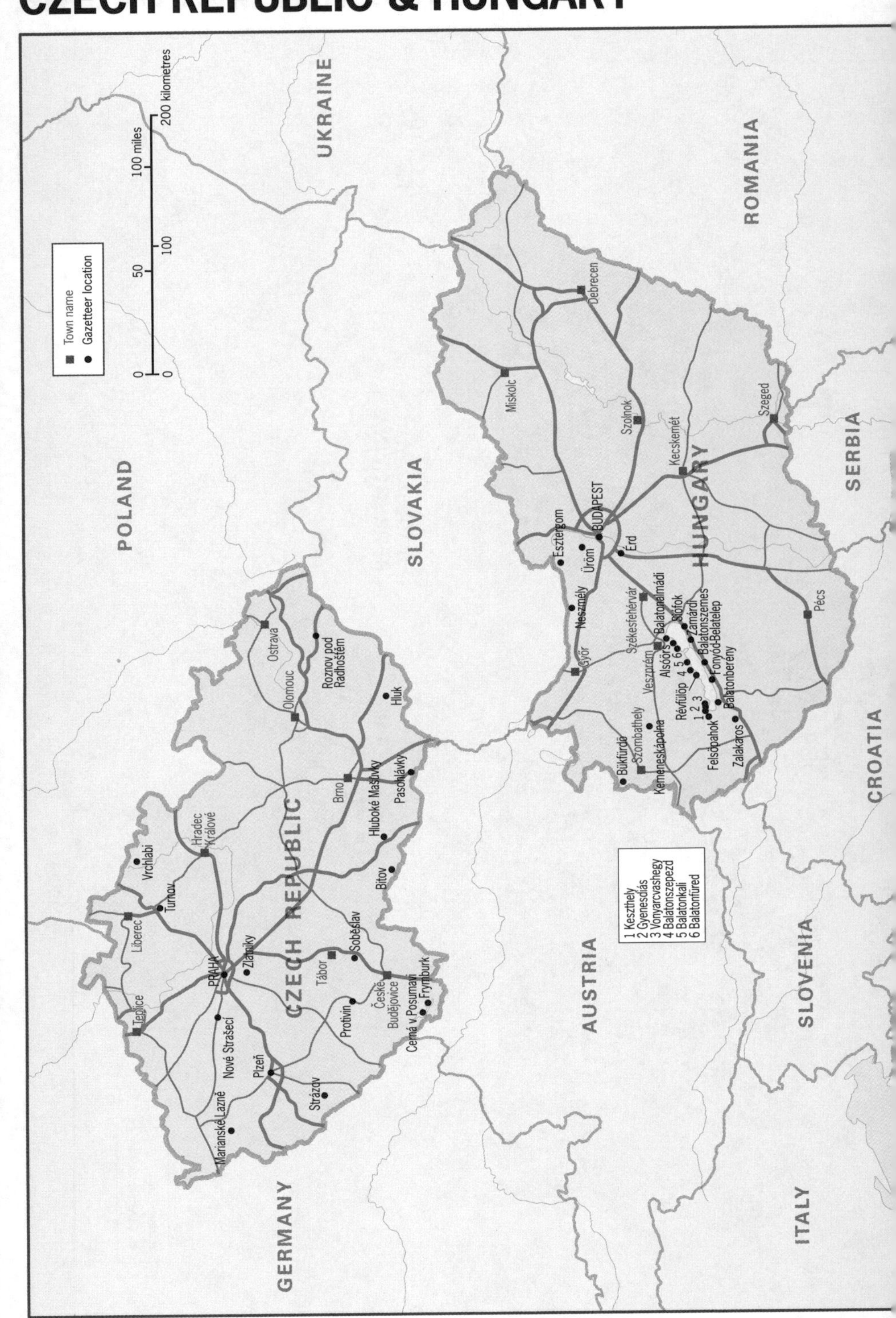

GREECE

MONTENEGRO
BULGARIA
MACEDONIA
ALBANIA
ITALY
TURKEY
GREECE
Kavála
Alexandroúpoli
Thessaloníki
Kozáni
Litóchoro
Dassia
Kérkyra
Igoumenítsa
Plataria
Ioánnina
Lárisa
Agiókambos
Vólos
Kato Gatzea
Stylida
Lamía
Itéa
Delfoí
(Delphi)
Rio
Pátra
Kato
Alissos
Marathonas
ATHÍNA
Lecheon
Kórinthos
Glifa
Epidavros
Town name
Gazetteer location
0
50
100 miles
0
100
200 kilometres
Serifos
Livadakia
Kalamáta
Pylos
Finikounda
Gytheio
Areópoli
Monemvasía
Gialova
Ródos
Ródos
Kríti
Chaniá
Réthymno
Irákleio
Siteia

POLAND

Town name
Gazetteer location
0 50 100 miles
0 50 100 150 kilometres
SWEDEN
LATVIA
LITHUANIA
DENMARK
RUSSIA
BELARUS
GERMANY
CZECH REPUBLIC
SLOVAKIA
UKRAINE
AUSTRIA
HUNGARY
ROMANIA
Słupsk
Sopot
Gdańsk
Elblag
Mielno
Koszalin
Świnoujście
Dziwnówek
Szczecin
Olsztyn
Gizycko
Mikolajki
Augustów
Białystok
Bydgoszcz
Toruń
Płock
WARSZAWA
Poznań
Kalisz
Łódź
Radom
Lublin
Chmielno
Wrocław
Jelenia Góra
Wolibórz
Częstochowa
Kielce
Katowice
Kraków
Przeworsk
Rzeszów
Zakopane

ROMANIA, BULGARIA & WESTERN TURKEY

SLOVAKIA
UKRAINE
Town name
Gazetteer location
0
50
100 miles
0
100
200 kilometres
HUNGARY
MOLDOVA
ROMANIA
SERBIA
KOSOVO
BULGARIA
MACEDONIA
LBANIA
GREECE
TURKEY
Satu Mare
Suceava
Oradea
Gilău
Cluj Napoca
Sóvata
Darmanesti
Bacău
Arad
Miniş
Blajel
Aurel Vlaicu
Sibiu
Cârţa
Timişoara
Cisnădioara
Bran
Braşov
Rucar
Galaţi
Tulcea
Murighiol
Piteşti
Ploieşti
BUCUREŞTI
Craiova
Constanţa
Vidin
Eforie
Ruse
Pleven
Veliko Tŭrnovo
Lyaskovets
Šumen
Varna
Dryanovo
SOFIYA
Burgas
Stara Zagora
Plovdiv
Harmanli
Edirne
İstanbul
Kocaeli (İzmit)
Bogazkale, Göreme, Sultanhanı
Bandırma
Çanakkale
Bursa
Eskişehir
Balıkesir
Afyon
İzmir
Çeşme
Selçuk
Denizli
Antalya
Bodrum

Index

A

C

F

G

H

I

M

N

O

P

U

V

The Automobile Association would like to thank the following photographers, companies and picture libraries for their assistance in the preparation of this book.

Abbreviations for the picture credits are as follows: (t) top; (b) bottom; (l) left; (r) right; (c) centre; (AA) AA World Travel Library.

Front Cover (t) AA/J Smith; Front Cover (bl) AA/I Dawson; Front Cover (br) AA/J Smith; Back Cover (l) AA/A Baker; Back Cover (c) AA/P Kenward; Back Cover (r) AA/T Carter;

1 AA/S Day; 2 AA/J Tims; 3t AA/M Bonnet; 3bl AA/A Mockford & N Bonetti; 3br AA/M Chaplow; 4 AA/I Cumming; 5 AA/J Smith; 6 AA/I Cumming; 8t AA/I Cumming; 8b AA/C Sawyer; 9l AA/K Paterson; 9r AA/M Bonnet; 10 AA/I Cumming; 11 AA/S McBride; 12 AA/I Cumming; 13 AA/M Bonnet; 14t AA/I Cumming; 14c AA/N Setchfield; 15 AA/J Tims; 16 AA/I Cumming; 17 AA/M Bonnet; 18t AA/I Cumming; 18b AA/W Voysey; 26 AA/I Cumming; 27 AA/M Bonnet; 28 AA/A Baker

Country opener pictures:
Austria AA/J Smith; Belgium AA/A Kouprianoff & AA/A Kouprianoff; Croatia AA/J Smith; Czech Republic AA/W Wyand; France AA/P Kenward & AA/J Tims; Germany AA/A Kouprianoff & AA/T Souter; Greece AA/I Cumming; Hungary AA/J Smith & AA/J Smith; Italy AA/J Tims; Luxembourg Royalty Free Photodisc; Netherlands AA/A Robinson; Poland AA/J Tims; Portugal AA/A Mockford and N Bonetti & AA/M Chaplow; Romania & Bulgaria AA/C Sawyer; AA/M Morris; Slovenia AA/J Smith; Spain & Andorra AA/M Bonnet; Switzerland AA/A Baker; Turkey AA/P Bennett

Every effort has been made to trace the copyright holders, and we apologise in advance for any accidental errors. We would be happy to apply any corrections in the following edition of this publication.

Readers' Report Form

Please send this form to:
Editor, AA Caravan & Camping Europe,
Lifestyle Guides,
The Automobile Association,
Fanum House,
Basingstoke RG21 4EA

fax: 01256 493312
e-mail: lifestyleguides@theAA.com

Please use this form to tell us about any site you have visited, whether it is in the guide or not currently listed. Feedback from readers helps us to keep our guide accurate and up to date. However, if you have a complaint to make during your visit, we recommend that you discuss the matter with the management there and then, so that they have a chance to put things right before your visit is spoilt. The AA does not undertake to arbitrate between you and the site's management, or to obtain compensation or engage in protracted correspondence.

Date:

Your name (block capitals)

Your address (block capitals)

....

....

....

....

....

....

e-mail address:

Name of site/park:

Comments (Please include the address of the site/park) ....

....

....

....

....

....

....

....

....

....

....

(please attach a separate sheet if necessary)

Please tick here if you DO NOT wish to receive details of AA offers or products ☐

PTO

Caravan & Camping Europe 2011

Have you bought this Guide before? Yes No

How often do you visit a caravan park or camp site? (circle one choice)

once a year twice a year 3 times a year

more than 3 times a year

How long do you generally stay at a park or site? (circle one choice)

one night up to a week 1 week

2 weeks over 2 weeks

Do you have a:

tent caravan motorhome

Which of the following is most important when choosing a site? (circle one choice)

location toilet/washing facilities personal recommendation

leisure facilities other ....

Do you prefer self-contained cubicled washrooms with WC, shower and washhand basin to open-plan separate facilities?

yes no don't mind

Do you buy any other camping guides? If so, which ones? ....

....

....

Please answer these questions to help us make improvements to the guide:

Have you read the introductory pages and features in this guide? Yes No

Do you use the location atlas in this guide? Yes No

Which of the following most influences your choice of site/park from this guide? (circle one choice)

gazetteer entry information and description photograph advertisement

Do you have any suggestions to improve the guide? ....

....

....

....

Thank you for returning this form

Readers' Report Form

Please send this form to:
Editor, AA Caravan & Camping Europe,
Lifestyle Guides,
The Automobile Association,
Fanum House,
Basingstoke RG21 4EA

fax: 01256 493312
e-mail: lifestyleguides@theAA.com

Please use this form to tell us about any site you have visited, whether it is in the guide or not currently listed. Feedback from readers helps us to keep our guide accurate and up to date. However, if you have a complaint to make during your visit, we recommend that you discuss the matter with the management there and then, so that they have a chance to put things right before your visit is spoilt. The AA does not undertake to arbitrate between you and the site's management, or to obtain compensation or engage in protracted correspondence.

Date:

Your name (block capitals)

Your address (block capitals)

....

....

....

....

....

....

e-mail address:

Name of site/park:

Comments (Please include the address of the site/park) ....

....

....

....

....

....

....

....

....

....

....

(please attach a separate sheet if necessary)

Please tick here if you DO NOT wish to receive details of AA offers or products ☐

PTO

Caravan & Camping Europe 2011

Have you bought this Guide before? Yes No

How often do you visit a caravan park or camp site? (circle one choice)
once a year twice a year 3 times a year
more than 3 times a year

How long do you generally stay at a park or site? (circle one choice)
one night up to a week 1 week
2 weeks over 2 weeks

Do you have a:
tent caravan motorhome

Which of the following is most important when choosing a site? (circle one choice)
location toilet/washing facilities personal recommendation
leisure facilities other ....

Do you prefer self-contained cubicled washrooms with WC, shower and washhand basin to open-plan separate facilities?
yes no don't mind

Do you buy any other camping guides? If so, which ones? ....
....
....

Please answer these questions to help us make improvements to the guide:

Have you read the introductory pages and features in this guide? Yes No

Do you use the location atlas in this guide? Yes No

Which of the following most influences your choice of site/park from this guide? (circle one choice)

gazetteer entry information and description photograph advertisement

Do you have any suggestions to improve the guide? ....
....
....
....

Thank you for returning this form